Renault Clio
Service and Repair Manual

A K Legg LAE MIMI & Peter Gill

Models covered (3906-384)

Renault Clio Hatchback, including special/limited editions
Petrol engines: 1.2 litre (1149cc), 1.4 litre (1390cc) & 1.6 litre (1598cc)
Diesel engines: 1.9 litre (1870cc) normally-aspirated

Does NOT cover 1.2 litre 16-valve, 2.0 litre 16-valve or 3.0 litre V6 petrol engines, or 1.9 litre turbo-diesel engine

ABCDE
FGHIJ
KLMNO
PQRST
1 2 3

A book in the **Haynes Service and Repair Manual Series**

ISBN **1 85960 906 6**

British Library Cataloguing in Publication Data
A catalogue record for this book is available from the British Library.

Printed by **J H Haynes & Co Ltd, Sparkford, Nr Yeovil, Somerset BA22 7JJ, England**

Haynes Publishing
Sparkford, Nr Yeovil, Somerset BA22 7JJ, England

Haynes North America, Inc
861 Lawrence Drive, Newbury Park, California 91320, USA

Editions Haynes S.A.
Tour Aurore - IBC 18 Place des Reflets,
92975 Paris La Defense 2, Cedex, France

Haynes Publishing Nordiska AB
Box 1504, 751 45 UPPSALA, Sverige

Contents

Contents

Advanced driving

Many people see the words 'advanced driving' and believe that it won't interest them or that it is a style of driving beyond their own abilities. Nothing could be further from the truth. Advanced driving is straightforward safe, sensible driving - the sort of driving we should all do every time we get behind the wheel.

An average of 10 people are killed every day on UK roads and 870 more are injured, some seriously. Lives are ruined daily, usually because somebody did something stupid. Something like 95% of all accidents are due to human error, mostly driver failure. Sometimes we make genuine mistakes - everyone does. Sometimes we have lapses of concentration. Sometimes we deliberately take risks.

For many people, the process of 'learning to drive' doesn't go much further than learning how to pass the driving test because of a common belief that good drivers are made by 'experience'.

Learning to drive by 'experience' teaches three driving skills:

- ☐ Quick reactions. (Whoops, that was close!)
- ☐ Good handling skills. (Horn, swerve, brake, horn).
- ☐ Reliance on vehicle technology. (Great stuff this ABS, stop in no distance even in the wet...)

Drivers whose skills are 'experience based' generally have a lot of near misses and the odd accident. The results can be seen every day in our courts and our hospital casualty departments.

Advanced drivers have learnt to control the risks by controlling the position and speed of their vehicle. They avoid accidents and near misses, even if the drivers around them make mistakes.

The key skills of advanced driving are **concentration,** effective all-round **observation, anticipation** and **planning.** When **good vehicle handling** is added to these skills, all driving situations can be approached and negotiated in a safe, methodical way, leaving nothing to chance.

Concentration means applying your mind to safe driving, completely excluding anything that's not relevant. Driving is usually the most dangerous activity that most of us undertake in our daily routines. It deserves our full attention.

Observation means not just looking, but seeing and seeking out the information found in the driving environment.

Anticipation means asking yourself what is happening, what you can reasonably expect to happen and what could happen unexpectedly. (One of the commonest words used in compiling accident reports is 'suddenly'.)

Planning is the link between seeing something and taking the appropriate action. For many drivers, planning is the missing link.

If you want to become a safer and more skilful driver and you want to enjoy your driving more, contact the Institute of Advanced Motorists on 0208 994 4403 or write to IAM House, Chiswick High Road, London W4 4HS for an information pack.

Working on your car can be dangerous. This page shows just some of the potential risks and hazards, with the aim of creating a safety-conscious attitude.

General hazards

Scalding

• Don't remove the radiator or expansion tank cap while the engine is hot.

• Engine oil, automatic transmission fluid or power steering fluid may also be dangerously hot if the engine has recently been running.

Burning

• Beware of burns from the exhaust system and from any part of the engine. Brake discs and drums can also be extremely hot immediately after use.

Crushing

• When working under or near a raised vehicle, always supplement the jack with axle stands, or use drive-on ramps. ***Never venture under a car which is only supported by a jack.***

• Take care if loosening or tightening high-torque nuts when the vehicle is on stands. Initial loosening and final tightening should be done with the wheels on the ground.

Fire

• Fuel is highly flammable; fuel vapour is explosive.

• Don't let fuel spill onto a hot engine.

• Do not smoke or allow naked lights (including pilot lights) anywhere near a vehicle being worked on. Also beware of creating sparks (electrically or by use of tools).

• Fuel vapour is heavier than air, so don't work on the fuel system with the vehicle over an inspection pit.

• Another cause of fire is an electrical overload or short-circuit. Take care when repairing or modifying the vehicle wiring.

• Keep a fire extinguisher handy, of a type suitable for use on fuel and electrical fires.

Electric shock

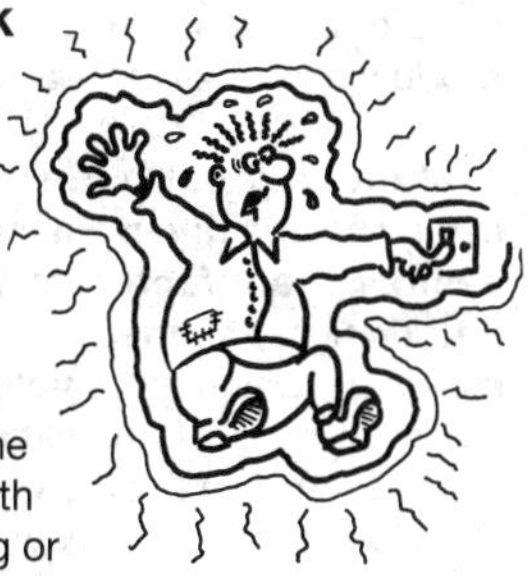

• Ignition HT voltage can be dangerous, especially to people with heart problems or a pacemaker. Don't work on or near the ignition system with the engine running or the ignition switched on.

• Mains voltage is also dangerous. Make sure that any mains-operated equipment is correctly earthed. Mains power points should be protected by a residual current device (RCD) circuit breaker.

Fume or gas intoxication

• Exhaust fumes are poisonous; they often contain carbon monoxide, which is rapidly fatal if inhaled. Never run the engine in a confined space such as a garage with the doors shut.

• Fuel vapour is also poisonous, as are the vapours from some cleaning solvents and paint thinners.

Poisonous or irritant substances

• Avoid skin contact with battery acid and with any fuel, fluid or lubricant, especially antifreeze, brake hydraulic fluid and Diesel fuel. Don't syphon them by mouth. If such a substance is swallowed or gets into the eyes, seek medical advice.

• Prolonged contact with used engine oil can cause skin cancer. Wear gloves or use a barrier cream if necessary. Change out of oil-soaked clothes and do not keep oily rags in your pocket.

• Air conditioning refrigerant forms a poisonous gas if exposed to a naked flame (including a cigarette). It can also cause skin burns on contact.

Asbestos

• Asbestos dust can cause cancer if inhaled or swallowed. Asbestos may be found in gaskets and in brake and clutch linings. When dealing with such components it is safest to assume that they contain asbestos.

Special hazards

Hydrofluoric acid

• This extremely corrosive acid is formed when certain types of synthetic rubber, found in some O-rings, oil seals, fuel hoses etc, are exposed to temperatures above 400°C. The rubber changes into a charred or sticky substance containing the acid. *Once formed, the acid remains dangerous for years. If it gets onto the skin, it may be necessary to amputate the limb concerned.*

• When dealing with a vehicle which has suffered a fire, or with components salvaged from such a vehicle, wear protective gloves and discard them after use.

The battery

• Batteries contain sulphuric acid, which attacks clothing, eyes and skin. Take care when topping-up or carrying the battery.

• The hydrogen gas given off by the battery is highly explosive. Never cause a spark or allow a naked light nearby. Be careful when connecting and disconnecting battery chargers or jump leads.

Air bags

• Air bags can cause injury if they go off accidentally. Take care when removing the steering wheel and/or facia. Special storage instructions may apply.

Diesel injection equipment

• Diesel injection pumps supply fuel at very high pressure. Take care when working on the fuel injectors and fuel pipes.

Warning: Never expose the hands, face or any other part of the body to injector spray; the fuel can penetrate the skin with potentially fatal results.

Remember...

DO

• Do use eye protection when using power tools, and when working under the vehicle.

• Do wear gloves or use barrier cream to protect your hands when necessary.

• Do get someone to check periodically that all is well when working alone on the vehicle.

• Do keep loose clothing and long hair well out of the way of moving mechanical parts.

• Do remove rings, wristwatch etc, before working on the vehicle – especially the electrical system.

• Do ensure that any lifting or jacking equipment has a safe working load rating adequate for the job.

DON'T

• Don't attempt to lift a heavy component which may be beyond your capability – get assistance.

• Don't rush to finish a job, or take unverified short cuts.

• Don't use ill-fitting tools which may slip and cause injury.

• Don't leave tools or parts lying around where someone can trip over them. Mop up oil and fuel spills at once.

• Don't allow children or pets to play in or near a vehicle being worked on.

Three petrol engines and one diesel engine are available in the Clio range. The petrol engines are in 1.2, 1.4, and 1.6 litre sizes, and the diesel engine is 1.9 litre. All petrol engines use a fuel-injection system, and diesel engines use an indirect injection system. The direct injection system on the F9QT engine is not covered in this Manual. All the engines are of excellent design and, provided regular maintenance is carried out, are unlikely to give trouble.

The Clio is available in 3- and 5-door Hatchback body styles, with a wide range of fittings and interior trim depending on the model specification.

Fully-independent front suspension is fitted, with the components attached to a subframe assembly, and the rear suspension is semi-independent, with a compact H-form torsion beam and trailing arms.

A five-speed manual gearbox and electronically-controlled four-speed automatic transmission are available.

A wide range of standard and optional equipment is available within the Clio range to suit most tastes, including an anti-lock braking system.

The Clio is conventional in design, and the DIY mechanic should find most servicing work straightforward.

Your Renault Clio Manual

The aim of this manual is to help you get the best value from your vehicle. It can do so in several ways. It can help you decide what work must be done (even should you choose to get it done by a garage), provide information on routine maintenance and servicing, and give a logical course of action and diagnosis when random faults occur. However, it is hoped that you will use the manual by tackling the work yourself. On simpler jobs, it may even be quicker than booking the car into a garage and going there twice, to leave and collect it. Perhaps most important, a lot of money can be saved by avoiding the costs a garage must charge to cover its labour and overheads.

The manual has drawings and descriptions to show the function of the various components, so that their layout can be understood. Then the tasks are described and photographed in a clear step-by-step sequence.

References to the 'left' or 'right' are in the sense of a person in the driver's seat, facing forward.

Project vehicles

The main project vehicle used in the preparation of this manual, and appearing in many of the photographic sequences, was a 1998 Renault Clio Alize fitted with the 1.4 litre K4J engine.

Acknowledgements

Thanks are due to Champion Spark Plug, who supplied the illustrations showing spark plug conditions. Certain other illustrations are the copyright of Renault (UK) Limited, and are used with their permission. Thanks are also due to Draper Tools Limited, who provided some of the workshop tools, and to all those people at Sparkford who helped in the production of this manual.

The following pages are intended to help in dealing with common roadside emergencies and breakdowns. You will find more detailed fault finding information at the back of the manual, and repair information in the main chapters.

If your car won't start and the starter motor doesn't turn

- ☐ If it's a model with automatic transmission, make sure the selector is in P or N.
- ☐ Open the bonnet and make sure that the battery terminals are clean and tight.
- ☐ Switch on the headlights and try to start the engine. If the headlights go very dim when you're trying to start, the battery is probably flat. Get out of trouble by jump starting (see next page) using a friend's car.

If your car won't start even though the starter motor turns as normal

- ☐ Is there fuel in the tank?
- ☐ Is there moisture on electrical components under the bonnet? Switch off the ignition, then wipe off any obvious dampness with a dry cloth. Spray a water-repellent aerosol product (WD-40 or equivalent) on ignition and fuel system electrical connectors like those shown in the photos. Pay special attention to the ignition coil wiring connector and HT leads.

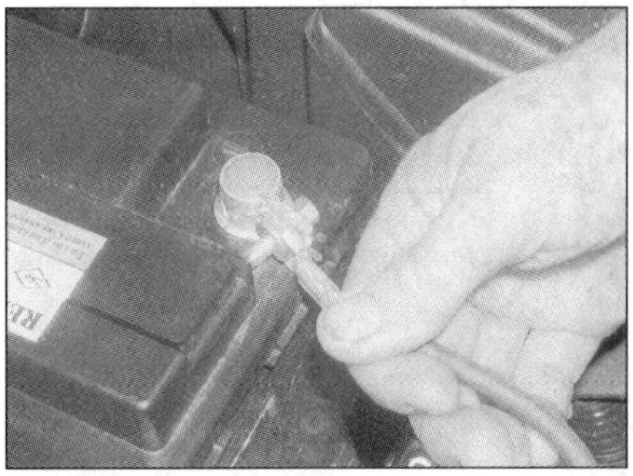

A Check the condition and security of the battery connections.

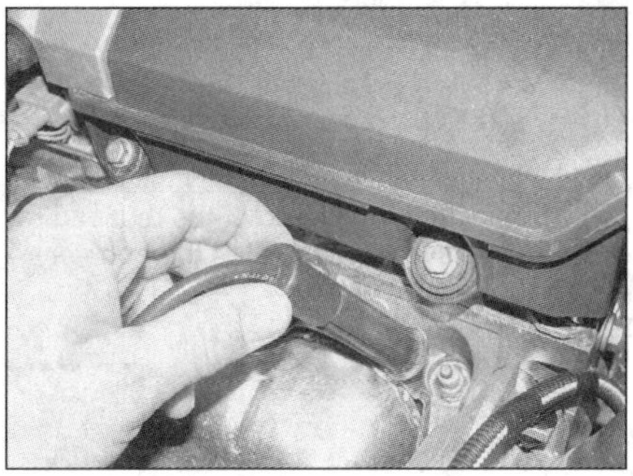

B Check that the spark plug HT leads or ignition coil wires are securely connected.

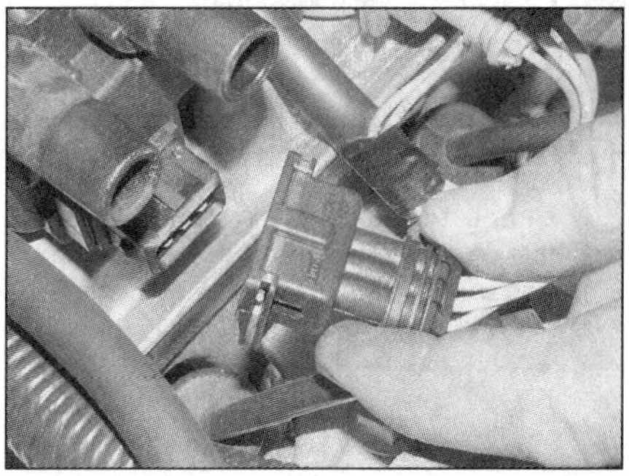

C Check that the ignition coil wiring plug is secure.

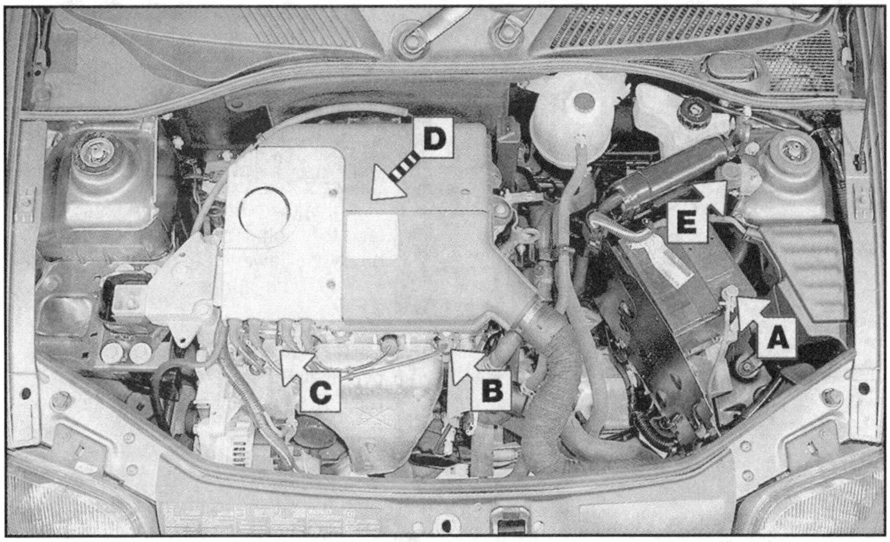

Check that all electrical connections are secure (with the ignition switched off). Spray the connector plugs with a water-dispersant spray like WD-40 if you suspect a problem due to damp. Diesel models do not usually suffer from damp starting problems, but check all visible connector plugs just in case.

D Check that the fuel injector wiring harness connector is secure.

E Check that the fuel cut-off switch has not been activated.

HAYNES HiNT *Jump starting will get you out of trouble, but you must correct whatever made the battery go flat in the first place. There are three possibilities:*

***1** The battery has been drained by repeated attempts to start, or by leaving the lights on.*

***2** The charging system is not working properly (alternator drivebelt slack or broken, alternator wiring fault or alternator itself faulty).*

***3** The battery itself is at fault (electrolyte low, or battery worn out).*

Jump starting

When jump-starting a car using a booster battery, observe the following precautions:

- ✔ Before connecting the booster battery, make sure that the ignition is switched off.
- ✔ Ensure that all electrical equipment (lights, heater, wipers, etc) is switched off.
- ✔ Take note of any special precautions printed on the battery case.
- ✔ Make sure that the booster battery is the same voltage as the discharged one in the vehicle.
- ✔ If the battery is being jump-started from the battery in another vehicle, the two vehicles MUST NOT TOUCH each other.
- ✔ Make sure that the transmission is in neutral (or PARK, in the case of automatic transmission).

1 Connect one end of the red jump lead to the positive (+) terminal of the flat battery

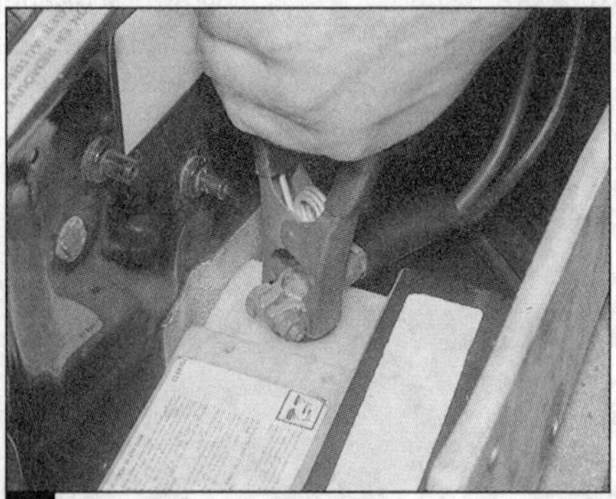

2 Connect the other end of the red lead to the positive (+) terminal of the booster battery.

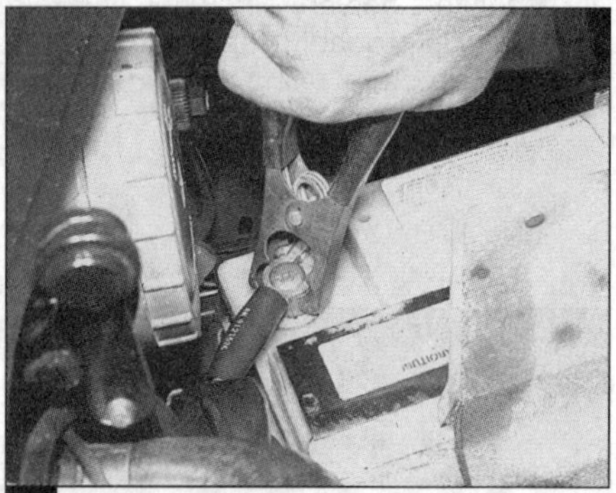

3 Connect one end of the black jump lead to the negative (-) terminal of the booster battery

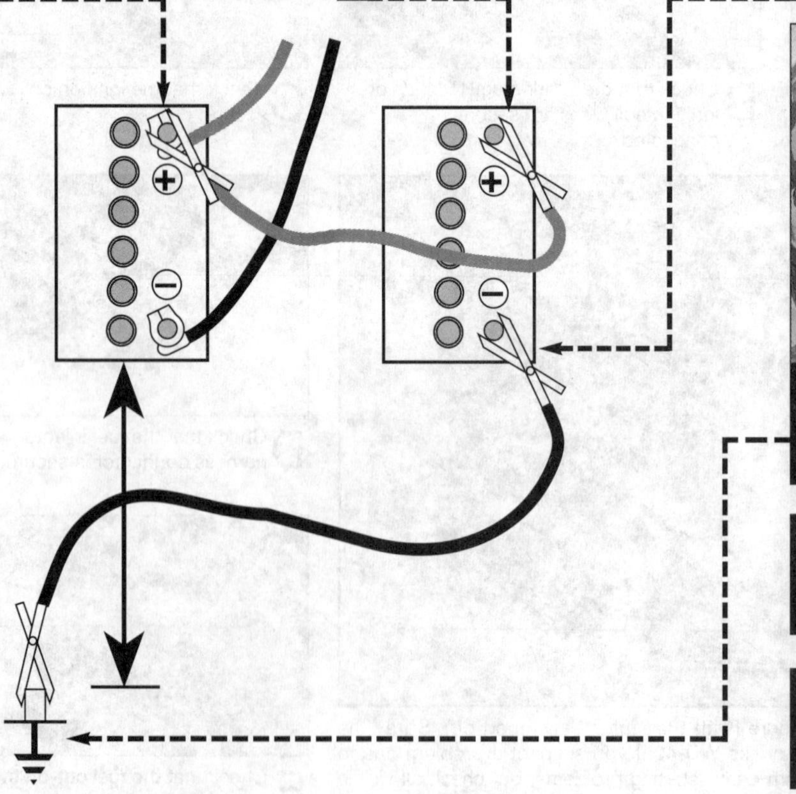

4 Connect the other end of the black jump lead to a bolt or bracket on the engine block, well away from the battery, on the vehicle to be started.

5 Make sure that the jump leads will not come into contact with the fan, drive-belts or other moving parts of the engine.

6 Start the engine using the booster battery and run it at idle speed. Switch on the lights, rear window demister and heater blower motor, then disconnect the jump leads in the reverse order of connection. Turn off the lights etc.

Wheel changing

Warning: Do not change a wheel in a situation where you risk being hit by other traffic. On busy roads, try to stop in a lay-by or a gateway. Be wary of passing traffic while changing the wheel – it is easy to become distracted by the job in hand.

Preparation

- ☐ When a puncture occurs, stop as soon as it is safe to do so.
- ☐ Park on firm level ground, if possible, and well out of the way of other traffic.
- ☐ Use hazard warning lights if necessary.
- ☐ If you have one, use a warning triangle to alert other drivers of your presence.
- ☐ Apply the handbrake and engage first or reverse gear.
- ☐ Chock the wheel diagonally opposite the one being removed – a couple of large stones will do for this.
- ☐ If the ground is soft, use a flat piece of wood to spread the load under the jack.

Changing the wheel

1 The spare wheel and tools are stored in the luggage compartment under the carpet. Unscrew the retainer securing the tool holder and spare wheel.

2 Lift out the tool holder.

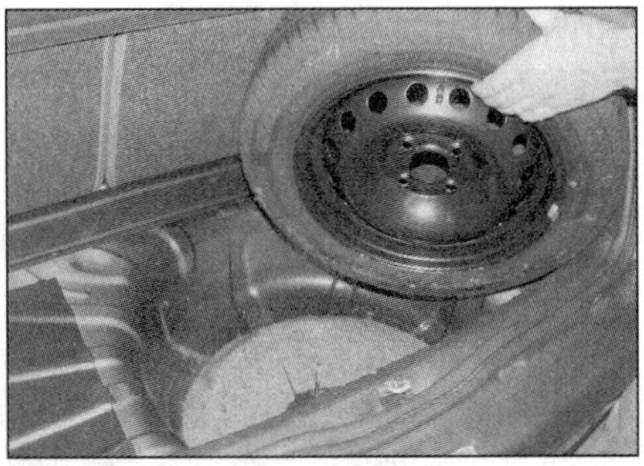

3 Lift out the spare wheel.

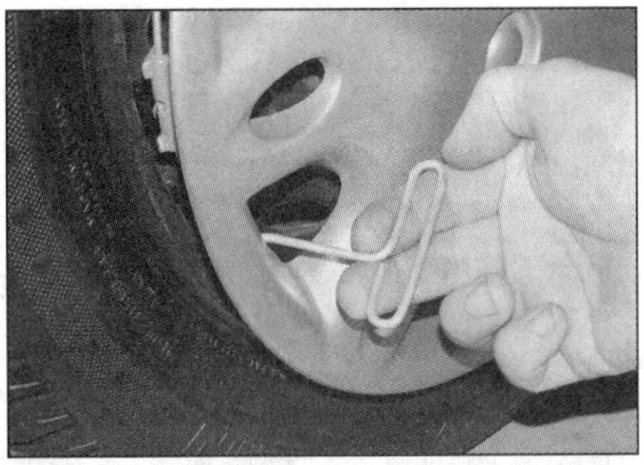

4 Use the hook provided to remove the wheel trim.

5 Slacken each wheel bolt by half a turn. For safety, chock the diagonally opposite wheel – a couple of large stones will do for this.

6 Locate the jack below the reinforced point on the sill (don't jack the vehicle at any other point of the sill) and on firm ground, then turn the jack handle clockwise until the wheel is raised clear of the ground.

7 Unscrew the wheel bolts using the brace provided, and remove the wheel. Fit the spare wheel, and screw in the bolts. Lightly tighten the bolts with the wheelbrace then lower the vehicle to the ground.

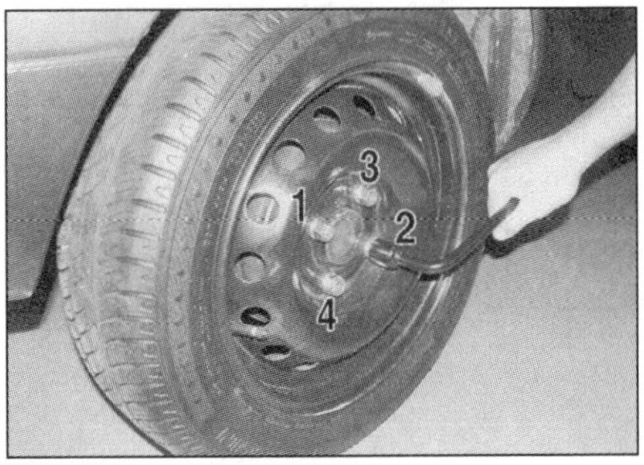

8 Securely tighten the wheel bolts in the sequence shown then refit the wheel trim. Stow the punctured wheel back in the spare wheel well. Note that the wheel bolts must be tightened to the specified torque at the earliest possible opportunity.

Finally . . .

- ☐ Remove the wheel chocks.
- ☐ Stow the jack and tools in the holder.
- ☐ Check the tyre pressure on the wheel just fitted. If it is low, or if you don't have a pressure gauge with you, drive slowly to the next garage and inflate the tyre to the right pressure.
- ☐ Have the damaged tyre or wheel repaired as soon as possible.

Identifying leaks

Puddles on the garage floor or drive, or obvious wetness under the bonnet or underneath the car, suggest a leak that needs investigating. It can sometimes be difficult to decide where the leak is coming from, especially if the engine bay is very dirty already. Leaking oil or fluid can also be blown rearwards by the passage of air under the car, giving a false impression of where the problem lies.

Warning: Most automotive oils and fluids are poisonous. Wash them off skin, and change out of contaminated clothing, without delay.

HAYNES HiNT *The smell of a fluid leaking from the car may provide a clue to what's leaking. Some fluids are distinctively coloured. It may help to clean the car carefully and to park it over some clean paper overnight as an aid to locating the source of the leak. Remember that some leaks may only occur while the engine is running.*

Sump oil

Engine oil may leak from the drain plug...

Oil from filter

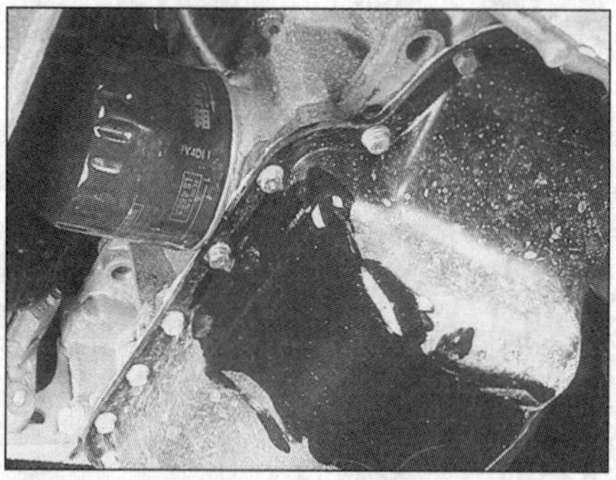

...or from the base of the oil filter.

Gearbox oil

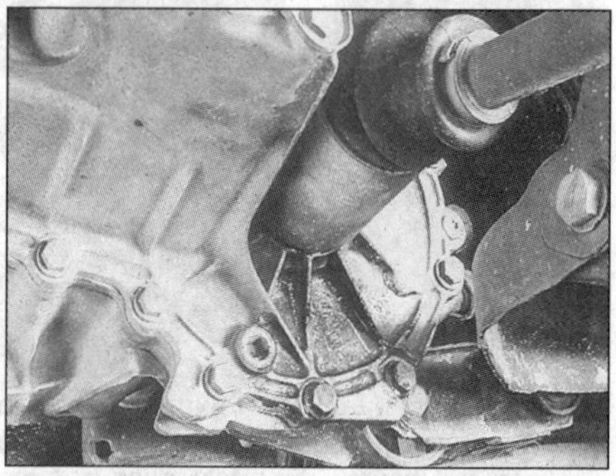

Gearbox oil can leak from the seals at the inboard ends of the driveshafts.

Antifreeze

Leaking antifreeze often leaves a crystalline deposit like this.

Brake fluid

A leak occurring at a wheel is almost certainly brake fluid.

Power steering fluid

Power steering fluid may leak from the pipe connectors on the steering rack.

Towing

When all else fails, you may find yourself having to get a tow home – or of course you may be helping somebody else. Long-distance recovery should only be done by a garage or breakdown service. For shorter distances, DIY towing using another car is easy enough, but observe the following points:

☐ Use a proper tow-rope – they are not expensive. The vehicle being towed must display an ON TOW sign in its rear window.

☐ Always turn the ignition key to the 'on' position when the vehicle is being towed, so that the steering lock is released, and that the direction indicator and brake lights will work.

☐ Before being towed, release the handbrake and select neutral on the transmission.

☐ On models with automatic transmission, do not exceed 25 mph and do not tow for more than 30 miles.

☐ Note that greater-than-usual pedal pressure will be required to operate the brakes, since the vacuum servo unit is only operational with the engine running.

☐ The driver of the car being towed must keep the tow rope taut at all times to avoid snatching.

☐ Make sure that both drivers know the route before setting off.

☐ Drive smoothly and allow plenty of time for slowing down at junctions.

☐ A towing eye is provided in the tool kit in the luggage compartment.

☐ To fit the towing eye at the front, screw it into the threaded hole located next to the left-hand headlight. Tighten the eye using the wheelbrace **(see illustrations)**.

☐ To fit the towing eye to the rear, prise the plastic cover from the rear bumper then screw the eye into the threaded hole. Tighten the eye using the wheelbrace **(see illustrations)**.

Screw the towing eye into the front threaded hole . . .

. . . and tighten it with the brace

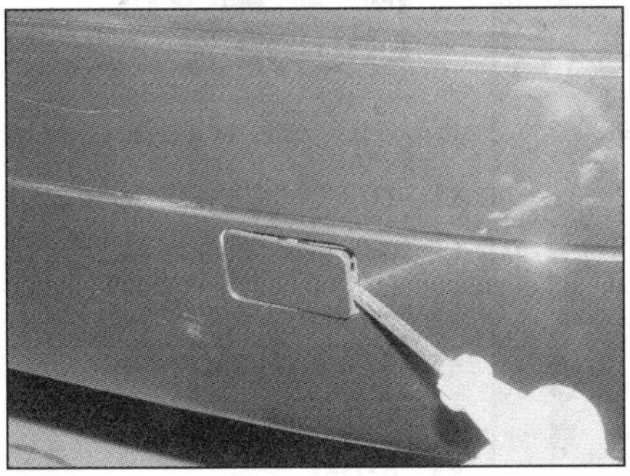

Prise the cover from the rear bumper . . .

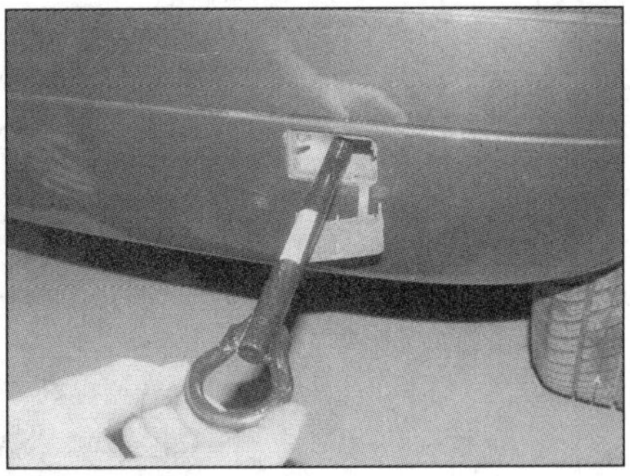

. . . then screw in the towing eye . . .

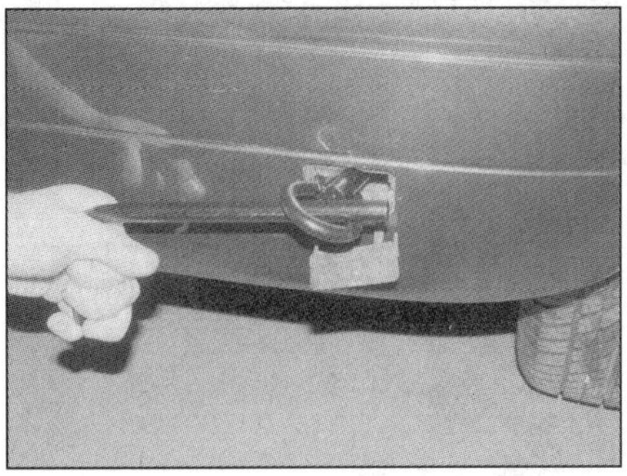

. . . and tighten with the brace

Introduction

There are some very simple checks which need only take a few minutes to carry out, but which could save you a lot of inconvenience and expense.

These 'Weekly checks' require no great skill or special tools, and the small amount of time they take to perform could prove to be very well spent, for example;

☐ Keeping an eye on tyre condition and pressures, will not only help to stop them wearing out prematurely, but could also save your life.

☐ Many breakdowns are caused by electrical problems. Battery-related faults are particularly common, and a quick check on a regular basis will often prevent the majority of these.

☐ If your car develops a brake fluid leak, the first time you might know about it is when your brakes don't work properly. Checking the level regularly will give advance warning of this kind of problem.

☐ If the oil or coolant levels run low, the cost of repairing any engine damage will be far greater than fixing the leak, for example.

Underbonnet check points

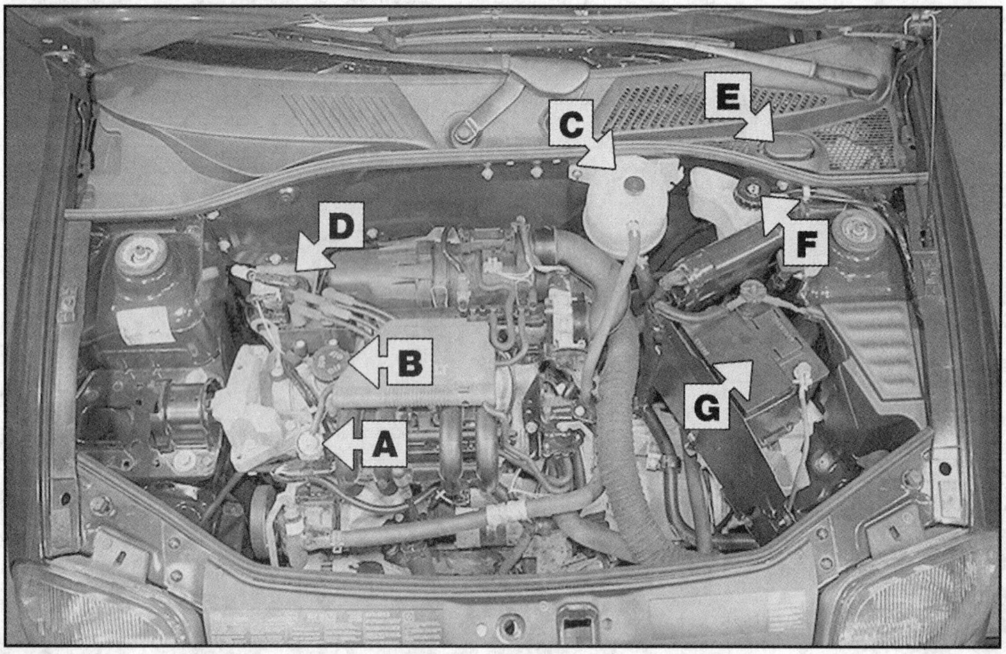

◀ 1.2 litre (D7F) petrol engine

A *Engine oil level dipstick*
B *Engine oil filler cap*
C *Coolant expansion tank*
D *Brake fluid reservoir*
E *Washer fluid reservoir*
F *Power steering fluid reservoir*
G *Battery*

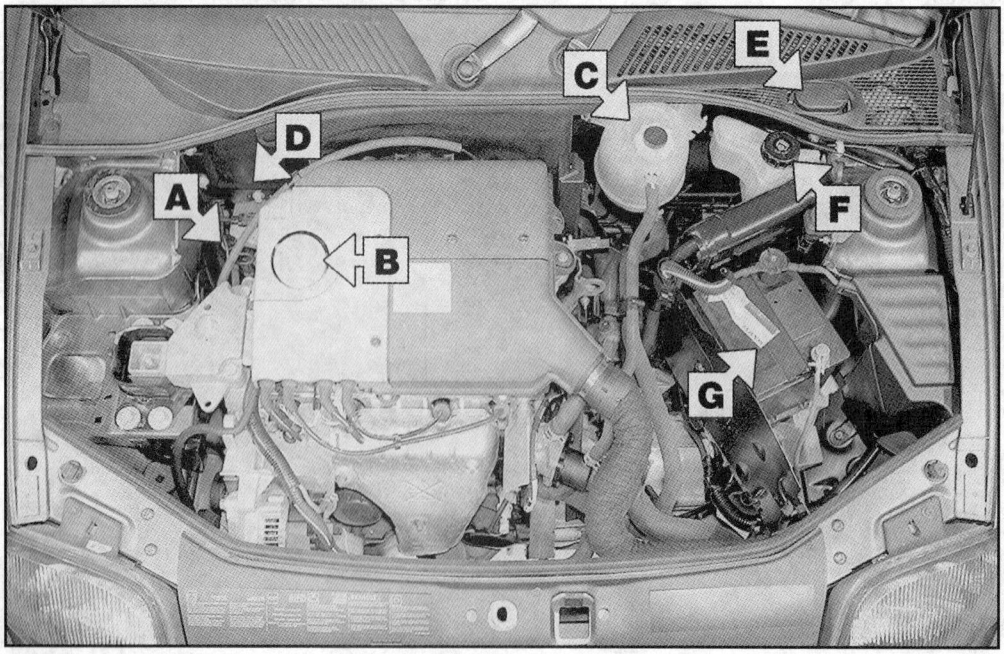

◀ 1.4 litre 8-valve (E7J) petrol engine

A *Engine oil level dipstick*
B *Engine oil filler cap*
C *Coolant expansion tank*
D *Brake fluid reservoir*
E *Washer fluid reservoir*
F *Power steering fluid reservoir*
G *Battery*

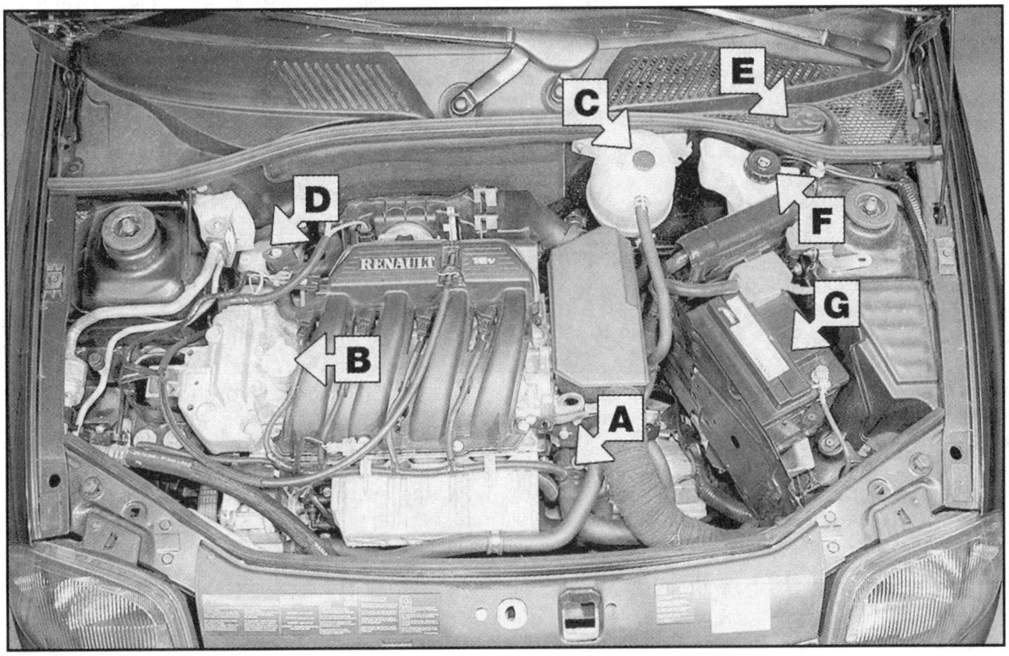

◀ **1.4 litre 16-valve (K4J) petrol engine**

A *Engine oil level dipstick*
B *Engine oil filler cap*
C *Coolant expansion tank*
D *Brake fluid reservoir*
E *Washer fluid reservoir*
F *Power steering fluid reservoir*
G *Battery*

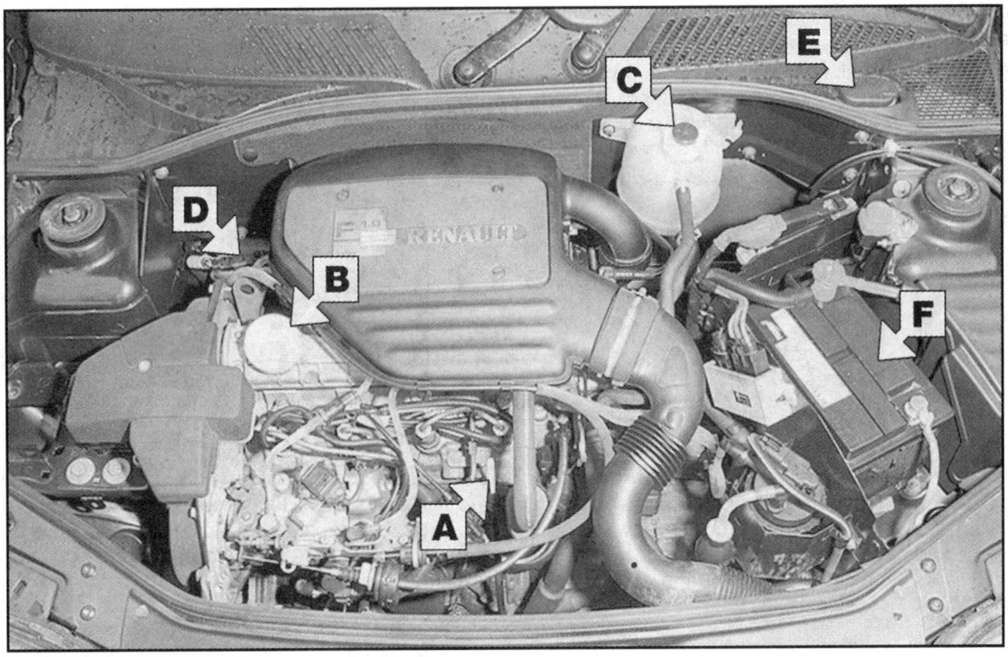

◀ **1.9 litre (F8Q) diesel engine**

A *Engine oil level dipstick*
B *Engine oil filler cap*
C *Coolant expansion tank*
D *Brake fluid reservoir*
E *Washer fluid reservoir*
F *Battery*

Engine oil level

Before you start

✔ Make sure that your car is on level ground.

✔ Check the oil level before the car is driven, or at least 5 minutes after the engine has been switched off.

> **HAYNES HiNT** ***If the oil is checked immediately after driving the vehicle, some of the oil will remain in the upper engine components, resulting in an inaccurate reading on the dipstick.***

The correct oil

Modern engines place great demands on their oil. It is very important that the correct oil for your car is used (See 'Lubricants and fluids').

Car Care

● If you have to add oil frequently, you should check whether you have any oil leaks. Place some clean paper under the car overnight, and check for stains in the morning. If there are no leaks, the engine may be burning oil.

● Always maintain the level between the upper and lower dipstick marks (see photo 3). If the level is too low severe engine damage may occur. Oil seal failure may result if the engine is overfilled by adding too much oil.

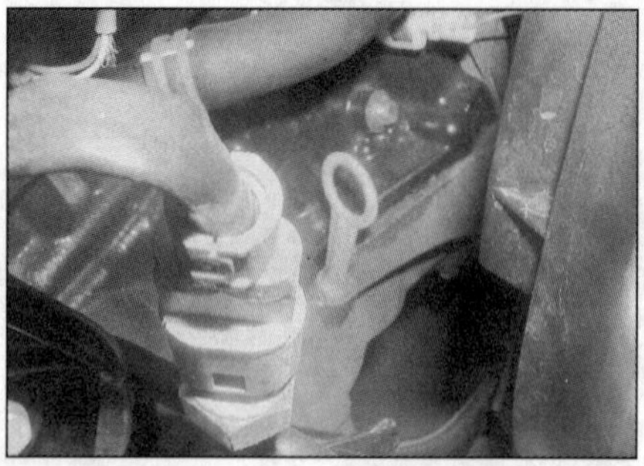

1 The dipstick is brightly coloured yellow and is located on the front of the engine (see *Underbonnet Check Points* for exact location). Withdraw the dipstick.

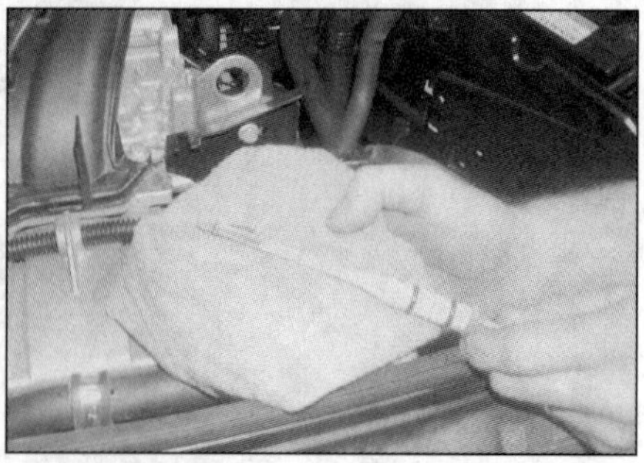

2 Using a clean rag or paper towel remove all oil from the dipstick. Insert the clean dipstick into the tube as far as it will go, then withdraw it again.

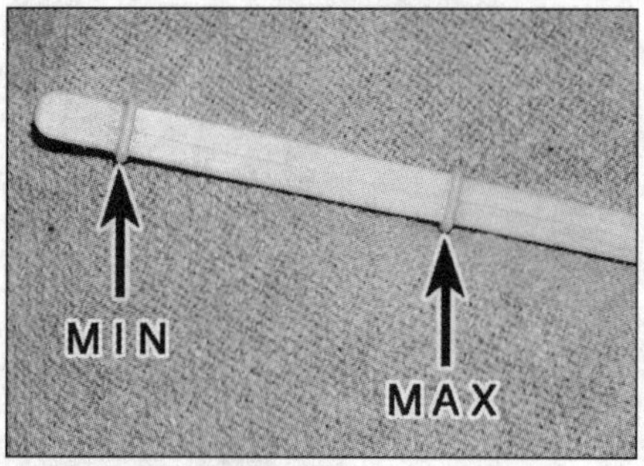

3 Note the oil level on the end of the dipstick, which should be between the upper (MAX) mark and lower (MIN) mark. Note that on some engines the MAX and MIN marks are indicated by notches. Approximately 1.0 litre of oil will raise the level from the lower mark to the upper mark.

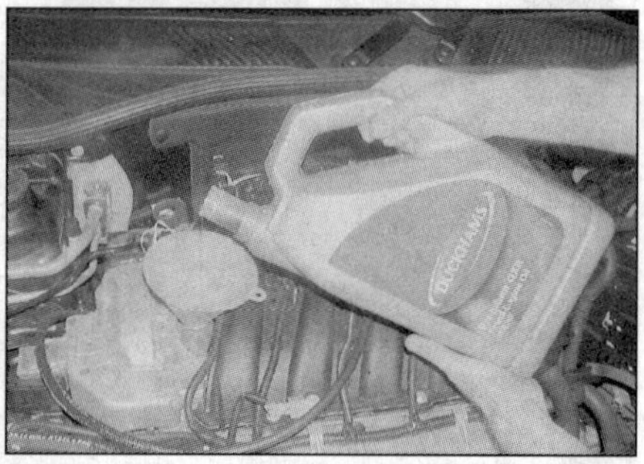

4 Oil is added through the filler cap. Twist the cap anti-clockwise and withdraw it. Top-up the level. A funnel may help to reduce spillage. Add the oil slowly, checking the level on the dipstick often. Do not overfill.

Coolant level

> ***Warning: DO NOT attempt to remove the expansion tank pressure cap when the engine is hot, as there is a very great risk of scalding. Do not leave open containers of coolant about, as it is poisonous.***

Car Care

● With a sealed-type cooling system, adding coolant should not be necessary on a regular basis. If frequent topping-up is required, it is likely there is a leak. Check the radiator, all hoses and joint faces for signs of staining or wetness, and rectify as necessary.

● It is important that antifreeze is used in the cooling system all year round, not just during the winter months. Don't top-up with water alone, as the antifreeze will become too diluted.

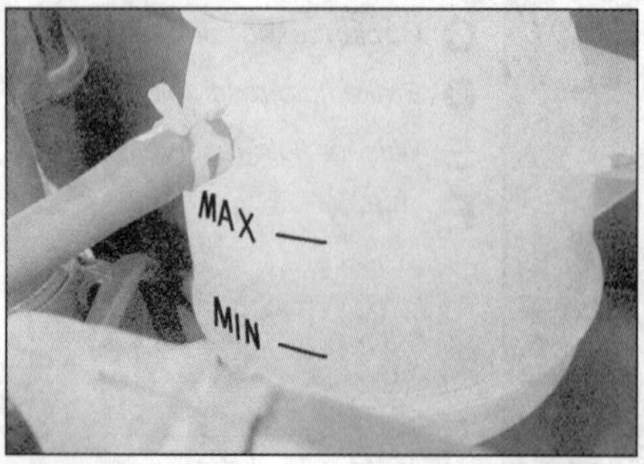

1 The coolant level varies with the temperature of the engine. When the engine is cold, the coolant level should be between the MIN and MAX marks (preferably near the MAX mark) on the side of the expansion tank. When the engine is hot, the level will rise.

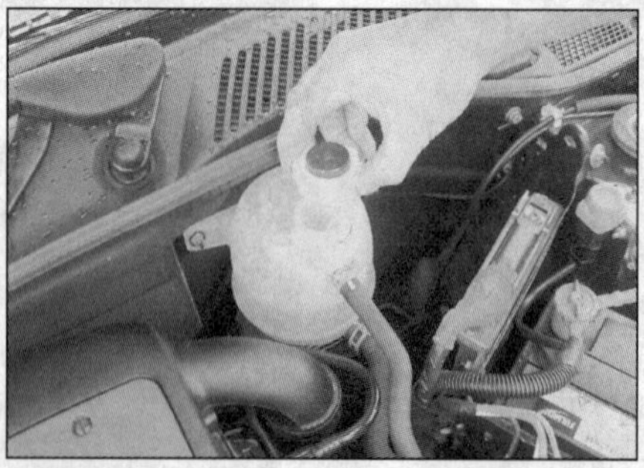

2 If topping-up is necessary, **wait until the engine is cold**. Slowly unscrew the expansion tank cap, to release any pressure present in the cooling system, and remove it.

3 Add a mixture of water and antifreeze to the expansion tank until the coolant is up to the MAX level mark. Refit the cap and tighten it securely.

Brake fluid level

Warning:

● ***Brake fluid can harm your eyes and damage painted surfaces, so use extreme caution when handling and pouring it.***

● ***Do not use fluid that has been standing open for some time, as it absorbs moisture from the air, which can cause a dangerous loss of braking effectiveness.***

HAYNES HiNT

• ***Make sure that your car is on level ground.***

• ***The fluid level in the reservoir will drop slightly as the brake pads wear down, but the fluid level must never be allowed to drop below the MIN mark.***

Safety First!

● If the reservoir requires repeated topping-up this is an indication of a fluid leak somewhere in the system, which should be investigated immediately.

● If a leak is suspected, the car should not be driven until the braking system has been checked. Never take any risks where brakes are concerned.

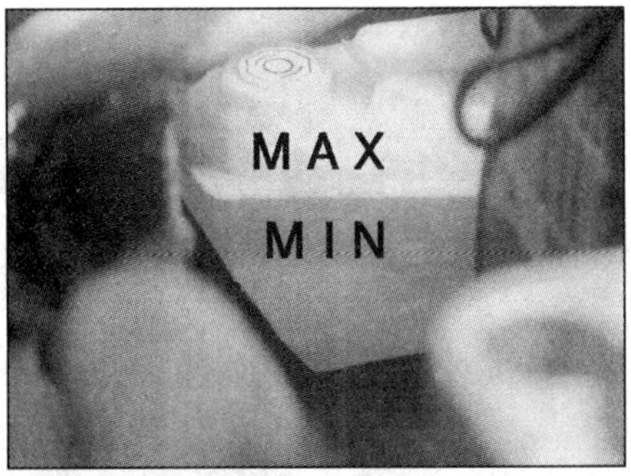

1 The MAX and MIN marks are indicated on the front of the reservoir. The fluid level must be kept between the marks at all times.

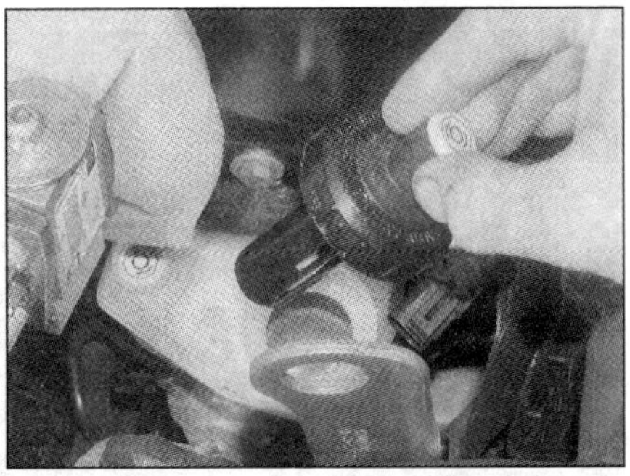

2 If topping-up is necessary, first wipe clean the area around the filler cap to prevent dirt entering the hydraulic system. Unscrew and remove the cap.

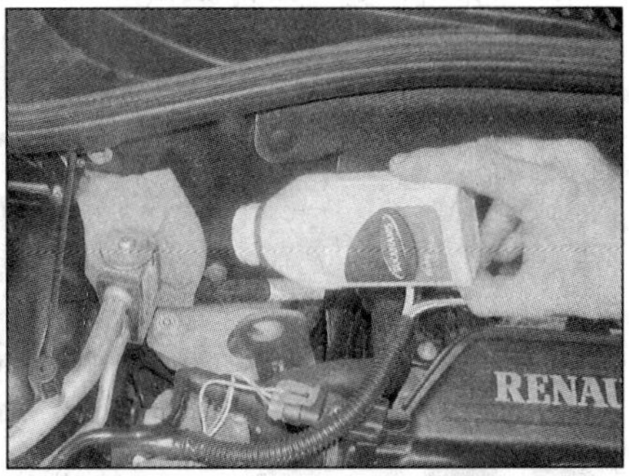

3 Carefully add fluid, taking care not to spill it onto the surrounding components. Use only the specified fluid; mixing different types can cause damage to the system. After topping-up to the correct level, securely refit the cap and wipe off any spilt fluid.

Screen washer fluid level

● Screenwash additives not only keep the windscreen clean during foul weather, they also prevent the washer system freezing in cold weather – which is when you are likely to need it most. Don't top up using plain water as the screenwash will become too diluted, and will freeze during cold weather. ***On no account use coolant antifreeze in the washer system – this could discolour or damage paintwork.***

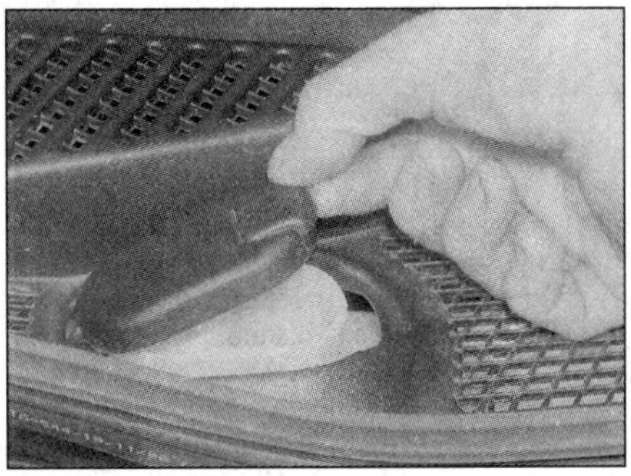

1 The reservoir for the windscreen and headlight washers (where fitted) is located on the rear left-hand side of the bulkhead. If topping-up is necessary, open the cap.

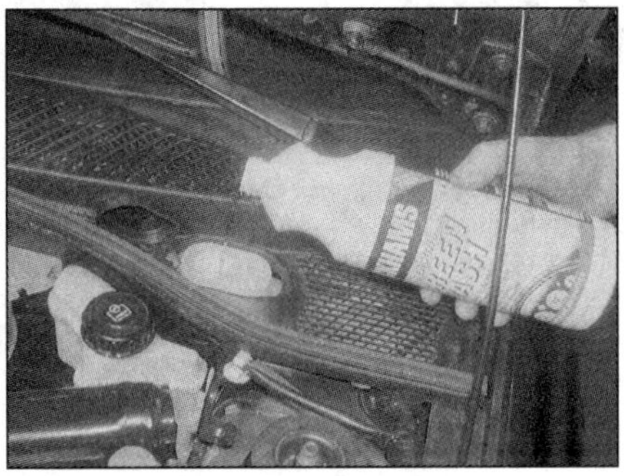

2 When topping-up the reservoir a screen-wash additive should be added in the quantities recommended on the bottle.

Tyre condition and pressure

It is very important that tyres are in good condition, and at the correct pressure - having a tyre failure at any speed is highly dangerous.

Tyre wear is influenced by driving style - harsh braking and acceleration, or fast cornering, will all produce more rapid tyre wear. As a general rule, the front tyres wear out faster than the rears. Interchanging the tyres from front to rear ("rotating" the tyres) may result in more even wear. However, if this is completely effective, you may have the expense of replacing all four tyres at once!

Remove any nails or stones embedded in the tread before they penetrate the tyre to cause deflation. If removal of a nail does reveal that the tyre has been punctured, refit the nail so that its point of penetration is marked. Then immediately change the wheel, and have the tyre repaired by a tyre dealer.

Regularly check the tyres for damage in the form of cuts or bulges, especially in the sidewalls. Periodically remove the wheels, and clean any dirt or mud from the inside and outside surfaces. Examine the wheel rims for signs of rusting, corrosion or other damage. Light alloy wheels are easily damaged by "kerbing" whilst parking; steel wheels may also become dented or buckled. A new wheel is very often the only way to overcome severe damage.

New tyres should be balanced when they are fitted, but it may become necessary to re-balance them as they wear, or if the balance weights fitted to the wheel rim should fall off. Unbalanced tyres will wear more quickly, as will the steering and suspension components. Wheel imbalance is normally signified by vibration, particularly at a certain speed (typically around 50 mph). If this vibration is felt only through the steering, then it is likely that just the front wheels need balancing. If, however, the vibration is felt through the whole car, the rear wheels could be out of balance. Wheel balancing should be carried out by a tyre dealer or garage.

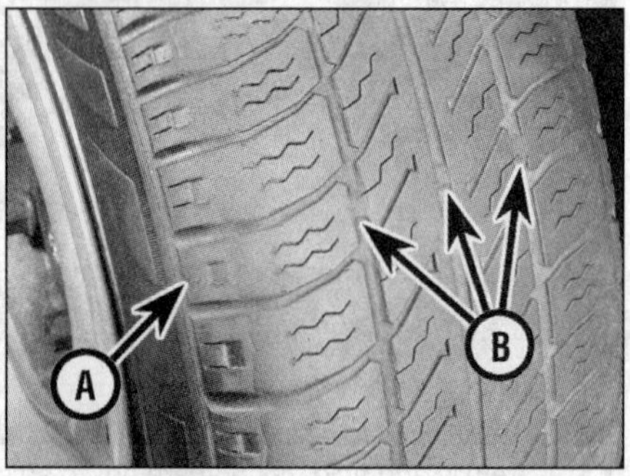

1 *Tread Depth - visual check*

The original tyres have tread wear safety bands (B), which will appear when the tread depth reaches approximately 1.6 mm. The band positions are indicated by a triangular mark on the tyre sidewall (A).

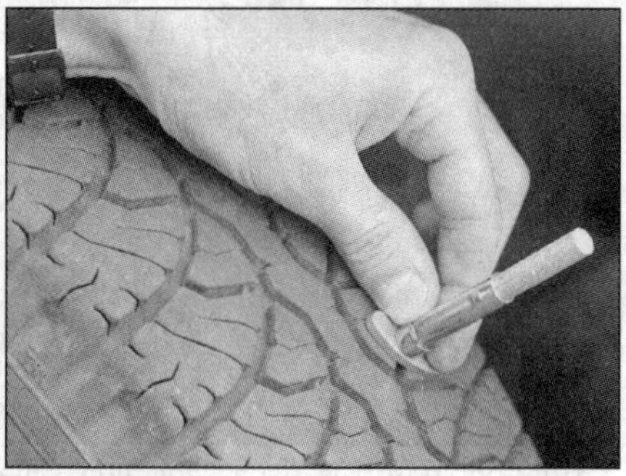

2 *Tread Depth - manual check*

Alternatively, tread wear can be monitored with a simple, inexpensive device known as a tread depth indicator gauge.

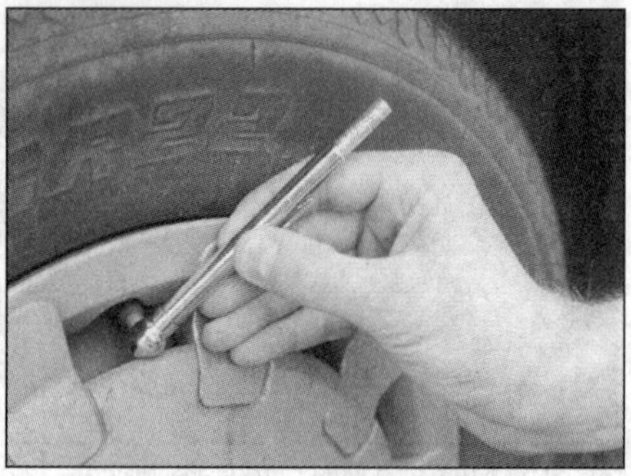

3 *Tyre Pressure Check*

Check the tyre pressures regularly with the tyres cold. Do not adjust the tyre pressures immediately after the vehicle has been used, or an inaccurate setting will result.

Tyre tread wear patterns

Shoulder Wear

Underinflation (wear on both sides)
Under-inflation will cause overheating of the tyre, because the tyre will flex too much, and the tread will not sit correctly on the road surface. This will cause a loss of grip and excessive wear, not to mention the danger of sudden tyre failure due to heat build-up.
Check and adjust pressures
Incorrect wheel camber (wear on one side)
Repair or renew suspension parts
Hard cornering
Reduce speed!

Centre Wear

Overinflation
Over-inflation will cause rapid wear of the centre part of the tyre tread, coupled with reduced grip, harsher ride, and the danger of shock damage occurring in the tyre casing.
Check and adjust pressures

If you sometimes have to inflate your car's tyres to the higher pressures specified for maximum load or sustained high speed, don't forget to reduce the pressures to normal afterwards.

Uneven Wear

Front tyres may wear unevenly as a result of wheel misalignment. Most tyre dealers and garages can check and adjust the wheel alignment (or "tracking") for a modest charge.
Incorrect camber or castor
Repair or renew suspension parts
Malfunctioning suspension
Repair or renew suspension parts
Unbalanced wheel
Balance tyres
Incorrect toe setting
Adjust front wheel alignment
Note: *The feathered edge of the tread which typifies toe wear is best checked by feel.*

Wiper blades

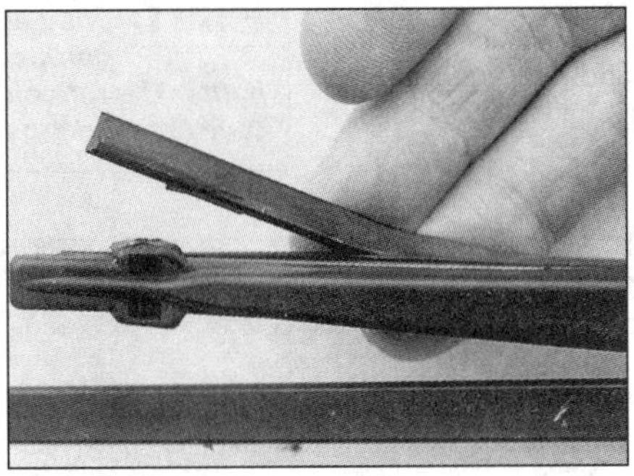

1 Check the condition of the wiper blades; if they are cracked or show any signs of deterioration, or if the glass swept area is smeared, renew them. For maximum clarity of vision, wiper blades should be renewed annually.

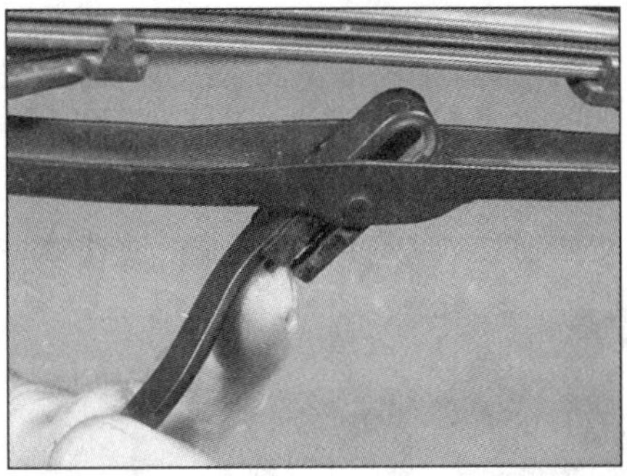

2 To remove a wiper blade, pull the arm fully away from the glass until it locks. Swivel the blade through 90°, then squeeze the locking clip, and detach the blade from the arm. When fitting the new blade, make sure that the blade locks securely into the arm, and that the blade is orientated correctly.

Battery

Caution: Before carrying out any work on the vehicle battery, read the precautions given in 'Safety first!' at the start of this manual.

✔ Make sure that the battery tray is in good condition, and that the clamp is tight. Any 'white' corrosion on the terminals or surrounding area can be removed with a solution of water and baking soda; thoroughly rinse all cleaned areas with water. Any metal parts damaged by corrosion should be covered with a zinc-based primer, then painted.

✔ Periodically (approximately every three months), check the charge condition of the battery as described in Chapter 5A.

✔ If the battery is flat, and you need to jump start your vehicle, see *Roadside Repairs*.

1 The battery is located on the left-hand side of the engine compartment. Where necessary, prise open the plastic cover for access to the positive terminal. The exterior of the battery should be inspected periodically for damage such as a cracked case or cover.

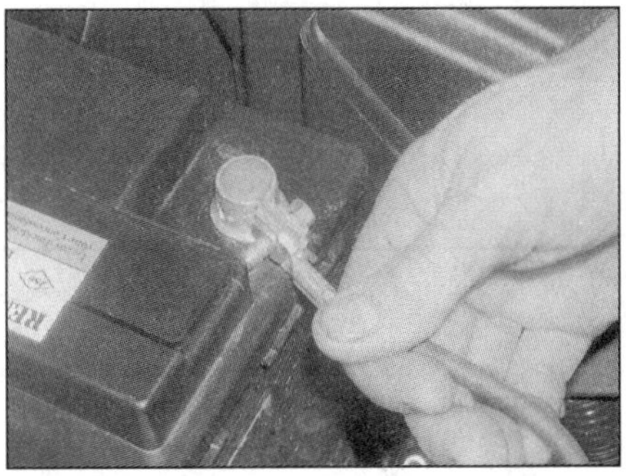

2 Check the tightness of battery clamps to ensure good electrical connections. You should not be able to move them. Also check each cable for cracks and frayed conductors.

HAYNES HiNT

Battery corrosion can be kept to a minimum by applying a layer of petroleum jelly to the clamps and terminals after they are reconnected.

3 If corrosion (white, fluffy deposits) is evident, remove the cables from the battery terminals, clean them with a small wire brush, then refit them. Automotive stores sell a tool for cleaning the battery post . . .

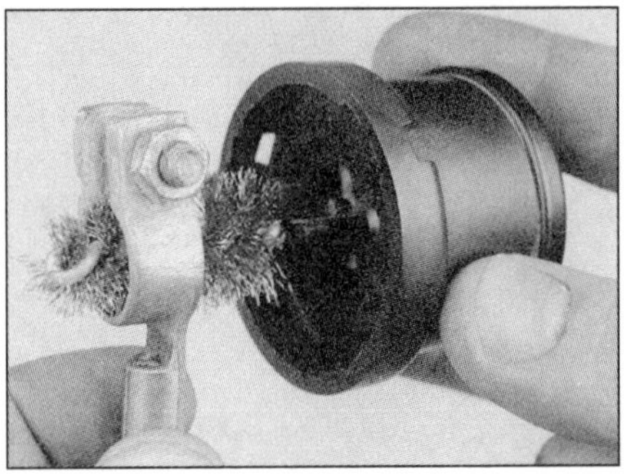

4 . . . as well as the battery cable clamps

Electrical systems

✔ Check all external lights and the horn. Refer to the appropriate Sections of Chapter 12 for details if any of the circuits are found to be inoperative.

✔ Visually check all accessible wiring connectors, harnesses and retaining clips for security, and for signs of chafing or damage.

HAYNES HiNT ***If you need to check your brake lights and indicators unaided, back up to a wall or garage door and operate the lights. The reflected light should show if they are working properly.***

1 If a single indicator light, stop-light or headlight has failed, it is likely that a bulb has blown and will need to be replaced. Refer to *Electrical fault finding* in Chapter 12 for details. If both stop-lights have failed, it is possible that the switch has failed (see Chapter 9).

2 If more than one indicator light or headlight has failed, it is likely that either a fuse has blown or that there is a fault in the circuit (see Chapter 12). The main fuses are located on the left-hand end of the instrument panel. Open the left-hand door then prise off the fusebox cover. The fuse locations are indicated by symbols on the rear of the cover. Additional fuses and relays are located in the left-hand side of the engine compartment.

3 To replace a blown fuse, remove it using the plastic tool provided. Fit a new fuse of the same rating, available from car accessory shops. It is important that you find the reason that the fuse failed (see *Electrical fault finding* in Chapter 12).

Lubricants and fluids

Petrol engine	Multigrade engine oil, viscosity range SAE 15W/40 to 15W/50, to ACEA A2-A3 *(Duckhams Fully Synthetic Engine Oil, QXR Premium Petrol Engine Oil, or Hypergrade Petrol Engine Oil)*
Diesel engine	Multigrade engine oil, viscosity range SAE 15W/40 to 15W/50, to ACEA B2-B3 *(Duckhams Fully Synthetic Engine Oil, QXR Premium Diesel Engine Oil, or Hypergrade Diesel Engine Oil)*
Cooling system	Ethylene glycol-based antifreeze – RX Glacéol type D coolant *(Duckhams Antifreeze and Summer Coolant)*
Manual gearbox	Elf Tranself TRX 75W/80W gear oil
Automatic transmission	Elf Renaultmatic D3 SYN, Dexron III ATF *(Duckhams ATF Autotrans III)*
Power steering reservoir	Elf Renaultmatic D2, Dexron II ATF *(Duckhams ATF Autotrans III)*
Brake fluid reservoir	Hydraulic fluid to SAE J1703F or DOT 4 *(Duckhams Universal Brake and Clutch Fluid)*

Choosing your engine oil

Engines need oil, not only to lubricate moving parts and minimise wear, but also to maximise power output and to improve fuel economy. By introducing a simplified and improved range of engine oils, Duckhams has taken away the confusion and made it easier for you to choose the right oil for your engine.

HOW ENGINE OIL WORKS

• Beating friction

Without oil, the moving surfaces inside your engine will rub together, heat up and melt, quickly causing the engine to seize. Engine oil creates a film which separates these moving parts, preventing wear and heat build-up.

• Cooling hot-spots

Temperatures inside the engine can exceed 1000° C. The engine oil circulates and acts as a coolant, transferring heat from the hot-spots to the sump.

• Cleaning the engine internally

Good quality engine oils clean the inside of your engine, collecting and dispersing combustion deposits and controlling them until they are trapped by the oil filter or flushed out at oil change.

OIL CARE - FOLLOW THE CODE

To handle and dispose of used engine oil safely, always:

OIL CARE
FOLLOW THE CODE
OIL BANK LINE
0800 66 33 66
www.oilbankline.org.uk

- ***Avoid skin contact with used engine oil. Repeated or prolonged contact can be harmful.***
- ***Dispose of used oil and empty packs in a responsible manner in an authorised disposal site. Call 0800 663366 to find the one nearest to you. Never tip oil down drains or onto the ground.***

DUCKHAMS ENGINE OILS

For the driver who demands a premium quality oil for complete reassurance, we recommend synthetic formula **Duckhams QXR Premium Engine Oils**.

For the driver who requires a straight-forward quality engine oil, we recommend **Duckhams Hypergrade Engine Oils**.

For further information and advice, call the Duckhams UK Helpline on 0800 212988.

DUCKHAMS

Tyre pressures (cold)

Note: *Pressures apply to original-equipment tyres, and may vary if any other make or type of tyre is fitted; check with the tyre manufacturer or supplier for correct pressures if necessary. The pressures are given on the inside of the fuel filler flap.*

	Front	Rear
1.2 litre models		
Normal use	29 psi (2.0 bar)	29 psi (2.0 bar)
Full load	32 psi (2.2 bar)	30 psi (2.1 bar)
1.4 and 1.9 litre models		
Normal use	32 psi (2.2 bar)	29 psi (2.0 bar)
Full load	33 psi (2.3 bar)	30 psi (2.1 bar)
1.6 litre models		
Normal use	33 psi (2.3 bar)	29 psi (2.0 bar)
Full load	35 psi (2.4 bar)	30 psi (2.1 bar)
Emergency spare wheel		
All models	61 psi (4.2 bar)	

Chapter 1 Part A:
Routine maintenance and servicing – petrol models

Contents

Degrees of difficulty

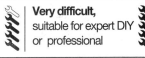

Easy, suitable for novice with little experience	**Fairly easy,** suitable for beginner with some experience	**Fairly difficult,** suitable for competent DIY mechanic	**Difficult,** suitable for experienced DIY mechanic	**Very difficult,** suitable for expert DIY or professional

Lubricants and fluids

Refer to *Weekly checks* on page 0•19

Capacities

Engine oil	Excluding oil filter	Including oil filter
1.2 litre D7F engine	3.5 litres	3.7 litres
1.4 litre E7J engine	2.7 litres	2.9 litres
1.4 litre K4J engine	4.25 litres	4.75 litres
1.6 litre K7M engine	3.5 litres	3.7 litres
1.6 litre K4M engine	4.25 litres	4.75 litres

Cooling system

1.2 litre D7F engine	5.0 litres
1.4 litre E7J engine	5.5 litres
1.4 litre K4J engine	5.7 litres
1.6 litre K7M engine	5.5 litres
1.6 litre K4M engine	5.7 litres
Manual gearbox	3.4 litres
Automatic transmission	6.0 litres
Power-assisted steering reservoir	
Models with mechanical pump	1.1 litres
Models with electric pump	0.7 litre
Fuel tank (All models)	50 litres

Cooling system

Antifreeze mixture:	Antifreeze	Water
Protection to –23°C	35%	65%
Protection to –40°C	50%	50%

Fuel system

Specified idle speed (non-adjustable):	
1.2 litre D7F engine	740 ± 50 rpm
All other engines	750 ± 50 rpm
Idle mixture CO content (non-adjustable)	0.5% maximum (0.3% at 2500 rpm)

Ignition system

Firing order	1-3-4-2
Location of No 1 cylinder	Flywheel end
Ignition timing	Controlled by ECU – see Chapter 5B
Spark plugs:	
1.2 litre D7F engine	Eyquem RFC 50 LZ 2E or NGK BKR 5 ES
1.4 litre:	
E7J engine	Champion RC 10 PYC or RC 10 YCL
K4J engine	Bosch RFC 50 LZ 2E
1.6 litre:	
K4M engine	Bosch RFC 50 LZ 2E
K7M engine	Eyquem RFC 50 LZ 2E
Spark plug electrode gap	0.9 mm

Brakes

Front disc brakes:	
Pad thickness (including backing):	
New	18.0 mm
Minimum thickness	6.0 mm
Rear disc brakes:	
Pad thickness (including backing):	
New	15.0 mm
Minimum thickness	6.0 mm
Rear drum brakes:	
Shoe thickness (including backing):	
New:	
1.2 litre D7F engine	4.85 mm
Other engine types:	
Leading	4.6 mm
Trailing	3.3 mm
Minimum thickness	2.0 mm

Torque wrench settings	Nm	lbf ft
Roadwheel bolts	90	66
Spark plugs	25 to 30	18 to 22
Sump:		
1.2 litre D7F engine	10	7
1.4 litre E7J engine	8	6
1.4 litre K4J engine:		
Stage 1	8	6
Stage 2	14	10
1.6 litre K7M engine	9	7
1.6 litre K4M engine:		
Stage 1	8	6
Stage 2	14	10

Maintenance schedule - petrol models

The maintenance intervals in this manual are provided with the assumption that you, not the dealer, will be carrying out the work. These are the minimum maintenance intervals recommended by us for vehicles driven daily. If you wish to keep your vehicle in peak condition at all times, you may wish to perform some of these procedures more often. We encourage frequent maintenance, because it enhances the efficiency, performance and resale value of your vehicle.

If the vehicle is driven in dusty areas, used to tow a trailer, or driven frequently at slow speeds (idling in traffic) or on short journeys, more frequent maintenance intervals are recommended.

When the vehicle is new, it should be serviced by a factory-authorised dealer service department, in order to preserve the factory warranty.

Note: *As from January 2001, Renault introduced servicing intervals based on 18 000 miles (30 000 km) instead of 12 000 miles (20 000 km). No information is available at the time of writing, but if necessary, consult a Renault dealer to confirm the interval applicable to your model.*

Every 250 miles (400 km) or weekly

- ☐ Refer to *Weekly Checks*

Every 6000 miles (10 000 km)

- ☐ Renew the engine oil and filter (Section 3)

Note: *Frequent oil and filter changes are good for the engine. We recommend changing the oil at the mileage specified here, or at least twice a year if the mileage covered is a less.*

Every 12 000 miles (20 000 km)

- ☐ Renew the pollen filter (Section 4)
- ☐ Power steering fluid level check (Section 5)
- ☐ Check the brake pad thickness and discs (Section 6)
- ☐ Check the operation of the handbrake (Section 7)
- ☐ Check the operation of the clutch (Section 8)
- ☐ Check the condition of the auxiliary drivebelts (Section 9)
- ☐ Check the condition of the seat belts (Section 10)
- ☐ Check the operation of all electrical systems (Section 11)
- ☐ Check the condition of the exhaust system and mountings (Section 12)
- ☐ Check the suspension and steering components (Section 13)
- ☐ Check all underbonnet components and hoses for fluid leaks (Section 14)
- ☐ Check the tightness of the roadwheel bolts (Section 15)
- ☐ Check the bodywork and underbody for damage and corrosion (Section 16)
- ☐ Check the front and rear shock absorbers (Section 17)

Every 36 000 miles (60 000 km)

In addition to all the items listed previously, carry out the following:

- ☐ Renew the spark plugs and check the ignition system (Section 18)
- ☐ Renew the air filter element (Section 19)
- ☐ Renew the fuel filter element (Section 20)
- ☐ Check the rear brake shoes and drums (Section 21)
- ☐ Check the manual transmission oil level (Section 22)
- ☐ Check the front wheel alignment (Section 23)
- ☐ Check the operation of the air conditioning system (Section 24)
- ☐ Carry out a road test (Section 25)
- ☐ Renew the timing belt (Section 26)

Note: *Although the normal interval for timing belt renewal is 72 000 miles (120 000 km), it is strongly recommended that the interval is halved to 36 000 miles (60 000 km) on vehicles which are subjected to intensive use, ie, mainly short journeys or a lot of stop-start driving. The actual belt renewal interval is therefore very much up to the individual owner, but bear in mind that severe engine damage may result if the belt breaks.*

Every 72 000 miles (120 000 km) or every 4 years, whichever comes first

In addition to all the items listed previously, carry out the following:

- ☐ Renew the brake fluid (Section 27)
- ☐ Renew the coolant (Section 28)

Every 4 years

- ☐ On models fitted with a self-contained airbag, renew the batteries (Section 29)

Underbonnet view of a 1.2 litre petrol model (D7F engine)

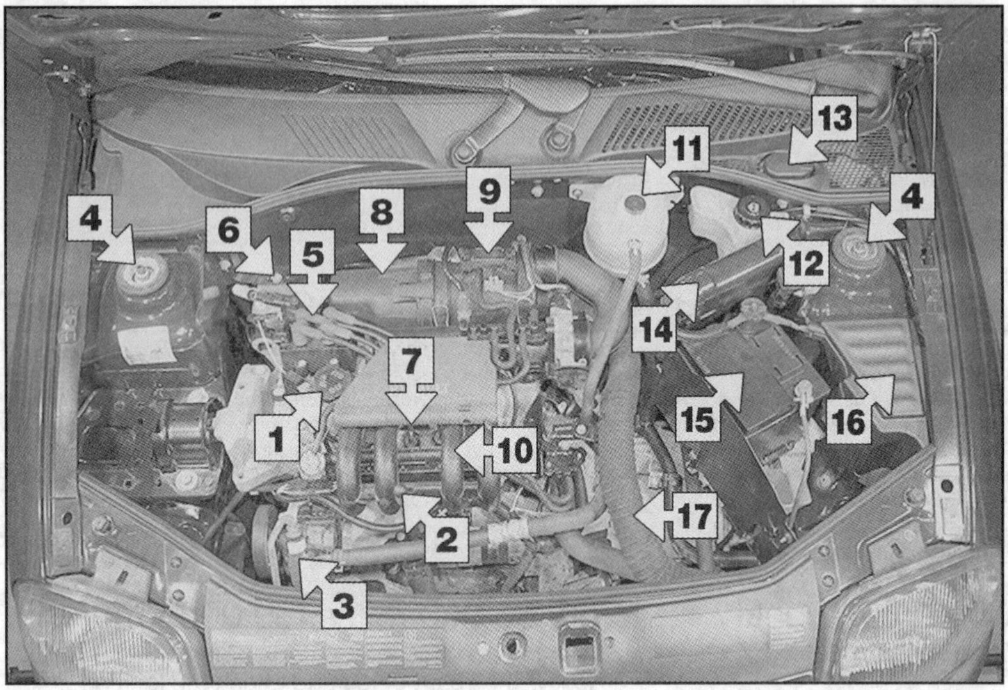

1. *Engine oil filler cap*
2. *Engine oil level dipstick*
3. *Power steering pump*
4. *Front suspension strut upper mountings*
5. *Ignition HT coils*
6. *Brake master cylinder fluid reservoir*
7. *HT lead removal tool*
8. *Air cleaner*
9. *Absolute air pressure MAP sensor*
10. *Inlet manifold*
11. *Coolant expansion tank*
12. *Power steering fluid reservoir*
13. *Windscreen/headlight washer fluid reservoir*
14. *Engine management ECU*
15. *Battery*
16. *Engine related fusebox*
17. *Air inlet duct*

Front underbody view of a 1.2 litre petrol model (D7F engine)

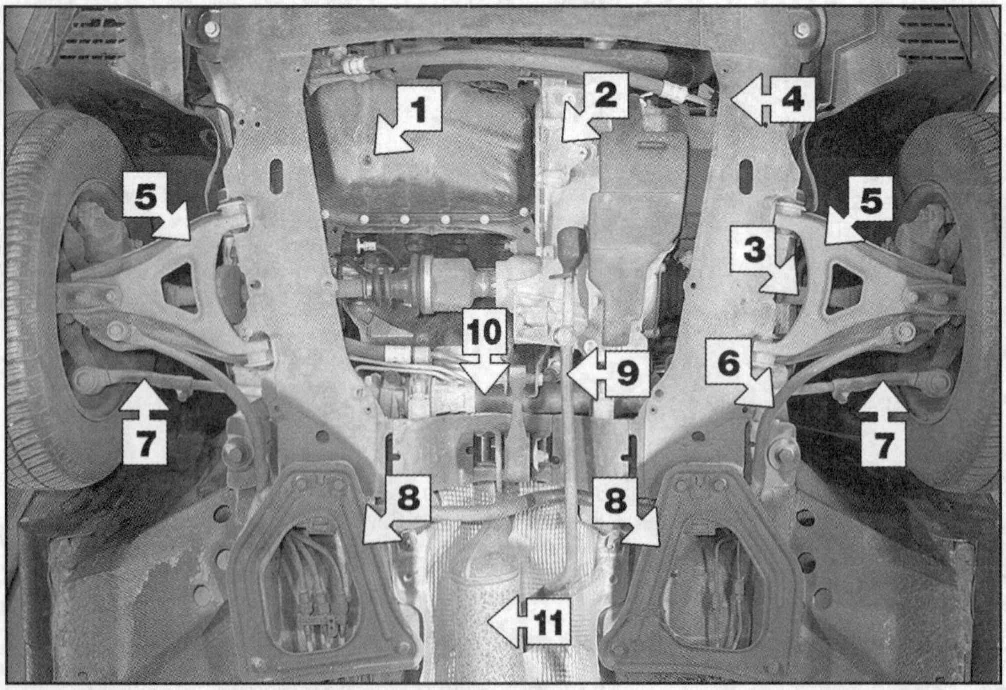

1. *Engine oil sump drain plug*
2. *Manual transmission*
3. *Driveshafts*
4. *Front suspension subframe*
5. *Front suspension lower arms*
6. *Front anti-roll bar*
7. *Track rod ends*
8. *Front subframe rear links*
9. *Gearchange rod*
10. *Power steering gear*
11. *Exhaust catalytic converter*

Rear underbody view of a 1.2 litre petrol model

1 Fuel tank
2 Handbrake cables
3 Fuel filter
4 Fuel feed and return lines
5 Rear brake compensator
6 Rear axle assembly
7 Rear coil springs
8 Exhaust rear silencer and tailpipe
9 Shock absorbers

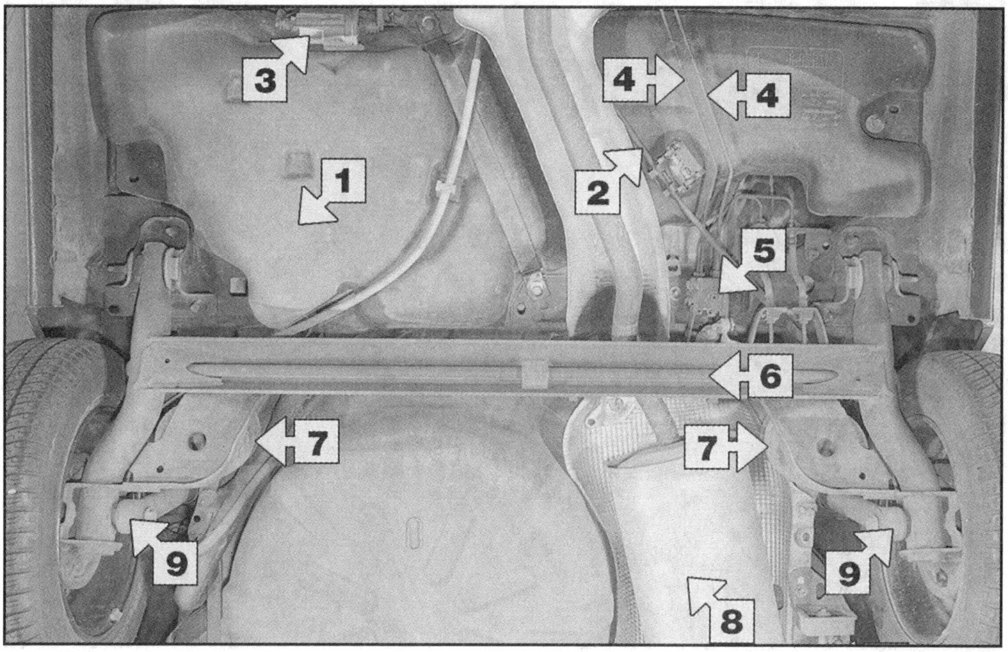

Underbonnet view of a 1.4 litre 8-valve petrol model (E7J engine)

1 Engine oil filler cap
2 Engine oil level dipstick
3 Ignition HT coils and leads
4 Alternator
5 Front suspension strut upper mountings
6 Brake master cylinder fluid reservoir
7 Air cleaner
8 Coolant expansion tank
9 Power steering fluid reservoir
10 Engine management ECU
11 Battery
12 Engine related fusebox
13 Air inlet duct
14 Exhaust manifold and hot air shroud
15 Oil filter

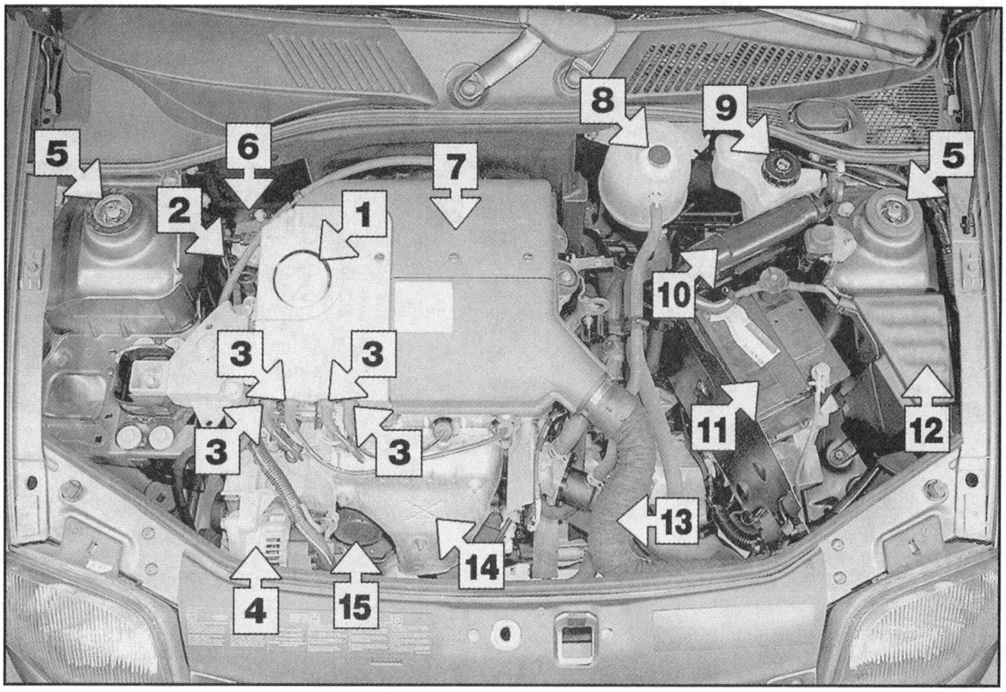

Front underbody view of a 1.4 litre 8-valve petrol model (E7J engine)

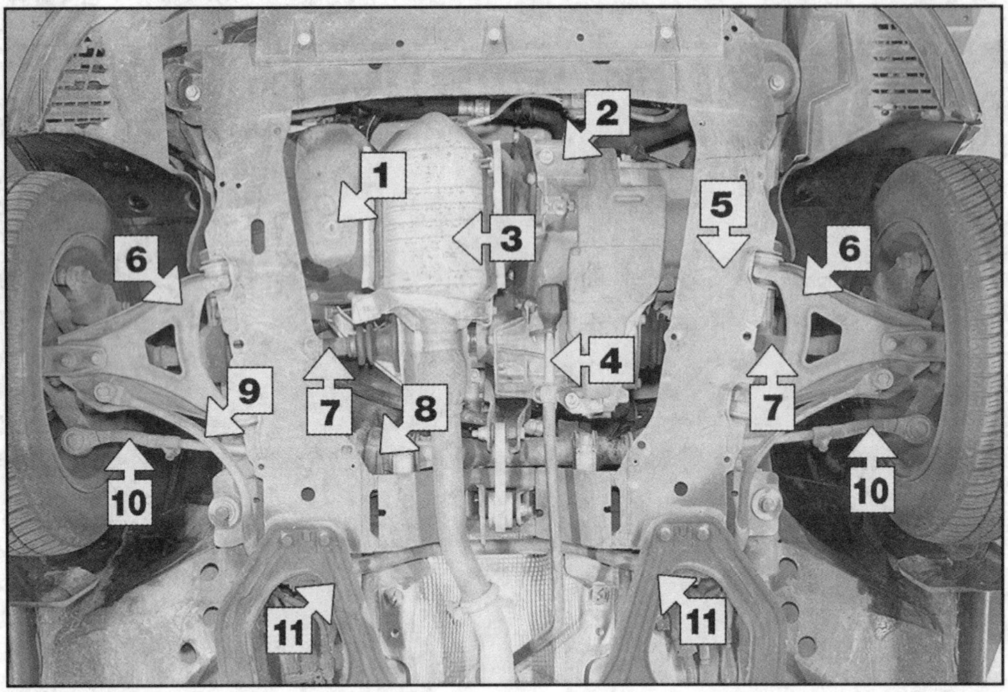

1 *Engine oil sump drain plug*
2 *Manual transmission*
3 *Exhaust catalytic converter*
4 *Gearchange rod*
5 *Front suspension subframe*
6 *Front suspension lower arms*
7 *Driveshafts*
8 *Power steering gear*
9 *Front anti-roll bar*
10 *Track rod ends*
11 *Front subframe rear links*

Underbonnet view of a 1.4 litre 16-valve petrol model (K4J engine)

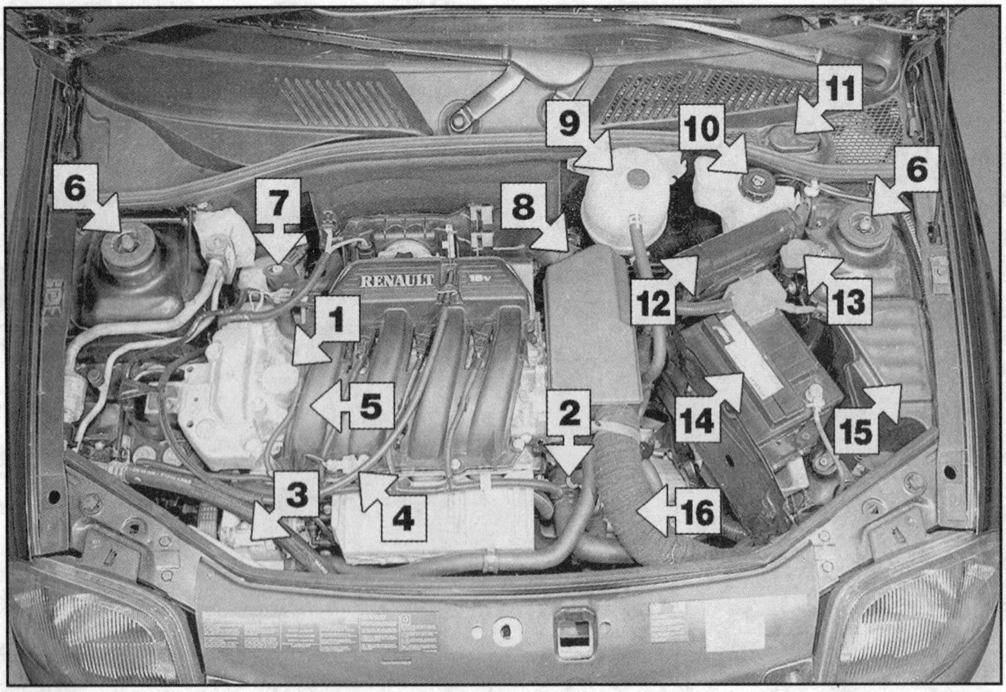

1 *Engine oil filler cap*
2 *Engine oil level dipstick*
3 *Power steering pump*
4 *Accelerator cable*
5 *Inlet manifold*
6 *Front suspension strut upper mountings*
7 *Brake master cylinder fluid reservoir*
8 *Air cleaner*
9 *Coolant expansion tank*
10 *Power steering fluid reservoir*
11 *Windscreen/headlight washer fluid reservoir*
12 *Engine management ECU*
13 *Fuel cut-off inertia switch*
14 *Battery*
15 *Engine related fusebox*
16 *Air inlet duct*

Front underbody view of a 1.4 litre 16-valve petrol model (K4J engine)

1 Engine oil sump drain plug
2 Manual transmission
3 Driveshafts
4 Front suspension subframe
5 Front suspension lower arms
6 Front anti-roll bar
7 Track rod ends
8 Front subframe rear links
9 Gearchange rod
10 Power steering gear
11 Exhaust catalytic converter

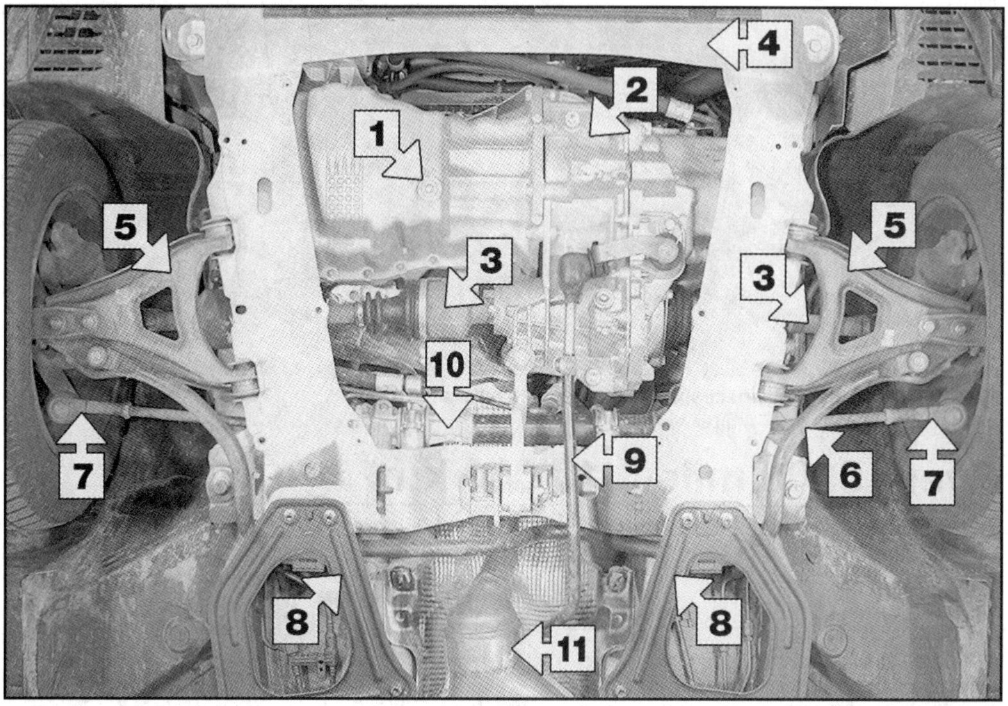

Maintenance procedures

1 Introduction

This Chapter is designed to help the home mechanic maintain his/her vehicle for safety, economy, long life and peak performance.

The Chapter contains a master maintenance schedule, followed by Sections dealing specifically with each task in the schedule. Visual checks, adjustments, component renewal and other helpful items are included. Refer to the accompanying illustrations of the engine compartment and the underside of the vehicle for the locations of the various components.

Servicing your vehicle in accordance with the mileage/time maintenance schedule and the following Sections will provide a planned maintenance programme, which should result in a long and reliable service life. This is a comprehensive plan, so maintaining some items but not others at the specified service intervals, will not produce the same results.

As you service your vehicle, you will discover that many of the procedures can – and should – be grouped together, because of the particular procedure being performed, or because of the proximity of two otherwise-unrelated components to one another. For example, if the vehicle is raised for any reason, the exhaust can be inspected at the same time as the suspension and steering components.

The first step in this maintenance programme is to prepare yourself before the actual work begins. Read through all the Sections relevant to the work to be carried out, then make a list and gather all the parts and tools required. If a problem is encountered, seek advice from a parts specialist, or a dealer service department.

2 Regular maintenance

If, from the time the vehicle is new, the routine maintenance schedule is followed closely, and frequent checks are made of fluid levels and high-wear items, as suggested throughout this manual, the engine will be kept in relatively good running condition, and the need for additional work will be minimised.

It is possible that there will be times when the engine is running poorly due to the lack of regular maintenance. This is even more likely if a used vehicle, which has not received regular and frequent maintenance checks, is purchased. In such cases, additional work may need to be carried out, outside of the regular maintenance intervals.

If engine wear is suspected, a compression test (refer to Chapter 2A or 2B as applicable) will provide valuable information regarding the overall performance of the main internal components. Such a test can be used as a basis to decide on the extent of the work to be carried out. If, for example, a compression test indicates serious internal engine wear, conventional maintenance as described in this Chapter will not greatly improve the performance of the engine, and may prove a waste of time and money, unless extensive overhaul work is carried out first.

The following series of operations are those most often required to improve the performance of a generally poor-running engine:

Primary operations

a) Clean, inspect and test the battery (refer to 'Weekly checks').
b) Check all the engine-related fluids (refer to 'Weekly checks').
c) Check the condition of the auxiliary drivebelt(s) (Section 9).
d) Check the condition of all hoses, and check for fluid leaks (Section 14).
e) Renew the spark plugs (Section 18).
f) Check the condition of the air filter, and renew if necessary (Section 19).
g) Check the fuel filter, and renew if necessary (Section 20).

If the above operations do not prove fully effective, carry out the following secondary operations:

Secondary operations

All items listed under *Primary operations*, plus the following:

a) Check the charging system (Chapter 5A).
b) Check the ignition system (Chapter 5B).
c) Check the fuel system (refer to Chapter 4A).

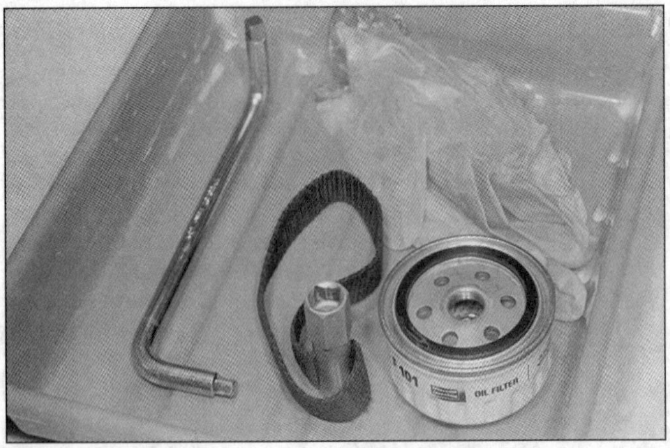

3.1 Tools and materials necessary for the engine oil change and filter renewal

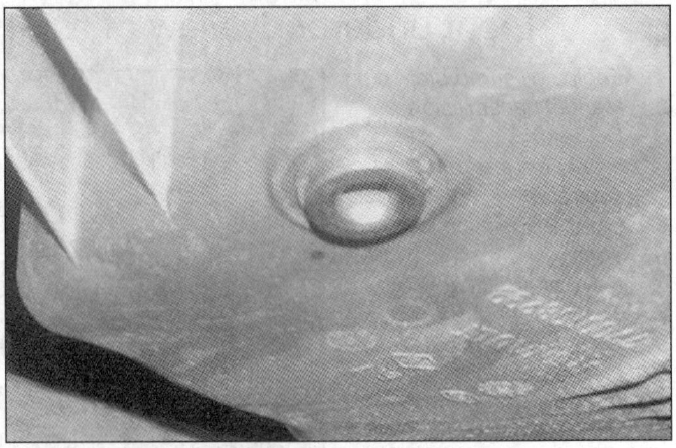

3.2 Engine oil drain plug – K4J engine

Every 6000 miles (10 000 km)

3 Engine oil and filter renewal

1 Before starting this procedure, gather together all the necessary tools and materials **(see illustration)**. Also make sure that you have plenty of clean rags and newspapers handy to mop up any spills. Ideally, the engine oil should be warm, as it will drain better and more built-up sludge will be removed with it. Take care, however, not to touch the exhaust or any other hot parts of the engine when working under the vehicle. To avoid any possibility of scalding, and to protect yourself from possible skin irritants and other harmful contaminants in used engine oils, it is advisable to wear rubber gloves when carrying out this work. Apply the handbrake, then jack up the front of the vehicle and support it on axle stands (see *Jacking and vehicle support*). Alternatively, raise the vehicle on a lift or drive it onto ramps. Whichever method is chosen, make sure that the car remains as level as possible, to enable the oil to drain fully. Remove the engine undertray where applicable.

2 Remove the oil filler cap from the valve cover, then position a suitable container beneath the sump. Clean the drain plug and the area around it, then slacken it half a turn using a special drain plug key (8 mm square) **(see illustration)**.

HAYNES HiNT ***If possible, try to keep the plug pressed into the sump while unscrewing it by hand the last couple of turns. As the plug releases from the threads, move it away sharply so the stream of oil issuing from the sump runs into the container, not up your sleeve.***

3 Allow some time for the old oil to drain, noting that it may be necessary to reposition the container as the oil flow slows to a trickle.

4 After all the oil has drained, wipe off the drain plug with a clean rag and renew its sealing washer. Clean the area around the drain plug opening, then refit and tighten the plug securely.

5 Move the container into position under the oil filter, located on the front of the cylinder block on all except D7F engines, or at the rear timing belt end corner of the engine on D7F engines **(see illustration)**.

6 On the K4J and K4M 16-valve engines, there is only limited room between the subframe and the sump, and it is very difficult to reach up to the oil filter. However, it is possible to gain access through this space, and it is not necessary to remove any body or engine components **(see illustration)**.

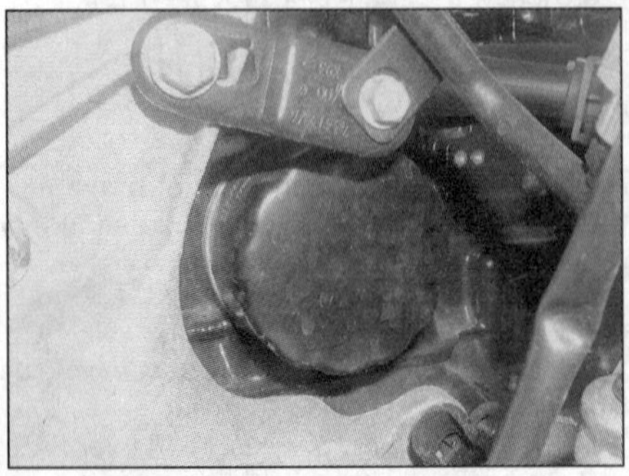

3.5 Oil filter location – K4J engine

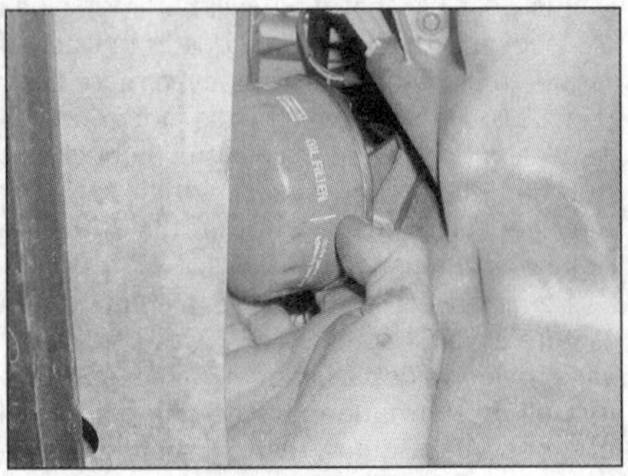

3.6 Removing the oil filter – K4J engine

7 Using an oil filter removal tool, slacken the filter initially. Loosely wrap some rags around the oil filter, then unscrew it and immediately position it with its open end uppermost to prevent further spillage of oil. Remove the oil filter from the engine compartment and empty the oil into the container.

8 Use a clean rag to remove all oil, dirt and sludge from the filter sealing area on the engine. Check the old filter to make sure that the rubber sealing ring hasn't stuck to the engine. If it has, carefully remove it.

9 Apply a light coating of clean oil to the sealing ring on the new filter, then screw it into position on the engine. Tighten the filter firmly by hand only – do not use any tools. Wipe clean the exterior of the oil filter.

10 Remove the old oil and all tools from under the car, then, where necessary, refit the undertray and lower the car to the ground.

11 Fill the engine with the specified quantity and grade of oil, as described in *Weekly checks*. Pour the oil in slowly, otherwise it may overflow from the top of the valve cover. Check that the oil level is up to the maximum mark on the dipstick, then refit and tighten the oil filler cap.

12 Start the engine and run it for a few minutes, checking that there are no leaks around the oil filter seal and the sump drain plug. Note that when the engine is first started, there will be a delay of a few seconds before the oil pressure warning light goes out while the new filter fills with oil. Do not race the engine while the warning light is on.

13 Switch off the engine and wait a few minutes for the oil to settle in the sump once more. With the new oil circulated and the filter now completely full, recheck the level on the dipstick and add more oil if necessary.

14 Dispose of the used engine oil safely with reference to *General repair procedures* in the *Reference* section of this manual.

4.2a Undo the screws . . .

4.2b . . . and unclip the cover from the pollen filter housing

4.3 Removing the pollen filter element. Note the direction arrows on the element and housing

Every 12 000 miles (20 000 km)

4 Pollen filter renewal

Note: *The pollen filter is not fitted to all models.*

1 With the bonnet open, remove the windscreen half-scuttle grille from the right-hand end of the bulkhead.

2 Undo the screws and unclip the cover from the pollen filter housing **(see illustrations)**.

3 Note the direction arrows on the filter and housing, then carefully extract the filter element by squeezing its central folds together **(see illustration)**.

4 Fit the new element using a reversal of the removal procedure, but make sure that the direction arrows are aligned with each other.

5 Power steering fluid level check

1 The power steering fluid reservoir is located on the rear left-hand corner of the engine compartment. The fluid level can be checked through the translucent reservoir, and should be between the MIN and MAX marks **(see illustration)**.

2 If topping-up is required, first wipe clean the filler cap and top of the reservoir, then unscrew and remove the cap, allowing any fluid to drain from the cap into the reservoir.

3 Top-up to the MAX level mark using the specified fluid given in *Lubricants and fluids* **(see illustration)**. On completion, refit and tighten the filler cap.

6 Brake pad and disc check

1 Firmly apply the handbrake, then jack up the front or of the vehicle (as applicable) and support it securely on axle stands (see *Jacking and vehicle support*). Remove the roadwheels.

2 For a quick check, the thickness of friction material remaining on each brake pad can be measured through the aperture in the caliper body **(see Haynes Hint)**. If any pad's friction material is worn to the specified thickness or less, all four pads must be renewed as a set. Pad wear warning contacts are fitted to the inboard pads, but this should not be used as an excuse for omitting a visual check.

3 For a comprehensive check, the brake pads should be removed and cleaned. This will allow the operation of the caliper to be checked, and the brake disc itself to be fully examined for condition on both sides. Refer to Chapter 9 for further information.

7 Handbrake check

1 The handbrake should be capable of holding the parked vehicle stationary, even on steep slopes, when applied with moderate force. The mechanism should be firm and positive in feel, with no trace of stiffness or sponginess from the cables, and should release immediately the handbrake lever is released. If the mechanism is faulty in any of these respects, it must be checked immediately as follows. **Note:** *On models with rear drum brakes, if the handbrake is not functioning correctly or is incorrectly adjusted, the rear brake self-adjust mechanism will not function. This will lead to the brake pedal travel becoming excessive as the shoe linings wear.*

2 According to model, handbrake adjustment is made either on the handbrake lever or beneath the vehicle on the cable adjuster nut. Where the adjustment is made on the lever, remove the trim (see Chapter 11, Section 27) for access to the nut and fully back it off.

3 Where the cable adjuster nut is beneath the vehicle, jack up the rear of the vehicle and support it on axle stands (see *Jacking and*

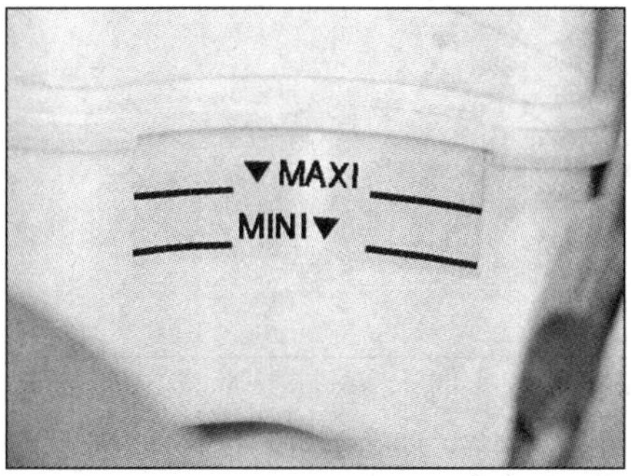

5.1 Level marks on the power steering fluid reservoir

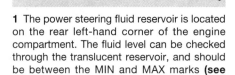

5.3 Topping-up the power steering fluid level

HAYNES HiNT

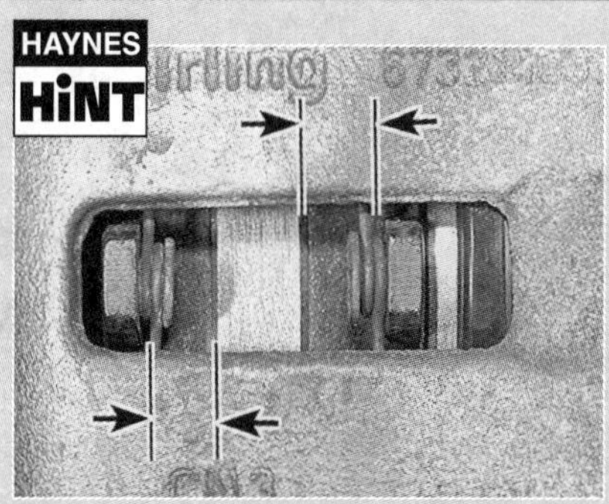

For a quick check, the thickness of friction material remaining on each brake pad can be measured through the aperture in the caliper body

7.3 Handbrake cable adjusting nut located beneath the vehicle

vehicle support). Undo the heat shield retaining nut(s) and lower the rear of the heat shield to gain access to the handbrake cable adjuster nut. Slacken the locknut, then fully slacken the cable adjuster nut **(see illustration)**.

Models with rear drum brakes

4 Remove both rear brake drums as described in Chapter 9.

5 Check that the knurled adjuster wheel on the adjuster strut is free to rotate in both directions. If it is seized, the brake shoes and strut must be removed and overhauled as described in Section 14 of Chapter 9.

6 If all is well, back off the adjuster wheel by five or six teeth so that the diameter of the brake shoes is slightly reduced.

7 Check that the handbrake cables slide freely by pulling on their front ends. Also check that the operating levers on the rear brake trailing shoes return to their correct positions, with their stop-pegs in contact with the edge of the trailing shoe web.

8 With the aid of an assistant, tighten the adjuster nut on the handbrake lever operating rod so that the lever on each rear brake assembly starts to move as the handbrake is moved between the first and second notch (click) of its ratchet mechanism. This is the case when the stop-pegs are still in contact with the shoes when the handbrake is on the first notch of the ratchet, but no longer contact the shoes when the handbrake is on the second notch. Once the adjustment is correct, hold the adjuster nut and securely tighten the locknut. Refit the catalytic converter heat shield retaining nuts.

9 Refit the brake drums as described in Chapter 9, then lower the vehicle to the ground.

10 With the vehicle standing on its wheels, repeatedly depress the footbrake to adjust the shoe-to-drum clearance. Whilst depressing the pedal, have an assistant listen to the rear drums to check that the adjuster strut mechanism is functioning; if this is so, a clicking sound will be heard from the adjuster strut as the pedal is depressed.

Models with rear disc brakes

11 Check that the handbrake cables slide freely by pulling on their front ends, and check that the operating levers on the rear brake calipers move smoothly.

12 Move both of the caliper operating levers as far rearwards as possible, then tighten the adjuster nut on the handbrake lever operating rod until all free play is removed from both cables. With the aid of an assistant, adjust the nut so that the operating lever on each rear brake caliper starts to move as the handbrake lever is moved between the first and second notch (click) of its ratchet mechanism. Once the handbrake adjustment is correct, hold the adjuster nut and securely tighten the locknut.

13 Refit the heat shield retaining nuts (where necessary), then lower the vehicle to the ground.

8 Clutch check

1 Check that the clutch pedal moves smoothly and easily through its full travel, and that the clutch itself functions correctly, with no trace of slip or drag. If the movement is uneven or stiff in places, check that the cable is routed correctly, with no sharp turns.

2 Inspect the ends of the clutch inner cable, both at the gearbox end and inside the car, for signs of wear and fraying.

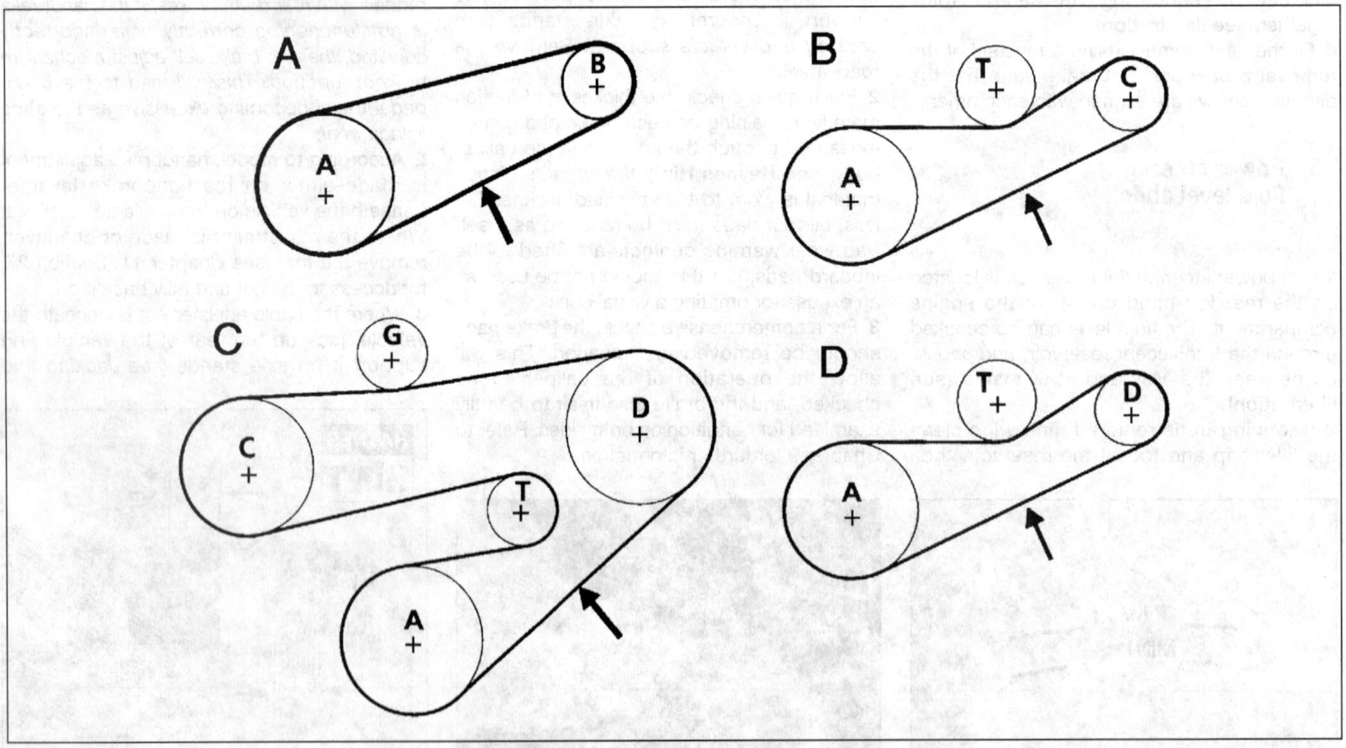

9.2a Auxiliary drivebelt configuration – D7F engine

A Alternator drivebelt
B Power steering pump drivebelt
C Alternator, PAS, and air conditioning compressor drivebelt
D Air conditioning compressor drivebelt

Pulley key: *Crankshaft (A), alternator (B), power steering pump (C), air conditioning compressor (D), roller (G) and tensioner (T)*

9 Auxiliary drivebelt check and renewal

Checking

1 The auxiliary drivebelt is located at the right-hand side of the engine.

2 Numerous different drivebelt configurations may be encountered, depending on engine type and whether the vehicle is equipped with air conditioning **(see illustrations)**.

3 Due to their function and material makeup, drivebelts are prone to failure after a period of time and should therefore be inspected and, where applicable, periodically adjusted.

4 Since the drivebelt is located very close to the right-hand side of the engine compartment, it is possible to gain better access by raising the front of the vehicle and removing the right-hand wheel, then removing the engine undercover (where applicable) and wheelarch liner from inside the wheelarch.

5 With the engine stopped, inspect the full length of the drivebelt for cracks and separation of the belt plies. It will be necessary to turn the engine (using a spanner or socket and bar on the crankshaft pulley bolt) in order to move the belt from the pulleys so that the belt can be inspected thoroughly. Twist the belt between the pulleys so that both sides can be viewed. Also check for

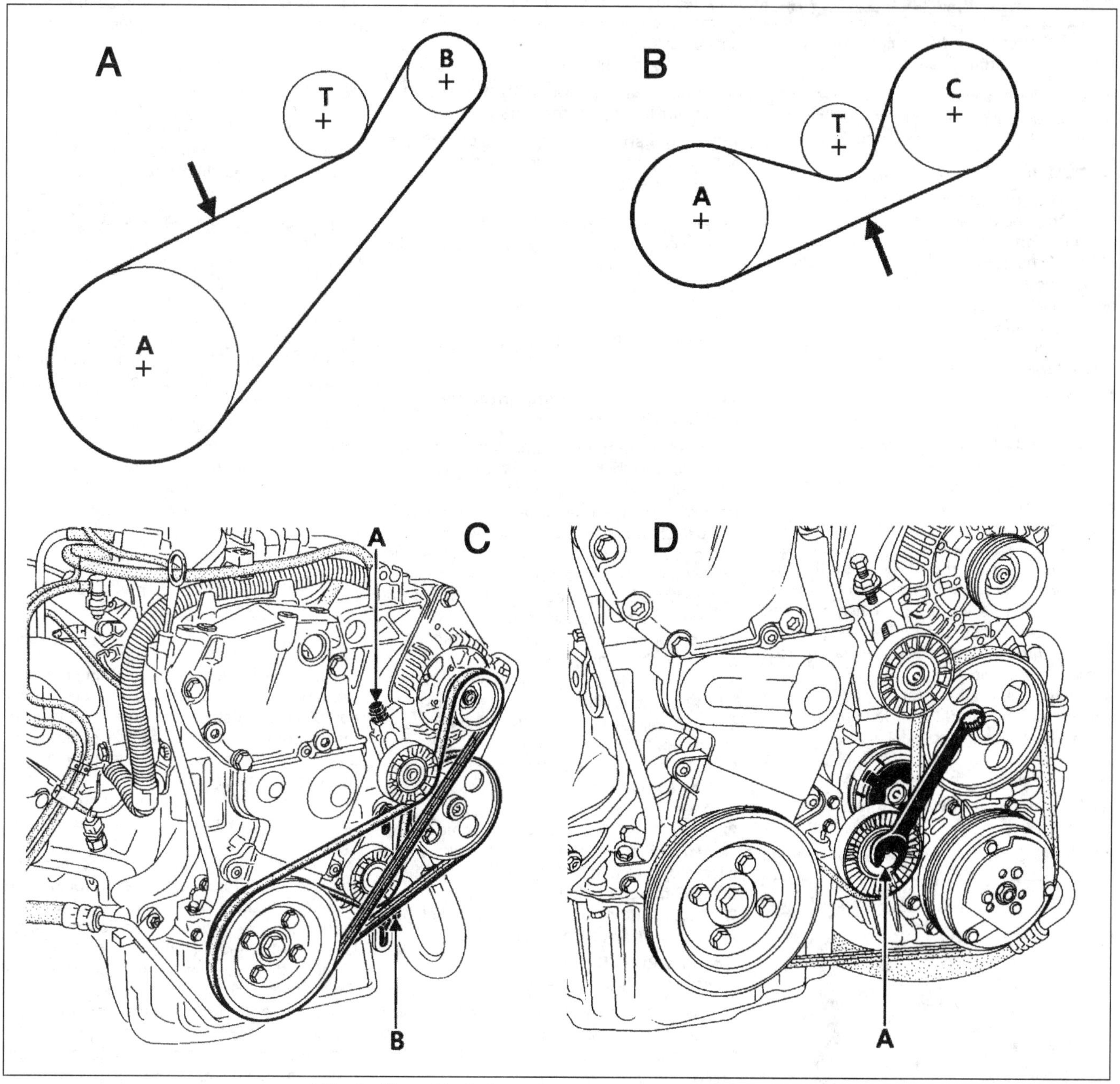

9.2b Auxiliary drivebelt configuration – E7J and K7M engines

A Alternator drivebelt
B Power steering pump drivebelt
C Alternator belt tension (A), and power steering pump belt tension (B)
D Spring tensioned tension roller (A)

Pulley key: *Crankshaft (A), alternator (B), power steering pump (C) and tensioner roller (T)*

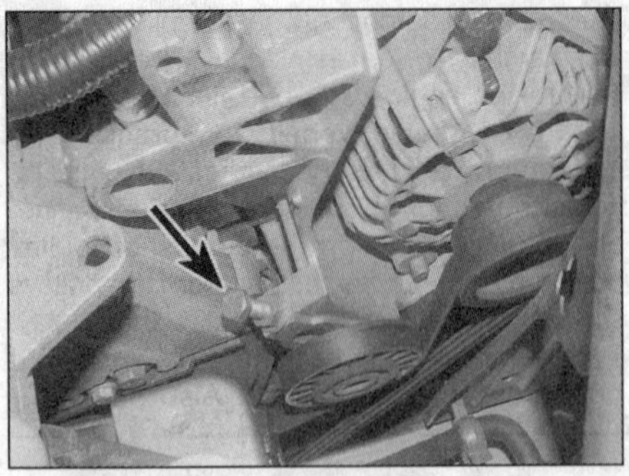

9.20 Alternator drivebelt tensioner adjustment bolt

fraying, and glazing which gives the belt a shiny appearance. Check the pulleys for nicks, cracks, distortion and corrosion.

Renewal - D7F engine

Note: *Where applicable, the tension of the belt is checked midway between the pulleys at the point indicated. The tension can only be checked and set using the Renault electronic measuring tool (Mot. 1273). If access to this equipment is not available, have the belt tension checked by a Renault dealer. The procedures in this Section assume that the Renault special tool is being used.*

Alternator

6 Remove the power steering pump drivebelt as described later in this Section.
7 Slacken the alternator mounting bolts, then move the alternator until the belt can be slipped from the pulleys.
8 Fit the belt around the pulleys, ensuring that the belt is of the correct type if it is being renewed. Take up the slack in the belt by swinging the alternator away from the engine and lightly tightening the mounting nuts and bolts. **Note:** *If necessary a threaded rod may be used through the bracket provided in order to tension the belt.*
9 Position the alternator to achieve the correct tension of 102 ± 7 Seem units, then tighten the mounting bolts fully.
10 On completion, where applicable, refit the power steering pump drivebelt.

PAS pump or air conditioning compressor

11 Working in the engine compartment, engage a suitable Allen key with the belt tensioner pulley centre bolt, then slacken the bolt. Use a spanner to release the tensioner pulley.
12 Slip the drivebelt from the pulleys.
13 Fit the belt around the pulleys, then take up the slack in the belt by turning the tensioner pulley with a spanner. Position the pulley to achieve the correct tension of 96 ± 5 Seem units for the PAS pump drivebelt, 104 ± 6 Seem units for the single air conditioning compressor drivebelt and 101 ± 6 Seem units for the combined compressor and PAS pump drivebelt.
14 Tighten the centre bolt.

10.3 Checking the security of the seat belt mountings

Combined alternator, PAS pump and air conditioning compressor

15 Using a spanner on the tensioner centre bolt, turn the tensioner clockwise to release the tension, then lift the drivebelt from the pulleys.
16 Fit the belt around the pulleys making sure that it is correctly located in the grooves. Turn the tensioner clockwise and engage the back of the belt, then release the tensioner to automatically tension the belt.

Renewal - E7J, K7M, K4J and K4M engines

Alternator or PAS pump (models without air conditioning)

17 If removing the PAS pump drivebelt, the alternator drivebelt must be removed first.
18 Apply the handbrake, then jack up the front of the car and support securely on axle stands (see *Jacking and vehicle support*). For improved access, remove the right-hand roadwheel, then remove the wheelarch liner, noting that it may be necessary to drill out the securing rivets on certain models.
19 Loosen the bolt securing the tensioner bracket to the engine.
20 Loosen the locknut and back off the tensioner adjustment bolt until the drivebelt can be removed from the pulleys **(see illustration)**.
21 Fit the drivebelt around the pulleys making sure that it is correctly located in the grooves.
22 Position the tensioner to achieve the correct tension of 101 ± 6 Seem units for the alternator drivebelt or 106 ± 6 Seem units for the PAS pump drivebelt.
23 Fully tighten the tensioner bracket bolt and the locknut for the adjustment bolt.

Combined PAS pump and air conditioning compressor

24 Using a spanner on the tensioner centre bolt, turn the tensioner clockwise to release the tension, then lift the drivebelt from the pulleys.
25 Fit the belt around the pulleys making sure that it is correctly located in the grooves. Turn the tensioner clockwise and engage the back of the belt, then release the tensioner to automatically tension the belt.

10 Seat belt check

1 Carefully examine the seat belt webbing for cuts, or any signs of serious fraying or deterioration. If the belt is of the retractable type, pull the belt all the way out of the inertia reel, and examine the full extent of the webbing.
2 Fasten and unfasten the belt, ensuring that the locking mechanism holds securely, and releases properly when intended. If the belt is of the retractable type, check also that the retracting mechanism operates correctly when the belt is released.
3 Check the security of all seat belt mountings and attachments which are accessible without removing any trim or other components **(see illustration)**.

11 Electrical systems check

1 Check the operation of all electrical equipment, ie, lights, direction indicators, horn, etc. Refer to the appropriate Sections of Chapter 12 for details if any of the circuits are found to be inoperative.
2 Note that stop-light switch adjustment is described in Chapter 9.
3 Visually check all accessible wiring connectors, harnesses and retaining clips for security, and for signs of chafing or damage. Rectify any faults found.

12 Exhaust system check

1 With the engine cold (at least an hour after the vehicle has been driven), check the complete exhaust system from the engine to the end of the tailpipe. Ideally, the inspection should be carried out with the vehicle on a hoist to permit unrestricted access, but if a hoist is not available, raise and support the vehicle safely on axle stands (see *Jacking and vehicle support*).
2 Check the exhaust pipes and connections for evidence of leaks, severe corrosion and damage. Make sure that all brackets and mountings are in good condition and tight. Leakage at any of the joints or in other parts of the system will usually show up as a black sooty stain in the vicinity of the leak.
3 Rattles and other noises can often be traced to the exhaust system, especially the brackets and mountings. Try to move the pipes and silencers. If the components can come into contact with the body or suspension parts, secure the system with new mountings or if possible, separate the joints and twist the pipes as necessary to provide additional clearance.

4 Run the engine at idling speed. Have an assistant place a cloth or rag over the rear end of the exhaust pipe, and listen for any escape of exhaust gases that would indicate a leak.
5 On completion, lower the car to the ground.
6 The inside of the exhaust tailpipe can be an indication of the running condition of the engine. The exhaust deposits here are an indication of the engine's state of tune. If the pipe is black and sooty, the engine is in need of a tune-up, including a thorough fuel system inspection and adjustment.

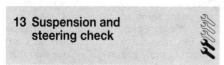

13 Suspension and steering check

Front suspension and steering check

1 Raise the front of the vehicle, and securely support it on axle stands (see *Jacking and vehicle support*).
2 Visually inspect the balljoint dust covers and the steering rack-and-pinion gaiters for splits, chafing or deterioration. Any wear of these components will cause loss of lubricant, together with dirt and water entry, resulting in rapid deterioration of the balljoints or steering gear.
3 On vehicles with power steering, check the fluid hoses for chafing or deterioration, and the pipe and hose unions for fluid leaks. Also check for signs of fluid leakage under pressure from the steering gear rubber gaiters, which would indicate failed fluid seals within the steering gear.
4 Grasp the roadwheel at the 12 o'clock and 6 o'clock positions, and try to rock it **(see illustration)**. Very slight free play may be felt, but if the movement is appreciable, further investigation is necessary to determine the source. Continue rocking the wheel while an assistant depresses the footbrake. If the movement is now eliminated or significantly reduced, it is likely that the hub bearings are at fault. If the free play is still evident with the footbrake depressed, then there is wear in the suspension joints or mountings.
5 Now grasp the wheel at the 9 o'clock and 3 o'clock positions, and try to rock it as before. Any movement felt now may again be caused by wear in the hub bearings or the steering track rod balljoints. If the outer balljoint is worn, the visual movement will be obvious. If the inner joint is suspect, it can be felt by placing a hand over the rack-and-pinion rubber gaiter and gripping the track rod. If the wheel is now rocked, movement will be felt at the inner joint if wear has taken place.
6 Using a large screwdriver or flat bar, check for wear in the suspension mounting bushes by levering between the relevant suspension component and its attachment point. Some movement is to be expected, as the mountings are made of rubber, but excessive wear should be obvious. Also check the condition of any visible rubber bushes, looking for splits, cracks or contamination of the rubber.

13.4 Check for wear in the hub bearings by grasping the wheel and trying to rock it

7 With the car standing on its wheels, have an assistant turn the steering wheel back-and-forth, about an eighth of a turn each way. There should be very little, if any, lost movement between the steering wheel and roadwheels. If this is not the case, closely observe the joints and mountings previously described. In addition, check the steering column universal joints for wear, and also check the rack-and-pinion steering gear itself.

Rear suspension check

8 Chock the front wheels, then jack up the rear of the vehicle and support securely on axle stands (see *Jacking and vehicle support*).
9 Working as described previously for the front suspension, check the rear hub bearings, the suspension bushes and the shock absorber mountings for wear.

14 Hose and fluid leak check

1 Visually inspect the engine joint faces, gaskets and seals for any signs of water or oil leaks. Pay particular attention to the areas around the valve cover, cylinder head, oil filter and sump joint faces. Bear in mind that, over a period of time, some very slight seepage from these areas is to be expected – what you are really looking for is any indication of a serious leak. Should a leak be found, renew the offending gasket or oil seal by referring to the appropriate Chapters in this manual.

HAYNES HiNT

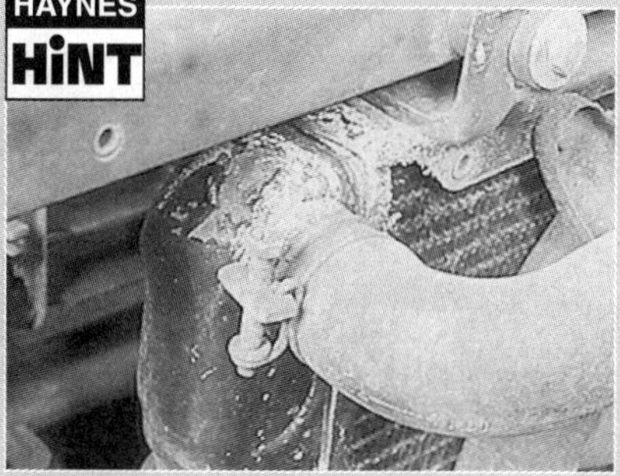

A leak in the cooling system will usually show up as white- or rust-coloured deposits on the area adjoining the leak.

2 Also check the security and condition of all the engine-related pipes and hoses, and all hydraulic and braking system pipes and hoses. Ensure that all cable ties or securing clips are in place, and in good condition. Clips which are broken or missing can lead to chafing of the hoses, pipes or wiring, which could cause more serious problems in the future.
3 Carefully check the radiator hoses and heater hoses along their entire length. Renew any hose which is cracked, swollen or deteriorated. Cracks will show up better if the hose is squeezed. Pay close attention to the hose clips that secure the hoses to the cooling system components. Hose clips can pinch and puncture hoses, resulting in cooling system leaks. If the crimped-type hose clips are used, it may be a good idea to replace them with standard worm-drive clips.
4 Inspect all the cooling system components (hoses, joint faces, etc) for leaks **(see Haynes Hint)**. Where any problems are found on system components, renew the component or gasket with reference to Chapter 3.
5 With the vehicle raised, inspect the fuel tank and filler neck for punctures, cracks and other damage. The connection between the filler neck and tank is especially critical. Sometimes a rubber filler neck or connecting hose will leak due to loose retaining clamps or deteriorated rubber.
6 Carefully check all rubber hoses and metal fuel lines leading away from the fuel tank. Check for loose connections, deteriorated hoses, crimped lines, and other damage. Pay particular attention to the vent pipes and hoses, which often loop up around the filler neck and can become blocked or crimped. Follow the lines to the front of the vehicle, carefully inspecting them all the way. Renew damaged sections as necessary. Similarly, whilst the vehicle is raised, take the opportunity to inspect all underbody brake fluid pipes and hoses.
7 From within the engine compartment, check the security of all fuel, vacuum and brake hose attachments and pipe unions, and inspect all hoses for kinks, chafing and deterioration.
8 Check the condition of the power steering fluid pipes and hoses and, where applicable, the automatic transmission fluid cooler pipes and hoses.

15 Roadwheel bolt check

1 Remove the wheel trims, where applicable, then slacken the roadwheel bolts slightly.
2 Tighten the bolts to the specified torque, using a torque wrench.

16 Bodywork and underbody condition check

1 Once the car has been washed and all tar spots and other surface blemishes have been cleaned off, carefully check all paintwork, looking closely for chips or scratches. Pay particular attention to vulnerable areas such as the front panels (bonnet and spoiler), and around the wheelarches. Any damage to the paintwork must be rectified as soon as possible to comply with the terms of the manufacturer's anti-corrosion warranties; check with a Renault dealer for details.

2 If a chip or light scratch is found which is recent and still free from rust, it can be touched-up using the appropriate touch-up stick which can be obtained from Renault dealers. Any more serious damage, or rusted stone chips, can be repaired as described in Chapter 11, but if damage or corrosion is so severe that a panel must be renewed, seek professional advice as soon as possible.

3 Always check that the door and ventilation opening drain holes and pipes are completely clear, so that water can drain out.

4 The wax-based underbody protective coating should be inspected annually, preferably just prior to Winter, when the underbody should be washed down as thoroughly as possible without disturbing the protective coating (see Chapter 11, Section 2, regarding the use of steam cleaners). Any damage to the coating should be repaired using a suitable wax-based sealer. If any of the body panels are disturbed for repair or renewal, do not forget to replace the coating and to inject wax into door panels, sills and box sections, to maintain the level of protection provided by the vehicle manufacturer.

17 Shock absorber check

1 Viewing over the roadwheels into the wheelarches, check for any signs of fluid leakage around the front and rear shock absorber bodies, or from the rubber gaiters around the piston rods. Should any fluid be noticed, the shock absorber is defective internally, and should be renewed. **Note:** *Shock absorbers should always be renewed in pairs on the same axle.*

2 The efficiency of the shock absorber may be checked by bouncing the vehicle at each corner. Generally speaking, the body will return to its normal position and stop after being depressed. If it rises and returns on a rebound, the shock absorber is probably suspect. Also examine the shock absorber upper and lower mountings for any signs of wear.

Every 36 000 miles (60 000 km)

18 Spark plug renewal and ignition system check

Note: *For models manufactured up to 31/03/1999 renew the spark plugs every 24 000 miles (40 000 km).*

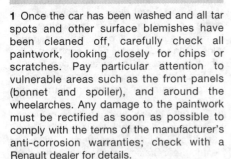

18.3a Unclip the plastic spark plug lead removal tool . . .

Warning: High voltages are produced by the electronic ignition system. Extreme care must be taken when working on the system with the ignition switched on. Persons with surgically-implanted cardiac pacemaker devices should keep well clear of the ignition circuits, components and test equipment.

1 The correct functioning of the spark plugs is vital for the correct running and efficiency of the engine. It is essential that the plugs fitted are appropriate for the engine, the suitable type being specified at the start of this Chapter. If the correct type of plug is used and the engine is in good condition, the spark plugs should not need attention between scheduled servicing intervals. Spark plug cleaning is rarely necessary, and should not be attempted unless specialised equipment is available, as damage can easily be caused to the firing ends.

2 To remove the plugs, first open the bonnet.

3 On models with the D7F engine, unclip the plastic spark plug lead tool from the HT lead cover on the top of the engine, then use the tool to disconnect the HT leads from the spark plugs **(see illustrations)**.

4 On E7J and K7M engines, carefully disconnect the HT leads from the spark plugs which are located on the front of the cylinder head **(see illustration)**. Pull on the end fittings and not the leads.

5 On K4J and K4M engines, remove the ignition HT coils from the top of the spark plugs as described in Chapter 5B **(see illustration)**.

6 It is advisable to remove any dirt from the spark plug recesses using a clean brush, a vacuum cleaner or compressed air before removing the plugs, to prevent the dirt dropping into the cylinders.

7 Unscrew the plugs using a spark plug spanner, suitable box spanner or a deep

18.3b . . . and use it to disconnect the HT leads – D7F engine

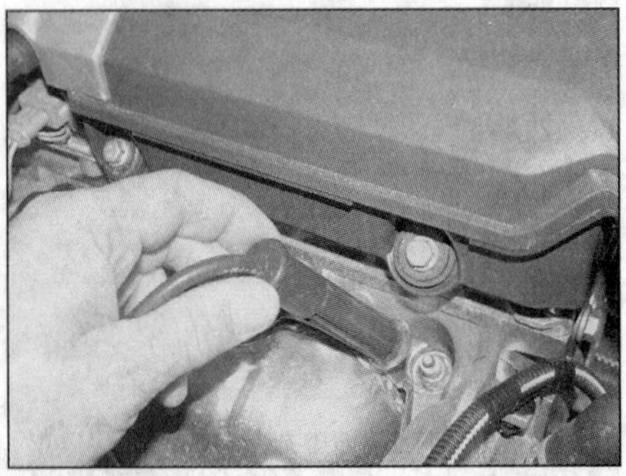

18.4 Disconnecting the HT leads from the spark plugs – E7J and K7M engines

18.5 Removing the ignition HT coils – K4J and K4M engines

socket and extension bar. Keep the socket in alignment with the spark plug, otherwise if it is forcibly moved to either side, the ceramic top of the spark plug may be broken off **(see illustrations)**. As each plug is removed, examine it as follows.

8 Examination of the spark plugs will give a good indication of the condition of the engine. If the insulator nose of the spark plug is clean and white, with no deposits, this is indicative of a weak mixture or too hot a plug (a hot plug transfers heat away from the electrode slowly, a cold plug transfers heat away quickly).

9 If the tip and insulator nose are covered with hard black-looking deposits, then this is indicative that the mixture is too rich. Should the plug be black and oily, then it is likely that the engine is fairly worn, as well as the mixture being too rich.

10 If the insulator nose is covered with light tan to greyish-brown deposits, then the mixture is correct and it is likely that the engine is in good condition.

11 If the spark plug has not completed its service interval, it may be refitted, however, it is recommended that it be re-gapped in order to maintain peak engine efficiency, and to allow for the slow increase in gap (approximately 0.025 mm per 1000 miles) which occurs in normal operation. If, due to engine condition, the spark plug is not serviceable, it should be renewed.

12 The spark plug gap is of considerable importance as, if it is too large or too small, the size of the spark and its efficiency will be seriously impaired. For best results, the spark plug gap should be set in accordance with the Specifications at the start of this Chapter.

13 To set it, measure the gap with a feeler blade, and then bend open, or closed, the outer plug electrode until the correct gap is achieved **(see illustration)**. The centre electrode should never be bent, as this may crack the insulation and cause plug failure, if nothing worse.

14 Special spark plug electrode gap measuring and adjusting tools are available from most motor accessory shops **(see illustration)**.

15 Before fitting the spark plugs, check that the threaded connector sleeves are tight, and that the plug exterior surfaces and threads are clean. Apply a little anti-seize compound to the threads.

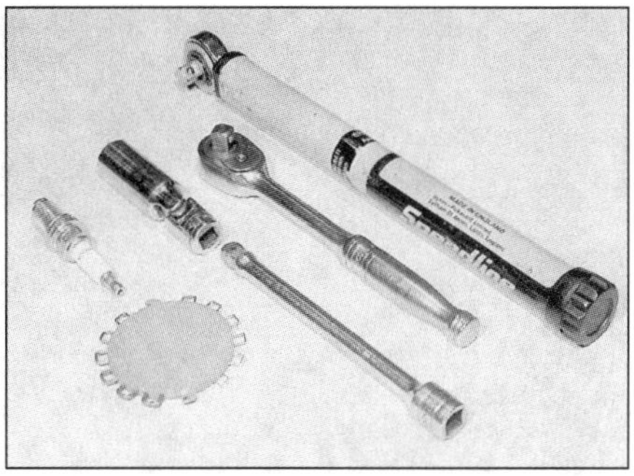

18.7a Tools required for spark plug removal, gap adjustment and refitting

16 Insert each spark plug into the cylinder head and screw them in by hand, taking extra care to enter the plug threads correctly **(see Haynes Hint)**.

17 Tighten the plugs to the specified torque using the spark plug socket and a torque wrench.

18 The spark plug (HT) leads, where applicable, should be checked whenever new spark plugs are fitted. On the D7F engine, open the lead holder and release the leads. On E7J and K7M engines, undo the screws and remove the lead holder located around the oil filter cap. Ensure that the leads are numbered before removing them, to avoid confusion when refitting. Check inside the end fitting for signs of corrosion, which will look like a white crusty powder. Push the end fitting back onto the spark plug, ensuring that it is a tight fit on the plug. Using a clean rag, wipe the entire length of the lead to remove any built-up dirt and grease. Once the lead is clean, check for burns, cracks and other damage. Do not bend the lead excessively, nor pull the lead lengthwise – the conductor inside might break. Disconnect the other end of the lead, and check for corrosion and a tight fit. If an ohmmeter is available, check the resistance of the lead. Check the remaining leads one at a time.

19 On models with the D7F engine, check that the HT leads are correctly located in the holder, then refit the plastic spark plug lead tool. Reconnect the HT leads to their respective spark plugs.

18.7b Using the special socket to remove the spark plugs – K4J engine

20 On E7J and K7M engines, reconnect the HT leads to their respective spark plugs and refit the holder.

21 On K4J and K4M engines, refit the ignition HT coils with reference to Chapter 5B.

19 Air filter element renewal

Note: *For models manufactured up to 31/03/1999 renew the air filter every 24 000 miles (40 000 km).*

Removal

D7F engine

1 Push down the air cleaner cover retaining clip on top of the air cleaner casing, and simultaneously twist the cover towards the rear of the engine compartment (anti-clockwise looking from the right-hand side of the car). Remove the cover from the air cleaner element housing **(see illustration)**.

HAYNES HiNT

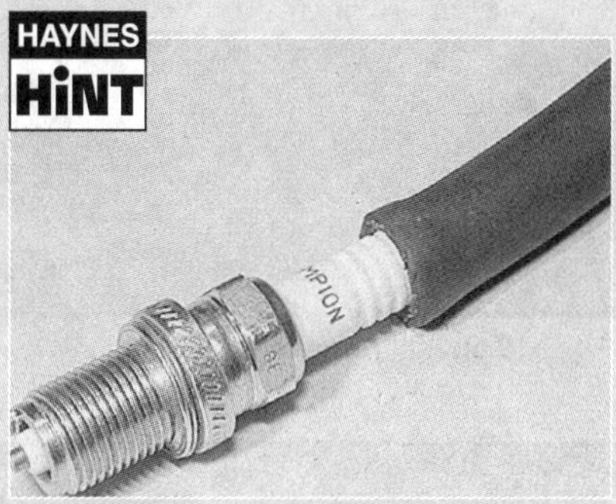

It is very often difficult to insert spark plugs into their holes without cross-threading them. To avoid this possibility, fit a short length of 5/16 inch internal diameter rubber hose over the end of the spark plug. The flexible hose acts as a universal joint to help align the plug with the plug hole. Should the plug begin to cross-thread, the hose will slip on the spark plug, preventing thread damage to the aluminium cylinder head

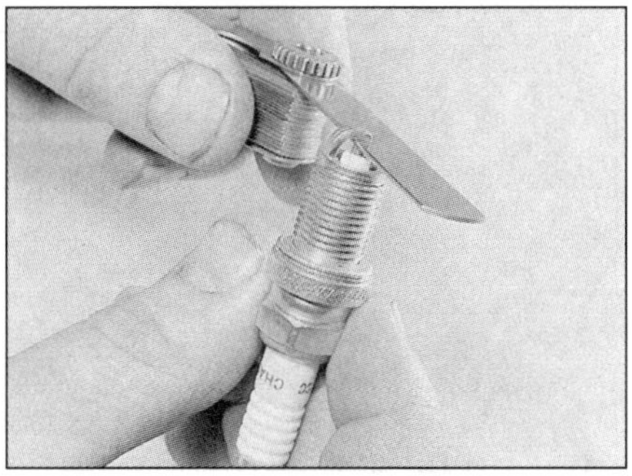

18.13 Measuring the spark plug gap with a feeler blade

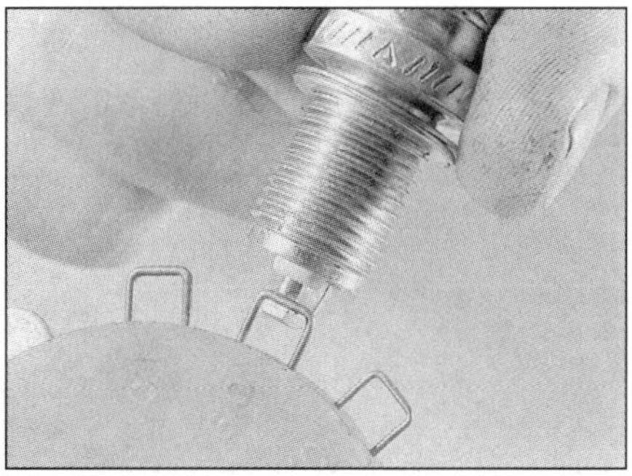

18.14 Measuring the spark plug gap with a wire gauge

1A

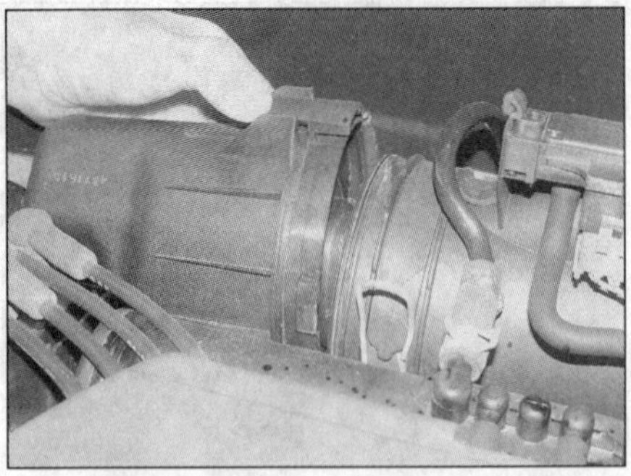

19.1 Removing the air cleaner cover – D7F engine

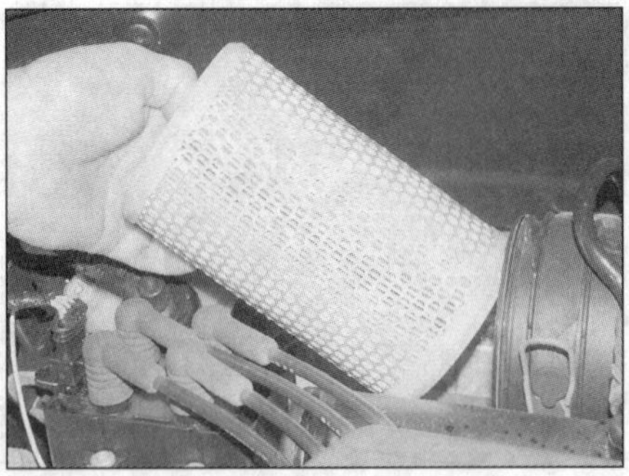

19.2 Removing the air cleaner element – D7F engine

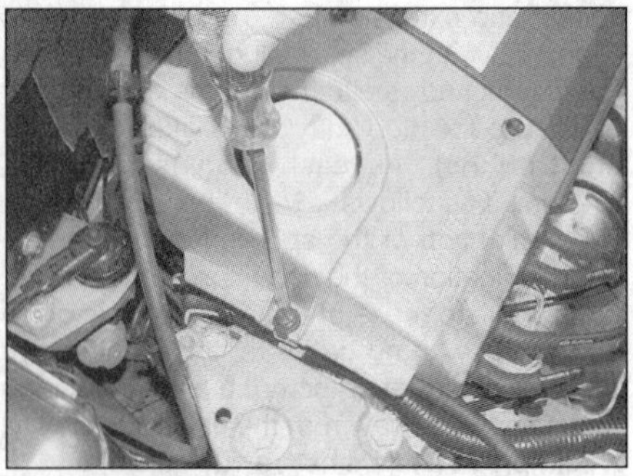

19.3a Undo the screws . . .

19.3b . . . and remove the HT lead holder . . .

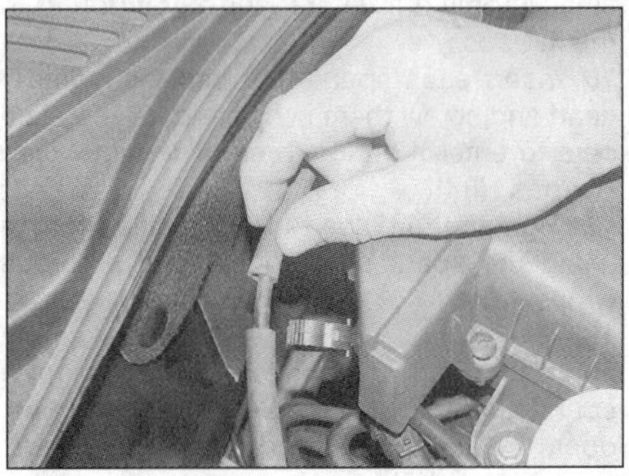

19.4 . . . then unclip the accelerator cable . . .

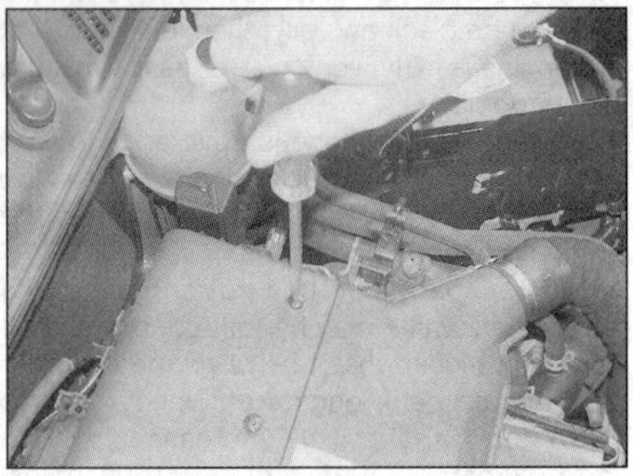

19.5a . . . undo the screws . . .

2 Withdraw the cylindrical-shaped element from the housing **(see illustration)**.

E7J and K7M engines

3 Undo the screws and remove the HT lead holder from around the oil filler cap **(see illustrations)**.

4 Unclip the accelerator cable from the rear of the air cleaner housing **(see illustration)**.

5 Undo the screws and remove the element cover from the housing, then withdraw the element **(see illustrations)**.

K4J and K4M engines

6 The air filter element is located at the left-hand rear of the engine. First unclip the air inlet duct from the air cleaner housing **(see illustration)**.

7 Undo the screws and unclip the element housing from the main body **(see illustrations)**.

8 Note how the element is fitted, then withdraw it from the housing **(see illustration opposite)**.

Refitting

9 Clean the inside of the air cleaner body and cover, being careful not to get dirt into the inlet duct.

10 Fit the new element using a reversal of the removal procedure.

19.5b . . . remove the cover . . .

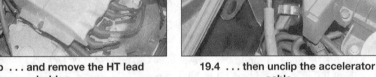

19.5c . . . and withdraw the element – E7J and K7M engines

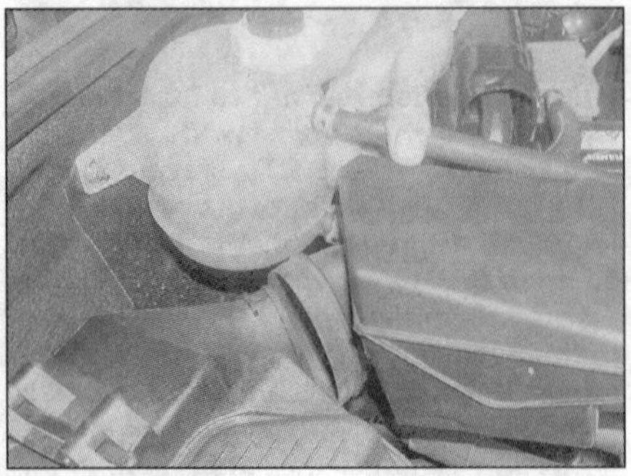

19.6 Unclip the air inlet duct . . .

19.7a . . . undo the screws . . .

19.7b . . . unclip the housing . . .

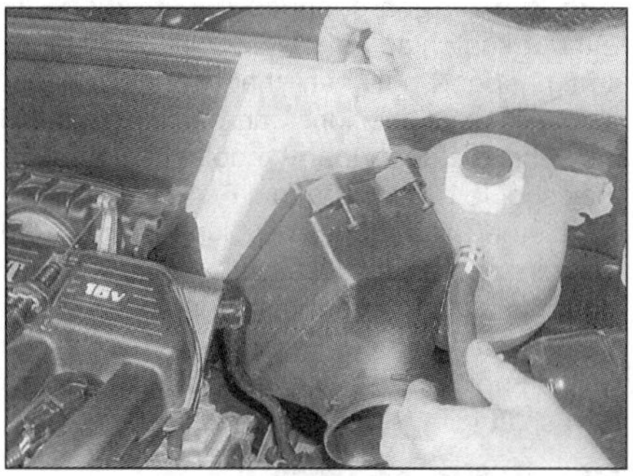

19.8 . . . then withdraw the element from the housing – K4J and K4M engines

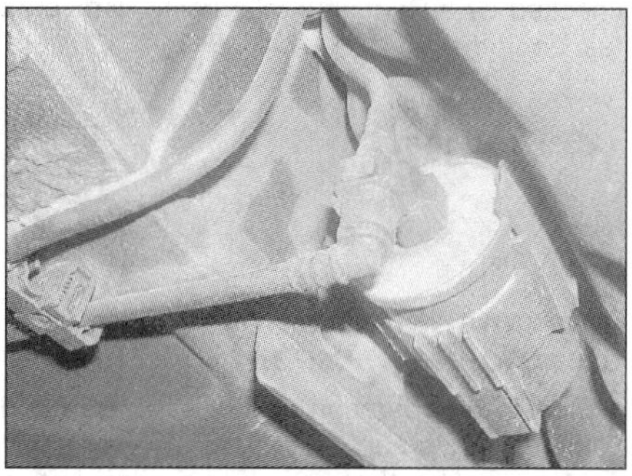

20.1 The fuel filter is located just in front of the fuel tank

20.2a Disconnect the fuel outlet hose to the engine . . .

20.2b . . . then disconnect the T-piece from the filter

20.2c Disconnecting the inlet fuel hose

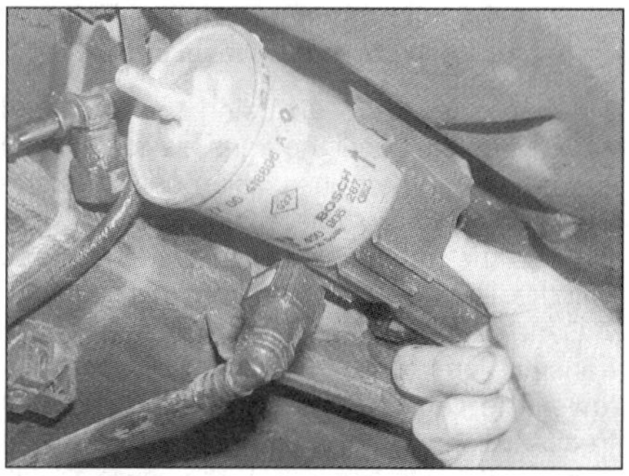

20.3 Removing the fuel filter from its holder. Note the direction arrow indicating fuel flow

20 Fuel filter renewal

Warning: Before carrying out the following operation refer to the precautions given in 'Safety first!' at the beginning of this manual and follow them implicitly. Petrol is a highly dangerous and volatile liquid and the precautions necessary when handling it cannot be overstressed

1 The fuel filter is located underneath the vehicle, just in front of the fuel tank **(see illustration)**. Chock the front roadwheels, then jack up the rear of the vehicle and support on axle stands (see *Jacking and vehicle support*). Clean the filter and its surroundings before starting work, to minimise the risk of dirt entering the fuel system.

2 Depressurise the fuel system with reference to Chapter 4A, then disconnect the hoses from the fuel filter **(see illustrations)**. The hoses are equipped with quick-release fittings to ease removal. Note the location of the sealing rings and plug the hose ends to minimise fuel loss.

3 Push the filter from its holder, noting which way round it is fitted. The arrow on the filter points in the direction of fuel flow (towards the throttle body/fuel rail) **(see illustration)**.

4 Slide the new filter into position making sure its arrow is pointing in the direction of fuel flow.

5 Ensure that the sealing rings are correctly located then reconnect the hoses to the fuel filter.

6 Start the engine and check the filter for signs of fuel leakage.

7 Lower the vehicle to the ground.

21 Rear brake shoe and drum check

1 Remove the rear brake drums, and check the brake shoes for signs of wear or contamination. At the same time, also inspect the wheel cylinders for signs of leakage, and the brake drum for signs of wear. Refer to the relevant Sections of Chapter 9 for further information.

22 Manual transmission oil level check

1 Either position the vehicle over an inspection pit, or jack up the front and rear of the vehicle and support it on axle stands (see *Jacking and vehicle support*). The vehicle must be level for the check to be accurate.

2 Remove the engine undertray or unclip the cover, as applicable, from the bottom of the transmission **(see illustration)**.

3 Clean the area around the filler/level plug located on the front facing side of the transmission, then unscrew and remove the plug **(see illustration)**.

4 The oil level should be up to the lower edge of the filler/level plug aperture **(see illustration)**.

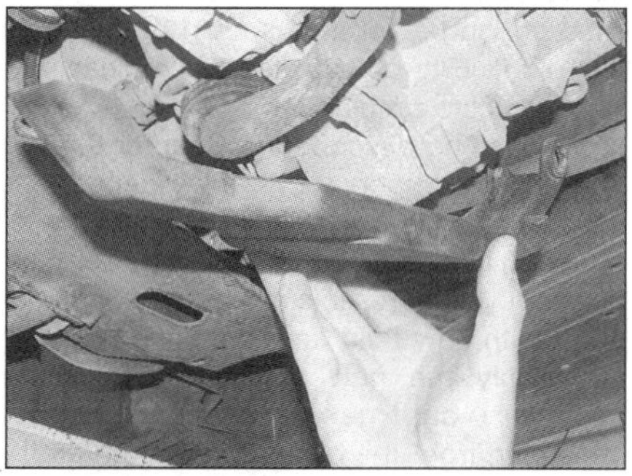

22.2 Unclipping the bottom cover from the transmission

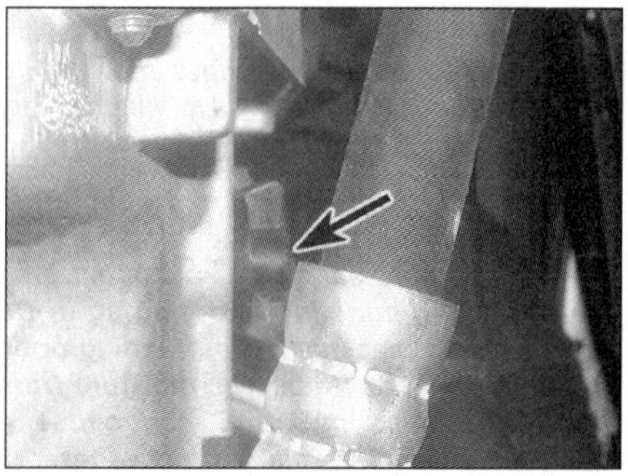

22.3 Transmission oil filler/level plug

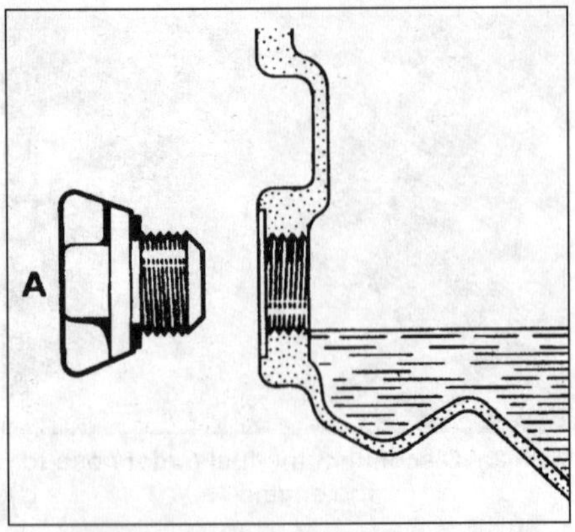

22.4 Manual transmission filler/level plug (A) - correct oil level shown

5 If necessary, top-up using the specified type of lubricant until the transmission oil level is correct. Fill the transmission until oil starts to flow out and allow excess oil to drain out.
6 Once the transmission oil level is correct, refit the filler/level plug and tighten it securely.
7 Refit the engine undertray cover or transmission bottom cover as applicable, then lower the vehicle to the ground. Note that frequent need for topping-up indicates a leak, possibly through an oil seal. The cause should be investigated and rectified.

23 Front wheel alignment check

Refer to the information given in Chapter 10.

24 Air conditioning system check

The air conditioning system must be checked by a Renault dealer using dedicated test equipment.

25 Road test

Instruments and electrical equipment

1 Check the operation of all instruments and electrical equipment.
2 Make sure that all instruments read correctly, and switch on all electrical equipment in turn, to check that it functions properly.

Steering and suspension

3 Check for any abnormalities in the steering, suspension, handling or road 'feel'.
4 Drive the vehicle, and check that there are no unusual vibrations or noises.
5 Check that the steering feels positive, with no excessive 'sloppiness', or roughness, and check for any suspension noises when cornering and driving over bumps.

Drivetrain

6 Check the performance of the engine, clutch, transmission and driveshafts.
7 Listen for any unusual noises from the engine, clutch and transmission.
8 Make sure that the engine runs smoothly when idling, and that there is no hesitation when accelerating.
9 Check that, where applicable, the clutch action is smooth and progressive, that the drive is taken up smoothly, and that the pedal travel is not excessive. Also listen for any noises when the clutch pedal is depressed.
10 Check that all gears can be engaged smoothly without noise, and that the gear lever action is smooth and not abnormally vague or 'notchy'.
11 On automatic transmission models, make sure that all gearchanges occur smoothly, without snatching, and without an increase in engine speed between changes. Check that all of the gear positions can be selected with the vehicle at rest. If any problems are found, they should be referred to a Renault dealer.
12 Listen for a metallic clicking sound from the front of the vehicle, as the vehicle is driven slowly in a circle with the steering on full-lock. Carry out this check in both directions. If a clicking noise is heard, this indicates wear in a driveshaft joint (see Chapter 8).

Check the operation and performance of the braking system

13 Make sure that the vehicle does not pull to one side when braking, and that the wheels do not lock prematurely when braking hard.
14 Check that there is no vibration through the steering when braking.
15 Check that the handbrake operates correctly, without excessive movement of the lever, and that it holds the vehicle stationary on a slope.
16 Test the operation of the brake servo unit as follows. Depress the footbrake four or five times to exhaust the vacuum, then start the engine. As the engine starts, there should be a noticeable 'give' in the brake pedal as vacuum builds up. Allow the engine to run for at least two minutes, and then switch it off. If the brake pedal is now depressed again, it should be possible to detect a hiss from the servo as the pedal is depressed. After about four or five applications, no further hissing should be heard, and the pedal should feel considerably harder.

26 Timing belt renewal

Refer to Chapter 2A or 2B.

Every 72 000 miles (120 000 km) or every 4 years

27 Brake fluid renewal

Note: *For models manufactured up to 31/03/1999 renew the air filter every 36 000 miles (60 000 km).*

Warning: Brake hydraulic fluid can harm your eyes and damage painted surfaces, so use extreme caution when handling and pouring it. Do not use fluid that has been standing open for some time, as it absorbs moisture from the air. Excess moisture can cause a dangerous loss of braking effectiveness.

1 The procedure is similar to that for the bleeding of the hydraulic system as described in Chapter 9, except that the brake fluid reservoir should be emptied by syphoning, using a clean poultry baster or similar before starting, and allowance should be made for the old fluid to be expelled when bleeding a section of the circuit.
2 Working as described in Chapter 9, open the first bleed screw in the sequence, and pump the brake pedal gently until nearly all the old fluid has been emptied from the master cylinder reservoir. Top-up to the MAX level with new fluid, and continue pumping until only the new fluid remains in the reservoir, and new fluid can be seen emerging from the bleed screw. Tighten the screw, and top the reservoir level up to the MAX level line.

HAYNES HiNT *Old hydraulic fluid is invariably much darker in colour than the new, making it easy to distinguish the two.*

3 Work through all the remaining bleed screws in the sequence until new fluid can be seen at all of them. Be careful to keep the master cylinder reservoir topped-up to above the MIN level at all times, or air may enter the system and greatly increase the length of the task.
4 When the operation is complete, check that all bleed screws are securely tightened, and that their dust caps are refitted. Wash off all traces of spilt fluid, and recheck the master cylinder reservoir fluid level.
5 Check the operation of the brakes before taking the car on the road.

28 Coolant renewal

Cooling system draining

Warning: Wait until the engine is cold before starting this procedure. Do not allow antifreeze to come in contact with your skin, or with the painted surfaces of the vehicle. Rinse off spills immediately with plenty of water. Never leave antifreeze lying around in an open container, or in a puddle in the driveway or on the garage floor. Children and pets are attracted by its sweet smell, but antifreeze can be fatal if ingested.

1 With the engine completely cold, remove the expansion tank filler cap. Turn the cap anti-clockwise, wait until any pressure remaining in the system is released, then unscrew it and lift it off.

2 Where applicable, remove the undershield, then position a suitable container beneath the radiator bottom hose connection.

3 Loosen the hose clip, pull off the hose and allow the coolant to drain into the container.

4 To assist draining, open the cooling system bleed screw(s). On the D7F engine without air conditioning, there are two bleed screws, one located in the hose leading from the thermostat housing to the heater matrix, and the other located in the hose leading from the heater matrix to the water pump. On the D7F engine with air conditioning, the bleed screw is located in the hose leading from the heater matrix to the water pump. On E7J and K7M engines, the bleed screw is located in the hose leading from the thermostat housing to the heater matrix **(see illustration)**. On K4J and K4M engines, the bleed screw is located on the thermostat housing.

5 When the flow of coolant stops, reposition the container below the cylinder block drain plug where fitted. Note that there is no plug fitted to the D7F engine. On the other engines, it is located either on the front left-hand side or rear right-hand side of the cylinder block. Remove the drain plug, and allow the coolant to drain into the container.

6 If the coolant has been drained for a reason other than renewal, then provided it is clean and less than two years old, it can be re-used.

7 Refit the radiator bottom hose and cylinder block drain plug on completion of draining.

Cooling system flushing

8 If coolant renewal has been neglected, or if the antifreeze mixture has become diluted, then in time, the cooling system may gradually lose efficiency, as the coolant passages become restricted due to rust, scale deposits, and other sediment. The cooling system efficiency can be restored by flushing the system clean.

9 The radiator should be flushed independently of the engine, to avoid unnecessary contamination.

Radiator flushing

10 Disconnect the top and bottom hoses and any other relevant hoses from the radiator, with reference to Chapter 3.

11 Insert a garden hose into the radiator top inlet. Direct a flow of clean water through the radiator, and continue flushing until clean water emerges from the radiator bottom outlet.

12 If after a reasonable period, the water still does not run clear, the radiator can be flushed with a good proprietary cleaning agent. It is important that the manufacturer's instructions are followed carefully. If the contamination is particularly bad, insert the hose in the radiator bottom outlet, and reverse-flush the radiator.

Engine flushing

13 To flush the engine, first refit the cylinder block drain plug.

14 Remove the thermostat as described in Chapter 3, then temporarily refit the top hose at its engine connection.

15 With the top and bottom hoses disconnected from the radiator, insert a garden hose into the radiator top hose. Direct a clean flow of water through the engine, and continue flushing until clean water emerges from the radiator bottom hose.

16 On completion of flushing, refit the thermostat and reconnect the hoses with reference to Chapter 3.

Cooling system filling

17 Before attempting to fill the cooling system, make sure that all hoses and clips are in good condition, and that the clips are tight. Note that an antifreeze mixture must be used all year round, to prevent corrosion of the engine components. Also check that the cylinder block drain plug is in place and tight.

18 Remove the expansion tank filler cap.

19 Open the cooling system bleed screw(s).

20 Slowly fill the system until the coolant level reaches the MAX mark on the expansion tank.

21 Close the bleed screw(s) when coolant free from air bubbles emerges.

22 Start the engine, and run it at a fast idle speed (do not exceed 1500 rpm) for approximately 4 minutes. Keep the level topped-up to the top of the expansion tank filler neck.

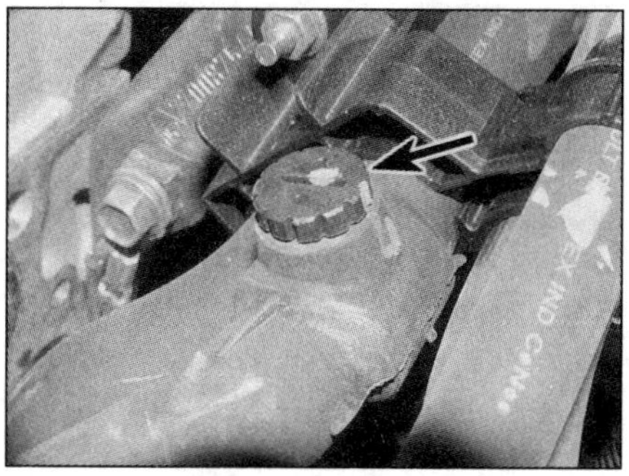

28.4 Cooling system bleed screw – E7J engine

23 Refit and tighten the expansion tank filler cap.

24 Allow the engine to run at 2500 rpm for approximately 10 minutes on D7F, E7J and K7M engines, or 20 minutes on K4J and K4M engines until the cooling fan cuts in and out.

25 Stop the engine and allow the engine to cool for at least 30 minutes.

26 Recheck the coolant level with reference to *Weekly checks*. Top-up the level if necessary and refit the expansion tank filler cap. Where applicable, refit the engine undershield.

Antifreeze mixture

27 The antifreeze should always be renewed at the specified intervals. This is necessary not only to maintain the antifreeze properties, but also to prevent corrosion which would otherwise occur as the corrosion inhibitors become progressively less effective.

28 Always use an ethylene-glycol based antifreeze which is suitable for use in mixed-metal cooling systems. The quantity of antifreeze and levels of protection are given in the Specifications.

29 Before adding antifreeze, the cooling system should be completely drained, preferably flushed, and all hoses checked for condition and security.

30 After filling with antifreeze, a label should be attached to the expansion tank, stating the type and concentration of antifreeze used, and the date installed. Any subsequent topping-up should be made with the same type and concentration of antifreeze.

31 Do not use engine antifreeze in the windscreen/tailgate washer system, as it will cause damage to the vehicle's paintwork. A screenwash additive should be added to the washer system in the quantities stated on the bottle.

Every 4 years

29 Airbag battery renewal

1 On models fitted with a self-contained airbag, the batteries must be renewed every 4 years. This work should be entrusted to a Renault dealer.

Chapter 1 Part B:
Routine maintenance and servicing – diesel models

Contents

Degrees of difficulty

Easy, suitable for novice with little experience	**Fairly easy,** suitable for beginner with some experience	**Fairly difficult,** suitable for competent DIY mechanic	**Difficult,** suitable for experienced DIY mechanic	**Very difficult,** suitable for expert DIY or professional

Lubricants and fluids

Refer to *Weekly checks* on page 0•19

Capacities

Engine oil

Excluding oil filter	4.7 litres
Including oil filter	5.2 litres
Difference between MAX and MIN dipstick marks	2.0 litres
Cooling system	7.4 litres
Manual gearbox	3.4 litres
Power-assisted steering reservoir	
Models with mechanical pump	1.1 litres
Models with electric pump	0.7 litre
Fuel tank	50 litres

Cooling system

Antifreeze mixture:	**Antifreeze**	**Water**
Protection to –23°C	35%	65%
Protection to –40°C	50%	50%

Fuel system

Idle speed:	
F8Q 630 engine	850 ± 25 rpm
F8Q 632 engine	825 ± 50 rpm
F8Q 662 engine	850 ± 50 rpm
Fast idle speed	Not adjustable (factory set)

Brakes

Front disc brakes:	
Pad thickness (including backing):	
New	18.0 mm
Minimum thickness	6.0 mm
Rear disc brakes:	
Pad thickness (including backing):	
New	15.0 mm
Minimum thickness	6.0 mm
Rear drum brakes:	
Shoe thickness (including backing):	
New:	
Leading	4.6 mm
Trailing	3.3 mm
Minimum thickness	2.0 mm

Torque wrench settings

	Nm	**lbf ft**
Roadwheel bolts	90	66
Sump drain plug	15	11

The maintenance intervals in this manual are provided with the assumption that you, not the dealer, will be carrying out the work. These are the minimum maintenance intervals recommended by us for vehicles driven daily. If you wish to keep your vehicle in peak condition at all times, you may wish to perform some of these procedures more often. We encourage frequent maintenance, because it enhances the efficiency, performance and resale value of your vehicle.

If the vehicle is driven in dusty areas, used to tow a trailer, or driven frequently at slow speeds (idling in traffic) or on short journeys, more frequent maintenance intervals are recommended.

When the vehicle is new, it should be serviced by a factory-authorised dealer service department, in order to preserve the factory warranty.

***Note:** As from January 2001, Renault introduced servicing intervals based on 18 000 miles (30 000 km) instead of 12 000 miles (20 000 km). No information is available at the time of writing, but if necessary, consult a Renault dealer to confirm the actual interval applicable to your model.*

Every 250 miles (400 km) or weekly

- ☐ Refer to *Weekly Checks*

Every 6000 miles (10 000 km)

- ☐ Renew the engine oil and filter (Section 3)

Note: *Frequent oil and filter changes are good for the engine. We recommend changing the oil at the mileage specified here, or at least twice a year if the mileage covered is a less.*

Every 12 000 miles (20 000 km)

- ☐ Renew the pollen filter (Section 4)
- ☐ Power steering fluid level check (Section 5)
- ☐ Check the brake pad thickness and discs (Section 6)
- ☐ Check the operation of the handbrake (Section 7)
- ☐ Check the operation of the clutch (Section 8)
- ☐ Check the condition of the auxiliary drivebelts (Section 9)
- ☐ Check the condition of the seat belts (Section 10)
- ☐ Check the operation of all electrical systems (Section 11)
- ☐ Check the condition of the exhaust system and mountings (Section 12)
- ☐ Check the suspension and steering components (Section 13)
- ☐ Check all underbonnet components and hoses for fluid leaks (Section 14)
- ☐ Check the tightness of the roadwheel bolts (Section 15)
- ☐ Check the bodywork and underbody for damage and corrosion (Section 16)
- ☐ Check the front and rear shock absorbers (Section 17)

Every 36 000 miles (60 000 km)

In addition to all the items listed previously, carry out the following:

- ☐ Renew the air filter element (Section 18)
- ☐ Renew the fuel filter element (Section 19)
- ☐ Check the rear brake shoes and drums (Section 20)
- ☐ Check the manual transmission oil level (Section 21)
- ☐ Check the front wheel alignment (Section 22)
- ☐ Check the operation of the air conditioning system (Section 23)
- ☐ Carry out a road test (Section 24)
- ☐ Renew the timing belt (Section 25)

Note: *Although the normal interval for timing belt renewal is 72 000 miles (120 000 km), it is strongly recommended that the interval is halved to 36 000 miles (60 000 km) on vehicles which are subjected to intensive use, ie, mainly short journeys or a lot of stop-start driving. The actual belt renewal interval is therefore very much up to the individual owner, but bear in mind that severe engine damage may result if the belt breaks.*

Every 72 000 miles (120 000 km) or every 4 years, whichever comes first

In addition to all the items listed previously, carry out the following:

- ☐ Renew the brake fluid (Section 26)
- ☐ Renew the coolant (Section 27)

Every 4 years

- ☐ On models fitted with a self-contained airbag, renew the batteries (Section 28)

Component location - diesel models

Underbonnet view of a 1.9 litre diesel model

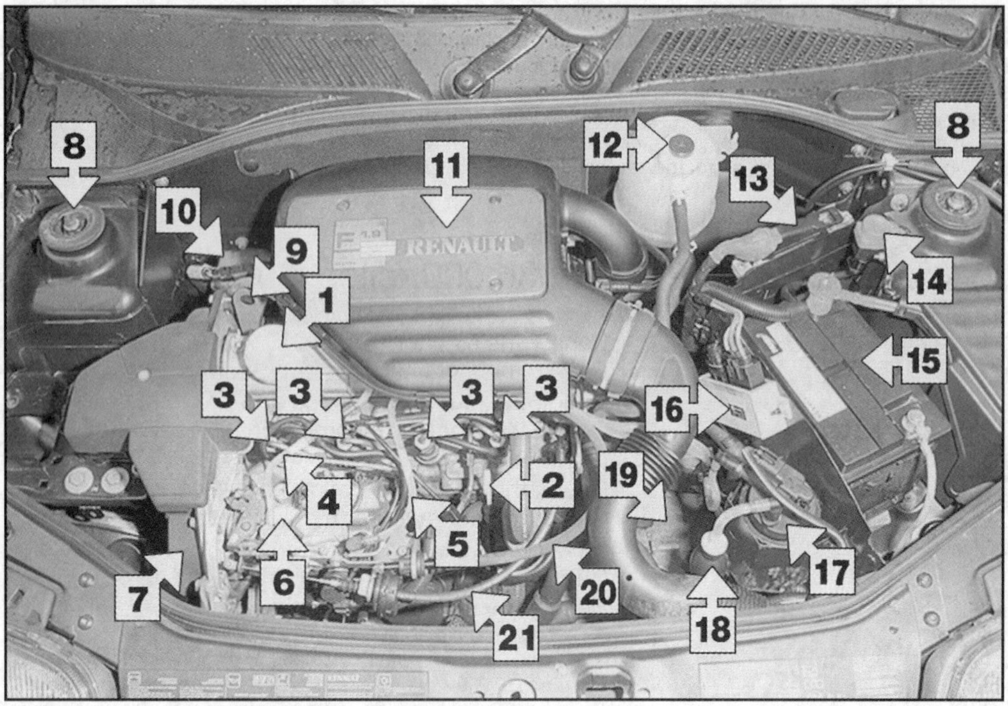

1 *Engine oil filler cap*
2 *Engine oil level dipstick*
3 *Fuel injectors*
4 *Fuel return pipe*
5 *Fuel supply pipe*
6 *Fuel injection pump*
7 *Auxiliary drive belt*
8 *Front suspension strut upper mountings*
9 *Engine lifting eye*
10 *Brake fluid reservoir*
11 *Air cleaner element*
12 *Coolant expansion tank*
13 *Fuel injection electronic control unit (ECU)*
14 *Fuel cut-off inertia switch*
15 *Battery*
16 *Pre/post-heating control unit*
17 *Fuel filter*
18 *Fuel system priming bulb*
19 *Manual gearbox*
20 *Accelerator cable*
21 *Fast idle control cable*

Front underbody view of a 1.9 litre diesel model

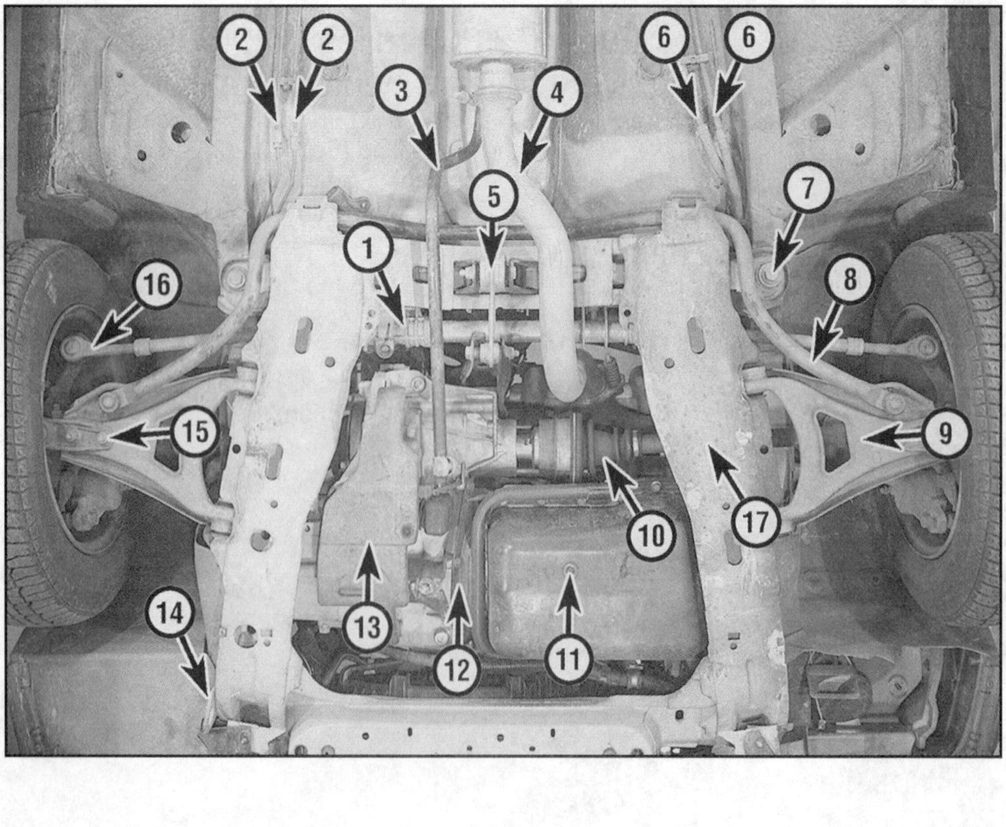

1 *Steering gear*
2 *Hydraulic brake pipes*
3 *Gearchange link rod*
4 *Exhaust downpipe*
5 *Rear engine mounting link*
6 *Fuel pipes*
7 *Subframe mounting bolt*
8 *Anti-roll bar*
9 *Front suspension lower arm*
10 *Right-hand driveshaft*
11 *Engine oil drain plug*
12 *Flywheel cover plate/engine-to-transmission bracing bracket*
13 *Transmission bottom cover*
14 *Front towing eye*
15 *Front lower arm balljoint*
16 *Steering track rod end*
17 *Front subframe*

Typical rear underbody view

1 *Fuel tank*
2 *Handbrake cables*
3 *Fuel filter (not fitted to diesel models)*
4 *Fuel feed and return lines*
5 *Rear brake compensator*
6 *Rear axle assembly*
7 *Rear coil springs*
8 *Exhaust rear silencer and tailpipe*

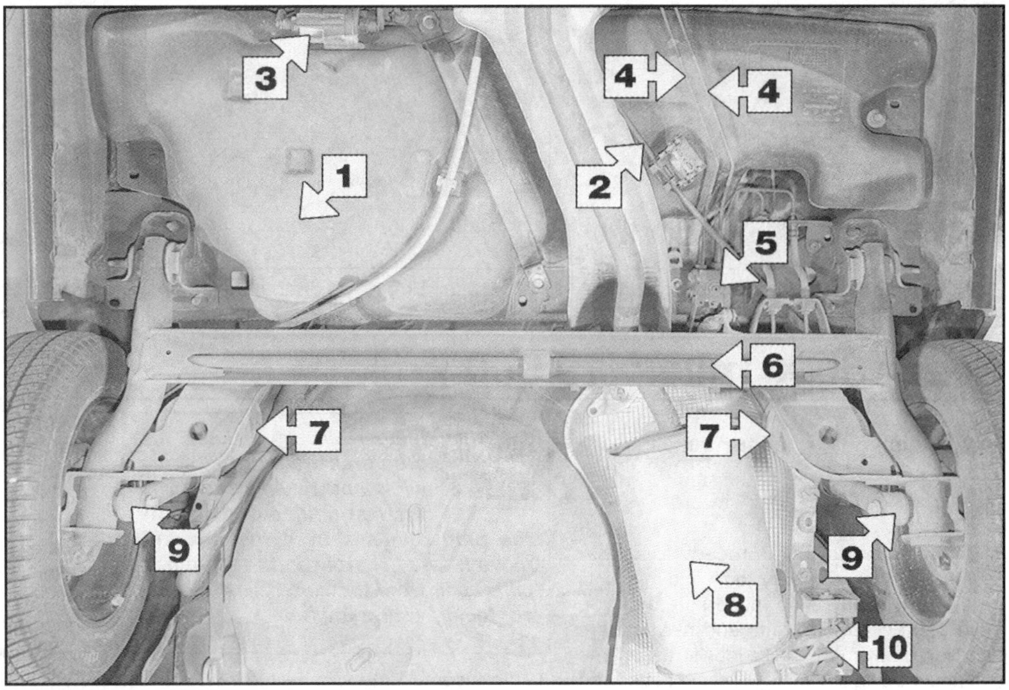

Maintenance procedures

1 Introduction

This Chapter is designed to help the home mechanic maintain his/her vehicle for safety, economy, long life and peak performance.

The Chapter contains a master maintenance schedule, followed by Sections dealing specifically with each task in the schedule. Visual checks, adjustments, component renewal and other helpful items are included. Refer to the accompanying illustrations of the engine compartment and the underside of the vehicle for the locations of the various components.

Servicing your vehicle in accordance with the mileage/time maintenance schedule and the following Sections will provide a planned maintenance programme, which should result in a long and reliable service life. This is a comprehensive plan, so maintaining some items but not others at the specified service intervals, will not produce the same results.

As you service your vehicle, you will discover that many of the procedures can – and should – be grouped together, because of the particular procedure being performed, or because of the proximity of two otherwise-unrelated components to one another. For example, if the vehicle is raised for any reason, the exhaust can be inspected at the same time as the suspension and steering components.

The first step in this maintenance programme is to prepare yourself before the actual work begins. Read through all the Sections relevant to the work to be carried out, then make a list and gather all the parts and tools required. If a problem is encountered, seek advice from a parts specialist, or a dealer service department.

2 Regular maintenance

If, from the time the vehicle is new, the routine maintenance schedule is followed closely, and frequent checks are made of fluid levels and high-wear items, as suggested throughout this manual, the engine will be kept in relatively good running condition, and the need for additional work will be minimised.

It is possible that there will be times when the engine is running poorly due to the lack of regular maintenance. This is even more likely if a used vehicle, which has not received regular and frequent maintenance checks, is purchased. In such cases, additional work may need to be carried out, outside of the regular maintenance intervals.

If engine wear is suspected, a compression test (refer to Chapter 2C) will provide valuable information regarding the overall performance of the main internal components. Such a test can be used as a basis to decide on the extent of the work to be carried out. If, for example, a compression test indicates serious internal engine wear, conventional maintenance as described in this Chapter will not greatly improve the performance of the engine, and may prove a waste of time and money, unless extensive overhaul work is carried out first.

The following series of operations are those most often required to improve the performance of a generally poor-running engine:

Primary operations

a) Clean, inspect and test the battery (refer to 'Weekly checks').
b) Check all the engine-related fluids (refer to 'Weekly checks').
c) Check the condition of the auxiliary drivebelt(s) (Section 9).
d) Check the condition of all hoses, and check for fluid leaks (Section 14).
e) Check the condition of the air filter, and renew if necessary (Section 18).
f) Check the fuel filter, and renew if necessary (Section 19).

If the above operations do not prove fully effective, carry out the following secondary operations:

Secondary operations

All items listed under *Primary operations*, plus the following:

a) Check the charging system (refer to Chapter 5A).
b) Check the pre-heating system (refer to Chapter 5C).
c) Check the fuel system (refer to Chapter 4B).

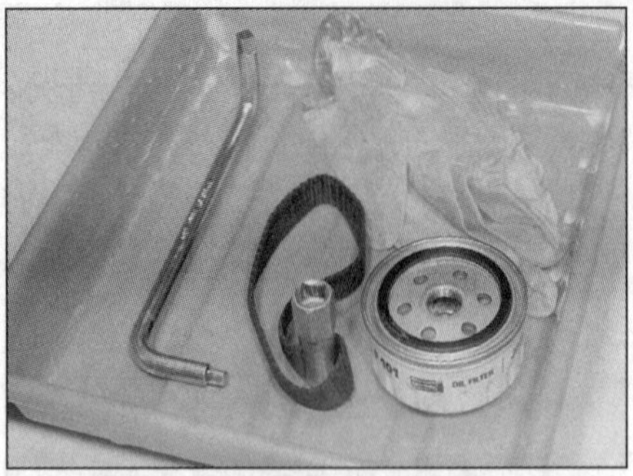

3.1 Tools and materials necessary for the engine oil change and filter renewal

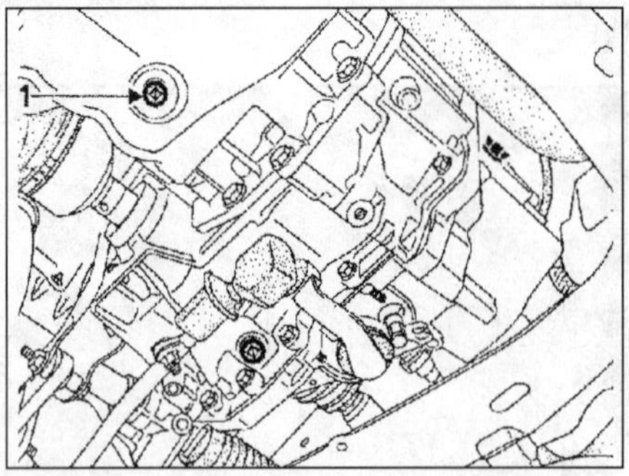

3.2a Engine oil drain plug (1)

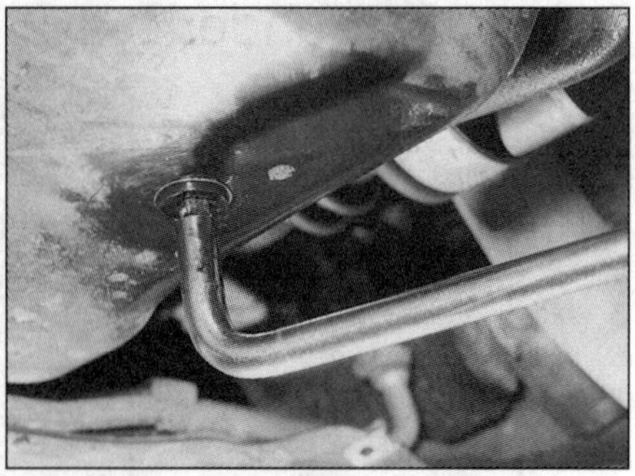

3.2b Using the special drain plug key to unscrew the sump drain plug

Every 6000 miles (10 000 km)

3 Engine oil and filter renewal

1 Before starting this procedure, gather together all the necessary tools and materials **(see illustration)**. Also make sure that you have plenty of clean rags and newspapers handy to mop up any spills. Ideally, the engine oil should be warm, as it will drain better and more built-up sludge will be removed with it. Take care, however, not to touch the exhaust or any other hot parts of the engine when working under the vehicle. To avoid any possibility of scalding, and to protect yourself from possible skin irritants and other harmful contaminants in used engine oils, it is advisable to wear rubber gloves when carrying out this work. Apply the handbrake, then jack up the front of the vehicle and support it on axle stands (see *Jacking and vehicle support*). Alternatively, raise the vehicle on a lift or drive it onto ramps. Whichever method is chosen, make sure that the car remains as level as possible, to enable the oil to drain fully. Remove the engine undertray where applicable.

2 Remove the oil filler cap from the valve cover, then position a suitable container beneath the sump. Clean the drain plug and the area around it, then slacken it half a turn using a special drain plug key (8 mm square) **(see illustrations)**.

HAYNES HiNT ***If possible, try to keep the plug pressed into the sump while unscrewing it by hand the last couple of turns. As the plug releases from the threads, move it away sharply so the stream of oil issuing from the sump runs into the container, not up your sleeve.***

3 Allow some time for the old oil to drain, noting that it may be necessary to reposition the container as the oil flow slows to a trickle.

4 After all the oil has drained, wipe off the drain plug with a clean rag and renew its sealing washer. Clean the area around the drain plug opening, then refit and tighten the plug to the specified torque setting.

5 Move the container into position under the oil filter, located on the front of the cylinder block **(see illustration)**.

6 Using an oil filter removal tool, slacken the filter initially **(see illustration)**. Loosely wrap some rags around the oil filter, then unscrew it and immediately position it with its open end uppermost to prevent further spillage of oil. Remove the oil filter from the engine compartment and empty the oil into the container.

7 Use a clean rag to remove all oil, dirt and sludge from the filter sealing area on the engine. Check the old filter to make sure that the rubber sealing ring hasn't stuck to the engine. If it has, carefully remove it.

8 Apply a light coating of clean oil to the sealing ring on the new filter, then screw it into position on the engine **(see illustration)**. Tighten the filter firmly by hand only – do not use any tools. Wipe clean the exterior of the oil filter.

9 Remove the old oil and all tools from under the car, then, where necessary, refit the undertray and lower the car to the ground.

10 Fill the engine with the specified quantity and grade of oil, as described in *Weekly checks*. Pour the oil in slowly, otherwise it may overflow from the top of the valve cover. Check that the oil level is up to the maximum mark on the dipstick, then refit and tighten the oil filler cap.

11 Start the engine and run it for a few minutes, checking that there are no leaks around the oil filter seal and the sump drain plug. Note that when the engine is first started, there will be a delay of a few seconds before the oil pressure warning light goes out while the new filter fills with oil. Do not race the engine while the warning light is on.

12 Switch off the engine and wait a few minutes for the oil to settle in the sump once more. With the new oil circulated and the filter now completely full, recheck the level on the dipstick and add more oil if necessary.

13 Dispose of the used engine oil safely with reference to *General repair procedures* in the *Reference* section of this manual.

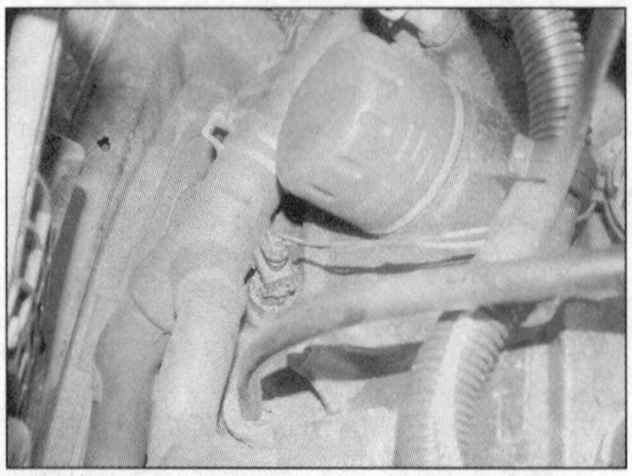

3.5 Oil filter location on the front of the engine

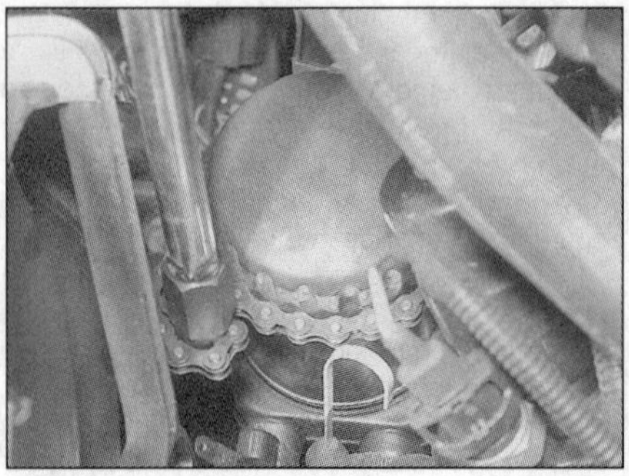

3.6 Slackening the oil filter with a removal tool

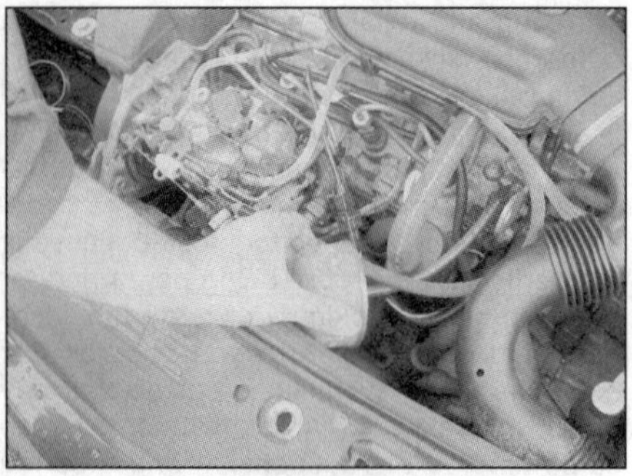

3.8 Fitting the new oil filter

4.2a Undo the screws . . .

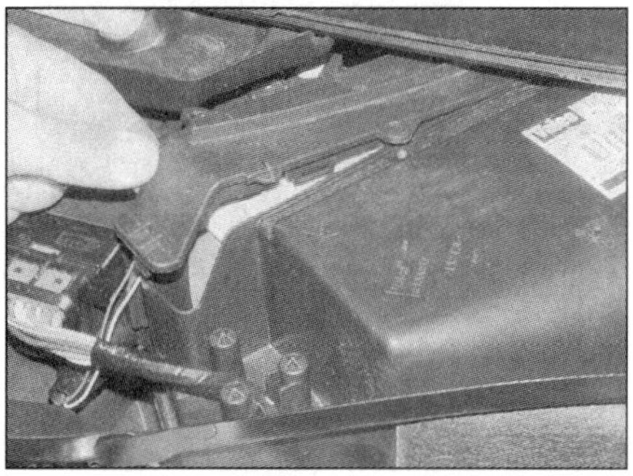

4.2b . . . and unclip the cover from the pollen filter housing

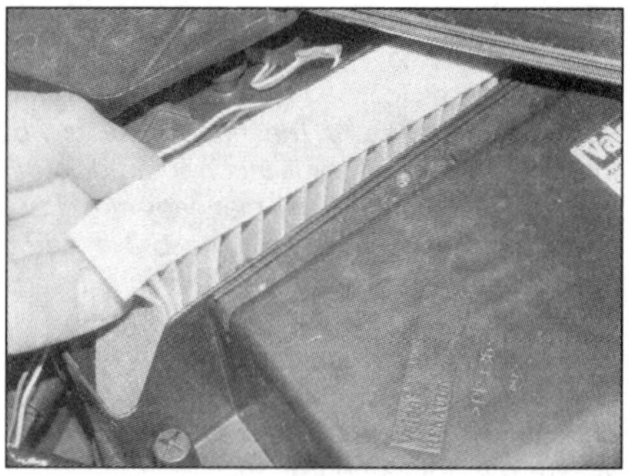

4.3 Removing the pollen filter element. Note the direction arrows on the element and housing

Every 12 000 miles (20 000 km)

4 Pollen filter renewal

Note: *On models manufactured up to 31/03/2000 renew the pollen filter every 6000 miles (10 000 km).*

1 With the bonnet open, remove the windscreen half-scuttle grille from the right-hand end of the bulkhead.

2 Undo the screws and unclip the cover from the pollen filter housing **(see illustrations)**.

3 Note the direction arrows on the filter and housing, then carefully extract the filter element by squeezing its central folds together **(see illustration)**.

4 Fit the new element using a reversal of the removal procedure, but make sure that the direction arrows are aligned with each other.

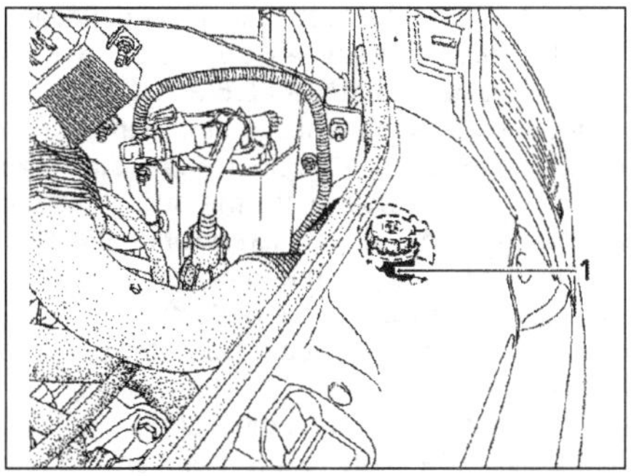

5.1a Power steering fluid reservoir on models with air conditioning (1)

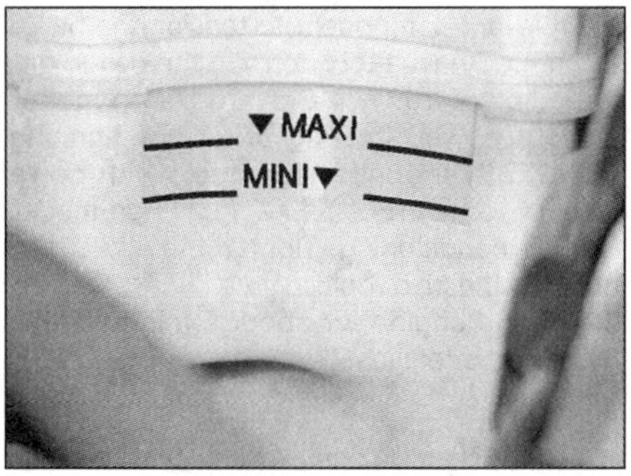

5.1b Level marks on the power steering fluid reservoir

5 Power steering fluid level check

1 The power steering fluid reservoir is located on the rear left-hand corner of the engine compartment on models without air conditioning. On models with air conditioning, the reservoir is located beneath the left-hand side of the engine compartment front crossmember, just in front of the fuel filter. The fluid level can be checked through the translucent reservoir, and should be between the MIN and MAX marks **(see illustrations)**.

2 If topping-up is required, first wipe clean the filler cap and top of the reservoir, then unscrew and remove the cap, allowing any fluid to drain from the cap into the reservoir.

3 Top-up to the MAX level mark using the specified fluid given in *Lubricants and fluids* **(see illustration)**. On completion, refit and tighten the filler cap.

6 Brake pad and disc check

1 Firmly apply the handbrake, then jack up the front or rear of the vehicle (as applicable) and support it securely on axle stands (see *Jacking and vehicle support*). Remove the roadwheels.

2 For a quick check, the thickness of friction material remaining on each brake pad can be measured through the aperture in the caliper body **(see Haynes Hint)**. If any pad's friction material is worn to the specified thickness or less, all four pads must be renewed as a set. Pad wear warning contacts are fitted to the inboard pads, but this should not be used as an excuse for omitting a visual check.

3 For a comprehensive check, the brake pads should be removed and cleaned. This will allow the operation of the caliper to be checked, and the brake disc itself to be fully examined for condition on both sides. Refer to Chapter 9 for further information.

5.3 Topping-up the power steering fluid level

7 Handbrake check

1 The handbrake should be capable of holding the parked vehicle stationary, even on steep slopes, when applied with moderate force. The mechanism should be firm and positive in feel, with no trace of stiffness or sponginess from the cables, and should release immediately the handbrake lever is

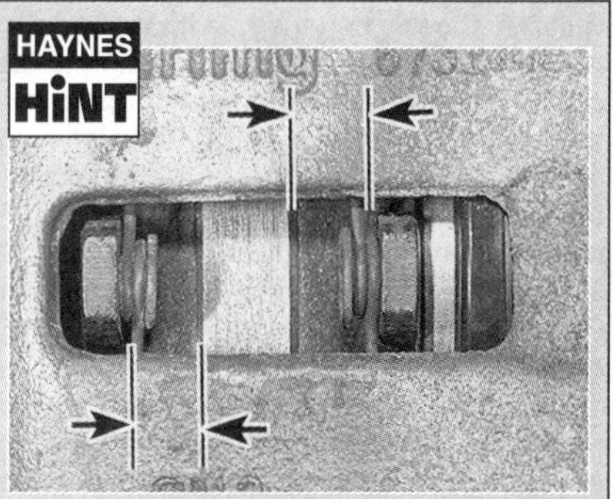

For a quick check, the thickness of friction material remaining on each brake pad can be measured through the aperture in the caliper body

released. If the mechanism is faulty in any of these respects, it must be checked immediately as follows. **Note:** *On models with rear drum brakes, if the handbrake is not functioning correctly or is incorrectly adjusted, the rear brake self-adjust mechanism will not function. This will lead to the brake pedal travel becoming excessive as the shoe linings wear.*

2 According to model, handbrake adjustment is made either on the handbrake lever or beneath the vehicle on the cable adjuster nut. Where the adjustment is made on the lever, remove the trim (see Chapter 11, Section 27) for access to the nut and fully back it off.

3 Where the cable adjuster nut is beneath the vehicle, jack up the rear of the vehicle and support it on axle stands (see *Jacking and vehicle support*). Undo the heat shield retaining nut(s) and lower the rear of the heat shield to gain access to the handbrake cable adjuster nut. Slacken the locknut, then fully slacken the cable adjuster nut **(see illustration)**.

Models with rear drum brakes

4 Remove both rear brake drums as described in Chapter 9.

5 Check that the knurled adjuster wheel on the adjuster strut is free to rotate in both directions. If it is seized, the brake shoes and strut must be removed and overhauled as described in Section 14 of Chapter 9.

6 If all is well, back off the adjuster wheel by five or six teeth so that the diameter of the brake shoes is slightly reduced.

7 Check that the handbrake cables slide freely by pulling on their front ends. Also check that the operating levers on the rear brake trailing shoes return to their correct positions, with their stop-pegs in contact with the edge of the trailing shoe web.

8 With the aid of an assistant, tighten the adjuster nut on the handbrake lever operating rod so that the lever on each rear brake assembly starts to move as the handbrake is moved between the first and second notch (click) of its ratchet mechanism. This is the case when the stop-pegs are still in contact with the shoes when the handbrake is on the first notch of the ratchet, but no longer contact the shoes when the handbrake is on the second notch. Once the adjustment is correct, hold the adjuster nut and securely tighten the locknut. Refit the catalytic converter heat shield retaining nuts.

9 Refit the brake drums as described in Chapter 9, then lower the vehicle to the ground.

10 With the vehicle standing on its wheels, repeatedly depress the footbrake to adjust the shoe-to-drum clearance. Whilst depressing the pedal, have an assistant listen to the rear drums to check that the adjuster strut mechanism is functioning; if this is so, a clicking sound will be heard from the adjuster strut as the pedal is depressed.

7.3 Handbrake cable adjusting nut located beneath the vehicle

Models with rear disc brakes

11 Check that the handbrake cables slide freely by pulling on their front ends, and check that the operating levers on the rear brake calipers move smoothly.

12 Move both of the caliper operating levers as far rearwards as possible, then tighten the adjuster nut on the handbrake lever operating rod until all free play is removed from both cables. With the aid of an assistant, adjust the nut so that the operating lever on each rear brake caliper starts to move as the handbrake lever is moved between the first and second notch (click) of its ratchet mechanism. Once the handbrake adjustment is correct, hold the adjuster nut and securely tighten the locknut.

13 Refit the heat shield retaining nuts (where necessary), then lower the vehicle to the ground.

8 Clutch check

1 Check that the clutch pedal moves smoothly and easily through its full travel, and that the clutch itself functions correctly, with no trace of slip or drag. If the movement is uneven or stiff in places, check that the cable is routed correctly, with no sharp turns.

2 Inspect the ends of the clutch inner cable, both at the gearbox end and inside the car, for signs of wear and fraying.

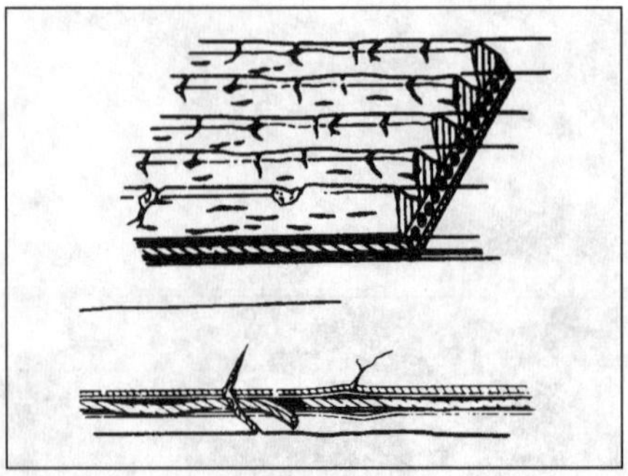

9.4 Checking for drivebelt wear – multi-ribbed type shown

9 Auxiliary drivebelt check and renewal

Checking

1 The auxiliary drivebelt is located on the front right-hand side of the engine.

2 Due to their function and material makeup, drivebelts are prone to failure after a period of time and should therefore be inspected, and if necessary adjusted periodically.

3 Since the drivebelt is located very close to the right-hand side of the engine compartment, it is possible to gain better access by raising the front of the vehicle and removing the right-hand wheel, then removing the engine undercover (where applicable) and wheelarch liner from inside the wheelarch.

4 With the engine stopped, inspect the full length of the drivebelt for cracks and separation of the belt plies **(see illustration)**. It will be necessary to turn the engine (using a spanner or socket and bar on the crankshaft pulley bolt) in order to move the belt from the pulleys so that the belt can be inspected thoroughly. Twist the belt between the pulleys so that both sides can be viewed. Also check for fraying, and glazing which gives the belt a shiny appearance. Check the pulleys for nicks, cracks, distortion and corrosion.

5 The tension of the belt is checked by pushing midway between the pulleys at the point indicated **(see illustration opposite)**. Renault technicians use a special spring-tensioned tool which applies a force of 30 N to the belt and then measures the deflection which should be between 2.5 and 3.5 mm on a cold engine, or between 3.5 and 4.5 mm on a hot engine. An alternative arrangement can be made by using a straight-edge, steel rule and spring balance. Hold the straight-edge across the two pulleys, then position the steel rule on the belt, apply the force with the spring balance, and measure the deflection.

6 If adjustment is necessary, loosen the alternator pivot bolt first, then loosen the locknut and adjustment bolt (if applicable).

7 To apply tension to the belt, on models without a separate belt tensioner/adjuster mechanism, insert a lever between the pulley end of the alternator (as applicable), and move the relevant component to tension the belt. If using the Renault tool, tension the belt to give a reading of 106 ± 4 Seem units on models without power steering or air conditioning, 104 ± 5 Seem units on models with power steering, and 115 ± 7 Seem units on models with air conditioning. Tighten the adjustment bolt and the pivot bolt.

8 Run the engine for about 5 minutes, then recheck the tension.

Renewal

9 To remove the belt, slacken the belt tension fully as described previously. Slip the belt off

the pulleys, then fit the new belt ensuring that it is routed correctly.
10 With the belt in position, adjust its tension as previously described.

10 Seat belt check

1 Carefully examine the seat belt webbing for cuts, or any signs of serious fraying or deterioration. If the belt is of the retractable type, pull the belt all the way out of the inertia reel, and examine the full extent of the webbing.
2 Fasten and unfasten the belt, ensuring that the locking mechanism holds securely, and releases properly when intended. If the belt is of the retractable type, check also that the retracting mechanism operates correctly when the belt is released.
3 Check the security of all seat belt mountings and attachments which are accessible without removing any trim or other components **(see illustration)**.

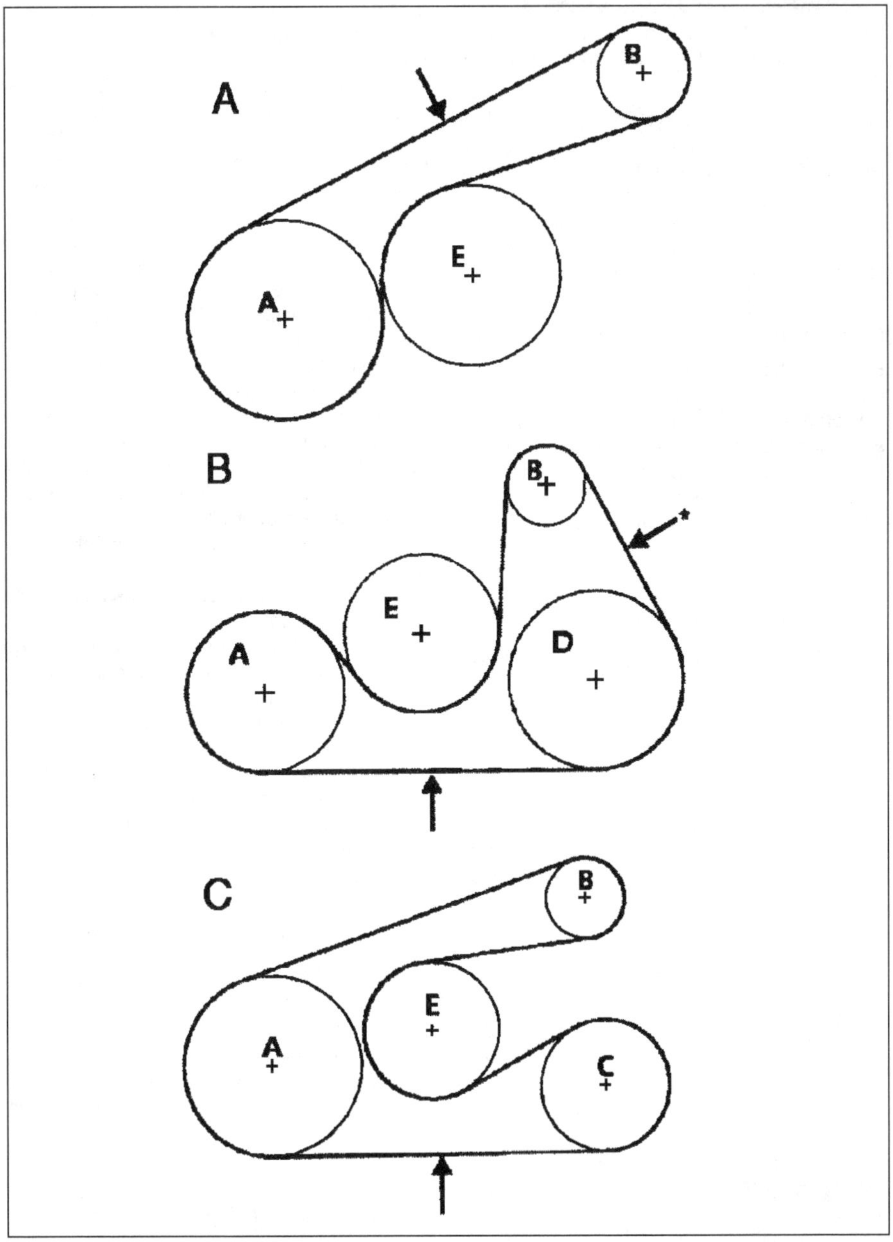

9.5 Auxiliary drivebelt configuration – F8Q engine

A Alternator and water pump drivebelt
B Alternator, water pump and air conditioning compressor drivebelt
C Alternator, water pump and power-assisted steering pump drivebelt

Pulley key: *Crankshaft (A), alternator (B), power steering pump (C), air conditioning compressor (D) and water pump (E)*

11 Electrical systems check

1 Check the operation of all electrical equipment, ie, lights, direction indicators, horn, etc. Refer to the appropriate Sections of Chapter 12 for details if any of the circuits are found to be inoperative.
2 Note that stop-light switch adjustment is described in Chapter 9.
3 Visually check all accessible wiring connectors, harnesses and retaining clips for security, and for signs of chafing or damage. Rectify any faults found.

12 Exhaust system check

1 With the engine cold (at least an hour after the vehicle has been driven), check the complete exhaust system from the engine to the end of the tailpipe. Ideally, the inspection should be carried out with the vehicle on a hoist to permit unrestricted access, but if a hoist is not available, raise and support the vehicle safely on axle stands (see *Jacking and vehicle support*).
2 Check the exhaust pipes and connections for evidence of leaks, severe corrosion and damage. Make sure that all brackets and mountings are in good condition and tight. Leakage at any of the joints or in other parts of the system will usually show up as a black sooty stain in the vicinity of the leak.
3 Rattles and other noises can often be traced to the exhaust system, especially the brackets and mountings. Try to move the pipes and silencers. If the components can come into contact with the body or suspension parts, secure the system with new mountings or if possible, separate the joints and twist the pipes as necessary to provide additional clearance.

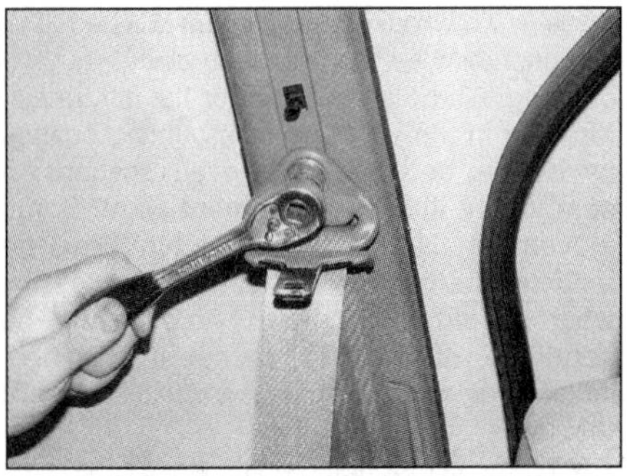

10.3 Checking the security of the seat belt mountings

4 Run the engine at idling speed. Have an assistant place a cloth or rag over the rear end of the exhaust pipe, and listen for any escape of exhaust gases that would indicate a leak.
5 On completion, lower the car to the ground.

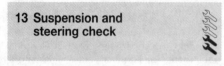

13 Suspension and steering check

Front suspension and steering check

1 Raise the front of the vehicle, and securely support it on axle stands (see *Jacking and vehicle support*).
2 Visually inspect the balljoint dust covers and the steering rack-and-pinion gaiters for splits, chafing or deterioration. Any wear of these components will cause loss of lubricant, together with dirt and water entry, resulting in rapid deterioration of the balljoints or steering gear.
3 On vehicles with power steering, check the fluid hoses for chafing or deterioration, and the pipe and hose unions for fluid leaks. Also check for signs of fluid leakage under pressure from the steering gear rubber gaiters, which would indicate failed fluid seals within the steering gear.
4 Grasp the roadwheel at the 12 o'clock and 6 o'clock positions, and try to rock it **(see illustration)**. Very slight free play may be felt, but if the movement is appreciable, further investigation is necessary to determine the source. Continue rocking the wheel while an assistant depresses the footbrake. If the movement is now eliminated or significantly reduced, it is likely that the hub bearings are at fault. If the free play is still evident with the footbrake depressed, then there is wear in the suspension joints or mountings.
5 Now grasp the wheel at the 9 o'clock and 3 o'clock positions, and try to rock it as before. Any movement felt now may again be caused by wear in the hub bearings or the steering track rod balljoints. If the outer balljoint is worn, the visual movement will be obvious. If the inner joint is suspect, it can be felt by placing a hand over the rack-and-pinion rubber gaiter and gripping the track rod. If the wheel is now rocked, movement will be felt at the inner joint if wear has taken place.
6 Using a large screwdriver or flat bar, check for wear in the suspension mounting bushes by levering between the relevant suspension component and its attachment point. Some movement is to be expected, as the mountings are made of rubber, but excessive wear should be obvious. Also check the condition of any visible rubber bushes, looking for splits, cracks or contamination of the rubber.
7 With the car standing on its wheels, have an assistant turn the steering wheel back-and-forth, about an eighth of a turn each way.

13.4 Check for wear in the hub bearings by grasping the wheel and trying to rock it

There should be very little, if any, lost movement between the steering wheel and roadwheels. If this is not the case, closely observe the joints and mountings previously described. In addition, check the steering column universal joints for wear, and also check the rack-and-pinion steering gear itself.

Rear suspension check

8 Chock the front wheels, then jack up the rear of the vehicle and support securely on axle stands (see *Jacking and vehicle support*).
9 Working as described previously for the front suspension, check the rear hub bearings, the suspension bushes and the shock absorber mountings for wear.

14 Hose and fluid leak check

1 Visually inspect the engine joint faces, gaskets and seals for any signs of water or oil leaks. Pay particular attention to the areas around the valve cover, cylinder head, oil filter and sump joint faces. Bear in mind that, over a period of time, some very slight seepage from these areas is to be expected – what you are really looking for is any indication of a serious leak. Should a leak be found, renew the offending gasket or oil seal by referring to the appropriate Chapters in this manual.
2 Also check the security and condition of all the engine-related pipes and hoses, and all hydraulic and braking system pipes and hoses. Ensure that all cable ties or securing clips are in place, and in good condition. Clips which are broken or missing can lead to chafing of the hoses, pipes or wiring, which could cause more serious problems in the future.
3 Carefully check the radiator hoses and heater hoses along their entire length . Renew any hose which is cracked, swollen or deteriorated. Cracks will show up better if the hose is squeezed. Pay close attention to the hose clips that secure the hoses to the cooling system components. Hose clips can pinch and puncture hoses, resulting in cooling system leaks. If the crimped-type hose clips are used, it may be a good idea to replace them with standard worm-drive clips.
4 Inspect all the cooling system components (hoses, joint faces, etc) for leaks **(see Haynes Hint)**. Where any problems are found on system components, renew the component or gasket with reference to Chapter 3.
5 With the vehicle raised, inspect the fuel tank and filler neck for punctures, cracks and other damage. The connection between the filler neck and tank is especially critical. Sometimes a rubber filler neck or connecting hose will leak due to loose retaining clamps or deteriorated rubber.
6 Carefully check all rubber hoses and metal fuel lines leading away from the fuel tank. Check for loose connections, deteriorated hoses, crimped lines, and other damage. Pay particular attention to the vent pipes and hoses, which often loop up around the filler neck and can become blocked or crimped. Follow the lines to the front of the vehicle, carefully inspecting them all the way. Renew damaged sections as necessary. Similarly, whilst the vehicle is raised, take the opportunity to inspect all underbody brake fluid pipes and hoses.
7 From within the engine compartment, check the security of all fuel, vacuum and brake hose attachments and pipe unions, and inspect all hoses for kinks, chafing and deterioration.
8 Check the condition of the power steering fluid pipes and hoses and, where applicable, the automatic transmission fluid cooler pipes and hoses.

A leak in the cooling system will usually show up as white- or rust-coloured deposits on the area adjoining the leak.

15 Roadwheel bolt check

1 Remove the wheel trims, where applicable, then slacken the roadwheel bolts slightly.
2 Tighten the bolts to the specified torque, using a torque wrench.

16 Bodywork and underbody condition check

1 Once the car has been washed and all tar spots and other surface blemishes have been cleaned off, carefully check all paintwork, looking closely for chips or scratches. Pay particular attention to vulnerable areas such as the front panels (bonnet and spoiler), and around the wheelarches. Any damage to the paintwork must be rectified as soon as possible to comply with the terms of the manufacturer's anti-corrosion warranties; check with a Renault dealer for details.
2 If a chip or light scratch is found which is recent and still free from rust, it can be touched-up using the appropriate touch-up stick which can be obtained from Renault dealers. Any more serious damage, or rusted stone chips, can be repaired as described in Chapter 11, but if damage or corrosion is so severe that a panel must be renewed, seek professional advice as soon as possible.
3 Always check that the door and ventilation opening drain holes and pipes are completely clear, so that water can drain out.
4 The wax-based underbody protective coating should be inspected annually, preferably just prior to Winter, when the underbody should be washed down as thoroughly as possible without disturbing the protective coating (see Chapter 11, Section 2, regarding the use of steam cleaners). Any damage to the coating should be repaired using a suitable wax-based sealer. If any of the body panels are disturbed for repair or renewal, do not forget to replace the coating and to inject wax into door panels, sills and box sections, to maintain the level of protection provided by the vehicle manufacturer.

17 Shock absorber check

1 Viewing over the roadwheels into the wheelarches, check for any signs of fluid leakage around the front and rear shock absorber bodies, or from the rubber gaiters around the piston rods. Should any fluid be noticed, the shock absorber is defective internally, and should be renewed. **Note:** *Shock absorbers should always be renewed in pairs on the same axle.*
2 The efficiency of the shock absorber may be checked by bouncing the vehicle at each corner. Generally speaking, the body will return to its normal position and stop after being depressed. If it rises and returns on a rebound, the shock absorber is probably suspect. Also examine the shock absorber upper and lower mountings for any signs of wear.

Every 36 000 miles (60 000 km)

18 Air filter element renewal

1 Undo the screws and lift the cover from the top of the air cleaner assembly **(see illustration)**.
2 Where applicable, release the clips, then lift the element from the main body **(see illustrations)**.
3 Clean the inside of the main body and cover, then insert the new filter element. Make sure it is located correctly – the bottom supports must locate in the groove, and the top clips (where applicable) must engage with the cut-outs.
4 Refit the cover and tighten the screws.

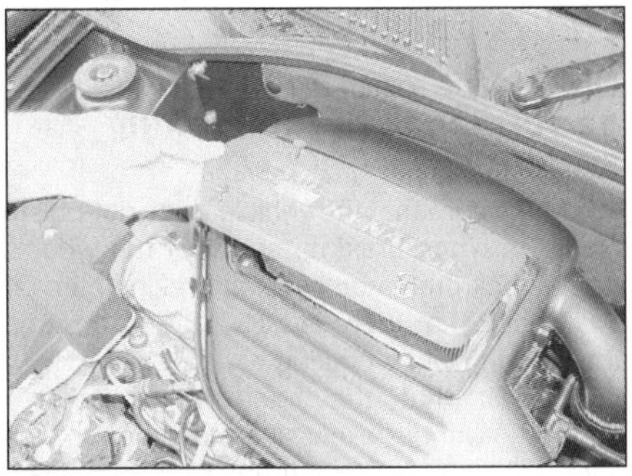

18.1 Removing the air filter element cover

18.2a Release the clips . . .

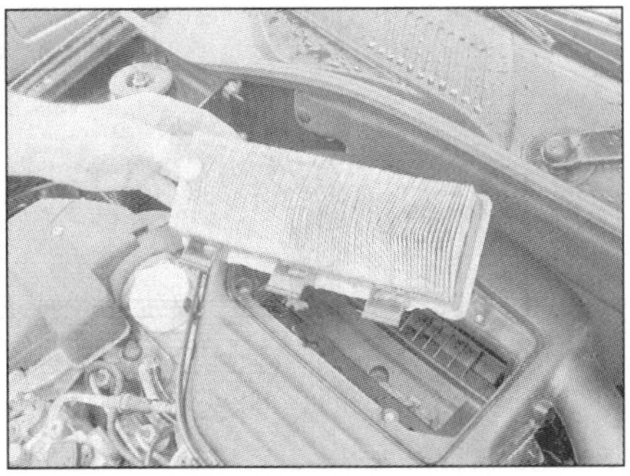

18.2b . . . and lift out the air filter element

19 Fuel filter renewal

1 The fuel filter is located in the left-hand side of the engine compartment, next to the battery **(see illustration)**. A water drain screw is provided on the base of the filter unit.
2 Place a suitable container beneath the drain screw. To make draining easier, a suitable length of tubing can be attached to the outlet on the screw to direct the fuel flow.
3 Loosen the fuel filter bleed screw **(see illustration)**, then open the drain screw by turning it anti-clockwise. On models where there is no bleed screw, loosen the fuel inlet union on the filter head.
4 Allow the entire contents of the filter to drain into the container, then securely tighten the drain screw and the bleed screw/fuel filter inlet union (as applicable).

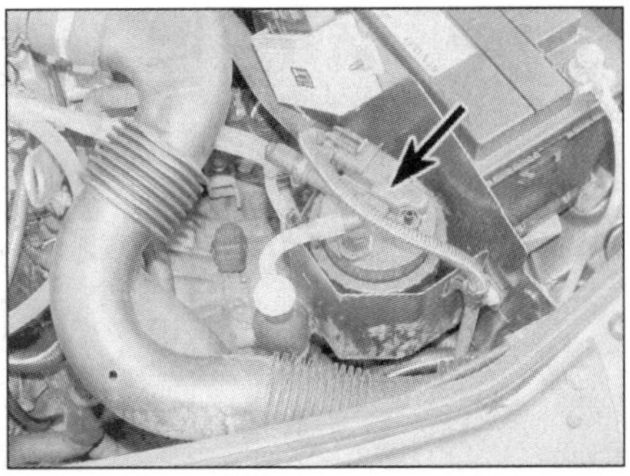

19.1 Fuel filter location

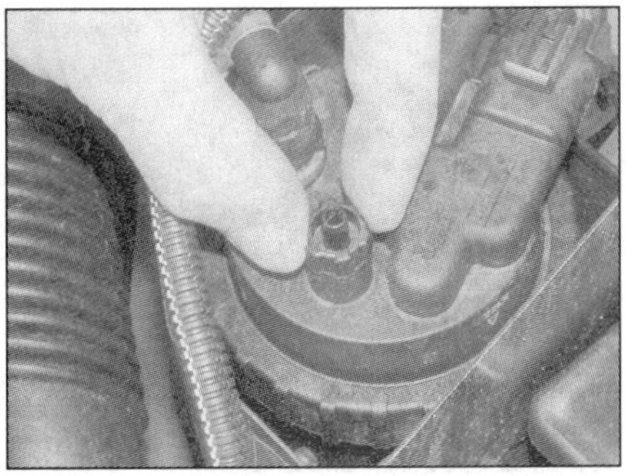

19.3 Loosening the fuel filter bleed screw

5 Unscrew the filter and remove it from the base of the fuel filter housing. Recover the filter sealing ring. To improve access, unscrew the retaining nuts and free the filter housing from its mounting bracket. If the filter is tight, use an oil filter removal tool to unscrew it.
6 Smear the sealing ring of the new filter with fuel and screw the new filter onto the housing. Tighten the filter firmly by hand only – **do not** use any tools.
7 Refit the filter housing to its mounting bracket and securely tighten the retaining nuts.

HAYNES HiNT ***Priming of the fuel system after filter renewal will be greatly improved if the filter element is filled with clean diesel fuel before securing it to the filter head. To avoid spillages of fuel, keep the filter upright during refitting.***

8 Prime and bleed the fuel system as described in Chapter 4B.

20 Rear brake shoe and drum check

1 Remove the rear brake drums, and check the brake shoes for signs of wear or contamination. At the same time, also inspect the wheel cylinders for signs of leakage, and the brake drum for signs of wear. Refer to the relevant Sections of Chapter 9 for further information.

21 Manual transmission oil level check

1 Either position the vehicle over an inspection pit, or jack up the front and rear of the vehicle and support it on axle stands (see *Jacking and vehicle support*). The vehicle must be level for the check to be accurate.
2 Remove the engine undertray or unclip the cover, as applicable, from the bottom of the transmission **(see illustration)**.
3 Clean the area around the filler/level plug located on the front facing side of the transmission, then unscrew and remove the plug **(see illustration)**.
4 The oil level should be up to the lower edge of the filler/level plug aperture **(see illustration)**.
5 If necessary, top-up using the specified type of lubricant until the transmission oil level is correct. Fill the transmission until oil starts to flow out and allow excess oil to drain out.
6 Once the transmission oil level is correct, refit the filler/level plug and tighten it securely.
7 Refit the engine undertray cover or transmission bottom cover as applicable, then lower the vehicle to the ground. Note that frequent need for topping-up indicates a leak, possibly through an oil seal. The cause should be investigated and rectified.

22 Front wheel alignment check

Refer to the information given in Chapter 10.

23 Air conditioning system check

The air conditioning system must be checked by a Renault dealer using dedicated test equipment.

24 Road test

Instruments and electrical equipment

1 Check the operation of all instruments and electrical equipment.
2 Make sure that all instruments read correctly, and switch on all electrical equipment in turn, to check that it functions properly.

Steering and suspension

3 Check for any abnormalities in the steering, suspension, handling or road 'feel'.
4 Drive the vehicle, and check that there are no unusual vibrations or noises.
5 Check that the steering feels positive, with no excessive 'sloppiness', or roughness, and check for any suspension noises when cornering and driving over bumps.

Drivetrain

6 Check the performance of the engine, clutch, transmission and driveshafts.
7 Listen for any unusual noises from the engine, clutch and transmission.
8 Make sure that the engine runs smoothly when idling, and that there is no hesitation when accelerating.
9 Check that, where applicable, the clutch action is smooth and progressive, that the drive is taken up smoothly, and that the pedal travel is not excessive. Also listen for any noises when the clutch pedal is depressed.
10 Check that all gears can be engaged smoothly without noise, and that the gear lever action is smooth and not abnormally vague or 'notchy'.
11 On automatic transmission models, make sure that all gearchanges occur smoothly, without snatching, and without an increase in engine speed between changes. Check that all of the gear positions can be selected with the vehicle at rest. If any problems are found, they should be referred to a Renault dealer.
12 Listen for a metallic clicking sound from the front of the vehicle, as the vehicle is driven slowly in a circle with the steering on full-lock. Carry out this check in both directions. If a clicking noise is heard, this indicates wear in a driveshaft joint (see Chapter 8).

Check the operation and performance of the braking system

13 Make sure that the vehicle does not pull to one side when braking, and that the wheels do not lock prematurely when braking hard.
14 Check that there is no vibration through the steering when braking.
15 Check that the handbrake operates correctly, without excessive movement of the lever, and that it holds the vehicle stationary on a slope.
16 Test the operation of the brake servo unit

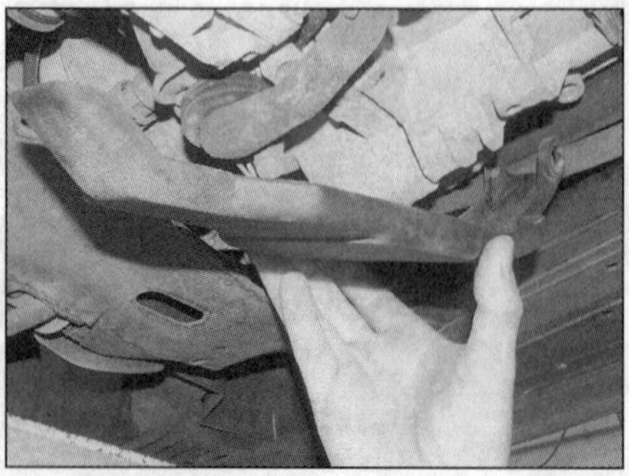

21.2 Unclipping the bottom cover from the transmission

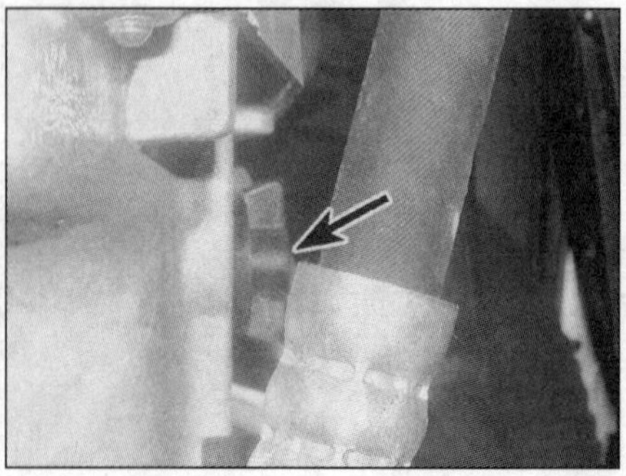

21.3 Transmission oil filler/level plug

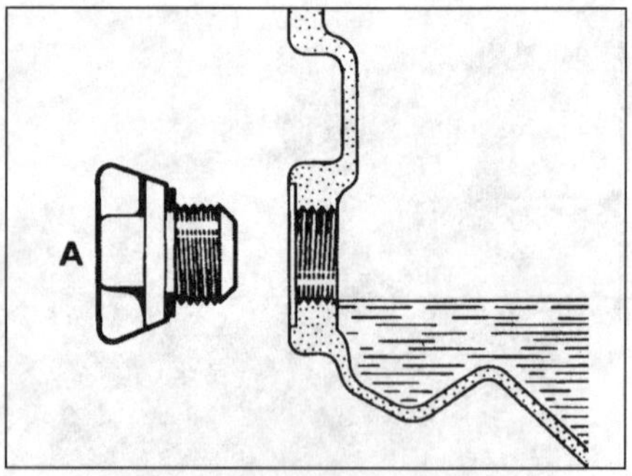

21.4 Manual transmission filler/level plug (A) – correct oil level shown

as follows. Depress the footbrake four or five times to exhaust the vacuum, then start the engine. As the engine starts, there should be a noticeable 'give' in the brake pedal as vacuum builds up. Allow the engine to run for at least two minutes, and then switch it off. If the brake pedal is now depressed again, it should be possible to detect a hiss from the servo as the pedal is depressed. After about four or five applications, no further hissing should be heard, and the pedal should feel considerably harder.

25 Timing belt renewal

Refer to Chapter 2C.

Every 72 000 miles (120 000 km) or every 4 years

26 Brake fluid renewal

Note: *For models manufactured up to 31/03/1999 renew the air filter every 36 000 miles (60 000 km).*

Warning: Brake hydraulic fluid can harm your eyes and damage painted surfaces, so use extreme caution when handling and pouring it. Do not use fluid that has been standing open for some time, as it absorbs moisture from the air. Excess moisture can cause a dangerous loss of braking effectiveness.

1 The procedure is similar to that for the bleeding of the hydraulic system as described in Chapter 9, except that the brake fluid reservoir should be emptied by syphoning, using a clean poultry baster or similar before starting, and allowance should be made for the old fluid to be expelled when bleeding a section of the circuit.

2 Working as described in Chapter 9, open the first bleed screw in the sequence, and pump the brake pedal gently until nearly all the old fluid has been emptied from the master cylinder reservoir. Top-up to the MAX level with new fluid, and continue pumping until only the new fluid remains in the reservoir, and new fluid can be seen emerging from the bleed screw. Tighten the screw, and top the reservoir level up to the MAX level line.

HAYNES HINT ***Old hydraulic fluid is invariably much darker in colour than the new, making it easy to distinguish the two.***

3 Work through all the remaining bleed screws in the sequence until new fluid can be seen at all of them. Be careful to keep the master cylinder reservoir topped-up to above the MIN level at all times, or air may enter the system and greatly increase the length of the task.

4 When the operation is complete, check that all bleed screws are securely tightened, and that their dust caps are refitted. Wash off all traces of spilt fluid, and recheck the master cylinder reservoir fluid level.

5 Check the operation of the brakes before taking the car on the road.

27 Coolant renewal

Cooling system draining

Warning: Wait until the engine is cold before starting this procedure. Do not allow antifreeze to come in contact with your skin, or with the painted surfaces of the vehicle. Rinse off spills immediately with plenty of water. Never leave antifreeze lying around in an open container, or in a puddle in the driveway or on the garage floor. Children and pets are attracted by its sweet smell, but antifreeze can be fatal if ingested.

1 With the engine completely cold, remove the expansion tank filler cap. Turn the cap anti-clockwise, wait until any pressure remaining in the system is released, then unscrew it and lift it off.

2 Where applicable, remove the undershield, then position a suitable container beneath the radiator bottom hose connection.

3 Loosen the hose clip, pull off the hose and allow the coolant to drain into the container.

4 To assist draining, open the cooling system bleed screw located on the thermostat housing.

5 When the flow of coolant stops, reposition the container below the cylinder block drain plug located at the rear right-hand side of the cylinder block. Unscrew the plug and drain the coolant into the container.

6 Flush the system if necessary as described in the following paragraphs, then refit the drain plug and secure the bottom hose. Use a new hose clip if necessary. Refill the system as described later in this Section.

Cooling system flushing

7 If coolant renewal has been neglected, or if the antifreeze mixture has become diluted, then in time, the cooling system may gradually lose efficiency, as the coolant passages become restricted due to rust, scale deposits, and other sediment. The cooling system efficiency can be restored by flushing the system clean.

8 The radiator should be flushed independently of the engine, to avoid unnecessary contamination.

Radiator flushing

9 Disconnect the top and bottom hoses and any other relevant hoses from the radiator, with reference to Chapter 3.

10 Insert a garden hose into the radiator top inlet. Direct a flow of clean water through the radiator, and continue flushing until clean water emerges from the radiator bottom outlet.

11 If after a reasonable period, the water still does not run clear, the radiator can be flushed with a good proprietary cleaning agent. It is important that the manufacturer's instructions are followed carefully. If the contamination is particularly bad, insert the hose in the radiator bottom outlet, and reverse-flush the radiator.

Engine flushing

12 To flush the engine, remove the thermostat as described in Chapter 3, and disconnect the bottom hose.

13 Insert a garden hose into the thermostat housing and direct a clean flow of water through the engine. Continue flushing until clean water emerges from the radiator bottom hose.

14 On completion, refit the thermostat and reconnect the bottom hose.

Cooling system filling

15 Before attempting to fill the cooling system, make sure that all hoses and clips are in good condition, and that the clips are tight. Note that an antifreeze mixture must be used all year round, to prevent corrosion of the engine components. Also check that the cylinder block drain plug is in place and tight.

16 Remove the expansion tank filler cap.

17 Open the cooling system bleed screw on the thermostat housing.

18 Slowly fill the system until the coolant level reaches the MAX mark on the expansion tank. Close the bleed screw when coolant free from air bubbles emerges.

19 Start the engine, and run it at a fast idle speed (approx 2500 rpm) for approximately 4 minutes. Keep the level topped-up to the top of the expansion tank filler neck.

20 Refit and tighten the expansion tank filler cap.

21 Allow the engine to run at 2500 rpm for approximately 10 minutes until the cooling fan cuts in and out.

22 Stop the engine and allow the engine to cool for at least 30 minutes.

23 Recheck the coolant level with reference to *Weekly checks*. Top-up the level if necessary and refit the expansion tank filler cap.

Antifreeze mixture

24 The antifreeze should always be renewed at the specified intervals. This is necessary not only to maintain the antifreeze properties, but also to prevent corrosion which would otherwise occur as the corrosion inhibitors become progressively less effective.

25 Always use an ethylene-glycol based antifreeze which is suitable for use in mixed-metal cooling systems. The quantity of antifreeze and levels of protection are given in the Specifications.

26 Before adding antifreeze, the cooling system should be completely drained, preferably flushed, and all hoses checked for condition and security.

27 After filling with antifreeze, a label should be attached to the expansion tank, stating the type and concentration of antifreeze used, and the date installed. Any subsequent topping-up should be made with the same type and concentration of antifreeze.

28 Do not use engine antifreeze in the windscreen/tailgate washer system, as it will cause damage to the vehicle's paintwork. A screenwash additive should be added to the washer system in the quantities stated on the bottle.

Every 4 years

28 Airbag battery renewal

1 On models fitted with a self-contained airbag, the batteries must be renewed every 4 years. This work should be entrusted to a Renault dealer.

Chapter 2 Part A:
1.2 litre petrol engine in-car repair procedures

Contents

Degrees of difficulty

Easy, suitable for novice with little experience	**Fairly easy,** suitable for beginner with some experience	**Fairly difficult,** suitable for competent DIY mechanic	**Difficult,** suitable for experienced DIY mechanic	**Very difficult,** suitable for expert DIY or professional

Specifications

General

Type	Four-cylinder, in-line, overhead camshaft
Designation	D7F
Bore	69.0 mm
Stroke	76.8 mm
Capacity	1149 cc
Firing order	1-3-4-2 (No 1 cylinder at flywheel end)
Direction of crankshaft rotation	Clockwise viewed from pulley end
Compression ratio	9.65 : 1
Camshaft endfloat	0.07 to 0.148 mm

Valve clearances (cold)

Inlet	0.10 mm
Exhaust	0.20 mm

Lubrication system

System pressure:	
At idle	0.8 bar
At 4000 rpm	3.5 bars
Oil pump type	Two-gear

Torque wrench settings

Torque wrench settings	Nm	lbf ft
Camshaft sprocket bolt	45	33
Connecting rod (big-end) cap:		
Stage 1	14	10
Stage 2	Angle-tighten a further 39°	
Crankshaft oil seal housing	9	7
Crankshaft pulley/sprocket bolt:		
Stage 1	20	15
Stage 2	Angle-tighten a further 90°	
Cylinder head bolts **(see illustration 11.33)**:		
Stage 1 – all bolts	20	15
Stage 2	Angle-tighten all bolts a further 90°	
Stage 3	Wait for at least 3 minutes	
Stage 4	Slacken bolts 1 and 2 fully	
Stage 5 Tighten bolts 1 and 2 to	20	15
Stage 6	Angle-tighten bolts 1 and 2 a further 200°	
Stage 7	Slacken bolts 3, 4, 5 and 6 fully	
Stage 8 Tighten bolts 3, 4, 5 and 6 to	20	15
Stage 9	Angle-tighten bolts 3, 4, 5 and 6 a further 200°	
Stage 10	Slacken bolts 7, 8, 9 and 10 fully	
Stage 11 Tighten bolts 7, 8, 9 and 10 to	20	15
Stage 12	Angle-tighten bolts 7, 8, 9 and 10 a further 200°	
Engine/transmission mountings (see Section 17):		
Left-hand mounting central nut	62	46
Left-hand mounting to body	21	16
Left-hand mounting to transmission	62	46
Rear mounting	62	46
Right-hand mounting central nut	105	77
Right-hand mounting to engine/body	62	46
Exhaust manifold	25	18
Flywheel bolts:		
Stage 1	17	13
Stage 2	Angle-tighten a further 110°	
Inlet manifold	15	11
Main bearing cap:		
Stage 1	20	15
Stage 2	Angle-tighten a further 80°	
Oil pump	9	7
Roadwheel bolts	90	66
Sump	10	7
Rocker shaft bolts	23	17
Timing belt tensioner bolt	50	37
Valve cover	11	8

1 General information

This Part of Chapter 2 is devoted to in-car repair procedures for the 1.2 litre petrol engine. Similar information covering the other engine types can be found in Parts B and C. All procedures concerning engine removal and refitting, and engine block/cylinder head overhaul can be found in Part D of this Chapter.

Refer to *Vehicle identification numbers* in the Reference Section at the end of this manual for details of engine code locations.

Most of the operations included in this Part are based on the assumption that the engine is still installed in the car. Therefore, if this information is being used during a complete engine overhaul, with the engine already removed, many of the steps included here will not apply.

Engine description

The engine is of four-cylinder, in-line, overhead camshaft type, mounted transversely in the front of the car.

The cylinder bores are machined directly into the cast-iron cylinder block. The crankshaft is supported within the cylinder block on five shell-type main bearings. Thrustwashers are fitted at the centre main bearing to control crankshaft endfloat.

The connecting rods are attached to the crankshaft by horizontally-split shell-type big-end bearings, and to the pistons by interference-fit gudgeon pins. The aluminium alloy pistons are of the slipper type, and are fitted with three piston rings, comprising two compression rings and a scraper-type oil control ring.

The overhead camshaft is mounted directly in the cylinder head, and is driven by the crankshaft via a toothed rubber timing belt which also drives the water pump. The camshaft operates the valves via rocker arms located on a rocker shaft bolted to the top of the cylinder head.

A semi-enclosed crankcase ventilation system is employed.

Lubrication is by pressure feed from a gear-type oil pump, which is driven directly from the timing end of the crankshaft.

Repair operations possible with the engine in the vehicle

The following operations can be carried out without having to remove the engine from the car.

a) Removal and refitting of the cylinder head.
b) Removal and refitting of the timing belt and sprockets.
c) Renewal of the camshaft oil seal.
d) Removal and refitting of the camshaft.
e) Removal and refitting of the sump.
*f) Removal and refitting of the connecting rods and pistons**
g) Removal and refitting of the oil pump.

h) Renewal of the crankshaft oil seals.
i) Renewal of the engine mountings.
j) Removal and refitting of the flywheel.

**Although the operation marked with an asterisk can be carried out with the engine in the car after removal of the sump, it is better for the engine to be removed in the interests of cleanliness and improved access. For this reason, the procedure is described in Part D of this Chapter.*

Caution: If the radio/cassette in your vehicle is equipped with an anti-theft system, make sure you have the correct activation code before disconnecting the battery.

2 Compression test - description and interpretation

Note: *A compression gauge will be required for this test.*

1 A compression check will tell you what mechanical condition the top end (pistons, rings, valves, head gasket) of the engine is in. Specifically, it can tell you if the compression is down due to leakage caused by worn piston rings, defective valves and seats or a blown head gasket. **Note:** *The engine must be at normal operating temperature, and the battery must be fully charged, for this check.*

2 Begin by cleaning the area around the spark plugs before you remove them (compressed air should be used, if available, otherwise a small brush or even a bicycle tyre pump will work). The idea is to prevent dirt from getting into the cylinders as the compression check is being done.

3 Remove all of the spark plugs from the engine (see Chapter 1A).

4 Disable the engine management system by removing the main engine protection fuse from the engine compartment fusebox.

5 Fit the compression gauge into the No 1 spark plug hole – the type of tester which screws into the plug thread is to be preferred **(see illustration)**.

6 Have an assistant hold the accelerator pedal fully depressed, while at the same time cranking the engine over several times on the starter motor. Observe the compression gauge – the compression should build-up quickly in a healthy engine. Low compression on the first stroke, followed by gradually-increasing pressure on successive strokes, indicates worn piston rings. A low compression reading on the first stroke, which does not build-up during successive strokes, indicates leaking valves or a blown head gasket (a cracked head could also be the cause). Deposits on the undersides of the valve heads can also cause low compression. Record the highest gauge reading obtained, then repeat the procedure for the remaining cylinders.

7 Add some engine oil (about three squirts from a plunger-type oil can) to each cylinder, through the spark plug hole, and repeat the test.

2.5 Carrying out a compression check

8 If the compression increases after the oil is added, the piston rings are worn. If the compression does not increase significantly, the leakage is occurring at the valves or head gasket. Leakage past the valves may be caused by burned valve seats and/or faces, or warped, cracked or bent valves.

9 If two adjacent cylinders have equally low compression, there is a strong possibility that the head gasket between them is blown. The appearance of coolant in the combustion chambers or the crankcase would verify this condition.

10 Actual compression pressures for the engines covered by this manual are not specified by the manufacturer. However, bearing in mind the information given in the preceding paragraphs, the results obtained should give a good indication of engine condition and what course of action, if any, to take.

3 Top Dead Centre (TDC) for No 1 piston - locating

1 Top dead centre (TDC) is the highest point in the cylinder that each piston reaches as the crankshaft turns. Each piston reaches TDC at the end of the compression stroke, and again at the end of the exhaust stroke; however, for the purpose of timing the engine, TDC refers to the position of No 1 piston at the end of its compression stroke. No 1 piston is at the flywheel end of the engine.

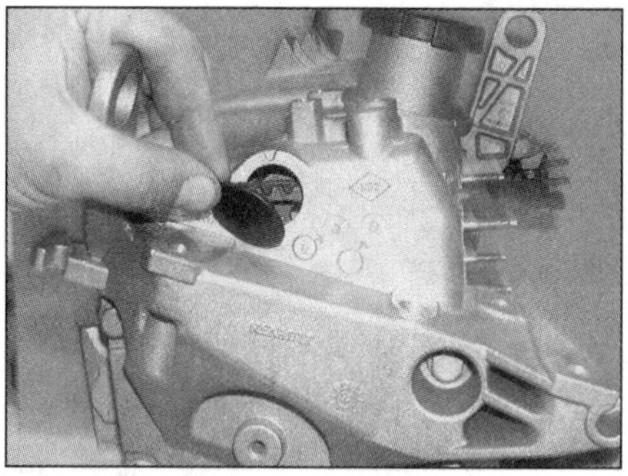

3.6a Remove the plug from the aperture in the lower engine mounting bracket/upper timing belt cover

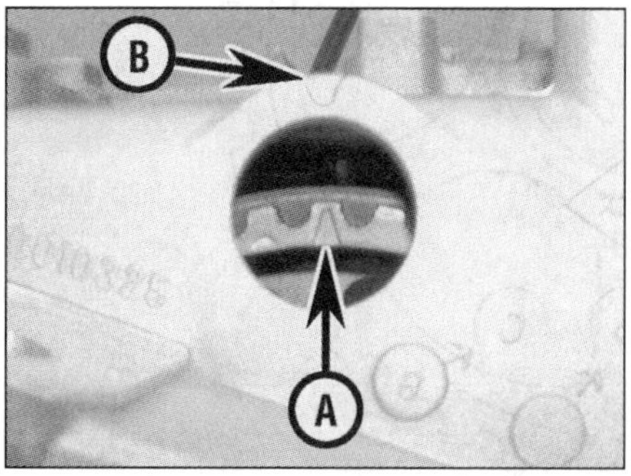

3.6b The TDC timing mark (A) on the camshaft sprocket should align with the reference mark (B) on the top of the lower engine mounting bracket/upper timing belt cover . . .

2 Apply the handbrake, then jack up the front right-hand side of the car and support it on axle stands. Remove the right-hand roadwheel.

3 Remove the plastic liners from within the right-hand wheelarch to give access to the crankshaft pulley bolt.

4 Remove the spark plugs as described in Chapter 1A.

5 Place a finger over the No 1 spark plug hole in the cylinder head (nearest the flywheel). Turn the engine in a clockwise direction, using a socket or spanner on the crankshaft pulley bolt, until pressure is felt in the No 1 cylinder. This indicates that No 1 piston is rising on its compression stroke.

6 Remove the plug from the aperture in the top of the lower engine mounting bracket/upper timing belt cover. Look through the aperture, and continue to turn the crankshaft until the TDC timing mark on the camshaft sprocket is aligned with the reference mark on the top of the bracket/timing belt cover. If the lower engine mounting bracket/upper timing belt cover has been removed, the reference mark on the camshaft sprocket should be aligned with the reference mark at the top of the valve cover **(see illustrations)**. **Note:** *The camshaft sprocket has five reference marks. Only the rectangular reference mark on one of the teeth*

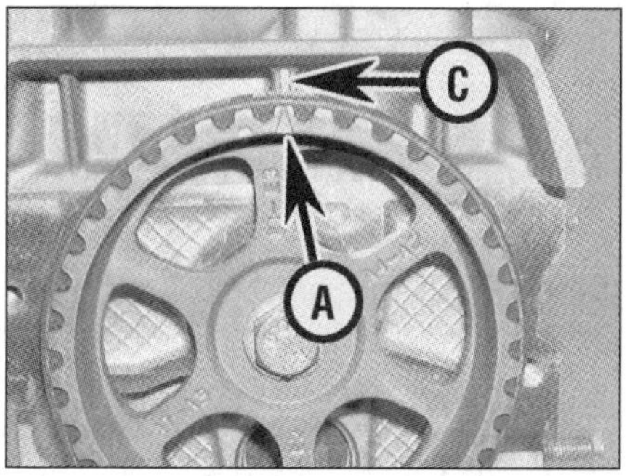

3.6c . . . or the reference mark (C) at the top of the valve cover

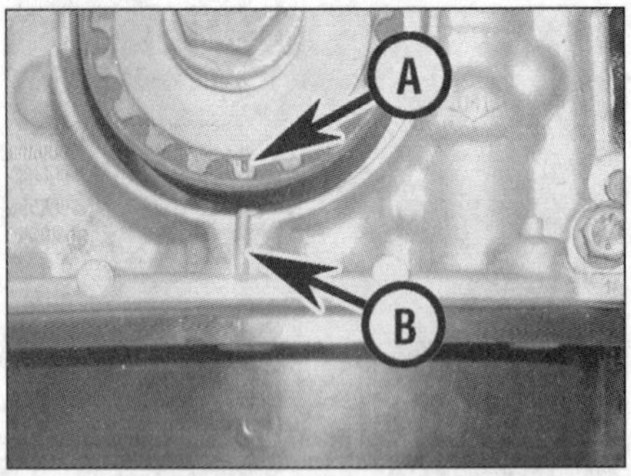

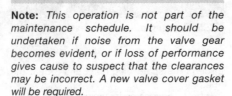

3.7 The timing mark (A) on the crankshaft sprocket should be aligned with the timing mark (B) on the oil pump flange

represents TDC. The other semi-circular marks are used to adjust the valve clearances. Due to parallax, it is tricky to see whether the reference marks are aligned when the lower engine mounting bracket/upper timing belt cover is fitted. Provided that the crankshaft sprocket timing mark is aligned with the mark on the oil pump flange (see paragraph 7), and the camshaft sprocket reference mark is visible through the hole in the engine mounting bracket/timing belt cover, No 1 piston is at TDC.

7 If the crankshaft pulley is now removed (see Section 5), the timing mark on the crankshaft sprocket should be aligned with the TDC mark at the bottom of the oil pump flange **(see illustration)**. If necessary, the flywheel may be locked to the cylinder block by inserting a suitable bolt through the special hole in the left-hand front of the block and locating it in the hole in the flywheel. Renault technicians use a special tool for this, and it is worth displaying a warning on the steering wheel as a precaution against someone attempting to start the engine with the tool in position.

4 Valve clearances – adjustment

Note: *This operation is not part of the maintenance schedule. It should be undertaken if noise from the valve gear becomes evident, or if loss of performance gives cause to suspect that the clearances may be incorrect. A new valve cover gasket will be required.*

1 Remove the inlet manifold, as described in Chapter 4A.

2 Unscrew the bolts, and remove the valve cover and gasket. Discard the gasket, a new one must be used on refitting.

3 Remove the spark plugs, with reference to Chapter 1A in order to make turning the engine easier. This however is not essential.

4 Draw the valve positions on a piece of paper, numbering them 1 to 4 inlet and exhaust according to their cylinders, from the flywheel end of the engine (ie, 1E, 1I, 2E, 2I and so on). The inlet valves are on the inlet manifold side of the cylinder head, and the exhaust valves are on the exhaust manifold side. As the valve clearances are adjusted, cross them off.

5 There are three methods of adjusting the valve clearances:

Method 1

6 Turn the crankshaft to bring No 1 piston to TDC on compression, as described in Section 3. Do not lock the crankshaft in position. Continue to turn the crankshaft until the first of the valve clearance adjustment marks (semi-circular marks) on the camshaft sprocket is aligned with the reference mark on the engine mounting bracket/upper timing belt cover, or the valve cover, as applicable (if necessary, temporarily refit the valve cover to check this) **(see illustration)**.

7 Insert a feeler blade of the correct thickness (see Specifications) between the No 1 cylinder exhaust valve stem and the end of the rocker arm. It should be a firm sliding fit. If adjustment is necessary, loosen the locknut on the rocker arm using a ring spanner, and turn the adjustment screw with a small screwdriver until the fit is correct **(see illustrations)**. Hold the adjustment screw, tighten the locknut and recheck the adjustment. Repeat the adjustment procedure on No 3 cylinder exhaust valve.

8 Turn the engine in a clockwise direction until the second valve clearance adjustment mark on the camshaft sprocket is aligned with the reference mark on the top of the timing belt cover or valve cover (as applicable) (see illustration 4.6). Adjust the valve clearances on No 1 inlet and No 3 inlet valves. Note that the valve clearances for the inlet and exhaust valves are different. Continue to adjust the valve clearances in the following sequence.

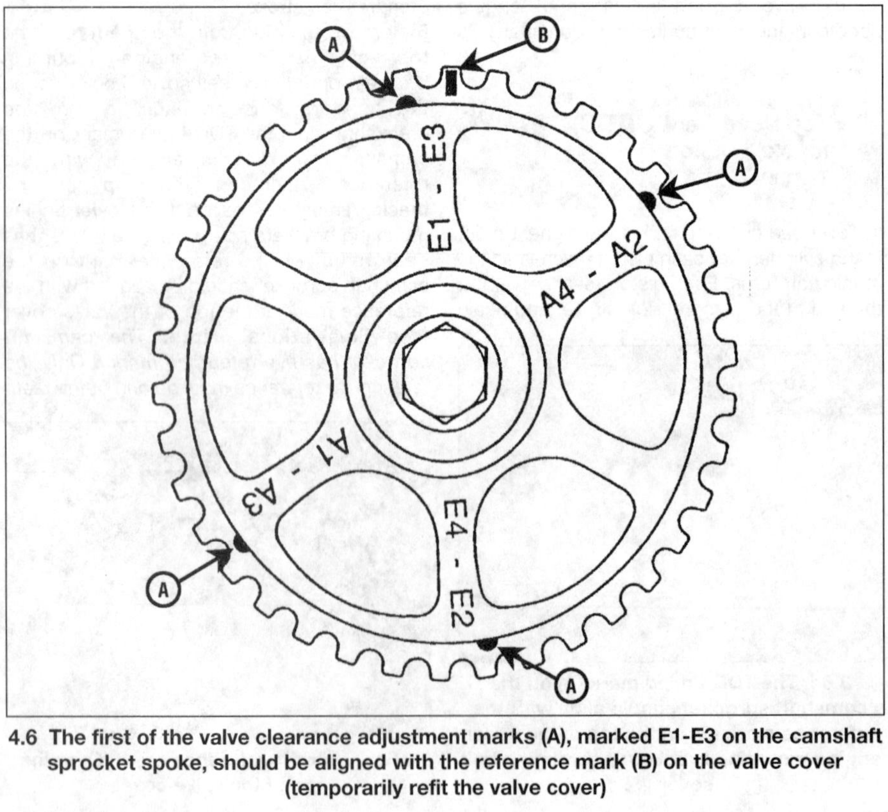

4.6 The first of the valve clearance adjustment marks (A), marked E1-E3 on the camshaft sprocket spoke, should be aligned with the reference mark (B) on the valve cover (temporarily refit the valve cover)

4.7a Check the valve clearance using a feeler blade . . .

4.7b . . . and adjust if necessary using a ring spanner and screwdriver

Valve clearance mark in alignment*	Valves to adjust
First	No 1 ex. and No 3 ex.
Second	No 1 in. and No 3 in.
Third	No 2 ex. and No 4 ex.
Fourth	No 2 in. and No 4 in.

** Turning crankshaft clockwise from camshaft sprocket TDC mark*

9 Remove the socket or spanner from the crankshaft pulley bolt.

10 Refit the spark plugs, with reference to Chapter 1A.

11 Refit the valve cover using a new gasket, and tighten the securing bolts to the specified torque in a spiral sequence (working from the centre outwards).

12 Refit the inlet manifold as described in Chapter 4A.

Method 2

13 Turn the crankshaft in a clockwise direction until No 1 exhaust valve is completely open (ie, the valve spring is completely compressed).

14 Insert a feeler blade of the correct thickness (see Specifications) between the No 3 cylinder inlet valve stem and the end of the rocker arm. It should be a firm sliding fit. If adjustment is necessary, loosen the locknut on the rocker arm using a ring spanner, and turn the adjustment screw with a screwdriver until the fit is correct. Tighten the locknut and recheck the adjustment, then repeat the adjustment procedure on No 4 cylinder exhaust valve. Note that the clearances for the inlet and exhaust valves are different.

15 Turn the engine in a clockwise direction until No 3 exhaust valve is completely open, then adjust the valve clearances on No 4 inlet and No 2 exhaust valves. Continue to adjust the valve clearances in the following sequence.

Exhaust valve fully open	Inlet valve to adjust	Exhaust valve to adjust
1E	3I	4E
3E	4I	2E
4E	2I	1E
2E	1I	3E

16 Remove the socket or spanner from the crankshaft pulley bolt.

17 Refit the spark plugs, with reference to Chapter 1A.

18 Refit the valve cover using a new gasket, and tighten the securing bolts to the specified torque in a spiral sequence (working from the centre outwards).

19 Refit the inlet manifold as described in Chapter 4A.

Method 3

20 Turn the crankshaft in a clockwise direction until the valves for cylinder No 1 are 'rocking'. The exhaust valve must be just closing and the inlet valve must be just opening. If necessary, turn the crankshaft backwards and forwards to confirm the correct position.

21 Insert a feeler blade of the correct thickness (see Specifications) between the No 4 cylinder inlet valve stem and the end of the rocker arm. It should be a firm sliding fit. If adjustment is necessary, loosen the locknut on the rocker arm using a ring spanner, and turn the adjustment screw with a screwdriver until the fit is correct. Tighten the locknut and recheck the adjustment, then repeat the adjustment procedure on No 4 exhaust valve. Note that the clearances for the inlet and exhaust valves are different.

22 Turn the engine in a clockwise direction until No 3 valves are 'rocking', then adjust the valve clearances on Nos 2 inlet and exhaust valves. Continue to adjust the valve clearances in the following sequence.

Exhaust valves 'rocking' in cylinder number	Adjust valves in cylinder number
1	4
3	2
4	1
2	3

23 Remove the socket or spanner from the crankshaft pulley bolt.

24 Refit the spark plugs, with reference to Chapter 1A.

25 Refit the valve cover using a new gasket, and tighten the securing bolts to the specified torque in a spiral sequence (working from the centre outwards).

26 Refit the inlet manifold as described in Chapter 4A.

5 Crankshaft pulley - removal and refitting

Removal

1 Apply the handbrake, then jack up the front of the car and support it securely on axle stands. Remove the right-hand front roadwheel.

2 Remove the plastic liner from inside the wheelarch for access to the crankshaft pulley.

3 Remove the auxiliary drivebelts with reference to Chapter 1A.

6.3 Removing the centre plastic timing belt cover

5.5 Removing the crankshaft pulley, complete with bolt and washer

4 The crankshaft must now be held stationary in order to loosen the crankshaft pulley bolt. To do this, have an assistant select first gear, and apply the footbrake firmly.

5 With the crankshaft held securely in place, unscrew the pulley bolt and recover the washer, then remove the pulley from the crankshaft **(see illustration)**.

Refitting

6 Refitting is a reversal of removal, bearing in mind the following points.

a) Ensure that the locating pin on the crankshaft sprocket engages with the corresponding hole in the pulley.

b) Tighten the pulley bolt to the specified torque, in the two stages given in the Specifications.

c) Refit and tension the auxiliary drivebelts as described in Chapter 1A.

6 Timing belt covers - removal and refitting

Lower engine mounting bracket/upper timing belt cover

1 Refer to Section 17.

Centre plastic cover

Removal

2 Remove the right-hand lower engine mounting bracket/upper timing belt cover, as described in Section 17.

3 Unscrew the two securing bolts and withdraw the centre plastic cover **(see illustration)**.

Refitting

4 Refitting is a reversal of removal, but refit the lower engine mounting bracket/upper timing belt cover as described in Section 17.

Lower plastic cover

Removal

5 Remove the crankshaft pulley as described in Section 5.

6 Unscrew the securing bolt, and remove the lower plastic cover **(see illustration)**.

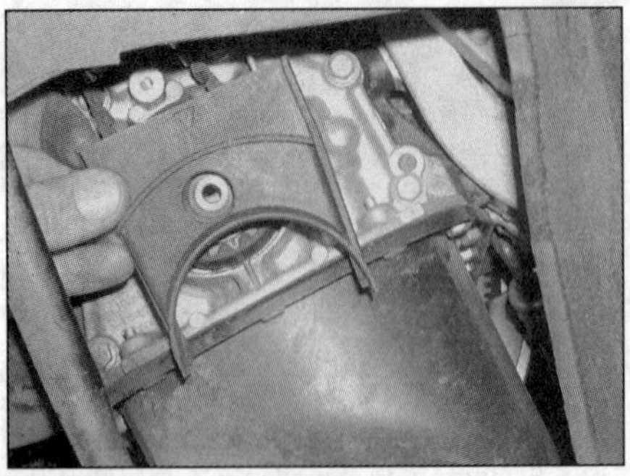

6.6 Removing the lower plastic timing belt cover

Refitting

7 Refitting is a reversal of removal, but refit the crankshaft pulley as described in Section 5.

7 Timing belt – removal, inspection, refitting and adjustment

Caution: If the timing belt breaks or slips in service, extensive engine damage may result. Renew the belt at the intervals specified in Chapter 1A, or earlier if its condition is at all doubtful.

Removal

1 Disconnect the battery negative lead.

2 To improve access, remove the bonnet as described in Chapter 11.

3 Remove the crankshaft pulley as described in Section 5.

4 Temporarily refit the crankshaft pulley bolt, and turn the crankshaft to bring No 1 piston to TDC, as described in Section 3. Lock the engine in this position with the special tool or a suitable bolt, as described in Section 3.

5 Carefully, position a trolley jack and a large block of wood under the sump to support the engine. Raise the jack to just take the weight of the engine.

6 Remove the right-hand upper engine mounting bracket, and the lower mounting bracket/timing belt cover, with reference to Section 17.

7.8 Slacken the timing belt tensioner nut and use a pair of angled long-nosed pliers to turn the tensioner pulley

7 Remove the two plastic outer timing belt covers with reference to Section 6.

8 Slacken the timing belt tensioner nut, and turn the tensioner pulley clockwise to relieve the belt tension **(see illustration)**. If necessary engage a pair of angled long-nosed pliers with the holes in the tensioner pulley to lever the pulley. Slip the timing belt from the sprockets and pulleys. With the timing belt removed, do not turn the crankshaft or the camshaft until the belt has been refitted.

Inspection

9 Check the timing belt carefully for any signs of uneven wear, splitting or oil contamination and renew it if there is the slightest doubt about its condition. If the engine is undergoing an overhaul and has covered more than 36 000 miles (60 000 km) since the original belt was fitted, it is advisable to renew the belt as a matter of course, regardless of its apparent condition.

10 If signs of oil contamination are found, trace the source of the oil leak and rectify it, then wash down the engine timing belt area and all related components to remove all traces of oil.

Refitting and adjustment

11 Ensure that the timing marks on the camshaft sprocket and crankshaft sprocket are still aligned with the relevant mark on the valve cover and the oil pump flange (see Section 3).

12 Fit the timing belt over the crankshaft and camshaft sprockets and around the water pump pulley, ensuring that the belt front run is taut, ie: all slack is on the tensioner pulley side of the belt, then fit the belt around the tensioner pulley. Where applicable, line up the two timing reference marks on the belt with the timing marks on the crankshaft and camshaft sprockets. Do not twist the belt sharply during refitting, and ensure that the belt teeth are correctly seated centrally in the sprockets and that the timing marks remain in alignment (see Section 3) **(see illustrations)**.

13 Renault recommend that a special timing belt tensioning tool (Tool Mot. 1273) is used to tension the belt. Alternatively, the following method can be used to tension the belt approximately, but in this case it is strongly recommended that the tension is checked using the Renault special tool at the earliest opportunity.

14 Engage a pair of angled long-nosed pliers with the two holes in the tensioner pulley, and use the pliers to turn the tensioner as necessary until the belt run between the tensioner and the crankshaft sprocket can just be twisted through 45° under moderate pressure with the thumb and forefinger, on the belt run between the water pump pulley and crankshaft sprocket.

15 Hold the tensioner in position using the pliers, and tighten the tensioner bolt to the specified torque **(see illustration)**.

16 Remove the locking tool, then temporarily refit the crankshaft pulley bolt, turn the crankshaft clockwise through two complete revolutions, and check that the timing marks are still aligned (see Section 3).

17 Refit the two plastic outer timing belt covers.

18 Refit the lower engine mounting bracket/timing belt cover, and the upper engine mounting bracket, with reference to Section 17.

19 Carefully lower the trolley jack and wooden block from under the sump.

20 Refit the crankshaft pulley as described in Section 5.

21 Refit the bonnet as described in Chapter 11.

22 Reconnect the battery negative lead.

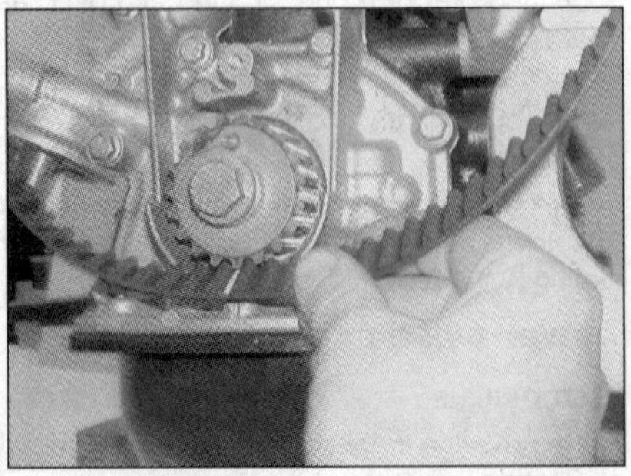

7.12a Align the timing reference marks on the belt with the timing marks on the crankshaft sprocket . . .

7.12b . . . and camshaft sprocket

7.15 Hold the belt tensioner in position and tighten the tensioner bolt to the specified torque

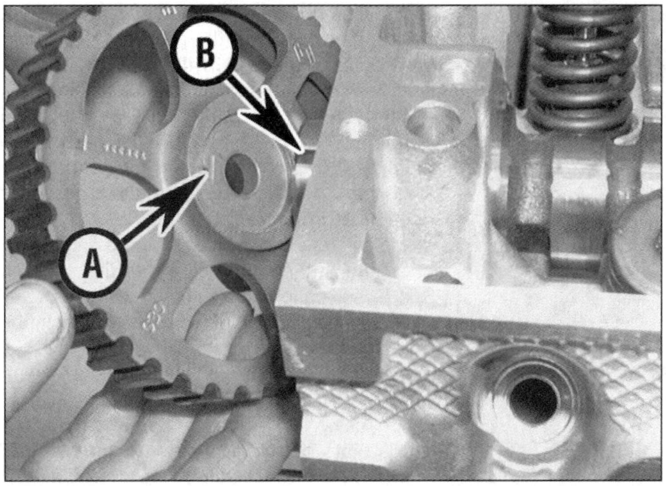

8.5 Ensure that the lug (A) on the sprocket engages with the cut-out (B) in the end of the camshaft

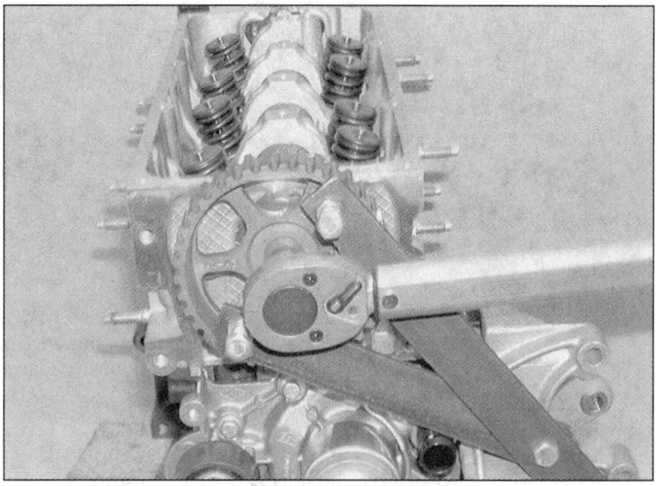

8.6 Preventing the camshaft sprocket from turning using an improvised tool whilst tightening the sprocket bolt

8 Timing belt tensioner and sprockets – removal, inspection and refitting

Camshaft sprocket

Removal

1 Remove the timing belt as described in Section 7. Note that there is no need to remove the timing belt completely, provided that it is slipped from the camshaft sprocket. **Do not** rotate the crankshaft or the camshaft until the timing belt has been refitted.

2 Slacken the camshaft sprocket retaining bolt and remove it, along with its washer. To prevent the camshaft from rotating, a tool can be fabricated from two lengths of steel strip (one long, the other short) and three nuts and bolts. One nut and bolt should form the pivot of a forked tool with the remaining two nuts and bolts at the tips of the forks to engage with the sprocket spokes (see illustration 8.6). Alternatively, if the valve cover and rocker shaft are removed, the camshaft can be held stationary using a suitable spanner on the flats provided on the timing belt end of the camshaft. **Do not** allow the camshaft to rotate as the sprocket bolt is being loosened.

3 Withdraw the sprocket from the camshaft.

Inspection

4 Clean the sprocket thoroughly, and renew it if it shows signs of wear, damage or cracks.

Refitting

5 Refit the sprocket, ensuring that the lug on the sprocket engages with the cut-out in the end of the camshaft **(see illustration)**.

6 Prevent the sprocket from rotating by using the method employed on removal, then tighten the sprocket securing bolt to the specified torque setting **(see illustration)**. **Do not** allow the camshaft to turn as the bolt is tightened.

7 Refit and tension the timing belt as described in Section 7.

Crankshaft sprocket

Removal

8 Remove the timing belt as described in Section 7. Note that there is no need to remove the timing belt completely, provided that it is slipped from the crankshaft sprocket. **Do not** rotate the crankshaft or the camshaft until the timing belt has been refitted.

9 Remove the sprocket from the end of the crankshaft.

Inspection

10 Clean the sprocket thoroughly, and renew it if it shows signs of wear, damage or cracks.

Refitting

11 Refit the sprocket to the crankshaft, ensuring that the lug on the sprocket engages with the cut-out in the end of the crankshaft. Note that the sprocket flange should be innermost, and the TDC mark on the sprocket should be aligned with the corresponding mark at the bottom of the oil pump flange **(see illustration)**.

12 Refit and tension the timing belt as described in Section 7.

Tensioner pulley

Removal

13 Remove the timing belt as described in Section 7. Note that there is no need to remove the timing belt completely. **Do not** rotate the crankshaft or the camshaft until the timing belt has been refitted.

14 Unscrew the securing nut and recover the washer, then withdraw the tensioner pulley from the stud on the water pump.

Inspection

15 Clean the tensioner pulley, but do not use any strong solvent which may enter the pulley bearing. Check that the pulley rotates freely, with no sign of stiffness or free play. Renew the assembly if there is any doubt about its condition or if there are any obvious signs of wear or damage.

Refitting

16 Fit the pulley to the stud on the water pump, ensuring that the direction of rotation arrow is visible on the outer face of the pulley, then fit the washer and the nut, but do not tighten the nut at this stage.

17 Refit and tension the timing belt as described in Section 7.

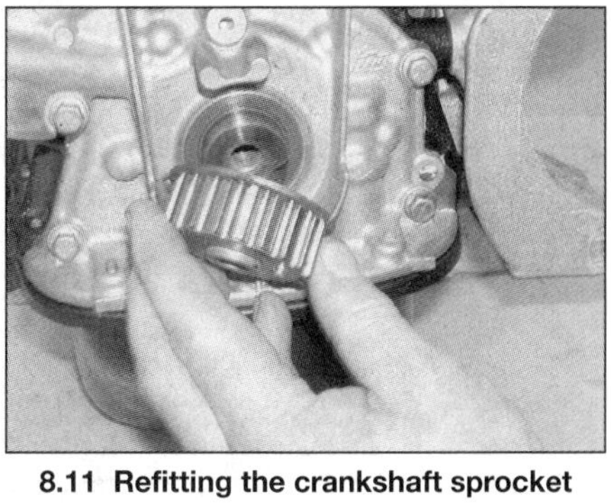

8.11 Refitting the crankshaft sprocket

Water pump pulley

18 The water pump pulley is integral with the water pump, and cannot be removed separately.

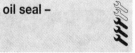

9 Camshaft oil seal – renewal

1 Remove the camshaft sprocket as described in Section 8.

2 Note the fitted depth of the seal, then prise out the old oil seal using a small screwdriver, taking care not to damage the surface of the camshaft. Alternatively, the oil seal can be removed by drilling two small holes diagonally opposite each other and inserting self-tapping screws in them. A pair of grips can then be used to pull out the oil seal, by pulling on each side in turn.

2A

9.4 Locate the oil seal over the camshaft . . .

9.5 . . . then drive the seal into position using a large socket or tube

3 Inspect the seal rubbing surface on the camshaft. If it is grooved or rough in the area where the old seal was fitted, the new seal should be fitted slightly less deeply, so that it rubs on an unworn part of the surface.
4 Wipe clean the oil seal seating, then dip the new seal in fresh engine oil, and locate it over the camshaft with its closed side facing outwards **(see illustration)**. Make sure that the oil seal lip is not damaged as it is located on the camshaft.
5 Using a metal tube (such as a large socket), drive the oil seal squarely into the bore to the depth noted before removal of the old seal (or less deeply if there is evidence of a wear groove on the camshaft) **(see illustration)**. A block of wood cut to pass over the end of the camshaft may be used instead.
6 Refit the camshaft sprocket as described in Section 8.

10 Camshaft - removal, inspection and refitting

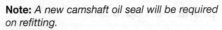

Note: *A new camshaft oil seal will be required on refitting.*

Removal

1 Remove the cylinder head as described Section 11, and place it on the workbench.
2 Progressively unscrew the bolts holding the rocker shaft and retaining plates to the cylinder head, and withdraw the rocker shaft assembly **(see illustration)**.
3 Slacken the camshaft sprocket retaining bolt and remove it, along with its washer. To prevent the camshaft from rotating, a tool can be fabricated from two lengths of steel strip (one long, the other short) and three nuts and bolts. One nut and bolt should form the pivot of a forked tool with the remaining two nuts and bolts at the tips of the forks to engage with the sprocket spokes (see illustration 8.6). Alternatively, the camshaft can be held stationary using a suitable spanner on the flats provided on the timing belt end of the camshaft. Remove the camshaft sprocket **(see illustration)**.
4 Using a dial gauge, measure the endfloat of the camshaft, and compare with that given in the Specifications **(see illustration)**. This will give an indication of the amount of wear in the thrustplate.
5 Remove the camshaft oil seal, with reference to Section 9.
6 Unscrew the two bolts and lift the thrustplate out from the slot in the cylinder head **(see illustrations)**. Note which way round the thrustplate is fitted so that it can be refitted in the same position.
7 Carefully withdraw the camshaft from the sprocket end of the cylinder head, taking care not to damage the bearing surfaces **(see illustration)**.

Inspection

8 Examine the camshaft bearing surfaces, and cam lobes for wear ridges and scoring. Renew the camshaft if any of these conditions are apparent.
9 Examine the condition of the bearing surfaces both on the camshaft and in the cylinder head. If the head bearing surfaces are worn excessively, the cylinder head will need to be renewed.

10.2 Withdrawing the rocker shaft assembly

10.3 Removing the camshaft sprocket bolt

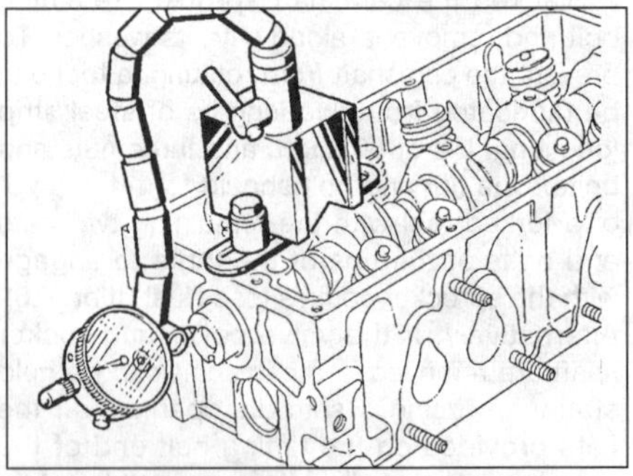

10.4 Measuring camshaft endfloat using a dial gauge

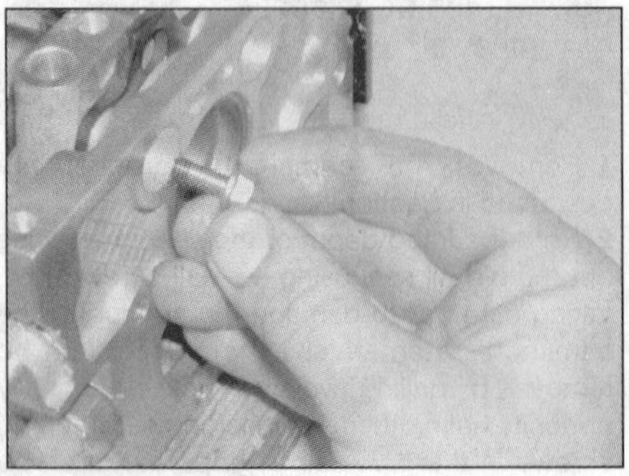

10.6a Unscrew the two bolts . . .

10.6b . . . and lift the thrustplate from the slot in the cylinder head

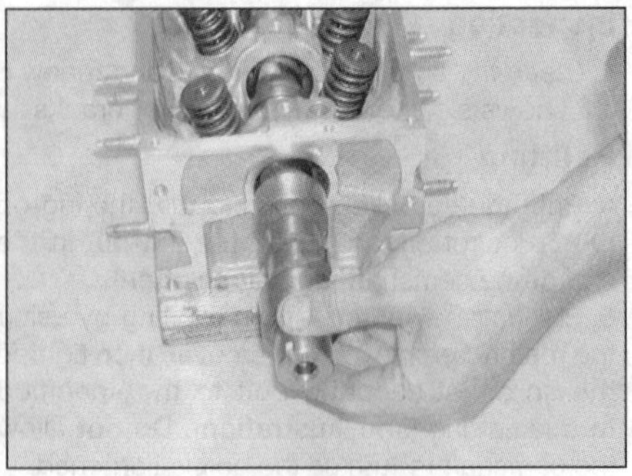

10.7 Removing the camshaft

11.13a Disconnect the coolant hoses from the water pump . . .

Refitting

10 Lubricate the bearing surfaces in the cylinder head and the camshaft journals, then insert the camshaft into the head.

11 Refit the thrustplate (if the original thrustplate is being refitted, ensure that it is fitted the correct way round, as noted before removal), then apply locking fluid to the threads of the retaining bolts, insert them, and tighten securely.

12 Measure the endfloat as described in paragraph 4, and make sure that it is within the limits given in the Specifications. Excessive endfloat can only be due to wear of the thrustplate or the camshaft.

13 Fit a new camshaft oil seal with reference to Section 9.

14 Refit the camshaft sprocket, making sure that the tab engages with the cut-out in the end of the camshaft. Hold the camshaft stationary using the method employed on removal, then insert the bolt and tighten it to the specified torque.

11.16 Disconnect the coolant hoses from the thermostat housing

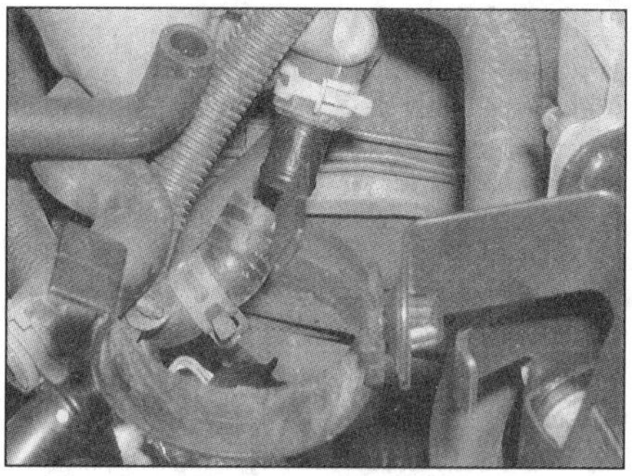

11.13b . . . and from the connector at the transmission end of the valve cover

15 Refit the rocker shaft assembly and retaining plates, then insert the bolts and tighten them to the specified torque.

16 Adjust the valve clearances as described in Section 4.

17 Refit the cylinder head as described in Section 11.

11 Cylinder head – removal and refitting

Note: *A new cylinder head gasket and a new valve cover gasket will be required on refitting.*

Removal

1 Apply the handbrake, then jack up the front of the vehicle and support securely on axle stands (see *Jacking and vehicle support*). Remove the front right-hand roadwheel and, where fitted, the engine compartment undertray.

2 Disconnect the battery negative lead.

3 To improve access, remove the bonnet as described in Chapter 11.

4 Drain the cooling system as described in Chapter 1A.

5 Remove the timing belt as described in Section 7. Make sure that the engine is adequately supported on the trolley jack.

6 Pull out the oil level dipstick then disconnect the brake servo vacuum pipe from the inlet manifold.

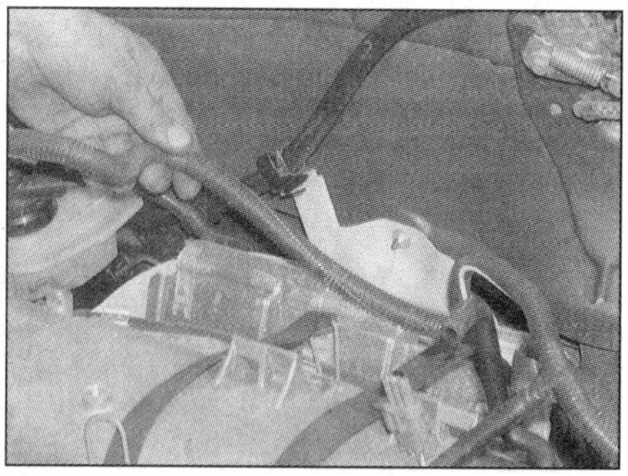

11.14 Release the wiring harness from the clips at the rear of the valve cover extension

7 Remove the air cleaner assembly and disconnect the accelerator cable as described in Chapter 4A.

8 Disconnect the fuel supply and return hoses located on the right-hand end of the cylinder head.

9 On models with air conditioning, loosen the bolts securing the compressor to the engine.

10 Disconnect the HT leads from the spark plugs. To do this, unclip the special tool located in the HT lead holder, engage its end with each lead and carefully pull to disconnect.

11 Disconnect the charcoal canister pipe and the fuel vapour hoses from the solenoid purge valve.

12 Disconnect the wiring from the ignition module, fuel injectors, idle speed stepper motor, throttle position potentiometer, and air temperature sensor (thermostat housing).

13 Release the hose clips, and disconnect the heater hoses from the water pump, and from the support at the transmission end of the valve cover **(see illustrations)**.

14 Release the wiring harness from the clips at the rear of the valve cover extension **(see illustration)**.

15 Remove the inlet manifold, throttle body and fuel rail as described in Chapter 4A.

16 Loosen the clips and disconnect the hoses from the thermostat housing **(see illustration)**.

17 Unscrew the securing bolts, and withdraw the valve cover and gasket. Note that one of the valve cover securing bolts is hidden under a rubber plug at the camshaft sprocket end of the cover **(see illustrations)**.

11.17a Remove the rubber plug . . .

11.17b . . . for access to one of the valve cover securing bolts

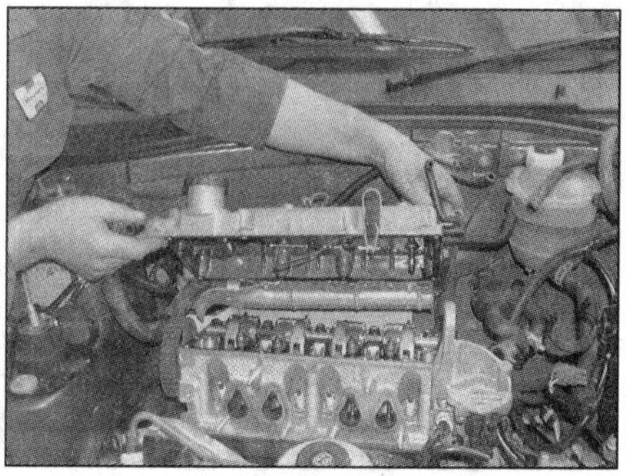

11.17c Removing the valve cover

11.19a Progressively unscrew . . .

11.19b . . . and then remove the cylinder head bolts

11.21 Lift the cylinder head from the cylinder block

18 Disconnect the exhaust downpipe from the manifold as described in Chapter 4A.

19 Working in the reverse order of the tightening sequence (see illustration 11.33), progressively unscrew (ie, slacken each bolt by one turn at a time) the cylinder head bolts. Withdraw the bolts **(see illustrations)**.

20 Release the cylinder head from the cylinder block and locating dowels by rocking it. Do not prise between the mating faces of the cylinder head and block, as this may damage the gasket faces.

21 Carefully lift the cylinder head from the block **(see illustration)**. Recover the cylinder head gasket, and discard it.

22 If desired, the camshaft can be removed as described in Section 10, and the cylinder head can be dismantled as described in Part D of this Chapter.

Refitting

23 The mating faces of the cylinder head and cylinder block/crankcase must be perfectly clean before refitting the head. Use a hard plastic or wood scraper to remove all traces of gasket and carbon. Also clean the piston crowns. Take particular care, as the soft aluminium alloy is damaged easily. Also, make sure that the carbon is not allowed to enter the oil and water passages – this is particularly important for the lubrication system, as carbon could block the oil supply to any of the engine components. Using adhesive tape and paper, seal the water, oil and bolt holes in the cylinder block/crankcase. To prevent carbon entering the gap between the pistons and bores, smear a little grease in the gap. After cleaning each piston, use a small brush to remove all traces of grease and carbon from the gap, then wipe away the remainder with a clean cloth. Clean all the pistons in the same way. Clean the head bolt hole threads in the cylinder block and remove all oil, if necessary using a syringe.

24 Check the mating surfaces of the cylinder block/crankcase and the cylinder head for nicks, deep scratches and other damage. If slight, they may be removed carefully with a file, but if excessive, machining may be the only alternative to renewal.

25 If warpage of the cylinder head gasket surface is suspected, use a straight-edge to check it for distortion. Refer to Part D of this Chapter if necessary.

26 Wipe clean the mating surfaces of the cylinder head and cylinder block/crankcase. Check that the two locating dowels are in position at each end of the cylinder block/crankcase surface.

27 Check that No 1 piston is still positioned at TDC with the camshaft and crankshaft sprocket marks correctly aligned (see Section 3). **Do not** rotate the camshaft and crankshaft until the timing belt has been refitted.

28 Fit the new cylinder head gasket to the cylinder block, ensuring that it locates correctly over the dowels, with the TOP marking visible on the inlet manifold side of the engine **(see illustration)**.

29 As necessary, reassemble the cylinder head with reference to Part D of this Chapter, and refit the camshaft as described in Section 10.

30 Lower the cylinder head into position, locating it on the dowels.

31 Apply a light film of clean engine oil to the threads of the **new** cylinder head bolts, and to the undersides of the bolt heads.

32 Carefully fit the new cylinder head bolts, and screw them in, by hand only, until finger-tight.

33 Tighten the cylinder head bolts to the specified torque in the sequence shown, and in the stages given in the Specifications at the beginning of this Chapter **(see illustration)**. The first three stages pre-compress the gasket, and the remaining stages form the main tightening procedure.

34 Reconnect the exhaust downpipe to the manifold with reference to Chapter 4A.

35 Refit the valve cover using a new gasket,

11.28 The cylinder head gasket TOP marking should be on the inlet manifold side of the engine

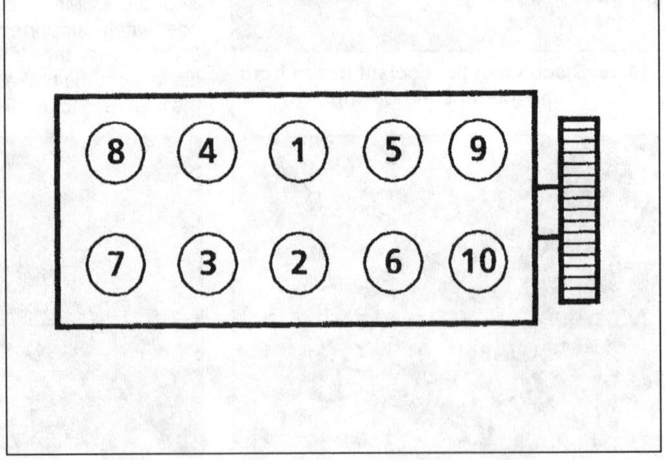

11.33 Cylinder head bolt tightening sequence

and tighten the securing bolts in a spiral sequence (working from the centre outwards).
36 Reconnect the hoses to the thermostat housing and tighten the clips.
37 Refit the inlet manifold, throttle body and fuel rail as described in Chapter 4A.
38 Refit the wiring harness to the clips at the rear of the valve cover extension.
39 Reconnect the heater hoses to the water pump and to the support at the transmission end of the valve cover, and tighten the clips.
40 Reconnect the wiring to the ignition module, fuel injectors, idle speed stepper motor, throttle position potentiometer, and air temperature sensor (thermostat housing).
41 Reconnect the charcoal canister pipe and the fuel vapour hoses to the solenoid purge valve.
42 Reconnect the HT leads to the spark plugs.
43 On models with air conditioning, tighten the compressor mounting bolts.
44 Reconnect the fuel supply and return hoses located on the right-hand end of the cylinder head.
45 Reconnect and adjust the accelerator cable, then refit the air cleaner assembly with reference to Chapter 4A.
46 Reconnect the brake servo vacuum pipe to the inlet manifold, and insert the oil level dipstick in its tube.
47 Refit the timing belt as described in Section 7.
48 Refill the cooling system as described in Chapter 1A.
49 Refit the bonnet with reference to Chapter 11.
50 Where applicable, refit the engine compartment undertray.
51 Refit the roadwheel and lower the vehicle to the ground, then reconnect the battery negative lead.

12 Sump and oil pick-up pipe – removal and refitting

Note: *A new sump gasket and a new oil pick-up pipe O-ring will be required on refitting.*

Removal

1 Disconnect the battery negative lead.
2 Apply the handbrake, then jack up the front of the vehicle and support it on axle stands (see *Jacking and vehicle support*). Remove the engine compartment undertray.
3 Drain the engine oil, with reference to Chapter 1A if necessary. Also pull out the oil level dipstick from its tube.
4 Disconnect the wiring from the oil level sensor, then unscrew and remove the sensor from the sump. If necessary use a half-moon wrench.
5 Unbolt the cover plate from the gearbox bellhousing **(see illustration)**.
6 Progressively unscrew and remove the sump securing bolts.

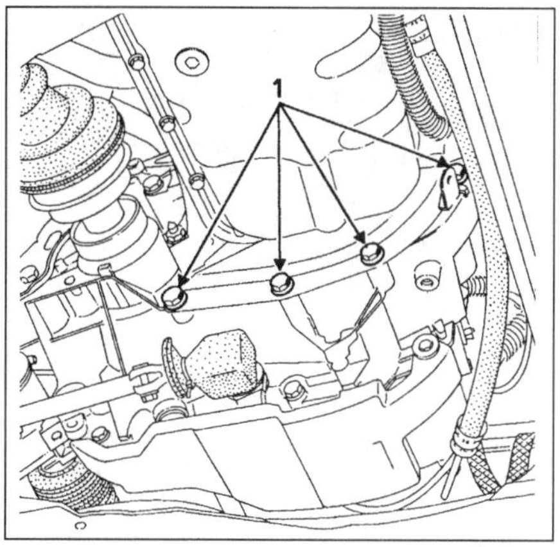

12.5 Gearbox bellhousing cover plate securing bolts (1)

7 Release the sump from the crankcase, then rotate it to the rear in order to release the oil pump strainer from the sump partition.
8 Lower the sump and withdraw it from under the vehicle. Where applicable, recover the gasket (note that the sump is sealed in production using sealant).
9 Unscrew the two bolts securing the oil pick-up pipe to the bottom of the oil pump. Remove the bolts, then withdraw the oil pick-up pipe and recover the O-ring **(see illustration)**.

Refitting

10 Clean all traces of sealant or gasket from the crankcase and sump mating faces, and wipe the mating faces dry.
11 Locate a new gasket on the sump, noting that the flat surface of the gasket should face the crankcase.
12 Refit the oil pick-up pipe to the bottom of the oil pump together with a new O-ring **(see illustration)**. Tighten the bolts securely.
13 Offer the sump onto the crankcase, rotating it as necessary over the oil pick-up pipe, and at the same time ensuring that the gasket remains in place. Insert the bolts and tighten them progressively in diagonal sequence to the specified torque.
14 Refit the gearbox bellhousing cover plate, and tighten the securing bolts.
15 Refit the oil level sensor to the sump and tighten securely, then reconnect the wiring.

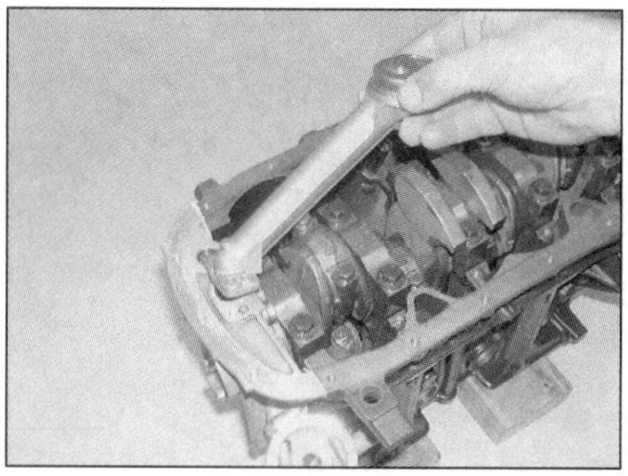

12.9 Removing the oil pick-up pipe (viewed with engine removed and inverted)

16 Refit the oil level dipstick to its tube.
17 Refit the engine compartment undertray, then lower the vehicle to the ground.
18 Reconnect the battery negative lead.
19 Refill the engine with oil as described in Chapter 1A.

13 Oil pump – removal and refitting

Note: *New main oil gallery and oil pump pick-up tube O-rings will be required on refitting, and RHODORSEAL 5661 sealant or a suitable alternative will be required.*

Removal

1 Remove the timing belt as described in Section 7.
2 Temporarily refit the right-hand lower engine mounting bracket/timing cover to the cylinder head, and tighten the securing bolts.
3 Connect a hoist and lifting tackle to the lifting eye on the right-hand lower engine mounting bracket/timing cover, and raise the hoist to just take the weight of the engine.
4 Working under the vehicle, withdraw the trolley jack and block of wood from under the sump, then remove the sump and pick-up pipe with reference to Section 12.
5 Withdraw the crankshaft sprocket from the crankshaft.
6 Unscrew the securing bolts, and withdraw the oil pump from the cylinder block **(see illustration)**.

2A

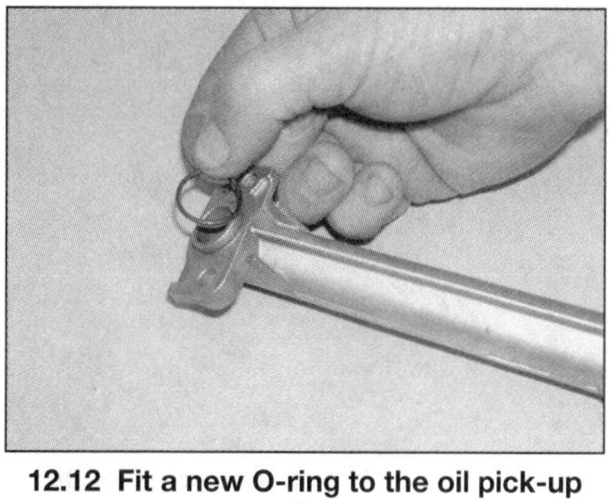

12.12 Fit a new O-ring to the oil pick-up pipe

13.6 Withdrawing the oil pump – viewed with engine removed and inverted

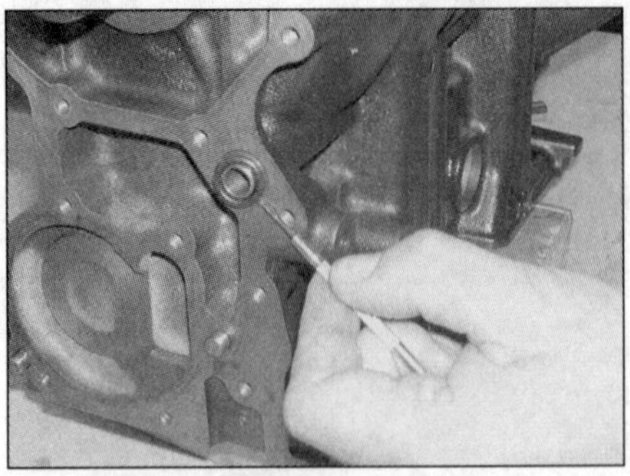
13.7 Recover the O-ring from the main oil gallery in the cylinder block

13.11 Apply a bead of sealant to the cylinder block mating face of the oil pump

13.12 Ensure that the flats on the crankshaft engage with the cut-outs (arrowed) in the oil pump rotor

7 Recover the O-ring from the main oil gallery in the cylinder block **(see illustration)**.
8 Prise the crankshaft oil seal from the oil pump.

Refitting

9 Commence refitting by thoroughly cleaning the mating faces of the oil pump and cylinder block.
10 Fit a new O-ring to the main oil gallery in the cylinder block.
11 Apply a thin bead of Rhodorseal 5661 (available from a Renault dealer), or a suitable equivalent, to the cylinder block mating face of the oil pump **(see illustration)**.
12 Slide the oil pump over the crankshaft, ensuring that the flats on the crankshaft engage with the cut-outs in the oil pump rotor, and that the positioning dowel engages with the hole in the oil pump **(see illustration)**. Wipe away any excess sealant.
13 Refit the oil pump securing bolts, and tighten progressively to the specified torque.
14 Fit a new crankshaft oil seal with reference to Section 15.
15 Refit the crankshaft sprocket, ensuring that the lug on the sprocket engages with the corresponding cut-out in the end of the crankshaft.
16 Refit the sump as described in Section 12.
17 Place the trolley jack and block of wood under the sump to support the engine, then disconnect the lifting tackle and hoist.
18 Unbolt the right-hand lower engine mounting bracket/timing cover, then refit and tension the timing belt as described in Section 7.

14 Oil pump - dismantling, inspection and reassembly

No spare parts are available for the oil pump, and no wear limit specifications are provided for the internal components. If wear or damage is suspected, a new pump assembly should be fitted.

15 Crankshaft oil seals - renewal

Timing belt end oil seal

1 Remove the crankshaft sprocket, as described in Section 8.
2 Note the fitted depth of the seal, then prise out the old oil seal using a small screwdriver, taking care not to damage the surface on the crankshaft. Alternatively, the oil seal can be removed by drilling two small holes diagonally opposite each other and inserting self-tapping screws in them. A pair of grips can then be used to pull out the oil seal, by pulling on each side in turn.
3 Inspect the seal rubbing surface on the crankshaft. If it is grooved or rough in the area where the old seal was fitted, the new seal should be fitted slightly less deeply, so that it rubs on an unworn part of the surface.
4 Wipe clean the oil seal seating, then dip the new seal in fresh engine oil, and locate it over the crankshaft with its closed side facing outwards. Make sure that the oil seal lip is not damaged as it is located on the crankshaft.
5 Using a metal tube, drive the oil seal squarely into the bore to the depth noted before removal of the old seal (or less deeply if there is evidence of a wear groove on the crankshaft). A block of wood cut to pass over the end of the crankshaft may be used instead.
6 Refit the crankshaft sprocket as described in Section 8.

Flywheel end oil seal

7 Remove the flywheel as described in Section 16.
8 Proceed as described in paragraphs 2 to 5.
9 Refit the flywheel with reference to Section 16.

16 Flywheel - removal, inspection and refitting

Note: *It is recommended that new flywheel bolts are used on refitting. Suitable thread-locking fluid will be required to coat the threads of the flywheel bolts.*

Removal

1 Remove the gearbox as described in Chapter 7A.
2 Remove the clutch as described in Chapter 6.
3 Mark the flywheel in relation to the crankshaft.
4 The flywheel must now be held stationary whilst the bolts are loosened. To do this, locate a long bolt in one of the transmission mounting bolt holes, and either insert a wide-bladed screwdriver in the starter ring gear, or use a piece of bent metal bar engaged with the ring gear. Alternatively, a suitable tool can be made up and bolted to the cylinder block (see illustration 16.8). Do not insert a bar or tool into the engine speed (flywheel) sensor teeth on the flywheel.
5 Unscrew the mounting bolts and withdraw the flywheel from the crankshaft **(see illustrations)**. Be careful not to drop it – it is heavy.

16.5a Unscrew the mounting bolts . . .

16.5b . . . and lift the flywheel from the crankshaft

16.8 Using a suitable tool to prevent the flywheel from turning when tightening the securing bolts

Inspection

6 Examine the flywheel for scoring of the clutch face, and for wear or chipping of the ring gear teeth. If the clutch face is scored, it may be possible to have the flywheel machined, but renewal is preferable. If the ring gear is worn or damaged, it may be possible to renew it separately, but this job is best left to a Renault dealer or engineering works. The temperature to which the new ring gear must be heated for installation is critical and, if not done accurately, the hardness of the teeth will be destroyed.

Refitting

7 Thoroughly clean the flywheel and crankshaft faces, then locate the flywheel on the crankshaft, making sure that any previously-made marks are aligned. Note that the flywheel bolts holes are offset, so the flywheel can only be fitted in one position.

8 Apply a few drops of locking fluid to the threads of the new flywheel bolts. Fit the bolts, and tighten them in a diagonal sequence to the specified torque in the two stages given in the Specifications. Prevent the flywheel from turning using the method used during removal **(see illustration)**.

9 Refit the clutch with reference to Chapter 6.

10 Refit the gearbox as described in Chapter 7A.

17 Engine/transmission mountings - inspection, removal and refitting

Inspection

1 Apply the handbrake, then jack up the front of the car and support it on axle stands (see *Jacking and vehicle support*). Where fitted, remove the engine compartment undershield.

2 Visually inspect the rubber pads on the two front and one rear engine/transmission mountings for signs of cracking and deterioration **(see illustration)**. Careful use of a lever will help to determine the condition of the rubber pads. If there is excessive movement in the mounting, or if the rubber has deteriorated, the mounting should be renewed.

3 Lower the vehicle to the ground.

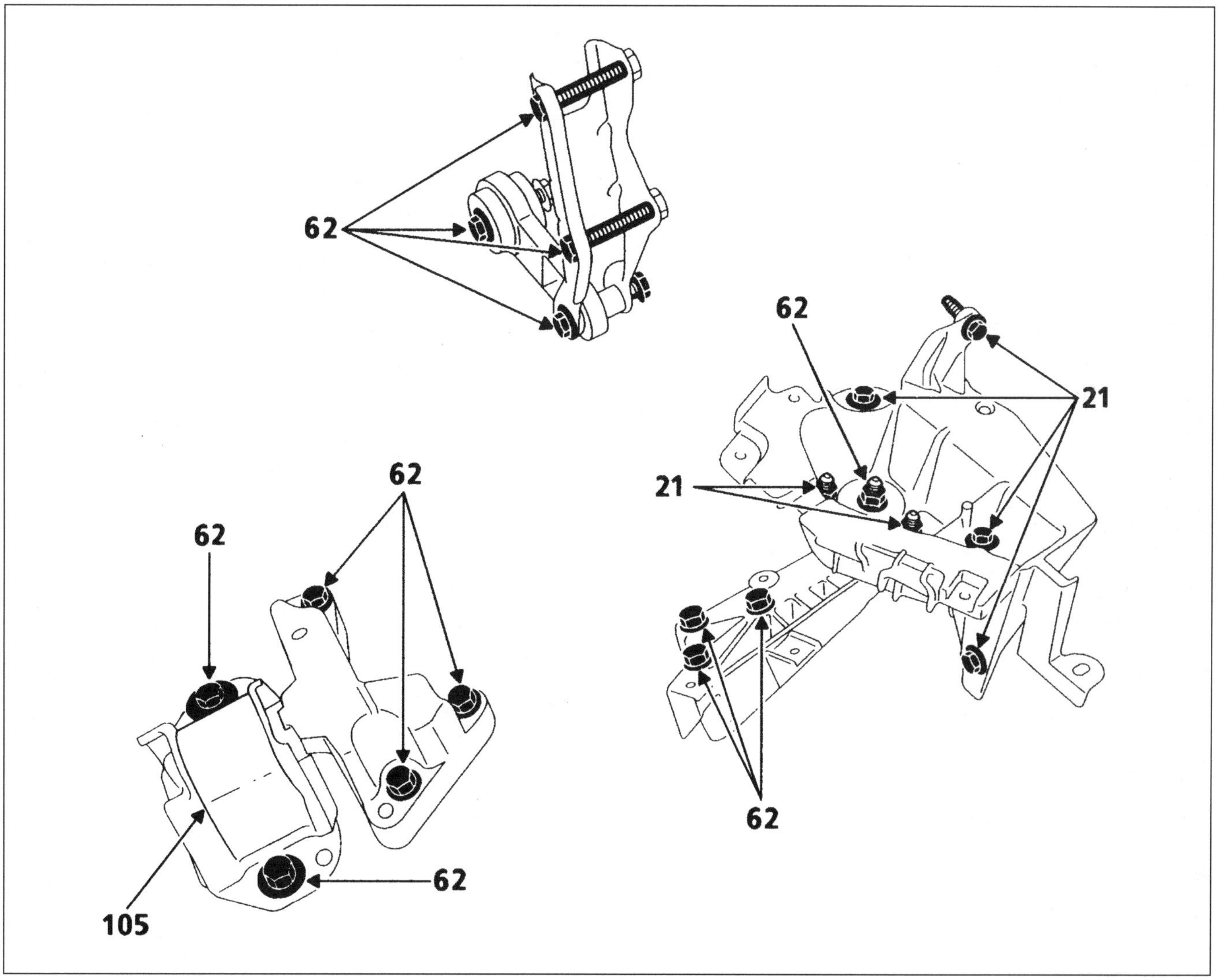

17.2 Torque wrench settings (in Nm) of the engine mountings

Renewal

Right-hand mounting

4 Support the right-hand end of the engine with a trolley jack and block of wood beneath the sump.

5 Unbolt the mounting brackets from the engine and inner wing panel.

6 Fit the new mounting using a reversal of the removal procedure, but tighten the nuts/bolts to the specified torque wrench settings (see illustration 17.2).

Left-hand mounting

7 Connect a suitable hoist and lifting tackle to the left-hand engine lifting bracket, and raise the hoist to just take the weight of the engine and gearbox.

8 Remove the battery as described in Chapter 5A.

9 Remove the fuel injection ECU as described in Chapter 4A, Section 13.

10 Release any wiring harnesses, cables, hoses, etc, from the mounting bracket/battery mounting.

11 Unbolt the battery mounting side plate from the bracket and remove it.

12 Carefully mark the position of the mounting bracket/battery mounting on the body to enable the bracket/mounting to be refitted in its original position.

13 Unscrew the two nuts securing the mounting bracket/battery mounting to the gearbox mounting, then unscrew the four bolts securing the bracket/battery mounting to the body, and withdraw the mounting.

14 Refitting is a reversal of removal, but tighten the mounting bracket/battery mounting bolts to the specified torque (see illustration 17.2).

Rear mounting

15 Apply the handbrake, then jack up the front of the vehicle, and support securely on axle stands (see *Jacking and vehicle support*). Remove the engine compartment undertray.

16 Working beneath the car, unscrew the bolts (counterhold the nuts with a second spanner or socket) securing the rear mounting link to the brackets on the subframe and cylinder block, noting the locations of any washers and spacers on the bolts. Withdraw the link from under the car.

17 If desired, unbolt and remove the brackets from the subframe and cylinder block.

18 Refitting is a reversal of the removal procedure, but tighten the securing nuts and bolts to the specified torque (see illustration 17.2).

Chapter 2 Part B:
1.4 and 1.6 litre petrol engine in-car repair procedures

Contents

Degrees of difficulty

Easy, suitable for novice with little experience	**Fairly easy,** suitable for beginner with some experience	**Fairly difficult,** suitable for competent DIY mechanic	**Difficult,** suitable for experienced DIY mechanic	**Very difficult,** suitable for expert DIY or professional

Specifications

General

Type	Four-cylinder, in-line, single-overhead (SOHC) or double-overhead (DOHC) camshaft engines
Designation:	
1.4 litre models:	
SOHC	E7J 764
DOHC	K4J 712, K4J 713
1.6 litre models:	
SOHC	K7M 744
DOHC	K4M 748
Bore:	
E7J engine	75.8 mm
K7M, K4J and K4M engines	79.5 mm
Stroke:	
E7J engine	77.0 mm
K4J engine	70.0 mm
K7M and K4M engines	80.5 mm
Capacity:	
E7J and K4J engines	1390 cc
K7M and K4M engines	1598 cc
Firing order	1-3-4-2 (No 1 cylinder at flywheel/driveplate end)
Direction of crankshaft rotation	Clockwise viewed from pulley end
Compression ratio:	
SOHC engines	9.5 : 1
DOHC engines	10 : 1

Valve clearances (cold)

SOHC engines:	
Inlet	0.10 mm
Exhaust	0.25 mm

Timing belt tension value (see text):

Fitting/checking value	30 ± 10% SEEM units
Minimum operating tension value	26 SEEM units

Camshaft

Endfloat:		
E7J engine	0.06 to 0.15 mm	
K7M engine	0.01 to 0.15 mm	
DOHC engines	0.08 to 0.178 mm	
Camshaft bearing journal diameters:		
DOHC engines:		
No 1 to No 5 bearings	24.979 to 25.000 mm	
No 6 bearing	27.979 to 28.000 mm	

Lubrication system

System pressure:		
At idle	1.0 bar	
At 4000 rpm (E7J) or 3000 rpm (K4J, K7M and K4M)	3.0 bar	
Oil pump clearances:	**Minimum**	**Maximum**
Gear to body	0.110 mm	0.249 mm
Gear endfloat	0.020 mm	0.086 mm

Torque wrench settings

Torque wrench settings	**Nm**	**lbf ft**
Camshaft sprocket bolt:		
E7J engines	55	41
K7M engines	45	33
DOHC engines:		
Stage 1	30	22
Stage 2	Angle-tighten a further 84°	
Connecting rod (big-end) cap – oiled:		
SOHC engines:		
Stage 1	10	7
Stage 2	45	33
DOHC engines	43	32
Crankshaft pulley bolt:		
SOHC engines:		
Stage 1	20	15
Stage 2	Angle-tighten a further 68° ± 6°	
DOHC engines:		
Stage 1	20	15
Stage 2	Angle-tighten a further 135° ± 15°	
Cylinder head bolts – E7J engines **(see illustration 9.82a)***:		
Stage 1 – all bolts	20	15
Stage 2	Angle-tighten all bolts a further 97° ± 2°	
Stage 3	Wait for at least 3 minutes	
Stage 4	Slacken bolts 1 and 2 fully	
Stage 5 Tighten bolts 1 and 2 to	20	15
Stage 6	Angle-tighten bolts 1 and 2 a further 97° ± 2°	
Stage 7	Slacken bolts 3, 4, 5 and 6 fully	
Stage 8 Tighten bolts 3, 4, 5 and 6 to	20	15
Stage 9	Angle-tighten bolts 3, 4, 5 and 6 a further 97° ± 2°	
Stage 10	Slacken bolts 7, 8, 9 and 10 fully	
Stage 11 Tighten bolts 7, 8, 9 and 10 to	20	15
Stage 12	Angle-tighten bolts 7, 8, 9 and 10 a further 97° ± 2°	
Cylinder head bolts – K7M engines **(see illustration 9.82a)***:		
Stage 1 – all bolts	20	15
Stage 2	Angle-tighten all bolts a further 100° ± 6°	
Stage 3	Wait for at least 3 minutes	
Stage 4	Slacken bolts 1 and 2 fully	
Stage 5 Tighten bolts 1 and 2 to	20	15
Stage 6	Angle-tighten bolts 1 and 2 a further 110° ± 6°	
Stage 7	Slacken bolts 3, 4, 5 and 6 fully	
Stage 8 Tighten bolts 3, 4, 5 and 6 to	20	15
Stage 9	Angle-tighten bolts 3, 4, 5 and 6 a further 110° ± 6°	
Stage 10	Slacken bolts 7, 8, 9 and 10 fully	
Stage 11 Tighten bolts 7, 8, 9 and 10 to	20	15
Stage 12	Angle-tighten bolts 7, 8, 9 and 10 a further 110° ± 6°	
Cylinder head bolts – DOHC engines **(see illustration 9.129b)***:		
Stage 1 – all bolts	20	15
Stage 2 – all bolts	Angle-tighten all bolts a further 240° ± 6°	

Torque wrench settings (continued)	Nm	lbf ft
Engine/transmission mountings (see Section 13):		
Right-hand mounting to engine/body	62	46
Right-hand mounting central nut	44	32
Left-hand mounting to transmission	62	46
Left-hand mounting to body	21	15
Left-hand mounting central nut	62	46
Rear mounting	62	46
Flywheel/driveplate bolts	53	39
Front suspension strut-to-hub carrier bolts	See Chapter 10	
Main bearing cap:		
E7J engine	64	47
K7M, K4J and K4M engines:		
Stage 1	25	18
Stage 2	Angle-tighten a further 47° ± 5°	
Oil pump:		
Mounting bolts	25	18
Sprocket bolts	10	7
Oil separator to cylinder head upper section	13	10
Roadwheel bolts	90	66
Rocker arm adjustment screw locknut	15	11
Rocker shaft bolts – oiled	23	17
Strengthening bracket/flywheel cover:		
On engine	50	37
On transmission	25	18
Subframe-to-underbody bolts:		
Front	62	46
Rear	105	77
Sump:		
E7J engines	8	6
K7M engines	9	7
DOHC engines:		
Stage 1	8	6
Stage 2	14	10
Timing belt idler pulley bolt	45	33
Timing belt tensioner pulley nut:		
SOHC engines	50	37
DOHC engines:		
Pre-tighten	7	5
Final	27	20
Valve cover bolts:		
SOHC engines	10	7
DOHC engines **(see illustration 8.49)**:		
Stage 1 (bolts 22, 23, 20, 13)	8	6
Stage 2 (bolts 1 to 12, 14 to 19, 21 to 24)	12	9
Stage 3 (bolts 22, 23, 20, 13)	Slacken completely	
Stage 4 (bolts 22, 23, 20, 13)	12	9

* **Note:** *There is no requirement to retighten the cylinder head bolts after the engine has first been run.*

2B

1 General information

How to use this Chapter

This Part of Chapter 2 is devoted to in-car repair procedures for the 1.4 and 1.6 litre petrol engines. Similar information covering the other engine types can be found in Parts B and C. All procedures concerning engine removal and refitting, and engine block/cylinder head overhaul can be found in Part D of this Chapter.

Refer to *Vehicle identification numbers* in the Reference Section at the end of this manual for details of engine code locations.

Most of the operations included in this Part are based on the assumption that the engine is still installed in the car. Therefore, if this information is being used during a complete engine overhaul, with the engine already removed, many of the steps included here will not apply.

Engine description

The engine is of four-cylinder, in-line, overhead camshaft type, mounted transversely in the front of the car. A single overhead camshaft is fitted to engines E7J and K7M, and double overhead camshafts are fitted to engines K4J and K4M.

On E7J and K7M engines, the overhead camshaft rotates in five plain bearings machined directly in the aluminium alloy cylinder head and is driven by the crankshaft via a toothed rubber timing belt, which also drives the water pump. The camshaft operates the valves via rocker arms located on a rocker shaft bolted to the top of the cylinder head.

On K4J and K4M engines, the overhead camshafts are each mounted in the cylinder head by six plain bearings with matching caps, and are driven by the crankshaft by a toothed rubber timing belt, which also drives the water pump. The camshafts operate the valves by hydraulic tappets and roller cam followers located below the camshafts in the cylinder head.

The cylinder block is of cast iron. Replaceable wet liners are fitted to the E-series engine, while the K-series engine has conventional dry liners bored directly into the cylinder block. The crankshaft is supported within the cylinder block on five shell-type main bearings. Thrustwashers are fitted at the upper centre main bearing to control crankshaft endfloat.

The connecting rods are attached to the crankshaft by horizontally-split shell-type big-end bearings and to the pistons by gudgeon pins which are an interference-fit in the connecting rods. The aluminium alloy pistons are fitted with three piston rings, comprising two compression rings and a scraper-type oil control ring.

A fully-enclosed crankcase ventilation system is employed.

Lubrication is by pressure feed from a gear-type oil pump, which is chain-driven direct from the crankshaft.

Repair operations possible with the engine in the vehicle

The following operations can be carried out without having to remove the engine from the car:

a) Removal and refitting of the cylinder head.
b) Removal and refitting of the timing belt and sprockets.
c) Renewal of the camshaft oil seal.
d) Removal and refitting of the camshaft.
e) Removal and refitting of the pressed-steel sump.
*f) Removal and refitting of the connecting rods and pistons. **
g) Removal and refitting of the oil pump.
h) Renewal of the crankshaft timing belt end oil seal.
i) Renewal of the engine mountings.

*** Note:** *Although the operation marked with an asterisk can be carried out with the engine in the car after removal of the sump, it is better for the engine to be removed, in the interests of cleanliness and improved access. For this reason, these procedures are described in Part D of this Chapter.*

Caution: If the radio/cassette in your vehicle is equipped with an anti-theft system, make sure you have the correct activation code before disconnecting the battery.

2 Compression test – description and interpretation

Note: *A compression gauge will be required for this test.*

1 A compression check will tell you what mechanical condition the top end (pistons, rings, valves, head gasket) of the engine is in. Specifically, it can tell you if the compression is down due to leakage caused by worn piston rings, defective valves and seats or a blown head gasket. **Note:** *The engine must be at normal operating temperature and the battery must be fully charged, for this check.*

2 Begin by cleaning the area around the spark plugs before you remove them (compressed air should be used, if available, otherwise a small brush or even a bicycle tyre pump will work). The idea is to prevent dirt from getting into the cylinders as the compression check is being done.

3 Remove all the spark plugs from the engine (see Chapter 1A).

4 Disable the engine management system by removing the engine protection fuse from the engine compartment fusebox.

5 Fit the compression gauge into the No 1 spark plug hole – the type of tester which screws into the plug thread is to be preferred.

6 Have an assistant hold the accelerator pedal fully depressed, while at the same time cranking the engine over several times on the starter motor. Observe the compression gauge – the compression should build-up quickly in a healthy engine. Low compression on the first stroke, followed by gradually-increasing pressure on successive strokes, indicates worn piston rings. A low compression reading on the first stroke, which does not build-up during successive strokes, indicates leaking valves or a blown head gasket (a cracked head could also be the cause). Deposits on the undersides of the valve heads can also cause low compression. Record the highest gauge reading obtained, then repeat the procedure for the remaining cylinders.

7 Add some engine oil (about three squirts from a plunger-type oil can) to each cylinder, through the spark plug hole and repeat the test.

8 If the compression increases after the oil is added, the piston rings are worn. If the compression does not increase significantly, the leakage is occurring at the valves or head gasket. Leakage past the valves may be caused by burned valve seats and/or faces, or warped, cracked or bent valves.

9 If two adjacent cylinders have equally low compression, there is a strong possibility that the head gasket between them is blown. The appearance of coolant in the combustion chambers or the crankcase would verify this condition.

10 Actual compression pressures for the engines covered by this manual are not specified by the manufacturer. However, bearing in mind the information given in the preceding paragraphs, the results obtained should give a good indication of engine condition and what course of action, if any, to take.

3.6a Remove the plug from the aperture in the lower engine mounting bracket/upper timing belt cover

3 Top Dead Centre (TDC) for No 1 piston – locating

1 Top Dead Centre (TDC) is the highest point in the cylinder that each piston reaches as the crankshaft turns. Each piston reaches TDC at the end of the compression stroke and again at the end of the exhaust stroke; however, for the purpose of timing the engine, TDC refers to the position of No 1 piston at the end of its compression stroke. No 1 piston is at the flywheel end of the engine.

2 Apply the handbrake, then jack up the front right-hand side of the car and support it on axle stands. Remove the right-hand roadwheel.

3 Remove the plastic liners from within the right-hand wheelarch to give access to the crankshaft pulley bolt.

4 Remove the spark plugs as described in Chapter 1A.

5 Place a finger over the No 1 spark plug hole in the cylinder head (nearest the flywheel) as the spark plugs are deeply recessed, or alternatively use the handle of a screwdriver. Turn the engine in a clockwise direction, using a socket or spanner on the crankshaft pulley bolt, until pressure is felt in the No 1 cylinder. This indicates that No 1 piston is rising on its compression stroke.

SOHC engines

6 Remove the plug from the aperture in the upper timing belt cover. Look through the aperture, and continue to turn the crankshaft until the TDC timing mark on the camshaft sprocket is aligned with the reference mark on the top of the bracket/timing belt cover. If the lower engine mounting bracket/upper timing belt cover has been removed, the reference mark on the camshaft sprocket should be aligned with the reference mark at the top of the valve cover **(see illustrations)**. **Note:** *The camshaft sprocket has five reference marks. Only the rectangular reference mark on one of the teeth represents TDC. The other semi-circular marks are used to adjust the valve clearances. Due to parallax, it is tricky to see whether the reference marks are aligned when the timing belt cover is fitted. Provided that the crankshaft sprocket timing mark is aligned with the mark on the oil pump flange, and the camshaft sprocket reference mark is visible through the hole in the engine mounting bracket/timing belt cover, No 1 piston is at TDC.*

7 If the crankshaft pulley is now removed, the timing mark on the crankshaft sprocket

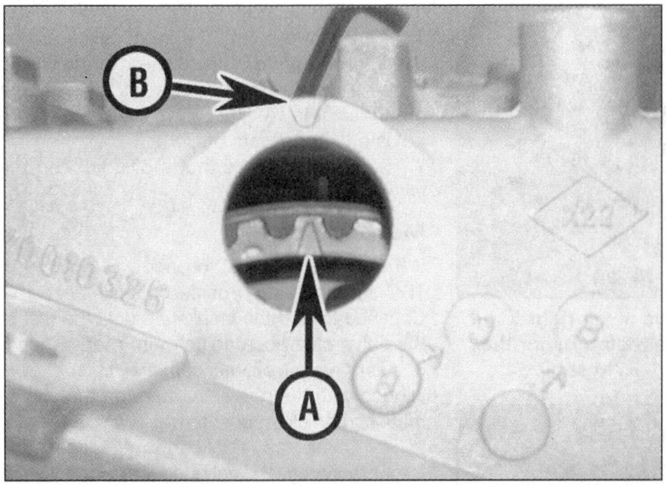

3.6b The TDC timing mark (A) on the camshaft sprocket should align with the reference mark (B) on the top of the lower engine mounting bracket/upper timing belt cover . . .

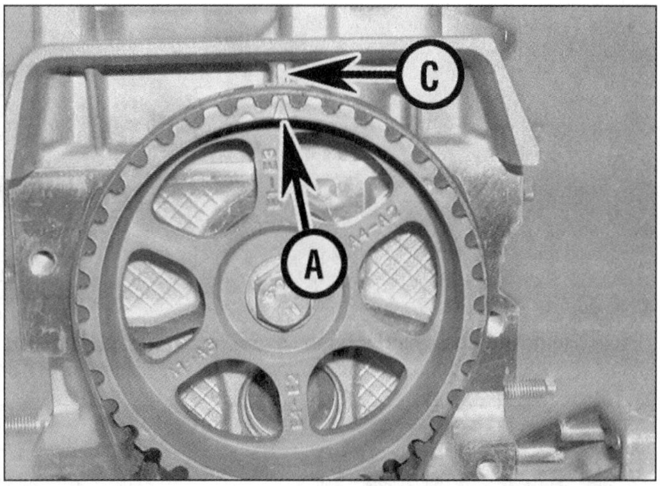

3.6c . . . or the reference mark (C) at the top of the valve cover

should be aligned with the TDC mark at the bottom of the oil pump flange **(see illustration)**.

DOHC engines

Note: *A TDC pin from a Renault dealer is required for this operation.*

8 Remove the air cleaner and resonator from the left-hand side of the engine with reference to Chapter 4A.

9 Using a screwdriver, pierce the centres of the two plastic plugs at the left-hand end of the cylinder head, and pull out the plugs **(see illustration)**. With No 1 piston approaching TDC, the grooves in the ends of the camshafts should be positioned approximately at 30° angle from the horizontal, with the offset below the centreline.

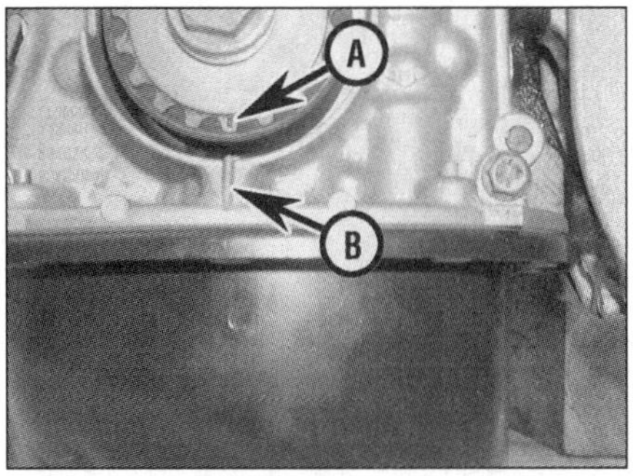

3.7 The timing mark (A) on the crankshaft sprocket should be aligned with the timing mark (B) on the oil pump flange

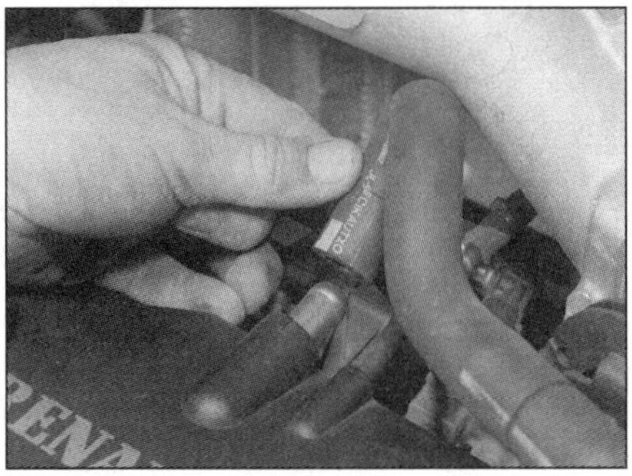

4.3a Disconnecting the large (to air cleaner) . . .

10 Unscrew the TDC plug from the left-hand front of the cylinder block, then fully screw in the TDC pin. **Note:** *If the pin is not available, an alternative method of determining the TDC position is to use a dial gauge on the top of piston No 1 after removing the spark plug.*

11 Carefully turn the crankshaft clockwise until the crankshaft web is in contact with the TDC pin. At this point, the No 1 piston is at TDC on its compression stroke, and the grooves in the ends of the camshafts will now be positioned horizontally. Renault technicians use a special tool to lock the camshafts in their TDC position. The tool is attached to the left-hand end of the cylinder head to hold the camshafts with their grooves horizontal, and a similar tool may be fabricated from metal plate if necessary.

12 Note that the crankshaft sprocket is not keyed to the crankshaft as is the normal arrangement, therefore if the crankshaft pulley/sprocket is removed it is important to have an accurate method of determining the TDC position of No 1 piston.

3.9 Using a screwdriver, prise the camshaft sealing plugs from the left-hand end of the cylinder head

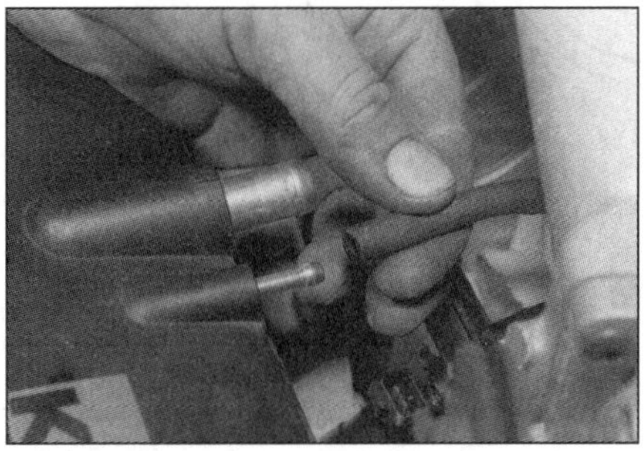

4.3b . . . and small (to inlet manifold) crankcase ventilation hoses from the cylinder head cover

4 Valve clearances – checking and adjustment

Note: *This operation applies to SOHC engines (E7J and K7M) only. It is not part of the maintenance schedule, but should be undertaken if noise from the valve gear becomes evident, or if loss of performance gives cause to suspect that the clearances may be incorrect. A new valve cover gasket will be required.*

1 Remove the air cleaner assembly with reference to Chapter 4A, then, where applicable disconnect the accelerator cable from the throttle housing. If necessary, unbolt the accelerator cable support from the cylinder head cover.

2 On the K7M engine, remove the ignition HT coils from the cylinder head cover with reference to Chapter 5B, then disconnect the HT leads from the spark plugs and unbolt the HT lead retainer from the cylinder head cover.

3 Disconnect the crankcase ventilation hoses from the cylinder head cover **(see illustrations)**.

4.4a Removing the cylinder head cover bolts

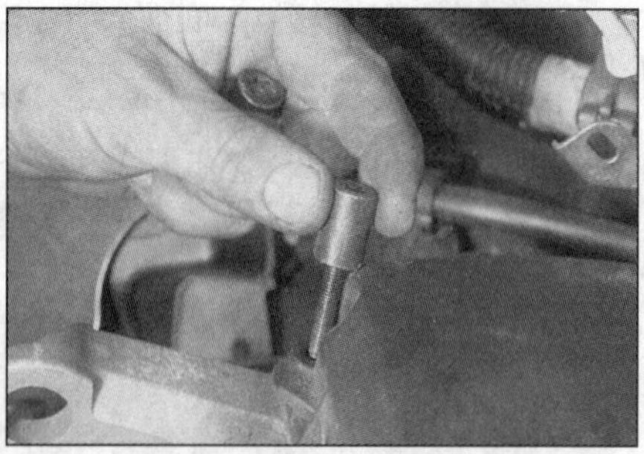
4.4b The cylinder head cover right-hand bolts have threads in their tops for the ignition HT coils – K7M engine

4.4c Removing the cylinder head cover . . .

4.4d . . . and gasket

4 Unscrew the bolts and remove the cylinder head cover and gasket. On the K7M engine, the right-hand bolts have threads in their tops, as the ignition coil is mounted on them **(see illustrations)**.

5 Remove the spark plugs (Chapter 1A) to make turning the engine easier.

6 Draw the valve positions on a piece of paper, numbering them 1 to 4 inlet and exhaust according to their cylinders, from the flywheel/driveplate end of the engine (ie, 1E, 1I, 2E, 2I and so on). The inlet valves are on the inlet manifold side of the cylinder head and the exhaust valves are on the exhaust manifold side. As the valve clearances are adjusted, cross them off.

7 There are three methods of adjusting the valve clearances:

Method 1

8 Turn the crankshaft to bring No 1 piston to TDC on compression, as described in Section 3. Continue to turn the crankshaft until the first of the valve clearance adjustment marks (semi-circular marks) on the camshaft sprocket is aligned with the reference mark on the engine mounting bracket/upper timing belt cover, or the valve cover, as applicable (if necessary, temporarily refit the valve cover to check this) **(see illustration)**.

9 Insert a feeler blade of the correct thickness (see Specifications) between the No 1 cylinder exhaust valve stem and the end of the rocker arm. It should be a firm sliding fit. If adjustment is necessary, loosen the locknut on the rocker arm using a ring spanner, and turn the adjustment screw with a small screwdriver until the fit is correct **(see illustrations)**. Hold the adjustment screw, tighten the locknut and recheck the adjustment. Repeat the adjustment procedure on No 3 cylinder exhaust valve.

10 Turn the engine in a clockwise direction until the second valve clearance adjustment mark on the camshaft sprocket is aligned with the reference mark on the top of the timing

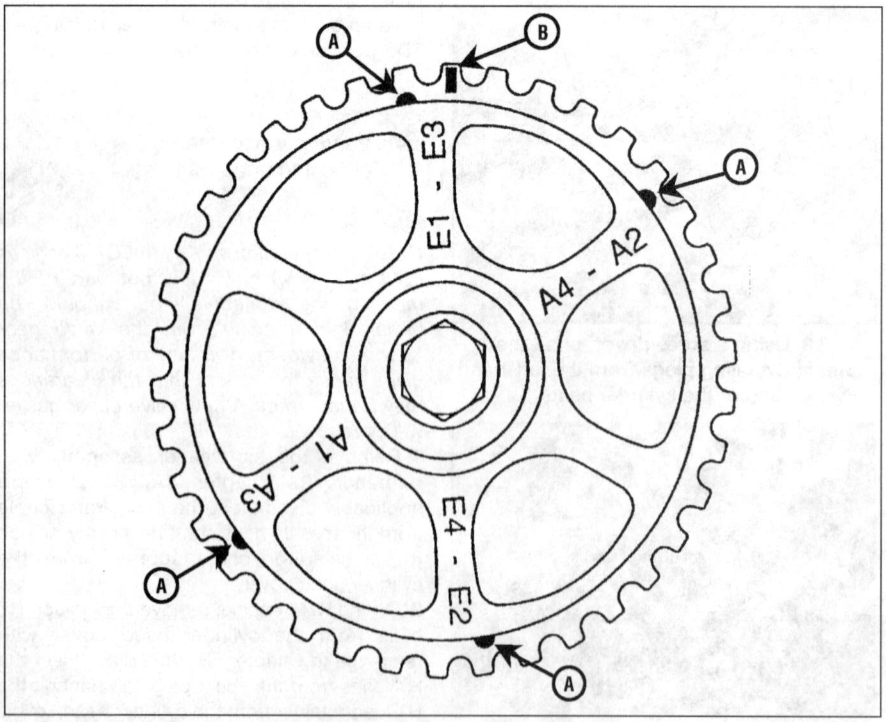

4.8 The first of the valve clearance adjustment marks (A), marked E1-E3 on the camshaft sprocket spoke, should be aligned with the reference mark (B) on the valve cover (temporarily refit the valve cover)

4.9a Loosening the rocker arm adjustment locknut

4.9b Turning the adjustment screw to alter the valve clearance

4.9c Tightening the adjustment locknut with a torque wrench

belt cover or valve cover (as applicable) (see illustration 4.8). Adjust the valve clearances on No 1 inlet and No 3 inlet valves. Note that the valve clearances for the inlet and exhaust valves are different. Continue to adjust the valve clearances in the following sequence.

Valve clearance mark in alignment*	Valves to adjust
First	No 1 ex. and No 3 ex.
Second	No 1 in. and No 3 in.
Third	No 2 ex. and No 4 ex.
Fourth	No 2 in. and No 4 in.

** Turning crankshaft clockwise from camshaft sprocket TDC mark*

11 Remove the socket or spanner from the crankshaft pulley bolt.

12 Refit the spark plugs, with reference to Chapter 1A.

13 Refit the valve cover using a new gasket, and tighten the securing bolts to the specified torque in a spiral sequence (working from the centre outwards).

14 Reconnect the crankcase ventilation hoses, HT leads and air cleaner assembly.

Method 2

15 Turn the crankshaft in a clockwise direction until No 1 exhaust valve is completely open (ie, the valve spring is completely compressed).

16 Insert a feeler blade of the correct thickness (see Specifications) between the No 3 cylinder inlet valve stem and the end of the rocker arm. It should be a firm sliding fit. If adjustment is necessary, loosen the locknut on the rocker arm using a ring spanner, and turn the adjustment screw with a screwdriver until the fit is correct. Tighten the locknut and recheck the adjustment, then repeat the adjustment procedure on No 4 cylinder exhaust valve. Note that the clearances for the inlet and exhaust valves are different.

17 Turn the engine in a clockwise direction until No 3 exhaust valve is completely open, then adjust the valve clearances on No 4 inlet and No 2 exhaust valves. Continue to adjust the valve clearances in the following sequence.

Exhaust valve fully open	Inlet valve to adjust	Exhaust valve to adjust
1E	3I	4E
3E	4I	2E
4E	2I	1E
2E	1I	3E

18 Remove the socket or spanner from the crankshaft pulley bolt.

19 Refit the spark plugs, with reference to Chapter 1A.

20 Refit the valve cover using a new gasket, and tighten the securing bolts to the specified torque in a spiral sequence (working from the centre outwards).

21 Reconnect the crankcase ventilation hoses, HT leads and air cleaner assembly.

Method 3

22 Turn the crankshaft in a clockwise direction until the valves for cylinder No 1 are 'rocking'. The exhaust valve must be just closing and the inlet valve must be just opening. If necessary, turn the crankshaft backwards and forwards to confirm the correct position.

23 Insert a feeler blade of the correct thickness (see Specifications) between the No 4 cylinder inlet valve stem and the end of the rocker arm. It should be a firm sliding fit. If adjustment is necessary, loosen the locknut on the rocker arm using a ring spanner, and turn the adjustment screw with a screwdriver until the fit is correct. Tighten the locknut and recheck the adjustment, then repeat the adjustment procedure on No 4 exhaust valve. Note that the clearances for the inlet and exhaust valves are different.

24 Turn the engine in a clockwise direction until No 3 valves are 'rocking', then adjust the valve clearances on Nos 2 inlet and exhaust valves. Continue to adjust the valve clearances in the following sequence.

Exhaust valves 'rocking' in cylinder number	Adjust valves in cylinder number
1	4
3	2
4	1
2	3

25 Remove the socket or spanner from the crankshaft pulley bolt.

26 Refit the spark plugs, with reference to Chapter 1A.

27 Refit the valve cover using a new gasket, and tighten the securing bolts to the specified torque in a spiral sequence (working from the centre outwards).

28 Reconnect the crankcase ventilation hoses, HT leads and air cleaner assembly.

5.8a Loosening the crankshaft pulley bolt

5 Timing belt – removal, inspection and refitting

Caution: If the timing belt breaks in service, extensive engine damage may result. Renew the belt at the intervals specified in Chapter 1A, or earlier if its condition is at all doubtful

Removal

1 Disconnect the battery negative lead (refer to *Disconnecting the battery* in the Reference Section).

2 Apply the handbrake, then jack up the front right-hand side of the vehicle and support on axle stands (see *Jacking and vehicle support*). Remove the right-hand roadwheel. Where fitted, remove the engine compartment undertray.

3 Remove the right-hand wheelarch liners, after pulling out the plastic retainers and removing the screws.

4 Remove the alternator and power steering pump drivebelts as applicable as described in Chapter 1A.

5 Set the engine at TDC for No 1 piston as described in Section 3.

6 Carefully, position a trolley jack and a large block of wood under the sump to support the engine. Raise the jack to just take the weight of the engine.

SOHC engines

7 Remove the right-hand upper engine mounting bracket, and the lower mounting bracket/timing belt cover, with reference to Section 13.

8 On manual transmission models, to prevent the crankshaft from rotating while the pulley centre bolt is unscrewed, have an assistant engage top gear and depress firmly the brake pedal. Alternatively, and on automatic transmission models, the crankshaft may be held stationary by unbolting the crankshaft speed/position sensor from the top of the transmission and wedging a screwdriver in the starter ring gear teeth through the sensor's opening in the bellhousing. Unscrew the crankshaft pulley bolt, then remove the pulley together with the hub, noting the key on the end of the crankshaft **(see illustrations)**.

5.8b Removing the crankshaft pulley bolt

5.8c Removing the crankshaft pulley

5.9a Timing cover lower mounting nut

5.9b Removing the timing cover

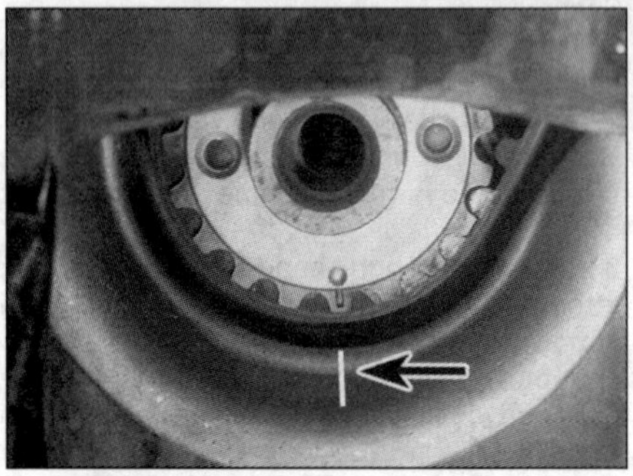

5.10 Mark the oil seal housing in line with the crankshaft sprocket timing mark

5.12a The arrows on the timing belt show its running direction

5.12b Removing the timing belt from the camshaft sprocket

Note: *The bolt is very tight.* Alternatively, the pulley may be unbolted from the hub first, then the hub bolt unscrewed.

9 Unbolt and remove the timing belt covers **(see illustrations)**.

10 Check that the TDC mark on the camshaft sprocket is pointing upwards and in line with the mark on the cylinder head cover. On some models there is also an alignment mark on the crankshaft timing belt end oil seal housing which must line up with the timing mark in the 6 o'clock position, opposite to the keyway, on the crankshaft sprocket – on later models, mark the housing as an aid to refitting **(see illustration)**.

11 Loosen the nut on the timing belt tensioner, turn the tensioner pulley clockwise to release the tension, then temporarily tighten the nut to hold the pulley away from the timing belt.

12 Check if the belt is marked with arrows to indicate its running direction, and mark it if necessary. Release the belt from the camshaft, water pump and crankshaft sprockets and remove it from the engine. If the belt is to be re-used, be careful not to kink or otherwise damage it **(see illustrations)**.

13 Clean the sprockets and tensioner and wipe them dry. Also clean the cylinder head and block behind the timing belt running area.

5.18 Turn the crankshaft until the slots in the camshafts are initially positioned at approximately a 30° angle from the horizontal, with the offsets below the centreline

DOHC engines

Note: *A Renault TDC pin is required for this operation.*

14 Remove the right-hand upper engine mounting bracket from the engine and body with reference to Section 13.

15 Remove the wiring loom from the right-hand end of the engine by disconnecting it over the inlet manifold and unbolting the support bracket at the right-hand front of the cylinder head. Also disconnect the vacuum pipe from the inlet manifold. Unclip the loom from the upper timing cover and position it to one side.

16 Unclip the fuel pipes from the lower timing cover.

17 Remove the air cleaner and resonator as described in Chapter 4A.

18 Using a screwdriver, pierce the centres of the two plastic plugs at the left-hand end of the camshafts, and pull the plugs from the cylinder head. With No 1 piston approaching TDC, the grooves in the ends of the camshafts should be as shown **(see illustration)**.

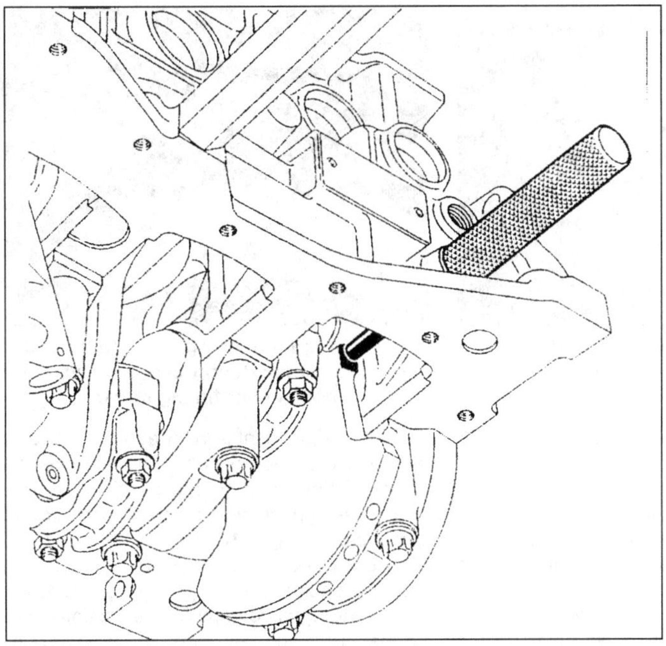

5.19 TDC pin on the left-hand front of the cylinder block

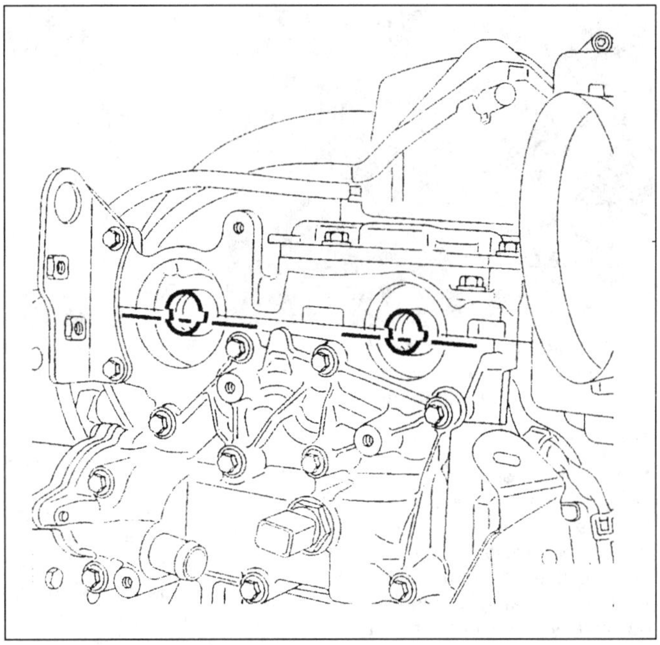

5.20a With the crankshaft at TDC the grooves in the end of the camshafts will be positioned horizontally

19 Unscrew the TDC plug from the left-hand front of the cylinder block, then fully screw in the TDC pin **(see illustration)**. **Note:** *If the pin is not available, an alternative method of determining the TDC position is to use a dial gauge on the top of piston No 1 after removing the spark plug.*

20 Carefully turn the crankshaft clockwise until the crankshaft web is in contact with the TDC pin. At this point, the No 1 piston is at TDC on its compression stroke, and the grooves in the ends of the camshafts will now be positioned horizontally. Renault technicians use a special tool to lock the camshafts in their TDC position, however, a length of metal bar may be fabricated **(see illustrations and Tool Tip)**.

21 Before loosening the crankshaft pulley bolt, note that the crankshaft sprocket is **not** keyed to the crankshaft as is the normal arrangement, therefore if the crankshaft pulley is removed it is important to have an accurate method of determining the TDC position of No 1 piston (refer to paragraph 19). Although the sprocket is not keyed to the crankshaft, there is still a groove in the crankshaft nose which is at the 12 o'clock position when piston No 1 is at TDC. To prevent the crankshaft from rotating while the pulley bolt is unscrewed, first remove the metal bar from the camshafts, then have an assistant engage top gear and depress firmly the brake pedal. Alternatively, and on automatic transmission models, the crankshaft may be held stationary by unbolting the crankshaft speed/position sensor from the top of the transmission and wedging a screwdriver in the starter ring gear teeth through the sensor's opening in the bellhousing. Unscrew the crankshaft pulley bolt, then remove the pulley/hub. **Note:** *The bolt is very tight*. The bolt may be re-used if its length from under the head to its end does not exceed 49.1 mm. If the length is greater than this, renew the bolt.

22 Unbolt the lower timing cover followed by the upper timing cover.

23 Loosen the nut on the timing belt tensioner, then turn the tensioner hub anti-clockwise to release the tension.

24 Check if the belt is marked with arrows to indicate its running direction, and if it is to be re-used, mark it to ensure correct refitting. Release the belt from the camshaft sprockets, water pump pulley, crankshaft sprocket, tensioner pulley and idler pulley and remove it from the engine.

25 Clean the sprockets, tensioner and idler and wipe them dry. Also clean the cylinder head and block behind the timing belt running area.

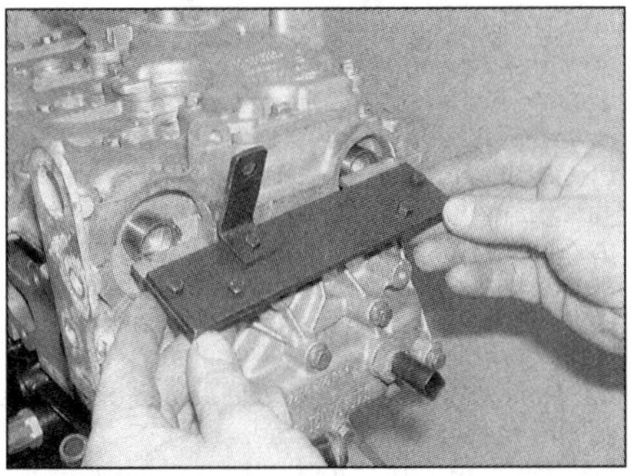

5.20b Engage the camshaft holding tool with the camshaft slots . . .

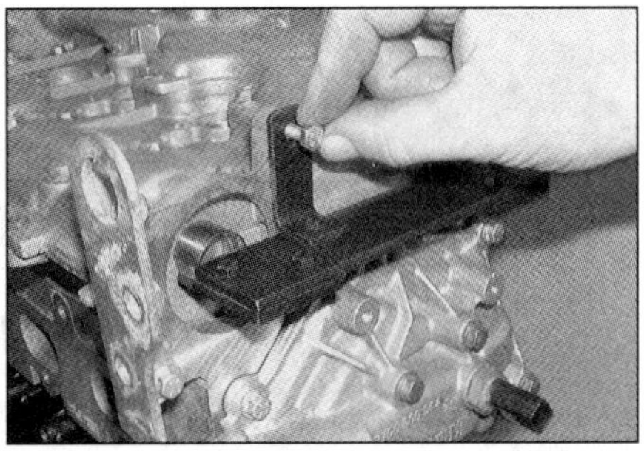

5.20c . . . and secure the tool using a suitable bolt screwed into the cylinder head

TOOL TIP

To make a camshaft holding tool, obtain a length of steel strip and cut it to length so that it will fit across the rear of the cylinder head. Obtain a second length of steel strip of suitable thickness to fit snugly in the slots in the camshafts. Cut the second strip into two lengths and drill accordingly so that they can be bolted to the first strip in the correct position to engage with the camshaft slots. Secure a suitably drilled small piece of steel angle to the first strip so that the tool can be bolted to the threaded hole in the cylinder head upper section.

5.29a Align the timing band on the inside of the belt with the crankshaft sprocket timing mark

5.29b The timing belt is also marked on its outside surface

5.29c Align the timing belt upper band with the camshaft sprocket and cylinder head cover timing marks

Inspection

Note: *Renault state that the timing belt must be renewed whenever it is removed, and also that the tensioner and idler pulley must be renewed whenever the timing belt is renewed.*

26 Examine the timing belt carefully for any signs of cracking, fraying or general wear, particularly at the roots of the teeth.

27 Renew the belt if there is any sign of deterioration of this nature, or if there is any oil or grease contamination. Renew any leaking oil seals. The belt **must** be renewed if it has completed the maximum mileage given in Chapter 1A.

28 Thoroughly clean the nose of the crankshaft and the bore of the crankshaft sprocket, and also the contact surfaces of the sprocket and pulley. This is necessary to prevent the possibility of the sprocket slipping in use.

Refitting

SOHC engines

29 Check the directional mark (arrows) and timing bands on the new timing belt. Fit the belt on the crankshaft sprocket so that one of the timing bands is aligned with the marks on the sprocket (in the 6 o'clock position, opposite to the keyway) and on the oil seal housing. The other timing band should be positioned so that it will locate on the camshaft sprocket in alignment with that sprocket's, and with the cylinder head cover's, timing marks. Having engaged the belt on the crankshaft sprocket, pull it taut over the water pump pulley and onto the camshaft sprocket, then position it over the tensioner pulley **(see illustrations)**.

30 With the belt fully engaged, slacken the tensioner nut and tension the belt, then retighten the nut **(see illustration)**. The tensioner is not spring-loaded, so it will have to be rotated manually to tension the belt. A screwdriver can be used as a lever between bolts in the holes in the tensioner hub, or use a two-pronged tool which engages in the holes in the tensioner. Check that the timing marks are still aligned correctly.

31 The belt tension must now be checked – this can be set or checked accurately only by using the Renault tool Mot. 1273 (SEEM C. Tronic 105.6). If this equipment is not available, set the belt's tension as carefully as possible using the method outlined below, then take the vehicle to a Renault dealer as soon as possible for the tension to be checked by qualified personnel using the special equipment. Do not take the vehicle on any long journeys or rev the engine to high speeds until the timing belt's tension has been checked and is known to be correct. Timing belt tension may be judged to be approximately correct when the belt can be twisted 90° with moderate pressure between the finger and thumb, checking midway between the pulleys on the belt's longest run. If the special tool is not available and there is any doubt about the tension of the timing belt, the vehicle should be taken to a Renault dealer as soon as possible for the tension to be checked by qualified personnel using the special equipment.

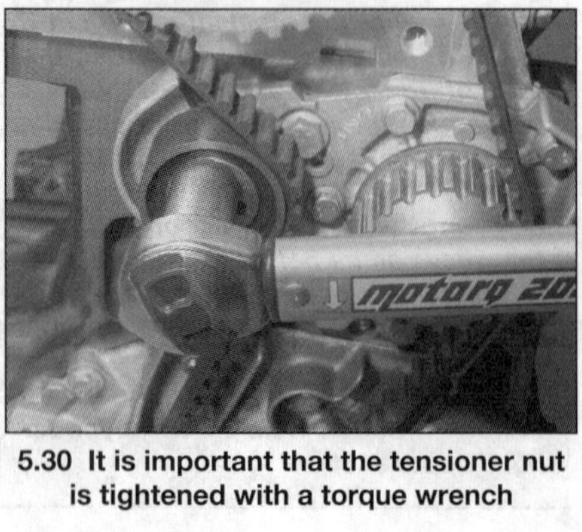

5.30 It is important that the tensioner nut is tightened with a torque wrench

5.33 Angle-tightening the crankshaft pulley bolt – K7M engine

32 If the adjustment is incorrect, the tensioner will have to be repositioned. The tensioner nut must be tightened to the specified torque wrench setting, since if it were to come loose, considerable engine damage would result.

33 Refit the crankshaft pulley and its bolt. Using a socket on the pulley bolt, turn the engine through two complete revolutions in its normal direction, then recheck the timing belt tension and make sure that the timing marks are still in alignment. Tighten the crankshaft pulley bolt to the specified torque (and angle where applicable) while the assistant holds the crankshaft stationary as described earlier in this Section **(see illustration)**.

34 Refit the lower timing belt cover and the right-hand upper engine mounting bracket, and tighten the retaining bolts securely. Lower the jack and block of wood from the sump.

35 Refit the alternator drivebelt followed by the power-assisted steering drivebelt and tension them as described in Chapter 1A.

36 Refit the right-hand wheelarch liners, and engine compartment undertray, then refit the roadwheel and lower the vehicle to the ground.

37 Reconnect the battery negative lead.

DOHC engines

38 Check that the lug on the rear of the tensioner is correctly located in the groove.

39 Check that the camshafts and No 1 piston are still at TDC. Fit the timing belt on the crankshaft sprocket, then locate it around the water pump and idler, over the camshafts and around the tensioner. Make sure that the belt is taut between the camshaft sprockets, and the correct way round if refitting the original.

40 Check that the idler retaining bolt is tightened to the specified torque.

41 With the belt fully engaged with the pulleys, slacken the tensioner nut and tension the belt. To do this, use an Allen key to turn the index finger on the tensioner 7.0 to 8.0 mm to the right of the static index, then retighten the nut to the specified torque **(see illustration)**. Check that the camshafts and crankshaft are still at TDC.

42 Refit the crankshaft pulley and tighten the bolt to the specified torque.

43 Remove the locking tool from the camshafts and the TDC pin from the cylinder block. Turn the crankshaft clockwise two

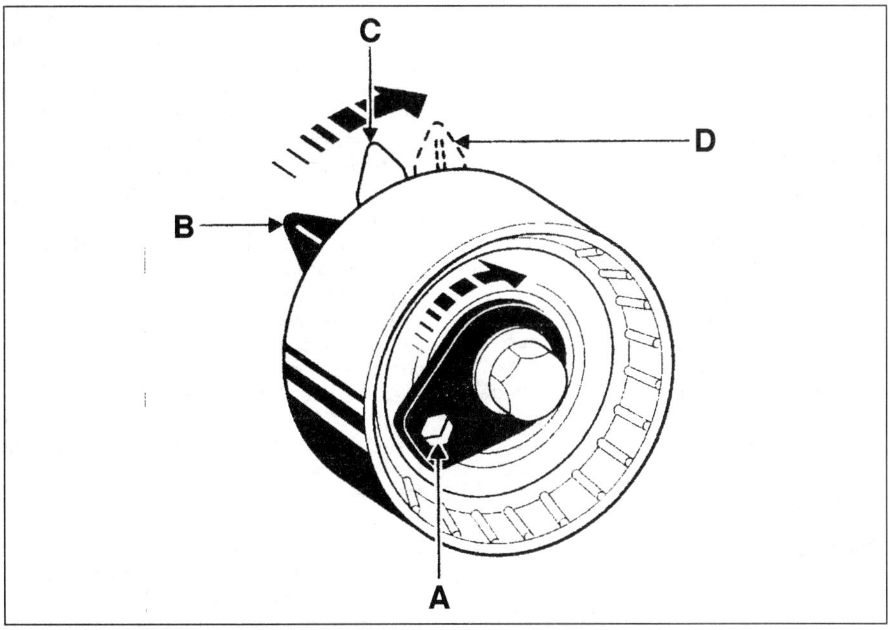

5.41 Timing belt tensioner pulley details

A Slot for Allen key in tensioner arm
B Position of moving index pointer in the at rest position
C Fixed index pointer
D Moving index pointer positioned 7.0 to 8.0 mm to the right of the fixed index pointer

complete turns, then reset the piston to TDC as described in earlier.

44 Remove the locking tool and TDC pin, then unscrew the tensioner bolt by one turn only. Using the Allen key, align the index finger with the static index. Tighten the tensioner bolt to the specified torque.

45 Turn the crankshaft two complete turns and recheck the TDC position and tensioner index setting.

46 Refit the upper timing cover and lower timing cover, and tighten the bolts securely.

47 Refit the TDC plug to the cylinder block and tighten securely.

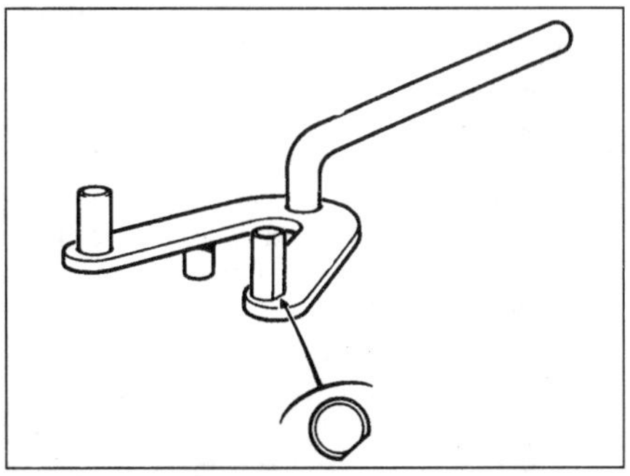

6.2a Tools for holding the camshaft sprocket – Renault tool Mot. 799-01 . . .

6.2b . . . and a home-made equivalent

6.2c Removing the camshaft sprocket bolt

6.4 Removing the crankshaft sprocket

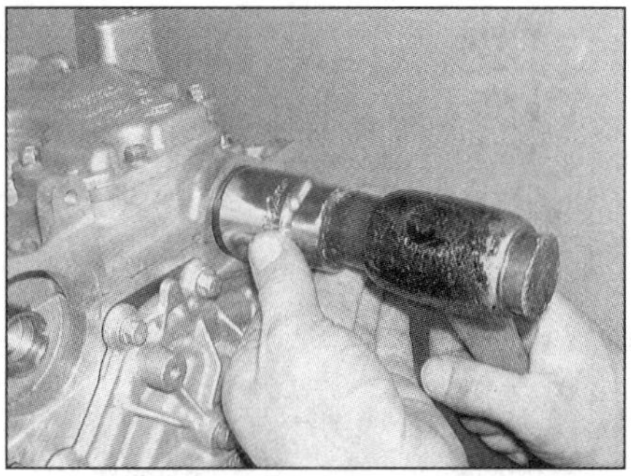

5.48 Fitting new plastic plugs to the cylinder head using a large socket

48 Fit two new plastic plugs in the cylinder head on the left-hand end of the camshafts. Renault technicians use special tools to drive the plugs into position, although suitable sockets or blocks of wood may be used instead **(see illustration)**.

49 Refit the air cleaner and resonator with reference to Chapter 4A.

50 Clip the fuel pipes to the lower timing cover.

51 Reconnect the vacuum pipe to the inlet manifold and attach the wiring loom to the upper timing cover. Refit the support bracket and tighten the bolts, reconnect the wiring and attach it to the support.

52 Refit the right-hand upper engine mounting bracket to the engine and body with reference to Section 13. Lower the jack and block of wood from the sump.

53 Refit the alternator drivebelt followed by the power-assisted steering drivebelt and tension them as described in Chapter 1A.

54 Refit the right-hand wheelarch liners, and engine compartment undertray, then refit the roadwheel and lower the vehicle to the ground.

55 Reconnect the battery negative lead.

6 Timing belt sprockets and tensioner – removal, inspection and refitting

Removal

SOHC engines

1 Remove the timing belt (see Section 5).

2 To remove the camshaft sprocket, hold the sprocket stationary using a home-made tool fabricated from two metal bars with one bolt and nut as a pivot and with two bolts at its tips inserted into the holes in the pulley, then unscrew the bolt. The Renault tool is also shown **(see illustrations)**.

3 Remove the sprocket from the end of the camshaft. Note that it has a tab on its inner face which locates in a slot in the end of the camshaft.

4 A puller may be necessary to remove the crankshaft sprocket if it is tight. Note that the key is incorporated in the pulley and is not separate **(see illustration and Tool Tip)**.

TOOL TIP

It is easy to make up a puller for the crankshaft sprocket using two bolts, a metal bar and the existing crankshaft sprocket bolt. By unscrewing the crankshaft sprocket bolt against the bar, the sprocket is drawn off the crankshaft

5 Unscrew the nut and withdraw the washer and tensioner pulley from the stud on the crankshaft timing belt end oil seal housing **(see illustrations)**.

DOHC engines

Caution: The timing belt sprockets are not keyed to the camshafts, neither is the crankshaft sprocket keyed to the crankshaft. Before starting work, make sure that you have the necessary tooling to accurately set the camshafts and crankshaft to TDC.

6 Remove the timing belt as described in Section 5.

7 Slide the crankshaft pulley from the nose of the crankshaft, noting which way round it is fitted.

8 Use a suitable tool to hold each camshaft sprocket stationary while the retaining nuts are loosened, then unscrew and remove the nuts and withdraw the sprockets from the camshafts.

9 To remove the tensioner, unscrew the centre nut and withdraw the unit from the stud on the water pump. Note the groove in the water pump cover for the tensioner lug.

10 To remove the idler, unscrew the centre bolt and withdraw it from the cylinder head.

Inspection

11 Inspect the teeth of the sprockets for signs of nicks and damage. Also examine the water pump pulley. The teeth are not prone to wear and should normally last the life of the engine.

12 Spin the tensioner pulley by hand and check it for any roughness or tightness. Do not attempt to clean it with solvent, as this may enter the bearing. If wear is evident, renew the tensioner. **Note:** *Renault state that the tensioner and idler pulley must be renewed whenever the timing belt is renewed.*

Refitting

SOHC engines

13 Locate the tensioner on the stud on the oil seal housing, then refit the nut and washer and tighten it finger-tight at this stage.

14 Slide the sprocket fully onto the crankshaft engaging the key with the groove in the crankshaft. Use a metal tube if necessary to tap it into position.

15 Locate the sprocket on the end of the camshaft, making sure that the tab locates in the special slot, then screw in the bolt. Tighten the bolt to the specified torque, holding the sprocket stationary using the method described in paragraph 2.

16 Fit a new timing belt as described in Section 5.

DOHC engines

17 Locate the idler on the cylinder head, then insert the bolt and tighten to the specified torque.

18 Locate the tensioner on the stud on the water pump cover, making sure that the lug engages the groove. Fit the nut loosely at this stage.

19 Locate the camshaft sprockets on the camshafts so that the Renault logo engraved spokes are at the 12 o'clock position. Fit the sprocket retaining nuts loosely at this stage. A clearance of between 0.5 and 1.0 mm should exist between the nuts and the sprockets.

20 Slide the crankshaft sprocket onto the nose of the crankshaft, making sure it is the correct way round.

21 Locate the timing belt on the crankshaft sprocket, around the water pump pulley and idler, then over the camshaft sprockets and around the tensioner.

22 With the belt fully engaged with the sprockets, tension the belt. To do this, use an Allen key to turn the index finger on the tensioner 7.0 to 8.0 mm to the right of the static index, then tighten the nut to the specified torque.

23 Refit the crankshaft pulley and tighten the bolt to the specified torque.

24 Check that the crankshaft is at TDC with the crank web touching the TDC pin. Check that the camshafts are both at TDC with the TDC tool in position on the left-hand end of the cylinder head.

25 The camshaft sprockets must now be held stationary while the retaining nuts are tightened in the specified stages. Renault technicians use a metal plate bolted to the cylinder head which clamps the two sprockets stationary, however, the tool used to hold the pulleys on removal can be used provided care is taken not to move the camshafts or crankshaft during the tightening procedure.

26 Remove the locking tool from the camshafts and the TDC pin from the cylinder block. Turn the crankshaft clockwise two complete turns, then reset the piston to TDC as described earlier.

27 Remove the locking tool and TDC pin, then unscrew the tensioner bolt by one turn only. Using the Allen key, align the index finger with the static index. Tighten the tensioner bolt to the specified torque.

6.5a Unscrew the nut and withdraw the washer . . .

6.5b . . . then remove the tensioner pulley

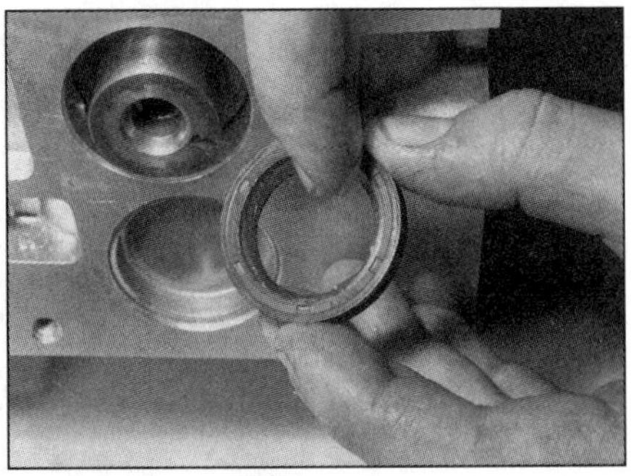

7.4a Smear a little grease on the oil seal . . .

28 Turn the crankshaft two complete turns and recheck the TDC position and tensioner index setting. If the camshafts do not align correctly, it will be necessary to loosen the camshaft sprocket retaining nuts, then repeat the tensioning procedure.

29 The remaining procedure is described in Section 5 for the timing belt refitting.

7 Camshaft oil seal – renewal

1 Remove the camshaft sprocket as described in Section 6.

2 Note the fitted position of the old oil seal. Using a small screwdriver, prise out the oil seal from the cylinder head.

3 Wipe clean the seating in the cylinder head.

4 Smear a little oil on the outer perimeter and sealing lip of the new oil seal. Locate the seal squarely in the cylinder head. Drive the seal into position using a metal tube or socket which has an external diameter slightly less than that of the bore in the cylinder head **(see illustrations)**. Make sure that the oil seal is the correct way round, with the lip facing inwards.

5 Refit the camshaft sprocket as described in Section 6.

8 Camshaft – removal, inspection and refitting

SOHC engines

Removal

1 Remove the cylinder head as described in Section 9 and place it on the workbench.

2 Progressively unscrew the bolts holding the rocker shaft and retaining plate to the cylinder head and withdraw the shaft **(see illustrations)**.

3 Hold the camshaft stationary using a spanner on the special flats provided on the camshaft, or with a suitable tool inserted through the sprocket holes, then unscrew the bolt and withdraw the pulley.

4 On the E7J engine, using a Torx key, unscrew the two bolts and remove the

7.4b . . . before driving it into the cylinder head with a suitable socket

distributor. There is no need to mark the distributor, as it is not possible to adjust its position. Although there is an elongated slot for one of the bolts, the other bolt locates in a single hole.

5 On the K7M engine, unbolt the cover and remove the gasket from the left-hand end of the cylinder head **(see illustrations)**.

6 Using a dial gauge, measure the endfloat of the camshaft and compare with that given in the Specifications. This will give an indication of the amount of wear in the thrustplate.

7 Unscrew the two bolts and lift the thrustplate out of the slot in the camshaft **(see illustrations)**.

8 Withdraw the camshaft from the pulley end of the cylinder head, taking care not to damage the bearing surfaces **(see illustration)**.

8.2a Unscrew the bolts . . .

8.2b . . . then withdraw the rocker shaft

8.5a Unscrew the bolts . . .

8.5b . . . and remove the cover from the left-hand end of the cylinder head – K7M engine

8.7a Unscrew the two bolts . . .

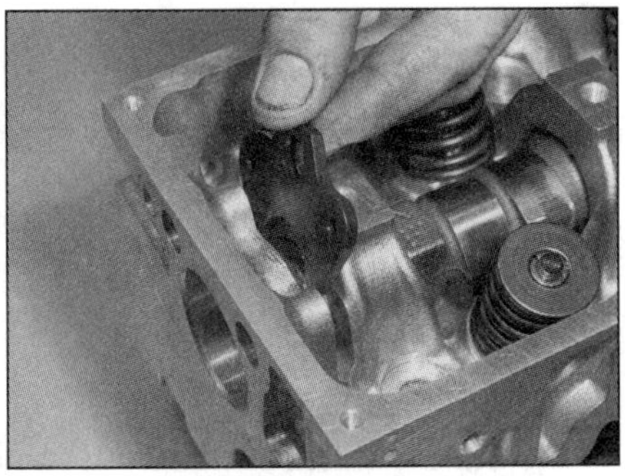

8.7b . . . and withdraw the thrustplate from the slot in the camshaft

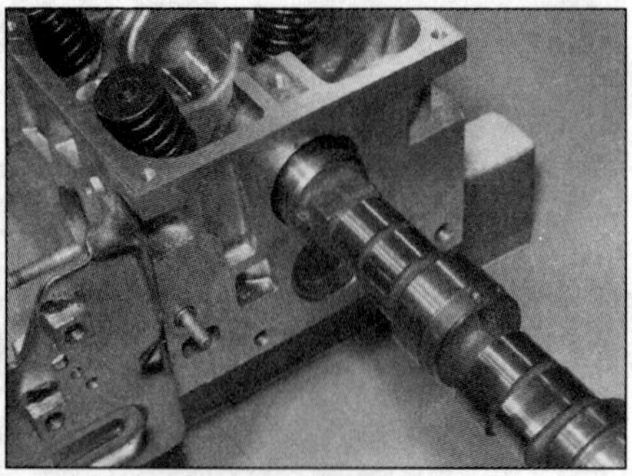
8.8 Removing the camshaft

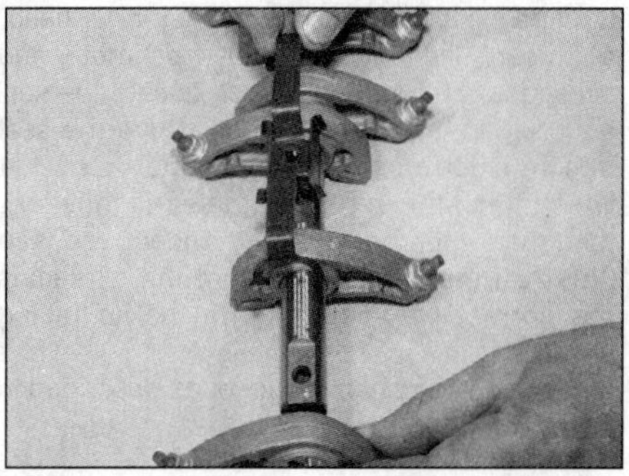
8.9 If necessary, the rockers may be removed from their shaft, but keep all the components in order

8.17 Tightening the rocker shaft mounting bolts

Inspection

9 Examine the camshaft bearing surfaces and cam lobes for wear ridges and scoring. Also examine the rocker shaft for wear. If necessary, the rocker shaft may be dismantled for inspection **(see illustration)**. Renew worn components as necessary.

10 Examine the condition of the bearing surfaces both on the camshaft and in the cylinder head. If the head bearing surfaces are worn excessively, a new cylinder head will be required.

Refitting

11 Lubricate the bearing surfaces in the cylinder head and the camshaft journals, then insert the camshaft into the head.

12 Refit the thrustplate, then insert and tighten the bolts.

13 Measure the endfloat as described in paragraph 6 and make sure that it is within the limits given in the Specifications. Excessive endfloat can only be due to wear of the thrustplate or the camshaft.

14 On the E7J engine, refit the distributor and tighten the two bolts using a Torx key.

15 On the K7M engine, refit the end cover with a new gasket and tighten the bolts.

16 Renew the oil seal (Section 7) then refit the camshaft sprocket, making sure that the tab engages with the cut-out in the end of the camshaft. Hold the camshaft stationary with a spanner on the special flats, then insert the bolt and tighten it to the specified torque.

17 Refit the rocker shaft and retaining plate, then insert the bolts in their original positions and tighten them to the specified torque **(see illustration)**. Note that the bolt threads and head contact surfaces must be oiled before inserting them. The hollow bolts are located at each end and in the middle.

18 Refit the cylinder head (see Section 9).

DOHC engines

Removal

19 Disconnect the battery negative (earth) lead and position it away from the terminal.

20 Remove the timing belt as described in Section 5.

21 Remove the camshaft sprockets as described in Section 6.

22 Disconnect the accelerator cable from the throttle housing with reference to Chapter 4A.

23 Disconnect the fuel supply and return hoses from the fuel rail with reference to Chapter 4A.

24 Remove the injector gallery protector, then disconnect the wiring from the injectors and coils and position it to one side.

25 Unbolt the inlet air duct unit, then remove the cooling system expansion bottle and position it to one side.

26 Unbolt the catalytic converter mountings and remove it from the exhaust manifold.

27 Remove the throttle body as described in Chapter 4A.

28 Disconnect the wiring from the oxygen sensor.

29 Unbolt and remove the exhaust manifold support strut and the engine lifting eye.

30 Disconnect the brake vacuum pipe from the inlet manifold.

31 Unbolt and remove the inlet manifold.

32 Remove the ignition coils as described in Chapter 5B.

33 Unbolt and remove the oil separator unit **(see illustration)**

34 Progressively unscrew the valve cover/bearing cap retaining bolts, then release the cover by using a copper mallet to tap the lugs at each rear corner and using a screwdriver to lever up the lugs on the front of the cover. Once the cover is free, lift it squarely from the cylinder head **(see illustration)**. The camshafts will rise up slightly under the pressure of the valve springs – be careful they don't tilt and jam. Remove the cover/bearing cap.

35 Identify each camshaft for location and TDC position, then carefully lift them from the cylinder head. The inlet camshaft should have the marking AM on it and the exhaust should have the marking EM. If these are not visible, identify the camshafts with dabs of paint. Remove the oil seals from the camshafts, noting their fitted positions.

36 Obtain a box with 16 compartments and mark the valve positions clearly on it. Remove each cam follower and place it in its compartment for safe-keeping **(see illustration)**.

37 Obtain a metal box with 16 compartments identified with the valve positions, and fill it with fresh engine oil. Carefully remove the hydraulic tappets from the cylinder head and

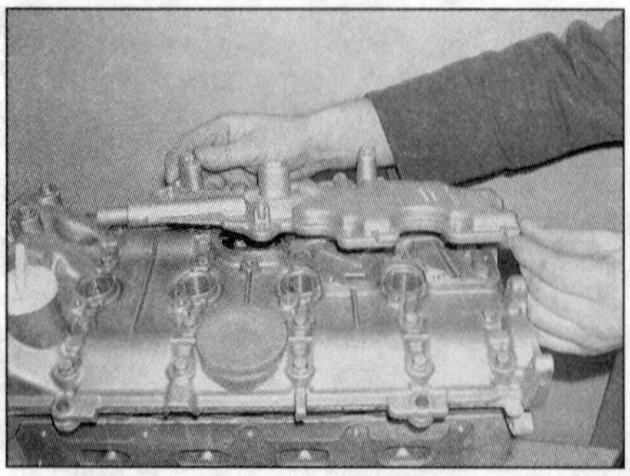
8.33 Undo the eight bolts and remove the oil separator housing

8.34 Removing the valve cover/bearing cap from the cylinder head

8.36 Lift out the cam followers and place them in a marked box or containers

place them in their correct compartments, making sure that they are completely immersed in the oil **(see illustration)**.

Inspection

38 Inspect the cam lobes and the camshaft bearing journals for scoring or other visible evidence of wear.

39 If the camshafts appear satisfactory, measure the bearing journal diameters and compare the figures obtained with those given in the Specifications. If the diameters are not as specified, consult a Renault dealer or engine overhaul specialist. Wear of the camshaft bearings will almost certainly be accompanied by similar wear of the bearings in the cylinder head, which will entail renewal of the cylinder head upper and lower sections together with the camshafts.

40 Inspect the rocker arms and hydraulic tappets for scuffing, cracking or other damage and renew any components as necessary. Also check the condition of the tappet bores in the cylinder head. As with the camshafts, any wear in this area will necessitate cylinder head renewal.

Refitting

41 Clean the sealant from the mating surfaces of the valve cover/bearing cap and cylinder head.

42 To prevent any possibility of the valves contacting the pistons when the camshafts are refitted, remove the TDC pin or dowel rod used to lock the crankshaft, and turn the crankshaft clockwise a quarter turn.

43 Lubricate the tappet bores in the cylinder head with clean engine oil.

44 If the hydraulic tappets have not been kept immersed in oil, the oil will drain from them and they will need to be re-primed before refitting. To check whether they require re-priming, depress the top of the tappet with a thumb – if the piston goes down, the tappet requires re-priming. Renault recommend that the tappets are immersed in diesel fuel and operated until they are primed.

45 Remove the hydraulic tappets from their compartments and insert them in their correct positions in the head.

46 One at a time, remove the rocker arms from their compartments and locate them on the hydraulic tappets and valve stems.

47 Lubricate the bearings and journals of the inlet and exhaust camshafts with fresh engine oil, then carefully locate them on the cylinder head in their correct positions and at TDC as previously noted. The grooves at the left-hand end of the camshafts must be horizontal **(see illustrations)**.

48 Check that the valve cover/bearing cap mating surfaces are clean and dry, then apply Loctite 518 (or a suitable alternative) to the cover surface using a roller **(see illustration)**. Make several applications until the colour is **reddish.**

49 Locate the valve cover/bearing cap on the cylinder head, insert the bolts, and progressively tighten them to the specified torque in the sequence and stages given in the Specifications **(see illustration)**. Make sure that the camshafts located correctly on the rockers and in the cover.

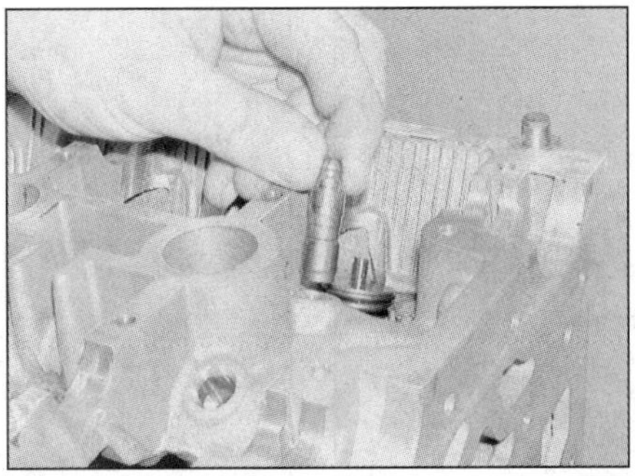

8.37 Lift out the tappets and place them upright in a marked box or containers filled with oil

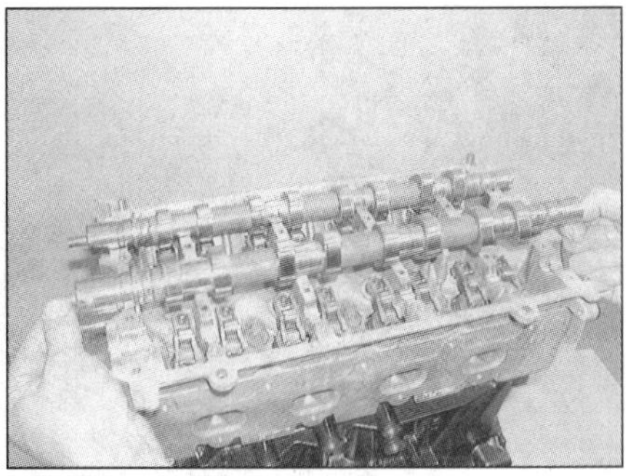

8.47a Refit the camshafts in the cylinder head . . .

8.47b Position the camshafts in their TDC position so that the grooves are horizontal and the offset is below the centreline

8.48 Apply an even coating of Loctite 518 gasket solution to the mating face of the valve cover/bearing cap

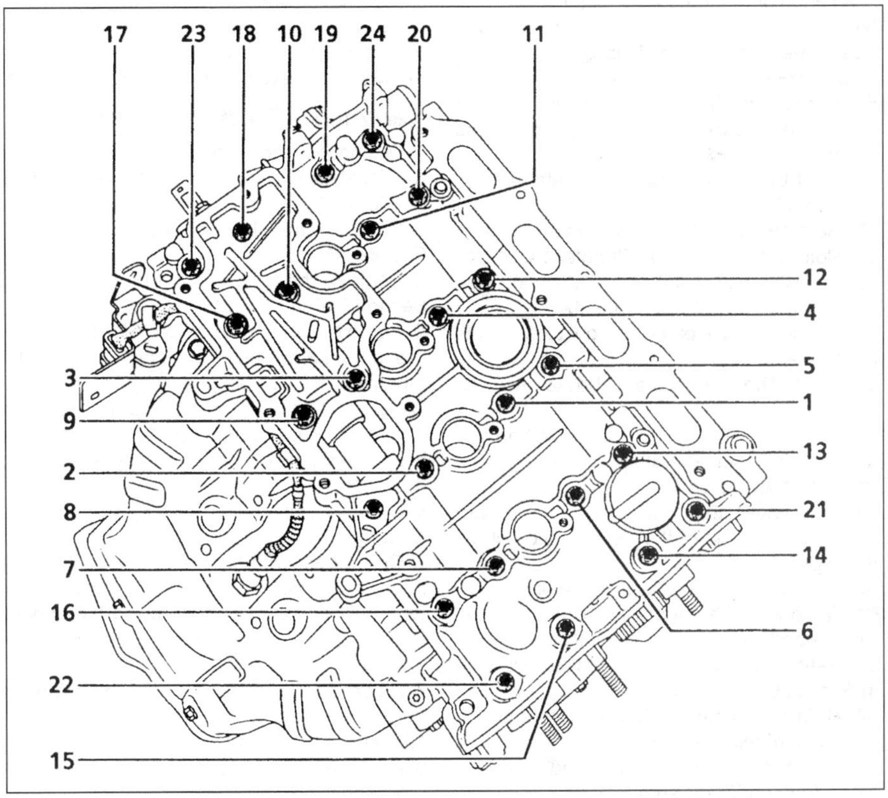

8.49 Valve cover/bearing cap retaining bolt identification

2B

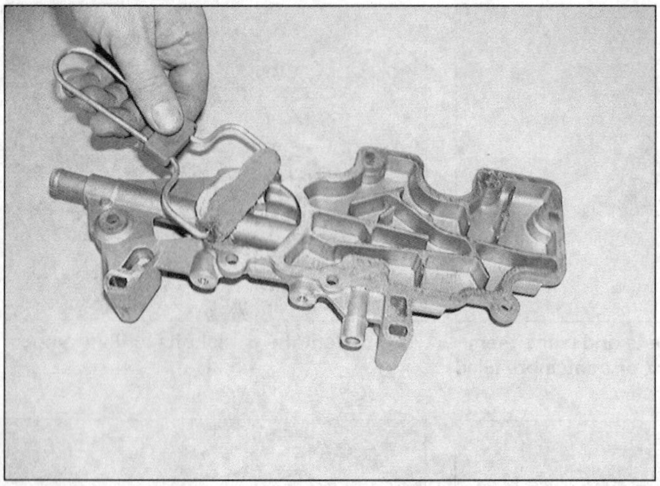

8.50 Apply an even coating of Loctite 518 gasket solution to the mating face of the oil separator housing

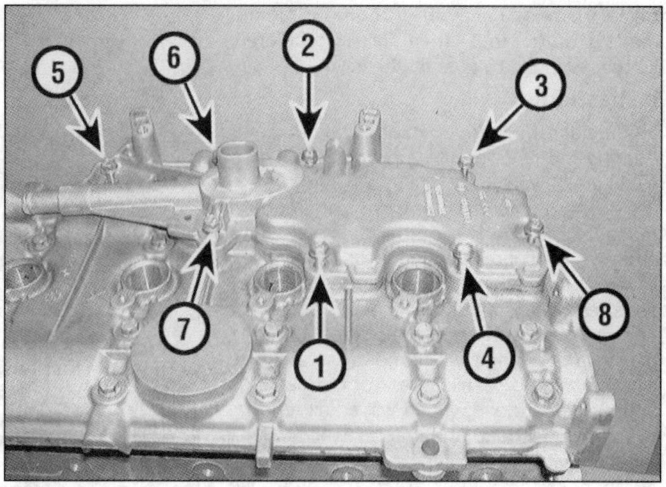

8.51 Oil separator housing retaining bolt tightening sequence

50 Check that the oil separator mating surfaces are clean and dry, then apply Loctite 518 (or a suitable alternative) to the separator surface using a roller **(see illustration)**. Make several applications until the colour is **reddish.**

51 Locate the oil separator on the valve cover, insert the bolts, and tighten them to the specified torque in the sequence shown **(see illustration)**.

52 Refit the ignition coils with reference to Chapter 5B.

53 Refit the engine lifting eye to the cylinder head and tighten the bolts securely.

54 Refit the support bracket to the right-hand side of the exhaust manifold, and tighten the bolts securely.

55 Reconnect the wiring to the oxygen sensor on the rear left-hand side of the engine.

56 Refit the throttle body with reference to Chapter 4A.

57 Refit the catalytic converter to the exhaust manifold with reference to Chapter 4A.

58 Refit the inlet manifold together with new seals with reference to Chapter 4A.

59 Reconnect the brake servo vacuum hose to the inlet manifold.

60 Refit the expansion bottle to the bulkhead.

61 Reconnect the wiring to the ignition coil and fuel injectors, and attach the wiring loom to the front of the engine.

62 Reconnect the fuel supply and return hoses to each end of the fuel rail, and tighten the clips.

63 Refit the injector gallery protector.

64 Reconnect the accelerator cable to the throttle body with reference to Chapter 4A.

65 Refit the camshaft sprockets as described in Section 6.

66 Refit the timing belt with reference to Section 5 of this Chapter.

67 Remove the trolley jack and block of wood from under the sump.

68 Reconnect the battery negative lead.

69 Refill the engine with fresh oil, with reference to Chapter 1A.

70 Refit the engine undertray and lower the vehicle to the ground.

9 Cylinder head – removal, inspection and refitting

Note: *In addition to any other parts required, have a new timing belt, cylinder head and cylinder head cover gaskets and (possibly) a set of new cylinder head bolts ready for reassembly. On DOHC engines, Renault state that the tensioner and idler pulley must be renewed whenever the timing belt is renewed.*

Removal – SOHC engines

1 Disconnect the battery negative lead (refer to *Disconnecting the battery* in the Reference Section).

2 Remove the bonnet as described in Chapter 11.

3 Remove the timing belt with reference to Section 5 of this Chapter.

4 Remove the engine undertray, then drain the cooling system including the cylinder block on the E7J engine, with reference to Chapter 1A (it is important to drain the block on the E7J engine, because if the wet cylinder liners are disturbed, the coolant will drain into the sump).

5 Drain the engine oil with reference to Chapter 1A.

6 On models with air conditioning, carefully position a trolley jack and a large block of wood under the sump to support the engine. Raise the jack to just take the weight of the engine.

7 Disconnect the wiring from the absolute pressure sensor on the inlet manifold. Also disconnect the brake servo vacuum pipe.

8 Disconnect the wiring from the stepper motor on the throttle body.

9 Remove the cover from the air cleaner then remove the air cleaner body as described in Chapter 4A.

10 Disconnect the wiring from the throttle position potentiometer.

11 Disconnect the accelerator cable from the throttle body with reference to Chapter 4A.

12 Disconnect the wiring from the air temperature sensor, then remove the air inlet duct.

13 Disconnect the wiring from the ignition coils, and also disconnect the wiring at the connector near the coils.

14 Disconnect the HT leads from the spark plugs, then unbolt the ignition coil from the top of the valve cover.

15 Disconnect the wiring and the vacuum pipes from the right-hand rear of the cylinder head.

16 Disconnect the crankcase ventilation hose from the rear of the valve cover.

17 Unbolt the engine lifting eye from the left-hand end of the cylinder head.

18 Disconnect the fuel inlet and return hoses from the throttle housing (E7J engine) or fuel rail (K7M).

19 Disconnect the wiring from the fuel injectors.

20 Unscrew the bolts and remove the cylinder head cover and gasket.

21 Disconnect the wiring from the temperature sensor on the thermostat housing at the left-hand end of the cylinder head.

22 Release the clips and disconnect the radiator top hose, heater hoses and expansion tank hose from the thermostat housing **(see illustration)**.

23 Unbolt the hot air shroud from the exhaust manifold, then unbolt the exhaust downpipe from the manifold with reference to Chapter 4A.

Models without air conditioning

24 Remove the alternator as described in Chapter 5A.

25 Remove the power steering pressostat mounting from the right-hand front of the cylinder block. Also disconnect the power steering pump wiring at the connector.

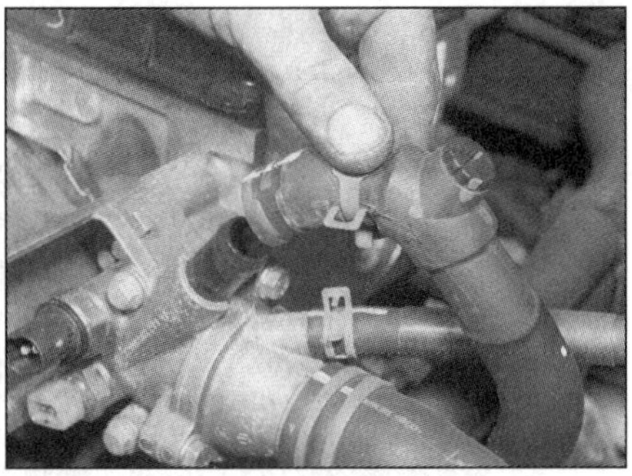

9.22 Disconnecting the heater hose from the thermostat housing

9.39a Removing a rocker shaft end bolt – the bolt is hollow for oil supply to the rockers

9.39b Slackening a cylinder head bolt

26 Refer to Chapter 10 and unbolt the power-assisted steering pump from the right-hand front of the cylinder block. Tie the pump to one side out of the way.

27 Unscrew the multi-function support mounting bolts and move it to one side.

Models with air conditioning

28 Remove the radiator grille as described in Chapter 11.

29 Remove the front bumper as described in Chapter 11. This procedure also includes removing the left-hand wheelarch liner.

30 Unscrew the centre lower and upper outer bolts and move the engine compartment front crossmember to one side.

31 Refer to Chapter 10 and unbolt the power-assisted steering pump from the right-hand front of the cylinder block. Tie to pump to one side out of the way.

32 Refer to Chapter 3 and unbolt the air conditioning compressor from the right-hand front of the cylinder block and tie it to one side. Do not disconnect the refrigerant pipes from the compressor.

33 Unscrew the multi-function support mounting bolts and move it to one side.

34 Unbolt the intermediate support from the right-hand end of the cylinder head.

All models

35 Remove the spark plugs as described in Chapter 1A.

36 Unbolt the support bracket securing the inlet manifold to the right-hand end of the cylinder head.

37 Unbolt the engine level dipstick tube from the right-hand end of the cylinder head.

38 Release the wiring loom from the clip on the right-hand end of the cylinder head.

39 Unbolt and remove the rocker shaft and retaining plate, then progressively slacken the cylinder head bolts in the **reverse** order to that shown in illustration 9.82a **(see illustrations)**. Remove all the bolts except the one positioned on the front right-hand corner, which should be unscrewed by only three or four threads.

40 The joint between the cylinder head, gasket and cylinder block must now be broken. On the E7J engine, it is important not to lift or disturb the 'wet' cylinder liners as the head is removed. To avoid this, pull the left-hand end of the cylinder head forward so as to swivel it around the single bolt still fitted, then move the head back to its original position. If this procedure is not followed on the E7J engine, there is a possibility of the cylinder liners moving and their bottom seals being disturbed, causing leakage after refitting the head.

41 Remove the remaining bolt and lift the head from the cylinder block, followed by the gasket. Note the locating dowel on the front right-hand corner of the block **(see illustrations)**.

42 Remove the inlet and exhaust manifolds with reference to Chapter 4A.

43 Note that on the E7J engine, the crankshaft must not be rotated with the cylinder head removed, otherwise the cylinder liners may be displaced. If it is necessary to turn the crankshaft (eg, to clean the piston crowns), clamp the liners using bolts and washers, or make up some retaining clamps out of flat metal bar, held in place with bolts screwed into the block **(see illustration)**.

Removal – DOHC engines

44 Disconnect the battery negative lead (refer to *Disconnecting the battery* in the Reference Section).

45 Remove the bonnet as described in Chapter 11.

46 Carefully, position a trolley jack and a large block of wood under the sump to support the engine. Raise the jack to just take the weight of the engine.

47 Remove the timing belt with reference to Section 5 of this Chapter.

48 Remove the engine undertray, then drain the cooling system with reference to Chapter 1A.

9.39c Removing a cylinder head bolt

9.41a Removing the cylinder head assembly

9.41b Removing the cylinder head gasket

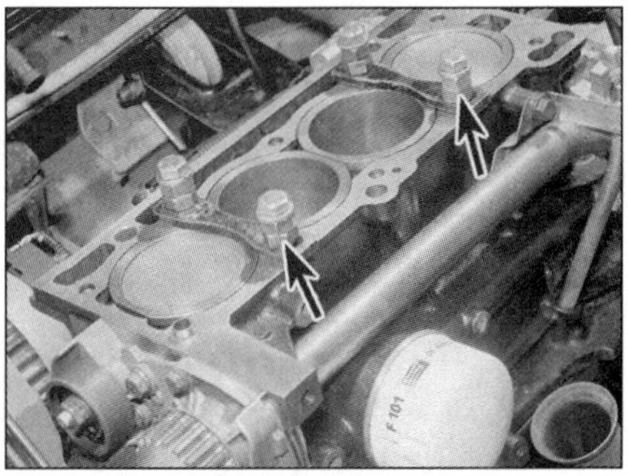

9.43 Clamps holding the liners in place – E7J engine

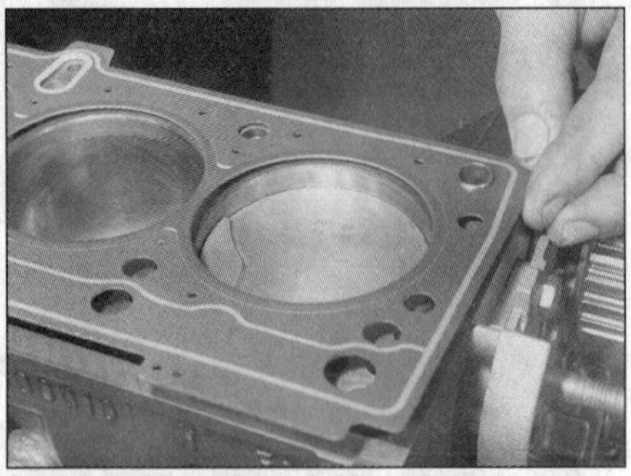

9.80 Place the new cylinder head gasket over the locating dowel on the block

49 Drain the engine oil with reference to Chapter 1A.

50 Disconnect the accelerator cable from the throttle body with reference to Chapter 4A.

51 Unbolt and remove the injector gallery protector.

52 Disconnect the fuel supply and return hoses from each end of the fuel rail.

53 Disconnect the engine wiring loom at the front of the engine, and also disconnect the wiring from the ignition coil and fuel injectors.

54 Refer to Chapter 3 and remove the expansion bottle from the bulkhead positioning it to one side, then unbolt and remove the inlet manifold with reference to Chapter 4A.

55 Refer to Chapter 4A and remove the catalytic converter from the exhaust manifold. Remove the throttle body as described in Chapter 4A. Disconnect the wiring for the oxygen sensor on the rear left-hand side of the engine.

56 Unscrew the bolts and remove the support bracket from the right-hand side of the exhaust manifold.

57 Unbolt the engine lifting eye from the cylinder head.

58 Disconnect the brake servo vacuum hose from the inlet manifold.

59 Remove the ignition coils with reference to Chapter 5B.

60 Unbolt the oil separator from the top of the valve cover.

61 Progressively unscrew the valve cover retaining bolts, then release the cover by using a copper mallet to tap the lugs at each rear corner and using a screwdriver to lever up the lugs on the front of the cover. Remove the cover.

62 Identify each camshaft for location and TDC position, then carefully lift them from the cylinder head. The inlet camshaft should have the marking AM on it and the exhaust should have the marking EM. If these are not visible, identify the camshafts with dabs of paint.

63 Obtain a box with 16 compartments and mark the valve positions clearly on it. Remove each cam follower and place it in its compartment for safe-keeping.

64 Obtain a metal box with 16 compartments identified with the valve positions, and fill it with fresh engine oil. Carefully remove the hydraulic tappets from the cylinder head and place them in their correct compartments, making sure that they are completely immersed in the oil.

65 Disconnect the wiring from the temperature sensor on the thermostat housing at the left-hand end of the cylinder head.

66 Release the clips and disconnect the radiator top hose, heater hoses and expansion tank hose from the thermostat housing.

67 Unbolt the wiring loom support bracket from the left-hand end of the cylinder head.

68 Unbolt the engine lifting eye from the left-hand end of the cylinder head.

69 Remove the spark plugs as described in Chapter 1A.

70 Progressively unscrew and remove the cylinder head bolts in the **reverse** order to that shown in illustration 9.129b.

71 Lift the head from the cylinder block, followed by the gasket.

Inspection

72 The mating faces of the cylinder head and block must be perfectly clean before refitting the head. Use a scraper to remove all traces of gasket and carbon and also clean the tops of the pistons. Take particular care with the aluminium cylinder head, as the soft metal is easily damaged. Also, make sure that debris is not allowed to enter the oil and water channels – this is particularly important for the oil circuit, as carbon could block the oil supply to the camshaft and cam followers or crankshaft bearings. Using adhesive tape and paper, seal the water, oil and bolt holes in the cylinder block. Clean the piston crowns in the same way.

> **HAYNES HiNT** ***To prevent carbon entering the gap between the pistons and bores, smear a little grease in the gap. After cleaning the piston, rotate the crankshaft so that the piston moves down the bore, then wipe out the grease and carbon with a cloth rag.***

73 Check the block and head for nicks, deep scratches and other damage. If slight, they may be removed carefully with a file. It may be possible to repair more serious damage by machining, but this is a specialist job.

74 If warpage of the cylinder head is suspected, use a straight-edge to check it for distortion. On the E7J engine, also check the protrusion of the cylinder liners. Either of these items can be associated with the head gasket blowing. Refer to Part D of this Chapter for further information.

75 Clean out all the bolt holes in the block using a pipe cleaner, or a rag and screwdriver. Make sure that all oil is removed, otherwise there is a possibility of the block being cracked by hydraulic pressure when the bolts are tightened.

76 Examine the bolt threads and the threads in the cylinder block for damage. If necessary, use the correct-size tap to chase out the threads in the block and use a die to clean the threads on the bolts. In view of the severe stresses to which they are subjected, owners may wish to renew the bolts as a matter of course whenever they are disturbed. If any of the bolts shows the slightest sign of wear or of damage, all the bolts should be renewed as a set. On DOHC engines, the bolts may be re-used if their length between the bolt head and end does not exceed 117.7 mm – if any one bolt is longer than this dimension, renew all the bolts as a set.

Refitting – SOHC engines

77 Refit the inlet and exhaust manifolds to the cylinder head, referring to Chapter 4A.

78 Check that No 1 piston is positioned at TDC, then wipe clean the faces of the head and block. On the E7J engine, remove the cylinder liner clamps.

79 Check that the locating dowel is in place on the front right-hand corner of the block.

80 Position the new gasket on the block and over the dowel – it can only be fitted one way round **(see illustration)**.

81 Lower the cylinder head onto the block. Oil the threads and under the heads of the cylinder head bolts, fit their washers, then insert the bolts – note that the shorter bolts are located on the inlet side of the head – and initially screw them in finger-tight **(see illustrations)**.

82 Tighten the cylinder head bolts to the

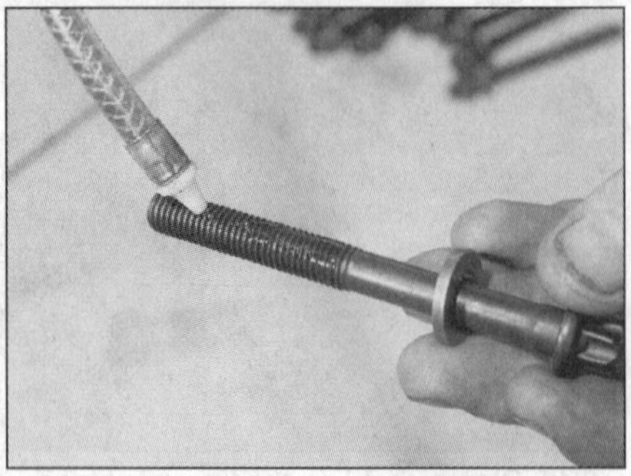

9.81a Oil the cylinder head bolts before . . .

9.81b . . . inserting them

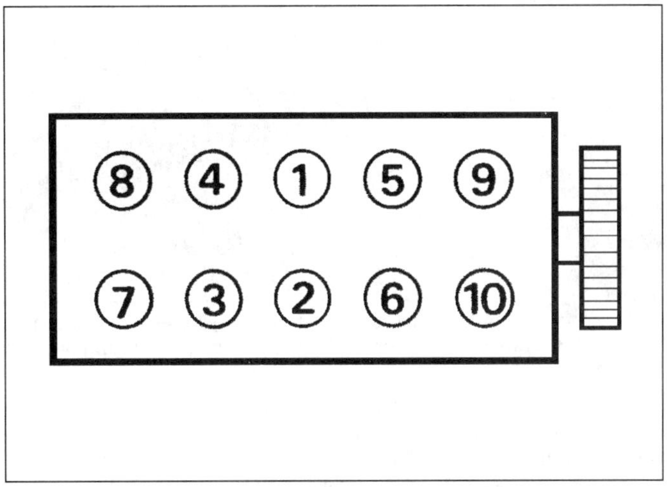

9.82a Cylinder head bolt tightening sequence

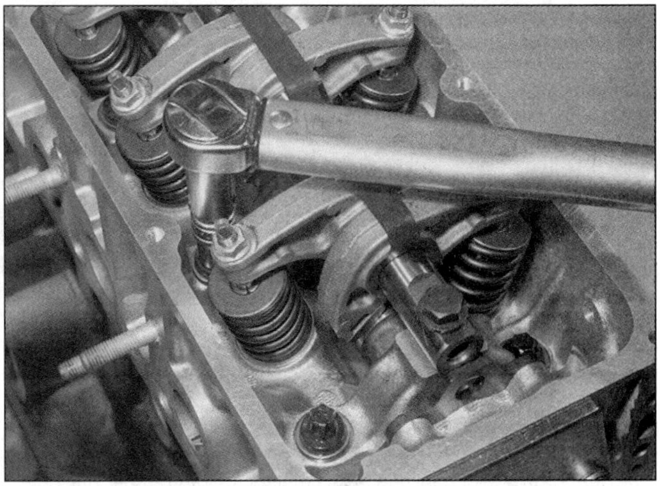

9.82b Torque-tightening a cylinder head bolt

specified torques in the sequence shown **(see illustrations)** and in the stages given in the Specifications at the beginning of this Chapter. The first stage pre-compresses the gasket and the subsequent stages are the main tightening procedure. When angle-tightening the bolts, put paint marks on the bolt heads and cylinder head as a guide for the correct angle, or obtain a special angle-tightening tool. Note that, provided the bolts are tightened exactly as specified, there will be no need to retighten them once the engine has been started and run after reassembly.

83 Refit the rocker shaft and retaining plate with reference to Section 8. If the cylinder head has been overhauled, it is worthwhile checking the valve clearances at this stage, to prevent any possibility of the valves touching the pistons when the timing belt is being fitted. Turn the crankshaft so that there are no pistons at TDC. Use a socket on the camshaft sprocket bolt to turn the camshaft and check the valve clearances. After carrying out the adjustment reposition the camshaft and pistons at TDC.

84 Refit the wiring loom to the clip on the right-hand end of the cylinder head.

85 Refit the engine level dipstick tube and tighten the bolt securely.

86 Refit the inlet manifold support bracket and tighten the bolts securely.

87 Refit the spark plugs with reference to Chapter 1A.

Models without air conditioning

88 Refit the multi-function support mounting and tighten the bolts.

89 Refit the power-assisted steering pump with reference to Chapter 10.

90 Refit the pressostat mounting and reconnect the wiring.

91 Refit the alternator with reference to Chapter 5A.

Models with air conditioning

92 Refit the intermediate support to the right-hand end of the cylinder head.

93 Refit the multi-function support mounting and tighten the bolts.

94 Refit the air conditioning compressor with reference to Chapter 3.

95 Refit the power steering pump with reference to Chapter 10.

96 Refit the engine compartment front crossmember.

97 Refit the front bumper and left-hand wheelarch liner with reference to Chapter 11.

98 Refit the radiator grille with reference to Chapter 11.

All models

99 Refit the exhaust downpipe to the manifold, and refit the hot air shroud with reference to Chapter 4A.

100 Reconnect the radiator top hose, heater hoses and expansion tank hose to the thermostat housing and tighten the clips.

101 Reconnect the wiring to the temperature sensor on the thermostat housing.

102 If not already done, adjust the valve clearances as described in Section 4 of this Chapter.

103 Refit the valve cover with a new gasket and tighten the bolts evenly to the specified torque wrench setting.

104 Reconnect the wiring to the fuel injectors.

105 Reconnect the fuel supply and return hoses to the throttle housing (E7J engine) or fuel rail (K7M engine).

106 Refit the engine lifting eye and tighten the bolts securely.

107 Reconnect the crankcase ventilation hose to the rear of the valve cover.

108 Reconnect the wiring and vacuum pipes to the right-hand rear of the cylinder head.

109 Refit the ignition coil to the valve cover and reconnect the HT leads to the spark plugs.

110 Reconnect the wiring to the ignition coils including the connector near the coils.

111 Refit the air inlet duct and reconnect the wiring to the air temperature sensor.

112 Reconnect the accelerator cable to the throttle body with reference to Chapter 4A.

113 Reconnect the wiring to the throttle position potentiometer.

114 Refit the air cleaner complete with reference to Chapter 4A.

115 Reconnect the wiring to the stepper motor on the throttle body.

116 Refit the brake vacuum pipe to the inlet manifold, then reconnect the wiring to the absolute pressure sensor.

117 Remove the trolley jack supporting the engine on models with air conditioning.

118 Fit a new timing belt with reference to Section 5 of this Chapter.

119 Refit the bonnet with reference to Chapter 11.

120 Refill the engine with fresh oil, with reference to Chapter 1A.

121 Reconnect the battery negative lead.

122 Refit the block drain plug on the E7J engine, then refill and bleed the cooling system with reference to Chapter 1A.

123 Refit the engine undertray and lower the vehicle to the ground.

Refitting – DOHC engines

124 It is recommended that No 1 piston is positioned half way up its cylinder before refitting the cylinder head as a safeguard against the valves touching the tops of the pistons. Turn the crankshaft clockwise until No 1 piston rises to the mid-cylinder position.

9.82c Angle-tightening a cylinder head bolt

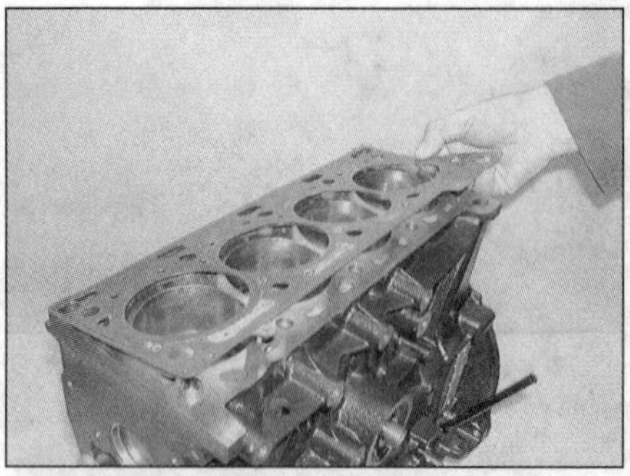

9.125 Locate a new cylinder head gasket on the cylinder block . . .

9.127 . . . and carefully lower the cylinder head into position

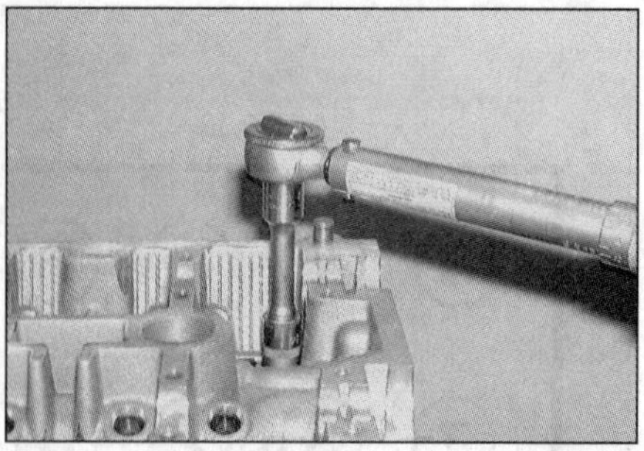

9.129a Tighten the cylinder head retaining bolts to the Stage 1 torque setting using a torque wrench

125 Position a new gasket on the block making sure it is the correct way up **(see illustration).**

126 If the lower inlet manifold was removed, it can be refitted at this stage with reference to Chapter 4A making sure that the timing end is flush with the end of the cylinder head before tightening the bolts.

127 Carefully lower the cylinder head onto the block making sure that the gasket is not displaced **(see illustration).**

128 If new bolts are being fitted, **do not** lubricate their threads, however if the old bolts are being refitted, lubricate their threads with fresh engine oil. Insert the bolts and initially screw them in finger-tight.

129 Tighten the cylinder head bolts to the specified torques in the sequence shown and in the stages given in the Specifications **(see illustrations)**. The first stage pre-compresses the gasket and the second stage is the main tightening procedure. When angle-tightening the bolts, put paint marks on the bolt heads and cylinder head as a guide for the correct angle, or obtain a special angle-tightening tool. Note that, provided the bolts are tightened exactly as specified, there will be no need to retighten them once the engine has been started and run after reassembly.

130 Refit the spark plugs with reference to Chapter 1A.

131 Refit the engine lifting eye to the left-hand end of the cylinder head.

132 Refit the wiring loom support bracket to the cylinder head and tighten the bolts.

133 Reconnect the radiator top hose, heater hoses and expansion tank to the thermostat housing and tighten the clips.

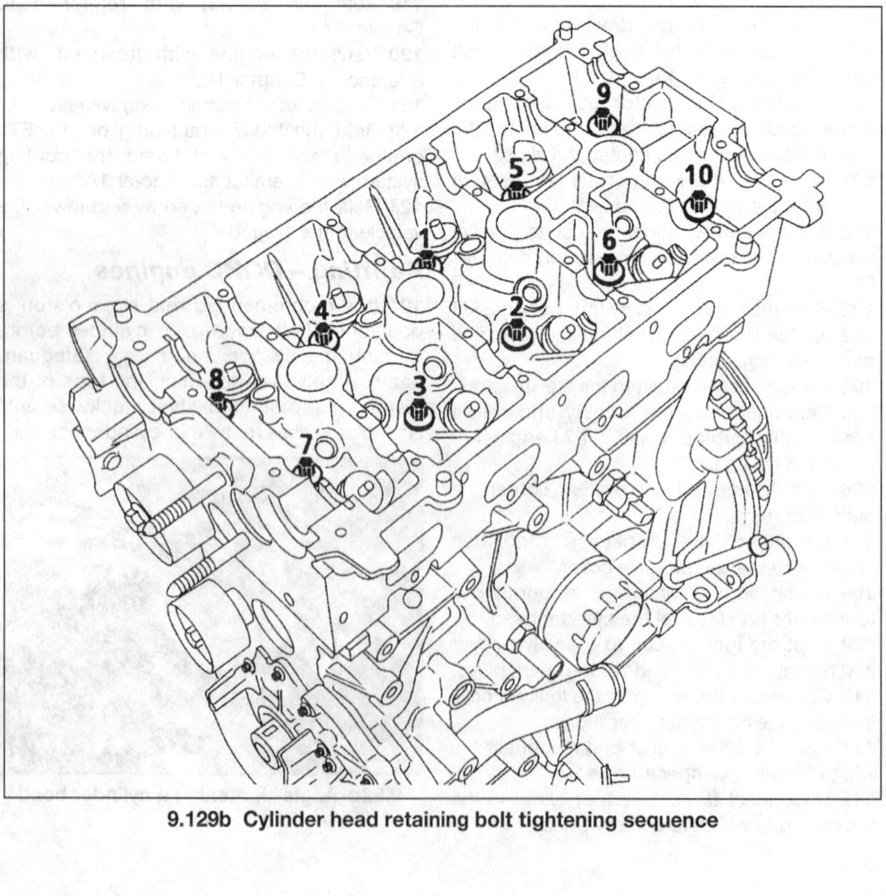

9.129b Cylinder head retaining bolt tightening sequence

134 Reconnect the wiring to the temperature sensor on the thermostat housing.

135 If the hydraulic tappets have not been kept immersed in oil, the oil will drain from them and they will need to be re-primed before refitting. To check whether they require re-priming, depress the top of the tappet with a thumb – if the piston goes down, the tappet requires re-priming. Renault recommend that the tappets are immersed in diesel fuel and operated until they are primed.

136 Remove the hydraulic tappets from their compartments and insert them in their correct positions in the head.

137 One at a time, remove the cam followers from their compartments and locate them on the hydraulic tappets and valve stems.

138 Lubricate the bearings and journals of the inlet and exhaust camshafts with fresh engine oil, then carefully locate them on the cylinder head in their correct positions and at TDC as previously noted. The grooves at the left-hand end of the camshafts must be horizontal.

139 Turn the crankshaft clockwise to position No 1 piston at TDC. Refer to Section 3 if necessary.

140 Check that the valve cover/bearing cap mating surfaces are clean and dry, then apply Loctite 518 (or a suitable alternative) to the cover surface using a roller. Make several applications until the colour is **reddish.**

141 Locate the valve cover on the cylinder head, insert the bolts, and tighten them to the specified torque in the sequence and stages given in the Specifications (see illustration 8.49).

142 Check that the oil separator mating surfaces are clean and dry, then apply

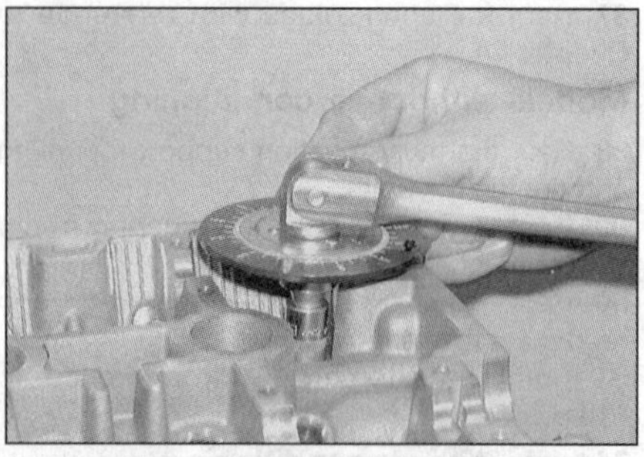

9.129c Using an angle tightening gauge to tighten the cylinder head retaining bolts through the Stage 2 angle

Loctite 518 (or a suitable alternative) to the separator surface using a roller. Make several applications until the colour is **reddish.**

143 Locate the oil separator on the valve cover, insert the bolts, and tighten them to the specified torque in the sequence shown (see illustration 8.51).

144 Refit the ignition coils with reference to Chapter 5B.

145 Refit the engine lifting eye to the cylinder head and tighten the bolts securely.

146 Refit the support bracket to the right-hand side of the exhaust manifold, and tighten the bolts securely.

147 Reconnect the wiring to the oxygen sensor on the rear left-hand side of the engine.

148 Refit the throttle body with reference to Chapter 4A.

149 Refit the catalytic converter to the exhaust manifold with reference to Chapter 4A.

150 Refit the inlet manifold together with new seals with reference to Chapter 4A.

151 Reconnect the brake servo vacuum hose to the inlet manifold.

152 Refit the expansion bottle to the bulkhead.

153 Reconnect the wiring to the ignition coil and fuel injectors, and attach the wiring loom to the front of the engine.

154 Reconnect the fuel supply and return hoses to each end of the fuel rail, and tighten the clips.

155 Refit the injector gallery protector.

156 Reconnect the accelerator cable to the throttle body with reference to Chapter 4A.

157 Refit the timing belt with reference to Section 5 of this Chapter.

158 Remove the trolley jack and block of wood from under the sump.

159 Refit the bonnet with reference to Chapter 11.

160 Reconnect the battery negative lead.

161 Refill the engine with fresh oil, with reference to Chapter 1A.

162 Refill and bleed the cooling system with reference to Chapter 1A.

163 Refit the engine undertray and lower the vehicle to the ground.

10 Sump – removal and refitting

Note: *An engine lifting hoist is required during this procedure.*

Removal

1 Disconnect the battery negative lead.

2 Jack up the front of the vehicle and support on axle stands. Remove the engine compartment undertray.

3 Drain the engine oil referring to Chapter 1A, then refit and tighten the drain plug using a new washer.

4 Remove both front roadwheels, then remove the right-hand wheelarch line.

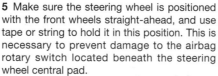

10.18a On DOHC engines, apply sealant to the joint areas of the oil seal housing . . .

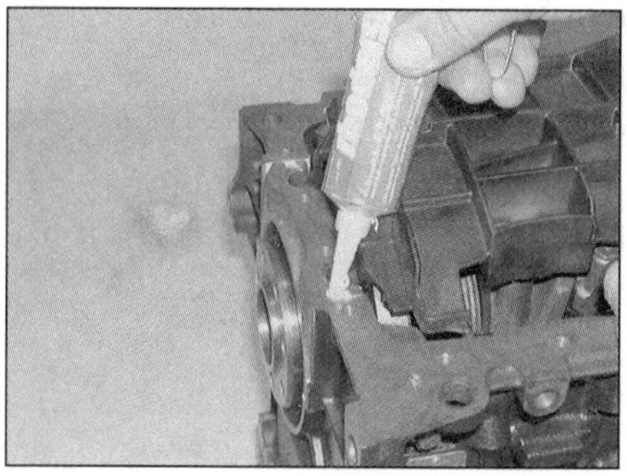

10.18b . . . and main bearing cap . . .

5 Make sure the steering wheel is positioned with the front wheels straight-ahead, and use tape or string to hold it in this position. This is necessary to prevent damage to the airbag rotary switch located beneath the steering wheel central pad.

6 Push back the gaiter and unscrew the bolt securing the steering column intermediate shaft to the steering gear pinion.

7 Refer to Chapter 10 and disconnect the front suspension lower arms from the hub carriers.

8 Unscrew the nuts and disconnect the track rod ends from the steering arms with reference to Chapter 10.

9 Detach the front suspension subframe tie-rods from the body. Also disconnect the gearchange rods from the transmission.

10 Loosen only the bolts securing the rear engine mounting link to the body.

11 Unscrew and remove the front bumper lower mounting fasteners.

12 Where necessary, unbolt and remove the exhaust manifold heatshield and remove the catalytic converter with reference to Chapter 4A.

13 Where necessary, unbolt the power-assisted steering pipe supports from the cylinder block. Also unbolt the multi-function support.

14 Unbolt the front suspension lower arms from the subframe with reference to Chapter 10.

15 Unscrew each subframe mounting bolt in turn and replace them with lengths of threaded rods and nuts. These are required to lower the subframe approximately 13.0 cm in order to remove the sump. With the rods in position, lower the subframe until the gap between the subframe and body is 9.0 cm at the rear mounting and 13.0 cm at the front mounting. As the subframe is being lowered, disconnect the steering gear pinion from the column intermediate shaft.

16 Unscrew the bolts securing the sump to the cylinder block. Tap the sump with a hide or plastic mallet to break the seal, then remove the sump. On SOHC engines, recover the half-moon gaskets from each end of the sump and discard them as new ones must be used on refitting. On DOHC engines, recover the gaskets.

Refitting

17 Thoroughly clean the mating surfaces of the sump and cylinder block.

18 On SOHC engines, apply a 3.0 mm bead of Rhodorseal 5661 sealant (available from Renault dealers) to the sump flanges making sure that the bead goes around the inner sides of the bolt holes and is approximately midway across the flange between the bolt holes. Do not apply any sealant to the half-moon areas of the sump. On DOHC engines apply some Rhodorseal 5661 sealant to the joint areas where the oil seal housing and main bearing cap meet the cylinder block, then locate a new gasket on the sump **(see illustrations)**.

19 Locate new half-moon gaskets in position, and lift the sump into position on the cylinder block. Insert the bolts and tighten them progressively to the specified torque. If the engine is removed from the car, use a straight-edge to maintain the alignment between the left-hand end of the sump and cylinder block **(see illustration)**.

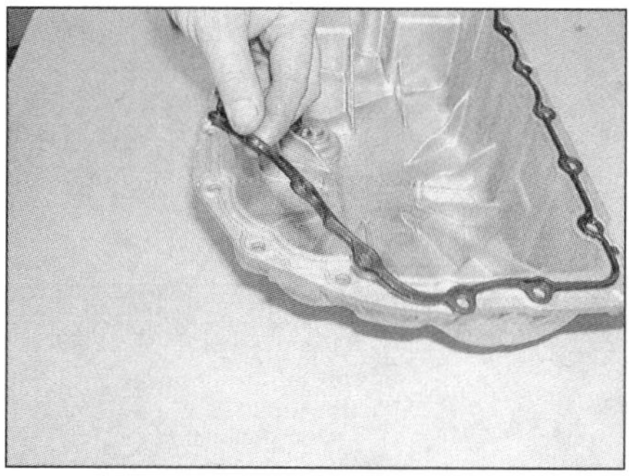

10.18c . . . then locate a new gasket on the sump

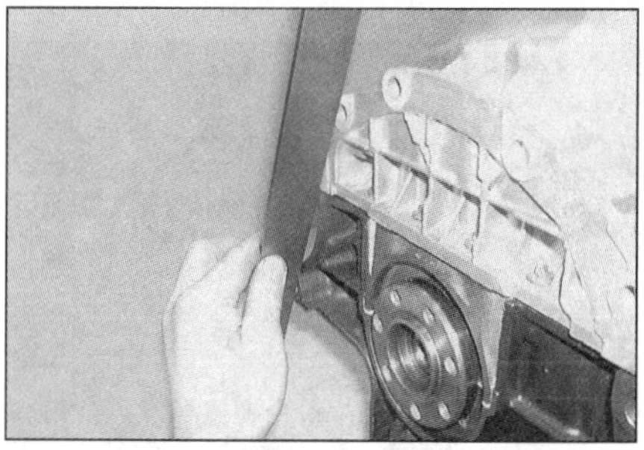

10.19 If the engine is removed, use a straight-edge to maintain the alignment between the left-hand end of the sump and cylinder block

11.4 Removing the oil seal housing from the cylinder block

11.5a Using a screwdriver to hold the oil pump sprocket when loosening the bolts

11.5b Removing the sprocket bolts from the oil pump

20 Raise the subframe and replace the threaded rods with the mounting bolts. As the subframe is being raised, make sure that the steering gear pinion locates in the column intermediate shaft correctly (see Chapter 10). Tighten the bolts to the specified torque (see Chapter 10).

21 Refit the front suspension lower arms to the subframe with reference to Chapter 10.

22 Refit the multi-function and power steering pipe supports.

23 Refit the catalytic converter and exhaust manifold heatshield with reference to Chapter 4A.

24 Refit and tighten the front bumper lower mounting fasteners.

25 Tighten the rear engine mounting link bolts to the specified torque.

26 Reconnect the gearchange rods to the transmission, and refit the front suspension subframe tie-rods to the body.

27 Refit the track rod ends to the steering arms with reference to Chapter 10.

28 Reconnect the front suspension lower arms to the hub carriers with reference to Chapter 10.

29 With the front roadwheels straight-ahead, refit and tighten the bolt securing the intermediate shaft to the steering gear pinion. Locate the gaiter over the shaft, then remove the tape or string from the steering wheel.

30 Refit the wheelarch liner and right-hand front roadwheel. Also refit the engine compartment undertray, then lower the vehicle to the ground.

31 Reconnect the battery negative lead.

32 Fill the engine with fresh oil with reference to Chapter 1A.

11.7 Slide off the oil seal spacer

11.8 Removing the oil pump sprockets and chain from the crankshaft

11.9a Unscrew the bolts . . .

11.9b . . . and remove the oil pump

11 Oil pump and sprockets – removal, inspection and refitting

SOHC engines

Removal

1 Remove the timing belt and the crankshaft sprocket, with reference to Sections 5 and 6.

2 Remove the sump referring to Section 10.

3 On the E7J engine, remove the Woodruff key (when fitted) from its slot in the crankshaft.

4 Unbolt the timing belt end oil seal housing from the cylinder block **(see illustration)**.

5 Unscrew the bolts securing the sprocket to the oil pump hub. Use a screwdriver through one of the holes in the sprocket to hold it stationary **(see illustrations)**.

6 Remove the sprocket from the oil pump.

7 Slide off the oil seal spacer **(see illustration)**.

8 Slide the drive sprocket from the crankshaft, then release both sprockets from the chain **(see illustration)**. **Note:** *The sprocket is not keyed to the crankshaft, but relies on the pulley bolt being tightened correctly to clamp the sprocket. It is most important that the pulley bolt is correctly tightened otherwise there is the possibility of the oil pump not functioning.*

9 Unscrew the two mounting bolts and withdraw the oil pump. If the two locating dowels are displaced, refit them in the cylinder block **(see illustrations)**.

Inspection

10 Unscrew the retaining bolts and lift off the pump cover and pick-up tube **(see illustrations)**.

11 Using a feeler gauge, check the clearance between each of the gears and the oil pump body. Also check the endfloat of both gears by measuring the clearance between the gears and the cover joint face. If any clearance is outside the tolerances given in the Specifications, the oil pump must be renewed **(see illustrations)**.

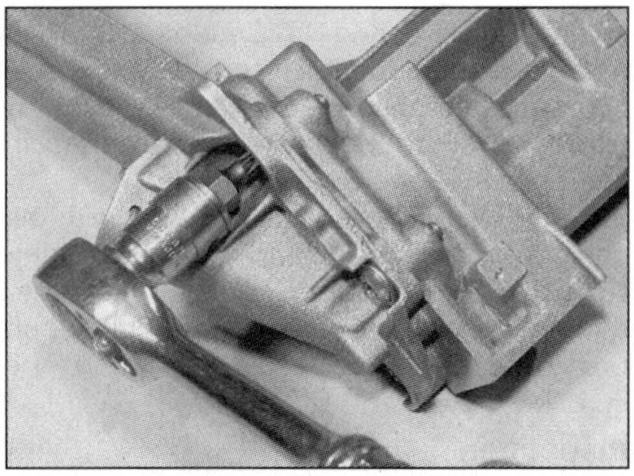

11.10a Unscrewing the bolts securing the cover and pick-up tube to the oil pump

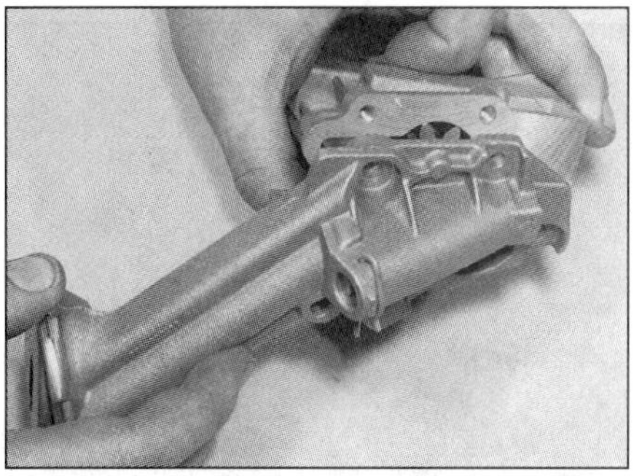

11.10b Removing the cover and pick-up tube

11.11a Measuring the oil pump gear-to-body clearance

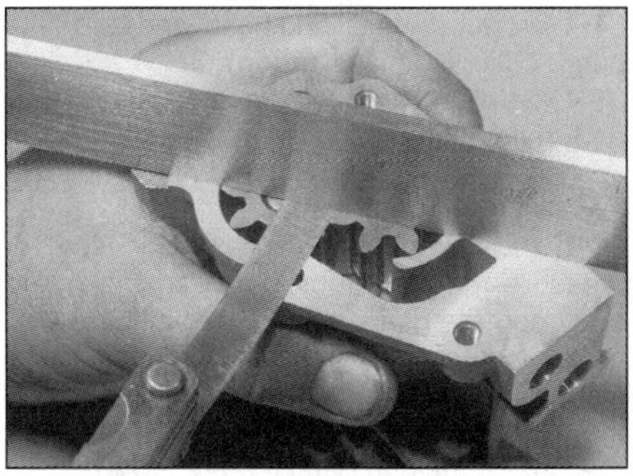

11.11b Measuring the oil pump gear endfloat

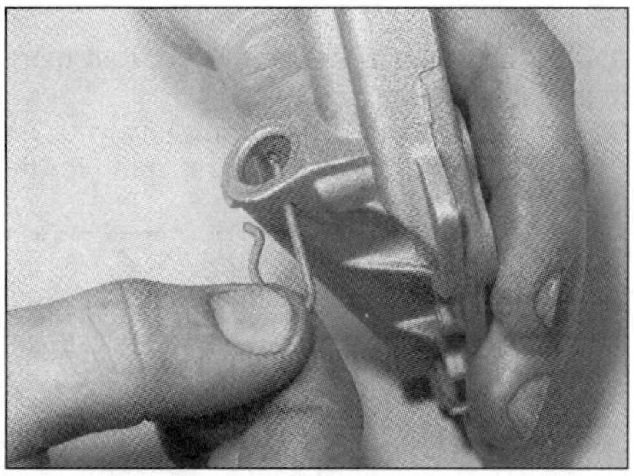

11.12a Extract the spring clip . . .

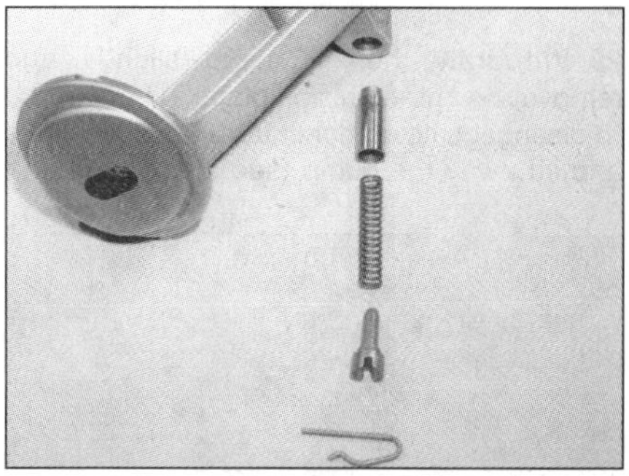

11.12b . . . and remove the end stop, spring and piston

12 Depress the relief valve end stop and extract the spring clip (with the piston at rest there is very little spring tension on the end stop, since the oil pressure release hole is located some way up the piston bore). Release the end stop and remove the spring and piston **(see illustrations)**.

13 Examine the relief valve piston and bore for signs of wear and damage. If evident, renew the oil pump complete.

14 If the components are serviceable, clean them and reassemble in the reverse order to dismantling. Before refitting the cover, fill the pump with fresh engine oil to assist circulation when the engine is first started. A new pump should also be primed with oil.

15 Examine the chain for excessive wear and renew it if necessary. Similarly check the sprockets.

Refitting

16 Wipe clean the oil pump and cylinder block mating surfaces.

17 Check that the two locating dowels are fitted in the cylinder block, then position the oil pump on them and insert the two mounting bolts. Tighten the bolts to the specified torque.

18 Slide the drive sprocket onto the crankshaft.

19 Engage the oil pump sprocket with the chain, then engage the chain with the crankshaft drive sprocket and locate the sprocket on the oil pump hub.

20 Align the holes, then insert the sprocket bolts and tighten them to the specified torque while holding the sprocket stationary with a screwdriver.

21 The timing belt end oil seal should be renewed whenever the housing is removed. Note the fitted position of the old seal, then prise it out with a screwdriver and wipe clean the seating. Smear the outer perimeter of the new seal with fresh engine oil and locate it squarely on the housing with its closed side facing outwards. Place the housing on a block of wood, then use a socket or metal tube to drive in the oil seal.

22 Clean all traces of sealant from the oil seal housing and block mating faces. Apply a 0.6 to 1.0 mm diameter bead of sealant to the housing, then refit it to the cylinder block and tighten the bolts securely. The sealant must be applied around the inner edges of the bolt holes **(see illustration)**.

23 Smear the oil seal with a little engine oil, then slide the spacer onto the crankshaft end. Turn the spacer slightly as it enters the oil seal, to prevent damage to the seal lip. If the spacer is worn where the old oil seal contacted it, it can be turned around so that the new oil seal contacts the unworn area.

24 On the E7J engine, refit the Woodruff key (when fitted) to its slot in the crankshaft.

25 Refit the sump (refer to Section 10).

26 Refit the crankshaft sprocket and fit the new timing belt with reference to Sections 6 and 5.

DOHC engines

Removal

27 To remove the oil pump alone, first remove the sump as described in Section 10.

28 Unscrew the oil pump mounting bolts and the additional bolt(s) securing the anti-emulsion plate to the crankcase **(see illustration)**.

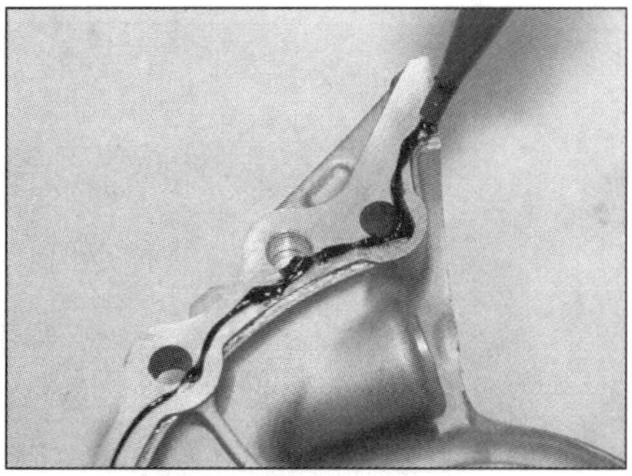

11.22 Apply sealant as directed to the oil seal housing

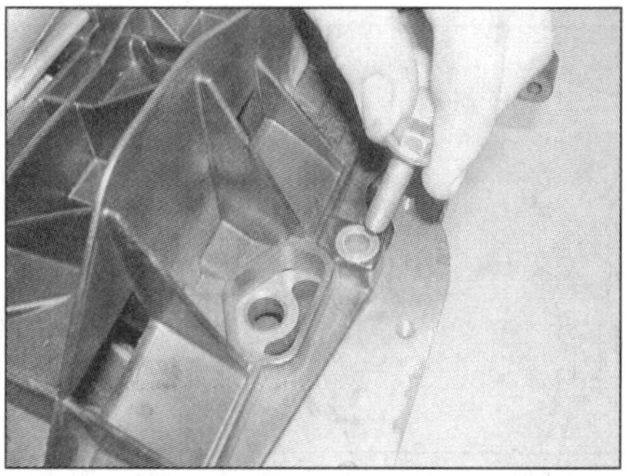

11.28 Unscrew the anti-emulsion plate retaining bolt(s)

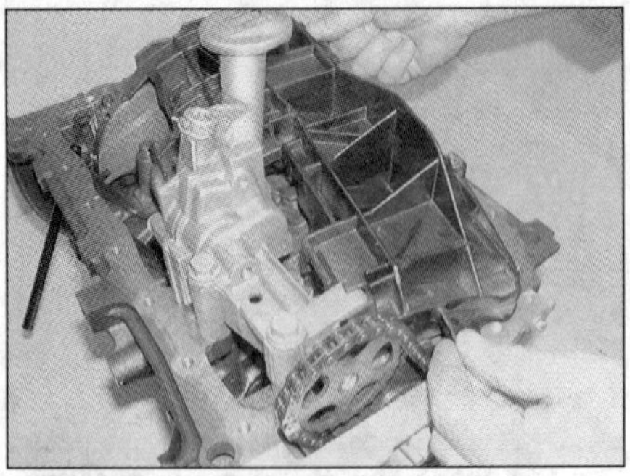

11.29a Remove the anti-emulsion plate . . .

11.29b . . . then tilt the pump to disengage its sprocket from the drive chain

29 Withdraw the oil pump slightly and remove the anti-emulsion plate. Tilt the pump to disengage its sprocket from the drive chain and lift away the pump **(see illustrations)**. If the locating dowels are displaced, refit them in their locations.

30 To remove the pump complete with its drive chain and sprockets, first remove the sump as described in Section 10, then remove the crankshaft timing belt end oil seal housing as described in Section 12.

31 Remove the oil pump as described in paragraphs 27 and 28 above.

32 Slide the drive sprocket together with the chain from the crankshaft **(see illustration)**. Note that the drive sprocket is not keyed to the crankshaft, but relies on the pulley bolt being tightened correctly to clamp the sprocket.

Inspection

33 Extract the retaining clip, and remove the oil pressure relief valve spring retainer, spring and plunger **(see illustrations)**.

34 Unscrew the retaining bolts, and lift off the pump cover **(see illustration)**.

35 Carefully examine the gears, pump body and relief valve plunger for any signs of scoring or wear. Renew the pump complete if excessive wear is evident.

36 If the components appear serviceable, measure the clearance between the pump body and the gears using feeler blades. Also measure the gear endfloat, and check the flatness of the end cover **(see illustrations)**. If the clearances exceed the specified tolerances, the pump must be renewed.

37 If the pump is satisfactory, reassemble the components in the reverse order of removal. Fill the pump with oil, then refit the cover and tighten the bolts securely **(see illustration)**.

Refitting

38 Wipe clean the oil pump and cylinder block mating surfaces.

11.32 Slide the drive sprocket together with the chain from the crankshaft

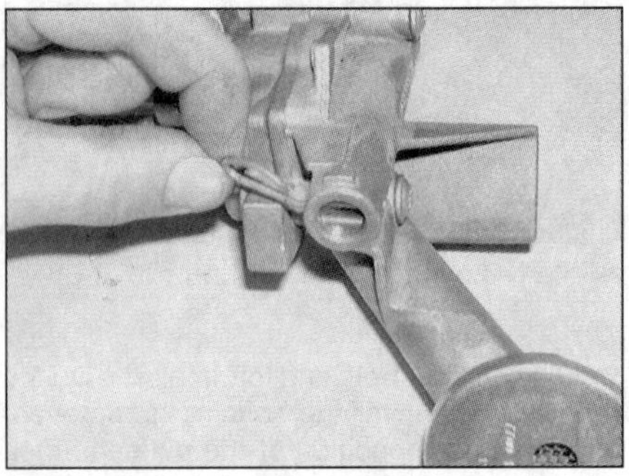

11.33a Extract the oil pressure relief valve retaining clip . . .

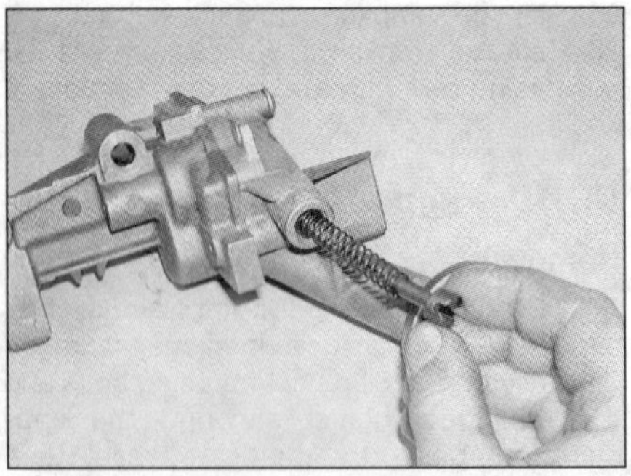

11.33b . . . remove the oil pressure relief valve spring retainer and spring . . .

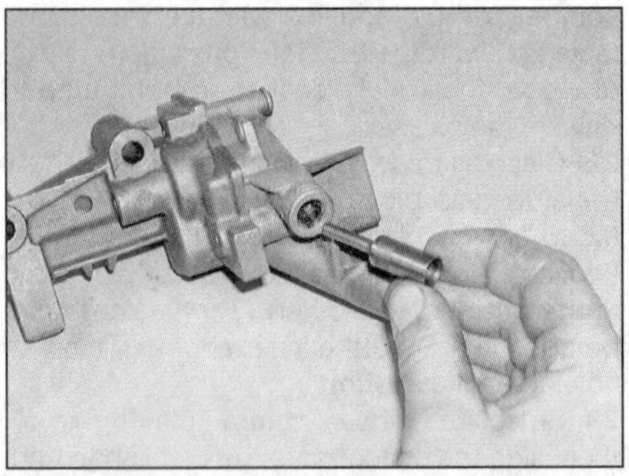

11.33c . . . followed by the plunger

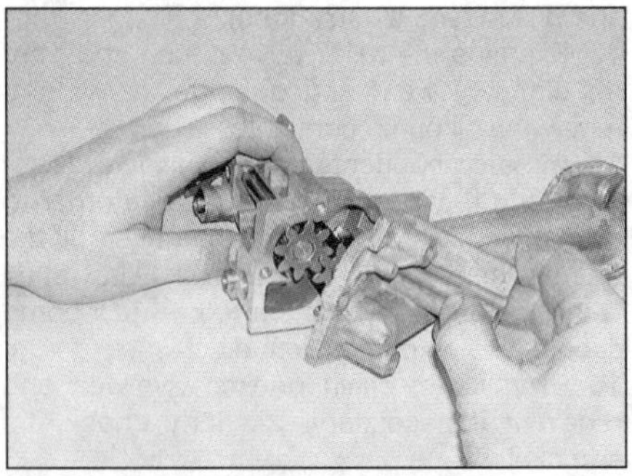

11.34 Unscrew the retaining bolts, and lift off the oil pump cover

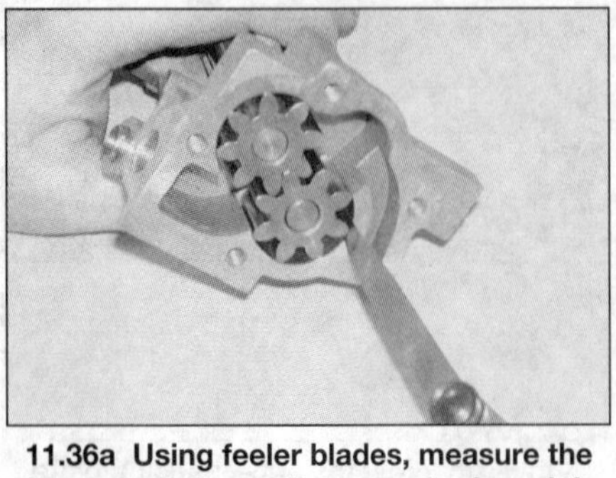

11.36a Using feeler blades, measure the clearance between the pump body and the gears . . .

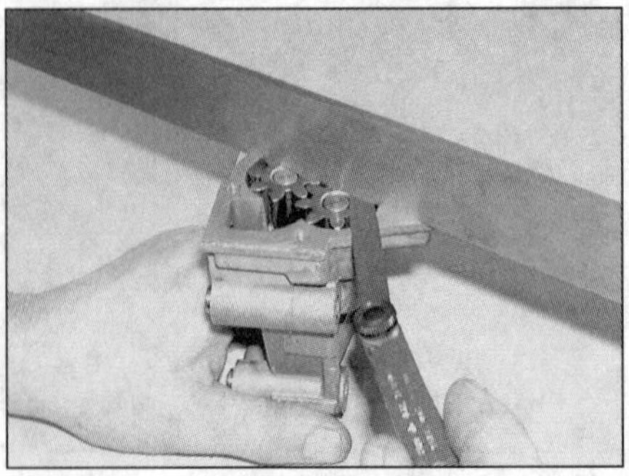

11.36b . . . and measure the gear endfloat

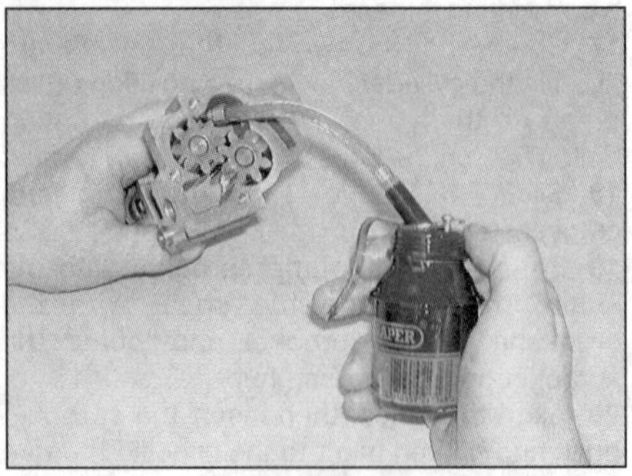

11.37 Fill the pump with oil, then refit the cover

39 Locate the drive sprocket onto the end of the crankshaft, ensuring that it is fitted with the projecting boss facing away from the crankshaft **(see illustration)**. Engage the pump with the dowels, fit the two retaining bolts and tighten them to the specified torque.
40 Refit the anti-emulsion plate and secure with the retaining bolt(s).
41 Refit the oil seal housing as described in Section 12.
42 Refit the sump as described in Section 10.

11.39 Ensure that the oil pump drive sprocket is fitted with the projecting boss facing away from the crankshaft

12 Crankshaft oil seals – renewal

Timing belt end oil seal

1 Remove the timing belt and the crankshaft sprocket with reference to Sections 5 and 6. An alternative, though longer, method is to remove the sump and oil seal housing, and fit the new oil seal on the bench.
2 Note the fitted position of the old seal, then prise it out of the oil seal housing using a screwdriver or suitable hooked instrument. An alternative method of removing the oil seal is to drill carefully two small holes opposite each other in the oil seal and insert self-tapping screws, then pull on the screws with grips. Take care not to damage the surface of the spacer or the seal housing.
3 With the oil seal removed, where applicable slide the spacer from the crankshaft, noting which way round it is fitted.
4 Examine the spacer for excessive oil seal wear and polish off any burrs or raised edges which may have caused the seal to fail in the first place. If necessary, the spacer can be refitted so that the new oil seal contacts an unworn area. Clean the oil seal seating in the housing.
5 Smear the lips and outer perimeter of the new seal with fresh engine oil and locate it over the crankshaft with its closed side facing outwards. Using hand pressure, press the oil seal squarely into the housing a little way, then use a socket or metal tube to drive the oil seal to the previously noted position – take great care not to damage the seal lips during fitting **(see illustration)**. Do not drive it in too far or it will have to be removed and possibly renewed.
6 Slide the spacer onto the crankshaft and carefully press it into the oil seal, while twisting it to prevent damage.
7 Wipe away any excess oil, then refit the crankshaft sprocket and fit the new timing belt with reference to Sections 6 and 5.

Flywheel/driveplate end oil seal

8 Renewal of the crankshaft left-hand oil seal requires the engine and transmission assembly to be removed as described in Chapter 2D so that the engine and transmission can be separated on the bench (see Chapter 7A or 7B), the clutch (where fitted – see Chapter 6) and the flywheel/ driveplate (see Section 14 of this Chapter) can be removed.
9 Prise out the old oil seal using a small screwdriver, taking care not to damage the surface on the crankshaft. Alternatively, the oil seal can be removed by drilling two small holes diagonally opposite each other and inserting self-tapping screws in them. A pair of grips can then be used to pull out the oil seal, by pulling on each side in turn.
10 Inspect the seal rubbing surface on the crankshaft. If it is grooved or rough in the area where the old seal was fitted, the new seal should be fitted slightly less deeply, so that it rubs on an unworn part of the surface.
11 Wipe clean the oil seal seating, then dip the new seal in fresh engine oil, and locate it over the crankshaft with its closed side facing outwards **(see illustration)**. Make sure that the oil seal lip is not damaged as it is located on the crankshaft.
12 Using a metal tube, drive the oil seal squarely into the bore until flush. A block of wood cut to pass over the end of the crankshaft may be used instead.
13 Refit the flywheel/driveplate with reference to Section 14. Refit the clutch as described in Chapter 6, reconnect the transmission to the engine and refit the engine/transmission unit as described in the relevant Chapters of this Manual.

13 Engine/transmission mountings – inspection and renewal

Inspection

1 Apply the handbrake, then jack up the front of the car and support it on axle stands (see *Jacking and vehicle support*). Where fitted, remove the engine compartment undershield.
2 Visually inspect the rubber pads on the two front and one rear engine/transmission mountings for signs of cracking and deterioration **(see illustration overleaf)**. Careful use of a lever will help to determine the condition of the rubber pads. If there is excessive movement in the mounting, or if the rubber has deteriorated, the mounting should be renewed.
3 Lower the vehicle to the ground.

12.5 Using a socket to drive the new crankshaft oil seal into the housing

12.11 Fitting a new crankshaft flywheel end oil seal

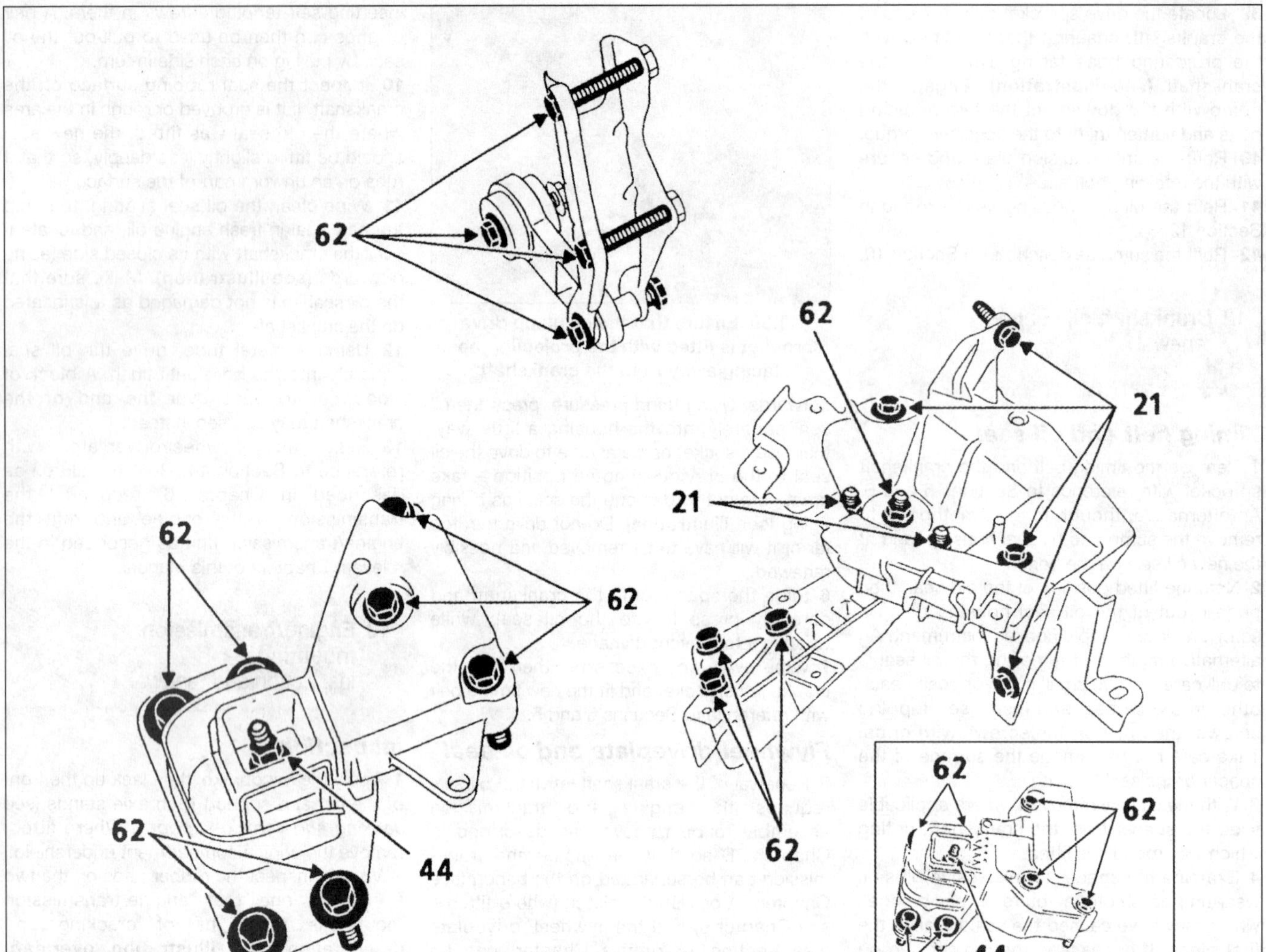

13.2 Torque wrench settings (in Nm) of the engine mountings

Inset shows right-hand mounting for K4J and K4M engines

Renewal

Right-hand front mounting

4 Support the right-hand end of the engine with a trolley jack and block of wood beneath the sump.

5 Unbolt the mounting brackets from the engine and inner wing panel **(see illustrations).**

6 Fit the new mounting using a reversal of the removal procedure, but tighten the nuts/bolts to the specified torque wrench settings.

Left-hand front mounting

7 Remove the air inlet ducts from the left-hand side of the engine as applicable, for access to the engine/transmission left-hand mounting. Remove the battery as described in Chapter 5A.

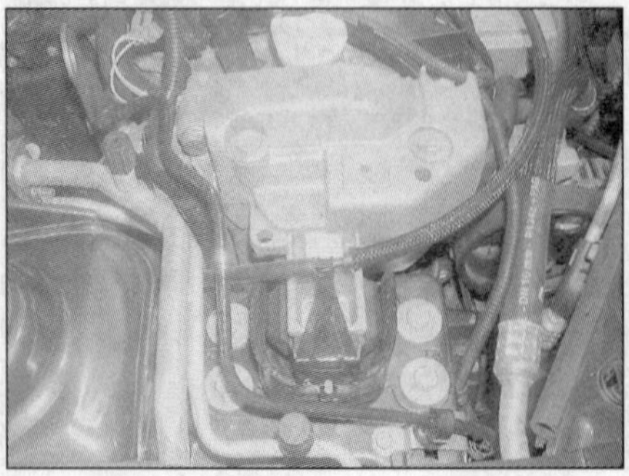

13.5a Right-hand engine mounting – K4J engine

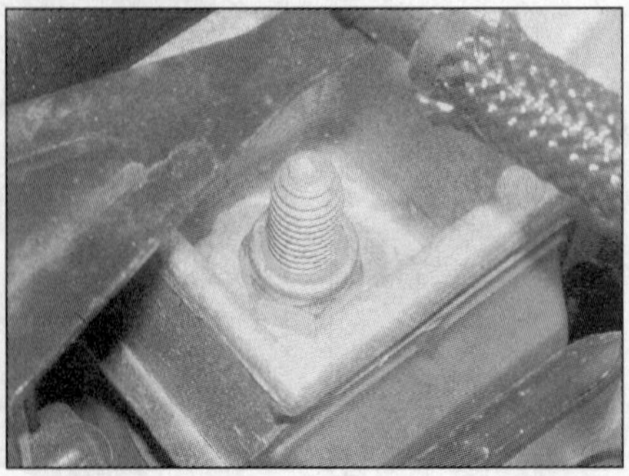

13.5b Central nut on the right-hand engine mounting – K4J engine

13.5c Right-hand engine mounting – E7J engine

8 Support the left-hand end of the transmission with a trolley jack and block of wood beneath the sump.
9 Unbolt the mounting brackets from the transmission and inner wing panel.
10 Fit the new mounting using a reversal of the removal procedure, but tighten the nuts/bolts to the specified torque wrench setting.

Rear mounting

11 Apply the handbrake, then jack up the front of the vehicle and support it on axle stands (see *Jacking and vehicle support*).
12 Unbolt the link bar from the transmission or bracket, and from the subframe **(see illustration)**.
13 Where applicable, unbolt the bracket from the transmission.
14 Fit the new mounting using a reversal of the removal procedure, but tighten the nuts/bolts to the specified torque setting.

13.12 Engine rear mounting link

14 Flywheel/driveplate – removal, inspection and refitting

Removal

Note: *Removal of the flywheel or driveplate requires the engine and transmission assembly to be removed as described in Chapter 2D so that the engine and transmission can separated on the bench.*

1 Remove the manual gearbox or automatic transmission as described in Chapter 7A or 7B.
2 On manual gearbox models, remove the clutch as described in Chapter 6.
3 Mark the flywheel/driveplate in relation to the crankshaft to aid refitting. Note that the flywheel/driveplate can only be refitted in one position, as the bolts are unequally spaced.
4 The flywheel/driveplate must now be held stationary while the bolts are loosened. To do this, locate a long bolt in one of the transmission-to-engine mounting bolt holes, and either insert a wide-bladed screwdriver in the starter ring gear, or use a piece of bent metal bar engaged with the ring gear.
5 Unscrew the mounting bolts, and withdraw the flywheel/driveplate; be careful – it is heavy.

Inspection

6 Examine the flywheel/driveplate for wear or chipping of the ring gear teeth. If the ring gear is worn or damaged, it may be possible to renew it separately, but this job is best left to a Renault dealer or engineering works. The temperature to which the new ring gear must be heated for installation is critical and, if not done accurately, the hardness of the teeth will be destroyed.
7 Check the flywheel/driveplate carefully for signs of distortion, and for hairline cracks around the bolt holes, or radiating outwards from the centre. If damage of this sort is found, it must be renewed.
8 Examine the flywheel for scoring of the clutch face. If the clutch face is scored, the flywheel may be machined until flat, but renewal is preferable.

Refitting

9 Clean the flywheel/driveplate and crankshaft mating surfaces, then locate the flywheel/driveplate on the crankshaft, making sure that any previously-made marks are aligned.
10 Apply a few drops of locking fluid to the mounting bolt threads, fit the bolts and tighten them in a diagonal sequence to the specified torque wrench setting.
11 Refit the clutch, if applicable (Chapter 6) and the manual gearbox or automatic transmission as described in Chapter 7A or 7B, then refit the engine/transmission assembly with reference to Chapter 2D.

Notes

Chapter 2 Part C: Diesel in-car engine repair procedures

Contents

Degrees of difficulty

Easy, suitable for novice with little experience	**Fairly easy,** suitable for beginner with some experience	**Fairly difficult,** suitable for competent DIY mechanic	**Difficult,** suitable for experienced DIY mechanic	**Very difficult,** suitable for expert DIY or professional

Specifications

General

Type	Four-cylinder, in-line, single overhead camshaft
Designation	F8Q 630, F8Q 662 and F8Q 632
Capacity	1870 cc
Bore	80.0 mm
Stroke	93.0 mm
Firing order	1-3-4-2 (No 1 cylinder at flywheel end)
Direction of crankshaft rotation	Clockwise viewed from timing belt end
Compression ratio	21.5:1
Maximum power output (typical)	47.0 kW (61 bhp) at 4500 rpm
Maximum torque (typical)	118 Nm (87 lbf ft) at 2250 rpm

Compression pressures

Engine warm – approximately 80°C:	
Minimum pressure	20 bars
Maximum difference between cylinders	4 bars

Camshaft

Drive	Toothed belt
Number of bearings	5
Camshaft endfloat	0.05 to 0.13 mm

Valve clearances

Inlet	0.20 ± 0.05 mm
Exhaust	0.40 ± 0.05 mm

Timing belt

Tension (approximate)	7.0 to 8.0 mm deflection under a load of 30 N	

Lubrication system

System pressure (at 80°C):		
At 1000 rpm	2.0 bars minimum	
At 3000 rpm	3.5 bars minimum	
Oil pump type	Two-gear	
Oil pump clearances:	**Minimum**	**Maximum**
Gear to body	0.10 mm	0.24 mm
Gear endfloat	0.02 mm	0.085 mm

Torque wrench settings

Torque wrench settings	Nm	lbf ft
Auxiliary shaft sprocket bolt	50	37
Camshaft bearing caps:		
8 mm diameter bolts	20	15
6 mm diameter bolts	10	7
Camshaft sprocket	50	37
Connecting rod (big-end) cap bolts	45 to 50	33 to 37
Crankshaft pulley bolt	90 to 100	66 to 74
Cylinder head bolts **(see illustration 9.39)***:		
Stage 1	30	22
Stage 2	Angle-tighten a further 80° ± 4°	
Stage 3	Wait for 3 minutes minimum	
Stage 4	Slacken bolts 1 and 2 fully	
Stage 5 Tighten bolts 1 and 2 to:	25	18
Stage 6	Angle-tighten bolts 1 and 2 a further 213° ±7°	
Stage 7	Slacken bolts 3 and 4 fully	
Stage 8 Tighten bolts 3 and 4 to:	25	18
Stage 9	Angle-tighten bolts 3 and 4 a further 213° ±7°	
Stage 10	Slacken bolts 5 and 6 fully	
Stage 11 Tighten bolts 5 and 6 to:	25	18
Stage 12	Angle-tighten bolts 5 and 6 a further 213° ±7°	
Stage 13	Slacken bolts 7 and 8 fully	
Stage 14 Tighten bolts 7 and 8 to:	25	18
Stage 15	Angle-tighten bolts 7 and 8 a further 213° ±7°	
Stage 16	Slacken bolts 9 and 10 fully	
Stage 17 Tighten bolts 9 and 10 to:	25	18
Stage 18	Angle-tighten bolts 9 and 10 a further 213° ±7°	
Engine/transmission mountings (see Section 14):		
Right-hand mounting to engine/body	62	46
Right-hand mounting central nut	44	32
Left-hand mounting to transmission	62	46
Left-hand mounting to body	21	15
Left-hand mounting central nut	62	46
Rear mounting	62	46
Flywheel bolts*	50 to 55	37 to 41
Fuel injection pump sprocket	50	37
Main bearing caps	60 to 65	44 to 48
Piston oil spray jet securing bolts	18 to 22	13 to 16
Sump bolts	12 to 15	9 to 11
Timing belt tensioner roller nut	50	37
Valve cover nuts/bolts	12	9

***Note:** *Use new bolts.*

1 General information

How to use this Chapter

This Part of Chapter 2 is devoted to in-car repair procedures for the 1.9 litre diesel engine. Similar information covering the other engine types can be found in Parts A and B. All procedures concerning engine removal and refitting, and engine block/cylinder head overhaul can be found in Part D of this Chapter.

Refer to *Vehicle identification numbers* in the Reference Section at the end of this manual for details of engine code locations.

Most of the operations included in this Part are based on the assumption that the engine is still installed in the car. Therefore, if this information is being used during a complete engine overhaul, with the engine already removed, many of the steps included here will not apply.

Engine description

The engine is of four-cylinder, in-line, single overhead camshaft type, mounted transversely at the front of the vehicle **(see illustration)**.

The cylinder block is of cast iron with conventional dry liners bored directly into the cylinder block. The crankshaft is supported in five shell-type main bearings. Thrust washers are fitted to No 2 main bearing to control crankshaft endfloat.

The connecting rods are attached to the crankshaft by horizontally split shell-type big-end bearings and to the pistons by gudgeon pins. The gudgeon pins are fully-floating and are retained by circlips. The aluminium alloy pistons are of the slipper type and are fitted with three piston rings, comprising two compression rings and a scraper-type oil control ring.

The single overhead camshaft is mounted directly in the cylinder head, and is driven by the crankshaft via a toothed timing belt.

The camshaft operates the valves via inverted bucket-type tappets, which operate in bores machined directly in the cylinder head. Valve clearance adjustment is by shims located externally between the tappet bucket and the cam lobe. The inlet and exhaust valves are mounted vertically in the cylinder head and are each closed by a single valve spring.

On some early engines an auxiliary shaft located alongside the crankshaft is also driven by the timing belt and actuates the oil pump via a skew gear. On later engines the oil pump is driven by chain from the crankshaft; no auxiliary shaft is fitted, but its sprocket is retained as an idler.

The fuel injection pump is driven by the timing belt and is described in further detail in Chapter 4B.

A semi-closed crankcase ventilation system is employed, and crankcase fumes are drawn from an oil separator on the cylinder block and passed via a hose to the inlet tract (see Chapter 4C for further details).

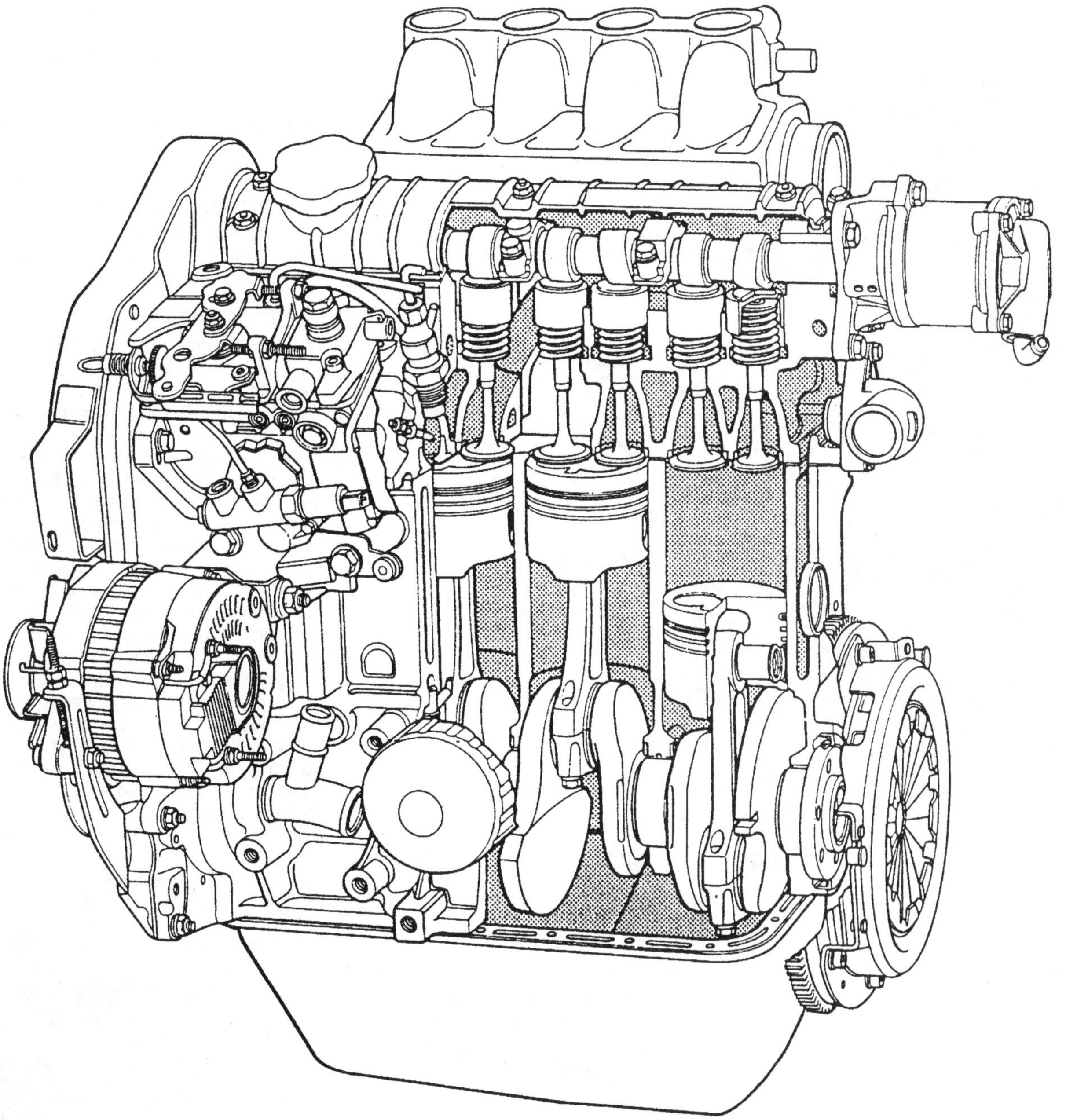

1.4 Cutaway view of the engine

Engine lubrication is by pressure feed from a gear-type oil pump located beneath the crankshaft. Engine oil is fed through an externally-mounted oil filter to the main oil gallery feeding the crankshaft, auxiliary shaft (where fitted) and camshaft **(see illustration)**. Oil spray jets are fitted to the cylinder block to supply oil to the underside of the pistons. An oil cooler is mounted between the oil filter and the cylinder block.

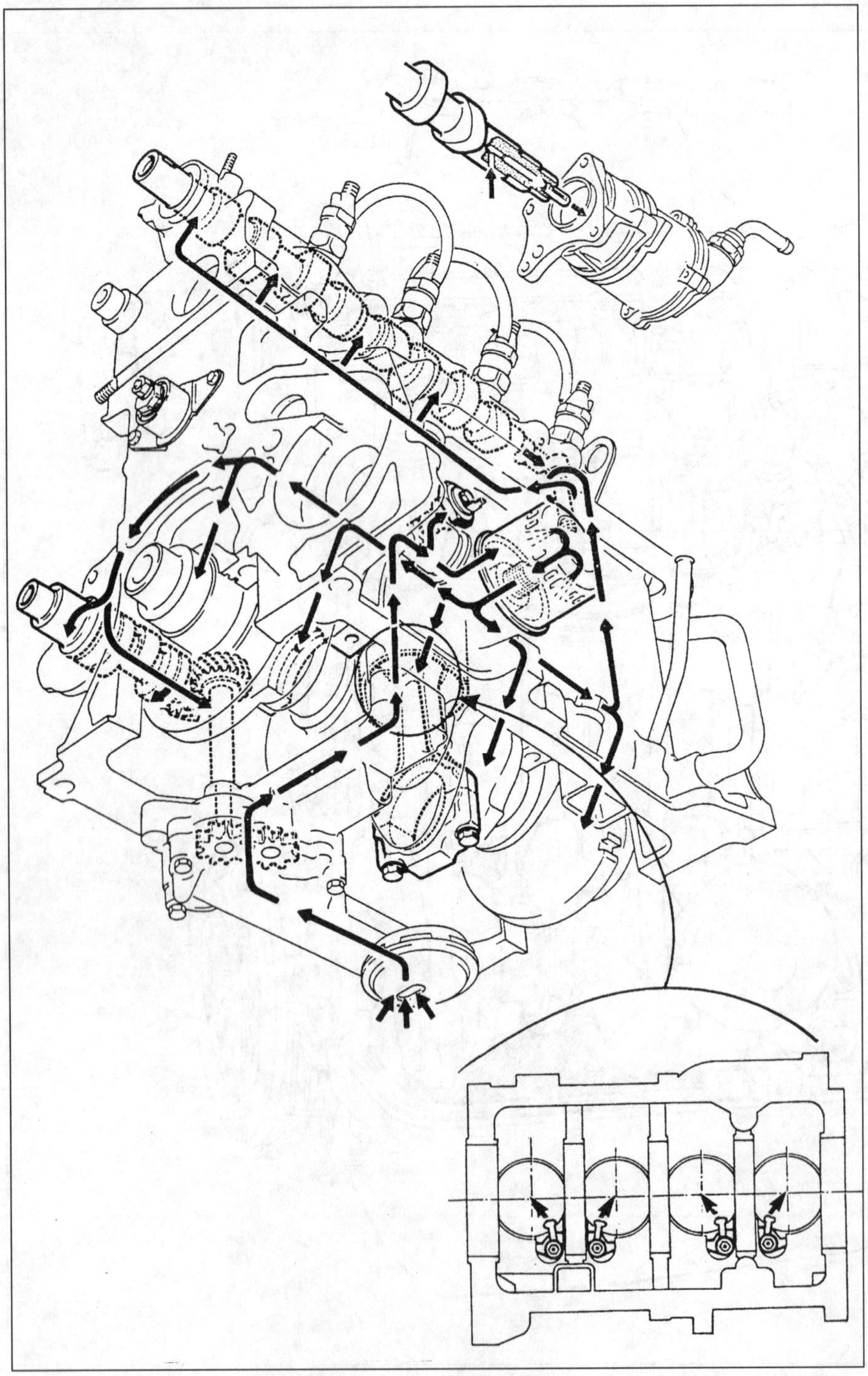

1.12 Engine lubrication circuit

Repair operations possible with the engine in the vehicle

The following operations can be carried out without having to remove the engine from the vehicle:

a) Removal and refitting of the cylinder head.
b) Removal and refitting of the timing belt and sprockets.
c) Renewal of the camshaft oil seals.
d) Removal and refitting of the camshaft.
e) Removal and refitting of the sump.
*f) Removal and refitting of the connecting rods and pistons.**
g) Removal and refitting of the oil pump.
h) Renewal of the crankshaft oil seals.
i) Renewal of the engine mountings.
j) Removal and refitting of the flywheel.

**Although the operation marked with an asterisk can be carried out with the engine in the car after removal of the sump, it is better for the engine to be removed in the interests of cleanliness and improved access. For this reason, the procedure is described in Chapter 2D.*

Caution: If the radio/cassette in your vehicle is equipped with an anti-theft system, make sure you have the correct activation code before disconnecting the battery.

2 Compression and leakdown tests – description and interpretation

Compression test

Note: *A compression tester specifically designed for diesel engines must be used for this test.*

1 When engine performance is down, or if misfiring occurs which cannot be attributed to a fault in the fuel system, a compression test can provide diagnostic clues as to the engine's condition. If the test is performed regularly it can give warning of trouble before any other symptoms become apparent.

2 A compression tester specifically intended for diesel engines must be used, because of the higher pressures involved. The tester is connected to an adaptor which screws into the glow plug or injector hole **(see illustration)**. It is unlikely to be worthwhile buying such a tester for occasional use, but it may be possible to borrow or hire one – if not, have the test performed by a garage.

3 Unless specific instructions to the contrary are supplied with the tester, observe the following points:

a) The battery must be in a good state of

2.2 Carrying out a compression test

charge, the air filter must be clean and the engine should be at normal operating temperature.

b) All the injectors or glow plugs should be removed before starting the test. If removing the injectors, also remove the fire seal washers (which must be renewed when the injectors are refitted – see Chapter 4B), otherwise they may be blown out.

c) It is advisable to disconnect the stop solenoid on the pump to reduce the amount of fuel discharged as the engine is cranked.

4 There is no need to hold the accelerator pedal down during the test because the diesel engine air inlet is not throttled.

5 The actual compression pressures measured are not so important as the balance between cylinders. Values are given in the Specifications.

6 The cause of poor compression is less easy to establish on a diesel engine than on a petrol one. The effect of introducing oil into the cylinders ('wet' testing) is not conclusive, because there is a risk that the oil will sit in the swirl chamber or in the recess on the piston crown instead of passing to the rings. However, the following can be used as a rough guide to diagnosis.

7 All cylinders should produce very similar pressures; any difference greater than that specified indicates the existence of a fault. Note that the compression should build-up quickly in a healthy engine; low compression on the first stroke, followed by gradually increasing pressure on successive strokes, indicates worn piston rings. A low compression reading on the first stroke, which does not build-up during successive strokes, indicates leaking valves or a blown head gasket (a cracked head could also be the cause). Deposits on the undersides of the valve heads can also cause low compression.

8 A low reading from two adjacent cylinders is almost certainly due to the head gasket having blown between them.

9 If the compression reading is unusually high, the cylinder head surfaces, valves and pistons are probably coated with carbon deposits. If this is the case, the cylinder head should be removed and decarbonised (see Chapter 2D, Section 9).

Leakdown test

10 A leakdown test measures the rate at which compressed air fed into the cylinder is lost. It is an alternative to a compression test and in many ways it is better, since the escaping air provides easy identification of where pressure loss is occurring (piston rings, valves or head gasket).

11 The equipment needed for leakdown testing is unlikely to be available to the home mechanic. If poor compression is suspected, have the test performed by a suitably-equipped garage.

3.3 View of the crankshaft pulley bolt with the lower wheelarch cover removed

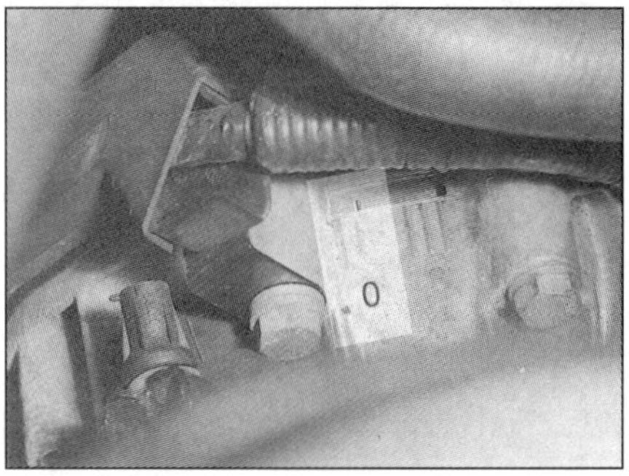

3.4 Flywheel timing mark aligned with TDC (0°) mark on bellhousing

3 Top dead centre (TDC) for number one piston - locating

Note: *If the special Renault tool mentioned in this Section is not available, an 8 mm diameter rod or drill bit can be used instead. On some engines, however, an 8 mm diameter rod may be too slack a fit in the blanking plug aperture in the cylinder block for the crankshaft position to be determined accurately – it will therefore be necessary in such cases to have a stepped pin made up, with an 8 mm diameter at its tip to engage in the crankshaft slot and a larger diameter as necessary to fit precisely in the cylinder block aperture.*

Caution: These timing pins are intended SOLELY for the purpose of checking the position of the crankshaft during various engine overhaul procedures. DO NOT use them as locking tools to prevent crankshaft rotation while the pulley or flywheel bolts are unscrewed or tightened

1 Top Dead Centre (TDC) is the highest point in the cylinder that each piston reaches as the crankshaft turns. Each piston reaches TDC at the end of the compression stroke and again at the end of the exhaust stroke; however, for the purpose of timing the engine, TDC refers to the position of No 1 piston at the end of its compression stroke. No 1 piston is at the flywheel end of the engine.

2 When No 1 piston is at TDC, the timing mark on the camshaft sprocket should be aligned with the pointer on the timing belt outer cover (the pulley mark can be viewed through the cut-out in the cover, below the pointer, using a mirror if necessary). Additionally, the timing mark on the flywheel should be aligned with the TDC mark on the gearbox bellhousing.

3 To align the timing marks, the crankshaft must be turned. This should be done by using a spanner on the crankshaft pulley bolt. Improved access to the pulley bolt can be obtained by jacking up the front right-hand corner of the vehicle and removing the roadwheel and the wheelarch lower liner (secured by plastic clips) **(see illustration)**. If desired, to enable the engine to be turned more easily, remove the glow plugs (Chapter 5C) or the fuel injectors (Chapter 4B).

4 Look through the timing aperture in the gearbox bellhousing and turn the crankshaft until the timing mark on the flywheel is aligned with the TDC (0°) mark on the bellhousing **(see illustration)**.

5 Unscrew the bolts and remove the plastic cover from the upper right-hand engine mounting bracket **(see illustration)**. Note the locations of any brackets which may be secured by the bolts.

6 Check that the timing mark on the camshaft sprocket is aligned with the pointer on the timing belt outer cover **(see illustration)**. The engine is now positioned with No 1 piston at TDC on its compression stroke.

7 It is possible to check the crankshaft position as follows. If necessary, remove the air cleaner housing assembly (Chapter 4B).

8 For absolute accuracy, the crankshaft position can be checked by inserting a timing pin – Renault tool Mot. 861 (early version) or

3.5 Removing the cover from the engine mounting bracket

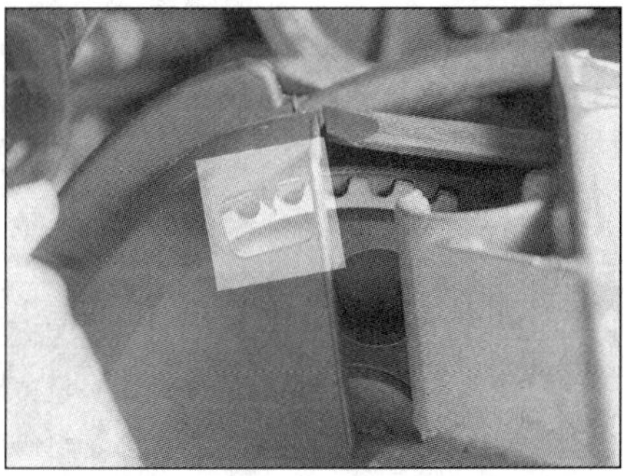

3.6 Camshaft sprocket timing mark aligned with pointer on timing belt cover

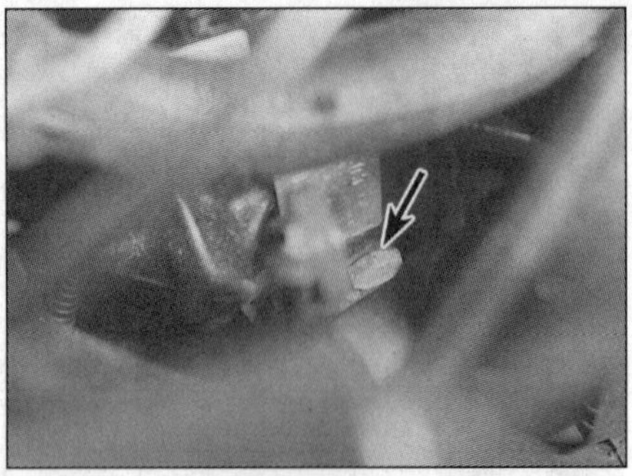

3.8a Remove the plug (arrowed) from the cylinder block . . .

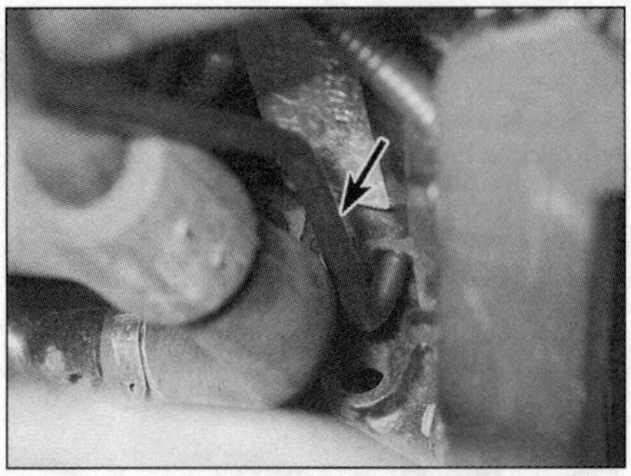

3.8b . . . and insert a suitable 8 mm rod (arrowed)

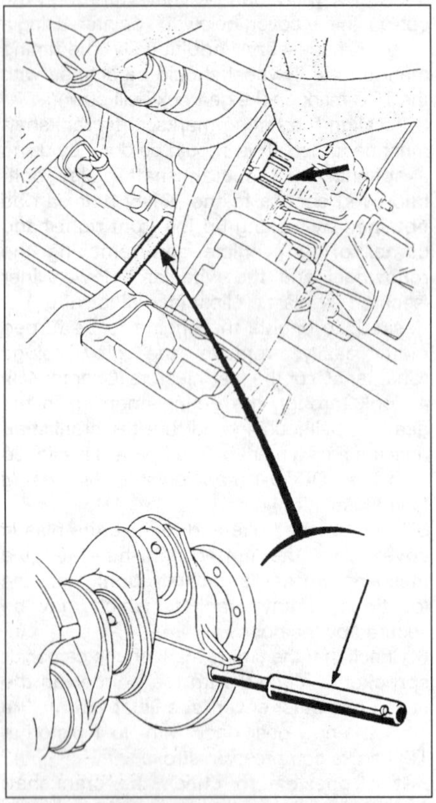

3.8c TDC mark on flywheel viewed through bellhousing aperture, and TDC locking tool engaged with crankshaft (arrowed)

Mot. 1054 (latest version). To do this, unscrew the blanking plug from the front left-hand end of the cylinder block, next to the base of the oil level dipstick tube, and insert the timing pin so that it engages in the timing slot provided for this purpose in the crankshaft, noting that it may be necessary to rock the crankshaft very slightly backwards or forwards to do this **(see illustrations)**. Once in place it should be impossible to turn the crankshaft – if the crankshaft will still move to-and-fro slightly, then the timing pin has entered a balance hole in the crankshaft instead of the timing slot. **Note:** *Do not attempt to rotate the engine whilst the timing pin is in place. If the engine is to be left in this state for a long period of time, it is a good idea to place warning notices inside the vehicle and in the engine compartment. This will reduce the possibility of the engine being accidentally cranked on the starter motor, which will cause severe damage if done with the timing pin in place.*

9 On completion, remove the timing pin and refit all removed components.

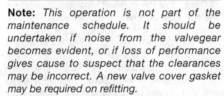

4 Valve clearances – checking and adjustment

Note: *This operation is not part of the maintenance schedule. It should be undertaken if noise from the valvegear becomes evident, or if loss of performance gives cause to suspect that the clearances may be incorrect. A new valve cover gasket may be required on refitting.*

Checking

1 Where necessary for improved access, unclip any hoses which are routed across the top of the valve cover, and move them to one side out of the way. If fuel lines are disconnected, cover open unions to prevent dirt ingress.

2 Where applicable, unscrew the securing bolts, and remove the upper timing belt/engine mounting plastic cover. Note the locations of any brackets secured by the bolts.

3 Unscrew the nuts from the valve cover, and withdraw the cover from the engine. Recover the gasket.

4 During the following procedure, the crankshaft must be turned, using a spanner on the crankshaft pulley bolt. Improved access to the pulley bolt can be obtained by jacking up the front right-hand corner of the vehicle and removing the roadwheel and the lower wheelarch cover (secured by plastic clips).

5 If desired, to enable the crankshaft to be turned more easily, remove the glow plugs (Chapter 5C) or the fuel injectors (Chapter 4B).

6 Draw the valve positions on a piece of paper, numbering them 1 to 8 from the flywheel end of the engine. Identify them as inlet or exhaust (ie, 1E, 2I, 3E, 4I, 5I, 6E, 7I, 8E) **(see illustration)**.

7 Turn the crankshaft until the valves of No 1 cylinder (flywheel end) are 'rocking'. The exhaust valve will be closing and the inlet valve will be opening. The piston of No 4 cylinder will be at the top of its compression stroke, with both valves fully closed. The clearances for both valves of No 4 cylinder may be checked at the same time.

8 Insert a feeler blade of the correct thickness (see Specifications) between the cam lobe and the shim on the top of the tappet bucket, and check that it is a firm sliding fit **(see illustration)**. If it is not, use the feeler blades to ascertain the exact clearance, and record this for use when calculating the new shim thickness required. Note that the inlet and exhaust valve clearances are different (see Specifications).

9 With No 4 cylinder valve clearances checked, turn the engine through half a turn so that No 3 valves are 'rocking', then check

3.8d Timing rod warning notice on the engine

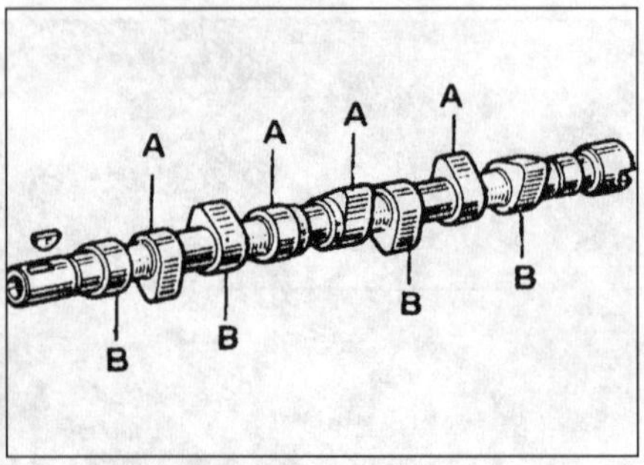

4.6 Cam lobe identification
A Inlet *B Exhaust*

4.8 Measuring a valve clearance

VALVES ROCKING ON CYLINDER	CHECK CLEARANCE ON CYLINDER

1	4
3	2
4	1
2	3

4.9 Valve clearance measurement

the valve clearances of No 2 cylinder in the same way. Similarly check the remaining valve clearances in the sequence shown **(see illustration)**.

Adjustment

Note: *A micrometer will be required for this operation.*

10 Where a valve clearance differs from the specified value, then the shim for that valve must be replaced with a thinner or thicker shim accordingly. The shim size is stamped on the bottom face of the shim, but it is prudent to use a micrometer to measure the true thickness of any shim removed, as it may have been reduced by wear **(see illustrations)**.

11 The size of shim required is calculated as follows. If the measured clearance is less than specified, subtract the measured clearance from the specified clearance, and deduct the result from the thickness of the existing shim. For example:

Sample calculation – clearance too small

Clearance measured (A) = 0.15 mm
Desired clearance (B) = 0.20 mm
Difference (B – A) = 0.05 mm
Shim thickness fitted = 3.70 mm
Shim thickness required = 3.70 – 0.05 = 3.65 mm

12 If the measured clearance is greater than specified, subtract the specified clearance from the measured clearance, and add the result to the thickness of the existing shim. For example:

Sample calculation – clearance too big

Clearance measured (A) = 0.50 mm
Desired clearance (B) = 0.40 mm
Difference (A – B) = 0.10 mm
Shim thickness fitted = 3.45 mm
Shim thickness required = 3.45 + 0.10 = 3.55 mm

13 The shims can be removed from their locations on top of the tappet buckets without removing the camshaft if the Renault tool

4.10a Shim thickness engraved on the underside

shown can be borrowed, or a suitable alternative fabricated **(see illustration)**.

14 To remove the shim, the tappet bucket has to be pressed down against valve spring pressure just far enough to allow the shim to be slid out. Theoretically, this could be done by levering against the camshaft between the cam lobes with a suitable screwdriver or similar tool to push the bucket down, but this is not recommended by the manufacturers. If this method is to be used, take great care not to damage the camshaft, cylinder head, or tappet bucket **(see illustration)**.

15 An arrangement similar to the Renault tool can be made by bolting a bar to the camshaft bearing studs and levering down against this with a stout screwdriver. The contact pad should be a triangular-shaped metal block with a lip filed along each side to contact the edge of the buckets. Levering down against this will open the valve and allow the shim to be withdrawn.

16 Make sure that the cam lobe peaks are uppermost when depressing a tappet, and rotate the buckets so that the notches are at

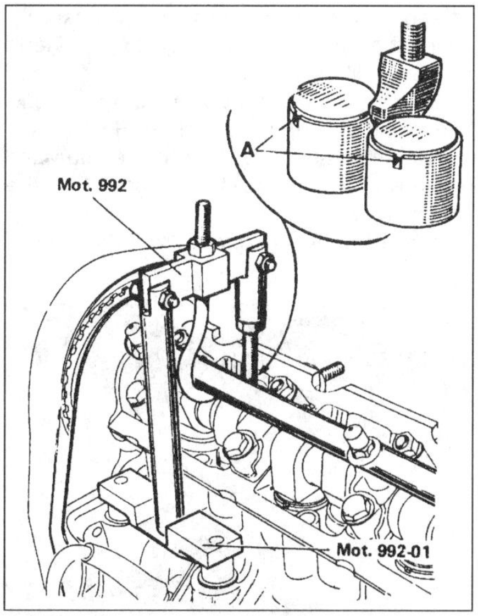

4.13 Renault tool for compressing tappet buckets to change shims

A *Notches positioned at right-angles to camshaft centre-line*

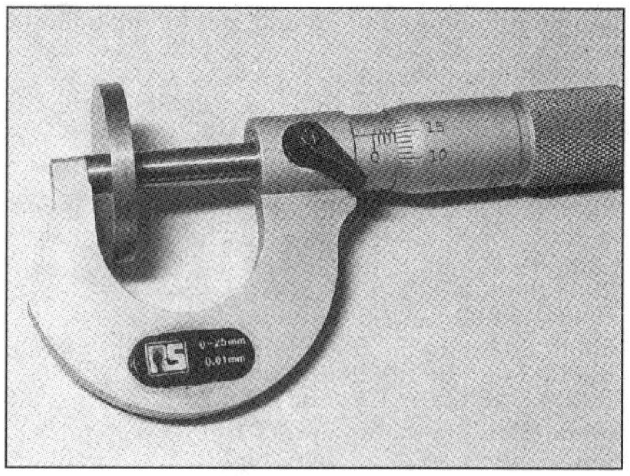

4.10b Measuring a shim using a micrometer

right-angles to the camshaft centre-line. When refitting the shims, ensure that the size markings face the tappet buckets (ie, face downwards).

17 If the Renault tool cannot be borrowed or a suitable alternative improvised, then it will be necessary to remove the camshaft to gain access to the shims, as described in Section 8.

18 Remove the spanner from the crankshaft pulley bolt.

19 Refit the valve cover, using a new gasket where necessary – tighten the retaining nuts evenly to the specified torque.

20 Where applicable, refit the fuel injectors (as described in Chapter 4B), or the glow plugs (Chapter 5C).

21 Refit/reconnect any hoses which were moved for access. If fuel lines were disconnected, reconnect them, then prime and bleed the fuel system as described in Chapter 4B.

22 Refit the upper timing belt/engine mounting plastic cover, fuel lines and any hoses as applicable. 2C

5 Timing belt – removal, inspection and refitting

Caution: If the timing belt breaks or slips in service, extensive engine damage may result. Renew the belt at the intervals specified in Chapter 1B, or earlier if its condition is at all doubtful. Make sure that the correct timing belt is obtained, as the tooth profile was changed on later models.

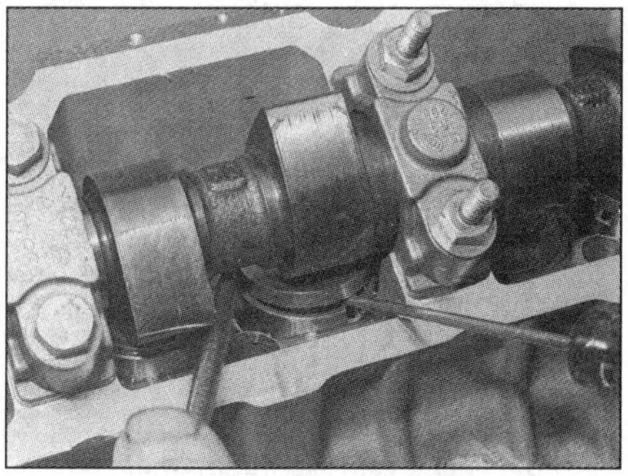

4.14 Removing a shim from a tappet bucket using screwdrivers

5.8 Unscrew the right-hand engine mounting securing bolts/nuts (arrowed)

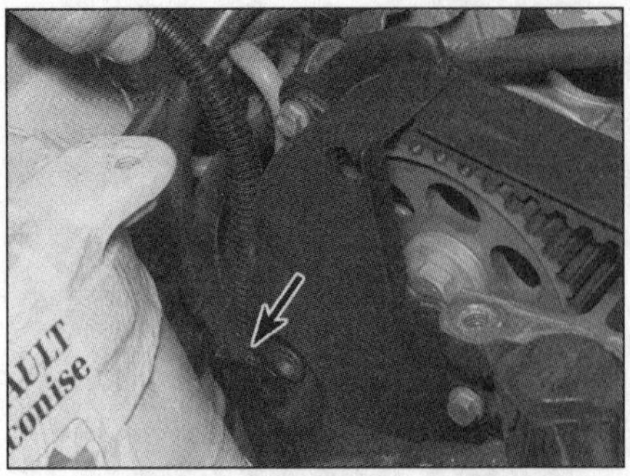

5.9a Note the location of any brackets (arrowed) secured by the bolts . . .

5.9b . . . and remove the timing belt cover from the camshaft sprocket

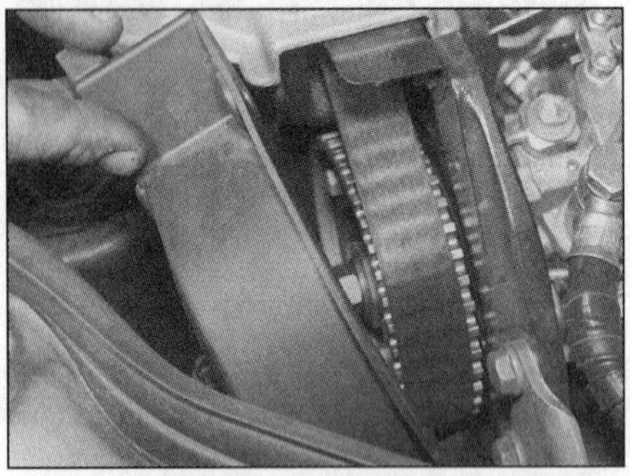

5.9c Removing the timing belt cover from the fuel injection pump sprocket

5.10a Unscrew the side . . .

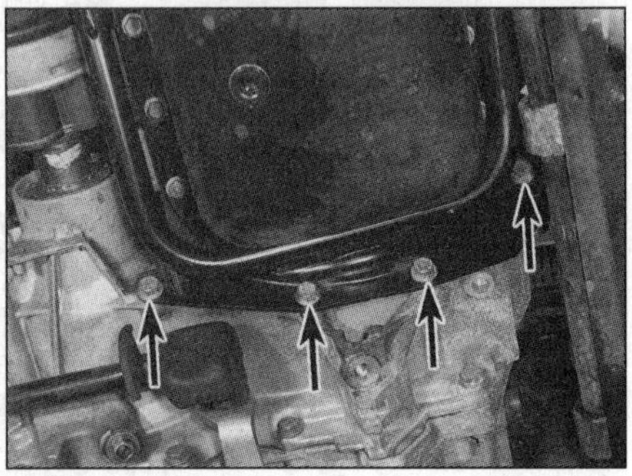

5.10b . . . and rear securing bolts (arrowed) . . .

Note: *A suitable tool will be required to check the timing belt tension on completion of refitting – see text. A suitable puller may be required to remove the crankshaft pulley.*

Removal

1 Disconnect the battery negative lead (refer to *Disconnecting the battery* in the Reference Section).

2 If the engine is to be supported by a hoist, remove the bonnet with reference to Chapter 11.

3 Apply the handbrake, then jack up the front right-hand side of the car and support on axle stands. Remove the roadwheel.

4 Remove the plastic wheelarch liner from within the right-hand wheelarch, to give access to the crankshaft pulley.

5 Remove the auxiliary drivebelt as described in Chapter 1A.

6 Set the engine to TDC as described in Section 3.

7 The right-hand upper engine mounting must be removed to enable the timing belt to be removed, therefore the engine must be supported. The assembly can be supported using a jack and a suitable block of wood to spread the load under the sump. Alternatively, connect a hoist and suitable lifting tackle to the engine lifting brackets.

8 Remove the plastic cover from the right-hand engine mounting, then unbolt and remove the mounting from the engine and body with reference to Section 14 **(see illustration)**.

9 Unbolt the timing covers from the engine, including the cover over the injection pump, noting the position of any brackets **(see illustrations)**.

10 Unscrew the crankshaft pulley bolt while holding the crankshaft stationary. To hold the crankshaft, working under the vehicle, remove the flywheel cover plate/engine-to-gearbox bracing bracket. Note the locations of any brackets secured by the bolts. Refit one of the cover plate-to-gearbox bolts to act as a fulcrum, and have an assistant insert a screwdriver or similar tool in the starter ring gear teeth **(see illustrations)**.

11 Remove the bolt and the pulley from the front of the crankshaft **(see illustrations)**. Use a puller if the pulley is tight.

12 Loosen the tensioner locknut, and if fitted back off the adjustment bolt located on the

5.10c . . . and remove the flywheel cover plate/engine-to-gearbox bracing bracket (arrowed)

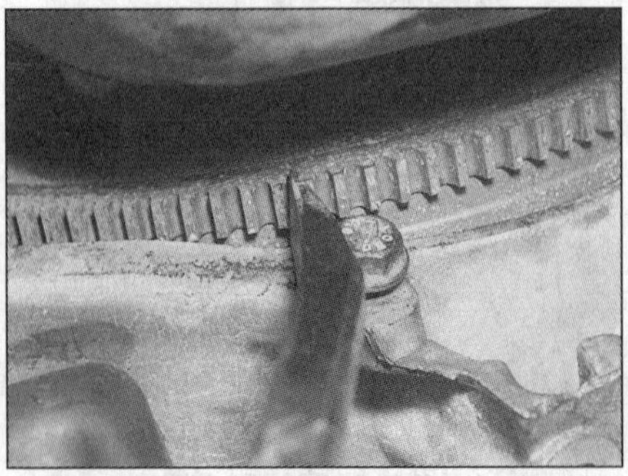

5.10d Insert a lever in the starter ring gear teeth

5.11a Remove the crankshaft pulley bolt . . .

5.11b . . . and the pulley

5.12 Loosen the timing belt tensioner adjuster nut

5.13a Running direction arrows on timing belt

inner timing cover. Move the timing belt tensioner back to relieve the tension from the belt **(see illustration)**, then re-tighten the locknut.

13 If the original belt is to be re-used (contrary to Renault's recommendation), check if the belt is marked with arrows to indicate its running direction, and if necessary mark it. Similarly, make accurate alignment marks on the belt, corresponding to the timing marks on the camshaft, fuel injection pump and crankshaft sprockets **(see illustrations)**. Check that there are 30 teeth between the timing marks on the camshaft and injection pump sprockets.

14 Release the belt from the camshaft sprocket, fuel injection pump sprocket, idler pulley, crankshaft sprocket and auxiliary shaft/idler sprocket, and remove it from the engine.

15 Do not turn the camshaft or the crankshaft whilst the timing belt is removed, as there is a risk of piston-to-valve contact. If it is necessary to turn the camshaft for any reason, before doing so, remove the TDC locking tool from the cylinder block, and turn the crankshaft anti-clockwise (viewed from the timing belt end of the engine) by a quarter turn to position all four pistons half way down their bores.

Inspection

16 Clean the sprockets, idler pulley and tensioner and wipe them dry, although do not apply excessive amounts of solvent to the idler and tensioner pulleys otherwise the bearing lubricant may be contaminated. Also clean the rear timing belt cover, and the front of the cylinder head and block.

17 Examine the timing belt carefully for any signs of cracking, fraying or general wear, particularly at the roots of the teeth. Renew the belt if there is any sign of deterioration of this nature, or if there is any oil or grease contamination. The belt must, of course, be renewed if it has completed the maximum mileage given in Chapter 1B

Refitting

18 Check that the crankshaft is positioned with No 1 piston at TDC, and locked in position using the tool through the hole in the cylinder block as described previously. If the pistons have been positioned halfway down their bores, turn the crankshaft clockwise until the TDC locking tool can be refitted.

19 Align the timing marks on the belt with those on the crankshaft, camshaft and fuel injection pump sprockets, ensuring that the running direction arrows on the belt are pointing clockwise (viewed from the timing belt end of the engine). Note that the belt

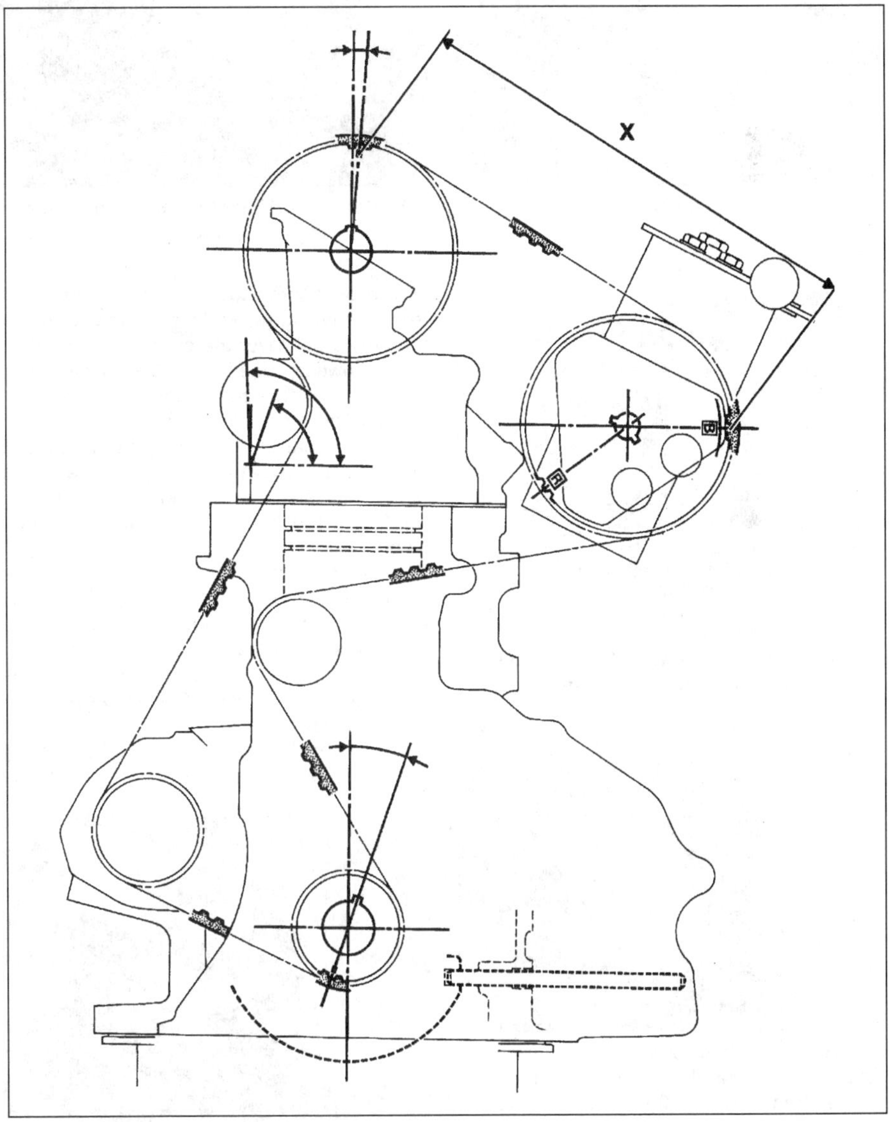

5.13b TDC timing marks on the toothed pulleys

X = 30 teeth

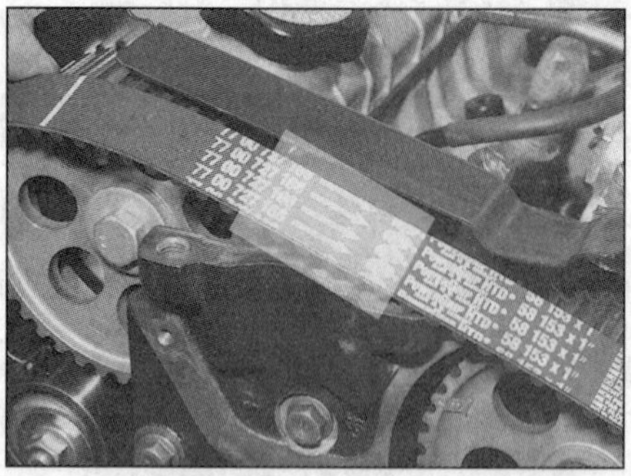

5.19a The running direction arrows on the belt must point clockwise

5.19b Align the timing marks on the belt with the crankshaft . . .

5.19c . . . camshaft . . .

5.19d . . . and injection pump sprocket marks

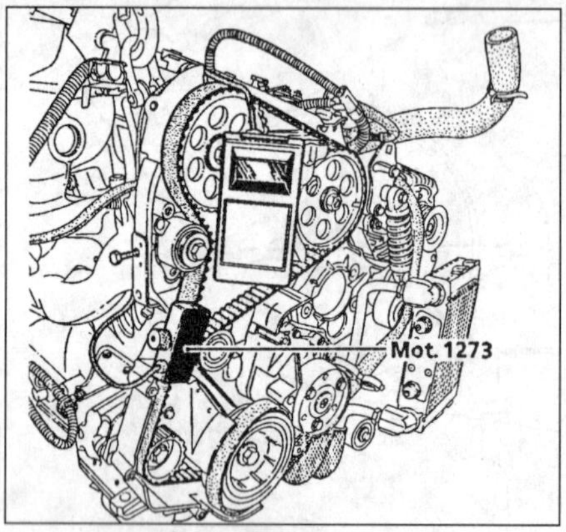

5.21a Using Renault tool Mot. 1273 to check the timing belt tension

5.21b Timing belt tension may be judged to be approximately correct when the belt can be twisted 45-90° with moderate pressure between the finger and thumb, checking midway between the pulleys on the belts longest run

should be marked with lines across its width to act as timing marks **(see illustrations)**. Fit the timing belt over the crankshaft sprocket first, followed by the idler pulley, fuel injection pump sprocket, camshaft sprocket, tensioner, and auxiliary shaft/idler sprocket.

20 Check that all the timing marks are still aligned and remove all slack from the timing belt by loosening the tensioner locknut then tightening the bolt fitted to the timing belt inner cover.

21 The belt tension must now be checked – this can be set or checked accurately **only** by using the Renault tool Mot. 1273 or Mot. 1505 **(see illustration)**. If this equipment is not available, set the belt's tension as carefully as possible using the method outlined here, then take the vehicle to a Renault dealer as soon as possible for the tension to be checked by qualified personnel using the special equipment. With experience, timing belt tension may be judged to be approximately correct when the belt can be twisted 45-90° with moderate pressure between the finger and thumb, checking midway between the pulleys on the belt's longest run.

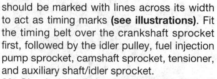

5.22 M6 bolt fitted to timing belt inner cover to adjust timing belt tension

22 If the adjustment is incorrect, the tensioner will have to be repositioned by loosening the tensioner nut and by screwing in or out the bolt fitted to the timing belt inner cover **(see illustration)**.

23 With the correct tension applied, retighten the tensioner nut to the specified torque. This torque is critical, since if the nut were to come loose, considerable engine damage would result. Loosen the bolt fitted to the timing belt inner cover so that it no longer bears on the tensioner roller bracket.

24 Remove the crankshaft timing pin, then refit the crankshaft pulley and securing bolt. Prevent the crankshaft turning using the method described previously and tighten the bolt to the specified torque.

25 Check that the crankshaft is still positioned with No 1 piston at TDC (by refitting temporarily the crankshaft timing pin), then remove the timing pin and turn the crankshaft two complete turns in the normal direction of rotation, returning it to the TDC position again. Re-insert the timing pin in the cylinder block.

26 Temporarily refit the timing belt outer cover which covers the camshaft sprocket and check that the pulley timing mark still aligns with the pointer on the cover, as noted before removal (see Section 3).

27 Recheck the belt tension as described previously. If the tension is incorrect, the setting and checking procedure must be repeated until the correct tension is achieved.

28 With the belt tensioned correctly, remove the M6 bolt from the timing belt inner cover and remove the timing pin from the cylinder block, if not already done. Refit the blanking plug to the cylinder block and tighten it securely, also the tensioner retaining bolt.

29 Check the fuel injection pump timing as described in Chapter 4B.

30 Refit the timing covers, ensuring that any brackets secured by the bolts are in position as noted before removal.

31 Refit the engine mounting rubber/movement limiter assembly to the body and the mounting upper bracket to the engine, as described in Section 14, and refit the plastic cover. Withdraw the jack or the lifting tackle, as applicable, used to support the engine.

33 Refit the auxiliary drivebelt as described in Chapter 1B.

34 Refit the plastic wheelarch liner to the right-hand wheelarch, then refit the roadwheel and lower the vehicle to the ground.

35 If removed, refit the bonnet with reference to Chapter 11.

36 Reconnect the battery negative lead (refer to *Disconnecting the battery* in the Reference Section).

6.2 Removing the crankshaft sprocket

6 Timing belt sprockets, idler pulley and tensioner – removal and refitting

Crankshaft sprocket

Note: *A suitable puller may be required for this operation.*

Removal

1 Remove the timing belt as described in Section 5.

2 It should be possible to simply pull the sprocket from the front of the crankshaft, however in some cases a puller may be required **(see illustration)**. It is a simple matter to make up a puller using two bolts, a metal bar and the existing crankshaft pulley bolt. By unscrewing the crankshaft pulley bolt, the sprocket is pulled from the end of the crankshaft.

3 Recover the Woodruff key if it is loose.

Refitting

4 Refitting is a reversal of removal. Note that the sprocket fits with the flange against the end of the cylinder block/rear timing belt cover.

5 Refit the timing belt as described in Section 5.

Auxiliary shaft sprocket

Removal

6 Remove the timing belt as described in Section 5.

7 Hold the sprocket stationary using a suitable gear-holding tool. Alternatively, an old timing belt can be wrapped around the sprocket and held firmly with a pair of grips.

6.8 Removing the auxiliary/idler shaft sprocket

8 Unscrew the securing bolt, then pull the sprocket from the end of the shaft **(see illustration)**. If necessary, use two levers or screwdrivers to free the sprocket (if necessary, a puller can be used as described previously for the crankshaft sprocket).

Refitting

9 Refitting is a reversal of removal. Tighten the sprocket securing bolt to the specified torque.

10 Refit the timing belt as described in Section 5.

Fuel injection pump sprocket

Note: *A suitable puller will be required for this operation.*

Caution: *Do not dismantle the MAA (Micro Angular Adjustment) type sprocket.*

Removal

11 Remove the timing belt as described in Section 5.

12 Hold the sprocket stationary using a suitable gear-holding tool. Alternatively, an old timing belt can be wrapped around the sprocket and held firmly with a pair of grips.

13 Unscrew the gold-coloured central securing nut. The nut acts as an extractor as it is being unscrewed **(see illustration)**.

14 Release the sprocket from the taper on the pump shaft.

15 Make a mark on the timing belt corresponding to the location of the fuel injection pump sprocket timing mark to aid alignment when refitting.

6.13 Unscrewing the fuel injection pump sprocket nut

16 Disengage the sprocket from the timing belt, remove the sprocket, and recover the Woodruff key from the end of the pump shaft if it is loose **(see illustrations)**.

Refitting

17 Refitting is a reversal of removal, bearing in mind the following points.

a) Ensure that the Woodruff key is correctly engaged with the pump shaft and sprocket.
b) Tighten the sprocket securing nut to the specified torque.
c) Refit and tension the timing belt as described in Section 5.
d) Before refitting the timing belt cover over the injection pump sprocket, check the injection timing as described in Chapter 4B.

Camshaft sprocket

Note: *This is an involved procedure due to the location of the upper engine mounting/fuel injection pump mounting bracket, which leaves insufficient clearance to remove the sprocket from the end of the camshaft. It is suggested that this procedure is read through thoroughly before beginning work.*

Removal

18 Disconnect the battery negative lead.

19 Remove the timing belt as described in Section 5.

20 Remove the plastic alternator shield **(see illustration)**.

21 Remove the alternator, with reference to Chapter 5A.

6.16a Make an alignment mark on the timing belt

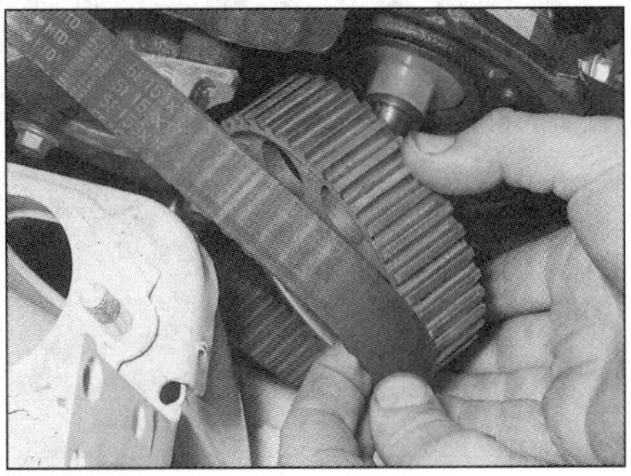

6.16b Disengage the sprocket from the timing belt

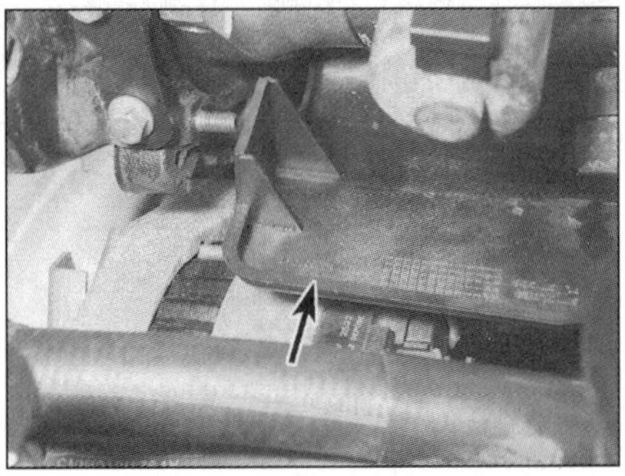

6.20 Remove the plastic alternator shield (arrowed)

6.22 Removing the alternator mounting bracket

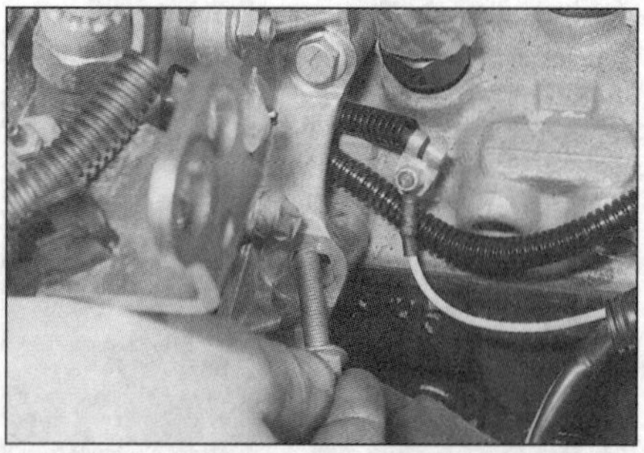

6.24 Removing one of the bolts securing the injection pump rear mounting bracket to the cylinder head

6.26 Remove the bolt (arrowed) securing the rear timing belt cover to the bracket

22 Unbolt the alternator mounting bracket from the cylinder block **(see illustration)**. Also remove the alternator drivebelt tensioner mounting if not already done.

23 Disconnect all cables, hoses, pipes and wiring from the fuel injection pump, to facilitate removal, with reference to Chapter 4B, Section 10.

24 Remove the bolts securing the injection pump rear mounting bracket to the cylinder head **(see illustration)**.

25 Unscrew the nuts and withdraw the bracket from the rear of the injection pump.

26 Remove the bolt securing the rear timing belt cover to the upper engine mounting/fuel injection pump mounting bracket **(see illustration)**.

27 Unscrew the three securing bolts, and remove the upper engine mounting/fuel injection pump mounting bracket, complete with the injection pump from the engine **(see illustrations)**. The assembly is removed by sliding it out towards the front of the vehicle. Note that it may not be possible to fully withdraw the upper two bolts from the bracket (due to limited clearance), in which case slide out the assembly with the bolts in position in their holes.

28 If not already done, remove the crankshaft TDC locking tool, and turn the engine a quarter of a turn anti-clockwise (viewed from the timing belt end of the engine) to position the pistons halfway down their bores. This is to avoid any possibility of piston-to-valve contact if the camshaft is inadvertently turned when loosening the sprocket bolt.

29 Unscrew the camshaft sprocket bolt. The sprocket can be held using a suitable socket and extension bar engaged with one of the rear timing belt cover securing bolts **(see illustration)**. Alternatively, use an old timing belt wrapped around the sprocket. Recover the washer.

30 Remove the bolt and washer and the sprocket from the front of the camshaft **(see illustrations)**. A puller may be required, in which case ensure that the legs of the puller act on the holes in the sprocket, **not** on the sprocket teeth.

31 Recover the Woodruff key from the end of the camshaft if it is loose **(see illustration)**.

Refitting

32 Ensure that the Woodruff key is in place in the end of the camshaft, then refit the camshaft sprocket, noting that the projecting hub fits towards the cylinder head.

33 Ensure that the washer is in place, then refit the sprocket bolt, and tighten it to the specified torque, holding the sprocket as during removal.

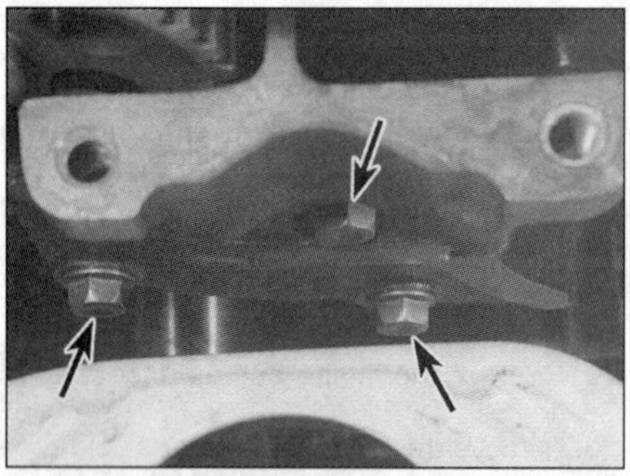

6.27a Unscrew the securing bolts (arrowed) . . .

6.27b . . . and withdraw the mounting bracket complete with the injection pump

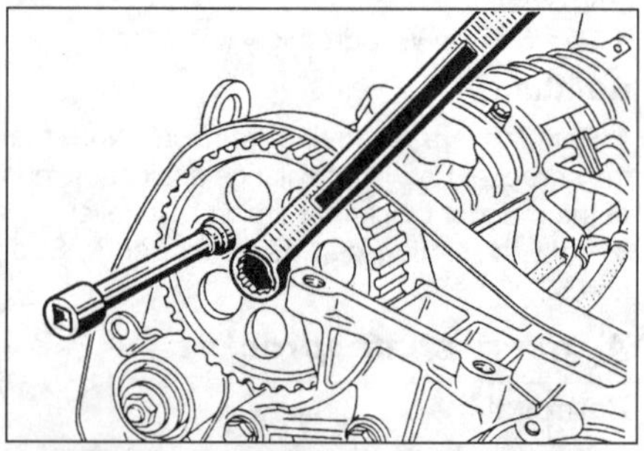

6.29 Using a socket and extension bar to counterhold the camshaft sprocket whilst unscrewing the sprocket bolt

6.30a Remove the bolt and washer . . .

6.30b . . . and the sprocket

6.31 Recover the Woodruff key from the end of the camshaft if it is loose

34 Refit the upper engine mounting/fuel injection pump mounting bracket, complete with the injection pump, and tighten the securing bolts. Where applicable, refit the upper two bolts to the holes in the bracket before the assembly is refitted.
35 Refit the bolt securing the rear timing belt cover to the upper engine mounting/fuel injection pump mounting bracket.
36 Refit the injection pump rear mounting bracket and tighten the securing bolts and nuts.
37 Reconnect all relevant cables, hoses, pipes and wiring to the fuel injection pump with reference to Chapter 4B, Section 10.
38 Refit the alternator mounting bracket to the cylinder block, and tighten the securing bolts. Also, where applicable, refit the alternator drivebelt tensioner mounting.
39 Refit the alternator, with reference to Chapter 5A.
40 Refit the plastic alternator shield.
41 Temporarily refit the outer timing belt cover which covers the camshaft sprocket, and check that the TDC mark on the camshaft sprocket is aligned with the pointer on the timing belt cover.
42 Turn the crankshaft clockwise (viewed from the timing belt end of the engine) until the crankshaft locking tool can be refitted (to position No 1 piston at TDC).
43 Refit and tension the timing belt, as described in Section 5.
44 Reconnect the battery negative lead.
45 Bleed the fuel system as described in Chapter 4B.

Idler pulley

Removal

46 Remove the timing belt as described in Section 5.
47 Unscrew the two securing bolts, and withdraw the idler pulley assembly, manipulating it out from the rear timing belt covers.

Refitting

48 Refitting is a reversal of removal, but check that the roller turns freely without binding or excessive play.
49 Refit and tension the timing belt as described in Section 5.

Tensioner

Removal

50 Remove the timing belt as described in Section 5.
51 Remove the securing nut and the washer, and the pivot bolt, and withdraw the tensioner assembly from the engine.

Refitting

52 Refitting is a reversal of removal, but check that the pulley turns freely without binding or excessive play.
53 Refit and tension the timing belt as described in Section 5.

7 Camshaft oil seals – renewal

Timing belt end oil seal

1 Remove the camshaft sprocket as described in Section 6.
2 Remove the Woodruff key from the end of the camshaft, if not already done. Note the fitted depth of the oil seal in the cylinder head.
3 Using a small screwdriver, prise out the oil seal from the cylinder head, taking care not to damage the surface of the camshaft. To ensure correct fitting, note the fitted position of the old oil seal.
4 Wipe clean the oil seal seating in the cylinder head, then dip the new seal in fresh engine oil, and locate it over the camshaft with its closed side facing outwards. Make sure that the oil seal lip is not damaged as it is located on the camshaft.
5 Using a tube of suitable diameter, drive the oil seal squarely into the housing to the previously noted depth. A block of wood cut to pass over the end of the camshaft may be used instead.
6 Refit the camshaft sprocket as described in Section 6.

Flywheel end oil seal

7 No oil seal is fitted to the flywheel end of the camshaft. The sealing is provided by a gasket between the cylinder head and the brake vacuum pump housing, and on certain models by an O-ring fitted between the vacuum pump and the housing. The gasket and the O-ring, where applicable, can be renewed after unbolting the vacuum pump from the cylinder head (see Chapter 9).

8 Camshaft and tappets – removal, inspection and refitting

Note: *A new camshaft oil seal should be fitted, and a new valve cover gasket may be required on refitting. Suitable sealant will be required for the camshaft bearing caps and the bearing cap bolts.*

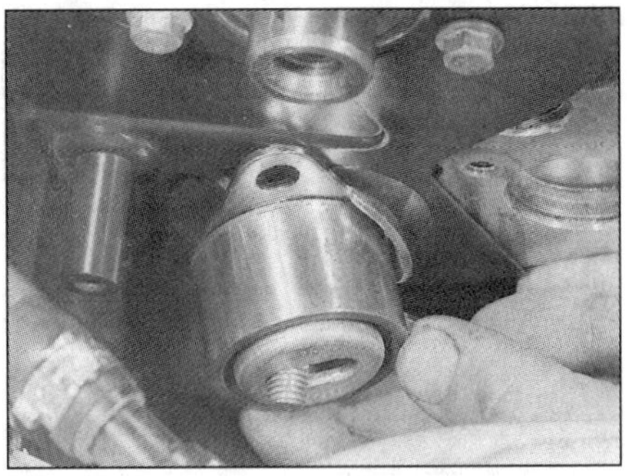

8.2 Withdraw the timing belt tensioner

Removal

1 Remove the camshaft sprocket as described in Section 6.
2 Remove the securing nut and bolt, and withdraw the timing belt tensioner from the engine **(see illustration)**.
3 Unscrew and remove the two bolts securing the upper rear timing belt cover to the cylinder head **(see illustration)**.
4 Unscrew the lower bolt(s) securing the upper rear timing belt cover to the cylinder block.
5 Remove the timing belt idler pulley securing bolt which also passes through the rear timing belt cover.
6 Manipulate the rear timing belt cover from the front of the camshaft and, where possible, withdraw the cover from the engine **(see illustration)**.
7 Remove the brake vacuum pump as described in Chapter 9.
8 Where necessary for improved access, unclip any hoses which are routed across the top of the valve cover, and move them to one side out of the way. If fuel lines are disconnected, cover open unions to prevent dirt ingress.
9 Unscrew the nuts from the valve cover, and withdraw the cover from the engine. Recover the gasket.
10 Using a dial gauge, measure the camshaft endfloat, and compare with the value given in the Specifications **(see illustration)**. This will give an indication of the amount of wear present on the thrust surfaces.
11 If the original camshaft is to be refitted, it

2C

8.3 Remove the bolts securing the rear timing belt cover to the cylinder head

8.6 Withdrawing the rear timing belt cover from the engine

8.10 Measuring the camshaft endfloat using a dial gauge

8.12a Number the camshaft bearing caps from the flywheel end of the engine

8.12b Identification mark on No 3 . . .

is advisable to measure the valve clearances at this stage, as described in Section 4, so that any shims required can be obtained before the camshaft is refitted.

12 Check the camshaft bearing caps for identification marks, and if none are present, make identifying marks so that they can be refitted in their original positions and the same way round. Number the caps from the flywheel end of the engine **(see illustrations)**.

13 Progressively slacken the bearing cap bolts and studs until the valve spring pressure is relieved. Remove the bolts and studs (noting their locations to ensure correct refitting), and the bearing caps themselves. Note that No 1 bearing cap is secured by 2 studs and 2 additional bolts **(see illustrations)**.

14 Lift out the camshaft together with the oil seal **(see illustration)**.

15 Remove the tappets, keeping each with its shim **(see illustration)**. Place them in a compartmented box, or on a sheet of card marked into eight sections, so that they may be refitted to their original locations. Write down the shim thicknesses – they will be needed later if any of the valve clearances are incorrect. The shim size is stamped on the bottom face of the shim, but it is prudent to use a micrometer to measure the true thickness of any shim removed, as it may have been reduced by wear.

Inspection

16 Examine the camshaft bearing surfaces and cam lobes for wear ridges, pitting or scoring. Renew the camshaft if evident.

17 Renew the oil seal at the end of the camshaft as a matter of course. Lubricate the lips of the new seal before fitting, and store the camshaft so that its weight is not resting on the seal.

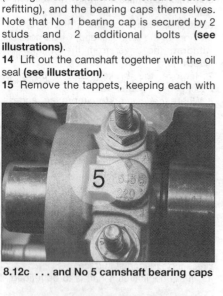

8.12c . . . and No 5 camshaft bearing caps

8.13a Removing a bearing cap bolt

18 Examine the camshaft bearing surfaces in the cylinder head and bearing caps. Deep scoring or other damage means that the cylinder head must be renewed.

19 Inspect the tappet buckets and shims for scoring, pitting and wear ridges. Renew as necessary.

Refitting

20 Ensure that the pistons are positioned half way down their bores, as described for sprocket removal in Section 6.

21 Oil the tappets and fit them to the bores from which they were removed. Fit the correct shim, numbered side downwards, to each tappet.

22 Oil the camshaft bearings. Place the camshaft with its oil seal onto the cylinder head. The oil seal must be positioned so that it is flush with the cylinder head face.

23 Apply sealant (CAF 4/60 THIXO, Rhodorseal 5661, or a suitable equivalent) to the cylinder head mating faces of the rear and front camshaft bearing caps (Nos 1 and 5) **(see illustration)**.

24 Refit the camshaft bearing caps to their original locations, ensuring that the oil seal is correctly located in the bearing cap.

25 Apply sealant to the threads of the bearing cap bolts and studs **(see illustration)**. Fit the bolts and studs, and tighten them progressively to the specified torque.

26 If a new camshaft has been fitted, measure the endfloat using a dial gauge, and check that it is within the specified limits.

27 Refit the brake vacuum pump with reference to Chapter 9.

8.13b Note that No 1 bearing cap is secured by 2 additional bolts

8.14 Lifting out the camshaft

8.15 Lift out the tappets

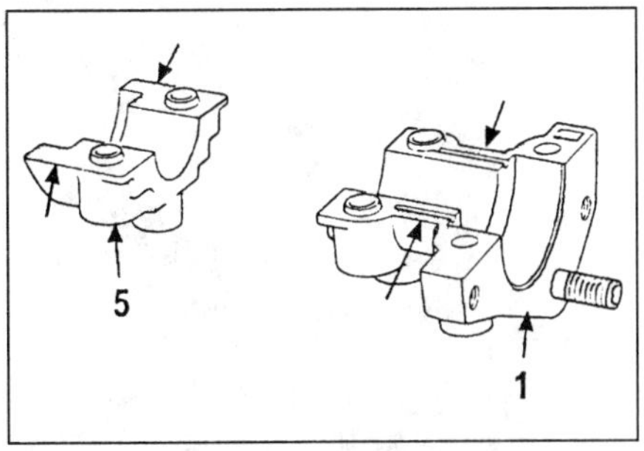

8.23 Apply sealant to the cylinder head mating faces (arrowed) of camshaft bearing caps Nos 1 and 5

8.25 Apply sealant to the threads of the bearing cap bolts and studs

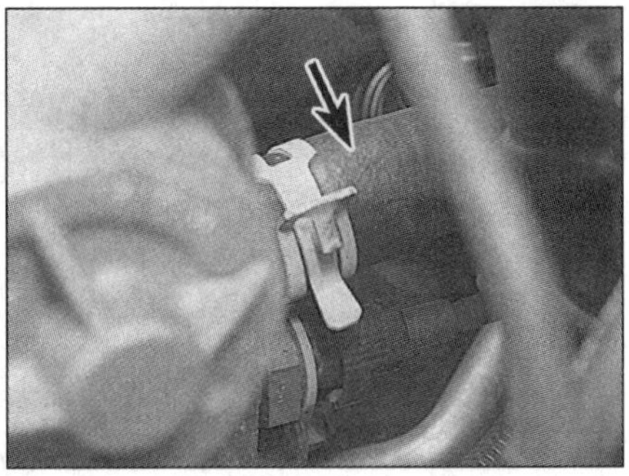

9.6 Coolant hose located on the left-hand end of the cylinder head

28 Refit the rear timing belt cover, then refit and tighten the securing bolts.

29 Refit and tighten the bolt securing the timing belt idler pulley assembly.

30 Refit the timing belt tensioner, ensuring that the peg on the cylinder block engages with the hole in the tensioner bracket.

31 Refit the camshaft sprocket as described in Section 6, ignoring the reference to bleeding the fuel system at this stage.

32 Check the valve clearances as described in Section 4, and take any corrective action necessary.

33 Refit the valve cover, using a new gasket if necessary, and tighten the securing nuts.

34 Refit/reconnect any hoses which were moved for access.

35 Reconnect the battery negative lead.

36 Bleed the fuel system as described in Chapter 4.

9 Cylinder head – removal, inspection and refitting

Note: *A new cylinder head gasket must be fitted, and a new valve cover gasket and cylinder head bolts may be required on refitting – see text.*

Removal

1 The following procedure describes removal and refitting of the cylinder head complete with manifolds and the fuel injection pump.

2 Disconnect the battery negative lead.

3 Drain the cooling system with reference to Chapter 1B. Also drain the cylinder block by unscrewing the drain plug located on the right-hand rear face of the engine. Refit the plug after draining.

4 Remove the timing belt as described in Section 5.

5 Either disconnect the exhaust downpipe from the exhaust manifold or remove the exhaust front section complete (Chapter 4B).

6 Note the location of the hoses on the outlet at the left-hand end of the cylinder head, then loosen the clips and disconnect them **(see illustration)**.

7 Disconnect the vacuum hose from the brake vacuum pump. To do this, Renault technicians use a U-shaped tool which enters the side of the adapter and releases the retainers **(see illustrations)**.

8 Disconnect the wiring from the EGR solenoid valve and air temperature sensors, then remove the air cleaner assembly with reference to Chapter 4B. At the same time unclip the fuel supply pipes from the housing.

9 Remove the air inlet duct from the engine compartment.

10 Disconnect the accelerator cable from the injection pump and supports with reference to Chapter 4B, and position it to one side.

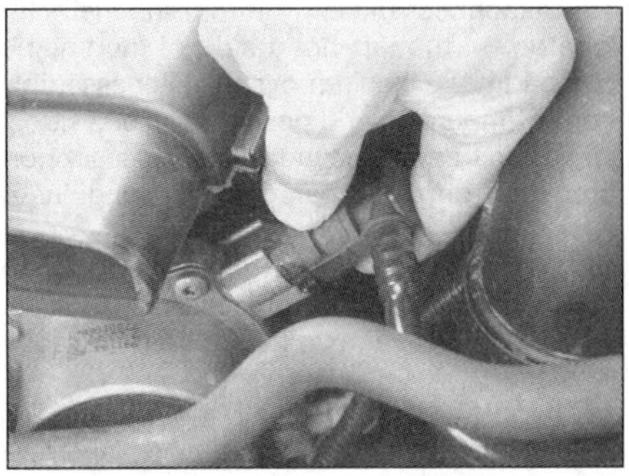

9.7a Disconnecting the brake vacuum hose

11 Disconnect the wiring from the heater plugs with reference to Chapter 5C.

12 Disconnect the wiring from the injector with the lift sensor.

13 Disconnect the wiring from the fast idle solenoid valve.

14 Disconnect the fuel supply and return hoses from the injection pump, and tape over the ends of the hoses and the apertures in the pump to prevent entry of dust and dirt. To release the supply hose, depress the top of the quick-release union, then squeeze together the bottom of the union and withdraw it upwards. To release the return hose, depress the perimeter of the union and separate it from the T-piece **(see illustrations)**.

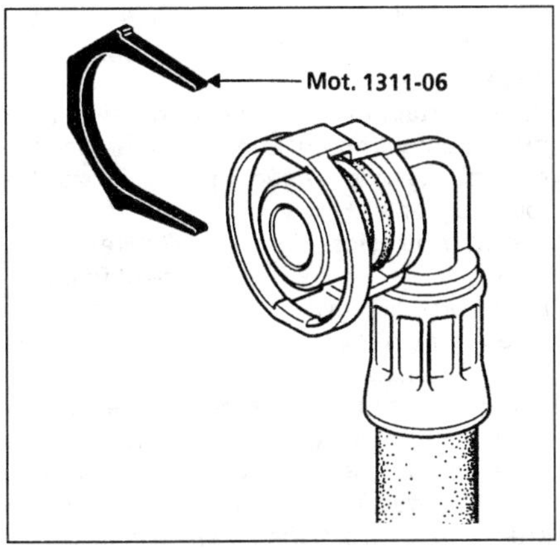

9.7b Tool for releasing the vacuum hose from the vacuum pump

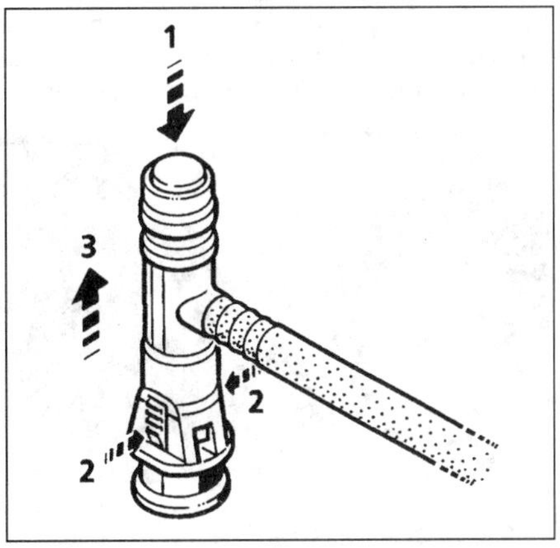

9.14a Disconnecting the quick-release fuel supply hose

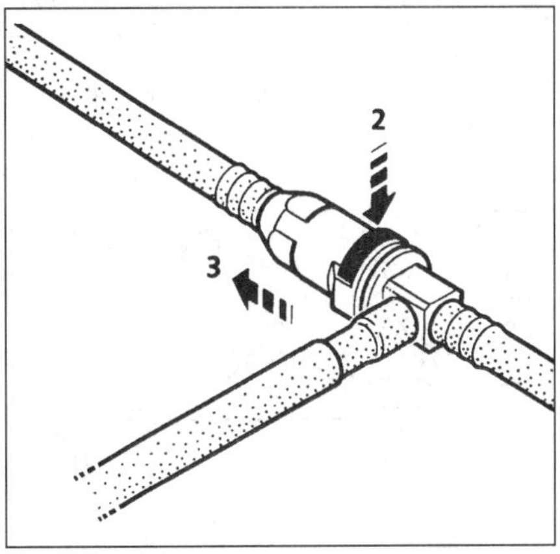

9.14b Disconnecting the quick-release return hose

9.20 Slackening a cylinder head bolt

9.22 Lifting the cylinder head assembly from the engine

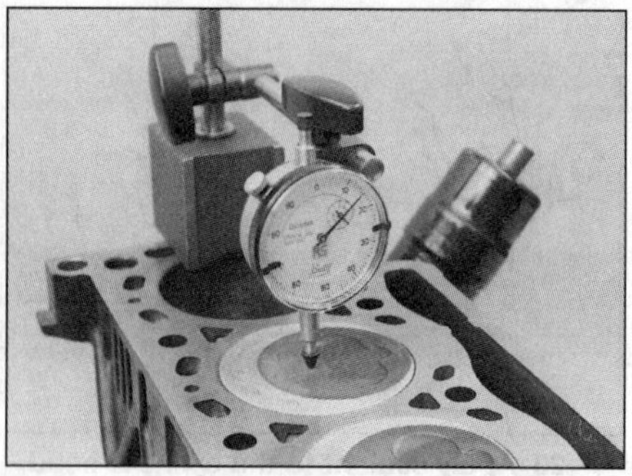

9.30 Measuring piston protrusion using a dial test indicator

15 Disconnect the wiring from the fuel filter located on the left-hand side of the engine compartment, then remove the filter assembly from its mounting and position it to one side.
16 Unbolt and remove the fuel pipe support bracket from the rear of the timing inner cover.
17 Loosen, but do not remove, the mounting bolts from the lower timing cover.
18 Unbolt and remove the auxiliary drivebelt tensioner.
19 If not already done, remove the TDC locking tool from the cylinder block, and turn the crankshaft anti-clockwise (viewed from the timing belt end of the engine) by a quarter turn to position all four pistons half way down their bores.
20 Progressively slacken the cylinder head bolts in the reverse sequence to that shown in illustration 9.39 **(see illustration)**. With all the bolts loose, remove them.
21 The cylinder head assembly complete with ancillaries is heavy, and it is advisable to attach a hoist and suitable lifting tackle to the lifting brackets on the cylinder head in order to lift it from the engine.
22 Lift the cylinder head (complete with manifolds, injection pump, and upper rear timing belt cover) upwards and off the cylinder block **(see illustration)**. If it is stuck, tap it upwards using a hammer and block of wood (taking care not to damage the fuel injection pump). **Do not** try to turn the cylinder head (it is located by two dowels), nor attempt to prise it free using a screwdriver inserted between the block and head faces.
23 If desired, the manifolds and injection pump can be removed from the cylinder head with reference to the relevant Sections of Chapter 4B.

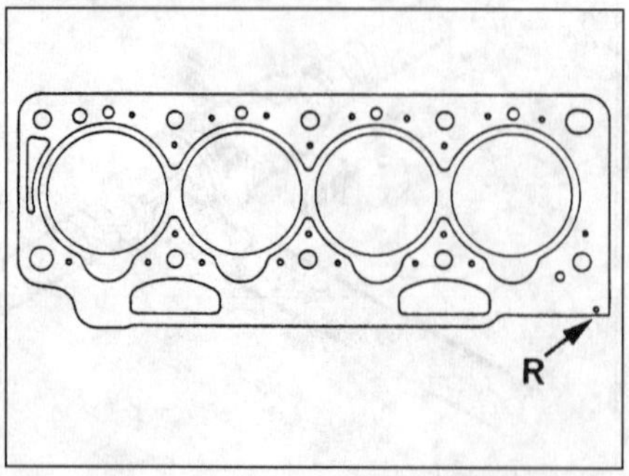

9.32a Location (R) of cylinder head gasket thickness identification hole(s)

Inspection

24 The mating faces of the cylinder head and block must be perfectly clean before refitting the head. Use a scraper to remove all traces of gasket and carbon, and also clean the tops of the pistons. Take particular care with the aluminium cylinder head, as the soft metal is damaged easily. Also, make sure that debris is not allowed to enter the oil and water channels – this is particularly important for the oil circuit, as carbon could block the oil supply to the camshaft or crankshaft bearings. Using adhesive tape and paper, seal the water, oil and bolt holes in the cylinder block. Clean the piston crowns in the same way.

HAYNES HiNT ***To prevent carbon entering the gap between the pistons and bores, smear a little grease in the gap. After cleaning the piston, rotate the crankshaft so that the piston moves down the bore, then wipe out the grease and carbon with a cloth rag.***

25 Check the block and head for nicks, deep scratches and other damage. If slight, they may be removed carefully with a file. Machining of the cylinder head or cylinder block is not recommended by the manufacturers.
26 If warpage of the cylinder head is suspected, use a straight-edge to check it for distortion. Refer to Chapter 2D if necessary.

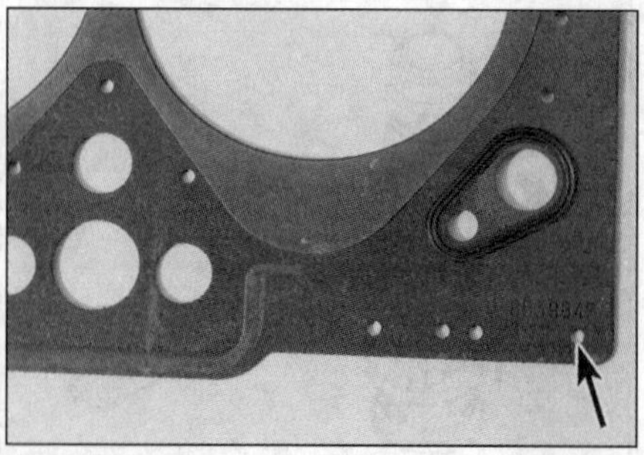

9.32b Cylinder head gasket thickness identification hole (arrowed) – 1 hole type shown (ignore remaining holes – see text)

27 Clean out the bolt holes in the block using a pipe cleaner, or a rag and screwdriver. Make sure that all oil is removed, otherwise there is a possibility of the block being cracked by hydraulic pressure when the bolts are tightened.
28 Examine the bolt threads and the threads in the cylinder block for damage. If necessary, use the correct-size tap to chase out the threads in the block, and use a die to clean the threads on the bolts.

Gasket selection

29 Turn the crankshaft to bring piston Nos 1 and 4 to just below the TDC position (just below the top face of the cylinder block). Position a dial test indicator (DTI) on the cylinder block and zero it on the block face. Transfer the probe to the centre of No 1 piston, then slowly turn the crankshaft back-and-forth past TDC, noting the highest reading produced on the indicator. Record this reading.
30 Repeat this measurement procedure on No 4 piston, then turn the crankshaft half a turn (180°) and repeat the procedure on Nos 2 and 3 pistons **(see illustration)**. Ensure that all measurements are taken along the longitudinal centreline of the crankshaft (this will eliminate errors due to piston slant).
31 If a dial test indicator is not available, piston protrusion may be measured using a straight-edge and feeler blades or vernier calipers. However, these methods are inevitably less accurate and cannot therefore be recommended.
32 Ascertain the greatest piston protrusion measurement and use this to determine the correct cylinder head gasket from the following table.

Piston protrusion	**Gasket identification**
Less than 0.868 mm	*2 holes*
0.868 to 1.000 mm	*1 hole*
More than 1.000 mm	*3 holes*

The identification holes are located at the front corner of the gasket, at the flywheel end **(see illustrations)**. **Note:** *The gasket thickness identification holes are located in an area 25 mm from the flywheel end of the gasket. Do not take into account any other holes outside this area.*

Cylinder head bolt examination

33 It is recommended that the cylinder head bolts are renewed as a matter of course whenever the cylinder head is removed.

Refitting

34 Where applicable, refit the manifolds and fuel injection pump to the cylinder head, with reference to the relevant Sections of Chapter 4B.
35 Turn the crankshaft clockwise (viewed from the timing belt end) until Nos 1 and 4 pistons pass bottom dead centre (BDC) and begin to rise, then position them halfway up their bores. Nos 2 and 3 pistons will also be at their mid-way positions, but descending their bores. Do not turn the crankshaft again until the timing belt is to be refitted (this is to prevent the possibility of piston-to-valve contact).
36 Ensure that the cylinder head locating dowels are fitted to the cylinder block, then fit the correct gasket the right way round on the cylinder block with the identification mark(s) at the front corner of the engine at the flywheel end **(see illustration)**.
37 Lower the cylinder head onto the block. Ensure that the upper rear timing belt cover engages correctly with the lower rear timing belt cover on the cylinder block. Where applicable, disconnect the lifting tackle and hoist. Ensure that the swirl chambers do not drop out of their locations in the cylinder head as it is lowered into position.
38 Lubricate the cylinder head bolt threads, and the undersides of the bolt heads with a little engine oil, then insert them, together with their washers. Screw the bolts into their threads as far as possible by hand.
39 Tighten the bolts in the order shown, and in the stages given in the Specifications **(see illustration)**.

Warning: The final tightening stages involve very high forces. Ensure that the tools used are in good condition. If the engine has been removed from the vehicle, it is recommended that the final tightening stages are carried out with the engine refitted to the vehicle (it may be necessary to remove the right-hand upper engine mounting bracket for access to one of the bolts with the engine in the vehicle).

40 Refit the auxiliary drivebelt tensioner and tighten the mounting bolt.
41 Tighten the lower timing cover mounting bolts.
42 Refit the fuel pipe support bracket to the rear of the timing inner cover.
43 Refit the fuel filter assembly and reconnect the wiring.
44 Reconnect the fuel supply and return hoses to the injection pump.
45 Reconnect the wiring to the fast idle solenoid valve.
46 Reconnect the wiring to the injector with the lift sensor.

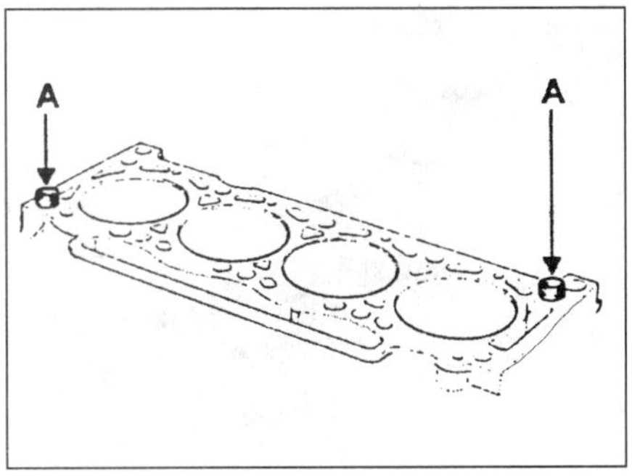

9.36 Cylinder head locating dowel locations (A)

47 Reconnect the wiring to the heater plugs with reference to Chapter 5C.
48 Reconnect the accelerator cable to the injection pump with reference to Chapter 4B.
49 Refit the air inlet duct and air cleaner assembly, and reconnect the wiring to the EGR solenoid valve and air temperature sensors. Secure the fuel supply pipes to the housing.
50 Reconnect the vacuum hose to the brake vacuum pump.
51 Reconnect the hoses to the outlet on the left-hand end of the cylinder head, and tighten the clips.
52 Reconnect/refit the exhaust front downpipe to the manifold with reference to Chapter 4B.
53 Refit the timing belt with reference to Section 5.
54 Refill and bleed the cooling system as described in Chapter 1B.
55 Reconnect the battery negative lead.
56 Prime and bleed the fuel system as described in Chapter 4B.

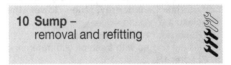

10 Sump – removal and refitting

Note: *An engine lifting hoist is required during this procedure.*

Removal

1 Disconnect the battery negative lead.
2 Jack up the front of the vehicle and support on axle stands. Remove the engine compartment undertray.

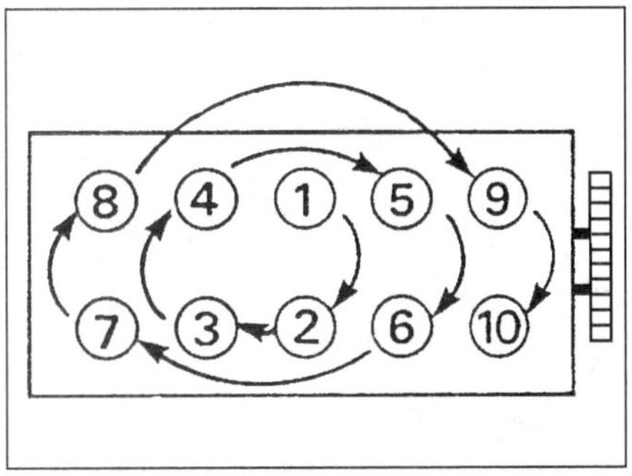

9.39 Cylinder head bolt tightening sequence

3 Drain the engine oil referring to Chapter 1B, then refit and tighten the drain plug using a new washer.
4 Remove both front roadwheels, then remove the right-hand wheelarch liner with reference.
5 Make sure the steering wheel is positioned with the front wheels straight-ahead, and use tape or string to hold it in this position. This is necessary to prevent damage to the airbag rotary switch located beneath the steering wheel central pad.
6 Push back the gaiter and unscrew the bolt securing the steering column intermediate shaft to the steering gear pinion.
7 Refer to Chapter 10 and disconnect the front suspension lower arms from the hub carriers.
8 Unscrew the nuts and disconnect the track rod ends from the steering arms with reference to Chapter 10.
9 Detach the front suspension subframe tie-rods from the body. Also disconnect the gearchange rods from the transmission.
10 Loosen only the bolts securing the rear engine mounting link to the body.
11 Unscrew and remove the front bumper lower mounting fasteners.
12 Remove the exhaust downpipe from the manifold with reference to Chapter 4B.
13 Unbolt the front suspension lower arms from the subframe with reference to Chapter 10.
14 Unscrew each subframe mounting bolt in turn and replace them with lengths of threaded rods and nuts. These are required to lower the subframe approximately 9.0 cm in order to remove the sump. With the rods in position, lower the subframe until the gap between the subframe and body is 7.0 cm at the rear mounting and 9.0 cm at the front mounting. As the subframe is being lowered, disconnect the steering gear pinion from the column intermediate shaft.
15 Unscrew the bolts securing the sump to the cylinder block. Tap the sump with a hide or plastic mallet to break the joint, then remove the sump. Recover the gasket and half-moon gaskets from each end of the sump and discard them as new ones must be used on refitting.

Refitting

16 Thoroughly clean the mating surfaces of the sump and cylinder block.
17 Apply some Rhodorseal 5661 sealant to the joint areas where the oil seal housing and main bearing cap meet the cylinder block, then locate a new gasket on the sump.
18 Locate new half-moon gaskets in position, and lift the sump into position on the cylinder block. Insert the bolts and tighten them progressively to the specified torque.
19 Raise the subframe and replace the threaded rods with the mounting bolts. As the subframe is being raised, make sure that the steering gear pinion locates in the column intermediate shaft correctly (see Chapter 10).

11.2 Removing the oil pump

11.7a Measuring the oil pump-to-body clearance

11.7b Measuring the oil pump gear endfloat

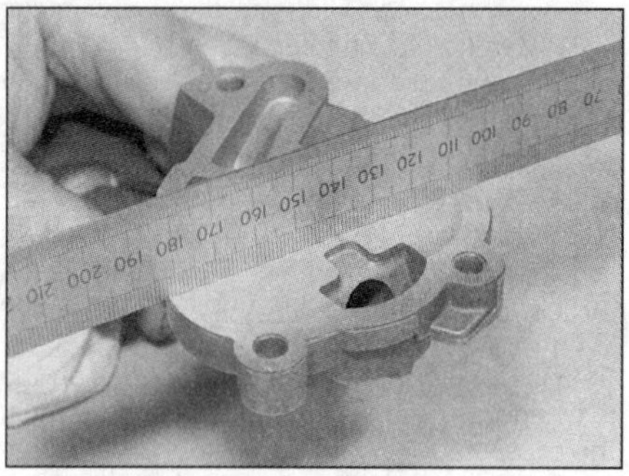
11.7c Checking the flatness of the oil pump cover

Tighten the bolts to the specified torque (see Chapter 10).

20 Refit the front suspension lower arms to the subframe with reference to Chapter 10.

21 Refit the exhaust downpipe to the manifold with reference to Chapter 4B.

22 Refit and tighten the front bumper lower mounting fasteners.

23 Tighten the rear engine mounting link bolts to the specified torque.

24 Reconnect the gearchange rods to the transmission, and refit the front suspension subframe tie-rods to the body.

25 Refit the track rod ends to the steering arms with reference to Chapter 10.

26 Reconnect the front suspension lower arms to the hub carriers with reference to Chapter 10.

27 With the front roadwheels straight-ahead, refit and tighten the bolt securing the intermediate shaft to the steering gear pinion. Locate the gaiter over the shaft, then remove the tape or string from the steering wheel.

28 Refit the wheelarch liner and right-hand front roadwheel. Also refit the engine compartment undertray, then lower the vehicle to the ground.

29 Reconnect the battery negative lead.

30 Fill the engine with fresh oil with reference to Chapter 1B.

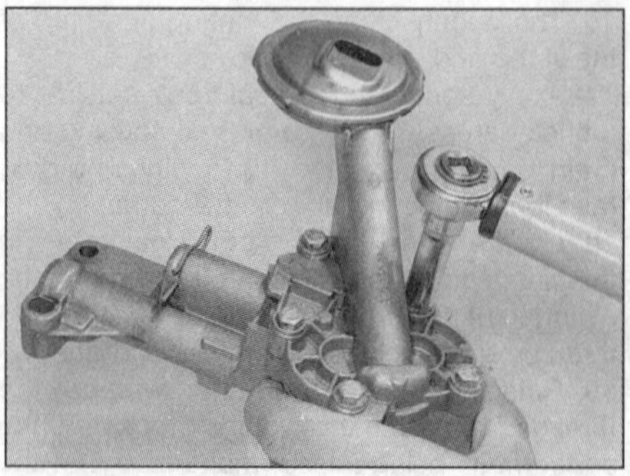
11.8a Tightening the oil pump cover bolts

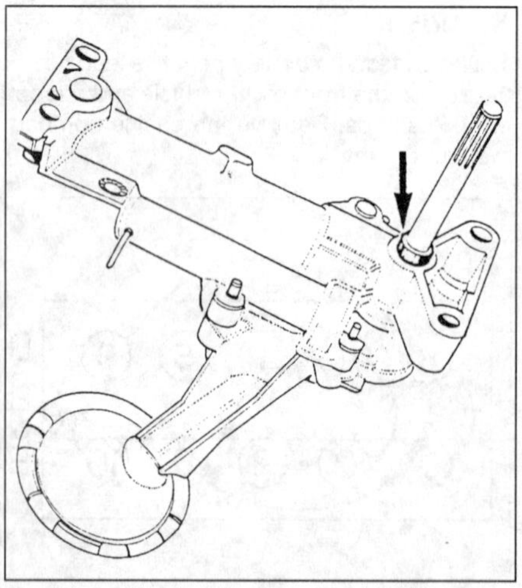
11.8b Dowel location (arrowed) in oil pump body

11 Oil pump – removal, inspection and refitting

Early engines with auxiliary shaft

Removal

1 Remove the sump (see Section 10).

2 Unscrew the four retaining bolts and withdraw the pump from the cylinder block and drivegear **(see illustration)**. Note the locating dowel which is fitted over the pump driveshaft.

3 If necessary, unscrew the two retaining bolts and remove the oil pump drivegear cover and sealing ring from the rear of the cylinder block. Withdraw the drivegear from the block; the drivegear can be removed by screwing a 12 mm bolt into its threads and using the bolt to pull out the gear. Discard the sealing ring; a new one should be used on refitting.

Inspection

4 Unscrew the retaining bolts and lift off the pump cover. Withdraw the idler gear and the drivegear/shaft. Mark the idler gear before removal, so that it can be refitted in its original position.

5 Extract the retaining clip and remove the oil pressure relief valve spring retainer, spring, spring seat and plunger.

6 Clean the components and carefully examine the gears, pump body and relief valve plunger for any signs of scoring or wear. Renew the complete pump assembly if excessive wear is evident (no spare parts are available).

7 If the components appear serviceable, measure the clearance between the pump body and the gears using feeler gauges. Also measure the gear endfloat and check the flatness of the end cover **(see illustrations)**. If the clearances exceed the specified tolerances, the pump must be renewed. There should be no discernible wear or distortion of the end cover.

8 If the pump is satisfactory, reassemble the components in the reverse order of removal. Fill the pump with oil, then refit the cover and tighten the bolts securely. Check that the locating dowel is in position where the driveshaft enters the oil pump body **(see illustrations)**. Prime the oil pump by filling it with clean engine oil whilst rotating the driveshaft.

Refitting

9 Where necessary, refit the pump drivegear to the cylinder block making sure it is correctly engaged with the auxiliary shaft. Refit the drivegear cover using a new sealing ring and securely tighten its retaining bolts.

10 Wipe clean the mating faces of the oil pump and cylinder block.

11 Ensure that the locating dowel is correctly

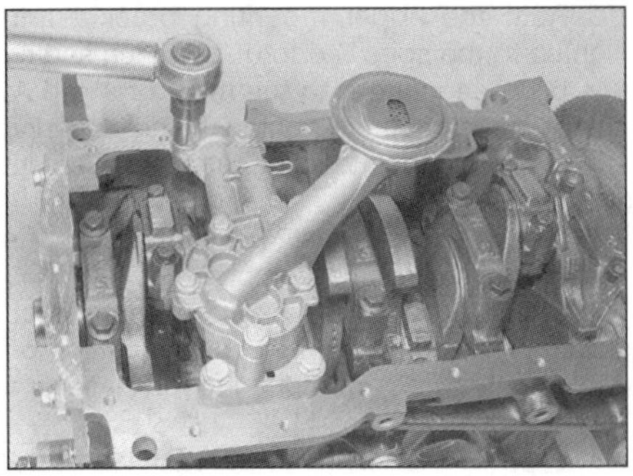

11.11 Tightening the oil pump securing bolts

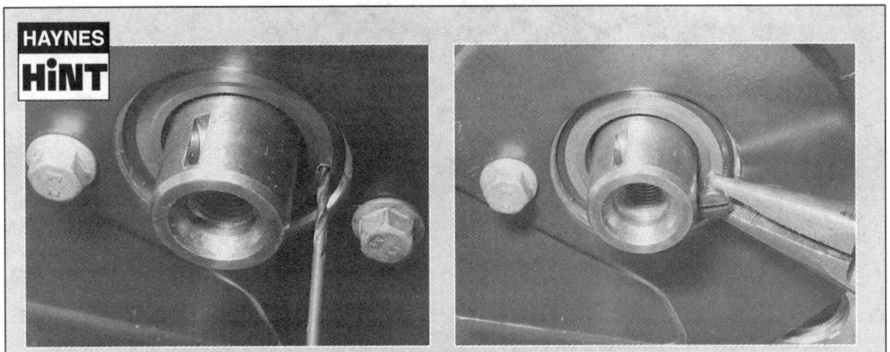

Oil seals can be removed by drilling a small hole and inserting a self-tapping screw. A pair of grips can then be used to pull out the oil seal by pulling on the screw. If difficulty is experienced, insert two screws diagonally opposite each other.

fitted to the oil pump then lift the pump into position, engaging the driveshaft with the drivegear splines and seat the pump fully in position. Refit the pump retaining bolts and tighten them securely **(see illustration)**.

12 Refit the sump as described in Section 10.

Engines without auxiliary shaft

Removal

13 To remove the oil pump alone, first remove the sump, referring to Section 10.

14 Unscrew the two mounting bolts and withdraw the oil pump, tilting it to disengage its sprocket from the drive chain. If the two locating dowels are displaced, refit them in their locations.

15 To remove the oil pump complete with its drive chain and sprockets, first remove the sump (Section 10), then unbolt the crankshaft timing belt end oil seal housing, as described in Section 12. Note the presence of the chain guide block and of its two locating dowels.

16 Unscrew the bolts securing the sprocket to the oil pump hub. Use a screwdriver through one of the holes in the sprocket to hold it stationary.

17 Slide the drive sprocket from the crankshaft and the driven sprocket from the oil pump. Withdraw both sprockets and the chain. Note that the drive sprocket is not keyed to the crankshaft, but relies on the pulley bolt being tightened correctly to clamp the sprocket. It is most important that the pulley bolt is correctly tightened otherwise there is the possibility of the oil pump not functioning.

18 Unbolt the oil pump as described in paragraph 14 above.

Inspection

19 Proceed as described in paragraphs 4 to 8 above.

Refitting

20 Wipe clean the oil pump and cylinder block mating surfaces.

21 Check that the two locating dowels are fitted in the cylinder block, then position the oil pump on them and insert the two mounting bolts. Tighten the bolts securely.

22 Engage the sprockets on the chain (if removed), then refit both sprockets and the chain as an assembly. Slide the drive sprocket fully onto the crankshaft and locate the driven sprocket on the oil pump hub.

23 Align the holes, then insert the sprocket bolts and tighten them securely while holding the sprocket stationary with a screwdriver.

24 Refit the oil seal housing as described in Section 12 – do not forget the chain guide block and its two locating dowels – and the sump (refer to Section 10).

12 Crankshaft oil seals – renewal

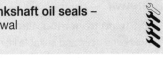

Timing belt oil seal

1 Remove the crankshaft sprocket, as described in Section 6.

2 Prise out the old oil seal using a small screwdriver, taking care not to damage the surface of the crankshaft. Alternatively, the oil seal can be removed by drilling two small holes diagonally opposite each other and inserting self-tapping screws in them. A pair of grips can then be used to pull out the oil seal, by pulling on each side in turn (see **Haynes Hint**).

3 Inspect the seal rubbing surface on the crankshaft. If it is grooved or rough in the area where the old seal was fitted, the new seal should be fitted slightly less deeply, so that it rubs on an unworn part of the crankshaft surface.

4 Wipe clean the oil seal seating, then dip the new seal in fresh engine oil, and locate it over the crankshaft with its closed side facing outwards. Make sure that the oil seal lip is not damaged as it is located on the crankshaft.

5 Using a tube of suitable diameter, drive the oil seal squarely into the housing until flush. A block of wood cut to pass over the end of the crankshaft may be used instead.

6 Refit the crankshaft sprocket as described in Section 6.

Flywheel end oil seal

7 Remove the flywheel as described in Section 13.

8 Renew the oil seal as described in paragraphs 2 to 5 inclusive.

9 Refit the flywheel with reference to Section 13.

13 Flywheel – removal, inspection and refitting

Note: *New flywheel bolts must be used on refitting.*

Removal

1 Remove the manual transmission as described in Chapter 7A.

2 Remove the clutch as described in Chapter 6.

3 Mark the flywheel in relation to the crankshaft to aid refitting.

4 The flywheel must now be held stationary while the securing bolts are loosened. To do this, locate a long bolt in one of the engine-to-gearbox mounting bolt holes and insert a wide-bladed screwdriver or length of bent metal bar in the starter ring gear or use a suitable locking tool **(see illustration)**.

5 Unscrew the securing bolts and withdraw the flywheel from the crankshaft.

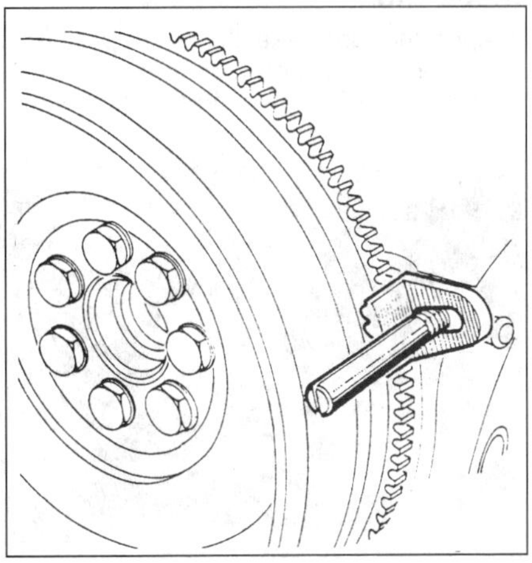

13.4 Tool bolted to cylinder block to hold flywheel stationary

2C

13.10a Fit new flywheel bolts . . .

13.10b . . . and tighten them to the specified torque. Note bar (arrowed) used to hold flywheel stationary

Inspection

6 Examine the flywheel for scoring of the clutch face and for wear or chipping of the ring gear teeth. If the clutch face is scored, the flywheel may be machined until flat, but renewal is preferable.

7 If the ring gear teeth are worn or damaged, the flywheel must be renewed.

Refitting

8 Clean the flywheel and crankshaft faces, then coat the locating face on the crankshaft with Loctite Autoform, or an equivalent compound.

9 Locate the flywheel on the crankshaft making sure that the previously made marks are aligned. The securing bolt holes are offset, so the flywheel cannot be fitted incorrectly.

10 Fit the new securing bolts, then tighten them in a diagonal sequence to the specified torque. Hold the flywheel stationary as during removal **(see illustrations)**.

11 Refit the clutch as described in Chapter 6.

12 Refit the gearbox with reference to Chapter 7A.

14 Engine mountings – renewal

Inspection

1 Apply the handbrake, then jack up the front of the car and support it on axle stands (see *Jacking and vehicle support*). Where fitted, remove the engine compartment undertray.

2 Visually inspect the rubber pads on the two front and one rear engine/transmission mountings for signs of cracking and deterioration. Careful use of a lever will help to determine the condition of the rubber pads. Check that all the mounting's fasteners are securely tightened; use a torque wrench to check if possible. If there is excessive movement in the mounting, or if the rubber has deteriorated, the mounting should be renewed.

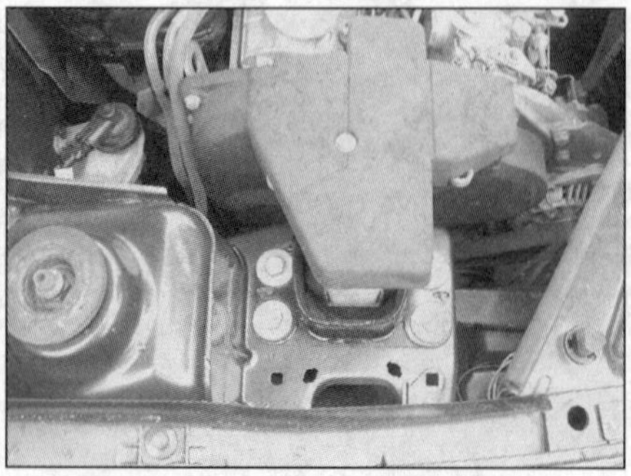

14.4 Right-hand engine mounting and plastic cover

Renewal

Right-hand front mounting

3 Connect a hoist and suitable lifting tackle to the engine lifting brackets to support the engine/transmission assembly while the mounting is removed. Alternatively, the assembly can be supported using a jack and a suitable block of wood to spread the load under the sump.

4 Unscrew the securing bolts and remove the timing belt upper/engine right-hand mounting plastic cover, noting the locations of any brackets secured by the bolts **(see illustration)**.

5 Ensure that the engine/gearbox assembly is adequately supported, then unscrew the nut securing the mounting upper bracket to the mounting rubber/movement limiter assembly on the body. On certain models it is necessary to counterhold the mounting threaded rod using a suitable Allen key or hexagon bit, whilst loosening the nut with an open-ended spanner.

6 Unscrew the three bolts securing the mounting upper bracket to the main bracket on the engine, then withdraw the bracket.

7 Unscrew the bolts securing the engine mounting rubber/movement limiter assembly to the body and withdraw the assembly.

8 With the mounting cover and upper bracket removed, remove the timing belt outer covers to reach the main bracket's mounting bolts on the engine. Unscrew the bolts and withdraw the main bracket; tighten the bolts securely on refitting.

9 Refit the mounting rubber/movement limiter assembly. Do not fully tighten the securing bolts at this stage.

10 Refit the upper mounting bracket and tighten to the specified torque wrench setting the bolts securing it to the main bracket. At this stage, do not fully tighten the nut securing the bracket to the mounting rubber/movement limiter assembly.

11 Remove the hoist or jack from the engine/transmission assembly.

12 Check that the engine/transmission assembly is settled in its central position on the mountings by attempting to rock it several times.

13 With the mounting centred, tighten to the specified torque wrench settings the body mounting bolts and the upper bracket-to-mounting rubber/movement limiter assembly nut **(see illustration opposite)**.

Left-hand front mounting

14 Remove the left-hand roadwheel.

15 Using a jack and block of wood, support the weight of the transmission/engine.

16 Unscrew the nut securing the lower mounting stud to the upper bracket. Using a soft-faced mallet, tap the stud to release it from the upper bracket.

17 Unbolt the upper mounting rubber and bracket.

18 Unbolt the lower mounting bracket from the transmission.

19 Fit the new mounting components using a reversal of the removal procedure, but before fully tightening the nut and bolts, attempt to rock the engine/transmission assembly several times to settle it on its mountings. With the engine settled, tighten the nuts and bolts to the specified torque wrench settings.

Rear mounting

20 With the vehicle raised and supported on axle stands, working beneath the car, unscrew the bolts securing the rear mounting link to the brackets on the subframe and cylinder block. Withdraw the link from under the car.

21 If necessary, unbolt and remove the brackets.

22 Refitting is a reversal of the removal procedure, but before fully tightening the bolts attempt to rock the engine/transmission assembly in order to settle the mountings. Tighten the mounting bolts to the specified torque.

15 Engine oil cooler – removal and refitting

Removal

1 Drain the cooling system as described in Chapter 1B.

2 Remove the oil filter with reference to Chapter 1B.

3 Loosen the clips, and disconnect the coolant hoses from the oil cooler.

4 Unscrew the oil filter mounting stud, which also secures the oil cooler to the adaptor on

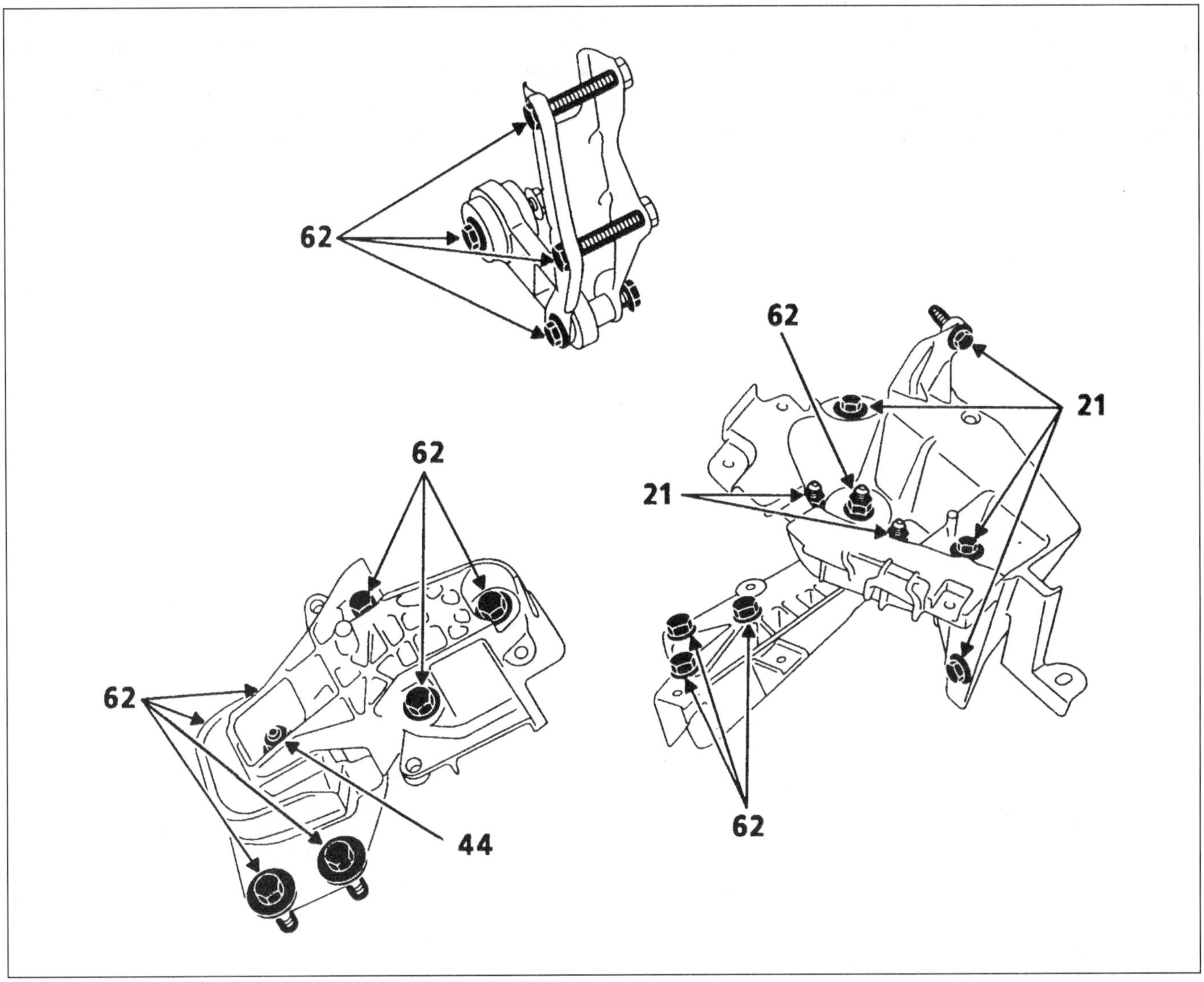

14.13 Torque wrench settings (in Nm) of the engine mountings

the front of the cylinder block, and withdraw the oil cooler from the engine. Recover the sealing ring **(see illustrations)**.

5 If necessary the adaptor may be removed by unscrewing the hollow bolt. Recover the O-ring and sealing washer.

Refitting

6 Refitting is a reversal of removal, but use a new sealing ring, O-ring and sealing washer.

16 Auxiliary shaft oil seal – renewal

Note: *This procedure applies only to those engines fitted with auxiliary shafts. There is no oil seal or gasket behind the idler pulley of those engines which do not have auxiliary shafts.*

1 Remove the auxiliary shaft sprocket as described in Section 6.

2 Make a note of the correct fitted depth of the seal then punch or drill two small holes opposite each other in the oil seal. Screw a self-tapping screw into each and pull on the screws with pliers to extract the seal. **Note:** *On some models it may be necessary to remove the timing belt lower inner cover to allow the seal to be withdrawn. If this is the case, remove the crankshaft sprocket and idler pulley (see Section 6) then unbolt the cover.*

3 Clean the seal housing and polish off any burrs or raised edges which may have caused the seal to fail in the first place.

15.4a Remove the oil filter mounting stud . . .

15.4b . . . then withdraw the oil cooler and recover the sealing ring

4 Lubricate the lips of the new seal with clean engine oil and ease it into position on the end of the shaft. Press the seal into its housing until it is positioned at the same depth as the original was prior to removal. If necessary, a suitable tubular drift, such as a socket, which bears only on the hard outer edge of the seal can be used to tap the seal into position. Take great care not to damage the seal lips during fitting and ensure that the seal lips face inwards. Note that if the surface of the shaft was noted to be badly scored, press the new seal slightly further into its housing so that its lip is running on an unmarked area of the shaft.

5 Refit the auxiliary shaft sprocket as described in Section 6 and fit the new timing belt as described in Section 5.

Chapter 2 Part D:
Engine removal and overhaul procedures

Contents

Degrees of difficulty

Easy, suitable for novice with little experience	**Fairly easy,** suitable for beginner with some experience	**Fairly difficult,** suitable for competent DIY mechanic	**Difficult,** suitable for experienced DIY mechanic	**Very difficult,** suitable for expert DIY or professional

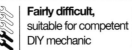

Specifications

General

Engine codes:	
1.2 litre petrol engine	D7F
1.4 litre petrol engine:	
SOHC	E7J
DOHC	K4J
1.6 litre petrol engine:	
SOHC	K7M
DOHC	K4M
Diesel engine	F8Q

Cylinder head

Height:	
D7F engine	113.5 mm
E7J, K7M engines	113.0 mm ± 0.05 mm
K4J and K4M engines	137.0 mm
F8Q engine	159.50 ± 0.20 mm
Maximum acceptable gasket face distortion	0.05 mm
Refinishing limit	No refinishing permitted
Swirl chamber protrusion (F8Q engine)	0.01 to 0.04 mm
Valve seat angle:	
D7F, E7J, K7M and F8Q engines:	
Inlet	120°
Exhaust	90°
K4J and K4M engines:	
Inlet and exhaust	89°
Valve seat width:	
D7F, E7J, K7M engines	1.7 mm ± 0.1 mm
K4J and K4M engines:	
Inlet	1.3 +1.4 –0 mm
Exhaust	1.4 +1.3 –0 mm
F8Q engine	1.8 mm
Valve depth below cylinder head gasket face:	
F8Q engine:	
Inlet	0.85 ± 0.09 mm
Exhaust	0.97 ± 0.09 mm

Valves

	Inlet	Exhaust
Head diameter:		
D7F engine	32.88 ± 0.12 mm	29.88 ± 0.12 mm
E7J and K7M engines	37.5 ± 0.1 mm	33.5 ± 0.1 mm
K4J and K4M engines	32.7 ± 0.12 mm	27.96 ± 0.12 mm
F8Q engine:		
Conventional valve seat	36.1 mm	31.5 mm
Stellite-coated valve	36.35 mm	31.5 mm
Stem diameter:		
D7F engine	5.98 +0 –0.015 mm	5.97 +0 –0.015 mm
E7J and K7M engines	7.0 mm	7.0 mm
K4J and K4M engines	5.484 ± 0.01 mm	5.473 ± 0.01 mm
F8Q engine	8.0 mm	8.0 mm
Valve spring free length:		
D7F engine	43.00 mm	
E7J and K7M engines:		
Black marking	46.64 mm	
Orange marking	44.93 mm	
K4J and K4M engines	41.30 mm	
F8Q engine	43.41 mm	

Auxiliary shaft (F8Q engine)

Endfloat	0.07 to 0.15 mm

Cylinder block

Bore diameter:	
D7F engine:	
Class A	69.000 to 69.015 mm
Class B	69.015 to 69.030 mm
E7J engine (wet liners)	75.8 mm +0.03 –0.00 mm
K7M, K4J and K4M engines	79.5 mm +0.03 –0.00 mm
F8Q engine:	
Class A or 1	80.000 to 80.015 mm
Class B or 2	80.015 to 80.030 mm
Wet liner dimensions – E7J engine:	
Liner height:	
Total	130.0 mm
From shoulder to top	91.5 mm +0.035 +0.005 mm
Cylinder block depth – from top to liner locating shoulder	91.5 mm –0.015 –0.055 mm
Liner protrusion – without O-ring	0.02 to 0.09 mm
Maximum difference in protrusion between adjacent liners	0.05 mm

Pistons and piston rings

Piston ring end gaps	Pre-adjusted
Piston ring thickness:	
Top compression ring:	
D7F engine	1.47 to 1.49 mm
E7J engine	1.75 mm
K7M engine	1.5 mm
K4J and K4M engines	1.2 mm
F8Q engine	2.0 mm
Second compression ring:	
D7F engine	1.47 to 1.49 mm
E7J engine	1.75 mm
K7M, K4J and K4M engines	1.5 mm
F8Q engine	2.0 mm
Oil control ring:	
D7F engine	2.47 to 2.49 mm
E7J engine	3.0 mm
K7M, K4J and K4M engines	2.5 mm
F8Q engine	3.0 mm
Piston clearance in liner/bore (suggested values):	
Petrol engines	0.045 to 0.065 mm
Diesel engines	0.015 to 0.030 mm

Connecting rods

Big-end bearing running clearance	0.014 to 0.053 mm
Big-end cap side play:	
D7F engine	0.210 to 0.453 mm
E7J engines	0.310 to 0.572 mm
K7M, K4J and K4M engines	0.310 to 0.604 mm
F8Q engine	0.220 to 0.400 mm

Crankshaft

Number of main bearings	5
Main bearing journal diameter:	
D7F engine:	
Standard	44.000 mm ± 0.01 mm
1st undersize	43.750 mm ± 0.01 mm
E7J engines:	
Standard	54.795 mm ± 0.01 mm
1st undersize	54.545 mm ± 0.01 mm
K7M engines:	
Standard	48.010 +0 –0.02 mm
1st undersize	47.760 +0 –0.02 mm
K4J and K4M engines:	
Standard	47.990 to 47.997 mm
1st undersize	47.997 to 48.003 mm
2nd undersize	48.003 to 48.010 mm
F8Q engine:	
Standard	54.795 ± 0.01 mm
1st undersize	54.545 ± 0.01 mm
Main bearing running clearance	0.020 to 0.058 mm
Crankpin (big-end) journal diameter:	
D7F engine:	
Standard	40.000 +0 –0.016 mm
1st undersize	39.750 mm +0 –0.016 mm
E7J engine:	
Standard	43.980 mm +0 –0.02 mm
1st undersize	43.730 mm +0 –0.02 mm
K7M engine:	
Standard	43.980 mm +0 –0.02 mm
1st undersize	43.790 mm +0 –0.02 mm
K4J and K4M engines:	
Standard	43.97 ± 0.01 mm
F8Q engine:	
Standard	48.00 mm
Undersize	47.75 mm +0.02 mm –0.00 mm
Crankshaft endfloat:	
D7F engine	0.060 to 0.235 mm
E7J engine:	
New	0.045 to 0.252 mm
Maximum	0.852 mm
K4J and K4M engines:	
New	0.045 to 0.252 mm
Maximum	0.852 mm
F8Q engine	0.070 to 0.230 mm

Torque wrench settings

Refer to Parts A, B, and C of this Chapter.

1 General information

Included in this part of Chapter 2 are the general overhaul procedures for the cylinder head, cylinder block/crankcase and internal engine components.

The information ranges from advice concerning preparation for an overhaul and the purchase of replacement parts, to detailed step-by-step procedures covering removal, inspection, renovation and refitting of internal engine parts.

The following Sections have been compiled based on the assumption that the engine has been removed from the car. For information concerning in-car engine repair, as well as the removal and refitting of the external components necessary for the overhaul, refer to Part A or B (petrol engines) or Part C (diesel engine) of this Chapter and to Section 7 of this Part.

Caution: If the radio/cassette in your vehicle is equipped with an anti-theft system, make sure you have the correct activation code before disconnecting the battery.

2 Engine overhaul – general information

It is not always easy to determine when, or if, an engine should be completely overhauled, as a number of factors must be considered.

High mileage is not necessarily an indication that an overhaul is needed, while low mileage does not preclude the need for an overhaul. Frequency of servicing is probably the most important consideration. An engine which has had regular and frequent oil and filter changes, as well as other required maintenance, will most likely give many thousands of miles of reliable service. Conversely, a neglected engine may require an overhaul very early in its life.

Excessive oil consumption is an indication that piston rings, valve stem oil seals and/or valves and valve guides are in need of attention. Make sure that oil leaks are not responsible before deciding that the rings and/or guides are bad. Perform a cylinder compression check to determine the extent of the work required.

Check the oil pressure with a gauge fitted in place of the oil pressure warning light switch and compare it with the value given in the Specifications. If it is extremely low, the main and big-end bearings and/or the oil pump are probably worn out.

Loss of power, rough running, knocking or metallic engine noises, excessive valve gear noise and high fuel consumption may also point to the need for an overhaul, especially if they are all present at the same time. If a complete tune-up does not remedy the situation, major mechanical work is the only solution.

An engine overhaul involves restoring the internal parts to the specifications of a new engine. During an overhaul, the pistons and rings are renewed and the cylinder bores are reconditioned. New main bearings, connecting rod bearings and camshaft bearings are generally fitted and, if necessary, the crankshaft may be reground to restore the journals. The valves are also serviced as well, since they are usually in less-than-perfect condition at this point. While the engine is being overhauled, other components, such as the distributor, starter and alternator, can be overhauled as well. The end result should be a like-new engine that will give many trouble-free miles. **Note:** *Critical cooling system components such as the hoses, drivebelts, thermostat and water pump MUST be renewed when an engine is overhauled. The radiator should be checked carefully, to ensure that it is not clogged or leaking. Also, it is a good idea to renew the oil pump whenever the engine is overhauled.*

Before beginning the engine overhaul, read through the entire procedure to familiarise yourself with the scope and requirements of the job. Overhauling an engine is not difficult if you follow all of the instructions carefully, have the necessary tools and equipment and pay close attention to all specifications; however, it can be time-consuming. Plan on the vehicle being tied up for a minimum of two weeks, especially if parts must be taken to an engineering works for repair or reconditioning. Check on the availability of parts and make sure that any necessary special tools and equipment are obtained in advance. Most work can be done with typical hand tools, although a number of precision measuring tools are required for inspecting parts to determine if they must be renewed. Often the engineering works will handle the inspection of parts and offer advice concerning reconditioning and renewal. **Note:** *Always wait until the engine has been completely disassembled and all components, especially the engine block, have been inspected before deciding what service and repair operations must be performed by an engineering works. Since the condition of the block will be the major factor to consider when determining whether to overhaul the original engine or buy a reconditioned unit, do not purchase parts or have overhaul work done on other components until the block has been thoroughly inspected.* As a general rule, time is the primary cost of an overhaul, so it does not pay to fit worn or substandard parts.

As a final note, to ensure maximum life and minimum trouble from a reconditioned engine, everything must be assembled with care and in a spotlessly-clean environment.

3 Engine removal – methods and precautions

If you have decided that an engine must be removed for overhaul or major repair work, several preliminary steps should be taken.

Locating a suitable place to work is extremely important. Adequate work space, with storage space for the vehicle, will be needed. If a garage is not available, at the very least a flat, level, clean work surface is required.

Cleaning the engine compartment and engine before beginning the removal procedure will help keep tools clean and organised.

An engine hoist or A-frame will also be necessary. Make sure the equipment is rated in excess of the combined weight of the engine and transmission. Safety is of primary importance, considering the potential hazards involved in lifting the engine out of the vehicle.

If the engine is being removed by a novice, an assistant should be available. Advice and aid from someone more experienced would also be helpful. There are many instances when one person cannot simultaneously perform all of the operations required when lifting the engine out of the vehicle.

Plan the operation ahead of time. Arrange for, or obtain, all of the tools and equipment you will need, prior to beginning the job. Some of the equipment necessary to perform engine removal and installation safely and with relative ease are (in addition to an engine hoist) a heavy-duty floor jack, complete sets of spanners and sockets as described in the *Tools and working facilities* section of this manual, wooden blocks and plenty of rags and cleaning solvent for mopping-up spilled oil, coolant and fuel. If the hoist must be hired, make sure that you arrange for it in advance and perform all of the operations possible without it beforehand. This will save you money and time.

Plan for the vehicle to be out of use for quite a while. An engineering works will be required to perform some of the work which the do-it-yourselfer cannot accomplish without special equipment. These places often have a busy schedule, so it would be a good idea to consult them before removing the engine, in order to accurately estimate the amount of time required to rebuild or repair components that may need work.

Always be extremely careful when removing and refitting the engine. Serious injury can result from careless actions. Plan ahead, take your time and you will find that a job of this nature, although major, can be accomplished successfully.

4 Petrol engine (1.2 litre) – removal and refitting

Removal

Note: *The following paragraphs describe the removal of the 1.2 litre petrol engine with gearbox upwards from the engine compartment; the gearbox is then separated from the engine on the bench.*

1 Remove the battery as described in Chapter 5A.

2 Apply the handbrake, then jack up the front of the vehicle and support it on axle stands (see *Jacking and vehicle support*). Remove both front roadwheels and both front wheelarch liners. Remove the engine compartment undertray.

3 Drain the cooling system as described in Chapter 1A.

4 Drain the gearbox oil with reference to Chapter 7A **(see illustration)**.

4.4 Gearbox oil drain plug

5 If necessary, drain the engine oil with reference to Chapter 1A.
6 Loosen the clips and remove the air intake duct from the engine compartment.
7 Remove the cooling system expansion tank and either attach it to the engine or remove it completely.
8 Unscrew the two mounting bolts securing the left-hand brake caliper to the swivel hub and disconnect the pad wear warning wiring. Tie the caliper to the coil spring, taking care not to strain the hose.
9 Unscrew the bolts securing the left-hand driveshaft inner rubber boot and metal ring to the transmission.
10 Unscrew the nut from the left-hand track rod end and disconnect it from the swivel hub steering arm using a balljoint separator tool.
11 Unscrew and remove fully both bolts securing the front suspension left-hand strut to the swivel hub (note that the nuts are on the rear of the carrier).
12 Support the inner end of the left-hand driveshaft, then carefully tilt the swivel hub outwards and lower the driveshaft from the gearbox. Tie the driveshaft to one side away from the gearbox. There may be some oil loss from the gearbox, so place a small container on the floor to catch it.
13 Working beneath the car, drive out the roll pin securing the right-hand driveshaft to the differential sun gear shaft **(see illustration)**. Note that if the original double roll pin is renewed, the new one will be of single coiled type.
14 Unscrew the two mounting bolts securing the right-hand brake caliper to the swivel hub and disconnect the pad wear warning wiring. Tie the caliper to the coil spring, taking care not to strain the hose.
15 Unscrew the nut from the right-hand track rod end and disconnect it from the swivel hub steering arm using a balljoint separator tool.
16 Unscrew and remove both bolts securing the front suspension left-hand strut to the swivel hub (note that the nuts are on the rear).
17 Carefully tilt the swivel hub outwards, then pull out the driveshaft and disconnect the inner end from the splines on the transmission sun gear shaft (refer to Chapter 8 if necessary). Tie the driveshaft to the steering gear.
18 Unscrew the bolt and remove the earth strap from the gearbox.
19 Pull back the rubber gaiter, then unscrew and remove the bolt and disconnect the gearchange rod from the lever on the gearbox.
20 Loosen only the bolt securing the rear engine mounting to the underbody, then unscrew and remove the bolt securing the mounting link to the gearbox. Swivel the link down from the gearbox.
21 Disconnect the accelerator cable from the throttle body with reference to Chapter 4A.
22 Disconnect the evaporative carbon canister hose from the solenoid valve on the inlet manifold.

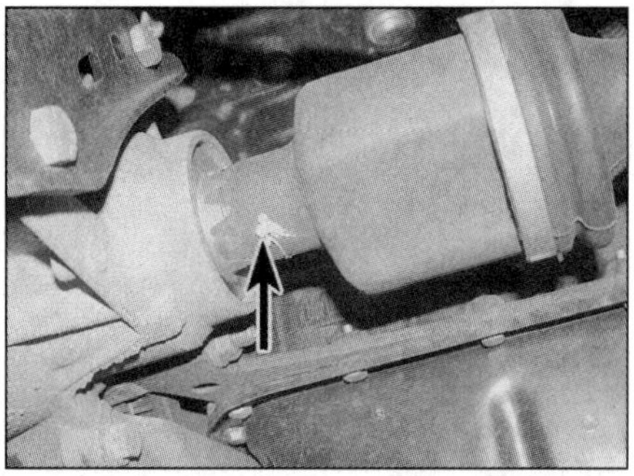

4.13 Roll pin securing the right-hand driveshaft to the differential sun gear shaft

23 Disconnect the brake vacuum servo unit hose from the inlet manifold.
24 Loosen the clip and disconnect the top hose from the radiator. If necessary, also disconnect it from the engine.
25 Disconnect the engine wiring harness at the left-hand side of the engine compartment and place it on the engine. To do this, remove the relay board, the fuse holders, and the fuse mounting and disconnect the wiring.
26 Note the location of the heater hoses on the bulkhead, then disconnect the quick-release clips and position the hoses to one side. There are two types of quick-release clips; on one type rotate the outer ring anti-clockwise to release it, and on the other type squeeze together the plastic tabs, then push the clip towards the bulkhead and release the clip.
27 Disconnect the wiring from the oxygen sensor and radiator cooling fan.
28 Loosen the clips and disconnect the fuel supply and return hoses from the throttle body housing or fuel rail.
29 At the left-hand side of the engine compartment, disconnect the wiring from the injection computer and impact switch, then unbolt the computer support plate.
30 On models with air conditioning, refer to Chapter 3 and remove the compressor from the engine without disconnecting the refrigerant lines. Tie the compressor to the side of the engine compartment.
31 Refer to Chapter 10 and remove the power steering pump from the engine without disconnecting the hydraulic fluid lines **(see illustration)**. Tie the pump to one side.
32 Disconnect the clutch cable from the transmission with reference to Chapter 6.
33 Remove the exhaust front downpipe and catalytic converter as described in Chapter 4A.
34 If necessary, remove the bonnet with reference to Chapter 11. Connect a hoist to the engine lifting eyes and take the weight of the engine/transmission assembly.
35 Unbolt the left-hand engine mounting from the gearbox and body with reference to Chapter 2A.
36 Mark the position of the right-hand engine mounting on the body, then unbolt and remove the mounting **(see illustration)**.

4.31 Power steering pump – D7F engine

37 Position a large piece of card over the radiator to protect it while removing the engine/gearbox. Depending on the type of hoist being used, it may be preferable to remove the radiator completely, with reference to Chapter 3.
38 With the help of an assistant, slowly lift the engine/transmission assembly from the engine compartment, taking care not to damage any components on the surrounding panels. When high enough, lift the assembly over the body front panel and lower to the ground.
39 If the engine is to be separated from the gearbox, first remove the wiring loom, noting its location and routing.
40 Separate the gearbox from the engine with reference to Chapter 7A.

Refitting

41 Refitting is a reversal of removal, with reference to the Chapters needed for removal, but tighten all nuts and bolts to the specified torque. Top-up the power steering fluid level as described in *Weekly checks*. Fill the engine with fresh oil and fill the cooling system with coolant with reference to Chapter 1A. Fill the manual gearbox with fresh oil with reference to Chapter 7A. Before taking the vehicle on the road, depress the brake pedal several times to bring the brake pads to their normal position.

4.36 Right-hand engine mounting – D7F engine

5.4 Unscrewing the drain plug from the manual transmission

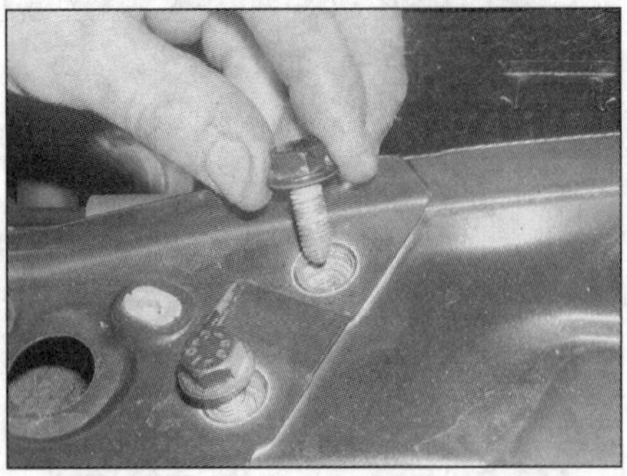

5.6a Unbolting the engine compartment front crossmember . . .

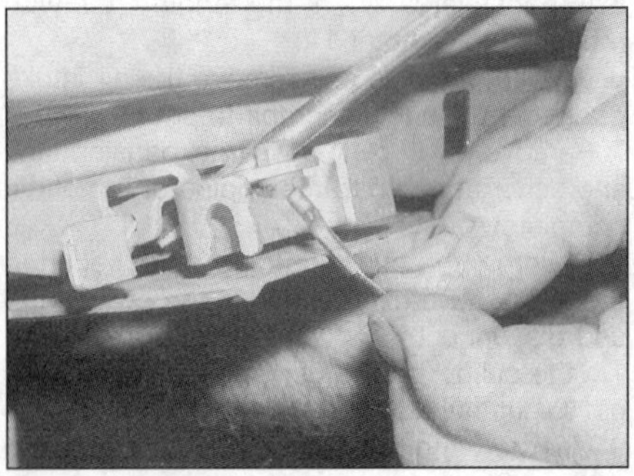

5.6b . . . and disconnecting the cable from the bonnet lock

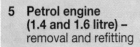

5 Petrol engine (1.4 and 1.6 litre) – removal and refitting

Note: *Renault recommend that the engine is removed downwards from the engine compartment together with the transmission and subframe. The engine/transmission can then be removed from the subframe and the transmission separated from the engine. This Section describes lowering the engine together with the subframe, however an alternative method is to remove the subframe first then lower the engine and transmission.*

Removal

1 Remove the battery as described in Chapter 5A.

2 Apply the handbrake, then jack up the front of the vehicle and support it on axle stands (see *Jacking and vehicle support*). Remove both front roadwheels and both front wheel-arch liners. Remove the engine compartment undertray.

3 Drain the cooling system as described in Chapter 1A.

4 Drain the manual gearbox oil (see Chapter 7A) or automatic transmission fluid (see Chapter 7B) **(see illustration).**

5 If necessary, drain the engine oil with reference to Chapter 1A.

6 Remove the radiator grille as described in Chapter 11, then unbolt the engine compartment front crossmember and disconnect the cable from the bonnet lock **(see illustrations).**

7 Remove the front bumper as described in Chapter 11 **(see illustration).**

8 Detach the front suspension subframe tie-rods from the body.

9 Unscrew the mounting bolts securing both front brake calipers (and where applicable the ABS sensors) to the swivel hubs and disconnect the pad wear warning wiring **(see illustrations).** Tie the calipers to the coil springs, taking care not to strain the hoses.

10 Unscrew and remove the bolts securing the front suspension struts to the swivel hubs (note that the nuts are on the rear) **(see illustrations).**

11 Working beneath the vehicle, unbolt and remove the heat shield located above the exhaust system on the underbody, then remove the gearchange selector rod with reference to Chapter 7A or the selector cable with reference to Chapter 7B.

12 Remove the exhaust front downpipe with reference to Chapter 4A.

13 Unbolt the earth strap from the transmission.

14 Remove the air inlet duct from the air cleaner with reference to Chapter 4A.

5.7 Removing the front bumper

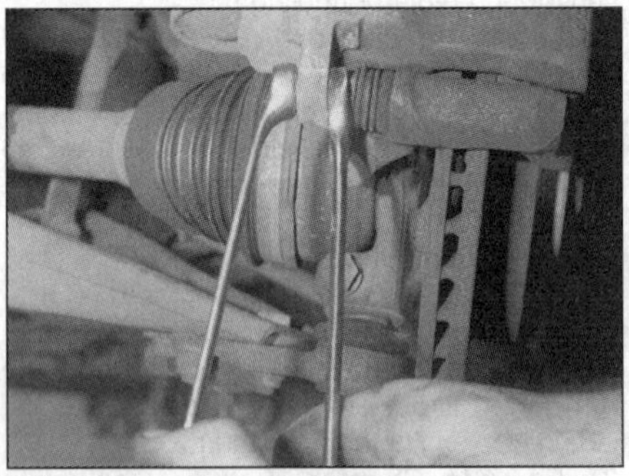

5.9a Unscrew the mounting bolts . . .

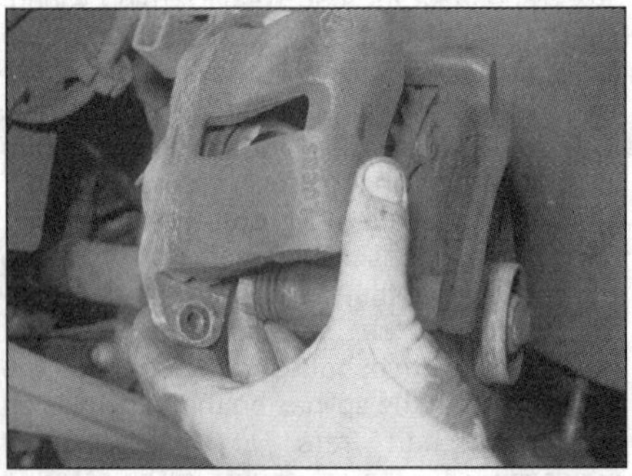

5.9b . . . remove the left-hand brake caliper . . .

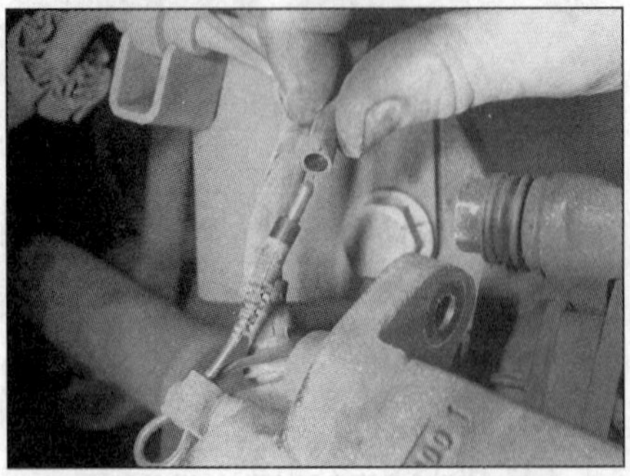

5.9c . . . and disconnect the pad wear warning wiring

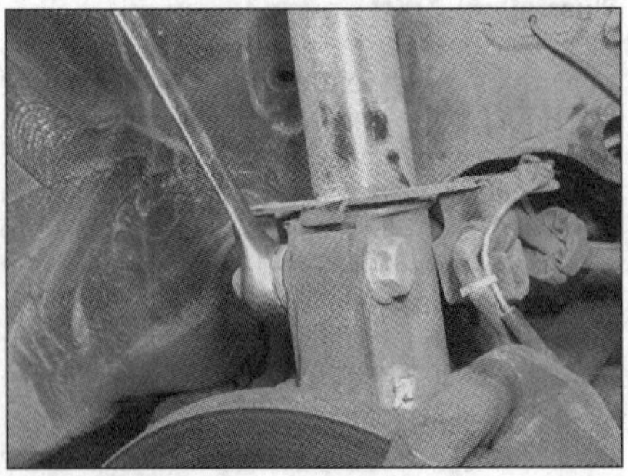

5.10a Unscrew the nuts . . .

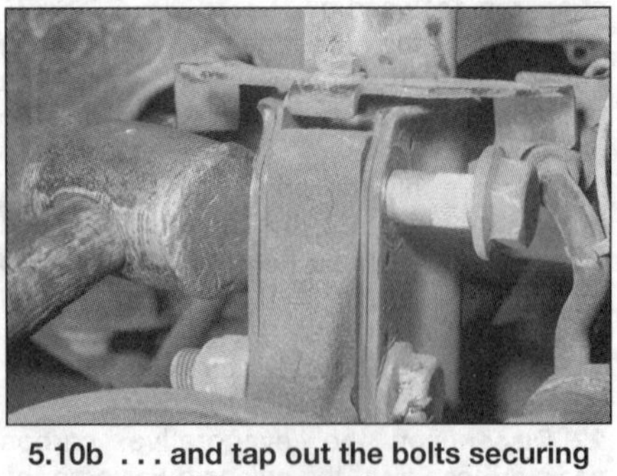

5.10b . . . and tap out the bolts securing the swivel hub to the bottom of the suspension strut

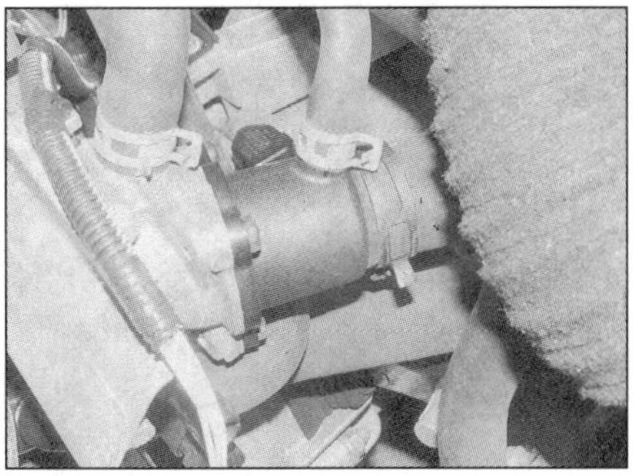

5.16 Coolant hoses to the thermostat housing – E7J engine

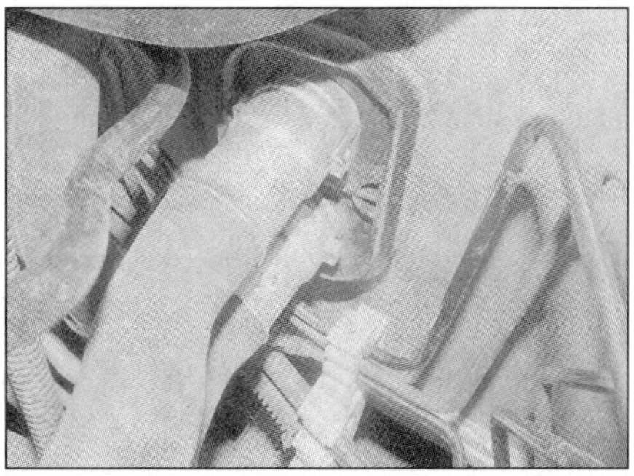

5.18 Heater hoses on the bulkhead

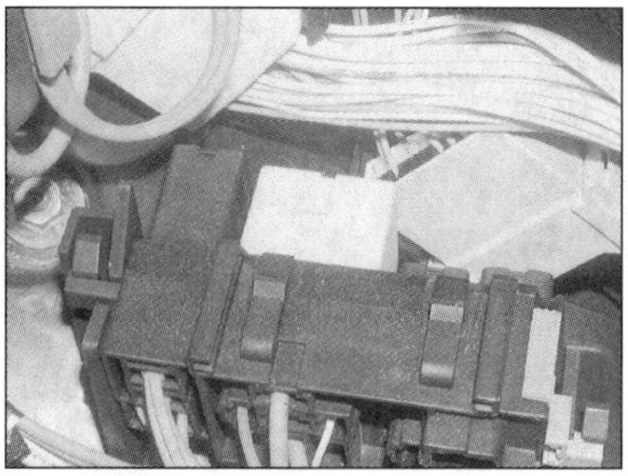

5.19 Engine wiring harness at the left-hand side of the engine compartment

15 At the left-hand side of the engine compartment, disconnect the wiring from the engine management computer and impact switch, then unbolt the computer support plate.

16 Disconnect the hoses from the expansion tank and remove the tank from the engine compartment. Where necessary, disconnect the hoses from the thermostat housing **(see illustration)**.

17 Disconnect the brake vacuum servo unit hose from the inlet manifold.

18 Note the location of the heater hoses on the bulkhead, then disconnect the quick-release clips and position the hoses to one side **(see illustration)**. There are two types of quick-release clips; on one type rotate the outer ring anti-clockwise to release it, and on the other type squeeze together the plastic tabs, then push the clip towards the bulkhead and release the clip.

19 Disconnect the engine wiring harness at the left-hand side of the engine compartment and place it on the engine. To do this, remove the relay board, the fuse holders, and the fuse mounting and disconnect the wiring **(see illustration)**.

20 Disconnect the evaporative carbon canister hose from the solenoid valve on the inlet manifold.

21 Disconnect the accelerator cable from the throttle body with reference to Chapter 4A **(see illustration)**.

22 On manual gearbox models, disconnect the clutch cable with reference to Chapter 6.

23 On automatic transmission models, disconnect the selector lever cable with reference to Chapter 7B.

24 Refer to Chapter 10 and remove the power steering pump from the engine without disconnecting the hydraulic fluid lines **(see illustration)**. Tie the pump to one side.

25 Remove the air cleaner assembly with reference to Chapter 4A.

26 Disconnect the fuel supply and return hoses from the fuel rail with reference to Chapter 4A.

27 Unbolt the radiator upper mountings from the engine compartment crossmember, then tie the radiator to the engine making sure that it is not damaged. If necessary, remove the electric fan assembly from the rear of the radiator **(see illustration)**. Note that the bottom radiator mountings are in the subframe which is lowered from the body later in this Section.

28 On models with air conditioning, refer to Chapter 3 and remove the compressor from the engine without disconnecting the refrigerant lines, and tie it to the side of the engine compartment. Also unbolt the condenser from the radiator and tie it to the bonnet **(see illustrations)**.

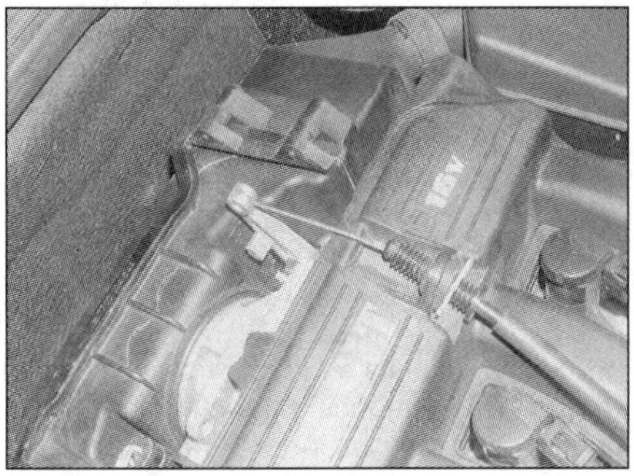

5.21 Accelerator cable – K4J engine

5.24 Power steering pump location

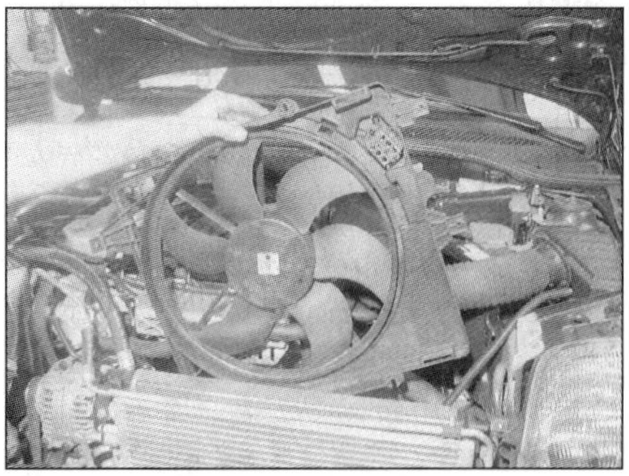

5.27 Removing the electric fan assembly from the rear of the radiator

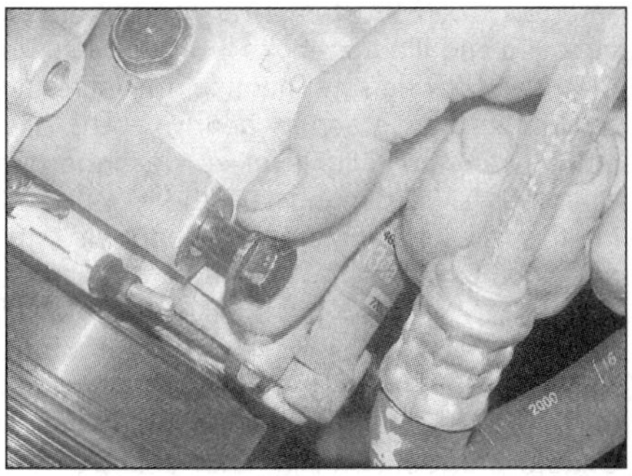

5.28a Unbolting the air conditioning compressor from the engine

5.28b Unbolt the air conditioning condenser from the radiator

5.28c Suspend the air conditioning condenser from the bonnet without disconnecting the refrigerant lines

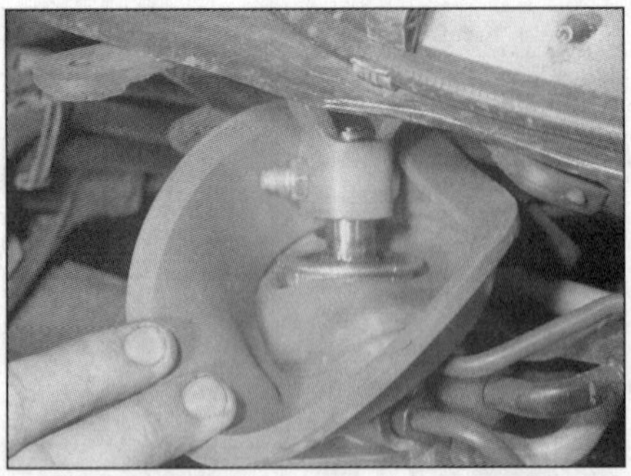

5.29 Pull back the rubber grommet, then remove the bolt securing the bottom of the steering inner column to the steering gear

5.37b Roll pin (arrowed) securing the right-hand driveshaft to the transmission sun gear

29 With the front wheels in the straight-ahead position, pull back the rubber grommet then unscrew the eccentric bolt securing the bottom of the steering inner column to the steering gear and separate the column (refer to Chapter 10 for more information) **(see illustration)**.

Caution: Where a driver's airbag is fitted, it is important that the airbag rotary switch beneath the steering wheel is not damaged. Before removing the column the steering wheel must be immobilised with the wheels straight using a steering wheel locking tool or by using adhesive tape to hold the steering wheel.

30 Using blocks of wood, support the engine on the subframe by inserting the blocks between the cylinder block, transmission, and subframe. Renault technicians use a special adjustable tool to support the right-hand rear of the engine, and a suitable screw-jack can be used instead of the block of wood if necessary.

Caution: Make sure the engine and transmission are adequately supported.

31 With the engine supported, unbolt and remove the right-hand engine mounting from the body and engine. As an added precaution, the engine and transmission may be supported by a hoist while removing the engine mountings.

32 Unbolt and remove the left-hand engine mounting from the body and transmission.

33 Unbolt and remove the subframe-to-underbody rear support plates **(see illustration)**.

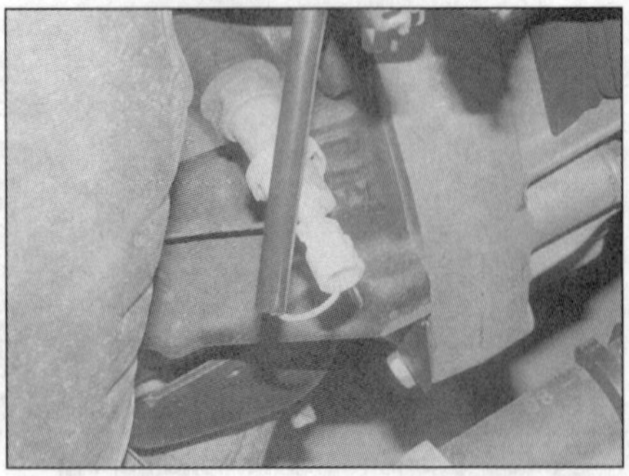

5.38a Wiring to the engine oil pressure switch – E7J engine

5.33 Subframe rear support plates

5.37c Using a punch to drive out the right-hand driveshaft roll pin

5.38b Wiring to the thermostat housing – E7J engine

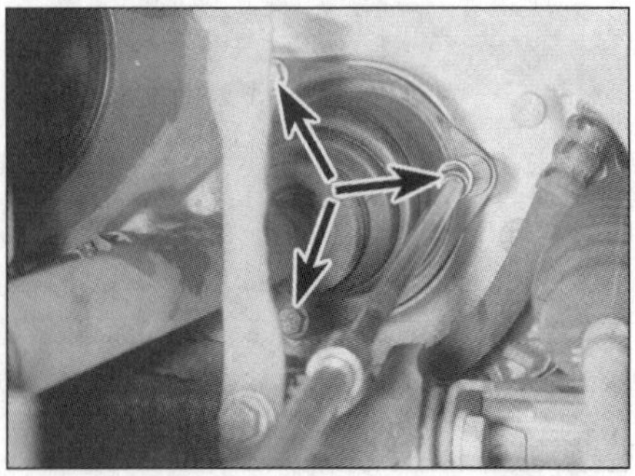

5.37a Removing the three bolts securing the left-hand driveshaft inner rubber boot and metal ring to the transmission

34 Loosen only one or two turns the subframe-to-body mounting bolts. **Do not** remove them.

35 Lower the front of the vehicle until the subframe can be supported on blocks of wood or axle stands.

36 Unscrew and remove the subframe mounting bolts, then with the help of some assistants, carefully raise the front of the vehicle while guiding it over the engine and transmission. If possible, move the vehicle away from the engine and transmission to facilitate working room. A trolley jack or hoist may be used to lift the vehicle.

37 Connect a hoist to the engine and transmission, then unscrew the bolts and separate the subframe. At the same time disconnect the driveshafts from the transmission with reference to Chapter 8 **(see illustrations)**.

38 If the engine is to be separated from the gearbox/transmission, first remove the wiring loom, noting its location and routing **(see illustrations)**.

39 Separate the gearbox/transmission from the engine with reference to Chapter 7A or 7B.

Refitting

40 Refitting is a reversal of removal, with reference to the Chapters needed for removal, but tighten all nuts and bolts to the specified torque. When attaching the subframe to the underbody, the use of 100 mm long rods temporarily screwed into the nuts will help alignment of the bolt holes. With the front of the subframe aligned, the rear bolts can be inserted, then the temporary rods can be removed and the front bolts inserted. Refer to Chapter 10 when connecting the steering column to the steering gear. Top-up the power steering fluid level as described in Chapter 1A. Fill the engine with fresh oil and fill the cooling system with coolant with reference to Chapter 1A. On manual gearbox models, refill the gearbox with oil with reference to Chapter 7A. On automatic transmission models, fill the automatic transmission with fresh fluid with reference to Chapter 7B. Before taking the vehicle on the road, depress the brake pedal several times to bring the brake pads to their normal position.

6 Diesel engine - removal and refitting

Note: *Renault recommend that the engine is removed downwards from the engine compartment together with the transmission and subframe. The engine/transmission can then be removed from the subframe and the transmission separated from the engine. This Section describes lowering the engine together with the subframe, however an alternative method is to remove the subframe first then lower the engine and transmission.*

Removal

1 Remove the battery as described in Chapter 5A.

2 Apply the handbrake, then jack up the front of the vehicle and support it on axle stands (see *Jacking and vehicle support*). Remove both front roadwheels and both front wheelarch liners. Remove the engine compartment undertray.

3 Drain the cooling system as described in Chapter 1B.

4 Drain the manual gearbox oil (see Chapter 7A) or automatic transmission fluid (see Chapter 7B).

5 If necessary, drain the engine oil with reference to Chapter 1A.

6 Detach the front suspension subframe tie-rods from the body.

7 Unscrew the mounting bolts securing both front brake calipers (and where applicable the ABS sensors) to the swivel hubs and disconnect the pad wear warning wiring. Tie the calipers to the coil springs, taking care not to strain the hoses.

8 Unscrew and remove the bolts securing the front suspension struts to the swivel hubs (note that the nuts are on the rear).

9 Remove the exhaust front downpipe with reference to Chapter 4D.

10 Unbolt the earth strap from the transmission **(see illustration)**.

11 Remove the front bumper as described in Chapter 11.

12 Remove the air inlet duct from the air cleaner with reference to Chapter 4B.

13 Disconnect the fuel supply and return hoses from the injection pump, and tape over the ends of the hoses and the apertures in the pump to prevent entry of dust and dirt. To release the supply hose, depress the top of the quick-release union, then squeeze together the bottom of the union and withdraw it upwards. To release the return hose, depress the perimeter of the union and separate it from the T-piece.

14 Identify and disconnect the wiring from the following components on the left-hand side of the engine compartment.

a) Fuel filter.
b) Pre-post heating relay unit.
c) ECU.
d) Inertia switch.

15 Unclip the fuel pipes from the air cleaner assembly and timing cover, then unclip the diesel filter assembly and position it to one side.

16 At the left-hand side of the engine compartment, disconnect the wiring from the injection ECU and impact switch, then unbolt the ECU support plate.

17 Disconnect the hoses from the expansion tank and remove the tank from the engine compartment.

18 Disconnect the brake vacuum servo unit hose from the inlet manifold.

19 Note the location of the heater hoses on the bulkhead, then disconnect the quick-release clips and position the hoses to one side. There are two types of quick-release clips; on one type rotate the outer ring anti-clockwise to release it, and on the other type squeeze together the plastic tabs, then push the clip towards the bulkhead and release the clip.

20 Disconnect the engine wiring harness at the left-hand side of the engine compartment and place it on the engine. To do this, remove the relay board, the fuse holders, and the fuse mounting and disconnect the wiring.

21 Disconnect the accelerator cable from the throttle body with reference to Chapter 4B.

22 On manual gearbox models, disconnect the clutch cable with reference to Chapter 6.

23 On automatic transmission models, disconnect the selector lever cable with reference to Chapter 7B.

24 Refer to Chapter 10 and remove the power steering pump from the engine without disconnecting the hydraulic fluid lines. Tie the pump to one side.

25 Unbolt the radiator upper mountings from the engine compartment crossmember, then tie the radiator to the engine making sure that it is not damaged. Note that the bottom radiator mountings are in the subframe which is lowered from the body later in this Section.

26 On models with air conditioning, refer to Chapter 3 and remove the compressor from the engine without disconnecting the refrigerant lines. Tie the compressor to the side of the engine compartment.

27 With the front wheels in the straight-ahead position, pull back the rubber grommet then unscrew the eccentric bolt securing the bottom of the steering inner column to the steering gear and separate the column (refer to Chapter 10 for more information).

Caution: Where a driver's airbag is fitted, it is important that the airbag rotary switch beneath the steering wheel is not damaged. Before removing the column the steering wheel must be immobilised with the wheels straight using a steering wheel locking tool or by using adhesive tape to hold the steering wheel.

28 Using blocks of wood, support the engine on the subframe by inserting the blocks between the cylinder block, transmission, and subframe. Renault technicians use a special adjustable tool to support the right-hand rear of the engine, and a suitable screw-jack can

6.10 Gearbox earth strap securing bolt (arrowed)

be used instead of the block of wood if necessary.

Caution: Make sure the engine and transmission are adequately supported.

29 With the engine supported, unbolt and remove the right-hand engine mounting from the body and engine. As an added precaution, the engine and transmission may be supported by a hoist while removing the engine mountings.

30 Unbolt and remove the left-hand engine mounting from the body and transmission.

31 Unbolt and remove the subframe-to-underbody rear support plates.

32 Loosen only one or two turns the subframe-to-body mounting bolts. **Do not** remove them.

33 Lower the front of the vehicle until the subframe can be supported on blocks of wood or axle stands.

34 Unscrew and remove the subframe mounting bolts, then with the help of some assistants, carefully raise the front of the vehicle while guiding it over the engine and transmission. If possible, move the vehicle away from the engine and transmission to facilitate working room. A trolley jack or hoist may be used to lift the vehicle.

35 Connect a hoist to the engine and transmission, then unscrew the bolts and separate the subframe. At the same time disconnect the driveshafts from the transmission with reference to Chapter 8 **(see illustrations)**.

36 If the engine is to be separated from the gearbox/transmission, first remove the wiring loom, noting its location and routing.

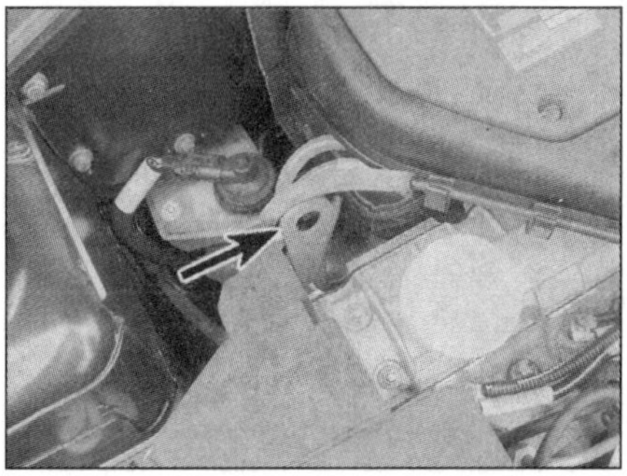

6.35a Right-hand engine lifting eye

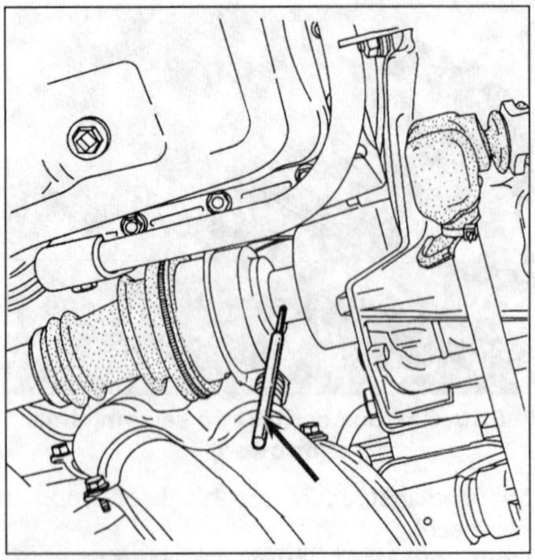

6.35b Using a pin punch (arrowed) to drive out the driveshaft roll pin

37 Separate the gearbox/transmission from the engine with reference to Chapter 7A or 7B **(see illustration)**.

Refitting

38 Refitting is a reversal of removal, with reference to the Chapters needed for removal, but tighten all nuts and bolts to the specified torque. When attaching the subframe to the underbody, the use of 100 mm long rods temporarily screwed into the nuts will help alignment of the bolt holes. With the front of the subframe aligned, the rear bolts can be inserted, then the temporary rods can be removed and the front bolts inserted. Refer to Chapter 10 when connecting the steering column to the steering gear. Top-up the power steering fluid level as described in Chapter 1B. Fill the engine with fresh oil and fill the cooling system with coolant with reference to Chapter 1A. On manual gearbox models, refill the gearbox with oil with reference to Chapter 7A. On automatic transmission models, fill the automatic transmission with fresh fluid with reference to Chapter 7B. Before taking the vehicle on the road, depress the brake pedal several times to bring the brake pads to their normal position.

7 Engine overhaul – dismantling sequence

1 It is much easier to disassemble and work on the engine if it is mounted on a portable engine stand. These stands can often be hired from a tool hire shop. Before the engine is mounted on a stand, the flywheel/driveplate should be removed from the engine, so that the engine stand bolts can be tightened into the end of the cylinder block.

2 If a stand is not available, it is possible to disassemble the engine with it blocked up on a sturdy workbench or on the floor. Be extra-careful not to tip or drop the engine when working without a stand.

3 If you are going to obtain a reconditioned engine, all the external components must be removed first, and be transferred to the replacement engine (just as they will if you are doing a complete engine overhaul yourself).

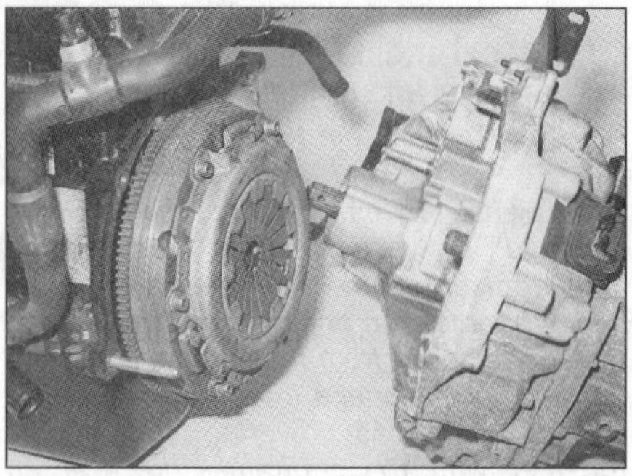

6.37 Separating the gearbox from the engine

Check with the engine supplier for details. Normally these components include:

Petrol engine models

a) Alternator and brackets.
b) HT leads and spark plugs (see Chapters 1A and 5B).
c) Thermostat and cover (see Chapter 3).
d) Fuel injection equipment.
e) Inlet and exhaust manifolds.
f) Oil filter.
g) Engine mountings, lifting brackets and hose brackets **(see illustration).**
h) Ancillary (power steering pump, air conditioning compressor) brackets **(see illustration).**
i) Oil filler tube and dipstick **(see illustrations).**
j) Coolant pipes and hoses **(see illustration).**
k) Flywheel (or driveplate where applicable) (see Chapter 2A or 2B).

7.3a Removing the front engine lifting bracket – K7M/K4J/K4M engine

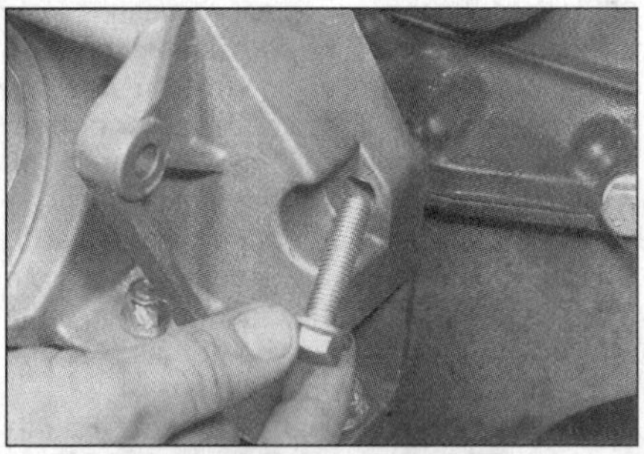

7.3b Removing the power-assisted steering pump bracket from the engine – K7M/K4J/K4M engine

7.3c On the K7M/K4J/K4M engine, unscrew the bolt . . .

7.3d . . . lift the oil filler tube and dipstick from the front cover . . .

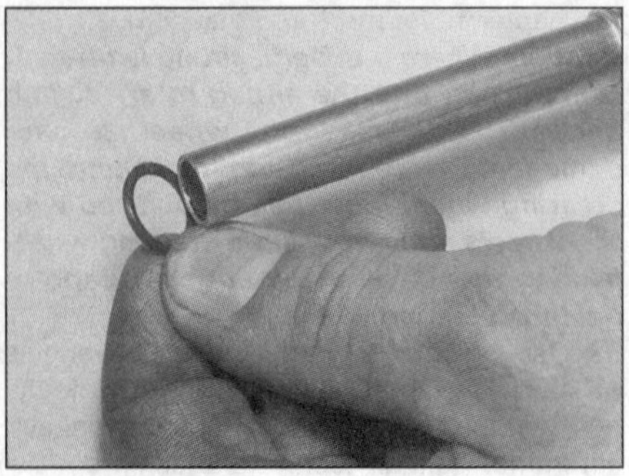

7.3e . . . and remove the sealing O-ring

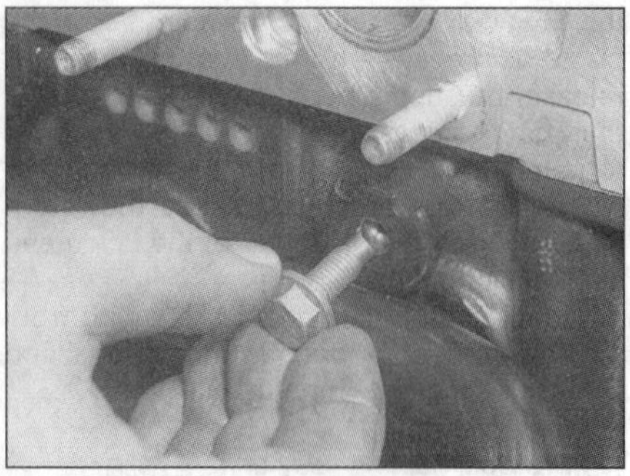

7.3f Unbolting the coolant pipe from the cylinder block

Diesel engine models

a) *Alternator mounting bracket.*
b) *Fuel injection pump and mounting bracket, fuel injectors and glow plugs (see Chapters 4B and 5C).*
c) *Thermostat and cover (see Chapter 3).*
d) *Inlet and exhaust manifolds (see Chapter 4B).*
e) *Oil cooler (see Chapter 2C).*
f) *Engine mountings, lifting brackets and hose brackets.*
g) *Ancillary (power steering pump, air conditioning compressor) brackets.*
h) *Oil pressure warning light switch and oil level sensor (where applicable) (see Chapter 5A).*
i) *Coolant temperature sensors (see Chapter 3).*
j) *Wiring harnesses and brackets.*
k *Oil filler tube and dipstick.*
l) *Coolant pipes and hoses (see Chapter 3).*
m) *Flywheel (see Chapter 2C).*

Note: *When removing the external components from the engine, pay close attention to details that may be helpful or important during refitting. Note the fitted position of gaskets, seals, spacers, pins, washers, bolts and other small items.*

4 If you are obtaining a 'short' motor (which, when available, consists of the engine cylinder block, crankshaft, pistons and connecting rods all assembled), then the cylinder head, sump, oil pump and timing belt will have to be removed also.

5 If you are planning a complete overhaul, the engine can be disassembled and the internal components removed in the following order:

a) *Inlet and exhaust manifolds.*
b) *Timing belt and pulleys and water pump **(see illustration)**.*
c) *Cylinder head **(see illustration)**.*
d) *Flywheel/driveplate.*
e) *Sump.*
f) *Oil pump.*
g) *Pistons.*
h) *Crankshaft.*

6 Before beginning the disassembly and overhaul procedures, make sure that you have all of the correct tools necessary. Refer to the *Tool and working facilities* at the end of this manual for further information.

7.5a Unbolting the water pump from the cylinder block – K7M/K4J/K4M engine

7.5b Removing the cylinder head – K7M/K4J/K4M engine

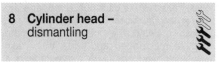

8 Cylinder head – dismantling

Note: *New and reconditioned cylinder heads are available from the manufacturers and from engine overhaul specialists. Due to the fact that some specialist tools are required for the dismantling and inspection procedures and new components may not be readily available, it may be more practical and economical for the home mechanic to purchase a reconditioned head rather than dismantle, inspect and recondition the original head.*

Petrol engines

1 Referring to Chapter 2A or 2B, as applicable, remove the camshaft(s).

Diesel engines

2 Remove the brake vacuum pump (see Chapter 9), the fuel injectors and injection pump, if removed with the cylinder head (Chapter 4B), and the camshaft and tappets (Chapter 2C).

All engines

3 Using a valve spring compressor, compress each valve spring in turn until the split collets can be removed. Release the compressor and lift off the cap, spring and spring seat. If, when the valve spring compressor is screwed down, the valve spring cap refuses to free and expose the split collets, gently tap the top of the tool, directly over the cap, with a light hammer. This will free the cap **(see illustrations)**.

4 Withdraw the oil seal from the top of the valve guide, then remove the valve through the combustion chamber **(see illustrations)**.

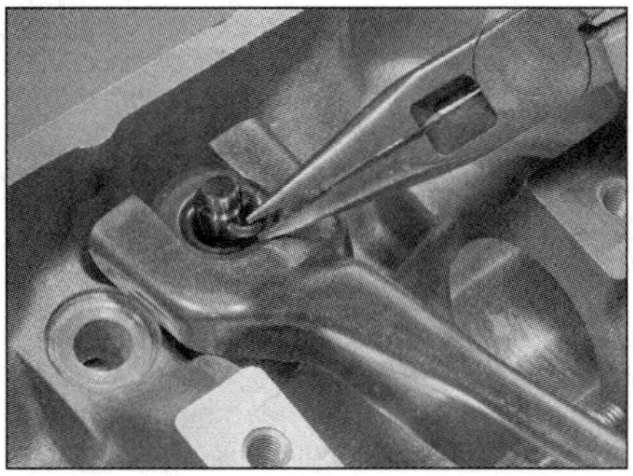

8.3a Removing the split collets . . .

8.3b . . . and lift off the cap and valve spring . . .

8.3c . . . followed by the spring seat

8.4a Removing the oil seal from the top of the valve guide

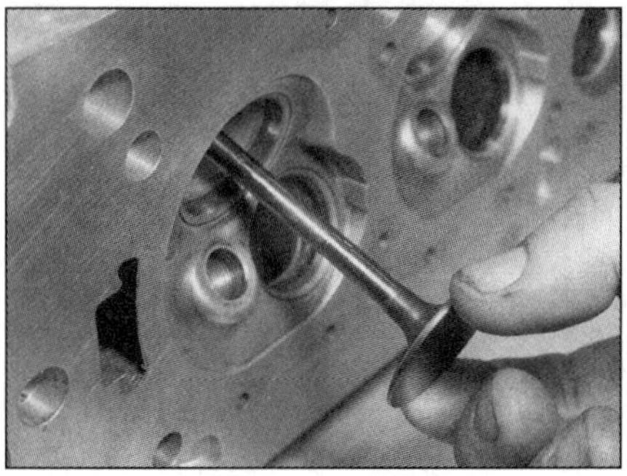

8.4b Withdrawing a valve from the combustion chamber

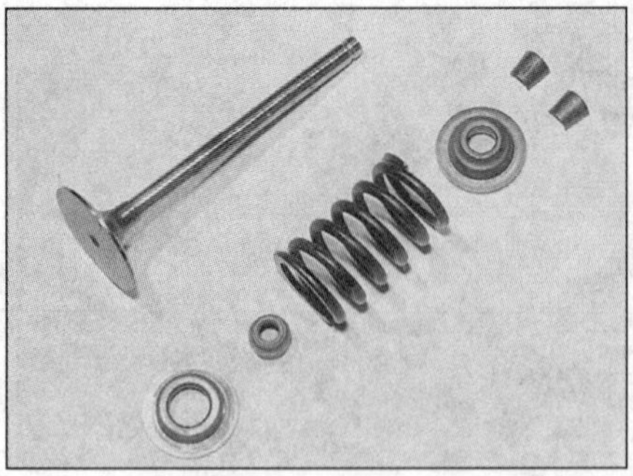

8.5a Valve components

8.5b Store the valve components in a labelled polythene bag

5 It is essential that the valves and associated components are kept in their correct sequence, unless they are so badly worn that they are to be renewed. If they are going to be kept and used again, place them in labelled polythene bags, or in a compartmented box **(see illustrations)**.

9 Cylinder head and valves – cleaning, inspection and renovation

1 Thorough cleaning of the cylinder head and valve components, followed by a detailed inspection, will enable you to decide how much valve service work must be carried out during the engine overhaul.

Cleaning

2 Scrape away all traces of old gasket material and sealing compound from the cylinder head. Take care not to damage the cylinder head surfaces.

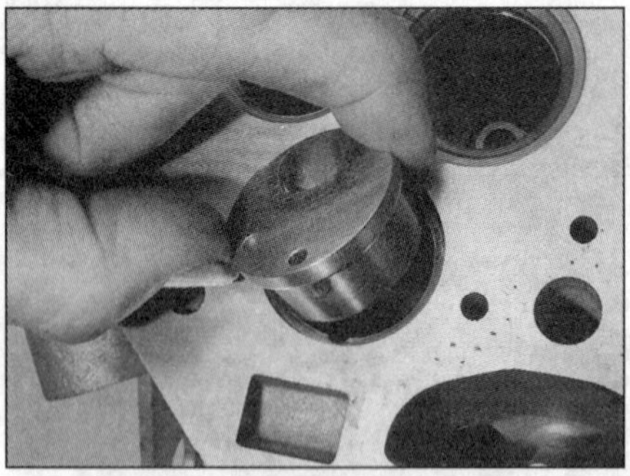

9.5 Removing a swirl chamber – F8Q engine

3 Scrape away the carbon from the combustion chambers and ports, then wash the cylinder head thoroughly with paraffin or a suitable solvent.

4 Scrape off any heavy carbon deposits that may have formed on the valves, then use a power-operated wire brush to remove deposits from the valve heads and stems.

5 On diesel engines, the swirl chambers should be removed from their locations if they are loose (if this is done, mark the swirl chambers so that they can be refitted in their original locations) **(see illustration)**.

6 If the head is extremely dirty, it should be steam-cleaned. On completion, make sure that all oil holes and oil galleries are cleaned.

Inspection and renovation

Note: *Be sure to perform all the following inspection procedures before concluding that the services of an engine overhaul specialist are required. Make a list of all items that require attention.*

Cylinder head

7 Inspect the head very carefully for cracks, evidence of coolant leakage and other damage. If cracks are found, a new cylinder head should be obtained.

8 Use a straight-edge and feeler gauge to check that the cylinder head surface is not distorted. On diesel engines, do not position the straight-edge over the swirl chambers, as these may be proud of the cylinder head face. If the specified distortion limit is exceeded, machining of the gasket face is not recommended by the manufacturers, so the only course of action is to renew the cylinder head. Check that the overall height of the cylinder head is as specified, which will indicate if the head has been machined in a mistaken attempt to compensate for surface distortion **(see illustrations)**.

9 Examine the valve seats in each of the combustion chambers. If they are severely pitted, cracked or burned, then they will need to be renewed or re-cut by an engine overhaul specialist. If they are only slightly pitted, this can be removed by grinding the valve heads and seats together with coarse, then fine, grinding paste as described below. Note that on diesel engines the valve seats can only be re-cut to a limited depth, to avoid decreasing the compression ratio. Using a dial test indicator, check that valve depth below the cylinder head gasket surface is within the limits given in the Specifications **(see illustration)**.

10 If the valve guides are worn, indicated by a side-to-side motion of the valve in the guide, new guides must be fitted. A dial gauge may be used to determine the amount of side play of the valve. Recheck the fit using a new valve if in doubt, to decide whether it is the valve or the guide which is worn. If new guides are to be fitted, the valves must be renewed in any case. Valve guides may be renewed using a press and a suitable mandrel, making sure that they are at the correct height. The work is best carried out by an engine overhaul specialist, since if it is not done skilfully, there is a risk of damaging the cylinder head.

11 On diesel engines, inspect the swirl chambers for burning or cracks. If required, the chambers can be renewed by an engine overhaul specialist. Using a dial test indicator check that the swirl chamber protrusion is within the limits given in the Specifications. Zero the dial test indicator on the gasket surface of the cylinder head, then measure the protrusion of the swirl chamber **(see illustrations)**.

12 Where applicable, check for wear the follower bores in the cylinder head. If excessive wear is evident, the cylinder head must be renewed.

13 Examine the camshaft bearing surfaces in the cylinder head (and bearing caps/carriers

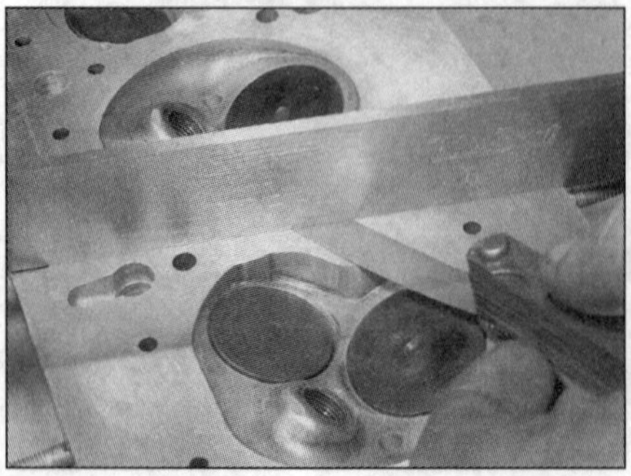

9.8a Checking the cylinder head surface for distortion with feeler blades

9.8b Checking the overall height of the cylinder head – F8Q engine

9.9 Measuring the valve depth – F8Q engine

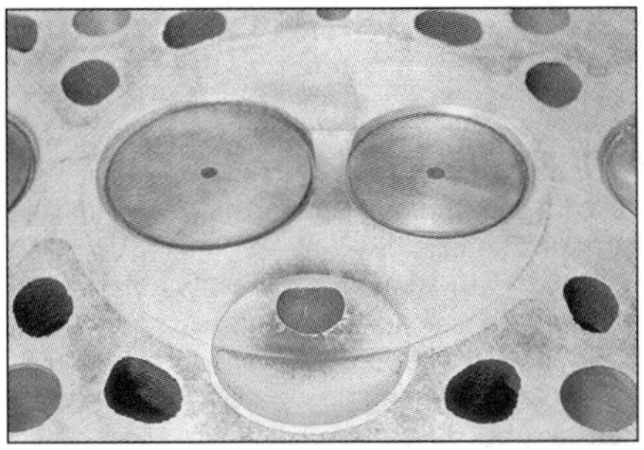

9.11a This swirl chamber shows the initial stages of cracking and burning – F8Q engine

9.11b Measuring the swirl chamber protrusion using a dial gauge – F8Q engine

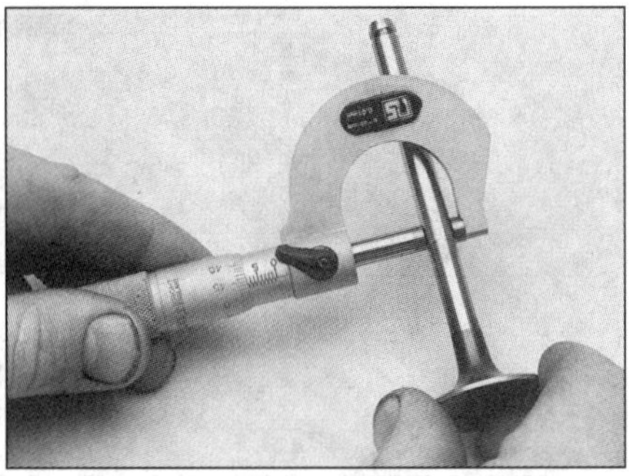

9.14 Measuring a valve stem using a micrometer

where applicable). Wear here can only be corrected by renewing the head. Also examine the camshaft as described in Chapter 2A, 2B or 2C.

Valves

14 Examine the head of each valve for pitting, burning, cracks and general wear and check the valve stem for scoring and wear ridges. Rotate the valve and check for any obvious indication that it is bent. Look for pits and excessive wear on the end of each valve stem. If the valve appears satisfactory at this stage, measure the valve stem diameter at several points using a micrometer **(see illustration)**. Any significant difference in the readings obtained indicates wear of the valve stem. Should any of these conditions be apparent, the valve(s) must be renewed. If the valves are in satisfactory condition, or if new valves are being fitted, they should be ground (lapped) into their respective seats to ensure a smooth gas-tight seal.

15 Valve grinding is carried out as follows. Place the cylinder head upside-down on a bench, with a block of wood at each end to give clearance for the valve stems.

16 Smear a trace of coarse carborundum paste on the seat face and press a suction grinding tool onto the valve head. With a semi-rotary action, grind the valve head to its seat, lifting the valve occasionally to redistribute the grinding paste **(see illustration)**. When a dull-matt even surface is produced on both the valve seat and the valve, wipe off the paste and repeat the process with fine carborundum paste. A light spring placed under the valve head will greatly ease this operation. When a smooth unbroken ring of light grey matt finish is produced on both the valve and seat, the grinding operation is complete. Be sure to remove all traces of grinding paste, using paraffin or a suitable solvent, before reassembly of the cylinder head.

Valve components

17 Examine the valve springs for signs of damage and discoloration and also measure their free length using vernier calipers or a steel rule **(see illustration)** or by comparing the existing spring with a new component.

18 Stand each spring on a flat surface and check it for squareness. If any of the springs are damaged, distorted or have lost their tension, obtain a complete new set of springs. It is normal to renew the springs as a matter of course during a major overhaul.

9.16 Grinding a valve to its seat – lift the valve to redistribute the paste

9.17 Checking a valve spring free length

19 Where applicable, check the followers and the shims for scoring, pitting (especially on the shims) and wear ridges. Renew any components as necessary. Some scuffing is to be expected and is acceptable provided that the followers are not scored.

Rocker arm components – D7F, E7J and K7M engines

20 Check the rocker arm contact surfaces for pits, wear, score marks or any indication that the surface-hardening has worn through. Dismantle the rocker shaft and check the rocker arm and rocker shaft pivot and contact areas in the same way. Measure the internal diameter of each rocker and check their fit on the shaft. Clean out the oil spill holes in each rocker using a length of wire. Renew the rocker arm or the rocker shaft itself if any are suspect.

Valve stem oil seals

21 The valve stem oil seals should be renewed as a matter of course.

10 Cylinder head – reassembly

1 On diesel engines, if the swirl chambers have been removed, refit them to their original locations.

2 Lubricate the valve stem oil seals with clean engine oil, then fit them by pushing into position in the cylinder head using a suitable socket or special tool **(see illustrations)**. Ensure that the seals are fully engaged with the valve guide.

10.2a Fitting the valve stem oil seals to the valve guides

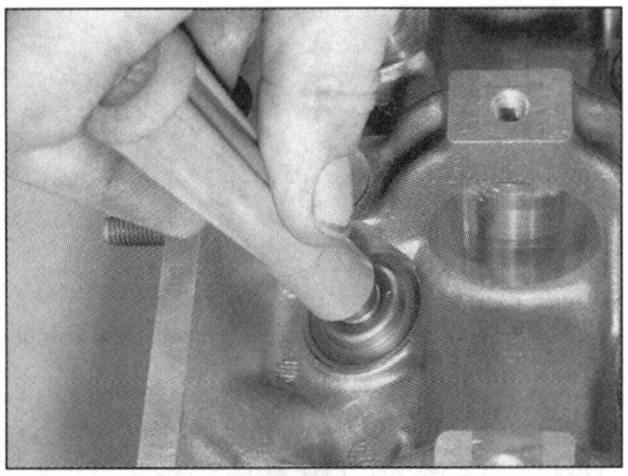

10.2b Using a special tool to fit the valve stem oil seals

10.3 Lubricate the valve stems before inserting the valves

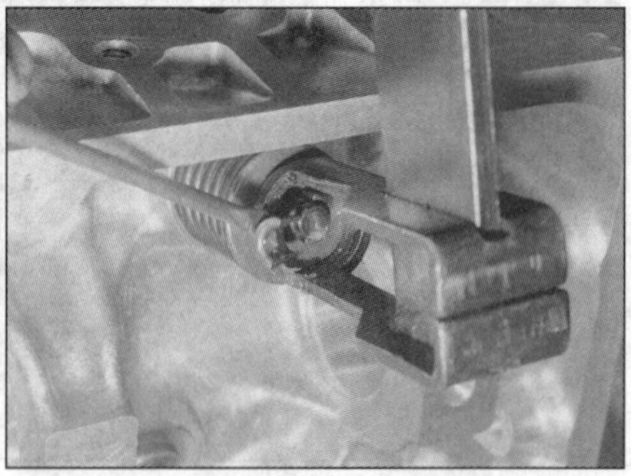

10.5 Use a little grease to hold the collets in place

3 Insert the valves into their original locations. If new valves are being fitted, insert them into the locations to which they have been ground. Take care not to damage the valve stem oil seal as each valve is fitted **(see illustration)**.

4 Locate the spring seat on the guide, followed by the spring and cap.

5 Compress the valve spring and locate the split collets in the recess in the valve stem. Release the compressor, then repeat the procedure on the remaining valves. Use a little grease to hold the collets in place **(see illustration)**.

6 With all the valves installed, place the cylinder head flat on the bench and, using a hammer and interposed block of wood, tap the end of each valve stem to settle the components.

7 The previously-removed components can now be refitted with reference to paragraphs 1 or 2 (as applicable) of Section 8.

11 Auxiliary shaft – removal and refitting

Note: *The following procedure is applicable only to early diesel engines. A new timing belt, auxiliary shaft oil seal, housing gasket (or suitable sealant, as applicable) and oil pump drivegear cover plate O-ring will be required on refitting.*

Removal

1 With the engine removed from the vehicle, proceed as follows.

2 Remove the timing belt (see Chapter 2C).

3 Remove the auxiliary shaft sprocket with reference to Chapter 2C.

4 Unbolt the timing belt lower inner cover and remove it.

5 Unscrew the four bolts and withdraw the auxiliary shaft housing **(see illustrations)**, then remove the gasket (if fitted). Note that the housing locates on two dowels.

6 Unscrew the two bolts and withdraw the oil pump drivegear cover plate/breather noting the location of the O-ring. Withdraw the drivegear from its location. Use a screwdriver or similar tool to hook the drivegear out if necessary **(see illustrations)**.

7 Unscrew the two bolts and washers and lift out the auxiliary shaft thrustplate and the auxiliary shaft **(see illustrations)**.

Inspection

8 Examine the auxiliary shaft and oil pump driveshaft for pitting, scoring or wear ridges on the bearing journals and for chipping or wear of the gear teeth. Renew as necessary.

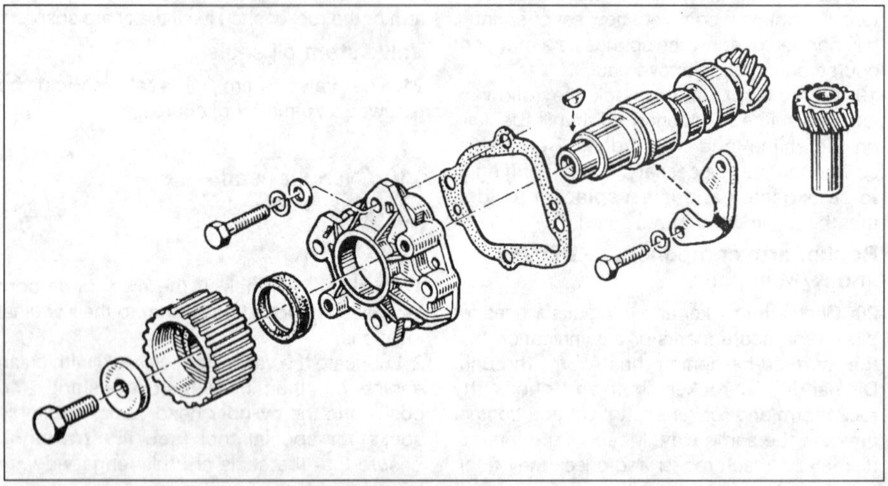

11.5a Auxiliary shaft components

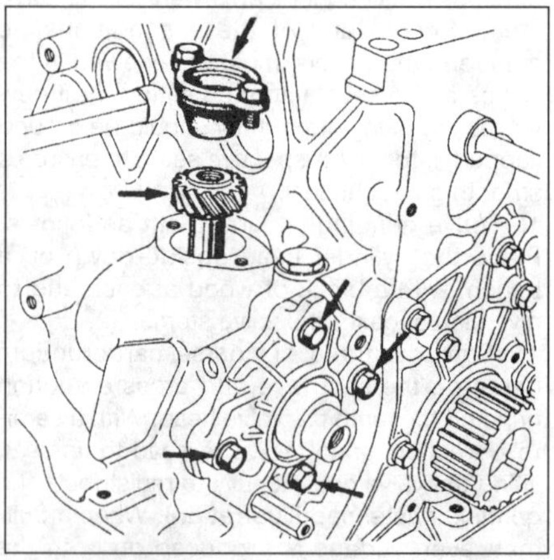

11.5b Auxiliary shaft housing retaining bolt locations, oil pump driveshaft and cover plate

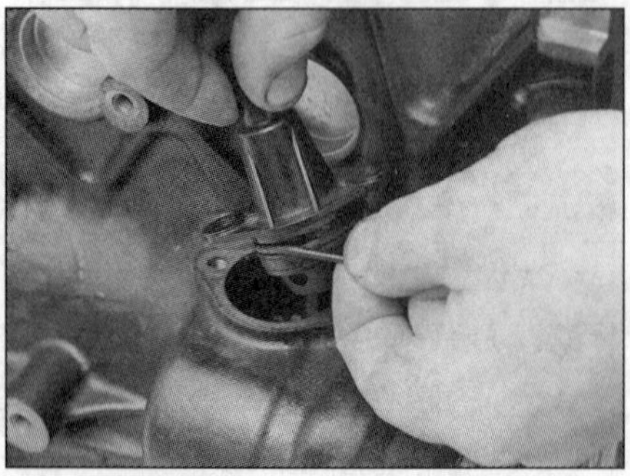

11.6a Removing the oil pump drivegear cover plate/breather and O-ring

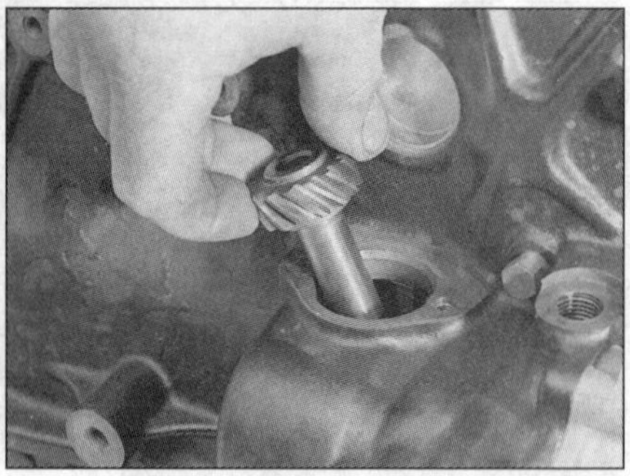

11.6b Removing the oil pump drivegear

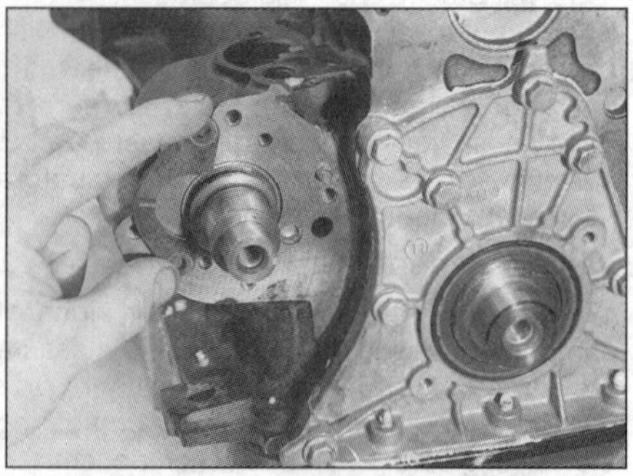

11.7a Removing the auxiliary shaft thrustplate . . .

11.7b . . . and the auxiliary shaft

11.9 Measuring the auxiliary shaft endfloat with a feeler blade

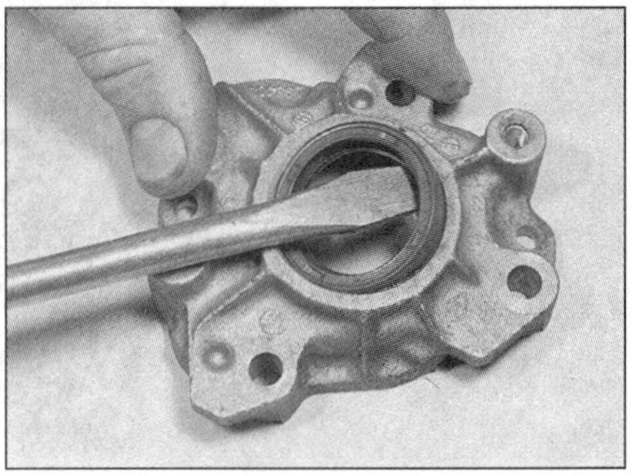

11.10a Prising the auxiliary shaft oil seal from the housing

11.10b Fitting a new auxiliary shaft oil seal

11.13 Auxiliary shaft gasket positioned over the dowels

11.14 Refitting the auxiliary shaft housing. Note tape around front of shaft

Check the auxiliary shaft bearings in the cylinder block for wear and, if worn, have these renewed by your Renault dealer or suitably-equipped engineering works. Wipe them clean if they are still serviceable.

9 Temporarily fit the thrustplate to its position on the auxiliary shaft and use a feeler gauge to check that the endfloat is as given in the Specifications **(see illustration)**. If it is greater than the upper tolerance, a new thrustplate should be obtained, but first check the thrust surfaces on the shaft to ascertain if wear has occurred here.

Refitting

10 Clean off all traces of the old gasket or sealant from the auxiliary shaft housing and prise out the oil seal with a screwdriver. Install the new oil seal using a block of wood, or a suitable socket and tap it in until it is flush with the outer face of the housing. The open side of the seal must be towards the engine **(see illustrations)**.

11 Liberally lubricate the auxiliary shaft and slide it into its bearings.

12 Place the thrustplate in position with its curved edge away from the crankshaft and refit the two retaining bolts, tightening them securely.

13 Place a new housing gasket in position over the dowels of the cylinder block **(see illustration)**. If a gasket was not used previously, apply a bead of CAF 4/60 THIXO sealant (or an alternative) to the housing mating face.

14 Wind a length of tape around the end of the auxiliary shaft, to prevent damage to the oil seal as the housing is refitted. Liberally lubricate the oil seal lips and then locate the housing in place, engaging it with the dowels **(see illustration)**. Refit and tighten the housing retaining bolts progressively in a diagonal sequence. Remove the tape from the end of the shaft.

15 Lubricate the oil pump drivegear and lower the gear into its location. Ensure that the splines on the drivegear engage with the oil pump.

16 Inspect the O-ring seal on the oil pump drivegear cover plate/breather and renew it if necessary. Fit the cover plate/breather and secure with the two retaining bolts.

17 Refit the timing belt lower inner cover to the cylinder block and tighten the bolts.

18 Refit the auxiliary shaft sprocket with reference to Chapter 2C.

19 Fit the new timing belt as described in Chapter 2C.

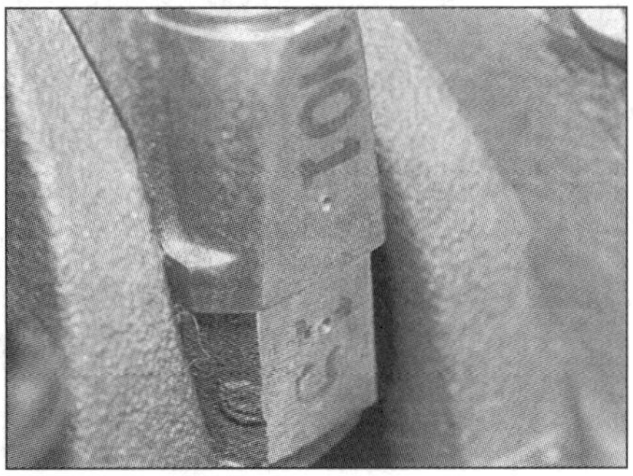

12.2 Big-end caps marked with a centre-punch

12 Piston/connecting rod assemblies - removal

2D

1 With the cylinder head, sump and oil pump removed (see Chapter 2A, 2B or 2C), proceed as follows. On the E7J engine, make sure the liner clamps are in position.

2 Rotate the crankshaft so that No 1 big-end cap (nearest the flywheel/driveplate position) is at the lowest point of its travel. If the big-end cap and rod are not already numbered, mark them with a centre-punch **(see illustration)**. Mark both cap and rod to identify the cylinder they operate in.

3 Before removing the big-end caps, check the amount of side play between the caps and the crankshaft webs **(see illustration)**.

4 Unscrew the big-end bearing cap nuts (E7J and K7M engines) or bolts (all other

12.3 Checking the side play between a big-end cap and the crankshaft web with a feeler blade

12.4 Removing a big-end bearing cap

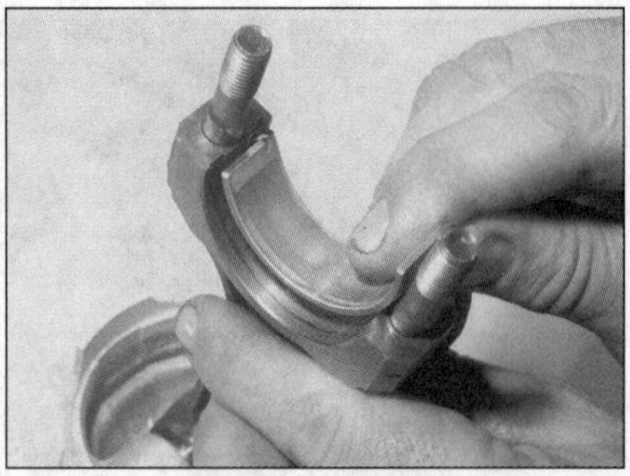

12.5 Removing a big-end bearing upper shell

engines). Withdraw the cap, complete with shell bearing, from the connecting rod. Strike the cap with a wooden or copper mallet if it is stuck **(see illustration)**.

5 If only the bearing shells are being attended to, push the connecting rod up and off the crankpin and remove the upper bearing shell **(see illustration)**. Keep the bearing shells and cap together in their correct sequence if they are to be refitted.

E7J engine

6 Remove the liner clamps and withdraw each liner, together with piston and connecting rod, from the top of the cylinder block. Mark the liners using masking tape, so that they may be refitted in their original locations.

7 Withdraw the piston from the bottom of the liner. Keep each piston with its respective liner if they are to be re-used.

8 Repeat the procedure for the remaining piston/connecting rod assemblies. Ensure that the caps and rods are marked before removal, as described previously and keep all components in order.

All other engines

9 Push the connecting rod up and remove the piston and rod from the bore. Note that if there is a pronounced wear ridge at the top of the bore, there is a risk of damaging the piston as the rings foul the ridge. However, it is reasonable to assume that a rebore and new pistons will be required in any case if the ridge is so pronounced.

10 Repeat the procedure for the remaining piston/connecting rod assemblies. Ensure that the caps and rods are marked before removal, as described previously, and keep all components in order.

13 Crankshaft - removal

1 Remove the timing belt, crankshaft sprocket, oil pump and flywheel/driveplate. The pistons/connecting rods must be free of the crankshaft journals, however it is not essential to remove them completely from the cylinder block.

2 Unbolt the timing belt lower inner cover (where fitted), then unscrew the securing bolts/ nuts and remove the crankshaft timing belt end oil seal housing and oil seal – refer if necessary to the relevant Sections of Parts A, B and C of this Chapter **(see illustration)**.

3 Before the crankshaft is removed, check the endfloat using a dial gauge in contact with the end of the crankshaft **(see illustration)**. Push the crankshaft fully one way and then zero the gauge. Push the crankshaft fully the other way and check the endfloat. The result can be compared with the specified amount and will give an indication as to whether new thrustwashers are required.

4 If a dial gauge is not available, feeler gauges can be used. First push the crankshaft fully towards the flywheel/driveplate end of the engine, then slip the feeler gauge between the web of No 2 crankpin and the thrustwasher of the centre main bearing (E7J, K4J, K7M and K4M engines), or between the web of No 1 crankpin and the thrustwasher of No 2 main bearing (all other engines).

5 Identification numbers should already be cast onto the base of each main bearing cap. If not, number the cap and crankcase using a centre-punch, as was done for the connecting rods and caps **(see illustration)**.

6 Unscrew the main bearing cap retaining bolts and withdraw the caps, complete with bearing shells **(see illustration)**. Tap the caps with a wooden or copper mallet if they are stuck. Note on the diesel engines, No 1 main bearing cap (flywheel/driveplate end) is secured by Allen bolts and sealed to the cylinder block using silicon sealant or butyl seals.

7 Carefully lift the crankshaft from the crankcase **(see illustration)**.

13.2 Unscrewing the nuts/bolts securing the crankshaft timing belt end oil seal housing – K7M/K4J/K4M engine

13.3 Checking the crankshaft endfloat with a dial gauge

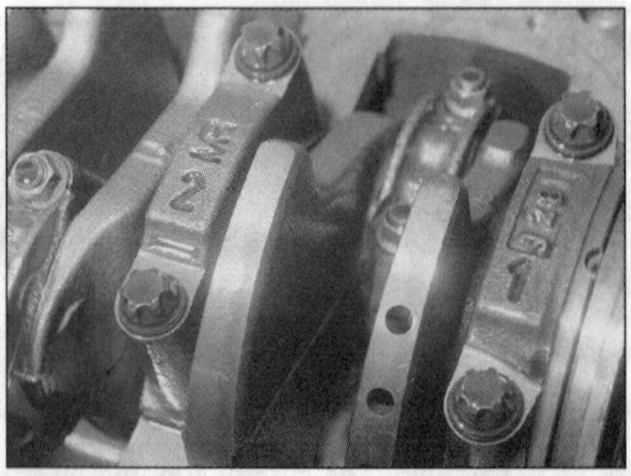

13.5 The main bearing caps are numbered for position

13.6 Removing a main bearing cap bolt

13.7 Lifting the crankshaft from the crankcase

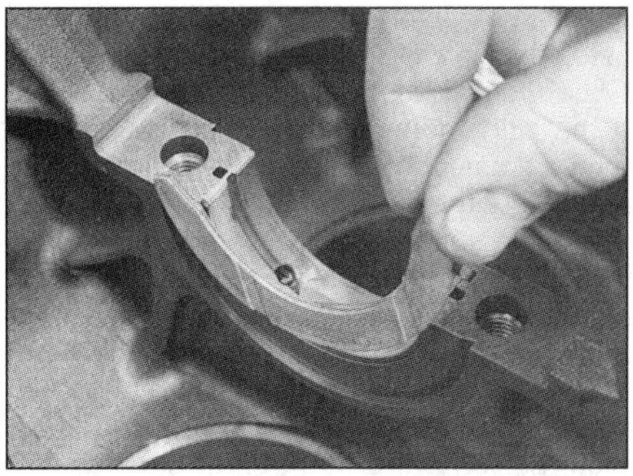

13.8 Removing the crankshaft thrustwashers

8 Remove the thrustwashers at each side of the centre main bearing (petrol engines) or No 2 main bearing (diesel engines), then remove the bearing shell upper halves from the crankcase **(see illustration)**. Place each shell with its respective bearing cap.

9 Remove the oil seal from the flywheel/driveplate end of the crankshaft.

14 Cylinder block/ crankcase and bores - cleaning and inspection

Cleaning

1 For complete cleaning, the core plugs should be removed. Drill a small hole in them, then insert a self-tapping screw and pull out the plugs using a pair of grips or a slide-hammer. Also remove all external components and sensors (if not already done), noting their locations. As applicable unbolt the drivebelt tensioner bracket, coolant pipe and oil cooler from the cylinder block. On diesel engines, remove the piston oil spray jets from the bottom of each bore by unscrewing the securing bolts **(see illustration)**.

2 Scrape all traces of gasket or sealant from the cylinder block, taking care not to damage the head and sump mating faces.

3 If the block is extremely dirty, it should be steam-cleaned.

4 After the block has been steam-cleaned, clean all oil holes and oil galleries one more time. Flush all internal passages with warm water until the water runs clear, dry the block thoroughly and wipe all machined surfaces with a light rust-preventative oil. If you have access to compressed air, use it to speed up the drying process and to blow out all the oil holes and galleries.

Warning: Wear eye protection when using compressed air.

5 If the block is not very dirty, you can do an adequate cleaning job with hot soapy water and a stiff brush. Take plenty of time and do a thorough job. Regardless of the cleaning method used, be sure to clean all oil holes and galleries very thoroughly, dry the block completely and coat all machined surfaces with light oil.

6 The threaded holes in the block must be clean to ensure accurate torque wrench readings during reassembly. Run the proper-size tap into each of the holes to remove rust, corrosion, thread sealant or sludge and to restore damaged threads. If possible, use compressed air to clear the holes of debris produced by this operation. Now is a good time to clean the threads on the head bolts and the main bearing cap bolts as well.

7 Refit the main bearing caps and tighten the bolts finger-tight.

8 After coating the mating surfaces of the new core plugs with suitable sealant, refit them in the cylinder block. Make sure that they are driven in straight and seated properly, or leakage could result. Special tools are available for this purpose, but a large socket, with an outside diameter that will just slip into the core plug, will work just as well.

9 On diesel engines, check the gauze filters and the oil holes in the piston oil spray jet securing bolts and the oil holes in the jets themselves for blockage **(see illustrations)**. Clean if necessary, then refit the jets and tighten the securing bolts to the specified torque wrench setting. Ensure the locating pegs on the jets engage with the corresponding holes in the cylinder block.

10 If the engine is not going to be reassembled right away, cover it with a large plastic bag to keep it clean and prevent it rusting.

Inspection

11 Visually check the block for cracks, rust and corrosion. Look for stripped threads in the threaded holes. If there has been any history of internal water leakage, it may be worthwhile having an engine overhaul specialist check the block with special equipment. If defects are found, have the block repaired, if possible, or renewed.

12 Check the cylinder bores/liners for scuffing and scoring. Normally, bore wear will show up in the form of a wear ridge at the top of the bore. This ridge marks the limit of piston travel.

13 Measure the diameter of each cylinder at the top (just under the ridge area), centre and bottom of the cylinder bore, parallel to the crankshaft axis.

14 Next measure each cylinder's diameter at the same three locations across the crankshaft axis. If the difference between any of the measurements is greater than 0.20 mm, indicating that the cylinder is excessively out-of-round or tapered, then remedial action must be considered.

15 Repeat this procedure for the remaining cylinders.

16 If the cylinder walls are badly scuffed or scored, or if they are excessively out-of-round or tapered, obtain new cylinder liners (E7J engine) or have the cylinder block rebored (all other engines). New pistons (oversize in the case of a rebore) will also be required.

17 If the cylinders are in reasonably good condition, then it may only be necessary to renew the piston rings.

18 If this is the case, the bores should be honed in order to allow the new rings to bed-in correctly and provide the best possible seal. The conventional type of hone has spring-loaded stones and is used with a power drill. You will also need some paraffin or honing oil and rags. The hone should be moved up and down the cylinder to produce a crosshatch pattern and plenty of honing oil should be used. Ideally, the crosshatch lines should intersect at approximately a 60° angle. Do not take off more material than is necessary to produce the required finish. If new pistons are being fitted, the piston manufacturers may specify a finish with a different angle, so their instructions should be followed. Do not withdraw the hone from the cylinder while it is still being turned, but stop it first (keep moving the drill up and down until

2D

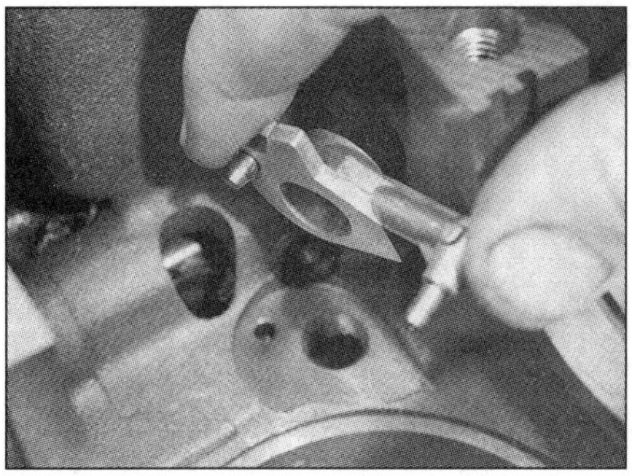

14.1 Removing a piston oil spray jet - F8Q engine

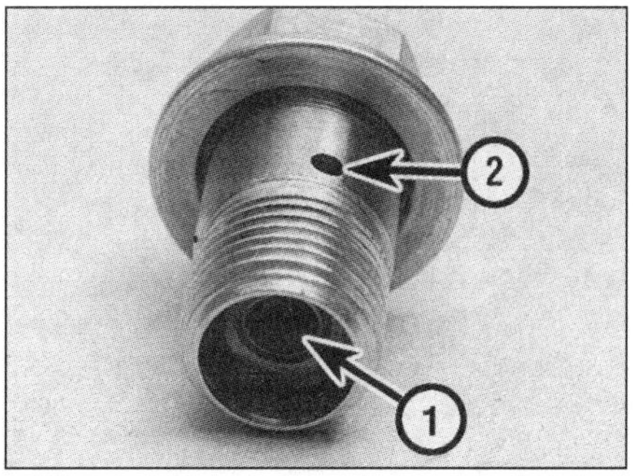

14.9a Check the gauze filters (1) and the oil holes (2) in the oil spray jet bolts . . .

14.9b . . . and the oil holes (arrowed) in the jets for blockage

14.19a Checking the liner protrusion with a dial gauge . . .

the hone stops). After honing a cylinder, wipe out all traces of the honing oil. If equipment of this type is not available, or if you are not sure whether you are competent to undertake the task yourself, an engine overhaul specialist will carry out the work at a moderate cost.

19 Before refitting the cylinder liners to the E7J engine, their protrusions must be checked as follows and new base O-rings fitted. Place the liner without a base O-ring in the cylinder block and press down to make sure that it is seated correctly. Using a dial gauge or straight-edge and feeler blade, check that the protrusion of the liner above the upper surface of the cylinder block is within the specified limits **(see illustrations)**. Check all of the liners in the same manner and record the protrusions. Note that there is also a limit specified for the difference of protrusion between two adjacent liners. If new liners are being fitted, it is permitted to interchange them to bring this difference within limits. The protrusions may be stepped upwards or downwards from the flywheel end of the engine.

20 Refit all external components and sensors in their correct locations, as noted before removal.

15 Piston/connecting rod assemblies – inspection and reassembly

Inspection

1 Before the inspection process can begin,

14.19b . . . and with feeler blades – E7J engine

the piston/connecting rod assemblies must be cleaned and the original piston rings removed from the pistons.

2 Carefully expand the old rings over the top of the pistons. The use of two or three old feeler blades will be helpful in preventing the rings dropping into empty grooves **(see illustration)**. Note that the oil control ring is in two sections.

3 Scrape away all traces of carbon from the top of the piston. A hand-held wire brush or a piece of fine emery cloth can be used once the majority of the deposits have been scraped away.

4 Remove the carbon from the ring grooves in the piston by cleaning them using an old ring. Break the ring in half to do this. Be very careful to remove only the carbon deposits; do not remove any metal, nor nick or scratch the sides of the ring grooves. Protect your fingers – piston rings are sharp.

5 Once the deposits have been removed, clean the piston/connecting rod assembly with paraffin or a suitable solvent and dry thoroughly. Make sure the oil return holes in the ring grooves are clear.

6 If the pistons and cylinder bores are not damaged or worn excessively and if the cylinder block does not need to be rebored or the liners renewed, the original pistons can be re-used. Normal piston wear appears as even vertical wear on the piston thrust surfaces and slight looseness of the top ring in its groove. New piston rings should always be used when the engine is reassembled.

7 Carefully inspect each piston for cracks around the skirt, at the gudgeon pin bosses and at the piston ring lands (between the piston ring grooves).

8 Look for scoring and scuffing on the sides of the skirt, holes in the piston crown and burned areas at the edge of the crown. If the skirt is scored or scuffed, the engine may have been suffering from overheating and/or abnormal combustion, which caused excessively-high operating temperatures. The cooling and lubricating systems should be checked thoroughly. Scorch marks on the sides of the pistons show that blow-by has occurred and the rings are not sealing correctly. A hole in the piston crown is an indication that abnormal combustion (pre-ignition, knocking or detonation) has been occurring. If any of the above problems exist, the causes must be corrected, or the damage will occur again. On petrol engines, the causes may include inlet air leaks, incorrect fuel/air mixture or incorrect ignition timing. On diesel engines incorrect injection pump timing or a faulty injector may be the cause.

9 Corrosion of the piston, in the form of small pits, indicates that coolant is leaking into the combustion chamber and/or the crankcase. Again, the cause must be corrected, or the problem may persist in the rebuilt engine.

10 If new rings are being fitted to old pistons, measure the piston ring-to-groove clearance by placing a new piston ring in each ring groove and measuring the clearance with a feeler gauge. Check the clearance at three or four places around each groove. No values are specified, but if the measured clearance is excessive – say greater than 0.10 mm – new pistons will be required. If the new ring is excessively tight, the most likely cause is dirt remaining in the groove.

11 Check the piston-to-bore/liner clearance by measuring the cylinder bore/liner diameter (see Section 14) and the piston diameter. Measure the piston across the skirt, at 90° to the gudgeon pin, approximately half way down the skirt **(see illustrations)**. Subtract the piston diameter from the bore/liner diameter to obtain the clearance. If this is greater than the figures given in the Specifications, the block will have to be rebored and new pistons and rings fitted. On the E7J engine, new pistons and liners are supplied in matched pairs.

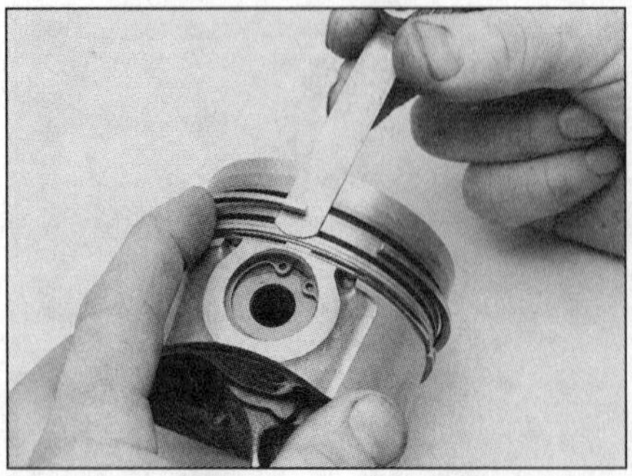

15.2 Removing a piston ring with the aid of a feeler blade

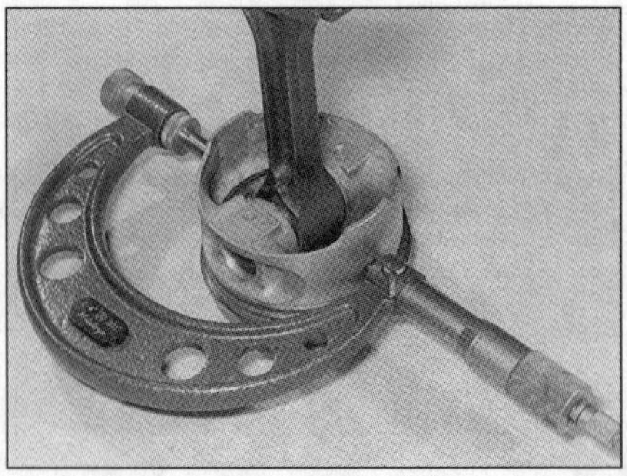

15.11a Measuring a piston diameter using a micrometer

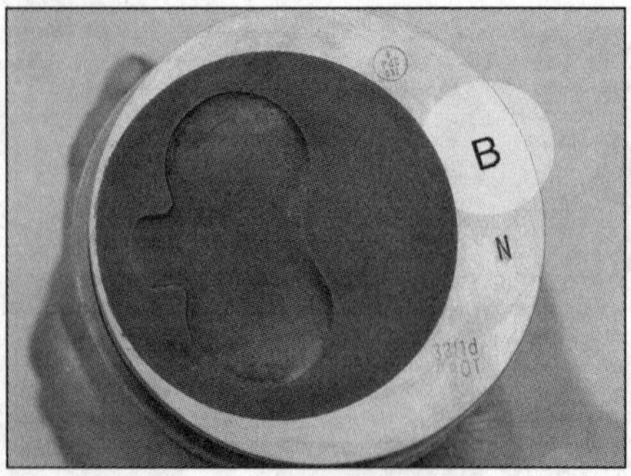

15.11b Piston diameter grade marked on piston crown

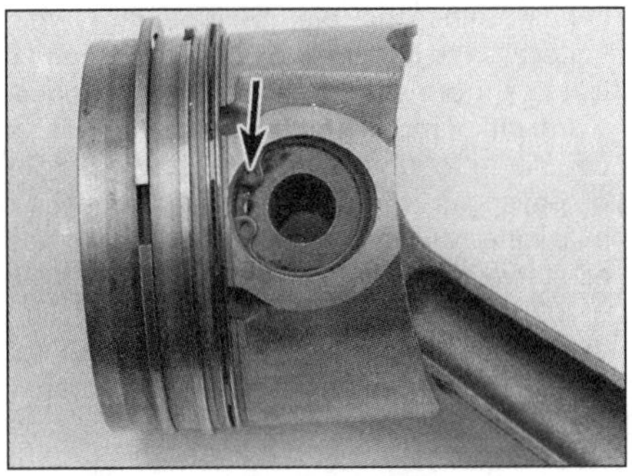

15.12a Gudgeon pin retaining circlip – arrowed

12 Check the fit of the gudgeon pin by twisting the piston and connecting rod in opposite directions. Any noticeable play indicates excessive wear, which must be corrected by separating the pistons and connecting rods as in the case for petrol engines. This operation must be entrusted to a Renault garage or engine overhaul specialist. Note in the case of the diesel engines, the gudgeon pins are secured by circlips, so the pistons and connecting rods can be separated without difficulty. Note the position of the piston relative to the rod before dismantling and use new circlips on reassembly **(see illustrations)**.

13 Before refitting the rings to the pistons, check their end gaps by inserting each of them in their cylinder bores. Use the piston to make sure that they are square **(see illustrations)**. No values are specified, but typical gaps would be of the order of 0.50 mm for compression rings, perhaps somewhat greater for the oil control rings. Renault rings are supplied pre-gapped; no attempt should be made to adjust the gaps by filing.

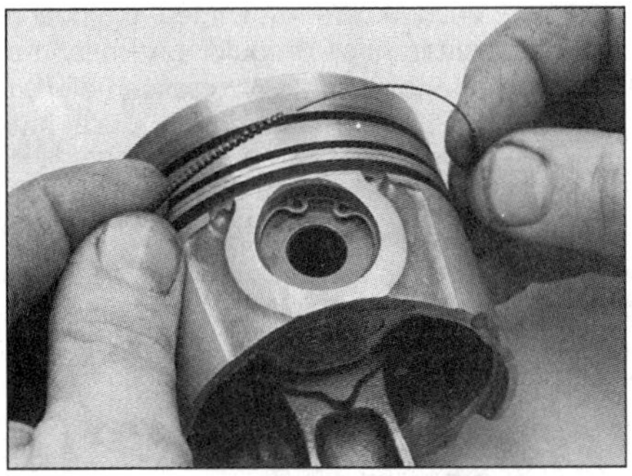

15.14a Fit the oil control ring expander . . .

15.14b . . . followed by the ring

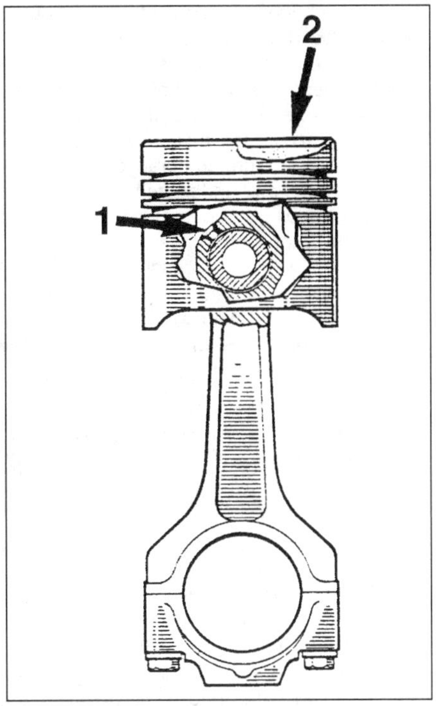

15.12b Oil hole (1) in connecting rod small-end should face away from combustion chamber (2) in piston crown – F8Q engine

Reassembly

14 Install the new rings by fitting them over the top of the piston, starting with the oil control scraper ring **(see illustrations)**. Use feeler blades in the same way as when removing the old rings. Note that the second compression ring is tapered and additionally stepped in the case of the K7M, K4J and K4M engines. Both compression rings must be fitted with the word TOP uppermost. Be careful when handling the compression rings; they will break if they are handled roughly or expanded too far. With all the rings in position, space the ring gaps at 120° to each other.

15 Note that on the E7J engine, if new piston and liner assemblies have been obtained, each piston is matched to its respective liner and they must not be interchanged.

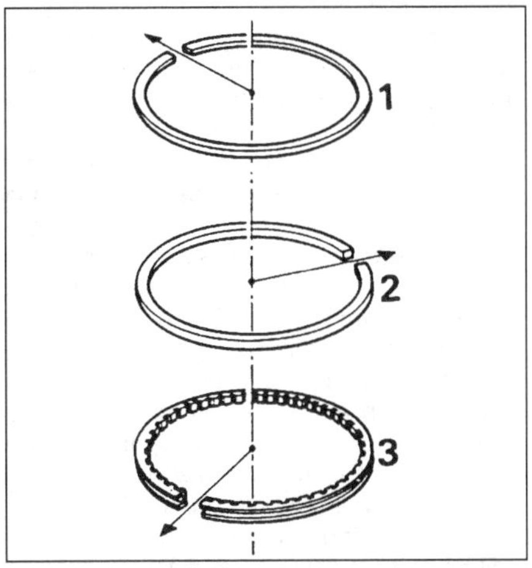

15.14c Position the piston ring end gaps 120° apart

1 Top compression ring
2 Lower compression ring
3 Oil control ring

15.13a Use the piston to push the rings into the cylinder bores . . .

15.13b . . . then measure the ring end gaps

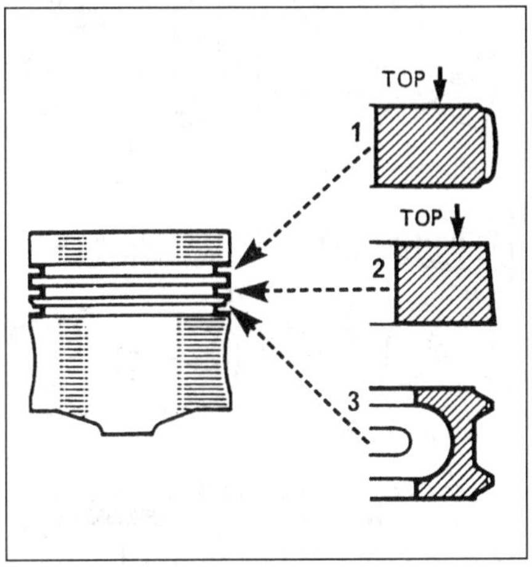

15.14d Piston ring profiles

1 Top compression ring
2 Lower compression ring
3 Oil control ring
Position the TOP markings as shown

16.4 Measuring a main bearing journal diameter using a micrometer

16 Crankshaft - inspection

1 Clean the crankshaft and dry it with compressed air if available. Be sure to clean the oil holes with a pipe cleaner or similar probe.

Warning: Wear eye protection when using compressed air.

2 Check the main and big-end bearing journals for uneven wear, scoring, pitting and cracking.

3 If the crankshaft has been reground, check for burrs around the crankshaft oil holes (the holes are usually chamfered, so burrs should not be a problem unless regrinding has been carried out carelessly). Remove any burrs with a fine file or scraper and thoroughly clean the oil holes as described previously.

4 Using a micrometer, measure the diameter of the main bearing and connecting rod journals and compare the results with the Specifications **(see illustration)**. By measuring the diameter at a number of points around each journal's circumference, you will be able to determine whether or not the journal is out-of-round. Take the measurement at each end of the journal, near the webs, to determine if the journal is tapered. If any of the measurements vary by more than 0.025 mm, the crankshaft will have to be reground and undersize bearings fitted.

5 Check the oil seal contact surfaces at each end of the crankshaft for wear and damage. If the seal has worn an excessive groove in the surface of the crankshaft, consult an engine overhaul specialist who will be able to advise whether a repair is possible or if a new crankshaft is necessary.

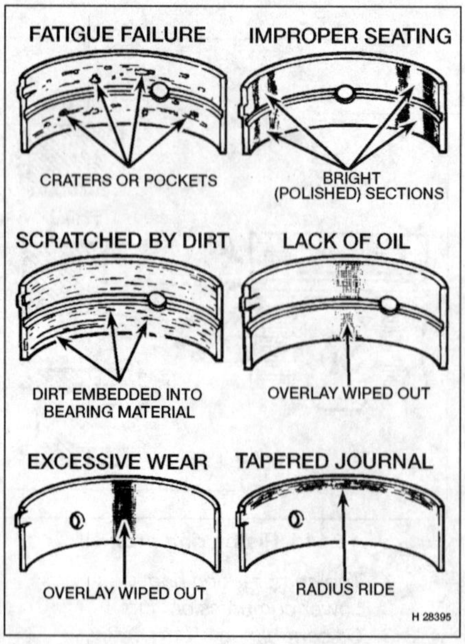

17.2 Typical bearing shell failures

17 Main and big-end bearings - inspection

1 Even though the main and big-end bearings should be renewed during the engine overhaul, the old bearings should be retained for close examination, as they may reveal valuable information about the condition of the engine. The size of the bearing shells is stamped on the back metal and this information should be given to the supplier of the new shells.

2 Bearing failure occurs because of lack of lubrication, the presence of dirt or other foreign particles, overloading the engine and corrosion. Regardless of the cause of bearing failure, it must be corrected before the engine is reassembled, to prevent it from happening again **(see illustration)**.

3 When examining the bearings, remove them from the engine block, the main bearing caps, the connecting rods and the rod caps and lay them out on a clean surface in the same general position as their location in the engine. This will enable you to match any bearing problems with the corresponding crankshaft journal.

4 Dirt and other foreign particles get into the engine in a variety of ways. Dirt may be left in the engine during assembly, or it may pass through filters or the crankcase ventilation system. It may get into the oil and from there into the bearings. Metal chips from machining operations and normal engine wear are often present. Abrasives are sometimes left in engine components after reconditioning, especially when parts are not thoroughly cleaned using the proper cleaning methods. Whatever the source, these foreign objects often end up embedded in the soft bearing material and are easily recognised. Large particles will not embed in the bearing and will score or gouge the bearing and journal. The best prevention for this cause of bearing failure is to clean all parts thoroughly and keep everything spotlessly-clean during engine assembly. Frequent and regular engine oil and filter changes are also recommended.

5 Lack of lubrication (or oil breakdown) has a number of interrelated causes. Excessive heat (which thins the oil), overloading (which squeezes the oil from the bearing face) and oil leakage (from excessive bearing clearances, worn oil pump or high engine speeds) all contribute to lubrication breakdown. Blocked oil passages, which usually are the result of misaligned oil holes in a bearing shell, will also oil-starve a bearing and destroy it. When lack of lubrication is the cause of bearing failure, the bearing material is wiped or extruded from the steel backing of the bearing. Temperatures may increase to the point where the steel backing turns blue from overheating.

6 Driving habits can have a definite effect on bearing life. Full-throttle, low-speed operation (labouring the engine) puts very high loads on bearings, which tends to squeeze out the oil film. These loads cause the bearings to flex, which produces fine cracks in the bearing face (fatigue failure). Eventually, the bearing material will loosen in pieces and tear away from the steel backing. Short-trip driving leads to corrosion of bearings, because insufficient engine heat is produced to drive off the condensed water and corrosive gases. These products collect in the engine oil, forming acid and sludge. As the oil is carried to the engine bearings, the acid attacks and corrodes the bearing material.

7 Incorrect bearing installation during engine assembly will lead to bearing failure as well. Tight-fitting bearings leave insufficient bearing oil clearance and will result in oil starvation. Dirt or foreign particles trapped behind a bearing shell result in high spots on the bearing which lead to failure.

8 If new bearings are to be fitted, the bearing running clearances should be measured before the engine is finally reassembled, to ensure that the correct bearing shells have been obtained (see Sections 19 and 20). If the crankshaft has been reground, the engineering works which carried out the work will advise on the correct size bearing shells to suit the work carried out. If there is any doubt as to which bearing shells should be used, seek advice from a Renault dealer.

18 Engine overhaul - reassembly sequence

Before starting, ensure all new parts have been obtained and all necessary tools are available. Read through the entire procedure to familiarise yourself with the work involved and to ensure all items necessary for engine reassembly are at hand. In addition to all normal tools and materials, a thread-locking compound will be needed. A tube of RTV sealing compound will also be required for the joint faces that are fitted without gaskets; it is recommended that Rhodorseal 5661 paste is used for the crankshaft main bearing cap and sump, and Loctite 518 for the water pump (E7J engine) and cylinder head end cover

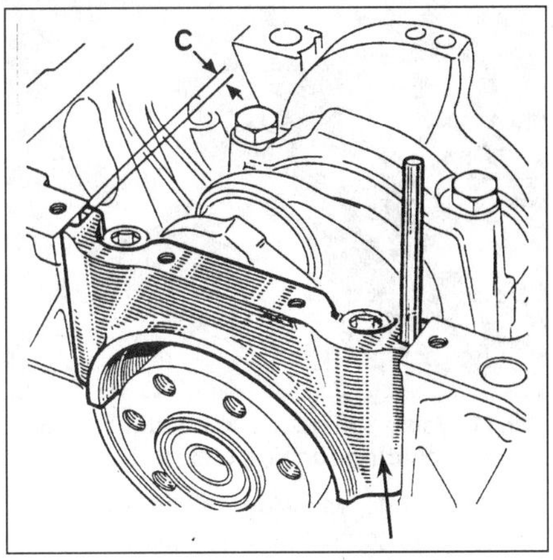

19.1 Measuring No 1 main bearing cap side seal grooves using a dowel rod

Bearing cap (arrowed)
C Seal groove measurement

(K7M, K4J and K4M engines). Both sealants are available from Renault dealers.

To save time and avoid problems, assembly can be carried out in the following order:

a) *Crankshaft.*
b) *Pistons/connecting rod assemblies.*
c) *Oil pump and sump.*
d) *Flywheel/driveplate.*
e) *Cylinder head.*
f) *Timing belt and sprockets.*
g) *Engine external components.*

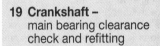

19 Crankshaft – main bearing clearance check and refitting

1 Before fitting the crankshaft and main bearings on the E7J petrol engine and diesel engines, decide whether the No 1 main bearing cap is to be sealed using butyl seals or silicone sealant. If butyl seals are to be used, it is necessary to determine the correct thickness of the seals to obtain from Renault. To do this, place the bearing cap in position without any seals and secure it with the two retaining bolts. Locate a twist drill, dowel rod or any other suitable implement which will just fit in the side seal groove **(see illustration)**. Now measure the implement – this dimension is the side seal groove size. If the dimension is less than or equal to 5 mm, a 5.10 mm thick side seal is needed. If the dimension is more than 5 mm, a 5.4 mm thick side seal is required. Having determined the side seal size and obtained the necessary seals, proceed as follows for the other types of engine as well. Note that silicone sealant is used instead of side seals when the engine is originally assembled at the factory.

Main bearing clearance check

2 Clean the backs of the bearing shells and the bearing recesses in both the cylinder block and main bearing caps.

3 Press the bearing shells into the caps and

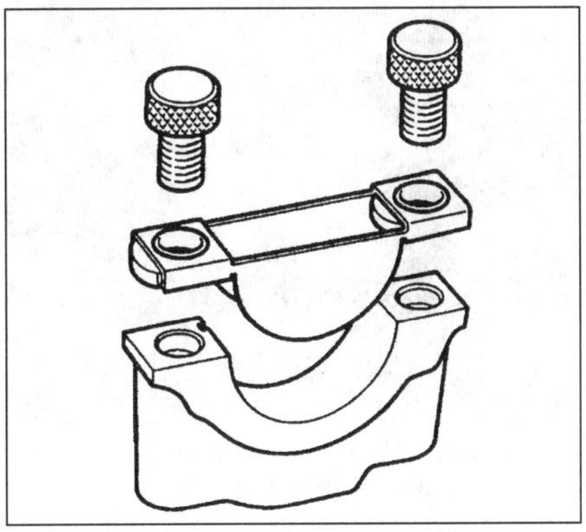

19.3a Tool for fitting main bearing shells – 1999-on K4J and K4M engines

cylinder block, ensuring that the tag on the shell engages in the notch in the cap. Note that on K4J and K4M engines from July 1999-on, tags are not incorporated in the shells and, to ensure correct fitting, it is recommended that the Renault tool Mot. 1493-01 is obtained **(see illustrations)**. Also note the following points.

a) *On the D7F engine, the shells with grooves are located on the cylinder block and the shells without grooves are located in the caps.*
b) *On the E7J engine, the shells without grooves are located in the caps, but note that No 5 upper shell incorporates a chamfer to lubricate the oil pump drive gear **(see illustration).***
c) *On the K7M engine, the shells with grooves are located at bearings 2 and 4 both on the cylinder block and in the caps, and the shells without grooves are located at bearings 1, 3 and 5 both on the cylinder block and in the caps **(see illustrations).***
d) *On the K4J and K4M engines, the shells with grooves are located on the cylinder block. Bearing caps 2 and 4 have grooved shells, and bearing caps 1, 3 and 5 have non-grooved shells **(see illustration).***

4 Note that if the original shells are being re-used, it is important that they are only refitted to their original locations in the block and caps.

5 Before the crankshaft can be permanently installed, the main bearing clearance should be checked; this can be done in either of two

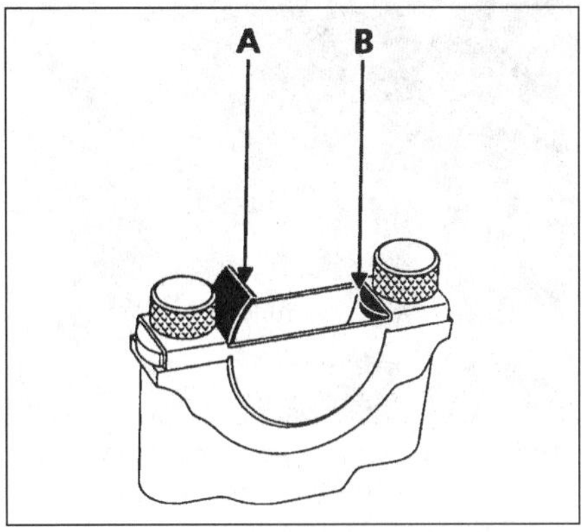

19.3b Press the bearing shell at (A) until it contacts (B)

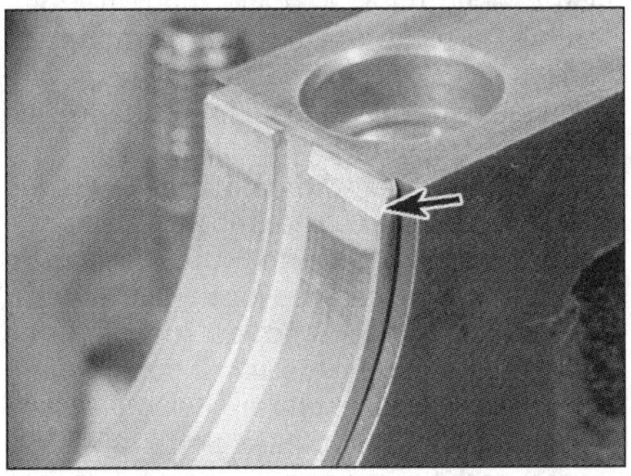

19.3c On the E7J engine, No 5 upper main bearing shell has an oil pump lubricating chamfer

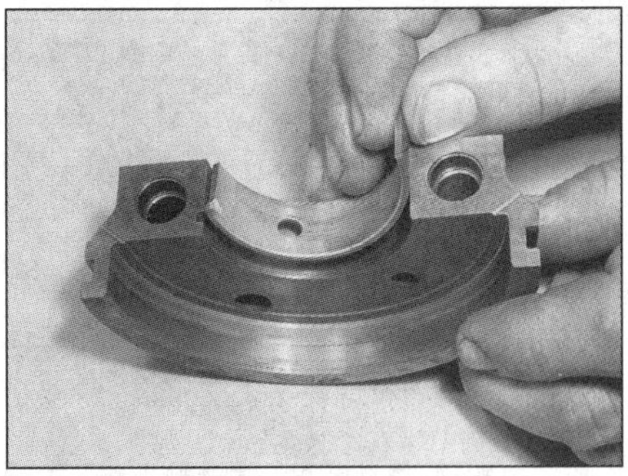

19.3d Fitting a shell to No 1 main bearing cap – K7M engine

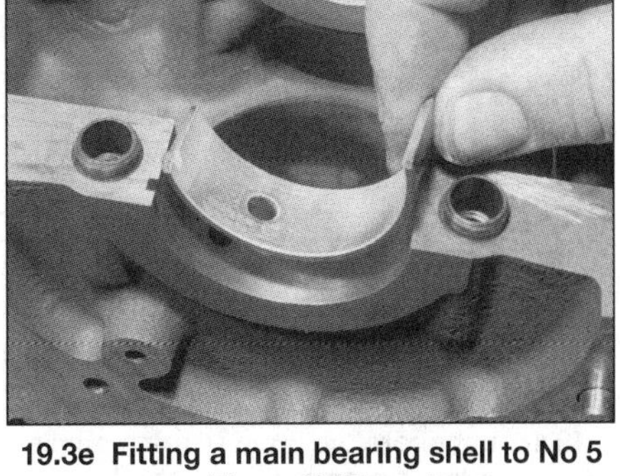

19.3e Fitting a main bearing shell to No 5 position – K7M engine

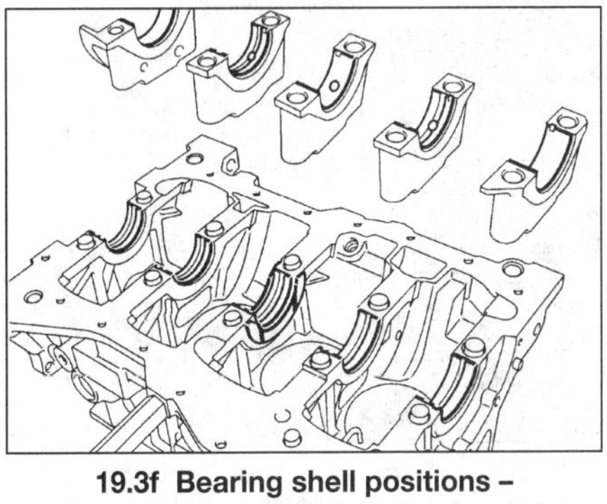

19.3f Bearing shell positions – K4J and K4M engines

19.6 Lay the crankshaft in position in the crankcase

19.7 Strip of Plastigauge placed on No 5 main bearing journal

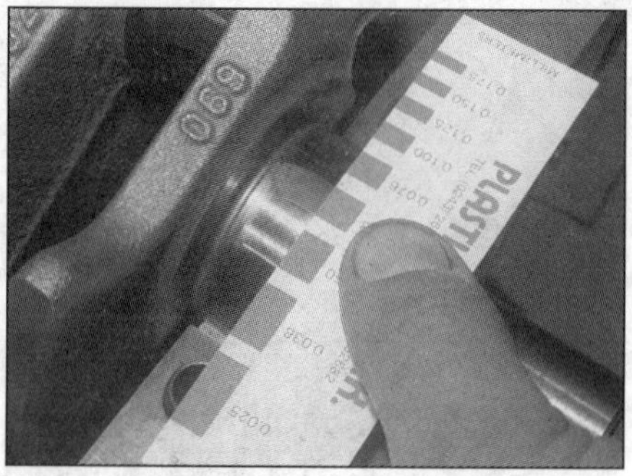

19.11 Using the gauge to check the main bearing running clearance

ways. One method is to fit the main bearing caps to the cylinder block, with the bearing shells in place. With the cap retaining bolts tightened to the specified torque, measure the internal diameter of each assembled pair of bearing shells using a vernier dial indicator or internal micrometer. If the diameter of each corresponding crankshaft journal is measured and then subtracted from the bearing internal diameter, the result will be the main bearing running clearance. The second (and more accurate) method is to use a product known as Plastigauge. This consists of a fine thread of perfectly-round plastic which is compressed between the bearing cap and the journal. When the cap is removed, the deformation of the plastic thread is measured with a special card gauge supplied with the kit. The running clearance is determined from this gauge. The procedure for using Plastigauge is as follows.

19.15a Smear a little grease on the crankshaft thrustwashers . . .

6 With the upper main bearing shells in place, carefully lay the crankshaft in position **(see illustration)**. Do not use any lubricant; the crankshaft journals and bearing shells must be perfectly clean and dry.

7 Cut several pieces of the appropriate-size Plastigauge (they should be slightly shorter than the width of the main bearings) and place one piece on each crankshaft journal axis **(see illustration)**.

8 With the bearing shells in position in the caps, fit the caps to their numbered or previously-noted locations. Take care not to disturb the Plastigauge.

9 Starting with the centre main bearing and working outward, tighten the main bearing cap bolts progressively to their specified torque setting and where applicable to the specified angle. Don't rotate the crankshaft at any time during this operation.

10 Remove the bolts and carefully lift off the main bearing caps, keeping them in order. Don't disturb the Plastigauge or rotate the crankshaft. If any of the bearing caps are difficult to remove, tap them from side-to-side with a soft-faced mallet.

11 Compare the width of the crushed Plastigauge on each journal to the scale printed on the gauge to obtain the main bearing running clearance **(see illustration)**.

12 If the clearance is not as specified, the bearing shells may be the wrong size (or badly worn if the original shells are being re-used). Before deciding that different size shells are needed, make sure no dirt or oil was trapped between the bearing shells and the caps or block when the clearance was measured. If the Plastigauge was wider at one end than at the other, the journal may be tapered.

13 Carefully scrape away all traces of the Plastigauge material from the crankshaft and bearing shells, using a fingernail or something similar which is unlikely to score the shells.

Final refitting

14 Carefully lift the crankshaft out of the cylinder block once more.

15 Using a little grease, stick the thrustwashers to each side of the centre main bearing (petrol engines) or No 2 main bearing (diesel engines). Ensure that the oilway grooves on each thrustwasher face outwards from the bearing location, towards the crankshaft webs **(see illustrations)**.

16 Liberally lubricate each bearing shell in the cylinder block and lower the crankshaft into position **(see illustration)**.

17 Lubricate the bearing shells, then fit the bearing caps in their numbered or previously-noted locations **(see illustration)**. Note the following points.

a) On the E7J engine, apply a thin coating of sealant to the outer corners of No 1 main bearing cap.

b) On the K7M, K4J and K4M engines, apply a thin coating of sealant to the complete contact faces of the No 1 main bearing cap ***(see illustrations).***

c) If fitting butyl seals to No 1 main bearing cap, fit the seals with their grooves facing outwards. Position the seals so that approximately 0.2 mm of seal protrudes at the bottom-facing side (the side towards the crankcase). Lubricate the seals with a

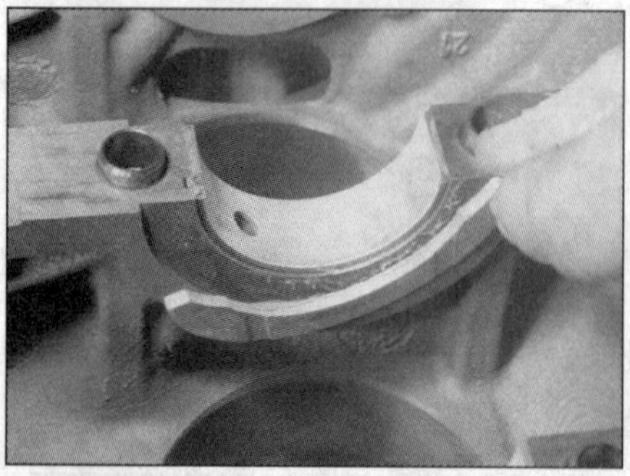

19.15b . . . and stick them to the centre main bearing – K7M/K4J/K4M engine

19.16 Lubricate the main bearing shells before fitting the crankshaft

19.17a Fitting No 5 main bearing cap – K7M/K4J/K4M engine

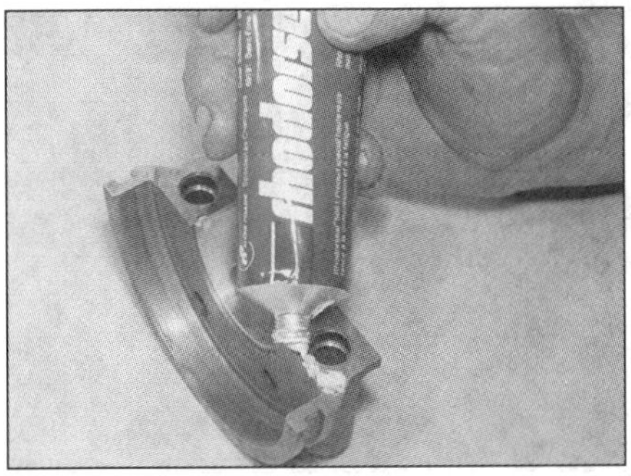

19.17b Apply sealant to the contact faces of No 1 main bearing cap . . .

little oil and apply a little sealant to the bottom corners of the cap prior to fitting it. When the cap is being fitted, use the bolts as a guide by just starting them in their threads, then pressing the cap firmly into position. When the cap is almost fully home, check that the seals still protrude slightly at the cylinder block mating face **(see illustration).**

d) *If silicone sealant is to be used on the No 1 main bearing, do not press the cap right down onto the crankshaft, but leave it raised so that the first few threads of the main bearing bolts can just be entered. Now inject the sealant into each of the cap side grooves until it enters the space below the cap and completely fills the grooves* **(see illustrations).**

18 Fit the main bearing cap bolts and tighten them progressively to the specified torque (and angle on certain engines) **(see illustrations)**.

19 Where butyl seals have been fitted to seal No 1 bearing cap, trim the protruding ends flush with the surface of the cylinder block sump mating face.

20 Where silicone sealant is to be used to seal No 1 main bearing cap, mix the sealant and the hardener as described in the instructions supplied with the kit. Inject the mixture into the bearing cap grooves, allowing the mixture to flow out slightly either side of the grooves and at the cylinder block sump mating face, to ensure that the grooves are completely filled. Allow the sealant to dry for a few minutes, then cut away surplus sealant from the joint face, both inside and outside the cylinder block and at the sump mating face.

19.17g Injecting sealant into the side grooves of No 1 main bearing cap

19.17c . . . before refitting the cap

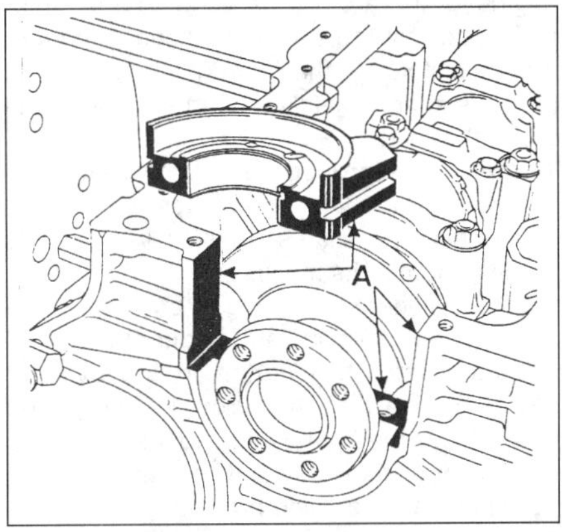

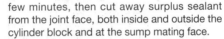

19.17e Clean the cylinder block and bearing cap mating faces (A) when using silicone sealant to seal No 1 main bearing cap . . .

21 Check that the crankshaft is free to turn. Some stiffness is normal if new components have been fitted, but there must be no jamming or tight spots.

22 Check the crankshaft endfloat with reference to Section 13.

23 Fit a new seal to the crankshaft timing belt end oil seal housing and refit the housing with reference to Chapter 2A, 2B or 2C.

24 Fit a new crankshaft flywheel/driveplate end oil seal, with reference to Chapter 2A, 2B or 2C.

19.18a Tighten the main bearing cap bolts to the specified torque . . .

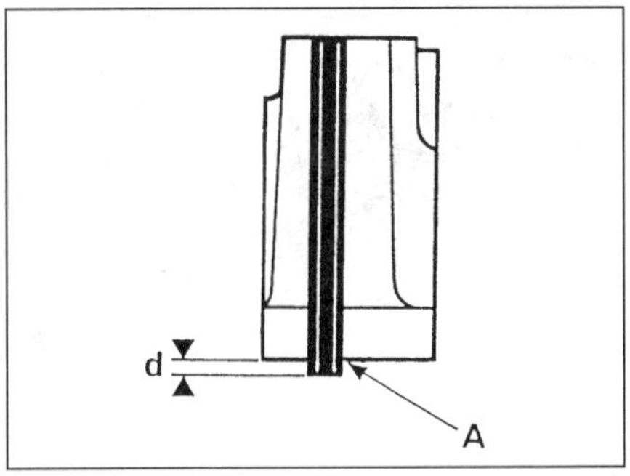

19.17d The butyl seals should protrude (d = 0.2 mm) beyond the lower face (A) of No 1 main bearing cap

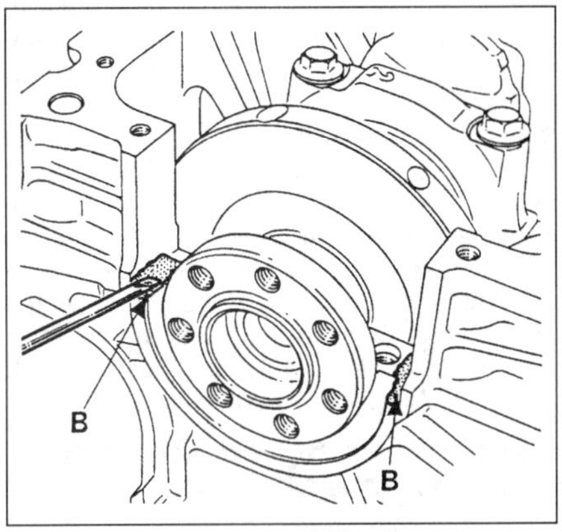

19.17f . . . and coat the lower faces of the cylinder block (B) with sealant

25 Where applicable, refit the timing belt lower inner cover.

26 On completion, refit the piston/connecting rod assemblies, the flywheel/driveplate, oil pump and the crankshaft sprocket, then fit a new timing belt.

20 Piston/connecting rods – refitting and big-end bearing clearance check

1 Clean the backs of the big-end bearing shells and the recesses in the connecting rods and big-end caps. If new shells are being

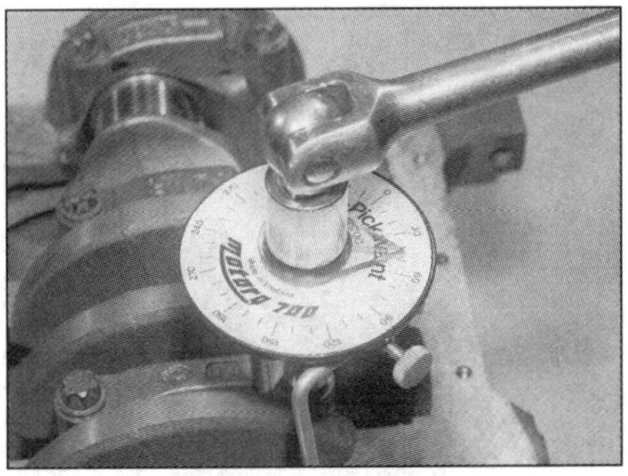

19.18b . . . and angle

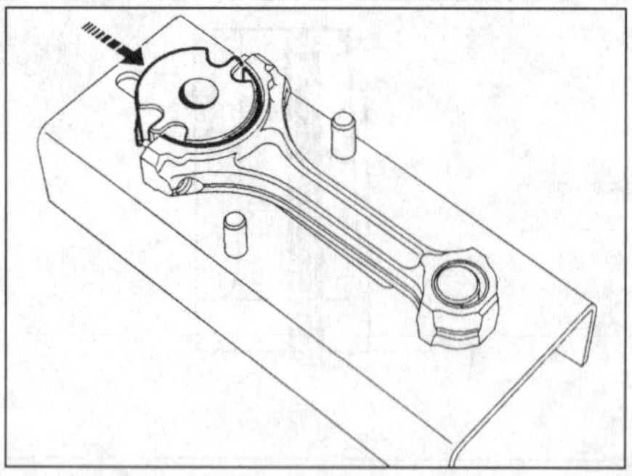

20.2 Using tool Mot. 1492 to fit the big-end shells

20.3 Fitting a liner base O-ring – E7J engines

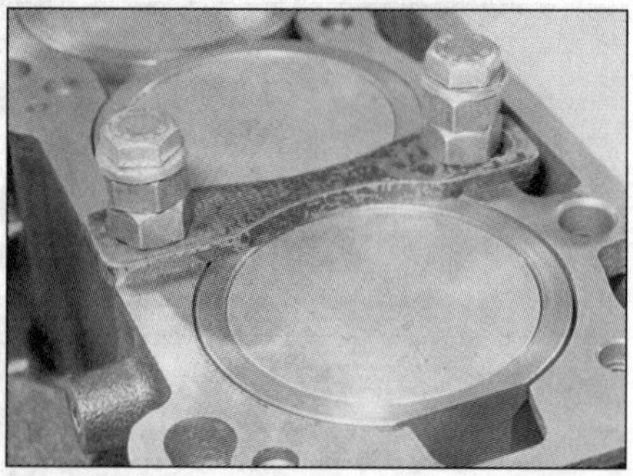

20.10 Clamp to hold the liners in place – E7J engines

fitted, ensure that all traces of the protective grease are cleaned off using paraffin. Wipe the shells and connecting rods dry with a lint-free cloth.

2 Press the big-end bearing shells into the connecting rods and caps in their correct positions. Make sure that the location tabs are engaged with the cut-outs in the connecting rods. Note that on K4J and K4M engines from July 1999-on, tags are not incorporated in the shells and, to ensure correct fitting, it is recommended that the Renault tool Mot. 1492 is obtained **(see illustration)**.

Refitting and big-end bearing clearance check

E7J petrol engine

3 Place the four liners face down in a row on the bench, in their correct order. Turn them as necessary so that the flats on the edges of liners 1 and 2 are towards each other and the flats on liners 3 and 4 are towards each other also. Fit the O-rings to the base of each liner **(see illustration)**.

4 Lubricate the pistons and piston rings, then place each piston and connecting rod assembly with its respective liner.

5 Starting with assembly No 1, make sure that the piston ring gaps are still spaced at 120° to each other. Clamp the piston rings using a piston ring compressor.

6 Insert the piston and connecting rod assembly into the bottom of the liner, ensuring that the arrow on the piston crown will be facing the flywheel/driveplate end of the engine. Using a block of wood or a hammer handle against the end of the connecting rod, tap the piston into the liner until the top of the piston is approximately 25 mm away from the top of the liner.

7 Repeat the procedure for the remaining three piston-and-liner assemblies.

8 Turn the crankshaft so that No 1 crankpin is at the bottom of its travel.

9 With the liner seal/O-ring in position, place No 1 liner, piston and connecting rod assembly into its location in the cylinder block. Ensure that the arrow on the piston crown faces the flywheel/driveplate end of the engine and that the flat on the liner is positioned as described previously.

10 With the liner/piston assembly installed, retain the liner using a bolt and washer screwed into the cylinder head bolt holes, or using liner clamps **(see illustration)**.

11 Repeat the above procedures for the remaining piston-and-liner assemblies.

12 To measure the big-end bearing running clearance, refer to the information contained in Section 19; the same general procedures apply. If the Plastigauge method is being used, ensure that the crankpin journal and the big-end bearing shells are clean and dry, then pull the connecting rod down and engage it with the crankpin. Place the Plastigauge strip on the crankpin, check that the marks made on the cap and rod during removal are next to each other, then refit the cap and retaining nuts. Tighten the nuts to the specified torque in two stages. Do not rotate the crankshaft during this operation. Remove the cap and check the running clearance by measuring the Plastigauge as previously described.

All other engines

13 Lubricate No 1 piston and piston rings and check that the ring gaps are spaced at 120° intervals to each other **(see illustration)**.

14 Fit a ring compressor to No 1 piston, then insert the piston and connecting rod into No 1 cylinder. On petrol engines, the V arrow must point to the flywheel end of the engine. On diesel engines, the combustion chamber recess in the piston crown should be on the oil filter side of the engine. With No 1 crankpin at its lowest point, drive the piston carefully into the cylinder with the wooden handle of a hammer, at the same time guiding the connecting rod onto the crankpin **(see illustrations)**.

15 To measure the big-end bearing running clearance, refer to the information contained in Section 19; the same general procedures apply. If the Plastigauge method is being used, ensure that the crankpin journal and the big-end bearing shells are clean and dry, then engage the connecting rod with the crankpin. Place the Plastigauge strip on the crankpin, fit the bearing cap in its previously-noted position, then tighten the nuts/bolts to the specified torque. Do not rotate the crankshaft during this operation. Remove the cap and check the running clearance by measuring the Plastigauge as previously described.

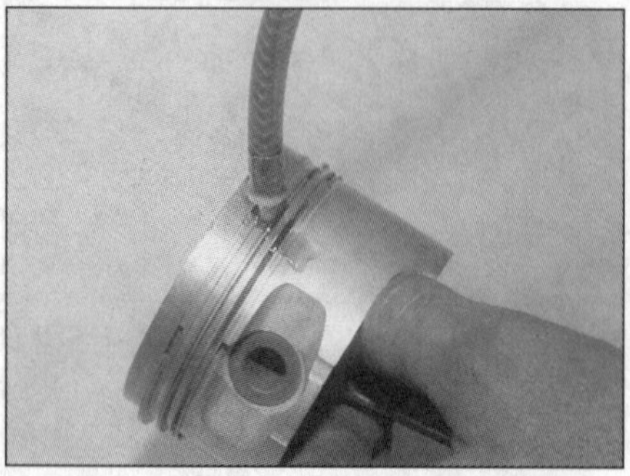

20.13 Lubricating the piston rings

20.14a Markings on the top of the piston – K7M/K4J/K4M engines

20.14b Using the wooden handle of a hammer to drive the piston into the bore

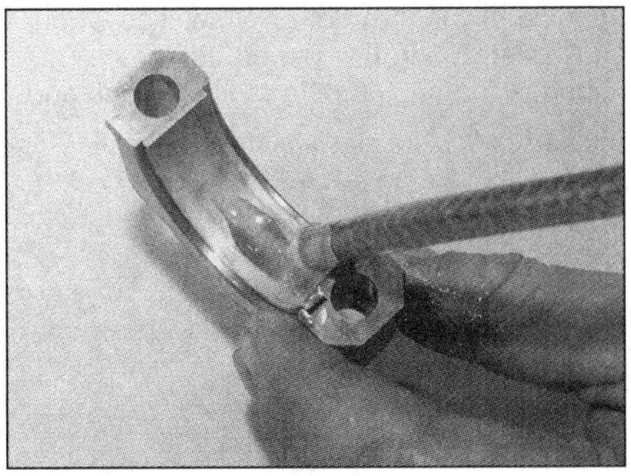

20.18a Lubricate both the cap . . .

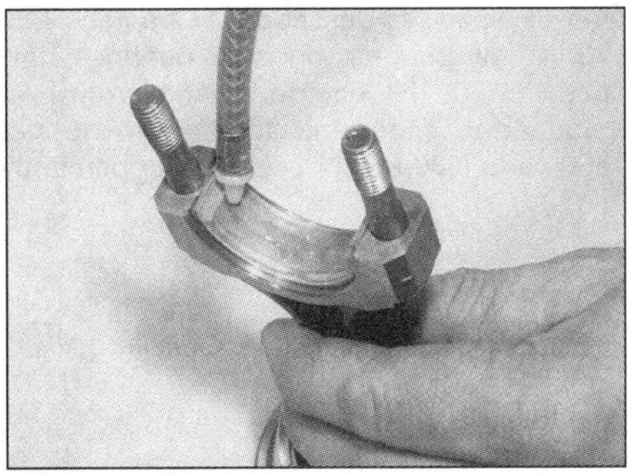

20.18b . . . and connecting rod shells before . . .

20.18c . . . refitting the cap . . .

16 Repeat the above procedures on the remaining piston/connecting rod assemblies.

Final refitting

17 Having checked the running clearance of all the crankpin journals and taken any corrective action necessary, clean off all traces of Plastigauge from the bearing shells and crankpin.

18 Liberally lubricate the crankpin journals and big-end bearing shells. Refit the bearing caps once more, ensuring correct positioning as previously described. Tighten the bearing cap nuts/bolts to the specified torque and turn the crankshaft each time to make sure that it is free before moving on to the next assembly. On the E7J engine, check that all the liners are positioned relative to each other, so that a 0.1 mm feeler gauge can pass freely through the gaps between the liners. If this is not the case, it may be necessary to interchange one or more of the complete piston/liner assemblies to achieve this clearance **(see illustrations)**.

19 On completion, refit the oil pump, sump and cylinder head as described in Chapter 2A, 2B or 2C.

21 Engine – initial start-up after overhaul

1 With the engine refitted in the vehicle, double-check the engine oil and coolant levels. Make a final check that everything has been reconnected and that there are no tools or rags left in the engine compartment.

Petrol-engined models

2 With the spark plugs removed and the engine management system disabled by removing the engine protection fuse from the engine compartment fusebox (fuse M – refer to the wiring diagrams at the end of Chapter 12 – note that this fuse also controls the supply to the seat belt tensioner and airbag systems, so refer also to the notes and warnings contained in Chapter 11), crank the engine on the starter motor until the oil pressure light goes out.

3 Refit the spark plugs and the fuse.

4 Start the engine, noting that this may take a little longer than usual, due to the fuel system being empty.

5 While the engine is idling, check for fuel, water and oil leaks. Where applicable, check the power steering pipe/hose unions for leakage. Do not be alarmed if there are some odd smells and smoke from parts getting hot and burning off oil deposits.

6 Keep the engine idling until hot water is felt circulating through the top hose, then switch it off.

7 After a few minutes, recheck the oil and water levels and top-up as necessary (see *Weekly checks*).

8 There is no requirement to retighten the cylinder head bolts.

9 If new pistons, rings or crankshaft bearings have been fitted, the engine must be run-in for the first 500 miles (800 km). Do not operate the engine at full-throttle, nor allow it to labour in any gear during this period. It is recommended that the oil and filter be changed at the end of this period.

Diesel-engined models

10 Prime the fuel system as described in Chapter 4B.

11 Prime the lubrication system by disconnecting the stop solenoid from the injection pump and by cranking the engine on the starter motor in 10 second bursts with pauses of 30 seconds in between. On completion, reconnect the stop solenoid (check that the oil pressure light goes out when the starter motor is being activated).

12 Fully depress the accelerator pedal, turn the ignition key to position M and wait for the pre-heating warning light to go out.

13 Start the engine. Additional cranking may be necessary to bleed the fuel system before the engine starts.

14 Once started, keep the engine running at fast tickover. Check that the oil pressure light goes out, then check that there are no leaks of oil, fuel and coolant. Where applicable, check the power steering pipe/hose unions for leakage. Do not be alarmed if there are some odd smells and smoke from parts getting hot and burning off oil deposits.

15 Keep the engine idling until hot coolant is felt circulating through the radiator top hose, indicating that the engine is at normal

20.18d . . . screwing on the nuts . . .

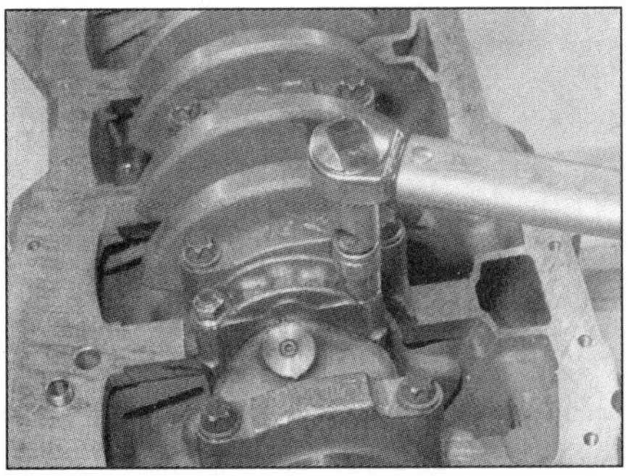

20.18e . . . and tightening the nuts

20.18f Checking the gap between the liners – E7J engines

operating temperature, then stop the engine and allow it to cool.

16 Recheck the oil and coolant levels and top-up if necessary (see *Weekly checks*).

17 Check the fuel injection pump timing and the idle speed as described in Chapter 4B.

18 If new pistons, rings or bearings have been fitted, the engine must be run-in at reduced speeds and loads for the first 500 miles (800 km) or so. Do not operate the engine at full throttle, or allow it to labour in any gear during this period. It is beneficial to change the engine oil and filter at the end of this period.

Chapter 3
Cooling, heating and air conditioning systems

Contents

Degrees of difficulty

Easy, suitable for novice with little experience	**Fairly easy,** suitable for beginner with some experience	**Fairly difficult,** suitable for competent DIY mechanic	**Difficult,** suitable for experienced DIY mechanic	**Very difficult,** suitable for expert DIY or professional

Specifications

General

Cooling system type	Pressurised, with belt-driven pump, front-mounted radiator and electric cooling fan
Engine codes:	
1.2 litre petrol engine	D7F
1.4 litre petrol engine:	
SOHC	E7J
DOHC	K4J
1.6 litre petrol engine:	
SOHC	K7M
DOHC	K4M
Diesel engine	F8Q
Cooling system pressure	1.2 bars
Air conditioning refrigerant type	R134a

Thermostat	**Starts to open**	**Fully open**
Opening temperatures	89°C	101°C
Travel (closed to fully open)	7.5 mm	
Type	Wax	

Torque wrench settings	**Nm**	**lbf ft**
Coolant pump bolts:		
E7J and K7M engines	22	16
K4M engines:		
Stage 1	8	6
Stage 2 (M6 bolts)	11	8
Stage 3 (M8 bolts)	22	16
Coolant pump nuts:		
E7J and K7M engines	10	7
Evaporator pressure sensor	8	6

Note: *Torque settings for other engine types were not specified at the time of writing*

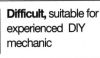

3

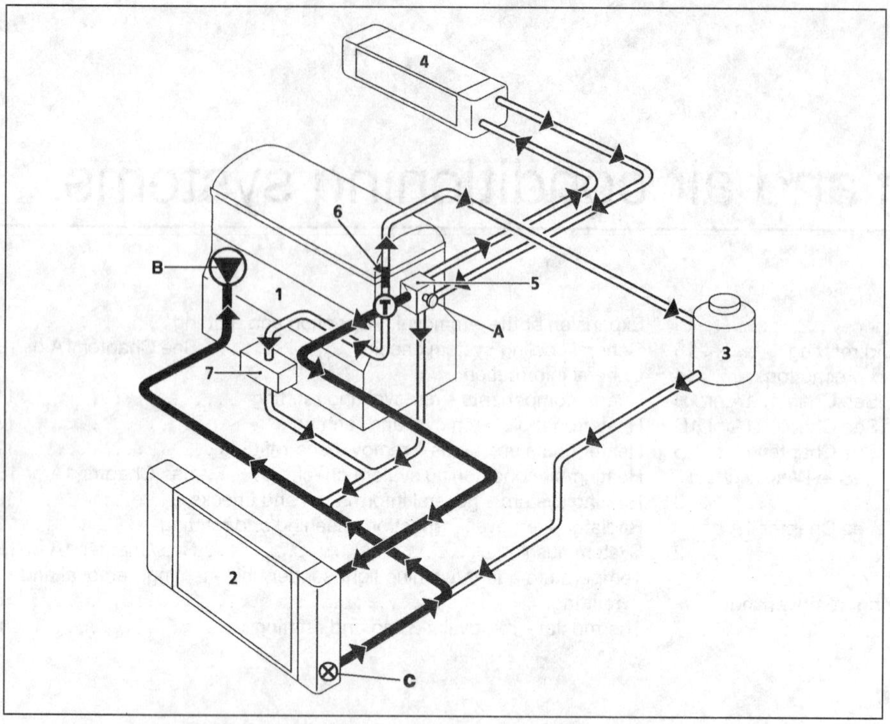

1.1a Cooling system schematic – F8Q engine

1 Cylinder block	*4 Heater matrix/radiator*	*A Bleed screw*
2 Radiator	*5 Thermostat mounting*	*B Water pump*
3 Hot Expansion bottle with permanent degassing	*6 3mm diameter restriction*	*C Fan thermostatic switch*
	7 Oil heat exchanger	*T Thermostat*

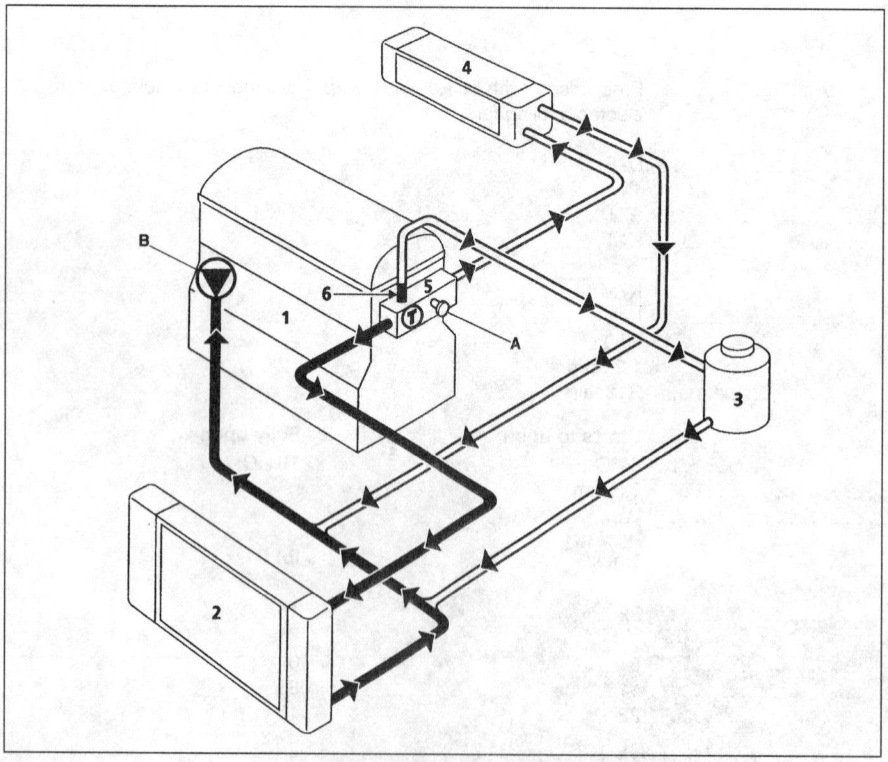

1.1b Cooling system schematic – K4J and K4M engines

see illustration 1.1a for key

1 General information

1 The cooling system is of the pressurised type. The main components are a belt-driven pump, an aluminium crossflow radiator, an expansion bottle, an electric cooling fan, a thermostat, and the associated hoses **(see illustrations)**.

2 The system functions as follows. When the engine is cold, coolant is pumped around the cylinder block and head passages. After cooling the cylinder bores, combustion surfaces and valve seats, the coolant passes through the heater and inlet manifold, and is returned to the water pump.

3 When the coolant reaches a predetermined temperature, the thermostat opens, and the hot coolant passes through the top hose to the radiator. As the coolant circulates through the radiator, it is cooled by the inrush of air when the car is in motion. The airflow is supplemented by the action of the electric cooling fan when necessary. Upon reaching the bottom of the radiator, the coolant returns to the pump via the radiator bottom hose, and the cycle is repeated.

4 As the coolant warms up, it expands; the increased volume is accommodated in an expansion bottle. The bottle is 'hot': the coolant circulates through the bottle all the time that the engine is running.

5 The electric cooling fan is mounted behind the radiator.

6 On petrol models, the fan is controlled at high speed by the injection ECU, if the coolant temperature is greater than 99°C the fan will operate. When the coolant temperature is lower than 96°C the fan stops operating.

7 On diesel models, the fan is controlled by a thermostatic switch located in the side of the radiator. At a predetermined coolant temperature, the switch contacts close, actuating the fan via a relay.

8 For details of the air conditioning system (when fitted) and the precautions associated with it, refer to Section 14.

Precautions

Caution: If the radio/cassette in your vehicle is equipped with an anti-theft system, make sure you have the correct activation code before disconnecting the battery.

Warning: Do not attempt to remove the expansion bottle filler cap, or to disturb any part of the cooling system, while the engine is hot, as there is a high risk of scalding. If the expansion bottle filler cap must be removed before the engine and radiator have fully cooled (even though this is not recommended), the pressure in the cooling system must first be relieved.

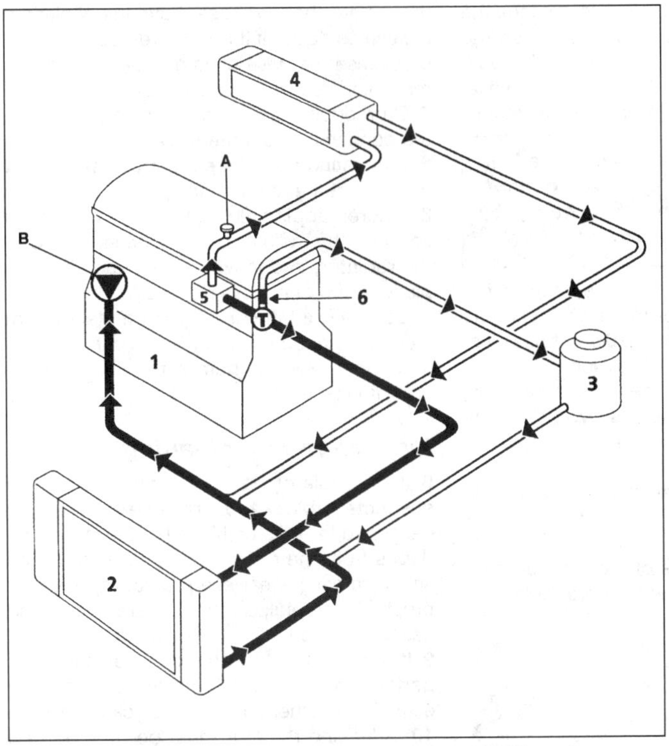

1.1c Cooling system schematic – E7J and K7M engines

see illustration 1.1a for key

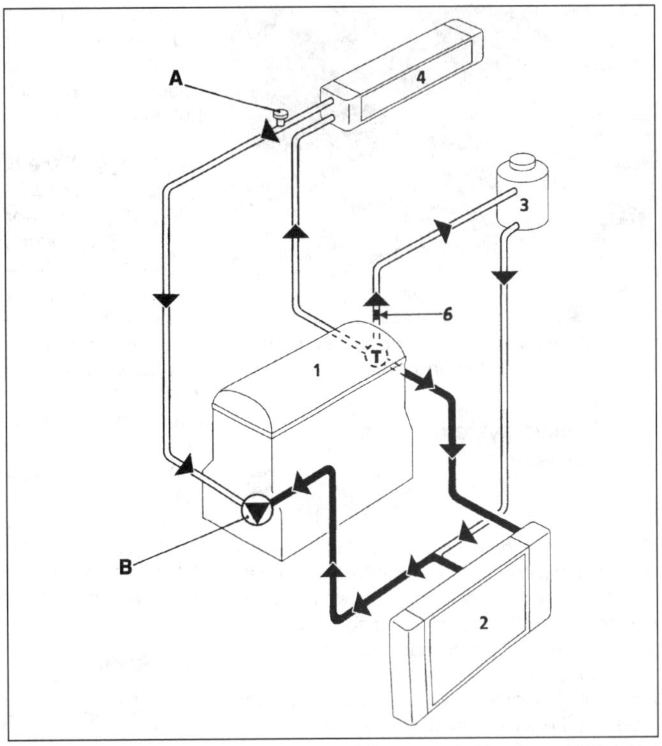

1.1d Cooling system schematic – D7F engine with air conditioning

see illustration 1.1a for key

Cover the cap with a thick layer of cloth to avoid scalding, and slowly unscrew the filler cap until a hissing sound is heard. When the hissing has stopped, indicating that the pressure has reduced, slowly unscrew the filler cap until it can be removed; if more hissing sounds are heard, wait until they have stopped before unscrewing the cap completely. At all times, keep well away from the filler cap opening, and protect your hands.

Warning: Do not allow antifreeze to come into contact with your skin, or with the painted surfaces of the vehicle. Rinse off spills immediately, with plenty of water. Never leave antifreeze lying around in an open container, or in a puddle in the driveway or on the garage floor. Children and pets are attracted by its sweet smell, but antifreeze can be fatal if ingested.

Warning: If the engine is hot, the electric cooling fan may start rotating even if the engine is not running. Be careful to keep your hands, hair, and any loose clothing well clear when working in the engine compartment.

Warning: Refer to Section 14 for precautions to be observed when working on models equipped with air conditioning.

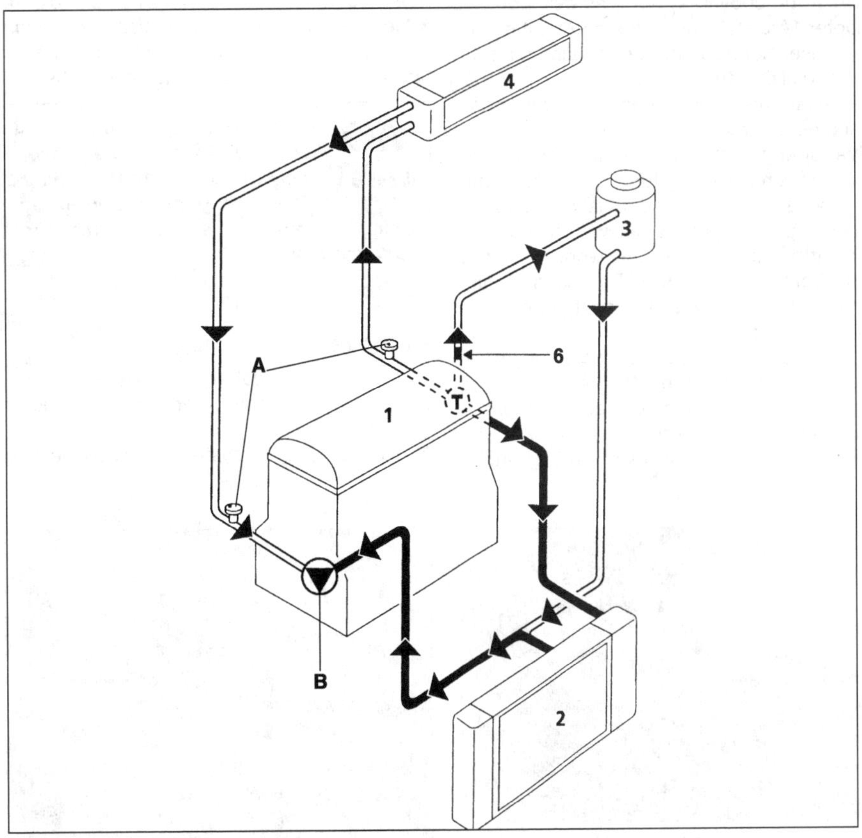

1.1e Cooling system schematic – D7F engines without air conditioning

see illustration 1.1a for key

3

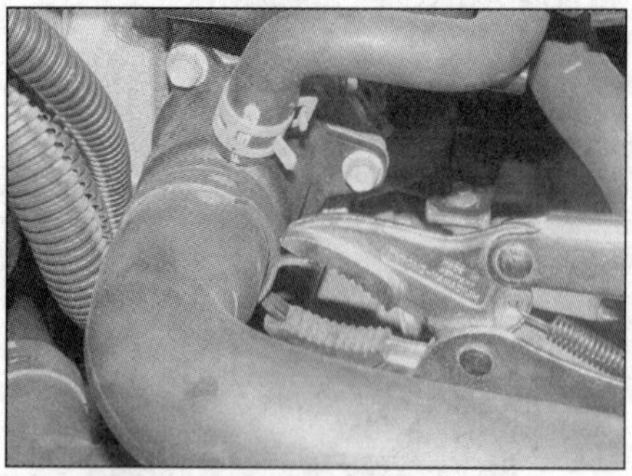

2.3 Releasing a spring hose clip using self-locking grips

2 Cooling system hoses - renewal

Note: *Refer to the warnings given in Section 1 of this Chapter before proceeding. Hoses should only be disconnected once the engine has cooled sufficiently to avoid scalding.*

1 The number, routing and pattern of hoses will vary according to model, but the same basic procedure applies. Before commencing work, make sure that the new hoses are to hand, along with new hose clips if needed. It is good practice to renew the hose clips at the same time as the hoses.

2 Drain the cooling system, as described in Chapter 1A or 1B, saving the coolant if it is fit for re-use. Squirt a little penetrating oil onto the hose clips if they are rusty.

3 Release the hose clips from the hose concerned. Three clip types are used: worm-drive, spring and 'sardine-can'. The worm-drive clip is released by turning its screw anti-clockwise. The spring clip is released by squeezing its tags together with pliers **(see illustration)**, at the same time working the clip away from the hose stub. The 'sardine-can' clip is not re-usable, and is best cut off with snips or side cutters.

4 Unclip any wires, cables or other hoses which may be attached to the hose being removed. Make notes for reference when reassembling if necessary.

5 Release the hose from its stubs with a twisting motion. Be careful not to damage the stubs on delicate components such as the radiator. If the hose is stuck fast, the best course is often to cut it off using a sharp knife, but again be careful not to damage the stubs.

HAYNES HiNT ***If the hose is stiff, use a little soapy water as a lubricant, or soften the hose by soaking it with hot water.***

6 Before fitting the new hose, smear the stubs with washing-up liquid or a suitable rubber lubricant to aid fitting. **Do not** use oil or grease, which may attack the rubber.

7 Fit the hose clips over the ends of the hose, then fit the hose over its stubs. Work the hose into position. When satisfied, locate and tighten the hose clips.

8 Refill the cooling system as described in Chapter 1A or 1B. Run the engine, and check that there are no leaks.

9 Recheck the tightness of the hose clips on any new hoses after a few hundred miles.

3 Radiator - removal, inspection, cleaning and refitting

Note: *If the radiator is to be removed for a period of more than 48 hours, precautions must be taken against internal corrosion. Either rinse the radiator with clean water and dry it thoroughly by blowing air through it, or fill it with coolant and plug the hose stubs.*

HAYNES HiNT ***If the reason for removing the radiator is concern over coolant loss, note that minor leaks may be repaired by using a radiator sealant with the radiator in situ.***

Removal

1 Disconnect the battery negative lead.

2 Remove the cooling fan as described in Section 6.

3 Drain the cooling system by disconnecting the radiator bottom hose. Save the coolant in a clean container if it is fit for re-use.

4 Release the hose clips and disconnect the remaining hoses from the radiator.

5 On models with air conditioning, separate the condenser from the radiator by removing the mounting bolts **(see illustration)**. **Do not** disconnect the refrigerant pipes.

6 Where applicable, unscrew the bolts securing the radiator plastic ducting/shield to the radiator, and leave the ducting/shield in place as the radiator is removed.

7 Carefully lift the radiator off its bottom mountings and remove it. Recover the rubber mountings; renew them if they are in poor condition **(see illustrations)**.

Inspection and cleaning

8 If the radiator has been removed due to suspected blockage, reverse-flush it as described in Chapter 1A or 1B. Clean dirt and debris from the radiator fins, using an airline (in which case, wear eye protection) or a soft brush. Be careful, as the fins are sharp, and easily damaged.

9 If necessary, a radiator specialist can perform a 'flow test' on the radiator, to establish whether an internal blockage exists.

10 A leaking radiator must be referred to a specialist for permanent repair. Do not attempt to weld or solder a leaking radiator, as damage to the plastic components may result.

11 If the radiator is to be sent for repair or renewed, remove all hoses and the cooling fan switch (where fitted).

12 Inspect the condition of the radiator mounting rubbers, and renew them if necessary.

Refitting

13 Refitting is a reversal of removal, bearing in mind the following points.

a) Take care not to damage the radiator fins during refitting.

b) Where applicable, refit the top crossmember and the bonnet catch with reference to Chapter 11.

c) On completion, refill the cooling system as described in Chapter 1A or 1B.

3.5 Undo the condenser retaining bolts from each end of the radiator (left-hand bolt arrowed)

3.7a Lower radiator rubber mounting (arrowed) . . .

3.7b . . . and upper radiator rubber mounting (arrowed)

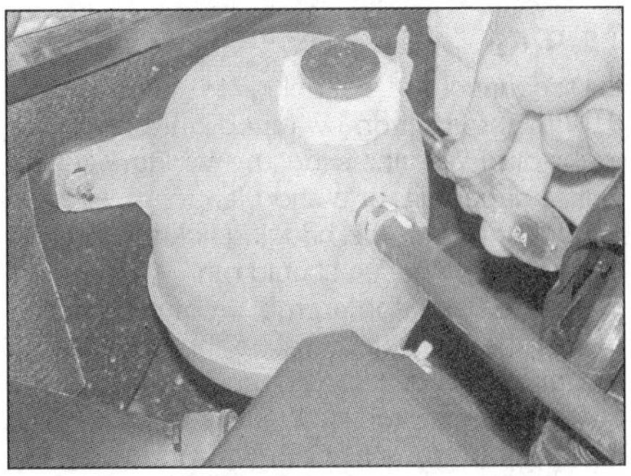

4.2a Undo the two retaining nuts . . .

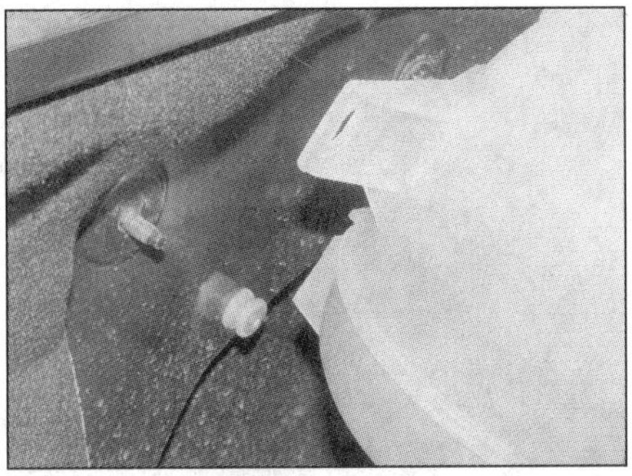

4.2b . . . and lift the expansion bottle, to remove it from the bulkhead

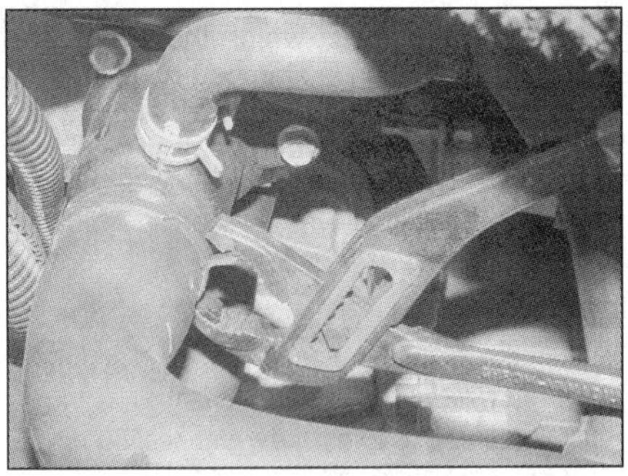

5.3 Releasing the clip securing the hose to the thermostat cover

4 Expansion bottle – removal, inspection and refitting

Removal

1 With the engine cold, drain some coolant from the system (see Chapter 1A or 1B) until the expansion bottle is empty.

2 Undo the two retaining nuts which secure the expansion bottle. Disconnect the hose (or hoses) and remove the bottle **(see illustrations)**.

Inspection

3 Clean the bottle and inspect it for cracks and other damage. Renew it if necessary. Also inspect the cap; if there is evidence that coolant has been vented through the cap, renew it.

Refitting

4 Refit by reversing the removal operations. Refill and bleed the cooling system as described in Chapter 1A or 1B.

5 Thermostat – removal, testing and refitting

1 The thermostat is located in the cylinder head outlet elbow housing on the left-hand side of the engine, above the gearbox bellhousing (see illustrations in Section 1).

Removal

Note: *A new thermostat sealing ring may be required on refitting – see text.*

2 Partially drain the cooling system, as described in Chapter 1A or 1B, so that the coolant level is below the thermostat location.

3 Where necessary, loosen the clip and disconnect the hose from the thermostat cover **(see illustration)**.

4 Unbolt the cover/thermostat assembly, noting that the thermostat may be integral with the cover. Recover the sealing ring from the housing **(see illustrations)**.

5 On some engine types, unbolt the cover and remove the thermostat, then remove the sealing ring from around the thermostat **(see illustrations)**.

Testing

6 To test whether the unit is serviceable, suspend it on a string in a saucepan of cold water, together with a thermometer. Heat the water, and note the temperature at which the thermostat begins to open. Continue heating the water until the thermostat is fully open, and then remove it from the water.

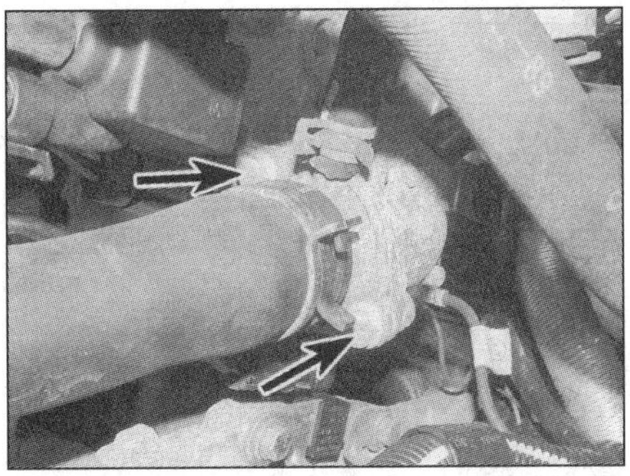

5.4a Undo the two retaining bolts (arrowed) . . .

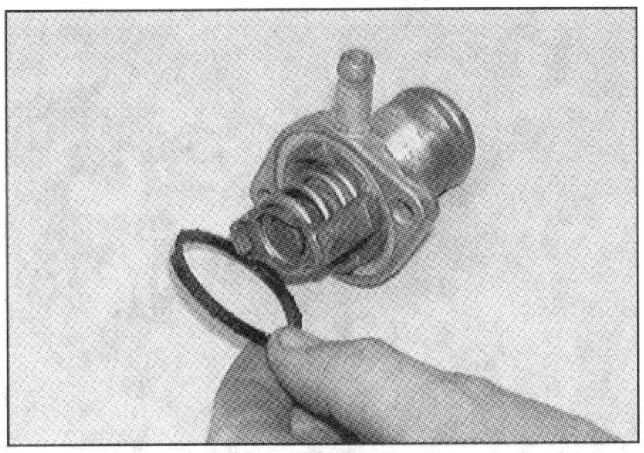

5.4b . . . and fit a new sealing ring to the thermostat/cover assembly on the D7F engine

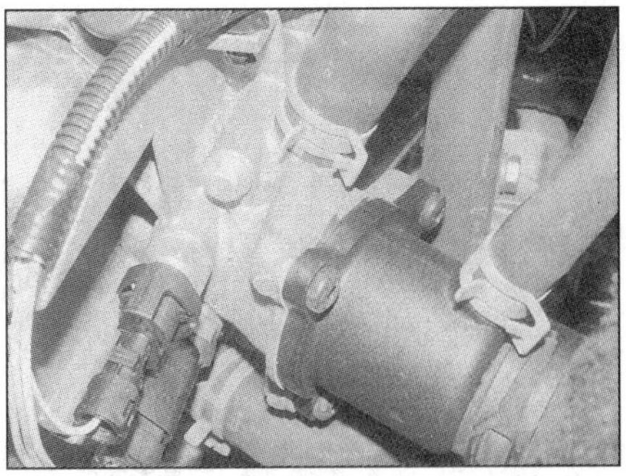

5.4c Thermostat housing on the K4J engine . . .

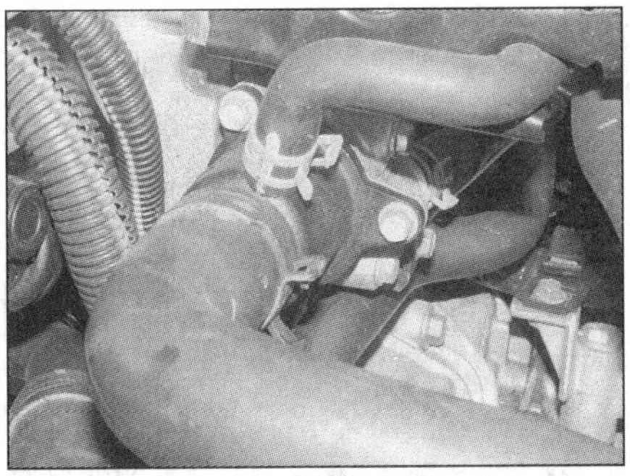

5.4d . . . and on the K4M engine

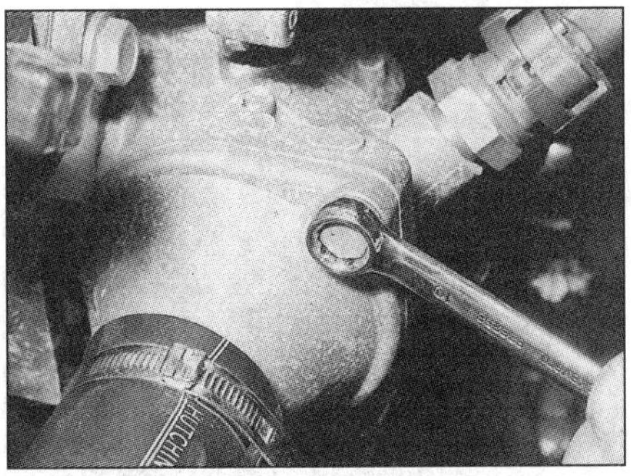

5.5a On diesel models, slacken and remove the retaining bolts . . .

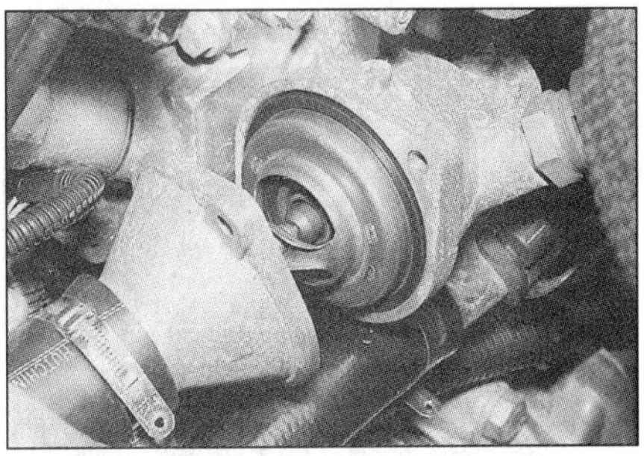

5.5b . . . then remove the thermostat housing cover (a gasket may be fitted on some engines) . . .

7 The temperature at which the thermostat should start to open is stamped on the unit. If the thermostat does not start to open at the specified temperature, does not fully open in boiling water, or does not fully close when removed from the water, then it must be discarded and a new one fitted.

Refitting

8 Refitting is a reversal of removal, bearing in mind the following points.

a) Where applicable renew the sealing ring.
b) On completion, refill the cooling system as described in Chapter 1A or 1B.

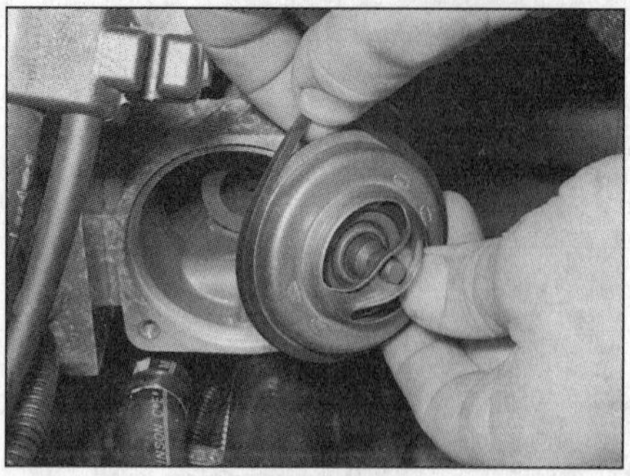

5.5c . . . and lift out the thermostat. Renew the sealing ring

6 Electric cooling fan assembly – removal and refitting

Removal

1 Disconnect the battery negative lead.
2 On models with the D7F engine, unscrew the bolts securing the fan assembly to the radiator **(see illustration)**, then release the wiring connector from fan frame, and disconnect it.
3 On other models, undo the grille retaining screws and carefully unclip the ends from the front edges of the wings. Remove the grille from the vehicle and lift off the rubber seal along the crossmember **(see illustration)**.
4 Remove the two radiator mounting bolts from the top crossmember. Note the position of each mounting brackets and remove them **(see illustrations)**.
5 Undo the four securing bolts and remove the crossmember from above the radiator **(see illustration)**. Move it to the rear of the engine bay leaving the bonnet release cable still connected.
6 Unclip the fan assembly from the radiator **(see illustration)**. Withdraw the fan assembly, disconnecting the wiring on removal.

Refitting

7 Refit by reversing the removal operations.

7 Electric cooling fan thermostatic switch (diesel models) – testing, removal and refitting

1 On diesel models, the cooling fan switch is located in the radiator. On petrol models the operation of the fan is controlled by the fuel injection ECU; see Section 1.

Testing

2 Disconnect the multi-plug for the fan switch.
3 With the ignition switched on, bridge the multi-plug terminals on the wiring harness with a paper clip or a short length of wire. Be careful not to let the bridging link touch earth (bare metal). The fan should run.
4 If there has been a problem of overheating due to the fan not operating, but it runs with the bridge in place, this suggests that the thermostatic switch is defective.
5 If the fan does not run with the bridge in place, there is a fault in the fan itself or in its supply circuit (including the fuse and, if applicable, the relay).
6 The switch can be tested further after removal by immersing it in a heated water bath like testing the thermostat (refer to Section 5), and using a continuity tester to check the temperature at which the switch contacts open and close.

Removal

Note: *Suitable sealant will be required to coat the switch threads on refitting.*
7 Drain the cooling system, as described in Chapter 1A or 1B.
8 Disconnect the multi-plug for the fan switch.
9 Unscrew the switch from the radiator and remove it.

Refitting

10 Apply a little sealant to the threads of the switch, and screw it into position.
11 Reconnect and secure the multi-plug.
12 Refill the cooling system as described in Chapter 1A or 1B.

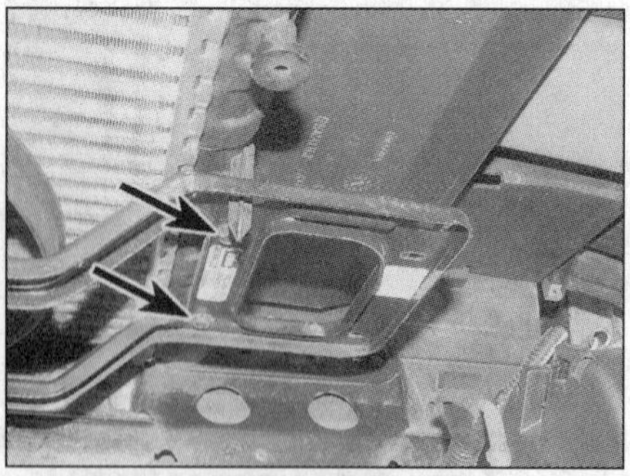

6.2 Undo the retaining bolts (arrowed) and lift out the fan assembly

6.3 Unclip the rubber seal from along the crossmember

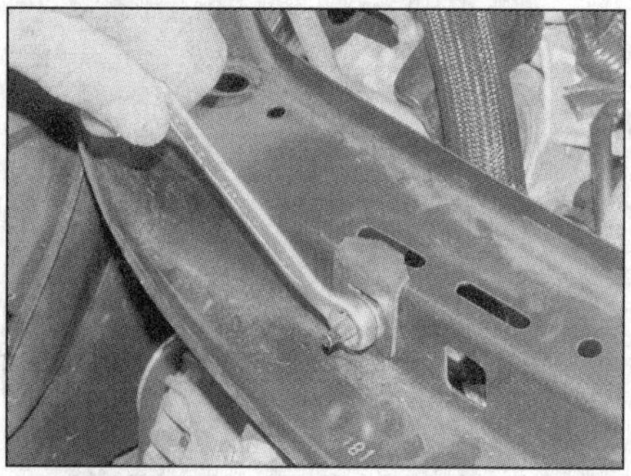

6.4a Slacken the two radiator mounting nuts . . .

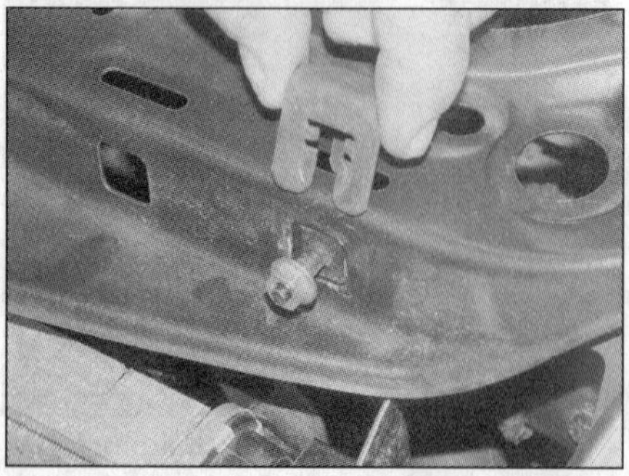

6.4b . . . and withdraw the brackets to release the radiator from the crossmember

6.5 Remove the crossmember retaining bolts

6.6 Lift fan assembly upwards to release it from the radiator retaining clips (arrowed)

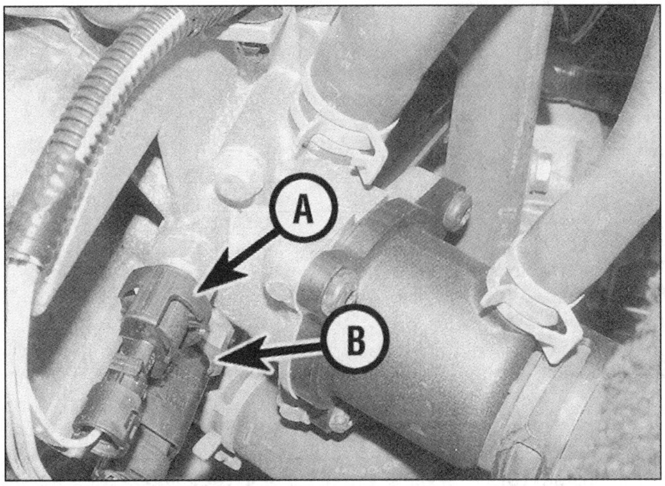

8.1a Temperature gauge sender (A) – K4J engine
Fuel injection system temperature sensor (B) is also visible

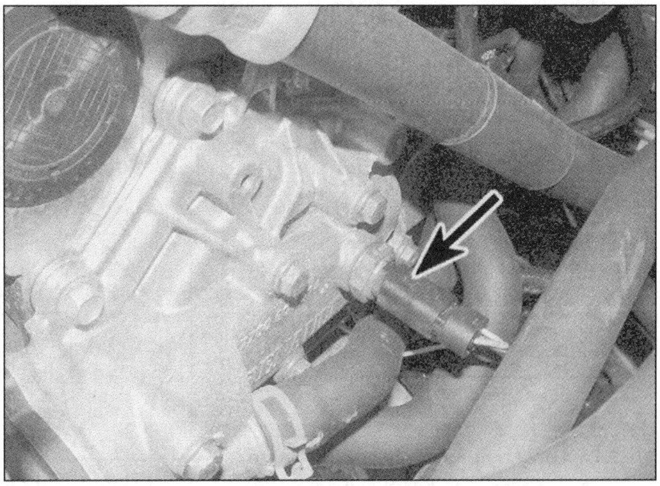

8.1b Temperature gauge sender unit (arrowed) in the thermostat housing – K4M engine

8 Temperature gauge/warning light sender unit – testing, removal and refitting

1 The location of the temperature gauge/warning light sender unit varies according to model. It is located in the thermostat housing or the left-hand of the cylinder head, above the gearbox bellhousing **(see illustrations)**. In all cases, the procedures are the same.

Testing

2 The temperature gauge is fed with a stabilised voltage from the instrument panel feed (via the ignition switch and a fuse). The gauge earth is controlled by the sender. The sender contains a thermistor – an electronic component whose electrical resistance decreases as its temperature rises. When the coolant is cold, the sender resistance is high, current flow through the gauge is reduced, and the gauge needle points towards the cold end of the scale. As the coolant temperature rises and the sender resistance falls, current flow increases, and the gauge needle moves towards the upper end of the scale. If the sender is faulty, it must be renewed.

3 The temperature warning light is fed with a voltage from the instrument panel. The light earth is controlled by the sender. The sender is effectively a switch, which operates at a predetermined temperature to earth the light and complete the circuit.

4 If the gauge develops a fault, first check the other instruments; if they do not work at all, check the instrument panel electrical feed. If the readings are erratic, there may be a fault in the voltage stabiliser, which will necessitate renewal of the stabiliser (the stabiliser is integral with the instrument panel printed circuit board – see Chapter 12). If the fault lies in the temperature gauge alone, check it as follows.

5 If the gauge needle remains at the 'cold' end of the scale when the engine is hot, disconnect the sender wiring plug, and earth the relevant wire to the cylinder head. If the needle then deflects when the ignition is switched on, the sender unit is proved faulty, and should be renewed. If the needle still does not move, remove the instrument panel (Chapter 12) and check the continuity of the wire between the sender unit and the gauge, and the feed to the gauge unit. If continuity is shown, and the fault still exists, then the gauge is faulty, and the gauge unit should be renewed.

6 If the gauge needle remains at the 'hot' end of the scale when the engine is cold, disconnect the sender wire. If the needle then returns to the 'cold' end of the scale when the ignition is switched on, the sender unit is proved faulty, and should be renewed. If the needle still does not move, check the remainder of the circuit as described previously.

7 The same basic principles apply to testing the warning light. The light should illuminate when the relevant sender wire is earthed.

Removal

Note: *Suitable sealant will be required to coat the sender threads on refitting.*

8 Drain the cooling system as described in Chapter 1A or 1B. Alternatively, remove the expansion bottle cap to depressurise the system, and have the new sender unit or a suitable bung to hand.

9 Disconnect the multi-plug and unscrew the sender unit **(see illustration)**.

Refitting

10 Apply a little sealant to the sender threads, and screw it into position. Reconnect the multi-plug.

11 Top-up or refill the cooling system, with reference to *Weekly checks,* Chapter 1A or 1B.

9 Coolant pump – removal and refitting

1 If the coolant pump is leaking, or is noisy in operation, it must be renewed.

K-type petrol engine

Note: *A tube of Loctite 518 sealant will be required on refitting.*

Removal

2 Disconnect the battery negative lead, then drain the cooling system as described in Chapter 1A.

3 Remove the timing belt and timing belt tensioner as described in Chapter 2B.

4 Slacken and remove the coolant pump retaining bolts, noting the locations of the different size bolts.

5 Withdraw the pump from the block, tapping it with a soft-faced mallet if it is stuck.

Refitting

6 Commence refitting by thoroughly cleaning the mating surfaces of the pump and cylinder block, ensuring that all traces of sealant are removed.

8.9 Disconnecting the multi-plug from the temperature gauge sender unit – D7F engine

3

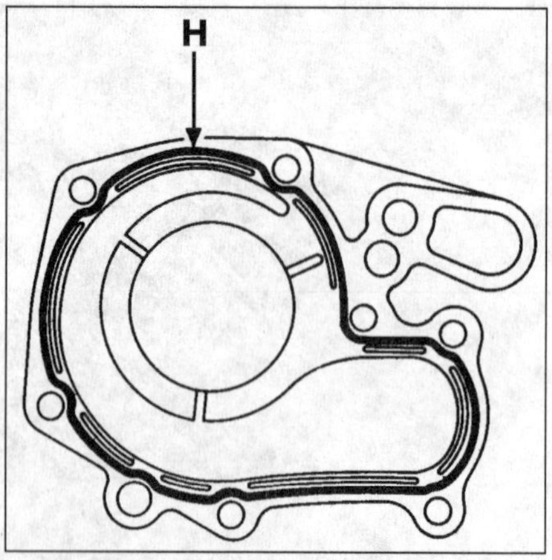

9.7a Apply a bead of sealant (H) to the coolant mating surface – K7M and E7J engines . . .

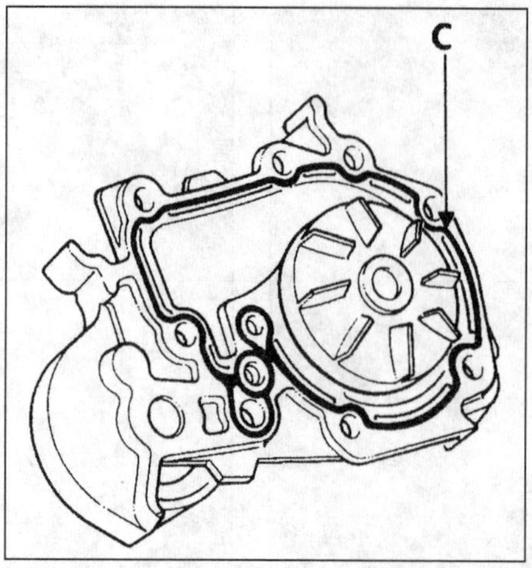

9.7b . . . . and a bead of sealant (C) – K4M engines

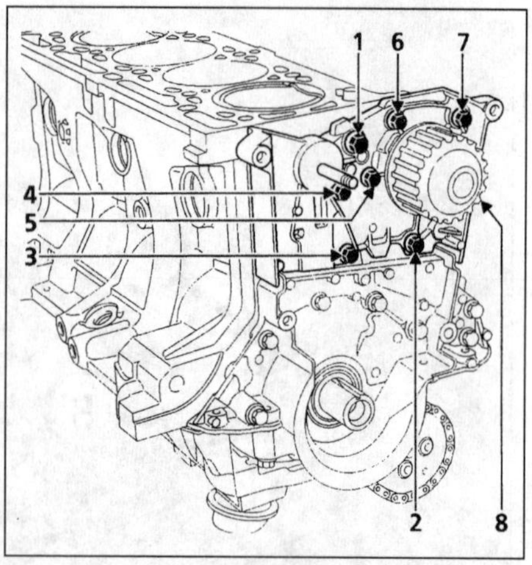

9.9 Coolant pump retaining bolt tightening sequence – K4M engine

7 Apply a 0.6 to 1.0mm wide band of Loctite 518 sealant to the pump mating face **(see illustrations).**

8 Locate the pump in position and refit the retaining bolts to their correct locations, tightening them to their specified torque. Note that a suitable thread sealant should be applied to the threads of bolts 1 and 4 for the K4M engine (see illustration 9.9).

9 On the K4M engine, work in the sequence shown **(see illustration)**, to tighten all the bolts to the specified stage 1 torque setting. Again working in sequence tighten the M6 bolts to the torque setting given for Stage 2, then tighten the M8 bolts to the setting given for Stage 3 (see Specifications at the start of this Chapter).

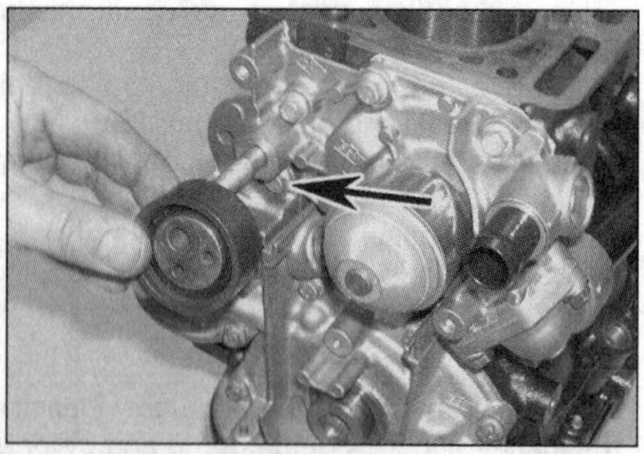

9.17 Remove the timing belt tensioner pulley for access to one of the pump securing bolts (arrowed) – D7F engine

10 Refit the timing belt tensioner and timing belt as described in Chapter 2B.

11 On completion, refill the cooling system as described in Chapter 1A.

D7F petrol engine

Note: *Suitable sealants will be required on refitting – see text.*

Removal

12 Disconnect the battery negative lead, then drain the cooling system as described in Chapter 1A.

13 Apply the handbrake, then jack up the front of the car and support securely on axle stands (see *Jacking and vehicle support*).

14 Remove the timing belt as described in Chapter 2A. Unscrew and remove the upper alternator mounting bolt, and slacken the lower bolt.

15 On models with power steering, proceed as follows.

a) *Where applicable, remove the power steering pump pulley.*
b) *Unscrew the two bolts securing the power steering fluid pipes to the cylinder block.*
c) *Unscrew and remove the bolts securing the power steering pump to the mounting bracket, then move the power steering pump and pipes to one side. Make sure that the pump is supported to avoid straining the pipes.*
d) *Unbolt the power steering pump bracket from the engine.*

16 Disconnect the coolant hoses from the coolant pump and, where applicable, unscrew the bolt securing the pump coolant pipe to the alternator mounting bracket.

17 Unscrew the nut and washer and remove the timing belt tensioner pulley (this is necessary for access to one of the coolant pump securing bolts) **(see illustration).**

18 Unbolt the coolant pump from the cylinder block. If the pump is stuck, strike it sharply with a plastic or hide mallet.

Refitting

19 Thoroughly clean all sealant from the mating faces of the coolant pump and the cylinder block.

20 If the water elbow has been removed from the pump, apply a thin bead of Loctite 518 or a suitable equivalent, to the sealing surface between the water elbow and the pump. Similarly, if the plastic pipe has been removed from the pump elbow, renew the O-ring – note that the plastic pipe is a push-fit in the elbow, and relies on the O-ring as the only form of sealing. Apply a bead of Rhodorseal 5661 (available from a Renault dealer), or similar sealant to the mating face of the coolant pump as shown **(see illustrations).**

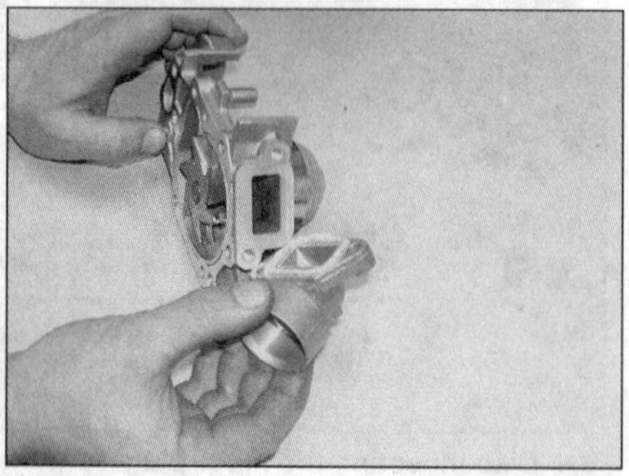

9.20a Apply a bead of sealant to the water elbow before refitting – D7F engine

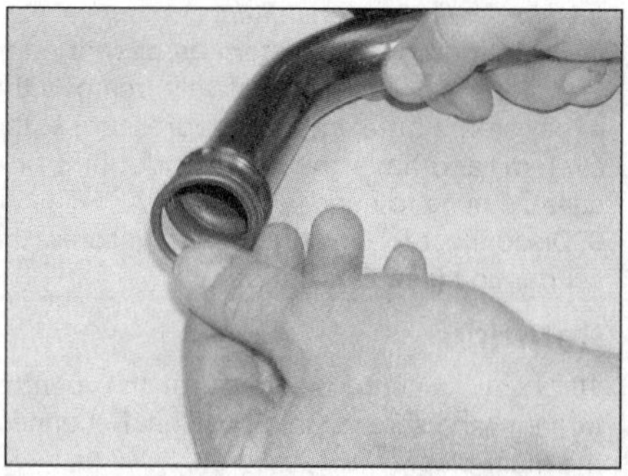

9.20b Renew the o-ring . . .

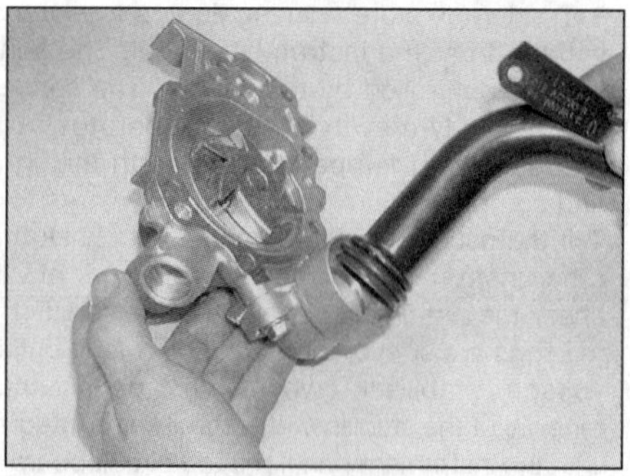

9.20c . . . then push the plastic pipe into the elbow . . .

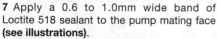

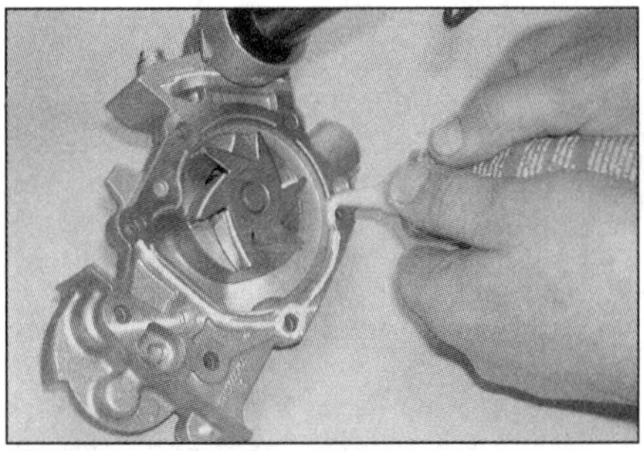

9.20d . . . and apply a bead of sealant to the water pump mating surface – D7F engine

21 Offer the pump into position in the cylinder block, ensuring that it engages with the locating dowels, then refit the bolts and tighten securely.

22 Further refitting is a reversal of removal, bearing in mind the following points.

a) Refit and tension the timing belt as described in Chapter 2A.

b) On completion, refill the cooling system as described in Chapter 1A.

E7J petrol engines

Note: *Suitable sealant will be required on refitting.*

Removal

23 Disconnect the battery negative lead, then drain the cooling system as described in Chapter 1A.

24 Remove the timing belt as described in Chapter 2B.

25 Unbolt the coolant pump from the front of the cylinder block **(see illustrations)**. If the pump is stuck, strike it sharply with a plastic or hide mallet.

Refitting

26 Clean the mating faces of the coolant pump and cylinder block, then apply a bead of sealant, 0.6 to 1.0 mm wide, around the inner perimeter of the cylinder block sealing face on the coolant pump (see illustration 9.7a).

27 Locate the coolant pump on the cylinder block, then insert the bolts and tighten them evenly.

28 Refit the timing belt as described in Chapter 2B. On completion, refill and bleed the cooling system as described in Chapter 1A.

Diesel engines

Note: *A new gasket will be required on refitting.*

Removal

29 Remove the auxiliary drivebelt as described in Chapter 1B, noting that the coolant pump pulley retaining bolts should be slackened before the belt is removed.

30 Drain the cooling system (see Chapter 1B).

31 Unscrew the retaining bolts, and remove the drivebelt pulley from the coolant pump **(see illustration)**.

32 Unscrew the retaining bolts, then manoeuvre the coolant pump out of position

9.25a Unscrew the securing bolts . . .

(see illustration). Note the correct fitted location of the pump locating dowels, and remove them for safe-keeping if they are loose. Recover the pump gasket and discard it; a new one must be used on refitting.

Refitting

33 Ensure that pump and cylinder block/housing mating faces are clean and dry, and that the locating dowels are correctly positioned.

34 Offer up the new gasket (dry) and fit the pump assembly, tightening its retaining bolts securely.

35 Refit the coolant pump pulley, refit the drivebelt and tension as described in Chapter 1B, then securely tighten the pulley retaining bolts.

36 Refill the cooling system as described in Chapter 1B.

10 Heating system – general information and checks

General information

1 The heater and fresh air ventilation unit works on the principle of mixing hot and cold air in the proportions selected by means of the left-hand (temperature) control knob. Coolant flows through the heater radiator all the time that the engine is running, regardless of the temperature selected.

2 Air distribution is selected by the central control knob. Additional control is possible by

9.31 Water pump pulley securing bolts (arrowed) – F8Q engine

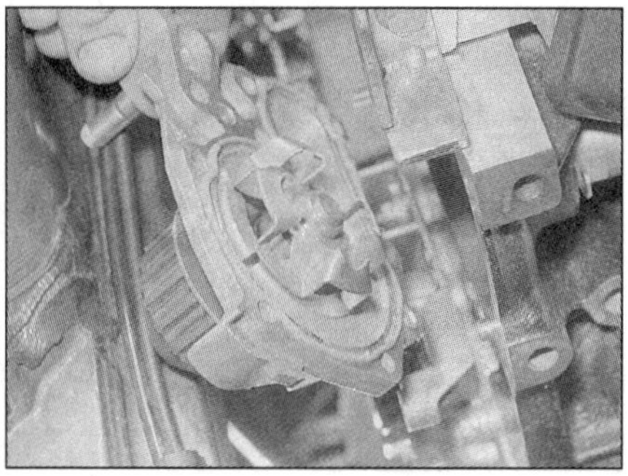

9.25b . . . and withdraw the water pump – E7J engine

opening, closing or redirecting individual vents in the facia panel.

3 A four-speed blower is controlled by the right-hand knob.

4 For details of the air conditioning system fitted to some models, refer to Section 14.

5 On some models, a recirculation switch enables the outside air supply to be closed off, while the air inside the vehicle is recirculated. This can be useful to prevent unpleasant odours entering from outside the vehicle – for instance, when driving in heavy traffic – but should only be used briefly, as the recirculated air inside the vehicle will soon become stale and may cause light misting.

Checks

6 Periodically check that all the controls operate as intended. Problems related to the temperature and air distribution controls may be due to cables being broken or disconnected (see Section 13).

7 If the blower does not operate at all, check the fuse and the blower multi-plug before condemning the motor. If one or two speeds do not work, the fault is almost certainly in the heater blower resistor (see Section 11).

8 Check the condition and security of the coolant hoses which feed the heater radiator. The radiator-to-hose joints are at the bulkhead under the bonnet. If water leaks inside the car seem to be coming from the heater, establish whether the leak is of coolant (indicating a leaking heater radiator) or of rainwater (indicating a defective scuttle seal). Cooling system antifreeze has a distinctive sweet smell.

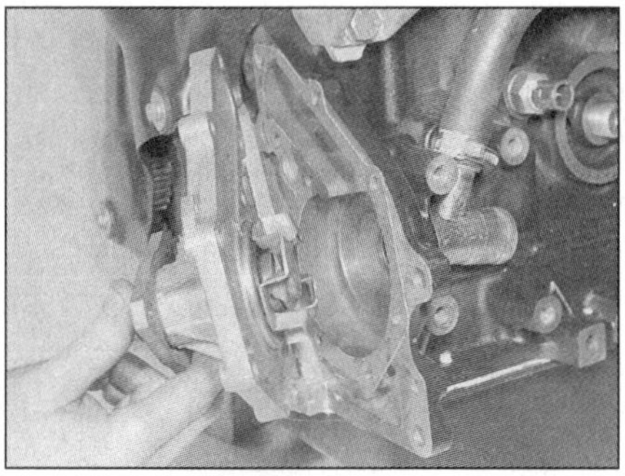

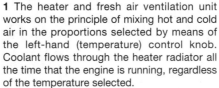

9.32 Removing the water pump

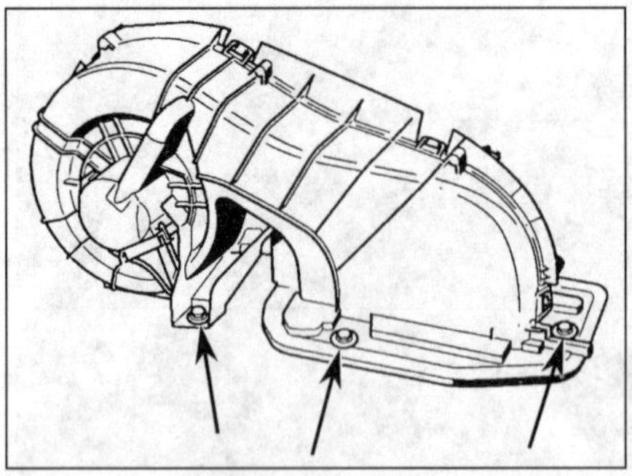

11.5 Undo the three heater blower securing bolts (arrowed)

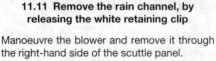

11.11 Remove the rain channel, by releasing the white retaining clip

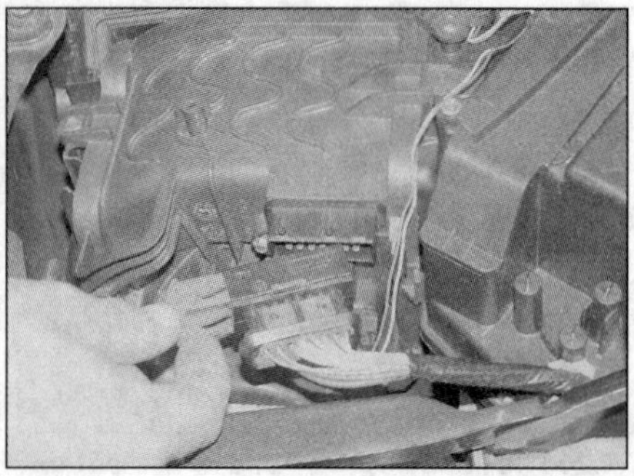

11.12 Disconnecting the multi-plug from the heater blower

11 Heater components - removal and refitting

Blower assembly - without air conditioning

Removal

1 Disconnect the battery negative lead.

2 Remove the windscreen wiper arms as described in Chapter 12, and the windscreen cowl panel as described in Chapter 11.

3 Where required, remove the windscreen wiper motor and linkage as described in Chapter 12.

4 Disconnect the multi-plug from the side of the blower assembly.

5 Remove the three bolts which secure the blower assembly in place **(see illustration)**. Manoeuvre the blower and remove it through the right-hand side of the scuttle panel.

6 If the motor is to be renewed, release the clips and separate the half-housings. Use new clips or screws (supplied with a new motor) on reassembly.

7 Check the condition of the seal at the base of the blower. Renew it if its condition is in doubt. **Note:** *If the seal is defective, rainwater entering the scuttle will leak into the passenger compartment.*

Refitting

8 Refit by reversing the removal operations.

Blower assembly - with air conditioning

Removal

9 Disconnect the battery negative lead.

10 Remove the windscreen wiper arms as described in Chapter 12, and the windscreen cowl panel as described in Chapter 11.

11 Unclip the rain channel from the lower corner of the windscreen, on the right-hand side **(see illustration)**.

12 Disconnect the multi-plug from the blower assembly **(see illustration)**.

13 Remove the four screws which secure the blower motor in place. Manoeuvre the blower motor and remove it from the scuttle panel **(see illustrations)**.

Refitting

14 Refit by reversing the removal operations.

Heater blower resistor

Removal

15 This resistor is located in the blower motor casing. It is switched into the circuit at low and intermediate speeds. If it fails, one or more speeds will not be operative.

16 Remove the blower assembly as described previously in this Section, and disconnect the wiring-plug from the resistor.

17 Remove the retaining screws, release the clips and withdraw the resistor.

Refitting

18 Refit by reversing the removal operations.

Air distribution unit

Removal

19 Remove the complete facia assembly as described in Chapter 11.

20 Undo the securing bolts from the facia mounting beam, and move it to one side.

21 If required, remove the blower assembly as described previously in this Section, to gain easier access.

22 Remove the two retaining bolts now accessible from inside the scuttle panel **(see illustration)**.

23 Clamp the coolant hoses where they pass through the bulkhead. Alternatively, drain the cooling system as described in Chapter 1A or 1B. Disconnect the hoses from the heater radiator stubs. **Note:** *There are two types of clips fitted for the heater hoses. One type twists and releases, for the other press at each side and then pull hose to release* ***(see illustrations)****.*

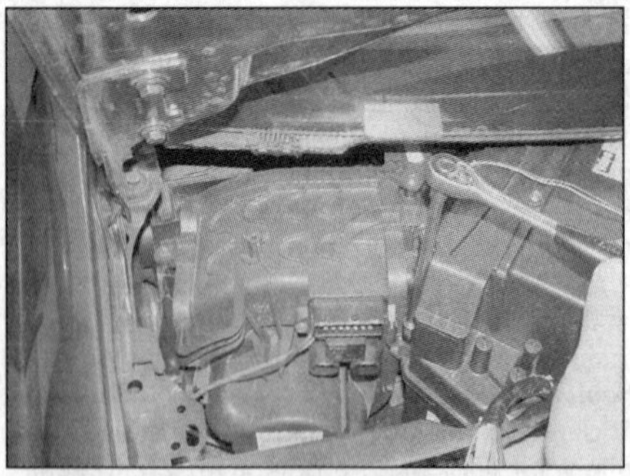

11.13a Removing one of the four heater blower securing screws

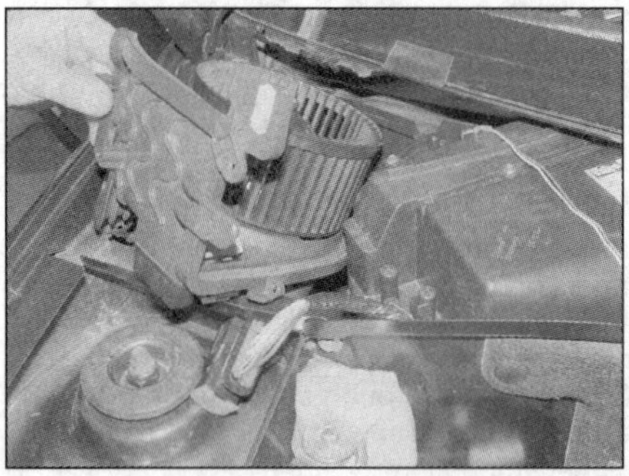

11.13b Removing the heater blower

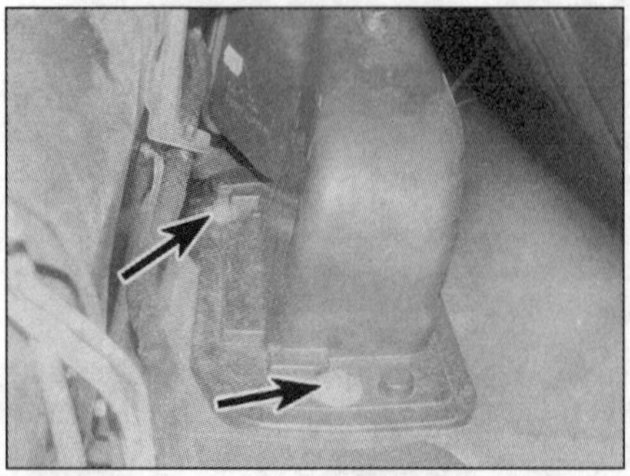

11.22 Undo the two heater unit retaining bolts (arrowed)

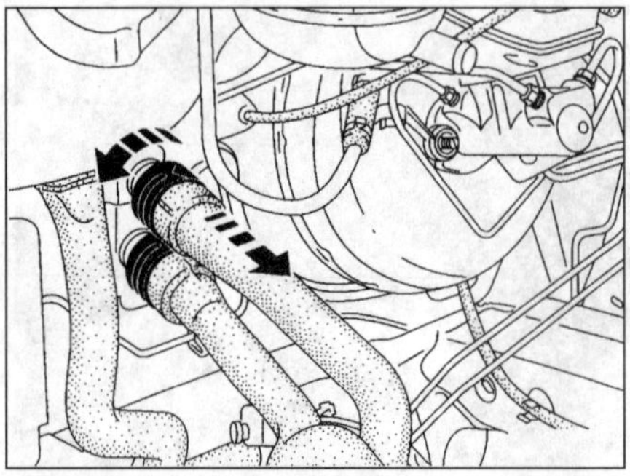

11.23a Quick release type of heater hose fittings, twist and release . . .

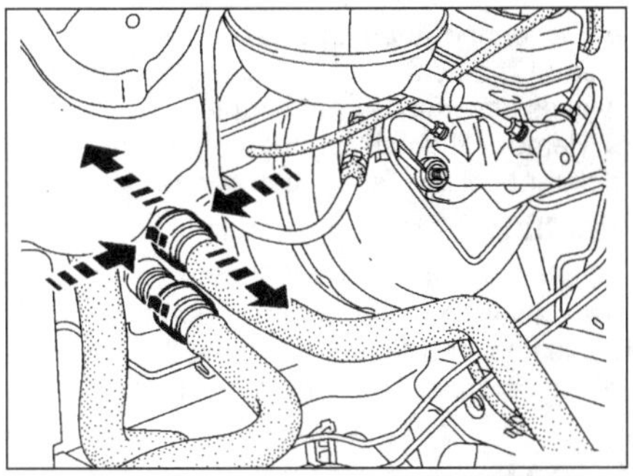

11.23b . . . and press at each side to release

24 Remove the air distribution unit, complete with control panel and cables (if still fitted), from inside the car. Be prepared for coolant spillage from the heater radiator.

Refitting

25 Refit by reversing the removal operations. Top up, or refill and bleed the cooling system as described in *Weekly checks,* Chapter 1A or 1B.

Heater radiator

Removal

26 Remove the air distribution unit as described previously in this Section.

27 Remove the foam seal and the closing plate from the heater radiator stubs **(see illustration)**.

28 Remove the two screws (if fitted), release the clips and withdraw the heater radiator **(see illustrations)**. Be careful not to damage the fins.

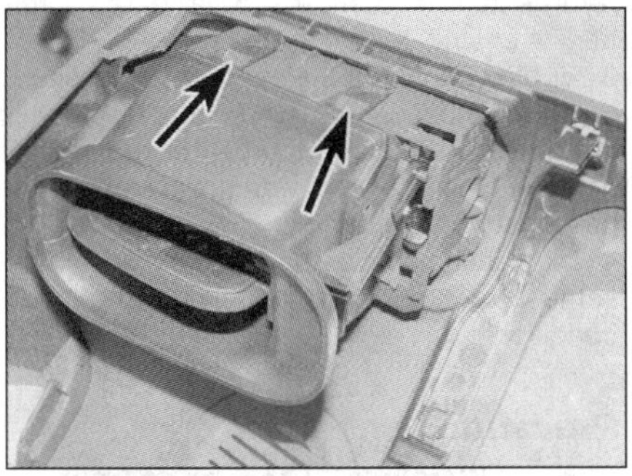

12.2a Release the clips arrowed . . .

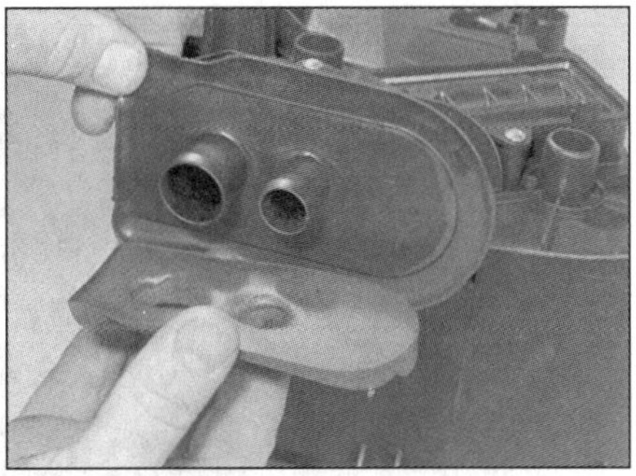

11.27 Removing the foam seal and the closing plate from the heater radiator stubs

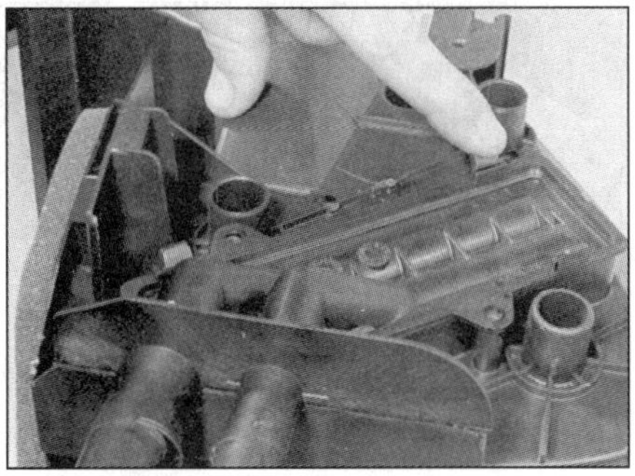

11.28b . . . release the clips . . .

Refitting

29 Refit by reversing the removal operations. If the clips were damaged during removal, secure the radiator using two screws in the holes provided.

12 Heater ducts and vents – removal and refitting

Removal

1 Remove the upper facia panel as described in Chapter 11.

2 The facia side vents are each clipped into the upper part of the facia – one at the side, unclip the retaining clips and withdraw the vents **(see illustrations)**.

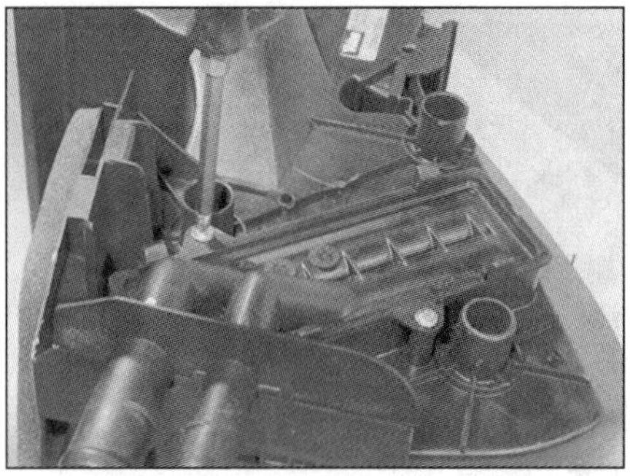

11.28a Remove the heater radiator securing screws, if fitted . . .

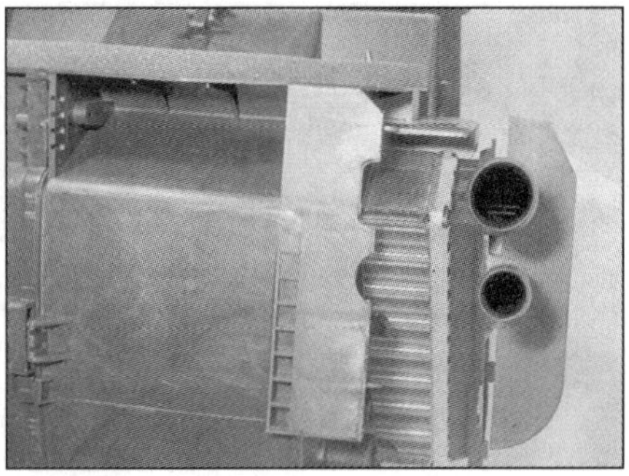

11.28c . . . and remove the heater radiator

3 Undo the retaining screws from the central vents, and withdraw them from the facia panel **(see illustrations)**.

Refitting

4 Refitting is a reversal of removal.

3

13 Heater controls – removal and refitting

Control panel and bulb

Removal

1 Disconnect the battery negative lead.

2 Remove the centre console as described in Chapter 11.

3 Remove the two screws which secure the

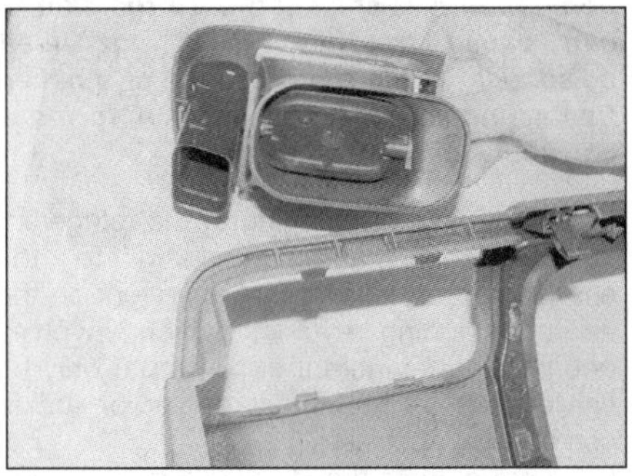

12.2b . . . and free the vent from the facia

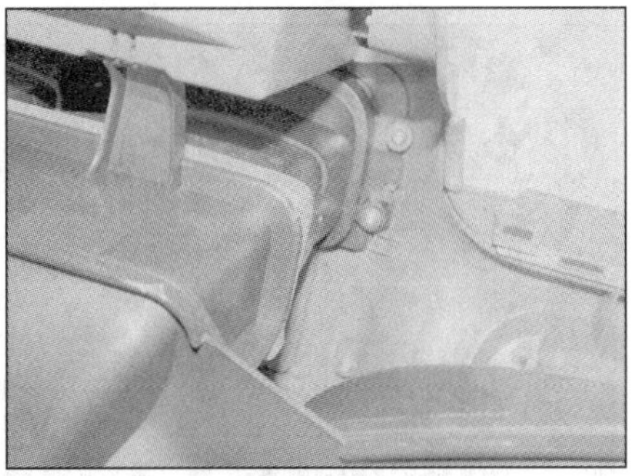

12.3a Remove the retaining screws – one from the left-hand side . . .

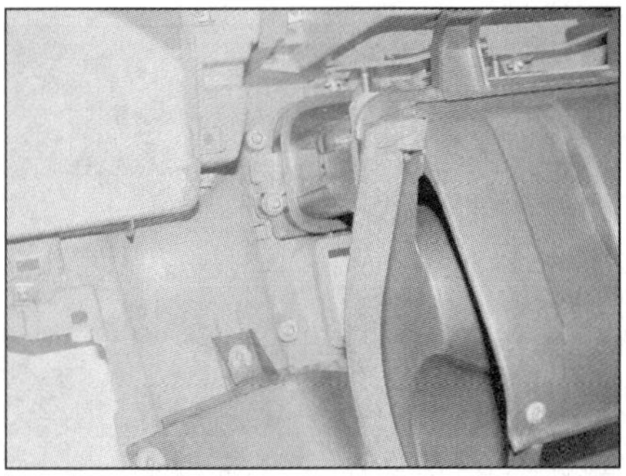

12.3b . . . and one from the right-hand side

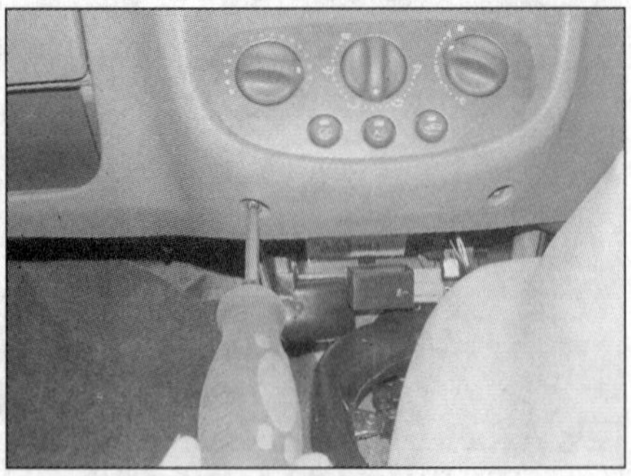

13.3a Removing the heater control panel screws . . .

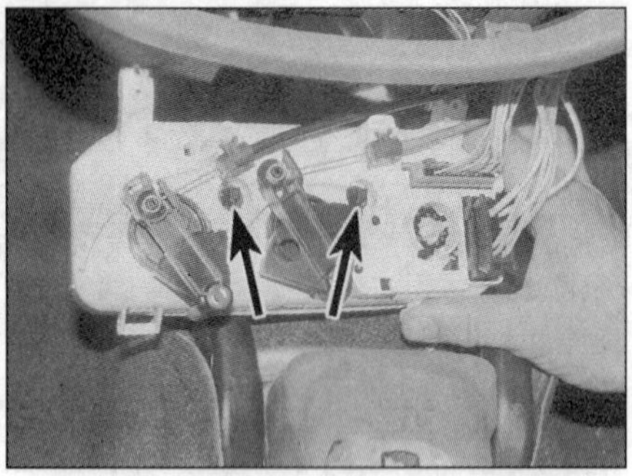

13.4a To renew the heater control panel bulbs (arrowed), free the bulbholder by twisting it a quarter of a turn with pliers . . .

heater control panel and withdraw the control panel **(see illustrations)**. (It may be necessary to disconnect the cables first, to give more room for removal of the control panel.)

13.7a Remove the heater control cable securing clip . . .

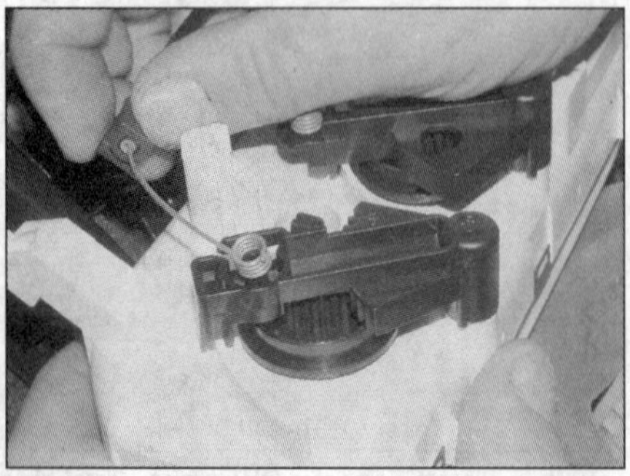

13.7b . . . and disconnect the cable from the lever

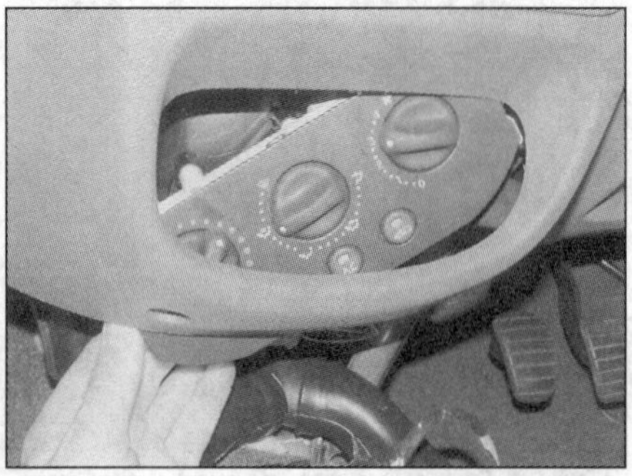

13.3b . . . and withdraw the heater control panel

13.4b . . . then separate the bulb and holder

4 If the reason for removing the panel is to renew the bulb, this can be done without further dismantling **(see illustrations)**. To remove the panel completely, disconnect the multi-plugs and the cables.

Refitting

5 Refit by reversing the removal operations. Check that the controls operate over their full range before securing the panel.

Control cables

Removal

6 Remove the control panel as described previously.

7 Unclip the outer cable securing clips from the back of the control panel. Disconnect each inner cable from its lever by turning the cable through 90° **(see illustrations)**.

13.9 Note – the upper cable colour is grey, and the lower cable is black

8 Disconnect the cables from the right-hand side of the heater unit assembly, in the same way as described in paragraph 7.

9 Remove the cables, noting that they are of different colours **(see illustration)**.

Refitting

10 Refitting is a reversal of removal. Connect the cables to the control levers. Fit the outer cable securing clips, and check the operation of the controls. Refit the control panel.

14 Air conditioning system – general information and precautions

General information

1 An air conditioning system is available on some models. It enables the temperature of incoming air to be lowered; it also dehumidifies the air, which makes for rapid demisting and increased comfort **(see illustration opposite)**.

2 The cooling side of the system works in the same way as a domestic refrigerator. Refrigerant gas is drawn into a belt-driven compressor, and passes into a condenser in front of the radiator, where it loses heat and becomes liquid. The liquid passes through an expansion valve to an evaporator, where it changes from liquid under high pressure to gas under low pressure. This change is accompanied by a drop in temperature, which cools the evaporator. The refrigerant returns to the compressor and the cycle begins again.

3 Air blown through the evaporator passes to the air distribution unit, where it is mixed with hot air blown through the heater radiator, to achieve the desired temperature in the passenger compartment.

4 The heating side of the system works in the same way as on models without air conditioning.

Precautions

Warning: The refrigerant is potentially dangerous, and should only be handled by qualified persons. If it is splashed onto the skin, it can cause frostbite. It is not itself poisonous, but in the presence of a naked flame (including a cigarette) it forms a poisonous gas.

5 Uncontrolled discharging of the refrigerant is dangerous, and damaging to the environment. It follows that any work on the air conditioning system which involves opening the refrigerant circuit **must** only be carried out by a Renault dealer or an air conditioning specialist.

6 Do not operate the air conditioning system if it is known to be short of refrigerant; the compressor may be damaged.

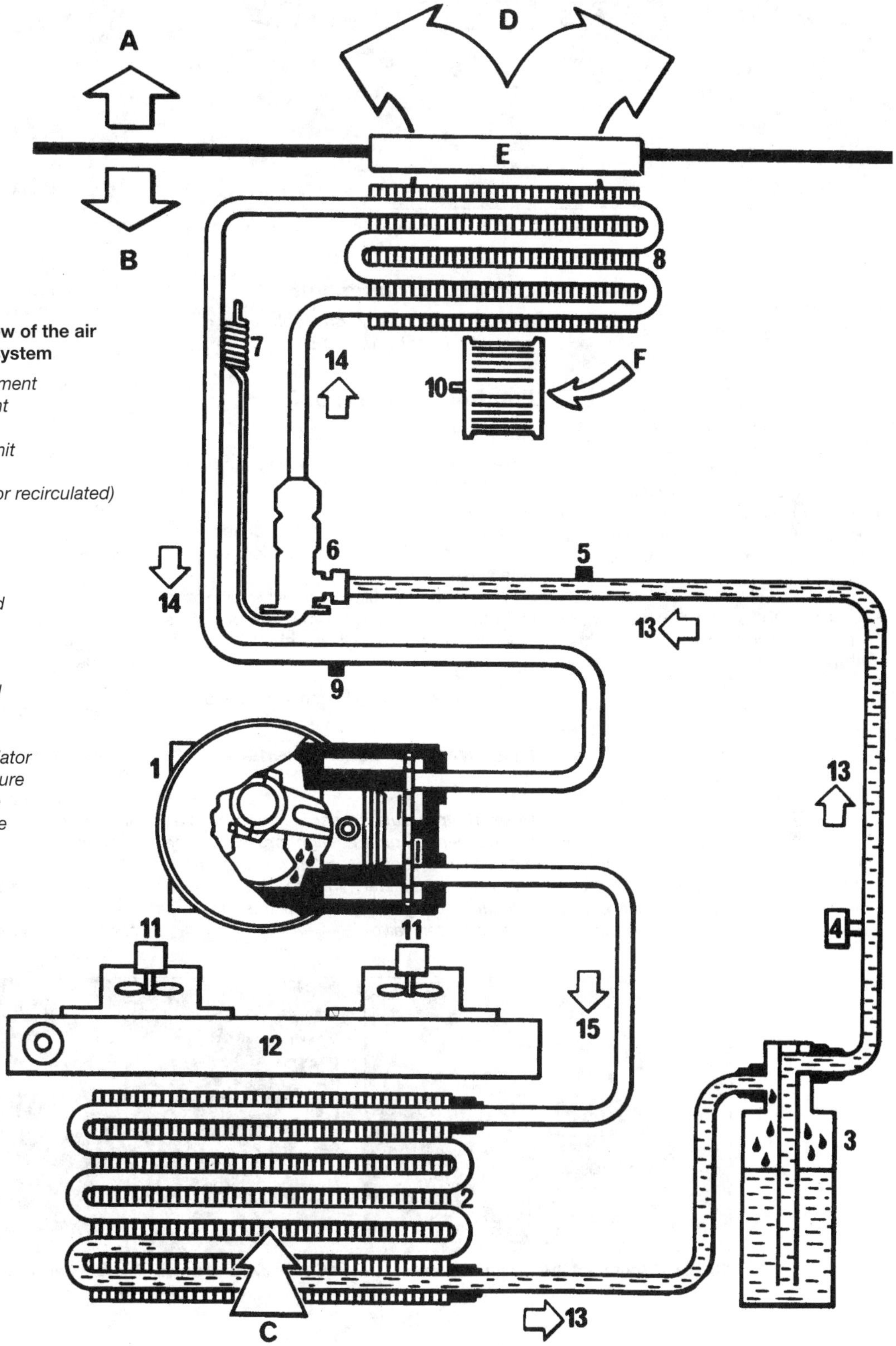

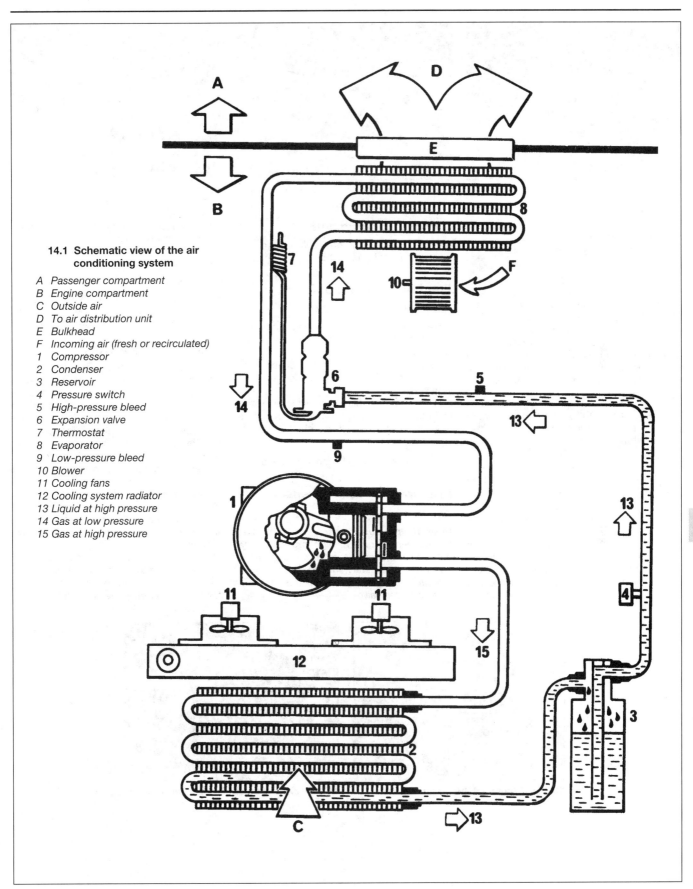

14.1 Schematic view of the air conditioning system

A Passenger compartment
B Engine compartment
C Outside air
D To air distribution unit
E Bulkhead
F Incoming air (fresh or recirculated)
1 Compressor
2 Condenser
3 Reservoir
4 Pressure switch
5 High-pressure bleed
6 Expansion valve
7 Thermostat
8 Evaporator
9 Low-pressure bleed
10 Blower
11 Cooling fans
12 Cooling system radiator
13 Liquid at high pressure
14 Gas at low pressure
15 Gas at high pressure

16.4 Disconnecting the air conditioning system electronic control unit . . .

16.5 . . . and unclip from the mounting bracket

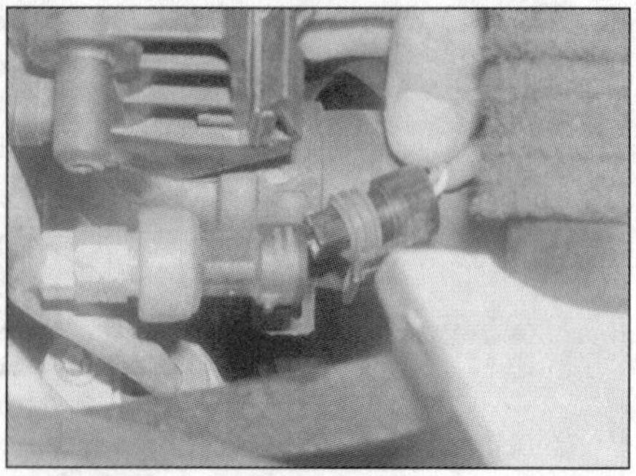

16.7 Disconnecting the wiring plug from the pressure sensor

15 Air conditioning system – checking and maintenance

1 Routine maintenance is limited to checking the tension and condition of the compressor drivebelt, as described in Chapter 1A or 1B.

2 Periodic recharging of the system will be required, since there is inevitably a slow loss of refrigerant. It is suggested that the system be inspected by a specialist every year, or at once if a loss of performance is noticed.

16 Air conditioning system – component removal and refitting

Warning: Do not attempt to open the refrigerant circuit. Refer to the precautions at the end of Section 14.

1 The only operations described here are those which can be carried out without discharging the refrigerant. All other operations must be referred to a specialist.

2 If necessary, the compressor can be unbolted and moved aside, without disconnecting its flexible hoses, after removing the drivebelt.

Compressor drivebelt

3 Refer to *Auxiliary drivebelt check and renewal* in Chapter 1A or 1B.

Electronic control unit

Removal

Note: *The control unit is located inside the driver's footwell, attached to the side of the heater unit.*

4 Disconnect the battery negative lead, then remove the multi-plug from the control unit **(see illustration)**.

5 Release the two clips, one either side, and slide the control unit downwards out of its mounting bracket **(see illustration)**.

Refitting

6 Refit by reversing the removal operations.

Evaporator pressure sensor

Removal

Note: *The pressure sensor is located beside the condenser on the high pressure pipe between the pressure relief valve and the dehydration canister. This can be removed without draining the system, as it is mounted on a 'schrader' valve.*

7 Disconnect the wiring connector from the sensor **(see illustration)**.

8 Slacken and remove the pressure sensor from the high pressure pipe.

Refitting

9 Refitting is a reversal of removal noting: The sensor is fitted with a seal, ensure it is in good condition and lubricate with P.A.G. SP10 oil.

Cooling fan relay/resistor

10 A two-speed cooling fan is fitted to models with air conditioning. The fan operates at low speed all the time that the air conditioning system is in use. If pressure rises in the refrigerant circuit or if the engine overheats, the fan operates at high speed.

11 The two fan speeds are obtained using a relay/resistor of 0.23 ohms. For low-speed operation, the resistor is switched in series with the fan motor. For high-speed operation, the resistor is bypassed.

12 Disconnect the wiring plug and unclip the resistor to disengage it from the cowling **(see illustrations)**. Refit by reversing the removal operations.

13 On most models, the resistor is located in the fan cowling to the left of the radiator. Its resistance can be checked without removing it, after disconnecting the multi-plug.

16.12a Disconnect the wiring connector . . .

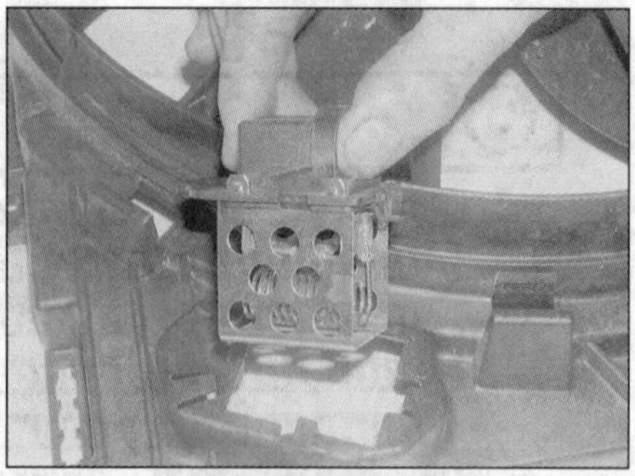

16.12b . . . and unclip the resistor from the cowling

Chapter 4 Part A: Petrol engine fuel and exhaust systems

Contents

Degrees of difficulty

Easy, suitable for novice with little experience	**Fairly easy,** suitable for beginner with some experience	**Fairly difficult,** suitable for competent DIY mechanic	**Difficult,** suitable for experienced DIY mechanic	**Very difficult,** suitable for expert DIY or professional

Specifications

System type

1.2 litre models (D7F engine):	
Engine code D7F 720	Sagem or Magneti Marelli semi-sequential multi-point injection with Magneti Marelli throttle body
Engine code D7F 702 and D7F 726	Siemens-Sirius sequential multi-point injection
1.4 litre models (E7J engine):	
Engine code E7J 780	Siemens-Fenix 5 semi-sequential multi-point injection with Pierburg throttle body
Engine code E7J 634	Siemens-Sirius sequential multi-point injection
1.4 litre models (K4J engine)	Siemens-Sirius sequential multi-point injection
1.6 litre models (K7M engine)	Siemens-Fenix 5 semi-sequential multi-point injection with Pierburg throttle body
1.6 litre models (K4M engine)	Siemens-Sirius sequential multi-point injection

Fuel system data

Fuel pressure regulator control pressure (all models):	
Zero vacuum	3.0 ± 0.2 bars
500 mbars vacuum	2.5 ± 0.2 bars
Fuel pump flow output (minimum):	
D7F, E7J 780, K7M engines	80 litres/hour at 3.0 bars fuel pressure
K4J engine	130 litres/hour at 3.5 bars fuel pressure
K4M engine	80 litres/hour at 3.0 bars fuel pressure
Air temperature sensor resistance:	
D7F 720 engine:	
At 0°C	5000 to 7000 ohms
At 20°C	1700 to 3300 ohms
At 40°C	800 to 1550 ohms
E7J 780 and K7M engines:	
At 0°C	7470 to 11 970 ohms
At 20°C	3060 to 4045 ohms
At 40°C	1315 to 1600 ohms
E7J 634 engine:	
At –10°C	10 450 to 8525 ohms
At 25°C	2120 to 1880 ohms
At 50°C	860 to 760 ohms
D7F 702/726, K4J and K4M engines:	
At 0°C	5290 to 6490 ohms
At 20°C	2400 to 2600 ohms
At 40°C	1070 to 1270 ohms

Fuel system data (continued)

Coolant temperature sensor resistance:	
D7F 720, E7J 780 and K7M engines:	
At 20°C	2600 to 3000 ohms
At 40°C	1100 to 1300 ohms
At 80°C	270 to 300 ohms
At 90°C	200 to 215 ohms
E7J 634 engine:	
At 25°C	2360 to 2140 ohms
At 50°C	770 to 850 ohms
At 80°C	275 to 290 ohms
At 110°C	112 to 117 ohms
D7F 702/726, K4J and K4M engines:	
At 20°C	3060 to 4045 ohms
At 40°C	1315 to 1600 ohms
At 80°C	300 to 370 ohms
At 90°C	210 to 270 ohms
Throttle potentiometer:	
D7F 720 engine:	
Voltage	5.0 volts
Resistance:	
Track A-B	1300 ohms (no load), 1300 ohms (full load)
Track A-C	1360 ohms (no load), 2350 ohms (full load)
Track B-C	2300 ohms (no load), 1260 ohms (full load)
D7F 702/726 engine:	
Voltage	5.0 volts
Resistance:	
Track A-B	1200 ohms (no load), 1200 ohms (full load)
Track A-C	1260 ohms (no load), 2200 ohms (full load)
Track B-C	2200 ohms (no load), 1260 ohms (full load)
E7J 780 engine:	
Voltage	5.0 volts
Resistance:	
Track 1-2	5400 ohms (no load), 2200 ohms (full load)
Track 1-3	4500 ohms (no load), 4460 ohms (full load)
Track 2-3	2160 ohms (no load), 5340 ohms (full load)
K7M engine:	
Voltage	5.0 volts
Resistance:	
Track 1-2	5440 ohms (no load), 2200 ohms (full load)
Track 1-3	4500 ohms (no load), 4460 ohms (full load)
Track 2-3	2160 ohms (no load), 5340 ohms (full load)
K4J and K4M engines:	
Voltage	5.0 volts
Resistance:	
Track A-B	1250 ohms (no load), 1250 ohms (full load)
Track A-C	1245 ohms (no load), 2230 ohms (full load)
Track B-C	2230 ohms (no load), 1245 ohms (full load)
E7J 634 engine:	
Type	Incorporated in throttle housing
Track resistance	4100 ± 800 ohms
Cursor resistance	1500 ± 150 ohms
Stepper motor:	
D7F engine:	
Voltage	12 volts
Resistance:	
Track A-D	100 ± 10 ohms
Track B-C	100 ± 10 ohms
E7J 780, K7M engines:	
Voltage	12 volts
Resistance:	
Track A-D	52.0 ± 5 ohms
Track B-C	52.0 ± 5 ohms
E7J 634 engine:	
Resistance	50.0 ohms
K4J and K4M engines:	
Resistance	53.0 ± 5 ohms

Fuel system data (continued)

Injector resistance	14.5 ± 1.0 ohms
TDC sensor resistance	220 ohms
Fuel tank level sender unit resistance at height of float pin (approx):	
At 164 mm	3.5 ± 3.5 ohms
At 143 mm	61 ± 7 ohms
At 110 mm	110 ± 10 ohms
At 81 mm	190 ± 16 ohms
At 52 mm	280 ± 20 ohms
At 47 mm	310 ± 10 ohms
Specified idle speed (non-adjustable):	
D7F engine	740 ± 50 rpm
E7J, K7M, K4J, K4M engines	750 ± 50 rpm
Idle mixture CO content (non-adjustable)	0.5% maximum (0.3% at 2500 rpm)

Recommended fuel

Minimum octane rating	95 RON unleaded. Leaded fuel must **not** be used

Torque wrench settings

Torque wrench settings	Nm	lbf ft
Exhaust manifold (D7F engine):		
Nut	25	18
Stud	10	7
Downpipe bolt	22	16
Exhaust manifold (E7J and K7M engines):		
Bolt	20	15
Exhaust manifold (K4J and K4M engines):		
Upstream oxygen sensor	45	33
Nut	18	13
Downpipe nuts	20	15
Heatshield	10	7
Fuel rail	10	7
Fuel tank	21	15
Inlet manifold (D7F engine):		
Nut	17	13
Stud	10	7
Inlet manifold (E7J and K7M engines):		
Bolt and nut	20	15
Inlet manifold (K4J and K4M engines):		
Bolt	10	7
Air cleaner securing bolt	9	7
Throttle body	15	11
Knock sensor	20	15
Throttle body	10	7

1 General information and precautions

The fuel system consists of a fuel tank which is mounted under the rear of the vehicle with an electric fuel pump immersed in it, a fuel filter and the fuel feed and return lines. The fuel pump supplies fuel to the fuel rail, which acts as a reservoir for the four fuel injectors which inject fuel into the inlet tracts. In addition, there is an Electronic Control Unit (ECU) and various sensors, electrical components and related wiring.

Refer to Section 6 for further information on the operation of each fuel injection system, and to Section 15 for information on the exhaust system.

Warning: Many of the procedures in this Chapter require the removal of fuel lines and connections, which may result in some fuel spillage. Before carrying out any operation on the fuel system, refer to the precautions given in 'Safety first!' at the beginning of this manual, and follow them implicitly. Petrol is a highly-dangerous and volatile liquid, and the precautions necessary when handling it cannot be overstressed

Note: *Residual pressure will remain in the fuel lines long after the vehicle was last used. When disconnecting any fuel line, first depressurise the fuel system as described in Section 7.*

Caution: If the radio/cassette in your vehicle is equipped with an anti-theft system, make sure you have the correct activation code before disconnecting the battery

2.1 Disconnect the wiring plug from the MAP sensor . . .

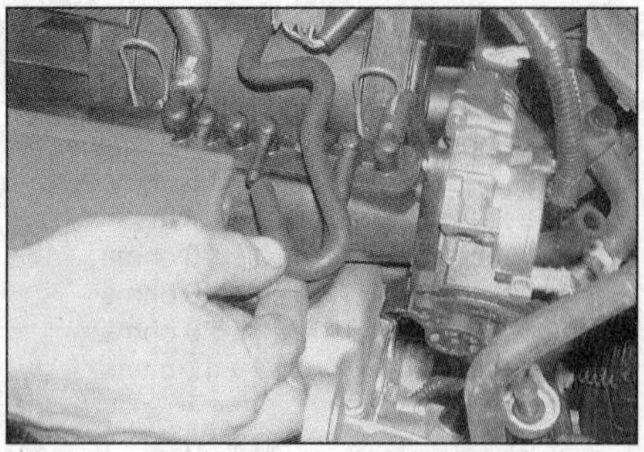

2.2 . . . then disconnect the MAP sensor vacuum hose from the inlet manifold – D7F engine

2.4a Removing the inlet air trunking . . .

2.4b . . . and the air cleaner-to-inlet manifold trunking – D7F engine

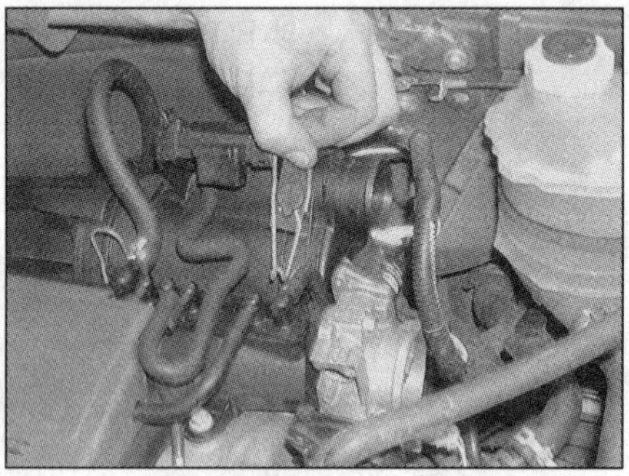

2.5a Release the rubber straps . . .

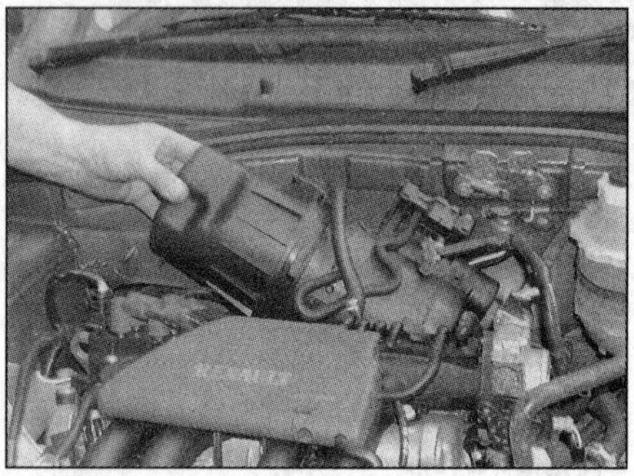

2.5b . . . then lift the air cleaner from the engine – D7F engine

2 Air cleaner assembly and inlet ducts – removal and refitting

Removal

D7F engine

1 Disconnect the wiring plug from the absolute pressure (MAP) sensor on top of the air cleaner housing **(see illustration)**.

2 Disconnect the MAP sensor vacuum hose from the inlet manifold **(see illustration)**.

3 Release the wiring harness from the clip on the air cleaner housing.

4 Release the clips, and disconnect the inlet air trunking from the air cleaner and the air intake pipe, then remove the inlet air trunking securing screw, disconnect the breather hoses from the trunking, and remove the trunking. Similarly, remove the air cleaner-to-inlet manifold trunking **(see illustrations)**.

5 Release the two rubber securing straps, then lift the air cleaner assembly from the engine. If necessary, remove the inlet duct from the front of the engine compartment **(see illustrations)**.

E7J and K7M engines

6 At the front of the engine compartment, detach the air inlet hose from the crossmember.

7 Unbolt and remove the air cleaner assembly from the top of the engine, and at the same time disconnect it from the air duct at the rear of the engine **(see illustrations)**.

8 Disconnect the wiring/hose from the air temperature and MAP sensors, then loosen the clips and remove the air inlet duct from the throttle body.

K4J and K4M engines

9 Release the rubber strap and remove the resonator box and duct from the air cleaner housing.

10 Undo the retaining screws then unhook the air cleaner housing and remove it from the inlet manifold.

11 Note how the air cleaner element is fitted, then remove it from the housing.

12 Unbolt the inlet duct plenum from the throttle body.

Refitting

13 Refitting is a reversal of removal.

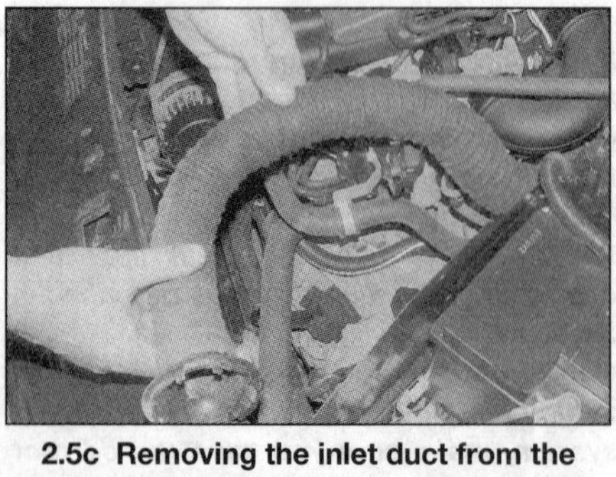

2.5c Removing the inlet duct from the front of the engine compartment – D7F engine

2.7a Unscrew the bolts . . .

2.7b . . . and remove the air cleaner assembly

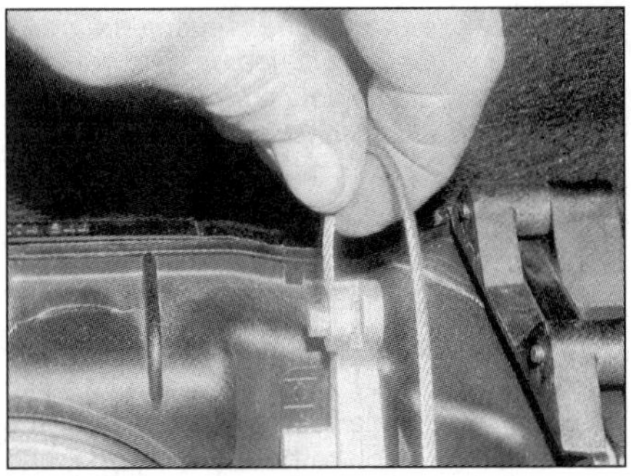

3.2 Disconnecting the accelerator cable from the quadrant

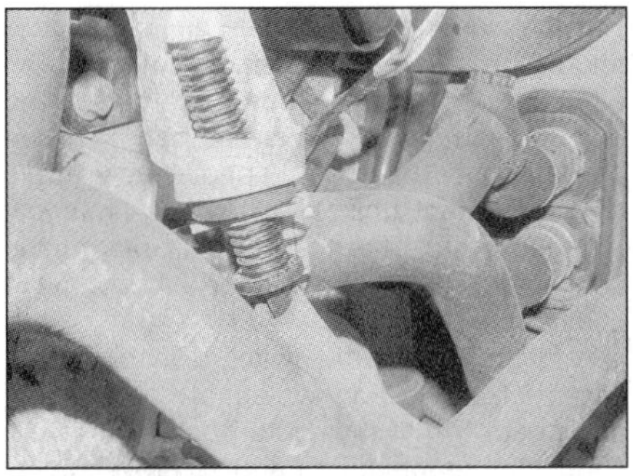

3.3a Accelerator cable adjustment ferrule and bracket – D7F engine

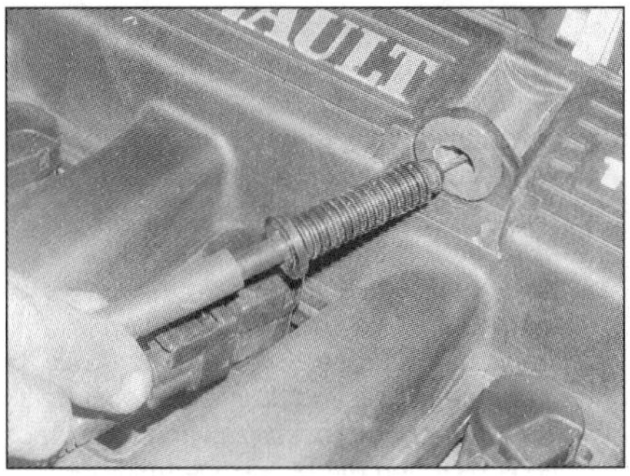

3.3b Removing the outer cable and ferrule from the support bracket – K4J engine

3 Accelerator cable – removal, refitting and adjustment

Removal

1 On E7J, K7M, K4J and K4M engines, remove the air cleaner and inlet ducts as described in Section 2.

2 On the throttle body/housing, turn the throttle quadrant by hand to release the cable tension. Disconnect the inner cable from the quadrant **(see illustration)**.

3 Remove the outer cable and ferrule from the support bracket **(see illustrations)**. If necessary, remove the spring clip from the end of the cable noting its position in the groove.

4 Working inside the car, remove the lower trim panel from under the steering column. Disconnect the cable from the accelerator pedal by squeezing the lugs of the cable end fitting.

5 Return to the engine compartment, release the outer cable from the bulkhead and withdraw the cable.

Refitting

6 Refitting is a reversal of removal, but adjust the cable if necessary as follows.

Adjustment

7 With the spring clip removed from the accelerator outer cable, ensure that the throttle quadrant is fully against its stop. Gently pull the cable out of its grommet until all free play is removed from the inner cable.

8 With the cable held in this position, refit the spring clip to the last exposed outer cable groove in front of the rubber grommet and washer **(see illustration)**. When the clip is refitted and the outer cable is released, there should be only a small amount of free play in the inner cable. **Note:** *The idle speed control motor opens the throttle slightly when the ignition is switched off. There must be enough slack in the cable to allow the throttle to close past this position, otherwise a stable idle speed will not be obtained.*

9 Have an assistant depress the accelerator pedal, and check that the throttle quadrant opens fully and returns smoothly to its stop.

4 Accelerator pedal – removal and refitting

Removal

1 Remove the lower trim panel from under the steering column.

2 Disconnect the cable from the top of the accelerator pedal by squeezing the lugs of the cable end fitting.

3 Remove the nut which secures the accelerator pedal pivot and bush to the bulkhead.

4 Withdraw the accelerator pedal.

5 Examine the pedal and pivot for signs of wear and renew as necessary.

Refitting

6 Refitting is a reversal of removal. Check the adjustment of the accelerator cable as described in Section 3.

5 Unleaded petrol – general information and usage

Note: *The information given in this Chapter is correct at the time of writing. If updated information is thought to be required, check with a Renault dealer. If travelling abroad, consult one of the motoring organisations (or a similar authority) for advice on the fuel available.*

The fuel recommended by Renault is given in the Specifications Section of this Chapter.

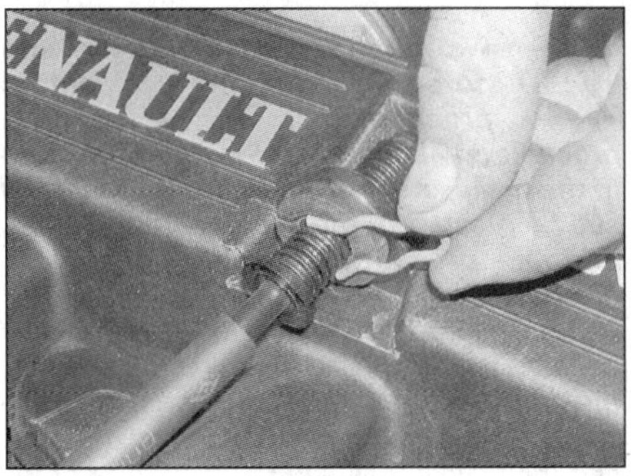

3.8 Fitting the spring clip to the ferrule on the outer cable

All petrol models are designed to run on fuel with a minimum octane rating of 95 (RON). All models have a catalytic converter, and so must be run on unleaded fuel **only**. Under no circumstances should leaded fuel be used, as this may damage the converter.

Super unleaded petrol (98 octane) can also be used in all models if wished, though there is no advantage in doing so.

6 Fuel injection systems – general information

Sagem and Magneti Marelli systems

1.2 litre models (D7F engines) are equipped with a Sagem or Magneti Marelli semi-sequential multi-point injection system with a Magneti Marelli throttle body. The system incorporates a closed-loop catalytic converter and an evaporative emission control system, and complies with the latest emission control standards. The system is of semi-sequential design with the injectors operating in pairs (1 and 4, then 2 and 3). There is one injection per revolution of the engine for each cylinder, ie, during the complete four-stroke cycle these take place on the induction **and** combustion strokes. The fuel injection side of the system operates as follows; refer to Chapter 5B for information on the ignition system.

4A

The fuel pump, immersed in the fuel tank, pumps fuel from the fuel tank to the fuel rail, via a filter mounted underneath the rear of the vehicle. Fuel supply pressure is controlled by the pressure regulator in the throttle body assembly. The regulator operates by allowing excess fuel to return to the tank. There are four injectors (one per cylinder) located in the inlet manifold downstream of the throttle valve. All the injectors are fed from the fuel rail.

The electrical control system consists of the ECU, along with the following sensors:

a) *Throttle potentiometer – informs the ECU of the throttle position, and the rate of throttle opening or closing.*
b) *Coolant temperature sensor – informs the ECU of engine temperature.*

c) *Inlet air temperature sensor – informs the ECU of the temperature of the air passing through the throttle body.*
d) *Lambda sensor – informs the ECU of the oxygen content of the exhaust gases (explained in greater detail in Part C of this Chapter).*
e) *Idle speed regulation stepper motor – controls the idle speed.*
f) *Crankshaft TDC sensor – informs the ECU of engine speed and crankshaft position.*
g) *Power steering pressure switch – informs the ECU when the power steering pump is working so the engine idle speed can be increased to prevent stalling.*
h) *Knock sensor – informs the ECU when pre-ignition ('pinking') is occurring (explained in greater detail in Part B of Chapter 5).*
i) *Manifold absolute pressure (MAP) sensor – informs the ECU of the engine load by monitoring the pressure in the inlet manifold.*
j) *Fuel vapour recirculation valve – operates the fuel evaporative control system (explained in greater detail in Part C of this Chapter).*

All the above information is analysed by the ECU and, based on this, the ECU determines the appropriate ignition and fuelling requirements for the engine. The ECU controls the fuel injector by varying its pulse width – the length of time the injector is held open – to provide a richer or weaker mixture, as appropriate. The mixture is constantly varied by the ECU, to provide the best setting for cranking, starting (with either a hot or cold engine), warm-up, idle, cruising, and acceleration. On automatic transmission models, information from sensors on the transmission is sent to the ECU for processing to determine the most efficient settings for the engine.

The ECU also has full control over the engine idle speed, via a stepper motor which is fitted to the throttle body. The motor pushrod rests against a cam on the throttle spindle. When the throttle is closed (accelerator pedal released), the ECU uses the motor to vary the opening of the throttle valve and so control the idle speed.

The ECU also controls the exhaust and evaporative emission control systems, which are described in detail in Part C of this Chapter.

If there is an abnormality in any of the readings obtained from either the coolant temperature sensor, the inlet air temperature sensor or the Lambda sensor, the ECU enters its back-up mode. In this event, the ECU ignores the abnormal sensor signal, and assumes a pre-programmed value which will allow the engine to continue running (albeit at reduced efficiency). If the ECU enters this back-up mode, the warning light on the instrument panel will come on, and the relevant fault code will be stored in the ECU memory.

If the warning light comes on, the vehicle should be taken to a Renault dealer at the earliest opportunity. A complete test of the engine management system can then be carried out, using a special electronic diagnostic test unit (XR25) which is simply plugged into the system's diagnostic connector (located beneath the ashtray on the centre console).

A fuel cut-off inertia switch is incorporated into the fuel injection system. In the event of an impact the switch cuts off the electrical supply to the fuel pump and so prevents fuel being expelled should the fuel pipes/hoses be damaged in an accident. The switch is located in the left-hand rear corner of the engine compartment.

Siemens-Fenix 5 system

1.4 and 1.6 litre models with SOHC engines (E7J and K7M) are equipped with a Siemens-Fenix 5 semi-sequential multi-point fuel injection/ignition system with a Pierburg throttle housing. This system operates as for the system described for the 1.2 litre engine.

Siemens-Sirius system

1.4 and 1.6 litre models with DOHC engines (K4J and K4M) are equipped with a Siemens-Sirius sequential multi-point fuel injection/ignition system. The system is of closed-loop type incorporating two oxygen sensors, one located upstream and the other downstream of the catalytic converter. An evaporative emission control system is fitted.

The multi-point injection system uses one injector and one ignition coil for each cylinder, and the injectors are operated individually and sequentially at the beginning of the inlet stroke. The electronic control unit (ECU) is able to determine which cylinder is on its inlet stroke without the use of a camshaft position sensor, however if the unit is renewed, the car must be taken for a road test lasting at least 25 minutes to enable the ECU to reprogram itself; the stepper motor must also be reset.

The system operates as for the system described for the 1.2 litre engine.

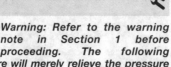

7 Fuel injection system – depressurisation

Warning: Refer to the warning note in Section 1 before proceeding. The following procedure will merely relieve the pressure in the fuel system – remember that fuel will still be present in the system components, and take precautions accordingly before disconnecting any of them.

Note: *The fuel system referred to in this Section includes the tank-mounted fuel pump, the fuel filter, the fuel injector(s) and the pressure regulator in the throttle body/fuel rail, and the metal pipes and flexible hoses of the fuel lines between these components. All these contain fuel which will be under pressure while the engine is running, and/or while the ignition is switched on. The pressure will remain for some time after the ignition has been switched off, and it must be relieved when any of these components are disturbed for servicing work.*

Method 1

1 Disconnect the battery negative lead (refer to *Disconnecting the battery* in the Reference Section).

2 Place a suitable container beneath the connection or union to be disconnected, and have a large rag ready to soak up any escaping fuel not being caught by the container.

3 Slowly loosen the connection or union nut to avoid a sudden release of pressure, and position the rag around the connection, to catch any fuel spray which may be expelled. Once the pressure is released, disconnect the fuel line. Plug the pipe ends, to minimise fuel loss and prevent the entry of dirt into the fuel system.

Method 2

4 Remove the fuel pump relay located in the engine compartment fuse/relay box (see Chapter 12).

5 Start the engine and allow it to idle until it stops due to lack of fuel. Operate the starter motor a couple more times, to ensure that all fuel pressure has been relieved.

6 Switch off the ignition and refit the fuel pump relay.

8 Fuel pump – removal and refitting

Warning: Refer to the warning note in Section 1 before proceeding.

Removal

1 Disconnect the battery negative lead (refer to *Disconnecting the battery* in the Reference Section).

2 Remove the rear seat, or rear seat cushion as described in Chapter 11, for access to the fuel pump cover.

3 Carefully prise the access cover from the floor to expose the fuel pump **(see illustration)**.

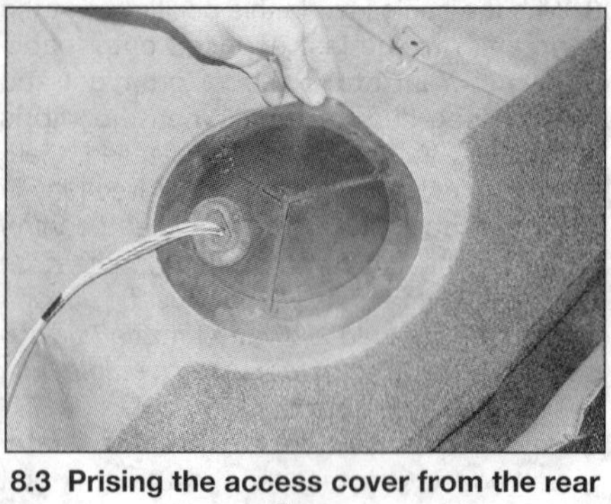

8.3 Prising the access cover from the rear floor

4 Disconnect the wiring connector from the fuel pump, and tape the connector to the vehicle body, to prevent it disappearing behind the tank **(see illustration)**.

5 Identify the fuel hoses for position; the green hose on the left-hand side is the supply to the engine compartment, and the red hose next to the wiring connector is the return (arrows on the top of the pump indicate the direction of fuel flow). The hoses are equipped with quick-release fittings to ease removal. To disconnect each hose, slide out the locking tab from the collar then compress the collar and detach the hose from the pump. Renault technicians use a special tool to compress the collar – without this tool, it is possible to use a small screwdriver **carefully** to press back the locking collar inside the end of the special end fitting. Disconnect both hoses from the top of the pump, then plug the hose ends to minimise fuel loss **(see illustration)**.

6 Noting the alignment arrows on the pump cover, locking ring and fuel tank, unscrew the locking ring and remove it from the tank. This can be accomplished by using a screwdriver on the raised ribs of the locking ring – carefully tap the screwdriver to turn the ring anti-clockwise until it can be unscrewed by hand. Alternatively a removal tool can be fabricated out of metal bar and two bolts **(see illustrations)**.

7 Carefully lift the fuel pump assembly out of the fuel tank, taking great care not to damage the fuel level gauge sender arm, or to spill fuel in the interior of the vehicle. Remove the rubber sealing ring and check it for deterioration; if it is in good condition, it may be re-used, however if

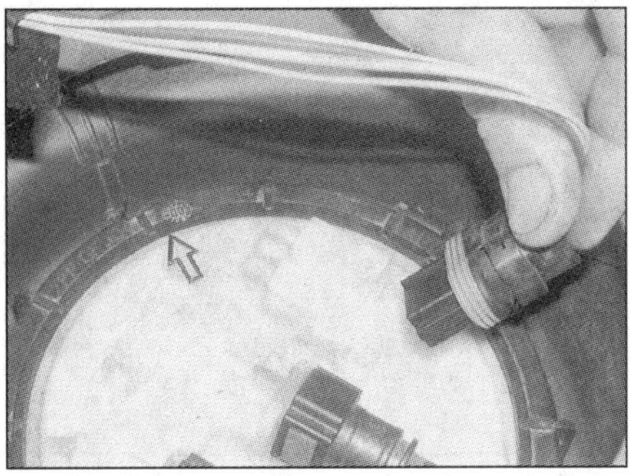

8.4 Disconnecting the wiring from the fuel pump

the pump is to remain out of the fuel tank for several hours, the locking ring should be refitted temporarily to prevent the sealing ring from distorting. If the sealing ring is unserviceable, obtain a new one **(see illustrations)**.

8 Note that the fuel pump/fuel gauge sender unit is only available as a complete assembly – no components are available separately.

Refitting

9 Ensure that the fuel pump pick-up filter is clean and free of debris. Fit the sealing ring to the top of the fuel tank.

10 Carefully manoeuvre the pump assembly into the fuel tank.

11 Align the arrow on the fuel pump cover with the arrow on the fuel tank (the arrow must point to the rear of the vehicle), then refit the locking ring. Securely tighten the locking ring, then recheck that the pump cover and tank marks are all correctly aligned.

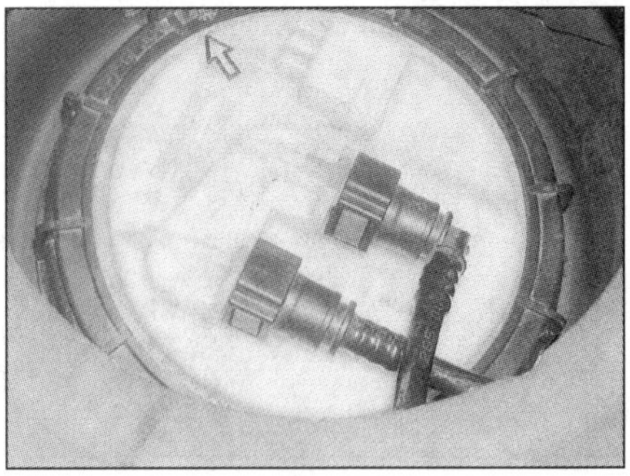

8.5 Fuel supply and return hoses on the fuel pump

12 Reconnect the feed and return hoses to the top of the fuel pump; it is not necessary to depress the collars when refitting the hoses. Check the hoses are securely in position.

13 Reconnect the wiring connector.

14 Reconnect the battery and start the engine. Check the fuel pump feed and return hoses for signs of leakage.

15 Refit the plastic access cover and the rear seat cushion.

9 Fuel gauge sender unit – testing, removal and refitting

Testing

1 The fuel gauge sender unit is supplied as part of the fuel pump assembly, however it is possible to test its operation and remove it.

8.6a Alignment arrows on the pump cover, fuel tank and locking ring

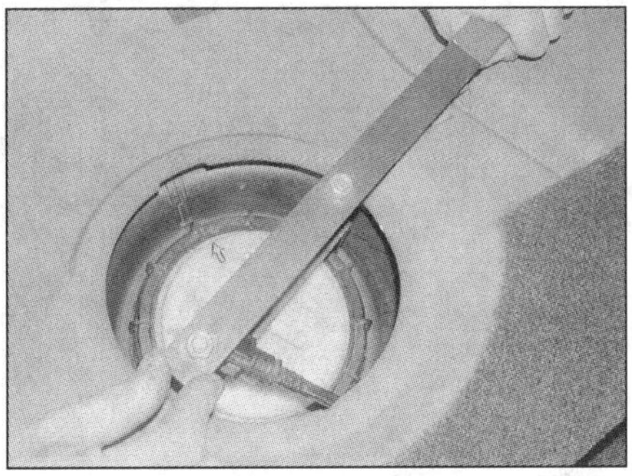

8.6b Using a home-made removal tool to unscrew the locking ring from the fuel tank

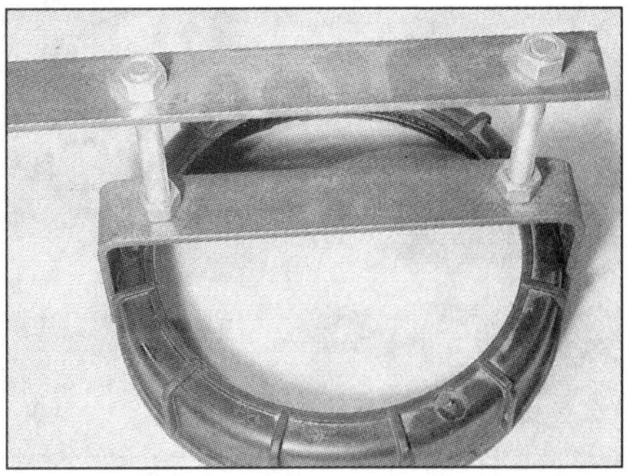

8.6c Home-made fuel pump locking ring removal tool

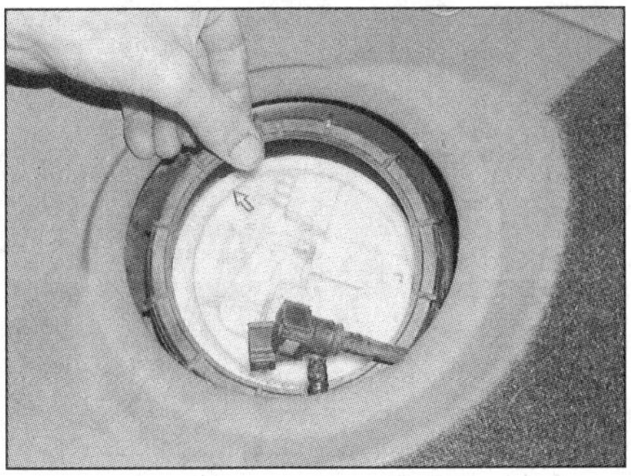

8.6d Removing the locking ring

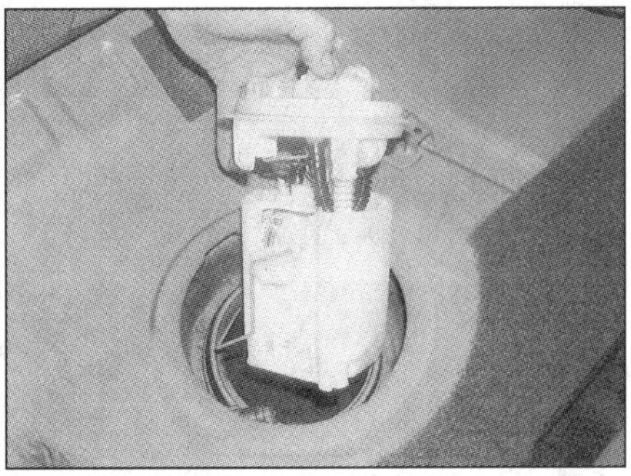

8.7a Removing the fuel pump from the tank

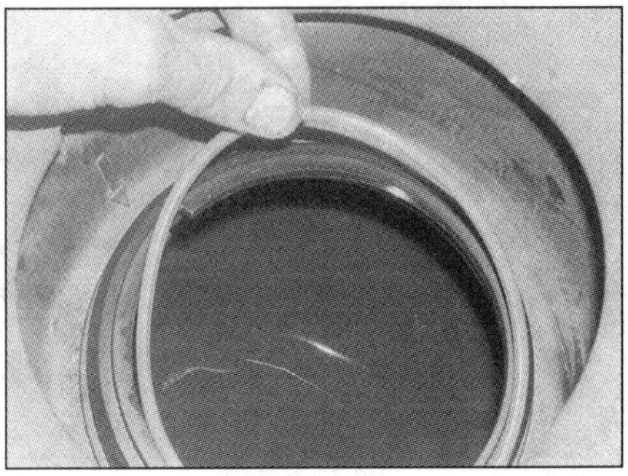

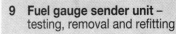

8.7b Removing the rubber sealing ring

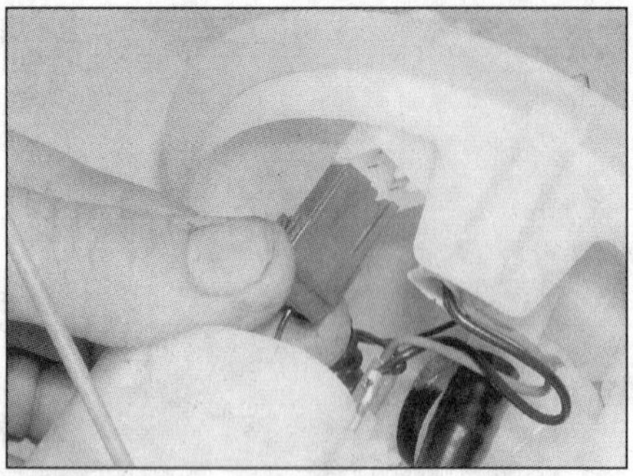
9.3 Disconnecting the wiring from the cover

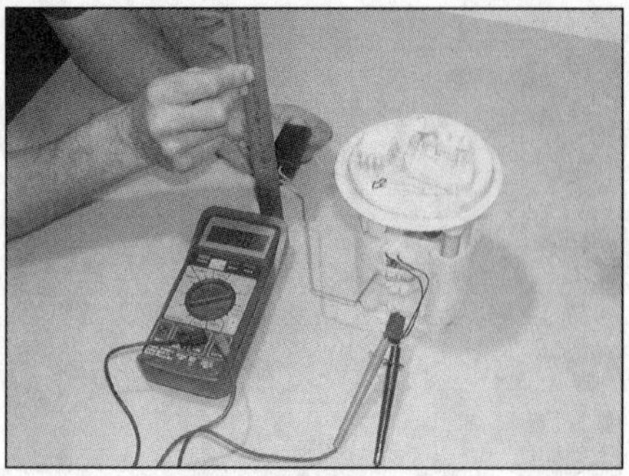
9.4 Testing the sender unit with an ohmmeter

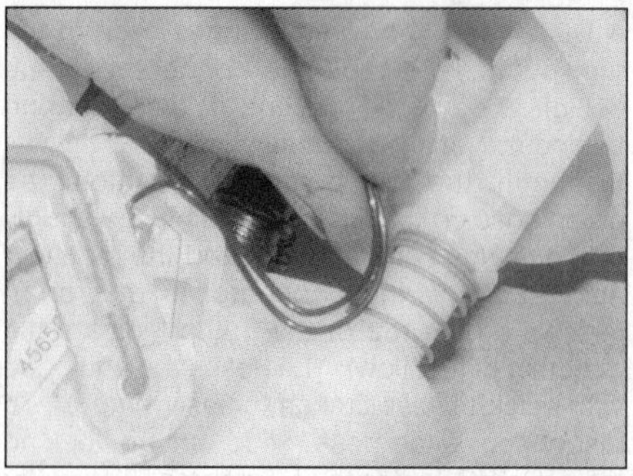
9.5a Remove the wiring from the clips . . .

2 To test the sender unit, first remove the pump as described in Section 8.

3 Disconnect the wiring plug from the cover and connect an ohmmeter to the two terminals **(see illustration)**.

4 With the pump assembly upright on the bench, measure the resistance of the sender unit at the different heights given in the Specifications **(see illustration)**. The resistances are approximate but is should be clear if the sender unit is not operating correctly.

Removal

5 To remove the sender unit, first release the wiring from the clips, then unclip and remove the cover from the main body **(see illustrations)**.

6 Using a screwdriver, prise off the gauze filter from the bottom of the unit. Also recover the O-ring seal from the spring location column **(see illustrations)**.

7 Carefully unclip the bottom section, then disconnect the wiring and slide out the sender unit and float **(see illustrations)**.

Refitting

8 Refitting is a reversal of removal, but test the unit before refitting the pump assembly to the tank.

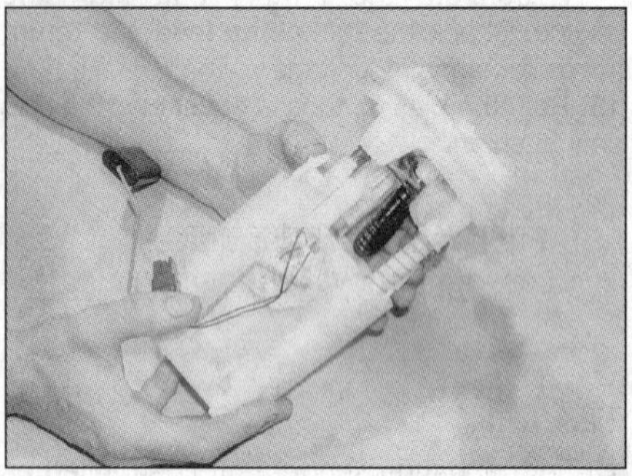
9.5b . . . then unclip the cover

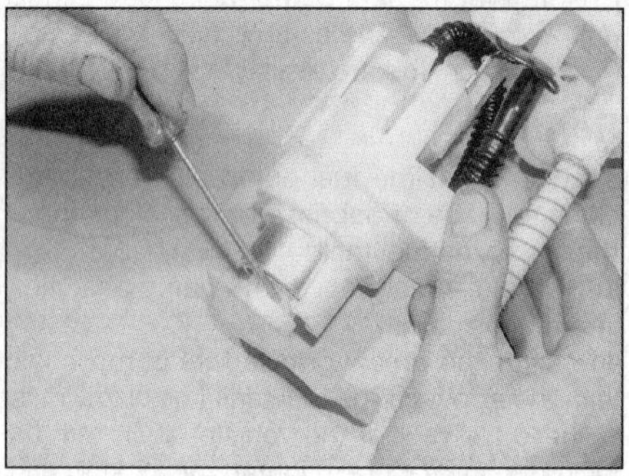
9.6a Insert a screwdriver . . .

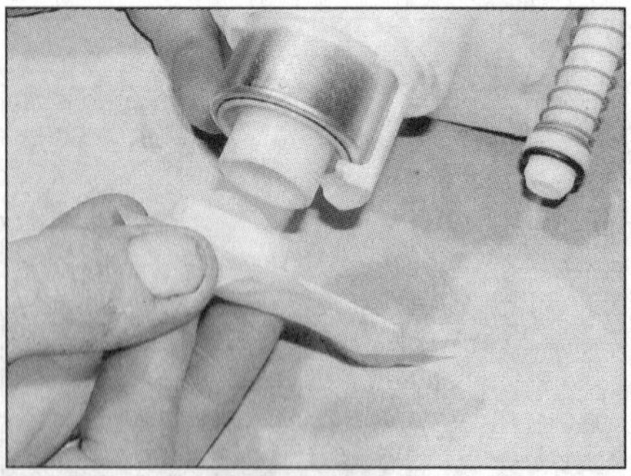
9.6b . . . prise off the gauze filter . . .

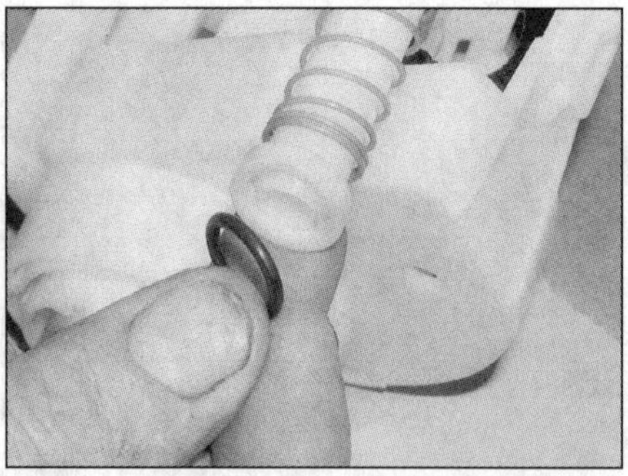
9.6c . . . and recover the O-ring seal

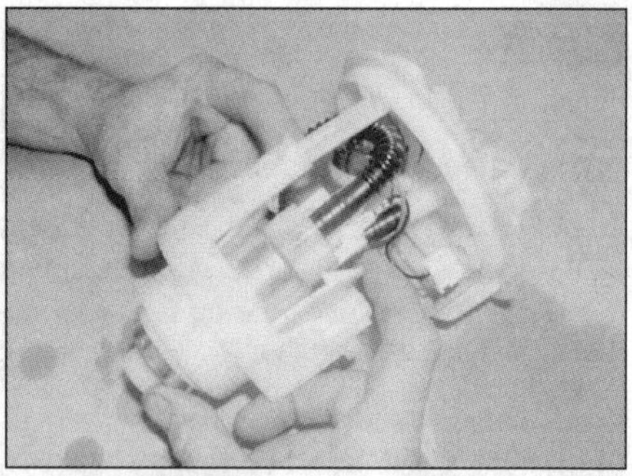
9.7a Unclip the bottom section . . .

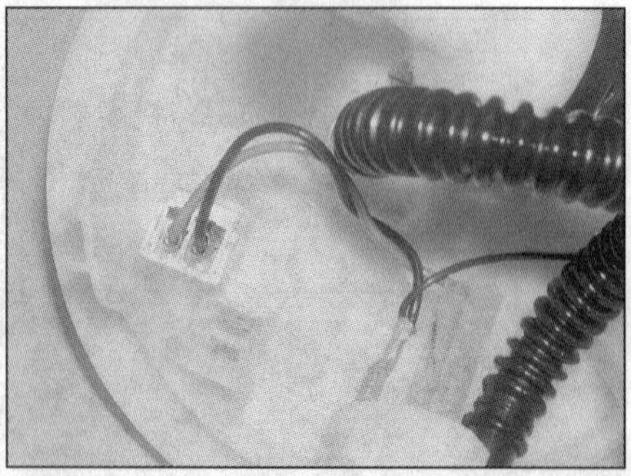
9.7b . . . then disconnect the wiring . . .

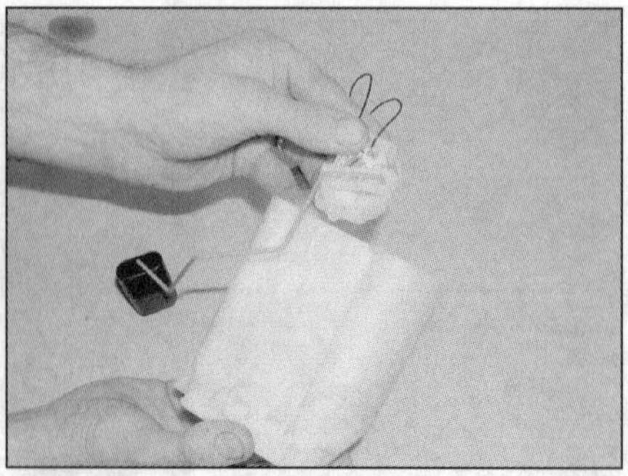
9.7c . . . and slide out the sender unit and float

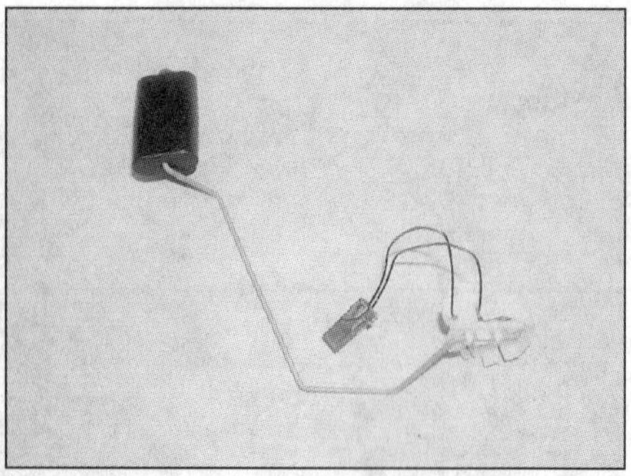
9.7d Sender unit and float removed

10 Fuel tank – removal and refitting

Warning: Refer to the warning note in Section 1 before proceeding

Removal

1 Before removing the fuel tank, all fuel must be drained from it. Since a drain plug is not provided, it is preferable to carry out the removal operation when the tank is nearly empty.

2 Remove the rear seat, or rear seat cushion (Chapter 11), for access to the fuel pump cover.

3 Using a screwdriver, carefully prise the plastic access cover from the floor to expose the fuel pump.

4 If there is any fuel remaining in the fuel tank, it can be removed by disconnecting the fuel delivery hose and connecting a suitable hose leading to a container outside the vehicle (refer to Section 8 for disconnecting the quick-release hose). Remove the fuel pump relay located in the engine compartment fuse/relay box (see Chapter 12), and connect a bridging wire between terminals 3 and 5 (the terminals with the thick wires). Allow the fuel pump to operate until the fuel flow is intermittent, then disconnect the bridging wire and refit the relay.

5 Disconnect the wiring connector from the fuel pump, and tape the connector to the vehicle body, to prevent it disappearing behind the tank.

6 Disconnect the battery negative lead (refer to *Disconnecting the battery* in the Reference Section).

7 Disconnect the return hose from the fuel pump with reference to Section 8.

8 Chock the front wheels then jack up the rear of the vehicle and support on axle stands (see *Jacking and vehicle support*). Remove the right-hand rear wheel.

9 Remove the exhaust system and relevant heat shield(s) with reference to Section 15. Also unbolt and remove the central exhaust mounting.

10 Disconnect the hose from the fuel filter and also disconnect the union with the fuel gallery.

11 Remove the heat shield from below the fuel tank and below the handbrake cables.

12 Note the position of the adjustment nut on the rear of the handbrake lever equaliser rod, then unscrew and remove it and detach the handbrake cables from the supports on the underbody. Position the cables to one side away from the fuel tank.

13 Disconnect the hoses from the fuel tank to the fuel gallery.

14 Disconnect the overflow pipe.

15 Separate the filler neck from the fuel tank, then unclip the handbrake cables from under the tank **(see illustrations)**.

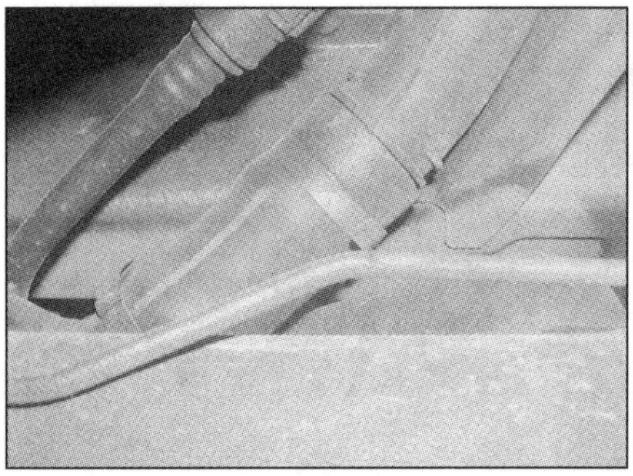

10.15a Filler neck connection to the tank

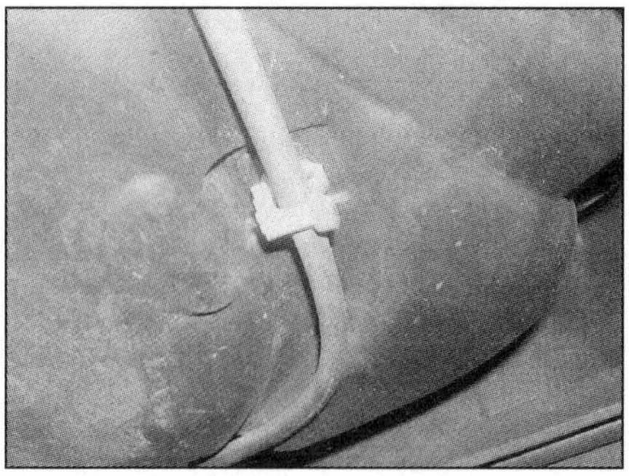

10.15b Handbrake cable clip on the bottom of the fuel tank

16 Place a trolley jack with an interposed block of wood beneath the tank, then raise the jack until it is supporting the weight of the tank.

17 Unscrew and remove the mounting bolts **(see illustrations)**, then slowly lower the fuel tank out of position, disconnecting any other relevant vent pipes as they become accessible (where necessary), and remove the tank from underneath the vehicle. Note that the tank must be slightly tilted to the right, and it may be necessary to bend the brake pipes to provide sufficient clearance. **Do not** bend the pipes excessively.

18 If the tank is contaminated with sediment or water, remove the fuel pump/sender unit (Section 8), and swill the tank out with clean fuel. The tank is injection-moulded from a synthetic material – if seriously damaged, it should be renewed. However, in certain cases, it may be possible to have small leaks or minor damage repaired. Seek the advice of a specialist before attempting to repair the fuel tank.

Refitting

19 Refitting is the reverse of the removal procedure, noting the following points:

a) *When lifting the tank back into position, take care to ensure that the hoses are not trapped between the tank and vehicle body.*
b) *As the tank is located on the underbody, make sure that the positioning holes are correctly aligned with each other. There are two rear holes and one front hole.*
c) *Ensure that all pipes and hoses are correctly routed. Make sure the sealing rings are in position in the quick-release fittings prior to fitting and make sure they are securely clipped in position.*
d) *On completion, refill the tank with a small amount of fuel, and check for signs of leakage prior to taking the vehicle out on the road.*

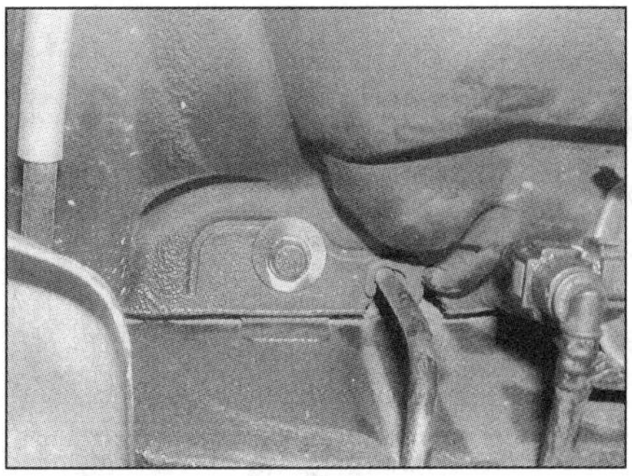

10.17a Fuel tank right-hand mounting bolt . . .

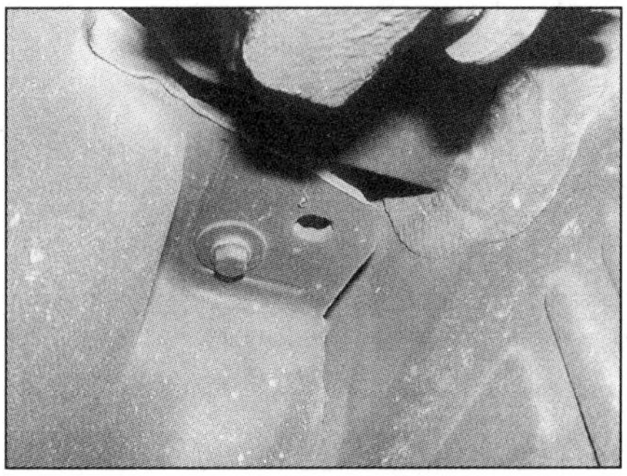

10.17b . . . and left-hand mounting bolt

11 Throttle body/housing – removal and refitting

Warning: Refer to the warning note in Section 1 before proceeding

Removal

1 Depressurise the fuel system with reference to Section 7.

2 Disconnect the battery negative lead (refer to *Disconnecting the battery* in the Reference Section) and proceed as described under the relevant heading.

D7F engine

Note: *The inlet air temperature sensor, idle speed control valve and throttle potentiometer are integral with the throttle housing, and cannot be renewed independently. A new seal will be required on refitting.*

3 Slacken the hose clips, and remove the air ducting connecting the air cleaner assembly to the throttle body.

11.4a Disconnect the wiring from the idle speed control valve . . .

11.4b . . . the air temperature sensor . . .

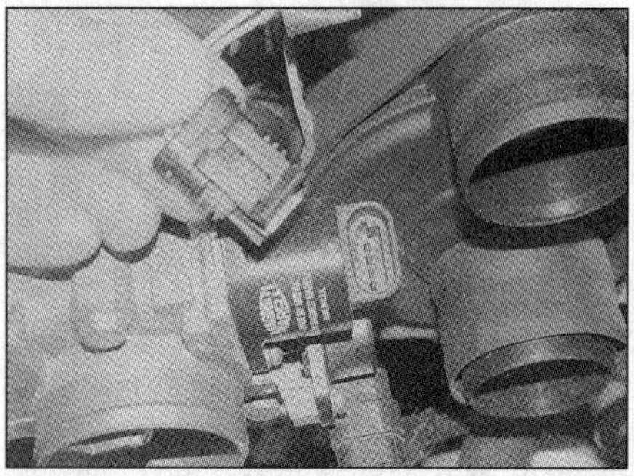

11.4c . . . and the throttle position sensor – D7F engine

4 Disconnect the wiring from the idle speed control valve, the air temperature sensor, and the throttle position sensor **(see illustrations)**.

5 Disconnect the accelerator cable from the throttle quadrant on the throttle housing, with reference to Section 3 if necessary **(see illustration)**.

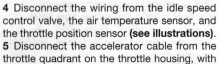

11.5 Disconnecting the accelerator cable from the throttle quadrant – D7F engine

6 Unscrew the three throttle housing securing bolts **(see illustration)**.

7 Unscrew the two bolts securing the bracing bracket to the cylinder head, or unscrew the bolts securing the bracing bracket to the throttle body bracket, then withdraw the throttle housing complete with the bracket(s). Recover the seal **(see illustrations)**.

8 Refitting is a reversal of removal, but use a new seal, and reconnect and if necessary adjust the accelerator cable.

E7J and K7M engines

9 Remove the air cleaner assembly as described in Section 2. Also remove the air inlet duct.

10 Disconnect the accelerator cable from the throttle quadrant.

11 Depress the retaining clips and disconnect the wiring connectors from the throttle potentiometer and idle control stepper motor **(see illustrations)**.

12 Unscrew and remove the bolts securing the throttle body assembly to the inlet manifold, then remove the assembly and gasket. Discard the gasket; a new one should be used on refitting.

K4J and K4M engines

13 Remove the air cleaner assembly as described in Section 2. Also remove the airbox from the throttle housing.

14 Disconnect the accelerator cable from the throttle quadrant.

15 Disconnect the wiring from the throttle potentiometer **(see illustration)**.

16 Unscrew the bolts securing the throttle body assembly to the inlet manifold, then

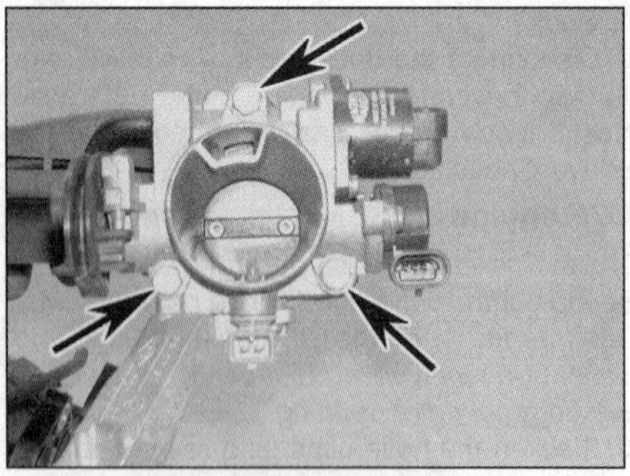

11.6 Throttle housing securing bolts (arrowed) – D7F engine

11.7a Throttle housing bracing bracket-to-cylinder head securing bolt (arrowed) – D7F engine

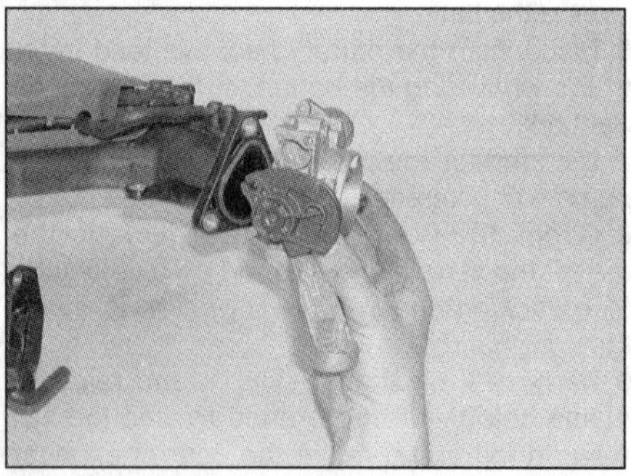

11.7b Withdraw the throttle housing . . .

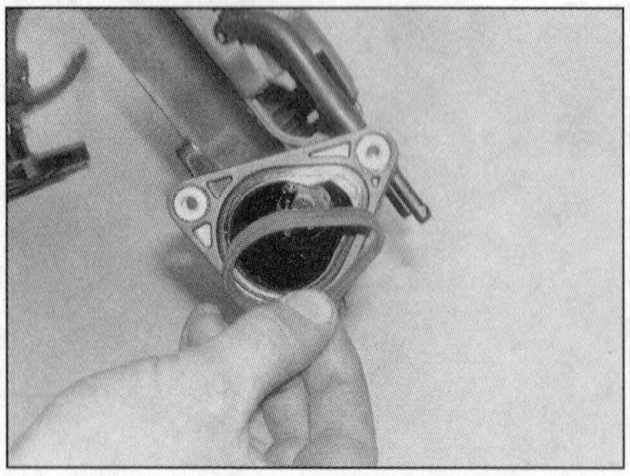

11.7c . . . and recover the seal – D7F engine

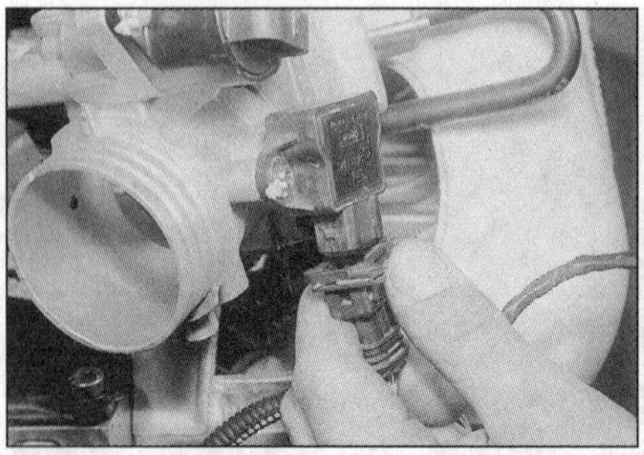

11.11a Disconnecting the throttle potentiometer wiring – E7J and K7M engines

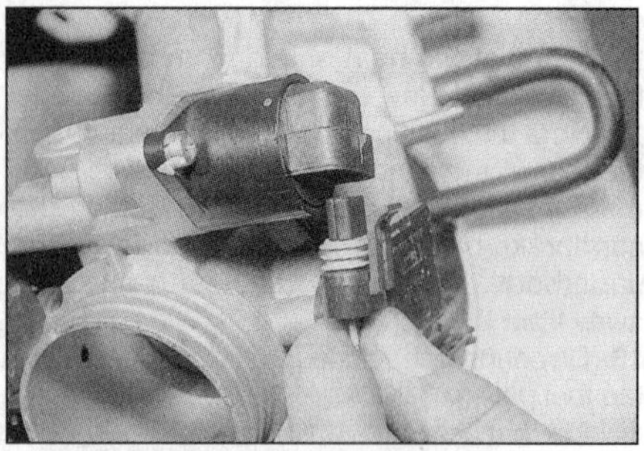

11.11b Disconnecting the idle control stepper motor wiring – E7J and K7M engines

remove the assembly and gasket/seal. Discard the gasket/seal; a new one should be used on refitting.

Refitting

17 Clean the mating faces of the throttle body/housing and inlet manifold.

18 Refitting is a reversal of removal, but fit a new gasket/seal and check the adjustment of the accelerator cable with reference to Section 3.

12 Fuel injection system – testing and adjustment

Testing

1 If a fault appears in the fuel injection system, first ensure that all the system wiring connectors are securely connected and free of corrosion. Ensure that the fault is not due to poor maintenance; ie, check that the air cleaner filter element is clean, the spark plugs are in good condition and correctly gapped, the cylinder compression pressures are correct, the ignition timing is correct, and that the engine breather hoses are clear and undamaged, referring to the relevant part of Chapters 1, 2 and 5 for further information.

2 If these checks fail to reveal the cause of the problem, the vehicle should be taken to a Renault dealer for testing. A diagnostic connector (located beneath the ashtray on the centre console) is incorporated in the engine management circuit, into which a special electronic diagnostic tester can be plugged. The tester will locate the fault quickly and simply, alleviating the need to test all the system components individually, which is a time-consuming operation that carries a risk of damaging the ECU. The Renault XR25 diagnostic tester is specific for Renault dealerships; at the time of writing there was no equivalent tester available. The tester uses a barchart configuration on a LCD screen; a fiche for the particular model is placed on the screen and each circuit can be checked instantly. There is no code output as such, so it is not possible for the home mechanic to determine a faulty area of the fuel injection system.

3 If the 'electronic incident' warning light illuminates on the instrument panel whilst driving, or remains illuminated longer than 3 seconds after switching on the ignition, a fault is indicated in one or more of the following components:

a) Manifold absolute pressure sensor.
b) Throttle potentiometer.
c) Injectors.
d) Idle speed stepper motor (where fitted).
e) Vehicle speed sensor (when the vehicle is moving).
f) EGR solenoid valve (where fitted).
g) Automatic transmission.

11.15 Disconnecting the wiring from the throttle potentiometer

4 Some individual components may be tested for resistance after removal using the information given in the Specifications, however other items (such as the idle speed stepper motor) cannot be checked and are not adjustable.

Adjustment

5 Experienced home mechanics with a considerable amount of skill and equipment (including a tachometer and an accurately calibrated exhaust gas analyser) may be able to check the exhaust CO level and the idle speed. However, if these are found to be in need of adjustment, the car *must* be taken to a suitably-equipped Renault dealer for further testing. Neither the mixture adjustment (exhaust gas CO level) nor the idle speed are adjustable, and should either be incorrect, a fault must be present in the fuel injection system.

13 Multi-point injection system components – removal and refitting

Fuel rail and injectors

Warning: Refer to the warning note in Section 1 before proceeding

Note: *If a faulty injector is suspected, before condemning the injector, it is worth trying the effect of one of the proprietary injector-cleaning treatments.*

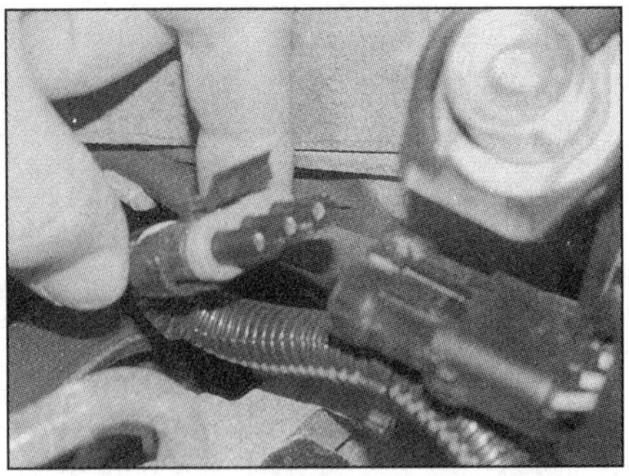

13.2 Separate the two halves of the fuel injection wiring connector – D7F engine

D7F engine

Note: *New O-rings will be required on refitting.*

1 Depressurise the fuel system as described in Section 7, then disconnect the battery negative lead.

2 Separate the two halves of the fuel injector harness wiring connector. The connector is located in front of the fuel pressure regulator **(see illustration)**.

3 Disconnect the vacuum pipe from the fuel pressure regulator **(see illustration)**.

4 Disconnect the fuel return pipe from the end of the fuel rail **(see illustration)**. Be prepared for fuel spillage. Plug or clamp the hose to prevent dirt entry and further fuel loss.

5 It is now necessary to disconnect the fuel feed hose from the fuel rail. To do this, a special tool will be required to release the connector. The appropriate Renault special tool (Mot. 1311-06) slides through the connector collar to release the securing lugs, but the same effect can be achieved using a small flat-bladed screwdriver to release the lugs. Note that some models have the Renault special tool built into the hose connection. Once the connector securing lugs have been released, the hose can be pulled from the end of the fuel rail **(see illustrations)**. Plug or clamp the hose to prevent dirt entry and further fuel loss.

6 Working underneath the manifold, unscrew the two bolts securing the fuel rail to the manifold **(see illustration)**.

13.3 Disconnecting the vacuum pipe from the fuel pressure regulator – D7F engine

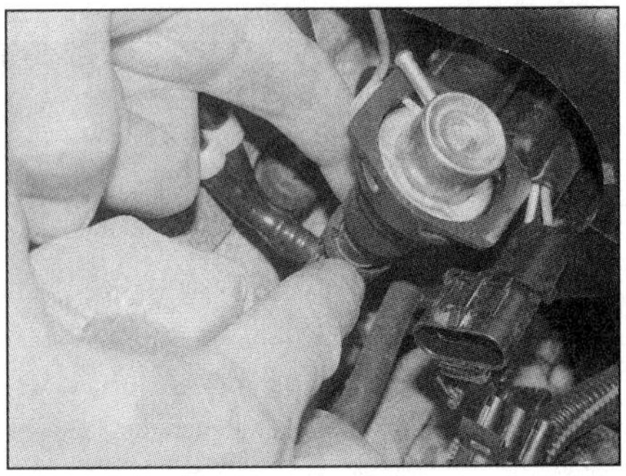

13.4 Release the securing clip, then disconnect the fuel return pipe from the fuel rail – D7F engine

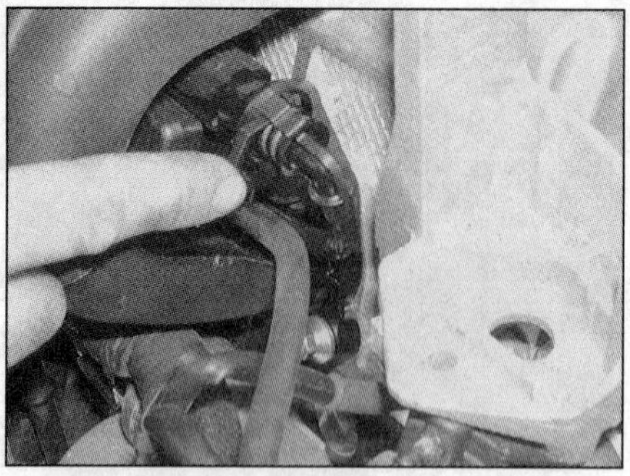

13.5a Push the built-in tool in to release the fuel feed hose connector securing lugs . . .

7 Carefully slide the fuel rail and injector assembly towards the right-hand side of the vehicle, between the manifold and cylinder head.

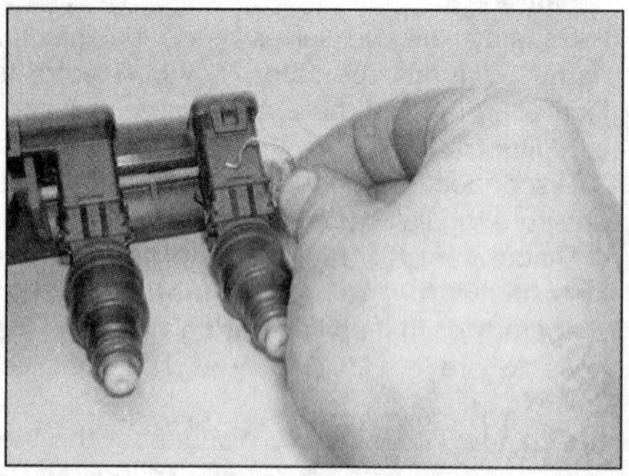

13.8a Release the injector wiring clips . . .

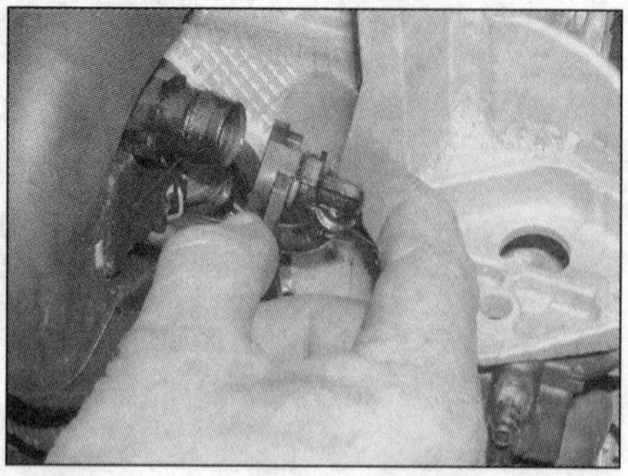

13.5b . . . then disconnect the hose from the fuel rail

8 To remove a fuel injector from the fuel rail, release the wiring clips from the injectors, and pull the wiring tube assembly from the top of the injectors. Release the relevant injector securing clip, and remove the fuel injector **(see illustrations).**

9 Refitting is a reversal of removal, but renew the O-rings at the top and bottom of each injector (check on availability before removing the old O-rings), and ensure that the fuel feed hose is securely reconnected (the connector should click securely into position).

E7J and K7M engines

10 Depressurise the fuel system as described in Section 7, then disconnect the battery negative lead.

11 Remove the air cleaner assembly as described in Section 2, then unbolt the

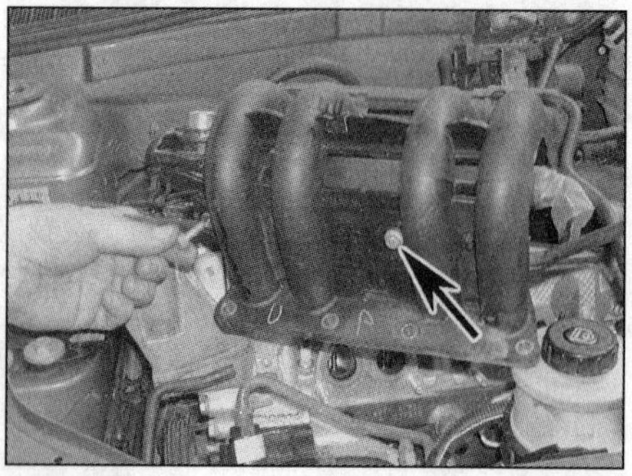

13.6 Unscrew the fuel rail securing bolts (arrowed) – viewed with inlet manifold removed

coolant expansion tank from the bulkhead and position it to one side **(see illustration).**

12 Disconnect the fuel feed and return hoses from the fuel rail **(see illustration).** The hoses have the same quick-release connectors as fitted to the fuel pump (see Section 8).

13 Disconnect the vacuum hose connecting the pressure regulator (on the fuel rail) to the inlet manifold.

14 Disconnect the wiring from the injectors and move the loom to one side **(see illustration).**

15 Unscrew and remove the mounting bolts and carefully ease the fuel rail together with the injectors from the inlet manifold **(see illustration).**

16 Note the fitted positions of the injectors, then remove the clips and ease the injectors from the fuel rail **(see illustrations).**

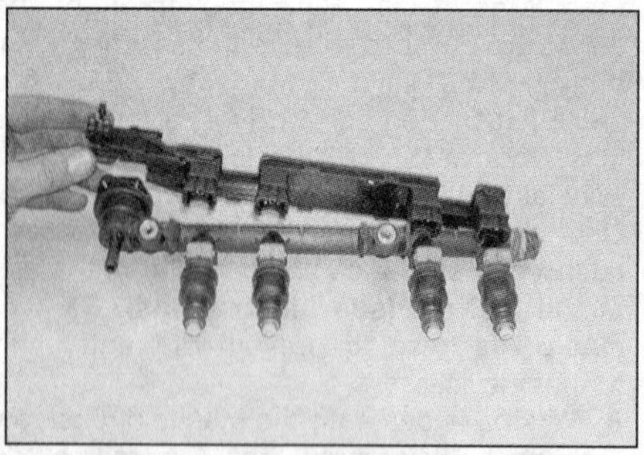

13.8b . . . and pull the wiring tube assembly from the top of the injectors – D7F engine

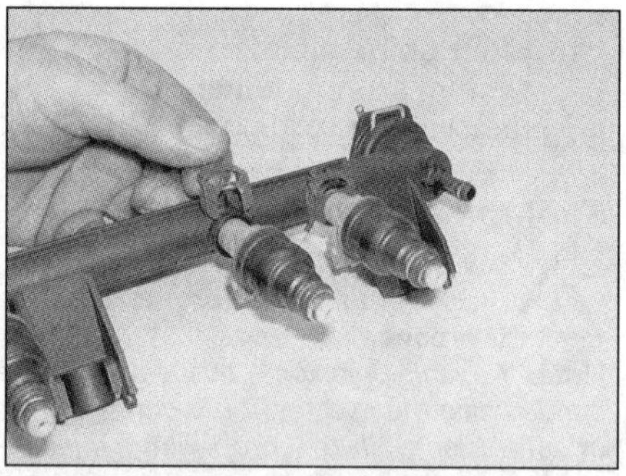

13.8c Release the injector securing clip . . .

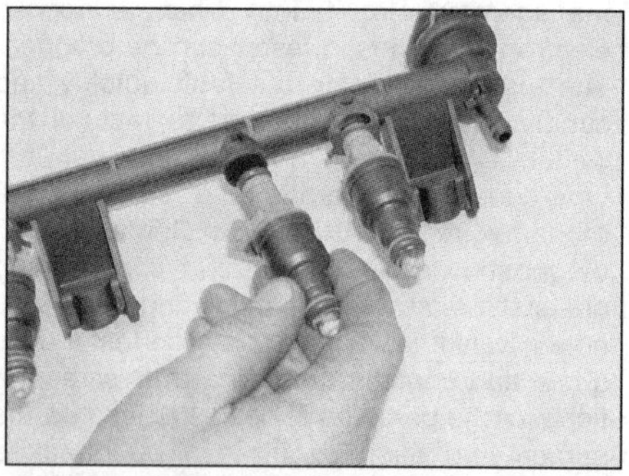

13.8d . . . and remove the fuel injector – D7F engine

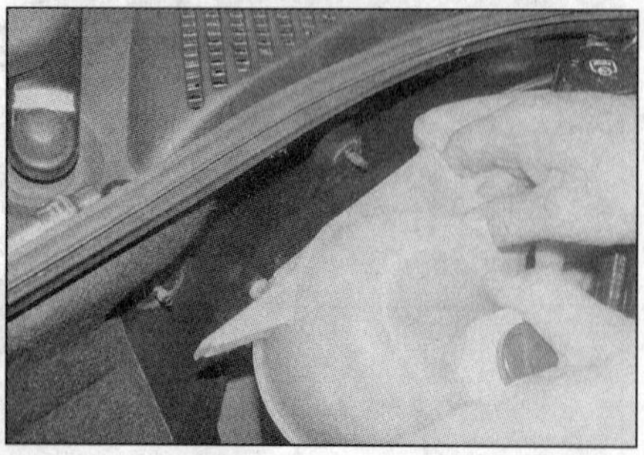

13.11 Unbolting the coolant expansion tank from the bulkhead – E7J and K7M engines

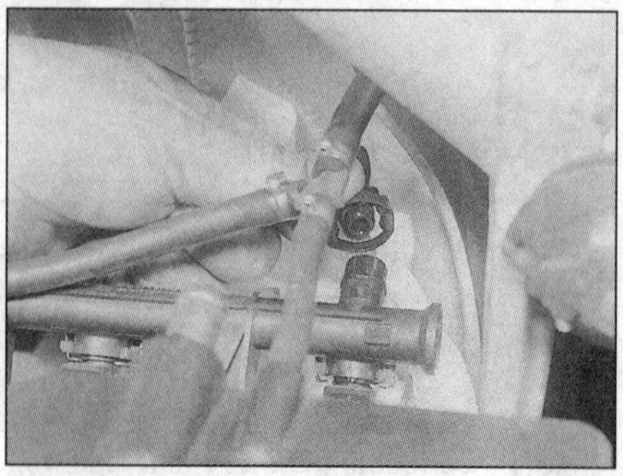

13.12 Disconnecting the fuel return hose from the fuel rail – E7J and K7M engines

13.14 Disconnecting the injector wiring – E7J and K7M engines

13.15 Removing the fuel rail mounting bolts – E7J and K7M engines

13.16a Remove the retaining clips . . .

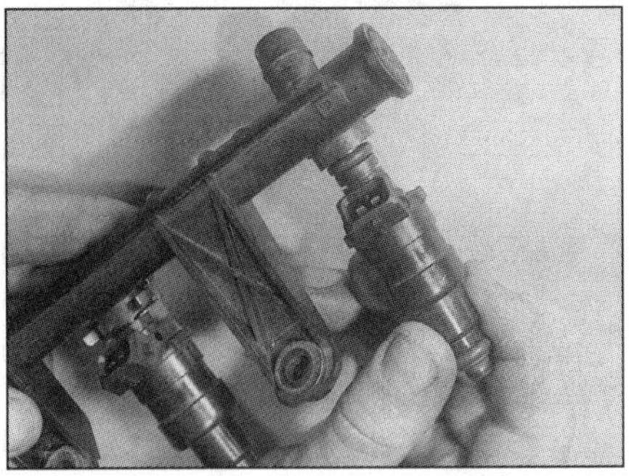

13.16b . . . and ease the injectors from the fuel rail – E7J and K7M engines

17 Remove the sealing rings from the grooves at each end of the injectors and obtain new ones.

18 Refitting is a reversal of the removal procedure, noting the following points:

a) *Renew all sealing rings, using a smear of engine oil to aid installation.*
b) *Refit the fuel rail assembly to the manifold, making sure the sealing rings remain correctly positioned, and tighten the retaining bolts to the specified torque.*
c) *On completion start the engine and check for fuel leaks.*

K4J and K4M engines

19 Depressurise the fuel system as described in Section 7, then disconnect the battery negative lead.

20 Remove the cover for access to the fuel rail.

21 Disconnect the fuel feed and return hoses from the fuel rail.

22 Disconnect the vacuum hose connecting the pressure regulator (on the fuel rail) to the inlet manifold.

23 Disconnect the wiring from the injectors and move the loom to one side.

24 Unscrew and remove the mounting bolts and carefully ease the fuel rail together with the injectors from the inlet manifold.

25 Note the fitted positions of the injectors, then remove the clips and ease the injectors from the fuel rail.

26 Remove the sealing rings from the grooves at each end of the injectors and obtain new ones.

27 Refitting is a reversal of the removal procedure, noting the following points:

a) *Renew all sealing rings, using a smear of engine oil to aid installation.*
b) *Refit the fuel rail assembly to the manifold, making sure the sealing rings remain correctly positioned, and tighten the retaining bolts to the specified torque.*
c) *On completion start the engine and check for fuel leaks.*

Fuel pressure regulator

⚠ ***Warning: Refer to the warning note in Section 1 before proceeding***

Removal

28 Disconnect the vacuum pipe from the regulator **(see illustration)**.

29 Place a wad of rag over the regulator to catch any spilled fuel, then extract the retaining spring and ease the regulator from the fuel rail.

30 Remove the sealing rings from the grooves in the pressure regulator and obtain new ones.

Refitting

31 On refitting, fit new sealing rings to the regulator grooves and apply a smear of engine oil to them to ease installation. Ease the regulator back into the end of the fuel rail and refit the retaining spring and vacuum pipe.

Throttle potentiometer

Removal

32 Remove the throttle housing as described in Section 11.

33 Undo the retaining screws and remove the potentiometer from the throttle housing.

Refitting

34 Refitting is a reverse of the removal procedure ensuring that the potentiometer is correctly engaged with the throttle spindle. **Note:** *Renault recommend that the potentiometer operation should be checked, whenever it is disturbed, using the XR25 diagnostic tester.*

Inlet air temperature sensor

Removal

35 The air temperature sensor is located on the air inlet duct to the throttle housing on SOHC engines, and on the upper section of the inlet manifold on DOHC engines. To remove it, first disconnect the wiring from the sensor **(see illustrations)**, then loosen the clips and remove the air inlet duct.

36 Unscrew and remove the inlet air temperature sensor from the air inlet duct.

Refitting

37 Refitting is a reversal of removal.

Coolant temperature sensor

38 The sensor is located on the thermostat housing or at the left-hand end of the cylinder

13.28 Fuel pressure regulator vacuum pipe – E7J and K7M engines

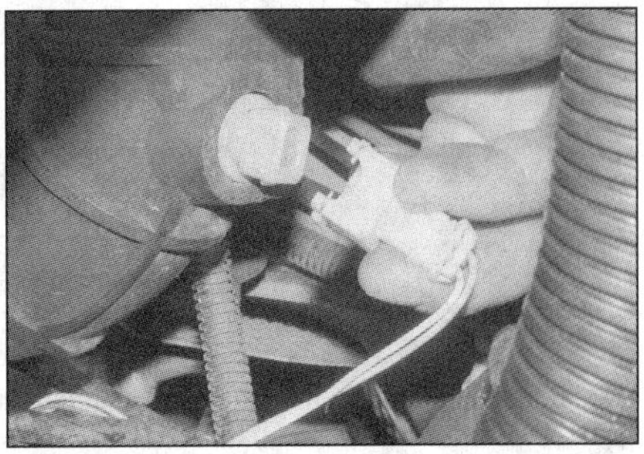

13.35a Disconnecting the wiring from the inlet air temperature sensor on the E7J engine . . .

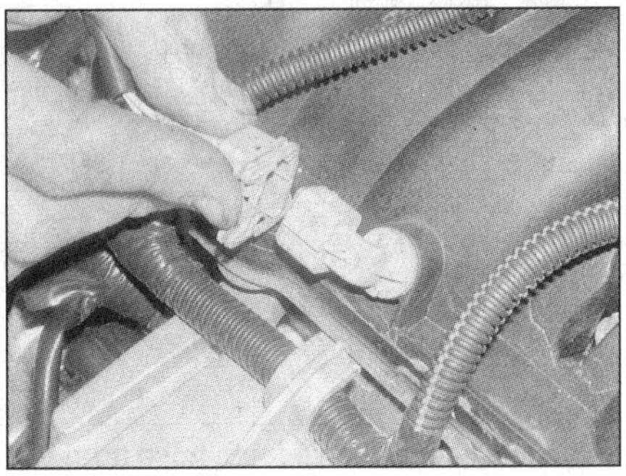

13.35b . . . and K4J engine

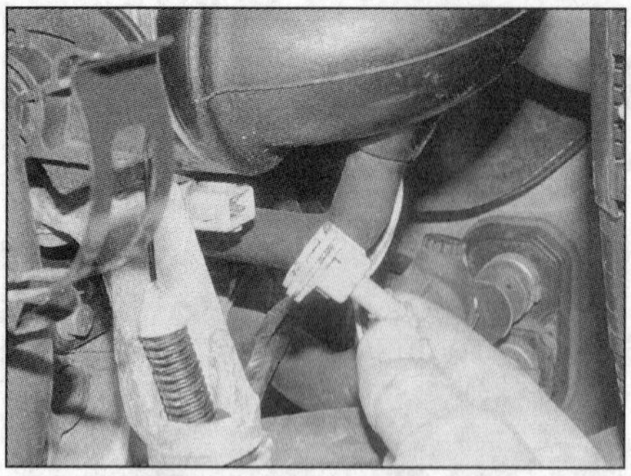

13.38 Disconnecting the wiring from the coolant temperature sensor

head above the gearbox bellhousing **(see illustration)**. Refer to Chapter 3, Section 8, for removal and refitting details.

Power steering pressure switch

Removal

39 The switch is screwed into the feed pipe from the power steering pump to the steering gear.

40 To remove the switch, disconnect the wiring connector.

41 Wipe clean the area around the switch then unscrew the switch and remove it from the pipe. Plug the pipe aperture to prevent excess fluid leakage and prevent dirt entry into the hydraulic system.

Refitting

42 Refitting is the reverse of removal. On completion check the power steering fluid level as described in Chapter 1A or 1B.

13.50a Disconnecting the wiring from the manifold absolute pressure sensor – D7F engine

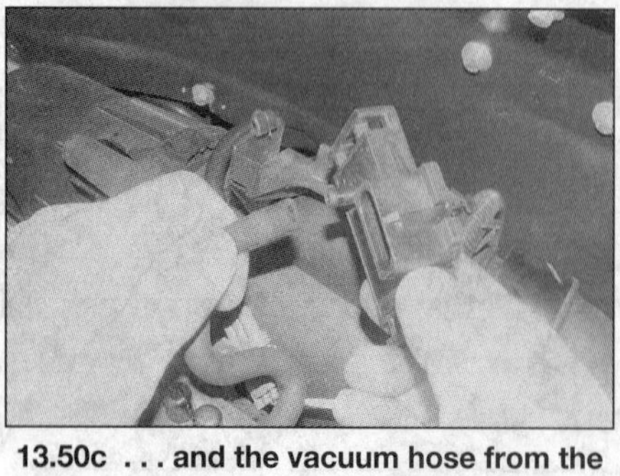

13.50c . . . and the vacuum hose from the manifold absolute pressure sensor – K4J engine

13.43a The knock sensor on the D7F engine . . .

Knock sensor

43 On the D7F, K4J and K4M engines the knock sensor is located on the front of the cylinder block **(see illustrations)**, however on E7J and K7M engines it is located on the rear of the cylinder block.

44 Refer to Chapter 5B for the removal and refitting procedures.

Idle speed control stepper motor

Removal

45 On the D7F engine, the idle speed control stepper motor is mounted on the top of the throttle housing on the left-hand side of the engine, however on E7J and K7M engines it is located on the rear of the throttle housing. On K4J and K4M engines the stepper motor is located on the top of the inlet plenum chamber on the right-hand rear side of the engine.

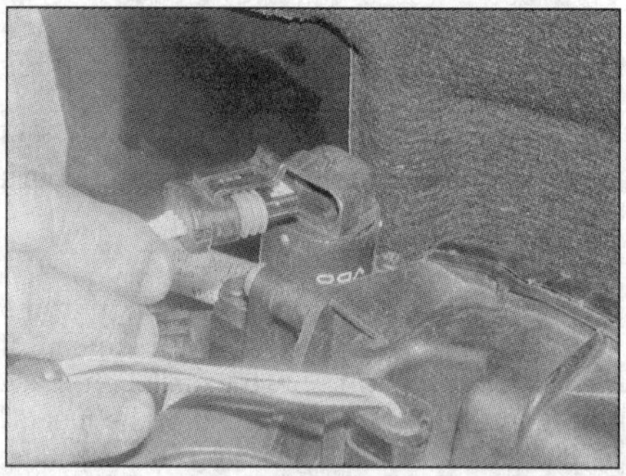

13.50b Disconnecting the wiring . . .

13.55 Fuse and relay box located on the left-hand side of the engine compartment

13.43b . . . and on the K4J engine

46 To remove the stepper motor, first remove the throttle housing as described in Section 11.

47 Undo the retaining screws and remove the stepper motor from the throttle housing. Recover the gasket and discard it; a new one should be used on refitting.

Refitting

48 Refitting is a reversal of the removal procedure using a new gasket.

Manifold absolute pressure (MAP) sensor

Removal

49 The manifold absolute sensor is mounted on the rear of the air cleaner.

50 Disconnect the wiring and vacuum hose from the sensor **(see illustrations)**.

51 Unscrew the mounting nuts and remove the sensor.

Refitting

52 Refitting is a reversal of removal.

Fuel injection system relay and fuel pump relay

Removal

53 These relays are located in the left-hand side of the engine compartment.

54 Remove the cover from the box.

55 Remove the relevant relay from the fuse/relay box **(see illustration)**.

Refitting

56 Refitting is the reverse of removal.

13.57 The crankshaft speed/position sensor is mounted on top of the transmission

13.60 Note the special bolts used to locate and secure the crankshaft speed/position sensor

Crankshaft TDC sensor

Removal

57 The sensor is mounted on the top of the transmission bellhousing at the left-hand end of the cylinder block **(see illustration)**.

58 To remove the sensor, remove the air cleaner housing as described in Section 2.

59 Trace the wiring back from the sensor to the wiring connector, and disconnect it from the main harness.

60 Unscrew the retaining bolts and remove the sensor **(see illustration)**.

Refitting

61 Refitting is a reversal of removal. Ensure that the sensor retaining bolts are securely tightened – note that only the special shouldered bolts originally fitted must be used to secure the sensor; these bolts locate the sensor precisely to give the correct air gap between the sensor tip and the flywheel/ driveplate.

Fuel cut-off inertia switch

Removal

62 The switch is located in the left-hand side of the engine compartment **(see illustration)**.

63 Unscrew and remove the switch retaining screws then disconnect its wiring connector and remove the switch from the engine compartment.

Refitting

64 Refitting is the reverse of removal. On completion, reset the switch by depressing its button.

Electronic control unit (ECU)

Removal

Note: *The ECU is electronically-coded to match the engine immobiliser. If the ECU is being removed to enable a new unit to be fitted, the new unit must be programmed with the vehicle code as described.*

65 The ECU is located in the left-hand side of the engine compartment, behind the battery. First disconnect the battery negative lead (refer to *Disconnecting the battery* in the Reference Section).

13.62 Fuel cut-off inertia switch

13.67 . . . then remove the upper bracket . . .

66 Unclip the power steering hydraulic fluid reservoir from the bulkhead and position it to one side **(see illustration)**.

67 Where applicable, unbolt the bracket from the top of the ECU and release the strap **(see illustration)**. Alternatively the bracket can remain on the ECU until the assembly is removed.

68 Undo the mounting screws and remove the ECU and mounting bracket **(see illustration)**.

69 Disconnect the wiring connector and remove the ECU from the engine compartment.

Refitting

70 Refitting is a reverse of the removal procedure ensuring that the wiring connector is securely reconnected. If a new ECU has been fitted, reprogramme it as follows. Turn the ignition on for a few seconds, then turn it off. Now remove the key to operate the immobiliser. After 10 seconds, the red immobiliser warning light should start to flash.

14.6 Remove the air ducting connecting the air cleaner assembly to the throttle body – D7F engine

13.66 Position the power steering hydraulic fluid reservoir to one side . . .

13.68 . . . followed by the ECU

14 Manifolds – removal and refitting

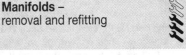

Inlet manifold

D7F, E7J and K7M engines

1 Disconnect the battery negative (earth) lead and position it away from the terminal.

2 Remove the air cleaner assembly as described in Section 2.

3 Remove the fuel rail and injectors as described in Section 13.

4 Apply the handbrake, then jack up the front of the vehicle and support it on axle stands (see *Jacking and vehicle support*). Remove the right-hand roadwheel and wheelarch liner.

5 On the right-hand side of the engine, unbolt the support strut located to the rear of the right-hand driveshaft.

6 Loosen the clips and remove the air inlet duct from between the air cleaner and throttle body **(see illustration)**.

7 Disconnect the accelerator cable from the throttle body with reference to Section 3 **(see illustration)**.

8 Disconnect the wiring from the throttle body.

9 Disconnect the brake servo vacuum hose.

10 Progressively unscrew and remove the

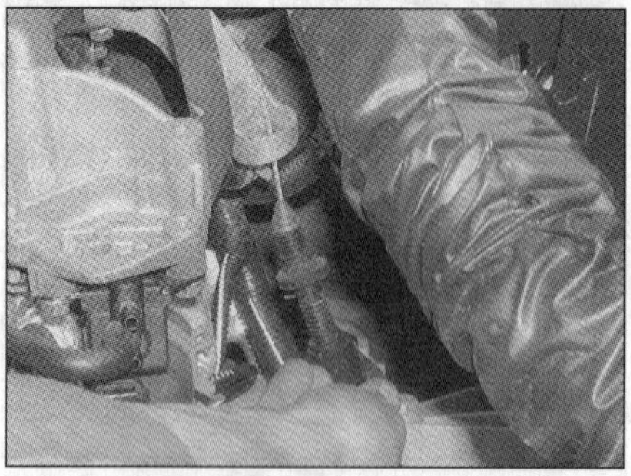

14.7 Disconnecting the accelerator cable – D7F engine

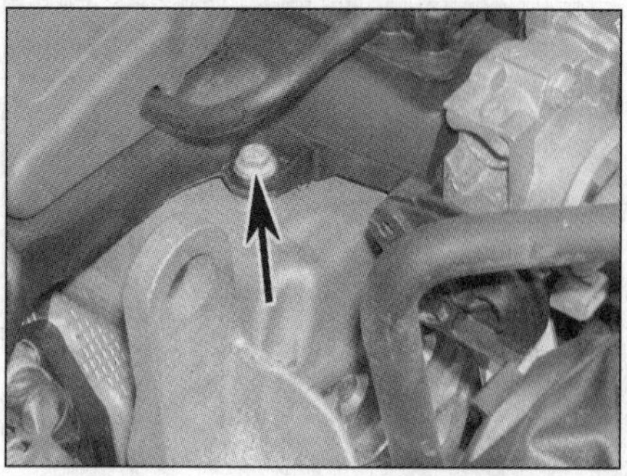

14.10a Unscrew the two bolts securing the inlet manifold to the top of the cylinder head . . .

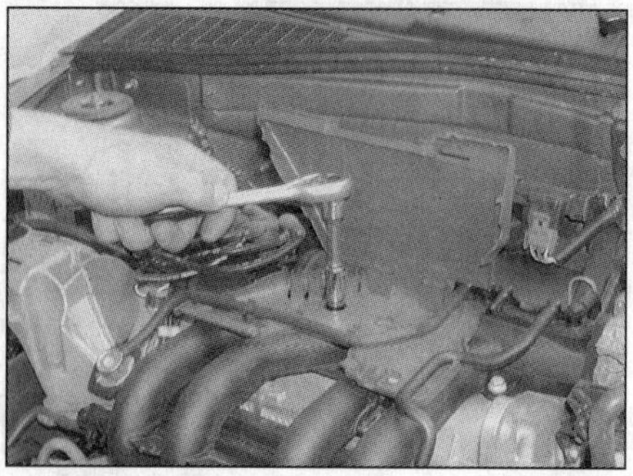

14.10b . . . noting that one of the bolts is accessed through the spark plug lead housing – D7F engine

bolts and nuts securing the inlet manifold to the cylinder head **(see illustrations)**. Also unscrew the bolts securing the support bracket.

11 Withdraw the inlet manifold from the cylinder head and recover the gasket or O-rings as applicable **(see illustration)**.

12 Refitting is a reversal of removal but use new O-rings or gasket (as applicable) and tighten the mounting nuts and bolts to the specified torque. Ensure that the cylinder head and manifold mating surfaces are clean.

K4J and K4M engines

13 Disconnect the battery negative (earth) lead and position it away from the terminal.

14 Remove the air cleaner assembly as described in Section 2.

15 Disconnect the wiring from the throttle potentiometer, absolute pressure sensor, ignition coils and air temperature sensor.

16 Disconnect the accelerator cable from the throttle body with reference to Section 3.

17 Unscrew and remove the throttle body mounting bolts and position the throttle body to one side.

18 Progressively unscrew and remove the bolts securing the inlet manifold to the cylinder head.

19 Withdraw the inlet manifold and recover the gasket.

20 Refitting is a reversal of removal but use a new gasket and tighten the mounting bolts to the specified torque. Ensure that the cylinder head and manifold mating surfaces are clean.

Exhaust manifold

D7F, E7J and K7M engines

21 Apply the handbrake, then jack up the front of the vehicle and support it on axle stands (see *Jacking and vehicle support*). Remove the engine undertray.

22 On the right-hand side of the engine, remove the multi-function support.

23 Disconnect the exhaust front downpipe from the exhaust manifold on the front of the engine with reference to Section 15.

24 Unscrew the nuts and remove the heat shield from the exhaust manifold **(see illustration)**.

25 Progressively unscrew the bolts and remove the exhaust manifold from the cylinder head **(see illustration)**. Recover the gasket.

26 Refitting is a reversal of removal but use a new gasket and tighten the mounting bolts to the specified torque. Ensure that the cylinder head and manifold mating surfaces are clean.

K4J and K4M engines

27 Apply the handbrake, then jack up the front of the vehicle and support it on axle stands (see *Jacking and vehicle support*). Remove the engine undertray.

28 Remove the air cleaner assembly as described in Section 2.

29 Remove the lambda/oxygen sensor as described in Chapter 4C, Section 2.

30 Unbolt the heat shield from the top of the exhaust manifold on the rear of the engine. Also remove the subframe heat shield.

31 Disconnect the exhaust front downpipe from the exhaust manifold with reference to Section 15.

32 Remove the catalytic converter from the exhaust manifold and exhaust intermediate section. Note that the subframe can be slightly lowered to make it easier to remove the catalytic converter without damaging the underbody heat shield.

33 Unbolt the support strut from between the exhaust manifold and cylinder block.

34 Unscrew the mounting nuts, then tilt the exhaust manifold as required and withdraw it from the studs on the cylinder head. Recover the gasket.

35 Refitting is a reversal of removal but use a new gasket and tighten the mounting nuts to the specified torque. Ensure that the cylinder head and manifold mating surfaces are clean.

15 Exhaust system – general information, removal and refitting

General information

1 On new vehicles the exhaust system consists of just two sections; the front downpipe (and catalytic converter where applicable) and the remaining system consisting of a resonator (except on D7F), tailpipe and silencer. The downpipe is attached to the rear section by a cone-and-socket clamp joint **(see illustration)**.

14.11 Removing the inlet manifold – D7F engine

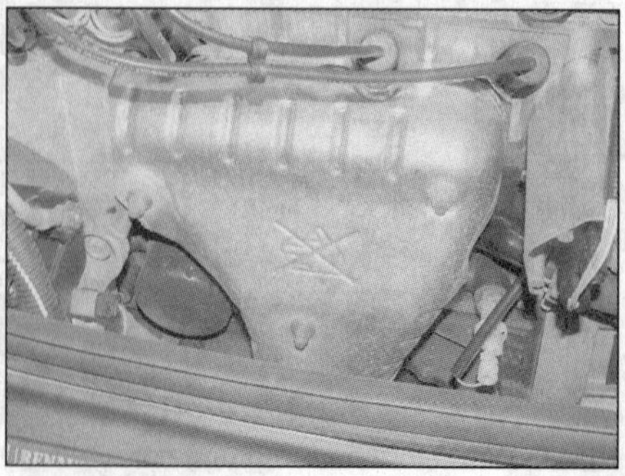

14.24 Heat shield on the exhaust manifold – E7J engine

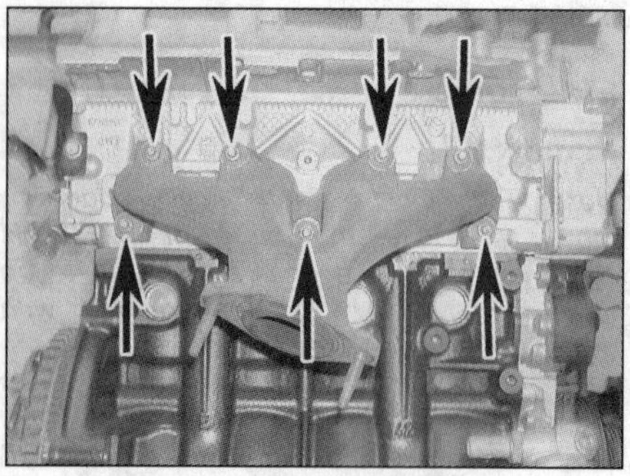

14.25 Exhaust manifold securing bolt locations – D7F engine

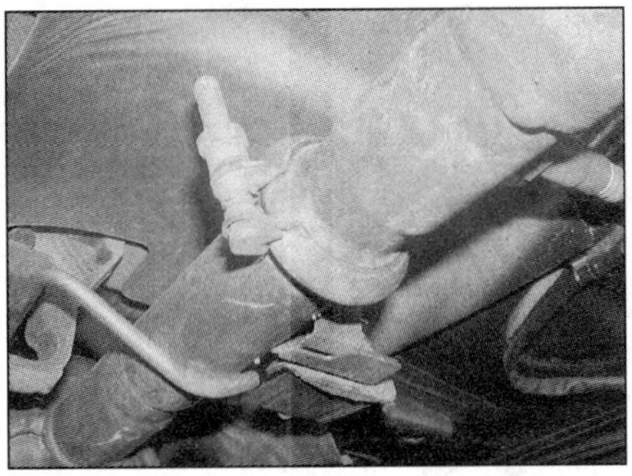

15.1 Exhaust system joint between the downpipe and rear section

15.2 Exhaust rubber mounting

2 The rear section of the exhaust is located above the rear suspension; the intermediate and tailpipe/silencer may be renewed separately by cutting the intermediate pipe with a hacksaw. The system is suspended throughout its entire length by rubber mountings **(see illustration)**.

Removal

3 To remove a part of the system, first jack up the front or rear of the car, and support it on axle stands (see *Jacking and vehicle support*). Alternatively, position the car over an inspection pit, or on car ramps. Where fitted, remove the engine compartment undertray.

Front downpipe and catalytic converter

4 Trace the wiring back from the lambda/oxygen sensor and disconnect it at the wiring connector. Free the wiring from any relevant retaining clips so the sensor is free to be removed with the front pipe.
5 Where applicable, unbolt the front pipe from the mounting bracket on the transmission.
6 Unscrew and remove the nuts/bolts securing the front pipe flange joint to the manifold, and recover the gasket.
7 Unscrew and remove the clamp and disconnect the front pipe and catalytic converter from the rear section. Withdraw the pipe from under the vehicle.

Intermediate pipe and resonator

8 Unscrew and remove the clamp bolts attaching the front pipe and catalytic converter to the rear section.
9 If the original rear section is fitted, it must be cut in half using either a hacksaw or pipe cutter. Locate the cutting area which is situated approximately midway between the rear silencer and intermediate mounting. The cutting point is marked with two circular punch marks on the side of the pipe. The punch marks are 90 mm apart and the exhaust section should be cut at the mid-point between the two punch marks. **Note:** *Ensure that the exhaust pipe is cut squarely, or else it will be difficult to obtain a gas-tight seal when the exhaust is refitted.*
10 With the intermediate pipe cut, withdraw the intermediate exhaust section from under the vehicle.
11 If the rear section is in two halves, unscrew the bolt and slide the clamp sleeve on to the rear section then release the rubber mountings and withdraw the intermediate section from under the vehicle.

Rear tailpipe and silencer

12 If the original rear section is fitted, follow the instructions given in paragraph 9.
13 If the rear section is in two halves, unscrew the bolt and slide the clamp sleeve on to the intermediate section then release the rubber mountings and withdraw the tailpipe and silencer from under the vehicle.

Heat shield(s)

14 The heat shields are secured to the underbody by various nuts and bolts. Each shield can be removed separately but note that they overlap making it necessary to loosen another section first. If a shield is being removed to gain access to a component located behind it, it may prove sufficient in some cases to remove the retaining nuts and/or bolts, and simply lower the shield, without disturbing the exhaust system. Otherwise remove the exhaust section as described earlier.

Refitting

15 Each section is refitted by reversing the removal sequence, noting the following points:

a) Ensure that all traces of corrosion have been removed from the joints.
b) Inspect the rubber mountings for signs of damage or deterioration, and renew as necessary.
c) When reconnecting the intermediate pipe to the tailpipe, apply a smear of exhaust system jointing paste (Renault recommend the use of Sodicam) to the sleeve inner surface, to ensure a gas-tight seal. Make sure both inner ends of the cut pipe are positioned squarely against the stop of the clamp sleeve. Position the sleeve bolt vertically on the left-hand side of the pipe and securely tighten the nut until it is heard to click; the clamp bolt has a groove in it to ensure that the nut is correctly tightened (equivalent to a tightening torque of approximately 25 Nm).
d) Prior to tightening the exhaust system fasteners, ensure that all rubber mountings are correctly located, and that there is adequate clearance between the exhaust system and vehicle underbody.

Notes

Chapter 4 Part B: Diesel engine fuel and exhaust systems

Contents

Degrees of difficulty

Easy, suitable for novice with little experience	**Fairly easy,** suitable for beginner with some experience	**Fairly difficult,** suitable for competent DIY mechanic	**Difficult,** suitable for experienced DIY mechanic	**Very difficult,** suitable for expert DIY or professional

Specifications

General

System type	Rear-mounted fuel tank, fuel injection pump with integral transfer pump, indirect injection
Firing order	1-3-4-2 (number 1 at flywheel end)
Fuel type	Diesel
Idle speed:	
F8Q 630 engine	850 ± 25 rpm
F8Q 632 engine	825 ± 50 rpm
F8Q 662 engine	850 ± 50 rpm
Maximum no-load speed:	
F8Q 630 engine	5100 ± 100 rpm
F8Q 632 engine	5175 ± 50 rpm
F8Q 662 engine	4600 ± 100 rpm
Fast idle speed	Not adjustable (factory set)

Injection pump

Type:	
F8Q 630 engine	Lucas 8448B 171 A/231A
F8Q 632 engine	Lucas EPIC
F8Q 662 engine	Lucas DPCN
Direction of rotation	Clockwise viewed from sprocket end

Sensor resistances

Air temperature sensor (F8Q 630/662 engine):	
0° C	7470 to 11 970 ohms
20° C	3060 to 4045 ohms
40° C	1315 to 1600 ohms
Air temperature sensor (F8Q 632 engine):	
–10° C	10 454 to 8623 ohms
25° C	2175 to 1928 ohms
50° C	857 to 763 ohms
80° C	325 to 292 ohms
TDC sensor (F8Q 630/662 engine)	220 ohms
Engine speed sensor (F8Q 632 engine)	760 ohms at 20° C
Positive flow solenoid valve (F8Q 632 engine)	31 ± 2 ohms
Negative flow solenoid valve (F8Q 632 engine)	31 ± 2 ohms
Advance solenoid valve (F8Q 632 engine)	31 ± 2 ohms
Electrical solenoid valve (F8Q 632 engine)	1.39 ± 0.1 ohms
Advance cam position sensor (F8Q 632 engine)	52 ± 4 ohms
Flow valve position sensor (F8Q 632 engine)	41 ± 4 ohms
Pump temperature thermistor (F8Q 632 engine)	2716 ± 60 ohms at 20° C

Injectors

Type	Pintle
Opening pressure	130 +5 –5 bars
Injector needle lift resistance (sensor type)	105 ohms

Fuel tank

Fuel tank level sender unit resistance at height of float pin (approx):

At 164 mm	3.5 ± 3.5 ohms
At 143 mm	61 ± 7 ohms
At 110 mm	110 ± 10 ohms
At 81 mm	190 ± 16 ohms
At 52 mm	280 ± 20 ohms
At 47 mm	310 ± 10 ohms

Torque wrench settings

Torque wrench settings	Nm	lbf ft
Advance solenoid valve	30	22
Altimetric solenoid valve	30	22
Fuel gauge sender unit	65	48
Fuel injectors to cylinder head	70	52
Fuel pipe union nuts and bolts	25	18
Fuel supply pipe union bolt	25	18
Fuel tank	21	15
Injection pump	22	16
Injection pump adjustment locking nut	90	66
Injection pump mounting nuts and bolts	25	18
Injection pump sprocket centre nut on F8Q 630 engine (gold-coloured):		
Stage 1	20	15
Stage 2	45	33
Injection pump sprocket centre nut on F8Q 632 engine	55	41
Injection pump sprocket securing nut	50	37
Injection pump timing hole blanking plug (Lucas)	5	4
Inlet/exhaust manifold mounting nuts	27	20
Inlet/exhaust manifold strut	25	18
Inlet/exhaust manifold stud	10	7

1 General information and precautions

General information

The fuel system consists of a rear-mounted fuel tank, a fuel filter with integral water separator, a fuel injection pump, injectors and associated components **(see illustrations)**. Before passing through the filter, the fuel is heated by an electric heating element which is fitted to the filter housing.

Fuel is drawn from the fuel tank to the fuel injection pump by a vane-type transfer pump incorporated in the fuel injection pump. Before reaching the pump, the fuel passes through a fuel filter, where foreign matter and water are removed. Excess fuel lubricates the moving components of the pump, and is then returned to the tank.

The fuel injection pump is driven at half crankshaft speed by the timing belt. The high pressure required to inject the fuel into the compressed air in the swirl chambers is

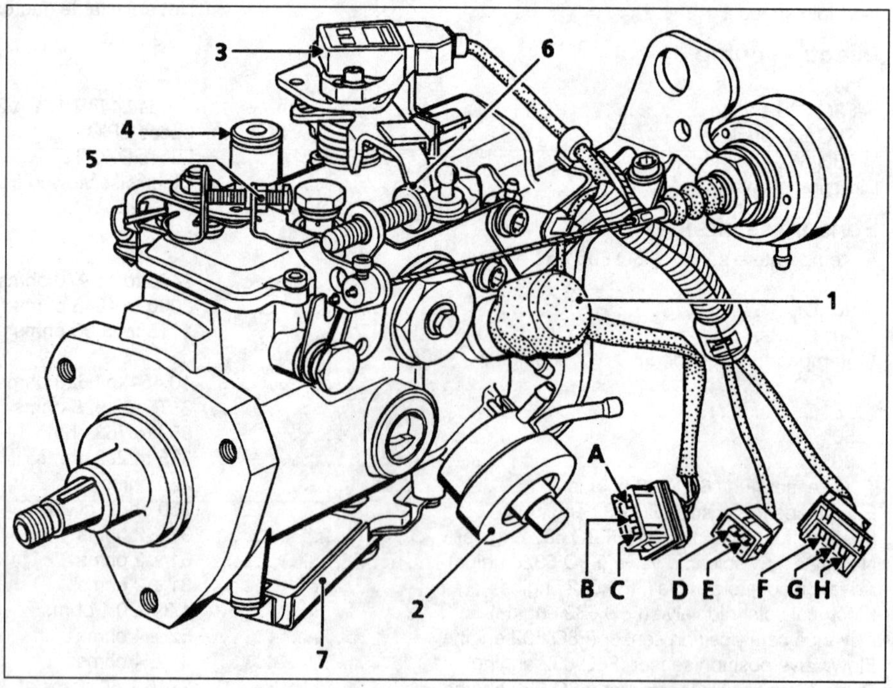

1.1a Early Lucas fuel injection pump components

1 Injection advance corrector
2 Boost pressure corrector
3 Accelerator lever potentiometer
4 Timing inspection plug
5 Idle adjustment screw
6 Anti-stall adjustment screw
7 Coded solenoid valve electronic unit
A Earth
B + after ignition feed
C Coded line
D Advance corrector control
E + after ignition feed
F Earth
G Accelerator lever signal
H Accelerator lever potentiometer 5V feed

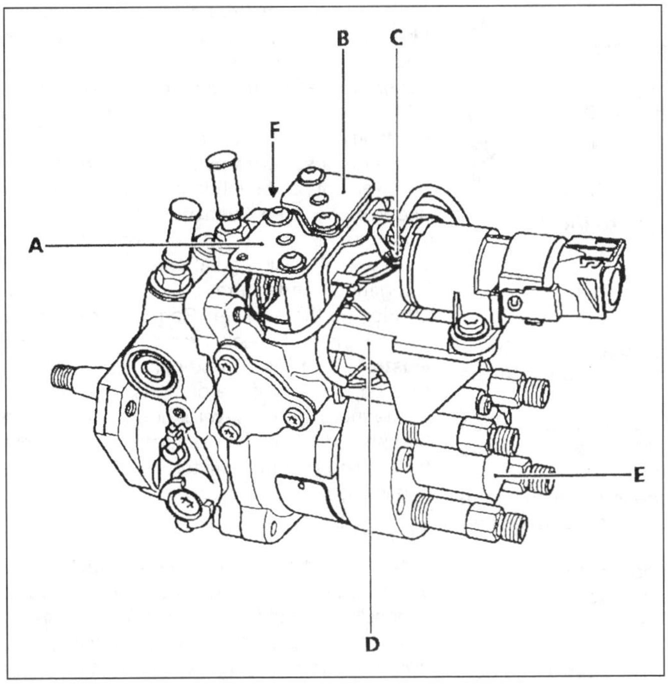

1.1b Lucas EPIC fuel injection pump components

A Advance solenoid valve
B Positive flow solenoid valve
C Negative flow solenoid valve
D Electrical solenoid valve
E Flow valve position sensor (cannot be removed)
F Advance valve position sensor (cannot be removed)

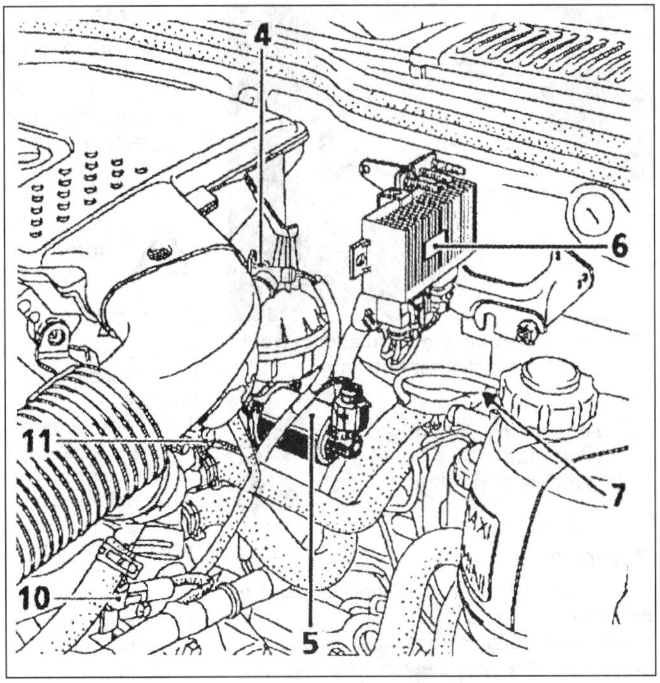

1.1c Lucas EPIC system components

4 Inlet air temperature sensor
5 EGR valve
6 Pre-post heating unit
7 Accelerator pedal position potentiometer
10 TDC sensor
11 Coolant temperature sensor

achieved by two opposed pistons forced together by rollers running in a cam ring. The fuel passes through a central rotor with a single outlet drilling which aligns with ports leading to the injector pipes.

The four fuel injectors inject a homogeneous spray of fuel into the swirl chambers located in the cylinder head. The injectors are calibrated to open and close at critical pressures to provide efficient and even combustion. Each injector needle is lubricated by fuel, which accumulates in the spring chamber.

To enable the engine to meet stringent exhaust emission regulations, fuel metering and injection timing is controlled electronically by an injection electronic control unit (ECU) located in the left-hand rear corner of the engine compartment. On early models, the injection pump has semi-electronic controls, however on later models fitted with the EPIC (Electronically Programmed Injection Control) injection pump, the controls are fully electronic. This highly sophisticated system is similar in operation to a full engine management system as used on petrol engine vehicles and uses similar sensors to provide data to the ECU on engine operating conditions. The sensors typically monitor coolant temperature, air temperature, fuel flow, engine speed, vehicle speed, atmospheric pressure, fuel temperature and accelerator pedal position. From the data received, the ECU controls injection pump fuel metering and injection advance, pre/post-heating system, idle speed, exhaust gas recirculation, the anti-theft system engine immobiliser, and the electric stop control. This allows precise control of all engine fuelling requirements providing optimum engine operation and minimal exhaust emissions under all engine operating conditions. Idle speed is dependent on coolant temperature, gear selected, battery voltage and electrical consumption. If one of the tracks in the accelerator pedal potentiometer is faulty, the idle speed is set at 1000 rpm, if both tracks are faulty, it is set to 1300 rpm. In 1st gear the idle speed is set to 850 rpm, in 2nd gear 875 rpm and in all other gears 900 rpm.

Provided that the specified maintenance is carried out, the fuel injection equipment will give long and trouble-free service. The injection pump itself may well outlast the engine. The main potential cause of damage to the injection pump and injectors is dirt or water in the fuel.

Servicing of the injection pump, injectors, and electronic equipment and sensors is very limited for the home mechanic, and any dismantling or adjustment other than that described in this Chapter must be entrusted to a Renault dealer or fuel injection specialist.

If a fault appears in the injection system, first ensure that all the system wiring connectors are securely connected and free of corrosion. Ensure that the fault is not due to poor maintenance; ie, check that the air cleaner filter element is clean, the cylinder compression pressures are correct, and that the engine breather hoses are clear and undamaged.

Should the fault persist, the vehicle should be taken to a Renault dealer who can test the system on the Renault XR25 diagnostic tester. The tester will locate the fault quickly and simply, alleviating the need to test all the system components individually, which is a time-consuming operation that carries a risk of damaging the ECU. The tester uses a bar chart configuration on a LCD screen; a fiche for the particular model is placed on the screen and each circuit can be checked instantly. It is also advisable to have any faulty components renewed by the dealer as in most instances the XR25 tester is required to reprogram the ECU in the event of component or sensor renewal.

Warning: Many of the procedures in this Chapter require the removal of fuel lines and connections, which may result in some fuel spillage. Before carrying out any operation on the fuel system, refer to the precautions given in 'Safety first!' at the beginning of this manual, and follow them implicitly. Fuel is a highly-dangerous and volatile liquid, and the precautions necessary when handling it cannot be overstressed

Caution: If the radio/cassette in your vehicle is equipped with an anti-theft system, make sure you have the correct activation code before disconnecting the battery

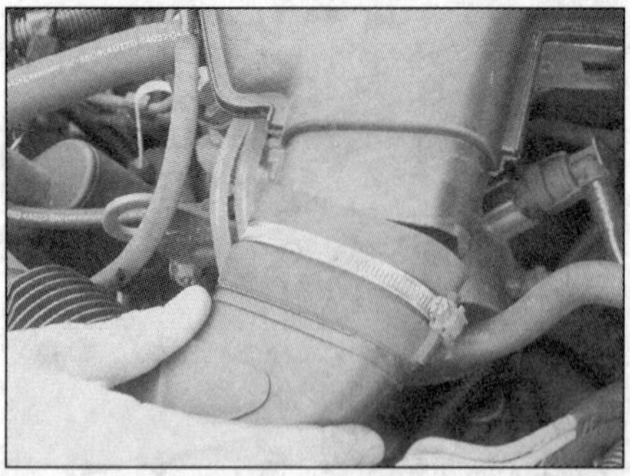

2.2 Disconnecting the air inlet duct from the air cleaner housing

2 Air cleaner housing assembly – removal and refitting

Removal

1 Remove the air cleaner filter element as described in Chapter 1B.
2 Loosen the clip and disconnect the air inlet duct from the air cleaner housing **(see illustration)**.
3 Reach down behind the engine and unscrew the lower mounting nuts, then unscrew the upper mounting bolts and lift the assembly from the inlet manifold. Disconnect the crankcase ventilation hose and remove the assembly.
4 Check the condition of the rubber mountings and renew them as necessary. Also check the hose and hose clip for condition.

Refitting

5 Refitting is a reversal of removal.

3 Fuel gauge sender unit – removal, testing and refitting

Warning: Refer to the warning note in Section 1 before proceeding.

Removal

1 Disconnect the battery negative lead (refer to *Disconnecting the battery* in the Reference Section).
2 Remove the rear seat, or rear seat cushion as described in Chapter 11, for access to the fuel gauge sender unit cover.
3 Carefully prise the access cover from the floor to expose the fuel gauge sender unit **(see illustration)**.
4 Disconnect the wiring connector, and tape it to the vehicle body, to prevent it disappearing behind the tank.
5 Identify the fuel hoses for position, then disconnect them. The hoses are equipped with quick-release fittings to ease removal. To disconnect each hose, slide out the locking tab from the collar then compress the collar and detach the hose from the pump. Renault technicians use a special tool to compress the collar – without this tool, it is possible to use a small screwdriver **carefully** to press back the locking collar inside the end of the special end fitting. Disconnect both hoses, then plug the hose ends to minimise fuel loss.
6 Noting the alignment arrows on the cover, locking ring and fuel tank, unscrew the locking ring and remove it from the tank. This can be accomplished by using a screwdriver on the raised ribs of the locking ring – carefully tap the screwdriver to turn the ring anti-clockwise until it can be unscrewed by hand. Alternatively a removal tool can be fabricated out of metal bar and two bolts **(see illustrations)**.
7 Carefully lift the fuel gauge sender unit out of the fuel tank, taking great care not to damage the gauge sender arm, or to spill fuel in the interior of the vehicle. Remove the rubber sealing ring and check it for deterioration **(see illustration)**; if it is in good condition, it may be re-used, however if the pump is to remain out of the fuel tank for several hours, the locking ring should be refitted temporarily to prevent the sealing ring from distorting. If the sealing ring is unserviceable, obtain a new one.

Testing

8 Note that the fuel gauge sender unit is only available as a complete assembly, however it is possible to test its operation and to remove it. To test the unit, disconnect the wiring plug from the cover and connect an ohmmeter to the two terminals.
9 With the pump assembly upright on the bench, measure the resistance of the sender unit at the different heights given in the Specifications. The resistances are approximate but is should be clear if the sender unit is not operating correctly.
10 To remove the sender unit, first release the wiring from the clips, then unclip and remove the cover from the main body.

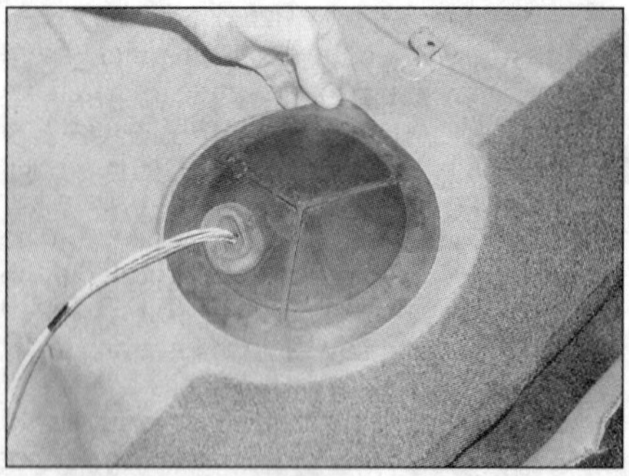

3.3 Prising the access cover from the rear floor

3.6a Alignment arrows on the cover, fuel tank and locking ring

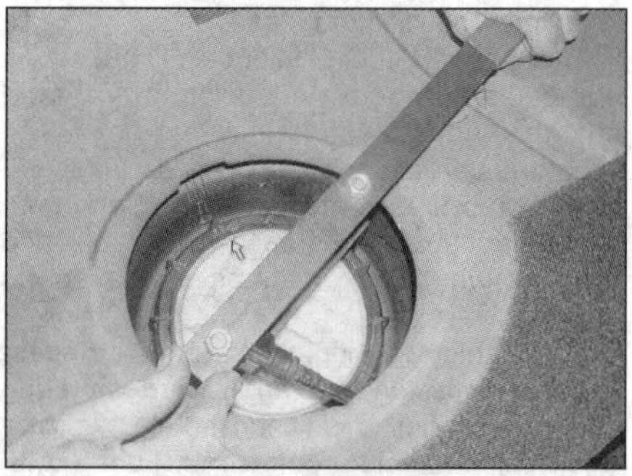

3.6b Using a home-made removal tool to unscrew the locking ring from the fuel tank

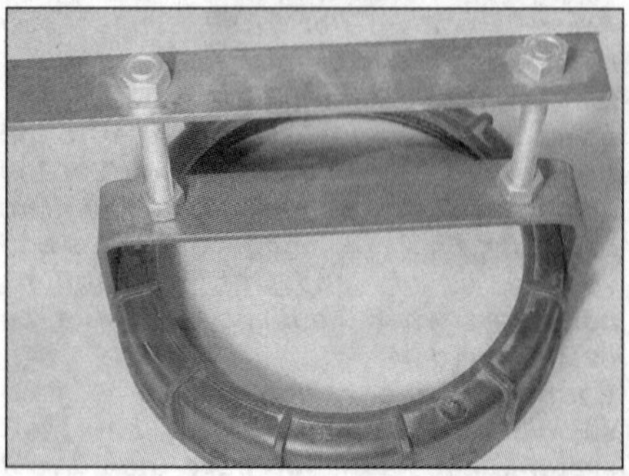

3.6c Home-made fuel pump locking ring removal tool

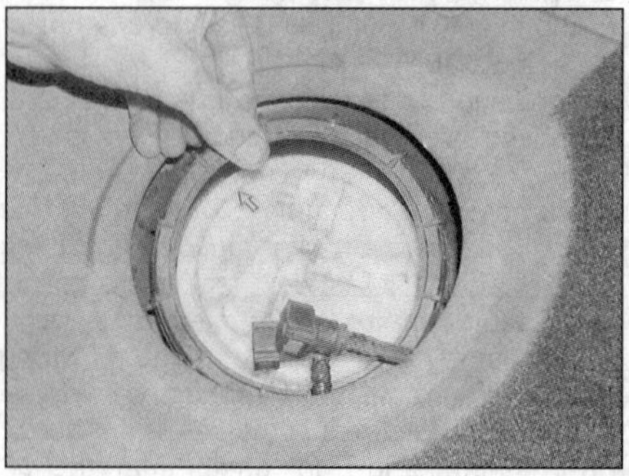

3.6d Removing the locking ring

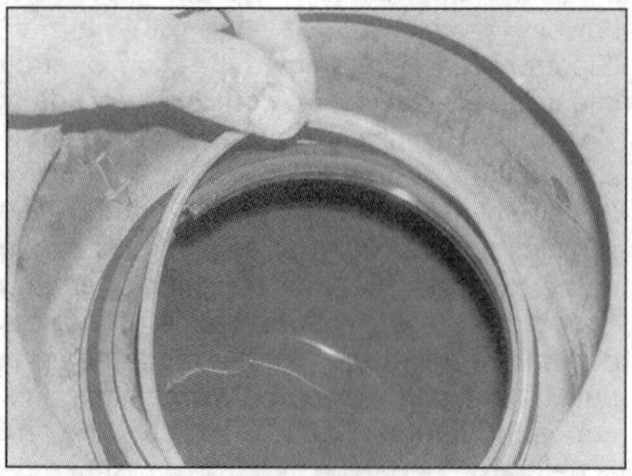

3.7 Removing the rubber sealing ring

11 Using a screwdriver, prise off the gauze filter from the bottom of the unit. Also recover the O-ring seal from the spring location column.

12 Carefully unclip the bottom section, then disconnect the wiring and slide out the sender unit and float.

Refitting

13 Refitting is a reversal of removal, but test the unit before refitting the sender unit to the tank.

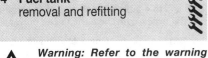

4 Fuel tank – removal and refitting

> **Warning: Refer to the warning note in Section 1 before proceeding.**

Removal

1 Before removing the fuel tank, all fuel must be drained from it. Since a drain plug is not provided, it is preferable to carry out the removal operation when the tank is nearly empty.

2 Remove the rear seat, or rear seat cushion (Chapter 11), for access to the fuel gauge sender unit cover.

3 Using a screwdriver, carefully prise the plastic access cover from the floor.

4 If there is any fuel remaining in the fuel tank, it can be removed by disconnecting the fuel delivery hose and connecting an external syphoning pump to the tank outlet union.

5 Disconnect the wiring connector from the sender unit, and tape the connector to the vehicle body, to prevent it disappearing behind the tank.

6 Disconnect the return hose from the fuel gauge sender unit with reference to Section 3.

7 Chock the front wheels then jack up the rear of the vehicle and support on axle stands (see *Jacking and vehicle support*). Remove the right-hand rear wheel.

8 Remove the exhaust system and relevant heat shield(s) with reference to Section 15. Also unbolt and remove the central exhaust mounting.

9 Remove the heat shield from below the fuel tank and below the handbrake cables.

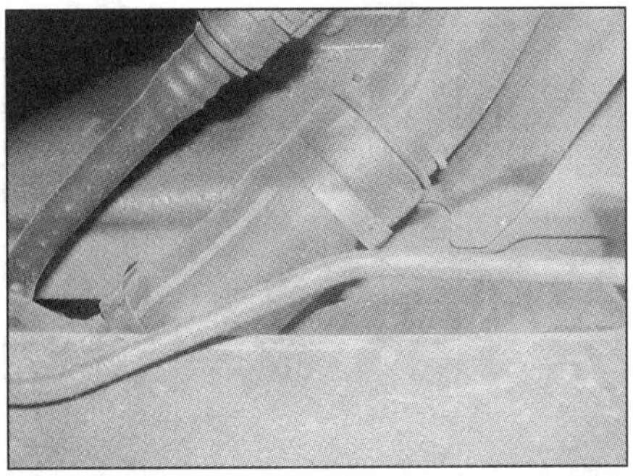

4.12a Filler neck connection to the tank

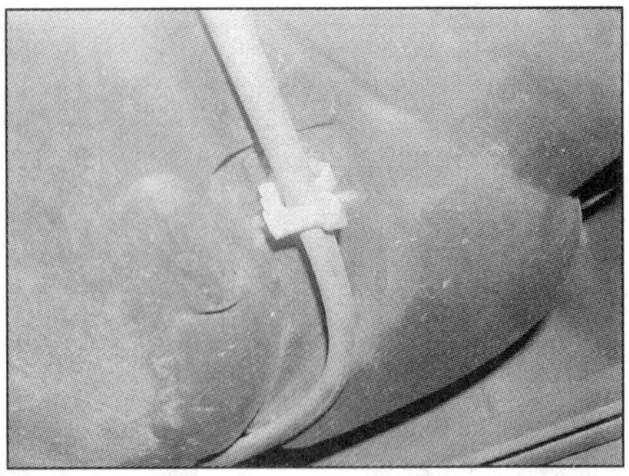

4.12b Handbrake cable clip on the bottom of the fuel tank

10 Note the position of the adjustment nut on the rear of the handbrake lever equaliser rod, then unscrew and remove it and detach the handbrake cables from the supports on the underbody. Unclip the cables and position them to one side away from the fuel tank.

11 Disconnect the overflow pipe.

12 Separate the filler neck from the fuel tank, then unclip the handbrake cables from under the tank **(see illustrations)**.

13 Place a trolley jack with an interposed block of wood beneath the tank, then raise the jack until it is supporting the weight of the tank.

14 Unscrew and remove the mounting bolts **(see illustrations)**, then slowly lower the fuel tank, disconnecting any other relevant vent pipes as they become accessible, and remove the tank from underneath the vehicle. Note that the tank must be slightly tilted to the right, and it may be necessary to bend the brake pipes to provide sufficient clearance. **Do not** bend the pipes excessively.

15 If the tank is contaminated with sediment or water, remove the sender unit (Section 3), and swill the tank out with clean fuel. The tank is injection-moulded from a synthetic material – if seriously damaged, it should be renewed. However, in certain cases, it may be possible to have small leaks or minor damage repaired. Seek the advice of a specialist before attempting to repair the fuel tank.

Refitting

16 Refitting is the reverse of the removal procedure, noting the following points:

a) When lifting the tank back into position, take care to ensure that the hoses are not trapped between the tank and vehicle body.

b) As the tank is located on the underbody, make sure that the positioning holes are correctly aligned with each other. There are two rear holes and one front hole.

c) Ensure that all pipes and hoses are correctly routed. Make sure the sealing rings are in position in the quick-release fittings prior to fitting and make sure they are securely clipped in position.

d) On completion, refill the tank with a small amount of fuel, and check for signs of leakage prior to taking the vehicle out on the road.

5 Accelerator cable – removal, refitting and adjustment

Removal

1 Working in the engine compartment, operate the accelerator lever on the fuel injection pump, and release the inner cable from the lever. Alternatively, on models with a press-fit balljoint cable end fitting, pull the cable end from the lever **(see illustrations)**.

2 Pull the cable outer ferrule from the grommet in the fuel injection pump bracket. Note that on models with a balljoint end fitting, it will be necessary to prise the balljoint from the rubber cable end fitting to enable the cable to pass through the pump bracket **(see**

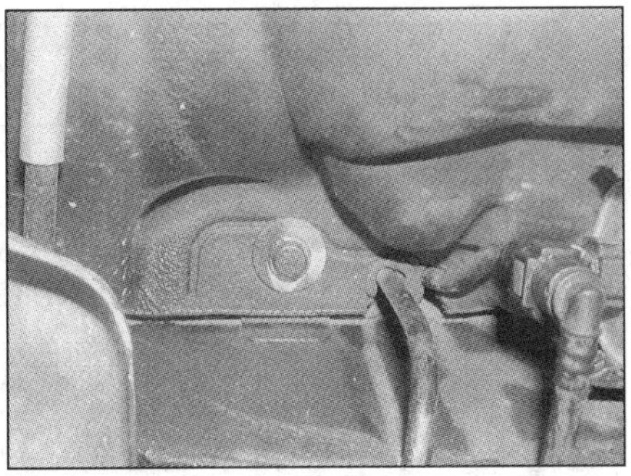

4.14a Fuel tank right-hand mounting bolt . . .

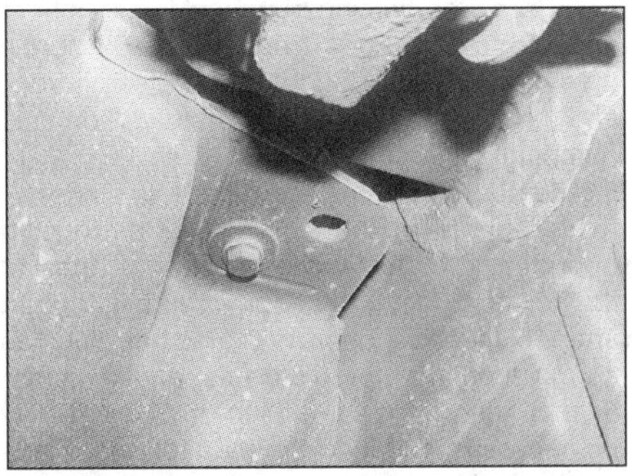

4.14b . . . and left-hand mounting bolt

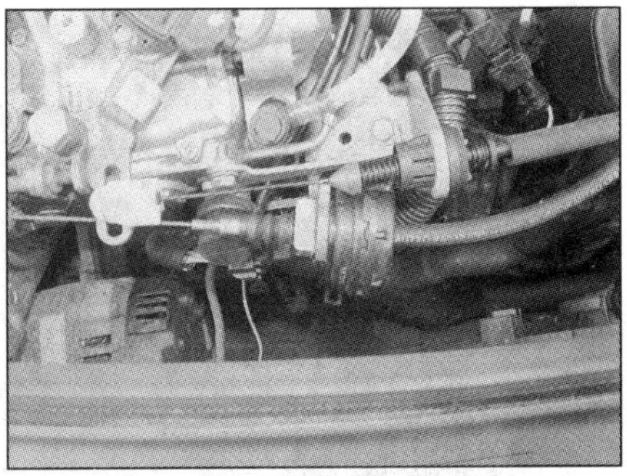

5.1a Accelerator cable on the injection pump

5.1b Disconnecting the accelerator cable from the injection pump lever

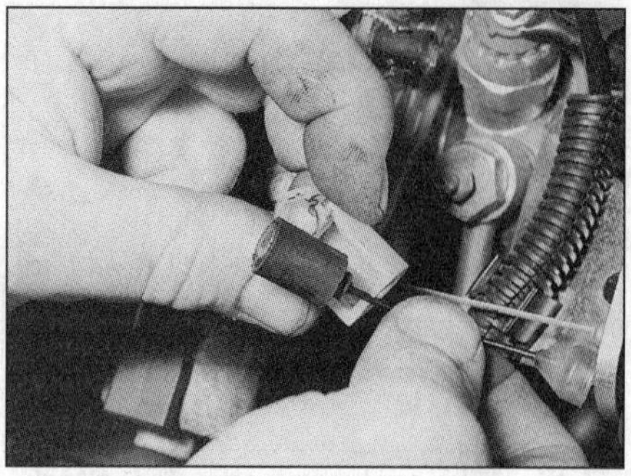

5.2a Remove the balljoint . . .

5.2b . . . to enable the cable to pass through the bracket on the early Lucas pump

illustrations). Where necessary remove the wiring harness plastic clip from the ferrule.

3 Working inside the vehicle, release the cable end fitting which is a push fit in the accelerator pedal rod.

4 Release the cable from the remaining clips and brackets in the engine compartment, noting its routing.

5 Withdraw the cable through the bulkhead into the engine compartment.

Refitting and adjustment

6 Refitting is a reversal of removal, ensuring that the cable is routed as noted before removal, and on completion, check the cable adjustment as follows.

7 Have an assistant fully depress the accelerator pedal, then check that the accelerator lever on the injection pump is touching the maximum speed adjustment screw. If adjustment is required, remove the spring clip from the adjustment ferrule, reposition the ferrule as necessary, then insert the clip in the next free groove on the ferrule.

8 With the accelerator pedal fully released, check that the accelerator lever is touching the anti-stall adjustment screw and that there is 1.0 mm freeplay in the cable.

6 Accelerator pedal – removal and refitting

Removal

1 Remove the nut which secures the accelerator pedal pivot bush **(see illustration)**.

6.1 Remove the nut (arrowed) which secures the accelerator pedal pivot bush

2 Disconnect the accelerator cable from the pedal as described in the previous Section.

3 Remove the pedal and bush.

Refitting

4 Refit by reversing the removal operations.

7 Fuel system – priming and bleeding

1 After disconnecting part of the fuel supply system or running out of fuel, it is necessary to prime the system and bleed off any air which may have entered the system components.

2 All models are fitted with a hand-operated priming bulb located next to the fuel filter, in the left-hand front corner of the engine compartment.

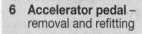

> **HAYNES HiNT** ***Priming of the fuel system after filter renewal will be greatly improved if the filter element is filled with clean diesel fuel before securing it to the filter head. To avoid spillages of fuel, keep the filter upright during refitting.***

3 To prime the system, loosen the bleed screw located on the filter head or on the injection pump inlet union.

4 Fit a piece of pipe to the bleed screw and place the open end in a container to catch the fuel. Pump the priming bulb until fuel free from air bubbles emerges from the bleed screw **(see illustration)**. Retighten the bleed screw, and remove the pipe and container. Continue pumping until firm resistance is felt.

5 Attempt to start the engine at this stage, by fully depressing the accelerator pedal and operating the starter motor. Do not operate the heater plugs. If the engine refuses to start after 15 seconds, operate the heater plugs as normal then attempt to start the engine again.

6 If air has entered the injector pipes, it may be necessary to bleed them as follows. Place wads of rag around the injector pipe unions at the injectors (to absorb spilt fuel), then slacken the unions. Crank the engine on the starter motor until fuel emerges from the unions, then stop cranking the engine and retighten the unions. Mop up spilt fuel.

> ***Warning: Be prepared to stop the engine if it should fire, to avoid fuel spray and spillage.***

7 Attempt to start the engine by fully depressing the accelerator pedal and operating the starter motor. Initially do not operate the heater plugs, however, if it refuses to start after 15 seconds, operate the heater plugs as normal then start the engine.

8 Idle and maximum speed – checking and adjustment

Caution: The maximum speed adjustment screw is sealed by the manufacturers at the factory using paint or a locking wire and a lead seal. There is no reason why it should require adjustment. Do not disturb the screw if the vehicle is still within the warranty period otherwise the warranty will be invalidated.

Note: *This adjustment requires the use of a tachometer.*

Note: *The following information is applicable to engine code F8Q 630 only. On engine codes F8Q 662 and F8Q 632, the idle speed is controlled by the system ECU and it is not possible to adjust it manually; the actual idle speed applied varies according to several inputs, including the gear engaged and the loading on the electrical system.*

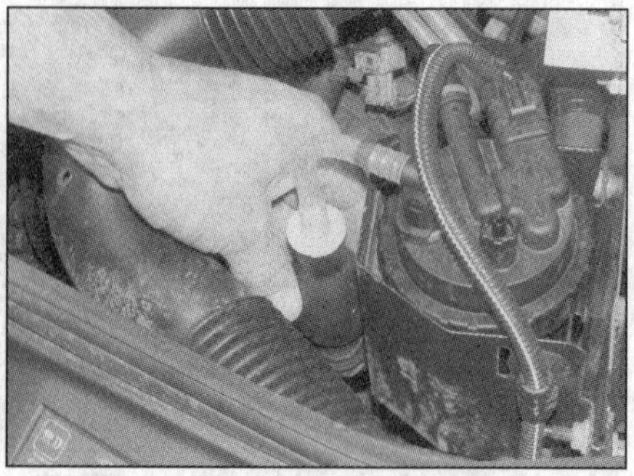

7.4 Pump the priming bulb to bleed the fuel system

Idle speed and residual flow adjustment

1 Run the engine to normal operating temperature, then make sure that the fast idle speed system is not operational (see sub-section later in this Section).
2 With the tachometer connected to the engine, check that the idle speed is as given in the Specifications.
3 If necessary, turn the idle speed adjustment screw on the injection pump as necessary **(see illustration)**.
4 Position a 4.0 mm thick shim between the load lever and the residual flow adjustment screw, and check the engine speed again. It should be 1250 ± 50 rpm. If necessary, adjust the residual flow adjustment screw as required.
5 Remove the shim then accelerate sharply twice, and check that the engine idles at the correct speed.
6 It is important to adjust the idle speed and residual flow correctly, since these adjustments affect the deceleration phase during normal running.

Fast idle speed

7 Fast idle speed is controlled by the ECU via a cable and LDA solenoid unit on the injection pump. The system is operational if the engine temperature is lower than 10°C when the ignition is switched on. The cut-off temperature varies according to the coolant temperature when the ignition is switched on, as shown in the following chart.

Coolant temperature (°C)	Cut-off temperature (°C)
15	20
5	20
0	25 (F8Q 630), 30 (F8Q 662)
–10	25 (F8Q 630), 40 (F8Q 662)
–20	35 (F8Q 630), 50 (F8Q 662)

8 The fast idle speed control system is also operational if the engine speed drops to 650 rpm and the vehicle speed is less than 15 mph, and also if the air conditioning is switched on.
9 The fast idle speed control system is cut-off if the engine speed is greater than 850 rpm.
10 The fast idle speed is adjusted at the factory and is not adjustable on the vehicle, however the cable adjustment can be checked as follows.
11 Disconnect the vacuum hose from the fast idle LDA, then check that there is free play of 2.0 ± 1.0 mm between the cable stop and the fast idle speed lever **(see illustration)**.
12 If necessary, loosen the cable stop nut and reposition the stop, then tighten the nut.

Maximum engine speed

13 Connect a tachometer to the engine, then briefly accelerate the engine to maximum speed. Check that the maximum speed is as given in the Specifications. If the speed is not correct, it will be necessary to have the injection pump adjusted at a Renault dealer or diesel specialist.

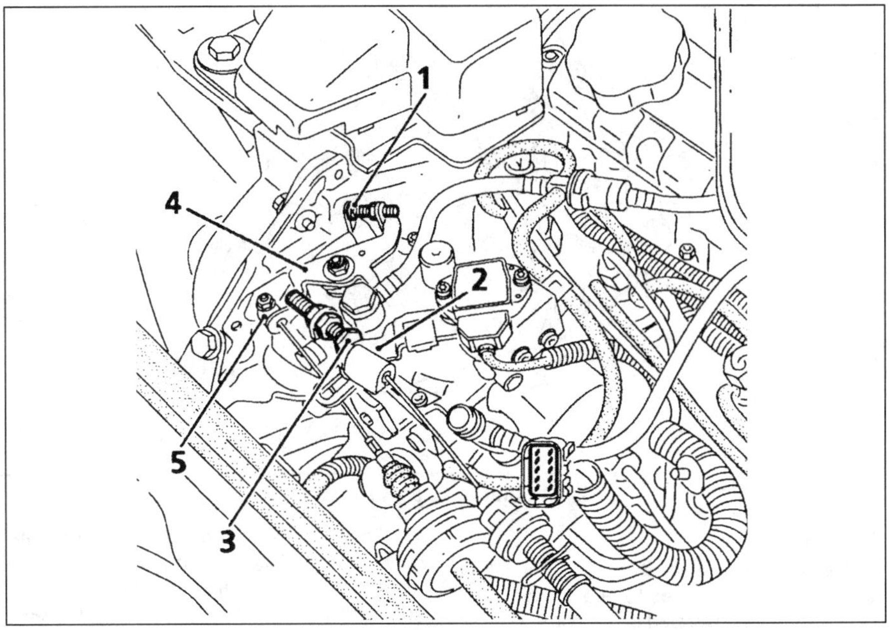

8.3 Adjustment screw locations on the early Lucas pump

1 Idle speed adjustment screw
2 Load lever
3 Residual flow adjustment screw (anti-stall)
4 Fast idle lever
5 Idle speed cable grip

9 Fuel injection pump components and ECU – removal and refitting

Warning: Refer to the warning note in Section 1 before proceeding.

Note: *After refitting the following components it is recommended that the ECU memory is checked and if necessary erased.*

Advance solenoid valve (F8Q 630)

Removal

1 The advance solenoid valve is located on the front-facing side of the injection pump.

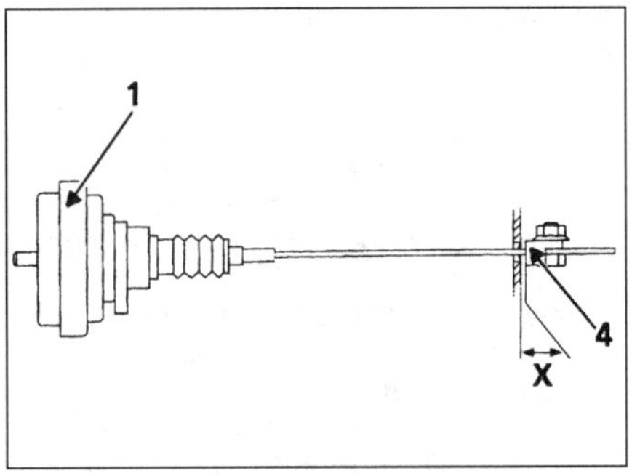

8.11 Fast idle speed adjustment

1 LDA
4 Cable stop
x = 2.0 ± 1.0 mm

2 The two wires for the valve must be removed from the multi-plug connector for the pump. To do this, first separate the connectors, then press the two tabs and remove the yellow guide. The wires can now be removed using a small screwdriver to prise the retaining tabs to one side. Release the wiring from the main loom.
3 Remove the cover from the valve, then unscrew and remove the valve from the pump.
4 Recover the return connection, seals and filter **(see illustration)**. Note that the filter must be renewed whenever the valve is removed.

4B

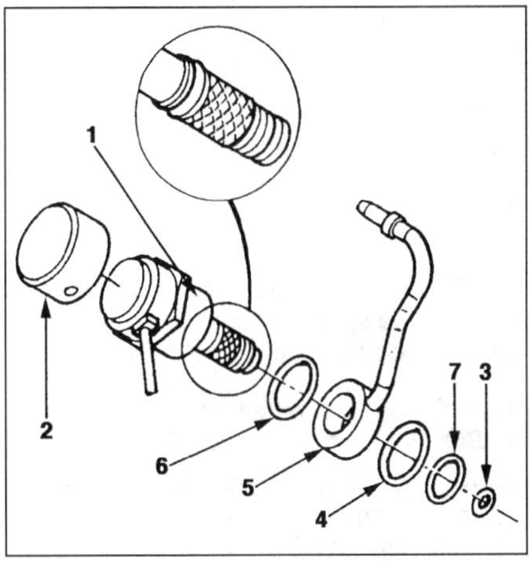

9.4 Advance solenoid valve – engine code F8Q 630

1 Solenoid valve
2 Protective cover
3 Small filter
4 Seal
5 Return connection
6 Seal
7 Seal

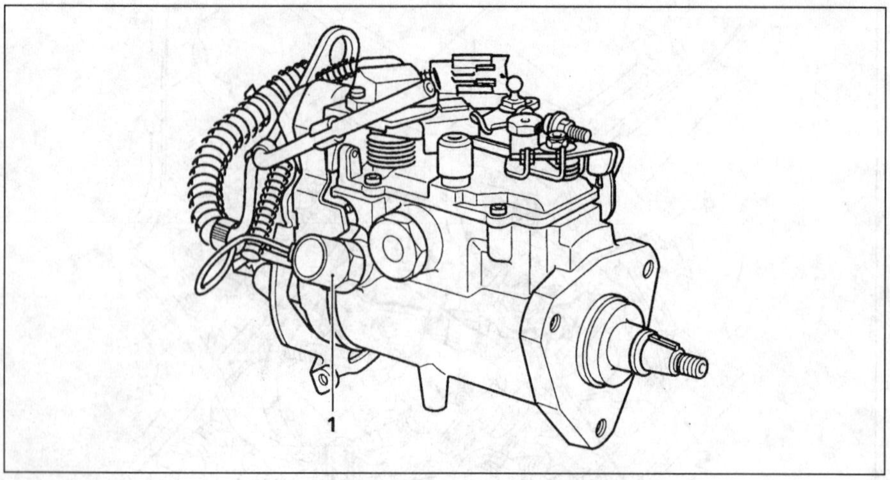

9.6 Altimetric solenoid valve (1)

Refitting

5 Refitting is a reversal of removal, but tighten the valve to the specified torque and bleed the fuel system as described in Section 7.

Altimetric solenoid valve (F8Q 630 and F8Q 662)

Removal

6 The altimetric corrector valve is located on the rear face of the injection pump, and its purpose is to reduce the fuel flow at altitudes above 1000 metres **(see illustration)**. First unscrew the unions and remove the high pressure pipes.

7 Remove the injector with the sensor with reference to Section 13.

8 The two wires for the valve must be removed from the multi-plug connector for the pump. To do this, first separate the connectors, then press the two tabs and remove the yellow guide. The wires can now be removed using a small screwdriver to prise the retaining tabs to one side. Release the wiring from the main loom.

9 Remove the cover from the valve, then unscrew and remove the valve from the pump.

10 Recover the small filter. Note that the filter must be renewed whenever the valve is removed.

Refitting

11 Refitting is a reversal of removal, but tighten the valve to the specified torque and bleed the fuel system as described in Section 7.

Load potentiometer (F8Q 630 and F8Q 662)

Note: *The following procedure is a delicate operation, and extra care must be taken to prevent damage to components. If a new unit is fitted, the 'full load' position must be reprogrammed into the ECU by a Renault dealer using specialist equipment.*

Removal

12 Disconnect the wiring from the injection pump.

13 Remove the wiring from the multi-plug connector as described in paragraph 8, then remove the wires from the plastic sheath.

14 Mark the potentiometer and bracket in relation to each other as a guide to refitting the unit.

15 Undo the mounting screws, then use a small screwdriver to release the slide contact from the lever. Turn the insert 90° to remove it.

16 With the load lever in the 'full load' position, turn the potentiometer 90° anti-clockwise and remove it.

Refitting

17 Refitting is a reversal of removal, but if a new unit has been fitted, have the 'full load' position reprogrammed into the ECU by a Renault dealer.

Advance and positive flow solenoid valves (F8Q 632)

Removal

18 The advance and positive flow solenoid valves are located on the top of the injection pump and are in one integral unit. To remove them, first disconnect the battery negative (earth) lead and position it away from the terminal.

19 Disconnect the main wiring plug from the connector.

20 Unbolt the connector body from its mounting, then pull out the plug by depressing the tabs.

21 Remove the pin plate, then carefully pull out the plastic clip and remove the pin holder.

22 Note the location of the 4 wires for the solenoid valve, then remove them together with the terminals. Renault technicians use a special tool for this, however a paper clip or similar tool may be used instead.

23 Unbolt the solenoid valve assembly from the injection pump and recover the 4 O-ring seals. Discard the seals as new ones must be fitted.

Refitting

24 Wipe clean the mating surfaces of the valve assembly and injection pump using lint-free cloth. Do not use any solvent.

25 Locate the new O-ring seals on the injection pump. Do not locate them on the solenoid valve assembly.

26 Locate the solenoid valve assembly on the pump, insert the bolts and hand-tighten them.

27 Tighten the bolts to the specified torque, tightening the inner bolts first then the outer bolts.

28 Refit the wires and terminals in their correct locations. Each terminal must be carefully pushed in then pulled back to lock the tabs.

29 Refit the pin holder and retain with the plastic clip, then refit the pin plate.

30 Reconnect the plug then refit the connector body and tighten the mounting bolts.

31 Reconnect the main wiring plug.

32 Reconnect the battery negative lead.

Negative flow and electrical solenoid valves (F8Q 632)

Removal

33 The negative flow and electrical solenoid valves are located on the lower part of the injection pump and are in one integral unit. To remove them, first disconnect the battery negative (earth) lead and position it away from the terminal.

34 Disconnect the main wiring plug from the connector.

35 Unbolt the connector body from its mounting, then pull out the plug by depressing the tabs **(see illustration opposite)**.

36 Remove the pin plate, then carefully pull out the plastic clip and remove the pin holder.

37 Note the location of the wires for the solenoid valve, then remove them together with the terminals. Renault technicians use a special tool for this, however a paper clip or similar tool may be used instead.

38 Unbolt the solenoid valve assembly and plastic mounting from the injection pump loosening the outer bolts first. As it is being removed note the position of the core and spring. Recover the 3 O-ring seals. Discard the seals as new ones must be fitted.

Refitting

39 Wipe clean the mating surfaces of the valve assembly and injection pump using lint-free cloth. Do not use any solvent.

40 Locate the new O-ring seals on the injection pump, using diesel fuel to hold them in position. Do not locate them on the solenoid valve assembly.

41 Refit the solenoid valve assembly together with core, spring and plastic mounting, making sure that the O-rings are not disturbed. Insert the inner bolts hand-tight while pressing the assembly onto the pump, then insert the outer bolts hand-tight. Tighten the bolts securely.

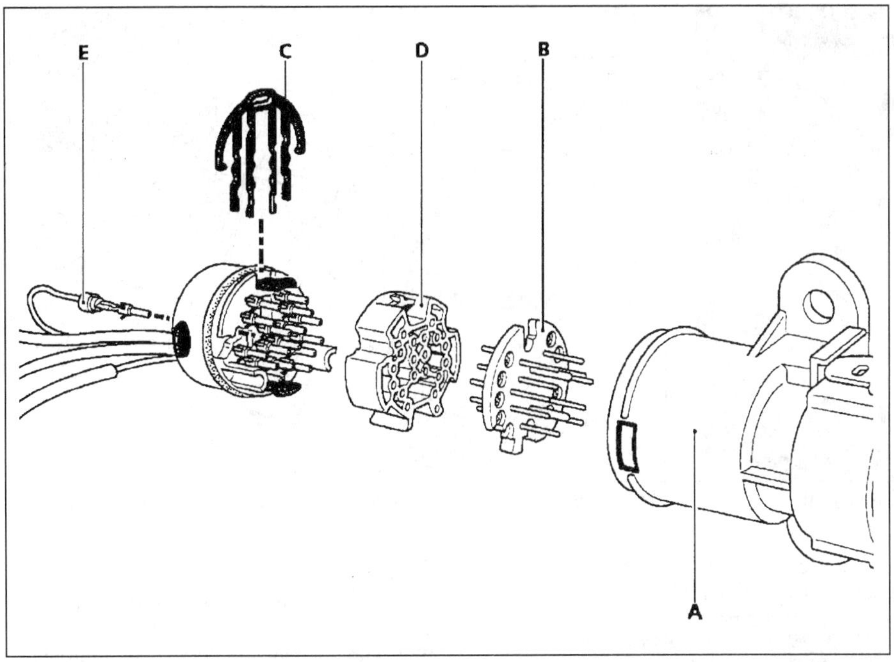

9.35 Pump connector components

A Holder *B Pin plate* *C Plastic clip* *D Pin holder* *E Terminals*

42 Refit the wires and terminals in their correct locations. Each terminal must be carefully pushed in then pulled back to lock the tabs.
43 Refit the pin holder and retain with the plastic clip, then refit the pin plate.
44 Reconnect the plug then refit the connector body and tighten the mounting bolts.
45 Reconnect the main wiring plug.
46 Reconnect the battery negative lead.

Accelerator potentiometer (F8Q 632)

Removal

47 The accelerator potentiometer is located beneath the brake master cylinder. It is connected to the accelerator pedal by cable **(see illustration)**.
48 Remove the unit from under the master cylinder, then prise open the plastic cover.
49 Turn the potentiometer segment slightly and unhook the cable end fitting.
50 Release the cable ferrule from the potentiometer.

Refitting

51 Refitting is a reversal of removal, but note that the engine management ECU should be checked by a Renault dealer for faults residing in its memory.

ECU (all engine codes)

Removal

***Note:** The ECU is electronically-coded to match the engine immobiliser. If the ECU is being removed to enable a new unit to be fitted, the new unit must be programmed with the vehicle code as described.*

52 The ECU is located in the left-hand side of the engine compartment, behind the battery. First disconnect the battery negative lead (refer to *Disconnecting the battery* in the Reference Section).
53 Unclip the power steering hydraulic fluid reservoir from the bulkhead and position it to one side **(see illustration)**.
54 Where applicable, unbolt the bracket from the top of the ECU and release the strap **(see illustration)**. Alternatively the bracket can remain on the ECU until the assembly is removed.
55 Undo the mounting screws and remove the ECU and mounting bracket **(see illustration)**.
56 Disconnect the wiring connector and remove the ECU from the engine compartment.

Refitting

57 Refitting is a reverse of the removal procedure ensuring that the wiring connector is securely reconnected. If a new ECU has been fitted, reprogramme it as follows. Turn the ignition on for a few seconds, then turn it off. Now remove the key to operate the immobiliser. After 10 seconds, the red immobiliser warning light should start to flash.

9.54 . . . then remove the upper bracket . . .

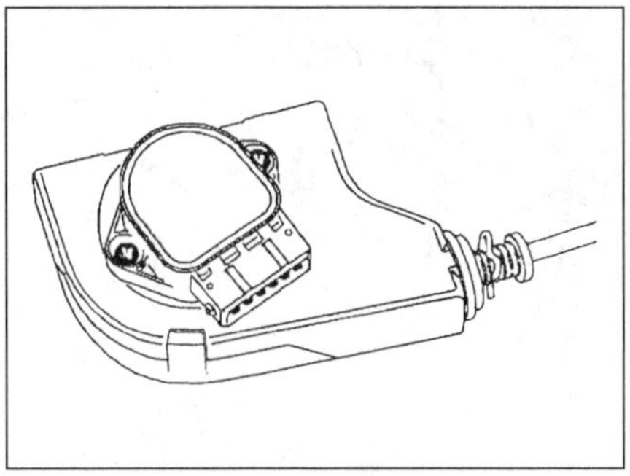

9.47 Accelerator potentiometer – engine code F8Q 632

9.53 Position the power steering hydraulic fluid reservoir to one side . . .

10 Fuel injection pump – removal and refitting

Warning: Refer to the warning note in Section 1 before proceeding.

Removal

1 Disconnect the battery negative (earth) lead and position it away from the terminal.
2 Apply the handbrake, then jack up the front of the vehicle and support securely on axle stands.

9.55 . . . followed by the ECU

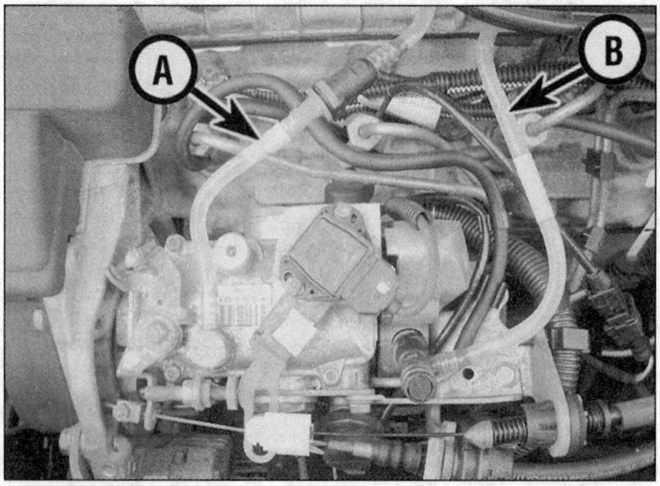

10.6 Fuel return hose (A) and supply hose (B)

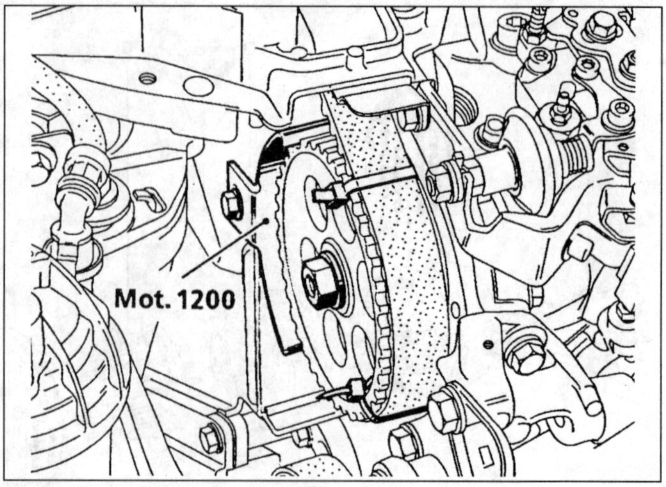

10.12 Renault sprocket holding tool in position – F8Q 630 engine

3 Remove the right-hand front roadwheel and the wheelarch liner for access to the crankshaft pulley bolt.

4 Unbolt the cover from the right-hand engine mounting, then unbolt the cover from over the injection pump sprocket.

5 Set the engine to TDC as described in Chapter 2C.

6 Unscrew the union bolt and remove the fuel supply pipe from the injection pump, then disconnect the fuel return pipe at the quick-release connector **(see illustration)**. Tape over or plug the apertures in the pump and the ends of the pipes.

7 Disconnect the wiring plug from the injection pump.

8 Disconnect the accelerator cable with reference to Section 5.

9 On the F8Q 630 engine, disconnect the vacuum hose from the LDA anti-stall device on the front of the injection pump.

10 Unscrew the union nuts on the injection pump and injectors and remove the injector pipes together from the engine.

11 Unscrew and remove the pump rear support mounting bolt.

12 Renault technicians use a special tool to hold the injection pump sprocket while the pump is removed **(see illustration)**. If it is not possible to obtain this tool, either make up an alternative tool or remove the timing belt as described in Chapter 2C.

HAYNES HiNT ***Use two plastic cable ties to secure the timing belt to the sprocket, if the sprocket is to remain in position.***

13 Make alignment marks between the pump and the mounting bracket. This will aid pump timing on refitting.

14 Hold the sprocket stationary then unscrew the central gold-coloured nut to release the sprocket from the pump shaft. On the F8Q 630 engine, the nut acts as an extractor when it is unscrewed. On the F8Q 632 engine, it may be necessary to use a puller to release the sprocket.

15 Unscrew the three pump securing bolts, and withdraw the pump from its mounting bracket, leaving the sprocket engaged with the timing belt, where applicable **(see illustrations)**. Access to the lower pump mounting bolt is most easily obtained from the rear of the pump, using a deep socket and extension.

16 Recover the Woodruff key from the end of the pump shaft if it is loose.

17 If desired, the rear pump mounting bracket can be unbolted from the rear of the pump.

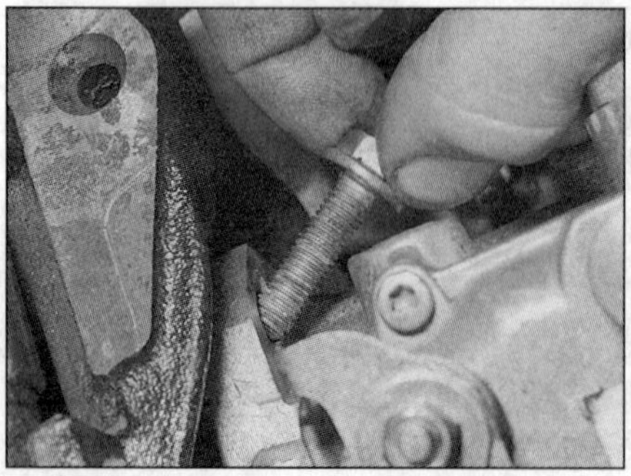

10.15a Remove the securing bolts . . .

10.15b . . . and withdraw the fuel injection pump

Refitting

18 Where applicable, refit the rear mounting bracket to the rear of the injection pump.

19 Clean the injection pump shaft thoroughly using suitable solvent to remove any traces of oil or grease.

20 Locate the Woodruff key in the end of the pump shaft.

21 Offer the injection pump to the mounting bracket, making sure that the previously made marks are correctly aligned. If the sprocket is still engaged with the timing belt, engage the pump shaft with the sprocket. Insert the mounting bolts and tighten to the specified torque.

22 Hold the sprocket stationary and tighten the centre nut to the specified torque. On engine code F8Q 630, tighten the gold-coloured central nut in the two stages given in the Specifications. It is important to pause between the two stages.

23 Remove the pump holding tool, or refit the timing belt with reference to Chapter 2C (as applicable).

24 Refit and tighten the pump rear support mounting bolt.

25 Carry out injection timing as described in Sections 11 and 12.

26 Refit the injector pipes to the injectors and pump and tighten the union nuts to the specified torque.

27 Reconnect the vacuum hose to the LDA anti-stall device.

28 Reconnect the accelerator cable with reference to Section 5.

29 Reconnect the wiring plug to the injection pump.

30 Reconnect the fuel supply and return pipes to the injection pump, tightening the supply union bolt to the specified torque.

31 Refit the covers over the injection pump sprocket and right-hand engine mounting.

32 Refit the wheelarch liner and the right-hand front roadwheel, then lower the vehicle to the ground.

33 Reconnect the battery negative lead.
34 Prime and bleed the fuel system as described in Section 7.
35 Start the engine, and check the idle speed setting, as described in Section 8.

11 Injection timing – checking methods and adjustment

1 Checking the injection timing is not a routine operation. It is only necessary after the injection pump has been disturbed.
2 Dynamic timing equipment does exist, but it is unlikely to be available to the home mechanic. The equipment works by converting pressure pulses in an injector pipe into electrical signals. If such equipment is available, use it in accordance with its maker's instructions.
3 Static timing as described in this Chapter will give a good result if carried out carefully. A dial test indicator will be needed, together with a probe and adaptor **(see illustration)**. Read through the procedures before starting work to find out what is involved.

12 Injection timing – checking and adjustment

Caution: Some of the injection pump settings and access plugs may be sealed by the manufacturers at the factory using paint or locking wire and lead seals. Do not disturb the seals if the vehicle is still within the warranty period otherwise the warranty will be invalidated. Also do not attempt the timing procedure unless accurate instrumentation is available. Suitable special tools for carrying out pump timing are available from motor factors, and a dial test indicator will be required regardless of the method used. Refer to the precautions given in Section 1 of this Chapter before proceeding.

1 Disconnect the battery negative (earth) lead and position it away from the terminal.
2 Apply the handbrake, then jack up the front right-hand corner of the vehicle until the wheel is just clear of the ground. Support the vehicle on an axle stand and engage 4th or 5th gear. This will enable the crankshaft to be turned easily by turning the right-hand wheel. Alternatively, the engine can be turned using an open-ended spanner on the crankshaft pulley bolt.
3 Turn the crankshaft to bring No 1 piston to TDC on the compression stroke, and fit the tool to lock the crankshaft in position, as described in Chapter 2C.

F8Q 630/662 engines

4 A dial test indicator will now be required, along with a suitable special probe (Renault tool Mot.1079, or an alternative available from

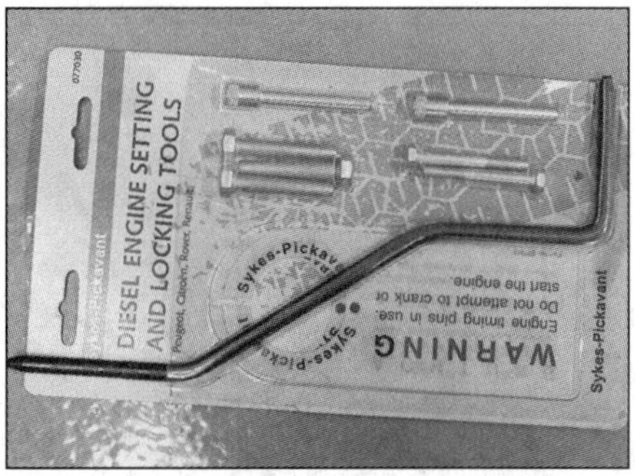

11.3 Tools for checking crankshaft position when setting injection timing on diesel engines

motor factors). Note that the probe of the Renault tool is 'waisted' to allow it to clear the pump rotor and rest on the timing shoulder **(see illustration)**.
5 Remove the inspection plug from the top of the pump, and recover the sealing washer. Position the timing probe in the aperture so that the tip of the probe rests on the rotor timing shoulder **(see illustrations)**.
6 Position the dial test indicator securely on the injection pump body, so that it can read the movement of the timing probe. Ensure that the gauge is positioned directly in line with the probe, with the gauge plunger at the mid-point of its travel.
7 Remove the crankshaft locking tool, then turn the crankshaft approximately a quarter-turn anti-clockwise (viewed from the timing belt end of the engine), and zero the dial test indicator. Check that the timing probe is seated on the timing shoulder.
8 Turn the crankshaft clockwise slowly until the crankshaft locking tool can be re-inserted (bringing the engine back to TDC). Only turn the engine clockwise – if it is turned anti-clockwise, repeat the setup procedure. To determine the exact timing position, maintain pressure on the crankshaft locking tool until it enters the TDC timing hole.
9 Read the dial test indicator; the reading should correspond to the value marked on a tag on the pump cover. If the reading is not as specified, proceed as follows.
10 Unbolt the cover from the right-hand engine mounting, then unbolt the cover from over the injection pump sprocket.

12.5a Unscrewing the timing inspection plug from the top of a Lucas pump

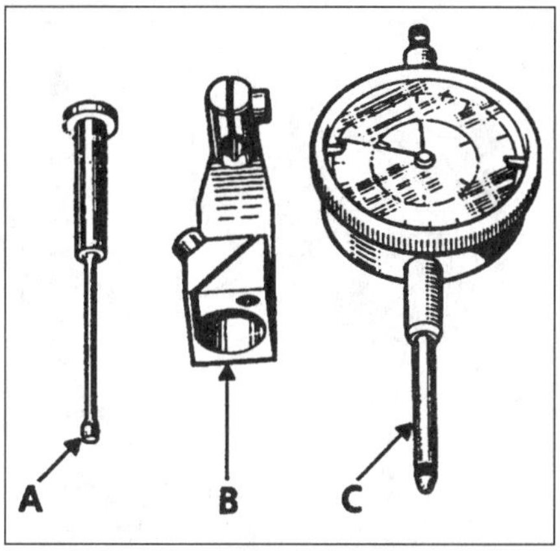

12.4 Components of Lucas injection pump timing tool set – Renault Mot. 1079

A Probe
B Adapter
C Dial test indicator (dial gauge)

11 Remove the crankshaft locking tool.
12 Withdraw the timing probe and lock the pump sprocket with the Renault special tool Mot. 1200-01 or an alternative tool.
13 The injection pump MAA-type sprocket (**M**icrometric **A**angular **A**djustment) consists of a hub and toothed rim which are locked together by a centre ring (left-hand thread) **(see illustration)**. The plate incorporates three holes into which a special tool (Renault Mot. 1358-01) is inserted to turn the pump shaft. First, the centre ring must be loosened

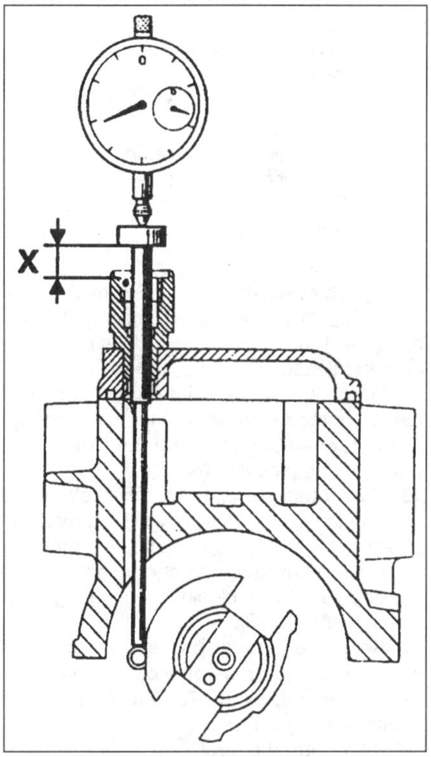

12.5b Timing probe details (Renault tool Mot. 1079) – Lucas pump

X = Timing value marked on pump

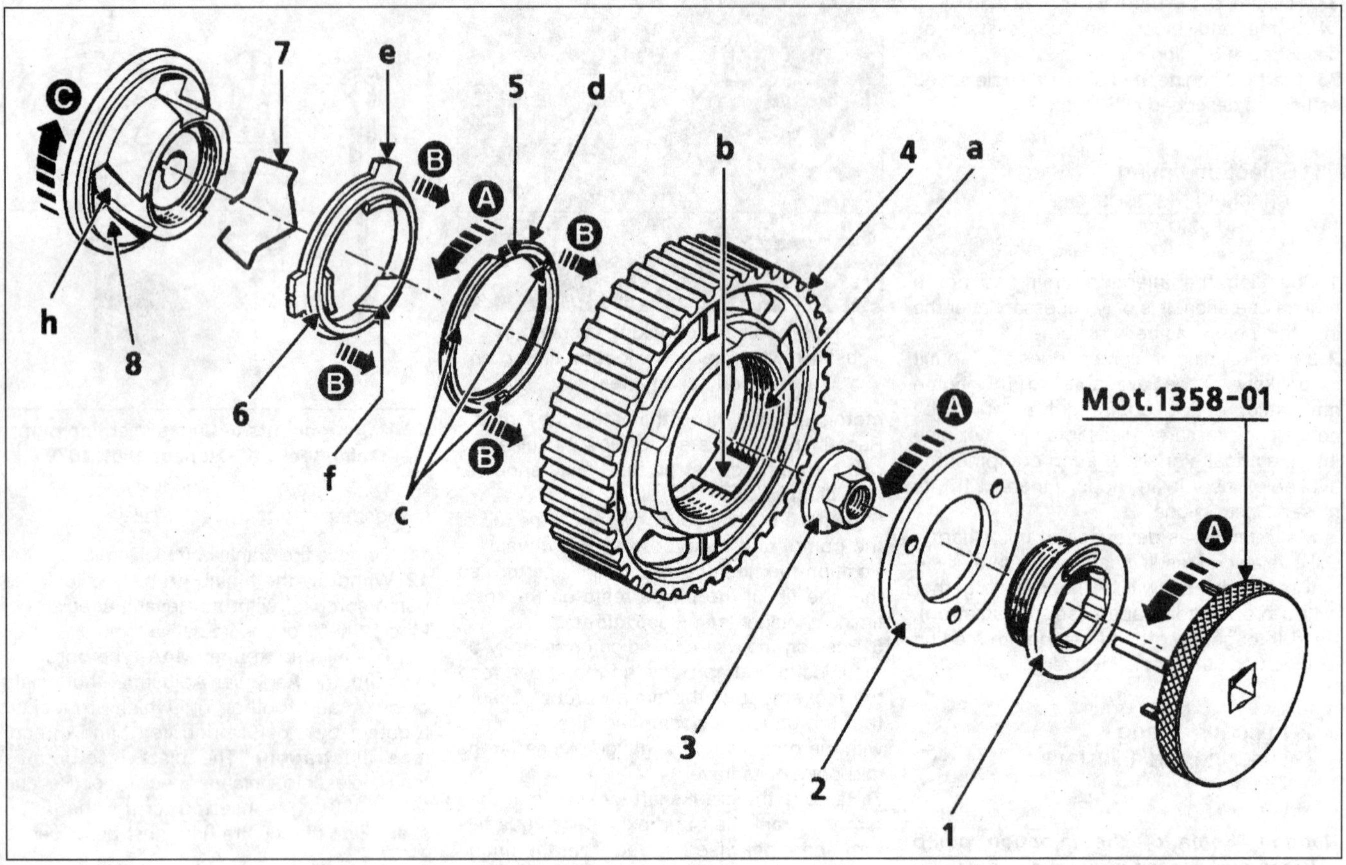

12.13 Exploded view of MAA-type sprocket

1 *Centre ring –* ***left-hand thread***
2 *Sprocket plate*
3 *Sprocket nut**
4 *Sprocket toothed rim*
5 *Micrometric advance ring*
6 *Angular adjustment ring*
7 *Centre bolt locking spring*
8 *Sprocket hub*
A *Anti-clockwise movement caused by tool operator*
B *Transverse movement of the rings*
C *Clockwise rotation exerted on the pump shaft*
a *Thread for item d*
b *Straight guide ramps for guide lugs e*
c *Slots for tool pins*
d *Thread for item a*
e *Guide lugs*
f *Helicoidal guide ramps for items h*
h *Helicoidal ramps for items f*
* *Gold-coloured extractor nut with integral washer shown*

(turn clockwise) using Renault tool Mot. 1359 or a suitable equivalent. The ring must be loosened sufficiently so that the adjacent flange can rotate freely.

14 Fit the special tool in the three holes and turn the plate assembly so that the three pins of the tool engage in the three slots in the advance ring **(see illustration)**.

15 Now rotate the plate assembly clockwise until the tool locks. This allows the sprocket to be set to the position for starting adjustment.

16 Remove the sprocket locking tool and turn the engine 2 turns clockwise (bringing No 1 piston back to TDC).

17 Refit the timing probe and dial test indicator and zero as previously described. Reset the engine to TDC and insert the crankshaft locking tool.

18 Now turn the tool Mot. 1358-01 anti-clockwise until the correct timing value is obtained on the dial gauge. If the timing value is exceeded, turn it fully back before making the adjustment again.

19 Remove the special tool, then tighten the centre ring (left-hand thread) to a torque of 20 Nm. The dial gauge should not move.

20 Remove the crankshaft locking tool.

21 Fit the tool Mot. 1200-01 (or alternative tool) to immobilise the sprocket, then tighten the centre ring to a torque of 90 Nm.

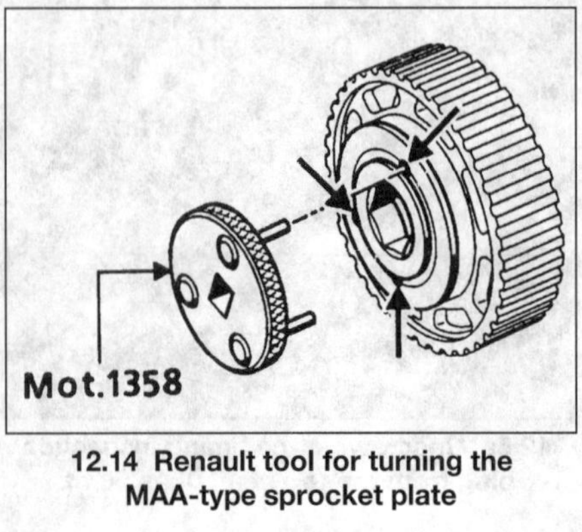

12.14 Renault tool for turning the MAA-type sprocket plate

22 Remove the sprocket locking tool, turn the engine 2 complete turns and check the pump timing once more.

Caution: If the correct injection timing cannot be obtained, check the alignment of the camshaft and injection pump sprockets (see illustration opposite). This alignment is correct if all timing marks are lined up and if there are 30 teeth between the camshaft sprocket mark and that of the injection pump.

23 When the timing is correct, remove the dial test indicator. Remove the probe from the inspection hole, and refit the inspection plug securely, ensuring that the sealing washer is in place.

24 Lower the vehicle to the ground and reconnect the battery negative lead.

25 Prime and bleed the fuel system (see Section 7).

26 Check and if necessary adjust the idle speed and anti-stall speed as described in Section 8.

F8Q 632 engine

Note: *Renault tools Mot. 1200-01, 1525, 1520 and 1522 are required for this procedure.*

27 Unbolt the diesel fuel filter and position it to one side, then remove the cover from the injection pump.

28 Fit Renault tool Mot. 1200-01 to the injection pump sprocket then loosen the sprocket retaining nut. Using tool Mot. 1525, release the sprocket from the pump shaft.

29 Fit the adjusting wheel tool Mot. 1522 to the end of the injection pump shaft.

30 Position a suitable container beneath the injection pump, then unscrew and remove the setting plug. Allow the diesel fuel to drain.

Caution: Do not loosen the two bolts securing the setting plug housing to the pump. If these are loosened, the injection pump will have to be returned to a diesel injection specialist for calibration.

31 While looking through the timing hole, slowly turn the pump shaft using the wheel tool until the timing groove appears. Using tool Mot. 1520, find the point where the setting pin engages with the groove in the pump shaft.

32 Carefully tighten the pump sprocket centre nut to lock the sprocket to the pump shaft.

33 Remove all of the tools and refit the setting plug.

34 Refit the cover to the injection pump, and refit the fuel filter.

35 Remove the crankshaft locking tool.

36 Lower the vehicle to the ground and reconnect the battery negative lead.

37 Prime and bleed the fuel system (see Section 7).

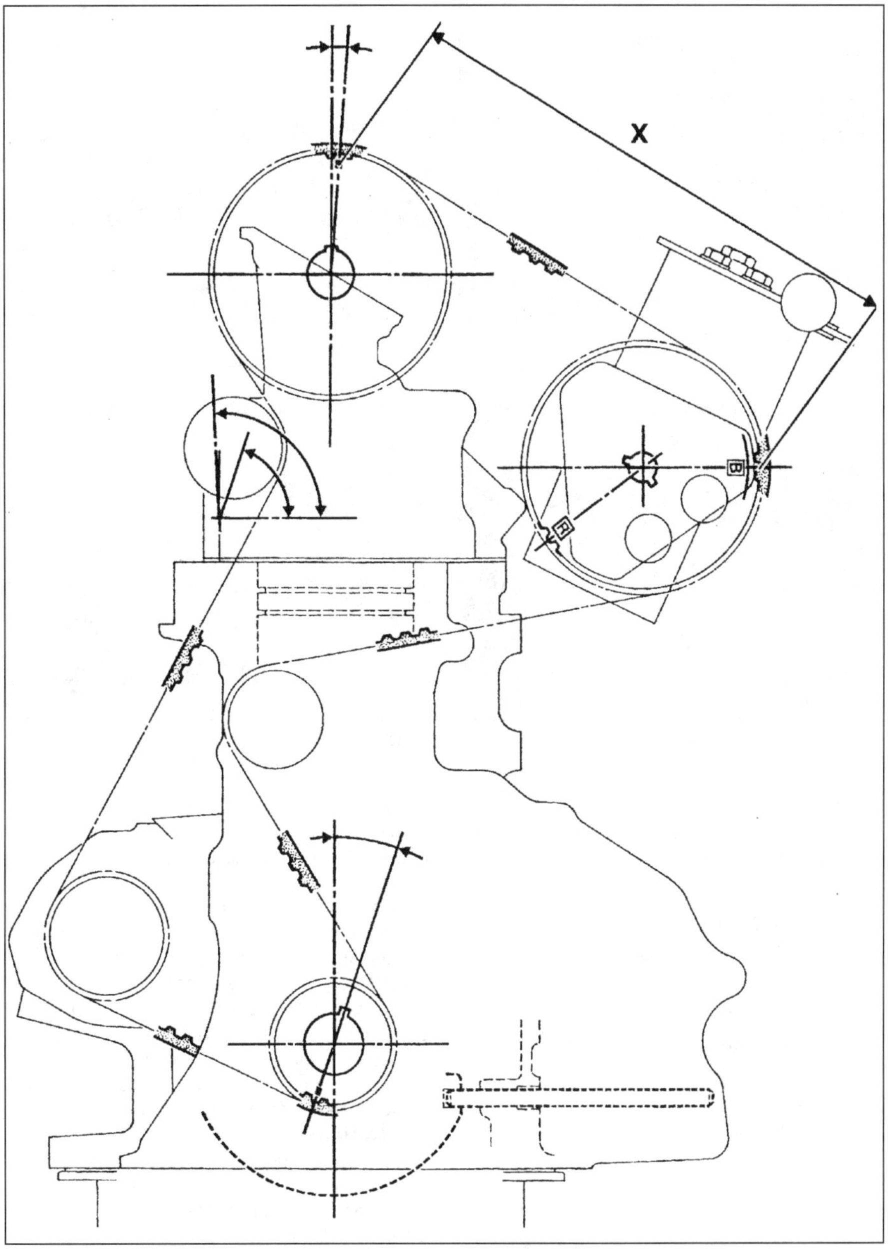

12.22 Alignment of timing marks on camshaft and injection pump sprockets (engine shown with No 1 cylinder at TDC)

X = 30 teeth

13 Fuel injectors – testing, removal and refitting

Warning: Exercise extreme caution when working on the fuel injectors. Never expose the hands or any part of the body to injector spray, as the high working pressure can cause the fuel to penetrate the skin, with possibly fatal results. You are strongly advised to have any work which involves testing the injectors under pressure carried out by a dealer or fuel injection specialist. Refer to the precautions given in Section 1 of this Chapter before proceeding.

Testing

1 Injectors do deteriorate with prolonged use and it is reasonable to expect them to need reconditioning or renewal after 60 000 miles (100 000 km) or so. Accurate testing, overhaul and calibration of the injectors must be left to a specialist. A defective injector which is causing knocking or smoking can be located without dismantling as follows.

2 Run the engine at a fast idle. Slacken each injector union in turn, placing rag around the union to catch spilt fuel and being careful not to expose the skin to any spray. When the union on the defective injector is slackened, the knocking or smoking will stop.

Removal

Note: *Take great care not to allow dirt into the injectors or fuel pipes during this procedure.*

3 Carefully clean around the injectors and injector pipe union nuts **(see illustration)**.

4 Pull the leak-off pipes from the injectors **(see illustration)**.

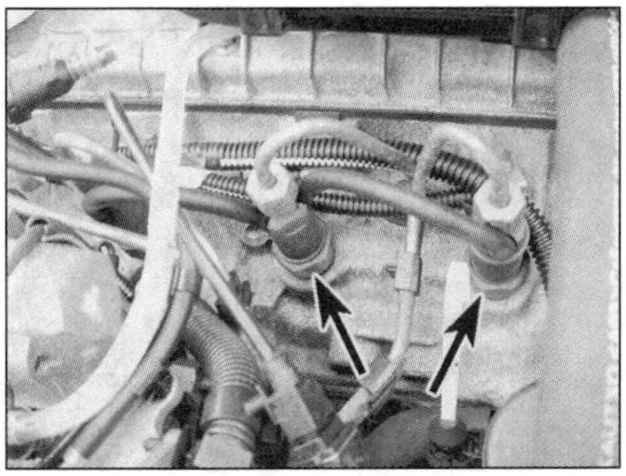

13.3 Two of the injectors

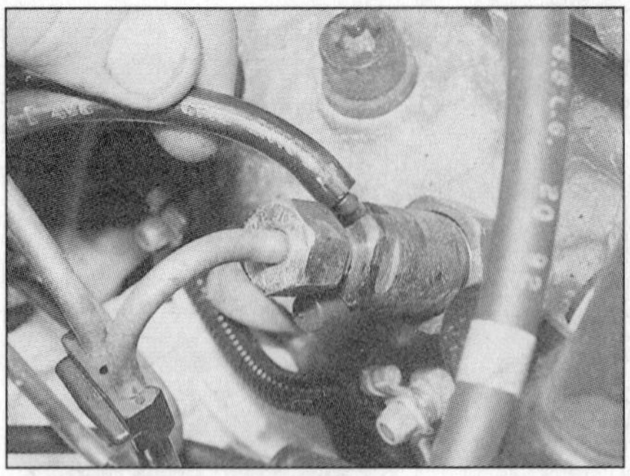

13.4 Pull the leak-off pipes from the fuel injectors

13.6 Disconnect the fuel pipes from the injectors

13.7b Unscrew the injectors . . .

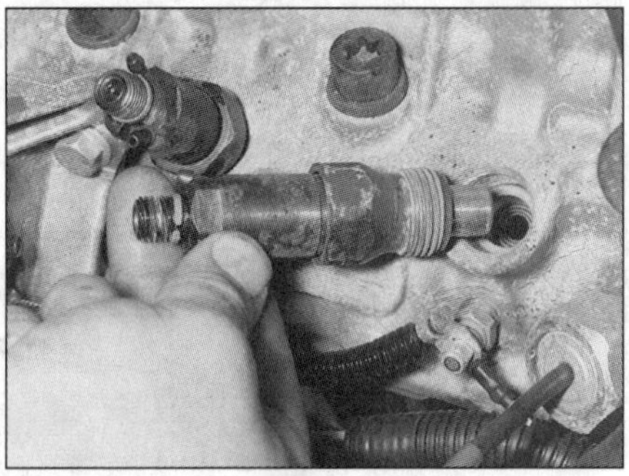

13.7c . . . and withdraw them from the cylinder head

5 Unscrew the union nuts securing the injector pipes to the fuel injection pump. Counterhold the unions on the pump, when unscrewing the nuts. Cover open unions to keep dirt out, using small plastic bags or fingers cut from discarded (but clean!) rubber gloves.

6 Unscrew the union nuts and disconnect the pipes from the injectors **(see illustration)**. If necessary the injector pipes may be completely removed. Note the locations of any clips attached to the pipes. Cover the ends of the injectors to prevent dirt ingress.

7 Unscrew the injectors using a deep socket or box spanner (27 mm across flats) and remove them from the cylinder head **(see illustrations)**. Note that No 3 injector incorporates a needle lift sensor, and it will be necessary to disconnect the wiring prior to removing it. Ideally, a deep socket with a slot for the wiring should be used.

8 Recover the copper washers and fire seal washers from the cylinder head. Also recover the sleeves if they are loose **(see illustrations)**.

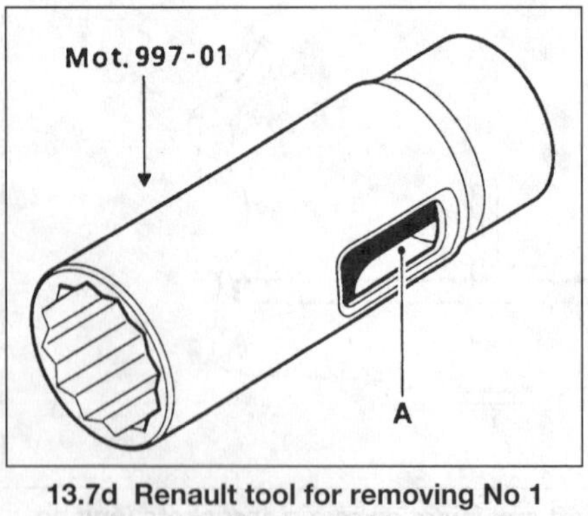

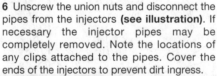

13.7d Renault tool for removing No 1 injector (with needle lift sensor)

A Cut-out for sensor wiring

13.8a Recover the copper washers . . .

13.8b . . . and the fire seal washers

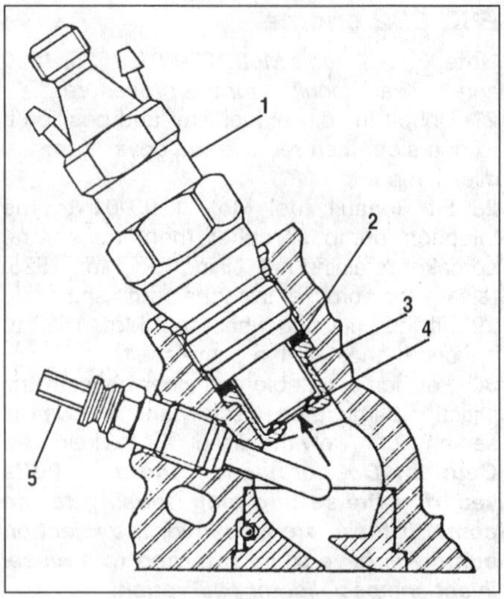

13.7a Cross-section of a fuel injector

1 Fuel injector
2 Copper washer
3 Sleeve
4 Fire seal washer
5 Glow plug

Refitting

9 Obtain new copper washers and fire seal washers. Also renew the sleeves if they are damaged.

10 Take care not to drop the injectors or allow the needles at their tips to become damaged. The injectors are precision-made to fine limits and must not be handled roughly. In particular, do not mount them in a bench vice.

11 Commence refitting by inserting the sleeves (if removed) into the cylinder head.

12 Fit the new fire seal washers to the cylinder head. Note that they should be fitted with the convex side downwards (towards the cylinder head) **(see illustration)**.

13 Fit the copper washers to the cylinder head.

14 Insert the injectors and tighten them to the specified torque.

15 Refit the injector pipes and tighten the union nuts. Position any clips attached to the pipes as noted before removal.

16 Reconnect the leak-off pipes.

17 Start the engine. If difficulty is experienced, bleed the fuel system as described in Section 7.

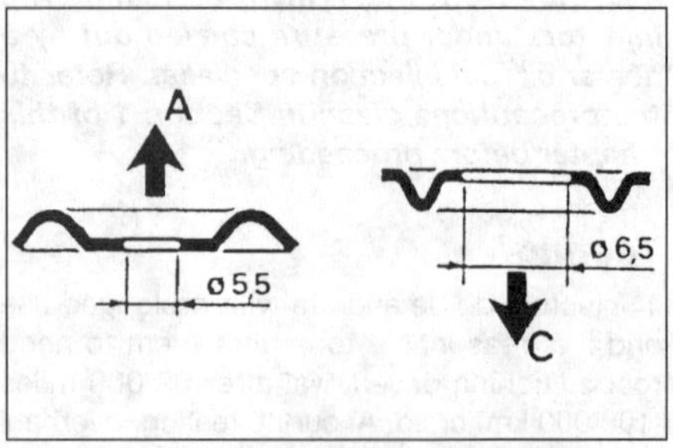

13.12 Fire seal washer fitting details

A Early type washer - convex side upwards
B Later type washer - convex side downwards

14 Manifolds – removal and refitting

Removal

1 Although the inlet and exhaust manifolds are separate, they are retained by the same nuts, since the stud holes are split between the manifold flanges.

2 Apply the handbrake, then jack up the front of the vehicle and support it on axle stands (see *Jacking and vehicle support*).

3 Remove the air cleaner assembly and gasket as described in Section 2.

4 On the F8Q 662/632 engines, remove the clip supporting the exhaust gas recirculation pipe, and also release the fuel supply pipe from the support on the timing cover.

5 Working from above, unscrew the two nuts securing the exhaust downpipe to the manifold.

6 Loosen **only** the nut on the clamp securing the downpipe to the exhaust intermediate section, then tilt the downpipe towards the transmission. Recover the gasket from between the manifold and downpipe.

7 Progressively unscrew the upper manifold mounting nuts working from above the engine, then unscrew the lower nuts working from beneath the engine. Note that access to the lower nut located above the starter motor requires the use of a socket and universal joint.

8 Withdraw the manifolds then recover the combined inlet and exhaust gasket.

Refitting

9 Refitting is a reversal of removal, but clean the mating surfaces of the manifold and cylinder head, and renew all gaskets. Tighten all nuts and bolts to the specified torque. Note that the central lower four mounting nuts and washers may be started on their studs before refitting the exhaust manifold as the manifold is slotted.

15 Exhaust system – general information and component renewal

General information

1 On new vehicles the exhaust system consists of just two sections; the front downpipe and the remaining system consisting of a catalytic converter, tailpipe and silencer. The downpipe is attached to the rear section by a cone-and-socket clamp joint **(see illustration)**.

2 The rear section of the exhaust is located above the rear suspension; the intermediate pipe/catalytic converter and tailpipe may be renewed separately by cutting the intermediate pipe with a hacksaw. The system is suspended throughout its entire length by rubber mountings **(see illustration)**.

Removal

3 To remove a part of the system, first jack up the front or rear of the car, and support it on axle stands (see *Jacking and vehicle support*). Alternatively, position the car over an inspection pit, or on car ramps. Where fitted, remove the engine compartment undertray.

Front downpipe

4 Remove the air cleaner assembly and gasket as described in Section 2.

5 Working from above, unscrew the two nuts securing the exhaust downpipe to the manifold.

6 Where applicable, unbolt the front pipe from the mounting bracket on the transmission.

7 Unscrew and remove the clamp and disconnect the front pipe and catalytic converter from the rear section. Withdraw the pipe from under the vehicle.

Catalytic converter and intermediate pipe

8 Unscrew and remove the clamp bolts attaching the front downpipe to the catalytic converter and rear section.

9 If the original rear section is fitted, it must be cut in half using either a hacksaw or pipe cutter. Locate the cutting area which is situated approximately midway between the rear silencer and intermediate mounting. The cutting point is marked with two circular punch marks on the side of the pipe. The punch marks are 90 mm apart and the exhaust section should be cut at the mid-point between the two punch marks. **Note:** *Ensure that the exhaust pipe is cut squarely, or else it will be difficult to obtain a gas-tight seal when the exhaust is refitted.*

10 With the intermediate pipe cut, withdraw the intermediate exhaust section from under the vehicle.

11 If the rear section is in two halves, unscrew the bolt and slide the clamp sleeve on to the rear section then release the rubber mountings and withdraw the intermediate section from under the vehicle.

Rear tailpipe and silencer

12 If the original rear section is fitted, follow the instructions given in paragraph 9.

13 If the rear section is in two halves, unscrew the bolt and slide the clamp sleeve on to the intermediate section then release the rubber mountings and withdraw the tailpipe and silencer from under the vehicle.

Heat shield(s)

14 The heat shields are secured to the underbody by various nuts and bolts. Each shield can be removed separately but note that they overlap making it necessary to loosen another section first. If a shield is being removed to gain access to a component located behind it, it may prove sufficient in some cases to remove the retaining nuts and/or bolts, and simply lower the shield, without disturbing the exhaust system. Otherwise remove the exhaust section as described earlier.

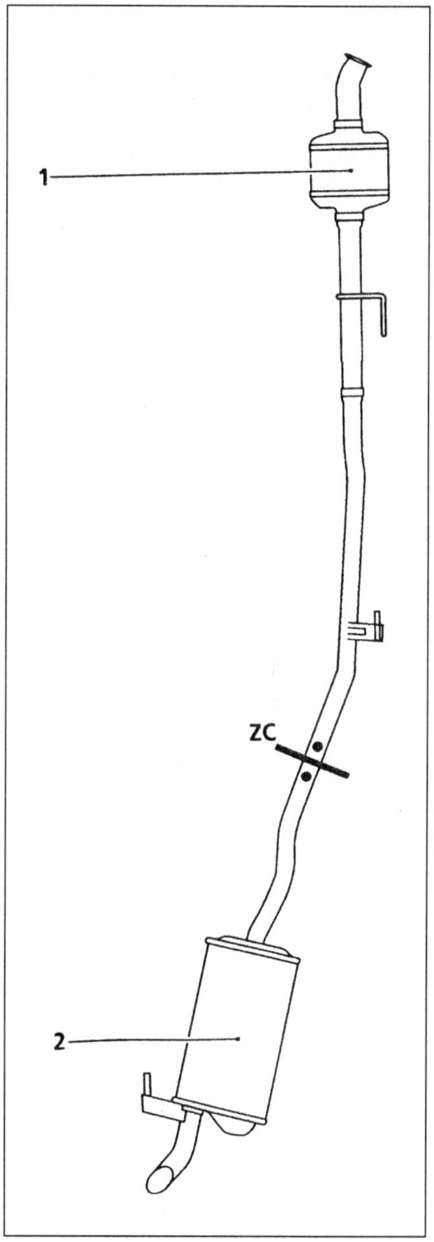

15.1 Exhaust system showing catalytic converter (1), silencer (2) and pipe cutting area (ZC)

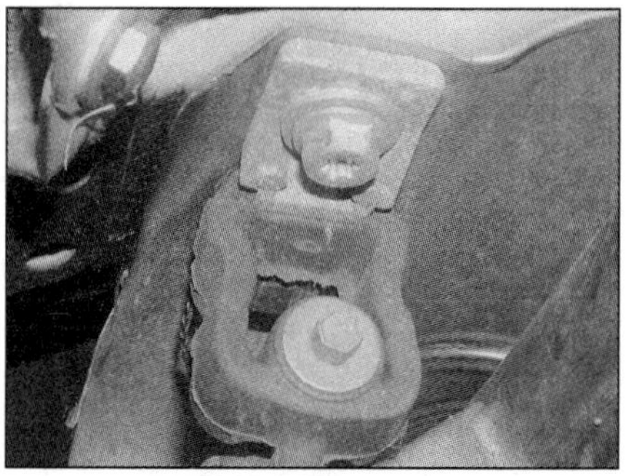

15.2 Exhaust rubber mounting

4B

Refitting

15 Each section is refitted by reversing the removal sequence, noting the following points:

a) *Ensure that all traces of corrosion have been removed from the joints.*

b) *Inspect the rubber mountings for signs of damage or deterioration, and renew as necessary.*

c) *When reconnecting the intermediate pipe to the tailpipe, apply a smear of exhaust system jointing paste (Renault recommend the use of Sodicam) to the sleeve inner surface, to ensure a gas-tight seal. Make sure both inner ends of the cut pipe are positioned squarely against the stop of the clamp sleeve. Position the sleeve bolt vertically on the left-hand side of the pipe and securely tighten the nut until it is heard to click; the clamp bolt has a groove in it to ensure that the nut is correctly tightened (equivalent to a tightening torque of approximately 25 Nm).*

d) *Prior to tightening the exhaust system fasteners, ensure that all rubber mountings are correctly located, and that there is adequate clearance between the exhaust system and vehicle underbody.*

Chapter 4 Part C: Emissions control systems

Contents

Degrees of difficulty

Easy, suitable for novice with little experience	**Fairly easy,** suitable for beginner with some experience	**Fairly difficult,** suitable for competent DIY mechanic	**Difficult,** suitable for experienced DIY mechanic	**Very difficult,** suitable for expert DIY or professional

Specifications

General

EGR solenoid valve resistance (diesel engines):	
F8Q 630 and F8Q 662	46 ± 5 ohms
F8Q 632 engine:	
Valve resistance	8 ± 0.5 ohms at 20°C
Sensor resistance	4000 ohms at 20°C
Lambda (oxygen) sensor voltage at 850°C (petrol engines):	
D7F 720, E7J 780, K7M engine:	
Rich mixture	>625 mV
Lean mixture	0 to 80 mV
D7F 702/726, K4J and K4M engines:	
Rich mixture	840 ± 70 mV
Lean mixture	20 ± 50 mV
Lambda (oxygen) sensor resistance at ambient temperature (petrol engines):	
D7F 720, E7J 780, K7M engines	3 to 15 ohms
D7F 702/726 engines:	
Upstream sensor	9.0 ohms
Downstream sensor	9.0 ohms
E7J 634 engine	6.0 ± 1.0 ohms (at 23°C)
K4J and K4M engines:	
Upstream sensor	9.0 ohms
Downstream sensor	3.4 ohms

Torque wrench setting	Nm	lbf ft
Lambda (oxygen) sensor	45	33

1 General information and precautions

1 All **petrol** engines are designed to use unleaded petrol and also have various other features built into the fuel system to help minimise harmful emissions. All models are equipped with a crankcase emissions control system, a catalytic converter and an evaporative emissions control system.

2 All **diesel** engine models are designed to meet strict emission requirements and are also equipped with a crankcase emissions control system. In addition to this, all models are fitted with an unregulated catalytic converter to reduce harmful exhaust emissions. To further reduce emissions, an exhaust gas recirculation (EGR) system is also fitted.

3 The emissions control systems function as follows.

Petrol models

Crankcase emissions control

4 To reduce the emission of unburned hydrocarbons from the crankcase into the atmosphere, the engine is sealed and the blow-by gases and oil vapour are drawn from inside the crankcase, and into the inlet manifold or throttle body to be burned by the engine during normal combustion **(see illustrations)**.

5 Under all conditions the gases are forced out of the crankcase by the (relatively) higher crankcase pressure.

6 The crankcase ventilation hoses and restrictors should be periodically cleaned to ensure correct operation of the system.

Exhaust emissions control

7 To minimise the amount of pollutants which escape into the atmosphere, all models are fitted with a catalytic converter in the exhaust system. The system is of the closed-loop type, in which a lambda (oxygen) sensor in the exhaust system provides the fuel injection/ignition system ECU with constant feedback, enabling the ECU to adjust the mixture to provide the best possible conditions for the converter to operate. On D7F, E7J, K7M and K4J engines the oxygen sensor is located in the exhaust downpipe, however on the K4M engine there are two sensors, one located on the top of the exhaust manifold and the other located downstream of the catalytic converter.

8 The lambda sensor has a heating element built-in that is controlled by the ECU through the sensor relay to bring the sensor's tip to an efficient operating temperature quickly. The sensor's tip is sensitive to oxygen and sends the ECU a varying voltage depending on the amount of oxygen in the exhaust gases; if the inlet air/fuel mixture is too rich, the exhaust gases are low in oxygen so the sensor sends a low-voltage signal, the voltage rising as the mixture weakens and the amount of oxygen rises in the exhaust gases. Peak conversion efficiency of all major pollutants occurs if the inlet air/fuel mixture is maintained at the chemically-correct ratio for the complete combustion of petrol of 14.7 parts (by weight) of air to 1 part of fuel (the 'stoichiometric' ratio). The sensor output voltage alters in a large step at this point, the ECU using the signal change as a reference point and correcting the inlet air/fuel mixture accordingly by altering the fuel injector pulse width.

Evaporative emissions control

9 To minimise the escape into the atmosphere of unburned hydrocarbons, an evaporative emissions control system is also fitted to all models **(see illustrations)**. The fuel tank filler cap is sealed and a charcoal canister is mounted on the front right-hand side of the engine compartment behind the bumper mounting. The canister collects the petrol vapours generated in the tank when the car is parked and stores them until they can be cleared from the canister (under the control of the fuel injection/ignition system ECU) via

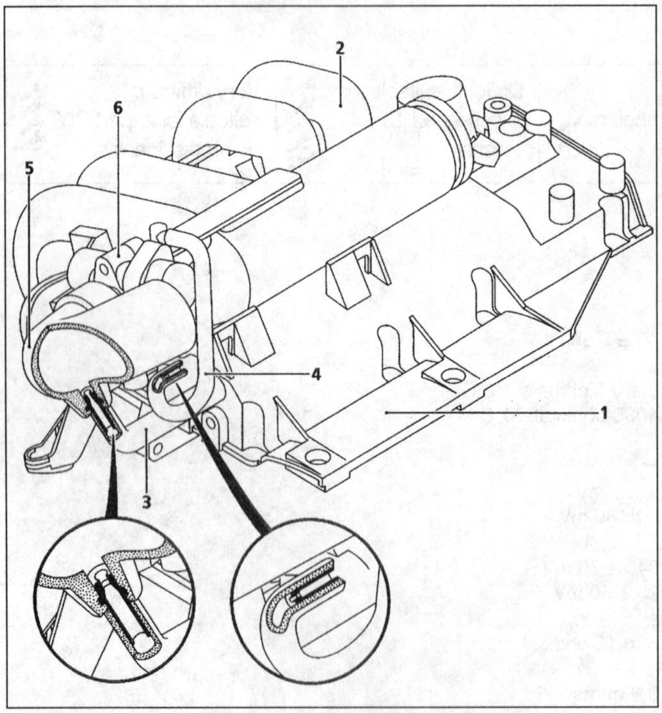

1.4a Crankcase emission control system – D7F engine

1 Cylinder head cover
2 Inlet manifold
3 Oil vapour re-breathing pipe connected upstream of the throttle body
4 Oil vapour re-breathing pipe connected downstream of the throttle body
5 Air pipe
6 Throttle body

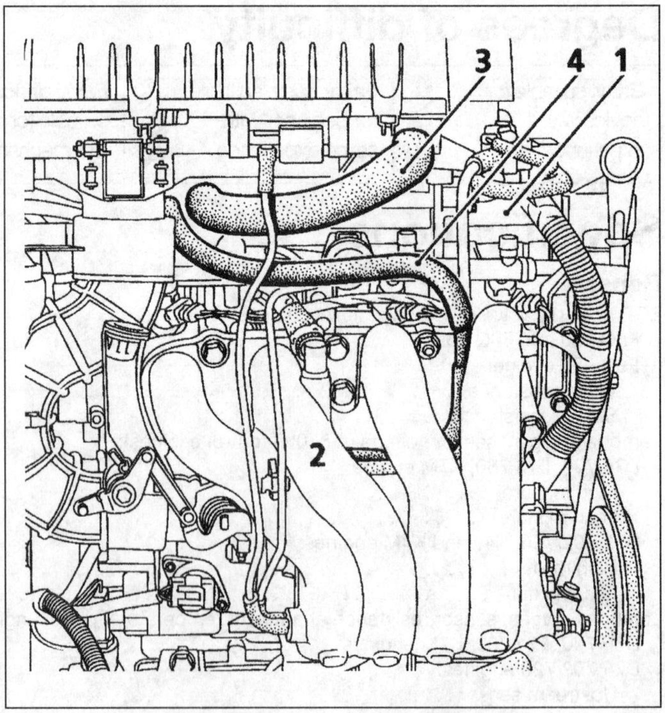

1.4b Crankcase emission control system – E7J and K7M engines

1 Cylinder head
2 Inlet manifold
3 Oil vapour re-breathing pipe upstream of the throttle body
4 Oil vapour re-breathing pipe downstream of the throttle body

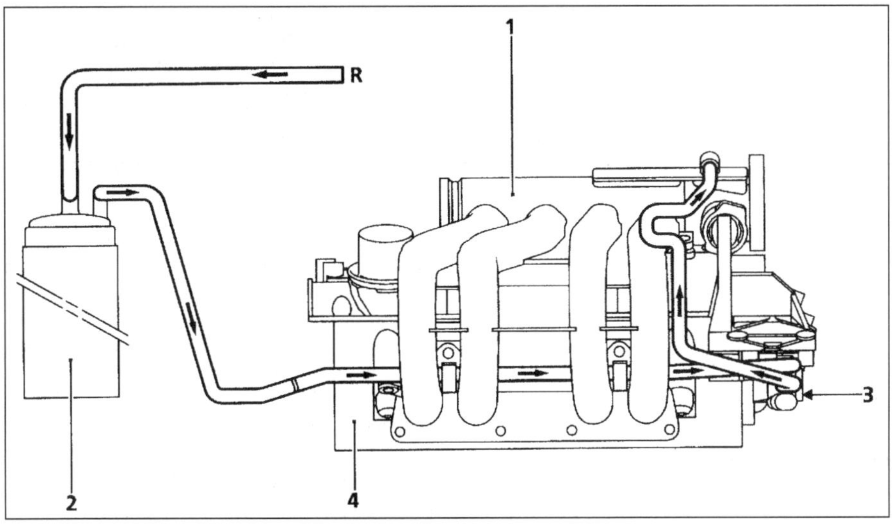

1.9a Evaporative emission control system – D7F engine

1 *Inlet manifold*
2 *Charcoal vapour canister*
3 *RCO control solenoid valve (purge valve)*
4 *Cylinder head*
R *Pipe from fuel tank*

the purge valve into the inlet manifold to be burned by the engine during normal combustion.

10 To ensure that the engine runs correctly when it is cold and/or idling and to protect the catalytic converter from the effects of an over-rich mixture, the purge control valve is not opened by the ECU until the engine has warmed-up, and the engine is under load; the valve solenoid is then modulated on and off to allow the stored vapour to pass into the inlet manifold.

Diesel models

Crankcase emissions control

11 To reduce the emission of unburned hydrocarbons from the crankcase into the atmosphere, the engine is sealed and the blow-by gases and oil vapour are drawn from inside the crankcase, through an oil separator located on the front left-hand side of the cylinder block, and into the inlet manifold to be burned by the engine during normal combustion **(see illustration)**.

12 There are no restrictors in the system hoses, since the minimal depression in the inlet manifold remains constant during all engine operating conditions.

Exhaust emissions control

13 To minimise the amount of pollutants which escape into the atmosphere, an unregulated catalytic converter is fitted in the exhaust system. The catalytic converter consists of a canister containing a fine mesh impregnated with a catalyst material, over which the exhaust gases pass. The catalyst speeds up the oxidation of harmful carbon monoxide, unburnt hydrocarbons and soot, effectively reducing the quantity of harmful products reaching the atmosphere. The catalytic converter operates remotely in the exhaust system, and there is no lambda sensor as fitted to the petrol engines.

Exhaust gas recirculation (EGR) system

14 The system is designed to recirculate small quantities of exhaust gas into the inlet tract, and therefore into the combustion process **(see illustration overleaf)**, reducing the level of oxides of nitrogen present in the final exhaust gas which is released into the atmosphere. The system is controlled by the engine management ECU which uses several sensors to determine when to switch the system on and off. The system is switched off at idle speed, if the air temperature is less than 16°C, if the coolant temperature is less than 45°C, or if the engine speed/load is greater than a specific threshold. The system is switched on when the vehicle reaches a speed of 17 mph.

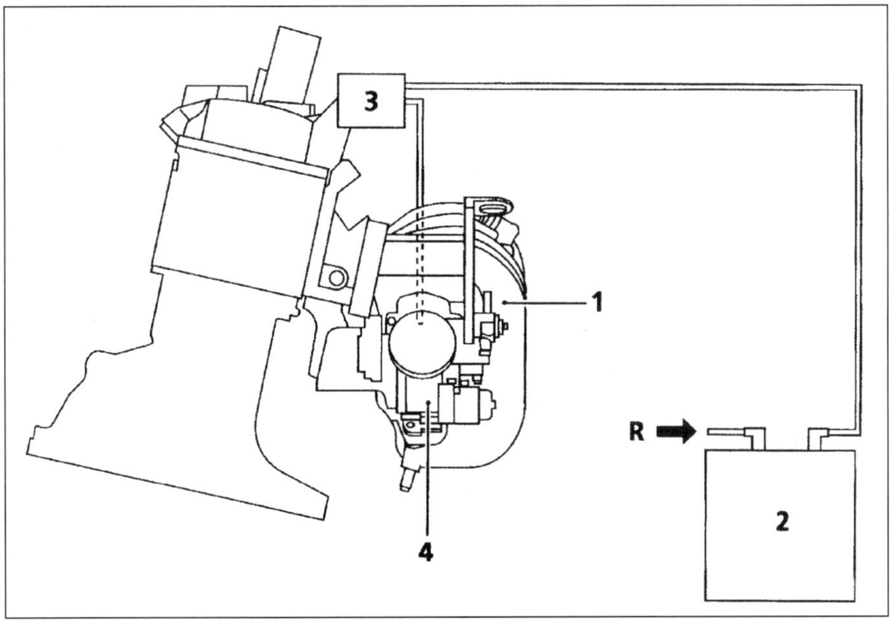

1.9b Evaporative emission control system – E7J and K7M engines

1 *Inlet manifold*
2 *Charcoal canister*
3 *RCO control solenoid valve (purge valve)*
4 *Throttle body*
R *Pipe from fuel tank*

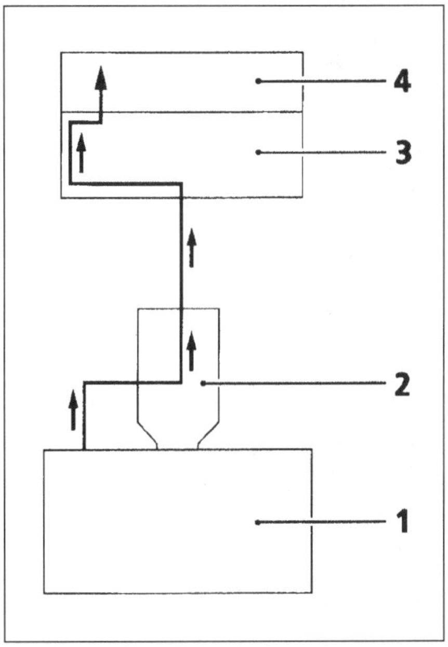

1.11 Crankcase emission control system – F8Q engine

1 *Engine*
2 *Oil decanter*
3 *Air filter*
4 *Inlet manifold*

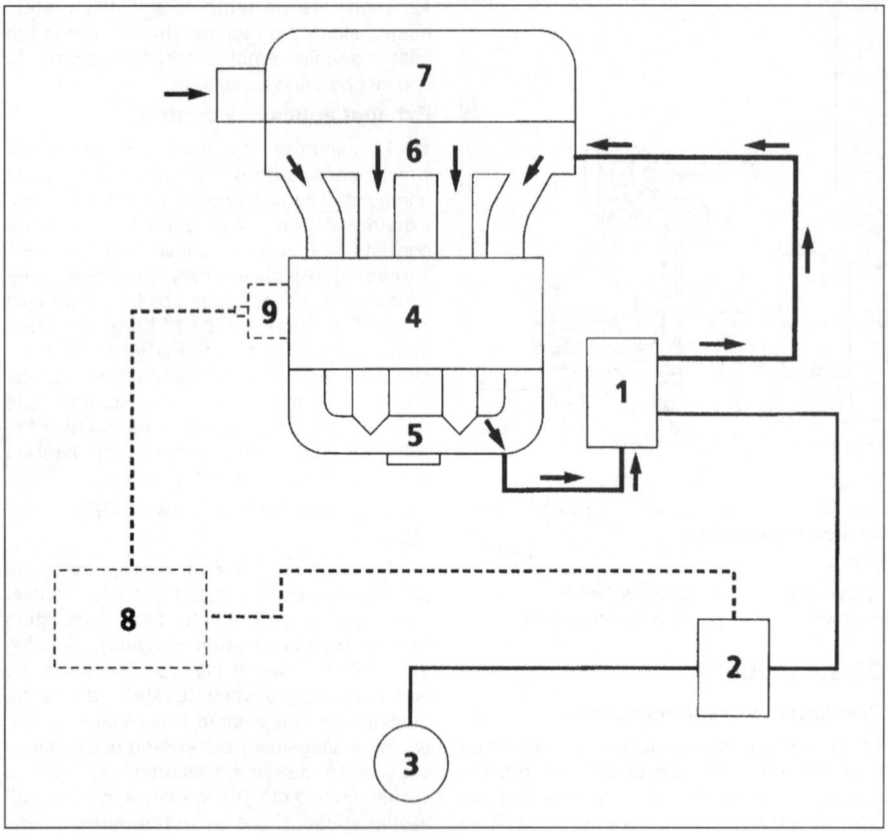

1.14 Exhaust gas recirculation system – F8Q 630 engine

1 EGR valve
2 EGR solenoid
3 Vacuum pump
4 Engine
5 Exhaust manifold
6 Inlet manifold
7 Air cleaner
8 ECU
9 Coolant temperature sensor

15 The volume of exhaust gas recirculated is controlled either by a vacuum- or electrically-operated exhaust gas recirculation (EGR) valve on the exhaust manifold, via a solenoid valve controlled by a microswitch mounted on the injection pump. On the vacuum-operated type fitted to the F8Q 630 engine, vacuum is supplied by the brake vacuum pump. The microswitch is also used to shut off the post-heating function and is controlled by the engine management ECU. A temperature valve fitted in the vacuum supply line cuts off the vacuum supply until the engine has warmed-up sufficiently. The electrically-operated type fitted to the F8Q 632 engine is regulated by the engine management ECU.

Catalytic converter – precautions

16 For long life and satisfactory operation of the catalytic converter, certain precautions must be observed. These are listed in Section 4 of this Chapter.

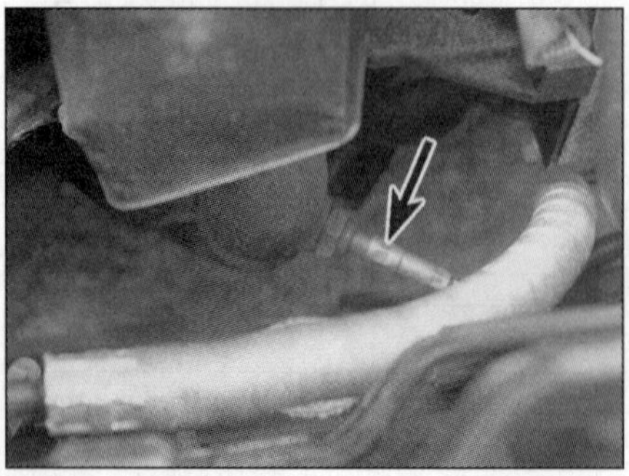

2.10a Lambda sensor viewed from inside the engine compartment – E7J engine

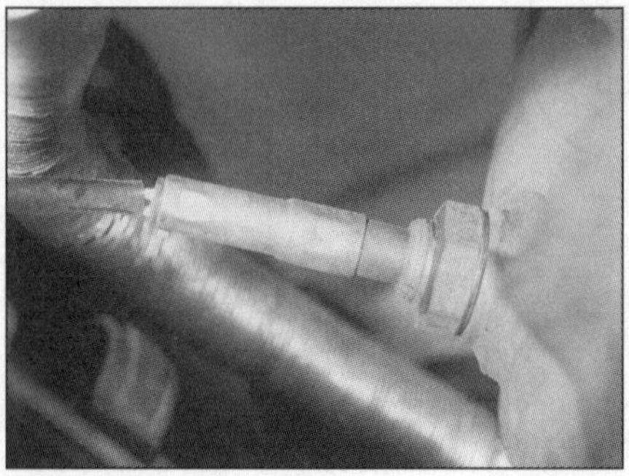

2.10b Lambda sensor viewed from under the engine – K7M engine

2 Petrol engine emissions control systems – testing and component renewal

Crankcase emissions control

Testing

1 There is no specific test procedure for the crankcase emissions control system. If problems are suspected (sometimes indicated by oil contamination of the air cleaner element), check that the hoses are clean internally, and that the restrictors are not blocked or missing.

Component renewal

2 This is self-evident. Mark the various hoses before disconnecting them, if there is any possibility of confusion on reassembly.

Exhaust emissions control

Testing

3 An exhaust gas analyser (CO meter) will be needed. The ignition system must be in good condition, the air cleaner element must be clean, and the engine must be in good mechanical condition.

4 Bring the engine to normal operating temperature, then connect the exhaust gas analyser in accordance with the equipment maker's instructions.

5 Run the engine at 2500 rpm for about 30 seconds, then allow it to idle and check the CO level (Chapter 1A Specifications). If the CO level is within the specified limits, the system is operating correctly.

6 If the CO level is higher than specified, try the effect of disconnecting the lambda sensor wiring. If the CO level rises when the sensor is disconnected, this suggests that the lambda sensor is OK and that the catalytic converter is faulty. If disconnecting the sensor has no effect, this suggests a fault in the sensor.

7 If a digital voltmeter is available, the lambda sensor output voltage can be measured. Voltage should alternate between 625 to 1100 mV (rich mixture) and 0 to 80 mV (lean mixture).

8 Renew the lambda sensor if it is proved faulty.

Lambda sensor – renewal

9 To remove the sensor on the K4M engine, trace the wiring from the sensor located on the exhaust manifold to the connector and disconnect it. Unscrew the sensor from the manifold using a deep socket.

10 On engines other than the K4M, raise the front of the vehicle and support it on axle stands (see *Jacking and vehicle support*). Remove the engine compartment undershield, where fitted, then disconnect the sensor wiring. Unscrew the sensor from the exhaust downpipe or catalytic converter (as applicable), and remove it **(see illustrations)**.

11 Clean the threads of the sensor (if it is to

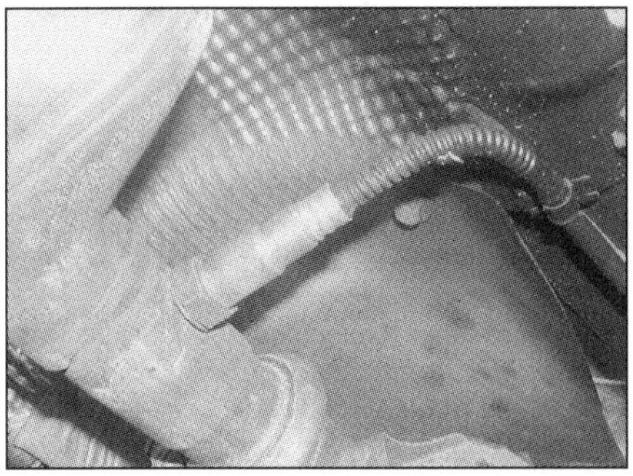

2.10c Downstream lambda sensor located on the catalytic converter – K4J engine

be refitted) and the threads in the exhaust pipe or manifold (as applicable).

12 Note that if the sensor wires are broken, the sensor must be renewed. No attempt should be made to repair them.

13 Apply high-temperature anti-seize compound to the sensor threads. Screw the sensor in by hand, then tighten it to the specified torque.

14 Reconnect the sensor wiring, and where applicable refit the undershield and lower the vehicle to the ground.

Catalytic converter – renewal

15 The catalytic converter is renewed as part of the exhaust system. Refer to Part A of this Chapter.

Evaporative emissions control

Testing

16 The operating principle of the system is that the solenoid valve is open only when the engine is warm with the throttle at least at the part-throttle position.

17 Bring the engine to normal operating temperature, then switch it off. Connect a vacuum gauge (range 0 to 1000 mbars) into the hose between the canister and the solenoid valve. Connect a voltmeter to the solenoid valve terminals.

18 Start the engine and allow it to idle. There should be no vacuum shown on the gauge, and no voltage present at the solenoid.

19 If manifold vacuum is indicated although no voltage is present, the solenoid valve may be stuck open. Temporarily disconnect the hoses from the solenoid valve and blow through the outlets to dislodge any particles of carbon.

20 If voltage is present at idle, there is a fault in the wiring or the computer.

21 Depress the accelerator slightly. Voltage should appear momentarily at the solenoid terminals, and manifold vacuum be indicated on the gauge.

22 If vacuum is not indicated even though voltage is present, either there is a leak in the hoses, or the valve is not opening.

23 If no voltage appears, there is a fault in the wiring or the computer.

Canister renewal

24 Working in the engine compartment,

2.10d Disconnecting the lambda sensor wiring

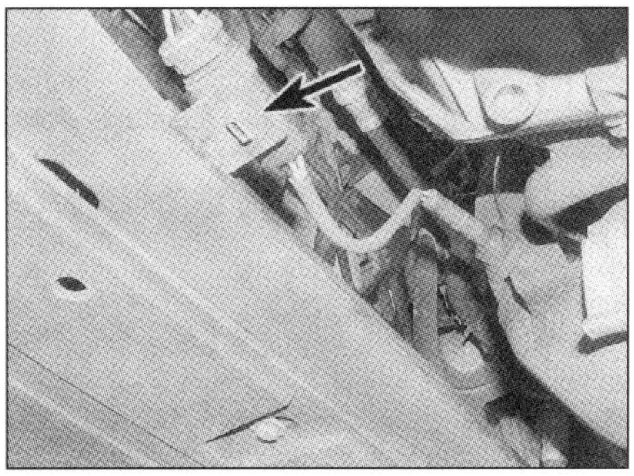

2.10f Lambda sensor wiring connector – E7J engine

disconnect the hose connecting the canister to the inlet manifold.

25 Apply the handbrake, then jack up the front of the vehicle and support it on axle stands (see *Jacking and vehicle support*). Remove the right-hand front roadwheel followed by the wheelarch liner for access to the canister which is located behind the bumper mounting **(see illustration)**.

26 Disconnect the fuel tank hose from the canister.

27 Unscrew the mounting bolts and lower the canister from under the front wing.

28 Dispose of the old canister safely, bearing in mind that it may contain liquid fuel and/or fuel vapour.

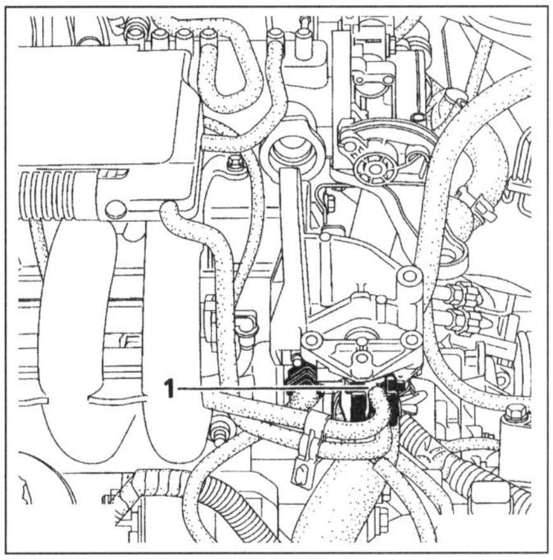

2.30a Evaporative emission solenoid valve (1) – D7F engine

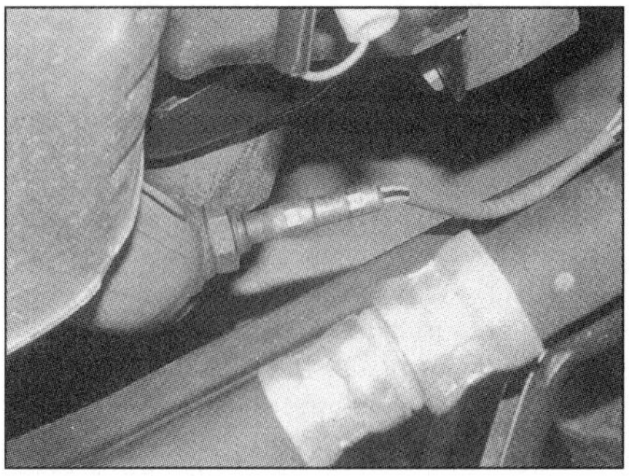

2.10e Lambda sensor on the exhaust downpipe – E7J engine

2.25 The evaporative emission canister is located behind the right-hand front bumper mounting

29 Fit the new canister using a reversal of the removal procedure. Make sure that the hoses are connected correctly.

Solenoid valve renewal

30 Depending on engine, the solenoid valve is located as follows **(see illustrations)**:

a) *D7F engine – at the front of the engine on the lifting bracket.*

b) *E7J, K4J, K7M and K4M engines – on top of the inlet manifold.*

31 Disconnect the hoses and multi-plug from the valve. Release the valve from its mountings and remove it.

32 Fit the new valve using a reversal of the removal procedure. Make sure that the hoses are connected correctly.

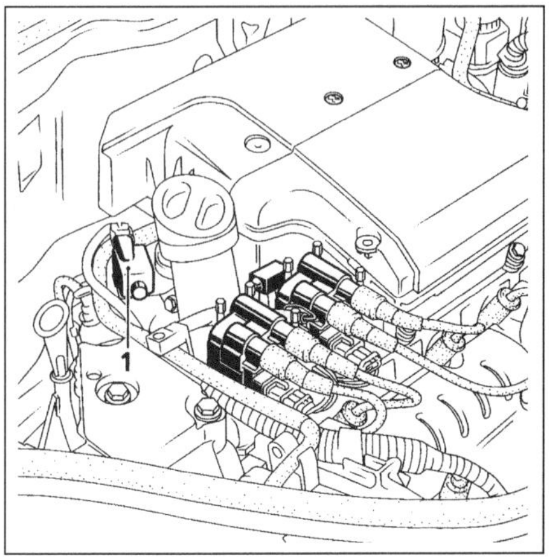

2.30b Evaporative emission solenoid valve (1) – E7J and K7M engines

3 Diesel engine emissions control systems - testing and component renewal

Crankcase emissions control

Testing

1 If the system is thought to be faulty, firstly, check that the hoses are unobstructed. On high mileage vehicles, particularly when regularly used for short journeys, a jelly-like deposit may be evident inside the system hoses and oil separators. If excessive deposits are present, the relevant component(s) should be removed and cleaned.

2 Periodically inspect the system components for security and damage, and renew them as necessary.

Component renewal

3 This is self-evident. Mark the various hoses before disconnecting them, if there is any possibility of confusion on reassembly.

Exhaust emissions control

Testing

4 The system can only be tested accurately using a suitable exhaust gas analyser (suitable for use with diesel engines).

Catalytic converter - renewal

5 The catalytic converter is renewed as part of the exhaust system. Refer to Part B of this Chapter.

Exhaust gas recirculation

Testing

Note: *The following procedure applies to the F8Q 630 engine only. Due to the need for Renault dedicated test equipment to test the valve fitted to the F8Q 632 and F8Q 662 engines, this work should be entrusted to a Renault dealer.*

6 Start the engine, and run it until it reaches normal operating temperature (the cooling fan should have cut in and out at least once).

7 With the engine idling, disconnect the vacuum hose from the recirculation valve. As the hose is disconnected, it should be possible to hear the valve click shut. If no click is heard, proceed as follows.

8 Check that vacuum is present at the recirculation valve end of the vacuum hose. If a vacuum gauge is available, check that the vacuum is at least 500 mbars. If vacuum is present, it is likely that the recirculation valve is faulty (jammed or pierced diaphragm). If no vacuum is present, carry out the following checks.

9 Check the security of all vacuum hose connections.

10 Check the electrical feed to the solenoid valve.

11 Check the operation of the temperature valve. This can be done by checking that vacuum will pass through the valve with the engine at normal operating temperature. Stop the engine and disconnect the temperature valve vacuum hoses at the recirculation valve and the solenoid valve, and check that it is possible to blow through the hoses. If not, it is likely that the temperature valve is faulty, or the hoses are obstructed.

12 Check the operation of the pre/post-heating systems as described in Chapter 5C.

EGR valve - renewal

13 The valve is located at the rear of the engine, and is bolted to the exhaust manifold. The valve is connected to the inlet manifold via a metal pipe bolted between the valve and the manifold.

14 Remove the air cleaner assembly as described in Chapter 4B.

15 Disconnect the vacuum hose from the valve.

16 Remove the securing bolts, and disconnect the valve pipe from the manifold. Recover the gasket.

17 Unbolt the valve body from the manifold, and recover the gasket. Remove the valve complete with the pipe.

18 If a new valve is to be fitted, unscrew the securing bolts or release the clamp, and transfer the pipe to the new valve, using a new gasket, where applicable.

19 Refitting is a reversal of removal, using new gaskets.

Solenoid valve - renewal

20 The valve is mounted behind the inlet manifold. To remove it, first remove the air cleaner assembly and upper inlet manifold plenum as described in Chapter 4B.

21 Disconnect the wiring plug and the vacuum hoses from the valve, noting the fitted locations of the hoses.

22 Unscrew the retaining nuts, and withdraw the valve complete with its bracket.

23 Refitting is a reversal of removal, ensuring that the vacuum hoses are securely reconnected.

4 Catalytic converter - general information and precautions

The catalytic converter is a reliable and simple device which needs no maintenance in itself, but there are some facts of which an owner should be aware if the converter is to function properly for its full service life.

Petrol models

a) *DO NOT use leaded petrol in a car equipped with a catalytic converter – the lead will coat the precious metals, reducing their converting efficiency and will eventually destroy the converter.*
b) *Always keep the ignition and fuel systems well-maintained in accordance with the manufacturer's schedule.*
c) *If the engine develops a misfire, do not drive the car at all (or at least as little as possible) until the fault is cured.*
d) *DO NOT push- or tow-start the car – this will soak the catalytic converter in unburned fuel, causing it to overheat when the engine does start.*
e) *DO NOT switch off the ignition at high engine speeds.*
f) *DO NOT use fuel or engine oil additives – these may contain substances harmful to the catalytic converter.*
g) *DO NOT continue to use the car if the engine burns oil to the extent of leaving a visible trail of blue smoke.*
h) *Remember that the catalytic converter operates at very high temperatures. DO NOT, therefore, park the car on dry undergrowth, over long grass or piles of dead leaves after a long run.*
i) *Remember that the catalytic converter is FRAGILE – do not strike it with tools during servicing work or drop it.*
j) *In some cases a sulphurous smell (like that of rotten eggs) may be noticed from the exhaust. This is common to many catalytic converter-equipped cars and once the car has covered a few thousand miles the problem should disappear.*
k) *The catalytic converter, used on a well-maintained and well-driven car, should last for between 50 000 and 100 000 miles – if the converter is no longer effective it must be renewed.*

Diesel models

a) *DO NOT use fuel or engine oil additives – these may contain substances harmful to the catalytic converter.*
b) *DO NOT continue to use the car if the engine burns oil to the extent of leaving a visible trail of blue smoke.*
c) *Remember that the catalytic converter operates at very high temperatures. DO NOT, therefore, park the car on dry undergrowth, over long grass or piles of dead leaves after a long run.*
d) *Remember that the catalytic converter is FRAGILE – do not strike it with tools during servicing work or drop it.*

Chapter 5 Part A:
Starting and charging systems

Contents

Degrees of difficulty

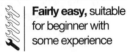

Easy, suitable for novice with little experience	**Fairly easy,** suitable for beginner with some experience	**Fairly difficult,** suitable for competent DIY mechanic	**Difficult,** suitable for experienced DIY mechanic	**Very difficult,** suitable for expert DIY or professional

Specifications

General

Engine codes:	
1.2 litre petrol engine	D7F
1.4 litre petrol engine:	
SOHC	E7J
DOHC	K4J
1.6 litre petrol engine:	
SOHC	K7M
DOHC	K4M
Diesel engine	F8Q

Battery

Type	Lead-acid, low-maintenance or 'maintenance-free'
Charge condition:	
Poor	12.5 volts
Normal	12.6 volts
Good	12.7 volts

Alternator

Type:	
D7F engine	AC Delco
All engines except D7F	Valeo
Output:	
D7F engine	80 amps
All engines except D7F:	
Without air conditioning	75 amps
With air conditioning	110 amps
Regulated voltage	13.5 volts

Oil level sensor

Resistance	6.0 to 20 ohms

1 General information and precautions

General information

The engine electrical system consists mainly of the charging and starting systems. Because of their engine-related functions, these components are covered separately from the body electrical devices such as the lights, instruments, etc (which are covered in Chapter 12). On petrol engine models, refer to Part B for information on the ignition system, and on diesel models, refer to Part C for information on the preheating system.

The electrical system is of the 12-volt negative earth type.

The battery is of the low maintenance or 'maintenance-free' (sealed for life) type, and is charged by the alternator, which is belt-driven from the crankshaft pulley.

The starter motor is of the pre-engaged type, incorporating an integral solenoid. On starting, the solenoid moves the drive pinion into engagement with the flywheel ring gear before the starter motor is energised. Once the engine has started, a one-way clutch prevents the motor armature being driven by the engine until the pinion disengages from the flywheel.

Further details of the various systems are given in the relevant Sections of this Chapter. While some repair procedures are given, the usual course of action is to renew the component concerned. The owner whose interest extends beyond mere component renewal should obtain a copy of the *Automobile Electrical & Electronic Systems Manual*, available from the publishers of this manual.

Precautions

Warning: It is necessary to take extra care when working on the electrical system, to avoid damage to semi-conductor devices (diodes and transistors), and to avoid the risk of personal injury. In addition to the precautions given in 'Safety first!' at the beginning of this manual, observe the following when working on the system:

Always remove rings, watches, etc, before working on the electrical system. Even with the battery disconnected, capacitive discharge could occur if a component's live terminal is earthed through a metal object. This could cause a shock or nasty burn

Do not reverse the battery connections. Components such as the alternator, electronic control units, or any other components having semi-conductor circuitry could be irreparably damaged

Never disconnect the battery terminals, the alternator, any electrical wiring or any test instruments with the engine running.

Do not allow the engine to turn the alternator when the alternator is not connected.

Never 'test' for alternator output by 'flashing' the output lead to earth.

Never use an ohmmeter of the type incorporating a hand-cranked generator for circuit or continuity testing.

Always ensure that the battery negative lead is disconnected when working on the electrical system.

If the engine is being started using jump leads and a slave battery, connect the batteries ***positive-to-positive*** and ***negative-to-negative*** (see *Jump starting* at the beginning of the manual). This also applies when connecting a battery charger.

Before using electric-arc welding equipment on the car, ***disconnect the battery, alternator and components such as the electronic control units*** to protect them from the risk of damage.

The radio/cassette unit fitted as standard equipment by Renault is equipped with a built-in security code, to deter thieves. If the power source to the unit is cut, the anti-theft system will activate.

Caution: If the radio/cassette in your vehicle is equipped with an anti-theft system, make sure you have the correct activation code before disconnecting the battery.

2 Electrical fault finding – general information

Refer to Chapter 12.

3 Battery – testing and charging

Testing

Standard and low maintenance battery

1 If the vehicle covers a small annual mileage, it is worthwhile checking the specific gravity of the electrolyte every three months to determine the state of charge of the battery. Use a hydrometer to make the check and compare the results with the following table (the temperatures quoted are ambient temperatures). Note that the specific gravity readings assume an electrolyte temperature of 15°C (60°F); for every 10°C (18°F) below 15°C (60°F) subtract 0.007. For every 10°C (18°F) above 15°C (60°F) add 0.007.

	Above 25°C	Below 25°C
Fully-charged	*1.210 to 1.230*	*1.270 to 1.290*
70% charged	*1.170 to 1.190*	*1.230 to 1.250*
Discharged	*1.050 to 1.070*	*1.110 to 1.130*

2 If the battery condition is suspect, first check the specific gravity of electrolyte in each cell. A variation of 0.040 or more between any cells indicates loss of electrolyte or deterioration of the internal plates.

3 If the specific gravity variation is 0.040 or more, the battery should be renewed. If the cell variation is satisfactory but the battery is discharged, it should be charged as described later in this Section.

Maintenance-free battery

4 In cases where a 'sealed for life' maintenance-free battery is fitted, topping-up and testing of the electrolyte in each cell is not possible. The condition of the battery can therefore only be tested using a battery condition indicator or a voltmeter.

5 Certain models may be fitted with a Delco type maintenance-free battery, with a built-in charge condition indicator. The indicator is located in the top of the battery casing, and indicates the condition of the battery from its colour. If the indicator shows green, then the battery is in a good state of charge. If the indicator turns darker, eventually to black, then the battery requires charging, as described later in this Section. If the indicator shows clear/yellow, then the electrolyte level in the battery is too low to allow further use, and the battery should be renewed. **Do not** attempt to charge, load or jump start a battery when the indicator shows clear/yellow.

All batteries

6 If testing the battery using a voltmeter, connect it to the terminals and compare the result with that given in the *Specifications*. The test is only accurate if the battery has not been subjected to any kind of charge for the previous six hours. If this is not the case, switch on the headlights for 30 seconds, then wait four to five minutes before testing the battery after switching off the headlights. All other electrical circuits must be switched off, so check that the doors and tailgate are fully shut when making the test.

7 If the voltage reading is less than 12.2 volts, then the battery is discharged, whilst a reading of 12.2 to 12.4 volts indicates a partially discharged condition.

8 If the battery is to be charged, remove it from the vehicle (Section 4) and charge it as described later in this Section.

Charging

Standard and low maintenance battery

Note: *The following is intended as a guide only. Always follow the maker's recommendations (often printed on a label attached to the battery) before charging a battery.*

9 Charge the battery at a rate equivalent to 10% of the battery capacity (eg, for a 45 Ah battery charge at 4.5A), and continue to charge the battery at this rate until no further rise in specific gravity is noted over a four-hour period.

10 Alternatively, a trickle charger charging at the rate of 1.5 amps can safely be used overnight.

11 Specially rapid 'boost' charges which are claimed to restore the power of the battery in 1 to 2 hours are not recommended, as they can cause serious damage to the battery plates through overheating.

12 While charging the battery, note that the temperature of the electrolyte should never exceed 37.8°C (100°F).

Maintenance-free battery

Note: *The following is intended as a guide only. Always follow the maker's recommendations (often printed on a label attached to the battery) before charging a battery.*

13 This battery type takes considerably longer to fully recharge than the standard type, the time taken being dependent on the extent of discharge, but it can take anything up to three days.

14 A constant voltage type charger is required, to be set, when connected, to 13.9 to 14.9 volts with a charger current below 25 amps. Using this method, the battery should be usable within three hours, giving a voltage reading of 12.5 volts, but this is for a partially discharged battery and, as mentioned, full charging can take considerably longer.

15 If the battery is to be charged from a fully discharged state (condition reading less than 12.2 volts), have it recharged by your Renault dealer or local automotive electrician, as the charge rate is higher and constant supervision during charging is necessary.

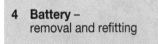

4 Battery – removal and refitting

Note: *Refer to the precautions given in 'Safety first!' and in Section 1 of this Chapter.*

Removal

1 The battery is located at the front left-hand corner of the engine compartment.

2 Disconnect the lead(s) at the negative (earth) terminal by unscrewing the retaining nut and removing the terminal clamp.

3 Disconnect the positive terminal lead(s) in the same way. Where necessary, flip open the cover for access to the terminal **(see illustration)**.

4 Unscrew the clamp bolt, remove the clamp assembly, then lift the battery from its location **(see illustration)**. Keep the battery in an upright position, to avoid spilling electrolyte on the bodywork.

Refitting

5 Refitting is a reversal of removal. Smear petroleum jelly on the terminals after reconnecting the leads to reduce corrosion. Always reconnect the positive lead first, and the negative lead last.

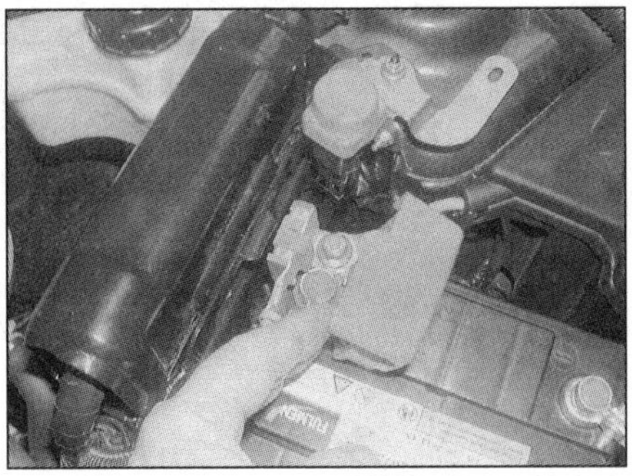

4.3 Open the cover for access to the positive battery terminal

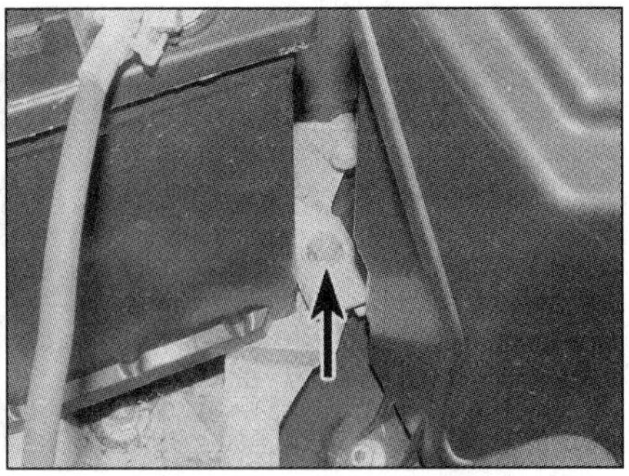

4.4 The battery retaining clamp bolt

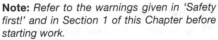

5 Charging system – testing

Note: *Refer to the warnings given in 'Safety first!' and in Section 1 of this Chapter before starting work.*

1 If the ignition warning light fails to illuminate when the ignition is switched on, first check the alternator wiring connections for security. If satisfactory, check that the warning light bulb has not blown, and that the bulbholder is secure in its location in the instrument panel (see Chapter 12). If the light still fails to illuminate, check the continuity of the warning light feed wire from the alternator to the bulbholder. If all is satisfactory, the alternator is at fault, and should be renewed or taken to an auto-electrician for testing and repair.

2 If the ignition warning light illuminates when the engine is running, stop the engine and check that the drivebelt is correctly tensioned (see Chapter 1A or 1B) and that the alternator connections are secure. If all is so far satisfactory, have the alternator checked by an auto-electrician for testing and repair.

3 If the alternator output is suspect even though the warning light functions correctly, the regulated voltage may be checked as follows.

4 Connect a voltmeter across the battery terminals and start the engine.

5 Increase the engine speed until the voltmeter reading remains steady; the reading should be between 13.2 and 14.8 volts.

6.7 Disconnecting the main cable from the alternator – D7F engine

6 Switch on as many electrical accessories (eg, the headlights, heated rear window and heater blower) as possible, and check that the alternator maintains the regulated voltage between 13.2 and 14.8 volts.

7 If the regulated voltage is not as stated, the fault may be due to worn brushes, weak brush springs, a faulty voltage regulator, a faulty diode, a severed phase winding, or worn or damaged slip rings. The alternator should be renewed or taken to an auto-electrician for testing and repair.

6 Alternator – removal and refitting

Removal

1 Disconnect the battery negative (earth) lead and position it away from the terminal.

D7F engine

2 Apply the handbrake, then jack up the front of the vehicle and support it on axle stands (see *Jacking and vehicle support*).

3 Remove the drivebelt(s) for the alternator, power-assisted steering pump and air conditioning compressor as applicable with reference to Chapter 1A.

4 On models with air conditioning, remove the radiator grille (Chapter 11), then unbolt and remove the radiator upper mountings.

5 Remove the electric cooling fan assembly as described in Chapter 3.

6 Lift the radiator from its lower mountings and position to provide access to the alternator.

7 Remove the cover (where fitted) from the alternator main terminal, then unscrew the retaining nut and disconnect the main cable. Also disconnect the wiring plug from the rear of the alternator **(see illustration)**.

8 Unscrew and remove the alternator upper mounting bolt, then support the alternator and unscrew the lower bolt. Withdraw the alternator from the engine **(see illustrations)**.

E7J and K7M engines

Note: *A engine hoist is required for this procedure.*

6.8a Unscrew the upper alternator mounting bolt . . .

6.8b . . . and the lower through-bolt, then remove the alternator – D7F engine

9 Apply the handbrake, then jack up the front of the vehicle and support it on axle stands (see *Jacking and vehicle support*).

10 Support the right-hand end of the engine using a suitable hoist. As a safety precaution, also position a axle stand and block of wood beneath the sump.

11 Unbolt the right-hand engine mounting from the engine and inner body with reference to Chapter 2B.

12 Remove the alternator drivebelt with reference to Chapter 1A. Briefly, this involves loosening the tensioner located on the right-hand end of the engine.

13 Remove the cover (where fitted) from the alternator main terminal, then unscrew the retaining nut and disconnect the main cable. Also disconnect the wiring plug from the rear of the alternator.

14 On models with air conditioning, unbolt the housing from the rear of the alternator.

15 Unscrew and remove the alternator lower mounting bolt, then support the alternator and unscrew the upper mounting bolt. Withdraw the alternator from the engine and remove it from the engine compartment.

K4J and K4M engines

16 Apply the handbrake, then jack up the front of the vehicle and support it on axle stands (see *Jacking and vehicle support*). Remove the front right-hand roadwheel

17 Remove the engine undertray, the right-hand front roadwheel, and the wheelarch liner from under the right-hand front wing.

18 Remove the radiator grille with reference to Chapter 11.

19 Loosen only the engine compartment front crossmember centre lower mounting bolts, then unbolt the crossmember from the inner body on both sides **(see illustrations)**. Position the crossmember on the engine, or alternatively unhook the bonnet lock cable and remove the crossmember completely.

20 Remove the protective cover from the fuel rail.

21 Remove the front right-hand headlight unit as described in Chapter 12, Section 9.

22 Remove the auxiliary drivebelt as described in Chapter 1A.

23 Remove the cover (where fitted) from the alternator main terminal, then unscrew the retaining nut and disconnect the main cable. Also disconnect the wiring plug from the rear of the alternator **(see illustration)**.

24 Remove the pulley from the power-assisted steering pump.

25 Disconnect the fuel supply pipe from the fuel rail, then disconnect the wiring from the fuel injector at the right-hand end of the engine.

26 Unscrew and remove the power-assisted steering mounting bolts, and release the fluid pipe leading to the pump at the multipurpose mounting.

27 Move the PAS pump to one side, and withdraw the alternator from the engine. If necessary to provide additional working room, the radiator and where fitted the air conditioning condenser may be unbolted and moved to one side with reference to the relevant Chapters of this Manual **(see illustrations)**. There is no need to drain the radiator or evacuate the refrigerant.

F8Q engine

28 Apply the handbrake, then jack up the front of the vehicle and support it on axle stands (see *Jacking and vehicle support*).

6.19a Unscrew the bolts from the front crossmember . . .

6.19b . . . then loosen the centre bolts and lift out the crossmember

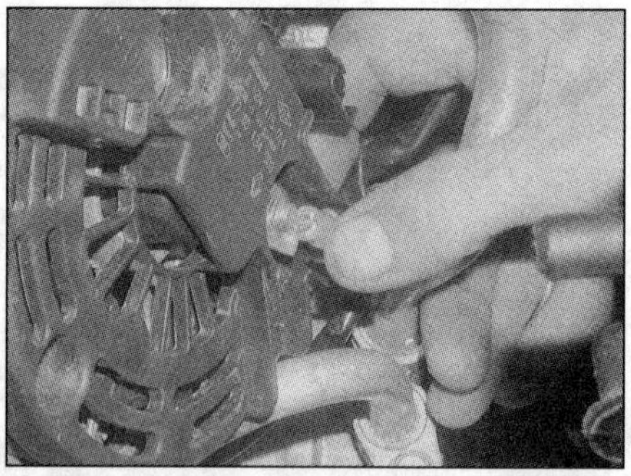

6.23a Disconnecting the main cable . . .

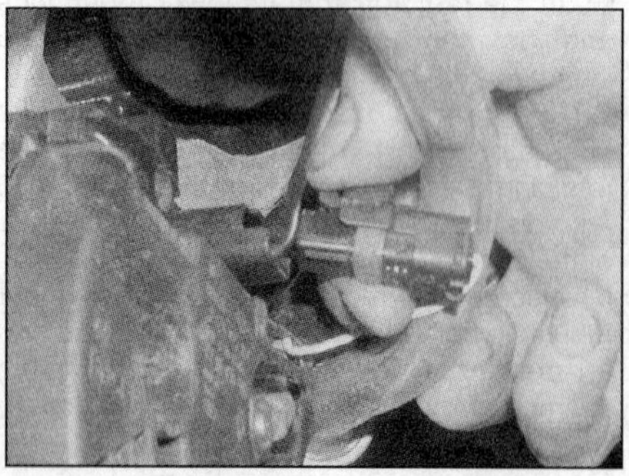

6.23b . . . and wiring plug from the rear of the alternator

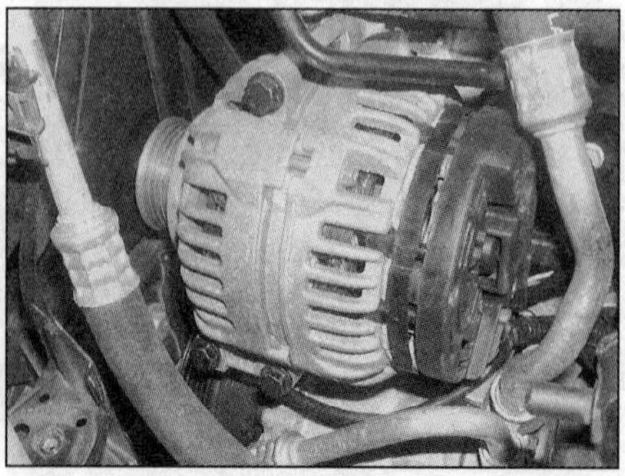

6.27a The alternator is located on the front right-hand side of the engine – K4M engine

6.27b Removing the alternator from the engine – K4M engine

Remove the engine undertray, the right-hand front roadwheel, and the wheelarch liner from under the right-hand front wing.

29 Remove the radiator grille with reference to Chapter 11.

30 Loosen only the engine compartment front crossmember centre lower mounting bolts, then unbolt the crossmember from the inner body on both sides. Position the crossmember on the engine.

31 Remove the alternator drivebelt with reference to Chapter 1B. Briefly, this involves loosening the tensioner located on the right-hand end of the engine.

32 Unbolt the tensioner mounting bracket from the engine.

33 Position a suitable container beneath the oil filter, then unscrew it from the front of the cylinder block. Keep the open end of the filter uppermost and lower it into the container.

34 Disconnect the wiring harness at the connector located above the oil filter position, release the harness from the support and position it to one side **(see illustration)**.

35 Loosen the mountings and lift the electric fan assembly from the rear of the radiator.

36 Remove the cover (where fitted) from the alternator main terminal, then unscrew the retaining nut and disconnect the main cable. Also disconnect the wiring plug from the rear of the alternator **(see illustrations)**.

37 Unscrew the mounting bolts and withdraw the alternator from the engine **(see illustration)**.

Refitting

38 Refitting is a reversal of removal. Refer to the relevant part of Chapter 1 for details of fitting and tensioning the drivebelts.

7 Alternator – testing

If the alternator is thought to be suspect, it should be removed from the vehicle and taken to an auto-electrician for testing. Most auto-electricians will be able to supply and fit brushes at a reasonable cost. However, check on the cost of repairs before proceeding as it may prove more economical to obtain a new or exchange alternator.

8 Alternator brush holder/regulator – renewal

Note: *Check on the availability of spare parts before attempting to renew the alternator brushes. The following typical procedure applies alternators with the brush holder/regulator mounted on the rear of the alternator. On other types, it is recommended that the alternator be taken to an automotive electrician for the work to be carried out.*

1 Remove the alternator as described in Section 6.

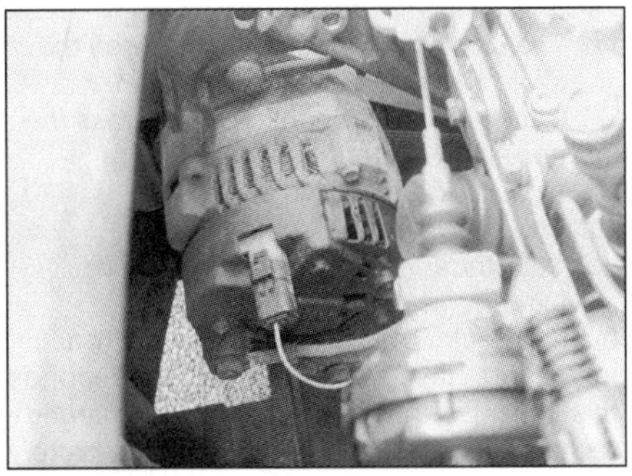

6.34 Alternator and wiring – F8Q engine

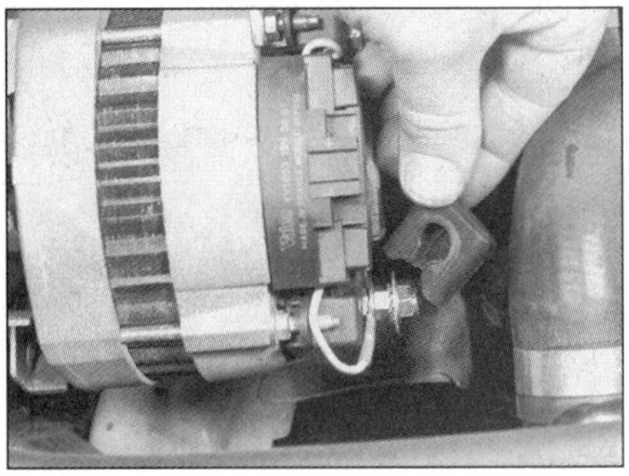

6.36a Remove the rubber cover . . .

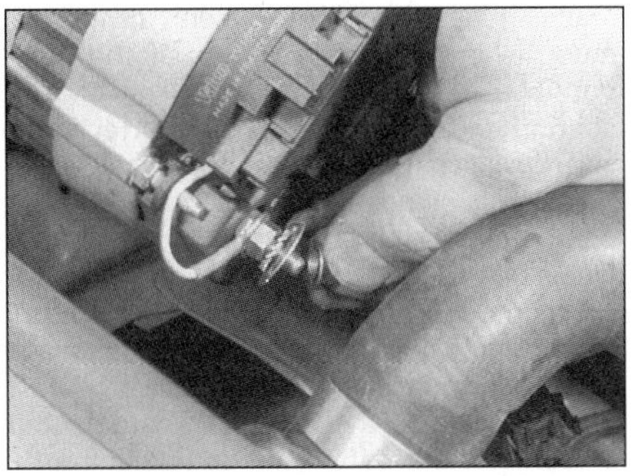

6.36b . . . then disconnect the alternator main feed wire – F8Q engine

6.36c Disconnecting the alternator wiring plug

2 Note the location of the brush holder/regulator assembly wire on the alternator B+ terminal. Unscrew the nut and disconnect the wire **(see illustration)**.

3 Unclip the plastic cover from the studs on the rear of the alternator, and remove the cover **(see illustration)**.

4 Unscrew the two screws securing the brush holder/regulator assembly to the rear of the alternator **(see illustration)**.

6.37 Removing the alternator – F8Q engine

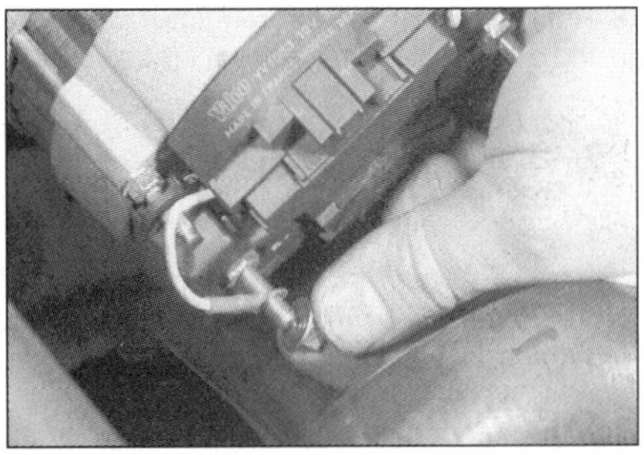

8.2 Disconnecting the brush holder/regulator assembly wire from the rear of the alternator

8.3 Removing the plastic cover from the rear of the alternator

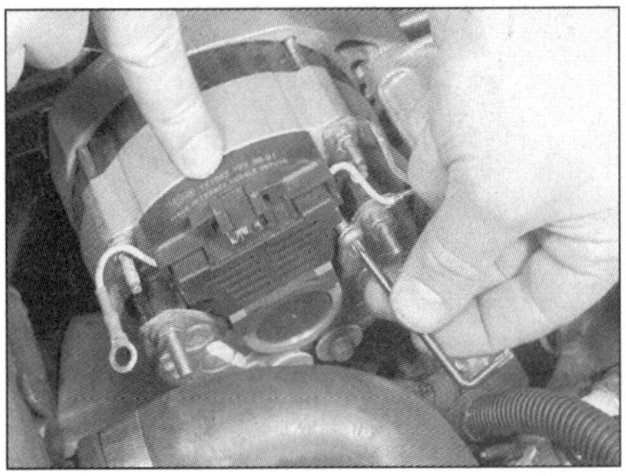

8.4 Unscrewing a brush holder/regulator assembly securing screw

8.5 Removing the brush holder/regulator assembly

5 Disconnect the remaining wire from the terminal on the rear of the alternator, then lift the brush holder/regulator assembly from the alternator **(see illustration)**.

6 Measure the protrusion of each brush from the brush holder **(see illustration)**. No minimum dimension is specified by the manufacturers, but as a rough guide, 5 mm should be regarded as a minimum. If either brush is worn below this dimension, the complete brush holder/regulator assembly must be renewed. If the brushes are still serviceable, clean them with a fuel-moistened cloth. Check that the brush spring tension is equal for both brushes and provides a reasonable pressure. The brushes must move freely in their holders.

7 Clean the alternator slip rings with a fuel-moistened cloth. Check for signs of scoring, burning or severe pitting on the surface of the slip rings. It may be possible to have the slip rings renovated by an electrical specialist.

8 Refit the brush holder/regulator assembly using a reversal of the removal procedure.

9 Starting system – testing

Note: *Refer to the precautions given in 'Safety first!' and in Section 1 of this Chapter before starting work.*

1 If the starter motor fails to operate when the ignition key is turned to the appropriate position, the following may be the possible causes:

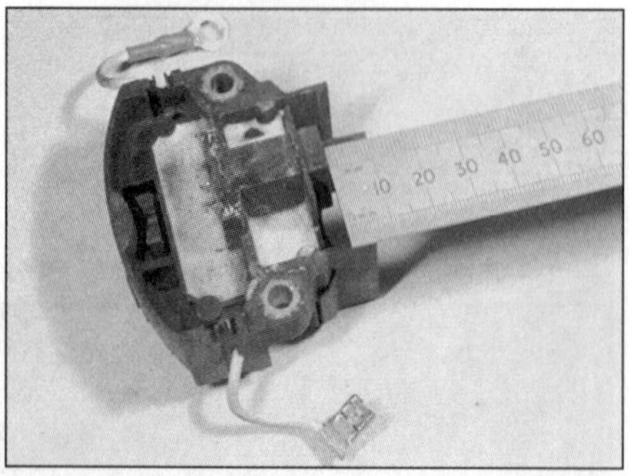

8.6 Measuring the alternator brush protrusion

a) The battery is faulty.
b) The electrical connections between the switch, solenoid, battery and starter motor are somewhere failing to pass the necessary current from the battery through the starter to earth.
c) The solenoid is faulty.
d) The starter motor is mechanically or electrically defective.

2 To check the battery, switch on the headlights. If they dim after a few seconds, this indicates that the battery is discharged – recharge (see Section 3) or renew the battery. If the headlights glow brightly, operate the ignition switch and observe the lights. If they dim, then this indicates that current is reaching the starter motor, therefore the fault must lie in the starter motor. If the lights continue to glow brightly (and no clicking sound can be heard from the starter motor solenoid), this indicates that there is a fault in the circuit or solenoid – see the following paragraphs. If the starter motor turns slowly when operated, but the battery is in good condition, then this indicates that either the starter motor is faulty, or there is considerable resistance somewhere in the circuit.

3 If a fault in the circuit is suspected, disconnect the battery leads (including the earth connection to the body), the starter/solenoid wiring and the engine/transmission earth strap. Thoroughly clean the connections, and reconnect the leads and wiring, then use a voltmeter or test lamp to check that full battery voltage is available at the battery positive lead connection to the solenoid, and that the earth is sound. Smear petroleum jelly around the battery terminals to prevent corrosion – corroded connections are amongst the most frequent causes of electrical system faults.

4 If the battery and all connections are in good condition, check the circuit by disconnecting the wire from the solenoid blade terminal. Connect a voltmeter or test lamp between the wire end and a good earth (such as the battery negative terminal), and check that the wire is live when the ignition switch is turned to the 'start' position. If it is, then the circuit is sound – if not the circuit wiring can be checked as described in Chapter 12.

5 The solenoid contacts can be checked by connecting a voltmeter or test lamp between the battery positive feed connection on the starter side of the solenoid and earth. When the ignition switch is turned to the 'start' position, there should be a reading or lighted bulb, as applicable. If there is no reading or lighted bulb, the solenoid is faulty and should be renewed.

6 If the circuit and solenoid are proved sound, the fault must lie in the starter motor. In this event, it may be possible to have the starter motor overhauled by a specialist, but check on the cost of spares before proceeding, as it may prove more economical to obtain a new or exchange motor.

10 Starter motor – removal and refitting

Removal

1 Disconnect the battery negative (earth) lead and position it away from the terminal.

D7F engine

2 The starter motor is located on the front of the cylinder block. Unscrew the nut and disconnect the main positive battery lead from the large terminal on the starter solenoid.

3 Disconnect the smaller trigger wire from the starter solenoid.

4 Support the starter motor, then unscrew and remove the two mounting bolts. The front bolt is on the motor side of the transmission flange, whereas the rear bolt is on the transmission side.

5 Withdraw the starter motor from the transmission.

E7J and K7M engines

6 Apply the handbrake, then jack up the front of the vehicle and support it on axle stands (see *Jacking and vehicle support*). Remove the right-hand front roadwheel. Also remove the engine undertray.

7 Unscrew and remove the bolt supporting the PAS fluid pipe and inlet manifold bracket from the transmission flange.

8 With reference to Chapter 8, detach the right-hand driveshaft from the transmission without disconnecting it at the wheel end. Briefly, to do this, the driveshaft roll pin must be driven out, then the upper bolt securing the hub carrier to the strut must be removed, and the lower bolt loosened only. Carefully tilt the hub carrier out while disconnecting the driveshaft, then lower the driveshaft away from the transmission to provide access to the starter motor.

9 Unscrew the nut and disconnect the main positive battery lead from the large terminal on the starter solenoid.

10 Disconnect the smaller trigger wire from the starter solenoid.

11 Support the starter motor, then unscrew the mounting bolts and lower it from under the vehicle.

K4J and K4M engines

12 Apply the handbrake, then jack up the front of the vehicle and support it on axle stands (see *Jacking and vehicle support*). Remove the right-hand front roadwheel. Also remove the engine undertray.

13 Remove the air inlet duct resonator with reference to Chapter 4A.

14 Refer to Chapter 8 and drive out the roll pin securing the right-hand driveshaft to the transmission sun gear.

15 Disconnect the steering right-hand track rod end with reference to Chapter 10, then unscrew and remove the upper bolt securing the hub carrier to the bottom of the

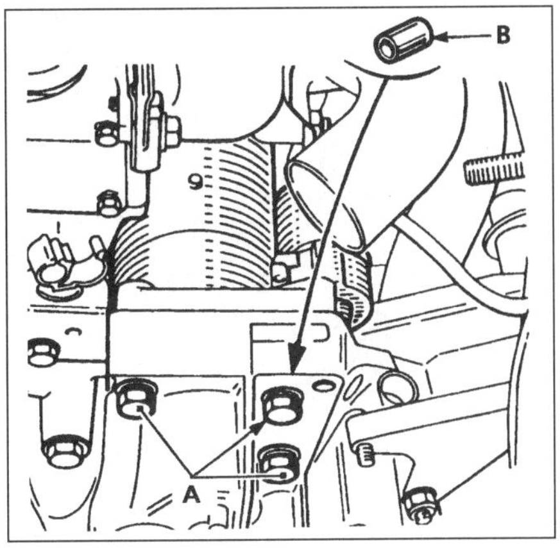

10.29 Starter motor securing bolts (A) and locating dowel (B)

suspension strut, noting which way round it is fitted. Loosen *only* the lower bolt.

16 Tilt outwards the hub carrier and detach the driveshaft from the sun gear.

17 Remove the battery as described in Section 4.

18 Disconnect the wiring loom from the engine management ECU and disconnect the wiring from the impact sensor located on the left-hand side of the engine compartment. Remove the ECU.

19 Remove the heat shield from over the catalytic converter below the exhaust manifold.

20 Disconnect the wiring from the oil level sensor and move the wiring loom to one side.

21 Unscrew the nut and disconnect the main positive battery lead from the large terminal on the starter solenoid.

22 Disconnect the smaller trigger wire from the starter solenoid.

23 Support the starter motor, then unscrew the mounting bolts and lower it from under the vehicle.

F8Q engine

24 Apply the handbrake, then jack up the front of the vehicle and support it on axle stands (see *Jacking and vehicle support*). Remove the engine undertray.

25 Remove the air cleaner inlet duct with reference to Chapter 4B.

26 Remove the battery and tray as described in Section 4.

27 Unscrew the engine management ECU and fuel filter support mounting bolts.

28 Disconnect the wiring at the two plugs, and move the support to one side.

29 Unscrew and remove the starter motor mounting bolts, and at the same time remove the heat shield **(see illustration)**.

30 Unscrew the nut and disconnect the main positive battery lead from the large terminal on the starter solenoid **(see illustration)**.

31 Disconnect the smaller trigger wire from the starter solenoid.

32 Withdraw the starter motor from the transmission **(see illustration)**. Recover the locating dowel which is fitted to the rear mounting bolt hole.

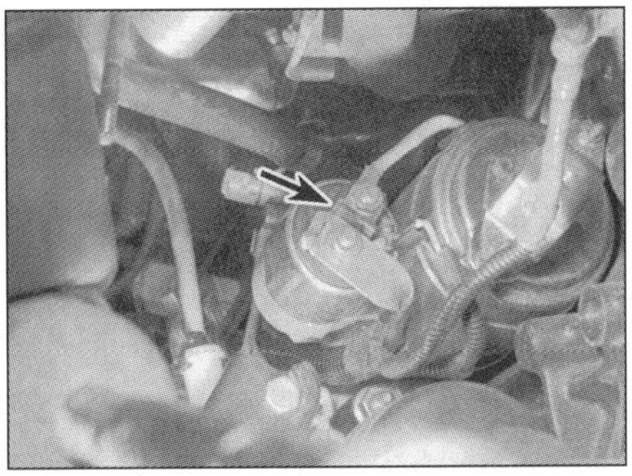

10.30 Starter motor wiring (arrowed) viewed from under the vehicle

Refitting

33 Refitting is a reversal of removal, tightening the mounting bolts securely.

11 Starter motor – brush renewal

Note: *The procedure described in this Section is for the Bosch starter motor, however, the procedure for other makes is similar.*

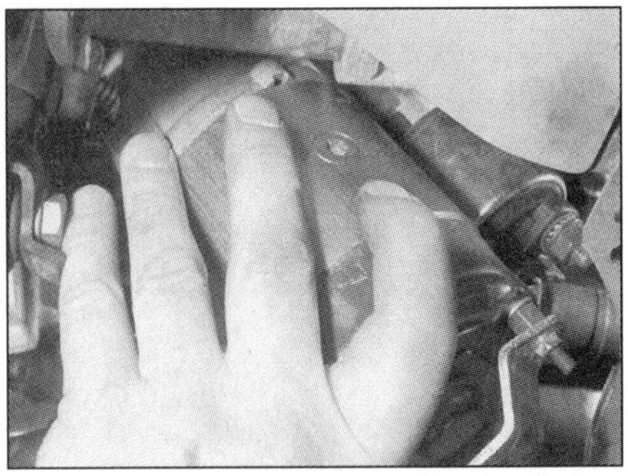

10.32 Removing the starter motor

1 With the starter motor removed from the vehicle as described in Section 10, proceed as follows **(see illustration)**.

2 Make alignment marks on the armature end cover and the motor body.

3 Where applicable, unscrew the two securing nuts, and remove the mounting bracket from the rear of the starter motor **(see illustration)**.

4 Unscrew the securing screws, and remove the armature shaft end cap **(see illustrations)**.

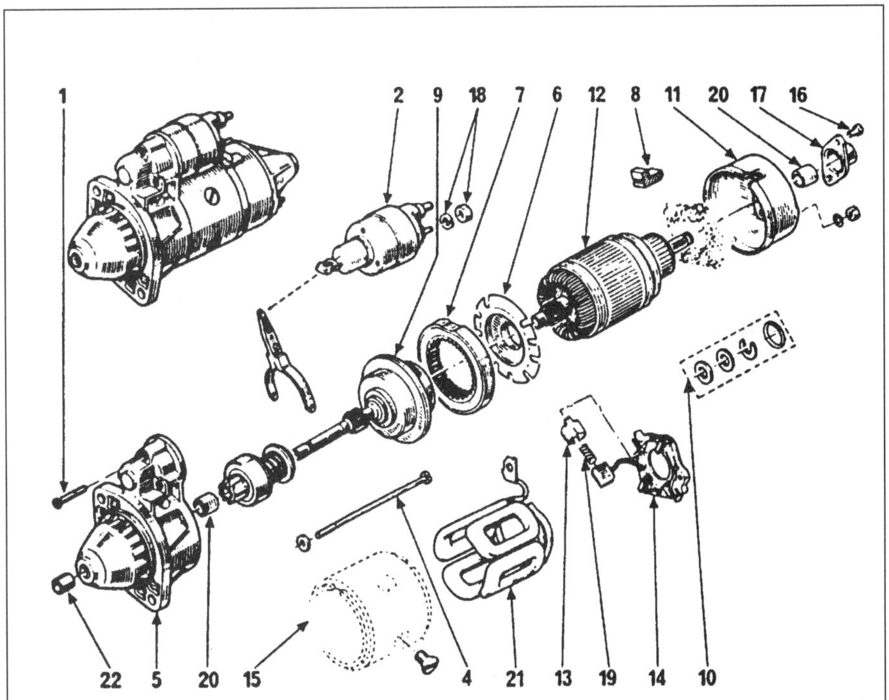

11.1 Exploded view of the Bosch reduction gear type starter motor

1 Bolt
2 Solenoid
4 Through-bolt
5 Drive end housing
6 Armature retaining plate
7 Ring gear
8 Rubber wiring grommet
9 Reduction gear assembly
10 Armature shaft end circlips and shims
11 Armature end cover
12 Armature
13 Brush holder
14 Brush holder plate
15 Motor body
16 End cap screw
17 Armature shaft end cap
18 Terminal nut and washer
19 Brush spring
20 Bush
21 Field windings
22 Bush

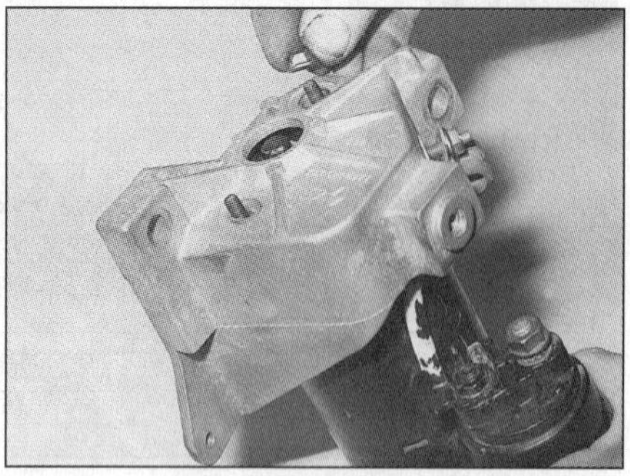

11.3 Removing the mounting bracket from the rear of the starter motor

11.4a Unscrew the securing screws . . .

11.4b . . . and remove the armature shaft end cap

5 Remove the circlip from the end of the armature shaft. Recover the washers and spacers, noting their orientation **(see illustrations)**.

6 Remove the nut securing the field wiring to the solenoid **(see illustration)**.

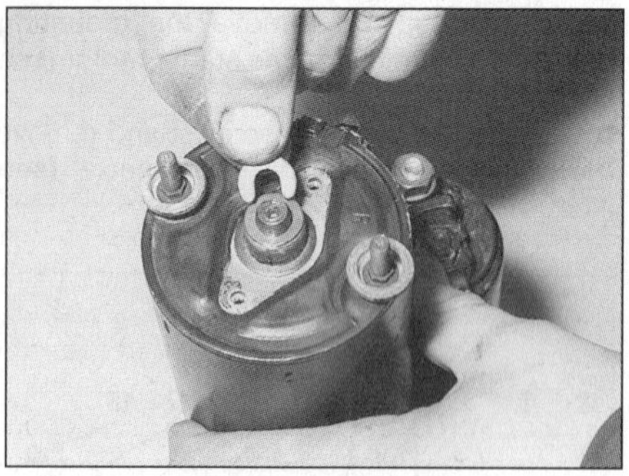

11.5a Remove the circlip . . .

7 Unscrew the two through-bolts and withdraw the armature end cover, along with the mounting bracket, when fitted **(see illustrations)**.

8 Withdraw the brush plate assembly from the rear of the starter motor, pulling the rubber wiring grommet from the motor casing as it is withdrawn.

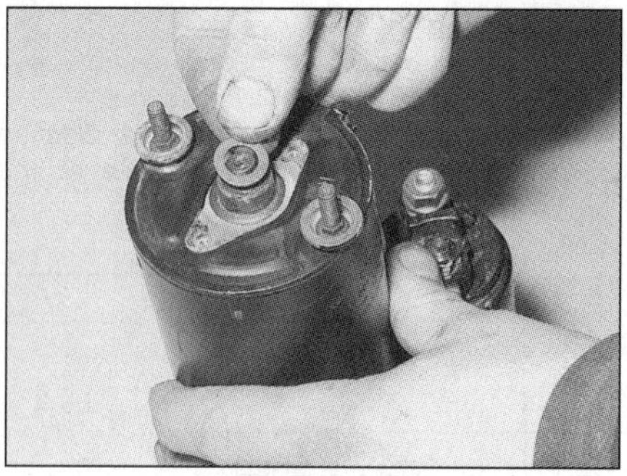

11.5b . . . and recover the washers and spacers

9 Withdraw the brushes and the springs from the brush holders, then unclip the brush holders from the brush plate **(see illustrations)**.

10 Examine the brushes for wear and damage. If they are damaged, or worn to the extent where the springs are unable to exert sufficient pressure to maintain good contact with the commutator, they should be renewed. If renewal is necessary, unsolder the old brushes, and solder new ones into place.

11 Clean the brush holder assemblies, and wipe the commutator with a petrol-moistened cloth. If the commutator is dirty, it may be cleaned with fine glass paper, then wiped with the cloth.

12 Fit the brush holders to the brush plate, then refit the springs and the brushes to the

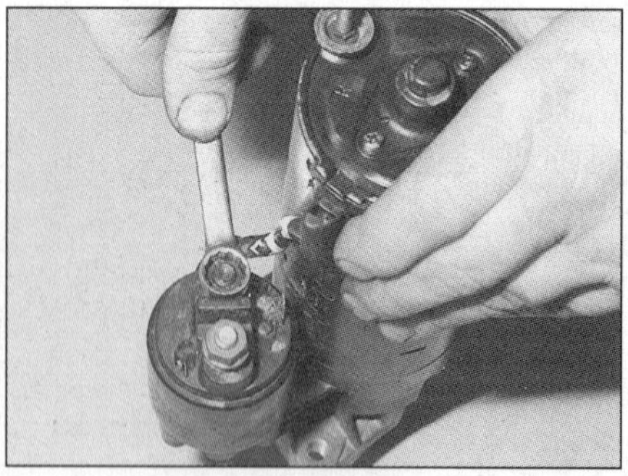

11.6 Remove the nut securing the field wiring to the solenoid

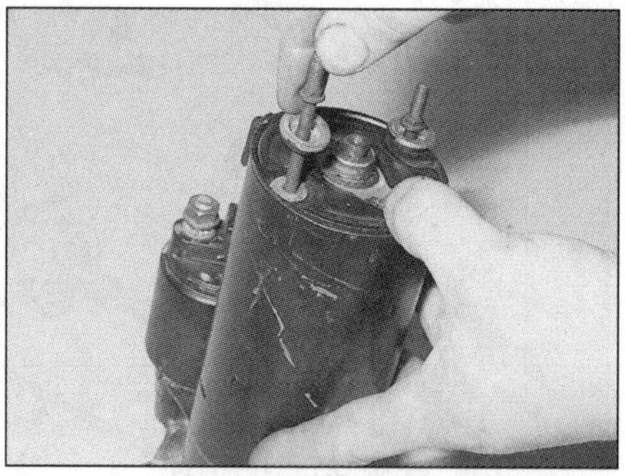

11.7a Unscrew the through-bolts . . .

11.7b . . . and withdraw the armature end cover

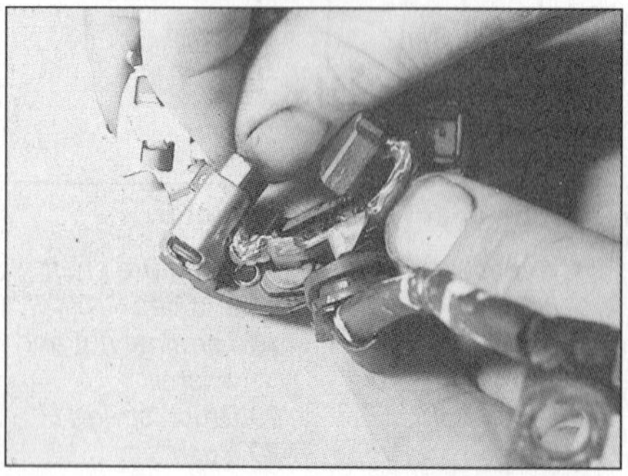

11.9a Withdraw the brushes . . .

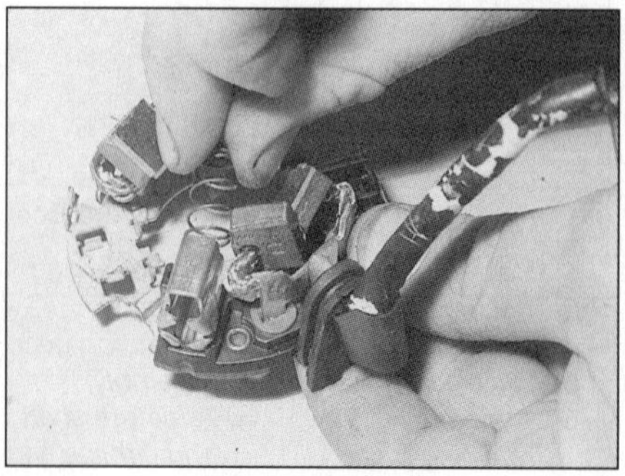

11.9b . . . springs . . .

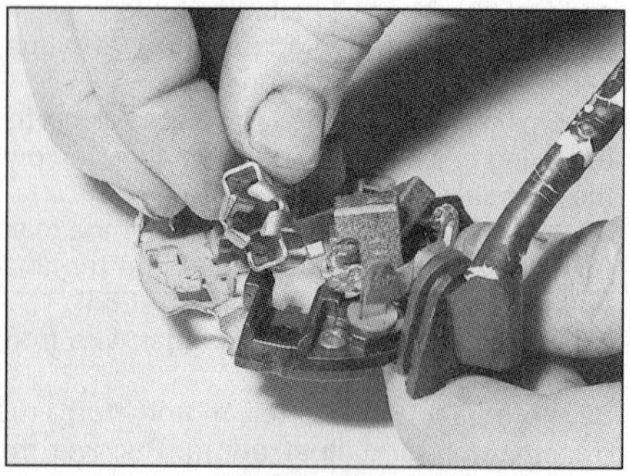

11.9c . . . and brush holders from the brush plate

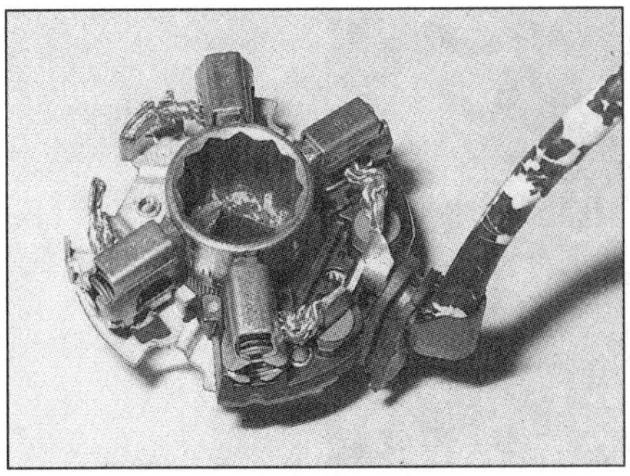

11.13 Use a socket to hold the brushes in position

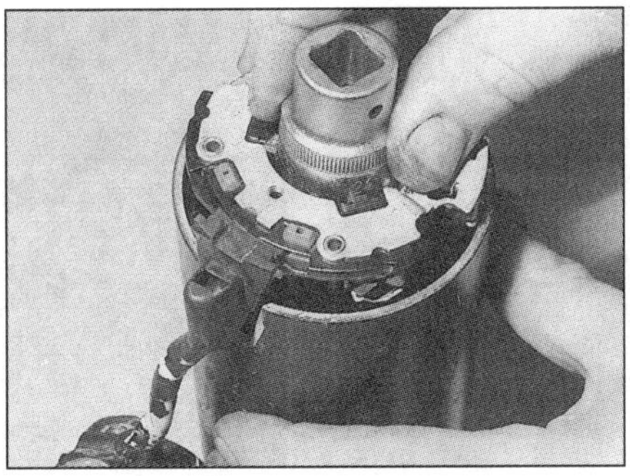

11.14 Fitting the brush plate over the armature shaft

brush holders. Ensure that the brushes move freely in their holders. Ensure that the brush springs provide adequate pressure on the brushes, and renew any worn springs.

13 Push the brushes into the brush holders, and use a socket to hold them in position **(see illustration)**.

14 Position the brush plate over the rear of the armature shaft, then withdraw the socket so that the brushes contact the commutator **(see illustration)**.

15 Further reassembly is a reversal of dismantling, bearing in mind the following points.

a) *Align the marks made on the end cover and the motor body before removal.*
b) *Ensure that the washers and spacers on the end of the armature shaft are fitted as noted before removal.*
c) *Refit the starter motor as described in Section 10.*

12 Ignition switch - removal and refitting

Removal

1 Disconnect the battery negative (earth) lead and position it away from the terminal.

2 Remove the steering wheel and steering column shrouds as described in Chapter 10. Make sure that the front wheels are in their straight-ahead position.

3 Remove the instrument panel as described in Chapter 12.

4 Remove the immobiliser antenna ring from the ignition switch.

5 Release the ignition switch wiring connector from its location beneath the steering column by pivoting it, then disconnect it **(see illustration)**. Note the routing of the wiring for correct refitting.

6 Unscrew and remove the small grub screw from the top of the ignition switch **(see illustration)**.

7 Insert the ignition key and turn it to position 3.

8 Depress the two pegs located under the switch housing, and withdraw the ignition switch together with the wiring **(see illustrations)**.

9 To separate the switch from the lock assembly, remove the two securing screws from the rear of the housing, and lift off the rear cover. The switch can now be withdrawn from the lock **(see illustrations)**.

Refitting

10 Refitting is a reversal of removal, but make sure the wiring is correctly routed.

13 Oil pressure warning light switch - removal and refitting

Removal

1 On all engines except the K7M, the oil pressure warning light switch is located at the lower front right-hand side of the cylinder block, next to the oil filter **(see illustration)**. On the K7M engine, it is located at the left-hand front of the cylinder block.

2 Apply the handbrake, then jack up the front of the vehicle and support on axle stands (see *Jacking and vehicle support*).

3 Disconnect the wiring from the switch.

12.5 Disconnecting a wiring connector from the ignition switch

12.6 Unscrewing the ignition switch grub screw

12.8a Depressing the ignition switch securing pegs

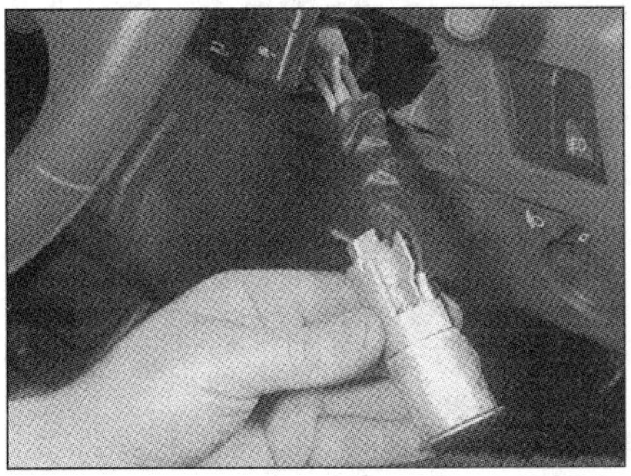

12.8b Withdrawing the ignition switch

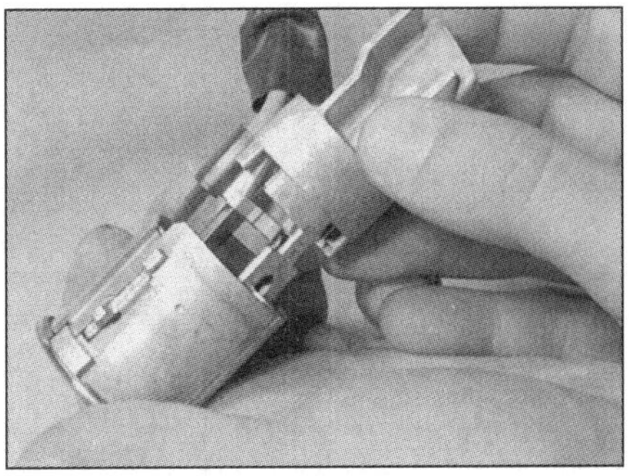

12.9a Removing the ignition switch rear cover . . .

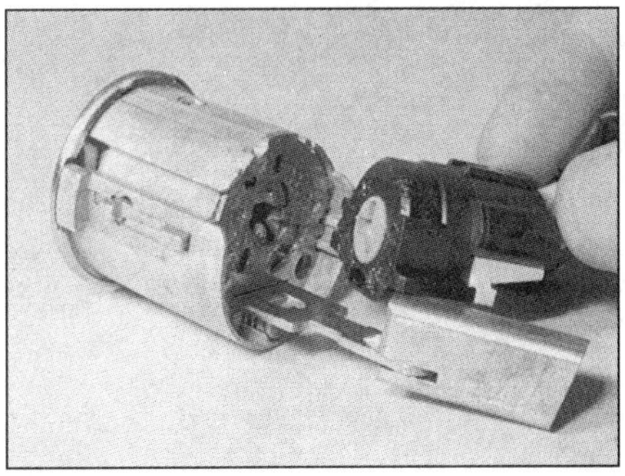

12.9b . . . and withdrawing the switch from the lock

5A

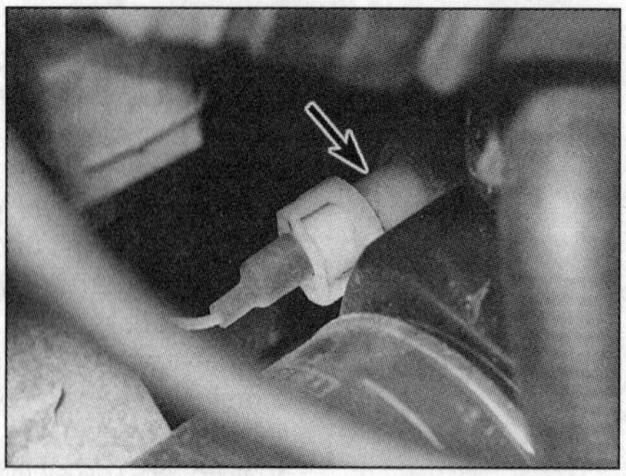

13.1 On all engines, except K7M, the oil pressure switch is located next to the oil filter

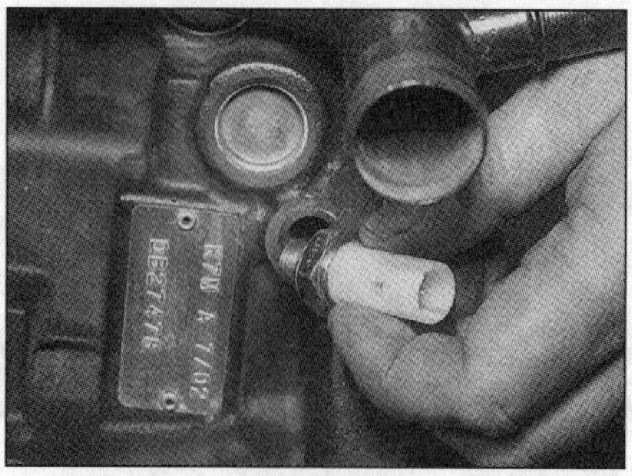

13.4 Removing the oil pressure switch – K7M engine

4 Unscrew the switch from the cylinder block, and recover the sealing washer **(see illustration)**. Be prepared for oil spillage, and if the switch is to be left removed from the engine, plug the hole in the cylinder block.

Refitting

5 Examine the sealing washer for signs of damage or deterioration, and if necessary renew it.

6 Refit the switch together with the washer, and tighten it securely. Reconnect the wiring.

7 Check and top-up the engine oil as described in *Weekly checks*.

14 Oil level sensor – removal and refitting

Removal

1 On all engines except K7M, the oil level sensor is located on the front of the cylinder block, below the oil filter **(see illustration)**. On the K7M engine it is located on the rear of the cylinder block below the manifolds.

2 Apply the handbrake, then jack up the front of the vehicle and support on axle stands (see *Jacking and vehicle support*). Remove the engine undertray.

3 Disconnect the wiring from the sensor.

4 Unscrew the sensor from the cylinder block, and recover the sealing washer **(see illustrations)**. If the sensor is to be left removed from the engine, plug the hole in the cylinder block.

Refitting

5 Examine the sealing washer for signs of damage or deterioration, and if necessary renew it.

6 Refit the sensor, complete with washer, and tighten it securely. Reconnect the wiring connector.

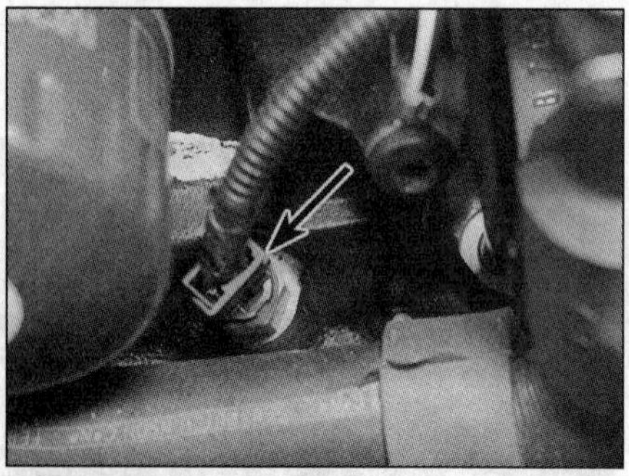

14.1 On all engines, except K7M, the oil level sensor is located below the oil filter

14.4a Unscrew the oil level sensor . . .

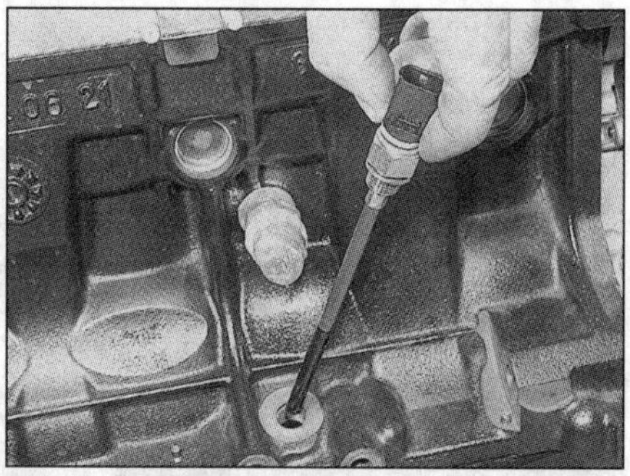

14.4b . . . and remove it from the cylinder block – K7M engine

Chapter 5 Part B:
Ignition system – petrol engines

Contents

Degrees of difficulty

Easy, suitable for novice with little experience	**Fairly easy,** suitable for beginner with some experience	**Fairly difficult,** suitable for competent DIY mechanic	**Difficult,** suitable for experienced DIY mechanic	**Very difficult,** suitable for expert DIY or professional

Specifications

General

Engine codes:	
1.2 litre petrol engine	D7F
1.4 litre petrol engine:	
SOHC	E7J
DOHC	K4J
1.6 litre petrol engine:	
SOHC	K7M
DOHC	K4M
Ignition system type:	
D7F, E7J and K7M engines	Fully-electronic, computer-controlled, with two dual output ignition coils serving cylinders 1 and 4, and 2 and 3
K4J and K4M engines	Fully-electronic, computer-controlled, with four individual ignition coils, one on each spark plug
Firing order	1-3-4-2
Location of No 1 cylinder	Flywheel end

Ignition timing	Controlled by the ECU

Ignition HT coil resistances measured at ignition connector

D7F 720 engine

Terminals 1 to 2	1.5 ohms
Terminals 1 to 3	1.0 ohms
Terminals 1 to 4	1.0 ohms
Terminals 2 to 3	1.0 ohms
Terminals 2 to 4	1.0 ohms
Terminals 3 to 4	0.6 ohms
HT terminal to HT terminal	8.0 ohms

D7F 702/726 engines

Terminals 1 to 2	2.0 ohms
Terminals 1 to 4, 2 to 3, 1 to 3 and 2 to 4	1.6 ohms
Terminals 3 to 4	1.1 ohms
HT terminal to HT terminal	7200 ohms

E7J 780 and K7M engines

Terminals 1 to 2	0.5 ohms
Terminals 1 to 3	1.0 ohms
Terminals 2 to 3	1.0 ohms
HT terminal to HT terminal	10 k ohms

E7J 634 and K7M engines

Primary resistance	0.5 ohms
Secondary resistance	11.0 ± 1.0 k ohms

Torque wrench settings

	Nm	lbf ft
Ignition coil	15	11
Knock sensor:		
D7F, E7J, K7M engines	25	18
K4J, K4M engines	20	15
Spark plugs	See Chapter 1A	

1 Ignition system – general information and precautions

General information

The ignition system is integrated with the fuel injection system to form a combined engine management system under the control of one ECU (see Chapter 4A for further information).

All engines are fitted with a distributorless ignition system, under the control of the ECU.

On SOHC engines the ignition system consists simply of two ignition HT coils, the crankshaft speed/position/TDC sensor and a knock sensor. Each coil supplies two cylinders (one coil supplies cylinders 1 and 4 and the other coil supplies cylinders 2 and 3). The ignition coils operate on the 'wasted spark' principle, ie, each spark plug sparks twice for every cycle of the engine, once on the compression stroke and once on the exhaust stroke.

On DOHC engines the ignition system uses one coil for each cylinder, with each coil mounted on the relevant spark plug. The coils are fed in series, two at a time, and the system operates on the 'wasted spark' principle as for SOHC engines.

The TDC sensor (see Chapter 4A) is used to determine piston position as well as engine speed.

The power module for the ignition is integrated in the engine management ECU. The ECU uses the inputs from the sensors to calculate the required ignition advance setting and coil charging time – an integral amplifier circuit within the ECU switches the ignition coil primary (LT) circuit.

The knock sensor is mounted on the cylinder block to inform the ECU when the engine is 'pinking'. Its sensitivity to a particular frequency of vibration allows it to detect the impulses which are caused by the shock waves set up when the engine starts to 'pink' (pre-ignite). The knock sensor sends an electrical signal to the ECU which retards the ignition advance setting until the 'pinking' ceases – the ignition timing is then gradually returned to the 'normal' setting. This maintains the ignition timing as close to the knock threshold as possible – the most efficient setting for the engine under normal running conditions.

Precautions

The following precautions must be observed, to prevent damage to the ignition system components and to reduce risk of personal injury.

a) Ensure the ignition is switched off before disconnecting any of the ignition wiring.

b) Ensure that the ignition is switched off before connecting or disconnecting any ignition test equipment, such as a timing light.

c) Do not earth the coil primary or secondary circuits.

Warning: Voltages produced by an electronic ignition system are considerably higher than those produced by conventional ignition systems. Extreme care must be taken when working on the system with the ignition switched on. Persons with surgically-implanted cardiac pacemaker devices should keep well clear of the ignition circuits, components and test equipment

Caution: If the radio/cassette in your vehicle is equipped with an anti-theft system, make sure you have the correct activation code before disconnecting the battery.

2 Ignition system – testing

1 The components of ignition systems are normally very reliable; most faults are far more likely to be due to loose or dirty connections, or to 'tracking' of HT voltage due to dirt, dampness or damaged insulation than to the failure of any of the system's components. Always check all wiring thoroughly before condemning an electrical component and work methodically to eliminate all other possibilities before deciding that a particular component is faulty.

2 The old practice of checking for a spark by holding the live end of a spark plug HT lead a short distance away from the engine is not recommended; not only is there a high risk of a powerful electric shock, but the HT coil or ECU may be damaged. However, if necessary each plug can be checked individually by removing it, then reconnecting the HT lead or coil (as applicable) and connecting the body of the spark plug to a suitable earthing point on the engine using a battery jumper lead. It is important to make a good earth connection if using this method. Never try to 'diagnose' misfires by pulling off one HT lead at a time.

Engine will not start

3 If the engine either will not turn over at all, or only turns very slowly, first check the battery and starter motor as described in Chapter 5A.

4 If the engine turns over at normal speed but will not start, the HT circuit of SOHC engines can be checked by connecting a timing light to an HT lead (following the manufacturer's instructions) and turning the engine over on the starter motor. If the light flashes, voltage is reaching the spark plugs, so these should be removed and checked. If the light does not flash, check the spark plug HT leads themselves with reference to Chapter 1. **Note:** *On DOHC engines, the coils are mounted on each individual spark plug, so it is not possible to use a conventional timing light to check the system.*

5 If there is still no spark on SOHC engines, use an ohmmeter to check the resistances of the coils at the coil multi-plug and compare with the information given in the Specifications. The tracks for each engine are as follows:

D7F engine

Track number	Allocation
1	Coil control for cylinders 1 and 4
2	Coil control for cylinders 3 and 2
3	+ after ignition
4	+ anti-interference condenser

E7J and K7M engines

Track number	Allocation
1	+ anti-interference condenser
2	+ after ignition
3	Coil control by ECU

6 If these checks fail to reveal the cause of the problem, the vehicle should be taken to a Renault dealer for testing. A wiring block connector is incorporated in the engine management circuit, into which a special electronic diagnostic tester can be plugged. The tester will locate the fault quickly and simply, alleviating the need to test all the system components individually, which is a time-consuming operation that carries a high risk of damaging the ECU. If necessary, the system wiring and wiring connectors can be checked as described in Chapter 12, ensuring that the ECU wiring connector is first disconnected with the ignition switched off.

Engine misfires

7 An irregular misfire suggests either a loose connection or intermittent fault in the primary circuit, or an HT fault on the circuit between the coil and spark plugs.

8 With the ignition switched off, check carefully through the system ensuring that all connections are clean and securely fastened.

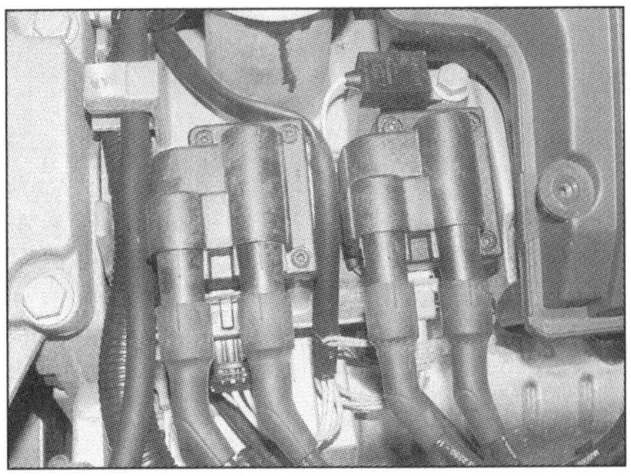
3.2 Ignition HT coils – E7J engine

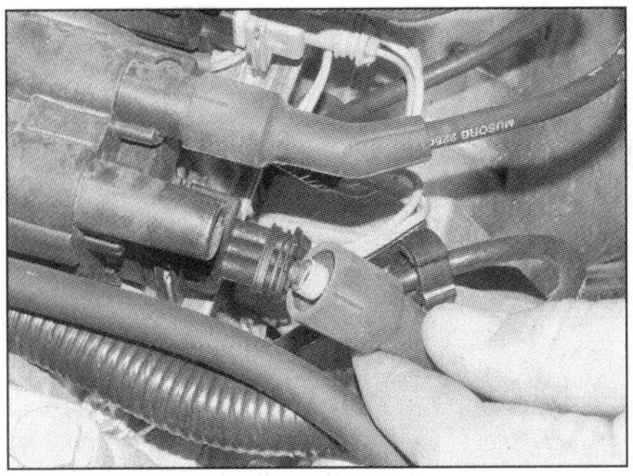
3.3a Disconnecting the HT leads from the coils . . .

3.3b . . . and from the spark plugs – E7J engine

9 Check that the HT coil and the spark plug HT leads (where applicable) are clean and dry.

10 Regular misfiring of one spark plug may be due to a faulty spark plug, faulty injector, a faulty HT lead or loss of compression in the relevant cylinder. Regular misfiring of cylinders 1 and 4 only, or 2 and 3 only suggests a fault on the relevant coil. Regular misfiring of all the cylinders suggests a fuel supply fault, such as a clogged fuel filter or faulty fuel pump.

3 Ignition HT coils – removal, testing and refitting

Removal

1 Disconnect the battery negative lead (refer to *Disconnecting the battery* in Reference).

D7F, E7J and K7M engines

2 The ignition HT coils are located on the right-hand end of the camshaft cover **(see illustration)**.

3 Note their location, then disconnect the spark plug HT leads from the spark plugs and from the coils **(see illustrations)**. If necessary, identify each lead to ensure correct refitting. On the D7F engine, the leads are located in a special retainer, and a tool for disconnecting the leads from the spark plugs is incorporated in the retainer.

4 Disconnect the wiring multi-plug from each coil **(see illustration)**.

5 Undo the mounting screws and remove the coils from the mounting plate – note the location of the suppressor **(see illustration)**. **Note:** *The base of each coil is different to ensure that they only locate in one position.*

K4J and K4M engines

6 The ignition coils are accessible through the holes in the inlet manifold. First, carefully disconnect the wiring from each coil. Take care not to damage the connectors **(see illustration)**.

7 Unscrew the mounting screws and withdraw each coil off of its spark plug **(see illustrations)**.

8 Check the condition of the O-rings where the coils enter the camshaft cover, and if necessary renew them.

Testing

9 On SOHC engines, each coil can be tested as described in the previous Section, using an ohmmeter to check for the resistances given in the Specifications **(see illustrations)**.

10 On DOHC engines, testing of the ignition

3.4 Disconnecting the wiring multi-plugs from the ignition coils

3.5 Note the location of the suppressor on one of the mounting screws

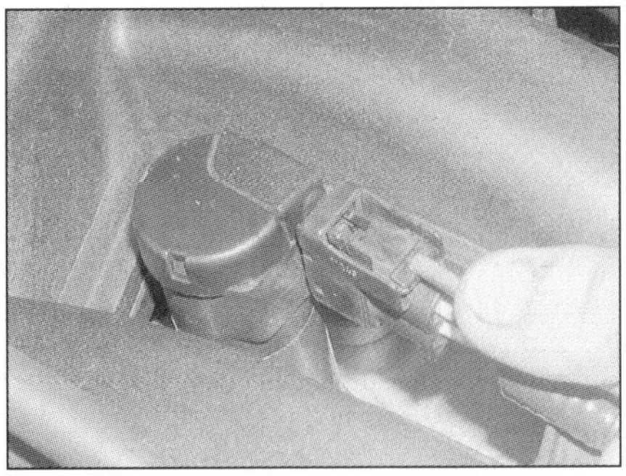
3.6 Disconnect the wiring from the ignition coil . . .

3.7a . . . then undo the mounting screws . . .

3.7b . . . and withdraw the coil off of its spark plug

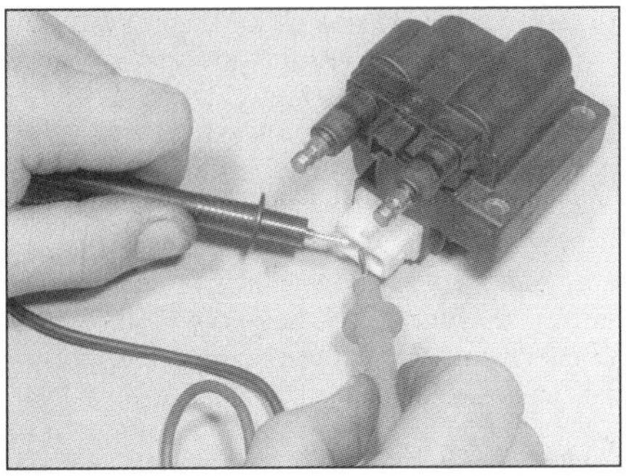
3.9a Testing an ignition coil's low tension circuits – K7M engine

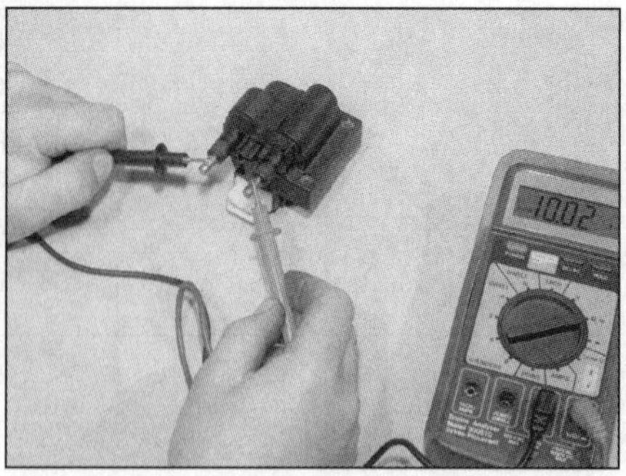

3.9b Testing an ignition coil's HT circuit – K7M engine

4.1 Knock sensor location – K4J engine

system should be carried out by a Renault dealer using specialised equipment connected to the engine management diagnostic socket.

Refitting

11 Refitting is a reversal of removal, but tighten the mounting bolts to the specified torque, and ensure that the wiring connectors and spark plug HT leads are correctly and securely refitted.

4 Knock sensor – removal and refitting

Removal

1 On the D7F engine the knock sensor is located on the front of the cylinder block, below the inlet manifold, next to the engine oil level dipstick tube. On E7J and K7M engines, it is located on the right-hand rear of the cylinder block. On K4J and K4M engines, it is located on the front, right-hand side of the cylinder block **(see illustration)**.

2 To remove the sensor, first disconnect the wiring, then unscrew it from the cylinder block.

Refitting

3 Refitting is a reversal of removal. Ensure that the sensor and its seating on the cylinder block or head are completely clean and tighten the sensor to the specified torque wrench setting. It is essential that these measures are scrupulously observed as if the sensor is not correctly secured to a clean mating surface it may not be able to detect the impulses caused by pre-ignition. If this were to happen the correction of ignition timing would not take place, with the consequent risk of severe engine damage.

5 Ignition timing – checking and adjustment

In this type of ignition system the ignition timing is constantly being monitored and adjusted by the engine management ECU and nominal checking values cannot be given. Therefore, it is not possible for the home mechanic to check the ignition timing. The only way in which the ignition timing can be checked is using special electronic test equipment, connected to the engine management system diagnostic connector (refer to Chapter 4A). No adjustment of the ignition timing is possible. Should the ignition timing be incorrect, then a fault must be present in the engine management system.

Chapter 5 Part C:
Pre/post-heating system – diesel engines

Contents

Degrees of difficulty

Easy, suitable for novice with little experience	**Fairly easy,** suitable for beginner with some experience	**Fairly difficult,** suitable for competent DIY mechanic	**Difficult,** suitable for experienced DIY mechanic	**Very difficult,** suitable for expert DIY or professional

Specifications

Glow plugs

Resistance:	
Except F8Q 632 engine	0.8 ohms
F8Q 632 engine	0.6 ohms

Coolant temperature sensor

F8Q 630/662 engine

Resistance at:	
20° C	3060 to 4045 ohms
40° C	1315 to 1600 ohms
80° C	300 to 370 ohms
90° C	210 to 270 ohms

F8Q 632 engine

Resistance at:	
–10° C	13588 to 11 332 ohms
25° C	2364 to 2140 ohms
50° C	850 to 773 ohms
80° C	290 to 275 ohms

Torque wrench settings	Nm	lbf ft
Glow plugs	20	15
Glow plug terminal nut	4	3

1 Pre/post-heating system – description and testing

Description

1 The pre-heating/post-heating system consists of glow plugs screwed into each swirl chamber, a control unit mounted on the left-hand side of the engine compartment next to the battery (F8Q 630 and F8Q 662 engines) or on the bulkhead (F8Q 632 engine), and a coolant temperature sensor located on the thermostat housing. The control unit is itself activated by the engine management ECU.

2 The glow plugs are supplied with current from the control unit in five phases, namely variable pre-heating, fixed pre-heating, starting heating, fixed post-heating and variable post-heating.

3 The variable pre-heating phase occurs when the ignition is switched on, and during this phase the pre-heating warning light is illuminated on the instrument panel. The period of pre-heating depends on the temperature of the coolant, battery voltage, and altitude. The maximum period of 15.5 seconds occurs if the coolant temperature is low, the battery voltage is less than 9.3 volts, and the altitude is higher than 2000 metres. The period varies from 15.5 seconds to zero seconds according to the temperature of the coolant, and when the temperature reaches 80°C, no pre-heating occurs.

4 The fixed pre-heating phase occurs immediately after the variable phase finishes, after the warning light has extinguished, and lasts for up to 8 seconds on F8Q 630/662 engines or 15 seconds on F8Q 632 engines. Normally, the driver will start the engine at some point during this phase.

5 During the period when the starter motor is in operation, the glow plugs are continuously supplied with current.

6 Fixed post-heating lasts for a period of 10 seconds after the engine has been started.

7 The variable post-heating phase occurs immediately after the fixed post-heating phase ends, and the period of post-heating depends on the temperature of the coolant, engine speed, and engine load which is determined by the load potentiometer on the injection pump lever. The maximum period of variable post-heating is 3 minutes, at which point the system is switched off. Variable post-heating will cease if the coolant

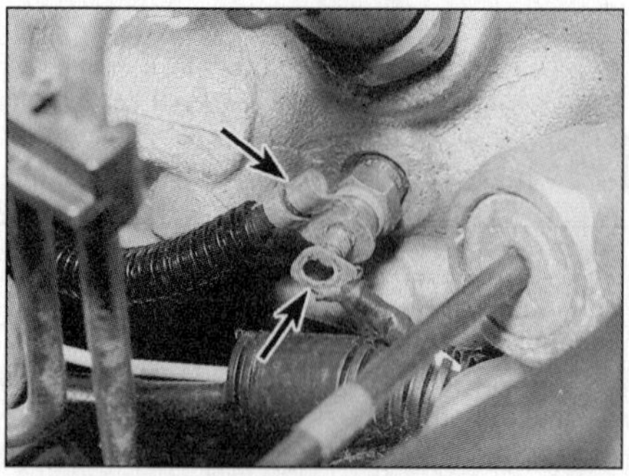
2.2 Disconnect the wiring (arrowed) from the glow plug terminal

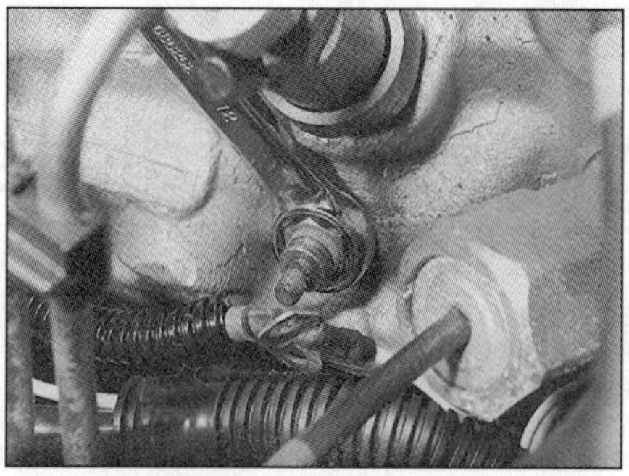
2.3a Unscrew the glow plug . . .

2.3b . . . and remove it from the cylinder head

temperature exceeds 60°C, if the full load occurs for more than 3 seconds, or if battery voltage is greater than 16 volts. It is reintroduced within the time limit of 3 minutes if the engine returns to idle speed or low load, or if the battery voltage is less than 15 volts.

8 If the coolant temperature sensor becomes faulty, the ECU uses the air temperature sensor to calculate the period of pre/post-heating.

Testing

9 If the system malfunctions, testing is best carried out by a Renault dealer using dedicated test equipment, however, some preliminary checks may be made as follows.

10 Connect a voltmeter or 12 volt test lamp between the glow plug supply cable and earth (engine or vehicle metal). Make sure that the live connection is kept clear of the engine and bodywork. Have an assistant switch on the ignition and check that voltage is applied to the glow plugs. Note the time for which the warning light is lit and the total time for which voltage is applied before the system cuts out, and compare to the times given in the description above.

11 If there is no supply at all, the relay, control unit or associated wiring is at fault.

12 To locate a defective glow plug, disconnect the main supply cable and the interconnecting wire or strap from the top of the glow plugs. Be careful not to drop the nuts and washers. Using an ohmmeter, check for continuity between each glow plug terminal and earth. The resistance of a glow plug in good condition is very low (less than 1 ohm), so if the test lamp does not light or the continuity tester shows a high resistance the glow plug is defective.

13 If an ammeter is available, the current draw of each glow plug can be checked. After an initial surge of around 15 to 20 amps, each plug should draw around 10 amps. Any plug which draws much more or less than 10 amps is probably defective.

14 As a final check, the glow plugs can be removed and inspected as described in Section 2.

15 If the pre/post-heating system is faulty, first check the wiring to each individual component. If this does not locate the fault, ideally each component should be replaced with known good units until the fault is located. If this is not possible, take the vehicle to a Renault dealer or diesel specialist who will have the diagnostic equipment necessary to pin-point the fault quickly.

Caution: If the radio/cassette in your vehicle is equipped with an anti-theft system, make sure you have the correct activation code before disconnecting the battery.

2 Glow plugs – removal, inspection and refitting

Removal

Caution: If the pre-heating system has just been energised, or if the engine has been running, the glow plugs may be very hot.

1 Disconnect the battery negative (earth) lead and position it away from the terminal (refer to *Disconnecting the battery* in the Reference Section).

2 Unscrew the nuts from the glow plug terminals, and recover the washers. Disconnect the wiring **(see illustration)**. Note that the main electrical feed wiring is connected to two of the plugs.

3 Unscrew the glow plugs and remove them from the cylinder head **(see illustrations)**.

Inspection

4 Inspect the glow plugs for physical damage. Burnt or eroded glow plug tips can be caused by a bad injector spray pattern. Have the injectors checked if this sort of damage is found.

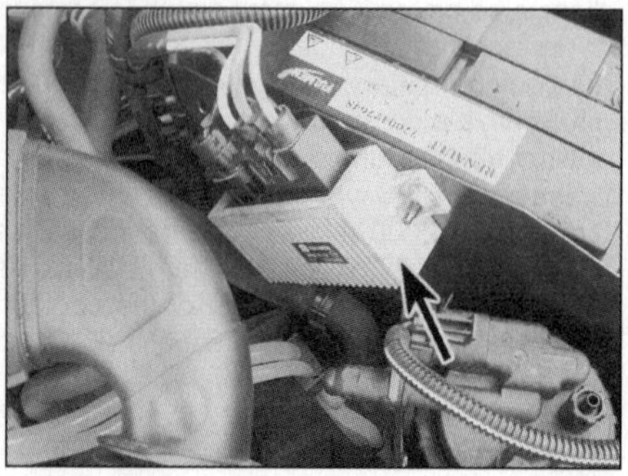
3.1 The pre/post-heating control unit

5 If the glow plugs are in good physical condition, check them electrically using a 12 volt test lamp or continuity tester with reference to the previous Section.

6 The glow plugs can be energised by applying 12 volts to them to verify that they heat up evenly and in the required time. Observe the following precautions:

a) Support the glow plug by clamping it carefully in a vice or self-locking pliers. Remember it will become red-hot.

b) Make sure that the power supply or test lead incorporates a fuse or overload trip to protect against damage from a short-circuit.

c) After testing, allow the glow plug to cool for several minutes before attempting to handle it.

7 A glow plug in good condition will start to glow red at the tip after drawing current for 5 seconds or so. Any plug which takes much longer to start glowing, or which starts glowing in the middle instead of at the tip, is defective.

Refitting

8 Refit by reversing the removal operations. Apply a smear of copper-based anti-seize compound to the plug threads and tighten the glow plugs to the specified torque. Do not overtighten, as this can damage the glow plug element.

3 Pre/post-heating system control unit – removal and refitting

Removal

1 The pre/post-heating control unit is located on a bracket next to the battery, on the left-hand side of the engine compartment **(see illustration)**. On models with the F8Q 632 engine, it is located on a bracket on the bulkhead. Before proceeding, make sure that the ignition is switched off.

2 Disconnect the wiring from the control unit.

3 Unscrew the mounting nuts/bolts and remove the control unit from the mounting bracket.

Refitting

4 Refitting is a reversal of removal.

4 Coolant temperature sensor - removal, testing, and refitting

Note: *Also refer to Chapter 3, Section 8.*

Removal

1 The coolant temperature sensor is located on the rear of the thermostat housing on the left-hand end of the cylinder head, below the brake vacuum pump.
2 Drain the cooling system as described in Chapter 1B. Alternatively, have the new sensor or a suitable bung to hand to quickly plug the hole and prevent liquid from being spilt while the sensor is being removed.
3 Disconnect the electrical connector, then unscrew the sensor. Recover the sealing ring.

Testing

Note: *A continuity tester or an ohmmeter will be required for testing.*
4 The sensor has two functions – the NTC (negative temperature coefficient) resistor informs the pre/post-heating control unit of the engine coolant temperature, and its switch interrupts the electrical supply to the EGR solenoid.
5 Connect a continuity tester or an ohmmeter to pins 1 and 4 of the sensor connector. There should be infinite resistance at room temperature, showing that the contacts of the thermoswitch are open.
6 Next suspend the sensor in a container of water (using string) so that it is immersed but not touching the sides or the base of the container. Dip a thermometer into the water, apply heat and then check that the contacts of the thermoswitch remain open up to 20°C but close at temperatures above 30°C. With the contacts closed, the ohmmeter must show zero resistance.
7 On all engines, connect an ohmmeter across the switch terminals 2 and 3. Heat the water and check that the resistance of the thermistor (coolant temperature sensor) is in accordance with the figures given in the Specifications.
8 If the results obtained are not as specified, the switch is proved faulty and should be renewed.

Refitting

9 Refitting is the reverse of removal, but fit a new sealing ring.
10 On completion, top up or refill and bleed the cooling system, as necessary, as described in Chapter 1B.

5 Fuel filter heating system - general information and component renewal

General information

1 The fuel filter is located in the left-hand front of the engine compartment. An electrically-operated heating element is fitted in the fuel filter housing, to prevent the fuel 'waxing' at low temperatures. The heater is controlled by an internal thermostat. When the fuel temperature is below 0°C, current to the heater warms the fuel in the filter housing and filter. When the fuel temperature reaches 8°C, current supply to the heater ceases.

Component renewal

Caution: Be careful not to allow dirt into the fuel system during the following procedures.

Fuel filter heating element

2 Remove the fuel filter as described in Chapter 1B.
3 Disconnect the wiring connector then unscrew the centre bolt and remove the heating element from the base of the fuel filter housing. Recover the sealing ring which is fitted between the element and filter housing and discard; a new one should be used on refitting.
4 On refitting, fit the new sealing ring to the groove in the heating element and refit the element to the filter housing, tightening the centre bolt securely.
5 Reconnect the wiring connector and fit the fuel filter as described in Chapter 1B.

Temperature switch

6 Disconnect the wiring connector from the temperature switch.
7 Wipe clean the area around the temperature switch and fuel filter housing. Position a container to catch any spilt fuel then slacken and remove the switch from the fuel filter housing. Recover the sealing washers which are fitted on each side of the fuel hose union and discard them; new ones must be used on refitting.
8 Refitting is the reverse of removal, positioning a new sealing washer on each side of the fuel hose union.

Chapter 6
Clutch

Contents

Degrees of difficulty

Easy, suitable for novice with little experience	**Fairly easy,** suitable for beginner with some experience	**Fairly difficult,** suitable for competent DIY mechanic	**Difficult,** suitable for experienced DIY mechanic	**Very difficult,** suitable for expert DIY or professional

Specifications

General

Clutch type	Single dry plate, diaphragm spring, cable-operated
Adjustment	Automatic
Engine codes:	
1.2 litre petrol engine	D7F
1.4 litre petrol engine:	
SOHC	E7J
DOHC	K4J
1.6 litre petrol engine:	
SOHC	K7M
DOHC	K4M
Diesel engine	F8Q

Clutch disc

Diameter:	
D7F and E7J engines	181.5 mm
All other engines	200.0 mm
Lining thickness (new, and in compressed position):	
D7F and E7J engines	6.7 mm
All other engines	6.8 mm
Number of springs	6

Torque wrench setting

	Nm	lbf ft
Clutch cover bolts	20	15

1 General information

All manual gearbox models are equipped with a cable-operated clutch. The unit consists of a steel cover which is dowelled and bolted to the rear face of the flywheel, and contains the pressure plate and diaphragm spring.

The clutch friction disc is free to slide along the gearbox splined input shaft. The disc is held in position between the flywheel and the pressure plate by the pressure of the diaphragm spring. Friction lining material is riveted to the disc, which has a spring-cushioned hub to absorb transmission shocks and help ensure a smooth take-up of the drive.

The clutch is actuated by a cable, controlled by the clutch pedal. The clutch release mechanism consists of a release arm and bearing which are in permanent contact with the fingers of the diaphragm spring.

Depressing the clutch pedal actuates the release arm by means of the cable. The arm pushes the release bearing against the diaphragm fingers, so moving the centre of the diaphragm spring inwards. As the centre of the spring is pushed in, the outside of the spring pivots out, so moving the pressure plate backwards and disengaging its grip on the friction disc.

When the pedal is released, the diaphragm spring forces the pressure plate into contact with the friction linings on the disc. The disc is now firmly sandwiched between the pressure plate and the flywheel, thus transmitting engine power to the gearbox.

Wear of the friction material on the disc is automatically compensated for by a self-adjusting mechanism. On early models, the mechanism consists of a serrated quadrant, a notched cam and a tension spring integrated into the top of the clutch pedal; on later models, the horizontal self-adjusting mechanism is separate, being attached to the clutch pedal by a short link. The mechanism functions as follows. One end of the clutch cable is attached to the quadrant, which is

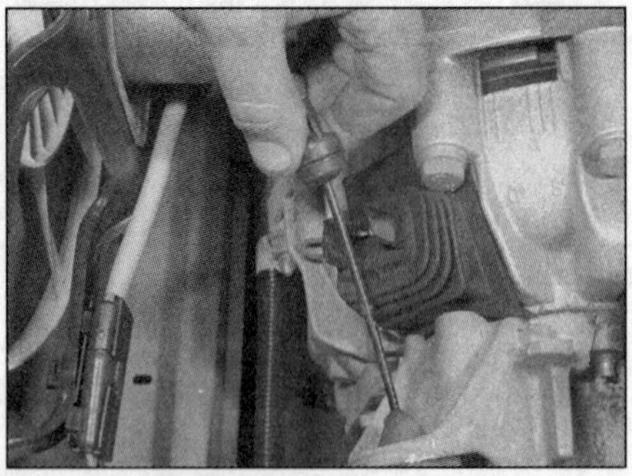
2.2a Disconnecting the clutch inner cable from the release fork

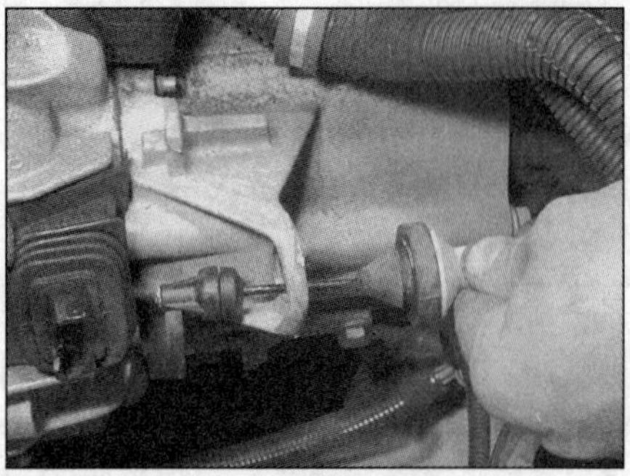
2.2b Withdrawing the clutch outer cable from the bracket on the bellhousing

2.3a Disconnecting the inner cable end from the quadrant (early type)

free to pivot, but is kept in tension by a spring. When the pedal is depressed, the notched cam contacts the quadrant, thus locking it and allowing the pedal to pull the cable and operate the clutch. When the pedal is released, the tension spring causes the notched cam to move free of the quadrant, and at the same time tension is maintained on the cable, keeping the release bearing in contact with the diaphragm spring. As the friction material on the disc wears, the self-adjusting quadrant will rotate when the pedal is released, and the pedal free play will be maintained between the notched cam and the quadrant.

2 Clutch cable – removal and refitting

Removal

1 In order to gain access to the clutch cable on the gearbox bellhousing, remove the air cleaner or air inlet ducting, according to model as described in Chapter 4A or 4B.

2 Disengage the inner cable from the release fork, then withdraw the outer cable from the bracket on the bellhousing **(see illustrations)**. ***Caution: Do not lift the release fork as it may become detached from the release bearing inside the bellhousing.***

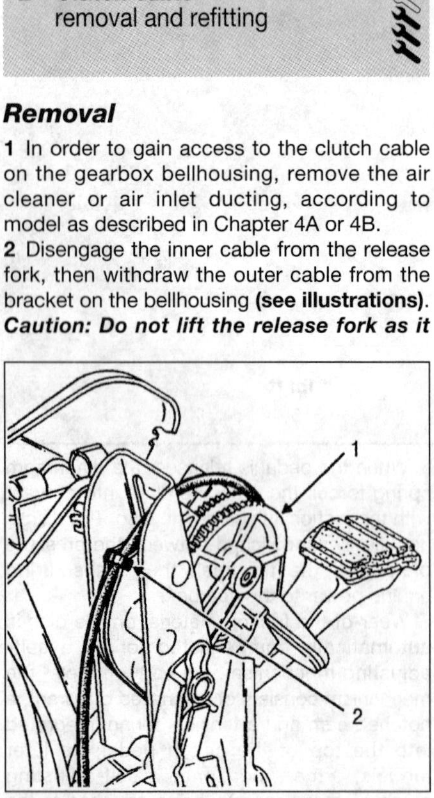

2.3b Clutch inner cable location on the self-adjusting quadrant (early type)

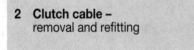

1 Quadrant 2 Guide

3 Working inside the car, remove the lower facia panel. Press the clutch pedal to the floor, then pull it up and free the inner cable end from the serrated quadrant on the self-adjusting mechanism. Where applicable, use a screwdriver to tap out the inner cable guide **(see illustrations)**.

4 With the inner cable released, push the outer cable out of its location in the bulkhead.

5 Pull the cable through into the engine compartment, detach it from the support clips and remove it from the car.

Refitting

6 To refit the cable, thread it through from the engine compartment, place it over the self-adjusting cam, and connect the inner cable end to the quadrant. Refit the inner cable guide where applicable.

7 Working in the engine compartment, slip the other end of the cable through the bellhousing bracket, and connect the inner cable to the release fork. Refit the cable to the support clips.

8 Depress the clutch pedal to draw the outer cable into its locating hole in the bulkhead, ensuring that it locates properly. At the same time, the inner cable guide (where fitted) will be automatically pulled onto the top of the pedal to hold the inner cable in position.

9 Depress the clutch pedal several times in order to allow the self-adjusting mechanism to set the correct free play.

10 When the self-adjusting mechanism on the clutch pedal is functioning correctly, there should be a minimum of 20 mm slack in the cable. To check this dimension, pull out the inner cable near the release fork on the gearbox **(see illustration)**. If there is less than the minimum slack in the cable, the self-adjusting quadrant should be checked for seizure or possible restricted movement.

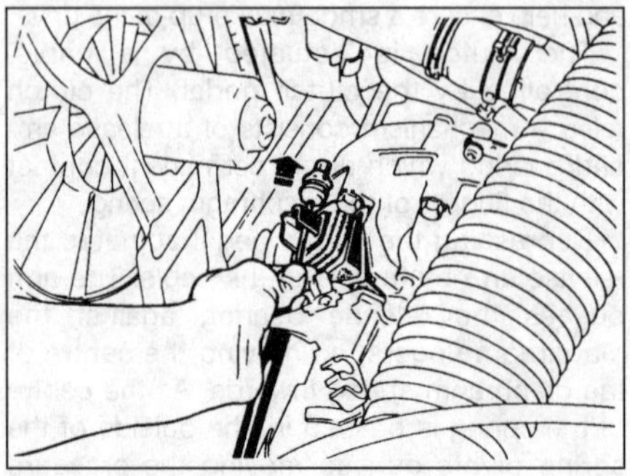
2.10 Checking the clutch inner cable slack at the release fork end

11 Depress the clutch pedal fully, and check that the total movement at the end of the release fork is as follows **(see illustration)**. This movement ensures that the clutch pedal stroke is correct. If not, make sure that the quadrant is free to turn, and that the spring has not lost its tension. If necessary, check the free length of the spring against a new one. Also check that the inner cable is not seizing in the outer cable.

12 Refit the lower facia panel, air cleaner and inlet ducting as applicable.

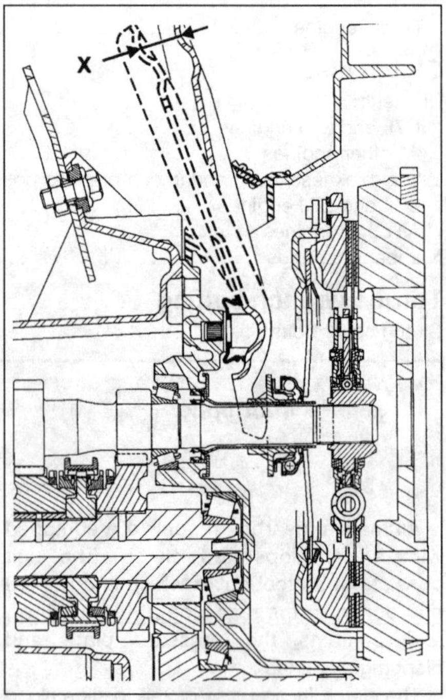

2.11 Checking the clutch release fork movement (X)

K4J and K4M engines: X = 27.0 to 31.6 mm
All other engines: X = 27.4 to 30.7 mm

3 Clutch pedal - removal and refitting

Models with integral adjusting mechanism

Removal

1 As applicable, remove the air cleaner or air inlet ducting as described in Chapter 4A or 4B, then disengage the inner cable from the release fork on the transmission.

Caution: Do not lift the release fork as it may become detached from the release bearing inside the bellhousing.

2 Working inside the car, remove the lower facia panel. Press the clutch pedal to the floor, then pull it up and free the inner cable end from the serrated quadrant on the self-adjusting mechanism **(see illustration)**. Use a screwdriver to tap out the inner cable guide.

3 Unscrew the nut from the end of the pedal pivot shaft.

4 Unscrew the bolts and remove the pedal support bracket **(see illustration)**.

5 Slide the pedal, complete with bushes and sleeve, off of the pedal pivot shaft **(see illustration)**.

6 With the pedal removed, unhook and remove the self-adjusting quadrant return spring. Note the fitted position of the self-adjusting components for correct refitting.

7 Remove the bushes and sleeve, then withdraw the self-adjusting quadrant assembly. Inspect these components and renew them if worn.

Refitting

8 Apply some multi-purpose grease to the bushes and sleeve, and to the bearing surfaces of the self-adjusting quadrant assembly and pedal shaft.

9 Locate the sleeve and plastic bushes in the clutch pedal. Reconnect the self-adjusting quadrant return spring.

10 Locate the pedal onto the pivot shaft and refit the support bracket, tightening the bolts securely.

11 Push the pedal shaft through from the right-hand side and refit the nut. Tighten the nut securely.

12 Refit the inner cable over the self-adjusting cam, and connect it to the quadrant. Refit the inner cable guide where applicable.

13 Working in the engine compartment, connect the inner cable to the release fork.

14 Depress the clutch pedal to draw the outer cable into its locating hole in the bulkhead, ensuring that it locates properly. At the same time, the inner cable guide (where fitted) will be automatically pulled onto the top of the pedal to hold the inner cable in position.

15 Depress the clutch pedal several times in order to allow the self-adjusting mechanism to set the correct free play.

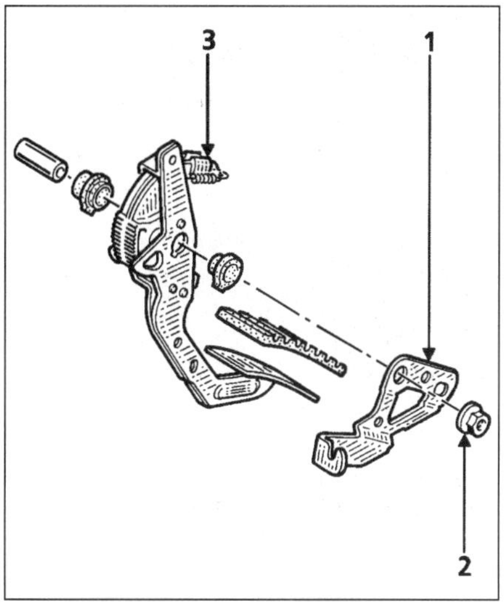

3.2 Clutch pedal components on early models

1 Clutch pedal support bracket
2 Pedal pivot shaft nut
3 Self-adjusting mechanism

16 Refit the lower facia panel, air cleaner and inlet ducting as applicable.

Models with separate adjusting mechanism

Removal

17 Working in the engine compartment, remove the air cleaner or air inlet ducting (as applicable) as described in Chapter 4A or 4B, then disengage the inner cable from the release fork on the transmission.

Caution: Do not lift the release fork as it may become detached from the release bearing inside the bellhousing.

18 Carefully prise the adjustment link bar from the top of the pedal using a screwdriver **(see illustration)**.

19 Unscrew and remove the pedal pivot bolt and withdraw the pedal.

Refitting

20 Apply some multi-purpose grease to the pedal pivot bush and upper link ball.

21 Locate the pedal on its bracket and insert the pivot bolt. Tighten the bolt securely.

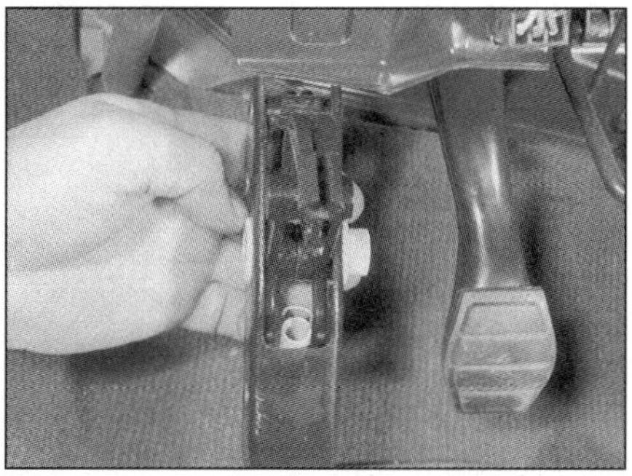

3.5 Removing the clutch pedal

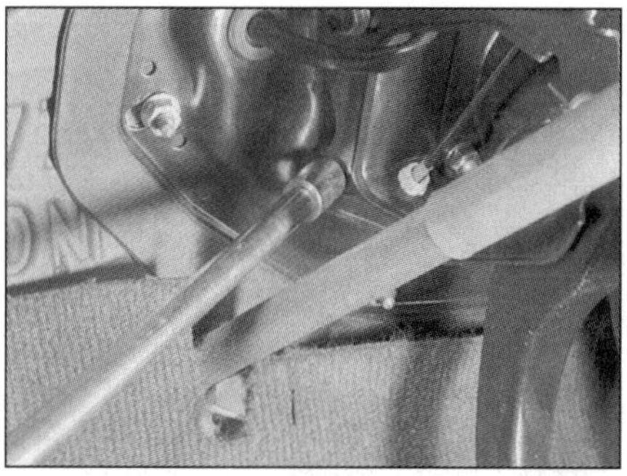

3.4 Removing the pedal shaft left-hand support bracket (right-hand drive shown)

22 Press the adjustment link bar onto the pedal upper ball.

23 If necessary, adjust the link bar so that the clutch pedal is the same height as the brake pedal. Tighten the lock nuts on completion.

4 Clutch cable adjusting mechanism - removal and refitting

Models with integral adjusting mechanism

1 The self-adjusting mechanism is integral with the clutch pedal. Refer to Section 3 for details.

Models with separate adjusting mechanism

Removal

2 Remove the clutch pedal as described in Section 3.

3 Working inside the car, remove the lower facia panel. Press the clutch pedal to the floor, then pull it up and free the inner cable

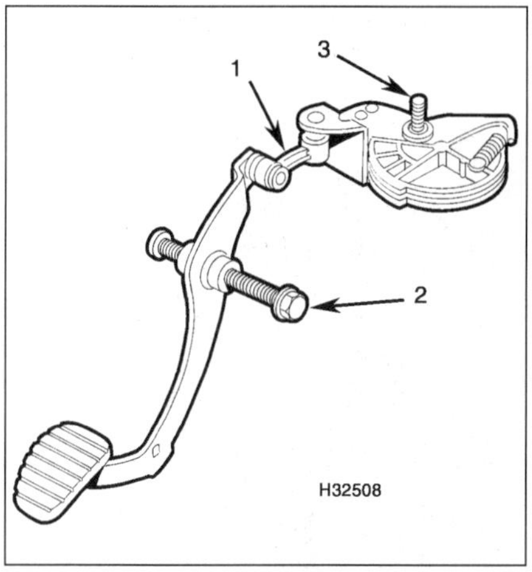

3.18 Clutch pedal components on later models

1 Link bar
2 Pedal pivot bolt
3 Self-adjusting mechanism retaining bolt

4.3a Self-adjusting mechanism showing return spring

4.3b Self-adjusting mechanism showing link

5.2 Mark the relationship of the clutch cover and flywheel before removing the pressure plate

end from the serrated quadrant on the self-adjusting mechanism **(see illustrations)**.

4 Unbolt and remove the adjusting mechanism.

Refitting

5 Refitting is a reversal of removal, but adjust the link bar so that the clutch pedal is the same height as the brake pedal. Tighten the lock nuts on completion.

5 Clutch assembly – removal, inspection and refitting

Warning: Dust created by clutch wear and deposited on the clutch components may contain asbestos which is a health hazard. DO NOT blow it out with compressed air or inhale any of it. DO NOT use petrol or petroleum-based solvents to clean off the dust. Brake system cleaner or methylated spirit should be used to flush the dust into a suitable receptacle. After the clutch components are wiped clean with rags, dispose of the contaminated rags and cleaner in a sealed, marked container.

Removal

1 Access to the clutch may be gained in one of two ways. Either the gearbox may be removed independently, as described in Chapter 7A, or the engine/gearbox unit may be removed as described in Chapter 2D, and the gearbox separated from the engine on the bench.

2 Having separated the gearbox from the engine, first use paint or a marker pen to mark the relationship of the clutch cover to the flywheel **(see illustration)**.

3 Unscrew and remove the clutch cover retaining bolts. Work in a diagonal sequence and slacken the bolts only a few turns at a time. Hold the flywheel stationary by positioning a screwdriver over the dowel on the cylinder block and engaging it with the starter ring gear **(see illustration)**.

4 Ease the pressure plate assembly off its locating dowels. Be prepared to catch the friction disc, which will drop out as the assembly is removed. Note which way round the disc is fitted.

Inspection

5 With the clutch assembly removed, clean off all traces of asbestos dust using a dry cloth. This is best done outside or in a well-ventilated area (refer to the warning at the beginning of this Section).

6 Examine the linings of the friction disc for wear or loose rivets, and the disc rim for distortion, cracks, broken torsion springs and worn splines **(see illustration)**. The surface of the friction linings may be highly glazed, but as long as the friction material pattern can be clearly seen, this is satisfactory. If there is any sign of oil contamination, indicated by shiny black discoloration, the disc must be renewed and the source of the contamination traced and rectified. This will be a leaking crankshaft oil seal, gearbox input shaft oil seal, or both. The renewal procedure for the crankshaft oil seal is given in the relevant part of Chapter 2. Renewal of the gearbox input shaft oil seal should be entrusted to a Renault garage, as it involves dismantling the gearbox and the renewal of the clutch release bearing guide tube using a press. The disc must also be renewed if the linings have worn down to, or just above, the level of the rivet heads.

7 Check the machined faces of the flywheel and pressure plate. If either is grooved, or heavily scored, renewal is necessary. The

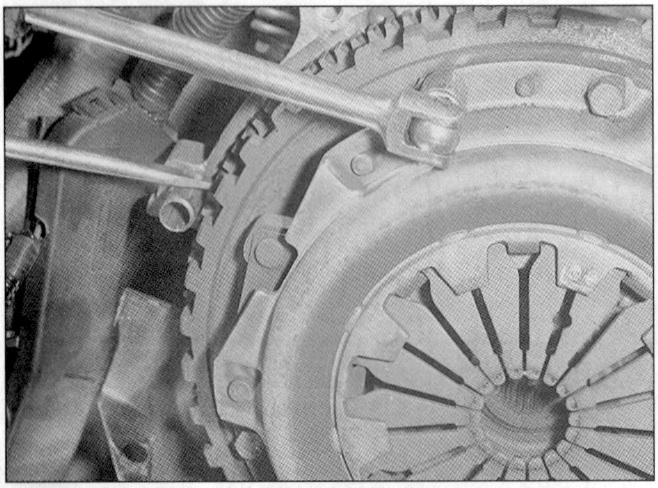

5.3 Unscrewing the clutch cover retaining bolts, showing a screwdriver engaged with the starter ring gear

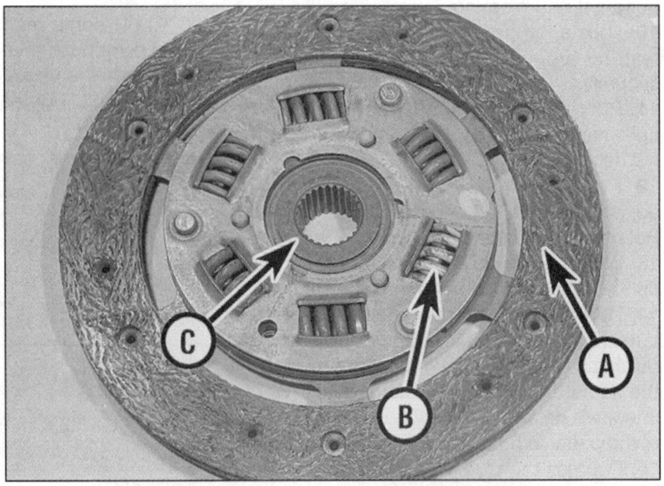

5.6 Inspect the friction disc linings (A), springs (B) and splines (C)

5.7a Check the machined face of the pressure plate (arrowed) . . .

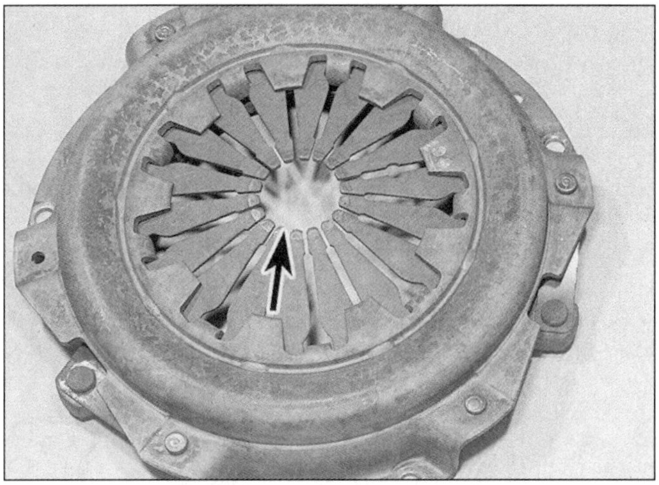

5.7b . . . and the diaphragm spring, paying particular attention to the tips (arrowed)

pressure plate must also be renewed if any cracks are apparent, or if the diaphragm spring is damaged or its pressure suspect **(see illustrations)**.

8 Take the opportunity to check the condition of the release bearing, as described in Section 6.

9 It is good practice to renew the friction disc, pressure plate and release bearing as an assembly.

Refitting

10 Before commencing the refitting procedure, apply a little high-melting-point grease to the splines of the gearbox input shaft. Distribute the grease by sliding the friction disc on and off the splines a few times. Remove the disc and wipe away any excess grease. Also smear a little grease to the guide tube on the gearbox.

11 It is important that no oil or grease is allowed to come into contact with the friction material of the friction disc or the pressure plate and flywheel faces. It is advisable to refit the clutch assembly with clean hands, and to wipe the pressure plate and flywheel faces with a clean dry rag before assembly begins.

12 Begin reassembly by placing the friction disc against the flywheel, with the side having the larger offset facing away from the flywheel **(see illustration)**.

13 Place the clutch cover assembly over the dowels, and where applicable, align it with the previously made mark. Refit the retaining bolts and tighten them finger-tight so that the friction disc is gripped, but can still be moved.

14 The friction disc must now be centralised so that, when the engine and gearbox are reconnected, the splines of the gearbox input shaft will pass through the splines in the centre of the friction disc hub. If this is not done accurately, it will be impossible to refit the gearbox.

15 Centralisation can be carried out quite easily by inserting a round bar through the hole in the centre of the friction disc, so that the end of the bar rests in the hole in the end of the crankshaft. Note that a plastic centralising tube is supplied with Renault clutch kits, making the use of a bar unnecessary.

16 If a bar is being used, move it sideways or up and down until the friction disc is centralised. Centralisation can be judged by removing the bar and viewing the disc hub in relation to the bore in the end of the crankshaft. When the bore appears exactly in the centre of the disc hub, all is correct.

17 If a non-Renault clutch is being fitted, an alternative and more accurate method of centralisation is to use a commercially-available clutch aligning tool obtainable from most accessory shops **(see illustration)**.

18 Once the friction disc is centralised, progressively tighten the cover bolts in a diagonal sequence to the correct torque setting **(see illustration)**. Remove the centralising tool.

19 The gearbox can now be refitted to the engine with reference to Chapter 7A or 2D as applicable.

6 Clutch release bearing - removal, inspection and refitting

Removal

1 Access to the clutch release bearing may be gained in one of two ways. Either the

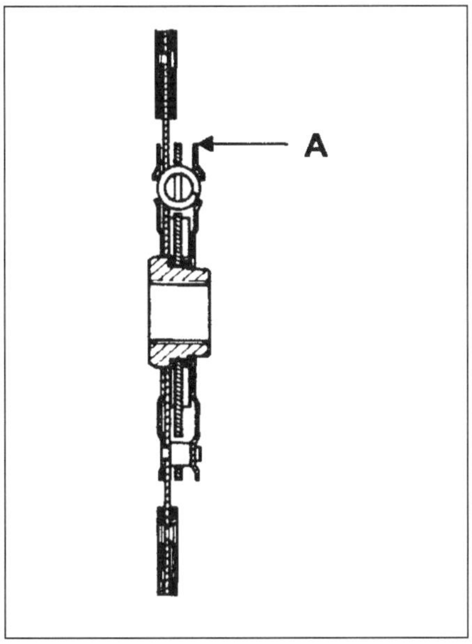

5.12 Clutch friction disc offset (A) faces away from flywheel

5.17 Using a clutch alignment tool to centralise the friction disc

5.18 Tightening the clutch cover bolts

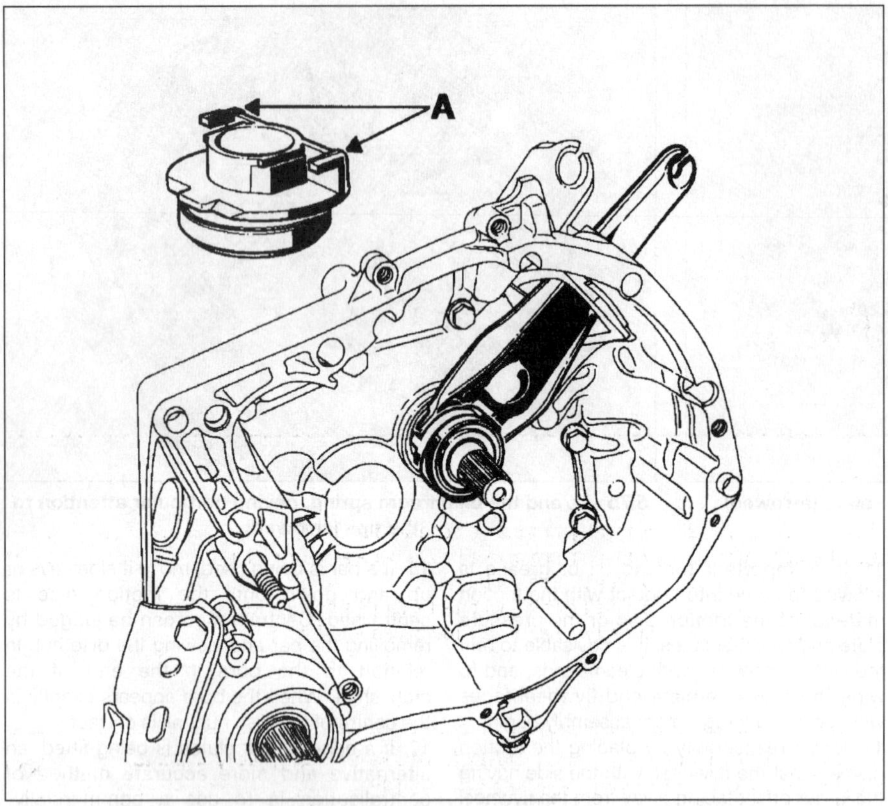

6.5 Clutch release components. Clip (A) on bearing carrier must engage with release fork

gearbox may be removed independently, as described in Chapter 7A, or the engine/gearbox unit may be removed as described in Chapter 2D, and the gearbox separated from the engine on the bench.

2 Having separated the gearbox from the engine, tilt the release fork and slide the bearing assembly off the gearbox input shaft guide tube. Note how the fork locates in the release bearing.

3 To remove the release fork, disengage the rubber cover and then pull the fork off its pivot ball stud.

Inspection

4 Check the bearing for smoothness of operation. Renew it if there is any roughness or harshness as the bearing is spun. It is good practice to renew the bearing as a matter of course during clutch overhaul, regardless of its apparent condition.

Refitting

5 Refitting the release fork and release bearing is a reversal of the removal procedure, but note the following points.

a) *Lubricate the release fork pivot ball stud, the release bearing-to-diaphragm spring contact areas and the guide tube sparingly with molybdenum disulphide grease.*

b) *Ensure that the release fork engages correctly with the lugs on the bearing* ***(see illustration).***

Chapter 7 Part A: Manual gearbox

Contents

Degrees of difficulty

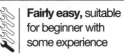

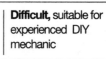

Easy, suitable for novice with little experience	**Fairly easy,** suitable for beginner with some experience	**Fairly difficult,** suitable for competent DIY mechanic	**Difficult,** suitable for experienced DIY mechanic	**Very difficult,** suitable for expert DIY or professional

Specifications

General

Type	Five forward speeds (all synchromesh) and reverse. Final drive differential integral with main gearbox
Engine codes:	
1.2 litre petrol engine	D7F
1.4 litre petrol engine:	
SOHC	E7J
DOHC	K4J
1.6 litre petrol engine:	
SOHC	K7M
DOHC	K4M
Diesel engine	F8Q

Designation

K4M engines	JB3
All other engines	JB1

Gear ratios

1st	3.4 : 1
2nd	1.9 : 1
3rd	1.3 : 1
4th	1.0 : 1
5th	0.8 : 1
Reverse	3.6 : 1
Final drive	4.1 : 1

Torque wrench settings	Nm	lbf ft
Engine to gearbox tie bar	65	48
Gearbox bellhousing to engine	45	33
Rear engine mounting to gearbox	See relevant part of Chapter 2	
Starter motor mounting bolt	45	33

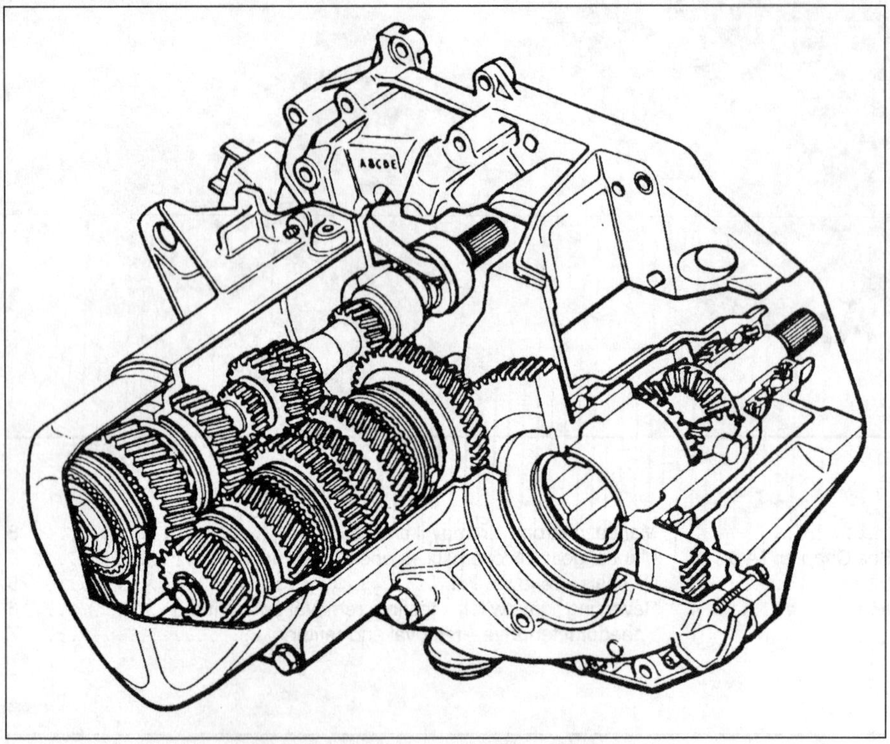

1.1a Cutaway view of the gearbox

1 General information

The gearbox is equipped with five forward gears, one reverse gear and a final drive differential, incorporated in one casing bolted to the left-hand end of the engine. The gearbox type code is stamped on an identification plate attached to the top of the gearbox **(see illustrations)**.

Drive is transmitted from the crankshaft via the clutch to the input shaft which rotates in sealed ball-bearings, and has a splined extension to accept the clutch friction disc. From the input shaft, drive is transmitted to the output shaft, which rotates in a roller bearing at its right-hand end, and a sealed ball-bearing at its left-hand end. From the output shaft, drive is transmitted to the differential crownwheel, which rotates with the differential case and planetary gears, thus driving the side gears and driveshafts. The rotation of the planetary gears on their shaft allows the inner roadwheel to rotate at a slower speed than the outer roadwheel when the car is cornering.

The input and output shafts are arranged side by side, parallel to the crankshaft and driveshafts, so that their gear pinion teeth are in constant mesh. In the neutral position, the output shaft gear pinions rotate freely, so that drive cannot be transmitted to the crownwheel. Synchromesh is provided on all forward speeds. Gear selection is via a floor-mounted lever and rod mechanism.

The gearbox selector rod causes the appropriate selector fork to move its respective synchro-sleeve along the shaft, in order to lock the gear pinion to the synchro-hub. Since the synchro-hubs are splined to

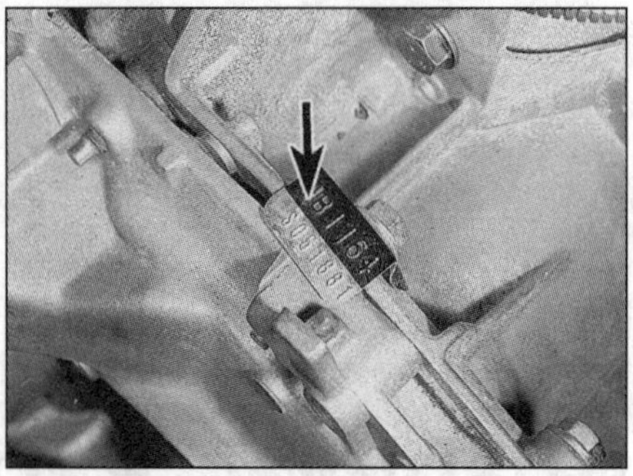

1.1b The identification number starts with the gearbox type code

the output shaft, this locks the pinion to the shaft, so that drive can be transmitted. To ensure that gearchanging can be made quickly and quietly, a synchromesh system is fitted to all forward gears, consisting of baulk rings and spring-loaded fingers, as well as the gear pinions and synchro-hubs. The synchromesh cones are formed on the mating faces of the baulk rings and gear pinions.

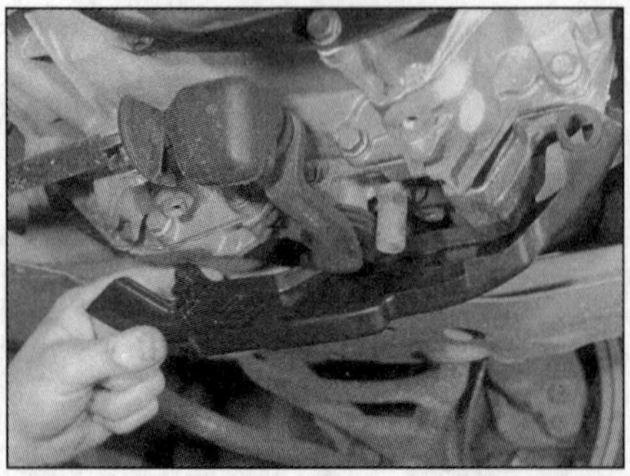

2.2 Removing the plastic cover from the bottom of the gearbox

2.3 Oil filler plug on the front of the gearbox

2 Gearbox oil – draining and refilling

Note: *The filler plug is also used as the level plug.*

1 This operation is much quicker and more efficient if the car is first taken on a journey of sufficient length to warm the engine/gearbox up to operating temperature.

2 Park the car on level ground, switch off the ignition and apply the handbrake firmly. For improved access, jack up the front of the car and support it securely on axle stands (see *Jacking and vehicle support*), or alternatively position the vehicle over an inspection pit or on car ramps. Remove the engine compartment undertray or the small cover from the bottom of the gearbox (as applicable) **(see illustration)**. Note that, to ensure accuracy, the car must be level when checking the oil level.

3 Remove all traces of dirt from around the drain and filler plugs, then unscrew the filler/level plug from the front face of the gearbox **(see illustration)**.

4 Position a suitable container under the gearbox, then unscrew the drain plug and allow the oil to drain completely into the container **(see illustrations)**. If the oil is hot, take precautions against scalding. Clean both the filler/level and the drain plugs, being especially careful to wipe any metallic particles off the magnetic inserts. The sealing washers should be renewed whenever they are disturbed.

5 When the oil has finished draining, clean the drain plug threads and those of the gearbox casing, and refit the drain plug, tightening it securely.

2.4a Unscrew the drain plug . . .

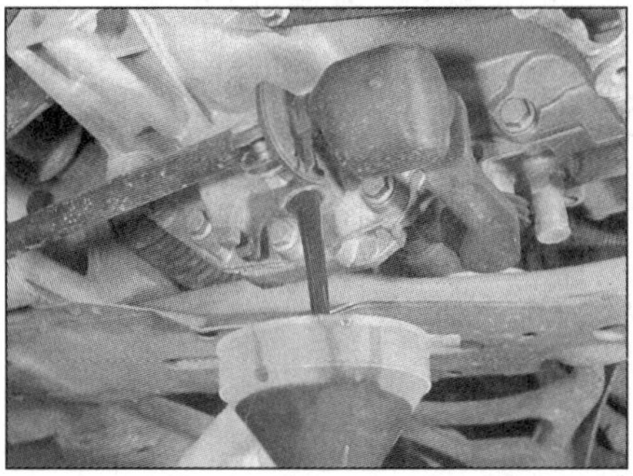

2.4b . . . and drain the oil

6 Refilling the gearbox is an extremely awkward operation. Above all, allow plenty of time for the oil level to settle properly before checking it. Note that the car must be level when checking the oil level.
7 Refill the gearbox with the exact amount of the specified type of oil, then check the oil level as described in Chapter 1A or 1B. When the level is correct, refit the filler level plug with a new sealing washer and tighten securely.
8 Refit the plastic cover to the gearbox or the engine undertray (as applicable), then lower the vehicle to the ground.

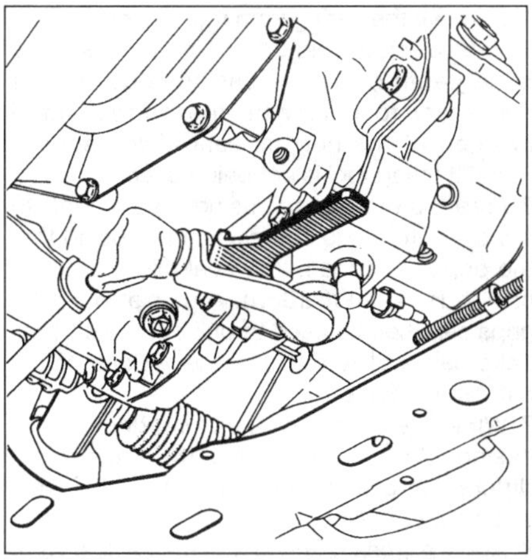

3.3b Using the Renault tool B.Vi. 1133 to hold the gearchange lever in position

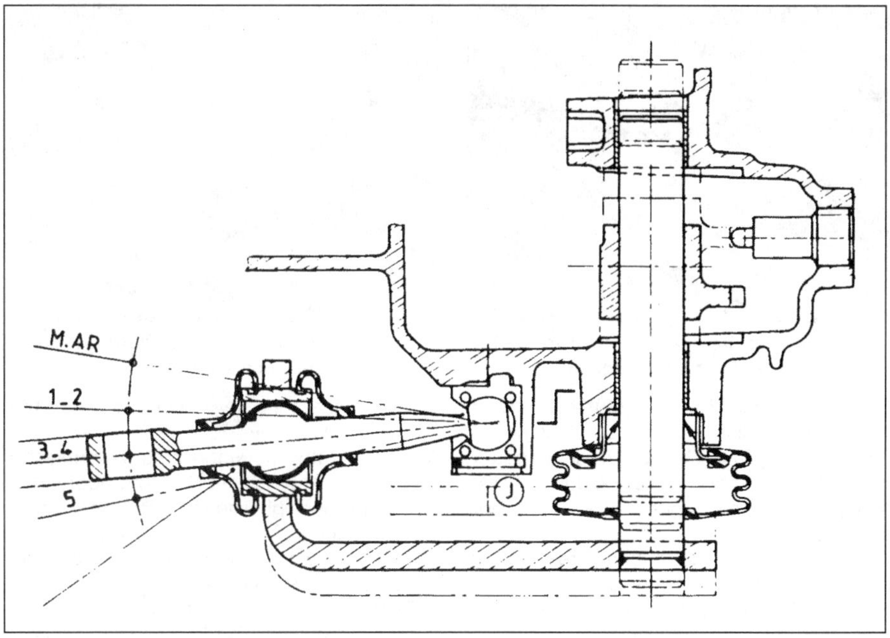

3.3a Gear positions for the gearbox lever

3 Gearchange mechanism - adjustment

Note: *A special Renault service tool (B.Vi. 1133) will be required to accurately adjust the gearchange linkage.*

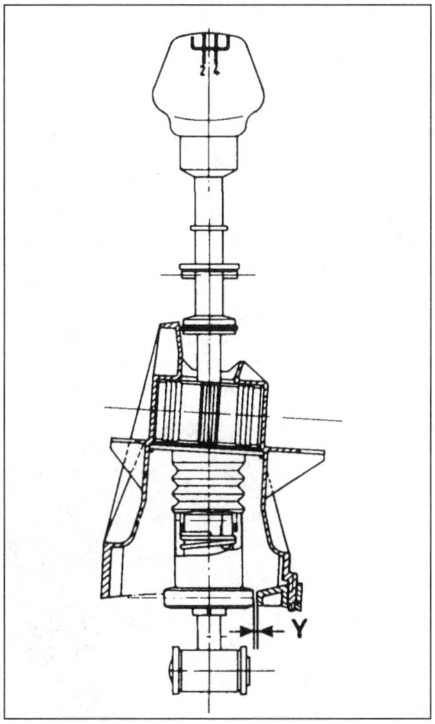

3.4 The clearance (Y) between the gear lever and housing should be between 7.0 and 10.0 mm

1 Firmly apply the handbrake, then jack up the front of the vehicle and support it securely on axle stands (see *Jacking and vehicle support*). As applicable, remove the engine compartment undertray or unclip the small cover from the bottom of the gearbox.
2 Unbolt the heat shields from the underbody to gain access to the bottom of the gear lever.
3 Select 1st gear at the gearbox by moving the lever to the appropriate position. To hold the lever securely in position, fit the Renault tool B.Vi. 1133 as shown **(see illustrations)**. In the absence of the special tool, a suitable alternative can be made from a flat metal bar or a piece of wood.
4 Using a feeler gauge, check that the clearance between the reverse stop-ring on the gear lever and the inclined plane on the right-hand side of the gear lever housing is between 7.0 and 10.0 mm **(see illustration)**.
5 If adjustment is necessary, loosen the clamp bolt at the gearbox end of the gearchange rod so that the rod can be moved **(see illustration)**.

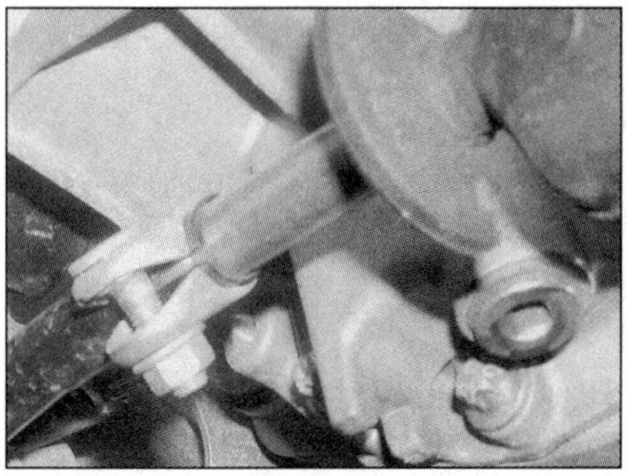

3.5 Adjustment clamp at the gearbox end of the gearchange rod

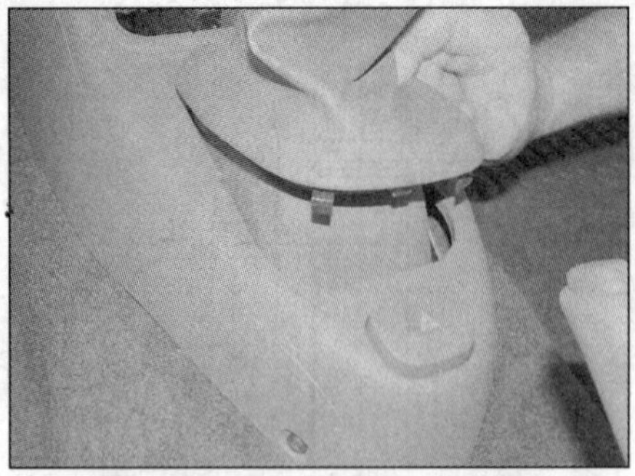

4.1 Removing the gearchange lever gaiter from the centre console

4.8a Pull back the rubber boot on the gearchange rod . . .

6 Move the gear lever so that the reverse stop-ring is against the inclined plane on the housing, then insert a 9.0 mm feeler gauge between the ring and plane. Hold the lever in this position, then tighten the clamp bolt securely.
7 Remove the holding tool, then recheck the clearance as described in paragraph 4.
8 Check that all gears can be selected, then refit the heat shields, plastic cover or undertray before lowering the vehicle to the ground.

4 Gearchange mechanism – removal and refitting

Removal

1 Working inside the vehicle, carefully prise the gearchange lever gaiter out of the centre console **(see illustration)**. Pull the knob off the top of the gearchange lever and remove it with the gaiter.
2 Firmly apply the handbrake, then jack up the front of the vehicle and support it on axle stands (see *Jacking and vehicle support*). As applicable, remove the engine compartment undertray or unclip the small cover from the bottom of the gearbox.
3 Unbolt and remove the exhaust heat shields for access to the bottom of the gear lever. If necessary, unscrew the clamp bolt and separate the exhaust system, then support the exhaust on an axle stand.
4 Unscrew the nut, then remove the washer and disconnect the gearchange rod from the bottom of the gear lever.
5 Unscrew the mounting nuts securing the gear lever base assembly to the floor, then lower the assembly and remove it from under the car. If the exhaust is still in position, it will be necessary to push it to one side while removing the gear lever assembly.
6 Remove the frame from the base.
7 Mount the gear lever in a soft-jawed vice, then extract the circlip and separate the base and gaiter.
8 To remove the gearchange rod, release the rubber gaiter and unscrew the bolt at the front of the rod. Note the location of the bush and spacer **(see illustrations)**. Remove the rod from the gearbox.
9 To separate the gearchange clevis, first mark it in relation to the main rod, then loosen the clamp bolt and separate the two sections.
10 Examine all components for signs of wear or damage, and renew as necessary.

Refitting

11 Lubricate all the pivot points with multi-purpose grease.
12 Where the gearchange rod has been dismantled, locate the clevis on the rod in its previously-noted position, and tighten the clamp bolt securely. Where new components are being fitted, locate the clevis on the rod so that approximately 7.0 to 8.0 mm of the knurled section is visible. Make sure that the clevis is offset towards the gearbox.
13 Attach the clevis to the gearchange lever and refit the bolt making sure that the bush and spacer are in their correct positions. Tighten the bolt to the specified torque.
14 Reassemble the gear lever components using a reversal of the removal procedure. Make sure the circlip is secure.
15 Lift the gear lever assembly into position in the floor aperture, then locate the frame and refit the mounting nuts. Tighten the nuts securely.
16 Connect the gearchange rod to the bottom of the gear lever, making sure that the bushes are correctly located and that the nut is positioned on the left-hand side. Refit the washer, then tighten the nut securely.
17 Check and adjust the gearchange with reference to Section 3.
18 Refit the heat shields, plastic cover and undertray, and exhaust system components as applicable, then lower the car to the ground.
19 Refit the gaiter and gear lever knob to the centre console. The knob should be bonded to the lever using suitable adhesive.

4.8b . . . unscrew and remove the bolt . . .

4.8c . . . and recover the bush from inside the lever

5 Oil seals – renewal

Right-hand driveshaft oil seal

Note: *New driveshaft-to-differential side gear roll pins may be required on refitting (see Chapter 8).*
1 Apply the handbrake, then jack up the front of the car and support it on axle stands (see *Jacking and vehicle support*). Remove the right-hand wheel.
2 Drain the gearbox oil as described in Section 2.
3 Referring to Chapter 8, disconnect the driveshaft from the gearbox. Note that it is not necessary to remove the driveshaft completely, the shaft can be left attached to the hub assembly and slid off from the differential gear splines as the hub assembly is pulled outwards. **Note:** *Do not allow it to hang down under its own weight, as this could damage the constant velocity joints/gaiters.*
4 Remove the O-ring from the side gear shaft.
5 Wipe clean the old oil seal, and measure its fitted depth below the casing edge. This is necessary to determine the correct fitted position of the new oil seal, if the special Renault fitting tool is not being used.
6 Free the old oil seal, using a small drift to tap the outer edge of the seal inwards so that the opposite edge of the seal tilts out of the casing **(see illustration)**. A pair of pliers or grips can then be used to pull out the oil seal. Take care not to damage the splines of the differential side gear.
7 Wipe clean the oil seal seating in the casing. Wrap tape around the end of the differential gear splines to prevent the new seal being damaged.
8 Apply a smear of grease to the sealing lip of the new oil seal and, making sure its sealing lip is facing inwards, carefully slide it onto the

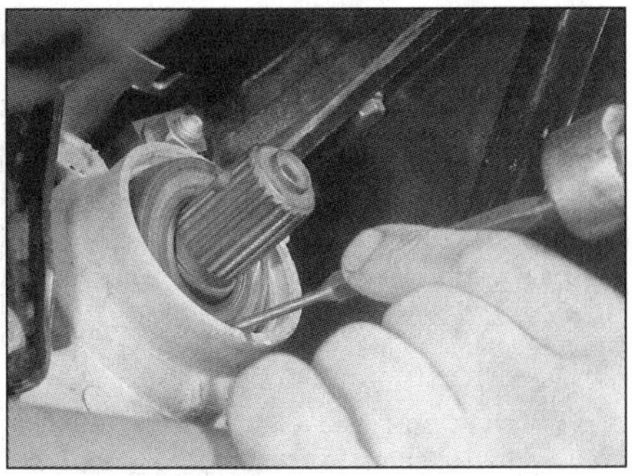
5.6 Tap the bottom of the driveshaft oil seal with a small drift to remove it

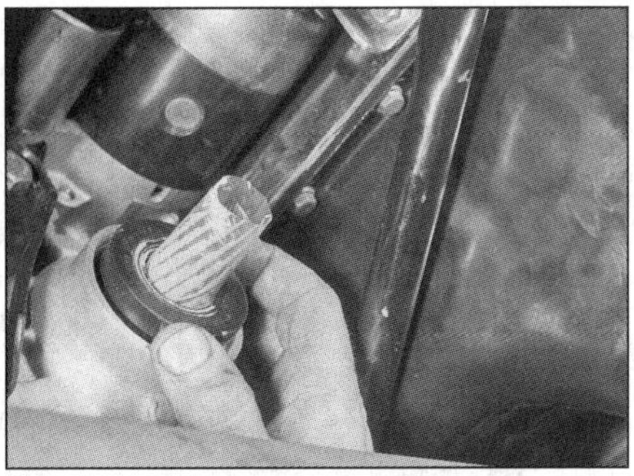
5.8a Locate the new oil seal carefully over the output shaft splines . . .

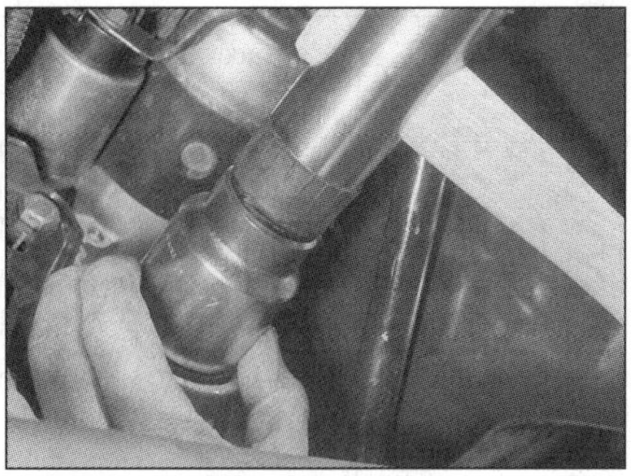
5.8b . . . and press into position with a socket or metal tube

differential gear shaft. Press the seal squarely into the gearbox until it is positioned at the same depth as the original was prior to removal. If necessary, the seal can be tapped into position using a piece of metal tube or a socket which bears only on the hard outer edge of the seal **(see illustrations)**.

9 Remove the tape from the end of the differential shaft, and slide a new O-ring into position.

10 Reconnect the driveshaft to the gearbox as described in Chapter 8.

11 Refill the gearbox with oil as described in Section 2.

12 Refit the roadwheel and lower the car to the ground. Tighten the wheel bolts to the specified torque (Chapter 1A or 1B).

Left-hand driveshaft oil seal

13 On the left-hand side of the gearbox, there is no oil seal as the seal is formed by the driveshaft gaiter. If oil is leaking from the left-hand driveshaft-to-gearbox joint, renew the gaiter as described in Chapter 8.

Input shaft oil seal

14 It is not possible to renew the input shaft oil seal without first dismantling the gearbox. The guide tube assembly is a press-fit in the housing, and is removed inwards. Oil seal renewal should therefore be entrusted to a Renault dealer or gearbox overhaul specialist.

6 Reversing light switch – testing, removal and refitting

Testing

1 The reversing light circuit is controlled by a plunger-type switch that is screwed into the left-hand side of the gearbox casing, next to the driveshaft inner joint. If a fault develops in the circuit, first ensure that the circuit fuse has not blown.

2 To test the switch, disconnect the wiring connector, and use a multimeter (set to the resistance function) or a battery-and-bulb test circuit to check that there is continuity between the switch terminals only when reverse gear is selected. If this is not the case, and there are no obvious breaks or other damage to the wires, the switch is faulty, and must be renewed.

Removal

3 Firmly apply the handbrake, then jack up the front of the vehicle and support it on axle stands (see *Jacking and vehicle support*).

4 Where fitted, remove the engine compartment undertray.

5 Disconnect the wiring, then unscrew the switch from the gearbox. Recover the sealing washer.

Refitting

6 Fit a new sealing washer to the switch, then screw it back into the gearbox casing and tighten it securely. Reconnect the wiring, and test the operation of the circuit. Where fitted, refit the engine compartment undertray, then lower the vehicle to the ground. If any oil was lost when the switch was removed, check the oil level as described in Chapter 1A or 1B.

7 Speedometer drive – removal and refitting

Note: *The speedometer drive is taken from the right-hand side of the gearbox, just above the driveshaft. On some later models, it is not possible to remove the drive – this later type can be identified by the plastic cable connection to the gearbox instead of the clip-type connection on earlier models.*

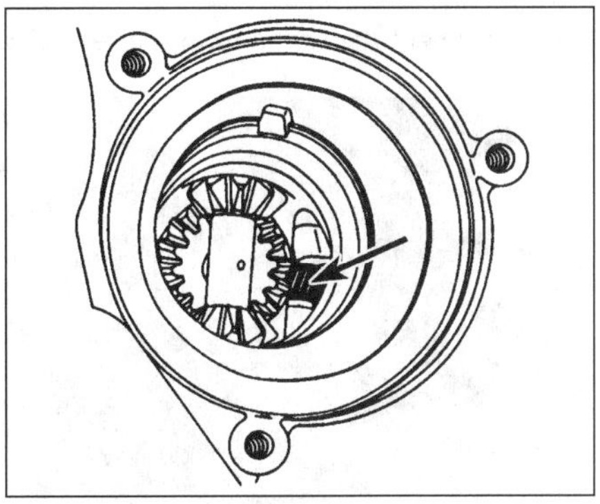
7.3 View of the speedometer drivegear (arrowed) with the differential side gear removed

Removal

1 Disconnect the left-hand driveshaft at the gearbox end – refer to Chapter 8. Note that it is not necessary to remove the driveshaft completely; the shaft can be left attached to the hub assembly and slid off from the differential gear splines as the hub assembly is pulled outwards. **Note:** *Do not allow it to hang down under its own weight, as this could damage the constant velocity joints/gaiters.*

2 Extract the circlip and thrustwasher, then withdraw the left-hand side gear from the differential. The side gear also acts as the driveshaft spider housing.

3 Turn the differential until the planetary gears are in a vertical plane so that the speedometer drivegear is visible **(see illustration)**.

4 Pull out the clip and disconnect the vehicle speed sensor from the outside of the gearbox **(see illustration)**.

5 Using long-nosed pliers from the outside of the gearbox, extract the speedometer drivegear shaft vertically.

6 Using the same pliers, extract the speedometer drivegear from inside the differential housing, being very careful not to drop it.

7 Examine the drivegear teeth for wear and damage. Renew it if necessary. Note that if the drivegear teeth on the differential are worn or damaged, it will be necessary to dismantle the gearbox – this work should be entrusted to a Renault dealer.

Refitting

8 Using long-nosed pliers, insert the speedometer drivegear into its location.

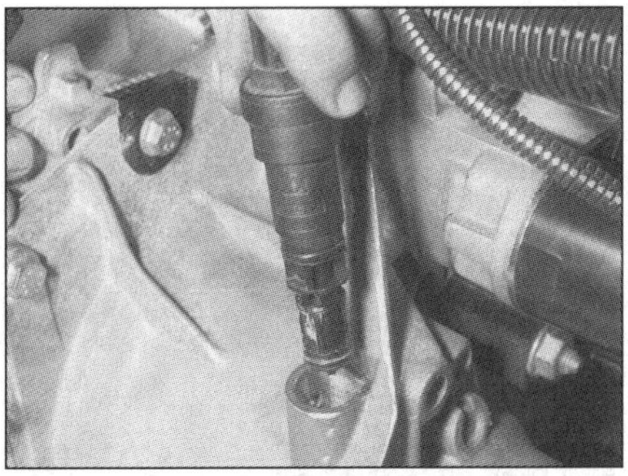
7.4 Removing the vehicle speed sensor from the gearbox

7.9 Notches in the speedometer drivegear engage with the shaft

8.11a Unscrew the lower front nut . . .

8.11b . . . and upper bolts securing the gearbox to the engine, noting the location of the wiring harness bracket

9 From outside the gearbox, refit the drivegear shaft. Make sure that it engages correctly with the gear location notches **(see illustration)**.

10 Refit the vehicle speed sensor and secure with its clip.

11 Insert the differential side gear, then refit the thrustwasher and circlip.

12 Reconnect the left-hand driveshaft with reference to Chapter 8.

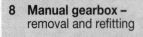

8 Manual gearbox – removal and refitting

Note: *This Section describes the removal of the gearbox, leaving the engine in position in the car. Alternatively, the engine and gearbox can be removed together, as described in Chapter 2D, then separated on the bench. New right-hand driveshaft-to-differential side gear roll pins may be required on refitting, and suitable sealant will be required to seal the ends of the roll pins.*

Removal

1 Apply the handbrake, then jack up the front of the vehicle and support it on axle stands (see *Jacking and vehicle support*). As applicable, remove the engine compartment undertray or unclip the small cover from the bottom of the gearbox. Remove both front roadwheels.

2 Remove the battery as described in Chapter 5A.

3 On petrol engine models, disconnect the wiring from the engine management ECU with reference to Chapter 4A.

4 On diesel engine models, disconnect the wiring from the post/pre-heating control unit and the fuel filter.

5 Disconnect the wiring from the impact sensor. Tie the wiring to one side.

6 Remove the inlet air duct leading to the air cleaner.

7 Unbolt and remove the battery shield plate.

8 Disconnect the clutch cable and position it to one side with reference to Chapter 6.

9 Unscrew the mounting bolts and remove the TDC sensor from the top of the gearbox bellhousing. Position the sensor to one side.

10 Unbolt the earth cables from the gearbox casing.

11 Unscrew the gearbox-to-engine bolts but leave one upper bolt finger-tight until just before the gearbox is removed. Also unscrew and remove the front lower nut securing the gearbox to the engine, noting the location of the wiring harness support **(see illustration)**.

12 Remove the right-hand driveshaft as described in Chapter 8.

13 Remove the left-hand driveshaft together with the hub carrier with reference to Chapters 8 and 10. There is no need to separate the driveshaft from the hub carrier.

14 Unbolt and remove the subframe-to-inner wing panel brace from the left-hand side.

15 Remove the starter motor as described in Chapter 5A.

16 Disconnect the wiring from the reversing light switch and from the speedometer sensor.

17 Remove the exhaust front downpipe as described in Chapter 4A or 4B.

18 Remove the gearchange mechanism control rod from the gear lever and gearbox with reference to Section 4.

19 Unscrew the nut securing the gearbox to the rear of the cylinder block. The nut is located above the right-hand gearbox output shaft **(see illustration)**.

20 Unscrew the engine rear mounting bolt securing the mounting to the rear of the gearbox. Swivel the mounting link away from the gearbox **(see illustration)**.

21 Where applicable, unbolt the engine-to-gearbox tie rod bracket from the gearbox flange.

22 Unbolt the steering gear from the subframe with reference to Chapter 10. To improve access, temporarily wedge a block of wood between the rear of the engine and the bulkhead to tilt the engine forward.

23 Attach a suitable hoist to the engine and take its weight.

24 Remove the left-hand engine mounting complete with brackets with reference to Chapter 2A, 2B or 2C.

25 Lower the engine and gearbox as far as possible without straining the coolant hoses.

26 Support the front suspension subframe with a trolley jack and length of wood, then unscrew the mounting bolts and lower the subframe to the ground.

27 Support the gearbox with a trolley jack,

8.11c Gearbox-to-engine upper mounting bolts

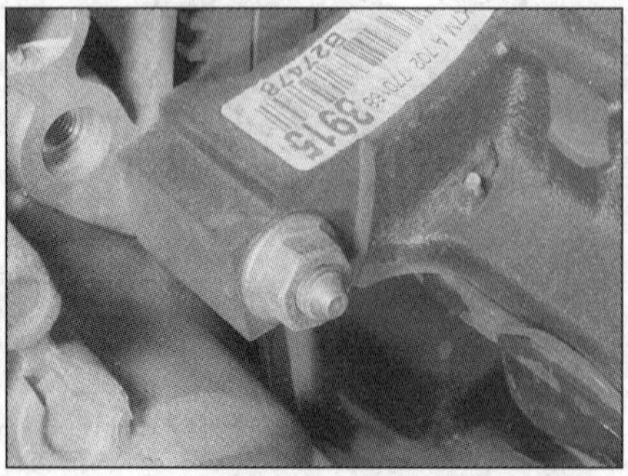

8.19 Gearbox-to-engine lower rear mounting nut

8.20 Rear mounting link swivelled downwards

then remove the final engine-to-gearbox bolt and, with the help of an assistant, withdraw the gearbox from the engine. Do not allow the gearbox to hang on the input shaft and keep the gearbox in line with the engine until the input shaft has cleared the clutch.

Refitting

28 Refitting is a reversal of removal, noting the following additional points.

a) *Before assembling the gearbox to the engine, make sure that the release fork is correctly engaged with the release bearing. To ensure the fork remains engaged, tie it to the gearbox bellhousing.*
b) *Make sure that the location dowels are correctly positioned in the gearbox.*
c) *Apply a little high-melting-point grease to the splines of the gearbox input shaft. Do not apply too much, otherwise there is the possibility of the grease contaminating the clutch friction disc.*
d) *Make sure that the locating dowel for the starter motor is correctly fitted.*
e) *Use new roll pins, where applicable, when reconnecting the right-hand driveshaft, and seal the ends using a suitable sealant.*
f) *Check the gearbox oil level with reference to Chapter 1A or 1B.*
g) *Tighten all nuts and bolts to the specified torque.*

9 Manual gearbox overhaul – general information

Overhauling a manual gearbox is a difficult and involved job for the DIY home mechanic. In addition to dismantling and reassembling many small parts, clearances must be precisely measured and, if necessary, changed by selecting shims and spacers. Gearbox internal components are also often difficult to obtain, and in many instances, extremely expensive. Because of this, if the gearbox develops a fault or becomes noisy, the best course of action is to have the unit overhauled by a specialist repairer, or to obtain an exchange reconditioned unit.

Nevertheless, it is not impossible for the more experienced mechanic to overhaul a gearbox, provided the special tools are available and the job is done in a deliberate step-by-step manner so that nothing is overlooked.

The tools necessary for an overhaul include internal and external circlip pliers, bearing pullers, a slide-hammer, a set of pin punches, a dial test indicator, and possibly a hydraulic press. In addition, a large, sturdy workbench and a vice will be required.

During dismantling of the gearbox, make careful notes of how each component is fitted, to make reassembly easier and more accurate.

Before dismantling the gearbox, it will help if you have some idea what area is malfunctioning. Certain problems can be closely related to specific areas in the gearbox, which can make component examination and replacement easier. Refer to the *Fault finding* Section at the end of this manual for more information.

Chapter 7 Part B:
Automatic transmission

Contents

Degrees of difficulty

Easy, suitable for novice with little experience	**Fairly easy,** suitable for beginner with some experience	**Fairly difficult,** suitable for competent DIY mechanic	**Difficult,** suitable for experienced DIY mechanic	**Very difficult,** suitable for expert DIY or professional

Specifications

General

Type	Electrically-controlled with four forward speeds and reverse. Final drive differential integral with transmission

Designation

All models	DP0

Ratios

1st	2.73 : 1
2nd	1.50 : 1
3rd	1.00 : 1
4th	0.71 : 1
Reverse	2.46 : 1
Final drive	3.04 : 1

Torque wrench settings	Nm	lbf ft
Drain plug	25	18
Driveplate-to-torque converter nuts	30	22
Engine-to-transmission bolts/nuts	45	33
Fluid cooler bolt	50	37
Modular connector mounting plate bolts	20	15
Multi-function switch mounting bolts	10	7
Topping-up overflow	35	26

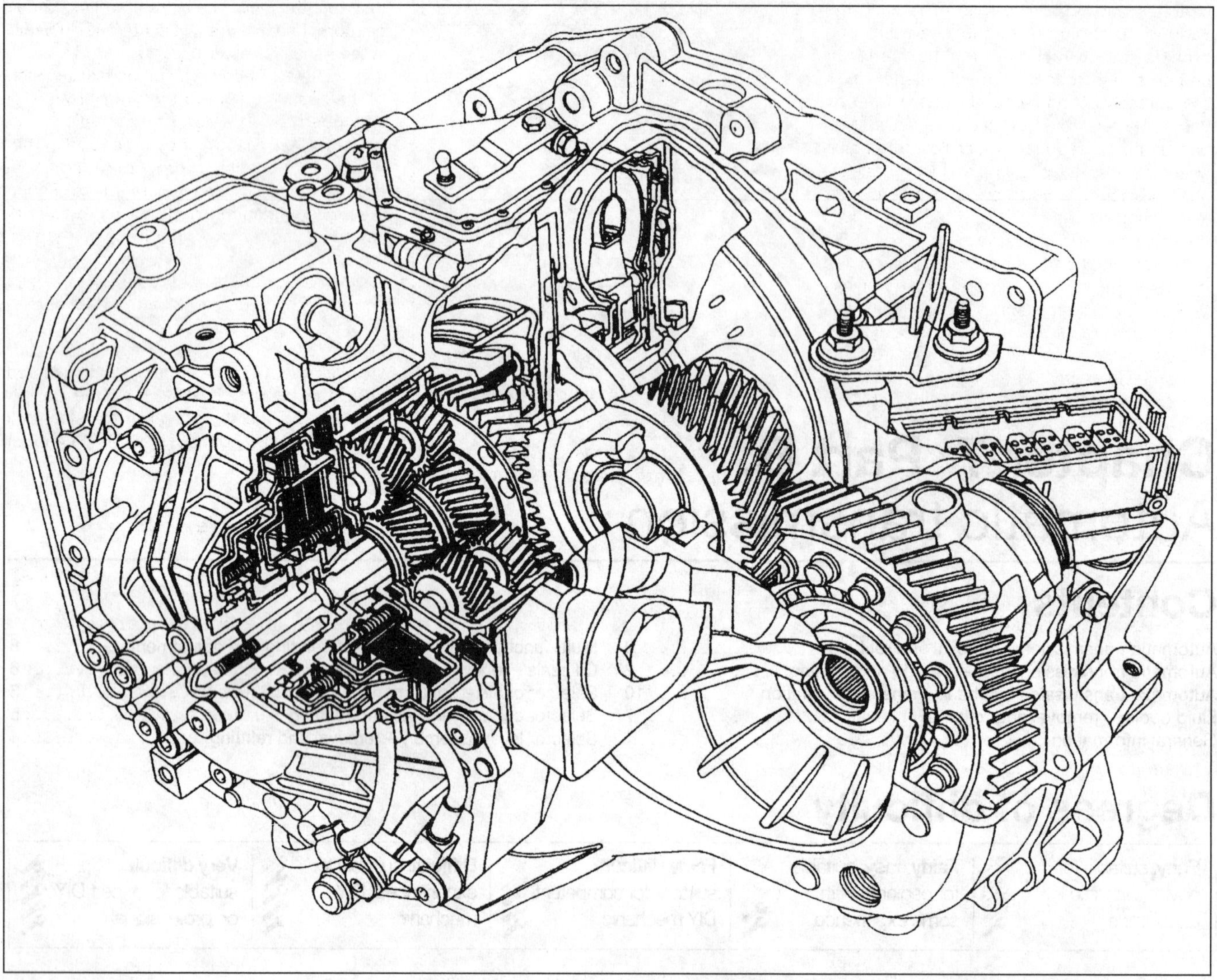

1.1 Cutaway view of the DP0 transmission unit

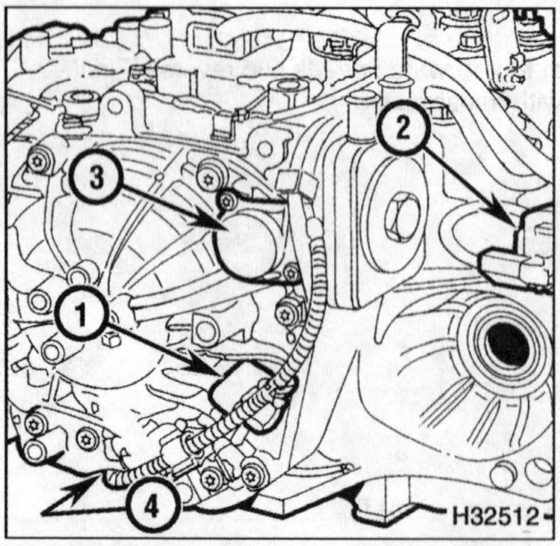

1.2 Sensor locations on the automatic transmission

1 *Input speed sensor*
2 *Output speed sensor*
3 *Fluid cooler flow control solenoid*
4 *Line pressure sensor*

1 General information

Automatic transmission models are fitted with the fully automatic four-speed, electronically controlled DP0-type transmission **(see illustration)**.

The transmission consists of a torque converter, an epicyclic geartrain, hydraulically-operated clutches and brakes, and an electronic control unit incorporated into the engine management ECU. Sensors fitted to the transmission include an input speed sensor, output speed sensor, fluid cooler flow control solenoid valve and a line pressure sensor **(see illustration)**.

The torque converter provides a fluid coupling between the engine and transmission, and acts as an automatic clutch, also providing a degree of torque multiplication when accelerating. The torque converter incorporates a lock-up function whereby the engine and transmission can be directly coupled by means of a small clutch unit inside the torque converter. The lock-up function is controlled by the ECU according to vehicle operating conditions.

The epicyclic geartrain provides the forward gears or reverse gear, depending on which of its component parts are held stationary or allowed to turn. The components of the geartrain are held or released by brakes and clutches which are activated by a hydraulic control unit. A fluid pump within the transmission provides the necessary hydraulic pressure to operate the brakes and clutches.

Impulses from switches and sensors connected to the transmission throttle and selector linkages are directed to the ECU computer module, which determines the ratio to be selected from the information received. The computer activates solenoid valves, which in turn open or close ducts within the hydraulic control unit. This causes the clutches and brakes to hold or release the various components of the geartrain, and provide the correct ratio for the particular engine speed or load. The information from the computer module can be overridden by use of the selector lever, and a particular gear can be held if required, regardless of engine speed. The selector lever also incorporates a shift-lock feature, which prevents the selector lever being moved from the P position unless the brake pedal is depressed.

The automatic transmission fluid is cooled by passing it through a cooler located on the top of the transmission. Coolant from the cooling system passes through the cooler.

Due to the complexity of the automatic transmission, any repair or overhaul work must be left to a Renault dealer with the necessary special equipment for fault diagnosis and repair. The contents of the following Sections are therefore confined to supplying general information, and any service information and instructions that can be used by the owner.

2 Automatic transmission fluid - draining and refilling

Note: *The transmission is a 'sealed-for-life' unit and fluid renewal is not required. The following procedure should only be necessary if there is any reason to believe that the fluid may be contaminated, or if repair work requiring the fluid to be drained is to be carried out. The transmission fluid filling and level checking procedure is particularly complicated, and the home mechanic would be well-advised to take the vehicle to a Renault dealer for the draining and refilling work carried out. To ensure accuracy, special test equipment is necessary to measure the fluid temperature when carrying out the level check. However, the following procedure is given for those who have access to this equipment.*

Draining

1 Take the vehicle on a short run, to warm the transmission up to normal operating temperature.

2 Park the car on level ground, then switch off the ignition and apply the handbrake firmly. Jack up the front of the car and support it securely on axle stands (see *Jacking and vehicle support*). Note that, when refilling and checking the fluid level, the car must be level to ensure accuracy.

3 Remove the engine compartment undertray.

4 Position a suitable container under the transmission. Unscrew the transmission drain plug and allow the fluid to drain completely into the container. Note that the drain plug and level checking plug are incorporated into one unit – the drain plug is the larger of the two hexagonal headed plugs forming the draining/level checking unit **(see illustrations)**.

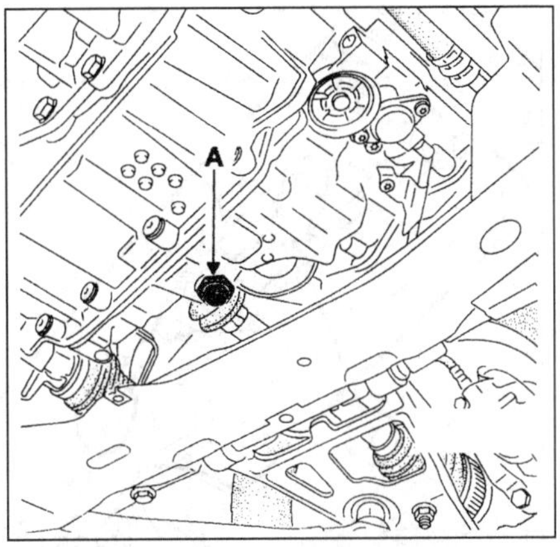

2.4a Combined drain plug and level checking plug unit (A)

Warning: If the fluid is hot, take precautions against scalding.

5 When the fluid has finished draining, clean the drain plug threads and those of the transmission casing. Fit a new sealing washer to the drain plug, and refit the plug to the transmission, tightening it securely.

Refilling

6 Refer to Chapter 4A and remove the air inlet duct from the engine compartment for access to the transmission filler plug. Unscrew the filler plug from the top of the transmission **(see illustration)**. Add 3.5 litres of the specified fluid to the transmission via the filler plug opening, using a clean funnel with a fine-mesh filter, then refit the plug.

7 Connect the Renault XR25 test meter to the diagnostic socket, and enter D14 then #04. With the selector lever in Park, run the engine at idle speed until the fluid temperature, as shown on the test meter, reaches 60° ± 1.0°C.

8 With the engine still running, unscrew the level plug from the centre of the draining/level checking unit. Allow the excess fluid to run out into a calibrated container drop-by-drop, then refit the plug. The amount of fluid should be more than 0.1 litre; if it is not, the fluid level in the transmission is incorrect.

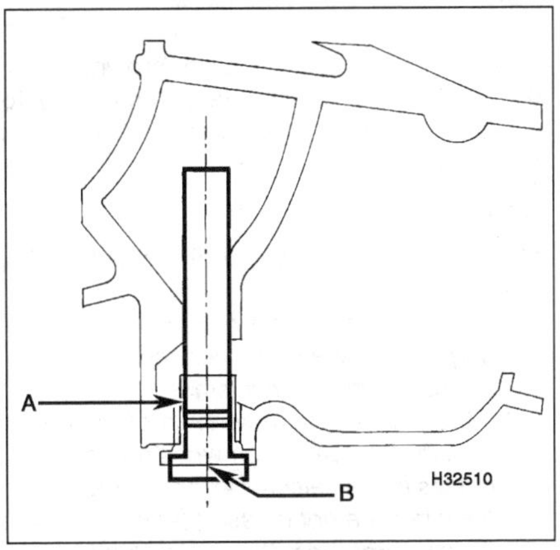

2.4b Cross-section of the combined drain/level plug unit

A Drain plug
B Level (overflow) plug

9 If the level is incorrect, add an extra 0.5 litre of the specified fluid to the transmission, as described in paragraph 6. Allow the transmission to cool down to 50°C, then repeat the checking procedure again as described in the previous paragraphs. Repeat the procedure as required until more than the specified amount of fluid is drained as described in the previous paragraphs, indicating that the transmission fluid level is correct, then securely tighten the level plug. Refit the engine undertray and the air cleaner duct.

10 With the XR25 test meter still connected, enter the command G74* then the date to reset the oil ageing counter in the electronic control unit. Disconnect the test meter on completion.

3 Selector cable - adjustment

1 Move the selector lever inside the car to the N position.

2 Disconnect the selector cable end fitting from the multi-function switch on top of the transmission. To improve access to the cable, remove the air cleaner inlet duct as described in Chapter 4A.

3 Check that the multi-function switch is in the N position, and if necessary set it accordingly.

4 Depress the tab on the side of the cable end fitting and suitably retain it in the released position.

5 Reconnect the selector cable to the multi-function switch then release the tab on the end fitting to lock the cable. Refit the air cleaner inlet duct as described in Chapter 4A.

6 Check that the selector lever moves freely, and that the starter motor will only operate with P or N selected. Also check that the Park function operates correctly.

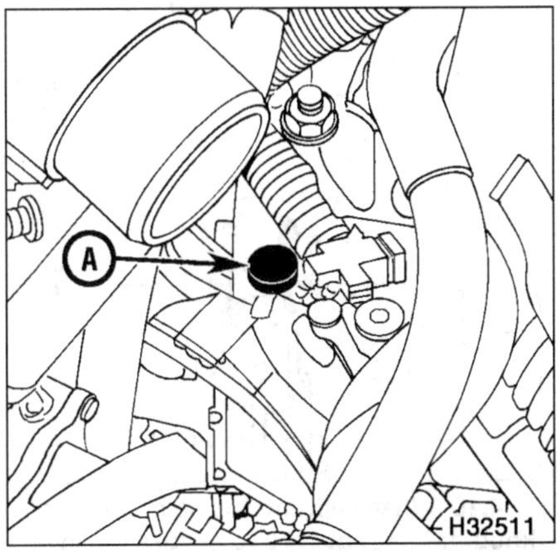

2.6 Transmission fluid filler plug (A)

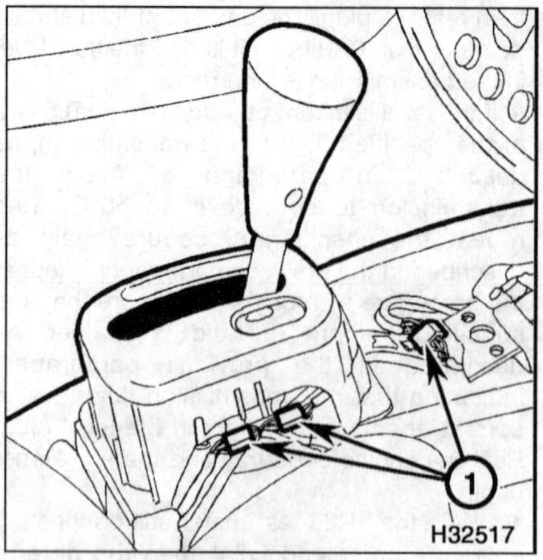

4.4 Wiring connectors (1) on the selector lever assembly

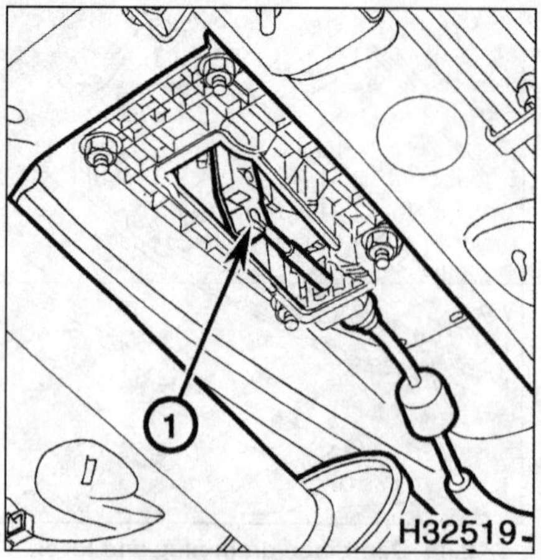

4.7a Selector cable end fitting (1) on the bottom of the selector lever

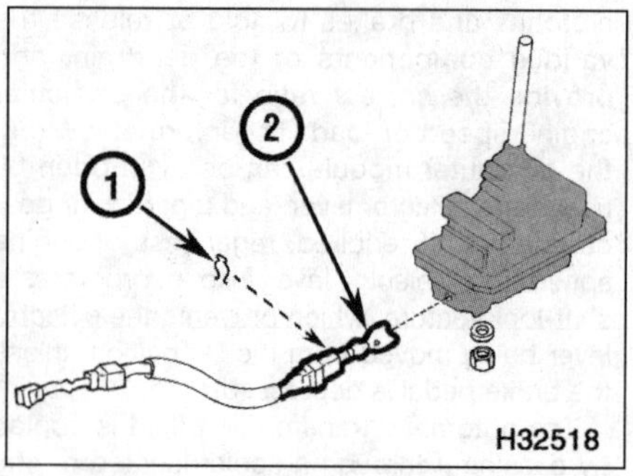

4.7b Selector cable retaining clip (1) and inner cable end fitting (2)

4 Selector lever assembly – removal and refitting

Removal

1 Apply the handbrake, then jack up the front of the vehicle and support it on axle stands (see *Jacking and vehicle support*).

2 Disconnect the battery negative (earth) lead and position it away from the terminal (refer to *Disconnecting the battery* in the Reference Section).

3 Remove the centre console as described in Chapter 11.

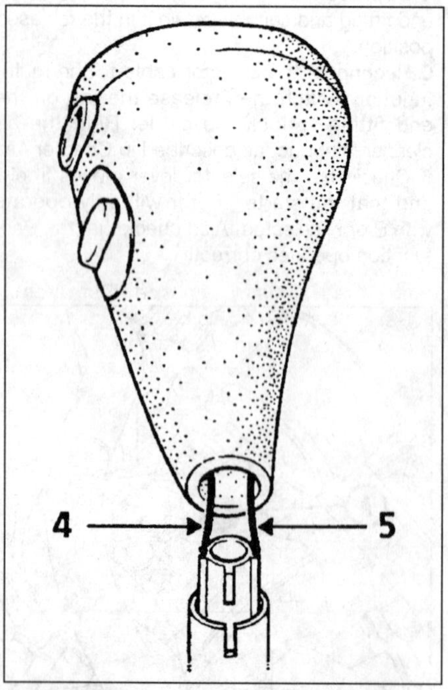

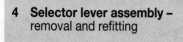

4.10 When refitting the selector lever knob, take great care to ensure the switch wires (4 and 5) are not crossed and are correctly routed down the lever guides

4 Disconnect the wiring from the selector lever assembly. There are two connectors under the right-hand side of the assembly, and one connector located just in front of the assembly **(see illustration)**.

5 Working under the vehicle, unclip the exhaust downpipe from its mounting, then unbolt the heat shields from the underbody for access beneath the selector assembly.

6 Remove the protector plate, then unscrew and remove the four mounting nuts securing the assembly to the floor. Recover the spacers.

7 Release the cable end fitting from its balljoint on the bottom of the lever, then prise out the clip and remove the outer cable from the assembly. Withdraw the assembly from under the vehicle **(see illustrations)**.

8 If necessary, the knob may be removed from the lever. To do this, undo the screw securing the knob to the lever and lift the knob to access the two wires. Identify the location of each wire, then disconnect them from the connector so that the knob may be removed separate. The wire locations are as follows.

Track	Colour
A1	Black
A2	Black
B1	White
B2	Light brown

9 Examine the selector lever assembly for signs of wear or damage and renew if necessary.

Refitting

10 Refitting is the reverse of removal, noting the following points.

a) *Prior to refitting, apply a smear of multi-purpose grease to the surfaces of the selector lever mechanism.*

b) *If the knob was removed, carefully feed the sport mode switch wires down the guides in the selector lever making sure the wires are not crossed* ***(see illustration).*** *Seat the control knob in position and tighten its retaining screw. Crimp new wiring connectors onto the ends of the switch wires and locate the connectors in the connector.*

c) *On completion check the operation of the selector lever and, if necessary, adjust the cable as described in Section 3.*

5 Selector cable – removal and refitting

Removal

1 Remove the selector lever assembly as described in Section 4.

2 Working in the engine compartment, remove the air cleaner inlet duct with reference to Chapter 4A.

3 Disconnect the selector cable end fitting from the multi-function switch on top of the transmission. Release the outer cable from the support bracket by turning the two locking rings in opposite directions. **Do not** move the orange ring as the locking rings are released. Note that if the orange ring breaks during removal, this will not adversely affect the operation of the cable and is not grounds for cable renewal.

4 Release the selector cable from all relevant retaining clips and withdraw it from under the vehicle.

5 Examine the cable for worn end fittings or a damaged outer casing, and for signs of fraying of the inner wire. The cable inner wire should move smoothly and easily through the outer casing. If the adjuster mechanism is thought to be faulty the cable must be renewed.

Refitting

6 Refitting is a reversal of removal, but adjust the cable as described in Section 3.

6 Oil seals – renewal

Differential oil seals

1 Disconnect the battery negative cable (refer to *Disconnecting the battery* in the Reference Section of this manual).

2 Apply the handbrake, then jack up the front

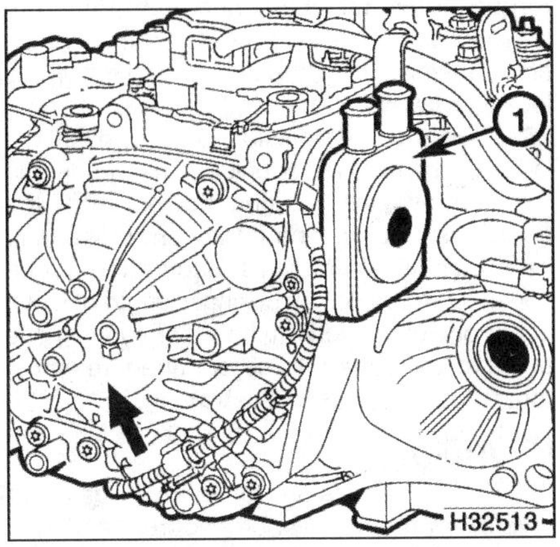

7.1 The fluid cooler (1) is located on the rear left-hand side of the transmission

Arrow indicates identification mark

of the car and support it on axle stands (see *Jacking and vehicle support*). Remove the relevant road wheel.

3 Drain the transmission fluid as described in Section 2.

4 Referring to Chapter 8, disconnect the complete driveshaft assembly from the transmission on the side being worked on. Note that it is not necessary to remove the driveshaft completely, as the shaft can be left attached to the hub assembly and freed from the transmission as the hub assembly is pulled outwards. **Note:** *Do not allow it to hang down under its own weight as this could damage the constant velocity joints/gaiters.*

5 Note the fitted depth of the old seal, then carefully lever the seal out of position using a flat-bladed screwdriver. Be careful not to drop the seal or its inner spring into the automatic transmission.

6 Wipe clean the oil seal seating in the casing and apply a smear of oil to the seal lip. Making sure the seal lip is facing inwards, carefully ease the new seal into position. Press the seal squarely into the transmission until it is positioned at the same depth as the original was prior to removal. If necessary the seal can be tapped into position using a piece of metal tube or a socket which bears only on the hard outer edge of the seal.

7 Refit the driveshaft assembly with reference to Chapter 8.

8 Refill the transmission with new fluid as described in Section 2.

9 Refit the roadwheel, lower the car to the ground and tighten the wheel bolts to the specified torque (Chapter 1A).

10 Reconnect the battery negative cable.

Torque converter seal

11 Remove the transmission from the engine as described in Section 9.

12 Remove the retaining strap and carefully slide the torque converter from the transmission shaft. Be prepared for fluid loss as the converter is removed.

13 Using a flat-bladed screwdriver carefully lever the seal out from the centre of the torque converter, taking great care not to mark the metal bush.

14 Press the new seal squarely into position making sure its sealing lip is facing inwards.

15 Lubricate the lip of the seal with clean transmission fluid and carefully slide the converter onto the transmission shaft.

16 Make sure the torque converter is correctly engaged with the transmission shaft splines then refit the transmission as described in Section 9.

7 Fluid cooler – removal and refitting

Removal

1 The fluid cooler is located on the rear left-hand side of the transmission **(see illustration)**. To gain access to the cooler, remove the air cleaner and inlet duct as described in Chapter 4A.

2 To minimise coolant loss, clamp the coolant hoses on either side of the fluid cooler. Alternately, drain the cooling system as described in Chapter 1A.

3 Loosen the clips and disconnect the hoses from the fluid cooler – be prepared for some coolant spillage. Wash off any spilt coolant immediately with cold water, and dry the surrounding area before proceeding further.

4 Slacken and remove the mounting bolt(s), and remove the fluid cooler from the transmission. There will be some loss of fluid, so some clean rags should be placed around the cooler to absorb spillage. Make sure that dirt is prevented from entering the hydraulic system.

5 Remove the sealing ring from each mounting bolt and the sealing rings fitted between the cooler and transmission. Discard all sealing rings; new ones must be used on refitting.

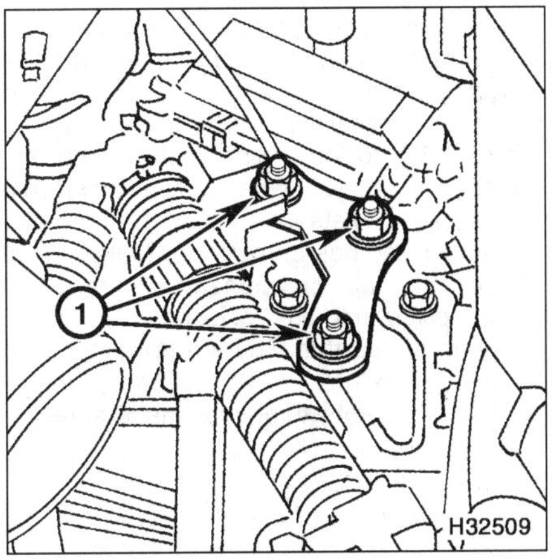

8.8 Modular connector mounting plate bolts (1)

Refitting

6 Lubricate the new seals with clean automatic transmission fluid, then fit the two new seals to the base of the fluid cooler, and a new seal to each mounting bolt.

7 Locate the fluid cooler on the top of the transmission housing, ensuring its lower seals remain in position. Refit the mounting bolt(s) and tighten them to the specified torque.

8 Reconnect the coolant hoses to the fluid cooler, and securely tighten their retaining clips. Remove the hose clamps.

9 Refit the air cleaner and inlet duct with reference to Chapter 4A.

10 On completion, top-up the cooling system and check the automatic transmission fluid level as described in Section 2.

8 Multi-function switch – removal, refitting and adjustment

Removal

1 Disconnect the battery negative lead (refer to *Disconnecting the battery* in the Reference Section of this manual).

2 The multi-function switch informs the electronic control unit of the selector lever position, prevents the starter motor operating when the transmission is in gear and also controls the reversing lights. The switch is located on the top of the transmission, below the air cleaner inlet duct.

3 Move the selector lever to position D.

4 To gain access to the switch, remove the air cleaner inlet duct with reference to Chapter 4A.

5 Pull out the locking tab and disconnect the transmission wiring harness modular connector.

6 Disconnect the selector cable end fitting from the multi-function switch lever.

7 Remove the lever then undo the two multi-function switch mounting bolts.

8 Undo the three mounting bolts and release the modular connector mounting plate from the top of the transmission **(see illustration)**.

9 Trace the switch wiring back to the modular connector plate and disconnect the 12-pin socket from the connector plate. Remove the multi-function switch from the transmission.

Refitting

10 Reconnect the multi-function switch wiring to the modular connector plate, then refit the plate and attach the connector. Tighten the mounting bolts.

11 Position the multi-function switch on the transmission and refit the two mounting bolts, finger tight only at this stage.

12 Reconnect the selector cable end fitting to the multi-function switch lever.

13 With the gear selector lever and multi-function switch in position N, connect an ohmmeter across the two test terminals on the side of the multi-function switch.

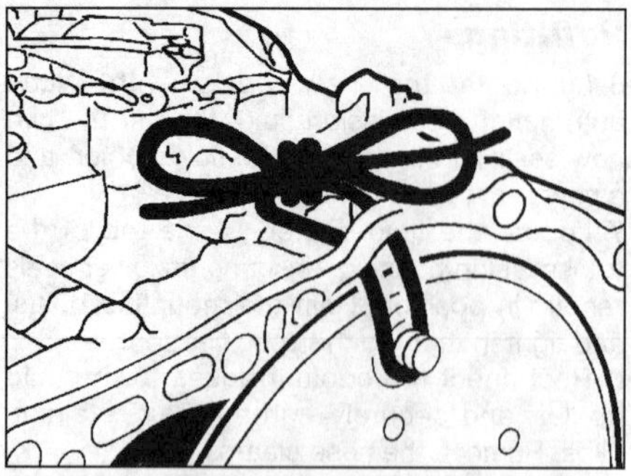
9.26 Torque converter secured in the transmission with string tied through the TDC sensor aperture

14 Turn the switch body until the internal switch contacts close and 0 ohms is indicated on the ohmmeter. Hold the switch body in this position and tighten the two retaining bolts.
15 Refit the air cleaner inlet duct with reference to Chapter 4A, then reconnect the battery negative lead.
16 Check that the starter motor will only operate with P or N selected.

9 Automatic transmission - removal and refitting

Note: *If a new transmission and/or torque converter is being fitted, note that the ECU auto-adaptive values must be re-set by a Renault dealer using the XR25 test equipment.*

Removal

1 Remove the battery and battery tray as described in Chapter 5A.
2 Apply the handbrake, then jack up the front of the vehicle and support it on axle stands (see *Jacking and vehicle support*). Remove the engine undertray and both front roadwheels.
3 Remove the air cleaner assembly and the inlet duct as described in Chapter 4A.
4 Disconnect the selector cable end fitting from the multi-function switch on top of the transmission. Release the outer cable from the support bracket by turning the two locking rings in opposite directions. **Do not** move the orange ring as the locking rings are released. Note that if the orange ring breaks during removal, this will not adversely affect the operation of the cable and is not grounds for cable renewal.
5 Pull out the locking tab and disconnect the transmission wiring harness modular connector. To prevent entry of dust and dirt, wrap a polythene bag over the connector.
6 Unscrew the engine wiring harness support bolts, and remove the support.
7 Unbolt the TDC sensor from the top of the transmission and place to one side.
8 Clamp the coolant hoses on either side of the fluid cooler. Alternately, drain the cooling system as described in Chapter 1A. Loosen the clips and disconnect the hoses from the cooler.
9 Disconnect the oxygen sensor wiring at the connector.
10 Remove both the left-hand and right-hand driveshafts as described in Chapter 8.
11 Unscrew the bolts securing the steering gear to the subframe and tie it to the bulkhead making sure that the power steering fluid pipes are not strained.
12 Disconnect the wiring from the input and output speed sensors on the transmission.
13 Remove the starter motor as described in Chapter 5A.
14 Unbolt the earthing cable from the transmission.
15 Remove the rear engine mounting as described in the relevant part of Chapter 2.
16 Remove the exhaust front downpipe as described in Chapter 4A.
17 Support the weight of the subframe on trolley jacks.
18 Support the weight of the engine with a suitable hoist attached to the lifting eyes.
19 Support the radiator by tying it to the engine compartment front crossmember, then unbolt and remove the subframe, lowering it to the ground.
20 The torque converter is attached to the driveplate by three nuts which are accessed through the starter motor aperture. Turn the engine as required to position the nuts in the aperture, then unscrew and remove them. **Note:** *The nuts must be renewed every time they are removed.* Where applicable, unbolt the access plate from the bottom of the transmission.
21 Support the weight of the transmission on a trolley jack, or (preferably) on a transmission cradle.
22 Unbolt and remove the transmission/engine left-hand mounting from the transmission and inner body panel.
23 Lower the transmission and engine as far as possible, but take care not to damage the air conditioning compressor (where fitted).
24 With the jack positioned beneath the transmission taking the weight, slacken and remove the remaining nut/bolts securing the transmission to the engine. Note the correct fitted positions of each nut/bolt, and the necessary brackets, as they are removed, to use as a reference on refitting. Make a final check that all components have been disconnected, and are positioned clear of the transmission so that they will not hinder the removal procedure.
25 With the bolts removed, make sure the torque converter is pushed fully onto the transmission shaft then move the trolley jack and transmission to the left, to free it from its locating dowels.
26 Once the transmission is free, lower the jack and manoeuvre the unit out from under the car. Remove the locating dowels from the transmission or engine if they are loose, and keep them in a safe place. Secure the torque converter in position by bolting a length of metal bar to one of the housing holes, or by tying one of the studs to the TDC sensor aperture on the top of the housing **(see illustration)**.

Refitting

27 The transmission is refitted using a reversal of the removal procedure, bearing in mind the following points.

a) *Remove the retaining bar and ensure that the torque converter is pushed fully onto the transmission. Apply a smear of high-melting point grease (Renault recommend the use of Molykote BR2) to the converter centring ring.*
b) *Ensure the locating dowels are correctly positioned prior to installation and clean the torque converter-to-driveplate stud threads.*
c) *Align the torque converter studs with the driveplate holes as the transmission is refitted. Apply thread locking compound (Renault recommend the use of Loctite Frenbloc) to the new retaining nuts and tighten them to the specified torque.*
d) *Tighten all nuts and bolts to the specified torque (where given).*
e) *Refit the driveshafts as described in Chapter 8.*
f) *Connect the selector cable and adjust as described in Sections 5 and 3.*
g) *On completion, top-up/refill the transmission with the specified type and quantity of lubricant, as described in Section 2.*

10 Automatic transmission overhaul - general information

In the event of a fault occurring with the transmission, it is first necessary to determine whether it is of an electrical, mechanical or hydraulic nature, and to do this, special test equipment is required. It is therefore essential to have the work carried out by a Renault dealer if a transmission fault is suspected.

Do not remove the transmission from the car for possible repair before professional fault diagnosis has been carried out, since most tests require the transmission to be in the vehicle.

Chapter 8
Driveshafts

Contents

Degrees of difficulty

Easy, suitable for novice with little experience	**Fairly easy,** suitable for beginner with some experience	**Fairly difficult,** suitable for competent DIY mechanic	**Difficult,** suitable for experienced DIY mechanic	**Very difficult,** suitable for expert DIY or professional

Specifications

General

Driveshaft type	Solid steel shafts, splined to inner and outer constant velocity joints, vibration damper fitted on some shafts
Lubricant type/specification	Special grease supplied in sachets with gaiter kits – joints are otherwise pre-packed with grease and sealed

Torque wrench settings

	Nm	lbf ft
Driveshaft retaining nut*:		
Nyloc type nut	250	185
ENKO self-locking nut with integral washer	280	207
Left-hand driveshaft gaiter retaining plate bolts – manual gearbox	25	18
Roadwheel bolts	90	66
Strut lower mounting bolts	105	77
Track rod end balljoint retaining nut	37	27

** Use new nuts*

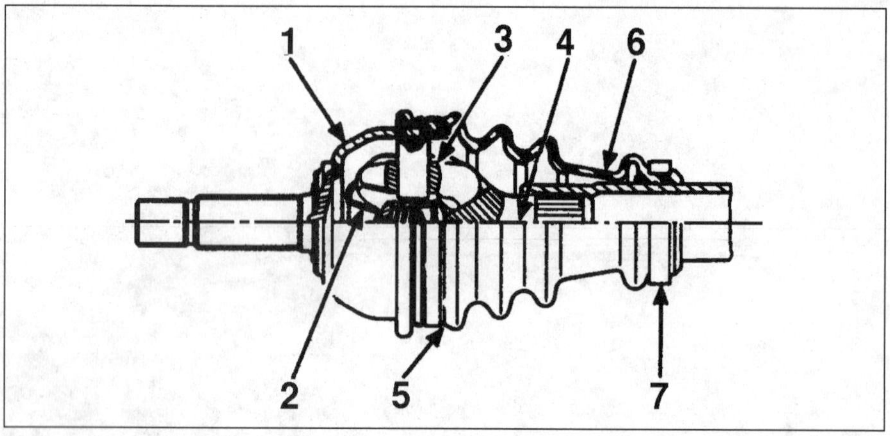

1.2 Sectional view of the spider-and-yoke type outer constant velocity joint

1 Outer member
2 Thrust plunger
3 Driveshaft spider
4 Driveshaft
5 Outer retaining clip
6 Gaiter
7 Inner retaining clip

1 General information

1 Drive is transmitted from the differential to the front wheels by means of two driveshafts.

2 Both driveshafts are fitted with a constant velocity (CV) joint at their outer ends, which are of the spider-and-yoke type **(see illustration)**. Each joint has an outer member, which is splined at its outer end to accept the wheel hub and is threaded so that it can be fastened to the hub by a large nut. The joint contains a spring-loaded plunger, which engages with the inner member. The complete assembly is protected by a thermoplastic flexible gaiter secured to the driveshaft and joint outer member.

3 On vehicles equipped with a manual gearbox, a different inner constant velocity joint arrangement is fitted to each driveshaft. On the right-hand side, the driveshaft is splined to engage with a tripod joint, containing needle roller bearings and cups. The tripod joint is free to slide within the yoke of the joint outer member, which is splined and retained by a roll pin to the differential side gear stub shaft (on most later models, the roll-pin is deleted, and the splined end of the driveshaft joint is sprung to retain it in the differential side gear stub shaft). A rubber flexible gaiter secured to the driveshaft and outer member protects the complete assembly. On the left-hand side, the driveshaft also engages with a tripod joint, but the yoke in which the tripod joint is free to slide is an integral part of the differential side gear. On this side, the gaiter is secured to the transmission casing with a retaining plate, and to a ball-bearing on the driveshaft with a retaining clip. The bearing allows the driveshaft to turn within the gaiter, which does not revolve.

2 Driveshaft – removal and refitting

Removal

Note: *When carrying out an operation on this assembly, it is essential to use the new Enko type self-locking nut without applying a coat of locking fluid to the splines of the stub axle. This type of nut is gradually being fitted in production across the whole vehicle range. The bearing and driveshaft kits are no longer supplied with the Nyloc type nut. If a Nyloc nut is fitted, then the driveshaft outer joint splines will have been coated with locking compound prior to refitting. Therefore it is likely that a puller/extractor will be required to draw the hub assembly off the driveshaft end on removal.*

Note: *Where applicable, new roll pins will be required on refitting. New driveshafts with no roll pins are used on later models, these have a spring built into the inner joint to prevent the joint coming of the differential splines.*

1 Remove the wheel trim/hub cap (as applicable), then slacken the driveshaft nut with the vehicle resting on its wheels. Also slacken the wheel bolts.

2 Chock the rear wheels of the car, firmly apply the handbrake, then jack up the front of the car and support it on axle stands (see *Jacking and vehicle support*). Remove the appropriate front roadwheel.

3 On models equipped with ABS, remove the wheel sensor as described in Chapter 9, Section 23.

4 Slacken and remove the driveshaft retaining nut. If the nut was not slackened with the wheels on the ground (see paragraph 1), refit at least two roadwheel bolts to the front hub, tightening them securely, then have an assistant firmly depress the brake pedal to prevent the front hub from rotating, whilst you slacken and remove the driveshaft retaining nut. Alternatively, a tool can be fabricated from two lengths of steel strip (one long, one short) and a nut and bolt; the nut and bolt forming the pivot of a forked tool **(see Tool Tip)**.

5 Unscrew the two bolts securing the brake caliper assembly to the swivel hub, and slide the caliper assembly off the disc. Using a piece of wire or string, tie the caliper to the front suspension coil spring, to avoid placing any strain on the hydraulic brake hose.

6 Slacken and remove the nut securing the steering gear track rod end balljoint to the swivel hub. Release the balljoint tapered shank using a universal balljoint separator **(see illustration)**.

7 Slacken and remove the two nuts from the bolts securing the swivel hub to the suspension strut, noting that the nuts are positioned on the rear side of the strut. Withdraw the upper bolt, but leave the lower bolt in position at this stage **(see illustration)**. Now proceed as described under the relevant sub-heading.

TOOL TiP

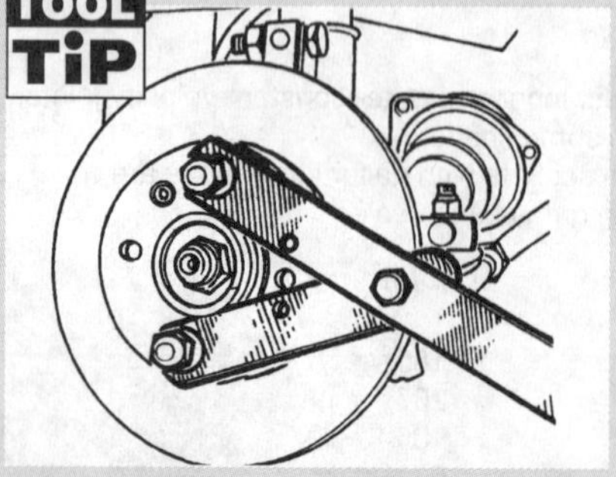

Using a fabricated tool to hold the front hub stationary whilst the driveshaft nut is slackened.

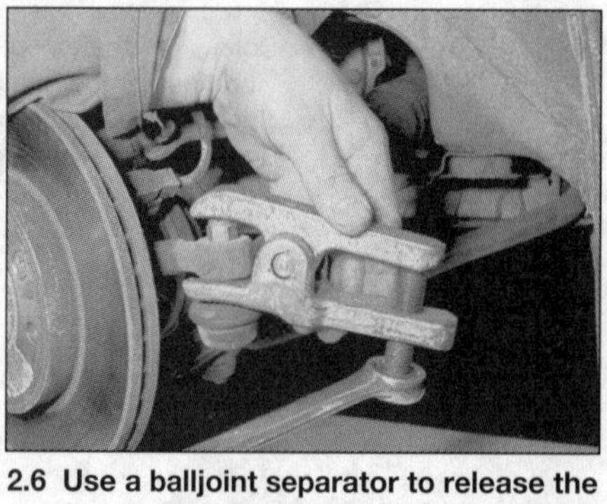

2.6 Use a balljoint separator to release the track rod end balljoint from the swivel hub

2.7 Withdraw the upper swivel hub-to-strut bolt, noting which way around it is fitted

2.9 On the left-hand driveshaft, remove the flexible gaiter retaining plate bolts . . .

2.10 . . . and release the tripod joint from the manual gearbox

Left-hand driveshaft – manual gearbox models

8 Drain the gearbox oil as described in Chapter 7A.

9 Slacken and remove the three bolts securing the flexible gaiter retaining plate to the side of the gearbox **(see illustration)**.

10 Pull the top of the swivel hub outwards until the driveshaft tripod joint is released from its yoke; be prepared for some oil spillage as the joint is withdrawn **(see illustration)**. Be careful that the rollers on the end of the tripod do not fall off.

11 Remove the lower bolt securing the swivel hub to the suspension strut. Taking care not to damage the driveshaft gaiters, release the outer constant velocity joint from the hub and remove the driveshaft. Note that it is likely the joint will be a tight fit in the hub splines (see Note at the start of this Section). Try tapping the joint out of position using a hammer and a soft metal drift, whilst an assistant supports the hub assembly. If this fails to move the joint, a suitable puller/extractor will be required to draw the hub assembly off the driveshaft end **(see illustration)**. Whilst the driveshaft is removed, support the hub assembly by refitting the bolts to the base of the strut.

Right-hand driveshaft – all models

Note: *On later models, the roll pin at the inner end of the driveshaft is deleted, and the splined end of the driveshaft joint is sprung to retain it in the differential side gear stub shaft – ignore the references to removing and refitting the roll pins when working on one of these vehicles.*

12 Where applicable, rotate the driveshaft until the double roll pin, securing the inner constant velocity joint to the side gear shaft, is visible. Using a hammer and a 5 mm diameter pin punch, drive out the double roll pin **(see illustration)**. New roll pins must be used on refitting.

13 Pull the top of the swivel hub outwards until the inner constant velocity joint splines are released from the side gear shaft. Remove the sealing ring (where fitted) from the side gear shaft splines.

14 Remove the driveshaft as described in paragraph 11.

Left-hand driveshaft – automatic transmission models

15 Pull the top of the swivel hub outwards, and disengage the inner constant velocity joint from the differential. Carefully use a lever to disengage the shaft as required.

16 Remove the driveshaft as described in paragraph 11.

Refitting

17 All new driveshafts supplied by Renault are equipped with cardboard or plastic protectors, to prevent damage to the gaiters. Even the slightest knock to the gaiter can puncture it, allowing the entry of water or dirt at a later date, which may lead to the premature failure of the joint. If the original driveshaft is being refitted, it is worthwhile making up some cardboard protectors as a precaution. They can be held in position with elastic bands. The protectors should be left on the driveshafts until the end of the refitting procedure.

Left-hand driveshaft – manual gearbox models

18 Wipe clean the side of the gearbox and the outer constant velocity joint splines.

19 Insert the tripod joint into the side gear yoke, keeping the driveshaft horizontal as far as possible. Align the gaiter retaining plate with its bolt holes. Refit the retaining bolts, and tighten them to the specified torque. Ensure that the gaiter is not twisted.

20 Ensure both the hub and driveshaft outer constant velocity joint splines are clean and dry.

21 Move the top of the swivel hub inwards, at the same time engaging the driveshaft with the hub.

22 Slide the hub fully onto the driveshaft splines, then insert the two suspension strut mounting bolts from the front side of the strut. Refit the washers and nuts to the rear of the bolts, and tighten them to the specified torque (see Chapter 10 Specifications).

23 Fit the new driveshaft Enko type **(see illustration)** retaining nut (see the note at the beginning of this Section), tightening it by hand only at this stage.

24 Reconnect the steering track rod balljoint to the swivel hub, and tighten its retaining nut to the specified torque (see Chapter 10 Specifications).

25 Clean the threads of the caliper bracket mounting bolts, and coat them with thread locking compound (Renault recommend Loctite Frenbloc – available from your Renault dealer). Slide the caliper into position, making sure the pads pass either side of the disc, and tighten the caliper bracket bolts to the specified torque setting (see Chapter 9 Specifications).

26 Using the method employed during removal to prevent the hub from rotating, tighten a new driveshaft retaining nut to the specified torque. Alternatively, lightly tighten the nut at this stage, and tighten it to the specified torque once the vehicle is resting on its wheels again.

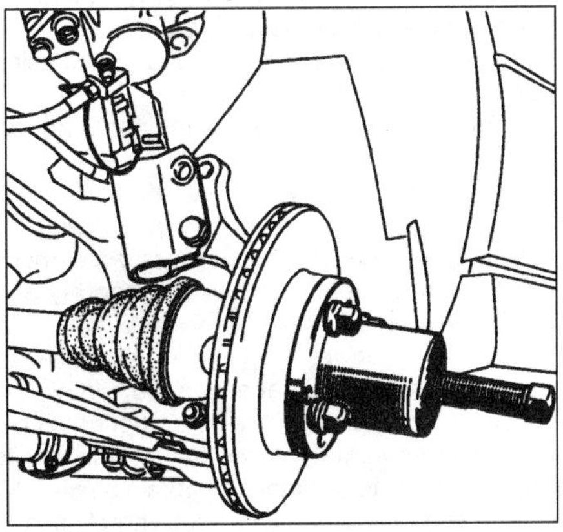

2.11 Using an extractor to press the driveshaft out of the front hub

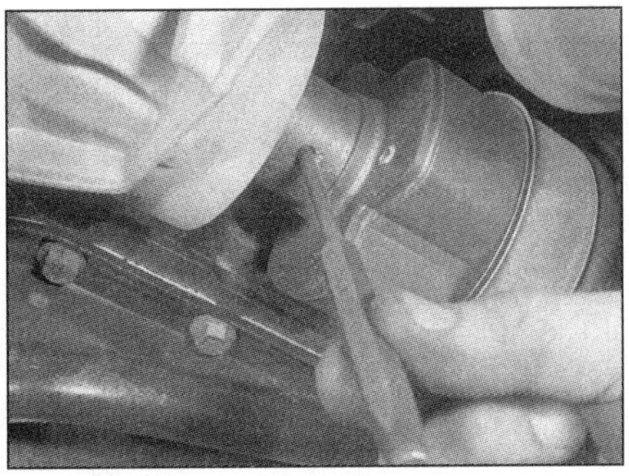

2.12 On the right-hand driveshaft, tap out the roll pins with a suitable pin punch

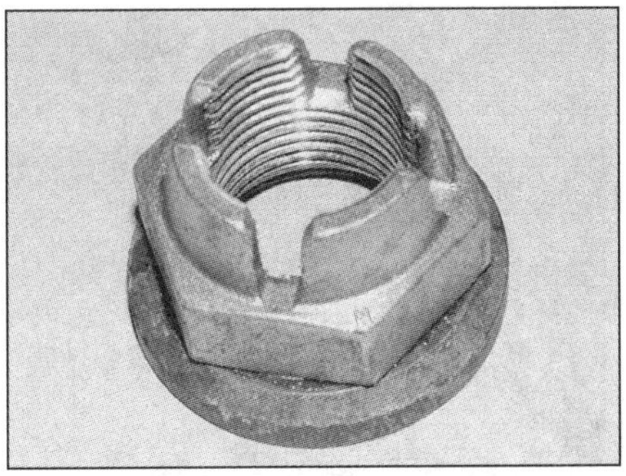

2.23 New Enko type driveshaft securing nut

2.30 Fit the new O-ring (where fitted) onto the side gear shaft . . .

27 Check that the hub rotates freely, then remove the protectors (where fitted) from the driveshaft, taking great care not to damage the flexible gaiters.

28 Refit the roadwheel. Lower the car to the ground and tighten the roadwheel bolts to the specified torque. If not already done, also tighten the driveshaft retaining nut to the specified torque.

29 Refill the gearbox with the specified type and amount of oil, and check the level using the information given in Chapter 1A or 1B.

Right-hand driveshaft – all models

30 Ensure that the inner constant velocity joint and side gear shaft splines are clean and dry. Apply a smear of molybdenum disulphide grease to the splines (Renault recommend the

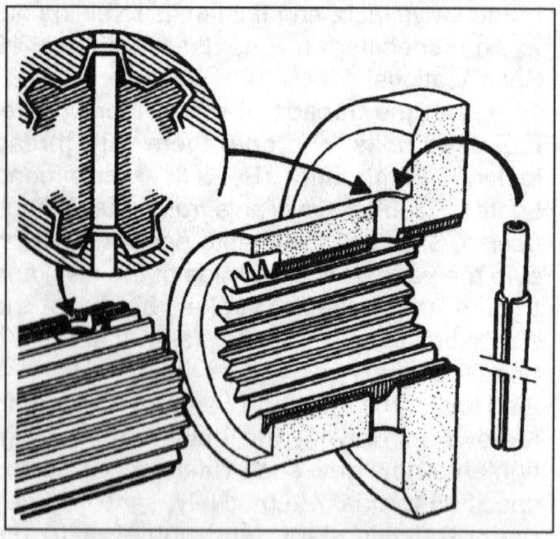

2.32a Right-hand driveshaft inner constant velocity joint roll pin arrangement

3.5 Removing the vibration damper from the driveshaft (where applicable)

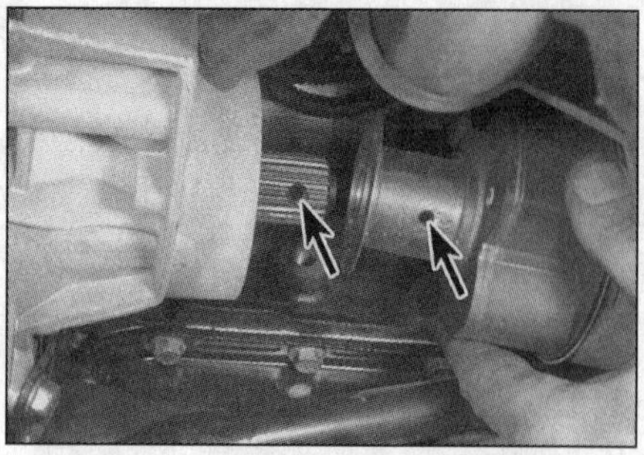

2.31 . . . and engage the driveshaft, ensuring that the roll pin holes (arrowed) are correctly aligned

use of Molykote BR2 – available from your Renault dealer). Where necessary, fit a new sealing ring over the end of the side gear shaft, and slide the O-ring along the shaft until it abuts the transmission oil seal **(see illustration)**.

31 Engage the driveshaft splines with those of the side gear shaft, where required, make sure that the roll pin holes are in alignment **(see illustration)**. Slide the driveshaft onto the side gear shaft until the roll pin holes are aligned.

32 Where applicable, drive in new roll pins with their slots 180° apart, then seal the ends of the pins with sealing compound (Renault recommend the use of CAF 4/60 THIXO or Rhodoseal 5661 – available from your Renault dealer) **(see illustrations)**.

33 Carry out the procedures described in paragraphs 20 to 28.

Left-hand driveshaft – automatic transmission

34 Ensure that the inner constant velocity joint and side gear shaft splines are clean and dry. Apply a smear of molybdenum disulphide grease to the splines (Renault recommend the use of Molykote BR2 – available from your Renault dealer).

2.32b On the right-hand driveshaft, tap the roll pins securely into position and seal their ends with sealing compound

3.9 Renault driveshaft gaiter repair kit

35 Engage the driveshaft inner constant velocity joint with the side gear shaft splines.

36 Carry out the procedures described in paragraphs 20 to 28.

3 Outer constant velocity joint gaiter (manual gearbox models) – renewal

Note: *The spider-and-yoke type joint is the most common type used, a suitable joint repair kit will be required.*

1 Remove the driveshaft as described in Section 2.

2 Cut through the gaiter retaining clip(s) or release the retaining spring and inner collar (as applicable), then slide the gaiter down the shaft to expose the outer constant velocity joint.

3 Scoop out as much grease as possible from the joint, and determine which type of constant velocity joint is fitted. Proceed as described under the relevant sub-heading.

Spider-and-yoke type joint

Note: *On some right-hand driveshafts, the vibration damper is an integral part of the driveshaft. If the gaiter is damaged on this type, then the complete driveshaft will need replacing.*

4 Remove the inner constant velocity joint, bearing and gaiter (as applicable), as described in Section 4 or 5 of this Chapter.

5 Where a vibration damper is fitted, check to see if it can be removed from the driveshaft. If it can, then clearly mark the position of the damper on the driveshaft, and use a puller or press to remove it from the inner end of the driveshaft, noting which way around it is fitted **(see illustration)**. Ensure that the legs of the puller or support plate rest only on the damper inner rubber bush, otherwise the damper will distort and break away from the outer metal housing as it is removed.

6 Slide the outer constant velocity joint gaiter off the inner end of the driveshaft.

7 Clean the outer constant velocity joint using paraffin or a suitable solvent, and dry it thoroughly. Carry out a visual inspection of the joint.

8 Check the driveshaft spider and outer member yoke for signs of wear, pitting or scuffing on their bearing surfaces. Also check that the outer member pivots smoothly and easily, with no traces of roughness.

9 If inspection reveals signs of wear or damage, it will be necessary to renew the driveshaft complete, since no components are available separately. If the joint components are in satisfactory condition, obtain a repair kit consisting of a new gaiter, retaining clips, and the correct type and quantity of grease **(see illustration)**.

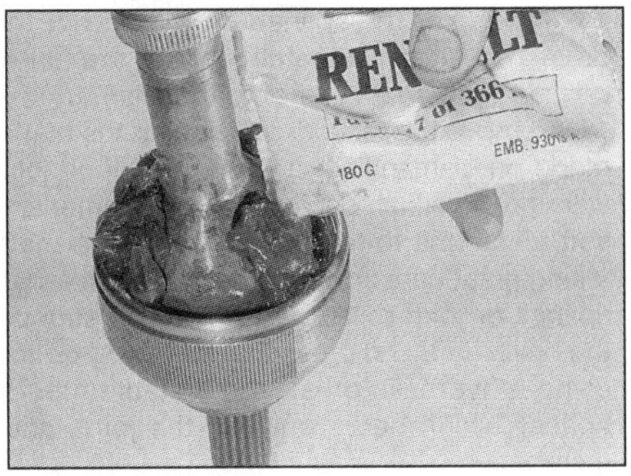

3.11 Pack the joint with the grease supplied in the repair kit . . .

10 Tape over the splines on the inner end of the driveshaft, then carefully slide the outer gaiter onto the shaft.

11 Pack the joint with the grease supplied in the repair kit. Work the grease well into the joint, and fill the gaiter with any excess **(see illustration)**.

12 Ease the gaiter over the joint, and ensure that the gaiter lips are correctly located in the grooves on the driveshaft and on the joint **(see illustration)**. With the coupling aligned with the driveshaft, lift the lip of the gaiter to equalise the air pressure.

13 Fit the large metal retaining clip to the gaiter. Remove any slack in the gaiter retaining clip by carefully compressing the raised section of the clip. In the absence of the special tool, a pair of pincers may be used. Secure the small retaining clip using the same procedure **(see illustrations)**. Check that the constant velocity joint moves freely in all directions before proceeding further.

14 To refit the vibration damper (where applicable), lubricate the driveshaft with a solution of soapy water. Press or drive the vibration damper along the shaft, using a tubular spacer which bears only on the damper inner bush, until it is aligned with the mark made prior to removal.

15 Refit the inner constant velocity joint components as described in Section 4 or 5 (as applicable), then refit the driveshaft to the vehicle as described in Section 2.

Ball-and-cage type joint

16 Using circlip pliers, expand the joint internal circlip. At the same time, tap the exposed face of the ball hub with a mallet to separate the joint from the driveshaft. Slide off the gaiter and rubber collar.

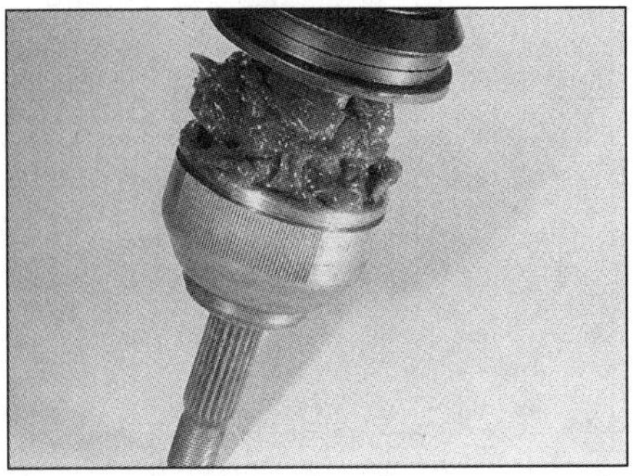

3.12 . . . then slide the gaiter into position over the joint

17 With the constant velocity joint removed from the driveshaft, clean the joint using paraffin, or a suitable solvent, and dry it thoroughly. Carry out a visual inspection of the joint.

18 Move the inner splined driving member from side-to-side, to expose each ball in turn at the top of its track. Examine the balls for cracks, flat spots or signs of surface pitting.

19 Inspect the ball tracks on the inner and outer members. If the tracks have widened, the balls will no longer be a tight fit. At the same time, check the ball cage windows for wear or cracking between the windows.

20 If on inspection any of the constant velocity joint components are found to be worn or damaged, it will be necessary to renew the complete driveshaft assembly, since no components are available separately. If the joint is in satisfactory condition, obtain a repair kit from your Renault dealer consisting of a new gaiter, rubber collar, retaining spring, and the correct type and quantity of grease.

21 Tape over the splines on the end of the driveshaft, then slide the rubber collar and gaiter onto the shaft. Locate the inner end of the gaiter on the driveshaft, and secure it in position with the rubber collar.

22 Remove the tape, then slide the constant velocity joint coupling onto the driveshaft until the internal circlip locates in the driveshaft groove.

23 Check that the circlip holds the joint securely on the driveshaft, then pack the joint with the grease supplied. Work the grease well into the ball tracks, and fill the gaiter with any excess.

24 Locate the outer lip of the gaiter in the groove on the joint outer member. With the coupling aligned with the driveshaft, lift the lip of the gaiter to equalise the air pressure. Secure the gaiter in position with the large retaining clip as described in paragraph 13.

25 Check that the constant velocity joint moves freely in all directions, then refit the driveshaft to the vehicle as described in Section 2.

4 Right-hand driveshaft inner gaiter (manual gearbox models) – renewal

Note: *On these models, two different types of inner constant velocity joint are used on the right-hand driveshaft: type RC 462 and type RC462 E. The RC 462 type has a roll pin to hold the driveshaft onto the splines of the differential. The RC462 E joint has no roll pin, this is held in position by a spring, fitted internally in the joint. A suitable joint repair kit will be required.*

1 Remove the driveshaft as described in Section 2.

2 Release the large outer retaining clip and the inner retaining clip, then slide the gaiter down the shaft to expose the joint.

3 Slide the outer member off the tripod joint. Be prepared to hold the rollers in place (where applicable), otherwise they may fall off the tripod ends as the outer member is withdrawn. If necessary, secure the rollers in place using tape after removal of the outer member. The rollers are matched to the tripod joint stems, and it is important that they are not interchanged.

4 On the RC 462 E Type joint (no roll pin type), remove the spring and cup from inside the outer member of the joint **(see illustration)**.

5 Using circlip pliers, extract the circlip securing the tripod joint to the driveshaft **(see illustration)**. Note that on some models, the joint may be staked in position; if so, relieve the staking using a file. Mark the position of the tripod in relation to the driveshaft, using a dab of paint or a punch.

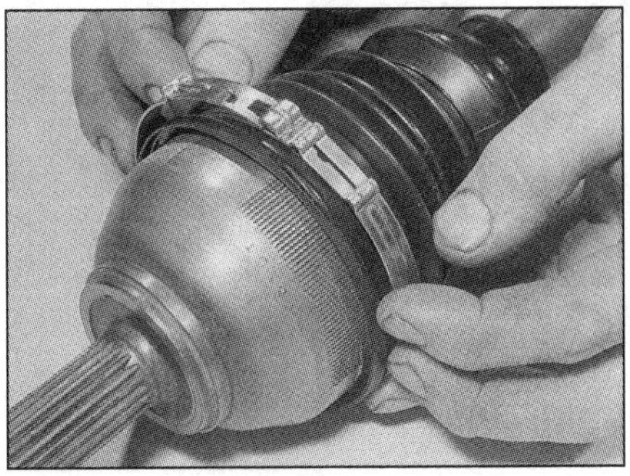

3.13a Fit the large gaiter retaining clip . . .

3.13b . . . and secure it in position by carefully compressing the raised section of the clip

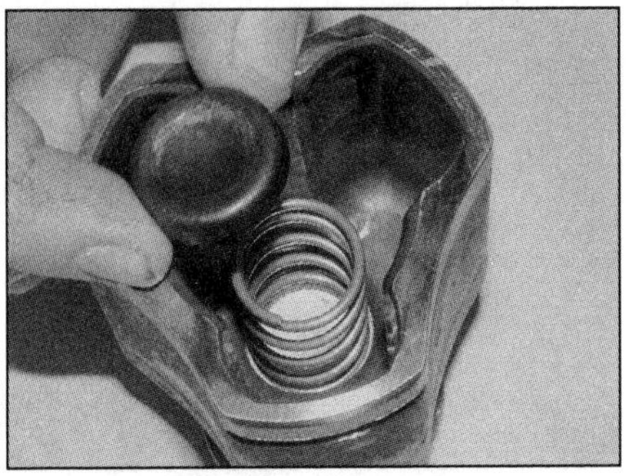

4.4 Spring and cup is fitted to the joint without a roll pin

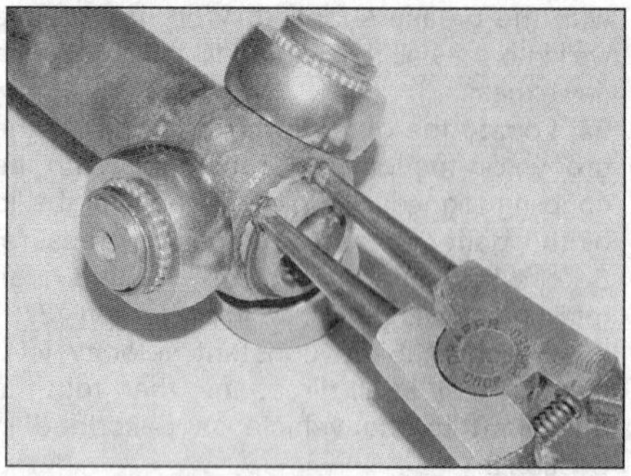

4.5 Remove the circlip . . .

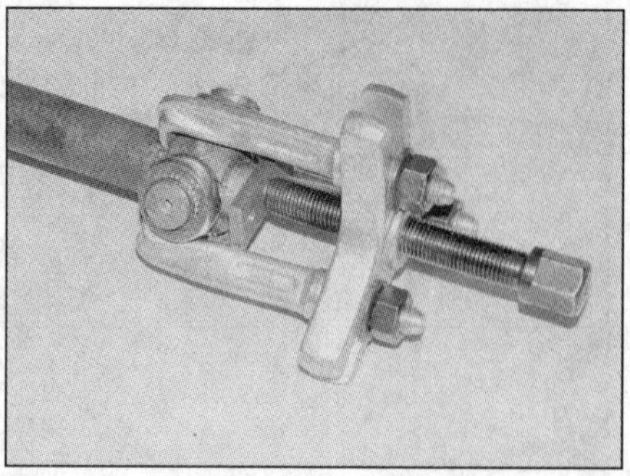

4.6 . . . and withdraw the tripod joint, using a puller if required

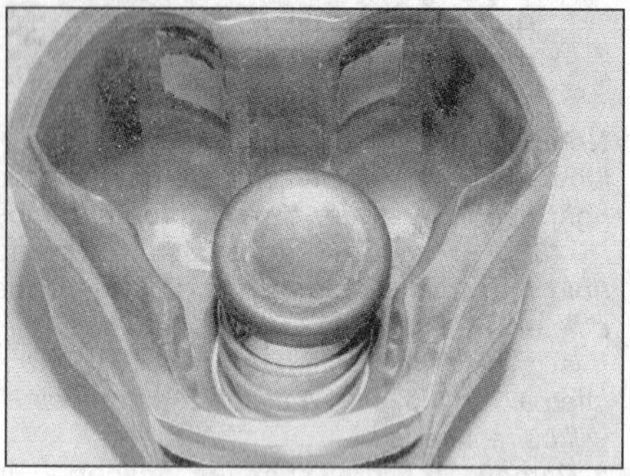

4.13a Refit the spring and cup into the outer part of the joint . . .

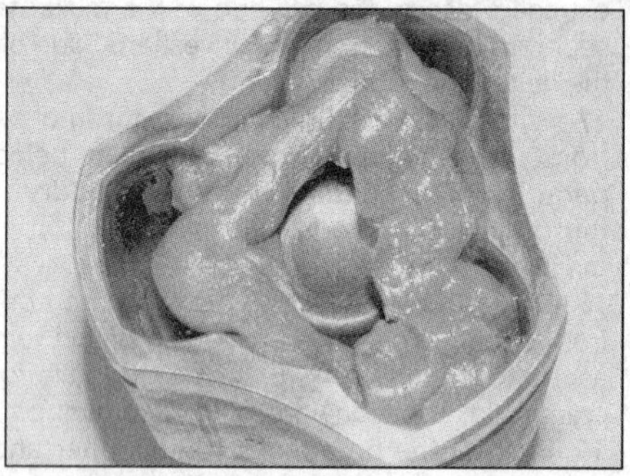

4.13b . . . and pack with the grease supplied in the repair kit

6 The tripod joint can now be removed **(see illustration)**. If it is tight, draw the joint off the driveshaft end using a puller. Ensure that the legs of the puller are located behind the joint inner member and do not contact the joint rollers. Alternatively, support the inner member of the tripod joint, and press the shaft out using a hydraulic press, again ensuring that no load is applied to the joint rollers.
7 With the tripod joint removed, slide the gaiter and inner retaining collar off the end of the driveshaft.
8 Wipe clean the joint components, taking care not to remove the alignment marks made on dismantling. **Do not** use paraffin or other solvents to clean this type of joint.
9 Examine the tripod joint, rollers and outer member for any signs of scoring or wear. Check that the rollers move smoothly on the tripod stems. If wear is evident, the tripod joint and roller assembly can be renewed, but it is not possible to obtain a replacement outer member. Obtain a new gaiter, retaining clips and a quantity of the special lubricating grease. These parts are available in the form of a repair kit from your Renault dealer.
10 Tape over the splines on the end of the driveshaft, then carefully slide the inner retaining clip and gaiter onto the shaft.
11 Remove the tape, then, aligning the marks made on dismantling, engage the tripod joint with the driveshaft splines. Use a hammer and soft metal drift to tap the joint onto the shaft, taking great care not to damage the driveshaft splines or joint rollers. Alternatively, support the driveshaft, and press the joint into position using a hydraulic press and suitable tubular spacer which bears only on the joint inner member.
12 Secure the tripod joint in position with the circlip, ensuring that it is correctly located in the driveshaft groove. Where no circlip is fitted, secure the joint in position by staking the end of the driveshaft in three places, at intervals of 120°, using a hammer and punch.
13 Refit the spring and cup in the outer member, then evenly distribute the grease contained in the repair kit around the tripod joint and inside the outer member **(see illustrations)**.
14 Pack the gaiter with the remainder of the grease and slide the two halves of the joint together **(see illustrations)**.
15 Slide the gaiter up the driveshaft. Locate the gaiter in the grooves on the driveshaft and outer member.
16 Fit the inner retaining clip into place over the inner end of the gaiter.
17 Using a blunt rod, carefully lift the outer lip of the gaiter to equalise the air pressure. With the rod in position, compress the joint until the dimension from the inner end of the gaiter to the flat end face of the outer member is as shown **(see illustrations)**. Hold the outer member in this position and withdraw the rod.
18 Slip the new retaining clip into place to secure the outer lip of the gaiter to the outer member. Remove any slack in the gaiter retaining clip by carefully compressing the raised section of the clip. In the absence of

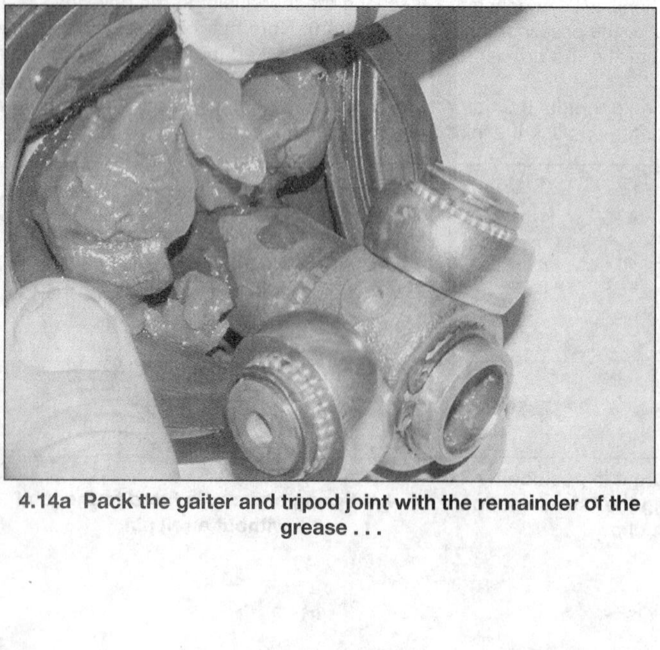

4.14a Pack the gaiter and tripod joint with the remainder of the grease . . .

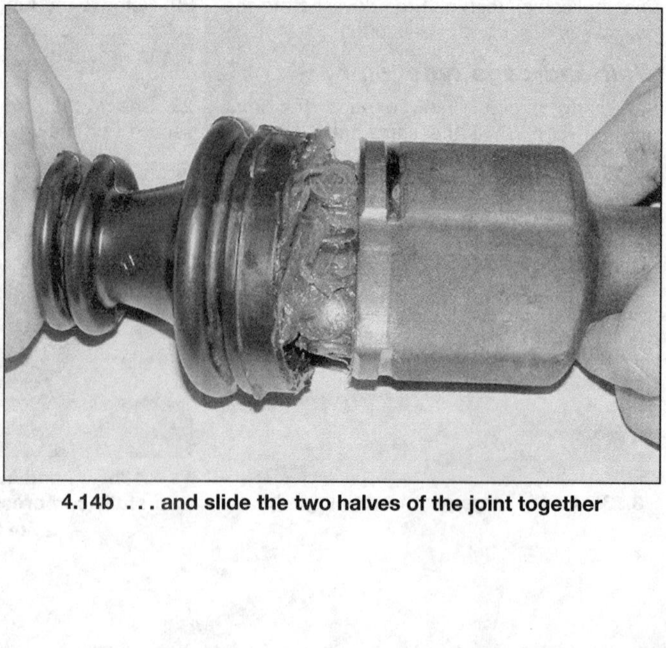

4.14b . . . and slide the two halves of the joint together

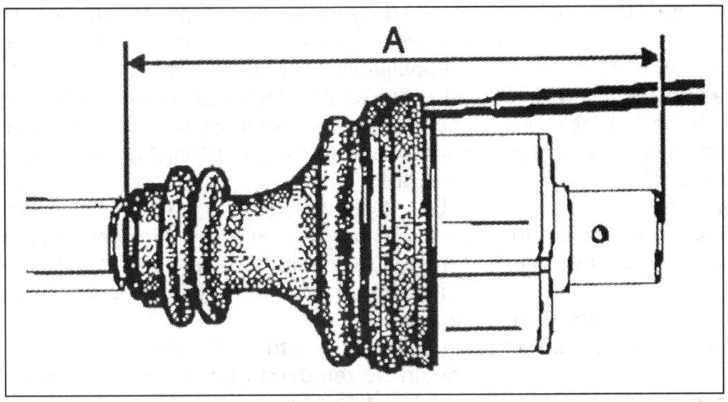

4.17a Fitting dimension for the right-hand driveshaft inner joint gaiter with roll pin – RC 462-type joint

A = 190 ± 1 mm

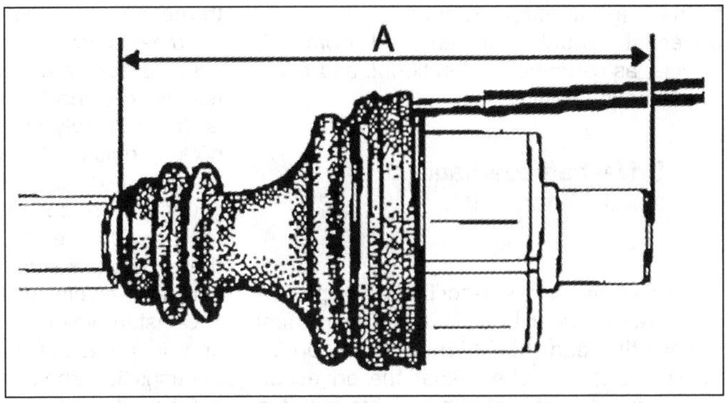

4.17b Fitting dimension for the right-hand driveshaft inner joint gaiter without roll pin – RC 462 E-type joint

A = 203 ± 1 mm

the special tool, a pair of pincers may be used **(see illustration)**. Secure the small retaining clip using the same procedure.

19 Check that the constant velocity joint moves freely in all directions, then refit the driveshaft as described in Section 2.

5 Left-hand driveshaft inner gaiter (manual gearbox models) – renewal

Note: *A suitable joint repair kit will be required.*

1 Remove the driveshaft as described in Section 2.

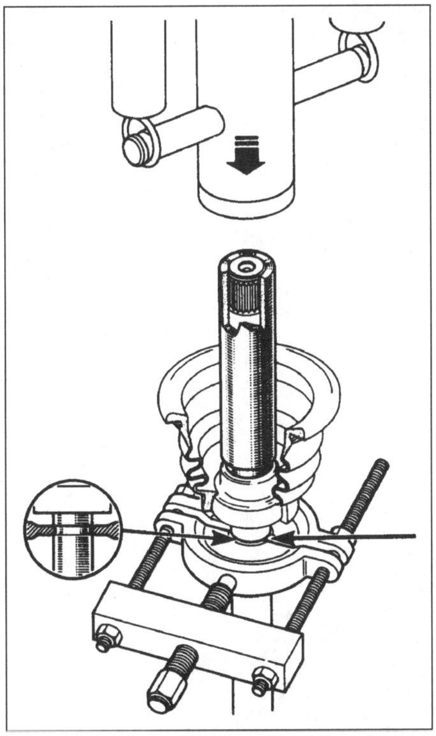

5.8a Pressing the inner bearing/gaiter onto the end of the left-hand driveshaft – manual gearbox models

2 Using circlip pliers, extract the circlip securing the tripod joint to the driveshaft. Note that on some models, the joint may be staked in position; if so, relieve the stakings using a file. Using a dab of paint or a hammer and punch, mark the position of the tripod joint in relation to the driveshaft, to use as a guide to refitting.

3 The tripod joint can now be removed. If it is tight, draw the joint off the driveshaft end using a puller. Ensure that the legs of the puller are located behind the joint inner member and do not contact the joint rollers. Alternatively, support the inner member of the tripod joint and press the shaft out of the joint, again ensuring that no load is applied to the joint rollers.

4 The gaiter and bearing assembly is removed in the same way, either by drawing the bearing off the driveshaft, or by pressing the driveshaft out of the bearing. Remove the retaining plate, noting which way round it is fitted.

5 Obtain a new gaiter, which is supplied complete with the small bearing.

6 Owing to the lip-type seal used in the bearing, the bearing and gaiter must be pressed into position. If a hammer and tubular drift are used to drive the assembly onto the driveshaft, there is a risk of distorting the seal.

7 Refit the retaining plate to the driveshaft, ensuring that it is fitted the correct way around.

8 Support the driveshaft, and press the gaiter bearing onto the shaft, using a tubular spacer which bears only on the bearing inner race. Position the bearing so that the distance from the end of the driveshaft to the inner face of the bearing is as shown **(see illustrations)**.

9 Align the marks made on dismantling, and engage the tripod joint with the driveshaft splines. Use a hammer and soft metal drift to tap the joint onto the shaft, taking care not to damage the driveshaft splines or joint rollers. Alternatively, support the driveshaft, and press the joint into position using a tubular spacer which bears only on the joint inner member.

10 Secure the tripod joint in position with the circlip, ensuring that it is correctly located in the driveshaft groove. Where no circlip is

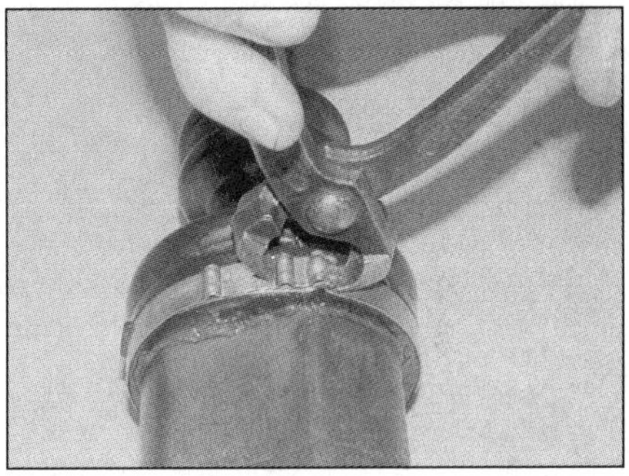

4.18 Using pincers to secure the gaiter retaining clip

fitted, secure the joint in position by staking the end of the driveshaft in three places, at intervals of 120°, using a hammer and punch.

11 Refit the driveshaft to the vehicle as described in Section 2.

6 CV joint gaiter renewal (automatic transmission models) – general information

At the time of writing, no information on driveshaft dismantling was available for these models, although the driveshafts are very similar in design to the manual gearbox models. If gaiter renewal is necessary, and

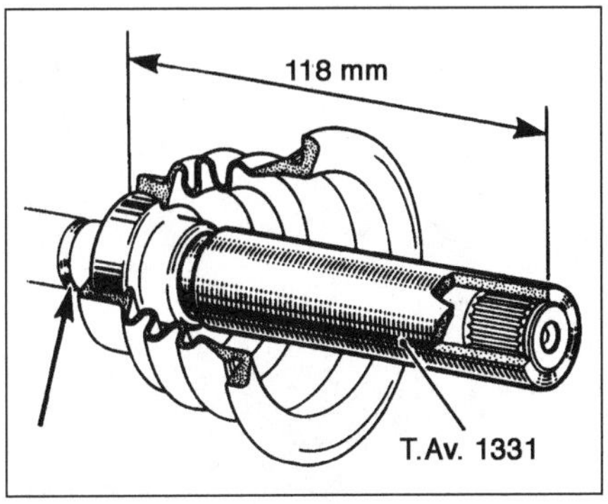

5.8b Fitting dimension for the left-hand driveshaft inner bearing/gaiter – manual gearbox models

further information required, then the driveshaft should be removed from the vehicle, as described in Section 2, and taken to a Renault dealer.

7 Driveshaft overhaul – general information

If any of the checks described in Chapter 1A or 1B reveal wear in a driveshaft joint, first remove the roadwheel trim or centre cap (as appropriate) and check that the driveshaft retaining nut is still correctly tightened; if in doubt, use a torque wrench to check it. Refit the centre cap or trim, and repeat the check on the other driveshaft.

Road test the vehicle, and listen for a metallic clicking from the front as the vehicle is driven slowly in a circle on full-lock. If a clicking noise is heard, this indicates wear in the outer constant velocity joint.

If vibration, consistent with road speed, is felt through the vehicle when accelerating, there is a possibility of wear in the inner constant velocity joints.

Constant velocity joints can be dismantled and inspected for wear as described in Sections 3, 4 and 5.

On models with a manual gearbox, wear in the outer constant velocity joint can only be rectified by renewing the driveshaft. This is necessary since no outer joint components are available separately. For the inner joint, the tripod joint and roller assembly is available separately, but wear in any of the other components will also necessitate driveshaft renewal.

On models equipped with automatic transmission, wear in either constant velocity joint will necessitate driveshaft renewal; no components for either joint are available separately.

On models with ABS, the reluctor ring should be removed from the old driveshaft and fitted to the new one. See Chapter 9, Section 23.

Chapter 9
Braking system

Contents

Degrees of difficulty

Easy, suitable for novice with little experience	**Fairly easy,** suitable for beginner with some experience	**Fairly difficult,** suitable for competent DIY mechanic	**Difficult,** suitable for experienced DIY mechanic	**Very difficult,** suitable for expert DIY or professional

Specifications

General

System type	Dual hydraulic circuit, split diagonally, with servo assistance (some versions fitted with ABS)	
Front brakes	Disc, with single-piston sliding caliper	
Rear brakes	Self-adjusting drum or disc, according to model	
Handbrake	Cable-operated, to rear wheels	

Front brakes

Disc diameter:		
All except 16-valve models	238 mm	
16-valve models	259 mm	
Disc run-out (all models)	0.07 mm maximum	
Disc thickness:	**New**	**Minimum**
Solid discs brakes	12.0 mm	10.5 mm
Vented disc brakes	20.0 mm	17.7 mm
Brake pad thickness (friction material and backing plate)	18.2	6.0 mm

Rear drum brakes

Drum diameter:		
Without ABS or air conditioning:		
New	180.25 mm	
Maximum diameter after machining	181.25 mm	
With ABS and/or air conditioning:		
New	203.20 mm	
Maximum diameter after machining	204.20 mm	
Brake shoe thickness (friction material and shoe):	**New**	**Minimum**
D7F engine models	4.85 mm	2.00 mm
All except D7F engine models:		
Leading shoe	4.60 mm	2.00 mm
Trailing shoe	3.30 mm	2.00 mm

Rear disc brakes

Brake pad thickness (friction material and backing plate):		
New	15.0 mm	
Minimum	6.0 mm	
Disc diameter	238 mm	
Disc thickness:		
New	8.0 mm	
Minimum	7.0 mm	
Disc run-out (all models)	0.07 mm maximum	

Anti-lock braking system (ABS)

Wheel sensor-to-reluctor ring clearance	0.10 to 1.90 mm
Sensor electrical resistance	1130 ohms (approx)

Torque wrench settings

Torque wrench settings	Nm	lbf ft
ABS system components:		
Hydraulic unit brake pipe union nuts	17	13
Wheel sensor retaining bolts	8 to 10	6 to 7
Brake caliper mounting bolts	100	74
Brake disc retaining screw	20	15
Flexible brake hose union	15	11
Front brake caliper guide pin bolts*	40	30
Master cylinder brake pipe union nuts	15	11
Master cylinder-to-servo unit nuts	18	13
Rear brake caliper frame retaining bolts	65	48
Rear brake compensator adjustment bolt	10	7
Rear brake compensator mounting bolts	18	13
Rear hub nut*:	175	129
Roadwheel bolts	90	66
Vacuum servo unit mounting nuts	23	17

Use new bolts or nuts

1 General information

The braking system is of the servo-assisted, dual circuit hydraulic type. The arrangement of the hydraulic system is such that each circuit operates one front and one rear brake from a tandem master cylinder. Under normal circumstances, both circuits operate in unison. However, in the event of hydraulic failure in one circuit, full braking force will still be available at two wheels.

All models are fitted with front disc brakes, but the rear brakes may be of drum or disc type, depending on model. All models fitted with ABS have rear disc brakes. (Refer to Section 22 for further information on ABS operation.)

The front disc brakes are actuated by single-piston sliding type calipers, which ensure that equal pressure is applied to each disc pad.

On models with rear drum brakes, the rear brakes incorporate leading and trailing shoes, which are actuated by twin-piston wheel cylinders (one cylinder per drum). The wheel cylinders incorporate integral pressure-regulating valves, which control the hydraulic pressure applied to the rear brakes. The regulating valves help to prevent rear wheel lock-up during emergency braking. As the brake shoe linings wear, footbrake operation automatically operates a self-adjuster mechanism, which effectively lengthens the strut between the shoes and reduces the lining-to-drum clearance.

On models with rear disc brakes, the brakes are actuated by single-piston sliding calipers which incorporate mechanical handbrake mechanisms. A load-sensitive pressure-regulating valve is connected into the brake lines to the rear calipers. The regulating valve is similar to that fitted to the rear wheel cylinders (on rear drum brake models), and helps to prevent rear wheel lock-up during emergency braking. It does this by varying the hydraulic pressure applied to the rear calipers in proportion to the load being carried by the vehicle.

On all models, the handbrake provides an independent mechanical means of rear brake application.

Note: *When servicing any part of the braking system, work carefully and methodically; also observe scrupulous cleanliness when overhauling any part of the hydraulic system. Always renew components (in axle sets, where applicable) if in doubt about their condition, and use only genuine Renault replacement parts, or at least those of known good quality. Note the warnings given in 'Safety first!' and at relevant points in this Chapter, concerning the dangers of asbestos dust and hydraulic fluid.*

Caution: If the radio/cassette in your vehicle is equipped with an anti-theft system, make sure you have the correct activation code before disconnecting the battery.

2 Brake pedal – removal and refitting

Removal

1 Remove the clutch pedal as described in Chapter 6.

2 Extract the spring clip, then withdraw the clevis pin securing the servo unit pushrod to the brake pedal **(see illustration)**. Note the spacer which is located on the inside of the pedal.

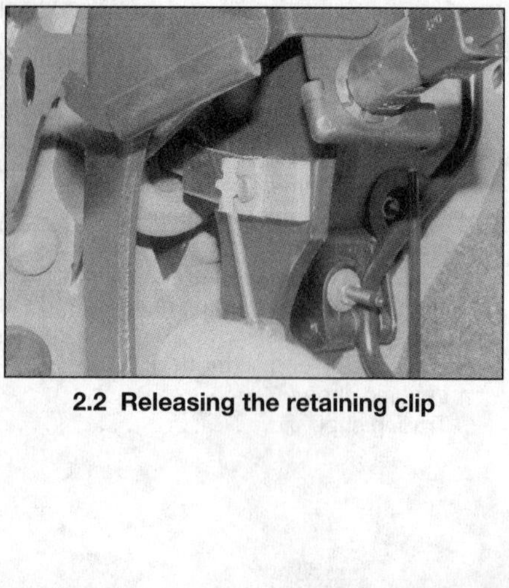

2.2 Releasing the retaining clip

3 Fully withdraw the pedal cross-shaft/bolt and manoeuvre the brake pedal out of the pedal mounting bracket, noting the fitted positions of the pivot bushes **(see illustration)**.

4 Inspect the bushes for signs of wear or damage, and renew as necessary.

Refitting

5 Apply a smear of multi-purpose grease to the contact surfaces of the pivot bushes (where fitted). Fit the bushes to the brake pedal, in the position noted on removal, and correctly locate the pedal.

6 Slide the pedal and bush assembly into position in the mounting bracket. Ensure that the pedal is correctly engaged with the servo pushrod, then insert the cross-shaft/bolt through the mounting bracket.

7 Position the spacer on the inside of the pedal **(see illustration)**. Refit the clevis pin, and secure it in position with the spring clip.

8 Refit the clutch pedal (see Chapter 6).

3 Vacuum servo unit – general information, testing, removal and refitting

General information

1 The vacuum servo unit can be removed from within the engine compartment. To do this the brake master cylinder will have to be removed first as described in Section 8. This procedure will mean that, depending on model, it will be necessary to remove the inlet

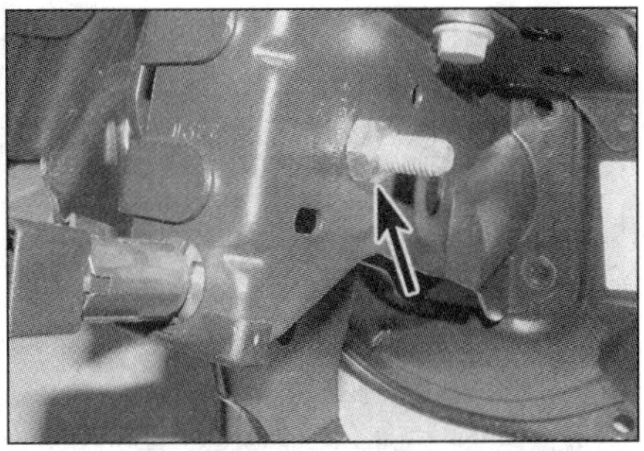

2.3 Withdraw the cross-shaft/bolt (arrowed) and manoeuvre the brake pedal out of the mounting bracket

manifold, heat shields, PAS reservoir, coolant expansion bottle, injection ECU and, on diesel models, the driveshaft. The removal and refitting of these components, can be found in their relevant Chapters. The removal procedure that is described in this Section is from inside the vehicle in the driver's footwell.

Testing

2 To test the operation of the servo unit, depress the footbrake several times to exhaust the vacuum, then start the engine whilst keeping the pedal firmly depressed. As the engine starts, there should be a noticeable 'give' in the brake pedal as the vacuum builds up. Allow the engine to run for at least two minutes, then switch it off. If the brake pedal is now depressed it should feel normal, but further applications should result in the pedal feeling firmer, with the pedal stroke decreasing with each application.

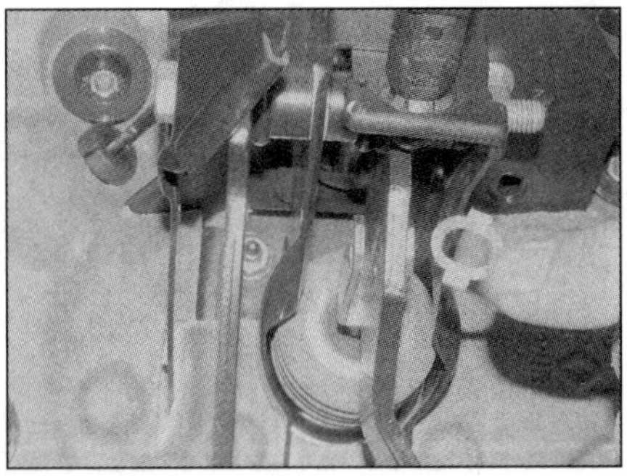

2.7 Ensure that the lugs on the spacer are correctly engaged with the pushrod

3 If the servo does not operate as described, inspect the servo unit check valve as described in Section 4. If the check valve is OK, try renewing the servo air filter (Section 5).

4 If the servo unit still fails to operate satisfactorily, the fault lies within the unit itself. Apart from external components, no spares are available, so a defective servo must be renewed.

Removal

Note: *A new master cylinder/servo O-ring seal will be required on refitting.*

5 Disconnect the battery negative lead (refer to *Disconnecting the battery* in the Reference Section).

6 Apply the handbrake, then jack up the front of the vehicle and support it on axle stands (see *Jacking and vehicle support*). Remove the right-hand front roadwheel and splash shield **(see illustration)**.

7 Undo the two master cylinder securing nuts to disengage it from the servo unit **(see illustration)**, discard the O-ring seal.

8 Disconnect the vacuum hose from the check valve on the servo unit **(see illustration)**.

9 Working inside the vehicle, disconnect the accelerator cable from the pedal. Undo the accelerator pedal securing nut and remove the pedal **(see illustration)**.

10 Disconnect the brake light switch wiring connector from above the brake pedal.

11 Remove the clutch pedal travel stop, and disconnect the clutch cable from its linkage on the top of the pedal assembly **(see illustrations)**.

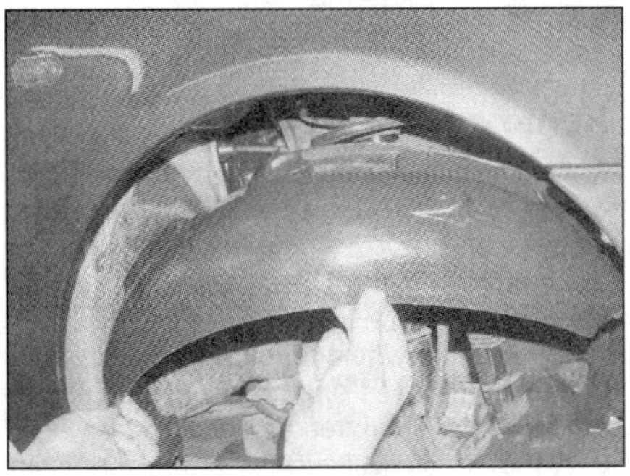

3.6 Removing the right-hand front splash shield

3.7 Removing the master cylinder securing nuts

3.8 Disconnect the vacuum hose from the servo unit

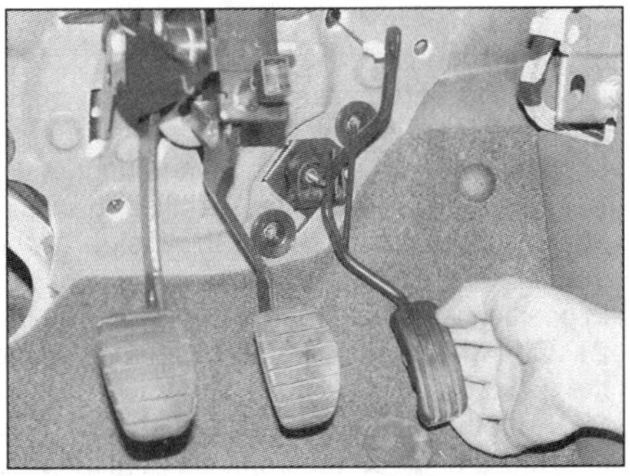

3.9 Removing the accelerator pedal

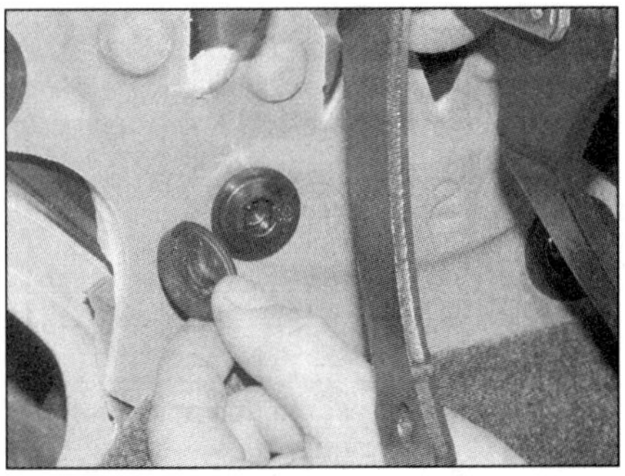

3.11a Unclip the clutch pedal stop . . .

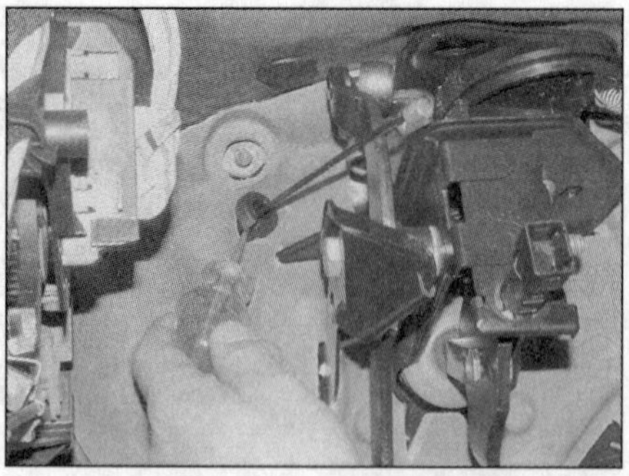

3.11b . . . and release the clutch cable

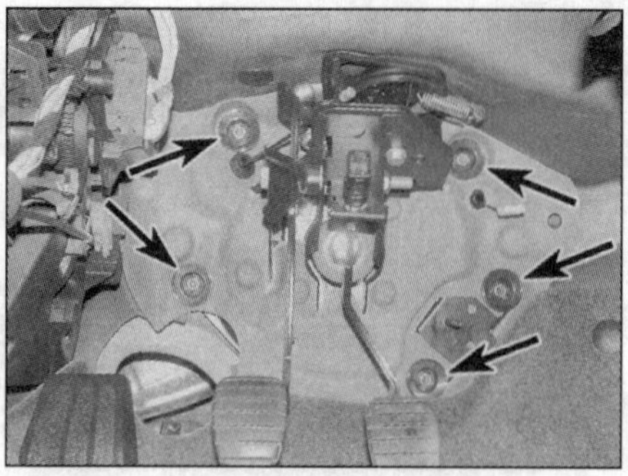

3.12a Remove the five retaining nuts (arrowed) . . .

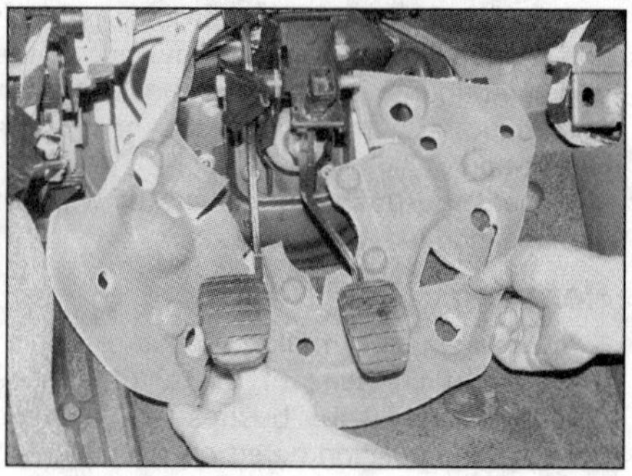

3.12b . . . and remove the soundproofing

3.13 Withdraw the assembly from the bulkhead – check the master cylinder does not foul the servo

12 Undo the five retaining nuts from around the pedal assembly, and remove the soundproofing **(see illustrations)**.

13 The pedal assembly, complete with mounting plate and servo, can be withdrawn from inside the footwell **(see illustration)**.

14 To remove the servo from the pedal assembly, remove the four nuts securing the servo unit to the pedal assembly mounting plate **(see illustration)**.

15 Extract the spring clip and withdraw the clevis pin securing the servo unit pushrod to the brake pedal. Note the spacer which is located on the inside of the pedal as described in Section 2.

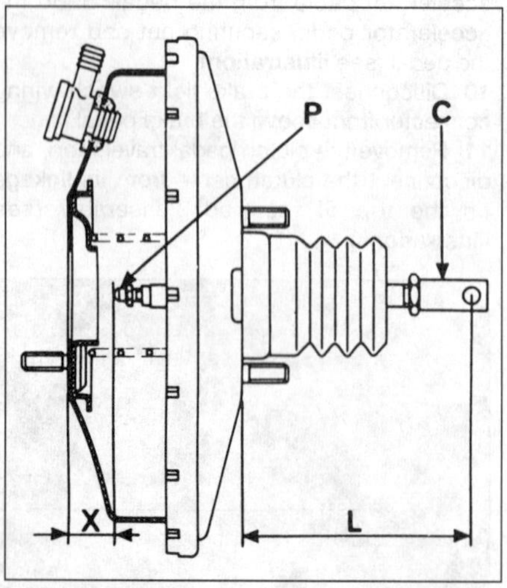

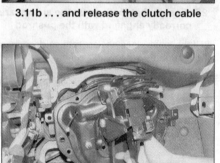

3.16 Vacuum servo unit adjustment dimensions

C Pushrod clevis *P Pushrod nut*
L = 104.8 mm *X = 22.3 mm*

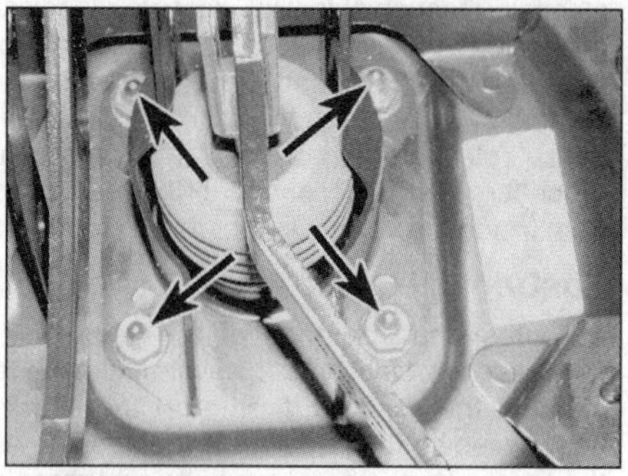

3.14 Remove the four securing nuts (arrowed) to release the servo from the pedal assembly

Refitting

16 Prior to refitting, check that the servo unit pushrod is correctly adjusted as follows. With the gasket removed, check the dimensions shown **(see illustration)**. If adjustment is necessary, dimension L can be altered by slackening the locknut and repositioning the pushrod clevis, and dimension X can be altered by repositioning the nut (P). After adjustment ensure that the clevis locknut is securely tightened.

17 Inspect the check valve sealing grommet for signs of damage or deterioration, and renew if necessary.

18 Fit a new O-ring seal to the rear of the master cylinder, and reposition the unit in the engine compartment.

19 Working inside the vehicle, refit the servo unit to the pedal assembly mounting plate. Ensure that the servo unit pushrod is correctly engaged with the brake pedal and tighten the four mounting nuts to their specified torque.

20 Position the spacer on the inside of the brake pedal. Refit the clevis pin, and secure it in position with the spring clip.

21 Offer the assembly into position, aligning the servo with the master cylinder.

22 Refit the soundproofing around the pedal assembly, and tighten the five mounting plate retaining nuts securely.

23 Reconnect the clutch cable to the pedal linkage, making sure the outer cable is located in the mounting plate correctly. Refit the clutch pedal travel stop.

24 Reconnect the brake light switch wiring connector, and refit the accelerator pedal and cable.

25 Working inside the engine bay, reconnect the vacuum hose to the servo unit check valve, and refit the master cylinder retaining nuts, tighten them to their specified torque.

26 Reconnect the battery.

27 Refit the splash shield and roadwheel, tighten the wheel bolts to their specified torque.

28 On completion, start the engine and check that there are no air leaks at the servo vacuum hose connection. Check the operation of the servo as described at the beginning of this Section.

4 Vacuum servo unit check valve – removal, testing and refitting

Removal

1 Apply the handbrake, then jack up the front of the vehicle and support it on axle stands (see *Jacking and vehicle support*). Remove the right-hand front roadwheel and splash shield.

2 Slacken the retaining clip, and disconnect the vacuum hose from the check valve on the servo unit (see illustration 3.8).

3 Withdraw the valve from its rubber sealing grommet, using a pulling and twisting motion. Remove the grommet from the servo.

Testing

4 Examine the check valve for signs of damage, and renew if necessary. The valve may be tested by blowing through it in both directions. Air should flow through the valve in one direction only – when blown through from the servo unit end of the valve. Renew the valve if this is not the case.

5 Examine the rubber sealing grommet and flexible vacuum hose for signs of damage or deterioration, and renew as necessary.

Refitting

6 Fit the sealing grommet into position in the servo unit.

7 Ease the check valve into position, taking care not to displace or damage the grommet. Reconnect the vacuum hose to the valve, and securely tighten its retaining clip.
8 On completion, start the engine and check that there are no air leaks.

5 Vacuum servo unit air filter – renewal

1 Working inside the car in the driver's footwell, ease the rubber cover off the rear of the servo unit, and move it up the pushrod.
2 Using a screwdriver or scriber, hook out the old air filter and remove it from the servo.
3 Make a cut in the new filter **(see illustration)**. Place the filter over the pushrod and into position in the servo end (check that it fills the complete opening to prevent any non-filtered air from passing through).
4 Refit the rubber cover, and check the operation of the brake pedal.

6 Hydraulic system – bleeding

Warning: Hydraulic fluid is poisonous; wash off immediately and thoroughly in the case of skin contact, and seek immediate medical advice if any fluid is swallowed or gets into the eyes. Certain types of hydraulic fluid are inflammable, and may ignite when allowed into contact with hot components; when servicing any hydraulic system, it is safest to assume that the fluid is inflammable, and to take precautions against the risk of fire as though it is petrol that is being handled. Finally, hydraulic fluid is hygroscopic (it absorbs moisture from the air) – old fluid may be contaminated and unfit for further use. When topping-up or renewing the fluid, always use the recommended type (see 'Lubricants and fluids'), and ensure that it comes from a freshly-opened, previously-sealed container.

HAYNES HiNT ***Hydraulic fluid is an effective paint stripper, and will attack plastics; if any is spilt, it should be washed off immediately using copious quantities of fresh water.***

Note: *On models with ABS, if any part of the hydraulic system is disconnected, the system must be fully bled before the vehicle is used. Failure to do so can result in air entering the hydraulic return pump. If the return pump draws in air, it will prove very difficult and even impossible to bleed out.*
Caution: On models equipped with ABS, disconnect the battery before disconnecting any braking system hydraulic union and do not reconnect the battery until after the hydraulic system has been bled. Failure to do this could lead to air entering the hydraulic unit. If air enters the hydraulic unit pump, it will prove very difficult (in some cases impossible) to bleed the unit.

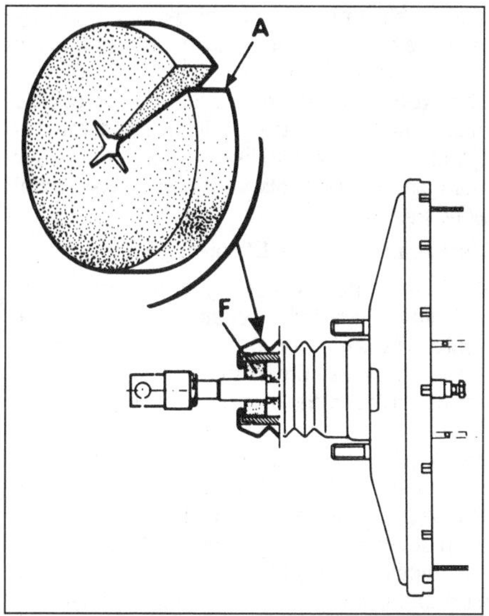

5.4 Vacuum servo unit air filter renewal

A Cut the new filter as shown
F Correct fitted position of filter in servo unit

General

1 The correct operation of any hydraulic system is only possible after removing all air from the components and circuit; this is achieved by bleeding the system.
2 During the bleeding procedure, add only clean, unused hydraulic fluid of the recommended type; never re-use fluid that has already been bled from the system. Ensure that sufficient fluid is available before starting work.
3 If there is any possibility of incorrect fluid being already in the system, the system must be flushed completely with uncontaminated, correct fluid, and new seals should be fitted to the various components.
4 If air has entered the hydraulic system because of a leak, ensure that the fault is cured before proceeding further.
5 Park the vehicle on level ground, switch off the engine and select first or reverse gear (or P on automatic transmission models). Chock the wheels and release the handbrake.
6 Check that all pipes and hoses are secure, unions tight and bleed screws closed. Clean any dirt from around the bleed screws.
7 Unscrew the master cylinder reservoir cap and top the master cylinder reservoir up to the MAX level line; refit the cap loosely. Remember to maintain the fluid level at least above the MIN level line throughout the procedure, or there is a risk of further air entering the system.
8 There are a number of one-man, do-it-yourself brake bleeding kits currently available from motor accessory shops. It is recommended that one of these kits is used whenever possible, as they greatly simplify the bleeding operation, and also reduce the risk of expelled air and fluid being drawn back into the system. If such a kit is not available, the basic (two-man) method must be used, which is described in detail below.
9 If a kit is to be used, prepare the vehicle as described previously, and follow the kit manufacturer's instructions. The procedure may vary slightly according to the type of kit being used; general procedures are as outlined below in the relevant sub-section.
10 Whichever method is used, the same sequence must be followed (paragraphs 11 and 12) to ensure the removal of all air from the system.

Bleeding sequence

Note: *The engine must not be running when bleeding the brakes.*
11 If the system has been only partially disconnected, and suitable precautions were taken to minimise fluid loss, it should be necessary only to bleed that part of the system (ie, the primary or secondary circuit).
12 If the complete system is to be bled, then it should be done working in the following sequence:

Non-ABS models

a) Right-hand rear brake.
b) Left-hand front brake.
c) Left-hand rear brake.
d) Right-hand front brake.

ABS models

a) Left-hand front brake.
b) Right-hand front brake.
c) Left-hand rear brake.
d) Right-hand rear brake.

Bleeding

Basic (two-man) method

13 Collect a clean glass jar, a suitable length of plastic or rubber tubing which is a tight fit over the bleed screw, and a ring spanner to fit the screw. The help of an assistant will also be required.
14 Remove the dust cap from the first screw in the sequence. Fit the spanner and tube to the screw, place the other end of the tube in the jar, and pour in sufficient fluid to cover the end of the tube.
15 Ensure that the master cylinder reservoir fluid level is maintained at least above the MIN level line throughout the procedure.
16 Have the assistant fully depress the brake pedal several times to build up pressure, then maintain it on the final stroke.
17 While pedal pressure is maintained, unscrew the bleed screw (approximately one turn) and allow the compressed fluid and air to flow into the jar. The assistant should maintain pedal pressure, following it down to the floor if

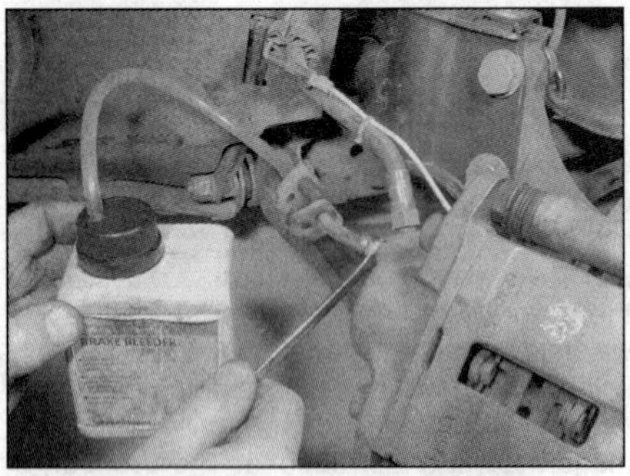

6.21 Bleeding a front brake caliper

necessary, and should not release it until instructed to do so. When the flow stops, tighten the bleed screw again. Have the assistant release the pedal slowly.

18 Repeat the steps given in paragraphs 16 and 17 until the fluid emerging from the bleed screw is free from air bubbles. Remember to recheck the fluid level in the master cylinder reservoir every five strokes or so. If the master cylinder has been drained and refilled, and air is being bled from the first screw in the sequence, allow approximately five seconds between strokes for the master cylinder passages to refill.

19 When no more air bubbles appear, tighten the bleed screw securely, remove the tube and spanner, and refit the dust cap. Do not overtighten the bleed screw.

20 Repeat the procedure on the remaining screws in the sequence until all air is removed from the system and the brake pedal feels firm.

Using a one-way valve kit

21 As their name implies, these kits consist of a length of tubing with a one-way valve fitted, to prevent expelled air and fluid being drawn back into the system; some kits include a translucent container, which can be positioned so that the air bubbles can be more easily seen flowing from the end of the tube **(see illustration)**.

22 The kit is connected to the bleed screw, which is then opened. The user returns to the driver's seat and depresses the brake pedal with a smooth, steady stroke and slowly releases it; this is repeated until the expelled fluid is clear of air bubbles.

23 Note that these kits simplify work so much that it is easy to forget the master cylinder reservoir fluid level; ensure that this is maintained at least above the MIN level line at all times.

Using a pressure-bleeding kit

24 These kits are usually operated by the reservoir of pressurised air contained in the spare tyre, although it may be necessary to reduce the pressure in the tyre to lower than normal; refer to the instructions supplied with the kit.

25 By connecting a pressurised, fluid-filled container to the master cylinder reservoir, bleeding can be carried out simply by opening each screw in turn (in the specified sequence) and allowing the fluid to flow out until no more air bubbles can be seen in the expelled fluid.

26 This method has the advantage that the large reservoir of fluid provides an additional safeguard against air being drawn into the system during bleeding.

27 Pressure-bleeding is particularly effective when bleeding 'difficult' systems, or when bleeding the complete system at the time of routine fluid renewal.

All methods

28 When bleeding is complete and firm pedal feel is restored, wash off any spilt fluid, tighten the bleed screws securely and refit their dust caps.

29 Check the hydraulic fluid level, and top-up if necessary (see *Weekly checks*).

30 Discard any hydraulic fluid that has been bled from the system; it will not be fit for re-use.

31 Check the feel of the brake pedal. If it feels at all spongy, air must still be present in the system, and further bleeding is required. Failure to bleed satisfactorily after several repetitions of the bleeding procedure may be due to worn master cylinder seals.

7 Hydraulic pipes and hoses – renewal

Note: *Before starting work, refer to the warning at the beginning of Section 6 concerning the dangers of hydraulic fluid.*

1 If any pipe or hose is to be renewed, minimise fluid loss by removing the master cylinder reservoir cap and then tightening it down onto a piece of polythene (taking care not to damage the sender unit) to obtain an airtight seal. Alternatively, flexible hoses can be sealed, if required, using a proprietary brake hose clamp; metal brake pipe unions can be plugged (if care is taken not to allow dirt into the system) or capped immediately they are disconnected. Place a wad of rag under any union that is to be disconnected, to catch any spilt fluid.

2 If a flexible hose is to be disconnected, unscrew the brake pipe union nut before removing the spring clip which secures the hose to its mounting bracket **(see illustrations)**.

3 To unscrew the union nuts, it is preferable to obtain a brake pipe spanner of the correct size (11 mm/13 mm split ring); these are available from motor accessory shops. Failing this, a close-fitting open-ended spanner will be required, though if the nuts are tight or corroded, their flats may be rounded off if the spanner slips. In such a case, a self-locking wrench is often the only way to unscrew a stubborn union, but it follows that the pipe and the damaged nuts must be renewed on reassembly. Always clean a union and surrounding area before disconnecting it. If disconnecting a component with more than one union, make a careful note of the connections before disturbing any of them.

4 If a brake pipe is to be renewed, it can be obtained, cut to length and with the union nuts and end flares in place, from Renault dealers. All that is then necessary is to bend it to shape, following the line of the original, before fitting it to the car. Alternatively, most motor accessory shops can make up brake pipes from kits, but this requires very careful measurement of the original to ensure that the replacement is of the correct length. The safest answer is usually to take the original to the shop as a pattern.

5 On refitting, do not overtighten the union nuts. The specified torque wrench settings (where given) are not high, and it is not necessary to exercise brute force to obtain a sound joint.

6 Ensure that the pipes and hoses are correctly routed with no kinks, and that they are secured in the clips or brackets provided. In the case of flexible hoses, make sure that they cannot contact other components during movement of the steering and/or suspension assemblies.

7 After fitting, remove the polythene from the reservoir (or remove the plugs or clamps, as applicable), and bleed the hydraulic system as described in Section 6. Wash off any spilt fluid, and check carefully for fluid leaks.

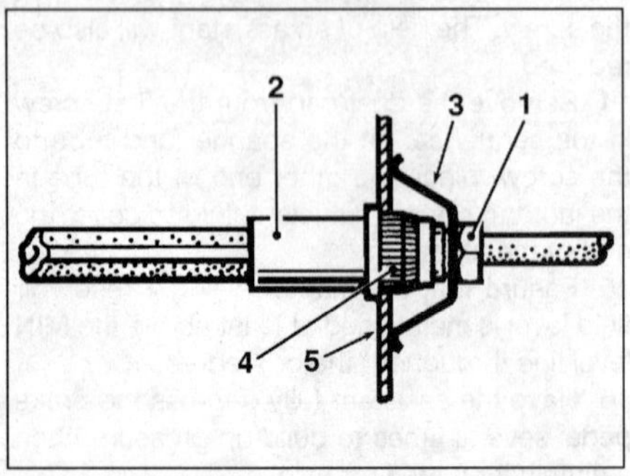

7.2a Hydraulic pipe connection to a flexible hose

1 Union nut
2 Flexible hose
3 Spring clip support
4 Splined end fitting
5 Bodywork

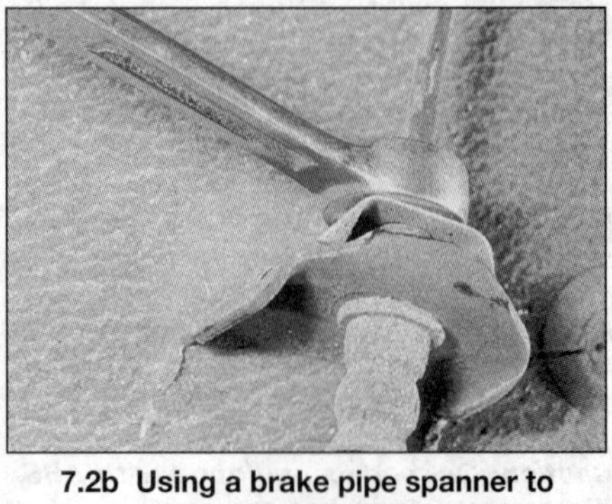

7.2b Using a brake pipe spanner to unscrew a hydraulic union nut

8 Master cylinder - removal and refitting

Caution: On models equipped with ABS, disconnect the battery before disconnecting any braking system hydraulic union and do not reconnect the battery until after the hydraulic system has been bled. Failure to do this could lead to air entering the hydraulic unit. If air enters the hydraulic unit pump, it will prove very difficult (in some cases impossible) to bleed the unit (see Section 6).

Note: *Before starting work, refer to the warning at the beginning of Section 6 concerning the dangers of hydraulic fluid.*

Removal

1 Disconnect the battery negative lead (refer to *Disconnecting the battery* in the Reference Section)

2 Apply the handbrake, then jack up the front of the vehicle and support it on axle stands (see *Jacking and vehicle support*).

3 On right-hand drive models, remove the right-hand front roadwheel and splash shield.

4 On left-hand drive models, remove the left-hand front roadwheel and splash shield.

5 On left-hand drive models, also remove the injection ECU (depending on model) from the inner wing. Also release the PAS reservoir and move it to one side.

6 On all models, remove the master cylinder reservoir cap, having disconnected the sender unit wiring connector, and syphon the hydraulic fluid from the reservoir. **Note:** *Do not syphon the fluid by mouth, as it is poisonous; use a syringe or an old antifreeze hydrometer.* Alternatively, open any convenient pair of bleed screws in the system (one in each hydraulic circuit) and gently pump the brake pedal to expel the fluid through plastic tubes connected to the screws (see Section 6).

7 Once drained, remove the reservoir from the master cylinder by pulling it upwards.

8 Wipe clean the area around the brake pipe unions on the side of the master cylinder, and place absorbent rags beneath the pipe unions to catch any surplus fluid. Make a note of the correct fitted positions of the unions, then unscrew the union nuts and carefully withdraw the pipes **(see illustration)**. Plug or tape over the pipe ends and master cylinder orifices, to minimise the loss of brake fluid and to prevent the entry of dirt into the system. Wash off any spilt fluid immediately with cold water.

9 Undo the two vacuum pipe retaining bracket nuts.

10 Slacken and remove the two nuts securing the master cylinder to the vacuum servo unit **(see illustration)**, then withdraw the master cylinder from the engine compartment. Remove the O-ring seal from the rear of the master cylinder, and discard it.

11 It is not possible to obtain internal components for the master cylinder, therefore

8.8 Slackening the brake fluid pipe unions in the master cylinder

if it is faulty, it must be renewed as a complete unit. The reservoir mounting bush seals may be renewed if necessary. The O-ring seal fitted between the master cylinder and the vacuum servo must be renewed as a matter of course whenever the unit is removed, as a leak at this point will allow atmospheric pressure into the servo unit.

Refitting

12 Before refitting the master cylinder, check that the distance between the tip of the master cylinder end of the pushrod and the front of the servo unit, dimension X, is as shown (see illustration 3.16). If necessary, adjust by repositioning the pushrod nut P.

13 Remove all traces of dirt from the master cylinder and servo unit mating surfaces. Fit a new O-ring seal to the groove on the master cylinder body.

14 Fit the master cylinder to the servo, ensuring that the servo pushrod enters the master cylinder bore centrally. Refit the master cylinder mounting nuts, and tighten them to the specified torque.

15 Wipe clean the brake pipe unions, then refit them to the master cylinder ports. Tighten the union nuts to the specified torque.

16 Carefully align the reservoir with the mounting bush seals. Push the reservoir firmly into position.

17 On left-hand drive models, refit the injection ECU and power steering reservoir back into their correct position.

18 On all models, refill the master cylinder reservoir with new fluid, and bleed the hydraulic system as described in Section 6.

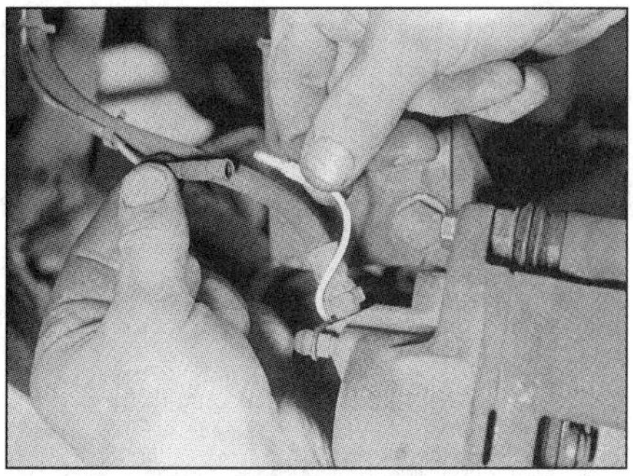

9.2 Disconnecting the pad wear sensor wiring connector - Girling caliper

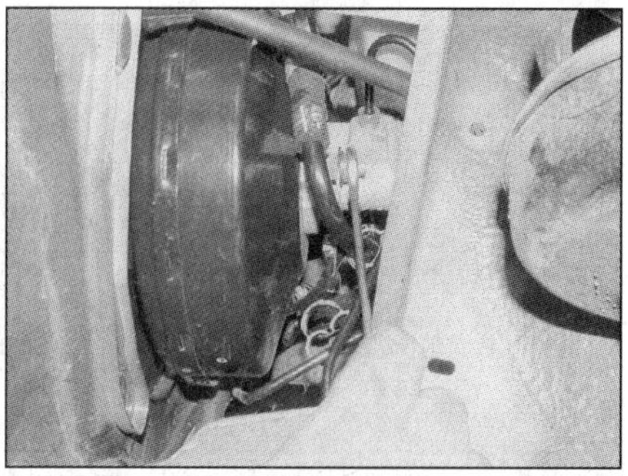

8.10 Removing the master cylinder securing nuts

9 Front brake pads - renewal

Warning: Renew both sets of front brake pads at the same time - never renew the pads on only one wheel, as uneven braking may result. Note that the dust created by wear of the pads may contain asbestos, which is a health hazard. Never blow it out with compressed air, and don't inhale any of it. An approved filtering mask should be worn when working on the brakes. DO NOT use petroleum-based solvents to clean brake parts - use brake cleaner or methylated spirit only.

1 Apply the handbrake, then jack up the front of the vehicle and support it on axle stands (see *Jacking and vehicle support*). Remove the front roadwheels.

2 Where fitted, trace the brake pad wear sensor wiring back from the inner pad, and disconnect it at the wiring connector **(see illustration)**.

3 Push the piston a short way into its bore by pulling the caliper outwards (do not overdo it, or the master cylinder reservoir may overflow).

Girling calipers

Note: *Suitable thread-locking compound will be required to coat the threads of the caliper guide pin bolt on refitting.*

4 Slacken and remove the caliper upper and lower guide pin bolts, using a slim open-ended spanner to prevent the guide pin itself from rotating **(see illustration)**. Discard the guide

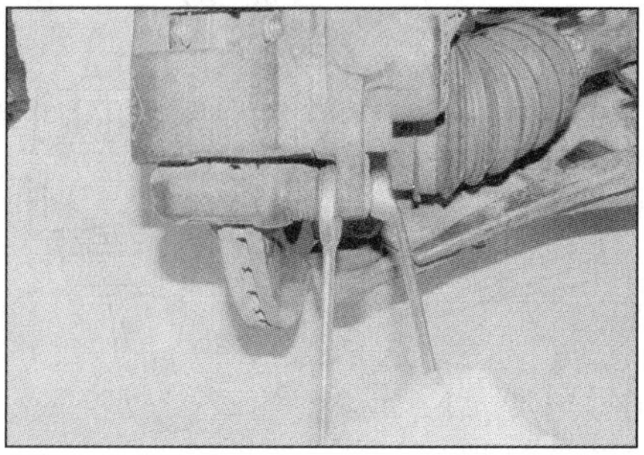

9.4 On Girling calipers, slacken the guide pin bolts whilst holding the guide pins with an open-ended spanner

9.11 Ensure that the brake pads are fitted the correct way round, with friction material facing the disc

pin bolts; new bolts must be used on refitting. If genuine Renault brake pads are purchased, the bolts will be supplied with the pad set.

5 With the guide pins removed, lift the caliper away from the brake pads and mounting bracket, and tie it to the suspension strut using a suitable piece of wire. Do not allow the caliper to hang unsupported on the flexible hose.

6 Withdraw the two brake pads from the caliper mounting bracket, and examine them.

7 First measure the thickness of each brake pad (friction material and backing plate). If any pad is worn at any point to the specified minimum thickness or less, all four pads must be renewed. Also, the pads should be renewed if any are fouled with oil or grease; there is no satisfactory way of degreasing friction material once contaminated. If any of the brake pads are worn unevenly or fouled with oil or grease, trace and rectify the cause before reassembly. New brake pads and spring kits are available from Renault dealers.

8 If the brake pads are still serviceable, carefully clean them using a clean, fine wire brush or similar, paying particular attention to the sides and back of the metal backing. Clean out the grooves in the friction material, and pick out any large embedded particles of dirt or debris. Carefully clean the pad locations in the caliper body/mounting bracket.

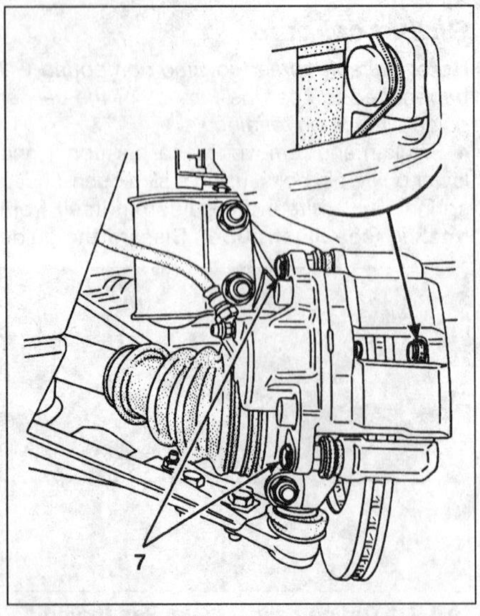

9.12 Girling caliper showing guide pin bolts (7) and correct fitted position of anti-rattle spring (Sec 9)

9 Prior to fitting the pads, check that the guide sleeves are free to slide easily in the caliper body, and check that the rubber guide sleeve gaiters are undamaged. Brush the dust and dirt from the caliper and piston, but *do not inhale it as it is injurious to health*. Inspect the dust seal around the piston for damage, and the piston for evidence of fluid leaks, corrosion or damage. If attention to any of these components is necessary, refer to Section 10. Also inspect the brake disc as described in Section 11.

10 If new brake pads are to be fitted, the caliper piston must be pushed back into the cylinder to make room for them. Either use a G-clamp or similar tool, or use suitable pieces of wood as levers. Provided that the master cylinder reservoir has not been overfilled with hydraulic fluid, there should be no spillage, but keep a careful watch on the fluid level while retracting the piston. If the fluid level rises above the MAX level line at any time, the surplus should be syphoned off (not by mouth – use an old syringe or antifreeze hydrometer) or ejected via a plastic tube connected to the bleed screw (see Section 6).

11 Install the pads in the caliper mounting bracket, ensuring that the friction material of each pad is against the brake disc. Where applicable, the pad with the wear sensor is fitted on the inside **(see illustration)**.

12 Position the caliper over the pads. Coat the threads of the new lower guide pin bolt with locking fluid, and fit the bolt. Apply locking fluid to the new upper guide pin bolt, press the caliper into position, and fit the bolt. Check that the anti-rattle springs are correctly located **(see illustration)**, then tighten the guide pin bolts to the specified torque, starting with the lower bolt.

13 Reconnect the brake pad wear sensor wiring connector, ensuring that the wire is correctly routed.

14 Depress the brake pedal several times to bring the pads into firm contact with the brake disc.

15 Repeat the above procedure on the other front brake caliper.

16 Refit the roadwheels, then lower the vehicle to the ground and tighten the bolts to the specified torque.

17 Check the hydraulic fluid level as described in *Weekly checks*.

18 If new pads have been fitted, full braking efficiency will not be obtained until the linings have bedded-in. Be prepared for longer stopping distances, and avoid harsh braking as far as possible for the first hundred miles or so after fitting new pads.

Bendix calipers

19 Extract the small spring clip from the pad retaining plate, and then slide the plate out of the caliper **(see illustrations)**.

20 Using pliers if necessary, withdraw the pads from the caliper. Make a note of the correct fitted position of the anti-rattle spring, and remove the spring from each pad.

21 First measure the thickness of each brake pad (friction material and backing plate). If any pad is worn at any point to the specified minimum thickness or less, all four pads must be renewed. Also, the pads should be renewed if any are fouled with oil or grease; there is no satisfactory way of degreasing friction material once contaminated. If any of the brake pads are worn unevenly or fouled with oil or grease, trace and rectify the cause before reassembly. New brake pads and spring kits are available from Renault dealers.

22 Note that there are two different types of brake pad available for the Bendix caliper. The correct pad type depends on the brake caliper bore/piston diameter. Calipers with a 45 mm diameter bore/piston require pads with symmetrical linings, whereas calipers with a 48 mm diameter bore/piston require pads with offset linings (groove in the friction material not central). The pad types can also be distinguished by the cut-outs in the upper corners of the friction material; symmetrical linings have two cut-outs, whereas the offset linings have only a single cut-out.

23 If the brake pads are still serviceable, carefully clean them using a clean, fine wire brush or similar, paying particular attention to the sides and back of the metal backing. Clean out the grooves in the friction material, and pick out any large embedded particles of dirt or debris. Carefully clean the pad locations in the caliper body/mounting bracket.

9.19a On Bendix calipers remove the spring clip . . .

9.19b . . . and remove the pad retaining plate

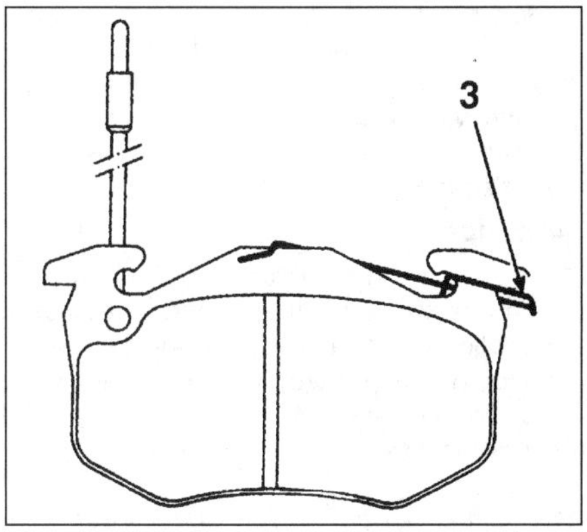

9.26 Anti-rattle spring (3) correctly fitted to Bendix inner brake pad

24 Prior to fitting the pads, check that the guide sleeves are free to slide easily in the caliper body, and check that the rubber guide sleeve gaiters are undamaged. Brush the dust and dirt from the caliper and piston, but *do not inhale it as it is injurious to health*. Inspect the dust seal around the piston for damage, and the piston for evidence of fluid leaks, corrosion or damage. If attention to any of these components is necessary, refer to Section 10. Also inspect the brake disc as described in Section 11.

25 If new brake pads are to be fitted, the caliper piston must be pushed back into the cylinder to make room for them. Either use a G-clamp or similar tool, or use suitable pieces of wood as levers. Provided that the master cylinder reservoir has not been overfilled with hydraulic fluid, there should be no spillage, but keep a careful watch on the fluid level while retracting the piston. If the fluid level rises above the MAX level line at any time, the surplus should be syphoned off (not by mouth – use an old syringe or antifreeze tester) or ejected via a plastic tube connected to the bleed screw (see Section 6).

26 Fit the anti-rattle springs to the pads, so that when the pads are installed in the caliper, the spring end will be located at the opposite end of the pad to the pad retaining plate **(see illustration)**.

27 Locate the pads in the caliper, ensuring that the friction material of each pad is against the brake disc, and the pad with the wear sensor is fitted on the inside. Also recheck that the anti-rattle spring ends are at the opposite end of the pad to which the retaining plate is to be inserted. On models with offset linings, looking at the pads from the front of the car, the innermost pad groove must be higher than the outer pad groove. Make sure that the pads are fitted correctly **(see illustrations)**.

28 Slide the retaining plate into place, and install the small spring clip at its inner end. It may be necessary to file an entry chamfer on the edge of the retaining plate, to enable it to be fitted without difficulty **(see illustration)**.

29 Reconnect the brake pad wear sensor wiring connector, ensuring that the wire is correctly routed.

30 Depress the brake pedal several times to bring the pads into firm contact with the brake disc.

31 Repeat the above procedure on the other front brake caliper.

32 Refit the roadwheels, then lower the vehicle to the ground and tighten the bolts to the specified torque.

33 Check the hydraulic fluid level as described in *Weekly checks*.

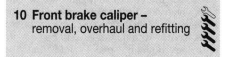

10 Front brake caliper – removal, overhaul and refitting

Note: *Before starting work, refer to the warnings at the beginning of Sections 6, 8 and 9 concerning the dangers of hydraulic fluid and asbestos dust.*

Removal

1 Apply the handbrake, then jack up the front of the vehicle and support it on axle stands (see *Jacking and vehicle support*). Remove the appropriate roadwheel.

2 Minimise fluid loss, either by removing the master cylinder reservoir cap and then tightening it down onto a piece of polythene to obtain an airtight seal (taking care not to damage the sender unit), or by using a brake hose clamp, a G-clamp or a similar tool with protected jaws to clamp the flexible hose.

Bendix caliper

3 Remove the brake pads as described in Section 9.

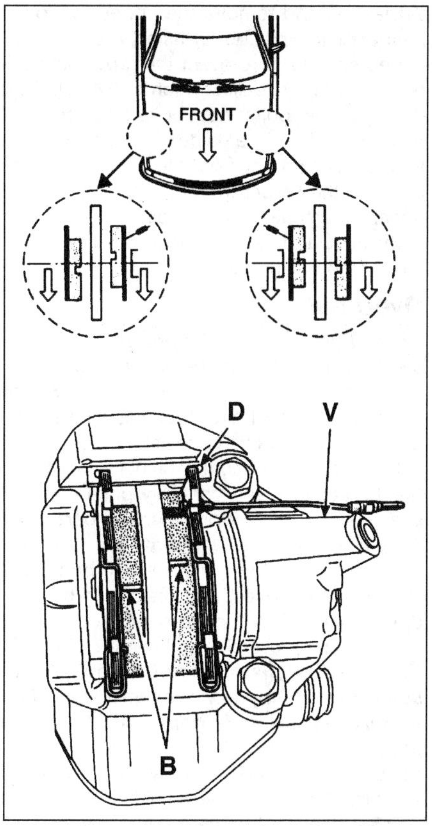

9.27a Correct fitting of Bendix offset lining brake pads

B Grooves
D Pad retaining plate spring clip location
V Bleed screw

4 Clean the area around the union, then loosen the brake hose union nut.

5 Slacken the two bolts securing the caliper assembly to the swivel hub, and remove them along with the mounting plate, noting which way around the plate is fitted. Lift the caliper assembly away from the brake disc, and unscrew it from the end of the brake hose.

Girling caliper

6 Clean the area around the hose union, then loosen the brake hose union nut **(see illustration)**.

9.27b Correct fitted positions of the Bendix offset lining brake pads

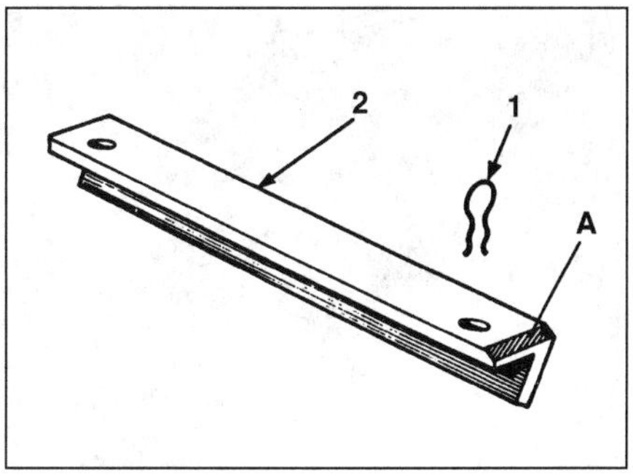

9.28 Bendix disc pad retaining plate (2) and spring clip (1) showing filed chamfer (A)

10.6 Slacken the front brake caliper hose union nut (arrowed) – Girling caliper

7 Slacken and remove the upper and lower caliper guide pin bolts, using a slim open-ended spanner to prevent the guide pin itself from rotating (see illustration in 9.4). Discard the guide pin bolts; new bolts must be used on refitting. With the guide pin bolts removed, lift the caliper away from the brake disc, then unscrew the caliper from the end of the brake hose. Note that the brake pads need not be disturbed, and can be left in position in the caliper mounting bracket.

Overhaul

Note: *Ensure that an appropriate caliper overhaul kit is obtained before starting work.*

8 With the caliper on the bench, wipe away all traces of dust and dirt, but avoid inhaling the dust, as it is injurious to health.

9 On the Girling caliper, using a small flat-bladed screwdriver, carefully prise the dust seal retaining clip out of the caliper bore.

10 On all calipers, withdraw the partially-ejected piston from the caliper body and remove the dust seal. The piston can be withdrawn by hand, or if necessary forced out by applying compressed air to the union bolt hole. ***Caution: The piston may be ejected with some force. Only low pressure should be required, such as is generated by a foot pump.***

11 Extract the piston hydraulic seal using a blunt instrument such as a knitting needle or a crochet hook, taking care not to damage the caliper bore.

12 Withdraw the guide sleeves or pins from the caliper body or mounting bracket (as applicable) and remove the rubber gaiters.

13 Thoroughly clean all components using only methylated spirit, isopropyl alcohol or clean hydraulic fluid as a cleaning medium. Never use mineral-based solvents, such as petrol or paraffin, which will attack the hydraulic system rubber components. Dry the components immediately, using compressed air or a clean, lint-free cloth. Use compressed air to blow clear the fluid passages.

14 Check all components and renew any that are worn or damaged. Check particularly the cylinder bore and piston; if they are scratched, worn or corroded in any way, they must be renewed (note that this means the renewal of the complete body assembly). Similarly check the condition of the guide sleeves or pins and their bores; they should be undamaged and (when cleaned) a reasonably tight sliding fit in the body or mounting bracket bores. If there is any doubt about the condition of a component, renew it.

15 If the assembly is fit for further use, obtain the appropriate repair kit; the components are available from Renault dealers, in various combinations.

16 Renew all rubber seals, dust covers and caps disturbed on dismantling as a matter of course; these should never be re-used.

17 Before commencing reassembly, ensure that all components are absolutely clean and dry.

18 Dip the piston and the new piston (fluid) seal in clean hydraulic fluid. Smear clean fluid on the cylinder bore surface.

19 Fit the new piston (fluid) seal, using only the fingers to manipulate it into the cylinder bore groove. Fit the new dust seal to the piston. Refit the piston to the cylinder bore using a twisting motion, ensuring that the piston enters squarely into the bore. Press the piston fully into the bore, then press the dust seal into the caliper body.

20 On the Girling caliper, install the dust seal retaining clip, ensuring that it is correctly seated in the caliper groove.

21 On all calipers, apply the grease supplied in the repair kit, or a good quality high-temperature brake grease or anti-seize compound to the guide sleeves or pins. Fit the sleeves or pins to the caliper body or mounting bracket. Fit the new rubber gaiters, ensuring that they are correctly located in the grooves on both the sleeve or pin, and body or mounting bracket (as applicable).

Refitting

Bendix caliper

22 Screw the caliper fully onto the flexible hose union nut. Position the caliper over the brake disc, then refit the two caliper mounting bolts (coated with thread-locking compound) and the mounting plate. Note that the mounting plate must be fitted so that its bend curves towards the caliper body; this is necessary to prevent the plate contacting the driveshaft gaiter when the steering is on full-lock. With the plate correctly positioned, tighten the caliper bolts to the specified torque setting.

23 Tighten the brake hose union nut to the specified torque, then refit the brake pads as described in Section 9.

Girling caliper

24 Screw the caliper body fully onto the flexible hose union nut. Check that the brake pads are still correctly fitted in the caliper mounting bracket.

25 Position the caliper over the pads. Coat the threads of the new lower guide pin bolt with locking fluid, and fit the bolt. Apply locking fluid to the new upper guide pin bolt, press the caliper into position, and fit the bolt.

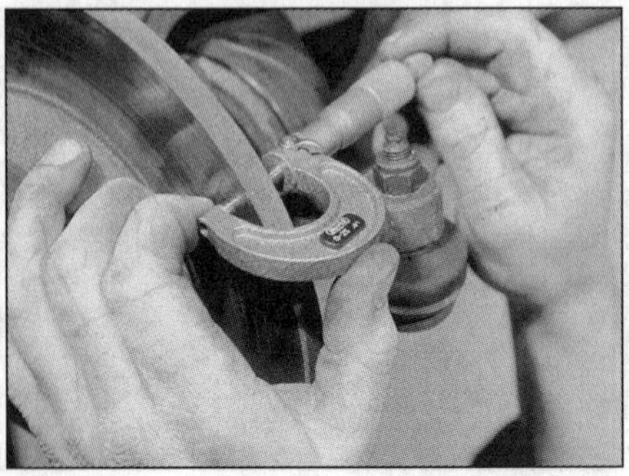

11.3 Measuring brake disc thickness with a micrometer

Check that the anti-rattle springs are correctly located (see illustration 9.12), then tighten the guide pin bolts to the specified torque, starting with the lower bolt.

26 Tighten the brake hose union nut to the specified torque.

All calipers

27 Remove the brake hose clamp or polythene, where fitted, and bleed the hydraulic system as described in Section 6. Providing the precautions described were taken to minimise brake fluid loss, it should only be necessary to bleed the relevant front brake.

28 Refit the roadwheel, then lower the vehicle to the ground and tighten the roadwheel bolts to the specified torque.

11 Front brake disc – inspection, removal and refitting

Note: *Before starting work, refer to the warning at the beginning of Section 9 concerning the dangers of asbestos dust. If either disc requires renewal, both should be renewed at the same time, to ensure even and consistent braking. In principle, new pads should be fitted also.*

Inspection

1 Chock the rear wheels, firmly apply the handbrake, jack up the front of the vehicle and support on axle stands (see *Jacking and vehicle support*). Remove the appropriate front roadwheel.

2 Slowly rotate the brake disc so that the full area of both sides can be checked; remove the brake pads, as described in Section 9, if better access is required to the inboard surface. Light scoring is normal in the area swept by the brake pads, but if heavy scoring is found, the disc must be renewed.

3 It is normal to find a lip of rust and brake dust around the disc's perimeter; this can be scraped off if required. If, however, a lip has formed due to wear of the brake pad swept area, the disc thickness must be measured using a micrometer **(see illustration).** Take measurements at several places around the disc at the inside and outside of the pad swept area; if the disc has worn at any point to the specified minimum thickness or less, it must be renewed.

4 If the disc is thought to be warped, it can be checked for run-out, ideally by using a dial gauge mounted on any convenient fixed point, while the disc is slowly rotated **(see illustration).** In the absence of a dial gauge, use feeler blades to measure (at several points all around the disc) the clearance between the disc and a fixed point such as the caliper mounting bracket. If the measurements obtained are at the specified maximum or beyond, the disc is excessively warped, and must be renewed; however, it is worth

checking first that the hub bearing is in good condition (Chapters 1A or 1B and 10). Also try the effect of removing the disc and turning it through 180° to reposition it on the hub; if run-out is still excessive, the disc must be renewed.

5 Check the disc for cracks (especially around the wheel bolt holes), and for any other wear or damage. Renew the disc if necessary.

Removal

Note: *Suitable thread-locking fluid will be required to coat the threads of the brake caliper mounting bolts on refitting.*

6 Unscrew the two bolts securing the brake caliper and bracket to the swivel hub, and slide the caliper assembly off the disc. Using a piece of wire or string, tie the caliper to the front suspension coil spring, to avoid placing any strain on the hydraulic brake hose **(see illustrations)**.

7 If the same disc is to be refitted, use chalk or paint to mark the relationship of the disc to the hub. Remove the two screws securing the brake disc to the hub **(see illustration)**, and remove the disc. If it is tight, lightly tap its rear face with a hide or plastic mallet.

Refitting

8 Refitting is the reverse of the removal procedure, noting the following points:

- a) *Ensure that the mating surfaces of the disc and hub are clean and flat.*
- b) *If applicable, align the marks made on removal.*
- c) *Securely tighten the disc retaining screws.*
- d) *If a new disc has been fitted, use a suitable solvent to wipe any preservative coating from the disc before refitting the caliper.*
- e) *Apply locking fluid to the threads of the brake caliper mounting bolts, and tighten them to the specified torque.*
- f) *Refit the roadwheel, then lower the vehicle to the ground and tighten the roadwheel bolts to the specified torque. On completion, depress the brake pedal several times to bring the brake pads into contact with the disc.*

12 Load-sensitive pressure-regulating valve – testing, removal and refitting

Testing

1 A load-sensitive pressure regulating valve is fitted into the hydraulic circuit to the rear brakes. The valve is mounted onto the underside of the rear of the vehicle and is attached to the rear axle. The valve measures the load on the rear axle, via the movement of the axle, and regulates the hydraulic pressure being applied to the rear brakes to help prevent rear wheels locking up under hard braking.

2 Specialist equipment is required to check the performance of the valve(s), therefore if the valve is thought to be faulty the car should be taken to a suitably-equipped Renault dealer for testing. Repairs are not possible and, if faulty, the valve must be renewed.

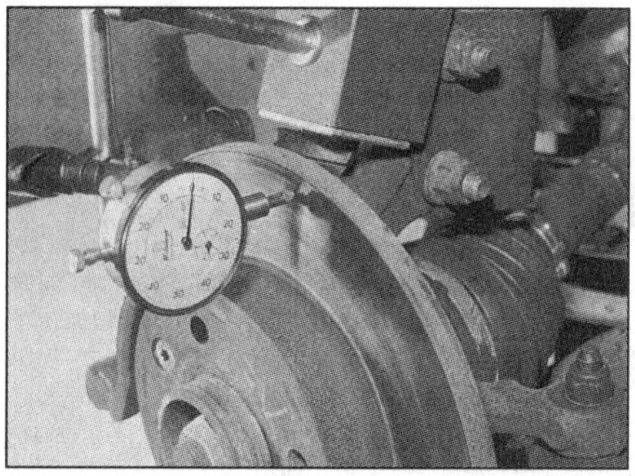

11.4 Measuring brake disc run-out with a dial gauge

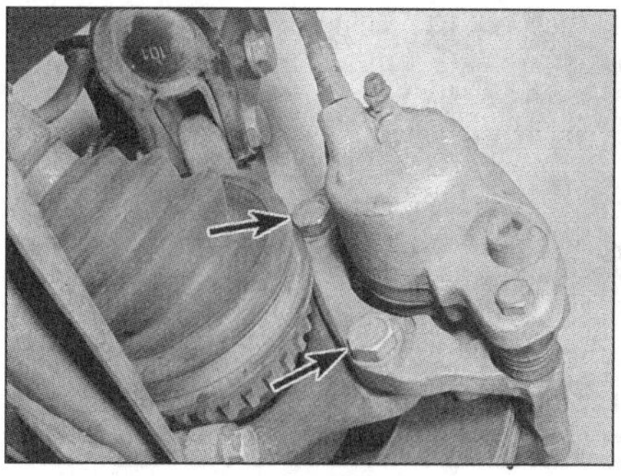

11.6a Undo the two bolts (arrowed) securing the caliper to the swivel hub . . .

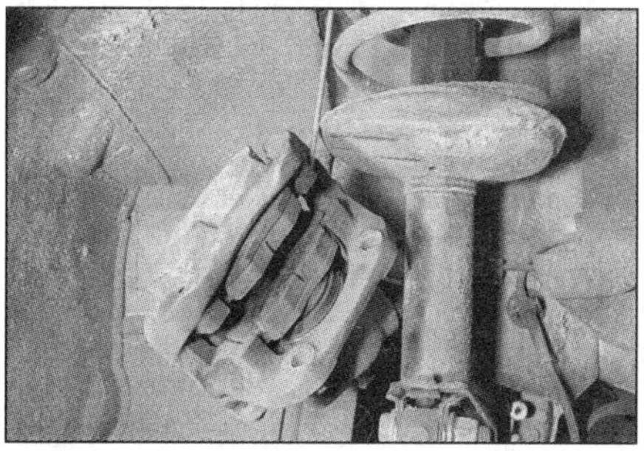

11.6b . . . then slide the caliper off the disc, and tie it to the suspension strut spring – Girling caliper

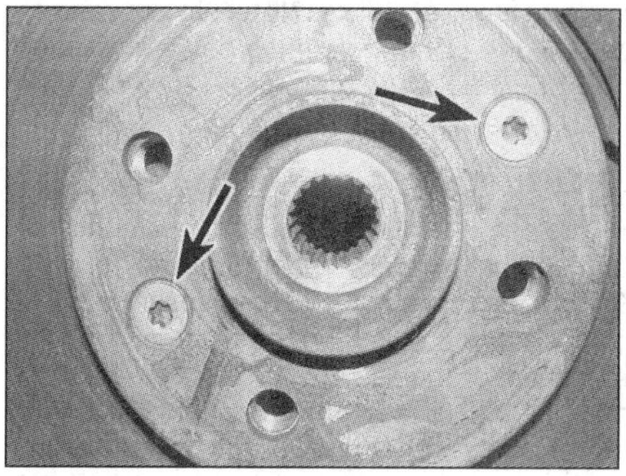

11.7 Remove the two brake disc retaining screws (arrowed)

Removal

Caution: On models equipped with ABS, disconnect the battery before disconnecting any braking system hydraulic union and do not reconnect the battery until after the hydraulic system has been bled. Failure to do this could lead to air entering the hydraulic unit. If air enters the hydraulic unit pump, it will prove very difficult (in some cases impossible) to bleed the unit (see Section 6).

Note: *Before starting work, refer to the warning at the beginning of Section 6 concerning the dangers of hydraulic fluid.*

3 Minimise fluid loss by first removing the master cylinder reservoir cap, and then tightening it down onto a piece of polythene, to obtain an airtight seal.

4 Check the front wheels then jack up the rear of the vehicle and support it on axle stands (see *Jacking and vehicle support*).

5 Wipe clean the area around the brake pipe unions on the valve, and place absorbent rags beneath the pipe unions to catch any surplus fluid. To avoid confusion on refitting, make alignment marks between the pipes and valve assembly.

6 Slacken the union nuts and disconnect the brake pipes from the valve **(see illustration)**. Plug or tape over the pipe ends and valve orifices, to minimise the loss of brake fluid, and to prevent the entry of dirt into the system. Wash off any spilt fluid immediately with cold water.

7 Slacken and remove the retaining bolts then unclip the valve link rod **(see illustration)** and remove the valve assembly from

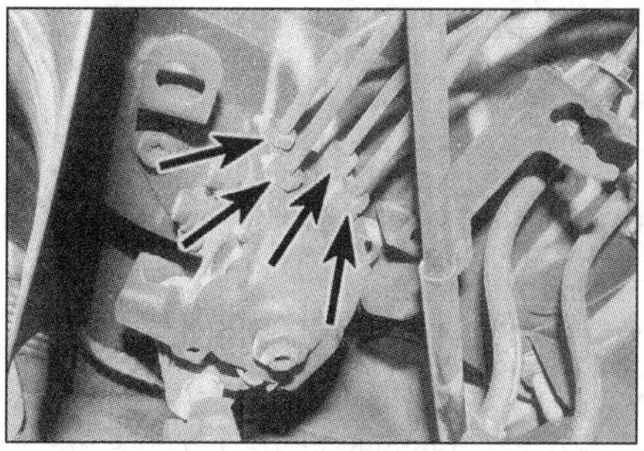

12.6 Disconnect the brake pipe unions (arrowed) from the load-sensitive pressure-regulating valve

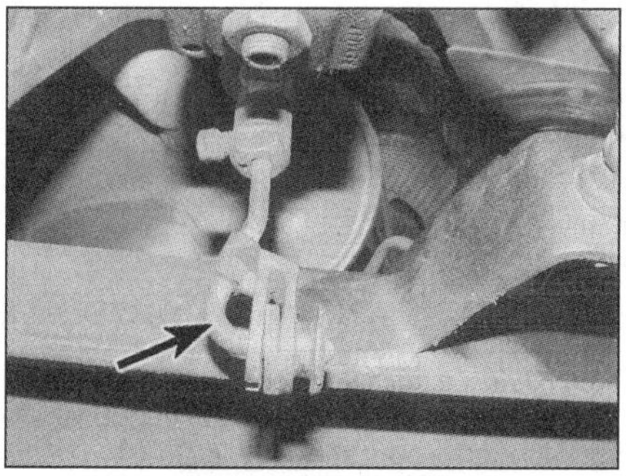

12.7 Unclip the linkage rod from the bracket on the axle

9

13.2 Lever out the cap from the centre of the brake drum . . .

underneath the vehicle. **Note:** *Do not slacken the link rod clamp bolt. If the bolt is slackened and the link rod length altered the valve will need to be adjusted on refitting.*

Refitting

8 Manoeuvre the valve assembly into position and tighten its retaining bolts securely.

9 Refit the brake pipes to their specific unions on the valve and tighten the union nuts to the specified torque setting.

10 Clip the valve link rod back into position in its retaining clip and lower the vehicle to the ground.

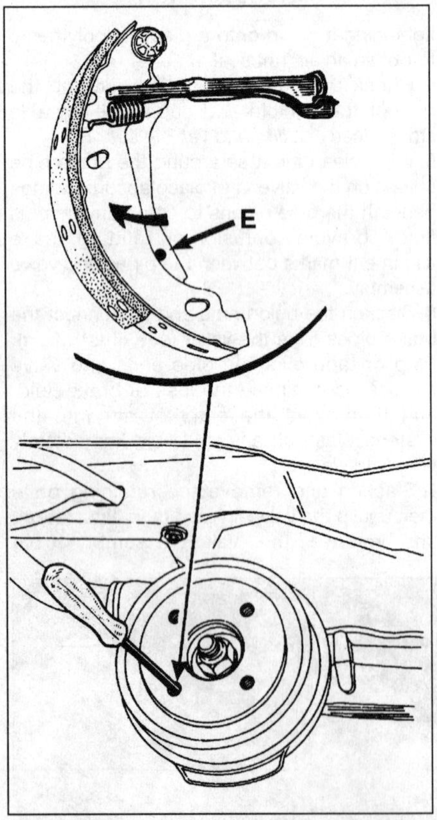

13.6 Using a screwdriver inserted through the brake drum to release the handbrake operating lever

E Handbrake operating lever stop-peg location

13.3 . . . then remove the rear hub nut

11 If a new valve assembly is being fitted, it will be noted that a spacer is fitted to the link rod; this is to adjust the link rod length. With the vehicle resting on its wheels, with a full tank of fuel and one person in the driver's seat, slacken the link rod clamp bolt and allow the valve spring to set the link rod length. Securely tighten the clamp bolt and remove the spacer from the link rod. Although not strictly necessary, it is recommended that the valve operation is tested by a Renault dealer.

12 Remove the polythene from the master cylinder reservoir and bleed the complete hydraulic system as described in Section 6.

13 Rear brake drum – removal, inspection and refitting

Note: *Before starting work, refer to the warning at the beginning of Section 14 concerning the dangers of asbestos dust. If either drum requires renewal or refinishing, both should be dealt with at the same time, to ensure even and consistent braking. In principle, new shoes should be fitted also. A new hub nut will be required on refitting.*

Removal

1 Chock the front wheels, engage reverse gear (or P) and release the handbrake. Jack up the rear of the vehicle and support it on axle stands (see *Jacking and vehicle support*). Remove the appropriate rear wheel.

2 Using a hammer and suitable large flat-bladed screwdriver, carefully tap and prise the cap out of the centre of the brake drum **(see illustration)**.

3 Using a socket and long bar, slacken and remove the rear hub nut, and withdraw the thrustwasher (where fitted) **(see illustration)**. Discard the hub nut; a new nut must used on refitting.

4 It should now be possible to withdraw the brake drum and hub bearing assembly from the stub axle by hand. It may be difficult to remove the drum due to the tightness of the hub bearing on the stub axle, or due to the brake shoes binding on the inner circumference of the drum. If the bearing is tight, tap the periphery of the drum using a hide or plastic mallet, or use a universal puller, secured to the drum with the wheel bolts, to pull it off. If the brake shoes are binding, proceed as follows.

5 First ensure that the handbrake is fully off. From underneath the vehicle, slacken the handbrake cable adjuster locknut, then back off the adjuster nut on the handbrake lever rod. Note that on most models, it will first be necessary to remove the mounting nut(s) and lower the exhaust heat shield to gain access to the adjuster nut.

6 Insert a screwdriver through one of the wheel bolt holes in the brake drum, so that it contacts the handbrake operating lever on the trailing brake shoe **(see illustration)**. Push the lever until the stop-peg slips behind the brake shoe web, allowing the brake shoes to retract fully. Withdraw the brake drum off the stub axle.

Inspection

7 Working carefully, remove all traces of brake dust from the drum, but *avoid inhaling the dust, as it is injurious to health.*

8 Scrub clean the outside of the drum, and check it for obvious signs of wear or damage such as cracks around the roadwheel bolt holes; renew the drum if necessary.

9 Examine carefully the inside of the drum. Light scoring of the friction surface is normal, but if heavy scoring is found, the drum must be renewed. It is usual to find a lip on the drum's inboard edge which consists of a mixture of rust and brake dust; this should be scraped away to leave a smooth surface which can be polished with fine (120 to 150 grade) emery paper. If the lip is due to the friction surface being recessed by wear, then the drum must be refinished (within the specified limits) or renewed.

10 If the drum is thought to be excessively worn or oval, its internal diameter must be measured at several points using an internal micrometer. Take measurements in pairs, the second at right-angles to the first, and compare the two to check for signs of ovality. Minor ovality can be corrected by machining; otherwise, renew the drum.

Refitting

11 If a new brake drum is to be installed, use a suitable solvent to remove any preservative coating that may have been applied to its interior.

12 Ensure that the handbrake lever stop-peg is correctly repositioned against the edge of the brake shoe web **(see illustration)**. Apply a smear of gear oil to the stub axle, and slide on the brake drum, being careful not to get oil onto the brake shoes or the friction surface of the drum. Fit the thrustwasher (where fitted) and a new hub nut; tighten the nut to the specified torque. Tap the hub cap into place in the centre of the brake drum.

13 Depress the footbrake several times to operate the self-adjusting mechanism.

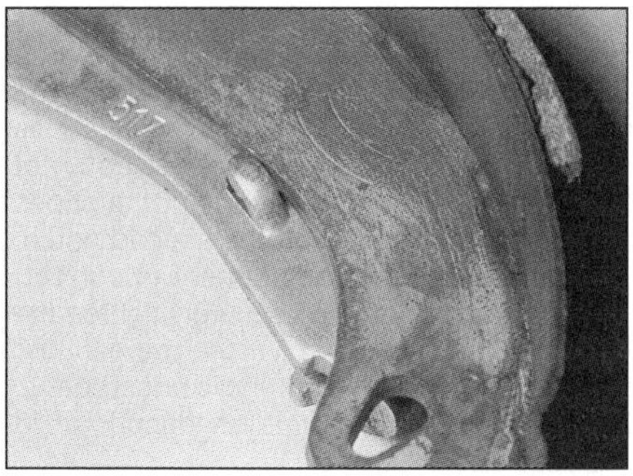

13.12 Check that the handbrake lever stop-peg is correctly positioned against the trailing shoe edge

14 Repeat the above procedure on the remaining rear brake assembly (where necessary), then adjust the handbrake as described in Chapter 1A or 1B.

15 On completion, refit the roadwheel(s), lower the vehicle to the ground and tighten the wheel bolts to the specified torque.

14 Rear brake shoes - inspection and renewal

Warning: *Brake shoes must be renewed on both rear wheels at the same time - never renew the shoes on only one wheel, as uneven braking may result. Also, the dust created by wear of the shoes may contain asbestos, which is a health hazard. Never blow it out with compressed air, and don't inhale any of it. An approved filtering mask should be worn when working on the brakes. DO NOT use petroleum-based solvents to clean brake parts - use brake cleaner or methylated spirit only.*

Inspection

1 Remove the brake drum as described in Section 13.

2 Working carefully, remove all traces of brake dust from the brake drum, backplate and shoes.

3 Measure the thickness of each brake shoe (friction material and shoe) at several points; if either shoe is worn at any point to the specified minimum thickness or less, all four shoes must be renewed as a set. Also, the shoes should be renewed if any are fouled with oil or grease; there is no satisfactory way of degreasing friction material once contaminated.

4 If any of the brake shoes are worn unevenly, or fouled with oil or grease, trace and rectify the cause before reassembly.

Renewal

Note: *Suitable high-temperature brake grease or anti-seize compound will be required to apply to the shoe contact surfaces on the brake backplate on refitting.*

5 The procedure now varies according to which make of brake is fitted.

Bendix brake shoes

6 Using a pair of pliers, remove the shoe retainer spring cups by depressing and turning them through 90°. With the cups removed, lift off the springs and withdraw the retainer pins.

7 Ease the shoes out one at a time from the lower pivot point, to release the tension of the return spring, then disconnect the lower return spring from both shoes **(see illustration)**.

8 Ease the upper end of both shoes out from their wheel cylinder locations, taking care not to damage the wheel cylinder seals, and disconnect the handbrake cable from the trailing shoe. The brake shoe and adjuster strut assembly can then be manoeuvred out of position and away from the backplate. Do not depress the brake pedal until the brakes are reassembled; wrap a strong elastic band around the wheel cylinder pistons to retain them.

9 With the shoe and adjuster strut assembly on the bench, make a note of the correct fitted positions of the springs and adjuster strut, to use as a guide on reassembly. Release the handbrake lever stop-peg (if not already done), then detach the adjuster strut bolt retaining spring from the leading shoe. Disconnect the upper return spring, then detach the leading shoe and return spring from the trailing shoe and strut assembly. Unhook the spring securing the adjuster strut to the trailing shoe, and separate the two.

10 If genuine Renault brake shoes are being installed, it will be necessary to remove the handbrake lever from the original trailing shoe and fit it to the new shoe. Secure the lever in position with the new retaining clip which is supplied with the brake shoes. All return springs should be renewed, regardless of their apparent condition; spring kits are also available from Renault dealers.

11 Withdraw the adjuster bolt from the strut, and carefully examine the assembly for signs of wear or damage, paying particular attention to the threads of the adjuster bolt and the knurled adjuster wheel, and renew if necessary. Note that left-hand and right-hand struts are not interchangeable - they are marked G (gauche/left) and D (droit/right) respectively. Also note that the strut adjuster bolts are not interchangeable; **the left-hand strut bolt has a left-hand thread**, and the right-hand bolt a right-hand thread. The left-hand bolt can be identified by the groove on its adjuster wheel collar. The right-hand bolt does not have a groove on the adjuster wheel collar, but the bolt itself is painted.

12 Ensure the components on the end of the strut are correctly positioned, then apply a little high melting-point grease to the threads of the adjuster bolt. Screw the adjuster wheel onto the bolt until only a small gap exists between the wheel and the head of the bolt, then install the bolt in the strut.

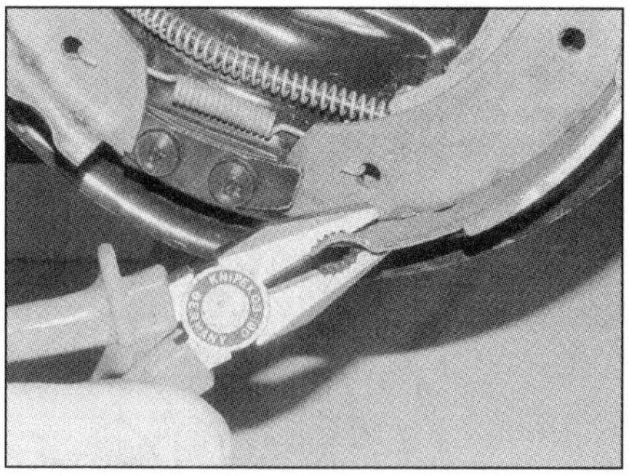

14.7 Ease the shoes out of the lower pivot point and disconnect the lower return spring

13 Fit the adjuster strut retaining spring to the trailing shoe, ensuring that the shorter hook of the spring is engaged with the shoe. Attach the adjuster strut to the spring end, then ease the strut into position in its slot in the trailing shoe.

14 Engage the upper return spring with the trailing shoe. Hook the leading shoe onto the other end of the spring, and lever the leading shoe down until the adjuster bolt head is correctly located in its groove. Once the bolt is correctly located, hook its retaining spring into the slot on the leading shoe.

15 Remove the elastic band fitted to the wheel cylinder. Peel back the rubber protective caps, and check the wheel cylinder for fluid leaks or other damage. Also check that both cylinder pistons are free to move easily. Refer to Section 15, if necessary, for information on wheel cylinder renewal.

16 Prior to installation, clean the backplate and apply a thin smear of high-temperature brake grease or anti-seize compound to all those surfaces of the backplate which bear on the shoes, particularly the wheel cylinder pistons and lower pivot point **(see illustration)**. Do not use too much, and don't allow the lubricant to foul the friction material.

17 Ensure that the handbrake lever stop-peg is correctly located against the edge of the trailing shoe.

18 Manoeuvre the shoe and strut assembly into position on the vehicle. Engage the upper ends of both shoes with the wheel cylinder pistons. Attach the handbrake cable to the

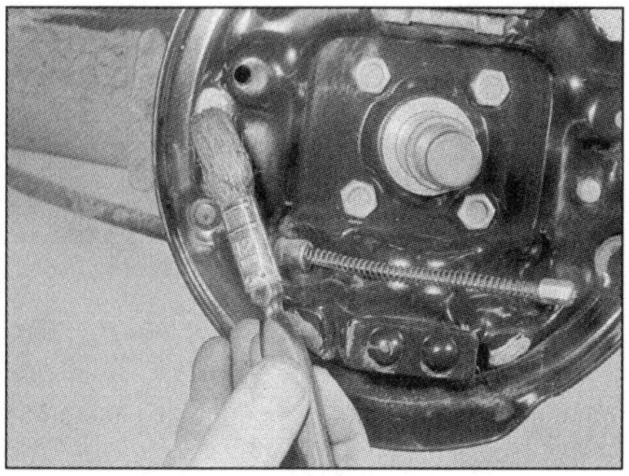

14.16 Apply a little high-melting point grease to shoe contact points on the backplate

9

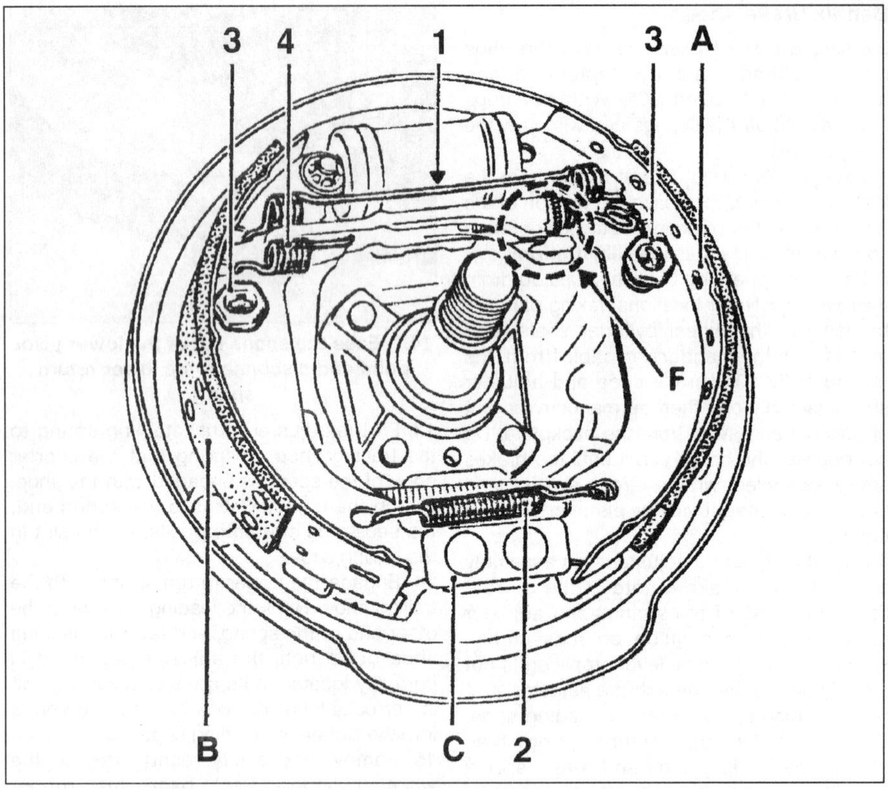

14.18 Correct fitted positions of Bendix rear brake components

A Leading shoe
B Trailing shoe
C Lower pivot point
F Adjuster strut mechanism
1 Upper return spring
2 Lower return spring
3 Retaining pin, spring and spring cup
4 Adjuster strut to trailing shoe spring

trailing shoe lever. Fit the lower return spring to both shoes, and ease the shoes into position on the lower pivot point **(see illustration)**.

19 Centralise the shoes relative to the backplate by tapping them. Refit the shoe retainer pins and springs, and secure them in position with the spring cups.

20 Using a screwdriver, turn the strut adjuster wheel until the brake drum will just pass over the brake shoes.

21 Slide the drum into position over the linings, but do not refit the hub nut yet.

22 Repeat the above procedure on the remaining rear brake.

23 Once both sets of rear shoes have been renewed, adjust the lining-to-drum clearance by repeatedly depressing the brake pedal. Whilst depressing the pedal, have an assistant listen to the rear drums, to check that the adjuster strut is functioning correctly; if this is so, a clicking sound will be emitted by the strut as the pedal is depressed.

24 Remove both the rear drums, and check that the handbrake lever stop-pegs are still correctly located against the edges of the trailing shoes, and that each lever operates smoothly. If all is well, with the aid of an assistant, adjust the handbrake cable so that the handbrake lever on each rear brake assembly starts to move as the handbrake is moved between the first and second notch (click) of its ratchet mechanism, ie, so that the stop-pegs are still in contact with the shoes when the handbrake is on the first notch of the ratchet, but no longer contact the shoes when the handbrake is on the second notch. Once the handbrake adjustment is correct, hold the adjuster nut and securely tighten the locknut. Where necessary, refit the exhaust system heat shield to the vehicle underbody.

25 Refit the brake drums as described in Section 13.

26 On completion, check the hydraulic fluid level as described in *Weekly checks*.

Girling brake shoes

27 Make a note of the correct fitted positions of the springs and adjuster strut, to use as a guide on reassembly.

28 Carefully unhook the lower return spring, and remove it from the brake shoes.

29 Using a pair of pliers, remove the leading shoe retainer spring cup by depressing it and turning through 90°. With the cup removed, lift off the spring, then withdraw the retainer pin and remove the shoe from the backplate. Unhook the adjusting lever spring, and remove it from the leading shoe **(see illustrations)**.

30 Detach the adjuster strut and upper return spring, then remove them from the trailing shoe.

31 Remove the trailing shoe retainer spring cup **(see illustration)**, spring and pin as described above, then detach the handbrake cable and remove the shoe from the vehicle. Do not depress the brake pedal until the brakes are reassembled; wrap a strong elastic band around the wheel cylinder pistons to retain them.

32 If genuine Renault brake shoes are being installed, it will be necessary to remove the adjusting lever from the original leading shoe and install it on the new shoe. All return springs should be renewed, regardless of their apparent condition; spring kits are also available from Renault dealers.

33 Withdraw the forked end from the adjuster strut. Carefully examine the assembly for signs of wear or damage, paying particular attention to the threads and the knurled adjuster wheel, and renew if necessary. Note

14.29a Remove the brake shoe retaining spring . . .

14.29b . . . and the adjusting lever return spring

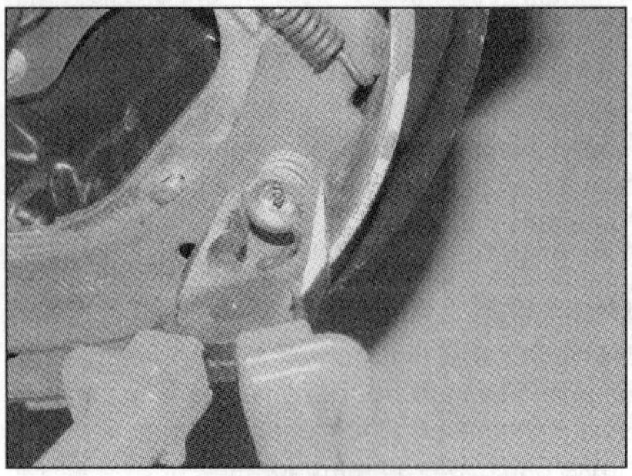

14.31 Removing the locking cup from the brake shoe retaining spring

that left-hand and right-hand struts are not interchangeable; the left-hand fork has a right-hand thread, and **the right-hand fork has a left-hand thread**. The forks can also be identified by their colour: the left-hand fork is silver, and the right-hand fork is gold.

34 Remove the elastic band fitted to the wheel cylinder. Peel back the rubber protective caps, and check the wheel cylinder for fluid leaks or other damage. Check that both cylinder pistons are free to move easily. Refer to Section 15, if necessary, for information on wheel cylinder renewal.

35 Prior to installation, clean the backplate and apply a thin smear of high-temperature brake grease or anti-seize compound to all those surfaces of the backplate which bear on the shoes, particularly the wheel cylinder pistons and lower pivot point. Do not allow the lubricant to foul the friction material.

36 Ensure that the handbrake lever stop-peg is correctly located against the edge of the trailing shoe.

37 Locate the upper end of the trailing shoe in the wheel cylinder piston, then refit the retainer pin and spring, and secure it in position with the spring cup. Connect the handbrake cable to the lever.

38 Screw in the adjuster wheel until the minimum strut length is obtained, then hook the strut into position on the trailing shoe. Rotate the adjuster strut forked end so that the cut-out of the fork will engage with the leading shoe adjusting lever **(see illustrations)**.

39 Fit the spring to the leading shoe adjusting lever, so that the shorter hook of the spring engages with the lever.

40 Slide the leading shoe assembly into position, ensuring that it is correctly engaged with the adjuster strut fork, and that the fork cut-out is engaged with the adjusting lever. Engage the upper end of the shoe in the wheel cylinder piston, then secure the shoe in position with the retainer pin, spring and spring cup.

41 Install the upper and lower return springs, then tap the shoes to centralise them on the backplate.

42 Using a screwdriver, turn the strut adjuster wheel until the brake drum will just pass over the brake shoes.

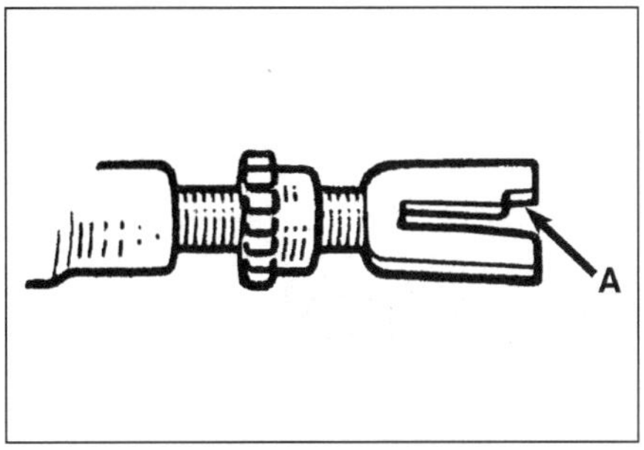

14.38a On Girling rear brakes, adjuster strut fork cut-out (A) must engage with leading shoe adjusting lever on refitting

14.38b Locating the adjusting lever in the cut-out in the adjuster strut fork

43 Slide the drum into position over the linings, but do not refit the hub nut yet.

44 Repeat the above procedure on the remaining rear brake.

45 Carry out the procedures described previously in paragraphs 23 to 26.

All brake shoes

46 If new shoes have been fitted, full braking efficiency will not be obtained until the linings have bedded-in. Be prepared for longer stopping distances, and avoid harsh braking as far as possible for the first hundred miles or so after fitting new shoes.

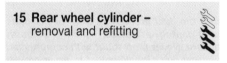

15 Rear wheel cylinder - removal and refitting

Note: *Before starting work, refer to the warnings at the beginning of Section 6 concerning the dangers of hydraulic fluid, and at the beginning of Section 14 concerning the dangers of asbestos dust.*

Removal

1 Remove the brake drum as described in Section 13.

2 Using pliers, carefully unhook the brake shoe upper return spring and remove it from the brake shoes. Pull the upper ends of the shoes away from the wheel cylinder to disengage them from the pistons.

3 Minimise fluid loss, either by removing the master cylinder reservoir cap and then tightening it down onto a piece of polythene to obtain an airtight seal (taking care not to damage the sender unit), or by using a brake hose clamp, a G-clamp or a similar tool with protected jaws to clamp the flexible hose at the nearest convenient point to the wheel cylinder **(see illustration)**.

4 Wipe away all traces of dirt around the brake pipe union at the rear of the wheel cylinder, and unscrew the union nut **(see illustration)**. Carefully ease the pipe out of the wheel cylinder, and plug or tape over its end to prevent dirt entry. Wipe off any spilt fluid immediately.

5 Unscrew the two wheel cylinder retaining bolts from the rear of the backplate **(see illustration)**. Remove the cylinder, taking care not to allow hydraulic fluid to contaminate the brake shoe linings.

6 It is not possible to overhaul the cylinder, since no components are available separately. If faulty, the complete wheel cylinder assembly must be renewed.

Refitting

7 Ensure the backplate and wheel cylinder mating surfaces are clean, then spread the brake shoes and manoeuvre the wheel cylinder into position.

8 Engage the brake pipe, and screw in the union nut two or three turns to ensure that the thread has started.

9 Insert the two wheel cylinder retaining bolts, and tighten them securely. Now fully tighten the brake pipe union nut.

10 Remove the clamp from the brake hose, or the polythene from the master cylinder reservoir (as applicable).

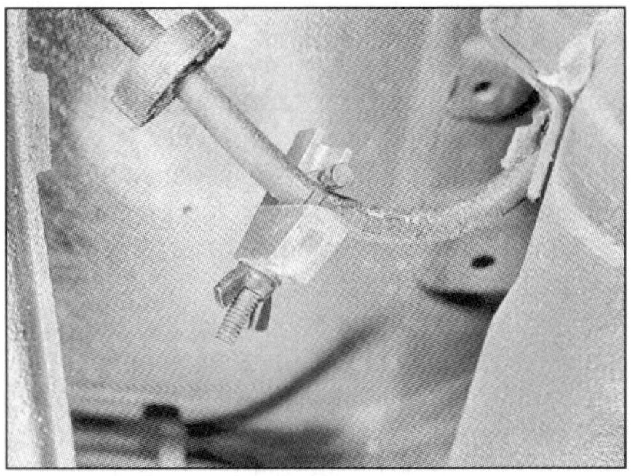

15.3 Brake hose clamp fitted to rear brake flexible hose

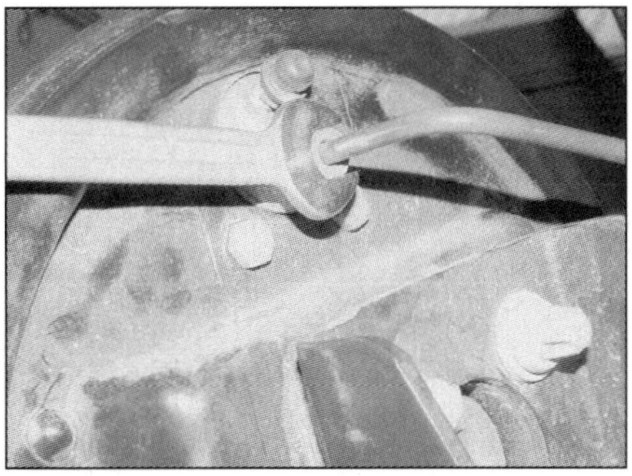

15.4 Unscrewing the union nut from the rear of the wheel cylinder

15.5 Undo the two wheel cylinder retaining bolts

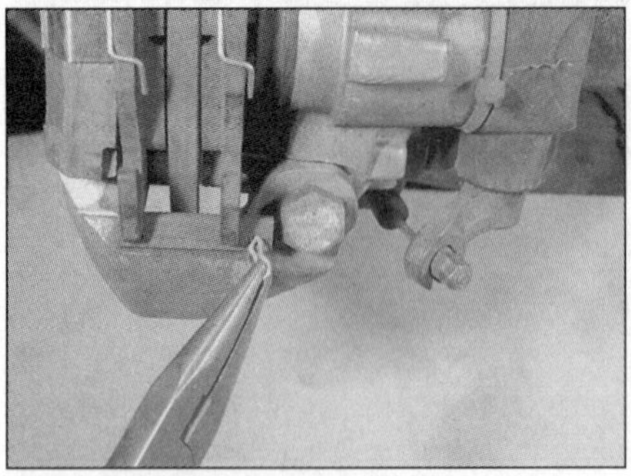

16.2a To remove rear brake pads, remove the spring clip . . .

16.2b . . . then withdraw the retaining plate from the caliper

16.3a Slide out the inner brake pad . . .

16.3b . . . undo the two retaining screws . . .

11 Ensure that the brake shoes are correctly located in the cylinder pistons. Carefully refit the brake shoe upper return spring, using a screwdriver to stretch the spring into position.

12 Refit the brake drum as described in Section 13.

13 Bleed the brake hydraulic system as described in Section 6. Providing suitable precautions were taken to minimise loss of fluid, it should only be necessary to bleed the relevant rear brake.

16 Rear brake pads – inspection and renewal

Warning: Renew both sets of rear brake pads at the same time – never renew the pads on only one wheel, as uneven braking may result. Note that the dust created by wear of the pads may contain asbestos, which is a health hazard. Never blow it out with compressed air, and don't inhale any of it. An approved filtering mask should be worn when working on the brakes. DO NOT use petroleum-based solvents to clean brake parts – use brake cleaner or methylated spirit only.

Inspection

1 Chock the front wheels, engage reverse gear (or P) and release the handbrake. Jack up the rear of the vehicle and support it on axle stands (see *Jacking and vehicle support*). Remove the rear wheels.

2 Extract the small spring clip from the pad retaining plate. Slide the plate out of the caliper **(see illustrations)**.

3 Withdraw the inner pad from the caliper, using pliers if necessary. Slacken and remove the two outer pad retaining screws, then withdraw the outer pad from the caliper **(see illustrations)**. Make a note of the correct fitted position of the anti-rattle springs, and remove the springs from each pad.

4 First measure the thickness of each brake pad (friction material and backing plate). If either pad is worn at any point to the specified minimum thickness or less, all four pads must be renewed. Also, the pads should be renewed if any are fouled with oil or grease; there is no satisfactory way of degreasing friction material once contaminated. If any of the brake pads are worn unevenly, or fouled with oil or grease, trace and rectify the cause before reassembly. New brake pads and spring kits are available from Renault dealers.

5 If the brake pads are still serviceable, carefully clean them using a clean, fine wire brush or similar, paying particular attention to the sides and back of the metal backing. Clean out the grooves in the friction material, and pick out any large embedded particles of dirt or debris. Clean the pad locations in the caliper body/mounting bracket.

6 Prior to fitting the pads, check that the guide sleeves are free to slide easily in the caliper body, and that the guide sleeve rubber gaiters are undamaged. Brush the dust and dirt from the caliper and piston, but *do not inhale it, as it is injurious to health.* Inspect the dust seal around the piston for damage, and the piston for evidence of fluid leaks, corrosion or damage. If attention to any of these components is necessary, refer to Section 17.

Renewal

7 If new brake pads are to be fitted, it will be necessary to retract the piston fully into the caliper bore by rotating it in a clockwise direction. This can be achieved using a suitable square-section bar, such as the shaft of a suitable screwdriver, which locates snugly in the caliper piston slots **(see illustration)**. Provided that the master cylinder reservoir has not been overfilled with hydraulic fluid, there should be no spillage, but keep a careful watch on the fluid level while retracting the piston. If the fluid level rises above the MAX level, the surplus should be syphoned off (not by mouth – use an old syringe or antifreeze tester), or ejected via a plastic tube connected to the bleed screw (see Section 6).

8 Position the caliper piston so that the small groove scribed across the piston points in the direction of the caliper bleed screw. This is necessary to ensure that the lug on the inner pad will locate with the caliper piston slot on installation **(see illustration)**.

9 Refit the anti-rattle springs to the pads, so that when the pads are installed in the caliper, the spring end will be located at the opposite end of the pad in relation to the pad retaining plate. The brake pad with the lug on its backing plate is the inner pad **(see illustration)**.

16.3c . . . and withdraw the outer brake pad

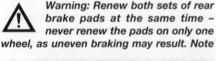

16.7 Retract the piston using a square-section bar

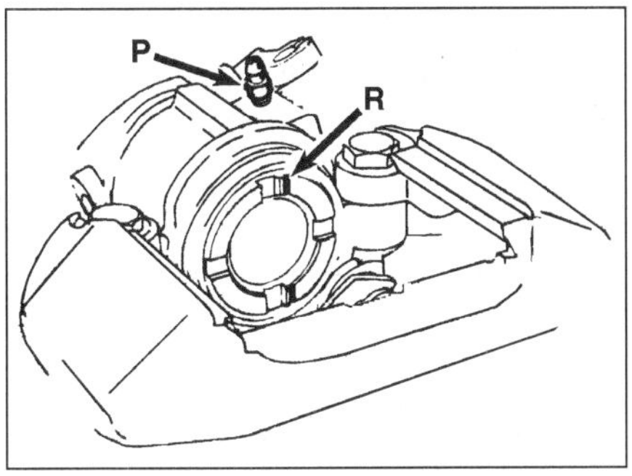

16.8 Prior to installing rear brake pads, align groove on caliper piston (R) with bleed screw (P)

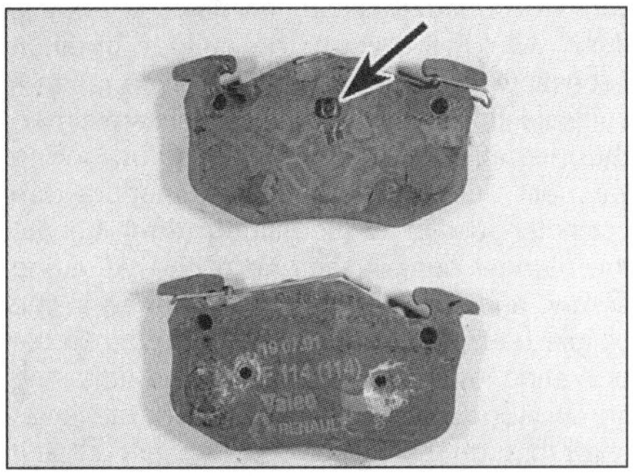

16.9 Inner brake pad can be identified by its locating lug (arrowed). Note correct fitted positions of anti-rattle springs

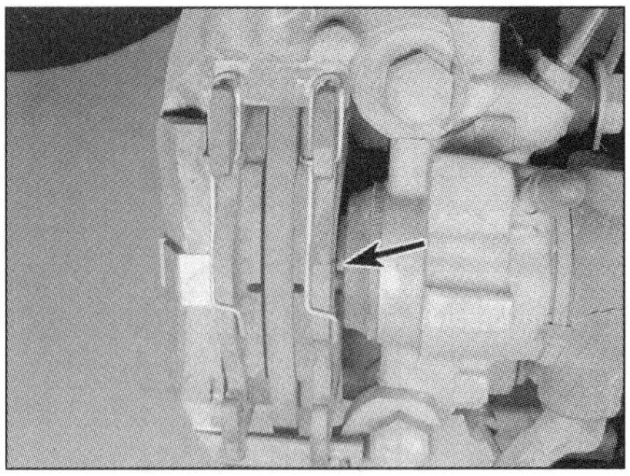

16.13 Ensure inner pad locating lug is correctly located in piston slot (arrowed)

10 Locate the outer brake pad in the caliper body, ensuring that its friction material is against the brake disc. Insert the retaining screws and tighten them securely.

11 Slide the inner pad into position in the caliper, ensuring that the lug on the pad backing plate is aligned with the slot in the caliper piston. Recheck that the anti-rattle spring ends on both pads are at the opposite end of the pad to which the retaining plate is to be inserted.

12 Slide the retaining plate into place, and install the small spring clip at its inner end. It may be necessary to file an entry chamfer on the edge of the retaining key, to enable it to be fitted without difficulty.

13 Depress the brake pedal repeatedly until the pads are pressed into firm contact with the brake disc. Check that the inner pad lug is correctly engaged with one of the caliper piston slots **(see illustration)**.

14 Repeat the procedure on the remaining rear brake caliper.

15 Check the handbrake cable adjustment as described in Chapter 1A or 1B, then refit the roadwheels and lower the vehicle to the ground. Tighten the roadwheel bolts to the specified torque.

16 Check the hydraulic fluid level as described in *Weekly checks*.

17 If new pads have been fitted, full braking efficiency will not be obtained until the linings have bedded-in. Be prepared for longer stopping distances, and avoid harsh braking as far as possible for the first hundred miles or so after fitting new pads.

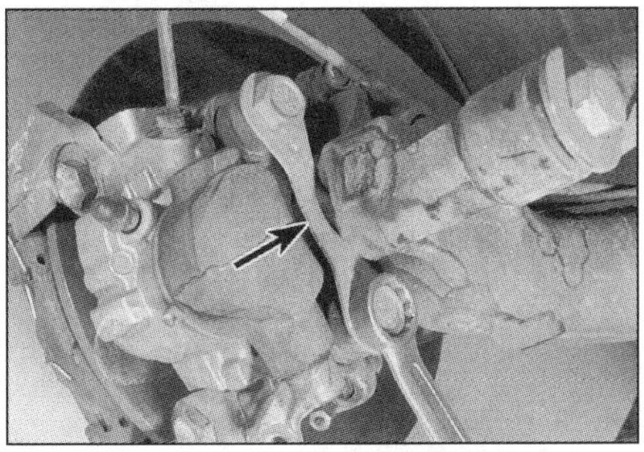

17.6 Remove the caliper mounting bolts, noting which way around the mounting plate is fitted (arrowed)

17 Rear brake caliper – removal, overhaul and refitting

Note: *Before starting work, refer to the warnings at the beginning of Section 6 concerning the dangers of hydraulic fluid, and at the beginning of Section 16 concerning the dangers of asbestos dust.*

Removal

1 Chock the front wheels, engage reverse gear (or P) and release the handbrake. Jack up the rear of the vehicle and support it on axle stands (see *Jacking and vehicle support*). Remove the relevant rear wheel.

2 Remove the brake pads as described in Section 16.

3 Free the handbrake inner cable from the caliper handbrake operating lever, then tap the outer cable out of its bracket on the caliper body.

4 Minimise fluid loss, either by removing the master cylinder reservoir cap and then tightening it down onto a piece of polythene to obtain an airtight seal (taking care not to damage the sender unit), or by using a brake hose clamp, a G-clamp or a similar tool with protected jaws to clamp the flexible hose at the nearest convenient point to the brake caliper.

5 Wipe away all traces of dirt around the brake pipe union on the caliper, and unscrew the union nut. Carefully ease the pipe out of position, and plug or tape over its end to prevent dirt entry. Wipe off any spilt fluid immediately.

6 Slacken the two bolts securing the caliper assembly to the trailing arm, and remove them along with the mounting plate, noting which way around the plate is fitted **(see illustration)**. Lift the caliper assembly away from the brake disc.

Overhaul

Note: *Ensure that a suitable caliper overhaul kit is obtained before starting work.*

7 With the caliper on the bench, wipe away all traces of dust and dirt, but avoid inhaling the dust, as it is injurious to health.

8 Using a small screwdriver, carefully prise out the dust seal from the caliper bore, taking care not to damage the piston **(see illustration)**.

9 Remove the piston from the caliper bore by rotating it in an anti-clockwise direction. This can be achieved using a suitable square-section bar, such as the shaft of a suitable screwdriver, which locates snugly in the caliper piston slots. Once the piston turns freely but does not come out any further, the piston can be withdrawn by hand, or if necessary pushed out by applying compressed air to the union bolt hole.

Caution: The piston may be ejected with some force – only low pressure should be required, such as is generated by a foot pump.

10 Using a blunt instrument such as a knitting needle or a crochet hook, extract the piston hydraulic seal, taking care not to damage the caliper bore.

11 Withdraw the guide sleeves from the caliper body, and remove the guide sleeve gaiters.

12 Inspect the caliper components as described in Section 10. Renew as necessary, noting that the inside of the caliper piston

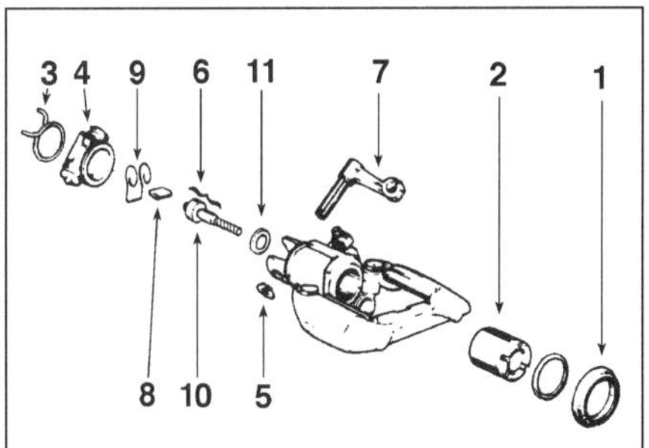

17.8 Exploded view of the rear brake caliper

1 *Dust seal*
2 *Piston*
3 *Retaining clip*
4 *Handbrake mechanism dust cover*
5 *Circlip*
6 *Spring washers*
7 *Handbrake operating lever*
8 *Plunger cam*
9 *Return spring*
10 *Adjusting screw*
11 *Thrustwasher*

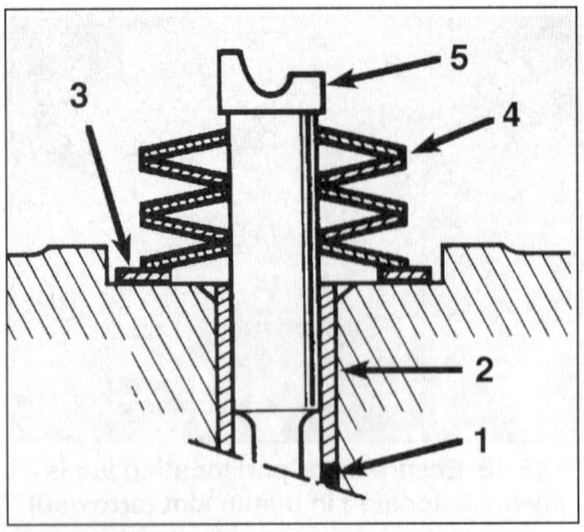

17.15 Correct fitted positions of rear brake caliper handbrake mechanism adjuster screw and associated components

1 O-ring
2 Adjusting screw bush
3 Thrustwasher
4 Correct arrangement of spring washers
5 Adjusting screw

must **not** be dismantled. If necessary, the handbrake mechanism can be overhauled as described in the following paragraphs. If it is not wished to overhaul the handbrake mechanism, proceed to paragraph 16.

13 Release the handbrake dust cover retaining clip, and peel the cover away from the rear of the caliper. Make a note of the correct fitted positions of the relative components to use as a guide on reassembly. Remove the circlip from the base of the operating lever shaft, then compress the adjusting screw spring washers, and withdraw the operating lever and dust cover from the caliper body. With the lever withdrawn, remove the return spring, plunger cam, adjusting screw, spring washers and thrustwasher from the rear of the caliper body. Using a suitable pin punch, carefully tap the adjusting screw bush out of the caliper body and remove the O-ring.

14 Clean all the handbrake components in methylated spirit, and examine them for wear. If there is any sign of wear or damage, the complete handbrake mechanism assembly should be renewed; a kit is available from your Renault dealer.

15 Ensure that all components are clean and dry. Install the O-ring, then press the adjusting screw bush into position until its outer edge is flush with the rear of the caliper body; if necessary, tap the bush into position using a suitable tubular drift. Fit the thrustwasher, then install the adjusting screw and spring washers, ensuring that the washers are correctly positioned **(see illustration)**. Locate the plunger cam in the end of the adjusting screw, and position the return spring in the caliper housing. Fit the new dust cover to the operating lever, then compress the adjusting screw spring washers and insert the lever shaft through the caliper body, ensuring that it is correctly engaged with the return spring and plunger cam. Secure the operating lever in position with the circlip, then release the spring washers and check the operation of the handbrake mechanism. Apply a smear of high-melting point grease to the operating lever shaft and adjusting screw. Slide the dust cover over the caliper body, and secure it in position with a cable tie.

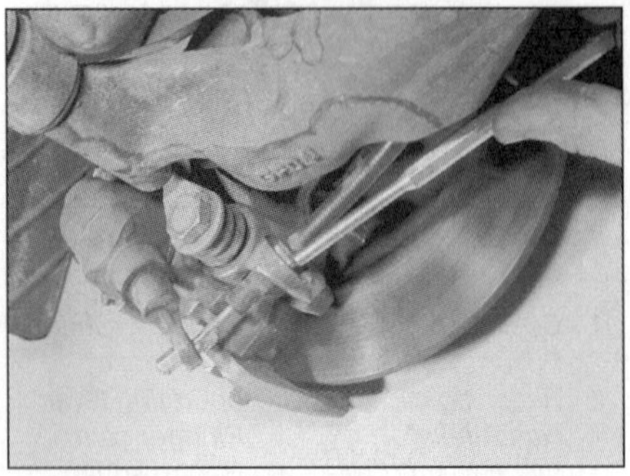

17.23 Tap the handbrake outer cable into position using a hammer and punch

16 Soak the piston and the new piston (fluid) seal in clean hydraulic fluid. Smear clean fluid on the cylinder bore surface.

17 Fit the new piston (fluid) seal, using only the fingers to manipulate it into the cylinder bore groove, and refit the piston assembly. Turn the piston in a clockwise direction, using the method employed on dismantling, until it is fully retracted into the caliper bore.

18 Fit the dust seal to the caliper, ensuring that it is correctly located in the caliper and also the groove on the piston.

19 Apply the grease supplied in the repair kit, or a good-quality high-temperature brake grease or anti-seize compound to the guide sleeves. Fit the guide sleeves to the caliper body, and fit the new gaiters, ensuring that the gaiters are correctly located in the grooves on both the guide sleeve and caliper body.

Refitting

20 Position the caliper over the brake disc. Refit the two caliper mounting bolts and the mounting plate, noting that the mounting plate must be fitted so that its bend curves towards the caliper body. With the plate correctly positioned, tighten the caliper bolts to the specified torque.

21 Wipe clean the brake pipe union. Refit the pipe to the caliper, and tighten its union nut securely.

22 Remove the clamp from the brake hose, or the polythene from the master cylinder reservoir (as applicable).

23 Insert the handbrake cable through its bracket on the caliper, and tap the outer cable into position using a hammer and a pin punch **(see illustration)**. Reconnect the inner cable to the caliper operating lever.

24 Refit the brake pads as described in Section 16.

25 Bleed the hydraulic system as described in Section 6. Note that, providing the precautions described were taken to minimise brake fluid loss, it should only be necessary to bleed the relevant rear brake.

26 Repeatedly apply the brake pedal to bring the pads into contact with the disc. Check and if necessary adjust the handbrake cable as described in Chapter 1A or 1B.

27 Refit the roadwheel, lower the vehicle to the ground and tighten the wheel bolts to the specified torque. On completion, check the hydraulic fluid level as described in *Weekly checks*.

18 Rear brake disc – inspection, removal and refitting

Note: *Before starting work, refer to the warning at the beginning of Section 16 concerning the dangers of asbestos dust. If either disc requires renewal, both should be renewed at the same time, to ensure even and consistent braking. A new rear hub nut will be required on refitting.*

Inspection

1 Chock the front wheels, engage reverse gear (or P) and release the handbrake. Jack up the rear of the vehicle and support it on axle stands (see *Jacking and vehicle support*). Remove the appropriate rear roadwheel.

2 Inspect the disc as described in Section 11.

Removal

3 Remove the brake pads as described in Section 16.

4 Remove the two caliper frame retaining bolts. Remove the frame from the caliper body.

5 Using a hammer and a large flat-bladed screwdriver, carefully tap and prise the cap out of the centre of the brake disc **(see illustration)**.

6 Using a socket and long bar, slacken and remove the rear hub nut and withdraw the thrustwasher. Discard the hub nut; a new nut must be used on refitting.

7 It should now be possible to withdraw the brake disc and hub bearing assembly from the stub axle by hand. It may be difficult to remove the disc, due to the tightness of the hub bearing on the stub axle. If the bearing is tight, tap the periphery of the disc using a hide or plastic mallet, or use a universal puller,

18.5 Prising out the rear disc hub cap

18.9a Refit the spacer to the rear of the brake disc . . .

secured to the disc with the wheel bolts, to pull it off. Remove the spacer from the rear of the disc, noting which way round it is fitted.

Refitting

8 Prior to refitting the disc, smear the stub axle shaft with gear oil. Be careful not to contaminate the friction surfaces with oil. If a new disc is to be fitted, use a suitable solvent to wipe any preservative coating from its surface.

9 Refit the spacer to the rear of the disc, noting that its slightly bigger protrusion should face the hub bearing. Slide the disc onto the stub axle, and tap it into position using a soft-faced mallet **(see illustrations)**.

10 Slide on the thrustwasher, then fit the new rear hub nut and tighten it to the specified torque **(see illustration)**. Tap the cap back into position in the centre of the disc.

11 Apply a few drops of locking fluid to the threads of the caliper frame retaining bolts. Offer up the frame and refit the bolts. Tighten both bolts to the specified torque **(see illustrations)**.

12 Refit the brake pads as described in Section 16.

13 Check the handbrake cable adjustment as described in Chapter 1A or 1B.

14 Refit the roadwheels and lower the vehicle to the ground. Tighten the roadwheel bolts to the specified torque.

19 Handbrake lever - removal and refitting

Removal

1 Chock the front wheels, engage reverse gear (or P) and release the handbrake. Jack up the rear of the vehicle and support it on axle stands (see *Jacking and vehicle support*).

2 Working from inside the vehicle, move the front seats as far forwards as possible. Undo the two retaining screws in the rear of the console and lift it off from around the handbrake lever **(see illustration)**.

3 On early models, unclip the plastic surround from around the handbrake lever, and slacken the adjuster locknut **(see illustration)**.

4 Working from underneath the vehicle, undo

18.9b . . . and slide the disc onto the stub axle

18.10 Tighten the new rear hub nut to the specified torque

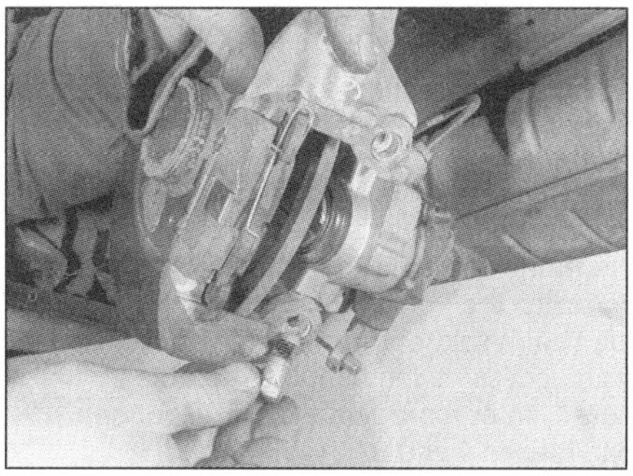

18.11a Apply locking fluid to the retaining bolts, then refit the caliper frame . . .

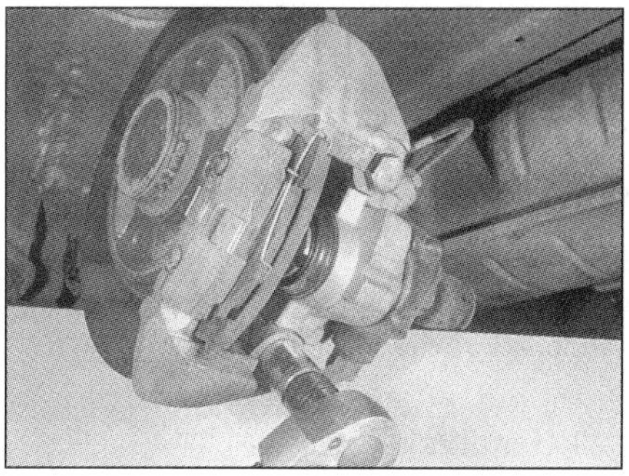

18.11b . . . and tighten the bolts

the nuts securing the exhaust system heat shield to the vehicle underbody. Manoeuvre the heat shield out from under the vehicle **(see illustration)**.

5 On later models, unscrew the handbrake cable adjuster locknut from the end of the handbrake linkage rod under the vehicle **(see illustration)**.

6 Disengage the cable equaliser plate from the end of the cable/linkage rod.

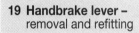

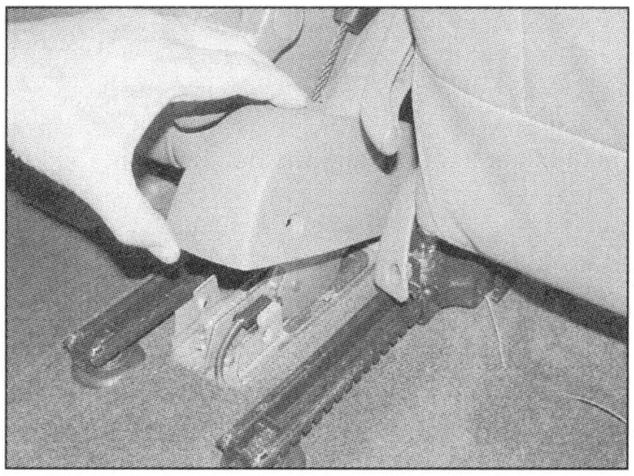

19.2 Remove the retaining screws and lift off the handbrake lever trim

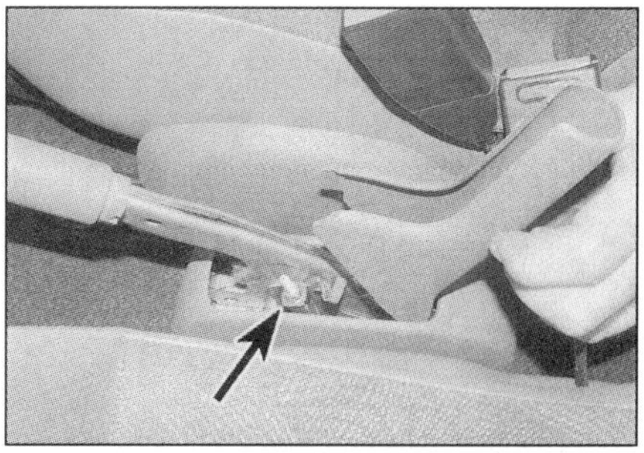

19.3 On some models, the handbrake adjuster nut is on the handbrake lever (arrowed)

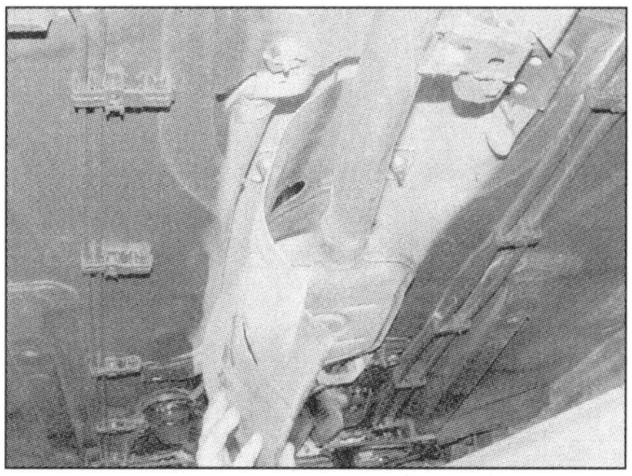

19.4 Withdrawing the heat shield from above the exhaust system

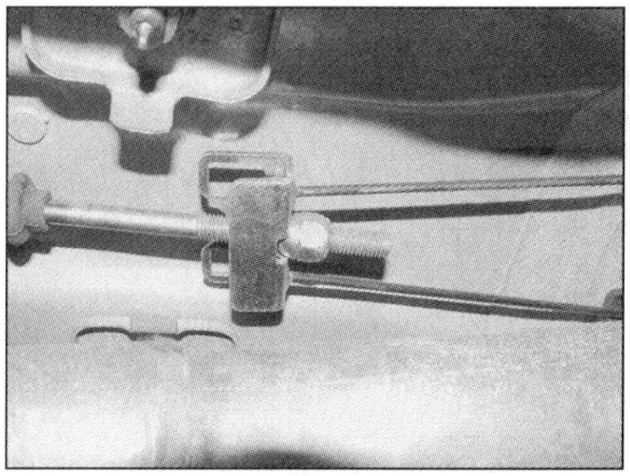

19.5 On some models, the handbrake adjuster nut is under the vehicle

9

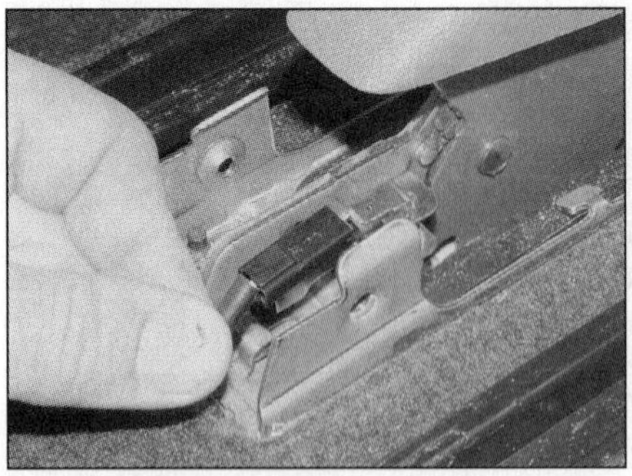

19.7a Disconnect the handbrake warning light switch wire . . .

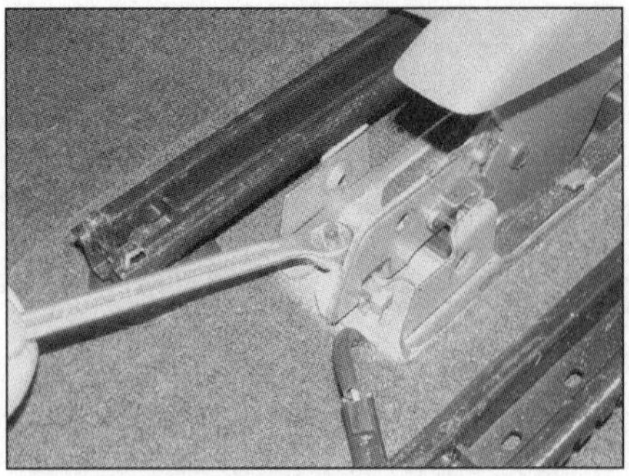

19.7b . . . then undo the handbrake lever mounting securing nuts

7 Working inside the vehicle, unscrew the two nuts securing the lever to the floor, and remove the assembly from the vehicle. Disconnect the handbrake warning light switch wire from the rear of the lever **(see illustrations)**.

Refitting

8 Refitting is a reversal of removal. Adjust the handbrake as described in Chapter 1A or 1B.

20 Handbrake cables - removal and refitting

Removal

1 The handbrake cable consists of two sections, a right- and left-hand section, which are linked to the lever assembly by an equaliser plate. Each section can be removed individually as follows.

2 Chock the front wheels, engage reverse gear (or P) and release the handbrake. Jack up the rear of the vehicle and support it on axle stands (see *Jacking and vehicle support*).

3 Working from underneath the vehicle, undo the nut(s) securing the exhaust system heat shield to the vehicle underbody. Manoeuvre the heat shield out from under the vehicle, to gain access to the handbrake cable adjuster nuts (later models) see Section 19, paragraphs 4 and 5.

4 On early models, unclip the plastic surround from around the handbrake lever inside the vehicle, to gain access to the handbrake adjuster nut, see Section 19, paragraph 3.

5 Slacken the adjuster locknut until there is sufficient slack in the cables to allow it to be disconnected from the equaliser plate **(see illustrations)**.

6 On models with rear drum brakes, remove the rear brake shoes from the appropriate side as described in Section 14. Using a hammer and pin punch, carefully tap the outer cable from the brake backplate **(see illustration)**.

7 On models with rear disc brakes, disengage the inner cable from the caliper handbrake lever. Using a hammer and pin punch, tap the outer cable out of its mounting bracket on the caliper **(see illustration)**.

8 Working along the length of the cable, remove any retaining bolts and screws, and free the cable from the retaining clips and ties **(see illustration)**. Remove the cable from under the vehicle.

Refitting

9 Refitting is a reversal of removal. Adjust the handbrake as described in Chapter 1A or 1B.

21 Stop-light switch - removal, refitting and adjustment

Removal

1 The stop-light switch is located on the pedal bracket beneath the facia.

2 To remove the switch, reach up behind the facia, disconnect the wiring connector and unscrew the switch from the bracket **(see illustrations)**.

Refitting and adjustment

3 Screw the switch back into position in the mounting bracket.

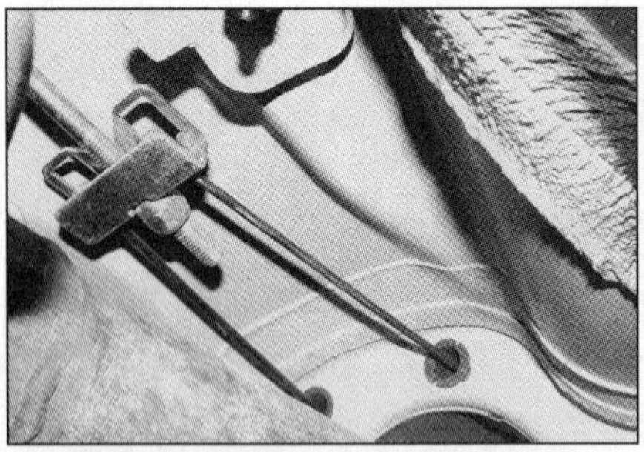

20.5a On later models, slacken the adjuster nut under the vehicle to release the equaliser plate . . .

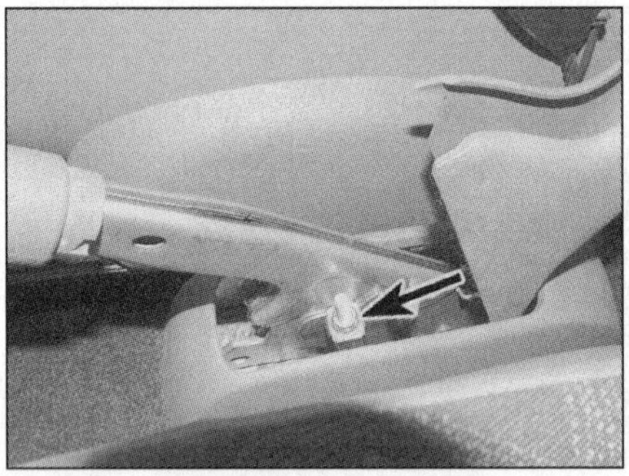

20.5b . . . on early models, the adjustment is on the handbrake lever

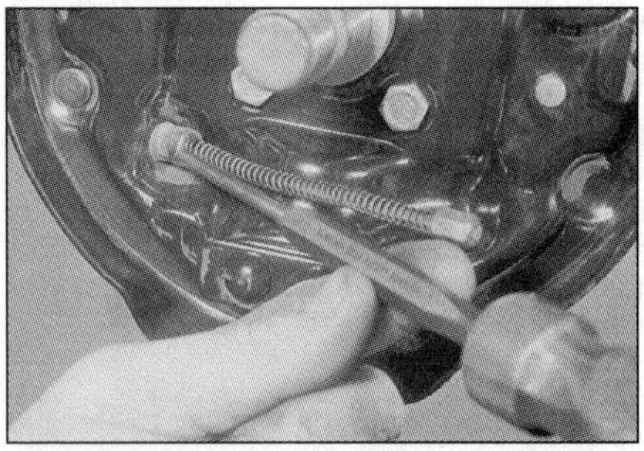

20.6 Drive the handbrake outer cable from the brake backplate (rear drum brake models)

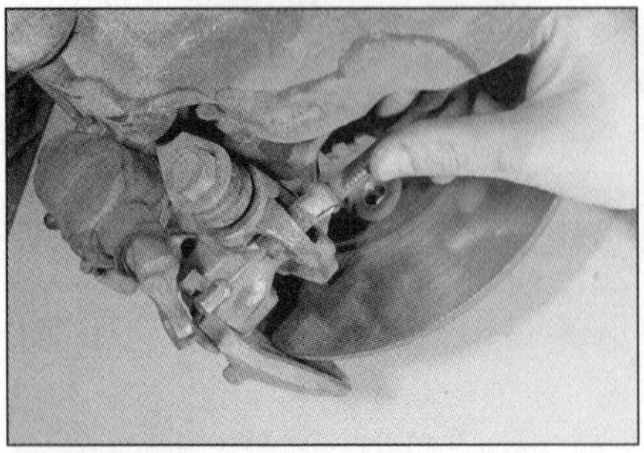

20.7 On rear disc brake models, disconnect the handbrake cable from the brake caliper

20.8 Release the handbrake cable from the retaining clips

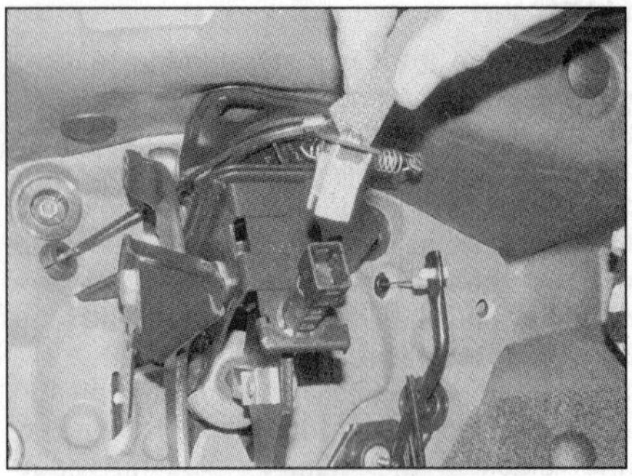

21.2a Disconnect the wiring connector . . .

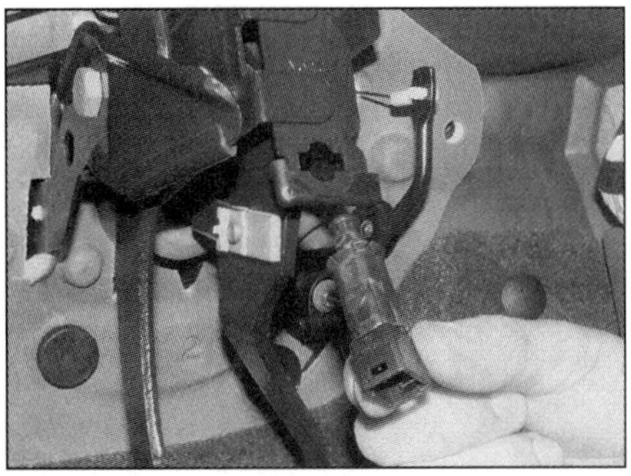

21.2b . . . and unscrew the stop-light switch (facia panel removed for clarity)

4 Connect a continuity tester (ohmmeter or self-powered test light) across the switch terminals. Screw the switch in until an open-circuit is present between the switch terminals (infinite resistance, or light goes out). Gently depress the pedal and check that continuity exists between the switch terminals (zero resistance, or light comes on) after the pedal has travelled approximately 5 mm. If necessary, reposition the switch until it operates as specified.
5 In the absence of a continuity tester, the same adjustment can be made by reconnecting the wiring to the switch and having an assistant observe the stop-lights (ignition on).
6 Once the stop-light switch is correctly adjusted, remake the original wiring connections, and recheck the operation of the stop-lights.

22 Anti-lock braking system (ABS) - general information

1 ABS is available as an option on certain Clio models. The purpose of the system is to prevent wheel(s) locking during heavy braking. This is achieved by automatic release of the brake on the relevant wheel, followed by reapplication of the brake **(see illustration)**.
2 The main components of the system are four wheel sensors (one per wheel), and a modulator block which contains the ABS computer, the hydraulic solenoid valves and accumulators, and an electrically-driven return pump.
3 The solenoids are controlled by the computer, which receives signals from the wheel sensors. The sensors detect the speed of rotation of a toothed ring, known as a reluctor ring, attached to the wheel hub. By comparing the speed signals from the four wheels, the computer can determine when a wheel is decelerating at an abnormal rate, and can therefore predict when a wheel is about to lock. During normal operation, the system functions in the same way as a non-ABS braking system does.
4 If the computer senses that a wheel is about to lock, the ABS system enters the 'pressure-maintain' phase. The computer operates the relevant solenoid valve in the modulator block; this isolates the brake on the wheel in question from the master cylinder, effectively sealing-in the hydraulic pressure.
5 If the speed of rotation of the wheel continues to decrease at an abnormal rate, the ABS system then enters the 'pressure-decrease' phase. The return pump operates and pumps the hydraulic fluid back into the master cylinder, releasing pressure on the brake. When the speed of rotation of the wheel returns to an acceptable rate, the pump stops and the solenoid valve opens, allowing hydraulic pressure to return and reapply the brake. This cycle can be carried out at up to 10 times a second.
6 The action of the solenoid valves and return pump creates pulses in the hydraulic circuit. When the ABS system is functioning, these pulses can be felt through the brake pedal.
7 The solenoid valves connected to the front calipers operate independently, but the valve connected to the rear brakes operates both simultaneously. Since the braking circuit is split diagonally, a separate mechanical plunger valve in the modulator block divides the rear solenoid valve hydraulic outlet into two separate circuits.
8 The operation of the ABS system is entirely dependent on electrical signals. To prevent the system responding to any inaccurate signals, a built-in safety circuit monitors all signals received by the computer. If an inaccurate signal or low battery voltage is detected, the ABS system is automatically shut down, and the warning lamp on the instrument panel is illuminated to inform the driver that the ABS system is not operational. Normal braking is unaffected.
9 If a fault does develop in the ABS system, the vehicle must be taken to a Renault dealer for fault diagnosis and repair. Check first, however, that the problem is not due to loose or damaged wiring connections, or badly-routed wiring picking up spurious signals from the ignition system.

Warning: If the ABS fuse is removed, be careful during road tests not to brake hard as the Electronic Braking Distributor Function is no longer activated (identical front and rear pressure), so there is a risk that the vehicle will spin.

23 Anti-lock braking system (ABS) components - removal and refitting

Caution: On models equipped with ABS, disconnect the battery before disconnecting any braking system hydraulic union and do not reconnect the battery until after the hydraulic system has been bled. Failure to do this could lead to air entering the hydraulic unit. If air enters the hydraulic unit pump, it will prove very difficult (in some cases impossible) to bleed the unit (see Section 6).

Hydraulic Unit

Note: *Before starting work, refer to the warning at the beginning of Section 6 concerning the dangers of hydraulic fluid.*

Removal

1 Disconnect the battery negative lead (refer to *Disconnecting the battery* in the Reference Section).
2 Detach the coolant expansion bottle and the PAS reservoir and move to one side.

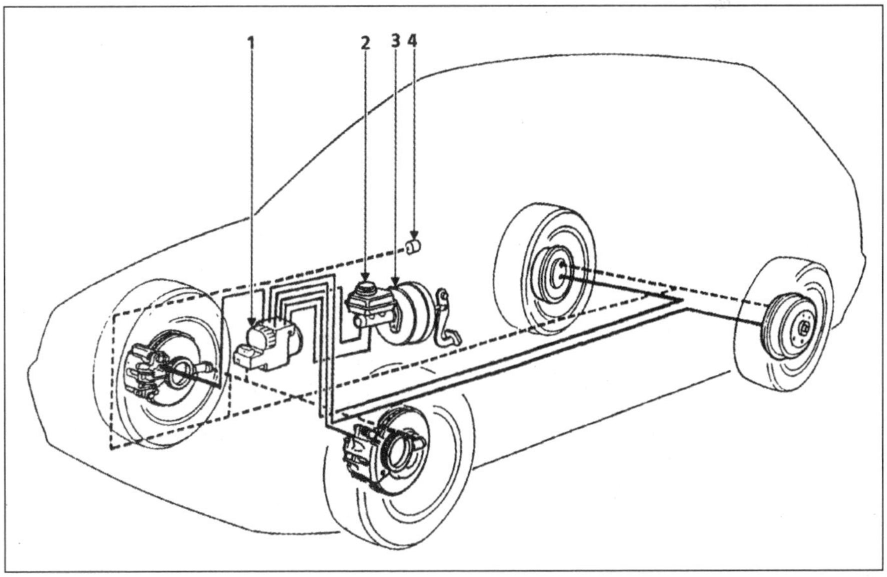

22.1 Location of the Bosch anti-lock braking system (ABS) components

1 Hydraulic assembly
2 Master cylinder
3 Brake servo
4 Brake fluid level warning light

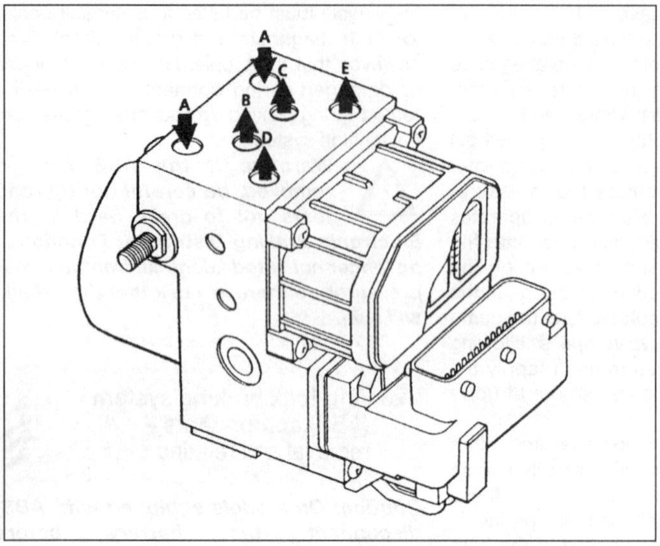

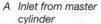

23.6 Hydraulic unit brake pipe union locations

A Inlet from master cylinder
B Rear left wheel
C Rear right wheel
D Front right wheel
E Front left wheel

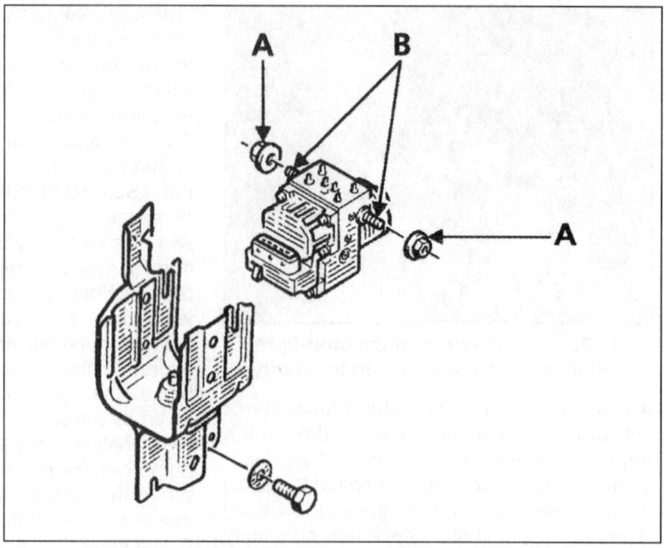

23.8 Unscrew the hydraulic unit retaining nuts (A), remove studs (B) for easier removal

3 Disconnect the large block connector from the hydraulic unit.

4 Undo the two securing bolts and release the earth leads (where fitted).

5 Remove the master cylinder reservoir filler cap. Place a piece of polythene over the filler neck, and securely refit the cap (taking care not to damage the sender unit). This will minimise brake fluid loss during subsequent operations. On all models, be prepared for some fluid spillage. As a precaution, place absorbent rags beneath the modulator brake pipe unions.

6 Wipe clean the area around the hydraulic unit brake pipe unions. Make a note of how the pipes are arranged, to use as a reference on refitting; the pipes may be colour-coded, and the hydraulic unit unions marked to aid refitting **(see illustration)**. Unscrew the union nuts and carefully withdraw the pipes. Plug or tape over the pipe ends and valve orifices, to minimise the loss of brake fluid and to prevent the entry of dirt into the system. Wash off any spilt fluid immediately with cold water.

7 Slacken and remove the upper mounting bolt, and the two lower mounting bolts from the hydraulic unit support bracket and withdraw from the engine compartment.

8 To remove the hydraulic unit from the support bracket, undo the two securing nuts (one at each side). If required remove the two studs to make removal of the unit easier **(see illustration)**.

Caution: Do not attempt to dismantle the hydraulic unit assembly. Overhaul of the unit is a complex job, and should be entrusted to a Renault dealer.

Refitting

9 Refitting is the reverse of the removal procedure, noting the following points:

a) Tighten the hydraulic unit mounting nuts securely.

b) Refit the brake pipes to the correct unions, and tighten the union nuts to the specified torque.

c) Ensure the wiring is correctly routed, and the connectors firmly pressed into position.

d) Before reconnecting the battery, bleed the complete braking system as described in Section 6. Ensure the system is bled in the correct order, to prevent air entering the return pump.

ABS computer

10 The computer is an integral part of the hydraulic unit assembly, and cannot be renewed separately. If renewal is necessary, the hydraulic unit must be renewed as a complete assembly, as described in this Section.

Front wheel sensor

Removal

11 Chock the rear wheels and apply the handbrake. Jack up the front of the vehicle and support it on axle stands (see *Jacking and vehicle support*). Remove the appropriate front roadwheel.

12 From inside the engine compartment, release the sensor wiring connector from its clip on the side of the suspension turret. Disconnect the connector, and remove the sensor wiring grommet from the wing valance.

13 Pull the sensor wiring lead through from under the wheelarch, and free the sensor wiring from its bracket on the suspension strut **(see illustration)**.

14 Remove the bolt securing the sensor to the swivel hub, and remove the sensor and lead assembly from the vehicle **(see illustrations)**.

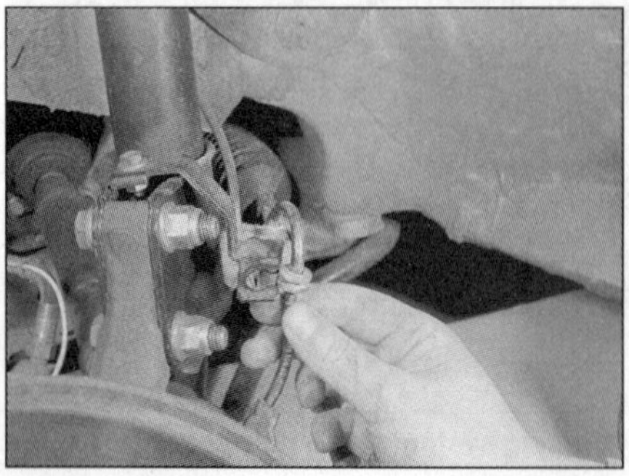

23.13 Release the sensor wiring from the suspension strut bracket . . .

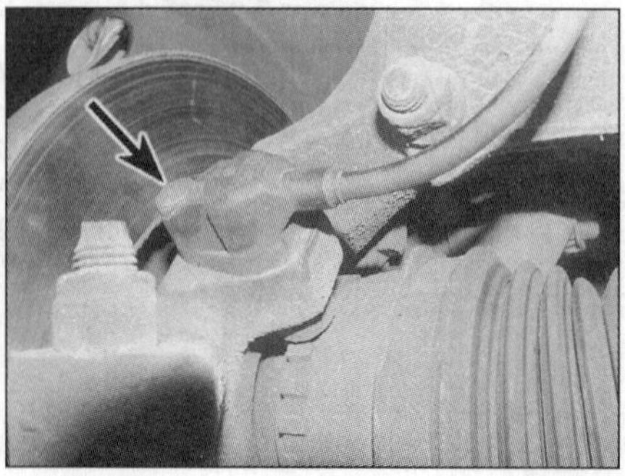

23.14a . . . undo the retaining screw (arrowed) . . .

23.14b . . . and withdraw the sensor from the swivel hub

23.17 Checking front wheel sensor-to-reluctor ring clearance

23.22 Rear wheel sensor wiring connectors are located on the left-hand side of the vehicle

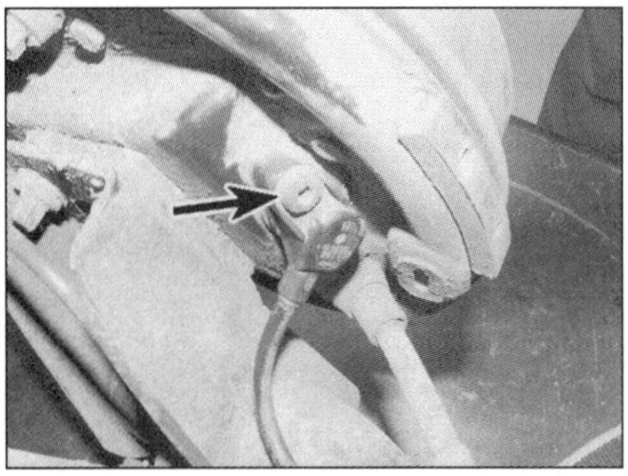

23.24 Remove the rear wheel sensor retaining bolt (arrowed) – rear drum brakes

Refitting

15 Prior to refitting, apply a thin coat of multi-purpose grease to the sensor tip.

16 Ensure that the sensor and swivel hub sealing faces are clean. Fit the sensor, using hand pressure only; in particular, do not hit it with a hammer. Fit the sensor retaining bolt, and tighten it to the specified torque.

17 Rotate the hub until one of the reluctor ring teeth is aligned with the sensor tip. Using feeler gauges, measure the air gap between the tooth and the sensor tip **(see illustration)**. Rotate the hub and repeat the check on several other teeth. If the air gap is not within the range given in the Specifications, then the advice of a Renault dealer must be sought to supply shims.

18 Ensure the sensor wiring is correctly routed, then clip it back into position in the strut bracket.

19 Feed the wiring through into the engine compartment, and reconnect the wiring connector. Refit the connector to its retaining clip, then refit the sealing grommet to the wing valance.

20 Refit the roadwheel. Lower the vehicle to the ground and tighten the roadwheel bolts to the specified torque.

Rear wheel sensor

Removal

21 Chock the front wheels, engage reverse gear (or P) and release the handbrake. Jack up the rear of the vehicle and support it on axle stands (see *Jacking and vehicle support*). Remove the appropriate roadwheel.

22 Trace the wiring back from the sensor, and disconnect the wiring from the main wiring loom **(see illustration)**.

23 Work back along the sensor wiring, and free it from any retaining clips.

24 Remove the bolt securing the sensor unit to the rear hub **(see illustration)**. Remove the sensor and lead assembly from the vehicle.

Refitting

25 Prior to refitting, apply a thin coat of multi-purpose grease to the sensor tip.

26 Ensure that the sensor and trailing arm sealing faces are clean. Fit the sensor, using hand pressure only; in particular, do not hit it with a hammer. Tighten the retaining bolt to the specified torque.

27 The rear sensors are not adjustable. If the air gap is not within the range given in the Specifications, then the advice of a Renault dealer must be sought.

28 Ensure that the sensor wiring is correctly routed and retained by all the necessary retaining clips. Reconnect the wiring connector, and clip it into its retaining bracket.

29 Refit the roadwheel. Lower the vehicle to the ground and tighten the roadwheel bolts to the specified torque.

Front reluctor ring

Note: *Check on the availability of a new reluctor ring before removal.*

Removal

30 The front reluctor rings are a press fit on the driveshaft outer constant velocity (CV) joints. They should not normally need any attention, but if damage is found such as chipped or missing teeth, they can be renewed as follows.

31 Remove the appropriate driveshaft as described in Chapter 8.

32 Using a heavy-duty puller, carefully draw the reluctor ring off the end of the CV joint.

Refitting

33 Ensure the mating surfaces of the reluctor ring and CV joint are clean and dry. Apply a thin coat of locking fluid to the inside of the ring.

34 Locate the reluctor ring on the CV joint, and tap the ring squarely onto the locating shoulder. Note that, to ensure the correct operation of the ABS system, it is important that the ring is correctly and squarely seated against the CV joint shoulder.

35 Refit the driveshaft to the vehicle as described in Chapter 8, then check the sensor tip air gap as described in paragraph 17 of this Section.

Rear reluctor ring

36 The rear reluctor rings are an integral part of the rear hub, and cannot be renewed separately. Examine the rings for signs of damage such as chipped or missing teeth, and renew as necessary. If renewal is necessary, the hub must be renewed as described in Chapter 10.

24 Vacuum pump (diesel engines) – removal and refitting

Removal

Note: *A new vacuum pump drive dog and gasket will be required before refitting.*

1 Release the air intake pipe from the air intake assembly on the top of the engine.

2 Undo the retaining clip and disconnect the vacuum hose from the pump.

3 Slacken and remove the four mounting bolts securing the pump to the end of the cylinder head, then remove the pump. Recover the pump gasket and discard it; a new one should be used on refitting.

Refitting

4 Ensure that the pump and cylinder head mating surfaces are clean and dry and fit the new gasket to the head.

5 Manoeuvre the pump into position, aligning its new drive dog with the camshaft slot, then refit the pump mounting bolts and tighten them securely.

25 Vacuum pump (diesel engines) – testing and overhaul

1 The operation of the braking system vacuum pump can be checked using a vacuum gauge.

2 Disconnect the vacuum pipe from the pump, and connect the gauge to the pump union using a suitable length of hose.

3 Start the engine and allow it to idle, then measure the vacuum created by the pump. As a guide, after one minute, a minimum of approximately 500 mm Hg should be recorded. If the vacuum registered is significantly less than this, it is likely that the pump is faulty. However, seek the advice of a Renault dealer before condemning the pump.

4 Overhaul of the vacuum pump is not possible, since no components are available separately for it. If faulty, the complete pump assembly must be renewed.

Chapter 10
Suspension and steering

Contents

Degrees of difficulty

Easy, suitable for novice with little experience	**Fairly easy,** suitable for beginner with some experience	**Fairly difficult,** suitable for competent DIY mechanic	**Difficult,** suitable for experienced DIY mechanic	**Very difficult,** suitable for expert DIY or professional

Specifications

General

Engine codes:	
1.2 litre petrol engine	D7F
1.4 litre petrol engine:	
SOHC	E7J
DOHC	K4J
1.6 litre petrol engine:	
SOHC	K7M
DOHC	K4M
Diesel engine	F8Q

Front suspension

Type	Independent, MacPherson struts, with coil springs and integral shock absorbers. Anti-roll bar fitted to all models
Hub bearing endfloat	0 to 0.05 mm
Front ride height (H1 minus H2):	
All models	95 ± 10.5 mm
Difference between left and right-hand side must not exceed	5.0 mm

Rear suspension

Type	Independent, incorporating trailing arms with telescopic dampers and separate coil springs.
Hub bearing endfloat	0 to 0.03 mm
Ride height (H4 minus H5):	
All models (except K4J and K4M)	–25 ± 10.5 mm
K4J engine types	–18 ± 7.5 mm
K4M engine types	8 ± 5.0 mm
Difference between left and right-hand side must not exceed	5.0 mm

Steering

Type	Rack-and-pinion, power-assisted on most models

Wheel alignment and steering angles

Front wheel camber angle at ride height (H1 minus H2) stated:	
D7F and K4M engine models:	
17 mm	0° 54’ ± 30’
89 mm	–0° 25’ ± 30’
115 mm	–0° 34’ ± 30’
179 mm	0° 05’ ± 30’
K4J engine models:	
94 mm	0° 27’ ± 30’
105 mm	–0° 22’ ± 30’
115 mm	–0° 34’ ± 30’
145 mm	0° 28’ ± 30’
All other models:	
17 mm	0° 16’ ± 30’
89 mm	–1° 10’ ± 30’
115 mm	–1° 20’ ± 30’
179 mm	–0° 45’ ± 30’
Maximum difference between left- and right-hand sides	1°
Castor angle at ride height (H5 minus H2) stated:	
K4J engine models:	
80 mm	2° 48’ ± 30’
100 mm	2° 18’ ± 30’
120 mm	1° 48’ ± 30’
130 mm	2° 00’ ± 30’
All other models:	
32 mm	4° 00’ ± 30’
51 mm	3° 30’ ± 30’
70 mm	3° 00’ ± 30’
89 mm	2° 30’ ± 30’
Maximum difference between left- and right-hand sides	1°
Steering axis inclination/kingpin inclination at ride height (H1 minus H2) stated:	
K4J engine models:	
94 mm	10° 50’ ± 30’
105 mm	11° 00’ ± 30’
115 mm	11° 20’ ± 30’
145 mm	12° 50’ ± 30’
All other models:	
17 mm	8° 30’ ± 30’
89 mm	10° 50’ ± 30’
115 mm	11° 20’ ± 30’
179 mm	12° 00’ ± 30’
Maximum difference between left- and right-hand sides	1°
Front wheel toe setting (vehicle unladen):	
K4J engine models	+0° 10’ ± 10’ (+1.0 mm ± 1.0 mm) toe-out
All models	+0° 16’ ± 20’ (+1.6 mm ± 2.0 mm) toe-out
Rear wheel camber setting (vehicle unladen):	
K4J engine models	–1° 00’ ± 15’
K4M engine models	–0° 57’ ± 20’
All other models	–0° 42’ ± 20’
Rear wheel toe setting (vehicle unladen):	
K4J engine models	–0° 15’ ± 10’ (–1.5mm ± 1.0mm) toe-in
K4M engine models	–0° 41’ ± 30’ (–4.0 mm ± 3.0 mm) toe-in
All other models	–0° 30’ ± 30’ (–3.0 mm ± 3.0 mm) toe-in

Tyres

Tyre size	165/70 R 13T, 165/60 R 14T, 165/65 R 14T or 175/70 R 13T (depending on model)
Pressures	See end of *Weekly checks*

Roadwheels

Type	Pressed-steel or aluminium alloy (depending on model)
Size	5B x 13, 5.5J x 14 and 6J x 14 (depending on model)
Maximum run-out at rim	1.2 mm
Maximum eccentricity on tyre bead locating surface	0.8 mm

Torque wrench settings

	Nm	lbf ft
Front suspension		
Anti-roll bar mounting clamp bolts	30	22
Anti-roll bar-to-lower arm bolt/nut	15	11
Driveshaft/hub nut*:		
Nyloc type nut	250	185
ENKO self-locking nut with integral washer	280	207
Engine tie-bar bolt	65	48
Lower arm balljoint clamp bolt	55	41
Lower arm balljoint retaining nuts	75	55
Lower arm pivot bolts	90	66
Strut upper mounting nut	60	44
Strut-to-swivel hub bolts	105	77
Rear suspension		
Hub nut*	175	129
Rear trailing arm mounting bracket-to-chassis securing bolts	60	44
Rear trailing arm-to-mounting bracket securing bolt	70	52
Shock absorber lower mounting bolt	105	77
Shock absorber upper mounting nut	20	15
Stub axle/back plate mounting bolts	55	41
Steering		
Intermediate shaft universal joint eccentric bolt	25	18
Manual steering gear mounting bolts	55	41
Power steering electric pump assembly mounting bolts	20	15
Power steering gear mounting bolts	50	37
Power steering pump mounting bolts	20	15
Steering column mounting bolts	20	15
Steering wheel bolt*	45	33
Track rod end balljoint – adjustment clamp bolt	18	13
Track rod end balljoint-to-swivel hub retaining nut	37	27
Track rod to steering rack – axial balljoint:		
SMI steering gear assembly	50	37
TRW steering gear assembly	80	59
Roadwheels		
Wheel bolts	90	66

**Renew every time*

1 General information

The independent front suspension is of the MacPherson strut type, incorporating coil springs and integral telescopic shock absorbers. The MacPherson struts are located by transverse lower suspension arms, which utilise rubber inner mounting bushes and incorporate a balljoint at the outer ends. The front swivel hubs, which carry the wheel bearings, brake calipers and the hub/disc assemblies, are bolted to the MacPherson struts and connected to the lower arms via the balljoints. A front anti-roll bar is fitted to all models. The anti-roll bar is rubber-mounted onto the subframe, and connects both the lower suspension arms.

The rear suspension incorporates a beam axle, trailing arms, coil springs and separate telescopic dampers. The front ends of the trailing arms are attached to the vehicle underbody by rubber bushes, and the rear ends are located by the shock absorbers, which are bolted to the underbody at their upper ends. The coil springs are mounted separately from the shock absorbers, and act directly between the axle and the underbody.

The steering column is connected by a universal joint to an intermediate shaft, which has a second universal joint at its lower end. The lower universal joint is attached to the steering gear pinion by means of an eccentric clamp bolt.

The steering gear is mounted onto the front subframe. It is connected by two track rods and balljoints to steering arms projecting rearwards from the swivel hubs. The track rod ends are threaded to enable wheel alignment adjustment.

Power-assisted steering is available on most larger-engine models. On diesel engine models equipped with air conditioning and power steering, an electrically-powered pump is used to power the steering hydraulic system; this is due to lack of space in the engine compartment to house both the air conditioning compressor and a belt-driven pump. All other models equipped with power steering are fitted with a traditional belt-driven pump, which is driven off the crankshaft pulley.

2 Front swivel hub assembly – removal and refitting

Note: *When carrying out an operation on this assembly, it is essential to use the new Enko type self-locking nut without applying a coat of locking fluid to the splines of the stub axle. This type of nut is gradually being fitted in production across the whole vehicle range. The bearing and driveshaft kits are no longer supplied with the Nyloc type nut. If a Nyloc nut is fitted, then the driveshaft outer joint splines will have been coated with locking compound prior to refitting. Therefore it is likely that a puller/extractor will be required to draw the hub assembly off the driveshaft end on removal.*

Removal

1 Chock the rear wheels, firmly apply the handbrake, then jack up the front of the vehicle and support it on axle stands *(see Jacking and vehicle support)*. Remove the appropriate front roadwheel.

2 Refit at least two roadwheel bolts to the front hub, and tighten them securely. Remove

2.3 Undo the mounting bracket bolts and slide the brake caliper off the disc

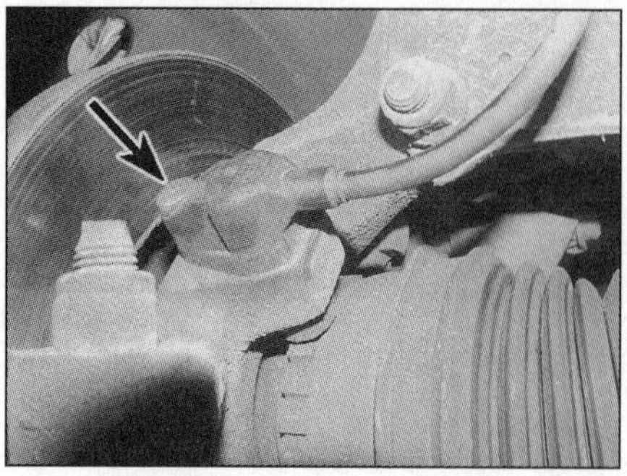

2.4 Front wheel sensor for ABS (arrowed)

the driveshaft nut (see Chapter 8, Section 2, paragraph 4, for full details). Discard the driveshaft nut; a new one should be used on refitting.

3 If the hub bearings are to be disturbed, remove the brake disc as described in Chapter 9. If not, unscrew the two bolts securing the brake caliper assembly to the swivel hub, and slide the caliper assembly off the disc **(see illustration)**. Using a piece of wire or string, tie the caliper to the front suspension coil spring, to avoid straining the brake hose.

4 On models equipped with ABS, undo the retaining bolt and withdraw the front wheel sensor from the swivel hub **(see illustration)**. Tie the sensor to the suspension strut, so that it does not get damaged during the remainder of the removal procedure.

5 Remove the nut securing the track rod end balljoint to the swivel hub. Release the balljoint tapered shank using a universal balljoint separator.

6 Remove the nut and clamp bolt securing the lower suspension arm to the swivel hub **(see illustration)**. Carefully lever the balljoint out of the swivel hub, taking care not to damage the balljoint or driveshaft gaiters. Note the plastic protector plate which is fitted to the balljoint shank.

7 Remove the two nuts from the bolts securing the swivel hub to the suspension strut, noting that the nuts are positioned on the rear side of the strut. Withdraw the bolts and support the swivel hub assembly.

8 Release the driveshaft joint from the hub, and remove the swivel hub assembly from the vehicle. **Note:** *Where Nyloc hub nuts are used, locking fluid is applied to the joint splines during assembly, so it is likely that they will be a tight fit in the hub. Use a hammer and soft metal drift to tap the joint out of the hub, or use a puller to draw the swivel hub assembly off the joint splines.*

Refitting

9 Ensure that the driveshaft joint and hub splines are clean and dry. If Nyloc hub nuts are fitted, then apply a coat of locking fluid to the joint splines.

10 Engage the joint splines with the hub, and slide the hub fully onto the driveshaft. Insert the two swivel hub-to-suspension strut mounting bolts from the front side of the strut, then refit the nuts to the bolts and tighten them to the specified torque.

11 Slide on the washer (where applicable) and fit the new driveshaft nut, tightening it by hand only at this stage.

12 Ensure that the plastic protector is still fitted to the lower arm balljoint **(see illustration)**, then locate the balljoint shank in the swivel hub. Refit the balljoint clamp bolt, and tighten its retaining nut to the specified torque.

13 Reconnect the track rod end balljoint to the swivel hub, and tighten its retaining nut to the specified torque.

14 On models equipped with ABS, refit the sensor to the hub, and tighten its retaining bolt to the specified torque (see Chapter 9).

15 Refit the brake disc (if removed), aligning the marks made on removal, and securely tighten its retaining screws. Slide the brake caliper assembly into position over the brake disc. Apply a few drops of locking fluid to the caliper bolt threads. Refit the bolts and tighten them to the specified torque (Chapter 9).

16 Insert and tighten two wheel bolts. Tighten the driveshaft nut to the specified torque (Chapter 8), using the method employed during removal to prevent the hub from rotating.

17 Check that the hub rotates freely, then refit the roadwheel and lower the vehicle to the ground. Tighten the roadwheel bolts to the specified torque.

2.6 Slackening the lower suspension arm balljoint clamp bolt and nut

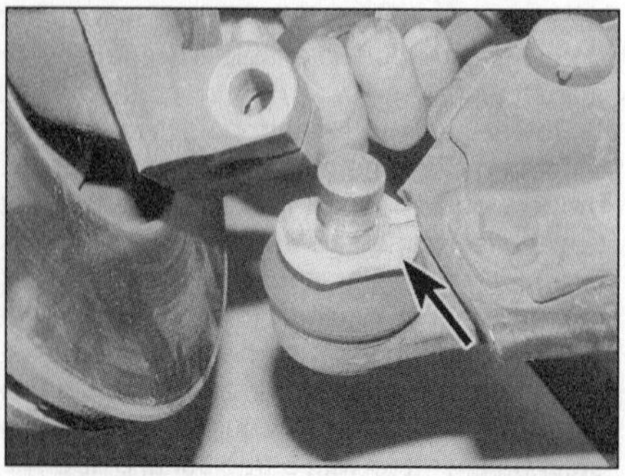

2.12 Make sure the plastic protector (arrowed) is fitted the correct way around

3 Front hub bearings - checking, removal and refitting

Note: *The bearing is a sealed, pre-adjusted and pre-lubricated, double-row roller type, and is intended to last the car's entire service life without maintenance or attention. Do not attempt to remove the bearing unless absolutely necessary, as it will be damaged during the removal operation. Never overtighten the driveshaft nut in an attempt to 'adjust' the bearing.*

A press will be required to dismantle and rebuild the assembly; if such a tool is not available, a large bench vice and suitable spacers (such as large sockets) will serve as an adequate substitute. The bearing's inner races are an interference fit on the hub; if the inner race remains on the hub when it is pressed out of the hub carrier, a suitable knife-edged bearing puller will be required to remove it.

Checking

1 Wear in the front hub bearings can be checked by measuring the amount of side play present. To do this, a dial gauge should be fixed so that its probe is in contact with the disc face of the hub. The play should be between 0 and 0.05 mm. If it is greater than this, the bearings are worn excessively, and should be renewed.

Removal

Note: *A new bearing circlip will be required on refitting.*

2 Remove the swivel hub assembly as described in Section 2.

3 Support the swivel hub securely on blocks or in a vice. Using a suitable tubular spacer which bears only on the inner end of the hub flange, press the hub flange out of the bearing. If the bearing outboard inner race remains on the hub, remove it using a suitable bearing puller (see note above).

4 Extract the bearing retaining circlip from the inner end of the swivel hub assembly **(see illustration)**.

5 Where necessary, refit the inner race in position over the ball cage, and securely support the inner face of the swivel hub. Using a suitable tubular spacer which bears only on the inner race, press the complete bearing assembly out of the swivel hub.

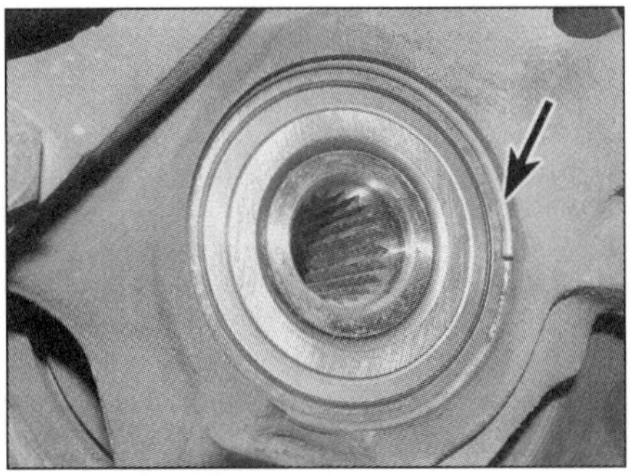

3.4 **Circlip fitted to retain the bearing in the hub assembly (arrowed)**

6 Thoroughly clean the hub and swivel hub, removing all traces of dirt and grease. Polish away any burrs or raised edges which might hinder reassembly. Check for cracks or any other signs of wear or damage, and renew the components if necessary. As noted above, the bearing and its circlip must be renewed whenever they are disturbed. A replacement bearing kit, which consists of the bearing, circlip and thrustwasher, is available from Renault dealers.

Refitting

7 On reassembly, check (if possible) that the new bearing is packed with grease. Apply a light film of oil to the bearing outer race and to the hub flange shaft.

8 Before fitting the new bearing, remove the plastic covers protecting the seals at each end, but leave the inner plastic sleeve in position to hold the inner races together.

9 Securely support the swivel hub, and locate the bearing in the hub. Press the bearing into position, ensuring that it enters the hub squarely, using a suitable tubular spacer which bears only on the outer race.

10 Once the bearing is correctly seated, secure it with the new circlip and remove the plastic sleeve. Apply a smear of grease to the seal lips.

11 Locate the bearing inner race over the end of the hub flange. Press the bearing onto the hub, using a tubular spacer which bears only on the inner race, until it seats against the thrustwasher/hub flange **(see illustration)**. Check that the hub flange rotates freely. Wipe off any excess oil or grease.

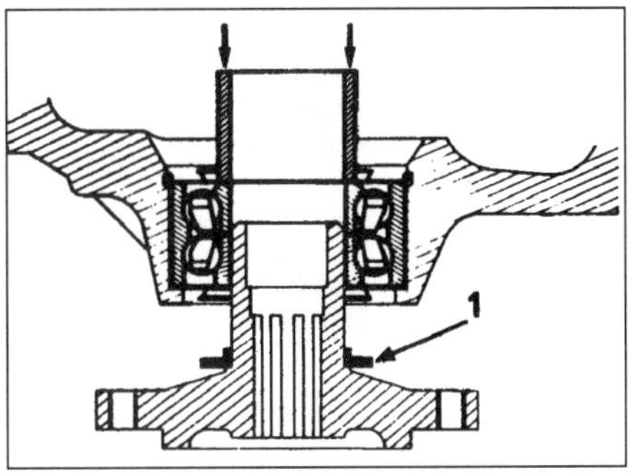

3.11 **Refitting the hub flange**

1 Thrustwasher (where applicable)

12 Refit the swivel hub assembly as described in Section 2.

4 Front strut – removal and refitting

Removal

1 Chock the rear wheels, firmly apply the handbrake, then jack up the front of the vehicle and support it on axle stands *(see Jacking and vehicle support)*. Remove the appropriate roadwheel.

2 Remove the two nuts from the bolts securing the swivel hub to the suspension strut, noting that the nuts are positioned on the rear side of the strut. Withdraw the bolts, and support the swivel hub assembly.

3 Unclip the brake pipe hose and ABS wiring from the strut assembly (where applicable).

4 From within the engine compartment, slacken the suspension strut upper mounting nut, holding the strut piston rod with an Allen key **(see illustration)**. Remove the nut.

5 Lower the assembly from under the wing, releasing the strut from the swivel hub. Withdraw the strut from under the wheelarch, taking care not to damage the driveshaft gaiter **(see illustration)**.

Refitting

6 Manoeuvre the strut assembly into position, taking care not to damage the driveshaft gaiter.

4.4 **Slacken the suspension strut upper mounting nut, holding the strut piston rod with an Allen key**

7 Insert the two swivel hub-to-suspension strut mounting bolts from the front side of the strut. Refit the nuts to the rear of the bolts, and tighten them to the specified torque **(see illustration)**.

8 Refit the upper mounting nut and tighten it to the specified torque.

9 Refit the roadwheel, lower the vehicle to the ground and tighten the roadwheel bolts to the specified torque.

5 Front strut – dismantling, inspection and reassembly

Warning: Before attempting to dismantle the front suspension strut, a suitable tool to hold the coil spring in compression must be obtained. Adjustable coil spring compressors are readily available, and are recommended for this operation. Any attempt to dismantle the strut without such a tool is likely to result in damage or personal injury.

Dismantling

1 With the strut removed from the vehicle as described in Section 4, clean away all external dirt. Mount the strut upright in a vice.

2 Remove the upper mounting rubber. Fit the spring compressor, and compress the coil spring until all tension is relieved from the upper mounting plate. Ensure that the compressor tool is securely located on the spring according to the tool manufacturer's instructions **(see illustration)**.

4.5 **Removing the front suspension strut**

4.7 **Tightening the swivel hub-to-strut nut and bolts. Note that the bolt heads face forwards**

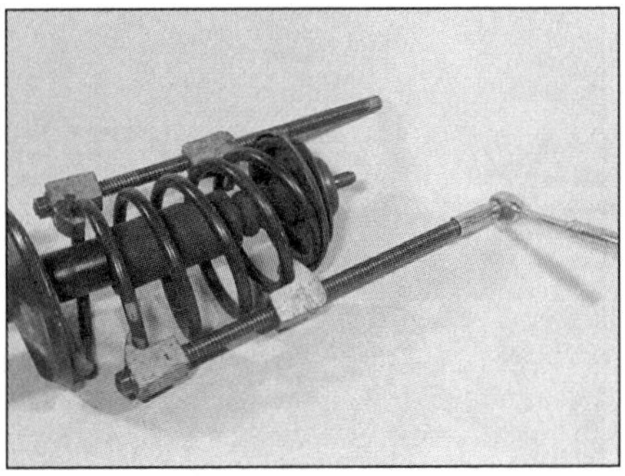

5.2 **Using spring compressors, compress the suspension strut coil spring**

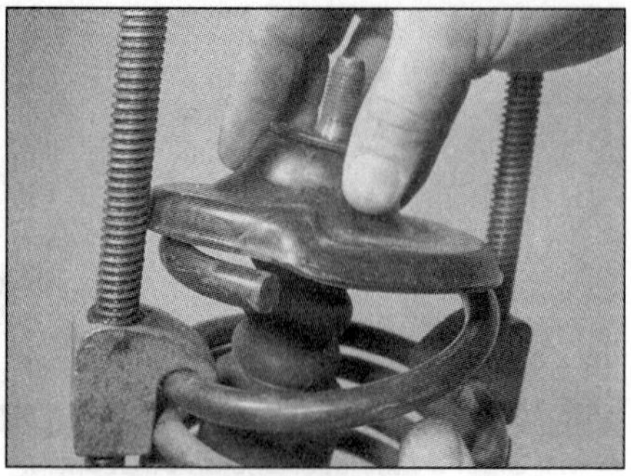

5.5 Remove the upper spring seat and coil spring

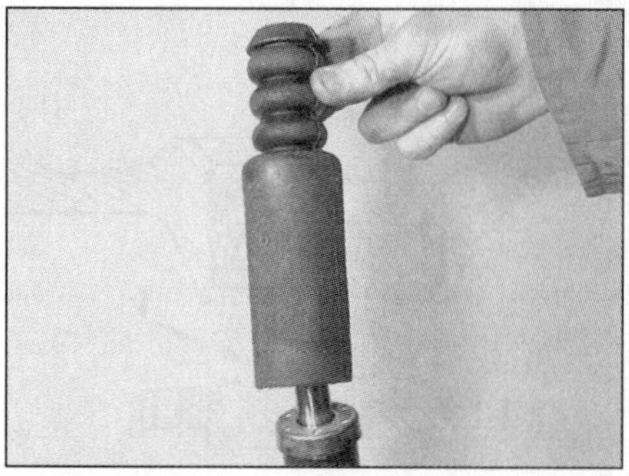

5.11 Refit the rubber dust cover to the strut piston

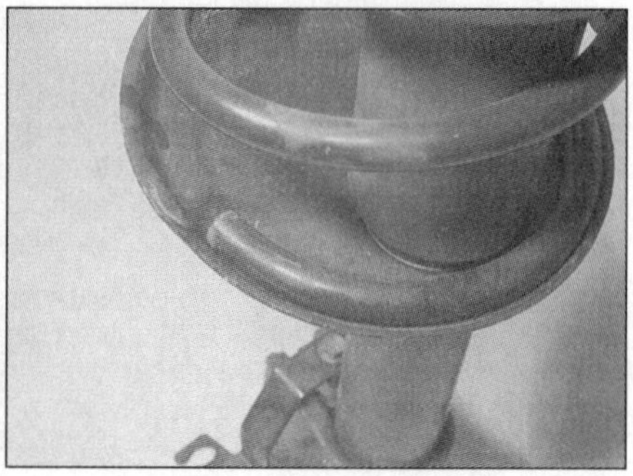

5.12 Coil spring lower end correctly located in spring seat

3 Slacken and remove the retaining nut from the top of the strut.

4 Remove the upper mounting plate, the bearing and the upper spring seat.

5 Carefully remove the coil spring, complete with the spring compressor, and store in a safe place for refitting **(see illustration)**. (It may be safer to release the spring compressor from the spring.)

6 Slide the rubber bump stop/dust cover off the strut piston.

Inspection

7 With the strut assembly now completely dismantled, examine all the components for wear, damage or deformation, and check the upper bearing for smoothness of operation. Renew any of the components as necessary.

8 Examine the strut for signs of fluid leakage. Check the strut piston for signs of pitting along its entire length, and check the strut body for signs of damage. Test the operation of the strut, while holding it in an upright position, by moving the piston through a full stroke and then through short strokes of 50 to 100 mm. In both cases, the resistance felt should be smooth and continuous. If the resistance is jerky or uneven, or if there is any visible sign of wear or damage, renewal is necessary.

9 If any doubt exists about the condition of the coil spring, gradually release the spring compressor (if not already done), and check the spring for distortion and signs of cracking. Since no minimum free length is specified by Renault, the only way to check the tension of the spring is to compare it to a new component. Renew the spring if it is damaged or distorted, or if there is any doubt as to its condition.

10 Inspect all other components for signs of damage or deterioration, and renew any that are suspect.

Reassembly

Note: *Apply grease between the ends of the spring and its stops.*

11 Ensure that all components are clean and dry. Slide the bump stop/dust cover into position over the strut piston **(see illustration)**.

12 Refit the compressed coil spring, followed by the upper spring seat. Ensure that both ends of the spring are correctly located in the spring seats **(see illustration)**.

13 Refit the strut bearing and upper mounting plate.

14 Slide the retaining collar (where fitted) onto the strut piston, and secure it in position with the retaining nut. Slowly and carefully release the spring compressor, watching to make sure that both ends of the spring remain correctly located in the spring seats.

15 Refit the strut to the vehicle as described in Section 4.

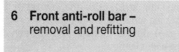

6 Front anti-roll bar – removal and refitting

Removal

1 Chock the rear wheels, apply the handbrake, then jack up the front of the vehicle and support it on axle stands *(see Jacking and vehicle support)*. Remove both front roadwheels.

2 Remove the exhaust downpipe as described in the relevant part of Chapter 4.

3 Working under the vehicle, undo the securing bolts from the two reinforcement plates (4 bolts each side) and remove the plates from the subframe **(see illustration)**.

4 Remove the nuts and bolts securing each end of the anti-roll bar to the lower suspension arms, noting the positions of the rubber mounting spacers **(see illustration)**.

5 Unbolt the anti-roll bar mounting clamps from the subframe **(see illustration)**.

6 Manoeuvre the anti-roll bar out from underneath the vehicle, and remove the rubber mounting bushes.

7 Carefully examine the anti-roll bar components for signs of wear, damage or deterioration, paying particular attention to the mounting bushes. Renew worn components as necessary.

Refitting

8 Fit the bushes onto the anti-roll bar, then manoeuvre the anti-roll bar into position underneath the vehicle. Do not tighten the mounting clamp bolts fully yet.

9 Secure the ends of the anti-roll bar to the lower suspension arms, ensuring that the rubber mounting spacers are correctly positioned. Fit the nuts and bolts, but do not tighten them fully yet.

10 Refit the exhaust downpipe.

11 Refit the reinforcement plates to the subframe.

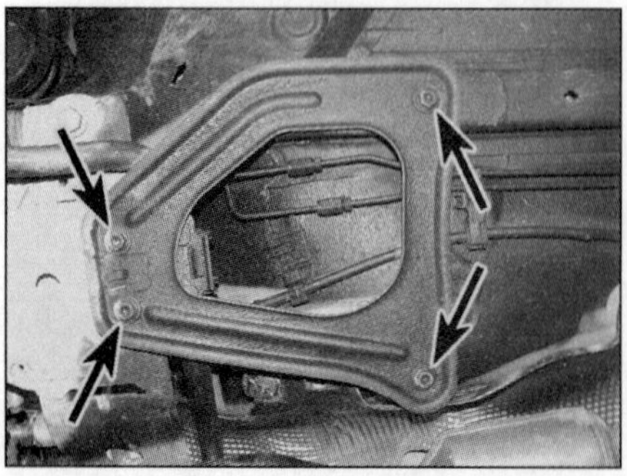

6.3 Undo the four securing bolts (arrowed) – left-hand reinforcement plate shown

6.4 Removing a front anti-roll bar mounting bolt

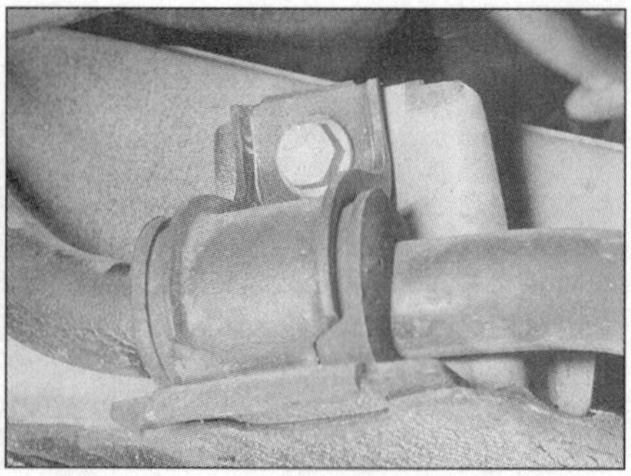

6.5 Front anti-roll bar mounting clamp

7.3a Where fitted, undo the support bar upper mounting bolt (arrowed) . . .

12 Refit the roadwheels, lower the vehicle to the ground and tighten the wheel bolts to the specified torque.

13 Tighten the anti-roll bar fastenings to the specified torque, starting with the mounting clamps.

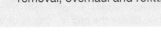

7 Front lower arm – removal, overhaul and refitting

Removal

1 Chock the rear wheels, apply the handbrake, jack up the front of the vehicle and support it on axle stands. *(see Jacking and vehicle support).* Remove the appropriate front roadwheel.

2 Disconnect the end of the anti-roll bar from the lower suspension arm, as described in the previous Section.

3 When applicable, remove the bolt securing the support bar to the front wing valance, and the nut securing it to the front pivot bolt. Remove the support bar from the vehicle **(see illustrations)**.

4 Remove the nut and clamp bolt securing the lower suspension arm balljoint to the swivel hub. Carefully lever the balljoint out of the swivel hub, taking care not to damage the balljoint or driveshaft gaiters. Remove the plastic protector plate which is fitted to the balljoint shank **(see illustrations)**.

5 Remove the two pivot nuts and bolts, and remove the lower suspension arm from the vehicle **(see illustration)**.

Overhaul

6 Clean the lower arm and the area around the arm mountings, then check for cracks, distortion or any other signs of damage. On some models, a brake disc cooling shield is clipped to the arm; this should also be removed. Check that the lower arm balljoint moves freely, without any sign of roughness, and that the balljoint gaiter is free from cracks and splits. Examine the shank of the pivot bolts for signs of wear or scoring. Renew worn components as necessary.

7 Inspect the lower arm pivot bushes. If they are worn, cracked, split or perished, they must be renewed. To renew the bushes, support the lower arm, and press the first bush out using a tubular spacer, such as a socket, which bears only on the hard, outer edge of the bush. **Note:** *Remove only one bush at a time from the arm, to ensure that each new bush is correctly positioned on installation.* Thoroughly clean the lower arm bore, removing all traces of dirt and grease, and polish away any burrs or raised edges which might hinder reassembly. Apply a smear of suitable grease to the outer edge of the new bush. Press the bush into position until the distance between the inner edges of the lower arm bushes is as shown **(see illustration)**. Wipe away surplus grease and repeat the procedure on the remaining bush.

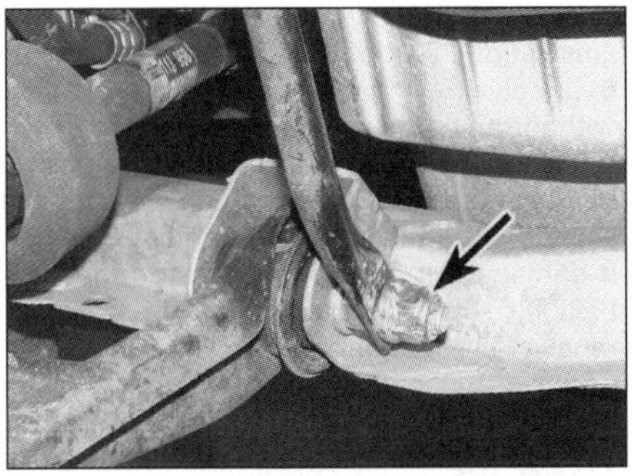

7.3b . . . and remove nut from the suspension arm pivot bolt (arrowed)

7.4b . . . then free the balljoint from the swivel hub, and remove the plastic protector plate

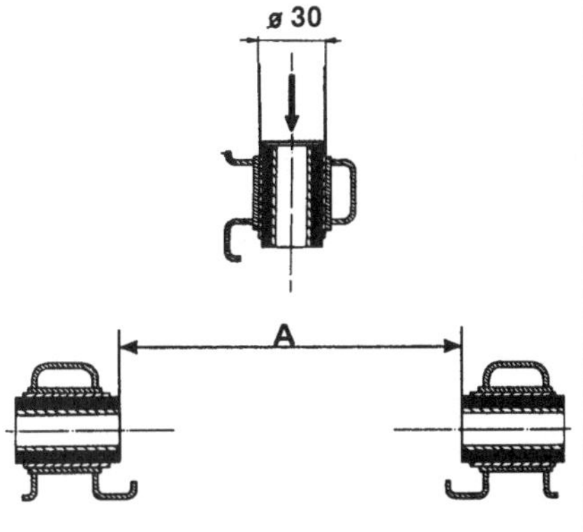

7.7 Front suspension lower arm pivot bush fitting dimension

A = 146.5

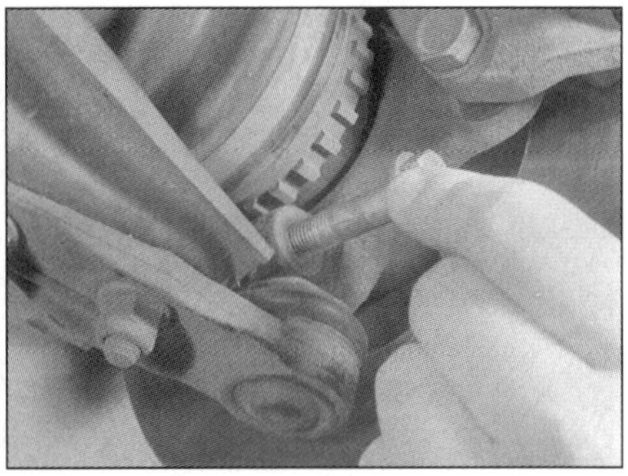

7.4a Remove the balljoint clamp bolt . . .

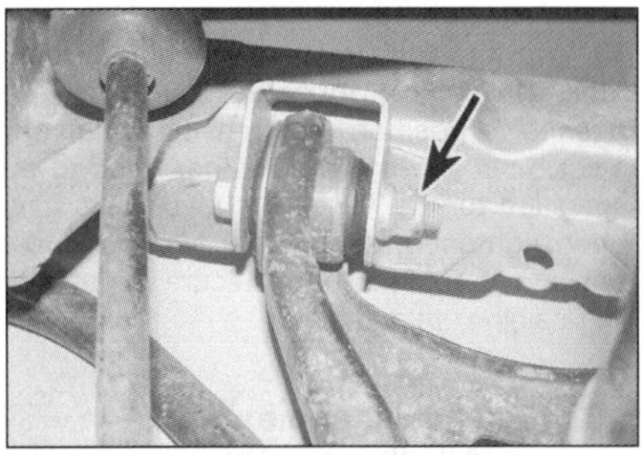

7.5 Undo the nut (arrowed) and withdraw the lower suspension arm pivot bolt (rear bolt shown)

Refitting

8 Offer up the lower suspension arm, and insert the two pivot bolts from the rear of the suspension arm. Refit the nuts, but tighten them by hand only at this stage.

9 Refit the plastic protector to the lower arm balljoint, then locate the balljoint shank in the swivel hub. Refit the balljoint clamp bolt, and tighten its retaining nut to the specified torque **(see illustration)**.

10 When applicable, refit the support bar on the front pivot bolt shank. Fit the retaining bolt and nut, tightening both by hand only at this stage.

11 Reconnect the end of the anti-roll bar to the lower suspension arm, ensuring that the rubber mounting spacers are correctly positioned. Do not fully tighten the fastenings yet.

12 Refit the roadwheel, lower the vehicle and tighten the roadwheel bolts to the specified torque.

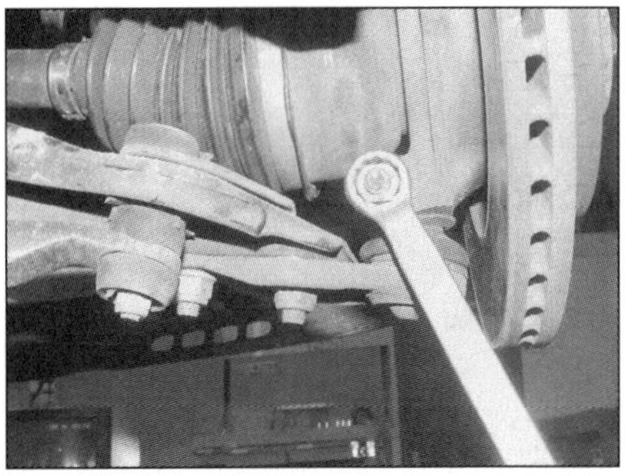

7.9 Tightening the balljoint clamp bolt

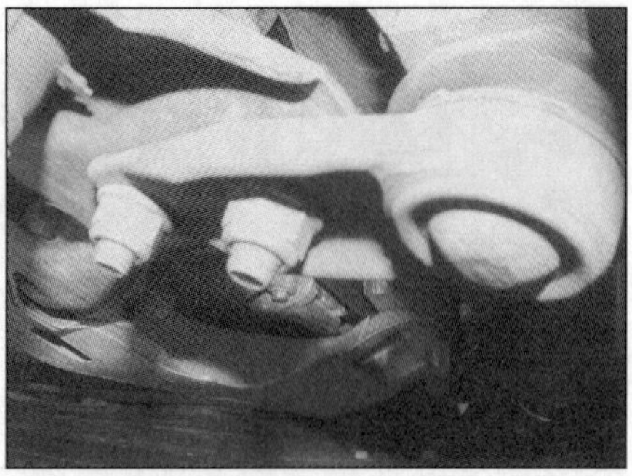

8.5 Front lower suspension arm balljoint retaining nuts

13 With the vehicle standing on its wheels, rock the vehicle to settle the lower arm bushes in position. Tighten the lower arm pivot bolts and the anti-roll bar fixing to the specified torque. When the pivot bolts have been tightened, secure the support bar in position (if applicable) by securely tightening its retaining nut and bolt.

8 Front lower arm balljoint – removal and refitting

Removal

1 Chock the rear wheels, apply the handbrake, jack up the front of the vehicle and support it on axle stands *(see Jacking and vehicle support)*. Remove the appropriate front roadwheel.
2 Disconnect the end of the anti-roll bar from the lower suspension arm, as described in Section 6.
3 Slacken the nut securing the support bar (where fitted) to the lower arm front pivot bolt, then slacken both the lower suspension arm pivot bolts.
4 Remove the nut and clamp bolt securing the lower suspension arm to the swivel hub. Carefully lever the balljoint out of the swivel hub, taking care not to damage the balljoint or driveshaft gaiters. Remove the plastic protector plate which is fitted to the balljoint shank.
5 Remove the two nuts and bolts securing the balljoint to the lower suspension arm **(see illustration)**. Remove the balljoint.
6 Check that the balljoint moves freely, without any sign of roughness or free play. Examine the balljoint gaiter for signs of damage and deterioration such as cracks or splits. Renew the complete balljoint assembly if damaged; it is not possible to renew the balljoint gaiter separately. The balljoint renewal kit obtainable from Renault dealers contains the balljoint, the plastic protector plate and all fixings.

Refitting

7 Fit the balljoint to the suspension arm. Insert the bolts and washers, and tighten the retaining nuts to the specified torque.
8 Fit the plastic protector to the balljoint shank, then locate the shank in the swivel hub. Refit the balljoint clamp bolt, and tighten its retaining nut to the specified torque.
9 Reconnect the end of the anti-roll bar to the lower suspension arm, ensuring that the rubber mounting spacers are correctly positioned. Do not fully tighten the fastenings yet.
10 Refit the roadwheel, lower the vehicle and tighten the roadwheel bolts to the specified torque.
11 With the vehicle standing on its wheels, rock the vehicle to settle the lower arm bushes in position. Tighten the lower arm pivot bolts and the anti-roll bar fixing to the specified torque. When the pivot bolts have been tightened, secure the support bar in position (if applicable) by securely tightening its retaining nut and bolt.

9 Rear hub bearings – checking, removal and refitting

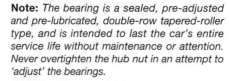

Note: *The bearing is a sealed, pre-adjusted and pre-lubricated, double-row tapered-roller type, and is intended to last the car's entire service life without maintenance or attention. Never overtighten the hub nut in an attempt to 'adjust' the bearings.*

Checking

1 Chock the front wheels and engage reverse gear (or P). Jack up the rear of the vehicle and support it on axle stands *(see Jacking and vehicle support)*. Remove the appropriate rear roadwheel, and fully release the handbrake.
2 Wear in the rear hub bearings can be checked by measuring the amount of side play present. To do this, a dial test indicator should be fixed so that its probe is in contact with the hub outer face. The play should be between 0 and 0.03 mm. If it is greater than this, the bearings are worn excessively and should be renewed.

Removal

3 Remove the rear brake disc or drum (as applicable), as described in Chapter 9.
4 Using circlip pliers, extract the bearing retaining circlip from the centre of the brake disc or drum **(see illustration)**.
5 Securely support the disc or drum hub. Press or drive the bearing out of the hub, using a suitable tubular tube as a drift **(see illustration)**.
6 Thoroughly clean the hub, removing all traces of dirt and grease. Polish away any burrs or raised edges which might hinder reassembly. Check the hub for cracks or any other signs of damage, and renew if necessary. The bearing and its circlip must be renewed whenever they are disturbed. A replacement bearing kit is available from Renault dealers, consisting of the bearing, circlip, spacer, thrustwasher, hub nut and grease cap.

Refitting

7 On reassembly, check (if possible) that the new bearing is packed with grease. Apply a light film of gear oil to the bearing outer race and stub axle.
8 Securely support the hub. Press the bearing into position, ensuring that it enters the hub squarely, using a suitable tube which presses only on the bearing outer race.
9 Ensure that the bearing is correctly seated against the hub shoulder, and secure it in position with the new circlip. Ensure that the circlip is correctly seated in its groove.
10 Refit the brake disc or drum as described in Chapter 9.

9.4 Extract the circlip . . .

9.5 . . . then drive the bearing out of the hub using a suitable tubular drift

10 Rear shock absorber – removal, testing and refitting

Removal

1 Chock the front wheels and engage reverse gear (or P). Jack up the rear of the vehicle and support it on axle stands *(see Jacking and vehicle support)*. Remove the appropriate rear roadwheel.
2 Using a jack, raise the trailing arm slightly until the shock absorber is slightly compressed. Remove the lower mounting bolt **(see illustration)**.
3 Working inside the luggage compartment,

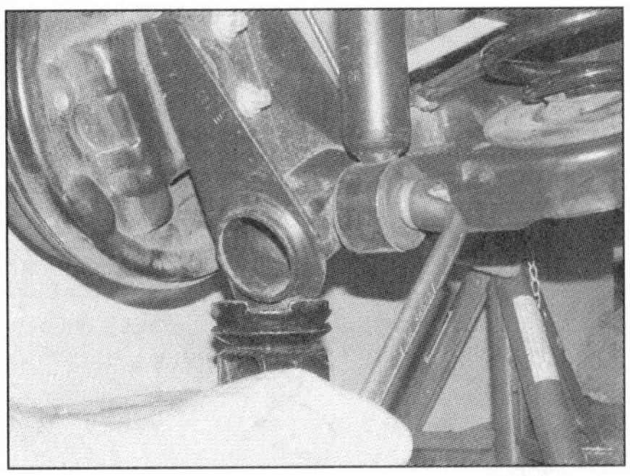

10.2 Removing the rear shock absorber lower mounting bolt

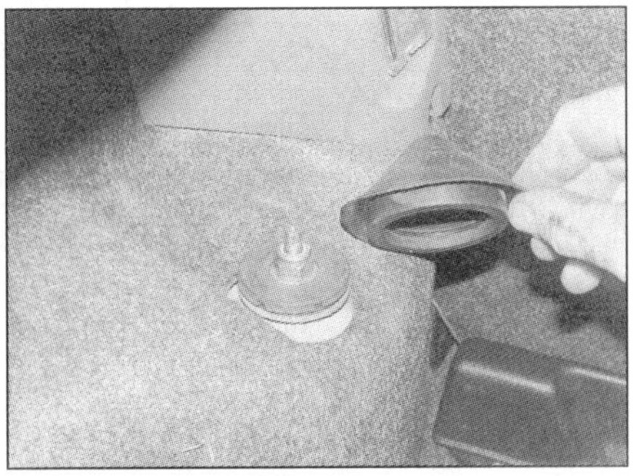

10.3a Unclip the upper shock absorber mounting cover . . . . .

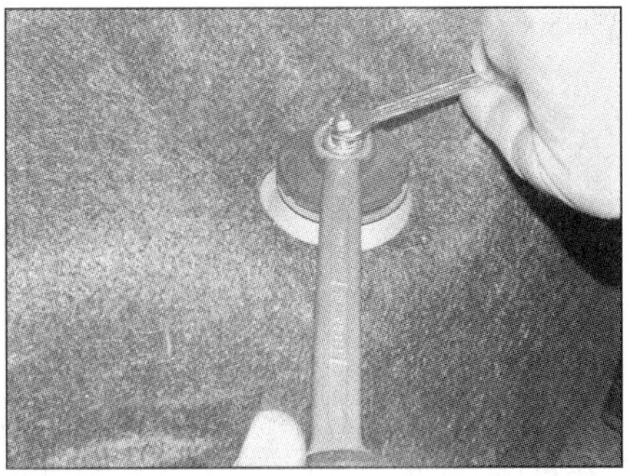

10.3b . . . . and slacken the retaining nut, holding the strut piston rod secure

unclip the cover from the shock absorber upper mounting. Slacken and remove the upper mounting nut **(see illustrations)**, and remove the shock absorber from the vehicle.

Testing

4 Mount the shock absorber in a vice, and test as described in Section 5 for the front suspension strut. Also check the rubber mounting bushes for damage and deterioration. Renew the shock absorber complete if any damage or wear is evident; the mounting bushes are not available separately. Inspect the mounting bolts for signs of wear or damage, and renew as necessary.

Refitting

5 Prior to refitting the shock absorber, mount it upright in the vice, and operate it fully through several strokes in order to prime it. (This is necessary even if a new unit is being fitted, as it may have been stored horizontally, and so need priming.) Apply a smear of multi-purpose grease to the shock absorber mounting bolts.
6 Offer up the shock absorber, then refit its upper mounting securing nut, tightening it by hand only at this stage.
7 Refit the lower shock absorber mounting bolt, again tightening it by hand only. Lower and remove the jack from under the trailing arm.
8 Refit the roadwheel, lower the vehicle to the ground and tighten the roadwheel bolts to the specified torque.
9 Rock the vehicle to settle the shock absorber mounting bushes in position, then tighten both the mounting bolts to the specified torque.

11 Rear coil spring - removal and refitting

Note: *Due to the design of the rear suspension, it is important that only one coil spring should be removed at a time. Note that the rear springs should be renewed in pairs, and if the springs are to be renewed, it is advisable to renew the spring damping rubbers at the same time.*

Removal

1 Chock the front wheels and engage reverse gear (or P). Jack up the rear of the vehicle and support it on axle stands. Remove the appropriate roadwheel.
2 Raise the relevant trailing arm slightly using a jack.
3 Unscrew and remove the bolt securing the lower end of the shock absorber to the trailing arm **(see illustration)**.
4 Carefully lower the jack supporting the trailing arm, and remove the coil spring and its damping rubbers from between the axle and underbody. Lever the trailing arm down slightly if necessary to remove the spring **(see illustration)**.

Refitting

5 Refitting is a reversal of removal, remembering the following points.
6 Ensure that the spring locates correctly on the damping rubbers, between the trailing arm and the under body. The spring has a coloured paint mark **(see illustration)**, which must be at the top and facing towards the rear of the vehicle.
7 Tighten the lower shock absorber bolt as described in Section 10.
8 If the coil spring is to be renewed, repeat the procedure on the other side of the vehicle.

12 Rear axle/trailing arm bushes - removal, overhaul and refitting

Removal

1 Chock the front wheels and engage reverse gear (or P). Jack up the rear of the vehicle and support it on axle stands. Remove both rear roadwheels.
2 On rear disc models, remove the rear brake calipers as described in Chapter 9.
3 If a new rear axle is to be installed, remove the brake discs or drums as described in Chapter 9.
4 On models equipped with ABS, remove the rear wheel sensors as described in Chapter 9, Section 23.
5 On non-ABS models, unhook the brake pressure-regulating valve link rod from the axle crossmember **(see illustration)**.
6 Use a brake hose clamp, a G-clamp or a similar tool with protected jaws to clamp the flexible hose at the nearest convenient point.

11.3 Removing the lower shock absorber mounting bolt

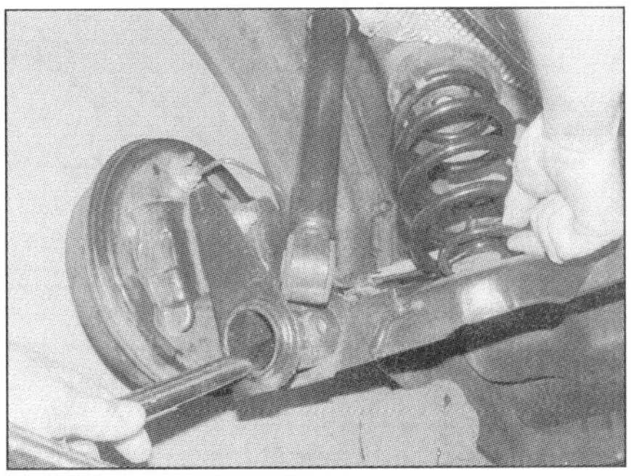

11.4 Lever the trailing arm downwards and remove the coil spring

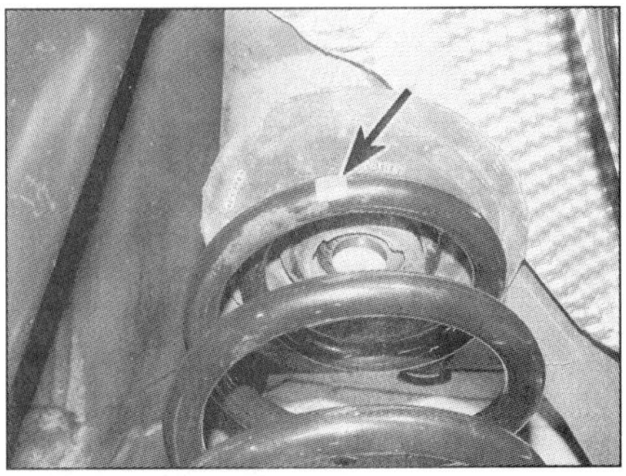

11.6 Coloured paint mark (arrowed) at the top, facing towards the rear of the vehicle

10

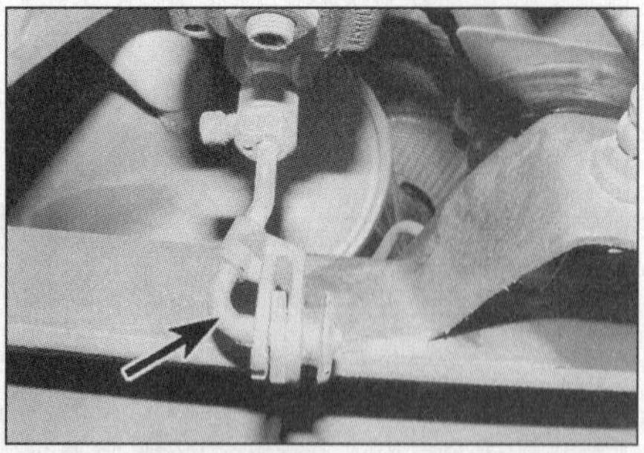

12.5 Unclip the pressure-regulating valve linkage rod (arrowed) from the axle crossmember

12.6 Disconnect the brake pipe connections from the axle crossmember

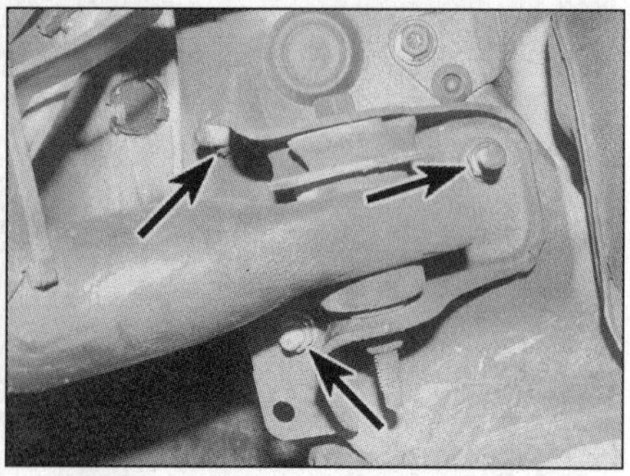

12.8 Slacken the three mounting nuts arrowed (left-hand side shown)

Disconnect the rear brake pipes at the flexible hose unions which are clipped to the axle crossmember **(see illustration)**. Remove the retaining clips, free the flexible hoses from the crossmember, and plug or tape over the union ends to prevent dirt entry. Wash off any spilt fluid immediately.

7 Disconnect the handbrake cables from the rear brakes as described in Chapter 9.

8 Slacken, but do not remove the nuts securing the front ends of the trailing arms to the vehicle underbody **(see illustration)**.

9 Remove the rear coil springs as described in Section 11.

10 Support the weight of the rear axle on a trolley jack.

11 The help of an assistant at this point will ease this task to ensure that the axle beam does not slip off the jack. Remove the six securing nuts (three each side) from the axle mountings to the vehicle body. Withdraw the axle from underneath the vehicle.

12 If necessary, the trailing arm bushes can be renewed, referring to the following paragraphs.

13 If a new axle is being fitted, remove the brake pipes from the original and fit them to the new axle. Also transfer the brake mounting brackets, using locking fluid on the threads of the retaining bolts.

Refitting

14 Place the rear axle on a trolley jack, and lift it into position underneath the vehicle. Insert the trailing arm mounting bolts from under the vehicle, ensuring that the mounting plate is correctly fitted. Refit the nuts and tighten them to the specified torque.

15 Refit the coil springs as described in Section 11.

16 Refit the brake hoses to the brackets on the crossmember, and secure them in position with the retaining clips. Reconnect the brake pipes to the hoses, and securely tighten the union nuts.

17 Where applicable, hook the brake pressure-regulating valve link rod onto its bracket on the axle crossmember.

18 Feed the handbrake cables along the trailing arms. Refit the handbrake cables as described in Chapter 9.

19 Refit the brake discs, brake calipers and ABS wheel sensors (as applicable); bleed the brake hydraulic system on completion. Refer to the relevant Sections of Chapter 9.

20 Refit the roadwheels, lower the vehicle to the ground and tighten the wheel bolts to the specified torque.

21 Check the rear underbody height as described in Section 13.

Trailing arm bush renewal

22 Examine all the axle components for wear and damage. If the trailing arm bushes require renewal, proceed as described below.

23 Make a note of the position of the bush in the trailing arm before removal, as the new bush will need to be fitted in the same position.

24 A special Renault tool is required for removal and refitting of the bushes, the tool is made up of three parts: T.Ar. 1454, T.Av. 1420 and T.Av. 1420-01 **(see illustration).** An alternative can be improvised using a long bolt, nut, washers, and a length of metal tubing or a socket.

25 Removal of the bush may be made easier if the bush housing in the trailing arm is heated using a heat gun, or similar. Do not use a naked flame, due to the close proximity of the fuel tank (if renewing the bushes while the axle is still on the vehicle).

26 Draw the bush from the trailing arm using the tool described in paragraph 24.

27 Refit the new bush using the special tool used on removal. Draw the new bush back into the trailing arm, ensuring that it is fitted in the correct position in the trailing arm.

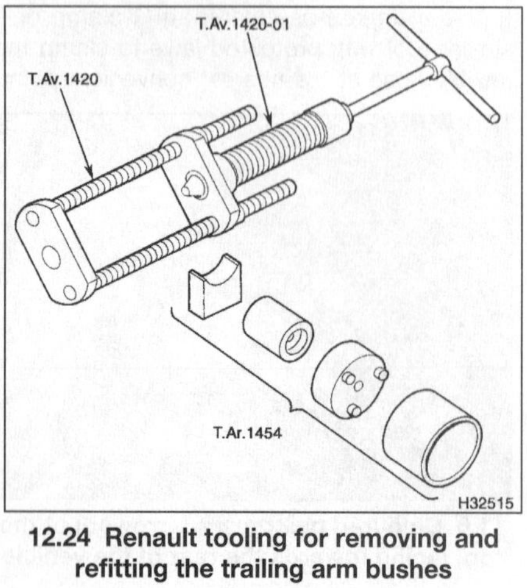

12.24 Renault tooling for removing and refitting the trailing arm bushes

13 Vehicle ride height - general information and checking

General information

1 The vehicle ride height measurements are used to ensure accuracy when checking the front suspension and steering angles (see Section 24). This is because the angles will vary slightly according to the ride height of the vehicle (see specifications). The ride height measuring points are as shown **(see illustration).** The front and rear ride heights can also be calculated as follows.

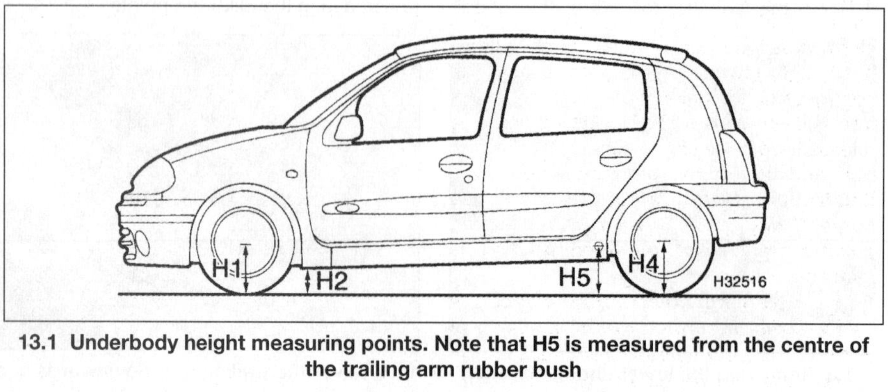

13.1 Underbody height measuring points. Note that H5 is measured from the centre of the trailing arm rubber bush

For values, refer to Specifications

Checking

2 To accurately check the ride height, position the unladen vehicle on a level surface, with the tyres correctly inflated and the fuel tank full.

Ride height

3 To check the front ride height, measure and record the dimensions H1 (centre of the wheel axis to the ground) and H2 (subframe to the ground) on both sides of the vehicle. Subtract H2 from H1 to find the rideheight checking dimension. Check that the dimensions are within the range given in the Specifications at the start of this Chapter.
4 To check the rear ride height, measure and record the dimensions H4 (centre of the wheel axis to the ground) and H5 (centre of the rear trailing arm bush to the ground) on both sides of the vehicle. Subtract H4 from H5 to find the ride height. Check that this dimension is within the range given in the Specifications at the start of this Chapter.
5 Note that the difference between the heights on each side must not exceed 5mm, with the driver's side slightly higher than the passenger side.
6 Note that no adjustment of the ride height is possible. If the ride height differs greatly from that specified, examine the suspension components for signs of wear or damage.
7 If further checks are required, take your vehicle to your local dealer who will have the specialised equipment to do this.

14 Steering wheel – removal and refitting

Note: *A new steering wheel retaining bolt will be required on refitting.*

Removal

1 Set the front wheels in the straight-ahead position. Release the steering lock by inserting the ignition key.
2 Remove the airbag (referring to warnings) as described in Chapter 12, Section 28.
3 Slacken but do not remove the steering wheel retaining bolt **(see illustration)**.
4 Mark the steering wheel and steering column shaft in relation to each other, then lift the steering wheel off the column splines. If it is tight tap the steering wheel near the centre, using the palm of the hand, or rock it from side-to-side whilst pulling upwards to release it from the shaft splines. Remove the bolt and lift off the steering wheel **(see illustration)**. ***Note:*** *Do not turn the airbag contact ring assembly or the steering column shaft whilst the steering wheel is removed.*

Warning: Do not refit the airbag to the steering wheel whilst the steering wheel is removed, as the system may be triggered. Whenever the steering wheel is removed, the airbag connector MUST be disconnected. It is fitted with a connector which short circuits when it is disconnected to avoid any incorrect triggering.

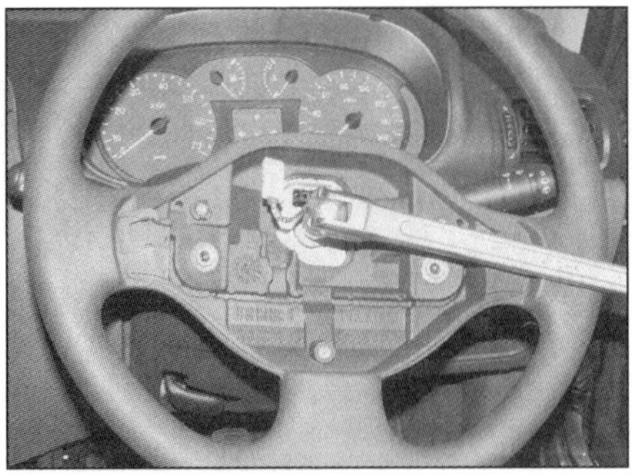
14.3 Slackening the steering wheel retaining bolt

14.4 Carefully lift off the steering wheel, leaving the wiring connector still in place

Refitting

5 Refitting is a reversal of removal, bearing in mind the following points.

a) *Align the marks made on the steering wheel and steering column shaft before removal.*
b) *Tighten the new retaining bolt to the specified torque.*
c) *Refit the airbag as described in Chapter 12.*

15 Steering column – removal, checking and refitting

Note: *A new steering wheel bolt will be required on refitting. For more information on removal of individual components, check in the relevant Chapters.*

Removal

1 Disconnect the battery negative lead.
2 Remove the steering wheel as described in Section 14.
3 Working underneath the steering column, undo the three retaining screws, then remove the upper shroud from the steering column **(see illustration)**. Pull the lower shroud down to release its retaining clips, and withdraw it from the steering column.
4 On models fitted with a radio/cassette player remote control switch, slide back the cover from the front of the switch assembly, and loosen the switch clamp screw.
5 Unclip the immobiliser antenna ring from around the ignition switch and disconnect the wiring connector.
6 Slacken the switch assembly clamp screw, then tap the screw sharply to release the locating cone. Slide the switch assembly off the steering column, disconnecting the wiring connectors as they become accessible.
7 Remove the upper facia trim panel and A-pillar trims as described in Chapter 11, Sections 27 and 29.
8 Undo the instrument panel securing screws and disconnect the wiring block connectors on removal.
9 Slide the retaining clip up and disconnect the wiring block connector for the ignition switch.
10 Chock the rear wheels, apply the handbrake, jack up the front of the vehicle and support it on axle stands *(see Jacking and vehicle support)*.
11 Working from underneath the vehicle, cut the retaining clip (where applicable), then fold the protective cover back from the steering gear to gain access to the lower universal joint clamp eccentric bolt **(see illustration)**.
12 Mark the relationship between the lower universal joint and the steering gear drive pinion, using a hammer and punch, white paint or similar. Remove the nut and clamp eccentric bolt securing the joint to the pinion.

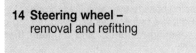

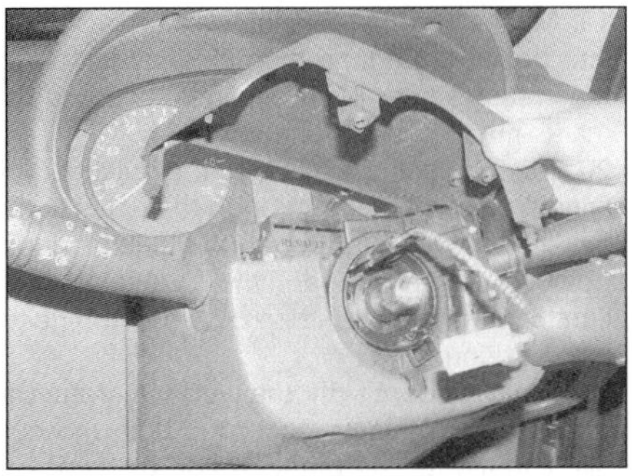
15.3 Removing the upper shroud from the steering column

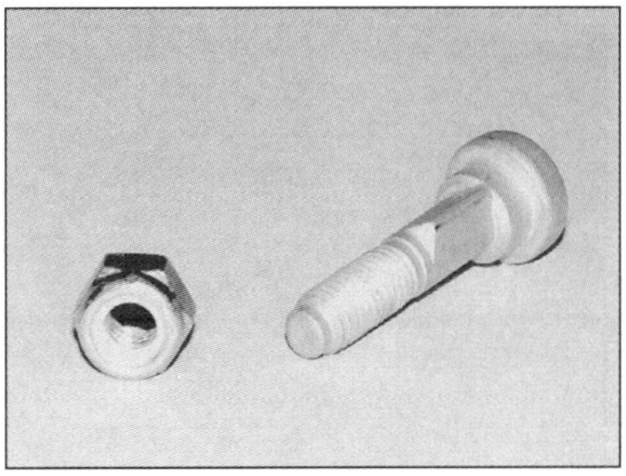
15.11 Lower universal joint clamp eccentric bolt

15.13 Undo the two upper securing screws (arrowed)

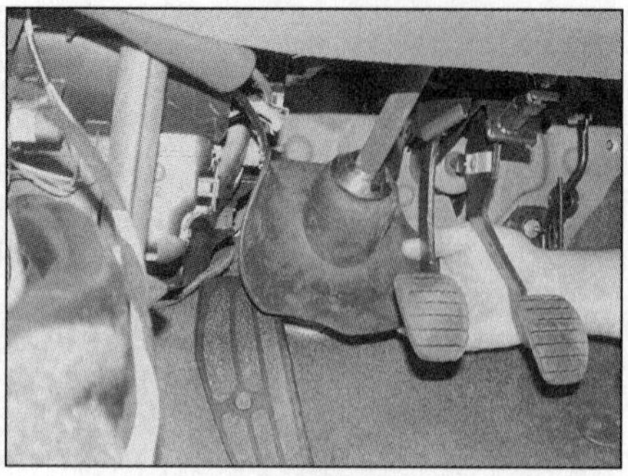

15.14 Releasing the lower gaiter from inside the vehicle

15.15 Removing the steering column from the vehicle

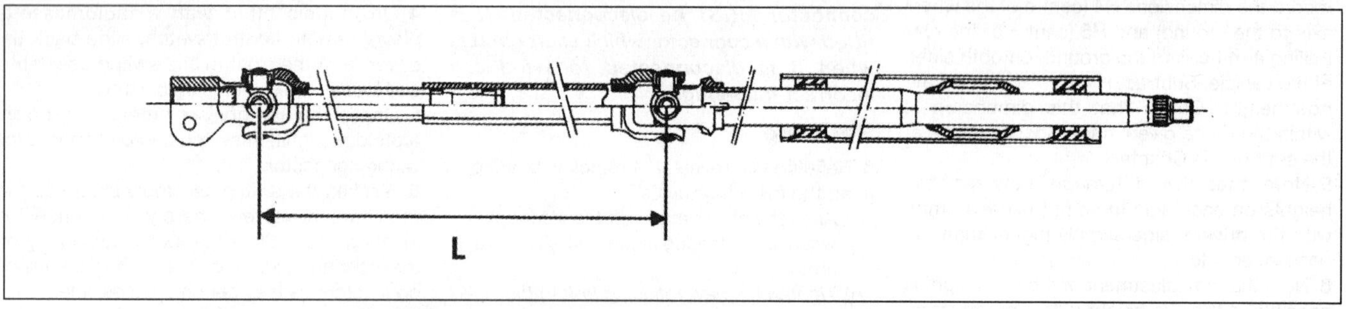

15.16 Steering column intermediate shaft checking dimension (L)

Right-hand drive models – L = 395.9 ± 1.5 mm *Left-hand drive models – L = 373.1 ± 1.5 mm*

13 From inside the vehicle, remove the two screws securing the top of the steering column **(see illustration)**.

14 Slacken and remove the four steering column mounting bolts. Release the steering column from its mountings and the facia panel, also release the steering column lower gaiter from the bulkhead **(see illustration)**.

15 Disengage the universal joint from the steering gear pinion, and remove the steering column assembly from the vehicle **(see illustration)**. Unclip any wiring from the steering column on removal.

Checking

16 The intermediate shaft attached to the bottom of the steering column incorporates a telescopic safety feature. In the event of a front-end crash, the shaft collapses and prevents the steering wheel injuring the driver. Before refitting the steering column, the length of the intermediate shaft must be checked **(see illustration)**. If the length is shorter than specified, the complete steering column must be renewed. Damage to the intermediate shaft is also implied if it is found that the clamp bolt at its base cannot be inserted freely when refitting the column.

17 Check the steering shaft for signs of free play in the column bushes, and check the universal joints for signs of damage or roughness in the joint bearings. If damage or wear is found on the steering shaft universal joints or shaft bushes, the column must be renewed as an assembly.

18 Refer to Chapter 12, Section 6, for information on ignition switch renewal.

15.20 Using a cable tie through the gaiter flaps to pull gaiter into position

Refitting

19 Manoeuvre the steering column assembly into position. Engage the universal joint with the steering gear pinion splines, aligning the marks made prior to removal.

20 Refit the column gaiter to the bulkhead by tying a piece of string through the holes in the gaiter and pulling it through the bulkhead into position from under the vehicle **(see illustration)**, cut the string off when the gaiter is in position.

21 From underneath the vehicle, refit the universal joint clamp eccentric bolt and nut, aligning it with the marks made on removal. Tighten the bolt to its specified torque. Relocate the protective cover on the steering gear, and secure it in position. Lower the vehicle to the ground.

22 Refit and tighten the steering column mounting bolts to their specified torque.

23 Refit the two screws securing the top of the steering column, and tighten them securely.

24 Reconnect the wiring block connector for the ignition switch, then refit the immobiliser antenna ring around the ignition switch.

25 Reconnect the wiring connectors to the instrument panel and refit the retaining screws.

26 Refit the upper facia trim panel and the A-pillar trims.

27 Ensuring that the wiring is correctly routed, reconnect the wiring connectors to the combination switch assembly. Locate the switch assembly on the top of the steering column. The rotary switch must be located correctly, check that the 0 mark on the rotary switch is pointing to the fixed reference mark on the housing. Do not tighten the securing screw until the upper and lower shrouds are fitted correctly, then tighten screw through the hole in the lower shroud.

28 Clip the lower shroud onto the steering column, and refit the upper shroud, tightening its retaining screws securely. Where applicable, refit the radio/cassette remote control switch.

29 Where applicable, refit the airbag as described in Chapter 12.

30 Refit the steering wheel as described in Section 14, and reconnect the battery negative terminal.

16 Steering gear rubber gaiter – renewal

1 Remove the track rod end balljoint as described in Section 22.
2 Mark the correct fitted position of the gaiter on the track rod. Release the retaining clips, and slide the gaiter off the steering gear housing and track rod end.
3 Thoroughly clean the track rod and the steering gear housing, using fine abrasive paper to polish off any corrosion, burrs or sharp edges which might damage the sealing lips of the new gaiter on installation.
4 Recover the grease from inside the old gaiter. If it is uncontaminated with dirt or grit, apply it to the track rod inner balljoint. If the old grease is contaminated, or it is suspected that some has been lost, apply some new molybdenum disulphide grease.
5 Grease the inside of the new gaiter. Carefully slide the gaiter onto the track rod, and locate it on the steering gear housing. Align the outer edge of the gaiter with the mark made on the track rod prior to removal, then secure it in position with new retaining clips.
6 Refit the track rod balljoint as described in Section 22.

17 Manual steering gear assembly – removal, inspection and refitting

Note: *A balljoint separator tool will be required for this operation*

Removal

1 Chock the rear wheels, apply the handbrake, jack up the front of the vehicle and support it on axle stands *(see Jacking and vehicle support)*. Remove both front roadwheels.
2 Remove the nuts securing the track rod balljoints to the swivel hubs. Release the balljoint tapered shanks using a universal balljoint separator.
3 Working from underneath the vehicle, cut the retaining clip, then fold the protective cover back from the steering gear to gain access to the lower universal joint clamp eccentric bolt.
4 Mark the relationship between the intermediate shaft universal joint and the steering gear drive pinion, using a hammer and punch, white paint or similar. Remove the nut and clamp eccentric bolt securing the joint to the pinion.
5 Remove the four nuts and bolts securing the steering gear assembly to the rear of the front subframe. Release the steering gear pinion from the universal joint, and manoeuvre the assembly sideways out of position.

Refitting

6 Manoeuvre the steering gear assembly into position. Engage the universal joint with the steering gear pinion splines, aligning the marks made prior to removal.
7 Insert the steering gear mounting bolts from the rear of the subframe. Refit the nuts and tighten them to the specified torque.
8 Refit the universal joint clamp eccentric bolt and nut, and tighten it to the specified torque. Relocate the protective cover on the steering gear, and secure it in position with a new cable tie (where applicable).
9 Reconnect the track rod balljoints to the swivel hubs, and tighten their retaining nuts to the specified torque.
10 Refit the roadwheels, lower the vehicle to the ground and tighten the wheel bolts to the specified torque.
11 Check the front wheel toe setting as described in Section 24.

Inspection

12 Renewal procedures for the gaiters, the track rod end balljoints and the track rods (complete with inner balljoints) are given in Sections 16, 22 and 23 respectively.
13 Examine the steering gear assembly for signs of wear or damage. Check that the rack moves freely over the full length of its travel, with no signs of roughness or excessive free play between the steering gear pinion and rack. Internal wear or damage can only be cured by renewing the steering gear assembly.
14 Overhaul of the steering rack and pinion assembly is not possible. The only components which can be renewed are the steering gear gaiters, the track rod balljoints and the track rods.

Rack pinion adjustment

15 If there is excessive free play of the rack in the steering gear housing, accompanied by a knocking noise, it may be possible to correct this by adjusting the rack pinion adjuster. On SMI steering racks, relieve the staking on the rack pinion adjusting nut. Using a 10mm Allen key, tighten the adjusting nut until the free play disappears (but by no more than 1 notch). Check that the rack still moves freely over its full travel, then secure the adjusting nut by staking it **(see illustration)**.

18 Power steering gear assembly – removal, inspection and refitting

Removal

1 Remove the battery as described in Chapter 5A.
2 Using brake hose clamps, clamp both the supply and return hoses near the power steering fluid reservoir. This will minimise fluid loss during subsequent operations. **Note:** *NEVER clamp the high pressure pipes.*
3 Chock the rear wheels, firmly apply the handbrake, jack up the front of the vehicle and support on axle stands (see *Jacking and vehicle support*). Remove the front roadwheels.
4 Remove the nuts securing the track rod balljoints to the swivel hubs. Release the balljoint tapered shanks using a universal balljoint separator.
5 Working from underneath the vehicle, cut the retaining clip, then fold the protective cover back from the steering gear to gain access to the lower universal joint clamp eccentric bolt.
6 Using a hammer and punch, white paint or similar, mark the relationship between the intermediate shaft universal joint and the steering gear drive pinion. Slacken and remove the nut and clamp eccentric bolt securing the joint to the pinion.
7 Disconnect the oxygen sensor and remove the exhaust downpipe as described in the relevant part of Chapter 4.

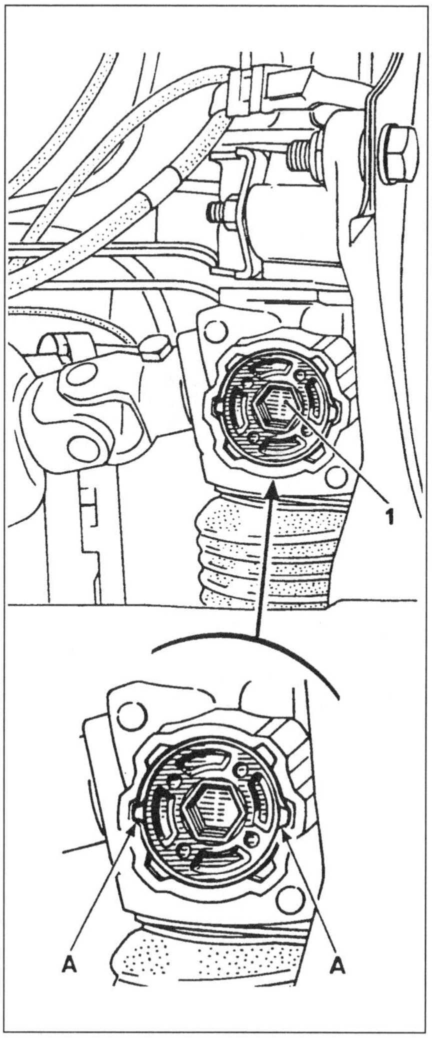

17.15 Steering rack thrust plunger adjustment

1 Adjusting nut *A Staking points*

8 Remove the bolt from the rear lower engine/transmission tie-bar **(see illustration)**, and pivot the engine and transmission assembly forwards. (Insert a retaining block to hold the engine/transmission forwards.)

9 Remove the nut securing the feed pipe support bracket to the steering gear housing. Mark the pipe unions to ensure they are correctly positioned on reassembly, then unscrew the feed and return pipe union nuts; be prepared for fluid spillage by placing a suitable container beneath the pipes whilst unscrewing the union nuts. The spilt fluid must be disposed of, and new fluid of the specified type (see *Lubricants and fluids*) used when refilling. Disconnect both pipes. Plug the pipe ends and steering gear orifices, to prevent excessive fluid leakage and the entry of dirt into the hydraulic system.

10 Remove the four mounting nuts and bolts securing the steering gear to the rear of the front subframe. Remove the mounting clamps and brackets from both ends of the steering gear. Where applicable, remove the two nuts to release the heat shield from the steering rack.

11 Release the steering gear pinion from the universal joint, and manoeuvre the assembly sideways out from the right-hand side of the vehicle.

Inspection

12 Examine the steering gear for signs of wear or damage **(see illustration)**. Check that the rack moves freely over the full length of its travel, with no signs of roughness or excessive free play between the pinion and rack. The steering gear must be renewed as an assembly if internal wear or damage is present. Track rod, track rod balljoint and steering gear gaiter renewal procedures are given in Sections 23, 22 and 16 respectively.

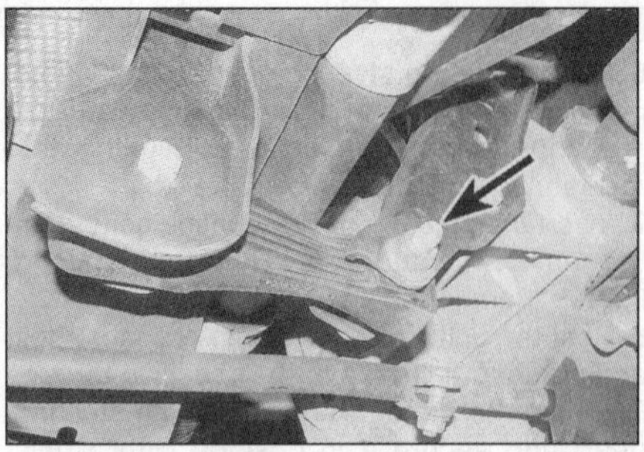

18.8 Remove the securing bolt and nut arrowed (type of tie-bar will vary, depending on model)

13 Inspect the steering gear fluid unions for signs of leakage, and check that the union nuts are securely tightened.

14 Examine the steering gear mounting rubbers for signs of damage and deterioration; renew as necessary.

Refitting

15 Manoeuvre the steering gear assembly into position. Aligning the marks made prior to removal, engage the universal joint with the steering gear pinion splines.

16 Locate the mounting brackets and clamps on the steering gear mounting rubbers, then insert the four steering gear mounting bolts from the rear of the subframe. Refit the nuts and tighten the mounting bolts to the specified torque.

17 Refit the exhaust downpipe (if removed) as described in the relevant Part of Chapter 4.

18 Refit the universal joint clamp eccentric bolt and nut, and tighten it to the specified torque. Relocate the protective cover on the steering gear, and secure it in position with a new cable tie (where applicable).

19 Wipe clean the feed and return pipe unions, then refit them to their respective positions on the steering gear. Tighten the union nuts.

20 Reconnect the track rod balljoints to the swivel hubs. Tighten their retaining nuts to the specified torque.

21 Refit the roadwheels, lower the vehicle to the ground and tighten the wheel bolts to the specified torque. Refit the battery.

22 Remove the hose clamps from the reservoir hoses. Top-up the reservoir and bleed the power steering hydraulic system as described in Section 21.

23 On completion, check the front wheel toe setting as described in Section 24.

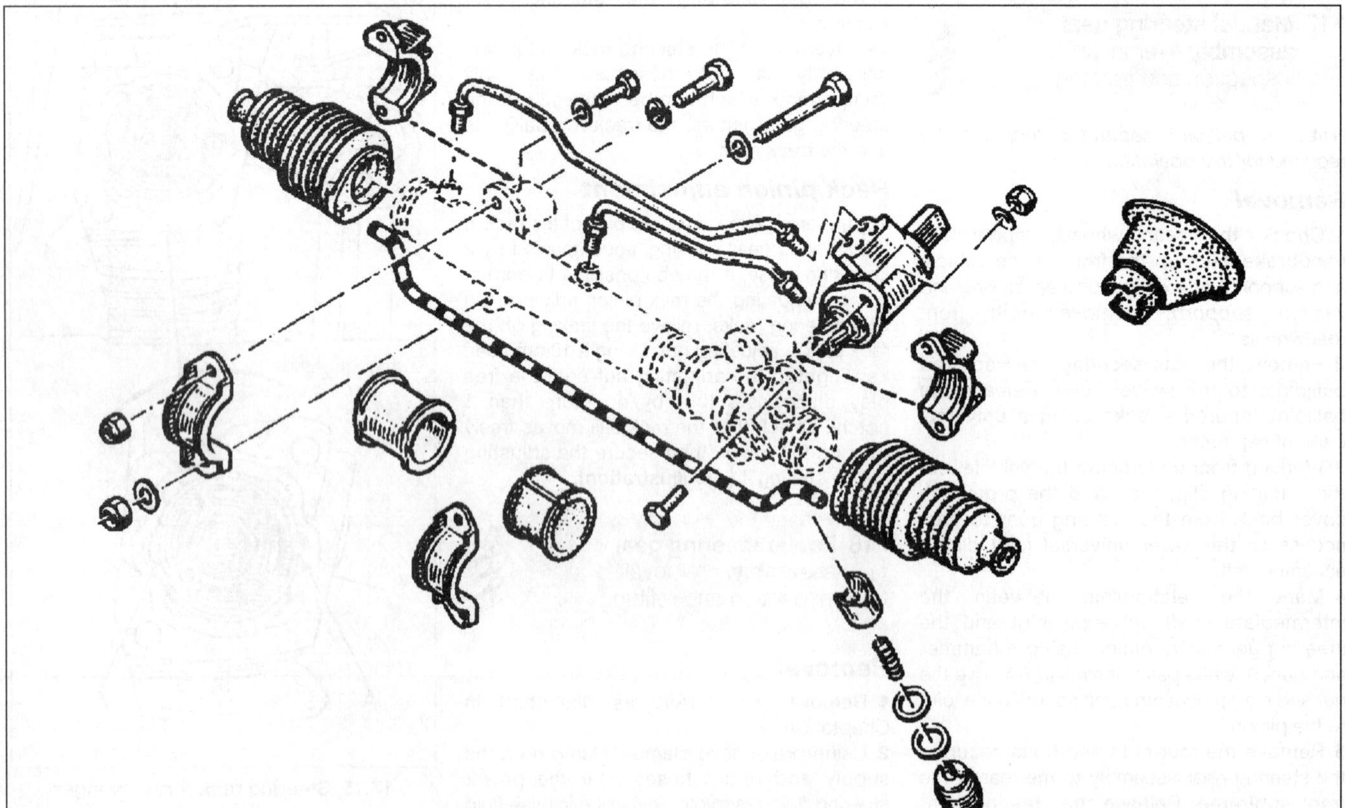

18.12 Power-assisted steering gear components

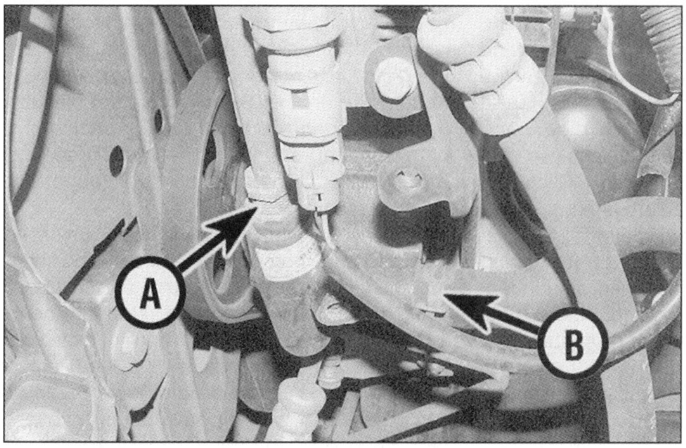

19.20a Power steering pump fluid supply hose (A) and feed pipe union (B) – K4J engine . . .

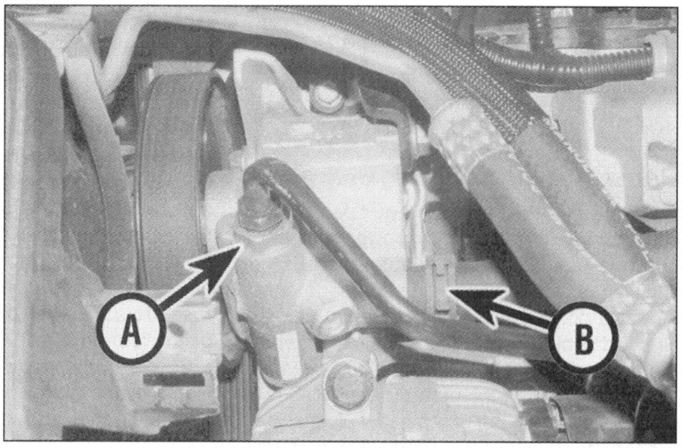

19.20b . . . and power steering pump fluid supply hose (A) and feed pipe union (B) – K4M engine

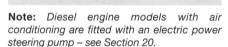

19 Mechanical power steering pump – removal and refitting

Note: *Diesel engine models with air conditioning are fitted with an electric power steering pump – see Section 20.*

D7F engines

Note: *The fluid pipe O-ring(s) should be renewed on refitting.*

Removal

1 Slacken the three bolts which secure the drivebelt pulley to the pump, then release the drivebelt tension as described in Chapter 1A or 1B. Disengage the drivebelt from the pump pulley.

2 Remove the pulley retaining bolts and washers, then remove the pulley from the pump, noting which way round it is fitted.

3 Using brake hose clamps, clamp the pump supply hose. This will minimise fluid loss during subsequent operations.

4 Mark the pipe unions to ensure that they are correctly positioned on reassembly, then unscrew the feed pipe union nut, and release the return pipe securing clip, or union nut (as applicable); be prepared for fluid spillage by placing a container beneath the pipe(s)/hose(s) whilst unscrewing the union nut(s). The spilt fluid must be disposed of, and new fluid of the specified type (see *Lubricants and fluids*) used when refilling. Disconnect both pipe(s)/hose(s), and plug the pipe/hose ends and pump unions (working quickly to minimise fluid loss), to prevent the entry of dirt into the hydraulic system.

5 Unscrew the three bolts securing the power steering pump to its mounting bracket, and remove the pump from the engine compartment.

Refitting

6 Manoeuvre the pump assembly back into position, and tighten the mounting bolts.

7 Renew the fluid pipe union O-ring(s). Refit the pipe(s)/hose(s) to the pump, using the marks made on removal to ensure that they are correctly reconnected. Tighten the union nut(s) and/or fit the hose clip, as applicable.

8 Refit the pulley to the pump, making sure it is the correct way around. Fit the pulley retaining bolts and washers.

9 Refit the drivebelt to the pulley, and adjust the drivebelt tension as described in Chapter 1A or 1B. Once the belt is correctly tensioned, tighten the pulley retaining bolts.

10 On completion, top-up and bleed the power steering hydraulic system as described in Section 21.

All other models

Note: *A new power steering fluid feed pipe O-ring will be required on refitting.*

Removal

11 Disconnect the battery negative lead.

12 To improve access to the pump, apply the handbrake, then jack up the front of the vehicle and support it on axle stands (see *Jacking and vehicle support*). To improve access even further, remove the right-hand wheel and wheelarch liner.

13 Undo the retaining screws and remove the radiator grille, unclipping it from the front edge of the wings.

14 Remove the right-hand headlight unit as described in Chapter 12, Section 9.

15 On diesel engine models without air conditioning, remove the front bumper as described in Chapter 11.

16 Remove the four crossmember upper mounting bolts, then slacken (do not remove) the two crossmember lower mounting bolts. Move the crossmember to the rear of the engine compartment without removing the bonnet release cable.

17 Release the drivebelt tension as described in Chapter 1A or 1B, then disengage the drivebelt from the pump pulley.

18 Where applicable, disconnect the PAS pressure switch connector and remove the high pressure hose mounting bracket.

19 Clamp the fluid supply hose as near to the power steering pump as possible, using a brake hose clamp. This will minimise fluid loss during subsequent operations.

20 Slacken the retaining clip, and disconnect the fluid supply hose from the rear of the pump. If the original Renault clip is still fitted, cut the clip and discard it; replace it with a standard worm drive hose clip on refitting. Slacken the union nut and disconnect the feed pipe from the pump **(see illustrations)**. Be prepared for some fluid spillage as the pipe and hose are disconnected; plug the hose and pipe ends and the pump unions, to minimise fluid loss and prevent the entry of dirt into the system.

21 On the E7J and K7M engines it may be necessary to remove the alternator as described in Chapter 5A.

22 On K4M engines the alternator is below the PAS pump, this will have to be protected against the ingress of the fluid when the pipes are removed.

23 Remove the bolts securing the power steering pump to its mounting bracket, on K4M engines it will be necessary to disconnect the fuel supply pipe from the fuel rail to gain access to the rear bolt. Remove the pump from the engine compartment.

Refitting

24 Refitting is a reversal of removal. Manoeuvre the pump into position. Refit the mounting bolts, ensuring that any spacers (where applicable) are correctly positioned, and tighten them.

25 Fit a new O-ring to the feed pipe union. Reconnect the pipe to the pump, and tighten the union nut. Refit the supply pipe to the pump, and tighten its retaining clip. Remove the brake hose clamp used to minimise fluid loss.

26 Refit the drivebelt as described in Chapter 1A or B. Top-up and bleed the power steering hydraulic system as described in Section 21.

27 Refit the headlight, grille and alternator as described in their relevant Chapters, then lower the vehicle to the ground.

28 Refit the roadwheels, lower the vehicle to the ground and tighten the wheel bolts to the specified torque.

20 Electric power steering pump – general information, removal and refitting

General information

1 On diesel engine models equipped with air conditioning, an electrically-powered steering pump is used. This is because there is not sufficient space in the engine compartment to mount a conventional belt-driven pump; the air conditioning compressor is situated where the power steering pump would be.
2 The operation of the pump is controlled by a pressure switch in the pump outlet pipe, and by either three or four relays, depending on model. The two power steering pump relays are situated in the engine compartment, mounted on the side of the left-hand suspension turret. On three-relay versions, the system control relay is fixed on the lid of the relay/junction box, which is mounted on the front of the left-hand suspension turret. On four-relay versions, there are two system control relays, both of which are also situated in the relay/junction box; one of them is fixed on the lid of the box, and the other is inside the bottom of the box.
3 Operation of the system is complex. If any fault develops, the vehicle should be taken to a Renault dealer for the fault to be diagnosed. The pump itself can be removed and refitted as follows.

Removal

Note: *New power steering fluid pipe O-rings will be required on refitting.*
4 Remove the battery as described in Chapter 5A.
5 Apply the handbrake, jack up the front of the vehicle and support it on axle stands (see *Jacking and vehicle support*). Remove the left-hand wheel and wheelarch liner.
6 Remove the left-hand headlamp as described in Chapter 12, Section 9.
7 Clamp the feed and return hoses as near to the power steering pump as possible, using brake hose clamps. This will minimise fluid loss during subsequent operations.
8 Mark the pipe unions to ensure they are correctly positioned on reassembly, then unscrew the feed and return pipe union nuts; be prepared for fluid spillage by positioning a container beneath the pipes. The spilt fluid must be disposed of, and new fluid of the specified type (see *Lubricants and fluids*) used when refilling. Disconnect both pipes, and plug the pipe ends and pump unions (working quickly to minimise fluid loss), to prevent the entry of dirt into the hydraulic system.
9 Remove the three pump mounting bracket bolts. Lift the pump up until its wiring connectors are accessible, then disconnect them from the base of the pump. Make a note of the locations of the wires, to ensure they are correctly reconnected on refitting. Remove the pump and reservoir assembly from the engine compartment.

Refitting

10 Manoeuvre the pump/reservoir assembly into position. Reconnect the wiring, using the notes made on removal.
11 Refit and tighten the three mounting bracket retaining bolts.
12 Renew the fluid pipe union O-rings. Refit the pipes to the pump, using the marks made on removal to ensure they are correctly reconnected, and tighten the union nuts.
13 Remove the hose clamps. Refit the battery as described in Chapter 5A.
14 Refit the roadwheels, lower the vehicle to the ground and tighten the wheel bolts to the specified torque.
15 Top-up and bleed the power steering hydraulic system as described in Section 21.

21 Power steering system – bleeding

1 This procedure will only be necessary when any part of the hydraulic system has been disconnected, or if air has entered because of leakage.
2 Remove the fluid reservoir filler cap, and top-up the fluid level to the maximum mark, using only the specified fluid. Refer to *Lubricants and fluids* for fluid specifications, and to *Chapter 1A or 1B* for details of the fluid reservoir markings.
3 With the engine stopped, slowly move the steering from lock-to-lock several times to expel trapped air, then top-up the level in the fluid reservoir. Repeat this procedure until the fluid level in the reservoir does not drop any further.
4 Start the engine. Slowly move the steering from lock-to-lock several times to expel any air remaining in the system. Repeat this procedure until bubbles cease to appear in the fluid reservoir.
5 If, when turning the steering, an abnormal noise is heard from the fluid pipes, it indicates that there is still air in the system. Check this by turning the wheels to the straight-ahead position and switching off the engine. If the fluid level in the reservoir rises, air is still present in the system, and further bleeding is necessary.
6 Once all traces of air have been removed, stop the engine and allow the system to cool. Once cool, check that the fluid level is up to the maximum mark on the power steering fluid reservoir; top-up if necessary.

22 Track rod end balljoint – removal and refitting

Note: *There are two types of track rod end locking arrangements: locknut type, and bolt and clamp type.*

Removal

Note: *A balljoint separator tool will be required for this operation.*
1 Apply the handbrake, then jack up the front of the vehicle and support it on axle stands (see *Jacking and vehicle support*). Remove the appropriate front roadwheel.
2 If the balljoint is to be re-used, use a straight-edge and a scriber, or similar, to mark its relationship to the track rod.
3 Holding the balljoint, unscrew its locknut or clamp **(see illustrations)**. If a locknut type is used, slacken it by half a turn only, do not move the locknut from this position as it will serve as a reference mark on refitting.
4 Remove the nut securing the track rod balljoint to the swivel hub. Release the balljoint tapered shank using a universal balljoint separator. If the balljoint is to be re-used, protect the threaded end of the shank by screwing the nut back on a few turns before using the separator **(see illustration)**.

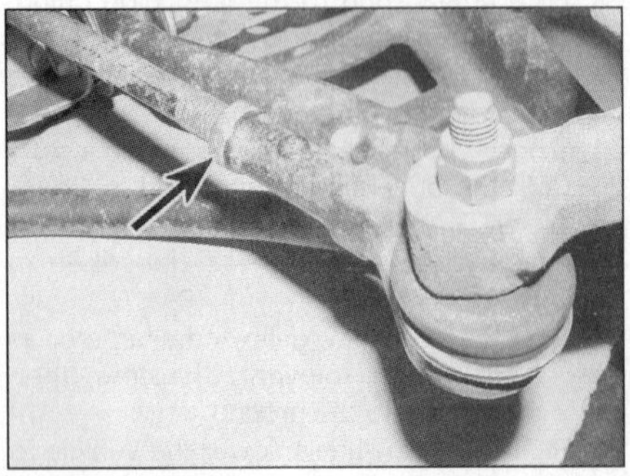

22.3a Lock nut (arrowed) used for locking one type of track rod end . . .

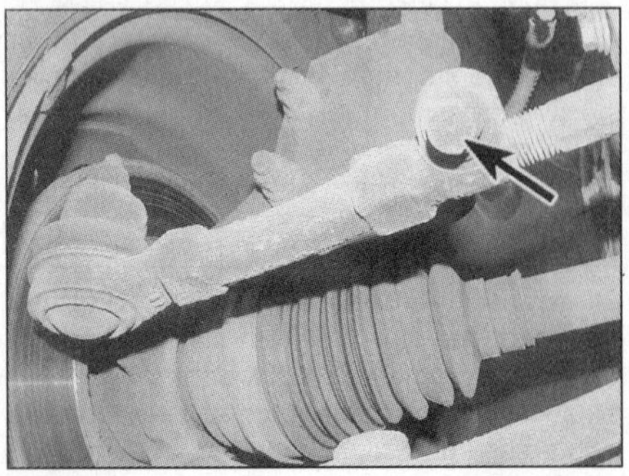

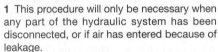

22.3b . . . and clamp type (arrowed) used for locking other types of track rod end

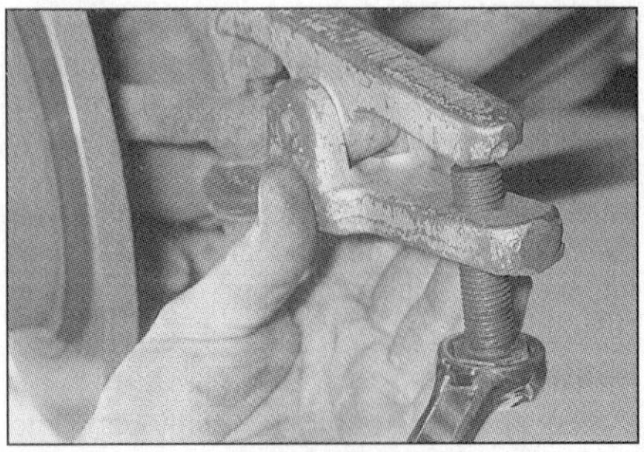

22.4 Using a universal balljoint separator to release the track rod balljoint from the swivel hub

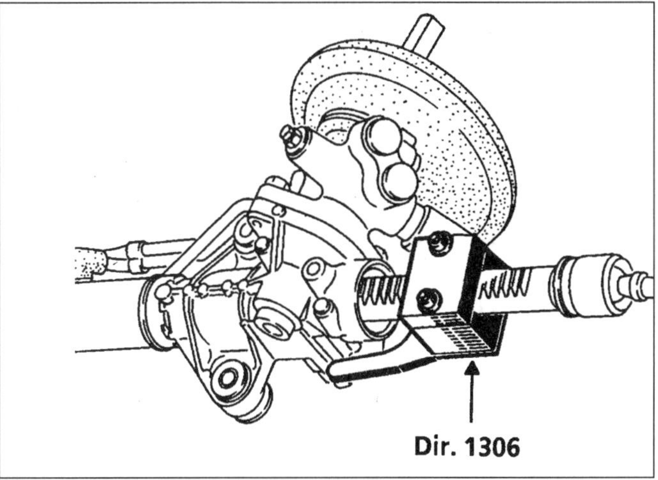

23.0a Steering rack secured with a retaining clamp

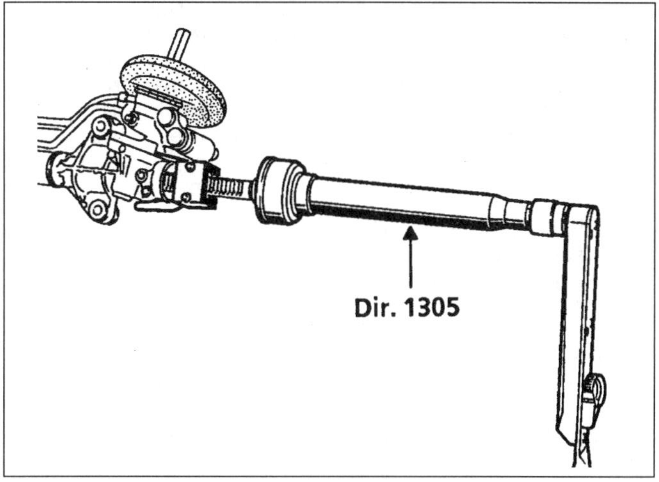

23.0b Track rod balljoints slackened with a special wrench

5 Counting the **exact** number of turns necessary to do so, unscrew the balljoint from the track rod end.

6 Count the number of exposed threads between the end of the balljoint and the locknut, and record this figure. If a new balljoint is to be fitted, unscrew the locknut from the old balljoint.

7 Carefully clean the balljoint and the threads. Renew the balljoint if its movement is sloppy or if it is too stiff, if it is excessively worn, or if it is damaged in any way. Carefully check the shank taper and threads. If the balljoint gaiter is damaged, the complete balljoint must be renewed; it is not possible to obtain the gaiter separately.

Refitting

8 If applicable, screw the locknut onto the new balljoint, and position it so that the same number of exposed threads are visible as was noted prior to removal.

9 Screw the balljoint into the track rod by the number of turns noted on removal. This should bring the balljoint locknut to within a quarter of a turn of the end of the track rod, with the alignment marks that were made (if applicable) on removal lined up.

10 Refit the balljoint shank to the swivel hub, and tighten the retaining nut to the specified torque. If difficulty is experienced due to the balljoint shank rotating, jam it by exerting pressure on the underside of the balljoint, using a tyre lever or a jack.

11 Refit the roadwheel, lower the vehicle to the ground and tighten the roadwheel bolts to the specified torque.

12 Check the front wheel toe setting as described in Section 24, then tighten the balljoint locknut/clamp bolt securely.

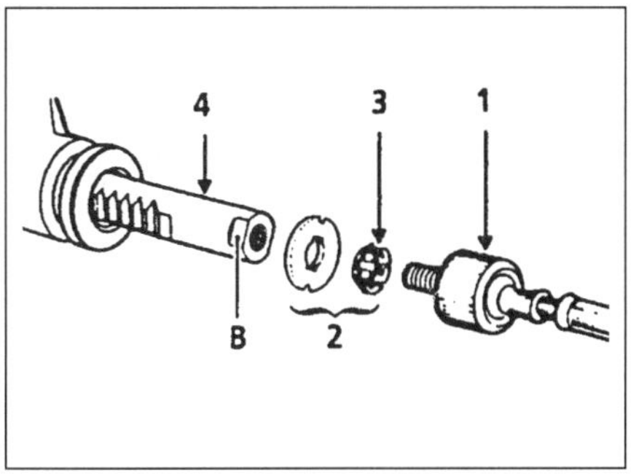

23.7 On models fitted with a SMI steering gear assembly, ensure the new lockwasher and locking ring are correctly assembled and fit them to the end of the track rod

1 Track rod
2 Locking ring
3 Lock washer
4 Steering gear
B Flats on steering end

23 Track rod and inner balljoint - removal and refitting

Note: *In order to safely remove the track rod, without the risk of damaging the steering rack, a special track rod wrench (Renault number Dir.1305) and rack retaining clamp (Renault number Dir.1306 for SMI steering rack or 1306-01 for TRW steering rack) will be required. The special wrench engages with the track rod inner balljoint housing allowing the track rod to be easily slackened/tightened, and the retaining clamp secures the rack to the steering gear housing to prevent any stress being exerted on the steering gear pinion assembly **(see illustrations)**. Note that without access to the special tools, track rod removal will be difficult, especially without causing damage.*

Note: *There are two different types of steering gear assemblies fitted to these vehicles; the steering racks are manufactured by either SMI or TRW; the type of rack fitted can be identified from the manufacturing markings cast onto the steering gear housing. If work is being carried out on a SMI steering rack note that a new track rod locking washer assembly must be used on refitting.*

Removal

1 Remove the track rod end balljoint as described in Section 22.

2 Cut the retaining clips, and slide the steering gear gaiter off the track rod. It is recommended that the gaiter is renewed, regardless of its apparent condition.

3 In the absence of the special tools, using a suitable pair of grips, unscrew the track rod inner balljoint from the steering rack end. Prevent the steering rack from turning by holding the balljoint lockwasher/steering rack with a second pair of grips.

Caution: Take care not to mark the surfaces of the rack and balljoint.

4 Remove the track rod assembly from the steering rack. On SMI steering gear assemblies, discard the lockwasher assembly; a new one must be used on refitting.

5 Examine the inner balljoint for signs of slackness or tight spots. Check that the track rod itself is straight and free from damage. If necessary, renew the track rod.

Refitting

6 Prior to refitting the track rod remove all traces of locking compound from the rack and track rod threads.

7 On models fitted with a SMI steering gear assembly, ensure the new lockwasher and locking ring are correctly assembled and fit them to the end of the track rod **(see illustration)**.

8 Apply a coat of locking compound (Renault recommend the use of Loctite Frenbloc – available from your Renault dealer) to the threads of the track rod then fit the track rod to the end of the steering rack. Using the method employed on removal, tighten the track rod inner balljoint to the specified torque, taking great care not to marks either the rack or the balljoint. On the SMI steering gear, whilst tightening the track rod ensure the tabs on the lock washer engage with the flats on the steering end.

9 Slide the new gaiter onto the track rod end, and locate it on the steering gear housing. Turn the steering from lock-to-lock to check that the gaiter is correctly positioned, then secure it with new retaining clips.
10 Refit the track rod end balljoint as described in Section 22.

24 Wheel alignment and steering angles – general information

General information

1 A car's steering and suspension geometry is defined in four basic settings **(see illustration)**. For this purpose, all angles are expressed in degrees (toe settings are also expressed as a measurement of length). The steering axis is defined as an imaginary line drawn through the axis of the suspension strut, extended where necessary to contact the ground.

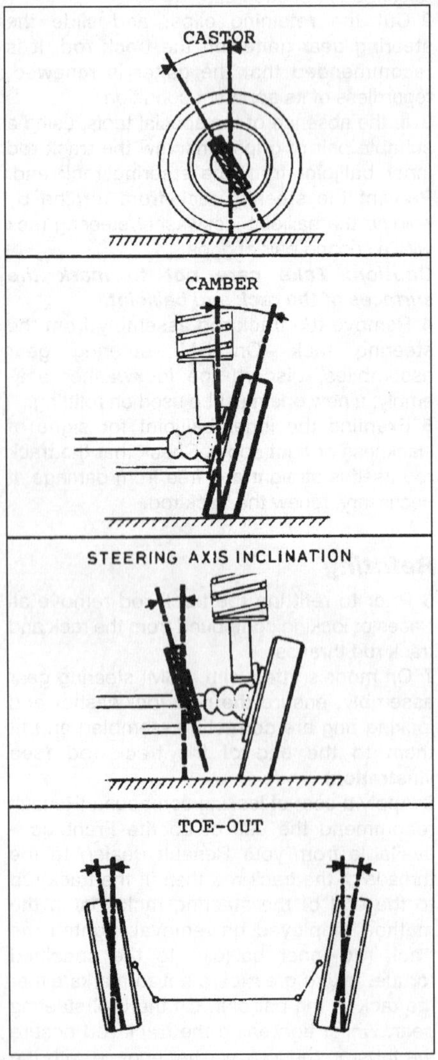

24.1 Wheel alignment and steering angles

2 Camber is the angle between each roadwheel and a vertical line drawn through its centre and tyre contact patch, when viewed from the front or rear of the car. Positive camber is when the roadwheels are tilted outwards from the vertical at the top; negative camber is when they are tilted inwards.
3 Camber is not adjustable. Values are given for reference only. Checking is possible using a camber checking gauge, but if the figure obtained is significantly different from that specified, the vehicle must be taken for careful checking by a professional. Wrong camber settings can only be caused by wear or damage to the body or suspension components.
4 Castor is the angle between the steering axis and a vertical line drawn through each roadwheel's centre and tyre contact patch, when viewed from the side of the car. Positive castor is when the steering axis is tilted so that it contacts the ground ahead of the vertical; negative castor is when it contacts the ground behind the vertical.
5 Castor is not adjustable. As with camber, values are given for reference only; deviation can only be due to wear or damage.
6 Steering axis inclination/SAI – also known as **kingpin inclination/KPI** – is the angle between the steering axis and a vertical line drawn through each roadwheel's centre and tyre contact patch, when viewed from the front or rear of the car.
7 SAI/KPI is not adjustable, and is given for reference only.
8 Toe is the amount by which the roadwheels point outwards or inwards, viewed from above. Toe-in is when the roadwheels point inwards, towards each other at the front, while toe-out is when they splay outwards from each other at the front. The value for toe can be expressed as an angle (taking the centre-line of the car as zero), or as a measurement of length (taking measurements between the inside rims of the wheels at hub height).
9 The front wheel toe setting is adjusted by screwing the balljoints in or out of their track rods to alter the effective length of the track rod assemblies.
10 Rear wheel toe setting is not adjustable, and is given for reference only. While it can be checked, if the figure obtained is significantly different from that specified, the vehicle must be taken for careful checking by a professional, as the fault can only be caused by wear or damage to the body or suspension components.

Checking – general

11 Due to the special measuring equipment necessary to check the wheel alignment, and the skill required to use it properly, the checking and adjustment of these settings is best left to a Renault dealer or similar expert. Most tyre-fitting shops now possess sophisticated checking equipment.
12 For accurate checking, the vehicle must be at the kerb weight specified in *Dimensions and weights* in the Reference Section.
13 Before starting work, check first that the tyre sizes and types are as specified, then check tyre pressures and tread wear. Also check roadwheel run-out, the condition of the hub bearings, the steering wheel free play and the condition of the front suspension components (Chapter 1A or 1B). Correct any faults.
14 Park the vehicle on level ground, with the front roadwheels in the straight-ahead position. Rock both ends to settle the suspension. Release the handbrake and roll the vehicle backwards 1 metre (3 feet), then forwards again, to relieve any stresses in the steering and suspension components.

Toe setting – checking and adjustment

Front wheels – checking

15 Two methods are available to the home mechanic for checking the front wheel toe setting. One method is to use a gauge to measure the distance between the front and rear inside edges of the roadwheels. The other method is to use a scuff plate, in which each front wheel is rolled across a movable plate which records any deviation, or scuff, of the tyre from the straight-ahead position as it moves across the plate. Such gauges are available in relatively-inexpensive form from accessory outlets. It is up to the owner to decide whether the expense is justified, in view of the small amount of use such equipment would normally receive.
16 Prepare the vehicle as described previously in paragraphs 12 to 14.
17 If the measurement procedure is being used, carefully measure the distance between the front edges of the roadwheel rims and the rear edges of the rims. Subtract the rear measurement from the front measurement, and check that the result is within the specified range. If not, adjust the toe setting as described in paragraph 19.
18 If scuff plates are to be used, roll the vehicle backwards, check that the roadwheels are in the straight-ahead position, then roll it across the scuff plates so that each front roadwheel passes squarely over the centre of its respective plate. Note the angle recorded by the scuff plates. To ensure accuracy, repeat the check three times, and take the average of the three readings. If the roadwheels are running parallel, there will of course be no angle recorded; if a deviation value is shown on the scuff plates, compare the reading obtained for each wheel with that specified. If the value recorded is outside the specified tolerance, the toe setting is incorrect, and must be adjusted as follows.

Front wheels – adjustment

Note: *There are two types of track rod end locking arrangements: locknut type, and bolt and clamp type.*

19 Apply the handbrake, jack up the front of the vehicle and support it securely on axle stands (see *Jacking and vehicle support*). Turn the steering wheel onto full-left lock, and record the number of exposed threads on the right-hand track rod end. Now turn the steering onto full-right lock, and record the number of threads on the left-hand side. If there are the same number of threads visible on both sides, then subsequent adjustment should be made equally on both sides. If there are more threads visible on one side than the other, it will be necessary to compensate for this during adjustment. **Note:** *It is important that, after adjustment, the same number of threads be visible on each track rod end.*

20 First clean the track rod threads; if they are corroded, apply penetrating fluid before starting adjustment. Release the rubber gaiter outboard clips, then peel back the gaiters and apply a smear of grease, so that both gaiters are free and will not be twisted or strained as their respective track rods are rotated.

21 Use a straight-edge and a scriber or similar to mark the relationship of each track rod to its balljoint. Holding each track rod in turn, unscrew its locknut or clamp fully.

22 Alter the length of the track rods, bearing in mind the note in paragraph 19, by screwing them into or out of the balljoints. Rotate the track rod using an open-ended spanner fitted to the flats provided. Shortening the track rods (screwing them onto their balljoints) will reduce toe-in and increase toe-out. Each complete turn of the track rod effectively adjusts the toe setting by 30' or 3 mm (depending on the method being used) **(see illustration)**.

23 When the setting is correct, hold the track rods and securely tighten the balljoint lock-nuts or clamps. Check that the balljoints are seated correctly in their sockets, and count the exposed threads. If the number of threads exposed is not the same on both sides, then the adjustment has not been made equally, and problems will be encountered with tyre scrubbing in turns; also, the steering wheel spokes will no longer be horizontal when the wheels are in the straight-ahead position.

24 When the track rod lengths are the same, lower the vehicle to the ground and recheck the toe setting; readjust if necessary. Ensure that the rubber gaiters are seated correctly and are not twisted or strained; secure them in position with new retaining clips.

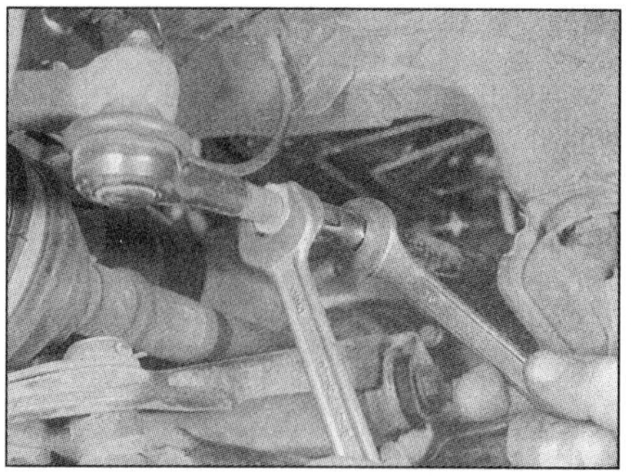

24.22 Adjusting the front wheel toe setting

Rear wheel toe setting

25 The procedure for checking the rear toe setting is same as described for the front in paragraph 17. However, no adjustment is possible.

Chapter 11
Bodywork and fittings

Contents

Degrees of difficulty

Easy, suitable for novice with little experience	**Fairly easy,** suitable for beginner with some experience	**Fairly difficult,** suitable for competent DIY mechanic	**Difficult,** suitable for experienced DIY mechanic	**Very difficult,** suitable for expert DIY or professional

Specifications

Torque wrench setting	**Nm**	**lbf ft**
Seat belt and seat belt height adjuster mountings	25	18

1 General information

The bodyshell and floorpan are manufactured from pressed-steel, and form an integral part of the vehicle's structure (monocoque), without the need for a separate chassis. The Clio is available in 3- and 5-door Hatchback body styles, with a Van version also available in some markets.

Various areas of the structure are strengthened to provide for suspension, steering and engine mounting points, and load distribution.

All models are fitted with front wings manufactured from a polymer compound, which can withstand an impact of up to 10 mph (16 km/h) without sustaining permanent damage.

Corrosion protection is applied to all new vehicles. Various anti-corrosion preparations are used, including galvanising, zinc phosphatisation, and PVC underseal. An 'anti-gravel' undercoat is applied to the front section of the bonnet, to prevent corrosion and paint chipping caused by stones and other road debris hitting the front of the vehicle. Protective wax is injected into the box sections and other hollow cavities.

Extensive use is made of plastic for peripheral components, such as the radiator grille, bumpers and wheel trims, and for much of the interior trim. Plastic wheelarch liners are fitted, to protect the metal body panels against corrosion due to a build-up of road dirt.

Interior fittings are to a high standard on all models, and a wide range of optional equipment is available throughout the range.

2 Maintenance – bodywork and underframe

The general condition of a vehicle's bodywork is the one thing that significantly affects its value. Maintenance is easy, but needs to be regular. Neglect, particularly after minor damage, can lead quickly to further deterioration and costly repair bills. It is important also to keep watch on those parts of the vehicle not immediately visible, for instance the underside, inside all the wheelarches, and the lower part of the engine compartment.

The basic maintenance routine for the bodywork is washing – preferably with a lot of water, from a hose. This will remove all the loose solids which may have stuck to the vehicle. It is important to flush these off in such a way as to prevent grit from scratching the finish. The wheelarches and underframe need washing in the same way, to remove any accumulated mud which will retain moisture and tend to encourage rust. Paradoxically enough, the best time to clean the underframe and wheelarches is in wet weather, when the mud is thoroughly wet and soft. In very wet weather, the underframe is usually cleaned of large accumulations automatically, and this is a good time for inspection.

Periodically, except on vehicles with a wax-based underbody protective coating, it is a good idea to have the whole of the underframe of the vehicle steam-cleaned, engine compartment included, so that a thorough inspection can be carried out to see what minor repairs and renovations are necessary. Steam-cleaning is available at many garages, and is necessary for the removal of the accumulation of oily grime, which sometimes is allowed to become thick in certain areas. If steam-cleaning facilities are not available, there are one or two excellent grease solvents available, which can be brush-applied; the dirt can then be simply hosed off. Note that these methods should not be used on vehicles with wax-based underbody protective coating, or the coating will be removed. Such vehicles should be inspected annually, preferably just prior to Winter, when the underbody should be washed down, and any damage to the wax coating repaired. Ideally, a completely fresh coat should be applied. It would also be worth considering the use of such wax-based protection for injection into door panels, sills, box sections, etc, as an additional safeguard against rust damage, where such protection is not provided by the vehicle manufacturer.

After washing paintwork, wipe off with a chamois leather to give an unspotted clear finish. A coat of clear protective wax polish will give added protection against chemical pollutants in the air. If the paintwork sheen has dulled or oxidised, use a cleaner/polisher combination to restore the brilliance of the shine. This requires a little effort, but such dulling is usually caused because regular washing has been neglected. Care needs to be taken with metallic paintwork, as special non-abrasive cleaner/polisher is required to avoid damage to the finish. Always check that the door and ventilator opening drain holes and pipes are completely clear, so that water can be drained out. Brightwork should be treated in the same way as paintwork. Windscreens and windows can be kept clear of the smeary film which often appears, by the use of proprietary glass cleaner. Never use any form of wax or other body or chromium polish on glass.

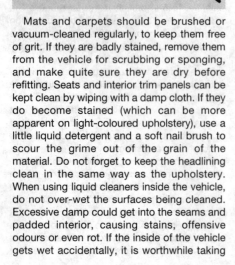

3 Maintenance – upholstery and carpets

Mats and carpets should be brushed or vacuum-cleaned regularly, to keep them free of grit. If they are badly stained, remove them from the vehicle for scrubbing or sponging, and make quite sure they are dry before refitting. Seats and interior trim panels can be kept clean by wiping with a damp cloth. If they do become stained (which can be more apparent on light-coloured upholstery), use a little liquid detergent and a soft nail brush to scour the grime out of the grain of the material. Do not forget to keep the headlining clean in the same way as the upholstery. When using liquid cleaners inside the vehicle, do not over-wet the surfaces being cleaned. Excessive damp could get into the seams and padded interior, causing stains, offensive odours or even rot. If the inside of the vehicle gets wet accidentally, it is worthwhile taking some trouble to dry it out properly, particularly where carpets are involved. *Do not leave oil or electric heaters inside the vehicle for this purpose.*

4 Minor body damage – repair

Repairs of minor scratches in bodywork

If the scratch is very superficial, and does not penetrate to the metal of the bodywork, repair is very simple. Lightly rub the area of the scratch with a paintwork renovator, or a very fine cutting paste, to remove loose paint from the scratch, and to clear the surrounding bodywork of wax polish. Rinse the area with clean water.

Apply touch-up paint to the scratch using a fine paint brush; continue to apply fine layers of paint until the surface of the paint in the scratch is level with the surrounding paintwork. Allow the new paint at least two weeks to harden, then blend it into the surrounding paintwork by rubbing the scratch area with a paintwork renovator or a very fine cutting paste. Finally, apply wax polish.

Where the scratch has penetrated right through to the metal of the bodywork, causing the metal to rust, a different repair technique is required. Remove any loose rust from the bottom of the scratch with a penknife, then apply rust-inhibiting paint, to prevent the formation of rust in the future. Using a rubber or nylon applicator, fill the scratch with bodystopper paste. If required, this paste can be mixed with cellulose thinners, to provide a very thin paste which is ideal for filling narrow scratches. Before the stopper-paste in the scratch hardens, wrap a piece of smooth cotton rag around the top of a finger. Dip the finger in cellulose thinners, and quickly sweep it across the surface of the stopper-paste in the scratch; this will ensure that the surface of the stopper-paste is slightly hollowed. The scratch can now be painted over as described earlier in this Section.

Repairs of dents in bodywork

When deep denting of the vehicle's bodywork has taken place, the first task is to pull the dent out, until the affected bodywork almost attains its original shape. There is little point in trying to restore the original shape completely, as the metal in the damaged area will have stretched on impact, and cannot be reshaped fully to its original contour. It is better to bring the level of the dent up to a point which is about 3 mm below the level of the surrounding bodywork. In cases where the dent is very shallow anyway, it is not worth trying to pull it out at all. If the underside of the dent is accessible, it can be hammered out gently from behind, using a mallet with a wooden or plastic head. Whilst doing this, hold a suitable block of wood firmly against the outside of the panel, to absorb the impact from the hammer blows and thus prevent a large area of the bodywork from being 'belled-out'.

Should the dent be in a section of the bodywork which has a double skin, or some other factor making it inaccessible from behind, a different technique is called for. Drill several small holes through the metal inside the area – particularly in the deeper section. Then screw long self-tapping screws into the holes, just sufficiently for them to gain a good purchase in the metal. Now the dent can be pulled out by pulling on the protruding heads of the screws with a pair of pliers.

The next stage of the repair is the removal of the paint from the damaged area, and from an inch or so of the surrounding 'sound' bodywork. This is accomplished most easily by using a wire brush or abrasive pad on a power drill, although it can be done just as effectively by hand, using sheets of abrasive paper. To complete the preparation for filling, score the surface of the bare metal with a screwdriver or the tang of a file, or alternatively, drill small holes in the affected area. This will provide a really good 'key' for the filler paste.

To complete the repair, see the Section on filling and respraying.

Repairs of rust holes or gashes in bodywork

Remove all paint from the affected area, and from an inch or so of the surrounding 'sound' bodywork, using an abrasive pad or a wire brush on a power drill. If these are not available, a few sheets of abrasive paper will do the job most effectively. With the paint removed, you will be able to judge the severity of the corrosion, and therefore decide whether to renew the whole panel (if this is possible) or to repair the affected area. New body panels are not as expensive as most people think, and it is often quicker and more satisfactory to fit a new panel than to attempt to repair large areas of corrosion.

Remove all fittings from the affected area, except those which will act as a guide to the original shape of the damaged bodywork (e.g. headlamp shells etc). Then, using tin snips or a hacksaw blade, remove all loose metal and any other metal badly affected by corrosion. Hammer the edges of the hole inwards, in order to create a slight depression for the filler paste.

Wire-brush the affected area to remove the powdery rust from the surface of the remaining metal. Paint the affected area with rust-inhibiting paint; if the back of the rusted area is accessible, treat this also.

Before filling can take place, it will be necessary to block the hole in some way. This can be achieved by the use of aluminium or plastic mesh, or aluminium tape.

Aluminium or plastic mesh, or glass-fibre matting is probably the best material to use for a large hole. Cut a piece to the approximate size and shape of the hole to be filled, then position it in the hole so that its edges are below the level of the surrounding bodywork. It can be retained in position by several blobs of filler paste around its periphery.

Aluminium tape should be used for small or very narrow holes. Pull a piece off the roll, trim it to the approximate size and shape required, then pull off the backing paper (if used) and stick the tape over the hole; it can be overlapped if the thickness of one piece is insufficient. Burnish down the edges of the tape with the handle of a screwdriver or similar, to ensure that the tape is securely attached to the metal underneath.

Bodywork repairs – filling and respraying

Before using this Section, see the Sections on dent, deep scratch, rust holes and gash repairs.

Many types of bodyfiller are available, but generally speaking, those proprietary kits which contain a tin of filler paste and a tube of resin hardener are best for this type of repair. A wide, flexible plastic or nylon applicator will be found invaluable for imparting a smooth and well-contoured finish to the surface of the filler.

Mix up a little filler on a clean piece of card or board – measure the hardener carefully (follow the maker's instructions on the pack), otherwise the filler will set too rapidly or too slowly. Using the applicator, apply the filler paste to the prepared area; draw the applicator across the surface of the filler to achieve the correct contour and to level the surface. As soon as a contour that approximates to the correct one is achieved, stop working the paste – if you carry on too long, the paste will become sticky and begin to 'pick-up' on the applicator. Continue to add thin layers of filler paste at 20-minute intervals, until the level of the filler is just proud of the surrounding bodywork.

Once the filler has hardened, the excess can be removed using a metal plane or file. From then on, progressively-finer grades of abrasive paper should be used, starting with a 40-grade production paper, and finishing with a 400-grade wet-and-dry paper. Always wrap the abrasive paper around a flat rubber, cork, or wooden block – otherwise the surface of the filler will not be completely flat. During the smoothing of the filler surface, the wet-and-dry paper should be periodically rinsed in water. This will ensure that a very smooth finish is imparted to the filler at the final stage.

At this stage, the 'dent' should be surrounded by a ring of bare metal, which in turn should be encircled by the finely 'feathered' edge of the good paintwork. Rinse the repair area with clean water, until all of the dust produced by the rubbing-down operation has gone.

Spray the whole area with a light coat of – this will show up any imperfections in the surface of the filler. Repair these imperfections with fresh filler paste or bodystopper, and once more smooth the surface with abrasive paper. If bodystopper is used, it can be mixed with cellulose thinners, to form a really thin paste which is ideal for filling small holes. Repeat this spray-and-repair procedure until you are satisfied that the surface of the filler, and the feathered edge of the paintwork, are perfect. Clean the repair area with clean water, and allow to dry fully.

The repair area is now ready for final spraying. Paint spraying must be carried out in a warm, dry, windless and dust-free atmosphere. This condition can be created artificially if you have access to a large indoor working area, but if you are forced to work in the open, you will have to pick your day very carefully. If you are working indoors, dousing the floor in the work area with water will help to settle the dust which would otherwise be in the atmosphere. If the repair area is confined to one body panel, mask off the surrounding panels; this will help to minimise the effects of a slight mis-match in paint colours. Bodywork fittings (e.g. chrome strips, door handles etc) will also need to be masked off. Use genuine masking tape, and several thicknesses of newspaper, for the masking operations.

Before commencing to spray, agitate the aerosol can thoroughly, then spray a test area (an old tin, or similar) until the technique is mastered. Cover the repair area with a thick coat of primer; the thickness should be built up using several thin layers of paint, rather than one thick one. Using 400 grade wet-and-dry paper, rub down the surface of the primer until it is really smooth. While doing this, the work area should be thoroughly doused with water, and the wet-and-dry paper periodically rinsed in water. Allow to dry before spraying on more paint.

Spray on the top coat, again building up the thickness by using several thin layers of paint. Start spraying at the top of the repair area, and then, using a side-to-side motion, work downwards until the whole repair area and about 2 inches of the surrounding original paintwork is covered. Remove all masking material 10 to 15 minutes after spraying on the final coat of paint.

Allow the new paint at least two weeks to harden, then, using a paintwork renovator or a very fine cutting paste, blend the edges of the paint into the existing paintwork. Finally, apply wax polish.

Plastic components

With the use of more and more plastic body components by the vehicle manufacturers (e.g. bumpers. spoilers, and in some cases major body panels), rectification of more serious damage to such items has become a matter of either entrusting repair work to a specialist in this field, or renewing complete components. Repair of such damage by the DIY owner is not really feasible, owing to the cost of the equipment and materials required for effecting such repairs. The basic technique involves making a groove along the line of the crack in the plastic, using a rotary burr in a power drill. The damaged part is then welded back together, using a hot air gun to heat up and fuse a plastic filler rod into the groove. Any excess plastic is then removed, and the area rubbed down to a smooth finish. It is important that a filler rod of the correct plastic is used, as body components can be made of a variety of different types (e.g. polycarbonate, ABS, polypropylene).

Damage of a less serious nature (abrasions, minor cracks etc) can be repaired by the DIY owner using a two-part epoxy filler repair. Once mixed in equal, this is used in similar fashion to the bodywork filler used on metal panels. The filler is usually cured in twenty to thirty minutes, ready for sanding and painting.

If the owner is renewing a complete component himself, or if he has repaired it with epoxy filler, he will be left with the problem of finding a suitable paint for finishing which is compatible with the type of plastic used. At one time, the use of a universal paint was not possible, owing to the complex range of plastics encountered in body component applications. Standard paints, generally speaking, will not bond to plastic or rubber satisfactorily, but suitable paints to match any plastic or rubber finish, can be obtained from dealers. However, it is now possible to obtain a plastic body parts finishing kit which consists of a pre-primer treatment, a primer and coloured top coat. Full instructions are normally supplied with a kit, but basically, the method of use is to first apply the pre-primer to the component concerned, and allow it to dry for up to 30 minutes. Then the primer is applied, and left to dry for about an hour before finally applying the special-coloured top coat. The result is a correctly-coloured component, where the paint will flex with the plastic or rubber, a property that standard paint does not normally posses.

5 Major body damage – repair

Where serious damage has occurred, or large areas need renewal due to neglect, it means that complete new panels will need welding-in, and this is best left to professionals. If the damage is due to impact, it will also be necessary to check completely the alignment of the bodyshell, and this can only be carried out accurately by a Renault dealer using special jigs. If the body is left misaligned, it is primarily dangerous, as the car will not handle properly, and secondly, uneven stresses will be imposed on the steering, suspension and possibly transmission, causing abnormal wear, or complete failure, particularly to such items as the tyres.

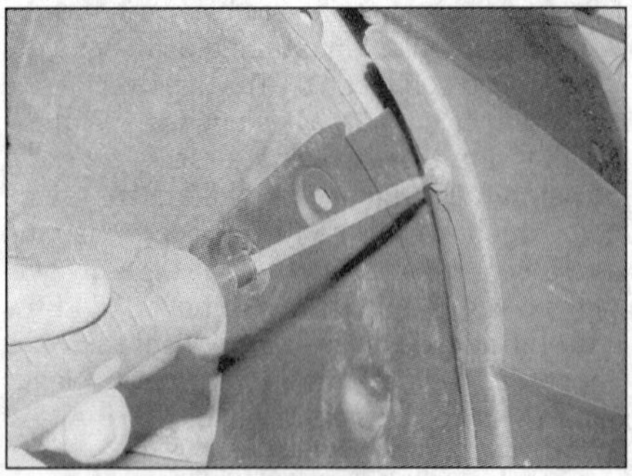
6.4 Unscrewing a front bumper front securing screw

6.6 Front bumper side securing bolt (arrowed), behind wheelarch splash shield

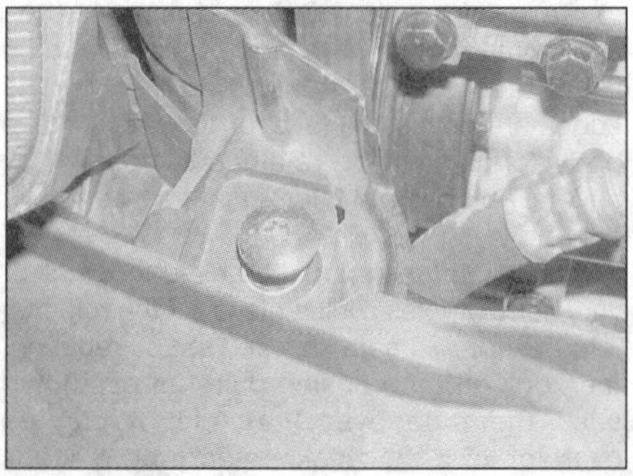
6.8 Front bumper upper securing screws, under the front grille

6 Bumpers – removal and refitting

Front bumper

Removal

1 On models fitted with front foglights, disconnect the battery negative lead.

2 To improve access, jack up the front of the car and support it securely on axle stands (see Jacking and vehicle support).

3 From under the front bumper, undo and remove the securing bolts from the splash shield below the radiator.

4 Working under the right-hand side of the car, undo the two retaining screws, and release the securing clips from the liner, under the front wheelarch **(see illustration)**.

5 Repeat the procedure given in paragraph 4, on the left-hand side of the car.

6 With the splash shields removed, undo the bumper side mounting bolts (one each side) **(see illustration)**.

7 Remove the radiator grille panel as described in Section 7.

8 Remove the now-exposed bumper upper mounting screws from under the grille **(see illustration)**.

9 Locate the front foglight wiring connectors **(see illustration)** and separate the two halves of the connector.

10 Have an assistant support one end of the bumper, then withdraw the bumper from the vehicle.

Refitting

11 Refitting is a reversal of removal. Refit the front grille with reference to Section 7.

Rear bumper

Removal

12 Disconnect the battery negative lead.

13 To improve access, chock the front wheels, then jack up the rear of the car and support it securely on axle stands (see *Jacking and vehicle support*).

14 Working under the rear wheelarches, remove the securing nut and retaining screws **(see illustration)**, and remove the splash shields from both sides of the car.

15 Remove the now-exposed bumper side-mounting bolts **(see illustration)** (one at each end of the bumper).

16 Working under the rear of the car, slacken the two lower securing bolts from the bumper **(see illustration)**.

17 Using a flat-bladed screwdriver, unclip the number plate light and disconnect the wiring **(see illustration)**.

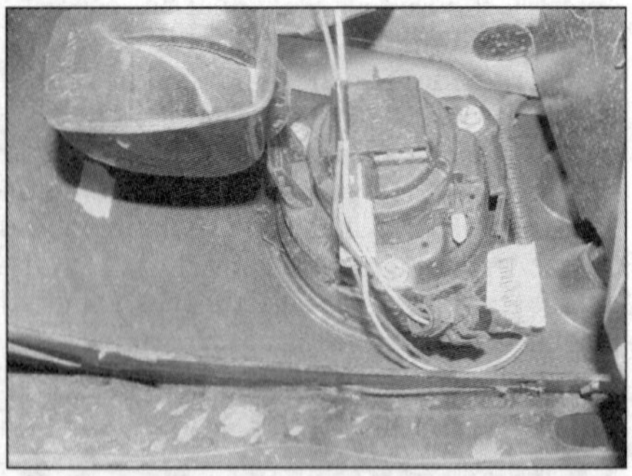
6.9 Front foglight wiring connector on the left-hand side of the bumper

6.14 Removing the splash shield retaining nut

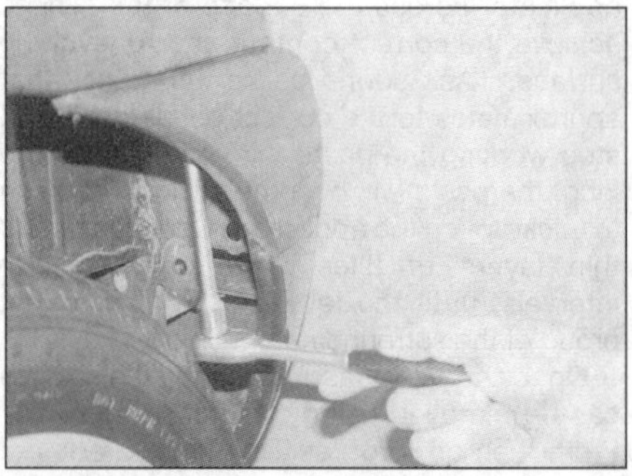
6.15 Removing the rear bumper side-mounting bolt

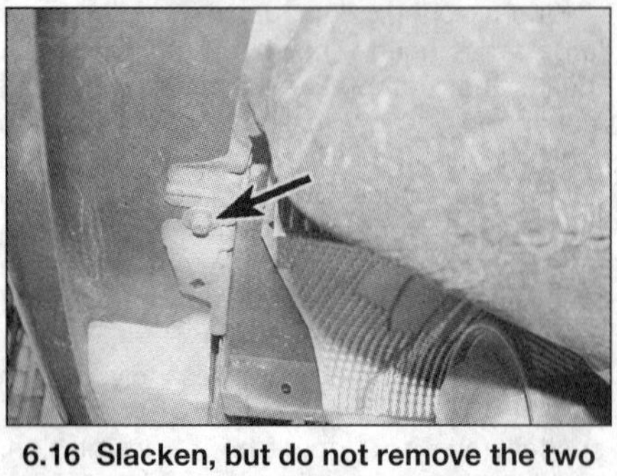
6.16 Slacken, but do not remove the two lower mounting bolts (left-hand bolt arrowed)

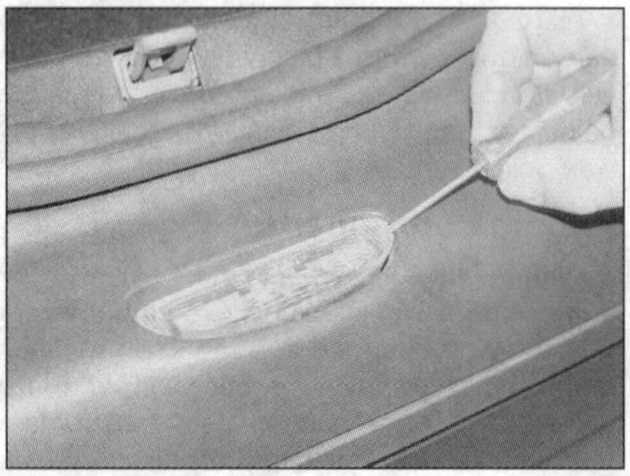
6.17 Unclipping the rear number plate light unit

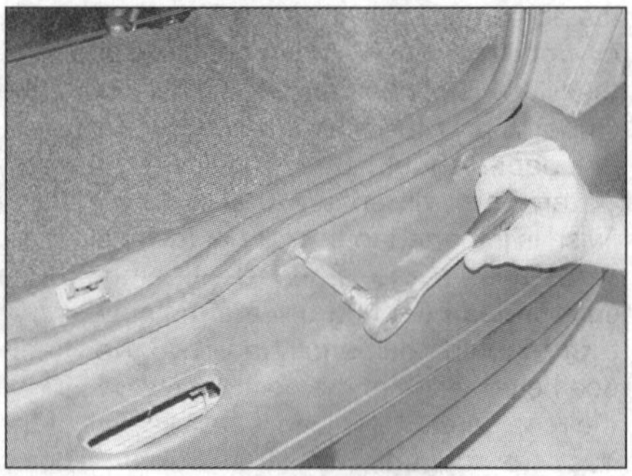
6.18 Unscrewing one of the four upper mounting bolts

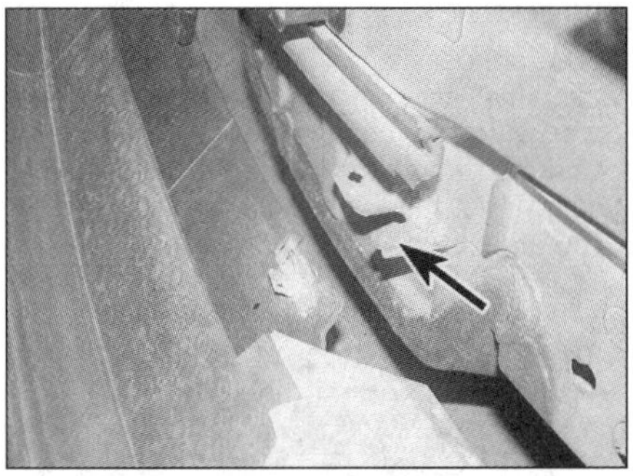

6.19 Withdraw the bumper from the lower mounting brackets (arrowed)

18 Undo and remove the four upper securing bolts from the bumper **(see illustration)**.
19 Have an assistant support the bumper, then withdraw the bumper from the rear of the vehicle **(see illustration)**.

Refitting

20 Refitting is a reversal of removal.

7 Radiator grille panel – removal and refitting

Removal

1 Open the bonnet.
2 Remove the retaining screws from around the grille **(see illustration)**.
3 Using a suitable screwdriver, carefully release the plastic securing clips (one at each

8.1 Removing the weather seal from along the scuttle panel

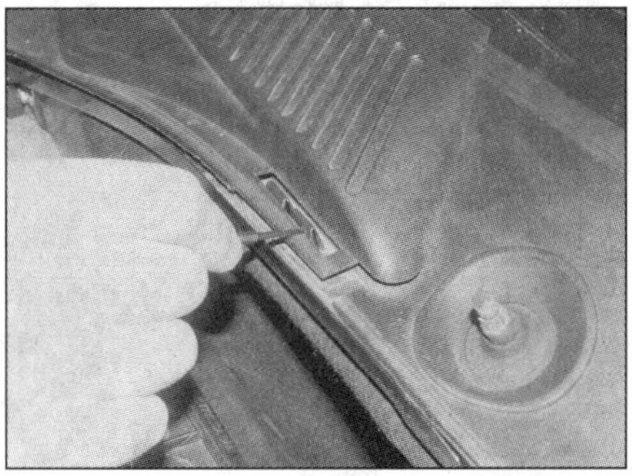

8.4a Unclip the right-hand windscreen cowl panel from the left-hand panel . . .

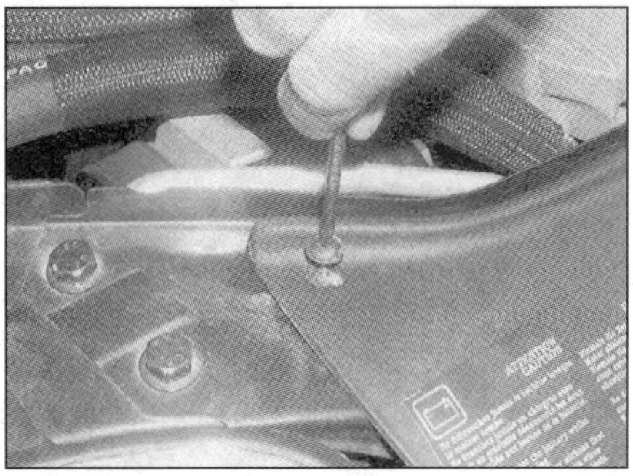

7.2 Unscrewing one of the grille retaining screws

end), and withdraw the grille panel from the front of the vehicle **(see illustration)**.

Refitting

4 Refitting is a reversal of removal.

8 Windscreen cowl panels – removal and refitting

Removal

Note: *The right-hand panel (as seen from the driver's seat) must be removed first, before removing the left-hand panel.*
1 Open the bonnet and remove the weatherseal from along the windscreen cowl panels **(see illustration)**.
2 Remove the windscreen wiper arms, as described in Chapter 12.

8.3 Releasing the securing clip from the windscreen cowl panel

8.4b . . . release the cowl panel from the windscreen . . .

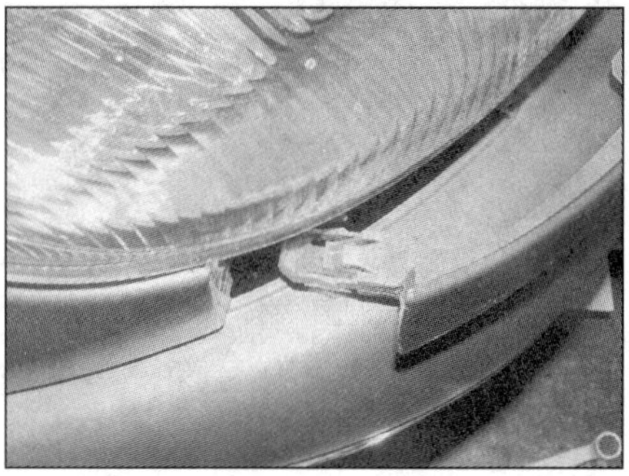

7.3 Unclip the grille from the edge of the front wing, below the headlight

3 Carefully release the cowl panel securing clips by pushing the centre pin down about 5mm **(see illustration)**. (One securing clip at each side, in the top of the inner wing.)
4 Unclip the panels at the centre, then release them from the lower part of the windscreen. Unclip the panels from the locating pin at the top edge of the inner wing, taking care not to damage the wing panel **(see illustrations)**.

Refitting

5 Refitting is a reversal of removal, bearing in mind the following points.
6 Check the two halves of the cowling are securely clipped together.
7 Ensure that the weatherseal is correctly located over the front of the panels, and that the panel securing clips are correctly engaged.
8 Refit the windscreen wiper arms with reference to Chapter 12.
9 Push the centre pin in the clip upwards by about 5mm, before refitting. Then when in place, push the centre pin down flush with the clip to secure.

9 Bonnet and hinges – removal and refitting

Bonnet

Removal

1 Have an assistant support the bonnet in the open position.

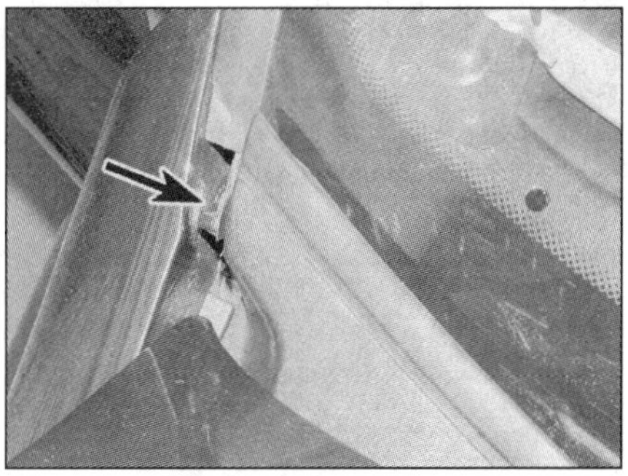

8.4c . . . then disengage it from the top corner of the wing panel (arrowed)

9.2a Unclip the washer hose from the bonnet hinge . . .

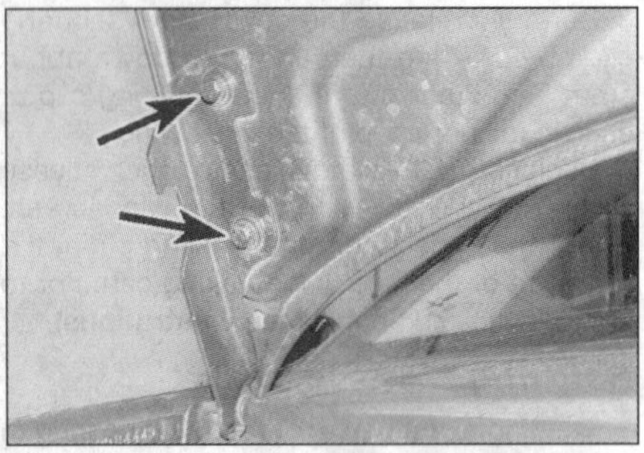

9.4 Undo the two bolts from the hinge (right-hand hinge arrowed)

2 Disconnect the windscreen washer hose from the left-hand bonnet hinge and the washer jet **(see illustrations)**.

3 If the original bonnet is to be refitted, mark the position of the hinges on the bonnet, to aid alignment on refitting.

9.2b . . . and disconnect the hose from the washer jet

4 Remove the bolts securing the bonnet to the hinges (two bolts at each side) **(see illustration)**, then carefully withdraw the bonnet from the car.

Refitting

5 Refitting is a reversal of removal, bearing in mind the following points.

6 Where applicable, align the hinges with the marks made on the bonnet before removal.

7 Close the bonnet (carefully, in case it fouls the surrounding bodywork), and check the alignment with the surrounding body panels.

8 If necessary, the alignment of the bonnet can be adjusted by altering the position of the bonnet on the hinges, using the elongated holes provided. The alignment of the front of the bonnet can also be adjusted by altering the position of the bonnet lock assembly, using the elongated bolt holes provided.

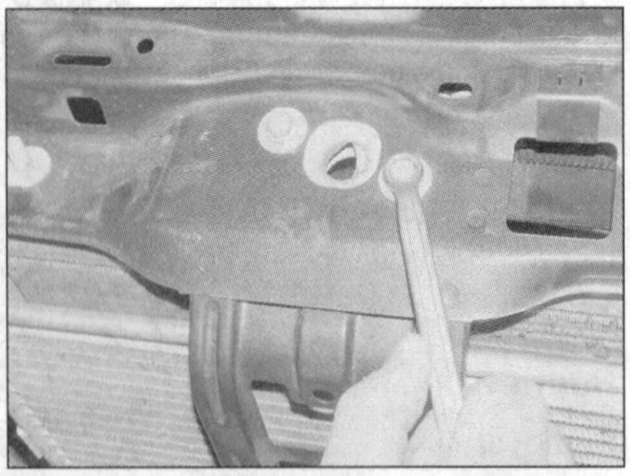

10.3a Undo the bonnet lock assembly securing bolts . . .

10.3b . . . then withdraw the lock assembly from the cross-panel

Hinges

9 The bonnet hinges are bolted to the inner wing panel, and can only be removed after the outer wing has been removed. This cannot easily be removed and may require special equipment, this can only be carried out accurately by a Renault dealer or bodyshop specialists.

10 Bonnet lock components – removal and refitting

Bonnet lock assembly

Removal

1 Open the bonnet.

2 Note and mark the position of the lock on the panel, to aid correct alignment when refitting.

3 Unscrew the two securing bolts, then lift the lock assembly from the panel **(see illustrations)**.

4 Release the outer cable from the lock assembly.

5 Disconnect the end of the inner release cable from the lock operating lever, and withdraw the lock assembly.

Refitting

6 Refitting is a reversal of removal, but align the assembly with the marks made on the panel before removal.

7 Make sure that the outer and inner cables are located correctly before closing the bonnet **(see illustration)**.

8 On completion, if necessary adjust the alignment of the bonnet with the surrounding body panels by altering the position of the lock/striker assembly, using the elongated bolt holes provided.

Bonnet lock striker

9 Open the bonnet. (The lock striker is bolted to the bonnet.)

10 Unclip the bonnet safety catch pull from the retaining clip **(see illustration)**.

11 Note and mark the position of the lock striker on the bonnet, to aid correct alignment when refitting.

12 Unscrew the two securing nuts **(see illustration)**, then remove the lock striker from the bonnet.

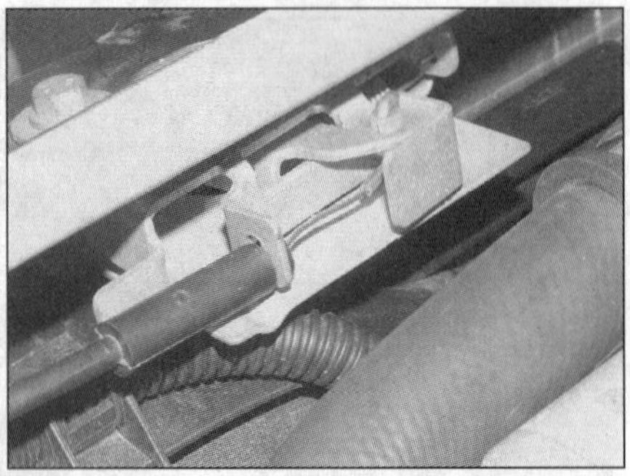

10.7 Check the cable is fitted correctly

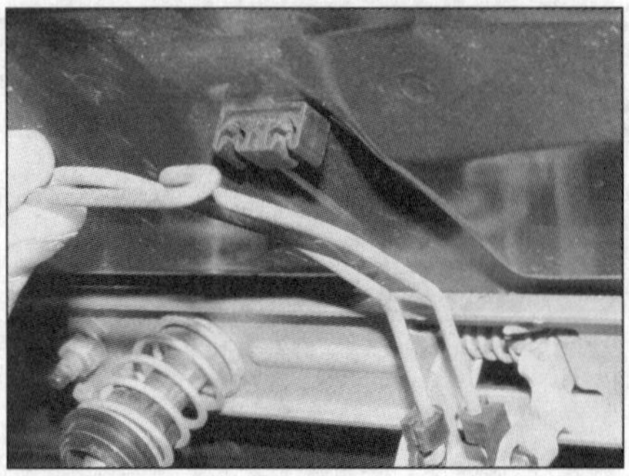

10.10 Unclipping the bonnet safety catch pull

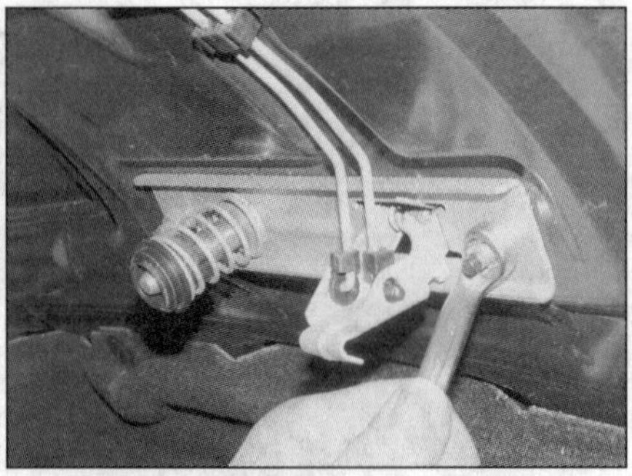

10.12 Removing the lock striker securing nuts

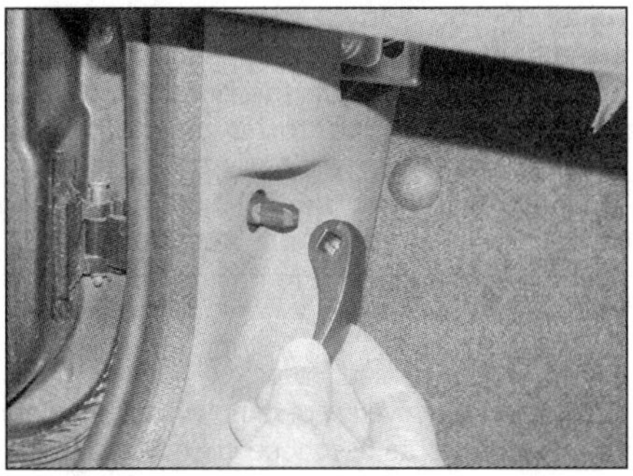
10.15 Withdraw the lever from the cable linkage assembly

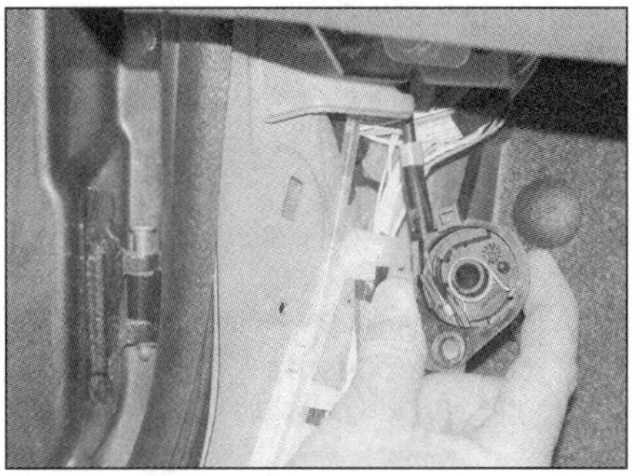
10.17 Unclip the assembly from the sill panel

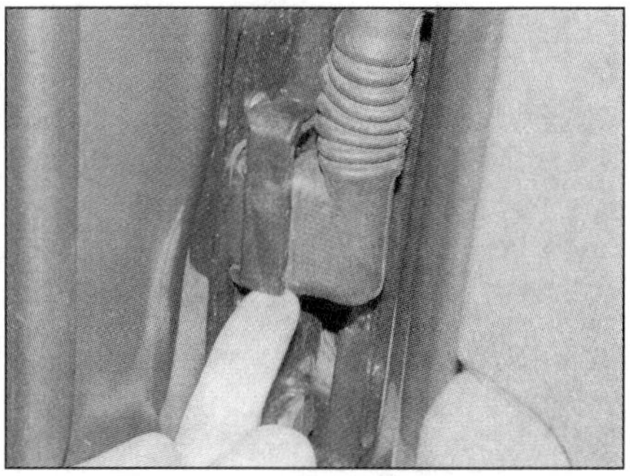
11.3a Slide the securing clip upwards . . .

Refitting

13 Refitting is a reversal of removal, but align the assembly with the marks made on the panel before removal.

14 On completion, if necessary adjust the alignment of the bonnet with the surrounding body panels by altering the position of the lock/striker assembly, using the elongated bolt holes provided.

Bonnet lock release cable/lever assembly

Removal

15 Working inside the vehicle, pull the bonnet release lever to disengage it from its linkage assembly **(see illustration)**.

16 Remove the left-hand side front sill panel, as described in Section 27.

17 Undo the retaining screw and unclip the release lever assembly from the body **(see illustration)**.

18 Working in the engine compartment, release the outer cable from the lock assembly and disconnect the inner cable from the lock operating lever (see illustration 10.7).

19 From inside the car, carefully pull the cable through the bulkhead grommet into the car, noting the cable routing.

Refitting

20 Refitting is a reversal of removal, but ensure that the bulkhead grommet is securely located in the bulkhead, and route the cable as noted during removal.

11 Doors and check straps – removal, refitting and adjustment

Doors

Removal

1 To remove a door, open it fully, and support it under its lower edge on blocks covered with pads of rag.

2 Disconnect the battery negative lead.

3 On the front doors, disconnect the door wiring connector by sliding the securing clip upwards, then pull the connector from its socket **(see illustrations)**.

4 On the rear doors (where applicable), disconnect the door wiring by unclipping the rubber grommet and disconnecting the wiring block connector **(see illustrations)**.

5 Unbolt the door check strap from the body **(see illustration)**.

6 Have an assistant support the door, then remove the securing clips from the hinge pins. Using a suitable tool and hammer, remove the two hinge pins from the hinges and withdraw the door from the car **(see illustrations)**.

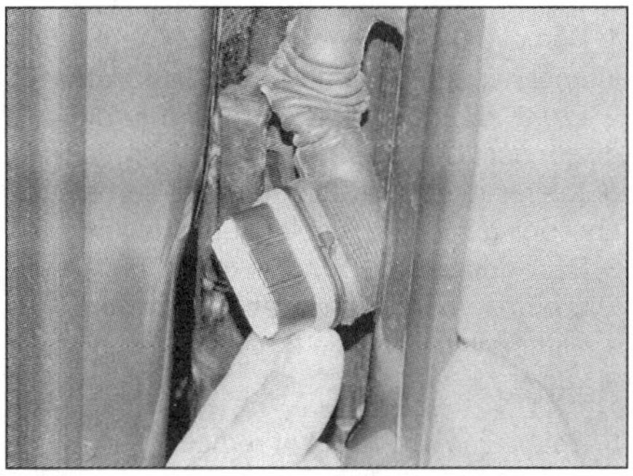
11.3b . . . and disconnect the block connector

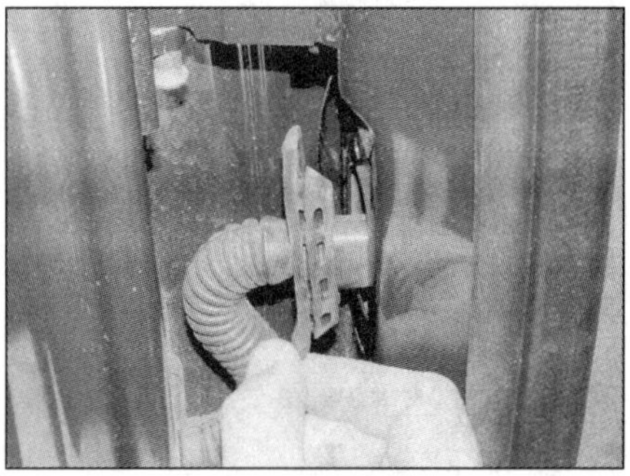
11.4a Unclip the rubber grommet from the door pillar . . .

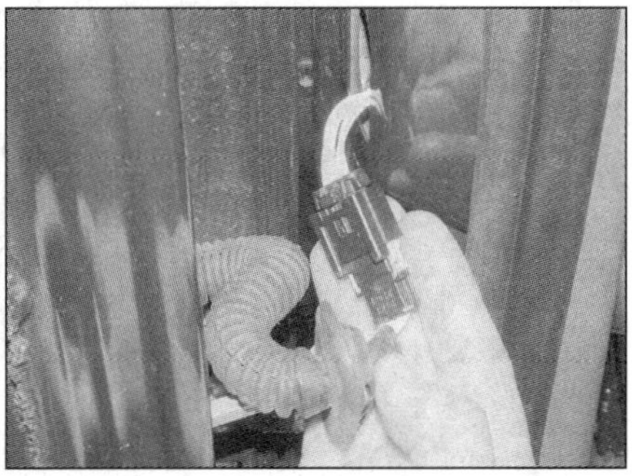
11.4b . . . and disconnect the wiring connector

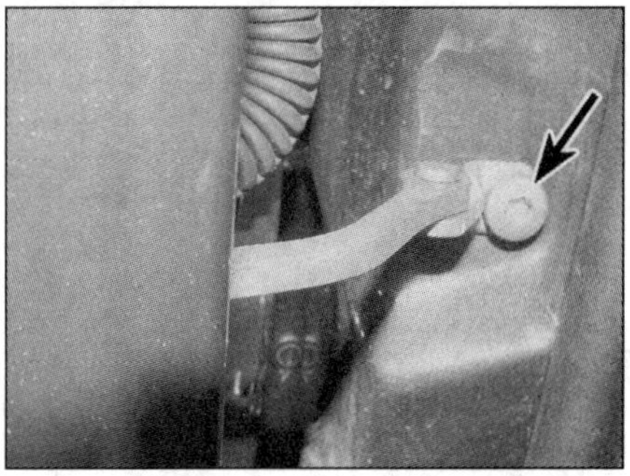
11.5 Door check strap securing screw (arrowed)

11.6a Remove the clip from the hinge pin . . .

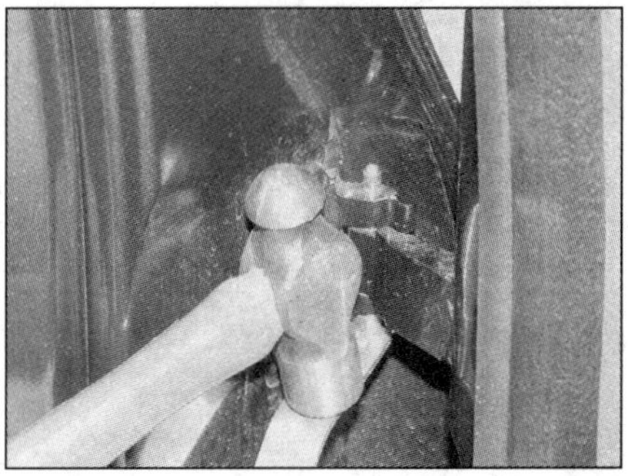
11.6b . . . then tap the hinge pin out using a forked tool

11.13 Undo the two check strap securing nuts (arrowed)

Refitting

7 Refitting is a reversal of removal.

Adjustment

8 The door hinges are welded onto the door frame and the body pillar, so that there is no provision for adjustment or alignment.

9 Door closure may be adjusted by altering the position of the lock striker on the body pillar, using a suitable Torx bit (see Section 12).

Door check straps

Removal

10 Open the door fully.

11 Unbolt the door check strap from the body.

12 Remove the door inner trim panel, as described in Section 27.

13 Working at the outer front edge of the door, unscrew the two nuts securing the check strap to the door **(see illustration)**.

14 Withdraw the check strap through the inside of the door.

Refitting

15 Refitting is a reversal of removal.

12 Door handle and lock components – removal and refitting

Door interior handle

Removal

1 Remove the single screw securing the door interior handle to the door **(see illustration)**.

2 Front doors, withdraw the handle and disconnect the operating cable from the rear of the handle by releasing the outer cable and unclipping the inner cable **(see illustration)**.

3 Rear doors, unclip the linkage rod from the rear of the door handle **(see illustration)**.

4 Withdraw the handle from the door.

Refitting

5 Refitting is a reversal of removal.

Front door exterior handle

Removal

6 Remove the door inner trim panel as described in Section 27.

7 Working inside the door, release the securing clip and disconnect the exterior handle operating rod from the lock or handle (if disconnecting from the handle, note the position of the rod for adjustment) **(see illustration)**.

8 Unscrew the two exterior handle securing nuts from inside the door **(see illustration)**, then tilt the handle and remove it from outside the door.

Refitting

9 Refitting is a reversal of removal, refit the door inner trim panel as described in Section 27.

Rear door exterior handle

Removal

10 Remove the door inner trim panel as described in Section 27.

11 Unclip the anti-theft cover from the door **(see illustration)**.

12 Working inside the door, release the securing clip and disconnect the exterior handle operating rod from the lock or handle (if disconnecting from the handle, note the position of the rod for adjustment) (see illustration 12.7).

13 Unscrew the two exterior handle securing nuts from inside the door **(see illustration)**, then tilt the handle and remove it from outside the door.

Refitting

14 Refitting is a reversal of removal, refit the door inner trim panel as described in Section 27.

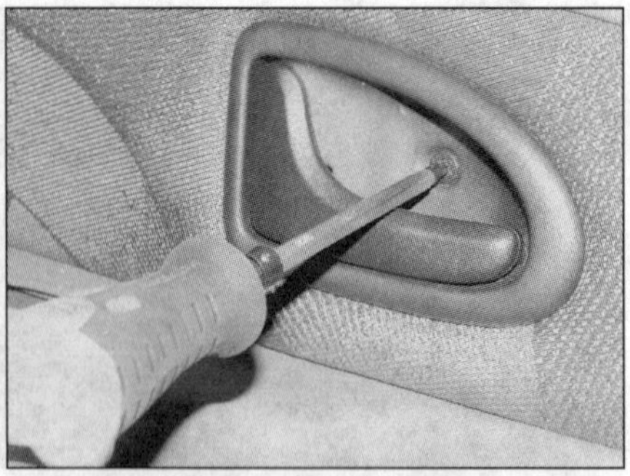

12.1 Remove the interior handle securing screw

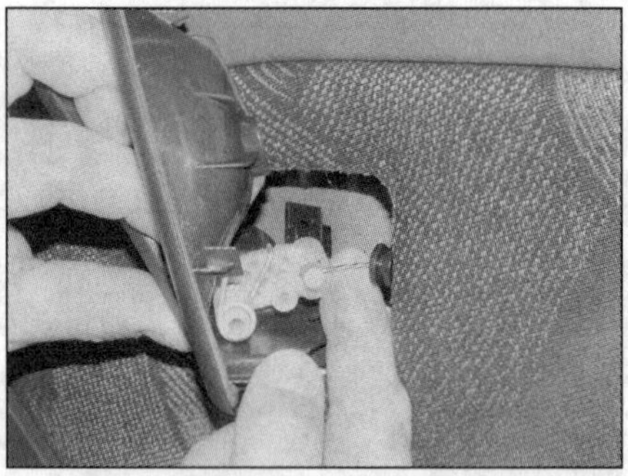

12.2 Disconnecting the operating cable from the front interior handle

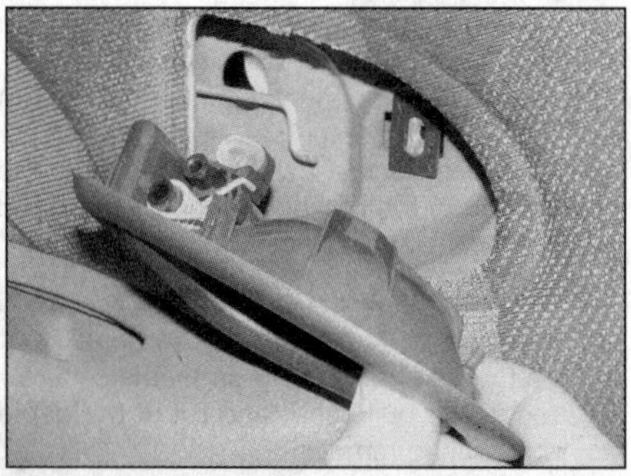

12.3 Disconnect the operating rod from the rear interior handle

12.7 Note the position of the retaining clip on the linkage rod before removal

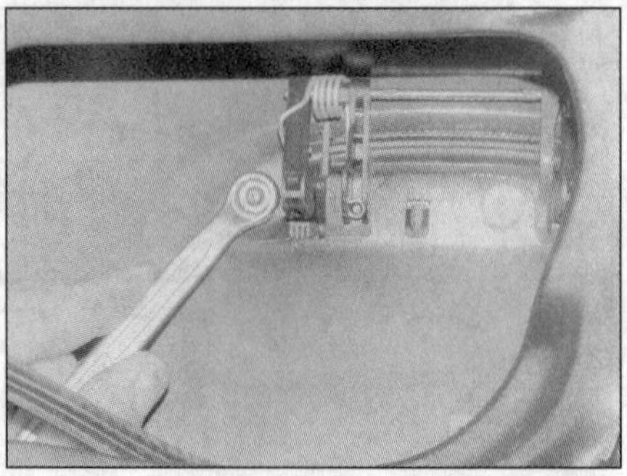

12.8 Removing the front door exterior handle securing nuts

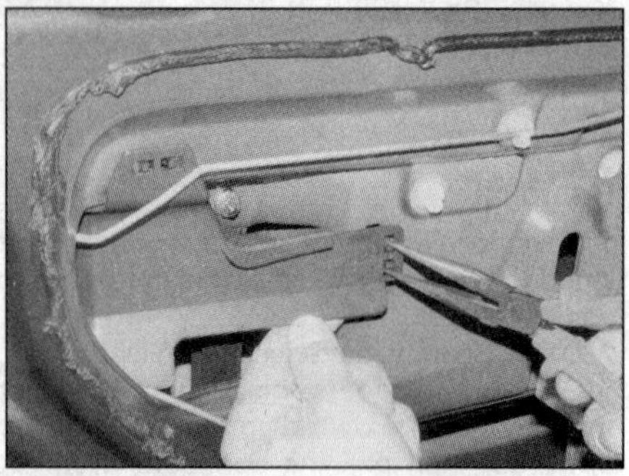

12.11 Unclipping the anti-theft cover from the door panel

12.13 Removing the rear door exterior handle securing nuts

12.16 Removing the three door lock securing screws

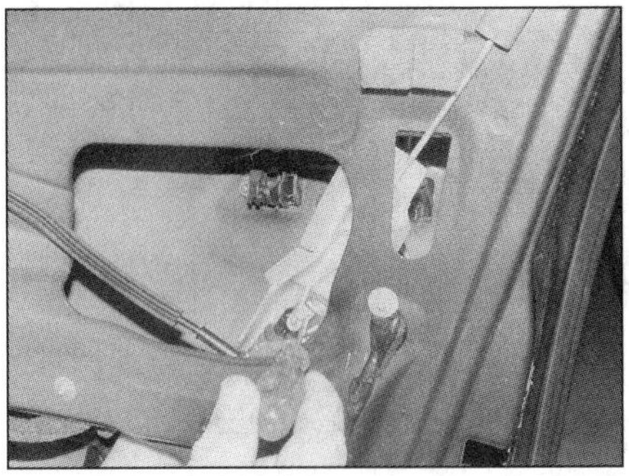

12.17 Releasing the door lock button/linkage rod retaining clip

Front door lock

Removal

15 Remove the door inner trim panel as described in Section 27.

16 Unscrew the three lock securing screws from the rear edge of the door **(see illustration)**.

17 Working inside the door, release the securing clips and disconnect the exterior handle operating rod and interior door handle cable from the lock assembly. Lift the lock button and operating rod from the door lock assembly **(see illustration)**.

18 On models fitted with central locking, disconnect the battery negative lead, if not already done, and disconnect the wiring plug(s) from the lock operating motor **(see illustration)**.

19 Twist the lock assembly, to release it from the control lever on the lock cylinder, then move the lock assembly downwards and out through the door aperture **(see illustration)**.

20 The anti-theft cover can be unclipped from the lock assembly when the lock assembly is removed **(see illustrations)**.

Refitting

21 Refitting is a reversal of removal, refitting the door inner trim panel as described in Section 27.

Rear door lock

Removal

22 Remove the door inner trim panel, as described in Section 27.

23 Unclip the anti-theft cover from the door (see illustration 12.11).

24 Working inside the door, release the securing clip, and disconnect the operating rod from the exterior door handle.

25 Unscrew the three lock securing screws from the rear edge of the door.

26 Disconnect the interior handle and lock button linkage rods and withdraw the lock assembly through the door aperture **(see illustration)**.

27 On models fitted with central locking, disconnect the battery negative lead. Disconnect the wiring plug from the lock operating motor as it is being withdrawn **(see illustration)**.

Refitting

28 Refitting is a reversal of removal, refitting the door inner trim panel as described in Section 27.

Front door lock cylinder

Removal

29 Remove the door inner trim panel, as described in Section 27.

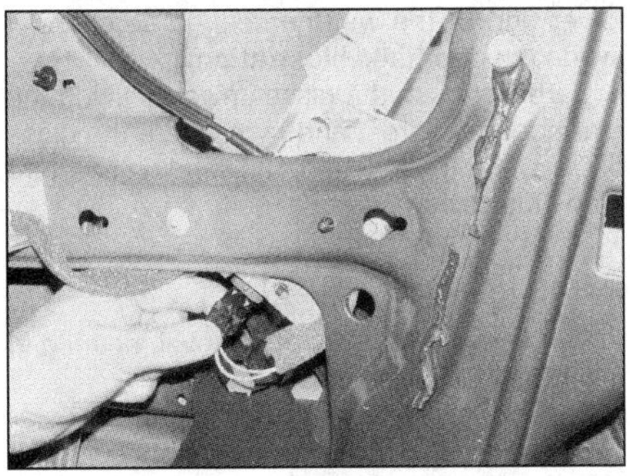

12.18 Disconnecting the wiring plug from the driver's door lock operating motor

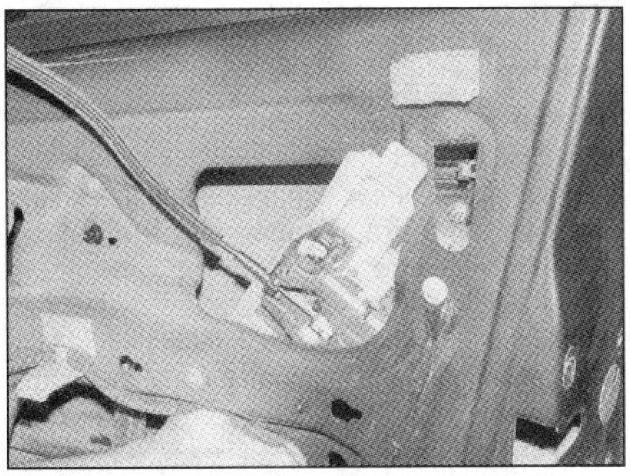

12.19 Removing a front door lock assembly from the door

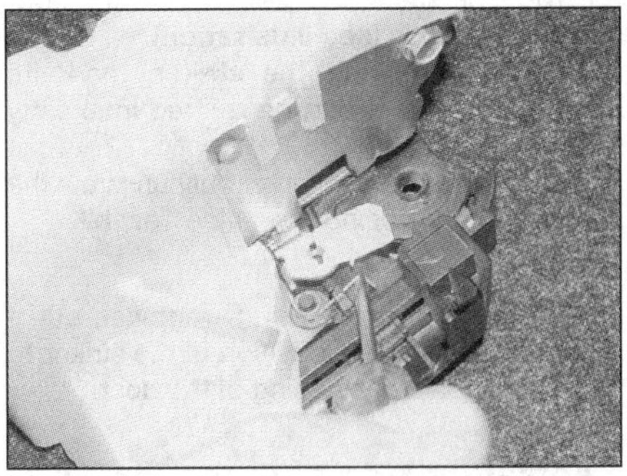

12.20a Unclip the spring from the lock assembly . . .

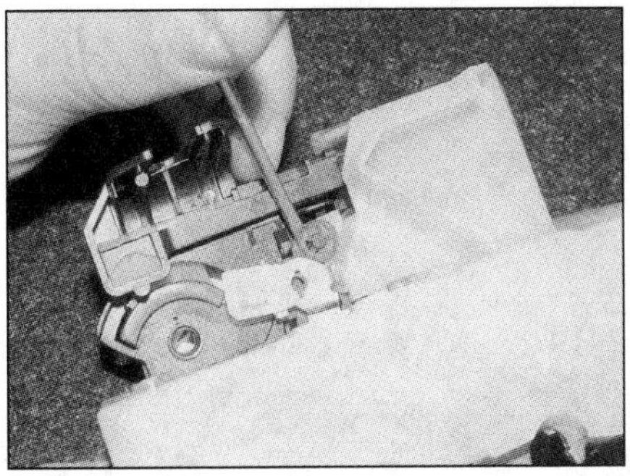

12.20b . . . then release the retaining clip to remove the anti-theft cover

12.26 Withdrawing a rear door lock from the door

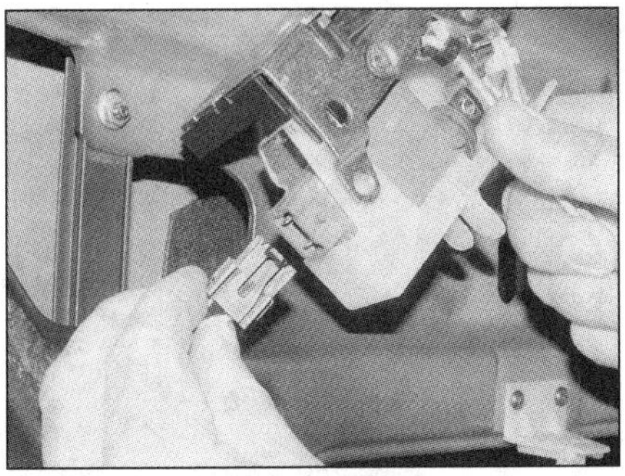

12.27 Disconnecting the wiring plug from the lock operating motor

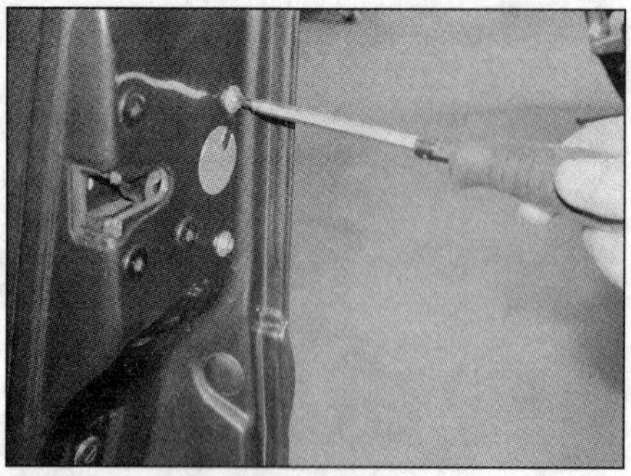

12.30a Undo the two securing screws . . .

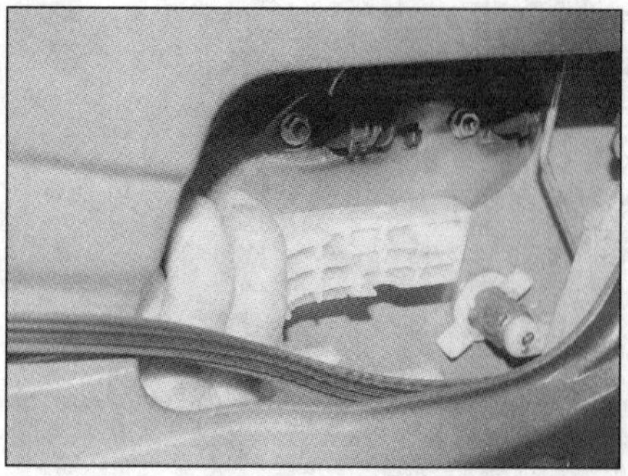

12.30b . . . and withdraw the anti-theft bracket

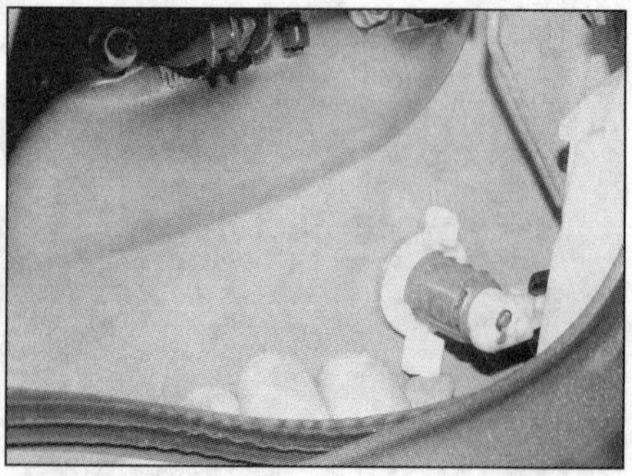

12.31a Remove the plastic retaining clip – turn anti-clockwise . . .

30 Unscrew the two securing screws from the rear edge of the door and from inside the door, remove the anti-theft bracket from around the lock cylinder **(see illustrations)**.

31 From inside the door, turn the retaining clip anti-clockwise to release the lock cylinder, then withdraw the lock cylinder from outside the door **(see illustrations)**.

Refitting

32 Refitting is a reversal of removal, bearing in mind the following points.

33 When refitting the lock cylinder, ensure that the lugs on the assembly engage with the corresponding cut-outs in the door panel.

34 Refit the door inner trim panel as described in Section 27.

Lock striker

Removal

35 The lock striker is screwed onto the door pillar on the body **(see illustration)**.

36 Before removing the striker, mark its position, so that it can be refitted in exactly the same place.

37 To remove the striker, simply unscrew the securing screws using a suitable Torx bit.

Refitting

38 Refitting is a reversal of removal, but if necessary, adjust the position of the striker to achieve satisfactory closing of the door.

Central locking components

39 Refer to Section 16.

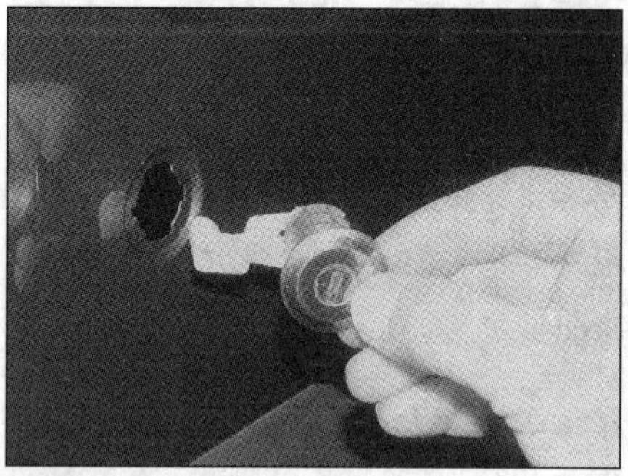

12.31b . . . and withdraw the lock cylinder

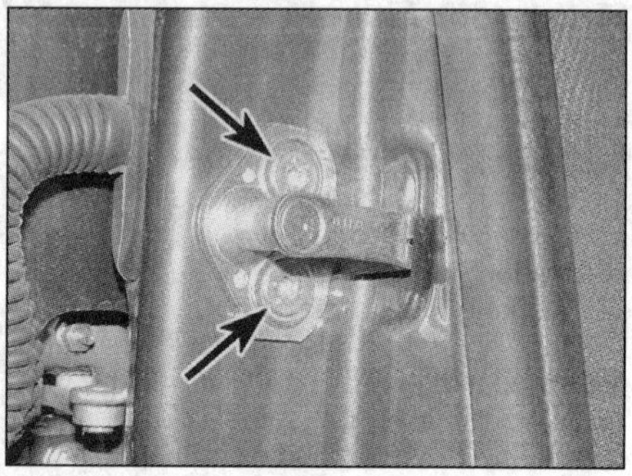

12.35 Lock striker securing screws (arrowed)

13 Door window glass and regulators – removal and refitting

Front door window

Removal

1 Remove the door inner trim panel, as described in Section 27.

2 Lower the window. On models with electric windows, temporarily reconnect the battery negative lead, and reconnect the wiring plug to the electric window operating switch, to enable the window to be lowered.

3 Carefully prise the weatherseal from the inner lower edge of the window aperture **(see illustration)**.

4 Remove the retaining clip from the rear of the window guide **(see illustration)**, then disengage the lug from the hole in the glass. Support the glass.

5 Working at the rear edge of the window glass, release the window pad guide (riveted to the rear upper edge of the glass). Carefully disengage the window pad guide from the lower end of the weatherseal/guide channel inside the door **(see illustration)**.

6 Carefully push the glass upwards tilting the rear edge forwards, and manipulate the glass out through the inside of the window aperture **(see illustration)**.

Refitting

7 Refitting is a reversal of removal, bearing in mind the following points.

8 Ensure that the guide plate at the rear upper edge of the glass is correctly engaged with the weatherseal/guide channel inside the door.

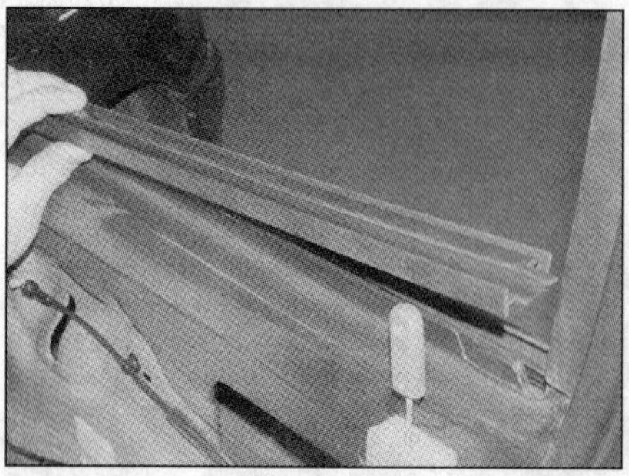

13.3 Unclip the inner sealing strip and remove it from the top of the door

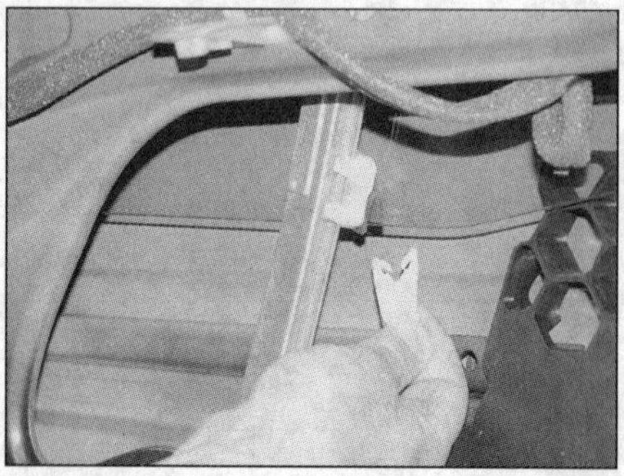

13.4 Removing the plastic clip securing the window glass to the guide block

13.5 Guide plate (arrowed) on front door window glass

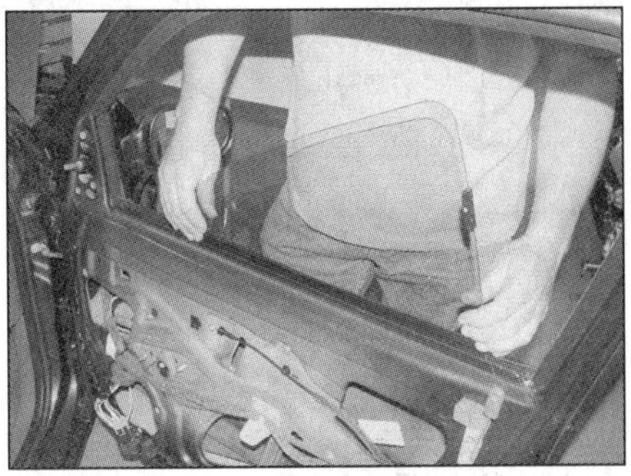
13.6 Removing the front door window glass

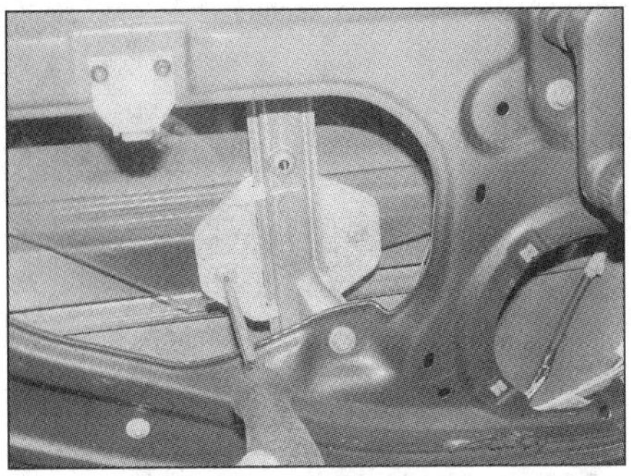
13.15 Removing a rear door window glass-to-regulator bracket securing screw

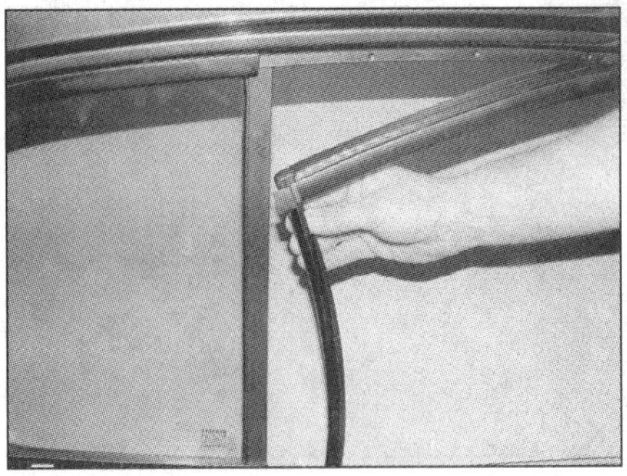
13.16 Removing the rubber seal from the window aperture

9 Before refitting the door inner trim panel, check the operation of the window mechanism, reconnecting the battery and the electric windows operating switch, or refitting the window winder handle, as applicable.
10 Refit the door inner trim panel as described in Section 27.

Rear door fixed window

Removal

11 Remove the door inner trim panel, as described in Section 27.
12 Lower the sliding window.
13 Carefully prise the inner and outer weatherseals from the lower edge of the window aperture.
14 Temporarily refit the window winder handle. Raise the window until the bolts securing the window glass to the regulator bracket are accessible.
15 If the original sliding glass is to be refitted, mark the positions of the two screws securing the window glass to the regulator bracket, then remove the screws and carefully lower the window glass into the door **(see illustration)**.
16 Carefully prise out the rubber guide seal from the window aperture in the door frame **(see illustration)**.
17 Remove the upper mounting bolt and lower mounting nut securing the window rear guide rail to the door. Support the fixed window glass, and carefully twist the guide rail and withdraw it through the window aperture **(see illustrations)**.
18 Carefully slide the fixed window glass from its location, complete with surrounding seal **(see illustration)**.

Refitting

19 Refitting is a reversal of removal, bearing in mind the following points.
20 When refitting the fixed window glass, ensure that the glass engages correctly with the seals around the edges of the window aperture.
21 Where applicable, refit the screws securing the sliding window glass to the regulator bracket in the positions marked before removal.
22 Make sure that the weatherseals are correctly located on the lower edge of the window aperture.
23 Before refitting the door inner trim panel, temporarily refit the window winder handle, and check the operation of the regulator mechanism. If necessary, the alignment of the glass can be adjusted by altering the position of the bolts securing the window glass to the regulator bracket, using the elongated holes provided.
24 Refit the door inner trim panel, as described in Section 27.

Rear door sliding window

Removal

25 Carry out the procedures in paragraphs 11 to 17, as described earlier in this Section.
26 With the fixed window glass left in position, carefully lift the sliding window glass out through the inside of the window aperture.

Refitting

27 Lower the window glass into the door, then refit as described earlier in this Section.

Front door regulator

Removal

28 Remove the door inner trim panel, as described in Section 27.
29 Remove the front door window glass as described earlier in this Section (or slide the glass up to the top of the window frame and tape in position).
30 On models fitted with electric windows, disconnect the wiring plug from the electric window motor **(see illustration)**.
31 Remove the three nuts securing the regulator assembly, and the two bolts securing the window guide rail to the door **(see illustrations)**.

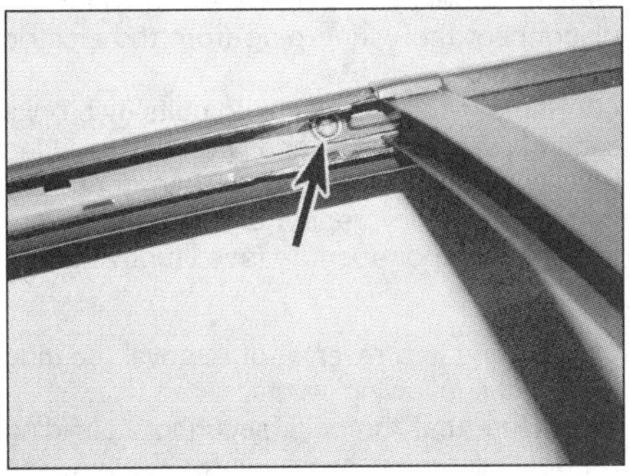
13.17a Remove the upper Torx screw inside the window channel (arrowed) . . .

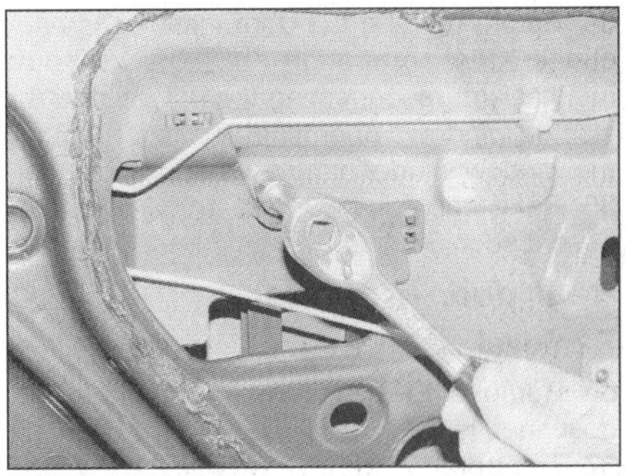
13.17b . . . and the lower securing nut, then withdraw the window guide rail

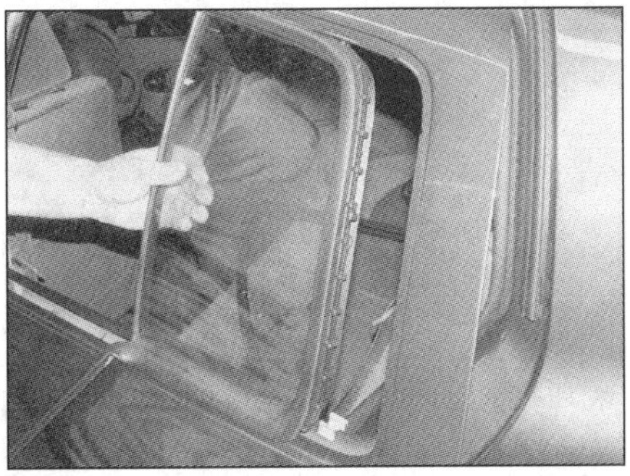
13.18 Removing the fixed rear window glass, complete with seal

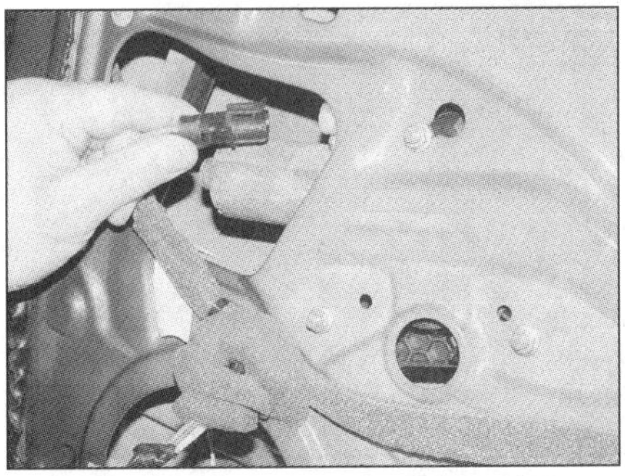
13.30 Disconnecting the wiring block connector from the electric window motor

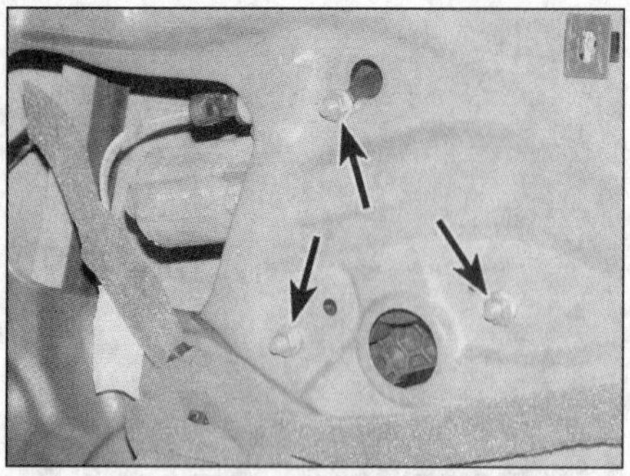

13.31a Remove the three motor securing nuts (arrowed) . . .

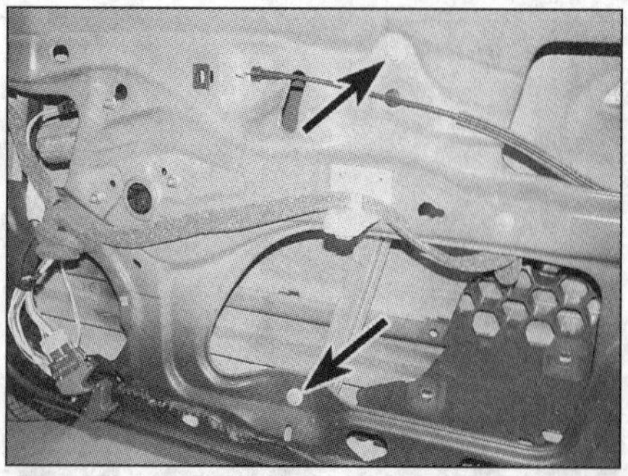

13.31b . . . and the two guide rail securing bolts (arrowed)

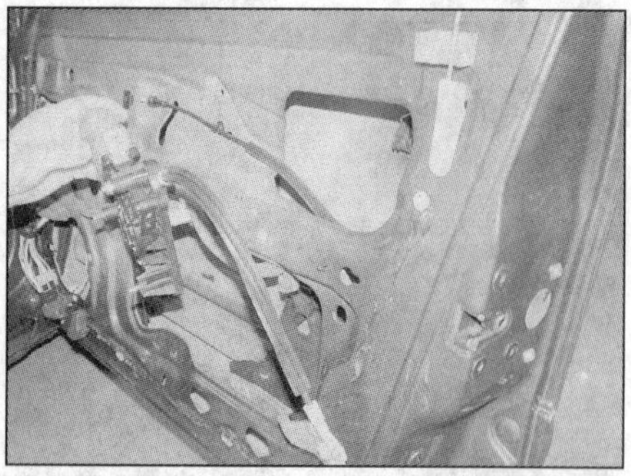

13.32 Removing the front door window regulator assembly

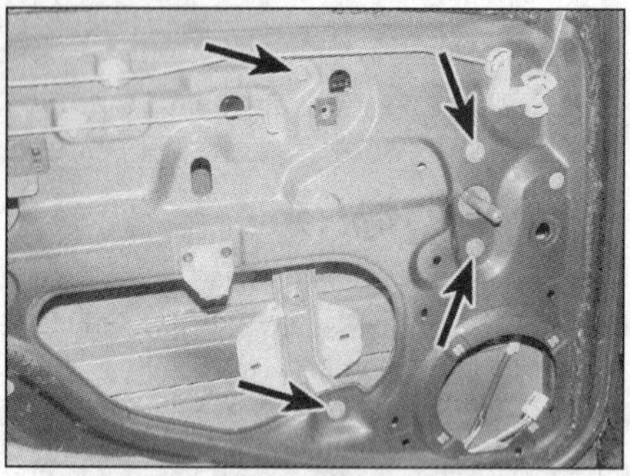

13.40a Rear door window regulator assembly securing bolts (arrowed)

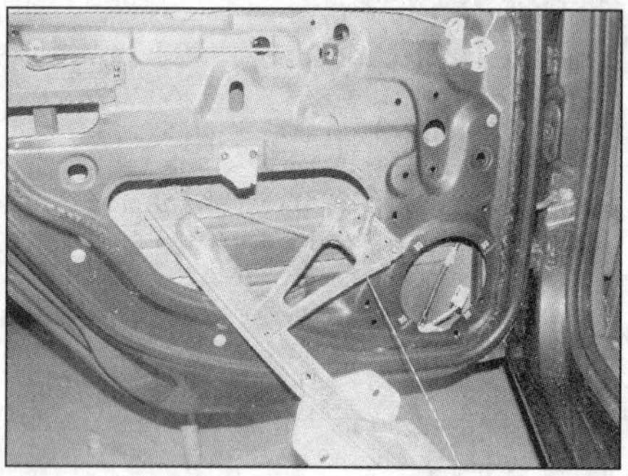

13.40b Removing the rear door window regulator mechanism

32 Carefully manipulate the window regulator assembly out through the lower aperture in the door **(see illustration)**.

Refitting

33 Refitting is a reversal of removal, bearing in mind the following points.

34 Before refitting the door inner trim panel, check the operation of the window mechanism, reconnecting the battery and the electric windows operating switch, or refitting the window winder handle, as applicable.

35 Refit the door inner trim panel as described in Section 27.

Rear door regulator

Removal

36 Remove the door inner trim panel, as described in Section 27.

37 Temporarily refit the window winder handle. Lower the window glass until the screws securing the window glass to the regulator bracket are accessible.

38 Mark the positions of the screws securing the window glass to the regulator bracket, then remove the screws and lower the window glass. To give more room for removal, slide the glass up to the top of the window frame and tape in position.

39 On models fitted with electric windows, disconnect the wiring plug from the electric window motor.

40 Remove the four securing bolts (two bolts securing the regulator, and two bolts securing the window guide rail), then carefully manipulate the regulator assembly out through the door aperture **(see illustrations)**.

Refitting

41 Refitting is a reversal of removal, bearing in mind the following points.

42 Ensure that the bolts securing the sliding window glass to the regulator bracket are refitted in their original positions marked before removal.

43 Before refitting the door inner trim panel, check the operation of the window mechanism, reconnecting the battery and the electric windows operating switch, or refitting the window winder handle, as applicable.

44 If necessary, the alignment of the glass can be adjusted by altering the position of the bolts securing the window glass to the regulator bracket, using the elongated holes provided.

45 Refit the door inner trim panel as described in Section 27.

Electric window components

46 The motors are an integral part of the window regulator assemblies, and cannot be renewed independently.

47 Removal and refitting of the regulator assemblies are described in this Section. Refer to Section 17 for the switches.

14 Tailgate, hinges and support struts – removal and refitting

Tailgate

Removal

1 Disconnect the battery negative lead.

2 Open the tailgate.

3 Undo the retaining screw from the right-hand side of the tailgate inner trim panel, then carefully pull the trim panel from the tailgate. If necessary, release the trim clips using a suitable forked tool.

4 Disconnect the wiring from the heated rear window, tailgate wiper motor, and central locking motor, as applicable.

5 Undo the rear spoiler securing screws and remove spoiler as described in Section 22. Disconnect the high-level stop-light and washer fluid hose, where applicable; be prepared for fluid spillage.

6 Release the wiring loom and hose grommets from the edge of the tailgate **(see illustration)**. Tie string to the wiring loom and hose, and pull them through the edge of the tailgate. Leave the string in position in the tailgate, to aid refitting.

7 Have an assistant support the tailgate. Disconnect the support struts from the tailgate by prising out the retaining clips using a screwdriver **(see illustration)**.

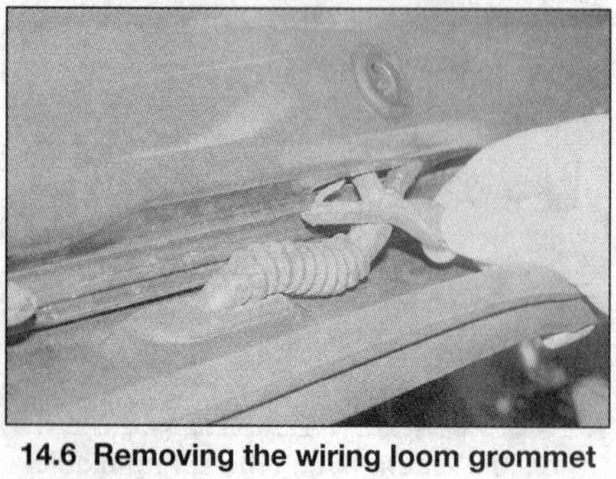

14.6 Removing the wiring loom grommet

14.7 Prising out a tailgate support strut securing clip

14.9 Undo the two tailgate securing nuts

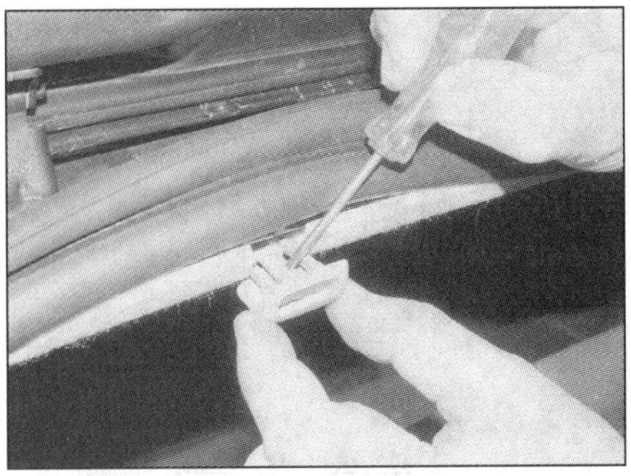

14.10a Prise out the plastic clip . . .

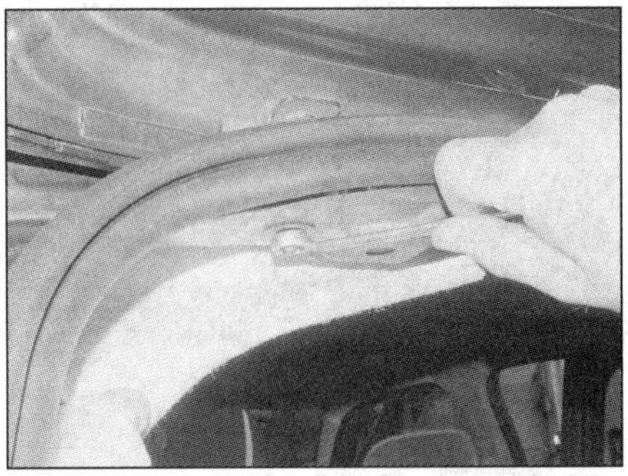

14.10b . . . and pull down the headlining to undo the hinge securing nuts

8 If the original tailgate is to be refitted, mark the positions of the securing nuts on the tailgate.
9 Unscrew the two nuts from under the spoiler **(see illustration)**, and carefully withdraw the tailgate from the vehicle.
10 To remove the hinges, prise the plastic clips from the headlining for access to the tailgate hinge securing nuts **(see illustrations)**.

Refitting

11 Refitting is a reversal of removal, but where applicable, fit the tailgate securing nuts in their original positions, as noted before removal. Do not fully tighten the tailgate securing nuts until the top of the tailgate is aligned correctly with the roof panel and the rear body pillars.
12 On completion, if adjustment of the tailgate lower edge alignment is required, adjust the tailgate lock striker on the lower body panel.
13 Alter the position of the lock striker on the body (by means of the elongated screw holes) to give correct alignment of the lower edge of the tailgate with the surrounding body panels.

Hinges

14 The tailgate hinges can be removed as described in paragraph 10.

Support struts

Removal

15 Open the tailgate, and have an assistant support it in the fully-open position.
16 Disconnect the support strut from the tailgate by prising out the securing clip using a suitable screwdriver (see illustration 14.7).
17 Repeat the procedure for the clip securing the strut to the body, and withdraw the strut from the vehicle.

Refitting

18 Refitting is a reversal of removal.

15 Tailgate lock components - removal and refitting

Lock

Removal

1 Disconnect the battery negative lead.
2 Open the tailgate.
3 Undo the retaining screw from the right-hand side of the tailgate inner trim panel, then carefully pull the trim panel from the tailgate. If necessary, release the trim clips using a suitable forked tool.
4 Unhook the linkage rod from the lock assembly **(see illustration)** and disconnect the wiring connector (where fitted).
5 Slacken and remove the two securing screws and remove the lock from the tailgate, withdrawing the linkage rod and wiring with it **(see illustrations)**.

Refitting

6 Refitting is a reversal of removal.

Lock cylinder

Removal

7 Proceed as described in paragraphs 1 to 3.
8 Unclip the lock control linkage rod and disconnect the wiring connector from the central locking motor. Also disconnect the drain tube from the lock assembly **(see illustration)**.
9 Undo the two lock securing screws, then unclip the lock cylinder assembly/motor from the plastic surround **(see illustrations)**.

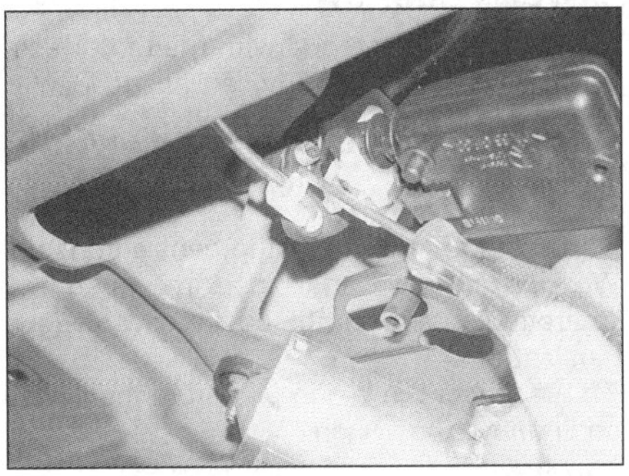

15.4 Unclipping the linkage rod from the lock cylinder

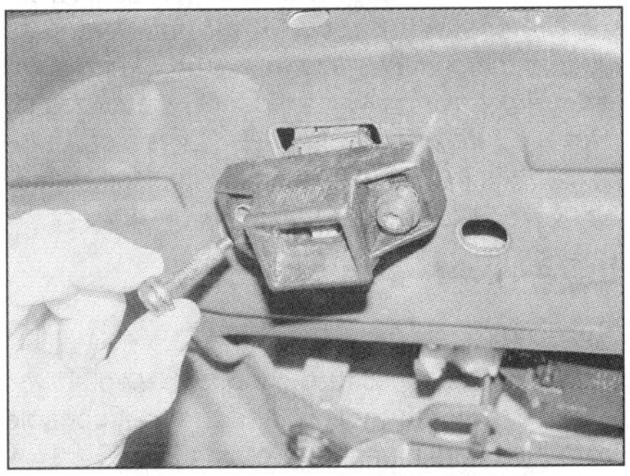

15.5a Remove the lock securing screws . . .

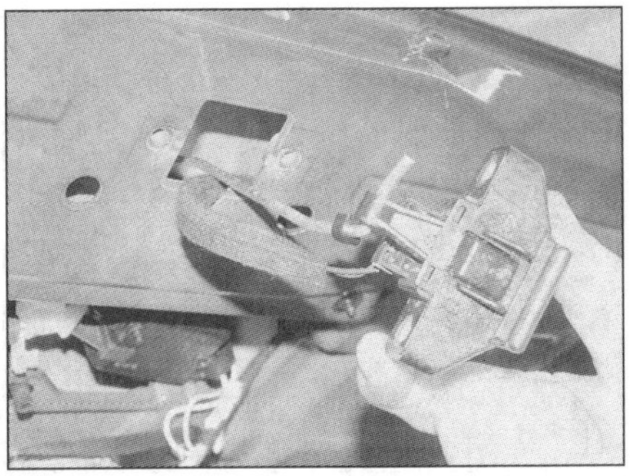

15.5b . . . and withdraw the lock

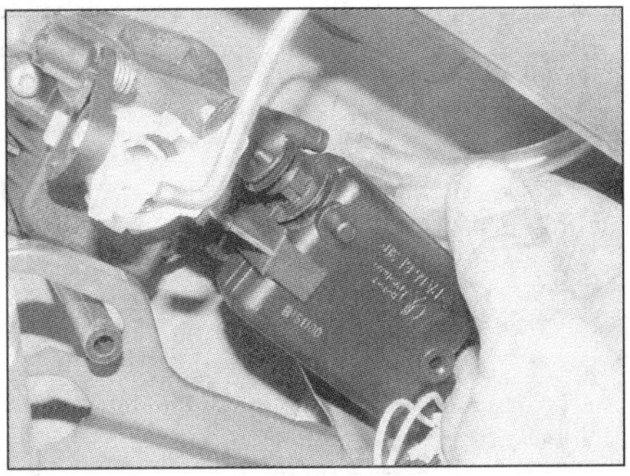

15.8 Disengaging the drain tube from the lock cylinder assembly

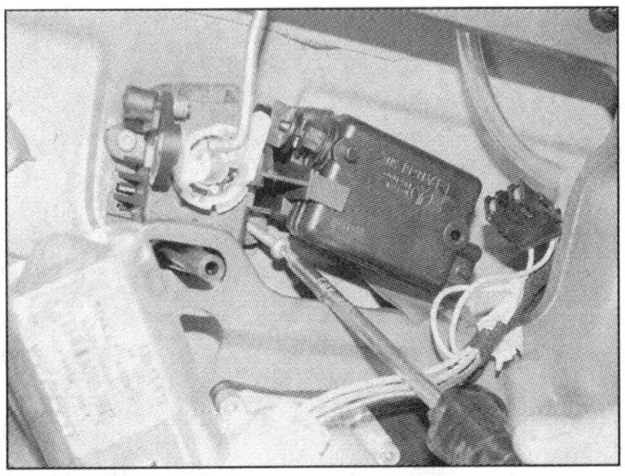

15.9a Undo the two retaining screws . . .

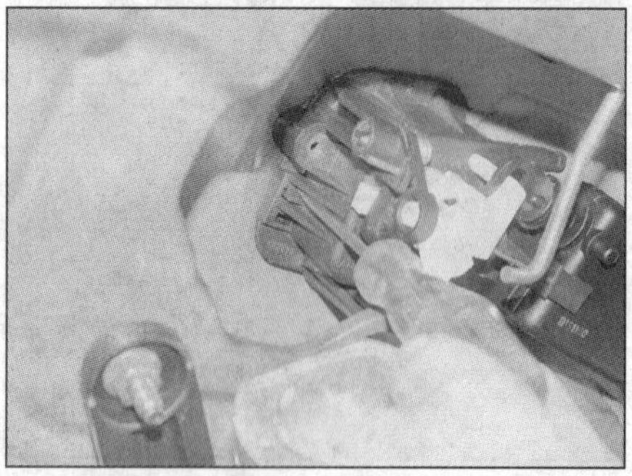

15.9b . . . then using a small screwdriver, unclip the lock cylinder assembly from the plastic surround

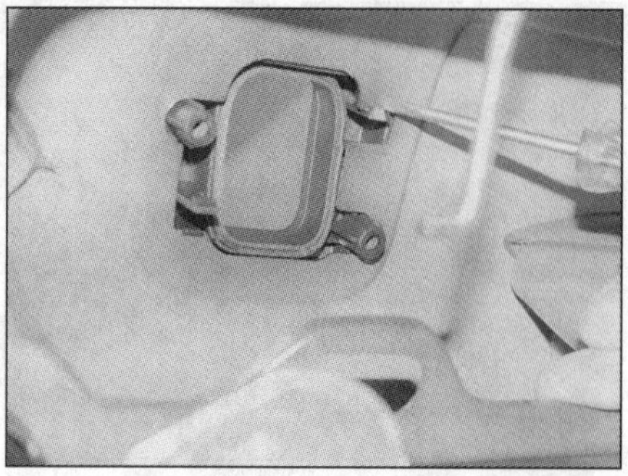

15.10a Unclipping the lock cylinder plastic surround . . .

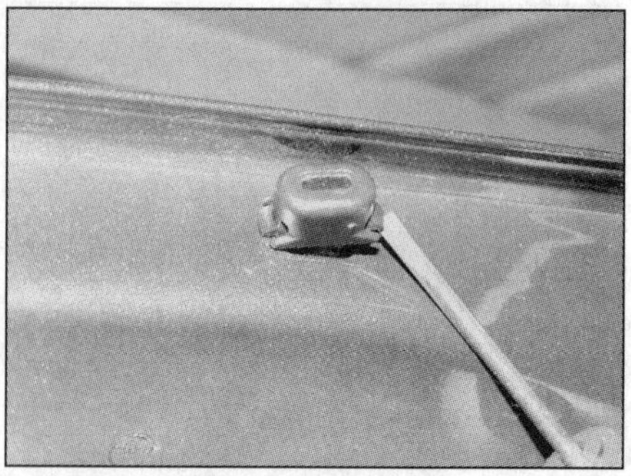

15.10b . . . and prising out the drain tube from the lower edge of the tailgate

10 The lock cylinder plastic surround and drain tube can be unclipped from the tailgate **(see illustration)**.

Refitting

11 Refitting is a reversal of removal.

Lock striker

Removal

12 The lock striker is attached to the lower body panel.

13 Remove the four securing screws, and withdraw the rear trim from the rear body panel.

14 Remove the mounting bolt now exposed and withdraw the lock striker assembly **(see illustration)**.

Refitting

15 Refitting is a reversal of removal, but if necessary adjust the position of the striker **(see illustration)** (by means of the elongated bolt hole) to achieve satisfactory alignment of the bottom of the tailgate with the surrounding body panels.

Central locking components

16 Refer to Section 16.

16 Central locking components – removal and refitting

Note: *There are two types of central locking, infra-red and radio frequency. In the infra-red type the receiver is fitted into the roof console, and can be removed as described in this Section. The radio frequency type is controlled by the Multi-timer unit, which also holds a number of relays. It is located under the left-hand side of the facia (as seen from the driver's seat) above the bonnet release lever. If there is a fault with this unit, then it will require checking by your local Renault dealer. (**Note:** There are four different types of Multi-timer units available, depending on the equipment level of the vehicle – see Chapter 12).*

15.14 Removing the mounting bolt from the tailgate lock striker

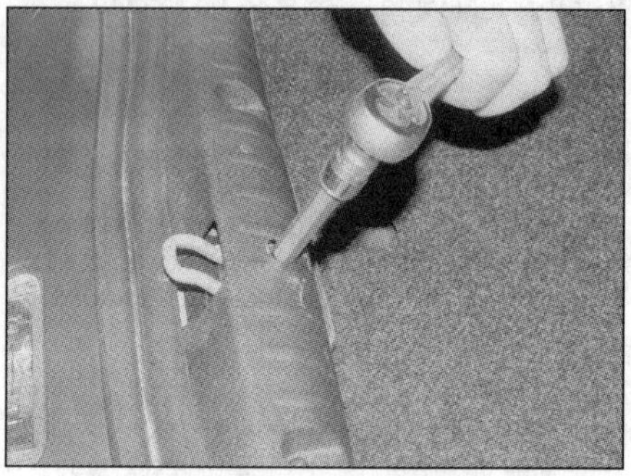

15.15 Adjusting the lock striker without removing the trim panel

Infra-red receiver

Removal

1 Disconnect the battery negative lead.

2 Unclip the interior light and the roof console from the headlining (see Section 27)

3 Carefully unclip the receiver unit, and pull it from its location in the roof console **(see illustration)**. Disconnect the wiring plug on removal of the unit.

Refitting

4 Refitting is a reversal of removal.

Driver's door switch

5 The switch is integral with the motor assembly, and cannot be removed independently.

Centre console-mounted switch

Removal

6 Pull the ashtray from the centre console. Working through the aperture, push the cigarette lighter from the centre console **(see illustrations)**.

7 Disconnect the wiring plug from the switch and remove the switch.

Refitting

8 Refit by reversing the removal operations.

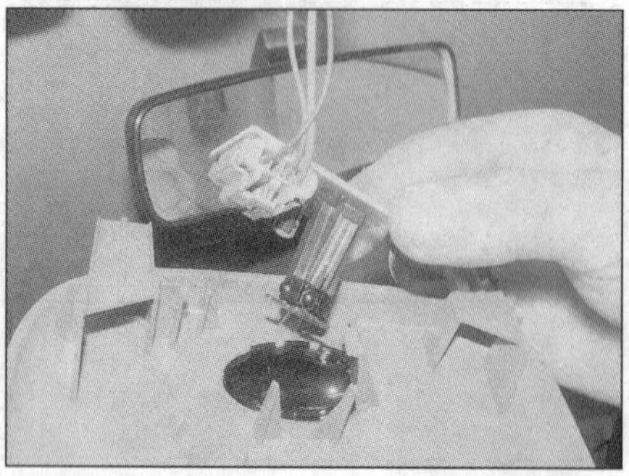

16.3 Unclipping the central locking remote control receiver (infra-red type)

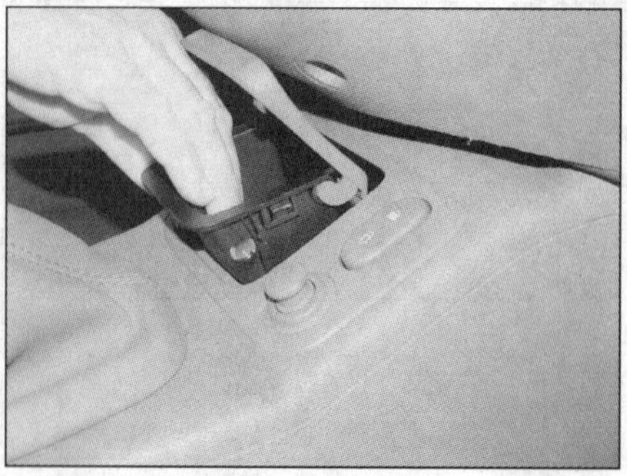

16.6a Remove the ashtray from the centre console . . .

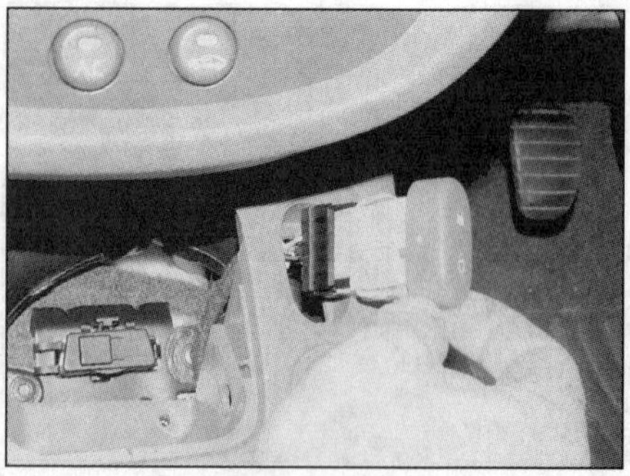

16.6b . . . and withdraw the central locking switch

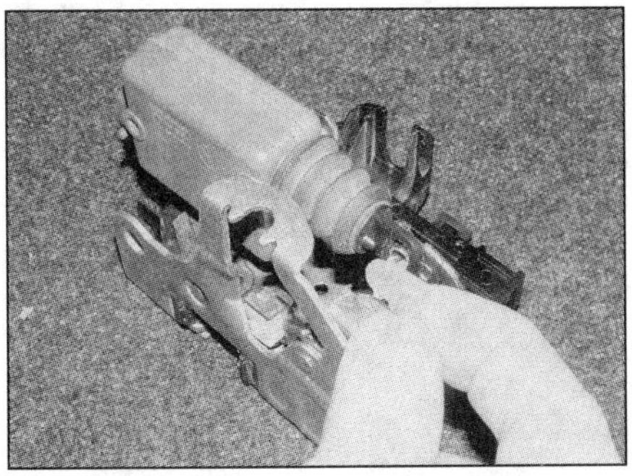

16.11 Removing the clip securing the lock operating rod to the central locking motor

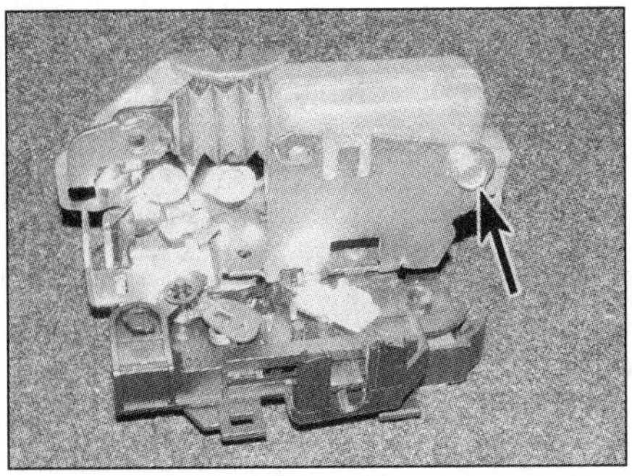

16.12 Motor securing screw (arrowed)

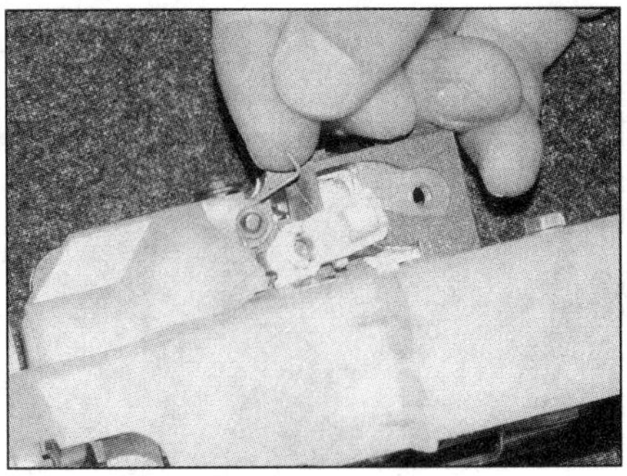

16.16a Release the spring clip . . .

Front door lock motor

Removal

9 Remove the door lock (see Section 12).

10 Unclip the spring and locking washer to release the anti-theft cover from the lock assembly (see illustrations 12.20a and 12.20b).

11 Remove the securing clip for the operating rod on the motor operating lever **(see illustration)**.

12 Undo the single bolt securing the motor to the lock assembly **(see illustration)**, then withdraw the motor from the operating lever.

Refitting

13 Refitting is a reversal of removal. Refit the door lock as described in Section 12.

Rear door lock motor

Removal

14 Remove the door lock (see Section 12).

15 Disconnect the linkage rods from the lock assembly.

16 Unclip the spring to release the anti-theft cover from the lock assembly **(see illustrations)**.

17 Undo the single bolt securing the motor to the lock assembly, then withdraw the motor from the operating lever **(see illustrations)**.

Refitting

18 Refitting is a reversal of removal. Refit the door lock as described in Section 12.

Tailgate lock motor

Removal

19 Disconnect the battery negative lead.

20 Open the tailgate. Remove the tailgate lock as described in Section 15.

21 Remove the single bolt securing the motor to the tailgate lock cylinder assembly, then withdraw the motor. Push the lock cylinder in, to release the motor operating lever **(see illustrations)**.

Refitting

22 Refitting is a reversal of removal. Refit the tailgate lock as described in Section 15.

17 Electric window components - removal and refitting

Switches in speaker housing

Removal

1 Disconnect the battery negative lead.

2 Unclip the speaker cover from the door trim panel.

3 Disconnect the wiring plug(s) and withdraw the switches out through the top of the door trim **(see illustrations)**.

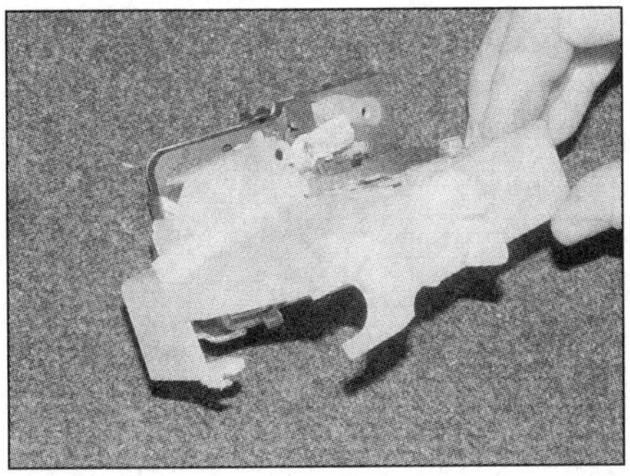

16.16b . . . and withdraw the anti-theft cover

16.17a Undo the bolt securing the central locking motor to the lock assembly . . .

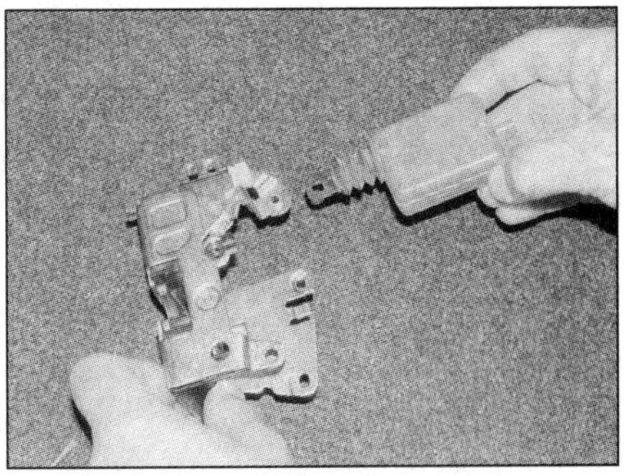

16.17b . . . then unhook the motor from the lock operating lever

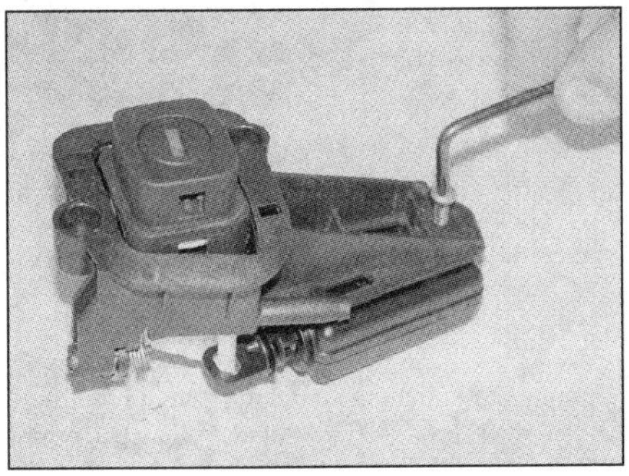

16.21a Remove the tailgate central locking motor securing screw . . .

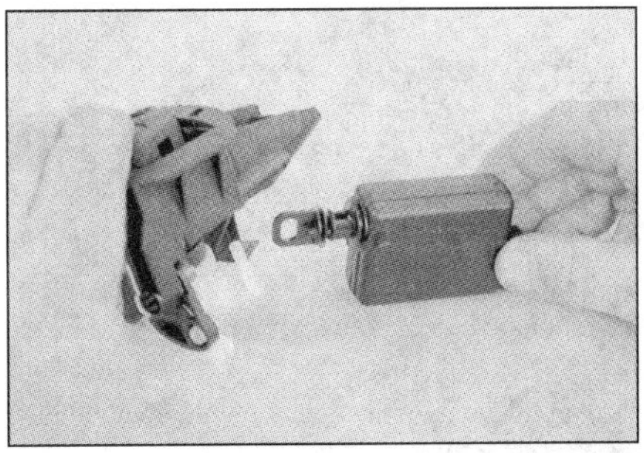

16.21b . . . then press the lock cylinder in, to release the motor from the operating lever

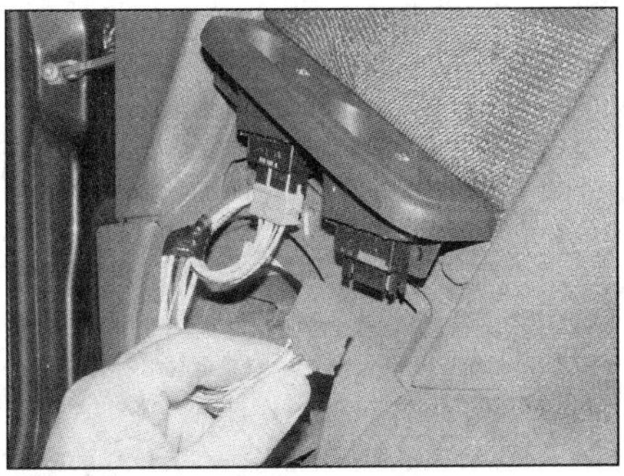

17.3a Disconnect the wiring plugs . . .

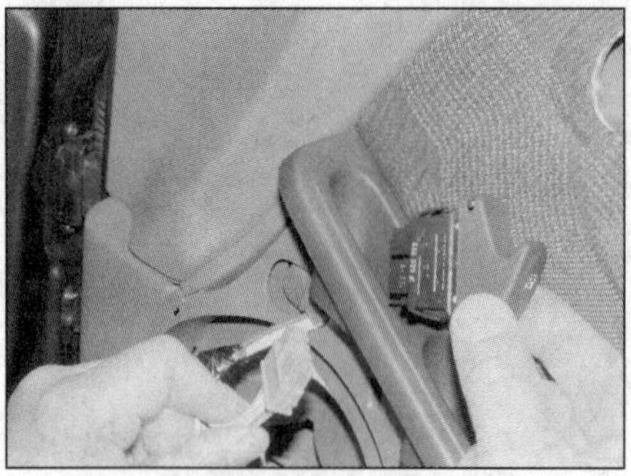

17.3b . . . and withdraw the switches from the door trim

Refitting

4 Refitting is a reversal of removal.

Switches in door handle

Removal

5 Disconnect the battery negative lead.

6 Remove the securing screw in the door grab handle, then carefully lift and pull back the handle to release it from the door.

7 Disconnect the wiring plug(s) and withdraw the switches out through the top of the trim.

Refitting

8 Refitting is a reversal of removal.

Operating motors

9 The motors are an integral part of the window regulator assemblies, and cannot be renewed independently.

10 Removal and refitting of the regulator assemblies are described in Section 13.

18 Mirrors – removal, refitting and glass renewal

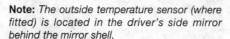

Note: *The outside temperature sensor (where fitted) is located in the driver's side mirror behind the mirror shell.*

Door mirror

Removal

1 On models fitted with electric mirrors, disconnect the battery negative lead.

2 Prise the plastic grommet from the front edge of the door to expose the mirror front lower securing screw **(see illustration)**.

3 Carefully prise the mirror trim panel from the front edge of the door **(see illustration)**.

4 Undo the two retaining screws now exposed and the one from behind the grommet **(see illustration)**.

5 On models fitted with electrically-operated mirrors, unplug the wiring connector from the mirror.

6 Withdraw the mirror from the door, by lifting it upwards and releasing it from the door frame **(see illustration)**.

Refitting

7 Refitting is a reversal of removal.

Glass renewal

8 Using a flat-bladed tool, carefully prise behind the top edge of the mirror glass.

9 Support the glass, and lever the tool forwards and the mirror glass will unclip from the mirror assembly **(see illustrations)**.

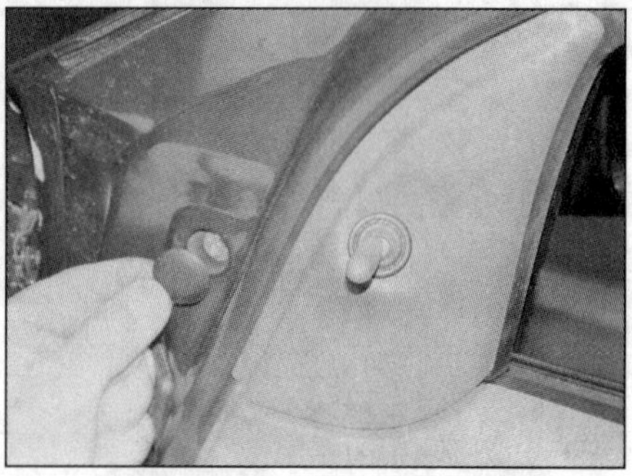

18.2 Unclipping the grommet to locate the mirror front securing screw

10 Take care not to drop the mirror glass as the clip is released.

11 To refit the glass, press the glass into position until it engages securely **(see illustration)**, taking care not to damage the glass.

Shell renewal

12 Remove the mirror glass as described in this Section.

13 Release the retaining clips from the inside of the mirror assembly and remove the mirror shell **(see illustrations)**.

Electric mirror switch

14 The switch is located in the driver's door armrest, with the electric window switches.

15 The procedure is as described for the electric window switches in Section 17.

Electric mirror motor

16 The motor is not available separately from

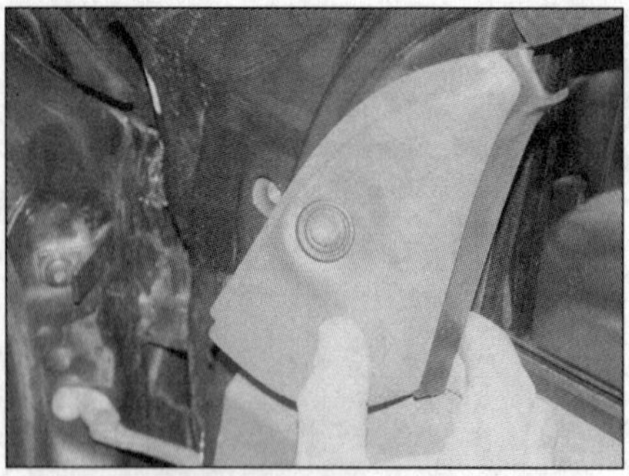

18.3 Removing the mirror trim panel (manual adjustable mirror)

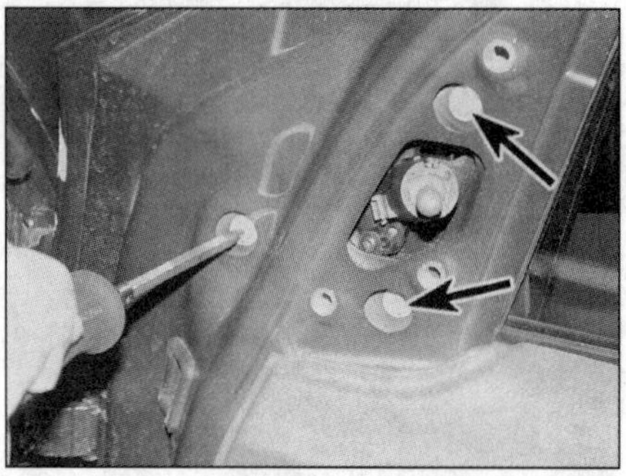

18.4 Undo the front securing screw and the two screws arrowed

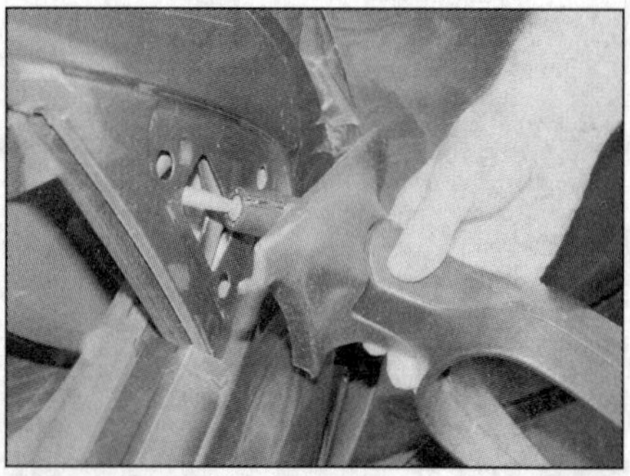

18.6 Withdrawing a manually-adjustable mirror

18.9a Carefully lever the mirror glass from its retaining clips . . .

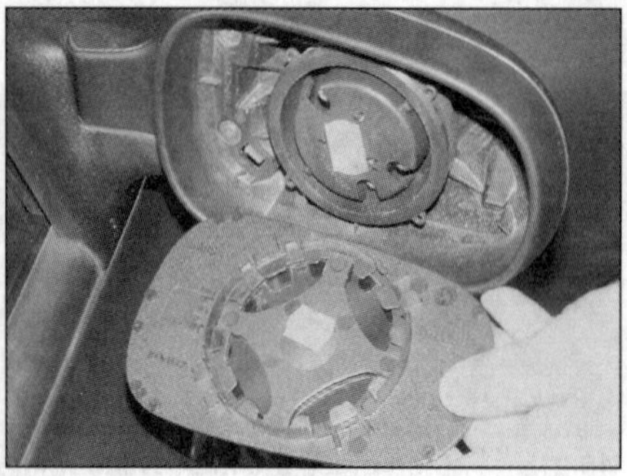

18.9b . . . and withdraw the glass

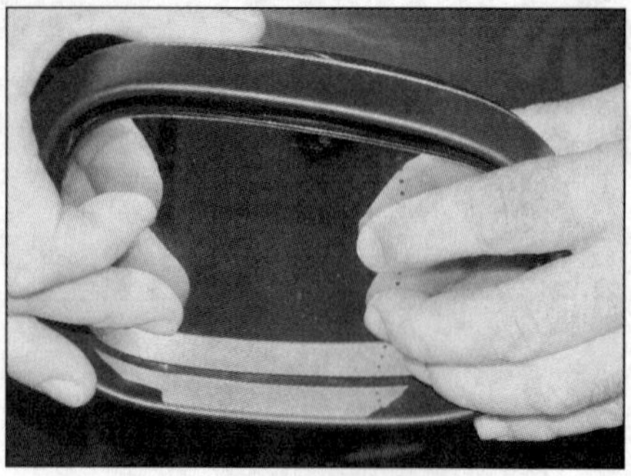

18.11 Carefully press the glass into position to secure the retaining clips

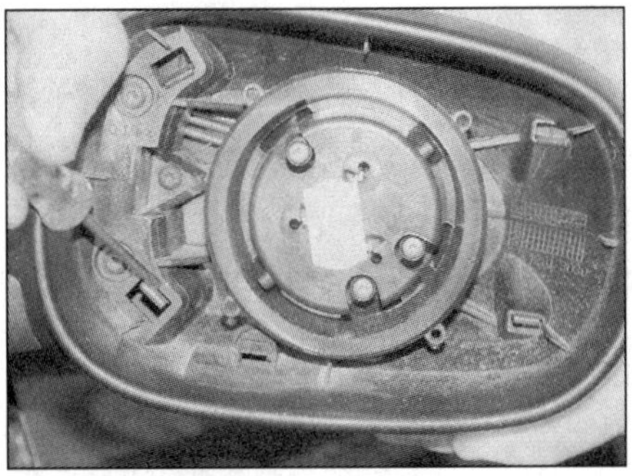

18.13a Releasing the retaining clips using a small screwdriver . . .

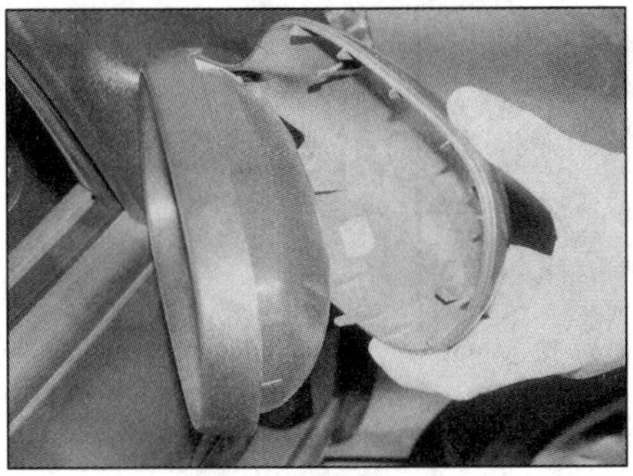

18.13b . . . and withdrawing the mirror shell

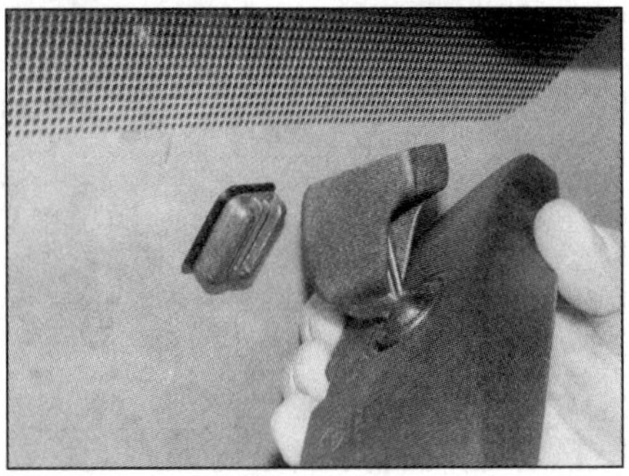

18.17 Lift the interior mirror from its mounting bracket

the mirror. If it is faulty, the complete mirror assembly must be renewed.

Interior mirror

Removal

17 The mirror can be removed by carefully lifting it upwards from the mounting bracket attached to the windscreen **(see illustration)**.

18 The mounting bracket is fixed to the windscreen using a special adhesive, and should not be disturbed unless absolutely necessary. Note that there is a risk of cracking the windscreen glass if an attempt is made to remove a securely-bonded mounting bracket.

Refitting

19 Refitting is a reversal of removal. If necessary, the special adhesive required to fix the mounting bracket to the windscreen can be obtained from a Renault dealer.

19 Windscreen and tailgate window glass – general information

1 The windscreen and the tailgate window glass are bonded in position using a special adhesive. Special tools, adhesives and expertise are required for successful removal and refitting of glass fixed by this method. Such work must therefore be entrusted to a Renault dealer, a windscreen specialist, or other competent professional.

20 Rear quarter window components – removal and refitting

1 The fixed rear quarter window glass is bonded in position using a special adhesive. Special tools, adhesives and expertise are required for successful removal and refitting of glass fixed by this method. Such work must therefore be entrusted to a Renault dealer, a windscreen specialist, or other competent professional.

21 Sunroof components – removal and refitting

Manual sunroof

Glass panel

1 Open the sunroof to its first stage, then press the red button on the handle to release it from the locating pin **(see illustration)**.

2 Lift the glass almost vertically, and unhook the hinges from the front of the sunroof frame **(see illustration)**. Lift the glass panel from the roof taking care not to damage it.

3 Refitting is a reversal of removal.

Handle and hinges

4 Remove the glass panel as described in paragraphs 1 and 2 of this Section.

5 Undo the two securing screws and remove the handle assembly from the glass panel.

6 Unclip the plastic covers, then undo the securing screws, and withdraw the hinges from the glass panel.

7 Refitting is a reversal of removal.

Electric sunroof

8 This type of sunroof is a complex piece of equipment, consisting of a large number of components. It is strongly recommended that the sunroof mechanism is not disturbed unless absolutely necessary. If the sunroof mechanism is faulty, or requires overhaul, consult a Renault dealer for advice.

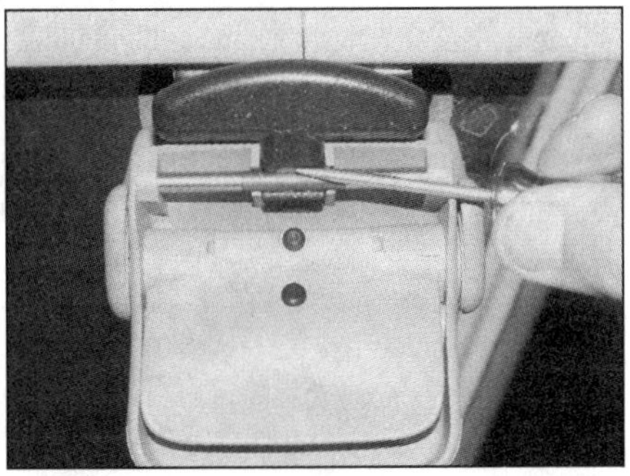

21.1 Press the red button in to release the handle assembly

21.2 Unhook the hinges from the front of the sunroof frame

22 Body exterior fittings – removal and refitting

Splash shields and wheelarch liners

1 Various plastic shields may be fitted to the wheelarches and various engine components to protect against road dirt and moisture.

2 The shields are secured by a combination of plastic clips, screws, nuts or pop-rivets. Removal and refitting should be self-evident. Take particular care not to break plastic clips when removing them. Renew any pop-rivets on refitting where necessary.

Rubbing strips

Note: *Take care not to damage the paintwork when removing the rubbing strips.*

Front door

3 Open the door, and remove the plastic cover from the rear edge of the door to expose the rubbing strip securing screw. Remove the screw (where fitted).

4 Working outside the door, unclip the end of the rubbing strip and push it towards the rear of the door **(see illustrations)**.

5 To refit a rubbing strip, align the clips in the strip with the corresponding holes in the door. Push the strip towards the front of the door to engage the holes.

6 On completion, refit the securing screw (where fitted) and its plastic cover.

Rear door

7 Open the door, and remove the plastic

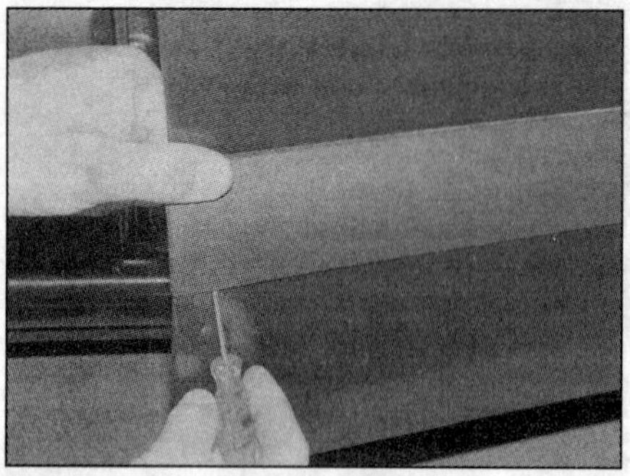

22.4a Use a small screwdriver to unclip the door rubbing strip . . .

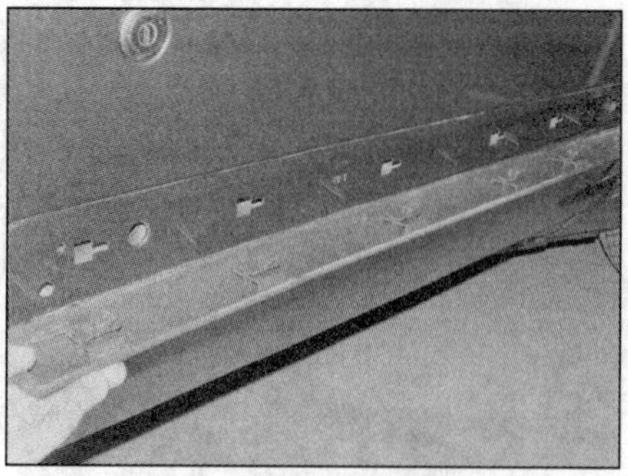

22.4b . . . then slide rubbing strip towards the rear of the door to remove

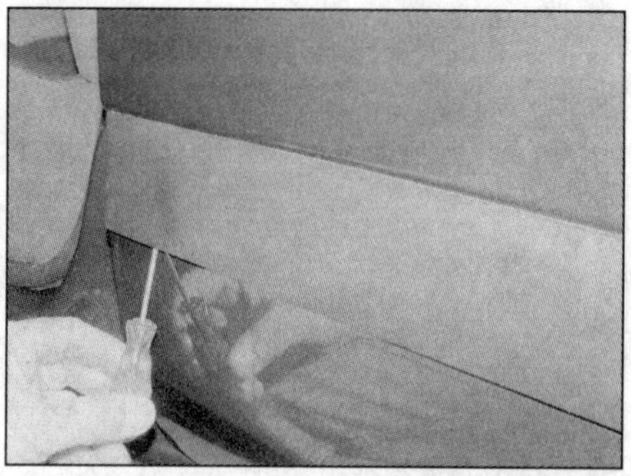

22.8 Using a small screwdriver to unclip the front of the door rubbing strip

cover from the front edge of the door to expose the rubbing strip securing screw. Remove the screw (where fitted).

8 Working outside the door, unclip the end of the rubbing strip and push it towards the front of the door **(see illustration)**.

9 To refit a rubbing strip, align the clips in the strip with the corresponding holes in the door. Push the strip towards the rear of the door to engage the holes.

10 On completion, refit the securing screw (where fitted) and its plastic cover.

Rear quarter panel (3-door)

11 Unclip the front retaining clip for the rubbing strip, then gently tap the rubbing strip towards the front of the vehicle to release it from its remaining clips **(see illustration)**. The retaining clips must be renewed before refitting. The rubbing strip can be removed without damaging the clips, by removing the inner trim panel first **(see illustration)**. See Section 27.

Badges

Removal

12 The various badges may be secured with adhesives. To remove them, either soften the adhesive using a hot air gun or hairdryer (taking care to avoid damage to the paintwork), or separate the badge from the body by 'sawing' through the adhesive using a length of nylon cord.

Refitting

13 Clean off all traces of adhesive using white spirit, then wash the area with warm soapy water to remove all traces of spirit, and allow to dry. Ensure that the surface to which the new badge is to be fastened is completely clean, and free from grease and dirt.

14 Use the hot air gun to soften the adhesive on the new badge, then press it firmly into position.

Tailgate spoiler

Removal

15 Open the tailgate, and remove the six spoiler securing screws (two at each end of the spoiler and two in the middle) **(see illustrations)**.

16 With the tailgate closed, carefully release the spoiler from its retaining clips by lifting it upwards from the tailgate, starting at the ends **(see illustration)**.

17 Disconnect the high-level stop-light wiring and washer hose **(see illustration)**, before withdrawing the spoiler.

Refitting

18 Refitting is a reversal of removal.

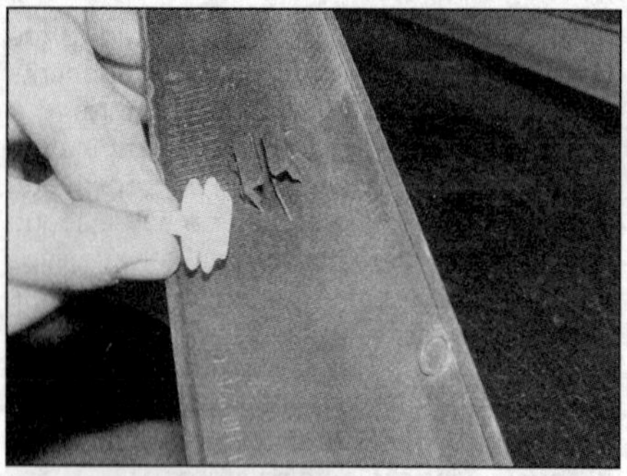

22.11a Retaining clip slides into the slot in the rubbing strip

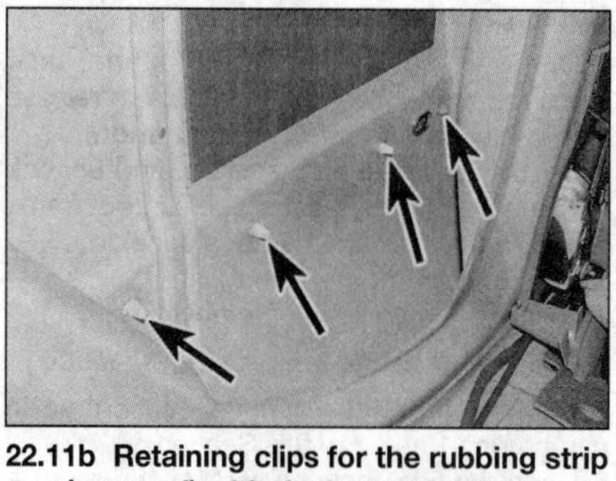

22.11b Retaining clips for the rubbing strip (arrowed) with the inner trim panel removed

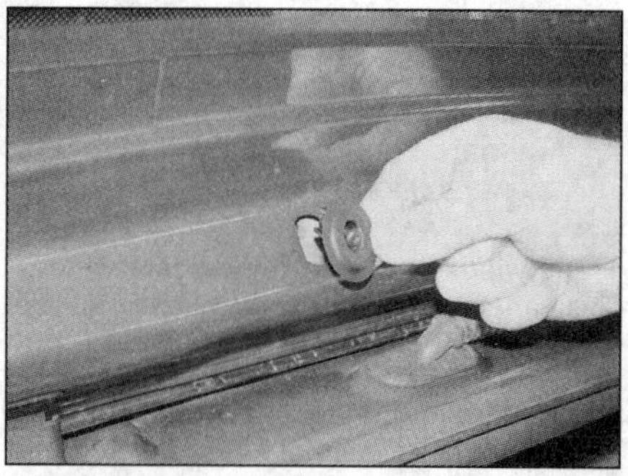

22.15a Unclipping a rubber grommet to access a retaining screw

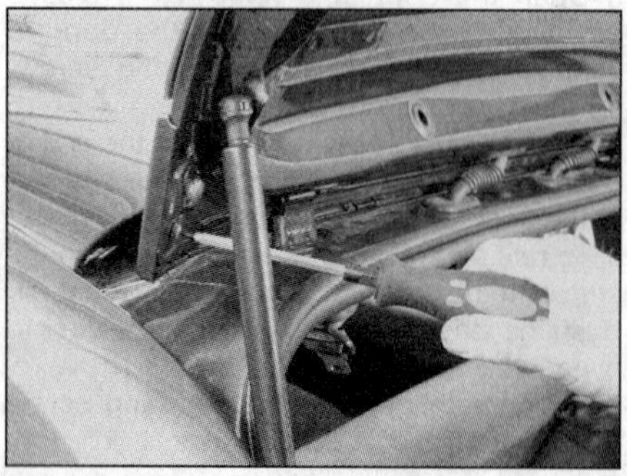

22.15b Unscrewing one of the retaining screws from the end of the spoiler

22.16 Unclipping the end of the spoiler from the tailgate

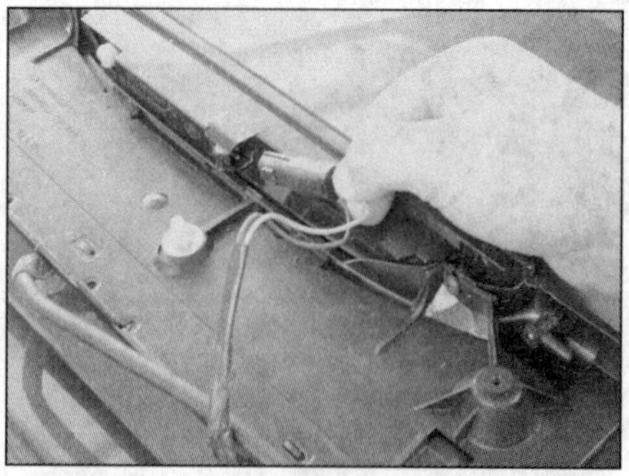

22.17 Disconnecting the wiring from the high-level stop-light in the spoiler

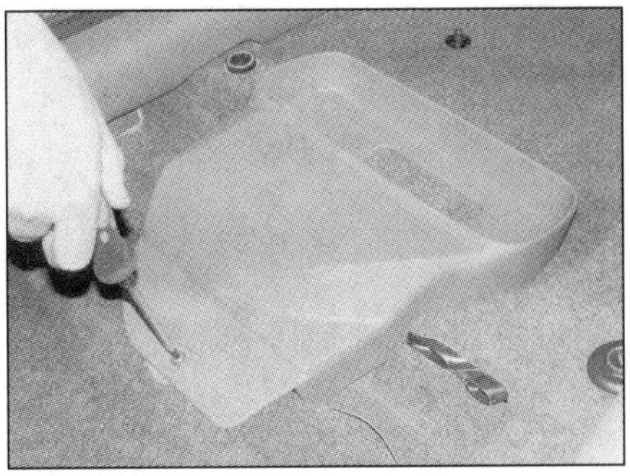
23.0 Undo the retaining screw to remove the storage tray

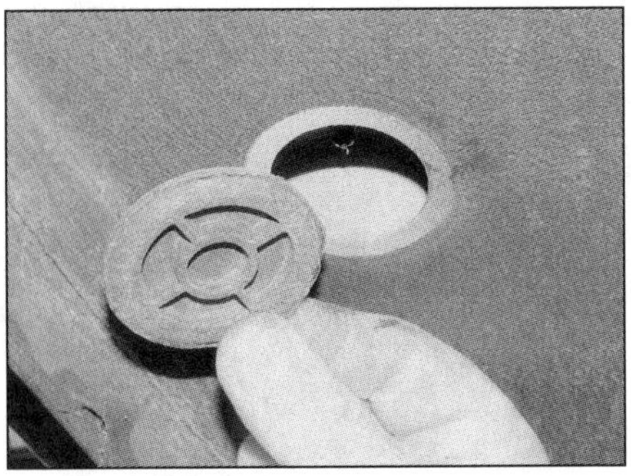
23.2a Prise out the rubber grommet . . .

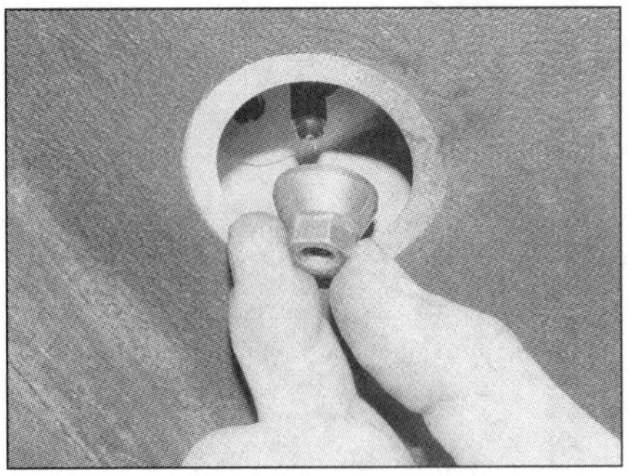
23.2b . . . and remove an outer seat securing nut

23 Seats – removal and refitting

Front seat

Warning: *On models fitted with seat belt pre-tensioners, before proceeding, de-activate the pre-tensioner system as described in Section 25.*

Removal

Note: *On some models, there is a storage tray fitted under the front passenger seat. This is held in place by one retaining screw* ***(see illustration).***

1 If desired, remove the seat side trim panels for improved access.

2 Working underneath the car, remove the rubber grommets (where fitted) and unscrew the four nuts securing the seat rails to the floor **(see illustrations)**. When removing the inner seat securing nuts, take care not to burn yourself if the exhaust is still hot.

3 Carefully lift the seat from the vehicle, disconnect any wiring on removal **(see illustration)**.

Refitting

4 Refitting is a reversal of removal, making sure the spacers are in place in the carpet before refitting.

Front seat runners

5 Remove the seat as described in this Section.

6 Undo the retaining screws (one on each side) and remove the seat side trim panels **(see illustration)**.

7 Slacken and remove the securing bolts (three each side) and withdraw the seat runners from the seat frame.

8 On three-door models, disconnect the control cable from the seat runner assembly.

Refitting

9 Refitting is a reversal of removal.

Rear seat cushion

Removal

10 Tilt the seat cushion forwards, then lift it to disengage the securing lugs from the holes in the floor **(see illustration)**.

Refitting

11 Refitting is a reversal of removal.

Rear seat back

Removal

12 Remove the luggage compartment carpet. Undo the two securing bolts from the rear luggage compartment reinforcement bar, and remove from the car **(see illustrations)**.

13 Slacken, but do not remove, the seat centre bracket front retaining bolt from the floor panel.

14 Release the securing catches at the top of the seat backs. Fold the seat backs forwards.

15 Remove the seat centre bracket rear retaining bolt from the floor panel and disengage the bracket from the front bolt **(see illustrations)**.

16 Working at the lower ends of the seat backs, lift out the locating pegs from the

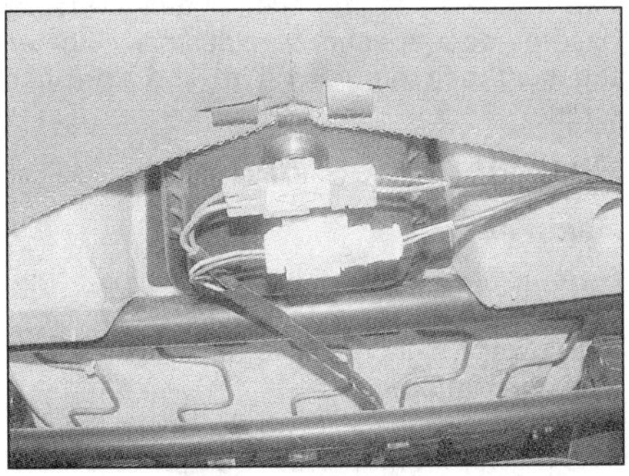
23.3 Wiring connectors under the front of the seat (where fitted)

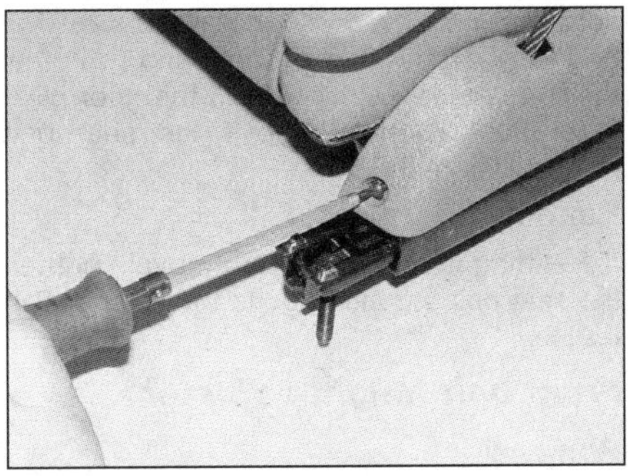
23.6 Undo the retaining screw to release the seat runner trim

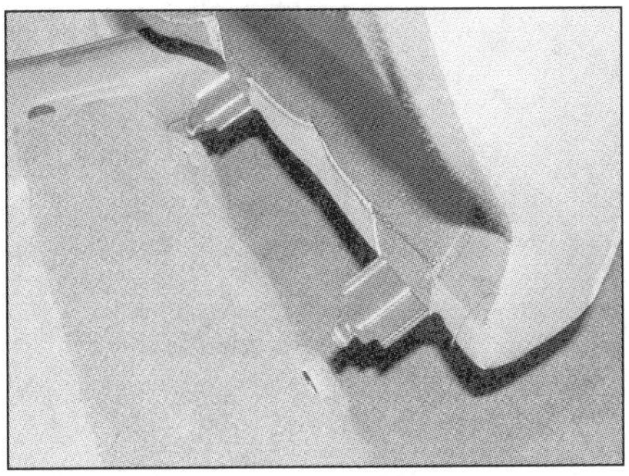
23.10 Disengaging the rear seat cushion from the floor panel

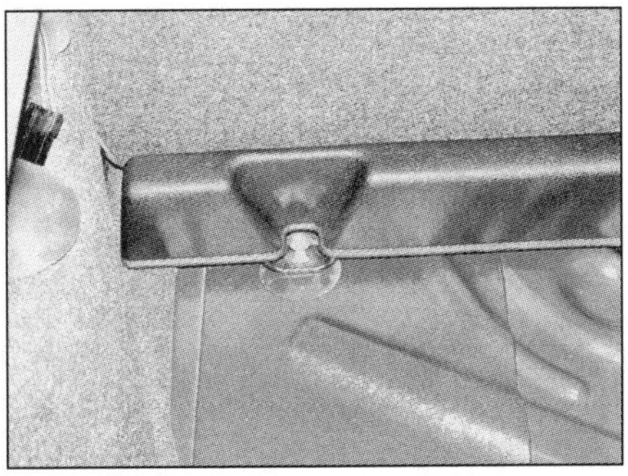
23.12a Undo the securing bolts – left-hand bolt arrowed . . .

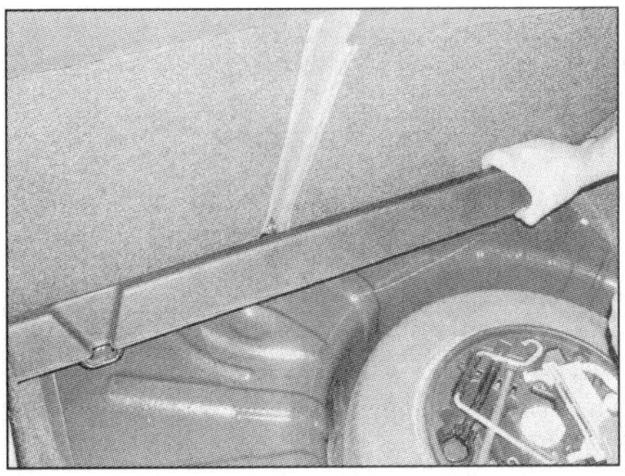
23.12b . . . and remove the reinforcement bar

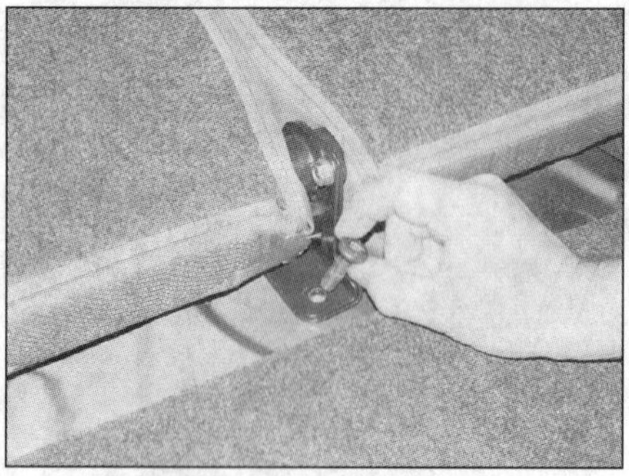
23.15a Remove the rear retaining bolt from the centre seat bracket . . .

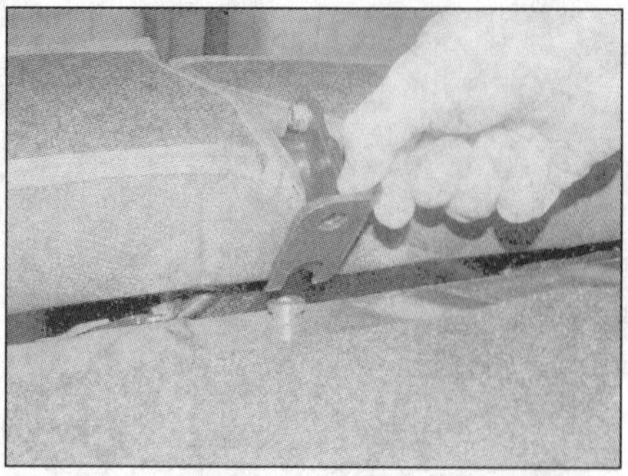
23.15b . . . then release the bracket from the front locating bolt

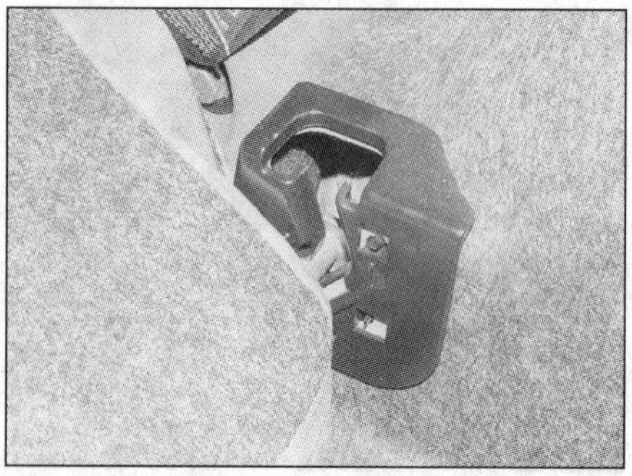
23.16 Lift the seat locating peg from the bracket on the wheelarch

brackets in front of the wheelarches **(see illustration)**, then withdraw the assembly from the car.

17 To split the two seat backs, undo the two securing nuts from the centre bracket. The seat covers can be unzipped for removal **(see illustrations)**.

Refitting

18 Refitting is a reversal of removal.

24 Seat belt components - removal and refitting

Warning: If the vehicle has been in an accident in which structural damage was sustained, all the seat belt components must be renewed.

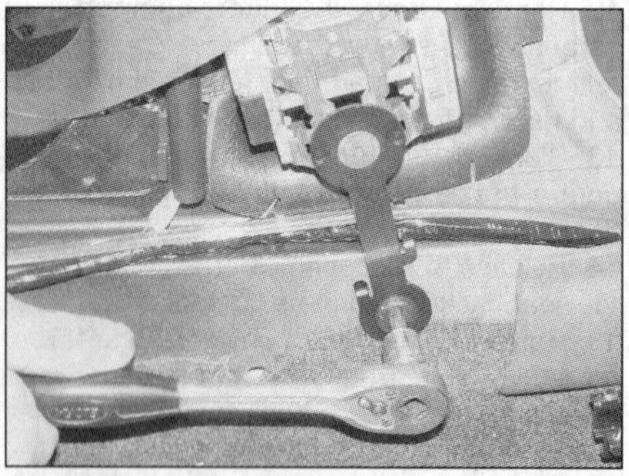
24.3 Undo the inertia reel mounting bolt

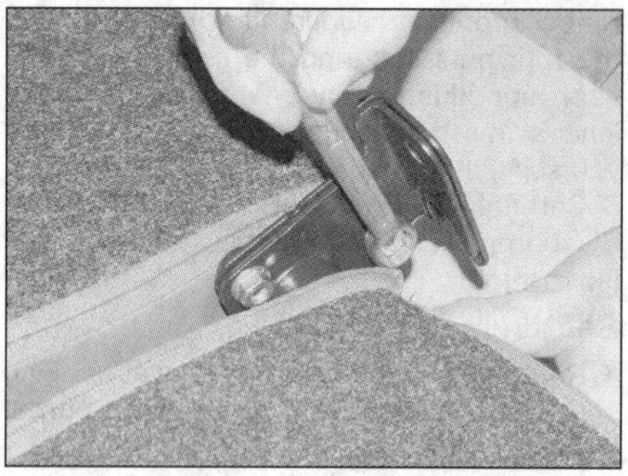
23.17a Undo the two securing nuts, to split the rear seat backs

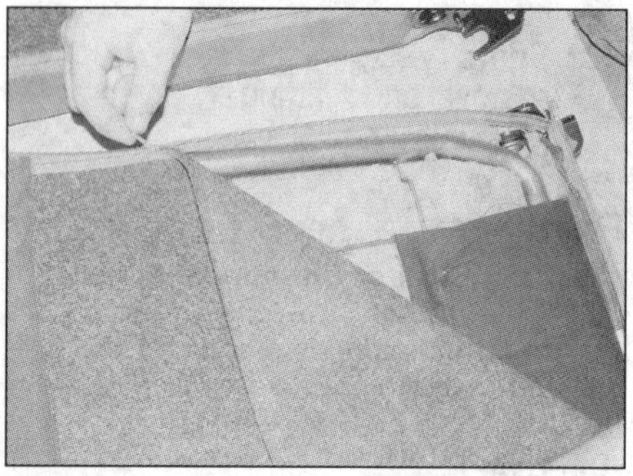
23.17b The seat covers can be unzipped from the seat backs

Front belt

Removal

1 Remove the footwell side/sill trim panels and B-pillar panel, as described in Section 27.

2 Undo the seat belt lower mounting bolt, if not already removed with the sill trims.

3 Unscrew the mounting bolt, and withdraw the inertia reel assembly from the door pillar **(see illustration)**. Remove the seat belt assembly from the car.

Refitting

4 Refitting is a reversal of removal. Tighten the seat belt mounting bolts to the specified torque.

Front belt height adjuster

Removal

5 Remove the B-pillar trim panel, as described in Section 27.

6 Unscrew the two securing bolts, and withdraw the adjuster from the pillar **(see illustration)**.

Refitting

7 Refitting is a reversal of removal. Ensure that the B-pillar trim panel locates correctly over the door aperture weatherseals. Tighten the seat belt mountings to the specified torque.

Rear inertia reel belt

Removal

8 Remove the rear seat cushion, with reference to Section 23, for access to the seat belt lower mounting bolt. Unscrew the bolt **(see illustration)**.

9 Fold the seat back forwards. Unclip the rear side sill trim from the rear quarter trim panel and undo the retaining screw **(see illustration)**.

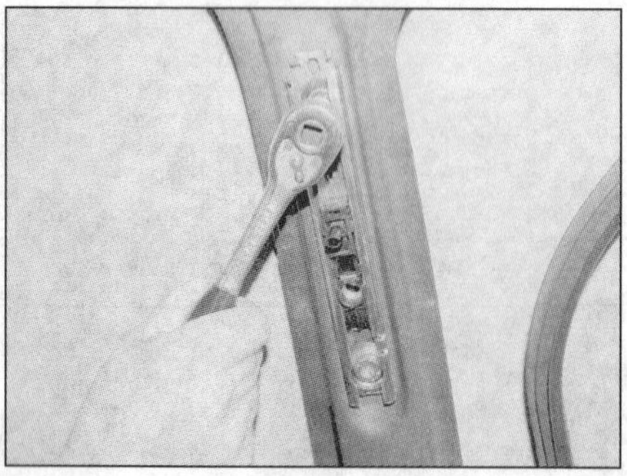
24.6 Remove the height adjuster mounting bolts

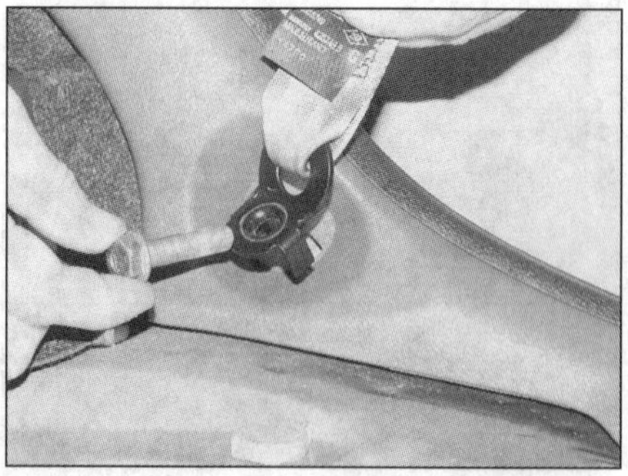
24.8 Removing the lower seat belt mounting bolt

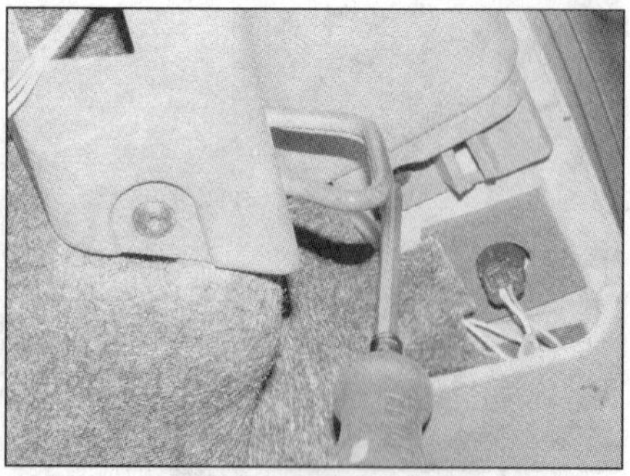
24.9 Undo the retaining screw from behind the sill trim

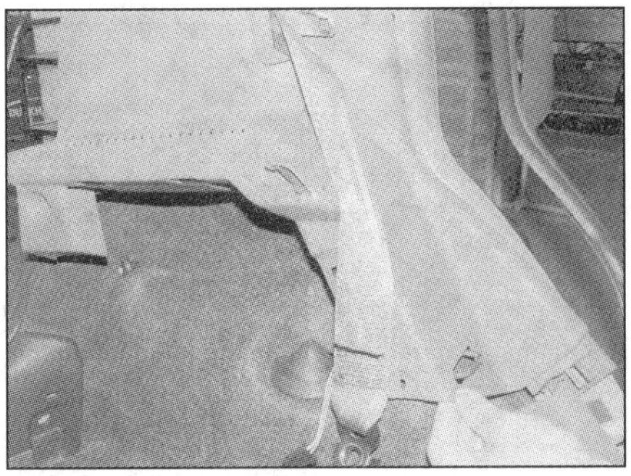

24.10 Remove the two retaining screws and withdraw the rear quarter trim panel

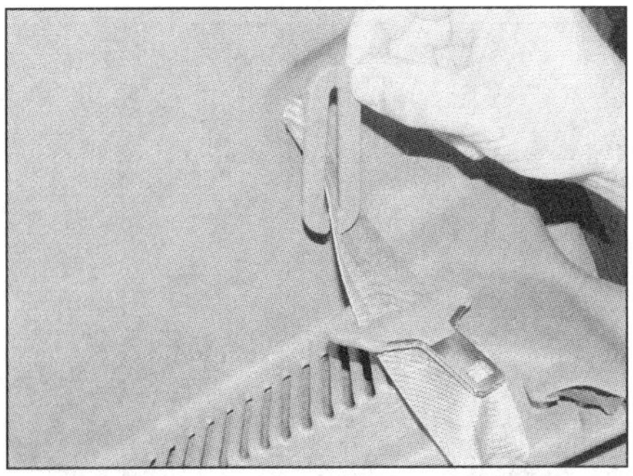

24.11 Unclipping the seat belt plastic surround

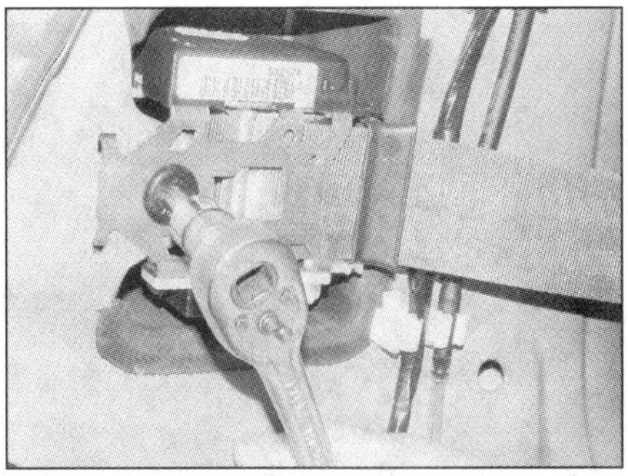

24.13 Undo the rear inertia reel mounting bolt

10 Unscrew the two remaining rear quarter trim panel retaining screws and pull the trim out from the body panel **(see illustration)**.

11 Unclip the seat belt surround from the rear quarter trim panel and feed the seat belt through the hole **(see illustration)**.

12 Disconnect the wiring connector from the luggage compartment light.

13 Unscrew the securing bolt and withdraw the inertia reel from its location **(see illustration)**.

14 The seat belt buckle can be unbolted from the floor, after removing the rear seat cushion for access **(see illustration)**.

Refitting

15 Refitting is a reversal of removal. Tighten the seat belt mountings to the specified torque.

Rear inertia reel centre belt

Removal

16 Carry out the procedures as described in paragraphs 9 to 12 in this Section (on the left-hand side of the car).

17 Unscrew the seat belt securing bolt from the rear of the headlining, then feed the seat belt through the hole in the rear quarter trim panel **(see illustrations)**.

18 Working in the luggage compartment, pull back the side trim to expose the inertia reel mounting bolt.

19 Undo the securing bolt and withdraw the inertia reel from its location **(see illustration)**.

20 Unbolt the metal guide bracket from the rear quarter body panel to release the seat belt **(see illustration)**.

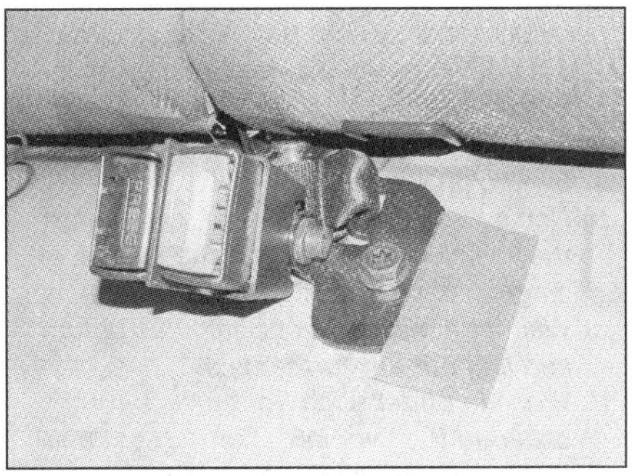

24.14 The rear seat belt buckles can be unbolted from the floor panel

21 The seat belt buckle can be unbolted from the floor, after removing the rear seat cushion for access.

Refitting

22 Refitting is a reversal of removal. Tighten the securing bolts to the specified torque.

25 Seat belt pre-tensioner system - general information and component renewal

General information

1 Seat belt pre-tensioners are fitted, to remove any slack from the front seat belts in the event of a frontal impact. The system is designed to reduce the chances of injury to the driver and front seat passenger in the event of an accident, due to the seat belts being slack.

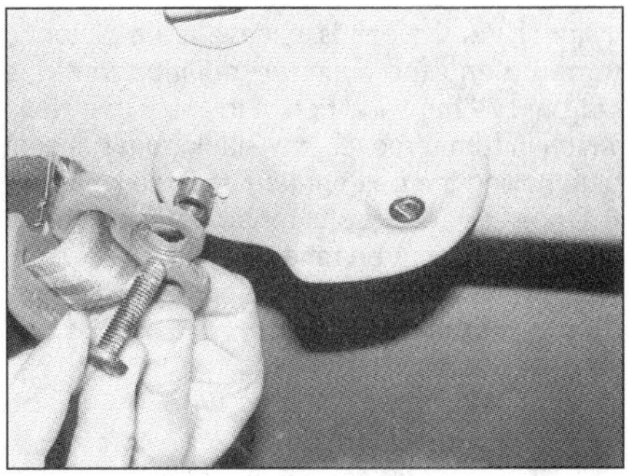

24.17a Unbolt the seat belt mounting from the roof panel . . .

2 The system consists of two special seat belt tensioner/stalk assemblies mounted directly on the front seats, and an electronic control unit.

3 Each tensioner/stalk assembly consist of a special buckle attached to a cable. The end of the cable is attached to a piston inside the tensioner cylinder.

4 The electronic control unit is mounted under the centre console, and incorporates a deceleration sensor and a trigger unit. If the sensor senses a deceleration greater than a predetermined limit, the trigger unit sends signals to the ignition modules in both seat belt tensioner units. Note that, on most models, the seat belt tensioner electronic control unit is integrated with the airbag electronic control unit.

5 When a tensioner ignition module is triggered, a small capsule is energised, which rapidly releases gas into the tensioner

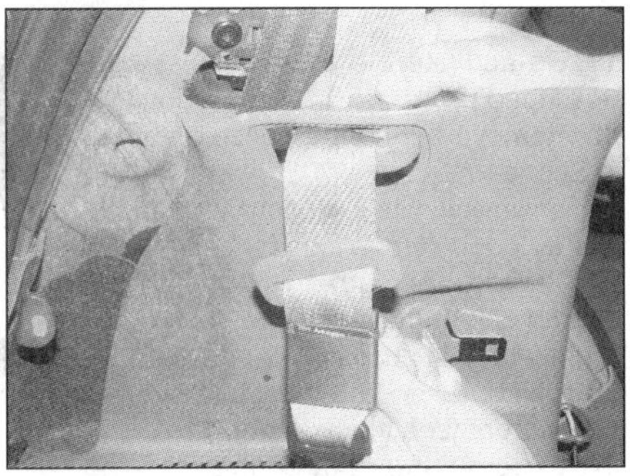

24.17b . . . then feed the belt through the rear quarter trim panel

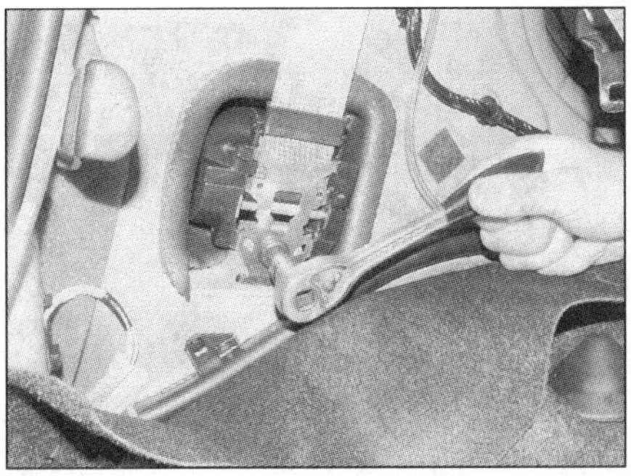

24.19 Undo the inertia reel mounting bolt for the centre seat belt

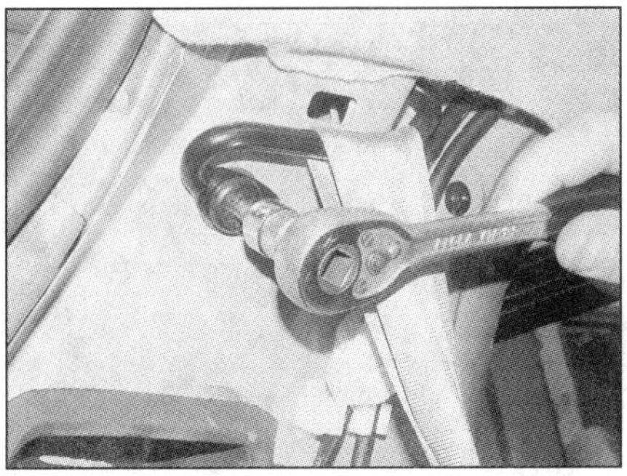

24.20 Unbolt the guide rail from the rear quarter body panel

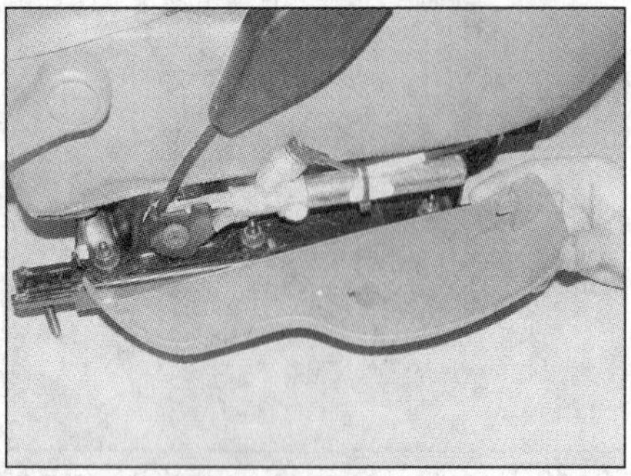

25.11 Remove screw and unclip trim panel from the seat runner

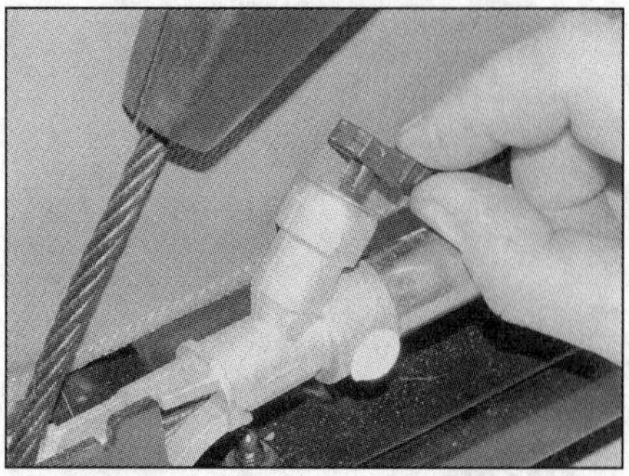

25.12 Disconnecting the wiring plug from the pre-tensioner assembly

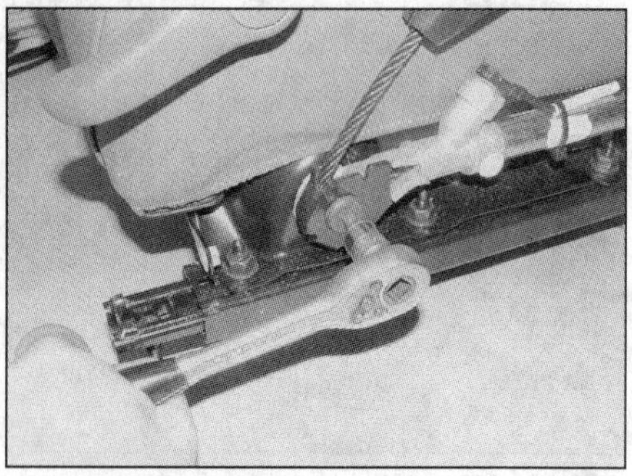

25.13 Unbolting the pre-tensioner assembly from the seat frame

cylinder. As the gas is released, the piston is forced along the cylinder, pulling the cable (approx. 70 mm) and hence the seat belt stalk, which in turn removes any slack from the seat belt, pulling the belt tight against the wearer.

6 Once a seat belt tensioner has been triggered, it must be renewed.

Warning: Do not expose the pre-tensioner system to excessive heat.

Warning: If any work is to be carried out under the vehicle (eg, exhaust renewal) or in the vicinity of the pre-tensioner system components which involves impacts or hammering, remove the pre-tensioner system fuse, then wait for at least five minutes before proceeding.

Warning: When installing any electrical accessories (such as loudspeakers or alarm systems) which emit a magnetic field, the components must not be fitted near the pre-tensioner control unit.

Warning: If an attempt has been made to steal the vehicle, if the vehicle has been stolen, or if the vehicle has been involved in an impact which did not trigger the pre-tensioners, the pre-tensioner system should be tested using Renault special test tool XRBAG.

Pre-tensioner system

Deactivation

Note: *Renault recommend that special test tool XRBAG (Ele. 1288) is used to test the operation of the system before reactivation.*

7 To de-activate the pre-tensioner system, in order to make the system safe, proceed as follows.

a) Switch off the ignition.
b) Remove the pre-tensioner fuse (refer to the vehicle handbook and the wiring diagrams in Chapter 12 for location).
c) Wait for a minimum of 5 minutes before carrying out any further work.
d) Working under each front seat in turn, separate the two halves of the seat belt pre-tensioner wiring connector.

Reactivation

8 To re-activate the pre-tensioner system after carrying out work, proceed as follows.

a) Before carrying out any further work, Renault recommend that the operation of the system is checked using Renault special test tool XRBAG (Ele. 1288).
b) Reconnect the pre-tensioner wiring connectors under the seats.
c) Refit the pre-tensioner fuse.

Pre-tensioner assembly

Removal

9 De-activate the pre-tensioner system as described previously in this Section.

10 Remove the seat as described in Section 23.

11 Undo the securing screw and remove trim panel from the seat **(see illustration)**.

12 Disconnect the wiring plug from the top of the pre-tensioner assembly **(see illustration)**, and feed the wiring through the trim panel (leave the wiring clipped in place under the seat)

13 Undo the securing bolt from the pre-tensioner assembly **(see illustration)**, then withdraw the tensioner assembly from the seat frame.

Warning: Do not expose the pre-tensioner assembly to shocks or excessive heat.

Warning: Before discarding a pre-tensioner assembly which has not been triggered, the assembly must be triggered using the appropriate Renault special equipment (Special tool Ele. 1287).

Refitting

14 Feed the pre-tensioner wiring through the slot in the seat trim panel, and reconnect the wring connector to the top of the pre-tensioner unit.

15 Refit the tensioner to the seat, ensuring that the pre-tensioner is correctly located, then refit and tighten the securing bolt.

16 Refit the trim panel to the seat frame.

17 Refit the seat as described in Section 23.

18 Re-activate the system as described previously in this Section.

Electronic control unit

Note: *On models with a 'central' airbag system, the pre-tensioner system shares the same control unit as the airbag system. If the control unit is to be removed on a model with a combined pre-tensioner/airbag control unit, before proceeding, de-activate the airbag system as described in Chapter 12, Section 28.*

Removal

19 De-activate the pre-tensioner system as described previously in this Section.

20 Remove the centre console as described in Section 28.

21 Undo the retaining screws and move the two air ducts to one side **(see illustration)**.

22 Remove the carpet to gain access to the control unit. It may be easier to cut the carpet slightly to gain access.

23 Disconnect the control unit wiring connectors **(see illustration)**.

24 Unscrew the control unit securing nuts. Lift the control unit, complete with the diagnostic socket bracket from the floor.

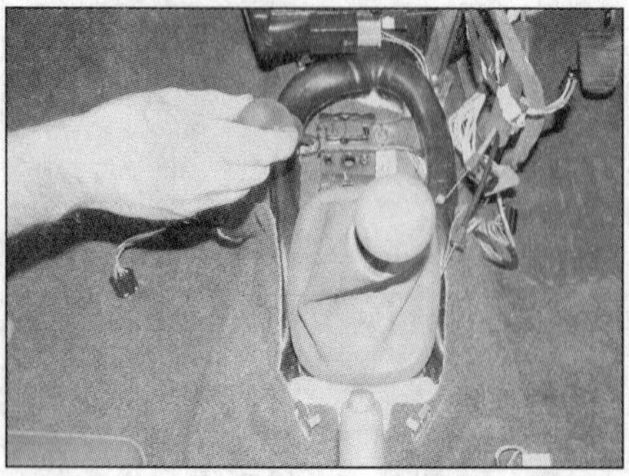

25.21 Unscrewing the air ducts from the control unit bracket

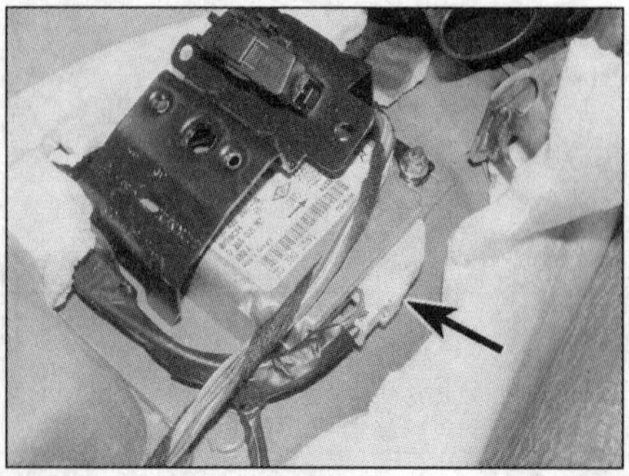

25.23 Release the retaining clip (arrowed) and remove the wiring connector

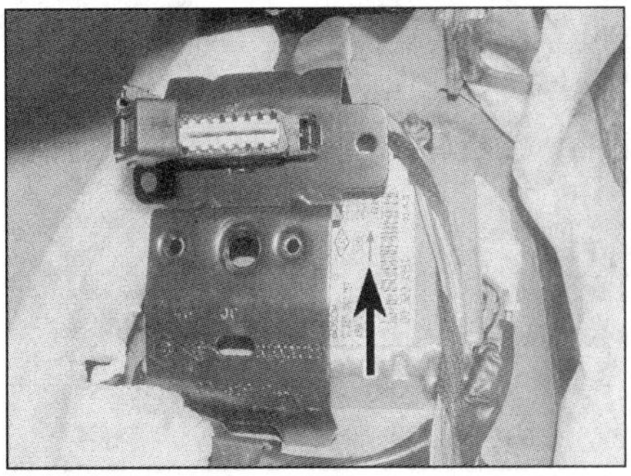

25.25 Arrow on the control unit (arrowed) must be pointing forwards

Refitting

25 Offer the control unit into position, noting that the arrow on top of the unit must face towards the front of the vehicle **(see illustration)**, then refit the securing nuts, and tighten them securely. **DO NOT** reconnect any of the wiring connectors until the securing nuts have been tightened.
26 Reconnect the control unit wiring connectors.
27 Refit the air ducts to the heater unit.
28 Refit the centre console as described in Section 28.
29 Re-activate the pre-tensioner system as described previously in this Section.

26 Interior trim - general information

Interior trim panels

Removal

1 The interior trim panels are all secured using either screws or various types of plastic fasteners.
2 Before removing a panel, study it carefully, noting how it is secured. Often, other panels or ancillary components (such as seat belt mountings, grab handles, etc) must be removed before a particular panel can be withdrawn.
3 Once any such components have been removed, check that there are no other panels overlapping the one to be removed. Usually, the sequence to be followed will become obvious on close inspection.

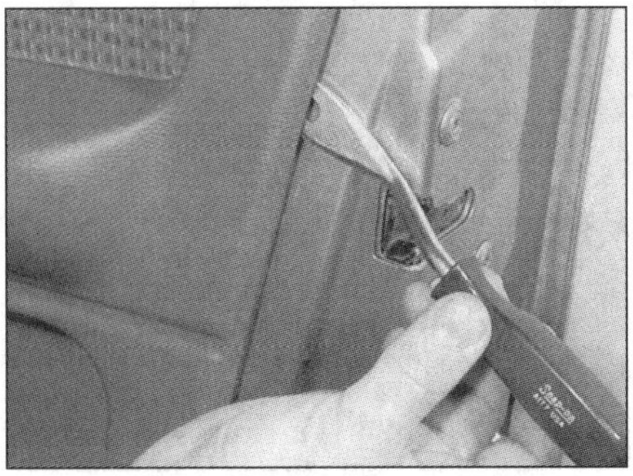

26.4 Suitable forked tool for releasing plastic trim panel securing clips

4 Remove all obvious fasteners, such as screws, many of which may have plastic covers fitted. If the panel cannot be freed, it is probably secured by hidden clips or fasteners on the rear of the panel. Such fasteners are usually situated around the edge of the panel, and can be prised up to release them. Note that plastic clips can break quite easily, so it is advisable to have a few replacement clips of the correct type available for refitting. Generally, the best way of releasing such clips is to use a suitable forked tool **(see illustration)**. If this is not available, an old, broad-bladed screwdriver with the edges rounded-off and wrapped in insulating tape will serve as a good substitute.
5 The following Section and the accompanying illustrations describe removal and refitting of all the major trim panels. Note that the type and number of fasteners used often varies during the production run of a particular model, so differences may be noted to the procedures provided for certain vehicles.
6 When removing a panel, **never** use excessive force, or the panel may be damaged. Always check carefully that all fasteners have been removed or released before attempting to withdraw a panel.

Refitting

7 When refitting, secure the fasteners by pressing them firmly into place. Ensure that all disturbed components are correctly secured, to prevent rattles. If adhesives were found at any point during removal, use white spirit to remove the old adhesive, then wash off the white spirit using soapy water. Use a suitable trim adhesive (a Renault dealer should be able to recommend a proprietary product) on reassembly.

Carpets

8 The carpet is not bonded and rests on the floor, it is held in position by the sill trim panels and other surrounding panels and components.
9 Carpet removal and refitting is reasonably straightforward, but very time-consuming, due to the fact that many of the adjoining trim panels must be removed first. It will also be necessary to remove components such as the seats and their mountings, the centre console, etc.

Headlining

10 The headlining is bonded to the rear section of the roof, and is also held in place by the grab handles, sun visors, sunroof trim, door pillar trim panels, rear quarter trim panels, weatherseals, etc. When all the fittings have been removed or prised clear, it can then be withdrawn out through the tailgate aperture.
11 Note that headlining removal requires considerable skill and patience if it is to be carried out without damage, and is therefore best entrusted to an expert.

27 Interior trim panels - removal and refitting

Front door inner trim panel

Removal

1 On models fitted with central locking, disconnect the battery negative lead.
2 Unclip the mirror inner trim panel and the speaker cover grille **(see illustrations)**.
3 On models fitted with manually-operated windows, note the position of the window winder handle with the window fully open, then pull the handle firmly to release it from the window regulator **(see illustration)**.

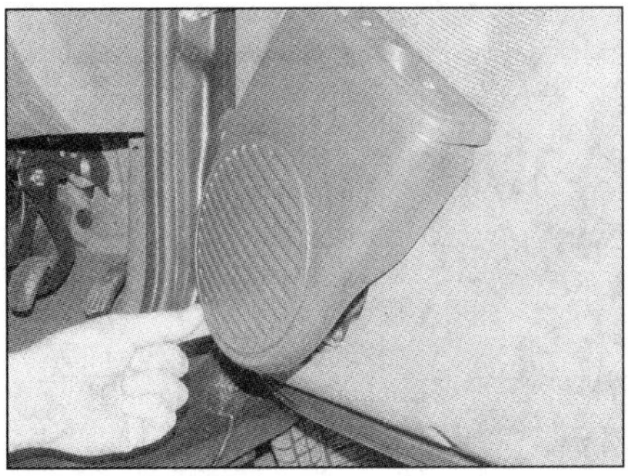

27.2a Unclipping the speaker grille on model with electric windows . . .

27.2b . . . and model with manual windows

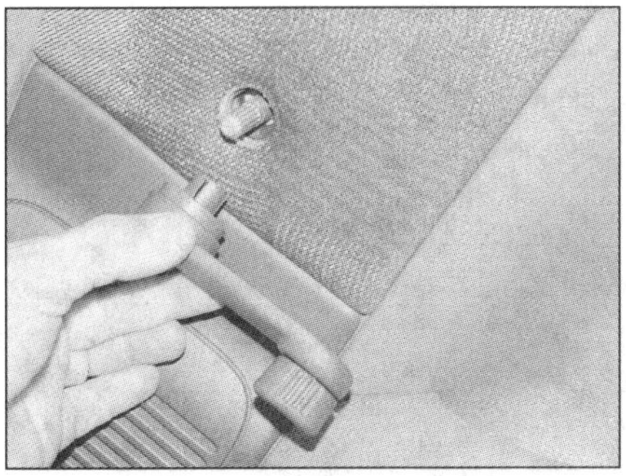

27.3 Pull winder handle to release from the window regulator splines

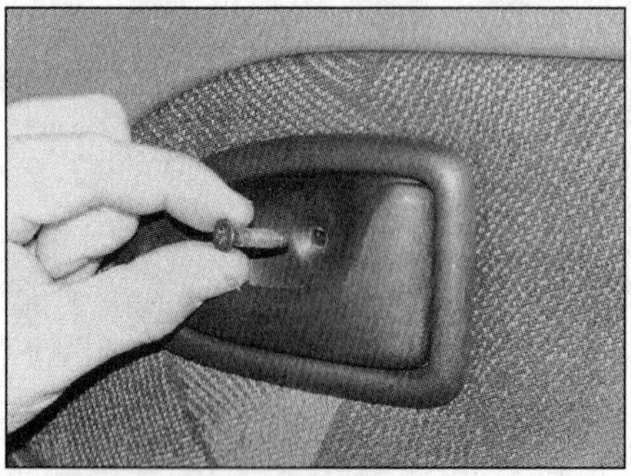

27.4a Remove the inner door handle securing screw . . .

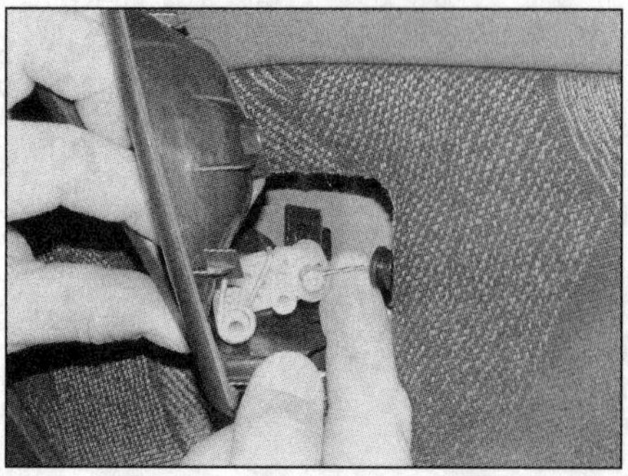

27.4b . . . then release the operating cable

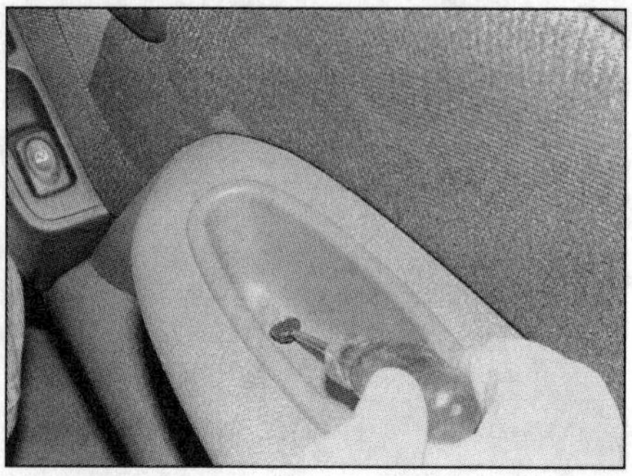

27.5a Prise the cover from the door grab handle to expose the securing screw

4 Remove the screw securing the inner door handle to the door. Withdraw the handle and disconnect the outer part of the operating cable from the rear of the handle, then unclip the inner cable **(see illustrations)**.

5 Remove the securing screw and cover, then carefully lift and pull back the grab handle to release it from the door **(see illustrations)**.

6 On models fitted with electric windows, disconnect the wiring plugs from the electric window switches. Also disconnect the wiring plug from the electric mirror switch, where applicable.

7 Remove the four securing screws and withdraw the speaker from the door, disconnect the wiring connector **(see illustration)**.

8 Slacken and remove the retaining screws from the lower edge of the door trim panel **(see illustration)**.

9 Carefully release the securing clips around the edge of the trim panel, preferably using a forked tool. Pull the trim panel from the door, and lift upwards of the inner weather strip to remove (noting that it is secured with sealing compound around its edge).

Refitting

10 Refitting is a reversal of removal, bearing in mind the following points.

11 When refitting the panel to the door, ensure that the sealing compound provides a good seal between the door and the panel. If necessary, apply new sealing compound of a suitable type (available from a Renault dealer).

12 Where applicable, refit the window winder handle in the position noted before removal.

Front door impact absorbers

13 With the door inner trim panel removed as described in this Section, remove the securing screw from the edge of the door, then using a flat-bladed screwdriver unclip the side impact absorber **(see illustrations)**. The impact absorber can then be withdrawn through the aperture in the door frame.

Refitting

14 Refitting is a reversal of removal.

Rear door inner trim panel

Removal

15 Remove the securing screw then carefully lift and pull forward the grab handle to release it from the door panel **(see illustration)**.

16 On models fitted with manual window winders, note the position of the window winder handle with the window fully open, then pull the handle firmly to release it from the window regulator **(see illustration)**.

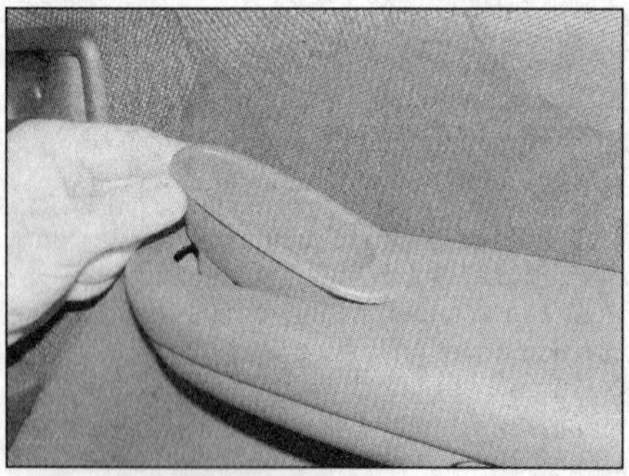

27.5b Withdrawing the front door grab handle

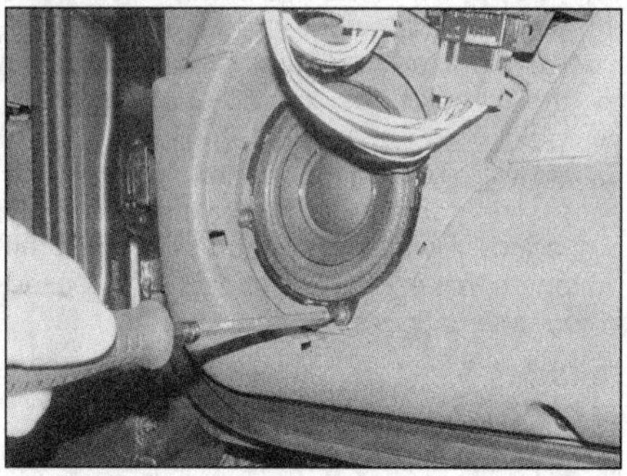

27.7 Removing the four speaker securing screws

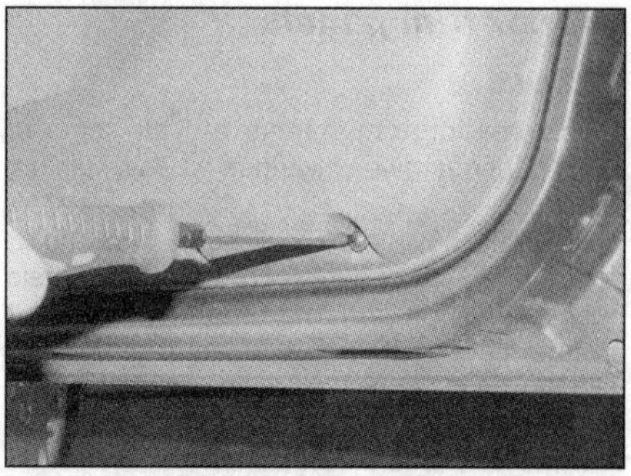

27.8 Removing one of the retaining screws from the lower edge of the door panel

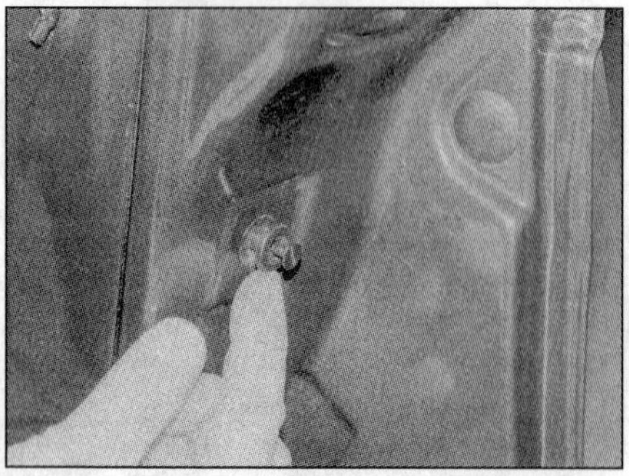

27.13a Remove the securing screw from the edge of the door . . .

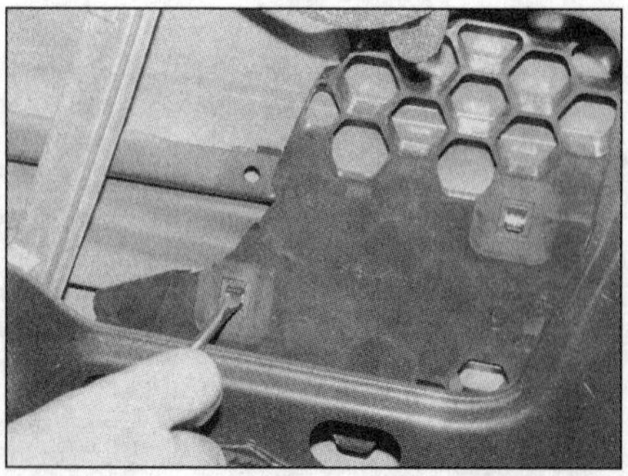

27.13b . . . and using a small screwdriver unclip the impact absorber

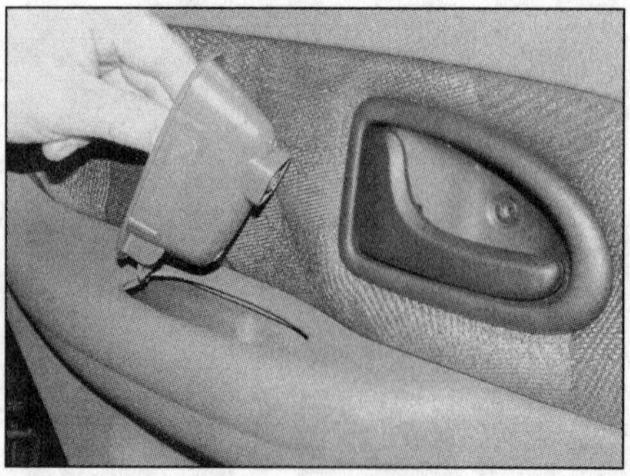

27.15 With the screw removed, lift the door grab handle out of the door trim panel

17 Remove the screw securing the inner door handle to the door. Withdraw the handle and disconnect the operating rod from the rear of the handle **(see illustrations)**.
18 On models fitted with electric windows, disconnect the wiring plugs from the electric window switches.
19 Turn the speaker cover anti-clockwise to remove, then undo the four securing screws and withdraw the speaker from the door panel, disconnect the wiring connector **(see illustrations)**.
20 Carefully release the securing clips around the edge of the trim panel, preferably using a forked tool. Pull the trim panel from the door, and lift upwards of the inner weather strip to remove (noting that it is secured with sealing compound around its edge). **Note:** *There is a spacer on the window regulator spindle, under the door trim panel* ***(see illustration)***.

Refitting

21 Proceed as described in paragraphs 10 to 12 in this Section.

Footwell side/sill trim panels

Removal

22 Remove the front seat as described in Section 23.
23 Carefully pull off the lower part of the door seals, taking care not to damage the seal.
24 For the front left-hand sill trim to be removed, the bonnet release lever will have to be unclipped first.

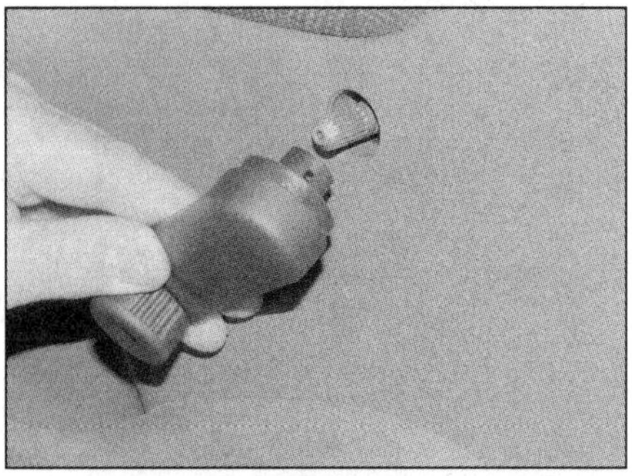
27.16 Removing the rear door window winder handle

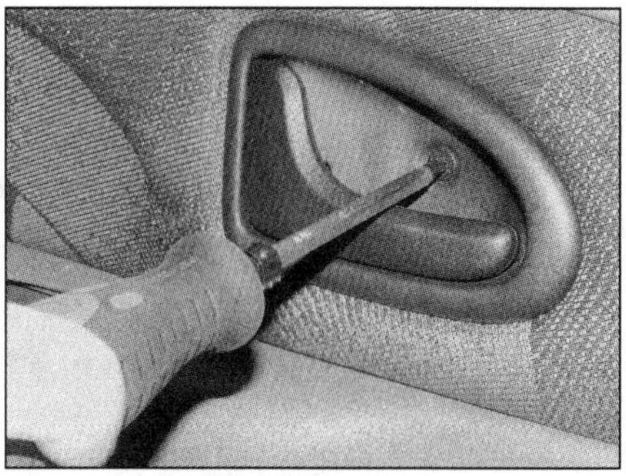
27.17a Remove the interior door handle securing screw . . .

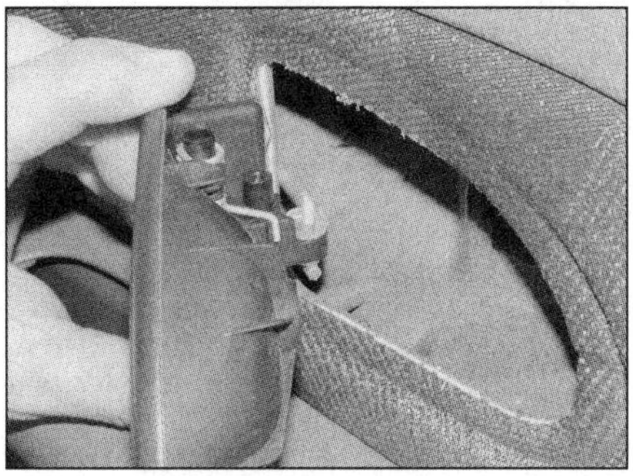
27.17b . . . then disconnect the operating rod

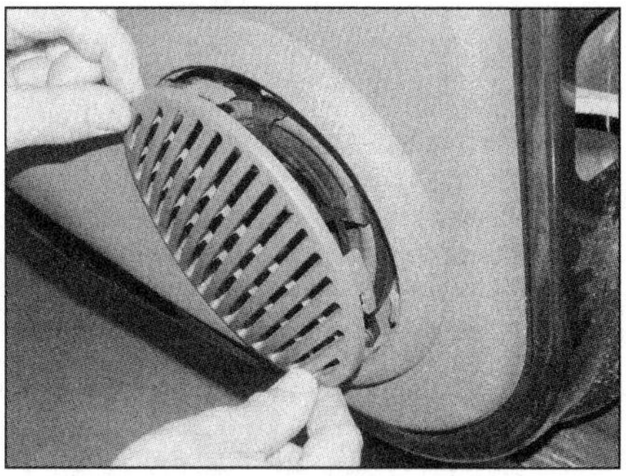
27.19a Turn the speaker cover anti-clockwise to remove . . .

25 On 3-door models, unscrew the bolt securing the seat belt mounting rail. Note the position of any washers and/or spacers. Carefully manipulate the rail to release the rear end from the trim panel **(see illustrations)**.
26 On 5-door models, unbolt the front and rear seat belt lower mountings **(see illustrations)**.

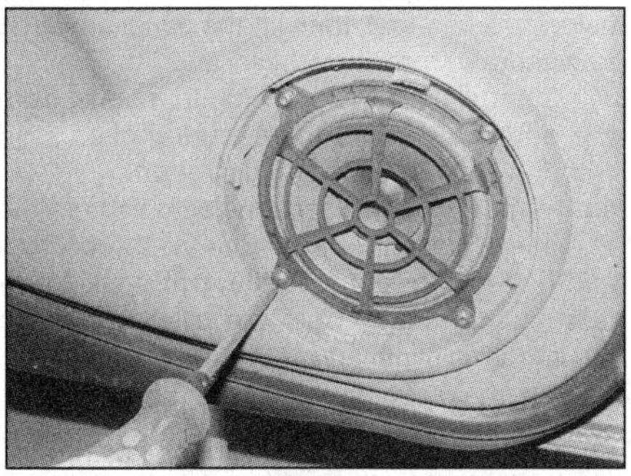
27.19b . . . then undo the four speaker retaining screws

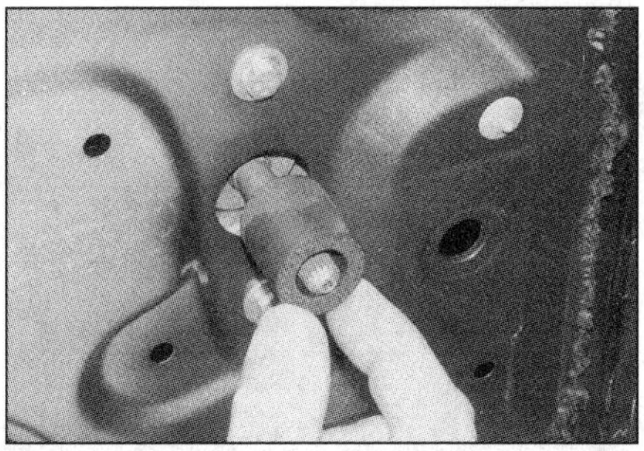
27.20 Make sure the spacer is fitted to the window regulator spindle, before refitting the door trim panel

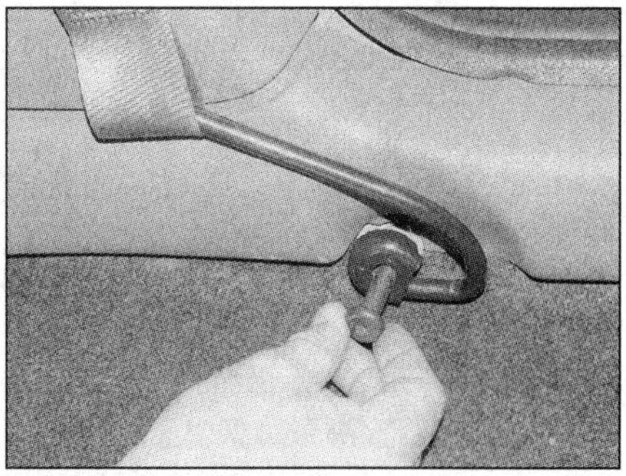
27.25a Remove the seat belt rail mounting bolt . . .

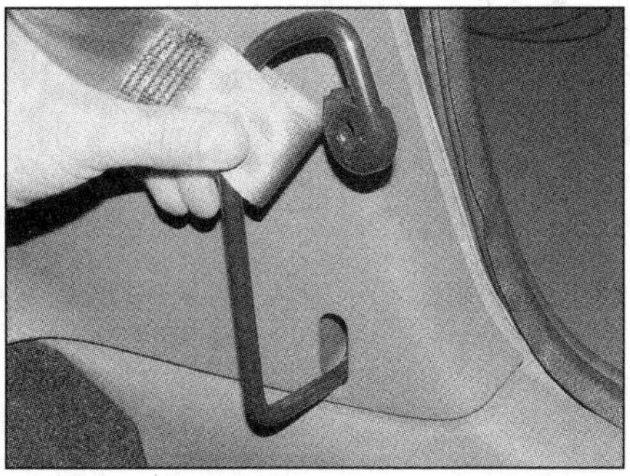
27.25b . . . then release the rail from the pillar – 3-door model

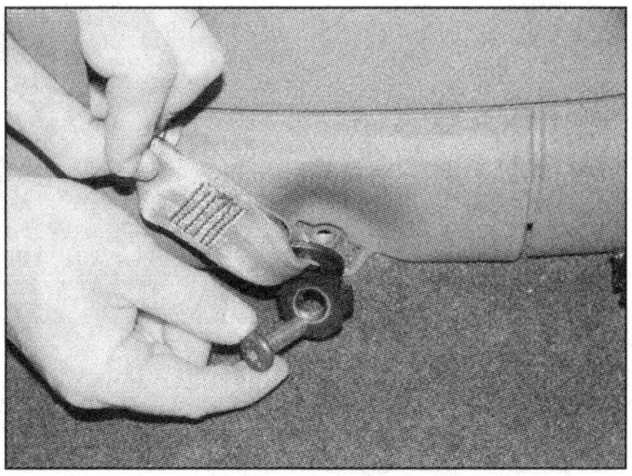
27.26a Removing the front seat belt lower mounting bolt – 5-door model

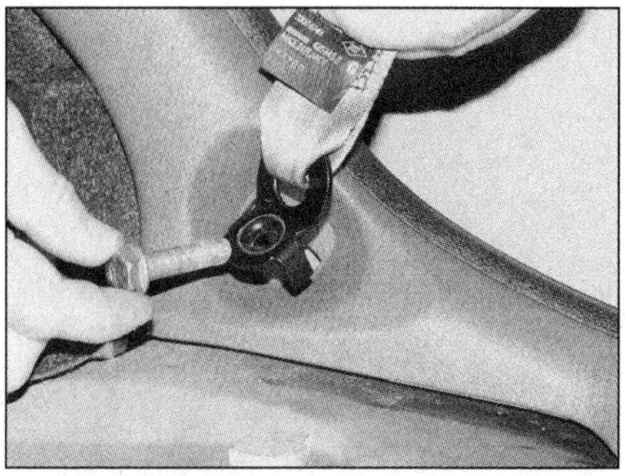
27.26b Removing the rear seat belt lower mounting bolt – 5-door model

11

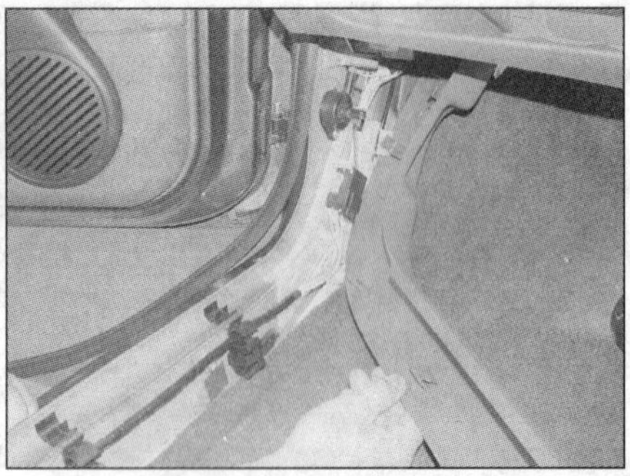

27.27 Removing a front footwell/side trim panel

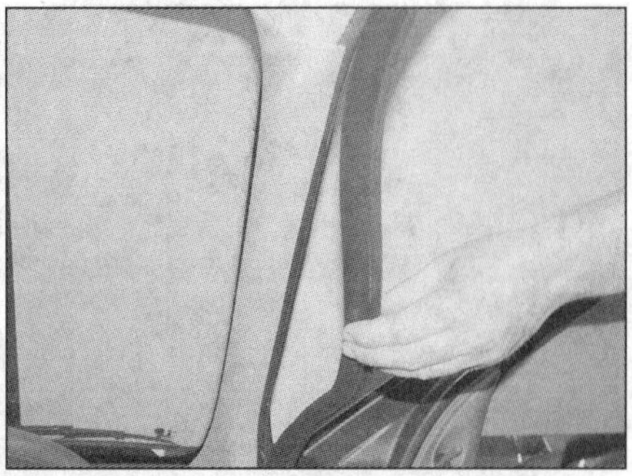

27.29 Take care not to damage the seal on removal

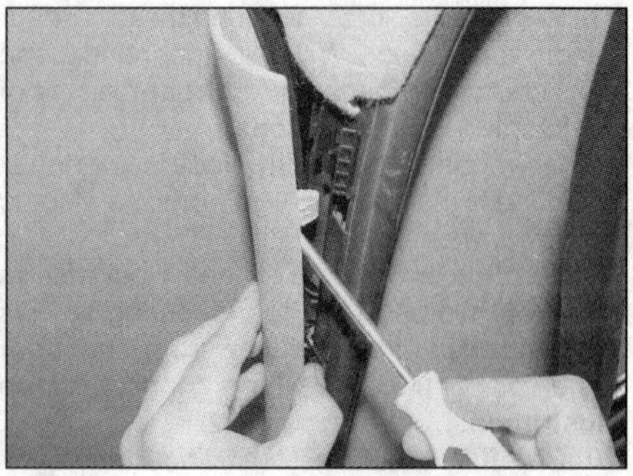

27.30 Unclipping the trim panel from the A-pillar

27 Carefully pull the panel from the body to release the securing clips, and withdraw the panel from the sill **(see illustration)**.

Refitting

28 Refitting is a reversal of removal. Ensure that the securing clips are correctly engaged, and tighten the seat belt mounting bolt to the specified torque.

A-pillar trim panel

Removal

29 Carefully pull the door seal away from the front windscreen pillar where it touches the trim panel, taking care not to damage the seal **(see illustration)**.

30 Carefully pull back the top of the panel from the pillar to release the securing clips. Withdraw the panel, lifting it upwards from the facia panel **(see illustration)**.

Refitting

31 Refitting is a reversal of removal.

B-pillar trim panel (5-door)

Removal

32 Remove the footwell side/sill trim panels as described previously in this Section.

33 Where applicable, prise the centre clip from the seat belt height adjustment knob, then pull the knob from the adjuster **(see illustration)**.

34 Prise off the cover, and unbolt the upper seat belt mounting **(see illustrations)**.

35 Unclip the seat belt trim and remove the retaining clip from above the upper mounting bolt **(see illustrations)**.

36 Carefully pull the panel from the pillar to release the securing clips, and withdraw the panel.

Refitting

37 Refitting is a reversal of removal. Ensure that the panel locates correctly with the door aperture weatherseals, and tighten the seat belt mountings to the specified torque.

Rear side/B-pillar trim panel (3-door)

Removal

38 Proceed as described in paragraphs 32 to 34.

39 Tilt the seat cushion forwards, then lift it to disengage the securing lugs from the holes in the floor.

40 Unscrew the bolt securing the seat belt mounting rail. Note the position of any washers and/or spacers. Carefully manipulate the rail to release the rear end from the trim panel (see illustrations 27.25a and 27.25b).

41 Carefully release the securing clips around the edge of the trim panel, preferably using a forked tool, then lift the panel upwards to withdraw from the vehicle.

42 Carefully pull the roof side trim panel from the body to release the securing clips, and withdraw the panel **(see illustration)**.

43 Remove the two securing screws from the B-pillar upper trim panel (one at the bottom and one at the top) **(see illustrations)**. Carefully pull the panel from the pillar to release the securing clips, and withdraw the panel.

Refitting

44 Refitting is a reversal of removal. Tighten the seat belt mountings to the specified torque.

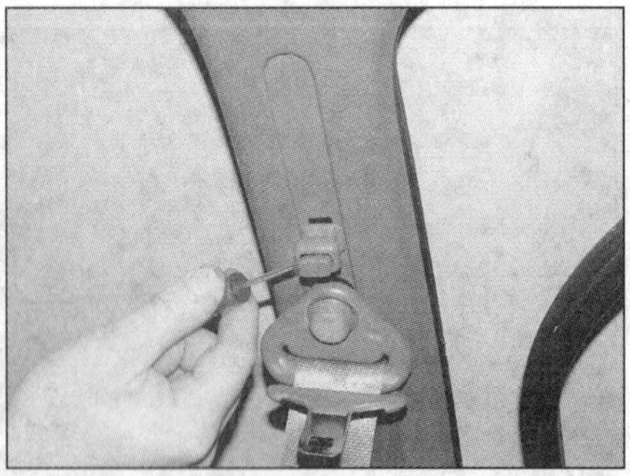

27.33 Prise the clip from the seat belt height adjustment knob, then pull the knob from the adjuster

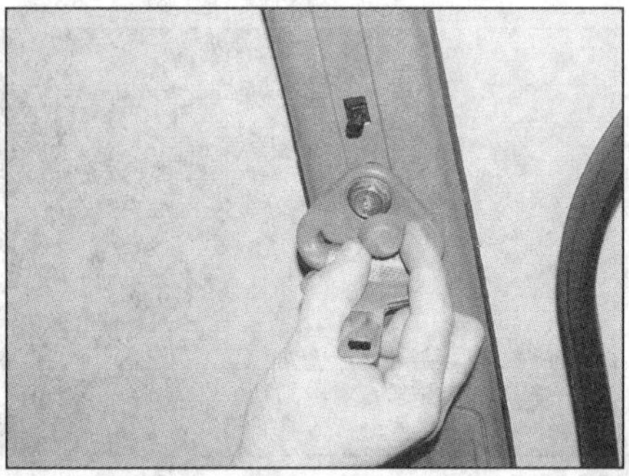

27.34a Prise off the cover . . .

27.34b . . . and remove the upper seat belt mounting bolt

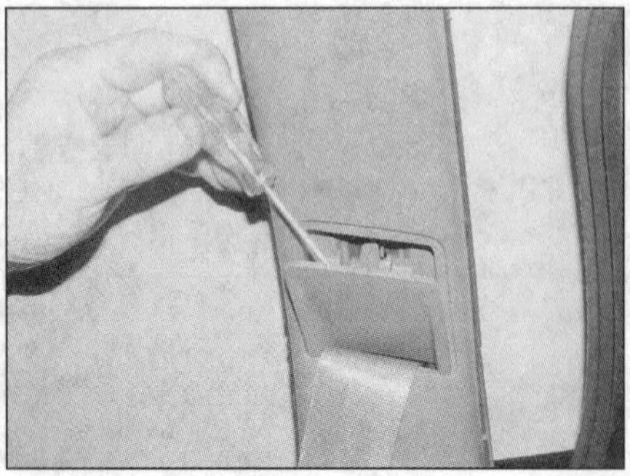

27.35a Unclip the plastic trim . . .

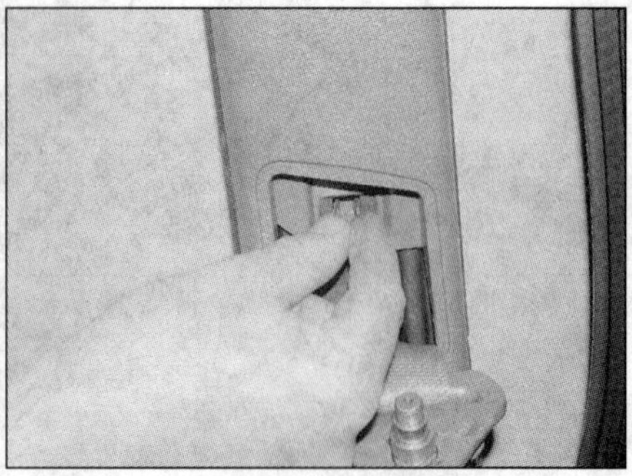

27.35b . . . and remove the retaining clip

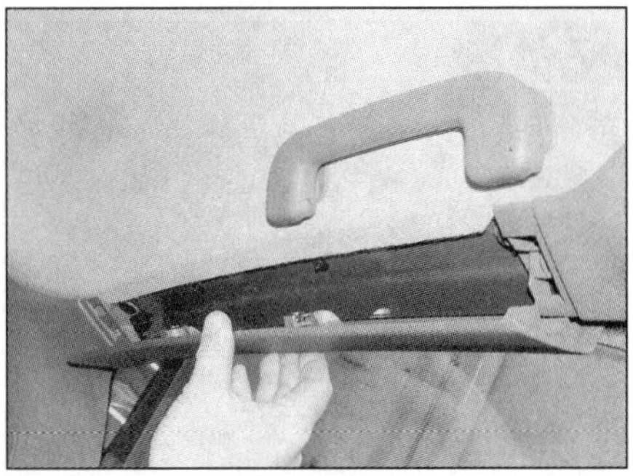
27.42 Removing the roof side trim panel

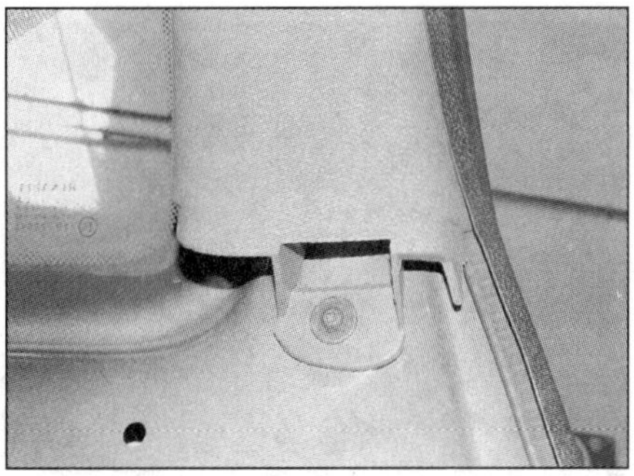
27.43a B-pillar trim lower retaining screw . . .

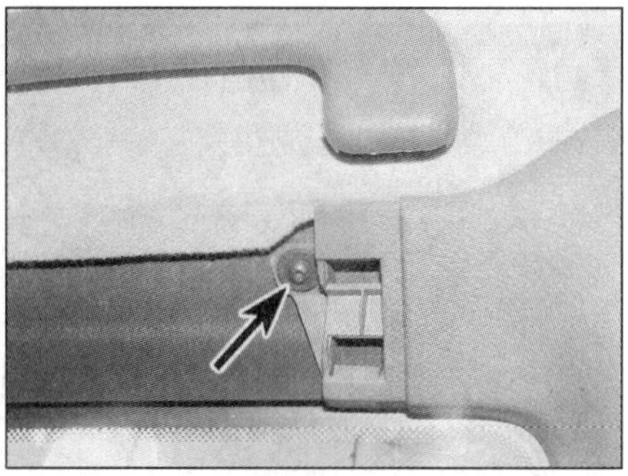
27.43b . . . and upper retaining screw (arrowed)

Roof side trim panel (3-door)

Removal

45 Carefully pull the roof side trim panel from the body to release the securing clips, and withdraw the panel (see illustration 27.42).

Refitting

46 Refitting is a reversal of removal.

Rear side shelf trim panels

Note: *See illustrations in Section 24, rear inertia belt removal.*

47 Carefully pull the rear door seal and the tailgate seal away from where it touches the trim panel, taking care not to damage the seals.

48 Unbolt the rear seat belt lower mounting.

49 Unclip the rear of the inner sill trim on 5-door models, to gain access to the screw at the front of the shelf trim panel. On 3-door models, remove the inner side trim and roof side trim panel as described in this Section and remove the securing screw and retaining clip from the shelf trim panel **(see illustrations)**.

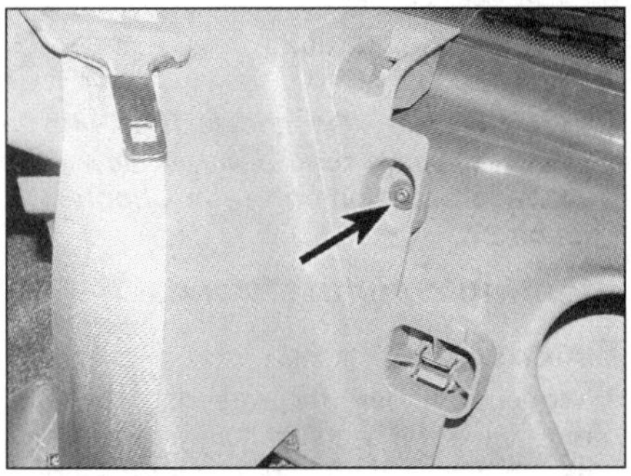
27.49a Rear shelf trim panel lower securing screw (arrowed) . . .

50 Undo the two remaining screws from the panel.

51 Unclip and disconnect the luggage compartment light and tailgate switch where fitted.

52 Carefully release the securing clips around the edge of the trim panel, preferably using a forked tool. Move the panel forwards to unhook it from the seat catch, then pass seat belt through the panel and withdraw from the vehicle.

Refitting

53 Refitting is a reversal of removal.

Rear wheelarch trim panel

Removal

54 Remove the rear seat backs as described in Section 23.

55 Remove the side shelf trim panels as described in this Section.

56 Remove the rear shock absorber upper mounting cover.

57 Unclip the seatback side anchor plate bracket.

58 Remove the luggage compartment rear trim panel as described in this Section.

59 Carefully pull the panel from the inner wheelarch and withdraw towards the front of the vehicle.

Refitting

60 Refitting is a reversal of removal. Tighten the seat belt mounting bolt to the specified torque.

Roof console panel

Removal

61 Remove the interior light assembly as described in Chapter 12, Section 10.

62 Unclip the console from the headlining, then slide it away from the windscreen to remove **(see illustration)**.

63 Where applicable, disconnect the wiring from the remote control central locking receiver and sunroof switch, then withdraw the panel.

Refitting

64 Refitting is a reversal of removal.

Luggage compartment rear trim panel

65 The luggage compartment rear trim panel has four securing screws, it can then be lifted upwards to release the retaining clips on the upper edge. Withdraw the trim panel from the rear of the luggage compartment.

Tailgate trim panel

66 The panel is secured by one retaining screw and a number of plastic clips around the panel. Carefully pull the panel from the tailgate to release the clips **(see illustration)**, or release the clips using a suitable forked tool.

Front seat trim panels

67 The seat side trim panels are secured by a single screw, then clipped in place. Removal and refitting are self-evident.

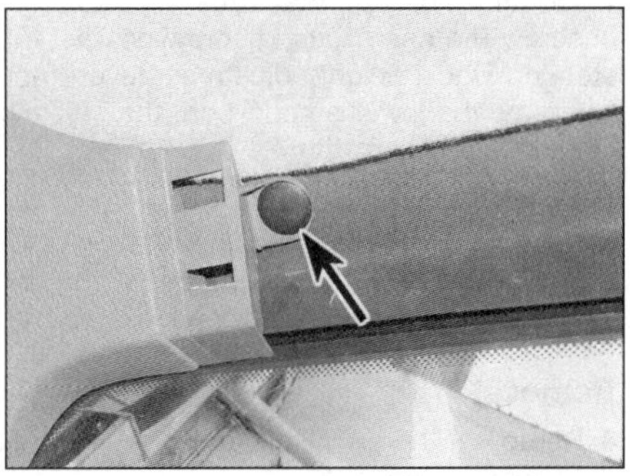
27.49b . . . and upper retaining clip (arrowed)

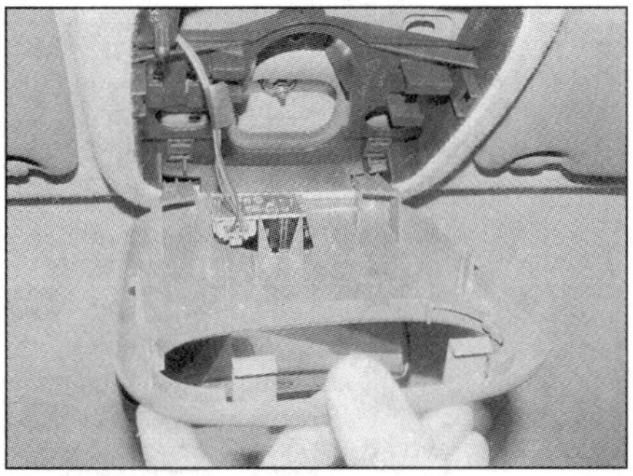
27.62 Withdrawing the roof console panel

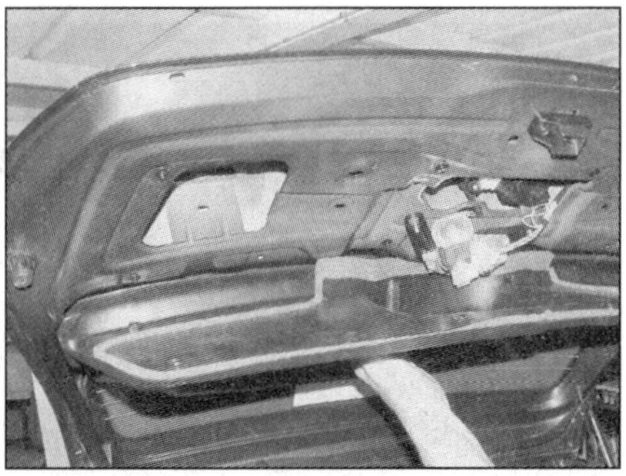
27.66 Removing the tailgate trim panel

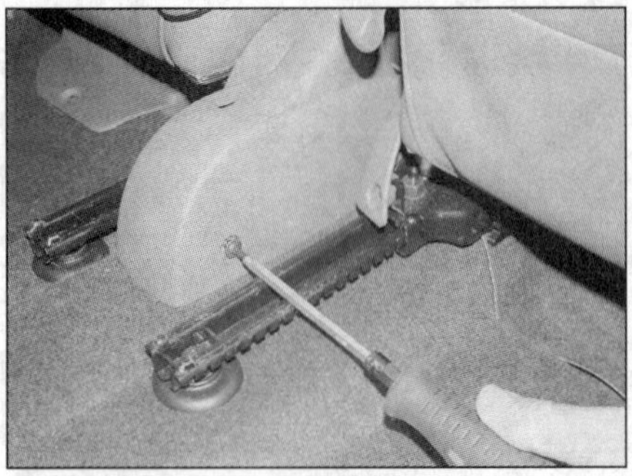

27.68 Removing the handbrake trim securing screws

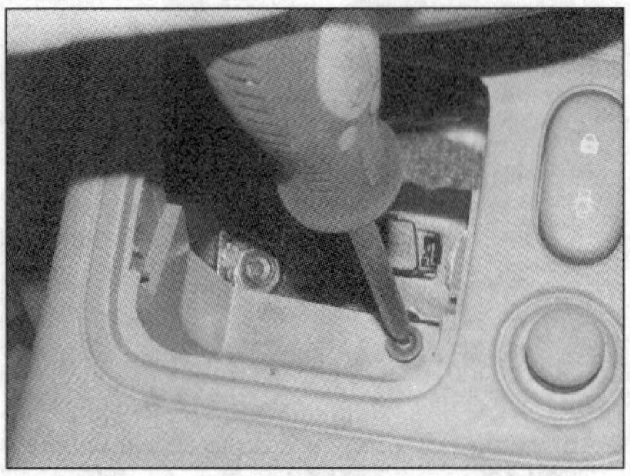

28.2 Removing the securing screw from under the ashtray

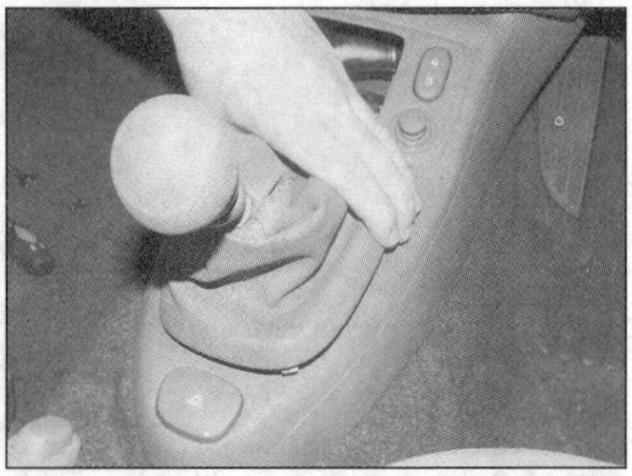

28.3 Unclipping the gear lever gaiter from the centre console

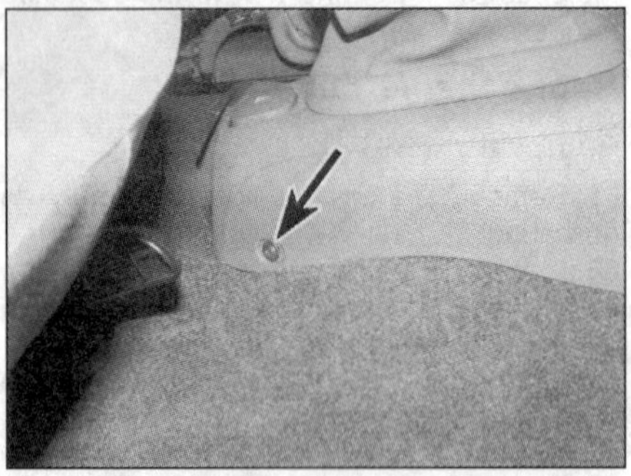

28.5a Remove the rear centre console securing screws (arrowed) . . .

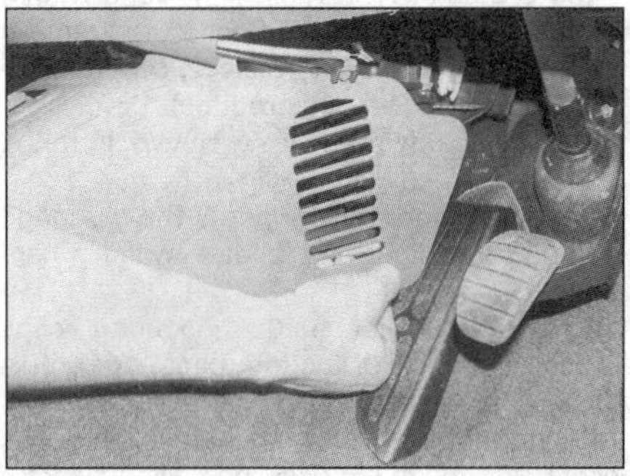

28.5b . . . and unclip the front of the centre console

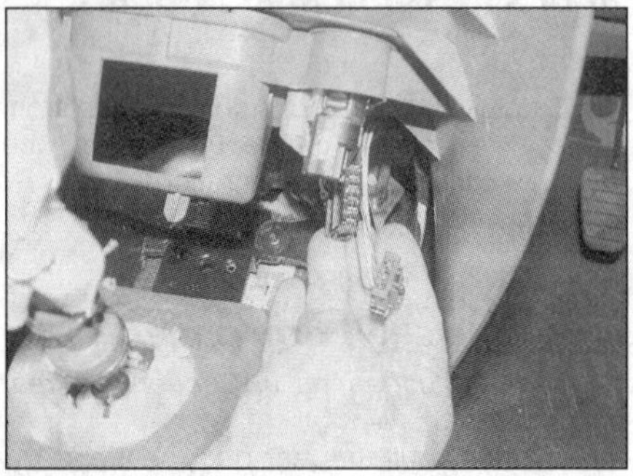

28.6 Withdraw the centre console and disconnect the wiring connectors

Handbrake lever trim

68 Move the two front seats as far forwards as possible. Undo the two securing screws from the rear of the handbrake trim, then push the trim forwards to remove **(see illustration)**.

28 Centre console – removal and refitting

Warning: On models fitted with seat belt pre-tensioners, de-activate the pre-tensioner system as described in Section 25.

Removal

1 Disconnect the battery negative lead.

2 Remove the ashtray from the centre console and undo the retaining screw from underneath **(see illustration)**.

3 On models fitted with a manual gearbox, unclip the gear lever gaiter from the centre console **(see illustration)**.

4 On models fitted with automatic transmission, unclip the selector lever surround from the centre console. Where applicable, undo the retaining screws.

5 Remove the two securing screws at the rear of the console, and release the securing clips (one each side) at the front of the console **(see illustrations)**. Withdraw the centre console from the floor, taking care not to strain any wiring.

6 Reach up under the centre console, and disconnect the wiring from the cigarette lighter and any switches mounted in the centre console **(see illustration)**.

7 Lift the centre console over the gear lever and gaiter (or selector lever surround and selector lever), and withdraw it from the car.

Refitting

8 Refitting is a reversal of removal.

29 Facia panels and components – removal and refitting

Warning: On models fitted with an airbag, read and follow the precautions given in Chapter 12, Section 27.

Steering column shrouds

Removal

1 Working under the steering column, unscrew the two securing screws nearest the steering wheel, then carefully lift the upper shroud from the steering column **(see illustration)**.

2 Working under the steering column, unscrew the one securing screw nearest the steering wheel height adjustment lever, then withdraw the lower shroud from the steering column **(see illustration)**.

Refitting

3 Refitting is a reversal of removal.

Upper facia trim panel

Removal

4 Remove the A-pillar trim panels as described in Section 27.

5 Remove the steering column shrouds as described in this Section.

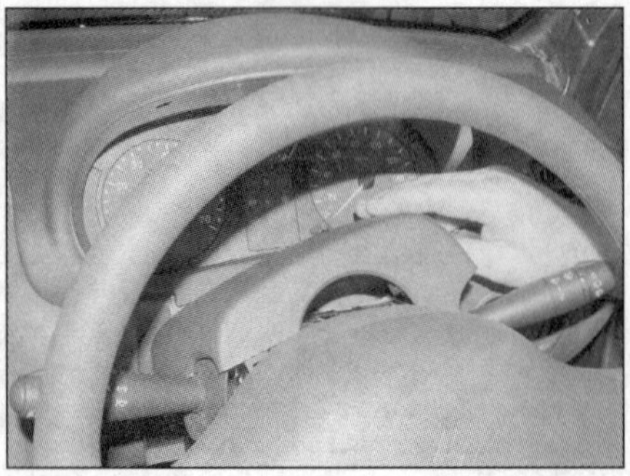

29.1 Remove the securing screws and withdraw the upper shroud

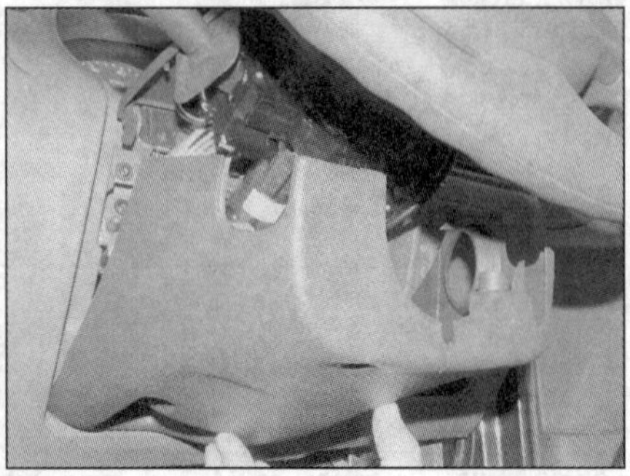

29.2 Unscrew the securing screw and withdraw the lower shroud

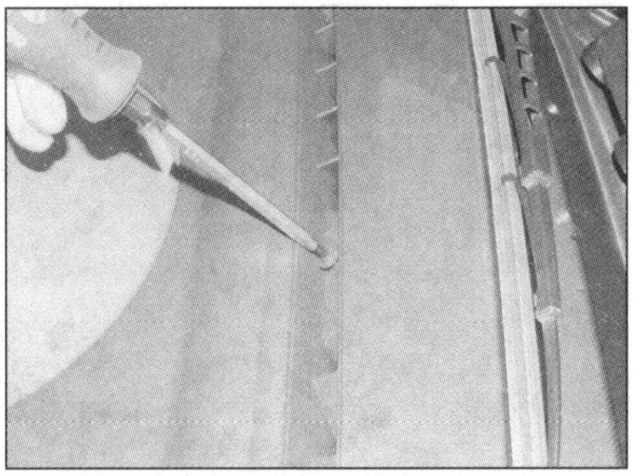

29.6a Unscrewing an upper facia trim panel top securing screw . . .

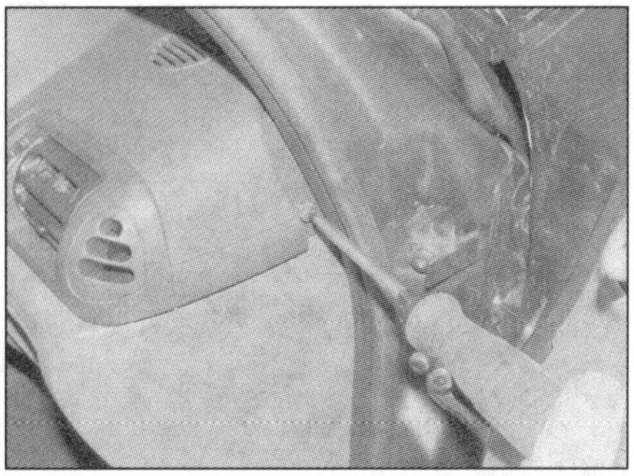

29.6b . . . and side securing screw

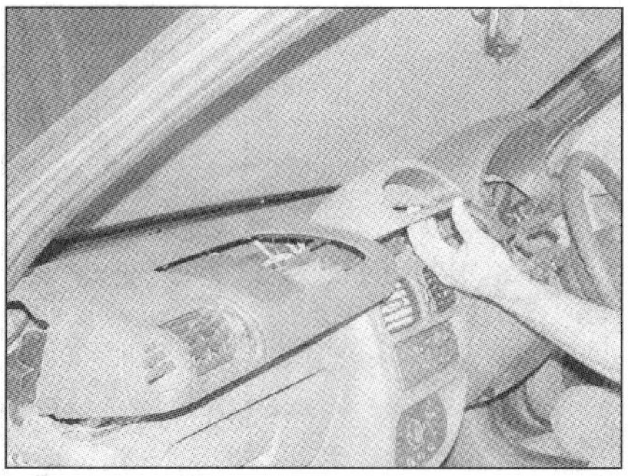

29.7 Removing the upper facia trim panel

6 Undo the seven securing screws (three along the top edge of the facia near to the windscreen, one at each end of the facia and two below the instrument panel) **(see illustrations)**.

7 Slide the upper facia panel towards you, away from the windscreen, to remove from the lower part of the facia **(see illustration)**.

Refitting

8 Refitting is a reversal of removal.

Heater ducts and vents

9 Refer to Chapter 3, Section 12.

Glovebox lid

Removal

10 Open the glovebox lid, and unclip the rubber stay.

11 Using a thin screwdriver, slide the two hinge pins inwards at the lower part of the glovebox lid.

12 Remove the glovebox lid from the facia.

Refitting

13 Refitting is a reversal of removal.

Complete facia assembly

Note: *This is an involved procedure, which is likely to take some time. It is advisable to make careful notes as the procedure progresses, to ensure correct refitting of all components, and correct routing of all wiring, etc. Specific details of fixings and components may vary from model to model, but the following will serve as a guide. Provided plenty of time is allowed, removal of the facia assembly should not present any problems.*

Removal

14 Disconnect the battery negative lead.

15 Remove the steering wheel as described in Chapter 10.

16 Remove the upper facia trim panel and steering column shrouds as described previously in this Section.

17 Unclip the immobiliser antenna ring from around the ignition switch and disconnect the wiring connector **(see illustration)**.

18 Undo the instrument panel securing screws and disconnect the wiring block connectors on removal **(see illustration)**.

19 Undo the two retaining screws from the central display (where fitted), and disconnect the wiring connectors **(see illustration)**.

20 Disconnect the wiring connector from the passenger airbag assembly (where fitted), then undo the six mounting screws to remove, as described in Chapter 12, Section 28.

21 Remove the four screws (each one securing earth wires) along the top of the reinforcement beam behind the facia **(see illustration)**.

22 Disconnect the wiring connectors from the tweeters at each end of the facia **(see illustration)**.

23 Using the special tool, remove the radio/cassette and disconnect the wiring as described in Chapter 12, Section 23.

24 Remove the centre console as described in Section 28.

25 Remove the two securing screws for the heater control unit **(see illustration)**, and unclip it from the facia (leaving it still connected to the cables and wiring).

26 Remove the steering column switches as described in Chapter 12, Section 6.

27 Unclip the trim from around the headlight height adjustment switch and disconnect the wiring connector.

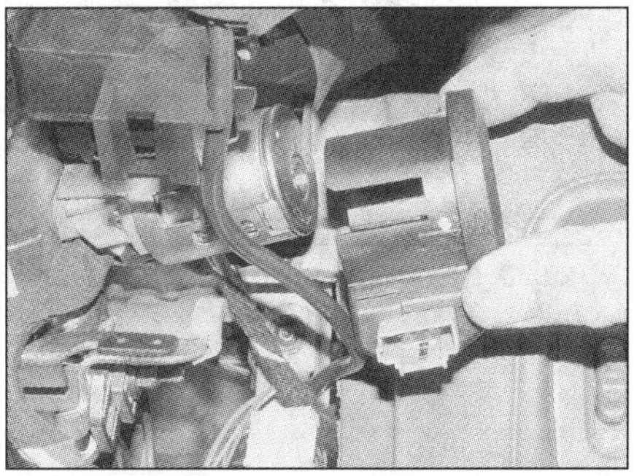

29.17 Unclipping the immobiliser antenna ring from the ignition switch

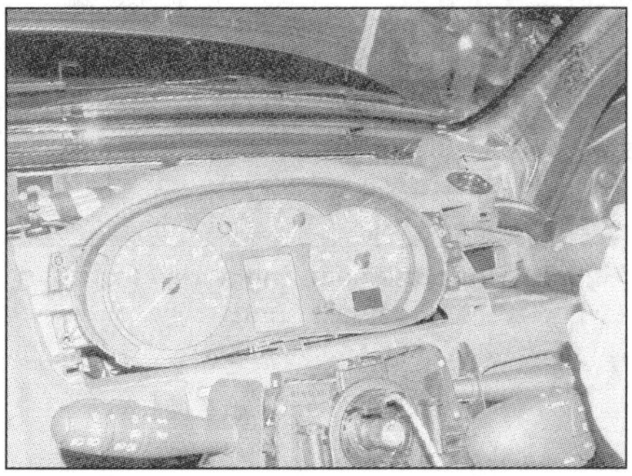

29.18 Removing an instrument panel securing screw

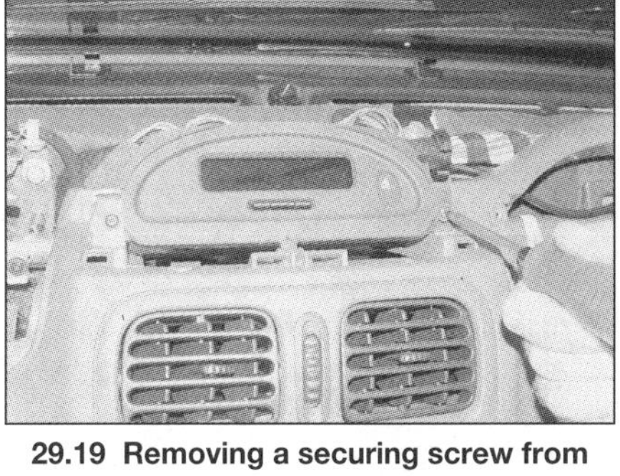

29.19 Removing a securing screw from the central display unit

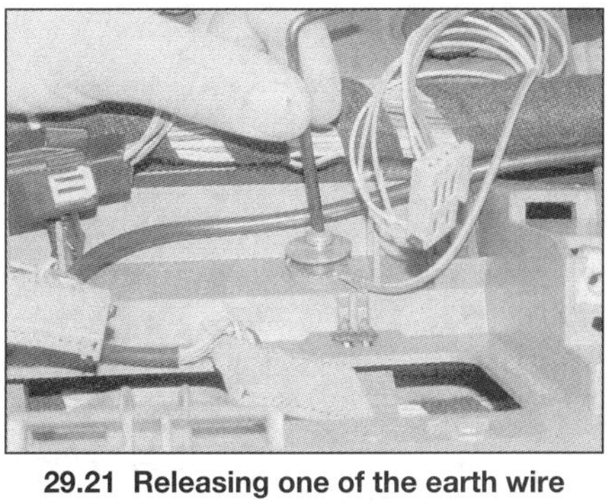

29.21 Releasing one of the earth wire retaining screws

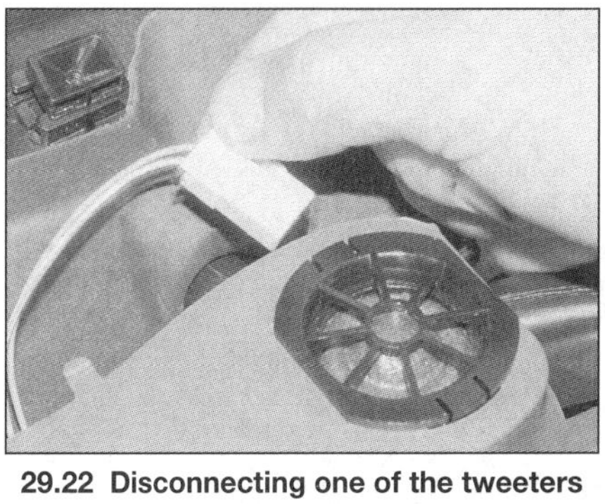

29.22 Disconnecting one of the tweeters

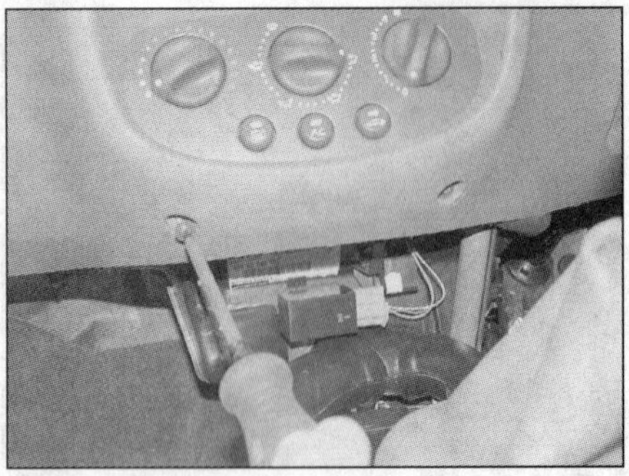
29.25 Undo the two heater panel securing screws

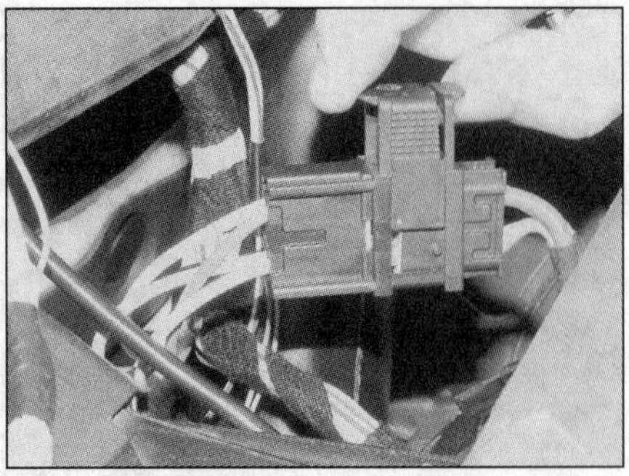
29.28 Disconnecting the ignition switch wiring block connector

29.30 Unclipping the fusebox cover

28 Slide the retaining clip up and disconnect the wiring block connector for the ignition switch **(see illustration)**.
29 Remove the steering column as described in Chapter 10.
30 Remove the cover from the fuse box at the end of the facia **(see illustration)**.
31 Unclip the covers from the lower edge of the facia panel and undo the securing screws (one at each end of the facia) **(see illustration)**.
32 Undo the facia lower securing screw from the heater unit at the centre **(see illustration)**.
33 Remove the two facia securing screws from above the steering column aperture **(see illustration)**.
34 Make a final check to ensure that all wires, cables and hoses are disconnected and moved clear of the facia.
35 With the aid of an assistant, carefully lift and withdraw the right-hand side of the facia assembly from the bulkhead first. Remove the facia from the car through one of the front doors.
36 If the facia is difficult to remove, do not use excessive force – check that all necessary wiring has been disconnected, and that the harnesses are not fouling surrounding components.

Refitting

37 Refitting is a reversal of removal, bearing in mind the following points.
38 As the facia assembly is offered to the bulkhead, ensure that none of the wiring harnesses, plugs, cables or hoses are trapped.
39 Ensure that all wiring connectors are securely reconnected, and that all connector securing clips are in place, where applicable.
40 On completion, check that all switches, lights and instruments function correctly.

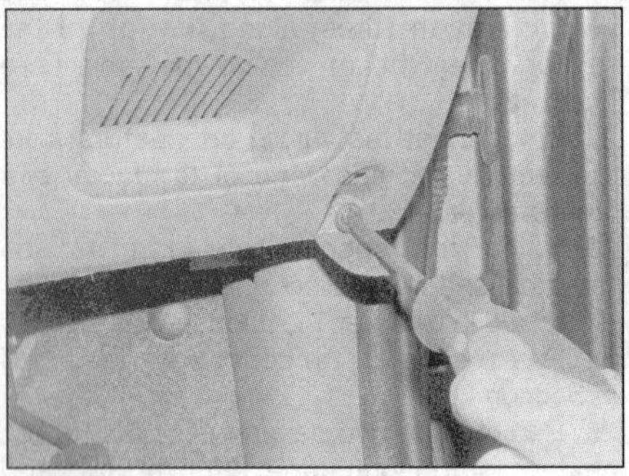
29.31 Removing one of the lower facia panel securing screws

29.32 Undo the securing screw from the heater unit

29.33 Removing one of the two facia securing screws

Chapter 12
Body electrical system

Contents

Degrees of difficulty

Easy, suitable for novice with little experience	**Fairly easy,** suitable for beginner with some experience	**Fairly difficult,** suitable for competent DIY mechanic	**Difficult,** suitable for experienced DIY mechanic	**Very difficult,** suitable for expert DIY or professional

Specifications

General

System type	12 volt, negative earth	

Torque wrench setting

	Nm	**lbf ft**
Airbag securing bolts	5	4

1 General information and precautions

Warning: *Before carrying out any work on the electrical system, read through the precautions given in 'Safety first!' at the beginning of this manual, and in Chapter 5A.*

The electrical system is of 12 volt negative earth type. Power for the lights and all electrical accessories is supplied by a lead/acid type battery, which is charged by the alternator.

This Chapter covers repair and service procedures for the various electrical components not associated with engine. Information on the battery, alternator and starter motor can be found in Chapter 5A.

It should be noted that, prior to working on any component in the electrical system, the battery negative terminal should first be disconnected, to prevent the possibility of electrical short-circuits and/or fires.

Caution: Before disconnecting the battery, refer to the information given in 'Disconnecting the battery' in the Reference Section of this manual.

2 Electrical fault finding – general information

Note: *Refer to the precautions given in 'Safety first!' and at the beginning of Chapter 5A before starting work. The following tests relate to testing of the main electrical circuits, and should not be used to test delicate electronic circuits (such as anti-lock braking systems), particularly where an electronic control module is used.*

General

1 A typical electrical circuit consists of an electrical component, any switches, relays, motors, fuses, fusible links or circuit breakers related to that component, and the wiring and connectors which link the component to both the battery and the chassis. To help to pinpoint a problem in an electrical circuit, wiring diagrams are included at the end of this Chapter.

2 Before attempting to diagnose an electrical fault, first study the appropriate wiring diagram, to obtain a more complete understanding of the components included in the particular circuit concerned. The possible sources of a fault can be narrowed down by noting whether other components related to the circuit are operating properly. If several components or circuits fail at one time, the problem is likely to be related to a shared fuse or earth connection.

3 Electrical problems usually stem from simple causes, such as loose or corroded connections, a faulty earth connection, a blown fuse, a melted fusible link, or a faulty relay (refer to Section 4 for details of testing relays). Visually inspect the condition of all fuses, wires and connections in a problem circuit before testing the components. Use the wiring diagrams to determine which terminal connections will need to be checked, in order to pinpoint the trouble-spot.

4 The basic tools required for electrical fault finding include a circuit tester or voltmeter (a 12 volt bulb with a set of test leads can also be used for certain tests); a self-powered test light (sometimes known as a continuity tester); an ohmmeter (to measure resistance); a battery and set of test leads; and a jumper wire, preferably with a circuit breaker or fuse incorporated, which can be used to bypass suspect wires or electrical components. Before attempting to locate a problem with test instruments, use the wiring diagram to determine where to make the connections.

5 To find the source of an intermittent wiring fault (usually due to a poor or dirty connection, or damaged wiring insulation), a 'wiggle' test can be performed on the wiring. This involves wiggling the wiring by hand, to see if the fault occurs as the wiring is moved. It should be possible to narrow down the source of the fault to a particular section of wiring. This method of testing can be used in conjunction with any of the tests described in the following sub-Sections.

6 Apart from problems due to poor connections, two basic types of fault can occur in an electrical circuit – open-circuit, or short-circuit.

7 Open-circuit faults are caused by a break somewhere in the circuit, which prevents current from flowing. An open-circuit fault will prevent a component from working, but will not cause the relevant circuit fuse to blow.

8 Short-circuit faults are caused by a 'short' somewhere in the circuit, which allows the current flowing in the circuit to 'escape' along an alternative route, usually to earth. Short-circuit faults are normally caused by a breakdown in wiring insulation, which allows a feed wire to touch either another wire, or an earthed component such as the bodyshell. A short-circuit fault will normally cause the relevant circuit fuse to blow.

3.2 Unclip the lower part of the fusebox cover to remove

Finding an open-circuit

9 To check for an open-circuit, connect one lead of a circuit tester or voltmeter to either the negative battery terminal or a known good earth.

10 Connect the other lead to a connector in the circuit being tested, preferably nearest to the battery or fuse.

11 Switch on the circuit, bearing in mind that some circuits are live only when the ignition switch is moved to a particular position.

12 If voltage is present (indicated either by the tester bulb lighting or a voltmeter reading, as applicable), this means that the section of the circuit between the relevant connector and the battery is problem-free.

13 Continue to check the remainder of the circuit in the same fashion.

14 When a point is reached at which no voltage is present, the problem must lie between that point and the previous test point with voltage. Most problems can be traced to a broken, corroded or loose connection.

Finding a short-circuit

15 To check for a short-circuit, first disconnect the load(s) from the circuit (loads are the components which draw current from a circuit, such as bulbs, motors, heating elements, etc).

16 Remove the relevant fuse from the circuit, and connect a circuit tester or voltmeter to the fuse connections.

17 Switch on the circuit, bearing in mind that some circuits are live only when the ignition switch is moved to a particular position.

18 If voltage is present (indicated either by the tester bulb lighting or a voltmeter reading, as applicable), this means that there is a short-circuit.

19 If no voltage is present, but the fuse still blows with the load(s) connected, this indicates an internal fault in the load(s).

Finding an earth fault

20 The battery negative terminal is connected to 'earth' – the metal of the engine/transmission unit and the car body – and most systems are wired so that they only receive a positive feed, the current returning via the metal of the car body. This means that the component mounting and the body form part of that circuit. Loose or corroded mountings can therefore cause a range of electrical faults, ranging from total failure of a circuit, to a puzzling partial fault. In particular, lights may shine dimly (especially when another circuit sharing the same earth point is in operation), motors (eg, wiper motors or the radiator cooling fan motor) may run slowly, and the operation of one circuit may have an apparently-unrelated effect on another. Note that on many vehicles, earth straps are used between certain components, such as the engine/transmission and the body, usually where there is no metal-to-metal contact between components, due to flexible rubber mountings, etc.

21 To check whether a component is properly earthed, disconnect the battery, and connect one lead of an ohmmeter to a known good earth point. Connect the other lead to the wire or earth connection being tested. The resistance reading should be zero; if not, check the connection as follows.

22 If an earth connection is thought to be faulty, dismantle the connection, and clean back to bare metal both the bodyshell and the wire terminal or the component earth connection mating surface. Be careful to remove all traces of dirt and corrosion, then use a knife to trim away any paint, so that a clean metal-to-metal joint is made. On reassembly, tighten the joint fasteners securely; if a wire terminal is being refitted, use serrated washers between the terminal and the bodyshell, to ensure a clean and secure connection. When the connection is remade, prevent the onset of corrosion in the future by applying a coat of petroleum jelly or silicone-based grease, or by spraying on (at regular intervals) a proprietary ignition sealer.

3 Fusebox – removal and refitting

Note: *Additional fuses are located in an auxiliary fusebox under the bonnet (see illustration 4.4).*

Removal

1 Disconnect the battery negative lead.

2 Unclip the fusebox cover from the left-hand side of the facia panel **(see illustration)**.

3 Unscrew the two securing screws from the fusebox **(see illustration)**.

4 Carefully lower the fusebox from under the facia.

Refitting

5 Refitting is a reversal of removal.

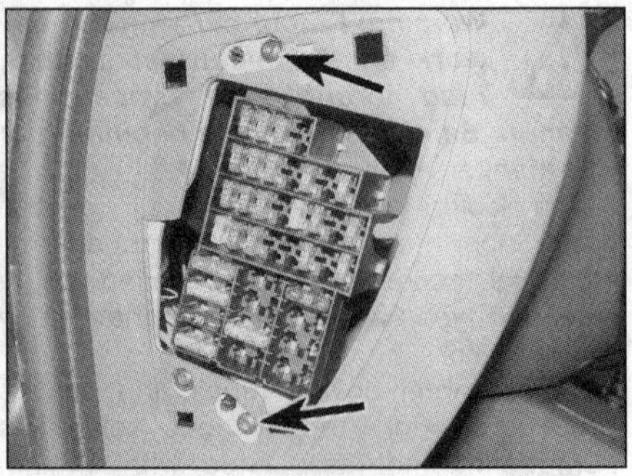

3.3 Undo the two securing screws (arrowed)

4.2 Most fuses are located behind the cover on the left-hand side of the facia

4.4 Other fuses located in the engine compartment fuse/relay box

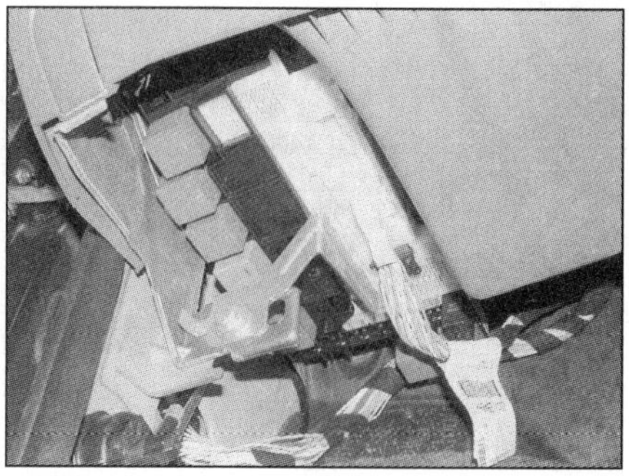

4.12a Location of the multi-timer control unit and relays

4 Fuses and relays – testing and renewal

Fuses

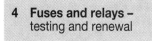

1 Fuses are designed to break a circuit when a predetermined current is reached, in order to protect components and wiring which could be damaged by excessive current flow. Any excessive current flow will be due to a fault in the circuit, usually a short-circuit (see Section 2).

2 The main fuses are located in the fusebox, in the left-hand side of the facia panel **(see illustration)**.

3 For access to the fuses, unclip the cover and withdraw from the facia. The circuits protected by the fuses are marked on a the inside of the fusebox cover.

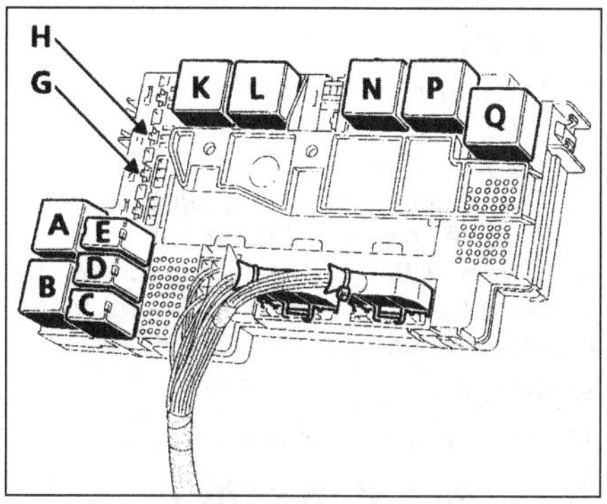

4.12b Identification of relays in the multi-timer unit

A Front foglight relay
B Heated rear window relay
C Indicator relay
D Drivers one-touch electric window raise relay
E Drivers one-touch electric window lower relay
G Running lights – side lights relay*
H Running lights – dipped headlights relay*
K Front wiper relay
L Rear wiper relay
N Central door locking relay
P Central door unlocking relay
Q After ignition relay
** Dipped headlights and sidelights illuminated after starting the engine (extreme cold).*

4 Additional fuses are located in an auxiliary fusebox under the bonnet **(see illustration)**, beneath a hinged cover behind the battery on the left-hand side of the engine compartment. For access to these fuses, lift the panel cover, then unclip the cover from the fusebox. The circuits protected by the fuses are marked on the inside of the panel cover. The fuse for the radio/cassette player is mounted on the rear of the unit.

5 A blown fuse can be recognised from its melted or broken wire.

6 To remove a fuse, first ensure that the relevant circuit is switched off.

7 Using the plastic tool provided on the fusebox cover, pull the fuse from its location.

8 Spare fuses are provided on the inside of the cover.

9 Before renewing a blown fuse, trace and rectify the cause, and always use a fuse of the correct rating. Never substitute a fuse of a higher rating, or make temporary repairs using wire or metal foil; more serious damage, or even fire, could result.

10 Note that the fuses are colour-coded as follows. Refer to the wiring diagrams for details of the fuse ratings and the circuits protected.

Colour	Rating
Orange	*5A*
Red	*10A*
Blue	*15A*
Yellow	*20A*
Clear or white	*25A*
Green	*30A*

Relays

11 A relay is an electrically-operated switch, which is used for the following reasons.

a) *A relay can switch a heavy current remotely from the circuit in which the current is flowing, therefore allowing the use of lighter gauge wiring and switch contacts.*
b) *A relay can receive more than one control input, unlike a mechanical switch.*
c) *A relay can have a 'timer' function – for example, the intermittent wiper relay.*

12 Most of the relays are located inside the vehicle, under the facia on the left-hand side **(see illustrations)**, along with the multi-timer unit (see Section 5).

13 Certain models have a relay box located in the engine compartment, on the left-hand side, in front of the suspension turret. The box contains relays for the fuel injection system and/or the power steering pump.

14 If a circuit controlled by a relay develops a fault, and the relay is suspect, operate the circuit. If the relay is functioning, it should be possible to hear the relay click as it is energised. If this is the case, the fault lies with the components or wiring in the system. If the relay is not being energised, then either the relay is not receiving a switching voltage, or the relay itself is faulty (do not overlook the relay socket terminals when tracing faults). Testing is by the substitution of a known good unit, but be careful; while some relays are identical in appearance and in operation, others look similar, but perform different functions.

5 Multi-timer unit – general information

1 The multi-timer unit is located under the left-hand side of the facia panel, along with the relays (see illustration 4.12a). If the multi-timer is to be replaced, remove all the relays first, then the multi-timer unit can be disengaged from the relay mounting unit **(see illustration)**. Note that

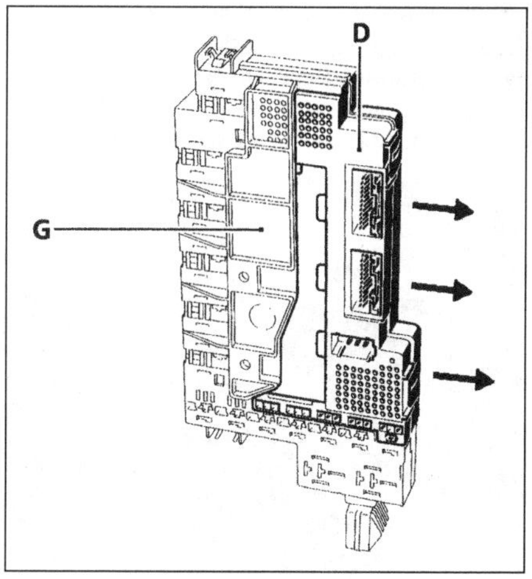

5.1 Unclip the multi-timer (D) from the relay mounting unit (G)

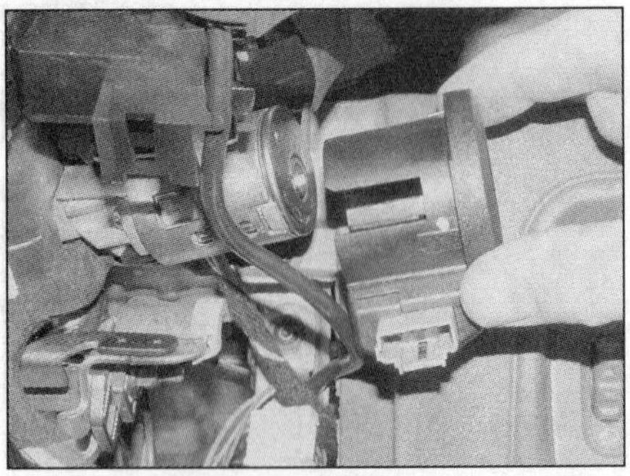

6.3 Unclip the immobiliser from around the ignition switch

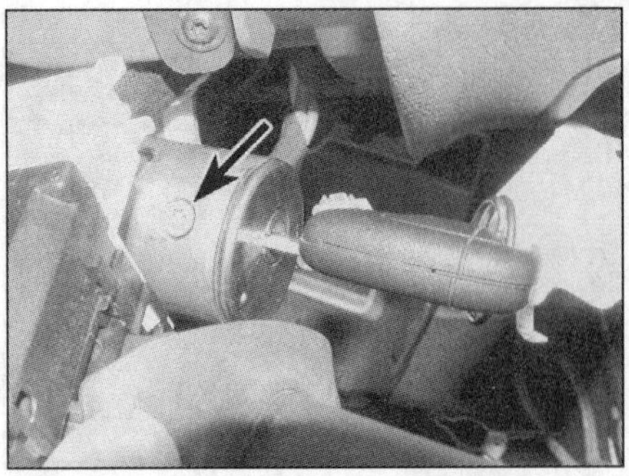

6.6 Unscrew the ignition switch grub screw (arrowed)

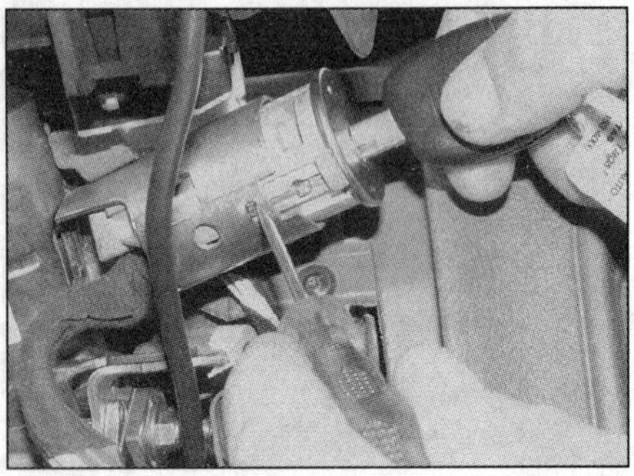

6.7 Depressing the ignition switch securing clip

once removed, the immobiliser, remote control, engine configuration, etc, will all need re-programming, if this is not done correctly it will prevent the vehicle from starting. Because of the specialised equipment required, this may have to be entrusted to your local Renault dealer.

2 There are four models of multi-timer units available, depending on the equipment level in the vehicle.

Level 1 – Basic model (no options) – Part number 7700 411 318

Controlling:

- the indicators and hazard warning lights.
- the front and rear wipers.
- the courtesy light (without timer).
- the lights 'on' reminder buzzer.
- the immobiliser.

Level 2 – Basic model (with options) – Part number 7700 411 319

Controlling (in addition to level 1):

- the central door locking with remote control.
- the front electric windows.
- the courtesy light timer (one bulb).

Level 3 – High specification model (no options) – Part number 7700 411 322

Controlling (in addition to levels 1 & 2):

- the variable front wiper timing.
- the one-touch front electric windows.
- the door/tailgate open warning light.
- the rear wiper in reverse gear.

Level 4 – High specification model (with options) – Part number 7700 411 321

Controlling (in addition to levels 1, 2 & 3):

- the running lights* (extreme cold).
- the headlight washers (extreme cold).
- the courtesy light timer (three bulbs).
- the door sill lighting timer (two bulbs).
- the overspeed warning (Arabia).
- dipped headlights and side lights illuminated after starting the engine (running lights).

6 Switches – removal and refitting

Ignition switch and immobiliser

Removal

1 Disconnect the battery negative lead.

2 Remove the steering column shrouds as described in Chapter 11, Section 29.

3 Disconnect the wiring connector from the immobiliser, and unclip it from around the ignition switch **(see illustration)**.

4 Follow the switch wiring behind the facia, and disconnect the wiring connectors. If necessary, remove the instrument panel as described in Section 12. Take note of the routing of the wiring.

5 Insert the ignition key into the switch, and turn it midway between A and M (or 3).

6 Using a Torx key, remove the grub screw securing the switch assembly to the steering column **(see illustration)**.

7 Using a screwdriver, depress the securing clip located at the bottom of the switch assembly, then pull the assembly from the steering column using the key **(see illustration)**. Feed the wiring through the steering column as the switch is withdrawn.

8 On some models, separate the switch from the lock assembly, by removing the two securing screws from the rear of the housing, and lifting off the rear cover. The switch can now be withdrawn from the lock.

Refitting

9 Refitting is a reversal of removal, bearing in mind the following points.

10 When refitting the switch to the lock assembly, make sure that the lugs on the lock engage with the cut-outs in the switch. Note that the switch will only fit in one position.

11 Ensure that the switch wiring is routed as noted before removal.

Lights/indicators/horn stalk switch

Removal

12 Disconnect the battery negative lead.

13 Remove the steering column shrouds as described in Chapter 11, Section 29.

14 Disconnect the wiring plug from the switch assembly **(see illustration)**.

15 Unscrew the two securing screws and withdraw the switch from the steering column **(see illustrations)**.

Refitting

16 Refitting is a reversal of removal.

Wash/wipe stalk switch

17 Proceed as just described for the lights/indicators/horn stalk switch.

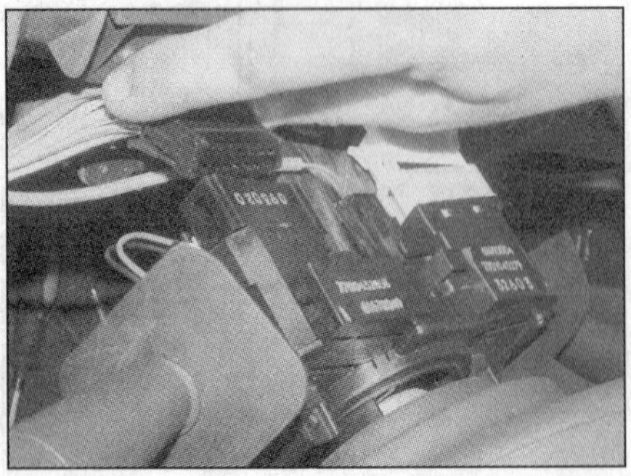

6.14 Disconnect the wiring plug from the switch

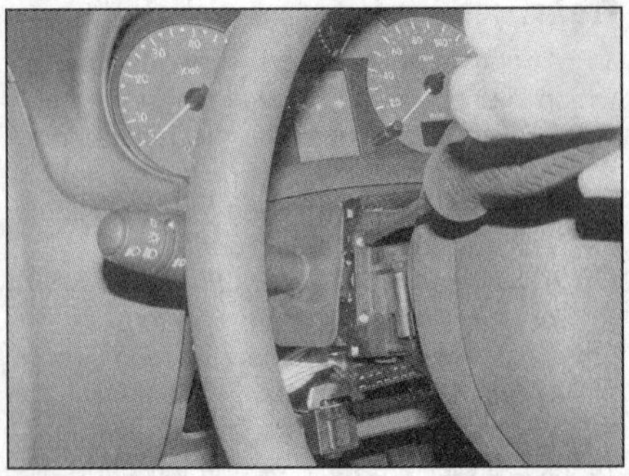

6.15a Unscrew the securing screws . . .

6.15b . . . and withdraw the stalk switch

Stalk switch assembly

Note: *Before removing the assembly, the position of the rotary switch MUST be noted. Either by ensuring the wheels are in the straight-ahead position or by checking that the 0 mark on the rotary switch is in line with the fixed reference mark (E)* ***(see illustration)****.*

Removal

18 Remove the steering wheel as described in Chapter 10.

19 Remove the steering column shrouds as described in Chapter 11, Section 29.

20 Disconnect the wiring plugs from the switches.

21 Where applicable, undo the radio/cassette remote control switch retaining screw from the bracket on the stalk switch assembly **(see illustration)**.

22 Loosen but do not remove the clamp screw, then tap with a screwdriver sharply to release the cone-shaped assembly from the column. Withdraw the assembly from the steering column **(see illustrations)**.

Refitting

Note: *Prior to refitting it is necessary to ensure that the contact unit is correctly centralised, with the wiring connector at the top of the unit, and that the front wheels are pointing in the straight-ahead position.*

23 Refitting is a reversal of removal. Refit the steering wheel and steering column shrouds as described in their relevant Chapters. **Note:** ***Do not*** *tighten the switch assembly clamp screw until the shrouds have been fitted* ***(see illustration).***

Radio/cassette player remote switch

Removal

24 Disconnect the battery negative lead.

25 Remove the radio/cassette player as described in Section 23. Disconnect the remote control switch wiring plug from the rear of the unit.

26 Where required, remove the steering column shrouds as described in Chapter 11, Section 29.

27 Unclip the cover, and undo the retaining screw from the switch on the stalk switch assembly **(see illustration)**.

28 Feed the wiring through from behind the facia, noting its routing, and remove the switch.

Refitting

29 Refitting is a reversal of removal, bearing in mind the following points.

30 Refit the radio/cassette player with reference to Section 23.

31 Ensure that the wiring is routed as noted during removal.

Heater-related switches

32 These switches are built into the heater control panel **(see illustration)**, remove the panel as described in Chapter 3, Section 13.

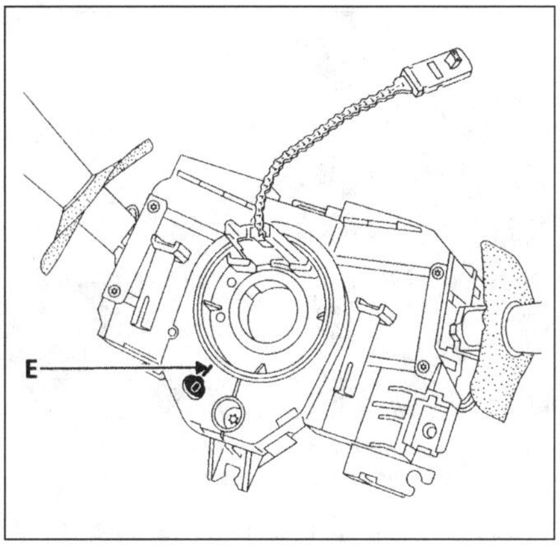

6.18a Valeo type of switch assembly

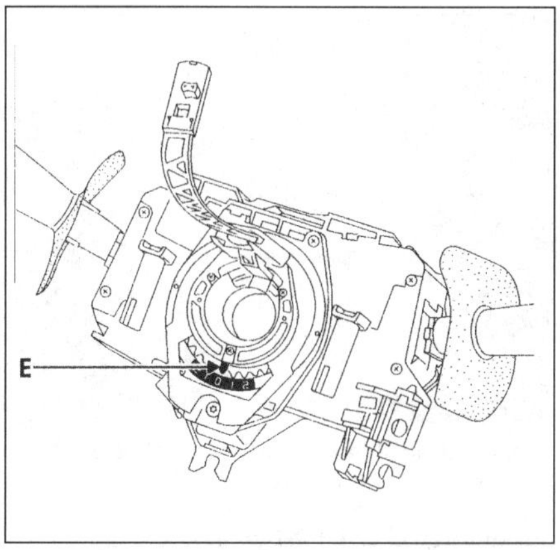

6.18b Lucas type of switch assembly

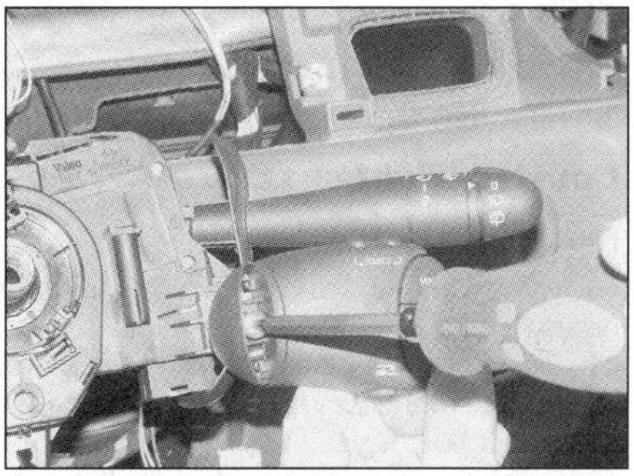

6.21 Remove the remote control retaining screw

6.22a Slacken screw, then tap gently . . .

6.22b . . . to release the switch assembly from the column

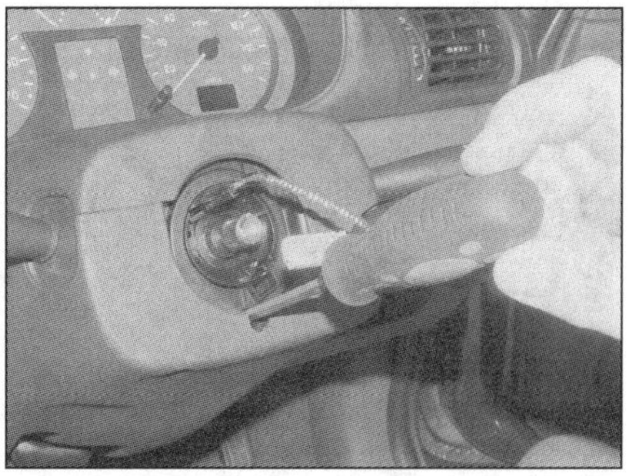

6.23 Tightening the switch clamp screw, after the shrouds have been fitted

6.27 Undo the retaining screw (arrowed) to remove the remote control switch

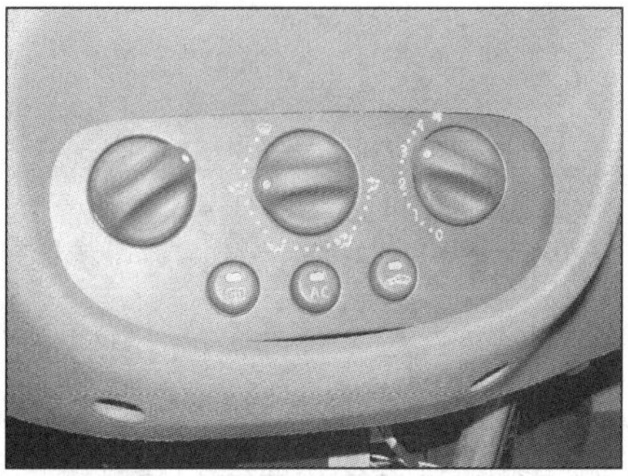

6.32 Switches are located in the heater control panel

6.33 Carefully prise the control panel from the facia

6.34 Disconnecting the wiring plug from the headlight control switch

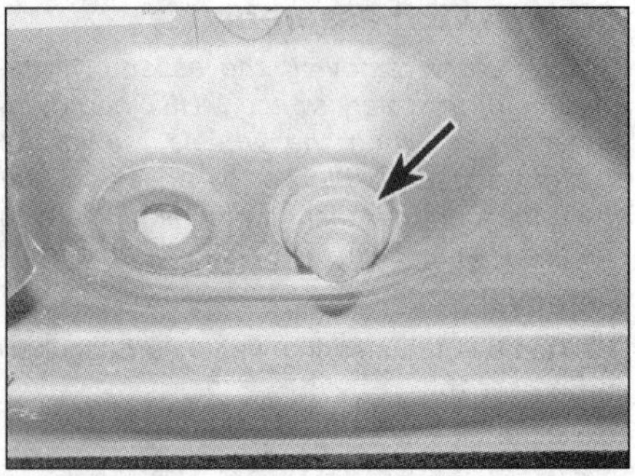

6.42 Unclip the rubber cover (arrowed) from the courtesy light switch

Headlight aim adjustment control

Removal

33 Using a screwdriver, carefully prise the control panel from the facia, taking care not to damage the facia trim **(see illustration)**.

34 Disconnect the wiring connector from the switch assembly **(see illustration)**, and unclip the switch from the control panel as required.

Refitting

35 Refitting is a reversal of removal.

Instrument panel illumination control

36 The switch (where fitted) is located in the same control panel as the headlight aim adjustment control.

37 To remove the switch, carry out the same procedure as described in paragraphs 33 and 34.

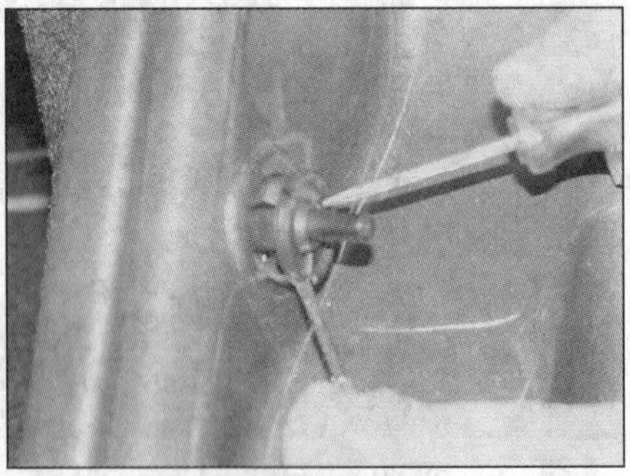

6.43 Using screwdrivers to release the switch from the door pillar

Central locking switches

38 Refer to Chapter 11, Section 16.

Electric window switches

39 Refer to Chapter 11, Section 17.

Courtesy light switches

Removal

40 The switches are located in the door pillars.

41 Disconnect the battery negative lead.

42 Pull the rubber cover from the switch **(see illustration)**.

43 Carefully prise the switch from the door pillar, and disconnect the wiring plug **(see illustration)**. Take care not to allow the wiring to drop down into the door pillar while the switch is removed – tape it to the door pillar if necessary.

Refitting

44 Refitting is a reversal of removal. **Note:** *Fit the rubber cover to the switch before refitting it into the pillar* ***(see illustration)****.*

Luggage compartment light switch

Removal

45 Disconnect the battery negative lead.

46 Open the tailgate. Pull the luggage compartment light switch from the rear shelf trim panel **(see illustration)**.

47 Disconnect the wiring plug from the switch **(see illustration)**.

Refitting

48 Refitting is a reversal of removal.

7 Bulbs (exterior lights) – renewal

General

1 Whenever a bulb is renewed, note the following points.

a) Disconnect the battery negative lead, or at least make sure that the lighting circuit is switched off, before starting work.

b) Remember that if the light has recently been in use, the bulb may be extremely hot.

c) Always check the bulb contacts and/or holder (as applicable). Ensure that there is clean metal-to-metal contact between the bulb contacts and the contacts in the holder, and/or the holder and the wiring plug. Clean off any corrosion or dirt before fitting a new bulb.

d) Ensure that the new bulb is of the correct rating and that it is completely clean before fitting; this applies particularly to headlight bulbs.

Headlight

Note: *Some headlights may vary slightly, depending on model.*

Note: *The headlight lenses are plastic and may melt if suitable bulbs are not fitted.*

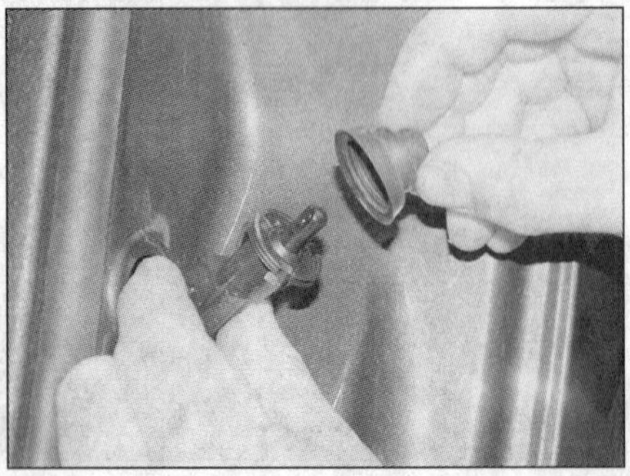

6.44 Fit the rubber cover to the switch before refitting the switch

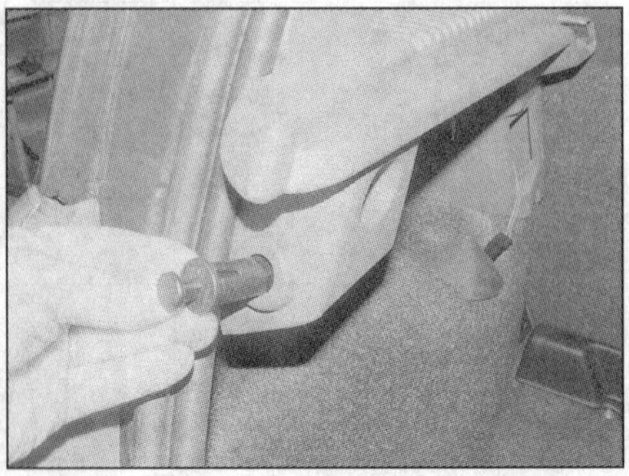

6.46 Release the switch from the trim panel

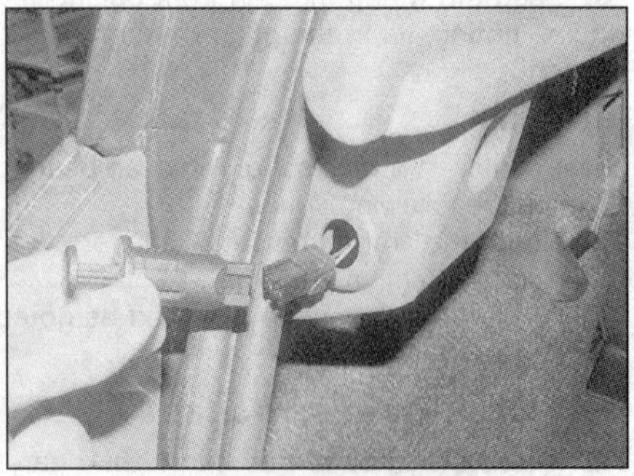

6.47 Disconnecting the wiring from the luggage compartment light switch

7.2 Disconnecting the wiring plug from the rear of the headlight

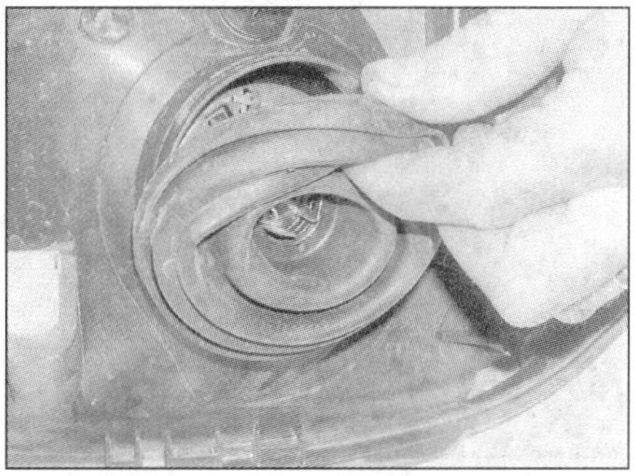

7.3 Unclip the rubber cover from the rear of the headlight unit

7.4a Release the spring clip . . .

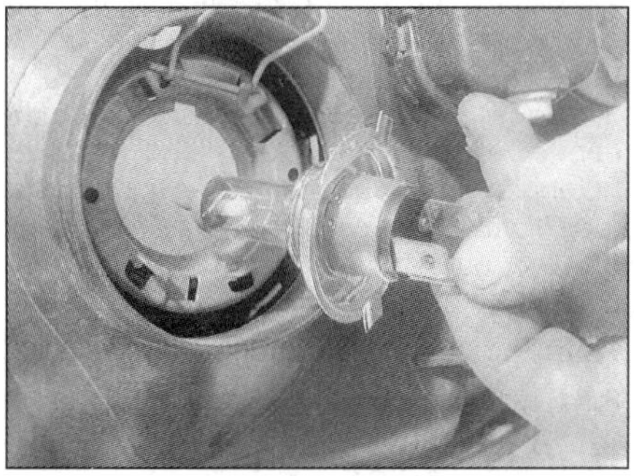

7.4b . . . and withdraw the headlight bulb

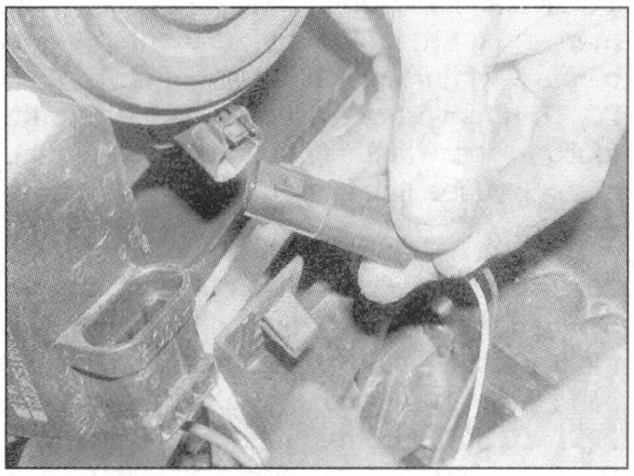

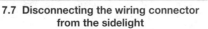

7.7 Disconnecting the wiring connector from the sidelight

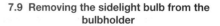

7.9 Removing the sidelight bulb from the bulbholder

Removal

2 Working in the engine compartment, pull the wiring plug from the rear of the headlight bulb **(see illustration)**.
3 Remove the rubber cover from the rear of the headlight **(see illustration)**.
4 Release the bulb retaining spring clip. Grasp the bulb by its contacts and carefully withdraw it from the headlight unit **(see illustration)**.

Refitting

5 When handling the new bulb, use a tissue or clean cloth to avoid touching the glass with the fingers; moisture and grease from the skin can cause blackening and rapid failure of this type of bulb.

> **HAYNES HiNT** ***If the headlight glass is accidentally touched, wipe it clean using methylated spirit.***

6 Refitting is a reversal of removal.

Front sidelight

Removal

7 Working in the engine compartment, pull the wiring plug from the rear of the sidelight bulbholder **(see illustration)**.
8 Twist the bulbholder anti-clockwise, and remove it from the rear of the headlight assembly.
9 The bulb is a push-fit (capless) in the bulbholder **(see illustration)**.

Refitting

10 Refitting is a reversal of removal, bearing in mind the following points.
11 Ensure that the rubber seal on the bulbholder is in good condition and is correctly fitted.

Front indicator

Removal

12 Working in the engine compartment, pull the wiring plug from the rear of the indicator bulbholder **(see illustration)**.
13 Twist the bulbholder anti-clockwise, and remove it from the rear of the indicator assembly.
14 The bulb is a bayonet fit in the bulbholder **(see illustration)**.

Refitting

15 Refitting is a reversal of removal.

Front indicator side repeater

Removal

16 Carefully prise the light unit from the front wing **(see illustration)**.

7.12 Disconnecting the wiring connector from the indicator

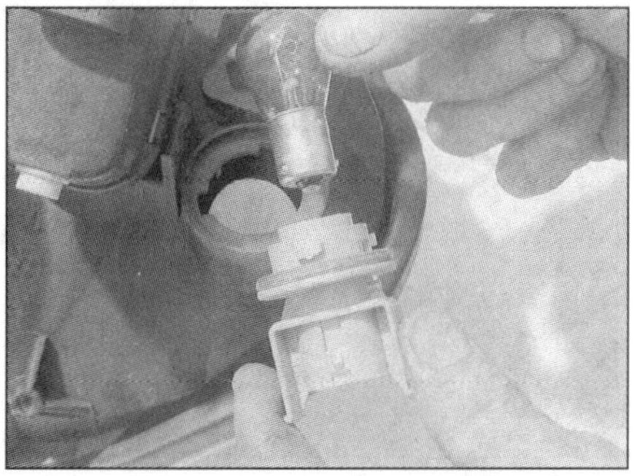

7.14 Removing a front direction indicator light bulb

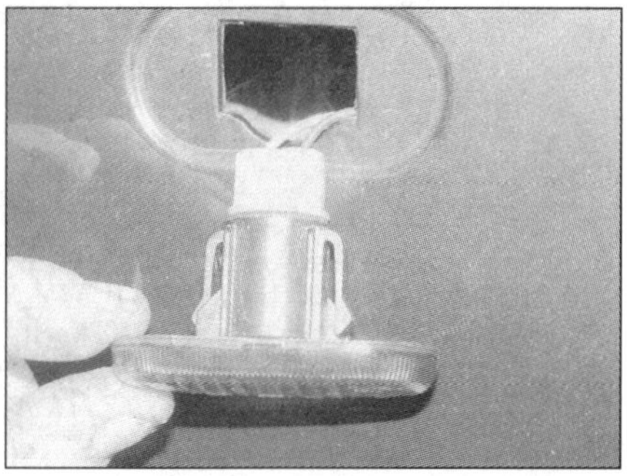

7.16 Direction indicator side repeater light removed from the wing

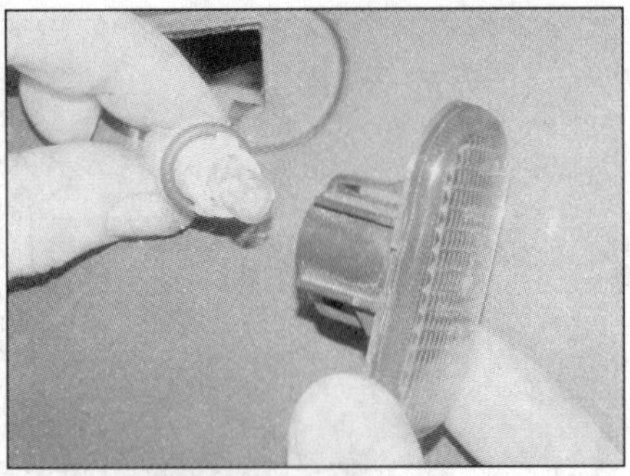

7.17 Twist the bulbholder to remove

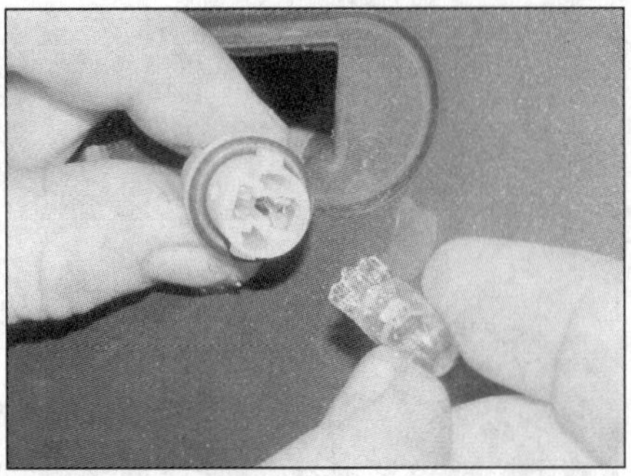

7.18 Removing the side repeater bulb

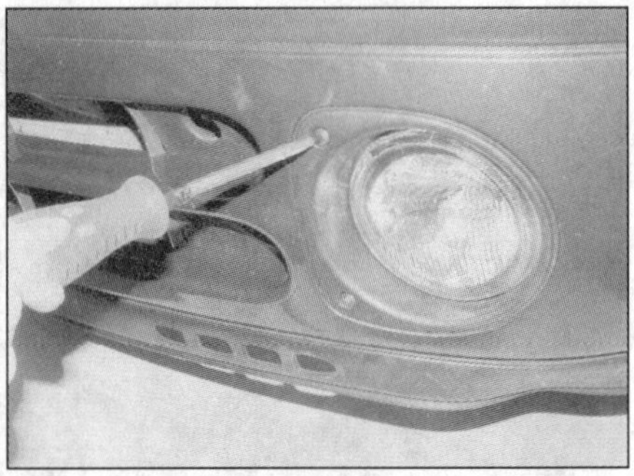

7.20 Unscrewing a front foglight securing screw

17 Twist the bulbholder anti-clockwise, and withdraw it from the rear of the light unit **(see illustration)**.

18 The bulb is a push-fit in the bulbholder **(see illustration)**.

Refitting

19 Refitting is a reversal of removal.

Front foglight

Removal

20 Unscrew the two securing screws, and remove the light from the front bumper **(see illustration)**.

21 Disconnect the wiring plug **(see illustration)**.

22 Twist the plastic cover anti-clockwise, and withdraw it from the rear of the light.

23 Disconnect the wiring from the rear of the bulb **(see illustration)**.

24 Release the bulb retaining spring clip, then grasp the bulb by its contacts and carefully withdraw it from the light unit.

25 To remove the plastic surround from the foglight, undo the three nuts on the rear of the assembly **(see illustration)**.

Refitting

26 When handling the new bulb, use a tissue or clean cloth to avoid touching the glass with the fingers; moisture and grease from the skin can cause blackening and rapid failure of this type of bulb. If the glass is accidentally touched, wipe it clean using methylated spirit.

27 Refitting is a reversal of removal.

Rear light cluster

Removal

28 Open the tailgate, and unscrew the rear light cluster securing nut **(see illustration)**.

29 Working outside the car, release the light cluster and lift it from the retaining lugs on the body. Disconnect the wiring plug.

30 Squeeze the securing clips towards the centre of the bulbholder, and pull the bulbholder from the rear of the light cluster **(see illustration)**.

31 The bulbs are a bayonet fit in their holders.

Refitting

32 Refitting is a reversal of removal.

High-level stop-light

Removal

33 Open the tailgate, and remove the rear spoiler as described in Chapter 11, Section 22.

34 Disconnect the wiring, and undo the two retaining screws to release the light unit from the rear spoiler **(see illustration)**.

7.21 Disconnecting a front foglight wiring plug

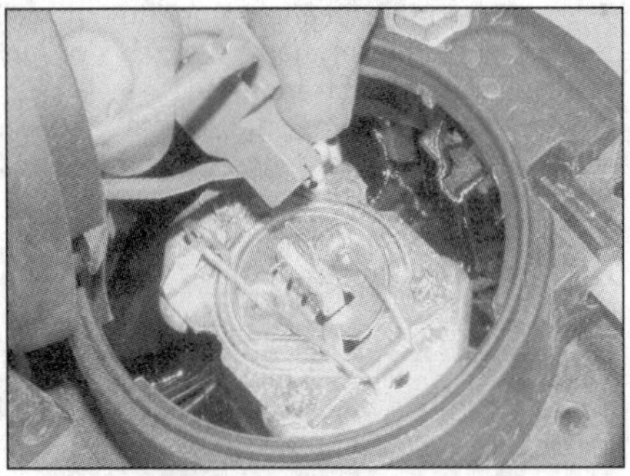

7.23 Disconnecting the wire connector from the foglight bulb

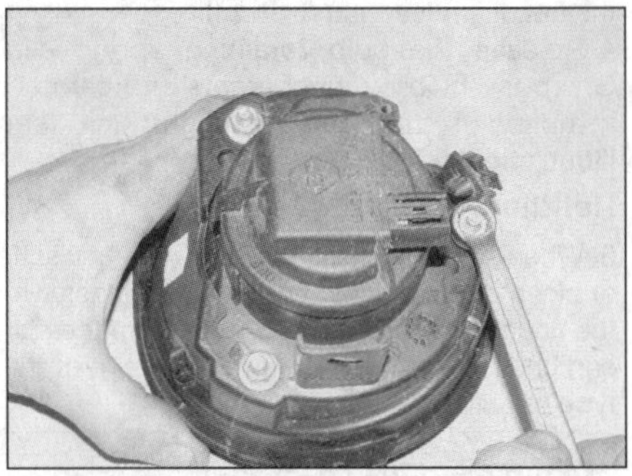

7.25 Removing the foglight surround securing nuts

7.28 Unscrewing a rear light cluster securing nut

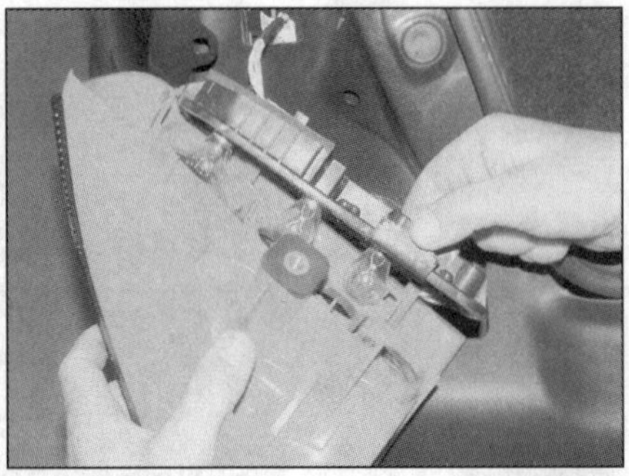

7.30 Squeeze the securing clips and remove the rear light cluster bulbholder

7.34 Disconnecting the wiring, from the high-level stop-light in the rear spoiler

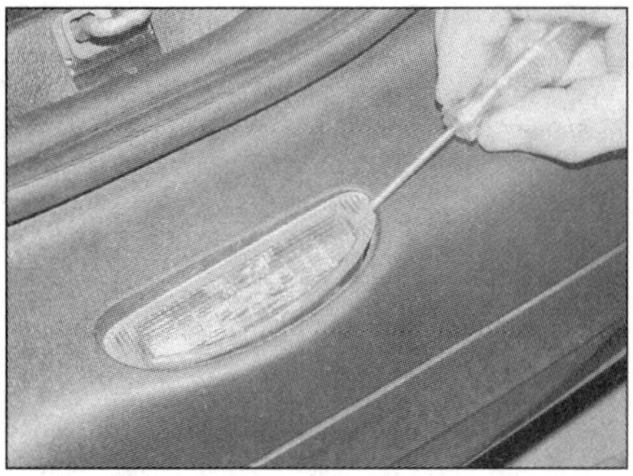

7.37 Using a screwdriver to release the number plate light from the bumper

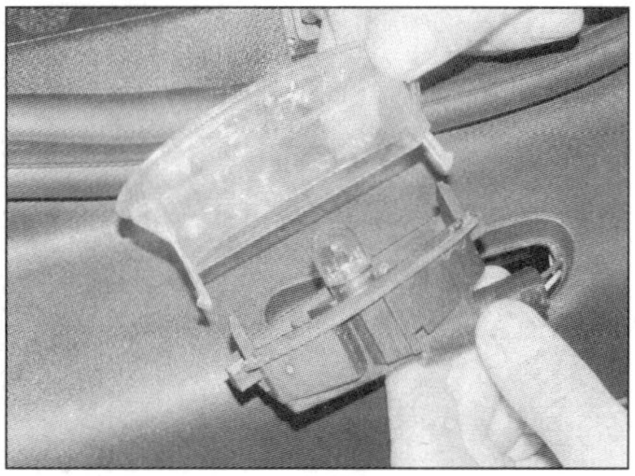

7.38 Unclip the lens to expose the bulb

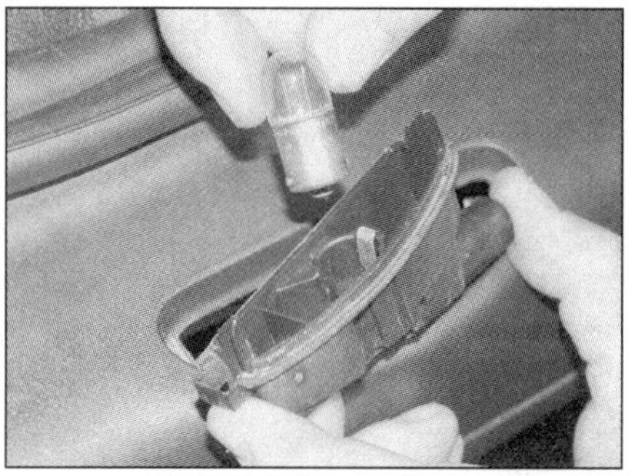

7.39 Removing the number plate light bulb

35 If the light unit is faulty, it will have to be renewed as a complete unit as it has an LED sealed unit.

Refitting

36 Refitting is a reversal of removal.

Rear number plate light

Removal

37 Using a screwdriver, carefully prise the number plate light assembly from its location in the bumper. Disconnect the wiring plug **(see illustration)**.

38 Release the securing tabs and unclip the lens from the light assembly **(see illustration)**.

39 The bulb is a bayonet fit in the holder **(see illustration)**.

Refitting

40 Refitting is a reversal of removal.

8 Bulbs (interior lights) – renewal

General

1 Refer to Section 7, paragraph 1.

Courtesy light

2 Unclip the interior light from the roof console for access to the bulb **(see illustration)**.

3 Release the lens from the light assembly and remove the festoon bulb **(see illustrations)**.

4 Refitting is a reversal of removal.

Luggage compartment light

5 Prise the light assembly from its location in the luggage compartment.

6 Unclip the lens, and remove the festoon bulb **(see illustrations)**.

7 Refitting is a reversal of removal.

Instrument panel and warning lights

8 The bulbs cannot be replaced on these instrument panels, as they are soldered LEDs.

Auxiliary display illumination

9 Refer to Section 14.

Cigarette lighter illumination

10 Remove the centre console as described in Chapter 11.

11 Disconnect the wiring from the cigarette lighter, and from any switches mounted under the console.

12 Working at the rear of the cigarette lighter, pull the plastic bulb assembly from the lighter.

13 Using a small screwdriver inserted through the rear of the bulb assembly, release the bulb and holder **(see illustrations)**.

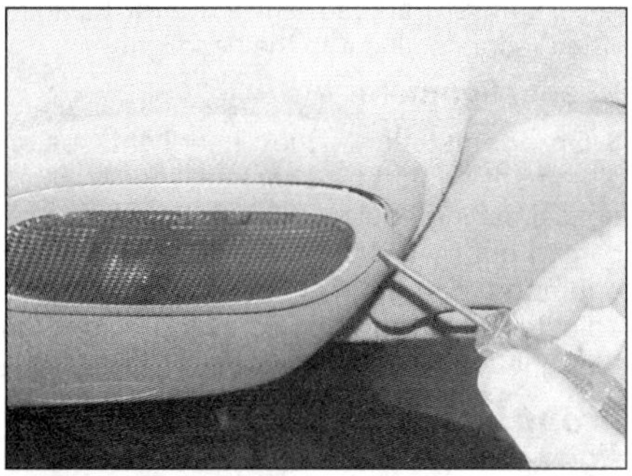

8.2 Unclipping the interior light from the roof console

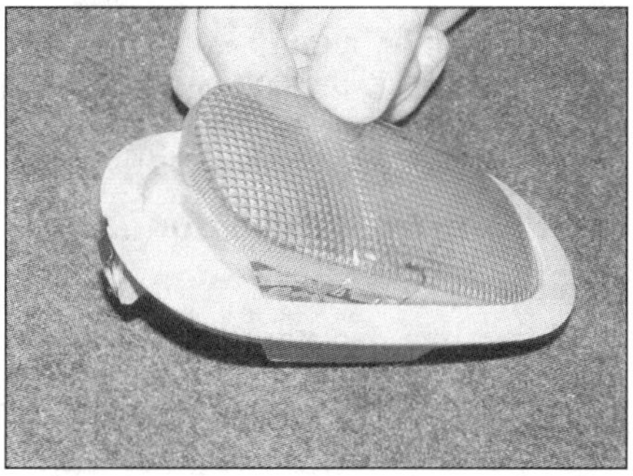

8.3a Release the lens from the light assembly . . .

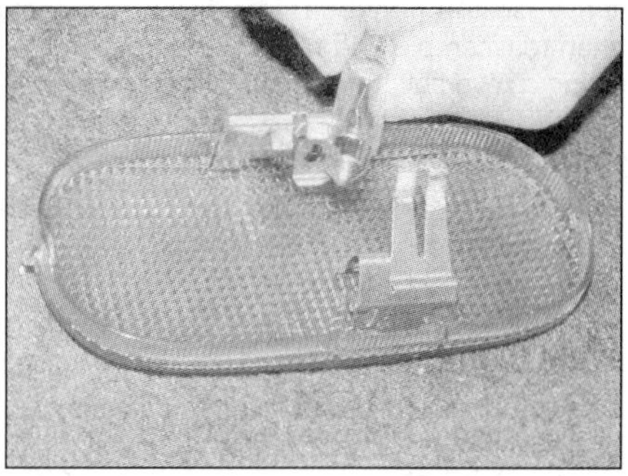

8.3b . . . and remove the festoon bulb

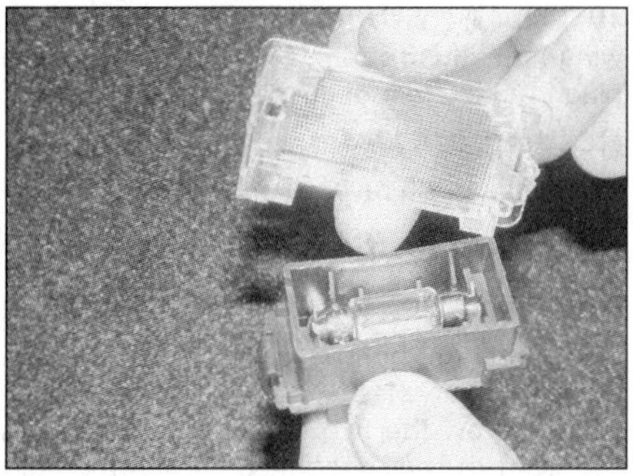

8.6a Unclip the lens from the boot light . . .

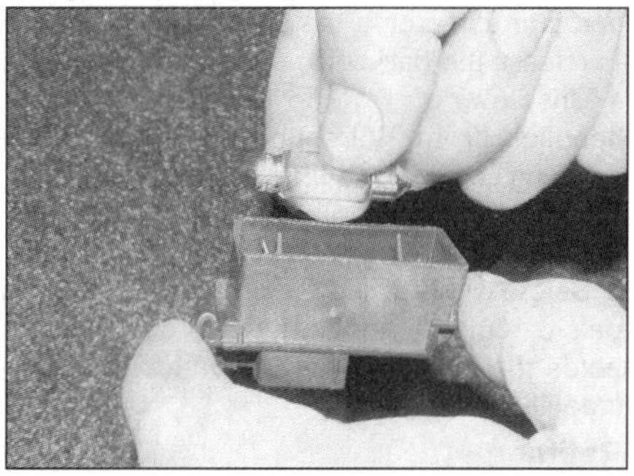

8.6b . . . and remove the festoon bulb

8.13a Insert a screwdriver to release the bulbholder . . .

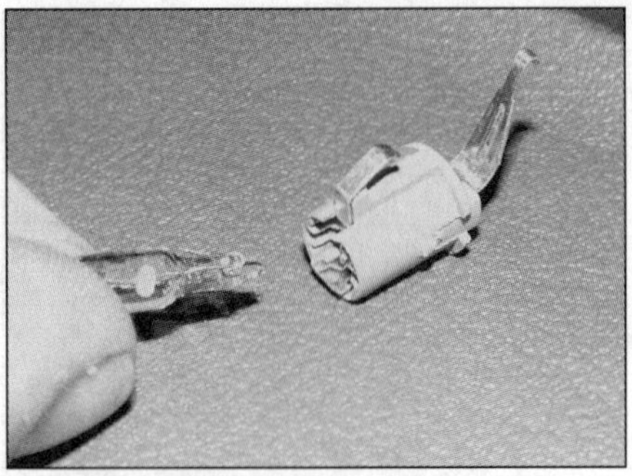

8.13b . . . then pull out the bulb from the holder

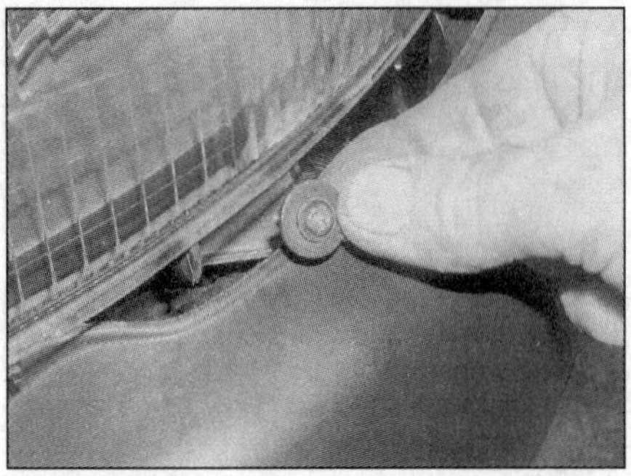

9.4 Removing one of the lower headlight securing screws

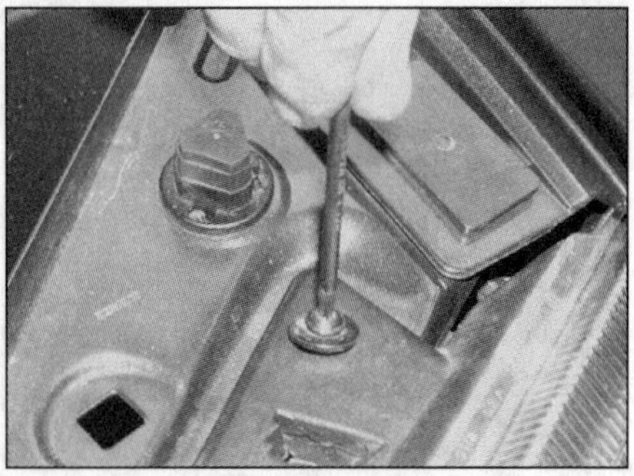

9.5 Unscrewing the upper headlight securing screw

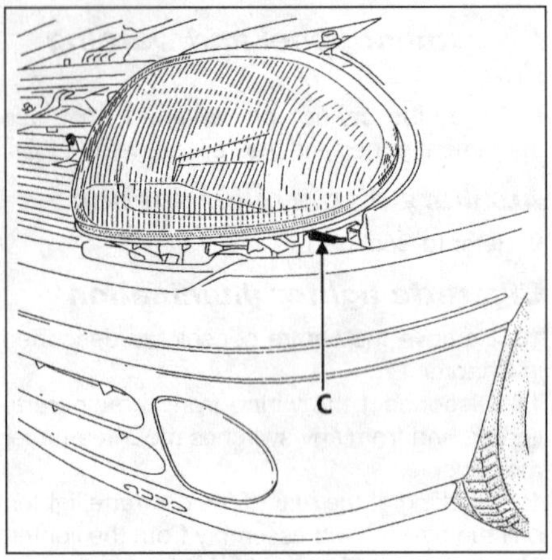

9.6a Cut the bracket at (C) . . .

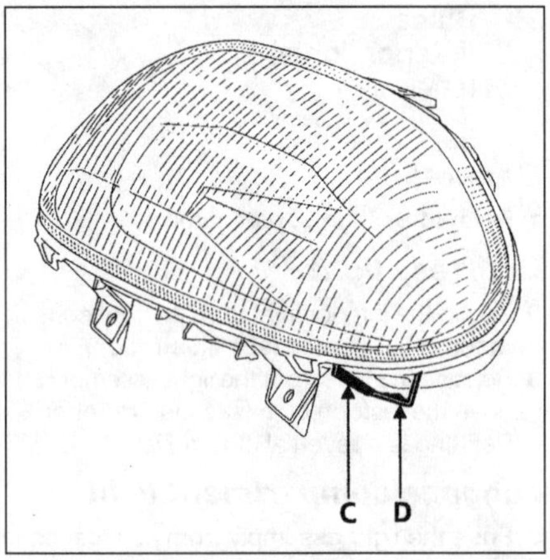

9.6b . . . then break off part (D) to help removal of headlight unit

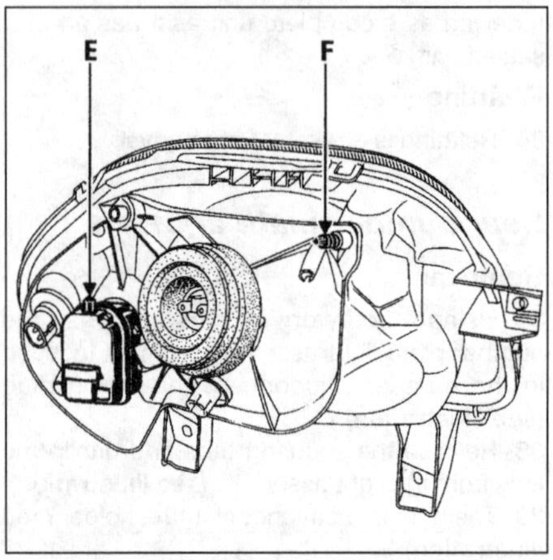

9.8 Adjust the height using bolt (E) and direction using bolt (F)

14 Push the new bulb into the bulbholder, then reassemble and refit the cigarette lighter using a reversal of the removal procedure.

Ashtray illumination

15 The ashtray shares the same illumination bulb as the cigarette lighter. Refer to paragraphs 10 to 14 for details.

Clock illumination

16 The clock is part of the instrument panel or the auxiliary display unit. Refer to Section 13 or 14 depending on specification of the vehicle.

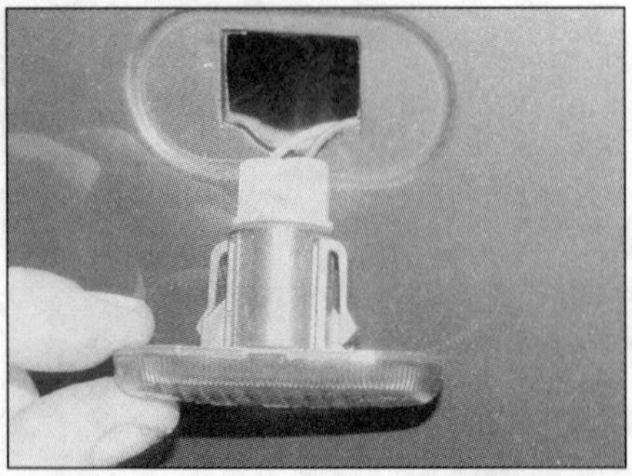

9.10 Removing the front direction indicator side repeater light

9 Exterior light units – removal and refitting

Headlight/front indicator unit

Removal

1 Remove the radiator grille panel, as described in Chapter 11.

2 Disconnect the wiring plugs from the rear of the headlight and sidelight bulbs.

3 On models fitted with a remote headlight aim adjustment control, free the actuator from the rear of the headlight, by twisting the actuator anti-clockwise and pulling it sharply to release the balljoint.

4 Unscrew and remove the two lower headlight/front direction indicator unit securing screws **(see illustration)**.

5 Unscrew the headlight/direction indicator unit upper securing screw **(see illustration)**.

6 Before withdrawing the headlight unit, use a pair of cutters and cut the bracket which holds the lower part of the unit to the wing **(see illustrations)**.

Refitting

7 Refitting is a reversal of removal, but where applicable, take care not to damage the headlight aim adjustment actuator balljoint when reconnecting it to the headlight.

Beam alignment

8 On completion, the headlight beam alignment should be checked, ideally using optical setting equipment. This check can be carried out by a Renault dealer or a suitably-equipped garage. The beam alignment is adjusted using the two screws provided on the light unit **(see illustration)**.

Front indicator side repeater light

Removal

9 Disconnect the battery negative lead.

10 Carefully prise the light unit from the front wing **(see illustration)**. Disconnect the wiring plug from the rear of the bulbholder.

Refitting

11 Refitting is a reversal of removal.

Front foglight

Removal

12 Open the bonnet and disconnect the battery negative lead.

13 Unscrew the two securing screws from the front of the foglight, then pull the light from the bumper **(see illustration)**, and disconnect the wiring plug.

9.13 Removing the foglight from the front bumper

Refitting

14 Refitting is a reversal of removal. If necessary, the vertical alignment of the beam can be adjusted by turning the adjustment screw **(see illustration)**.

Rear light cluster

Removal

15 Disconnect the battery negative lead.
16 Open the tailgate and unscrew the plastic nut from the rear of the light cluster.
17 Withdraw the light cluster from outside the car, taking care not to damage the retaining lugs at the bottom of the light, then disconnect the wiring plugs **(see illustration)**.
18 Where applicable, feed the wiring through the grommet in the bottom of the light cluster. Withdraw the assembly from the car.

Refitting

19 Refitting is a reversal of removal, bearing in mind the following points.
20 Where applicable, make sure that the wiring grommet is correctly positioned in the bottom of the light cluster.
21 Ensure that the retaining lugs at the base of the light cluster are correctly engaged with the corresponding holes in the body.
22 Make sure that the weatherseal is correctly located between the light cluster and the body.

High-level stop-light

Removal

23 Open the tailgate, and remove the rear

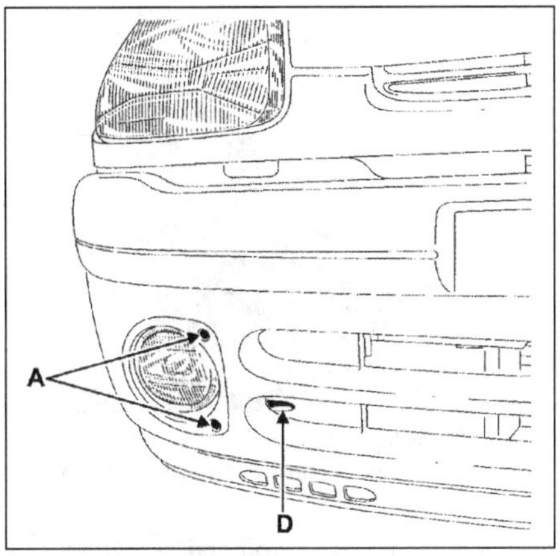

9.14 Front foglight securing screws (A), and beam adjustment screw (D)

spoiler as described in Chapter 11, Section 22.
24 Disconnect the wiring, and undo the two retaining screws to release the light unit from the rear spoiler.
25 If the light unit is faulty, it will have to be renewed as a complete unit as it has an LED sealed unit.

Refitting

26 Refitting is a reversal of removal.

Rear number plate light

Removal

27 Using a screwdriver, carefully prise the light unit from its location in the bumper.
28 Withdraw the light unit from the rear bumper and disconnect the wiring **(see illustration)**.

Refitting

29 Refitting is a reversal of removal.

10 Interior light units – removal and refitting

Courtesy light

1 Disconnect the battery negative lead.
2 Carefully prise the light assembly from its

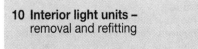

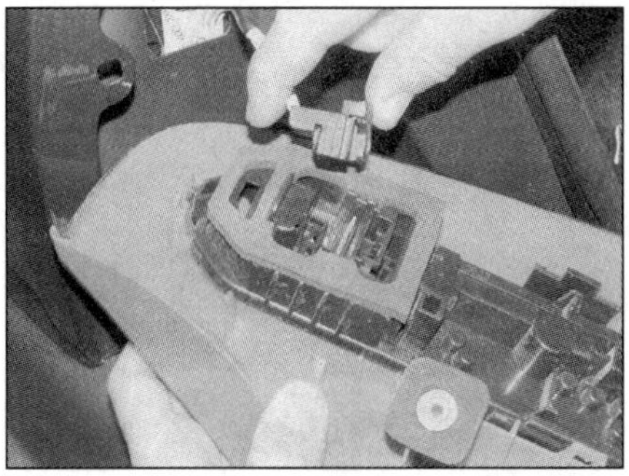

9.17 Disconnecting the wiring plug from the rear light unit

9.28 Disconnecting the wiring plug from the number plate light unit

location in the roof panel, and disconnect the wiring plugs **(see illustrations)**.
3 Refitting is a reversal of removal.

Luggage compartment light

4 Prise the light assembly from its location in the luggage compartment **(see illustration)**.
5 Disconnect the wiring plug as the light is withdrawn.
6 Refitting is a reversal of removal.

11 Headlight aim adjustment components – removal and refitting

Removal

1 Working in the engine compartment,

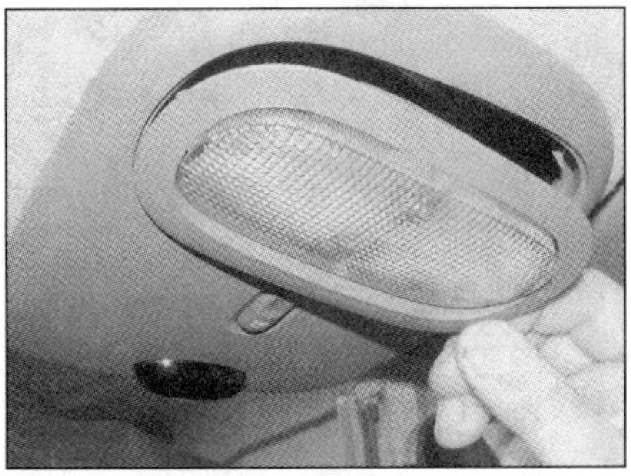

10.2a Release the courtesy light from the roof console . . .

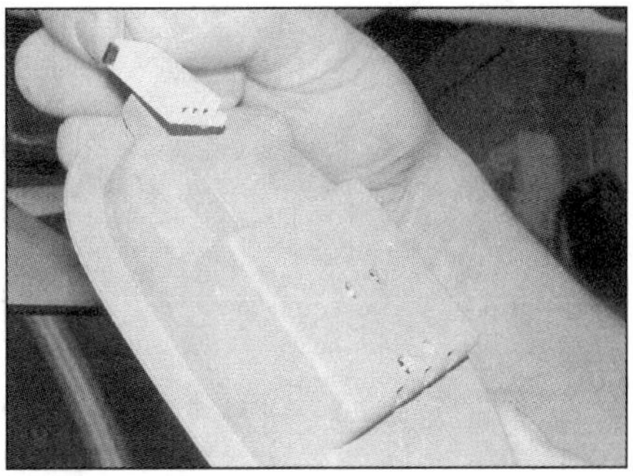

10.2b . . . and disconnect the wiring plug

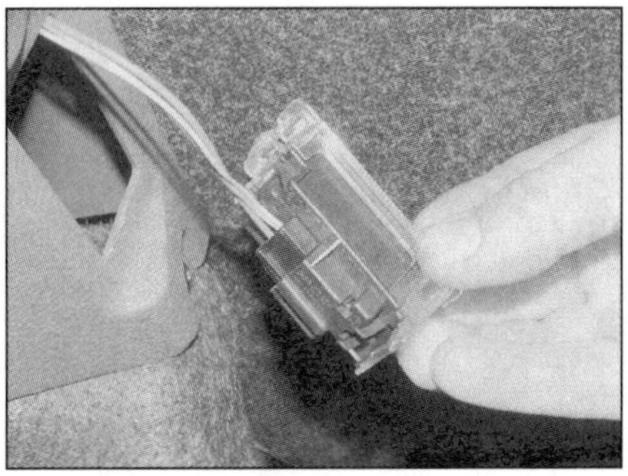

10.4 Unclip the luggage compartment light unit

11.1 Disconnecting the headlight adjuster wiring plug

11.2 Headlight aim adjustment actuator being removed from headlight assembly

disconnect the wiring connector from the rear of the headlight adjuster unit **(see illustration)**.

2 Release the actuator from the headlight by twisting anti-clockwise and pulling sharply to release the balljoint **(see illustration)**.

3 To remove the headlight aim adjustment control switch, refer to Section 6.

Refitting

4 Refitting is a reversal of removal, bearing in mind the following points.

5 Take care not to damage the actuator balljoints when reconnecting them to the headlights.

6 To set the beam alignment, refer to Section 9.

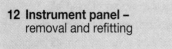

12 Instrument panel – removal and refitting

Removal

1 Disconnect the battery negative lead.

2 Remove the steering column shrouds and the facia upper trim panel, as described in Chapter 11, Section 29.

3 Unscrew the instrument panel securing screws **(see illustration)**.

4 Pull the instrument panel forwards from the facia, at the same time disconnecting the wiring plugs from the rear of the assembly **(see illustration)**.

5 Withdraw the panel from the facia.

Refitting

6 Refitting is a reversal of removal, ensuring that all wiring plugs are securely reconnected.

7 Where applicable, do not fully tighten the radio/cassette player remote control switch clamp screw until the steering column shrouds have been refitted.

13 Instrument panel components – general information

1 Depending on model specification, the instrument panel has the following functions:

- Electronic speedometer.
- Rev counter (tachometer).
- Fuel gauge.
- Engine coolant temperature gauge.
- Various warning light illuminations.
- Automatic transmission display.
- Display for total mileage, trip mileage, oil level and on-board computer (ADAC).
- Clock.
- Trip reset button.

2 The instrument panel is a sealed unit and the only part that can be replaced is the instrument glass. If any other components are faulty, the entire instrument panel has to be renewed.

3 The illumination bulbs cannot be renewed on these instrument panels, as they are soldered LEDs.

Self Test

4 On vehicles with a rev counter, there is a an automatic fault finding function. To access this function:

5 Vehicles without ADAC: Press and hold down the trip reset button on the instrument panel and switch the ignition on without starting the engine, release the trip reset button after approx 5 seconds.

6 Vehicles with ADAC: Press and hold down the ADAC button on the end of the wiper stalk and switch the ignition on without starting the engine, release the ADAC button after approx 5 seconds.

7 The system then checks the following functions simultaneously:

- The speedometer, by the needle moving at increments of 40 km/h.
- The rev counter, by the needle moving at increments of 1000 rpm.
- The fuel gauge, by the needle moving at increments of 1/4 of the scale.
- The coolant temperature gauge, by the needle moving at increments of 1/4 of the scale.
- The digital display, by making all the segments illuminate at once.

8 This will carry on checking the instruments until the ignition is switched off.

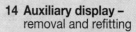

14 Auxiliary display – removal and refitting

Note: *On some models, there is an auxiliary display fitted in the top of the facia panel at the centre. This display is for the radio, temperature and clock. Models without a display are fitted with a storage tray* ***(see illustration)****.*

Removal

1 Disconnect the battery negative lead.

2 Remove the facia upper trim panel, as described in Chapter 11, Section 29.

12.3 Unscrew the instrument panel securing screws

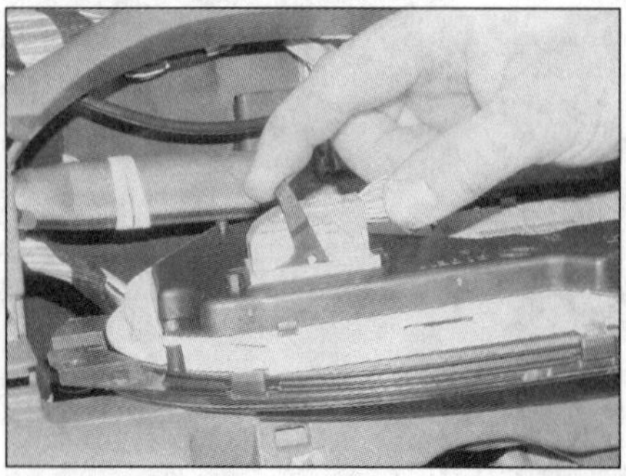

12.4 Disconnecting the wiring plugs

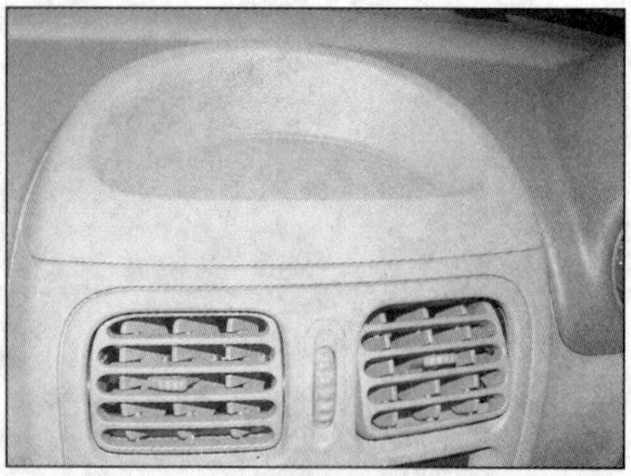

14.0 Storage tray fitted to lower specification models

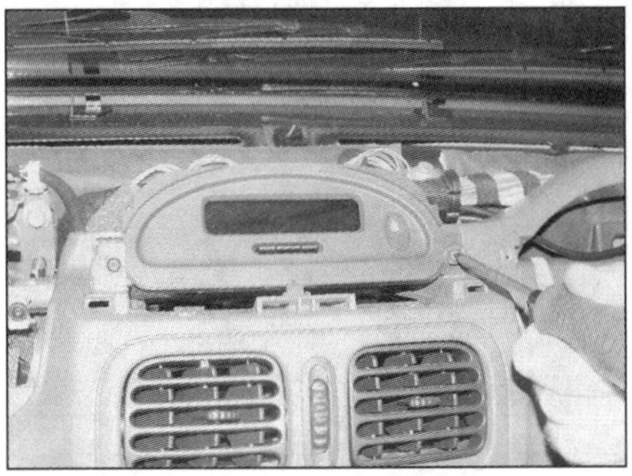

14.3 Unscrewing the auxiliary panel securing screws

3 Remove the two securing screws from the top of the auxiliary gauge panel **(see illustration)**, then pull the panel forwards from the facia.

4 Disconnect the wiring plugs from the rear of the panel **(see illustration)**, then withdraw the panel from the facia.

5 The components from the auxiliary panel can be unclipped from the surround trim panel **(see illustrations)** as required.

6 To renew a bulb, twist the appropriate bulbholder anti-clockwise, and withdraw it from the panel **(see illustration)**. The bulb can then be pulled out of the bulbholder.

Refitting

7 Refitting is a reversal of removal.

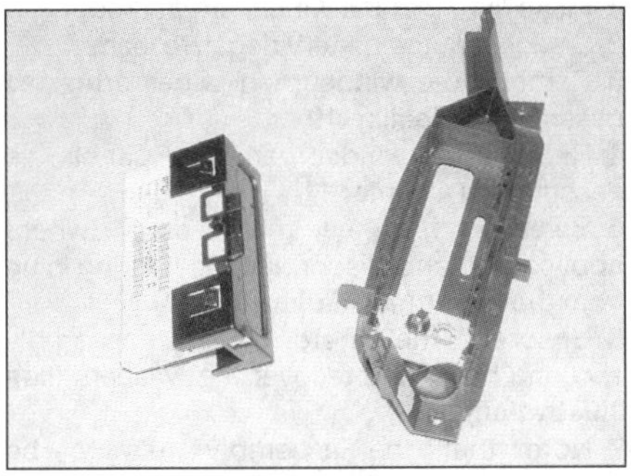

14.5b . . . from the surround trim panel

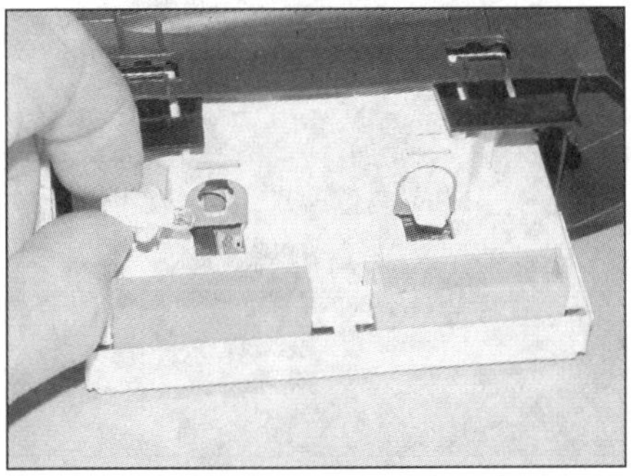

14.6 Withdrawing a bulb from the display unit

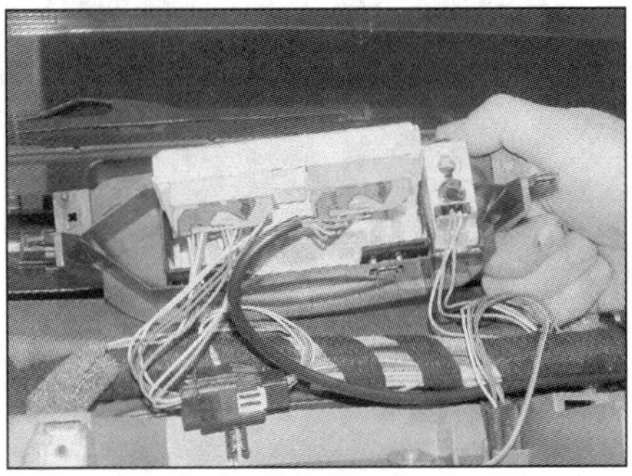

14.4 Disconnect the wiring plugs from the auxiliary panel

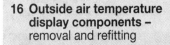

15 Clock – general information

1 The clock, depending on model specification, is either located in the instrument panel or the auxiliary display unit. Both the instrument panel and auxiliary unit are sealed units and if faulty must be renewed as a complete unit.

2 To remove either component refer to the relevant Sections.

3 If the clock is in the instrument panel, refer to Sections 12 and 13.

4 If the clock is in the auxiliary display unit, refer to Section 14.

16 Outside air temperature display components – removal and refitting

Instrument panel-mounted display

1 Proceed as described in Sections 12 and 13.

Auxiliary display

2 Proceed as described in Section 14.

Sensor

Removal

3 Where fitted, the sensor is mounted in the bottom of the exterior mirror on the driver's side.

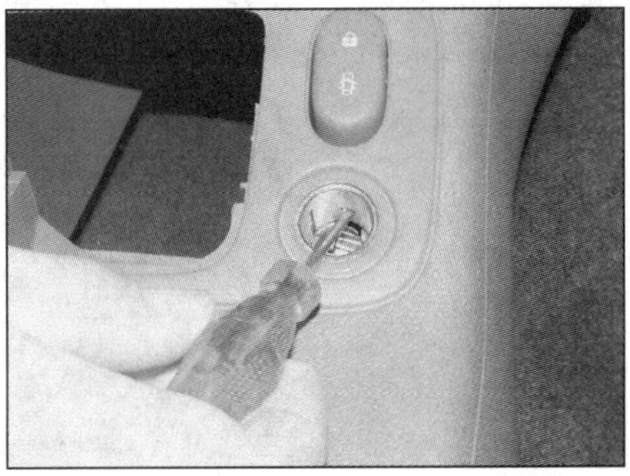

17.5a Using a screwdriver to release the retaining lugs . . .

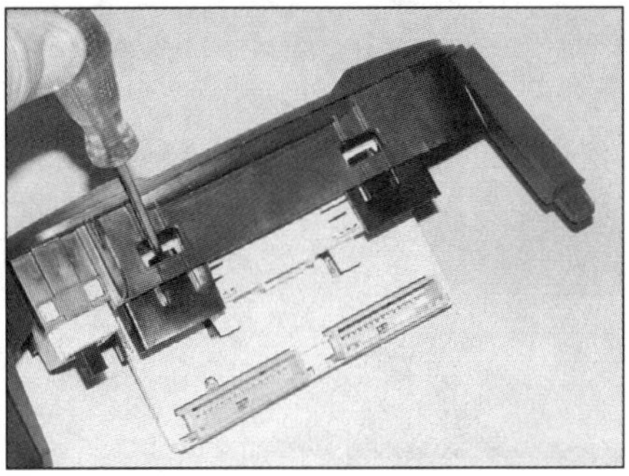

14.5a Unclipping the display unit . . .

4 Disconnect the battery negative lead.

5 Open the door, and carefully prise the mirror trim panel from the front edge of the door.

6 Unscrew the two screws securing the mirror cover panel to the door, then disconnect the sensor wiring plug.

7 Remove the mirror glass, as described in Chapter 11, Section 18.

8 Remove the single securing screw, and withdraw the sensor from the mirror, feeding the wiring through the mirror body.

Refitting

9 Refitting is a reversal of removal.

17 Cigarette lighter – removal and refitting

Removal

1 Disconnect the battery negative lead.

2 Remove the centre console as described in Chapter 11.

3 Disconnect the wiring from the cigarette lighter, and from any switches mounted under the console.

4 Remove the cigarette lighter from its housing.

5 Working through the cigarette lighter aperture, depress the retaining lugs, and prise the metal housing from the plastic surround. Push the housing out through the front of the assembly **(see illustrations)**.

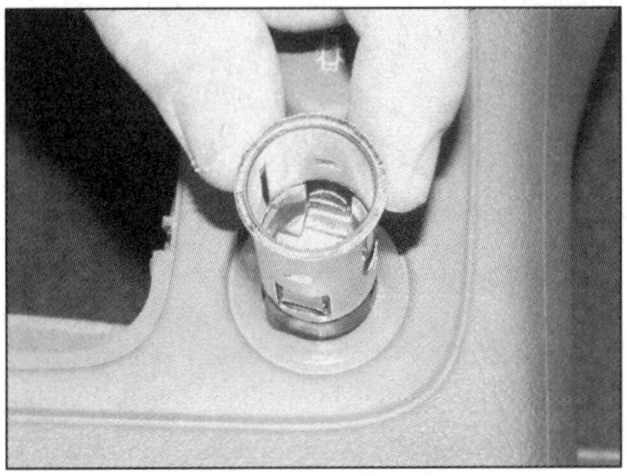

17.5b . . . and withdrawing the cigarette lighter metal housing

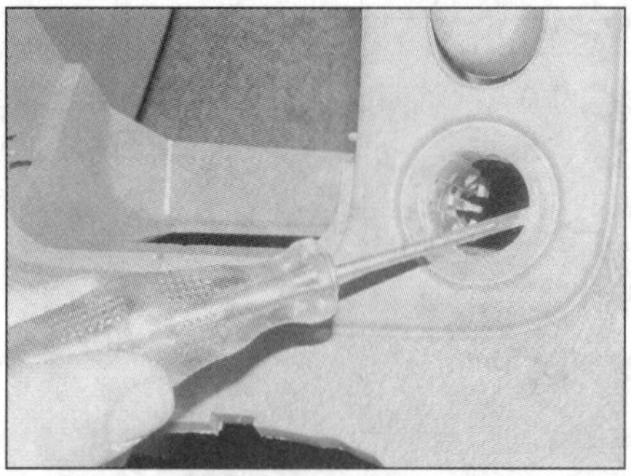

17.6a Using a screwdriver to release the retaining lugs . . .

6 Release the securing lugs and push the plastic surround out through the front of the mounting panel **(see illustrations)**.

Refitting

7 Refitting is a reversal of removal.

18 Horn – removal and refitting

Removal

1 The horn is located behind the left-hand side of the front bumper, below the headlight unit **(see illustration)**.
2 Disconnect the battery negative lead.
3 To gain access to the horn, remove the front wheelarch liner. Refer to Chapter 11, Section 22, if necessary.

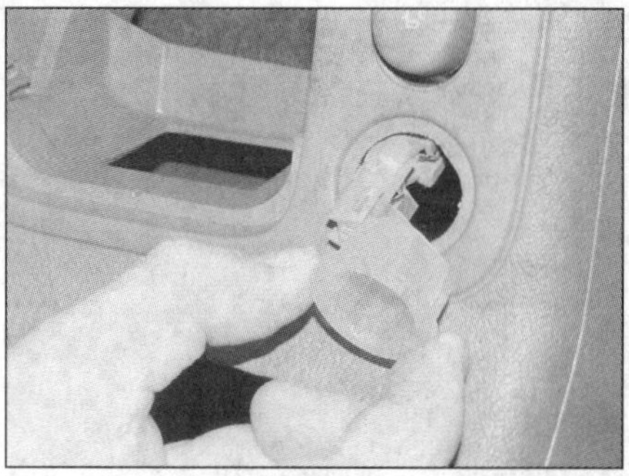

17.6b . . . and withdrawing the plastic surround

4 Disconnect the wiring from the horn.
5 Unscrew the securing nut, and withdraw the horn from its mounting bracket.

Refitting

6 Refitting is a reversal of removal.

19 Wiper arms – removal and refitting

Removal

1 The wiper motor should be in the parked position before removing the wiper arm. Mark the position of the blade on the glass with adhesive tape, as a guide to refitting.
2 If both windscreen wiper arms are to be removed, identify them so that they can be refitted in their original positions (the arms are of different lengths).
3 Lift the hinged cover or unclip the plastic cap, and remove the nut securing the arm to the spindle **(see illustrations)**.
4 Pull or prise the arm from the spindle, using a puller or screwdriver if necessary **(see illustration)**. Take care not to damage the trim or paintwork.

18.1 Horn location, viewed from above with the left-hand headlight removed

Refitting

5 Refitting is a reversal of removal. Position the arms so that the blades align with the tape applied to the glass before removal.

20 Windscreen wiper motor and linkage – removal and refitting

Removal

1 Make sure that the wipers are parked.
2 Disconnect the battery negative lead.
3 Remove the windscreen wiper arms, as described in Section 19.
4 Remove the windscreen cowl panels, as described in Chapter 11.
5 Release the securing clip (where applicable), and disconnect the wiring plug from the motor **(see illustration)**.
6 Unscrew the motor/linkage assembly securing bolts, and recover the washers **(see illustration)**.
7 Note that the assembly has to be disengaged from the locating peg at the rear of the scuttle panel **(see illustration)**.

19.3a Lift the hinged cover . . .

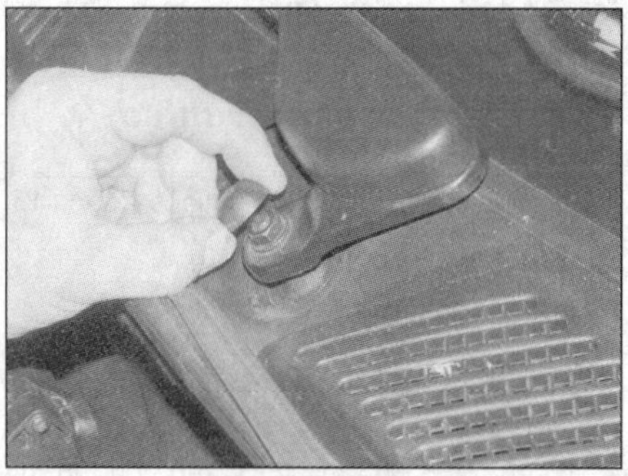

19.3b . . . or unclip the plastic cap . . .

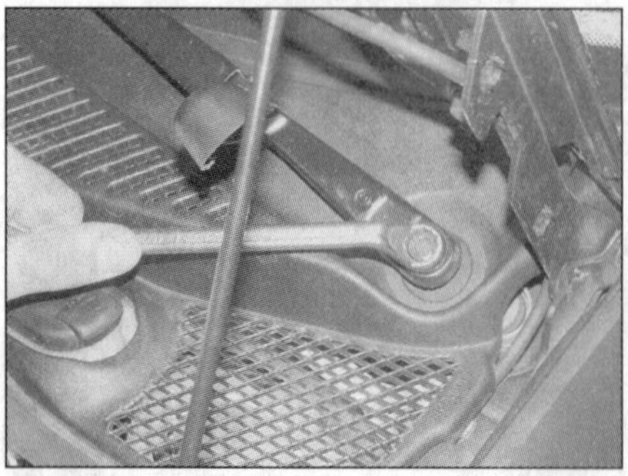

19.3c . . . and undo the wiper arm securing nut

19.4 Using a puller to remove the wiper arm

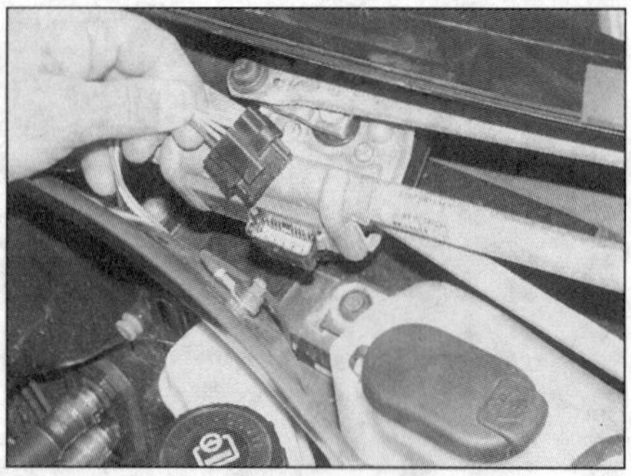

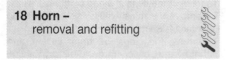

20.5 Disconnecting the windscreen wiper motor wiring plug

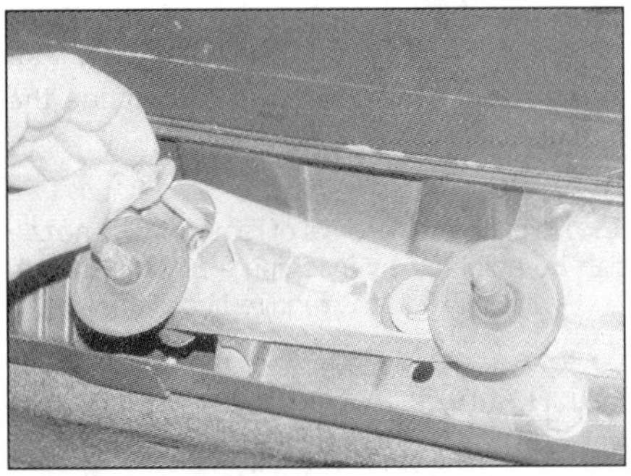

20.6 Unscrewing a windscreen wiper motor securing bolt

8 Manipulate the assembly out through the scuttle, taking care not to damage surrounding components.

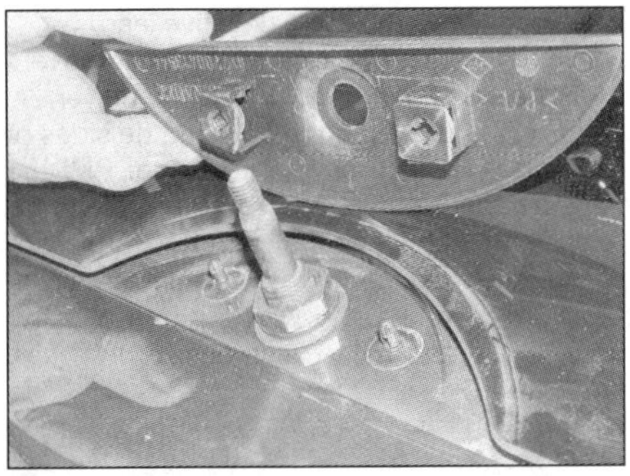

21.3a Unclip the plastic surround from the wiper spindle . . .

20.7 Locating peg (arrowed) at the rear of the scuttle panel

Refitting

9 Refitting is a reversal of removal, bearing in mind the following points.
10 Ensure that the assembly is mounted on the locating peg, before refitting the mounting bolts.
11 Refit the windscreen wiper arms with reference to Section 19.

21 Tailgate wiper motor and linkage - removal and refitting

Removal

1 Disconnect the battery negative lead.
2 Remove the tailgate wiper arm, as described in Section 19.
3 Unclip the plastic cover from around the wiper motor spindle, and remove the securing nut and washer **(see illustrations)**.
4 Open the tailgate, undo the retaining screw and unclip the tailgate interior trim panel.
5 Disconnect the wiper motor wiring plug **(see illustration)**.
6 Unscrew the three nuts securing the motor mounting bracket to the tailgate (use a screwdriver to hold the studs). Withdraw the motor assembly and retrieve the washers from the mounting studs **(see illustrations)**.

Refitting

7 Refitting is a reversal of removal.

22 Windscreen/tailgate washer system components - removal and refitting

Fluid reservoir

Removal

1 Disconnect the battery negative lead.
2 Remove the windscreen wiper arms as described in Section 19.
3 Remove the windscreen cowl panels as described in Chapter 11.
4 Disconnect the wiring plug from the top of the washer pump **(see illustration)**.
5 Unscrew the fluid reservoir securing bolt, then lift the reservoir sufficiently to disconnect the hoses from the pump **(see illustrations)**. Be prepared for fluid spillage.

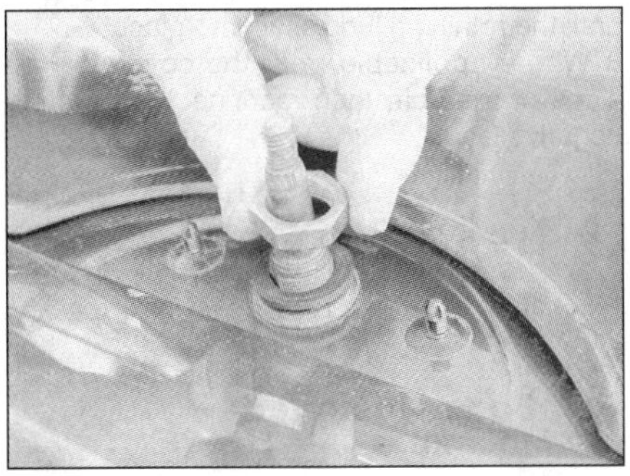

21.3b . . . and remove the securing nut and washer

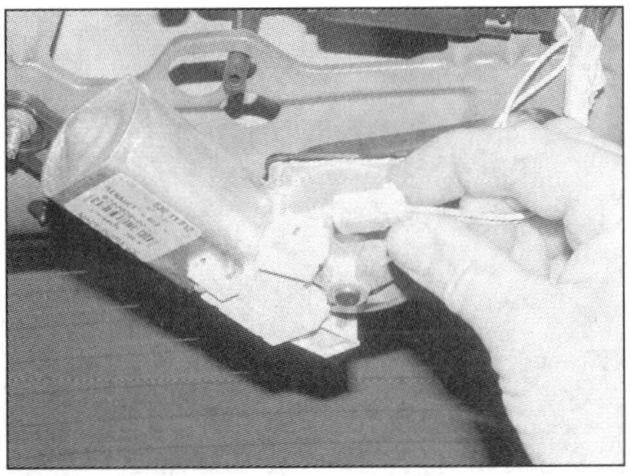

21.5 Disconnecting the wiring plug from the wiper motor

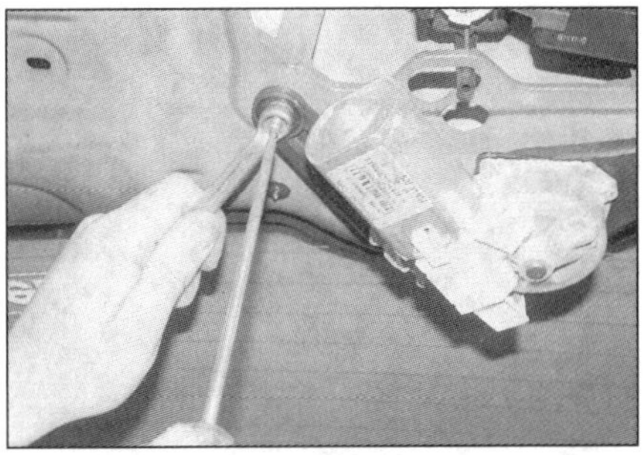

21.6a Using a screwdriver to hold the mounting studs, while unscrewing the securing nuts . . .

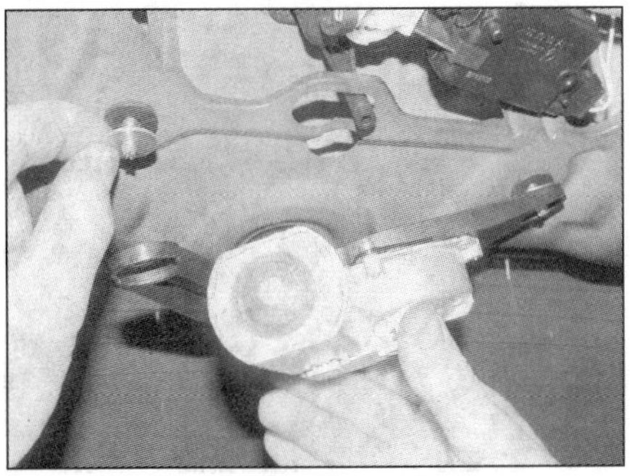

21.6b . . . and retrieving the washers as the motor is removed

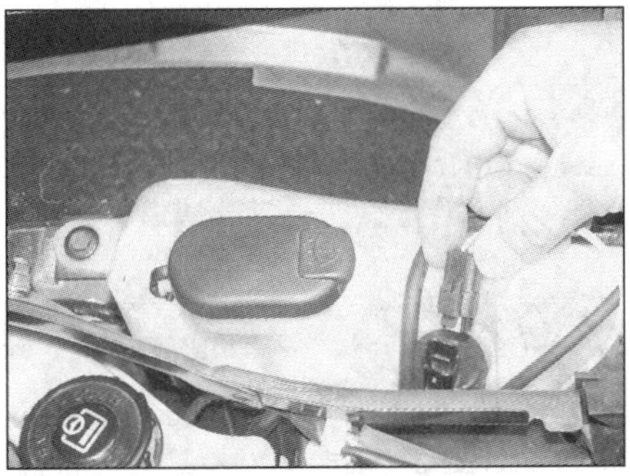

22.4 Disconnecting the wiring plug from the washer pump

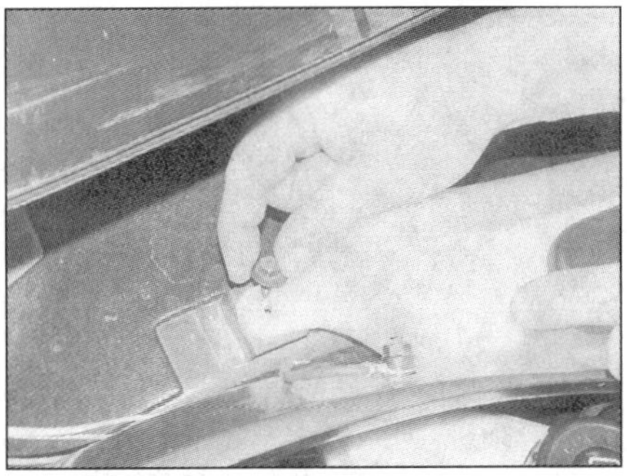

22.5a Unscrew the washer fluid reservoir securing bolt . . .

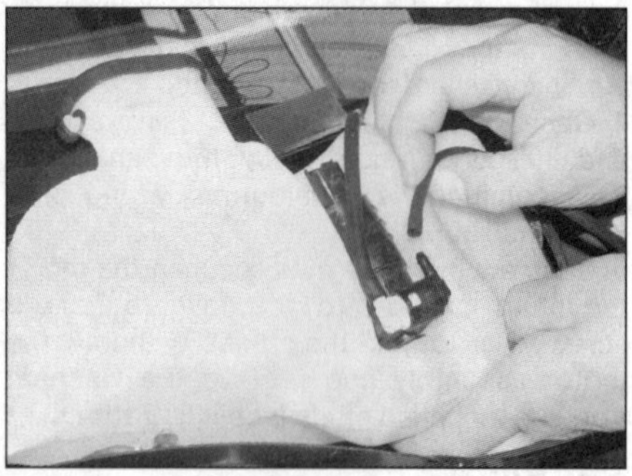

22.5b . . . and disconnect the two washer hoses (one for the front, and one for the rear)

6 Manipulate the reservoir out from the scuttle.

Refitting

7 Refitting is a reversal of removal. Refit the windscreen wiper arms with reference to Section 19.

Fluid pump

Removal

8 Remove the fluid reservoir as described in this Section.

9 Carefully disconnect the hoses from the pump, then pull the pump from the reservoir **(see illustration)**. Be prepared for fluid spillage. Note that one pump supplies the front and rear washer nozzles.

Refitting

10 Refitting is a reversal of removal. Check

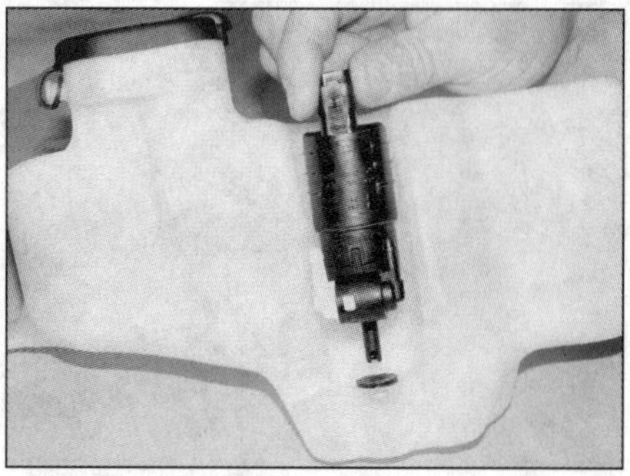

22.9 Carefully pull the pump from the sealing grommet in the reservoir

the sealing grommet in the fluid reservoir, before inserting the pump.

Windscreen washer nozzle

Removal

11 With the bonnet open, disconnect the fluid hose, then carefully prise the nozzle from the bonnet **(see illustrations)**. Take care not to damage the trim or paintwork.

Refitting

12 Refitting is a reversal of removal. The nozzle can be adjusted by inserting a pin into the jet, and swivelling it to the required position.

Tailgate washer nozzle

Removal

13 Remove the rear spoiler as described in Chapter 11.

14 Disconnect the fluid hose, then carefully prise the nozzle from the spoiler **(see illustration)**. Take care not to damage the trim or paintwork.

Refitting

15 Refitting is a reversal of removal. The nozzle can be adjusted by inserting a pin into the jet, and swivelling it to the required position.

23 Radio/cassette player – removal and refitting

Removal

1 All the radio/cassette players fitted to the Clio range have DIN standard fixings. A pair of removal clips, obtainable from in-car entertainment specialists, will be required for removal.

2 Disconnect the battery negative lead.

3 Where applicable, prise the plastic covers from the sides of the radio/cassette player.

4 Insert the clips into the holes at the sides of the unit until they snap into place. Pull the clips rearwards (away from the facia) to release the unit **(see illustration)**.

5 Withdraw the radio/cassette unit from the facia. Disconnect the wiring plugs and the aerial cable from the rear of the unit **(see illustration)**.

Refitting

6 Reconnect the wiring plugs and the aerial cable to the rear of the unit.

7 Push the unit into its housing in the facia until the retaining lugs snap into place.

8 Where applicable, refit the covers to the sides of the unit, then reconnect the battery negative lead.

24 Loudspeakers – removal and refitting

Front door-mounted loudspeakers

Removal

1 Disconnect the battery negative lead.

22.11a Disconnecting the hose from the washer nozzle . . .

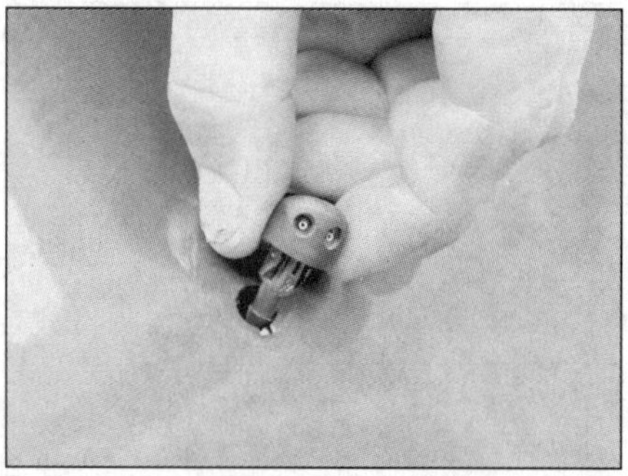

22.11b . . . and removing the washer nozzle from the bonnet

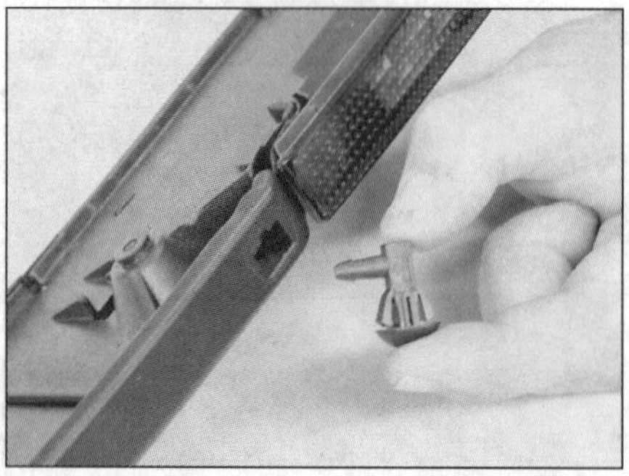

22.14 Removing the tailgate washer nozzle from the spoiler

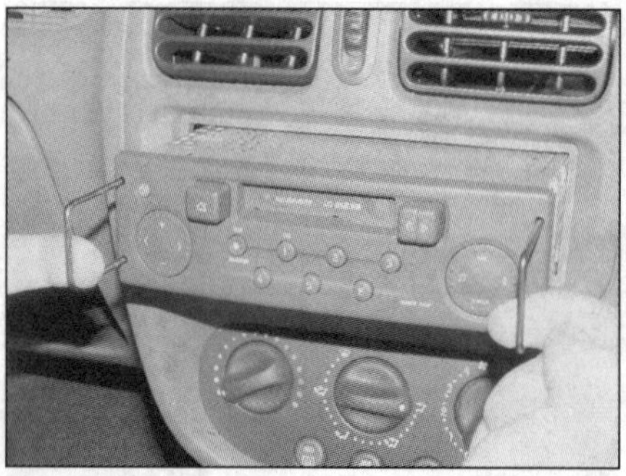

23.4 Using DIN standard removal clips to remove the radio/cassette player

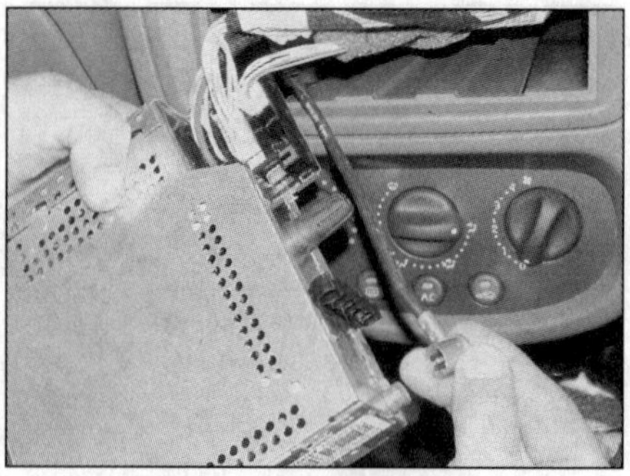

23.5 Disconnecting the radio/cassette player wiring plugs

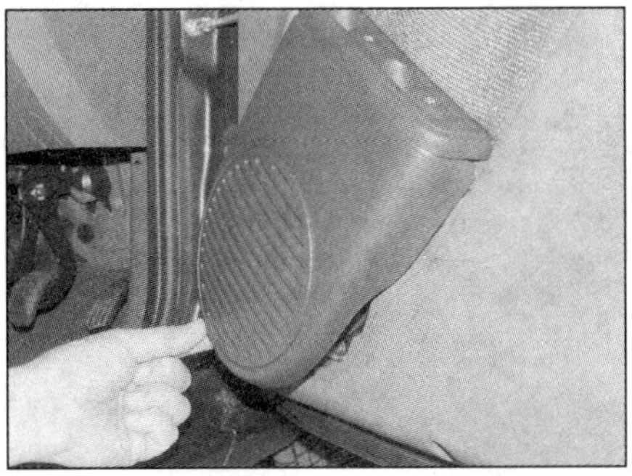

24.2a Unclipping the speaker grille from a vehicle with electric windows . . .

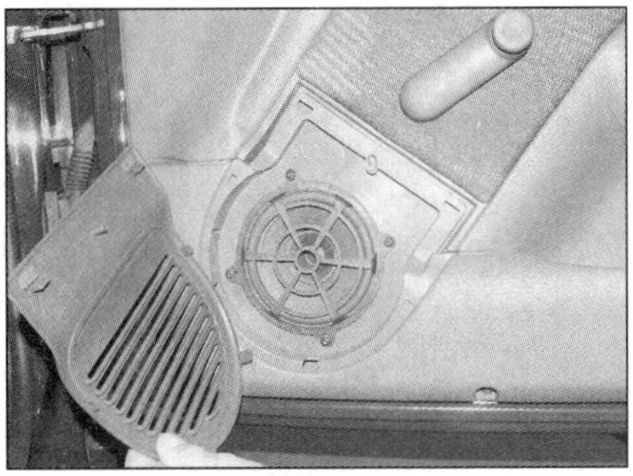

24.2b . . . and a vehicle with manual windows

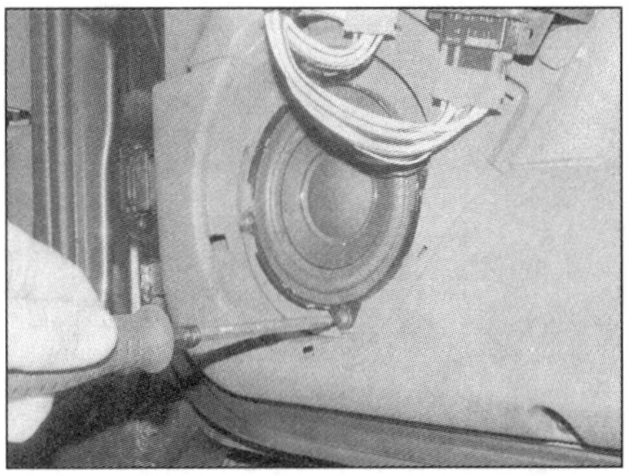

24.3 Undo the four speaker securing screws

2 Unclip the speaker grille from the speaker housing **(see illustrations).**
3 Remove the four securing screws, then withdraw the loudspeaker from the housing in the door **(see illustration)**.
4 Disconnect the wiring and remove the loudspeaker **(see illustration)**.

Refitting

5 Refitting is a reversal of removal.

Front facia-mounted loudspeakers

Removal

6 Disconnect the battery negative lead.
7 Remove the upper facia trim panel as described in Chapter 11.
8 Disconnect the wiring plug and withdraw the loudspeaker from the lower facia trim panel **(see illustrations)**.

Refitting

9 Refitting is a reversal of removal.

Rear door-mounted loudspeakers

Removal

10 Disconnect the battery negative lead.
11 Twist the speaker grille from the speaker housing **(see illustration).**
12 Remove the four securing screws, then withdraw the loudspeaker from the housing in the door **(see illustration)**.
13 Disconnect the wiring and remove the loudspeaker **(see illustration)**.

Refitting

14 Refitting is a reversal of removal.

25 Radio aerial – removal and refitting

Aerial assembly

Removal

1 Remove the courtesy light assembly, as described in Section 10.
2 Unclip the roof console from the headlining to expose the base of the aerial **(see illustration)**.

24.4 Disconnect the wiring from the speaker on removal

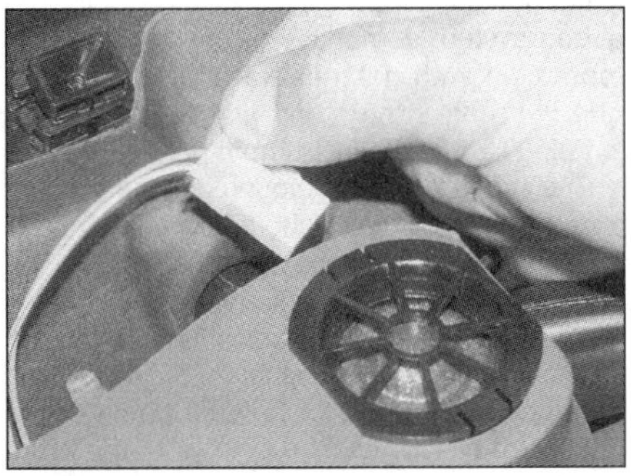

24.8a Disconnect the wiring plug . . .

24.8b . . . and unclip the speaker

24.11 Twist the speaker grille to remove

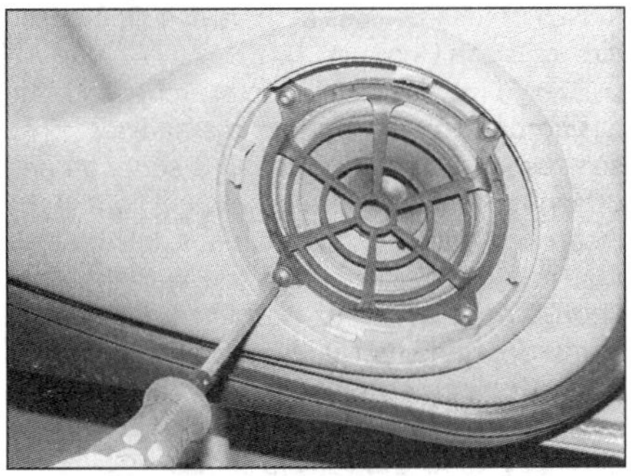

24.12 Undo the four speaker securing screws

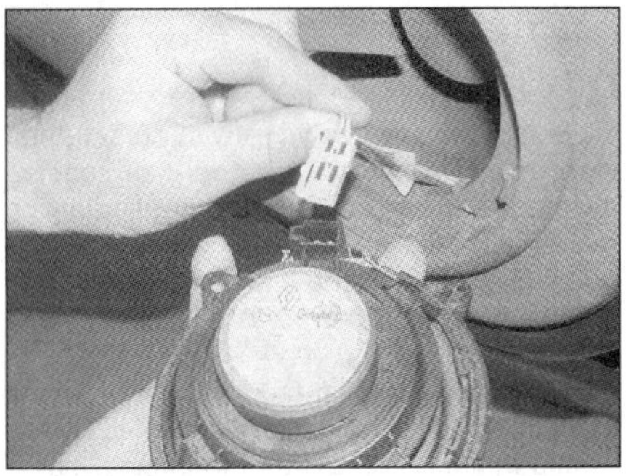

24.13 Disconnect the wiring plug from the speaker

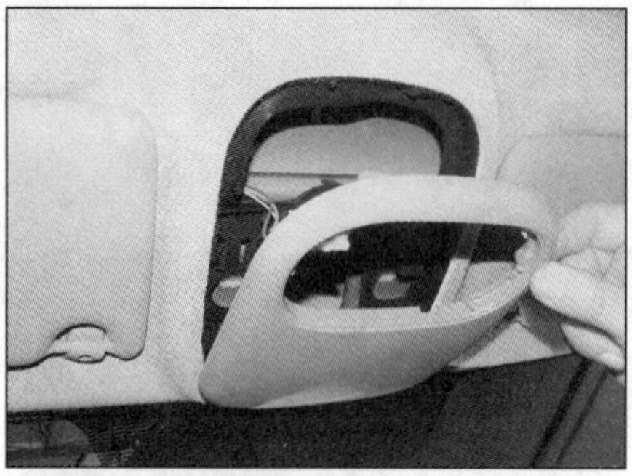

25.2 Unclip the roof console from the headlining

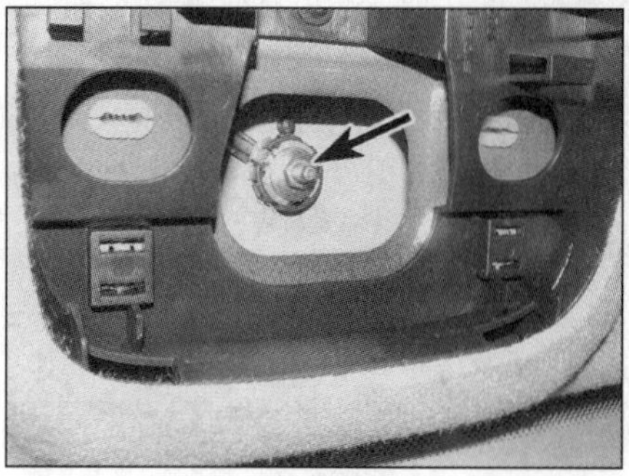

25.3 Radio aerial securing nut (arrowed)

25.4 Aerial mast will unscrew from the base

3 Unscrew the securing nut, and disconnect the aerial lead from the base of the aerial **(see illustration).** Lift the aerial from the roof panel.
4 The aerial mast can be unscrewed from the base of the aerial if required **(see illustration)**.

Refitting

5 Refitting is a reversal of removal.

Aerial lead

Removal

6 With the lead disconnected from the aerial as described previously in this Section, tie a length of string to the end of the lead.
7 Observe the routing of the lead. Remove the A-pillar trim panel and upper facia panel for access to the aerial lead, as described in Chapter 11, Section 27.
8 Remove the radio/cassette player and disconnect the aerial lead from the rear of the unit, as described in Section 23.
9 Pull the lower end of the lead. Feed the lead down the A-pillar, behind the facia, and out through the radio/cassette player aperture.
10 Untie the string from the lead, and leave it in position to aid refitting.

Refitting

11 Refitting is a reversal of removal, using the string to pull the lead into position. Take care not to damage the lead or surrounding components when feeding it through behind the facia.
12 Refit the radio/cassette player with reference to Section 23.

26 Anti-theft alarm system – general information

1 Certain models are fitted with an anti-theft alarm system, which uses various sensing systems and warning sirens, depending on model. No information was available for the alarm systems at the time of writing. Any faults should be referred to a Renault dealer for diagnosis.
2 All models are fitted with an engine immobiliser device which is activated by the coded ignition key. When the immobiliser is armed, the indicator light on the instrument panel will flash continuously. When the ignition is switched on, an antenna ring around the ignition switch interrogates and captures the code from the head of the key and transmits it to the multi-timer unit (see Section 5). If the multi-timer unit recognises the code, the engine can be started.

27 Airbag system – general information and precautions

Both a driver and passenger's airbag were fitted as standard to some models in the range; on other models they were available as an optional extra. Models fitted with a driver's airbag have the word AIRBAG stamped on the airbag unit, which is fitted to the centre of the steering wheel. Models also equipped with a passenger airbag also have the word AIRBAG stamped on the passenger airbag unit which is fitted to the passenger side of the facia. The airbag system comprises of the airbag unit(s) (complete with gas generators), the control unit (with an integral impact sensor) and a warning light in the instrument panel.

The airbag system is triggered in the event of a heavy frontal impact above a predetermined force; depending on the point of impact. The airbag is inflated within milliseconds and forms a safety cushion between the driver and steering wheel and (where fitted) the passenger and facia. This prevents contact between the upper body and wheel/facia and therefore greatly reduces the risk of injury. The airbag then deflates almost immediately. The control unit also operates the front seat belt pre-tensioner mechanisms at the same time as the airbag(s) (see Chapter 11).

Every time the ignition is switched on, the airbag control unit performs a self-test. The self-test takes approximately 3 seconds and during this time the airbag warning light in the instrument panel is illuminated. After the self-test has been completed the warning light should go out. If the warning light fails to come on, remains illuminated after the initial period or comes on at any time when the vehicle is being driven, there is a fault in the airbag system. The vehicle should be taken to a Renault dealer for examination at the earliest possible opportunity.

Precautions

Warning: Before carrying out any operations on the airbag system, to prevent the risk of injury if the system is triggered inadvertently when working on the vehicle, disconnect the battery and disable the system (wait for at least five minutes). This will allow the reserve power capacitors in the control unit to discharge. When operations are complete, make sure no one is inside the vehicle when the battery is reconnected then, with the driver's door open, switch the ignition on from outside the vehicle.

Warning: Before carrying out any operations in the vicinity of the airbag or steering wheel, to prevent the risk of injury if the system is triggered inadvertently when working on the vehicle, remove the airbag unit as described in Section 28.

Warning: Note that the airbag(s) must not be subjected to excess temperatures. When the airbag is removed, ensure that it is stored the correct way up to prevent possible inflation.

Warning: Do not allow any solvents or cleaning agents to contact the airbag assemblies. They must be cleaned using only a damp cloth.

Warning: The airbags and control unit are both sensitive to impact. If either is dropped or damaged they should be renewed.

Warning: Do not refit the airbag unit to the steering wheel once the steering wheel has been removed from the vehicle.

Warning: Do not attempt to test the airbag electrical circuit using anything except the Renault special test tool. Using a conventional multimeter or ohmmeter is likely to trigger the airbag.

Warning: If the airbag has been triggered, the control unit must be renewed.

Warning: If the airbag is to be renewed, the control unit (and batteries on models with a 'self-contained' airbag) must also be renewed.

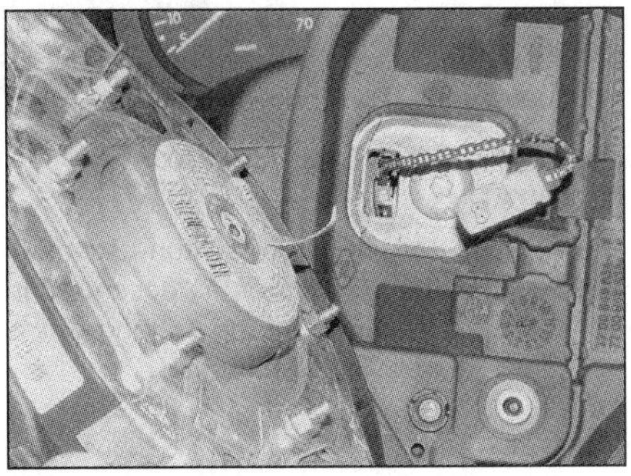

28.3 Disconnect the airbag wiring connector

Warning: On models fitted with a self-contained airbag, the batteries must be renewed every 4 years. This work should be entrusted to a Renault dealer.

Warning: Disconnect the airbag control unit wiring plug prior to using arc-welding equipment on the vehicle.

28 Airbag system components – removal and refitting

Note: *Refer to the warnings in Section 27 before carrying out the following operations.*

1 Disconnect the battery negative lead and wait for at least five minutes. This will allow the reserve power capacitors in the control unit to discharge and disable the airbag system (see Section 27).

Driver's airbag

Removal

2 Slacken and remove the two airbag retaining screws from the rear of the steering wheel, rotating the wheel as necessary to gain access to the screws.

3 Return the steering wheel to the straight-ahead position then carefully lift the airbag assembly away from the steering wheel and disconnect the wiring connector from the rear of the unit **(see illustration)**. Note that the airbag must not be knocked or dropped and should be stored the correct way up with its padded surface uppermost.

Refitting

4 Ensure that the wiring connector is securely reconnected and seat the airbag unit centrally in the steering wheel, making sure the wire does not become trapped. Fit the retaining screws and tighten them to the specified torque setting.

5 Ensuring no one is inside the vehicle, reconnect the battery. With the driver's door open, turn on the ignition switch and check the operation of the airbag warning light.

28.7a Unclip the locking tab . . .

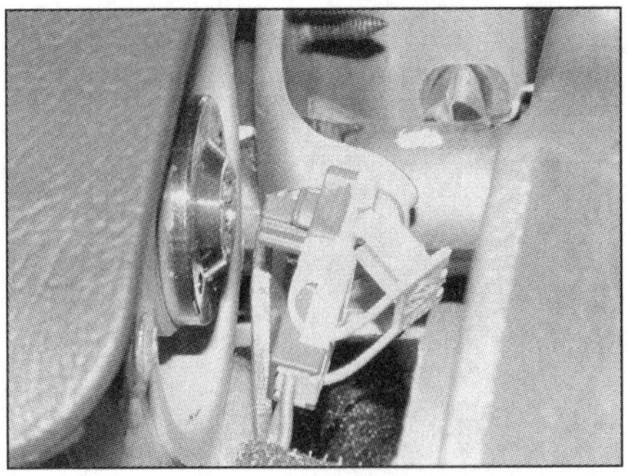

28.7b . . . and disconnect the wiring plug from the airbag

Passenger airbag

Removal

6 Remove the upper facia panel, referring to Chapter 11.

7 Unclip the centre locking tab from the wiring connector, then disconnect the wiring connector from the airbag unit **(see illustrations)**.

8 Slacken and remove the retaining screws, then release the airbag unit from its mountings and remove it from the facia **(see illustrations)**.

Refitting

9 Manoeuvre the airbag into position, then refit the mounting screws securely. Reconnect the wiring connector, ensuring that the wiring is correctly routed and retained by its locking tab.

10 Refit the upper facia panel as described in Chapter 11.

11 Ensuring no one is inside the vehicle, reconnect the battery. With the driver's door open, turn on the ignition switch and check the operation of the airbag warning light.

Airbag control unit

Removal

12 Remove the centre console as described in Chapter 11 to gain access to the control unit which is mounted in front of the gearchange/selector lever.

13 Undo the retaining screws and remove the heater ducting going to the rear footwell **(see illustration)**. If required, lift up the carpet to gain access to the control unit.

14 Release the retaining clip and disconnect the wiring connector **(see illustration)**. Unscrew the three retaining nuts and remove the control unit from the vehicle.

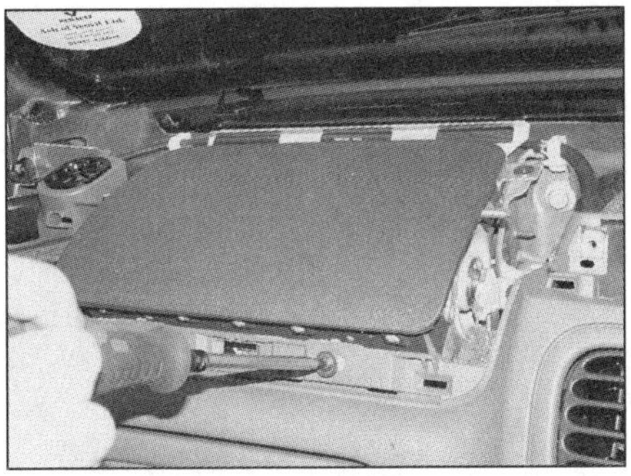

28.8a Undo the securing screws . . .

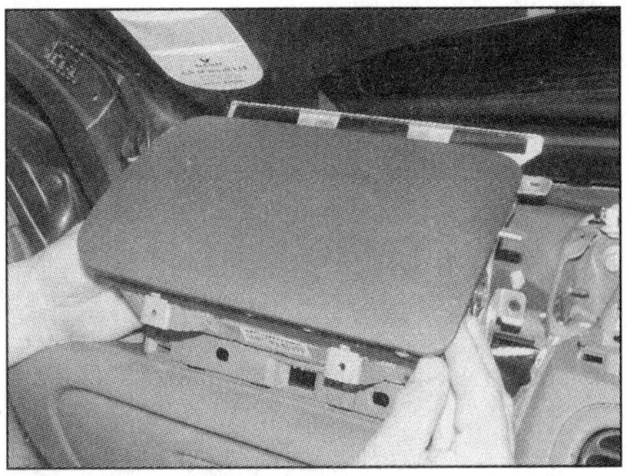

28.8b . . . and carefully remove the airbag

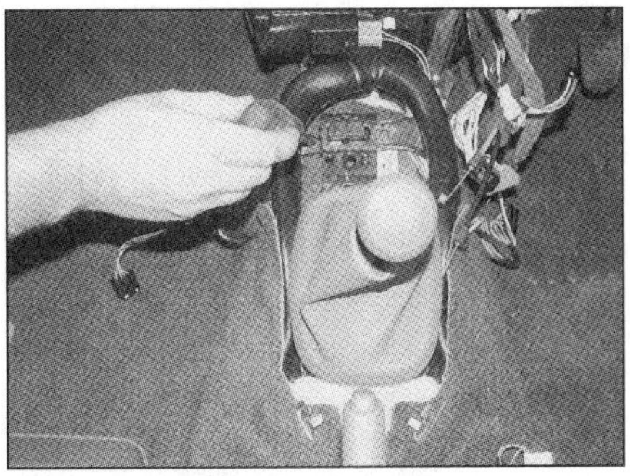

28.13 Unscrewing the air ducting from the control unit bracket

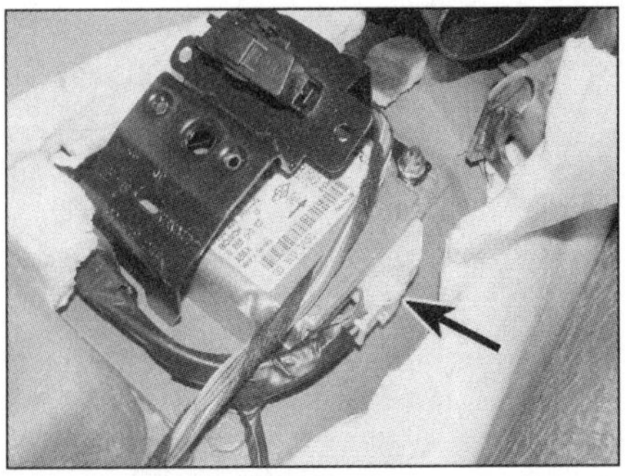

28.14 Release the retaining clip (arrowed) and remove the wiring connector

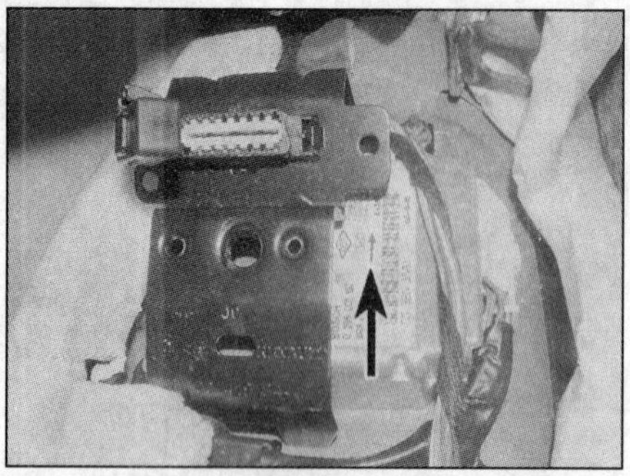

28.15 Arrow on the control unit (arrowed) must be pointing forwards

Refitting

15 Refit the control unit, making sure the arrow on the top of the unit is pointing towards the front of the vehicle **(see illustration)**. Refit the mounting nuts and tighten them securely.

16 Reconnect the wiring connector and refit the centre console as described in the relevant Section of Chapter 11.

17 Ensuring no one is inside the vehicle, reconnect the battery. With the driver's door open, turn on the ignition switch and check the operation of the airbag warning light.

Airbag contact unit/switch assembly

18 There are two types of switch assembly fitted, follow the procedures as described in Section 6 for the removal and refitting of the complete stalk switch assembly

Clio wiring diagrams

Diagram 1

Key to symbols

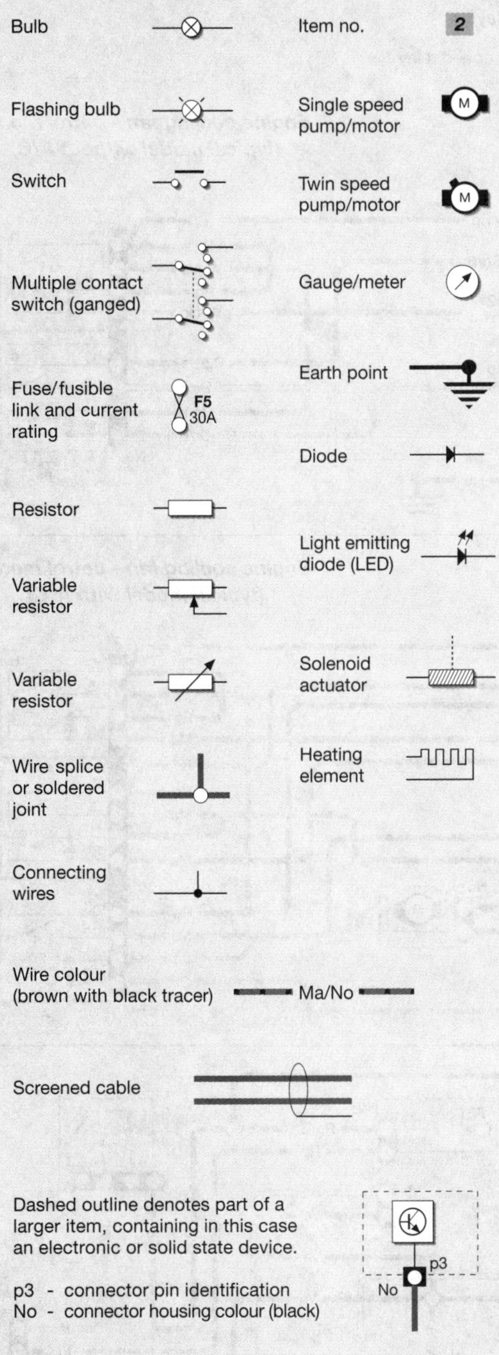

Passenger fusebox

Fuse	Rating	Circuit protected
F1	15A	Airbag, multi-timer unit
F2	15A	Stop lights, instrument panel, automatic transmission economy/performance switch and light, multi-timer unit, diagnostic socket
F3	15A	Heated rear screen, air conditioning ECU, automatic transmission ECU, rear screen wiper, reversing lights
F4	20A	Windscreen wiper
F5	10A	Anti-lock braking system
F6	10A	Multi-timer unit, air conditioning fan and control unit
F7	15A	Radio, cigar lighter, clock, heated rear screen
F8	15A	Horn
F9	10A	LH dipped beam
F10	10A	RH dipped beam
F11	10A	RH main beam
F12	10A	LH main beam
F13	20A	Dipped headlights (twin headlights)
F14	5A	Daytime running lights
F15	-	Spare
F16	-	Spare
F17	10A	Heated mirrors
F18	20A	Front fog lights
F19	-	Spare
F20	-	Spare
F21	5A	Multi-timer unit, diagnostic socket
F22	15A	Direction indicators and hazard warning lights
F23	15A	Rear fog lights
F24	-	Spare
F25	-	Spare
F26	10A	LH sidelights, switch lighting
F27	10A	RH sidelights, switch lighting
F28	2A	Immobiliser transponder, decoder unit
F29	20A	Accessories cut-off, interior lights, electric mirrors, radio, clock
F30	30A	Heated rear screen
F31	20A	Central locking
F32	30A	Electric windows
F33	20A	Headlight washer
F34	30A	Heater blower
F35	20A	Heated seats
F36	30A	Electric windows
F37	20A	Sunroof
F38	-	Spare
F39	-	Spare

Key to circuits

Diagram 1	Information for wiring diagrams.
Diagram 2	Starting, charging, engine cooling fan, diagnostic socket.
Diagram 3	Safety restraint system, electric power steering, horn, cigar lighter, Diesel fuel filter heater, heater blower.
Diagram 4	Typical air conditioning.
Diagram 5	Instrument cluster.
Diagram 6	Anti-lock brakes, front foglight, clock and external temperature gauge. Side, tail, number plate and headlights.
Diagram 7	Direction indicators, hazard warning, rear fog light, stop and reversing lights, headlight levelling.
Diagram 8	Interior light, luggage compartment light, heated rear window, front and rear wash/wipe, headlight washers.
Diagram 9	Electric mirrors, central locking, audio system, electric sunroof.
Diagram 10	Electric windows, Diesel engine management.
Diagram 11	Fuel injection (D7F 720 models).
Diagram 12	Fuel injection (D7F 726 models).
Diagram 13	Fuel injection (E7J 780/K7M 744 models).

H32308

Diagram 2

Wire colours

Ba	White	**No**	Black
Be	Blue	**Or**	Orange
Bj	Beige	**Rg**	Red
Cy	Clear	**Sa**	Pink
Gr	Grey	**Ve**	Green
Ja	Yellow	**Vi**	Mauve
Ma	Brown		

Key to items

1 Battery
2 Ignition switch
3 Starter motor
4 Alternator
5 Engine fusebox
6 Passenger fuse/relay/ multi-timer unit
7 Automatic transmission unit
a = starter inhibitor switch
8 Cooling fan switch
9 Cooling fan motor
10 Cooling fan resistor
11 Diagnostic socket
12 Engine relay unit
a = starter inhibitor relay
b = injection locking relay
c = cooling fan relay
d = percolation fan low speed relay

H32309

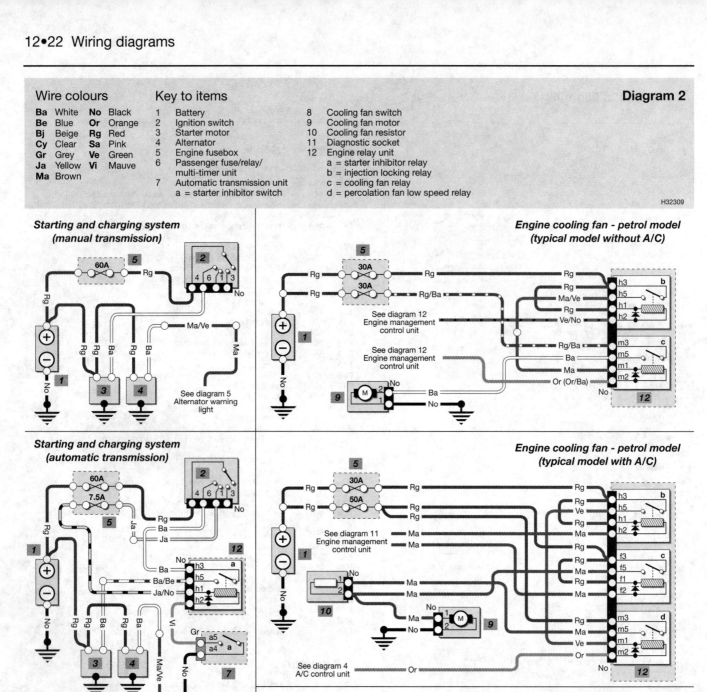

Starting and charging system (manual transmission)

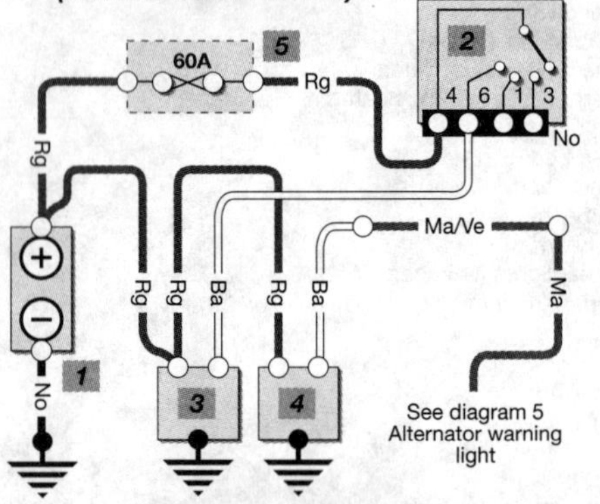

Engine cooling fan - petrol model (typical model without A/C)

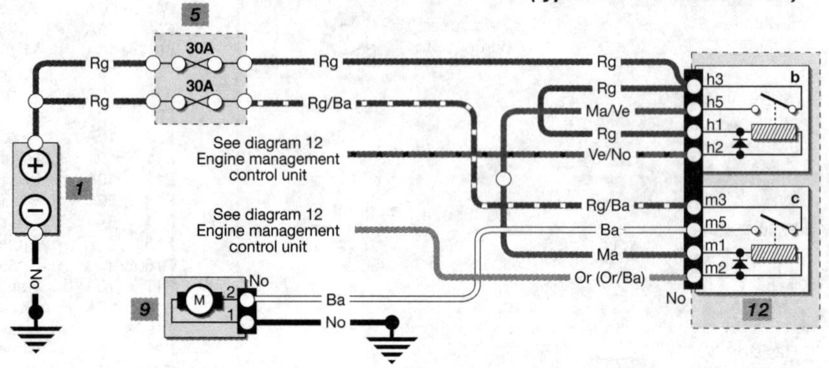

Starting and charging system (automatic transmission)

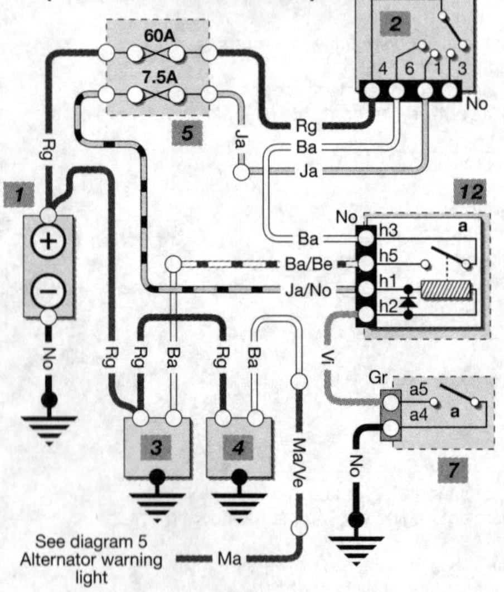

Engine cooling fan - petrol model (typical model with A/C)

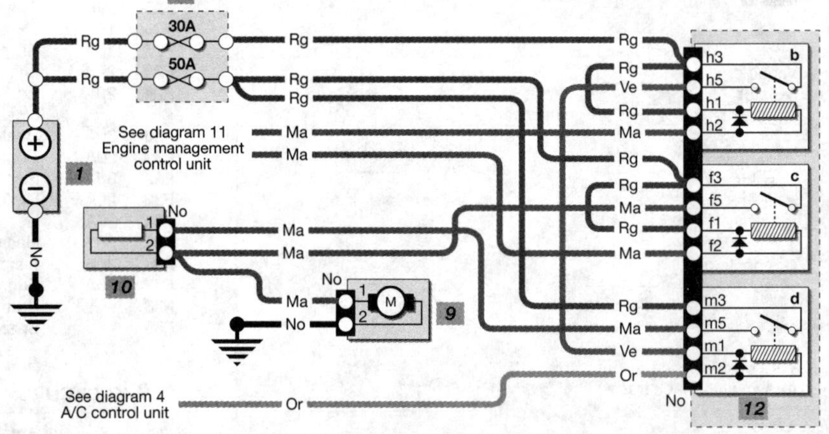

Engine cooling fan (Diesel engine)

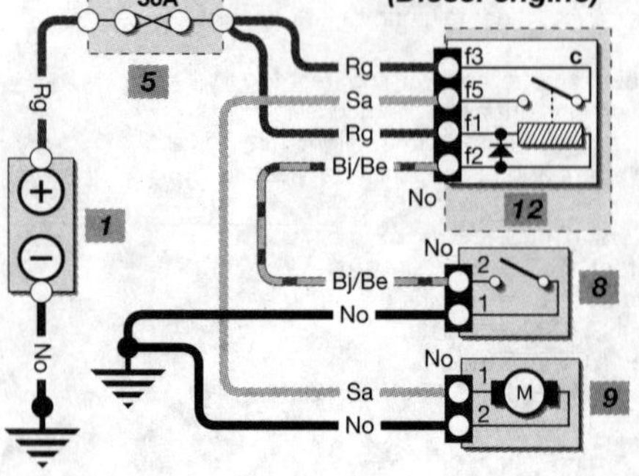

Diagnostic socket

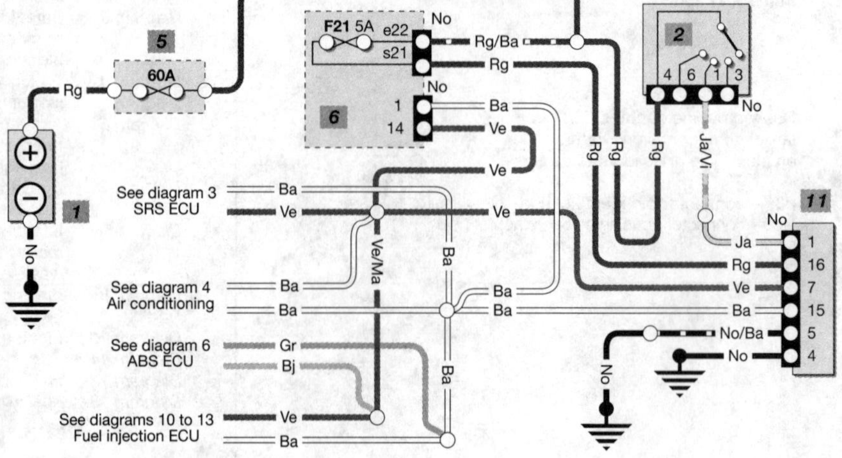

Diagram 3

Wire colours

Ba	White	**No**	Black
Be	Blue	**Or**	Orange
Bj	Beige	**Rg**	Red
Cy	Clear	**Sa**	Pink
Gr	Grey	**Ve**	Green
Ja	Yellow	**Vi**	Mauve
Ma	Brown		

Key to items

1 Battery
2 Ignition switch
5 Engine fusebox
6 Passenger fuse/relay/multi-timer unit
12 Engine relay unit
  e = power steering relay
  f = fuel filter heater relay
15 Power steering electric pump
16 SRS control unit
17 Driver's seatbelt pretensioner
18 Passenger's seatbelt pretensioner
19 Driver's airbag
20 Passenger's airbag
21 Horn/light switch
  a = horn
  b = side/headlight
22 Horn
23 Cigar lighter
24 Fuel filter heater element
25 Heater blower assembly
26 Heater blower switch
  a = blower switch
27 Interior lighting rheostat

H32310

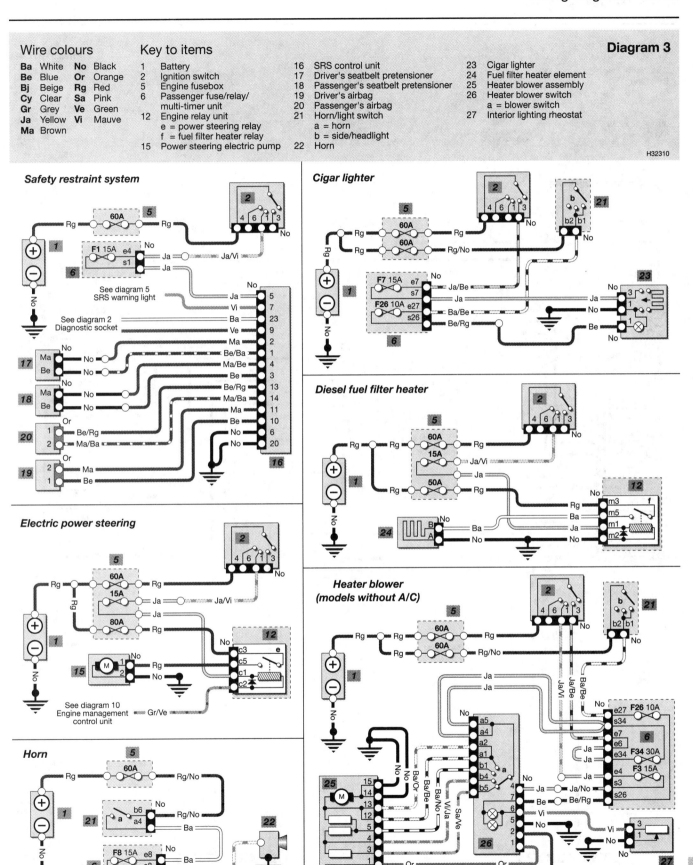

Safety restraint system

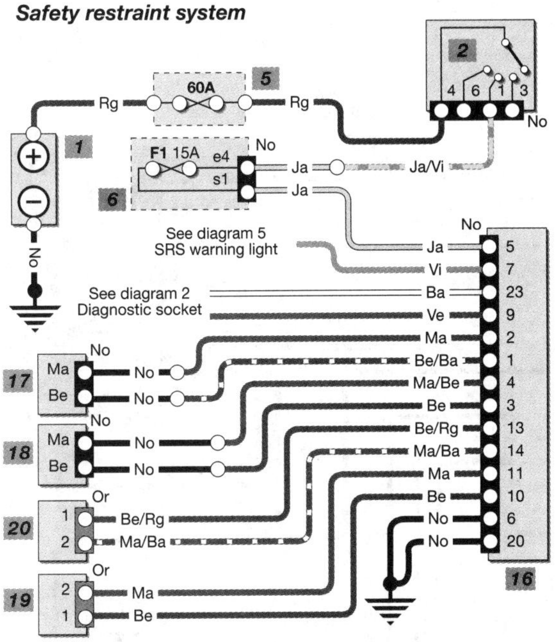

Cigar lighter

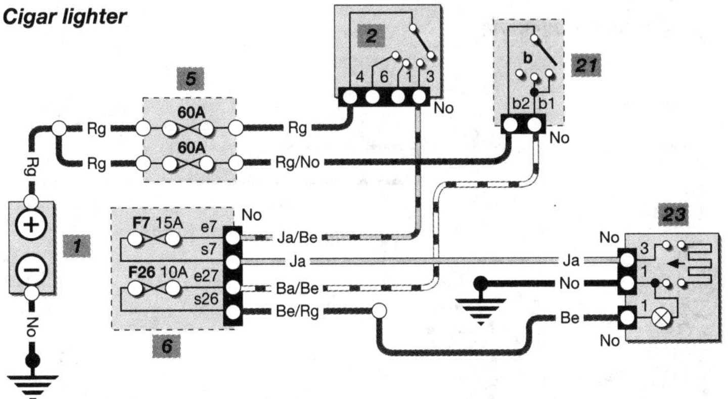

Diesel fuel filter heater

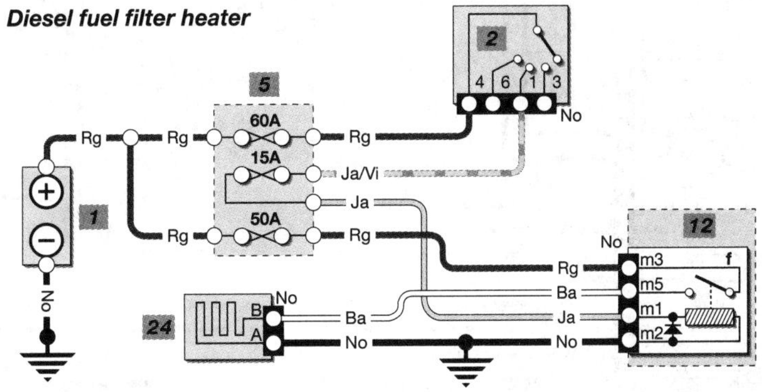

Electric power steering

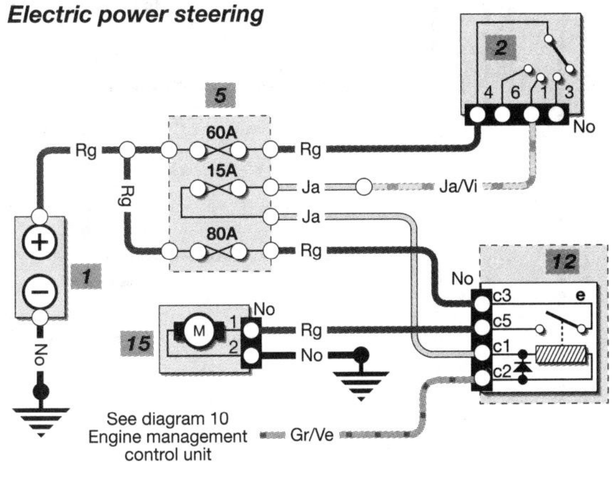

Horn

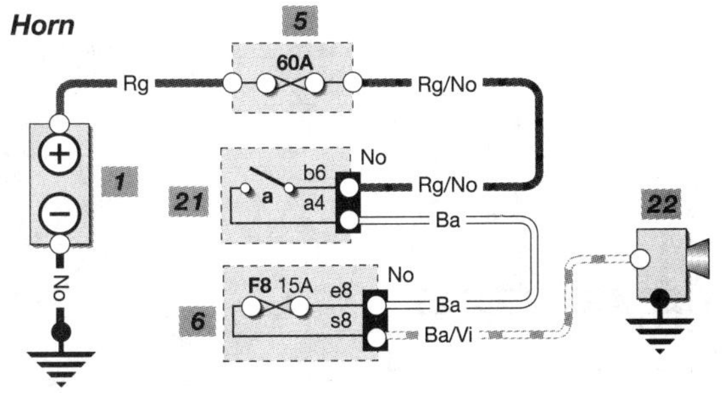

Heater blower (models without A/C)

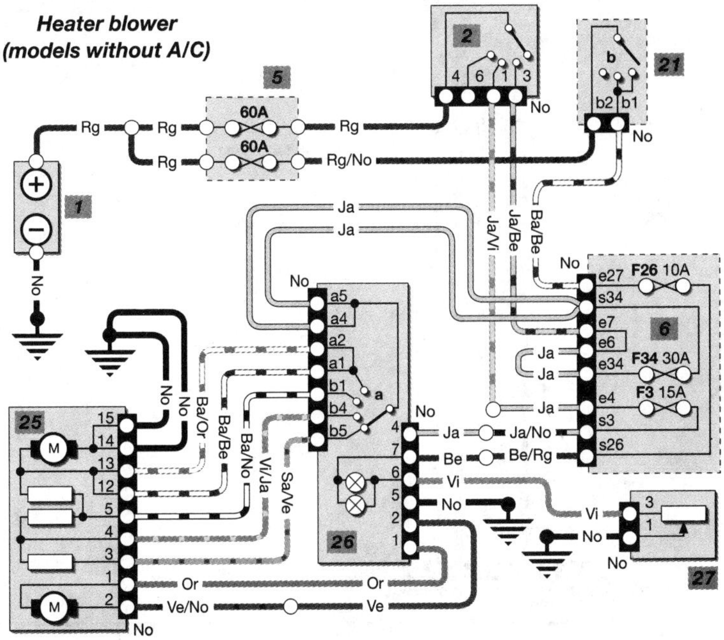

Diagram 4

Wire colours

Ba	White	**No**	Black
Be	Blue	**Or**	Orange
Bj	Beige	**Rg**	Red
Cy	Clear	**Sa**	Pink
Gr	Grey	**Ve**	Green
Ja	Yellow	**Vi**	Mauve
Ma	Brown		

Key to items

1 Battery
2 Ignition switch
5 Engine fusebox
6 Passenger fuse/relay/multi-timer unit
21 Horn/light switch
  b = side/headlight
25 Heater blower assembly
26 Heater blower switch
  a = blower switch
  b = a/c switch
  c = recirculation switch
  d = heated rear window switch
  e = heated rear window indicator
  f = recirculation indicator
  g = a/c indicator
27 Interior lighting rheostat
30 Air conditioning monitoring unit
31 Air conditioning three function pressure switch
32 Air conditioning clutch

H32311

Typical air conditioning

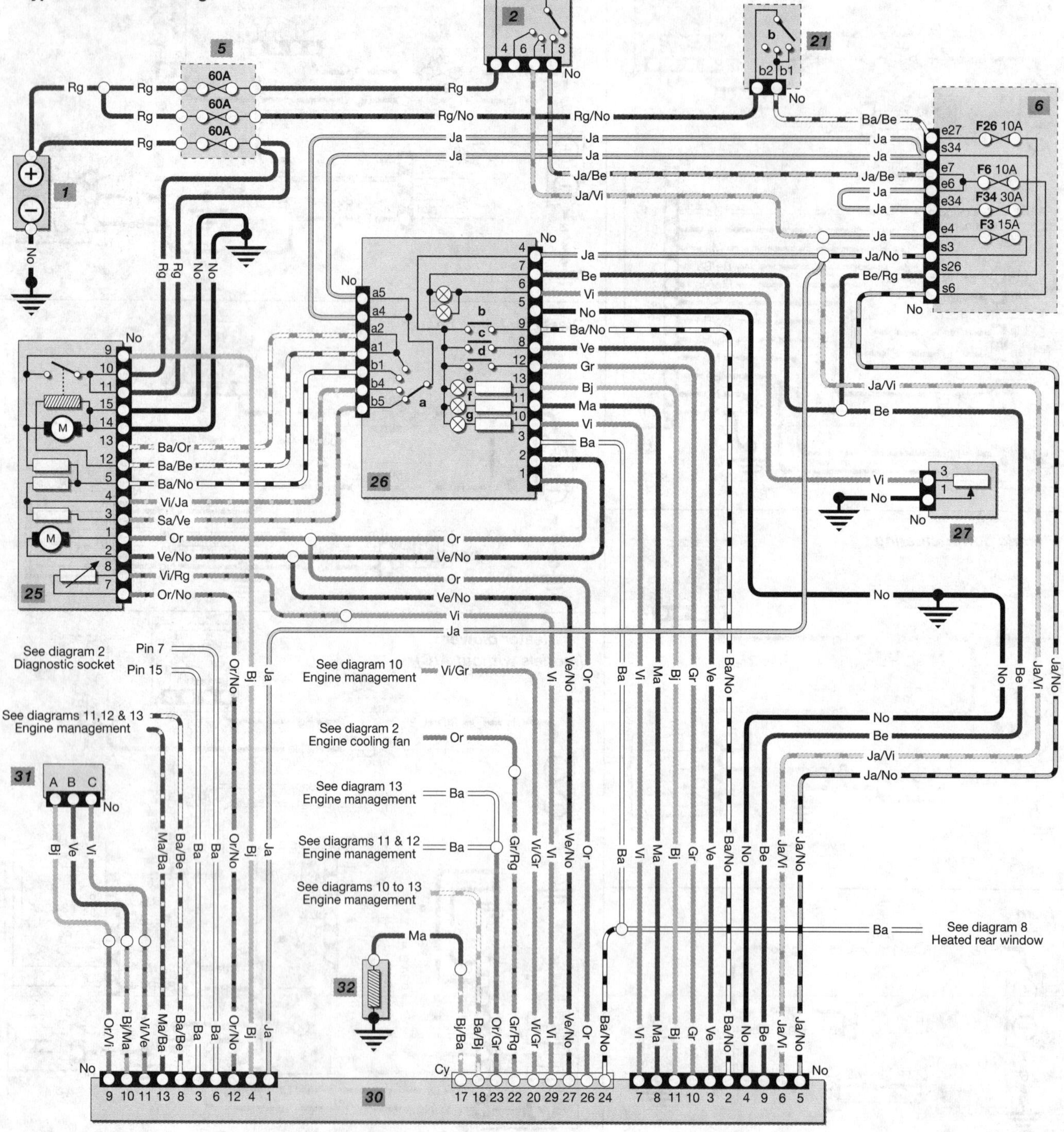

Wire colours

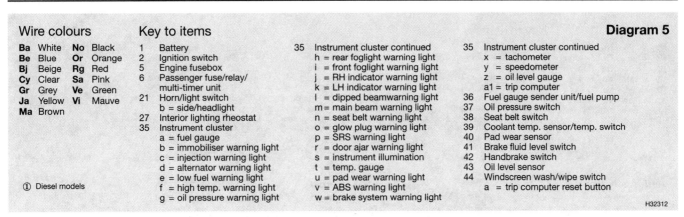

Ba	White	**No**	Black
Be	Blue	**Or**	Orange
Bj	Beige	**Rg**	Red
Cy	Clear	**Sa**	Pink
Gr	Grey	**Ve**	Green
Ja	Yellow	**Vi**	Mauve
Ma	Brown		

① Diesel models

Key to items

Diagram 5

1 Battery
2 Ignition switch
5 Engine fusebox
6 Passenger fuse/relay/multi-timer unit
21 Horn/light switch
  b = side/headlight
27 Interior lighting rheostat
35 Instrument cluster
  a = fuel gauge
  b = immobiliser warning light
  c = injection warning light
  d = alternator warning light
  e = low fuel warning light
  f = high temp. warning light
  g = oil pressure warning light

35 Instrument cluster continued
  h = rear foglight warning light
  i = front foglight warning light
  j = RH indicator warning light
  k = LH indicator warning light
  l = dipped beamwarning light
  m = main beam warning light
  n = seat belt warning light
  o = glow plug warning light
  p = SRS warning light
  r = door ajar warning light
  s = instrument illumination
  t = temp. gauge
  u = pad wear warning light
  v = ABS warning light
  w = brake system warning light

35 Instrument cluster continued
  x = tachometer
  y = speedometer
  z = oil level gauge
  a1 = trip computer
36 Fuel gauge sender unit/fuel pump
37 Oil pressure switch
38 Seat belt switch
39 Coolant temp. sensor/temp. switch
40 Pad wear sensor
41 Brake fluid level switch
42 Handbrake switch
43 Oil level sensor
44 Windscreen wash/wipe switch
  a = trip computer reset button

H32312

Instrument cluster

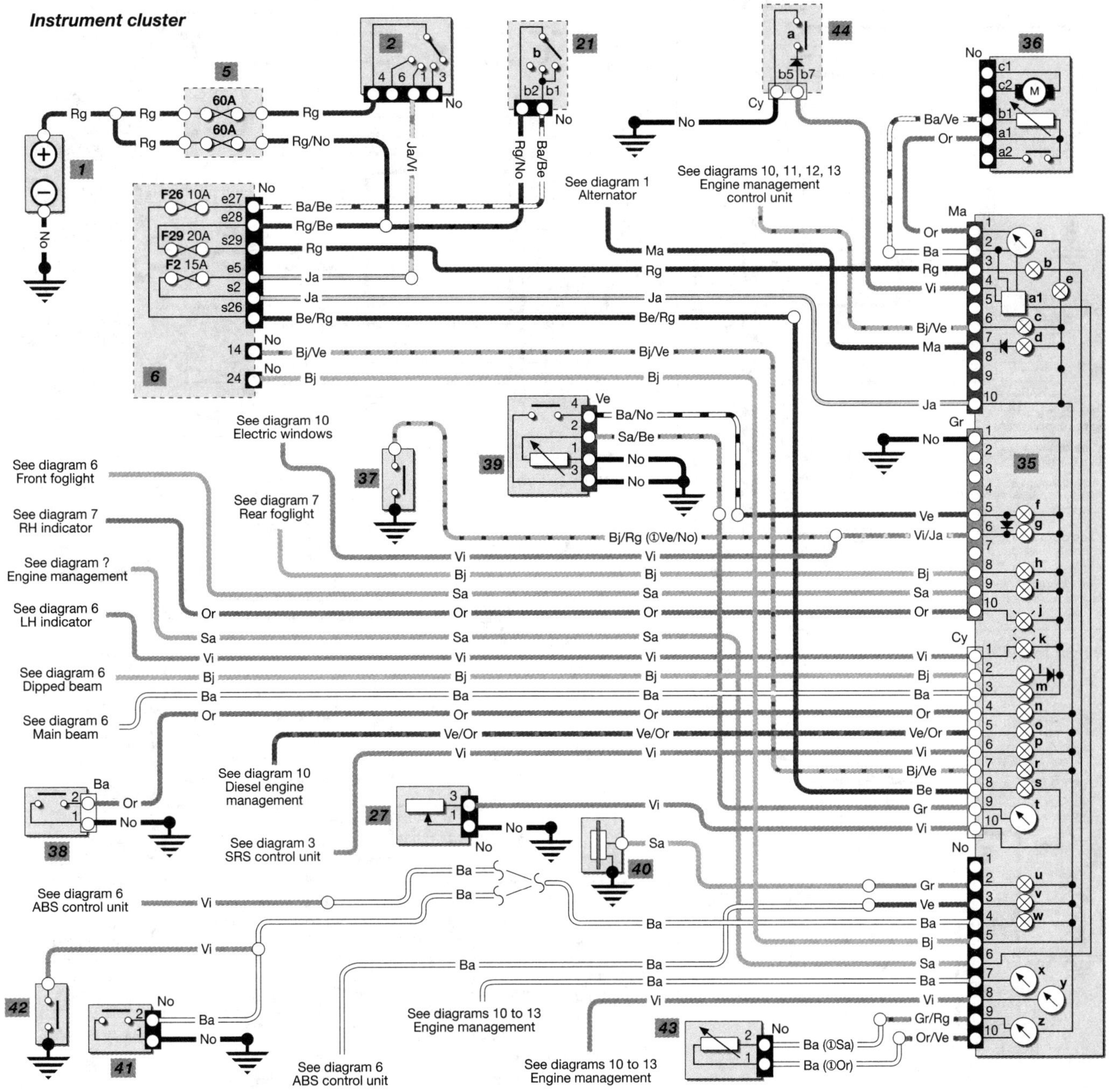

Diagram 6

Wire colours

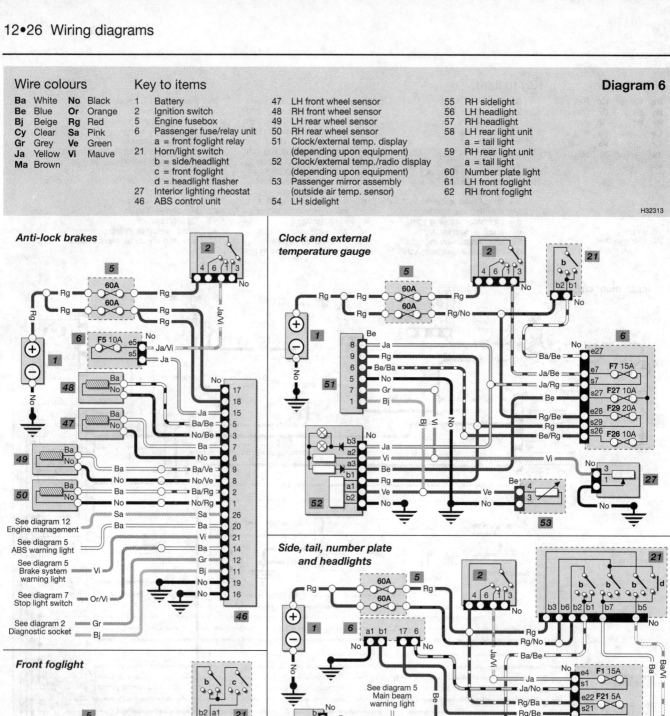

Ba	White	**No**	Black
Be	Blue	**Or**	Orange
Bj	Beige	**Rg**	Red
Cy	Clear	**Sa**	Pink
Gr	Grey	**Ve**	Green
Ja	Yellow	**Vi**	Mauve
Ma	Brown		

Key to items

1 Battery
2 Ignition switch
5 Engine fusebox
6 Passenger fuse/relay unit
  a = front foglight relay
21 Horn/light switch
  b = side/headlight
  c = front foglight
  d = headlight flasher
27 Interior lighting rheostat
46 ABS control unit
47 LH front wheel sensor
48 RH front wheel sensor
49 LH rear wheel sensor
50 RH rear wheel sensor
51 Clock/external temp. display (depending upon equipment)
52 Clock/external temp./radio display (depending upon equipment)
53 Passenger mirror assembly (outside air temp. sensor)
54 LH sidelight
55 RH sidelight
56 LH headlight
57 RH headlight
58 LH rear light unit
  a = tail light
59 RH rear light unit
  a = tail light
60 Number plate light
61 LH front foglight
62 RH front foglight

H32313

Anti-lock brakes

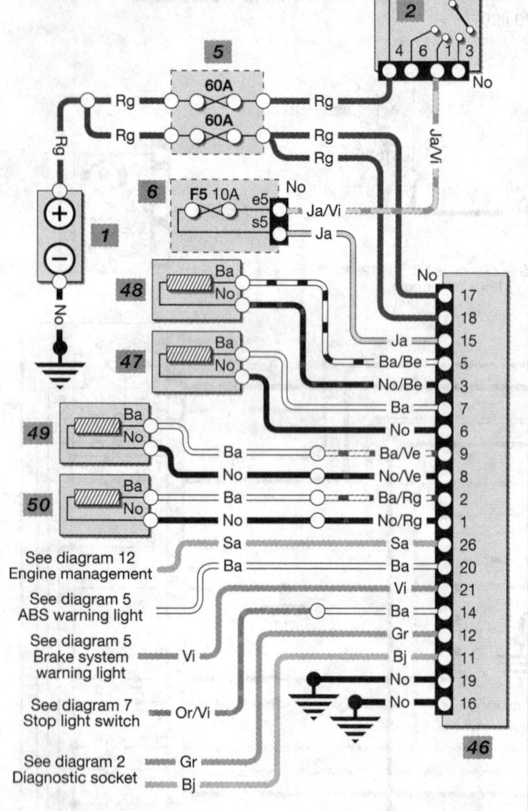

Clock and external temperature gauge

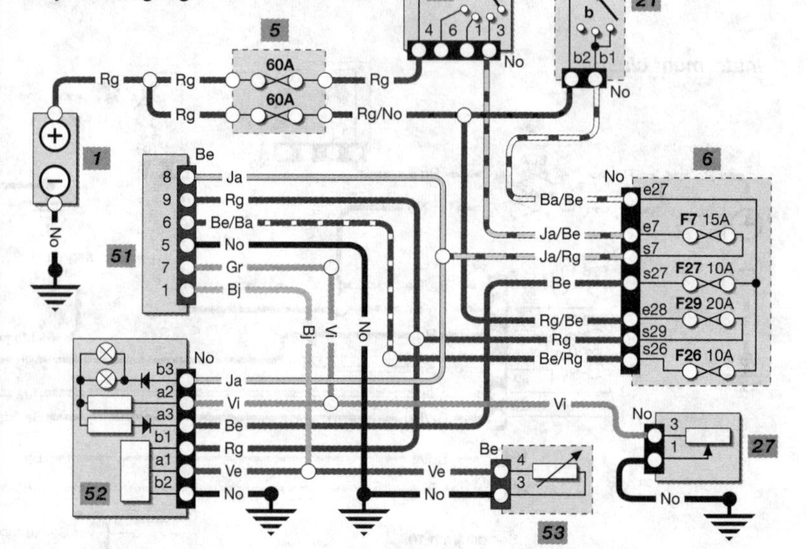

Front foglight

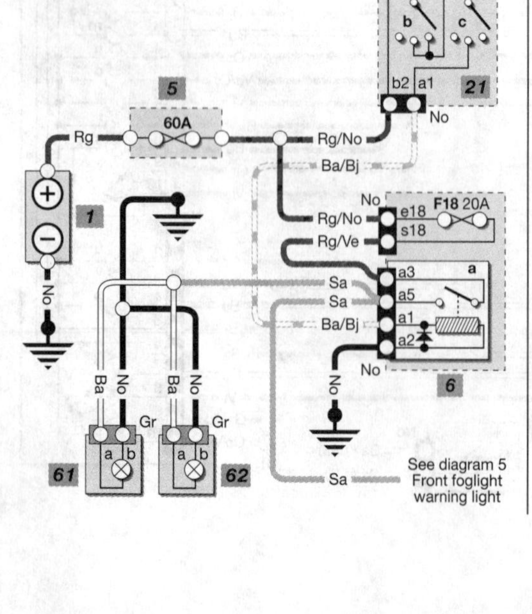

Side, tail, number plate and headlights

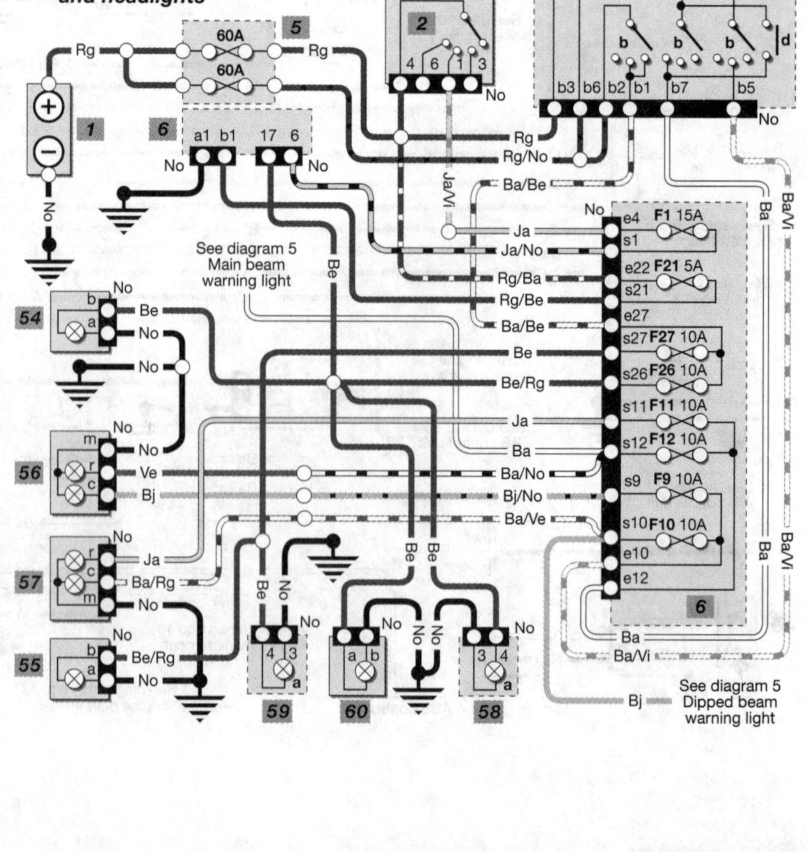

Diagram 7

Wire colours

Ba	White	**No**	Black
Be	Blue	**Or**	Orange
Bj	Beige	**Rg**	Red
Cy	Clear	**Sa**	Pink
Gr	Grey	**Ve**	Green
Ja	Yellow	**Vi**	Mauve
Ma	Brown		

Key to items

1 Battery
2 Ignition switch
5 Engine fusebox
6 Passenger fuse/relay/ /multi-timer unit
21 Horn/light switch
   b = side/headlight
   d = rear foglight
   e = direction indicator
56 LH headlight
57 RH headlight
58 LH rear light unit
   b = reversing light
   c = stop light
   d = direction indicator
   e = foglight
59 RH rear light unit
   b = reversing light
   c = stop light
   d = direction indicator
65 High level stop light
66 Reversing light switch (manual transmission)
67 Automatic transmission module
68 Automatic transmission control unit
69 Stop light switch
70 LH front indicator
71 RH front indicator
72 LH front indicator side repeater
73 RH front indicator side repeater
74 Hazard warning light switch
75 Headlight levelling control
76 LH headlight levelling motor
77 RH headlight levelling motor

H32314

Direction indicators and hazard warning light

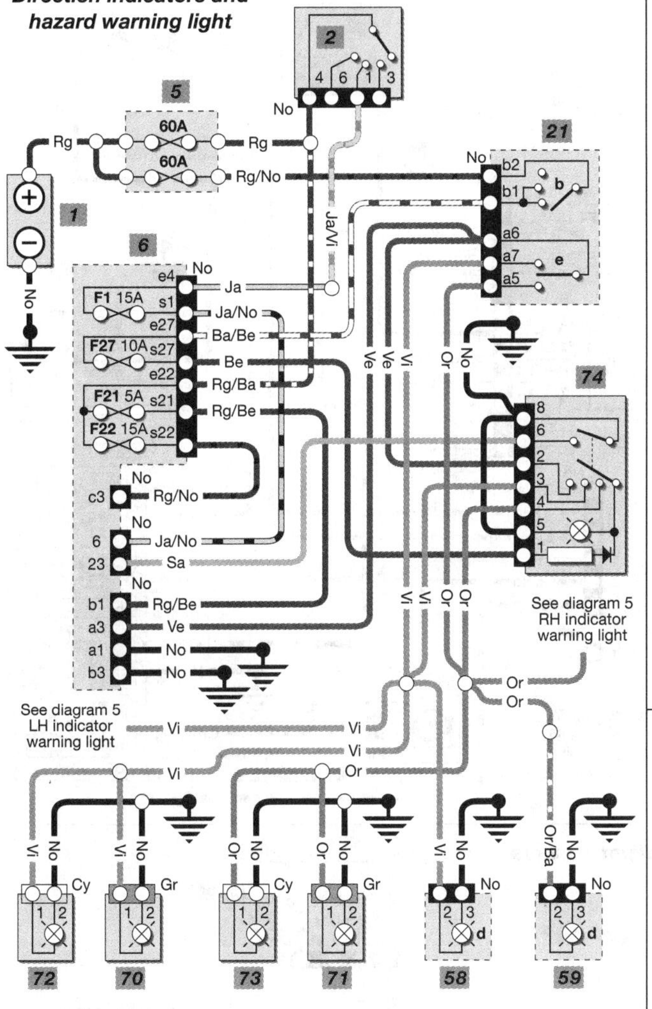

Stop and reversing lights

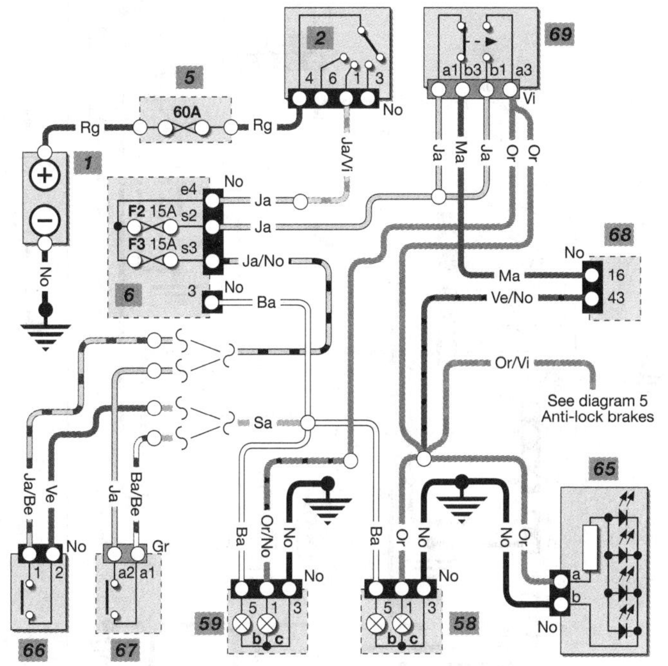

Headlight levelling

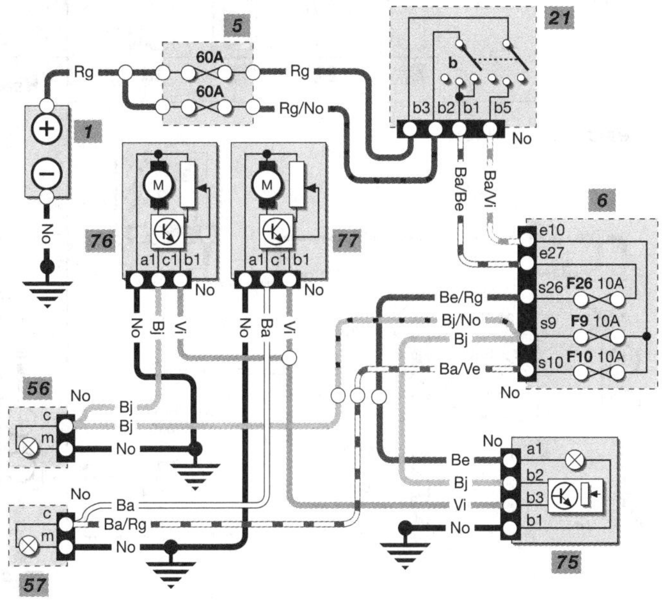

Rear foglight

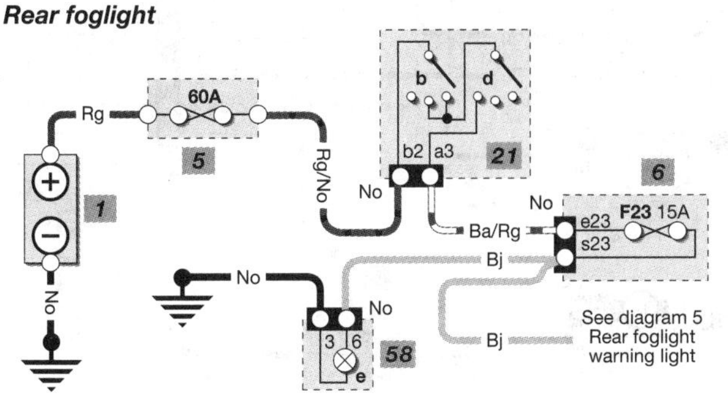

Diagram 8

Wire colours

Ba	White	**No**	Black
Be	Blue	**Or**	Orange
Bj	Beige	**Rg**	Red
Cy	Clear	**Sa**	Pink
Gr	Grey	**Ve**	Green
Ja	Yellow	**Vi**	Mauve
Ma	Brown		

Key to items

1 Battery
2 Ignition switch
5 Engine fusebox
6 Passenger fuse/relay/ /multi-timer unit
  b = heated rear window relay
44 Windscreen wash/wipe switch
  b = front wiper
  c = rear wash/wipe
  d = front washer
80 Infra-red receiver (if fitted)
81 Luggage compartment light
82 Luggage compartment light switch
83 Front courtesy light
84 Driver's door switch
85 Passenger's door switch
86 LH rear door switch
87 RH door switch
88 Front wiper motor
89 Rear wiper motor
90 Washer pump
91 Headlight washer pump
92 Headlight washer pump relay
93 Heated rear window

H32315

Interior light and luggage compartment light

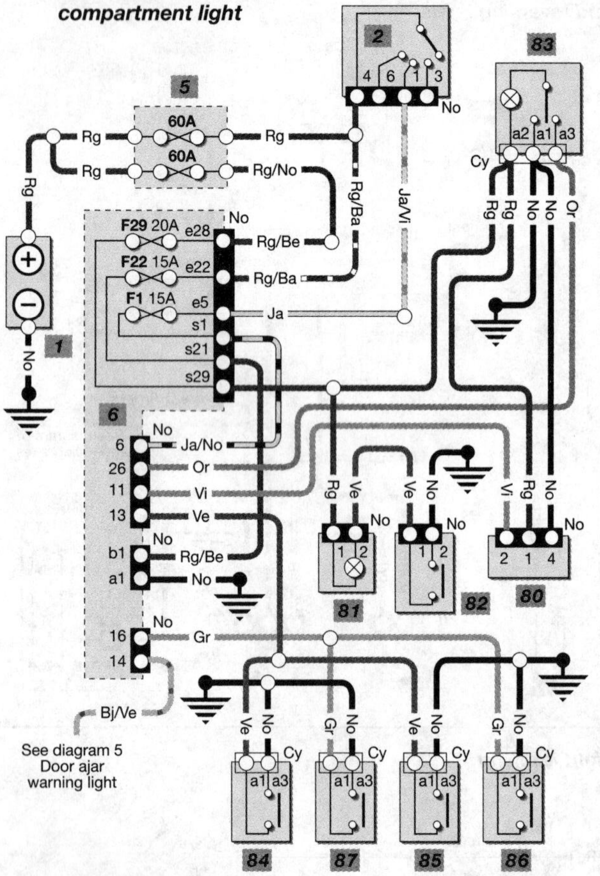

Front and rear wash/wipe

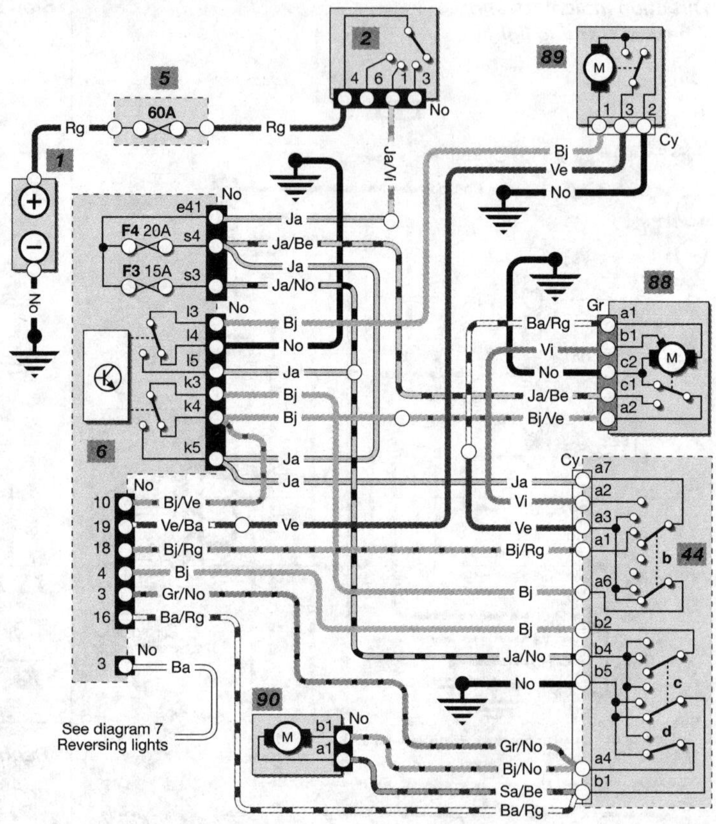

Heated rear window

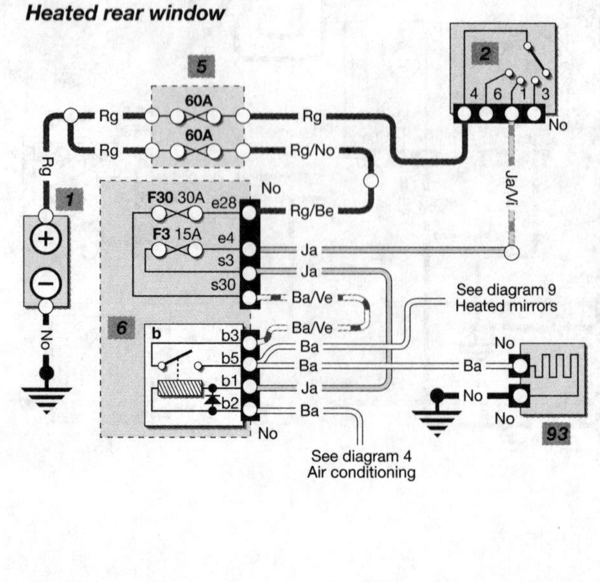

Headlight washers

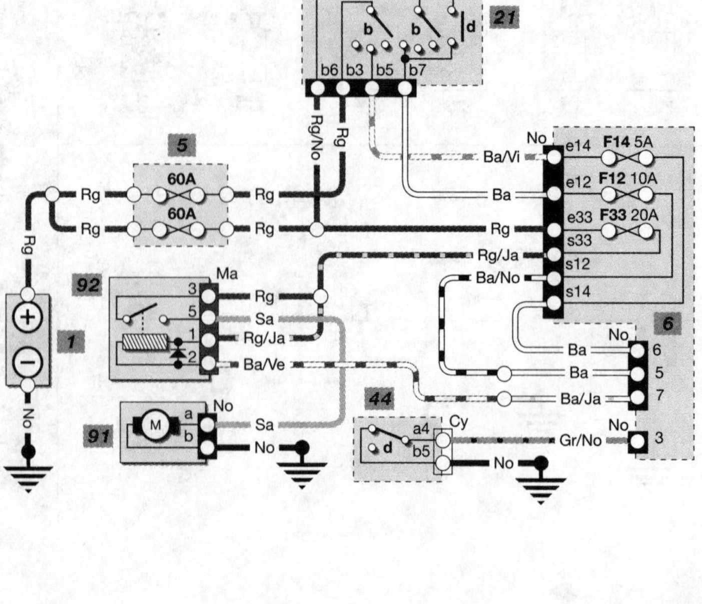

Diagram 9

Wire colours

Ba	White	**No**	Black
Be	Blue	**Or**	Orange
Bj	Beige	**Rg**	Red
Cy	Clear	**Sa**	Pink
Gr	Grey	**Ve**	Green
Ja	Yellow	**Vi**	Mauve
Ma	Brown		

Key to items

1 Battery
2 Ignition switch
5 Engine fusebox
6 Passenger fuse/relay/ /multi-timer unit
21 Horn/light switch
b = side/headlight
53 Passenger mirror assembly
80 Infra-red receiver
95 Mirror switch
96 Driver mirror assembly
97 Audio unit
98 LH front speaker
99 RH front speaker
100 LH front tweeter
101 RH front tweeter
102 Door lock switch
103 Tailgate lock motor
104 LH rear door lock motor
105 RH rear door lock motor
106 Driver's door lock motor
107 Passenger's door lock motor
108 Sunroof motor

H32316

Electric mirrors

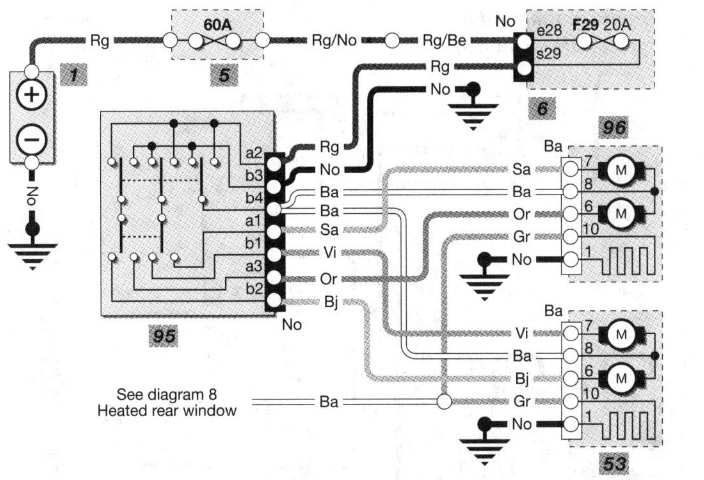

Audio system

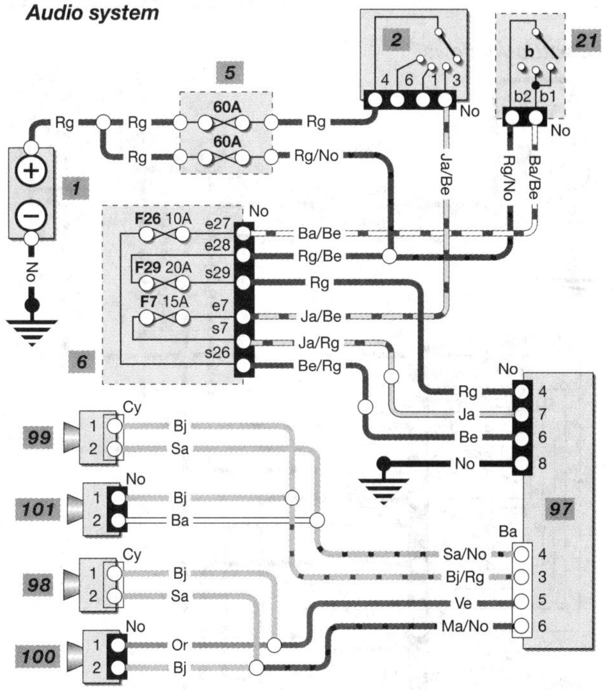

Central locking

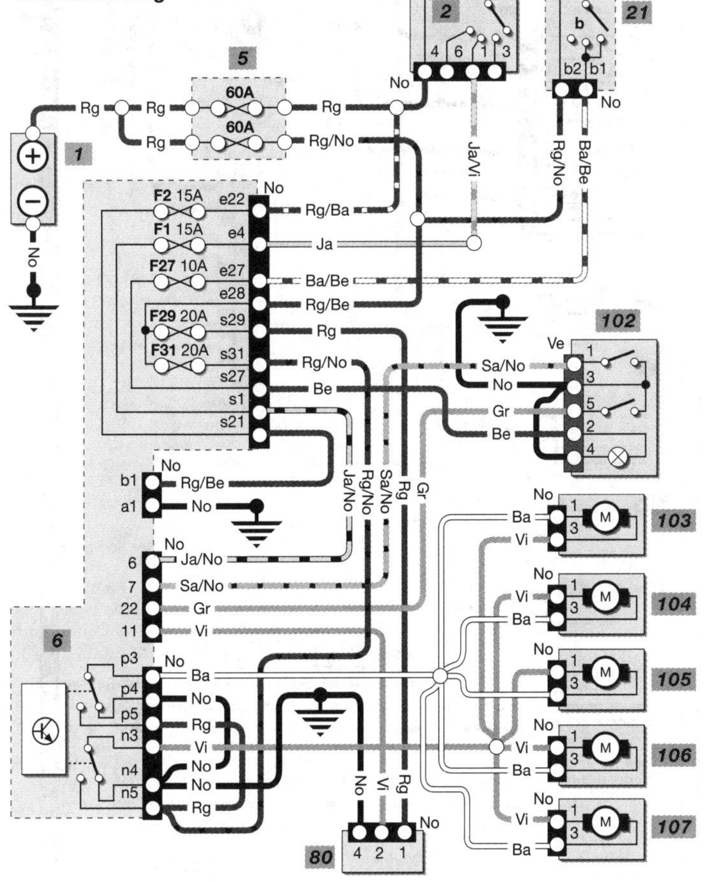

Electric sunroof

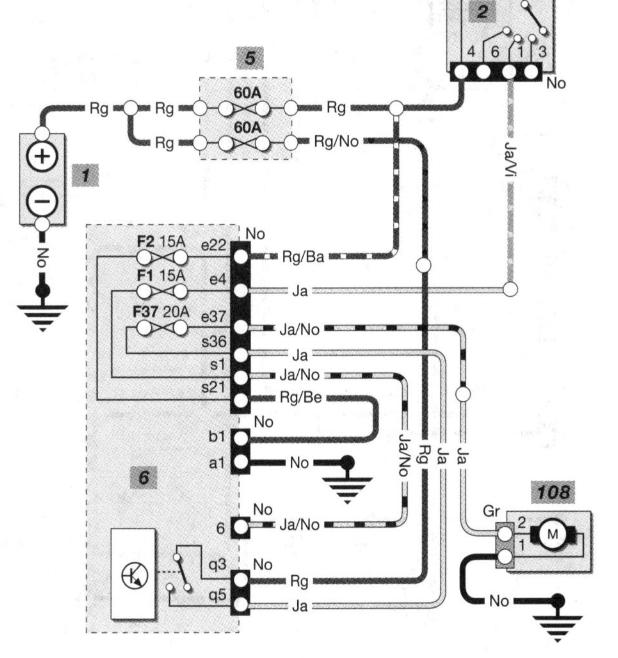

Diagram 10

Wire colours

Ba	White	**No**	Black
Be	Blue	**Or**	Orange
Bj	Beige	**Rg**	Red
Cy	Clear	**Sa**	Pink
Gr	Grey	**Ve**	Green
Ja	Yellow	**Vi**	Mauve
Ma	Brown		

Key to items

1 Battery
2 Ignition switch
5 Engine fusebox
6 Passenger fuse/relay/ /multi-timer unit
12 Engine compartment relay unit
  b = injection locking relay
  g = altitude relay
21 Horn/light switch
  b = side/headlight
84 Driver's door switch
85 Passenger's door switch
110 Driver's window motor
111 Passenger's window motor
112 Driver's window switch
113 Driver's switch for passenger window
114 Passenger's window switch
115 Engine management control unit
116 Pre-heater unit
117 Glow plugs
118 Speed sensor
119 Inertia switch
120 Pump unit
  a = boost compensator
  b = immobiliser
  c = throttle potentiometer
  d = advance solenoid
121 EGR solenoid valve
122 Fast idle solenoid valve
123 Needle lift sensor
124 Speed threshold sensor
125 Air temp. sensor
126 Coolant temp. sensor

H32317

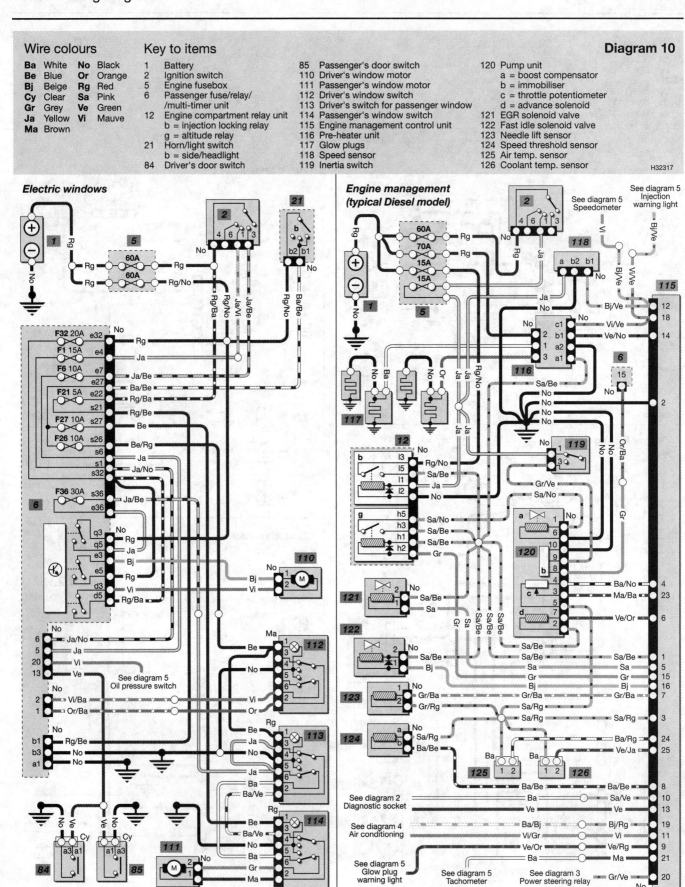

Electric windows

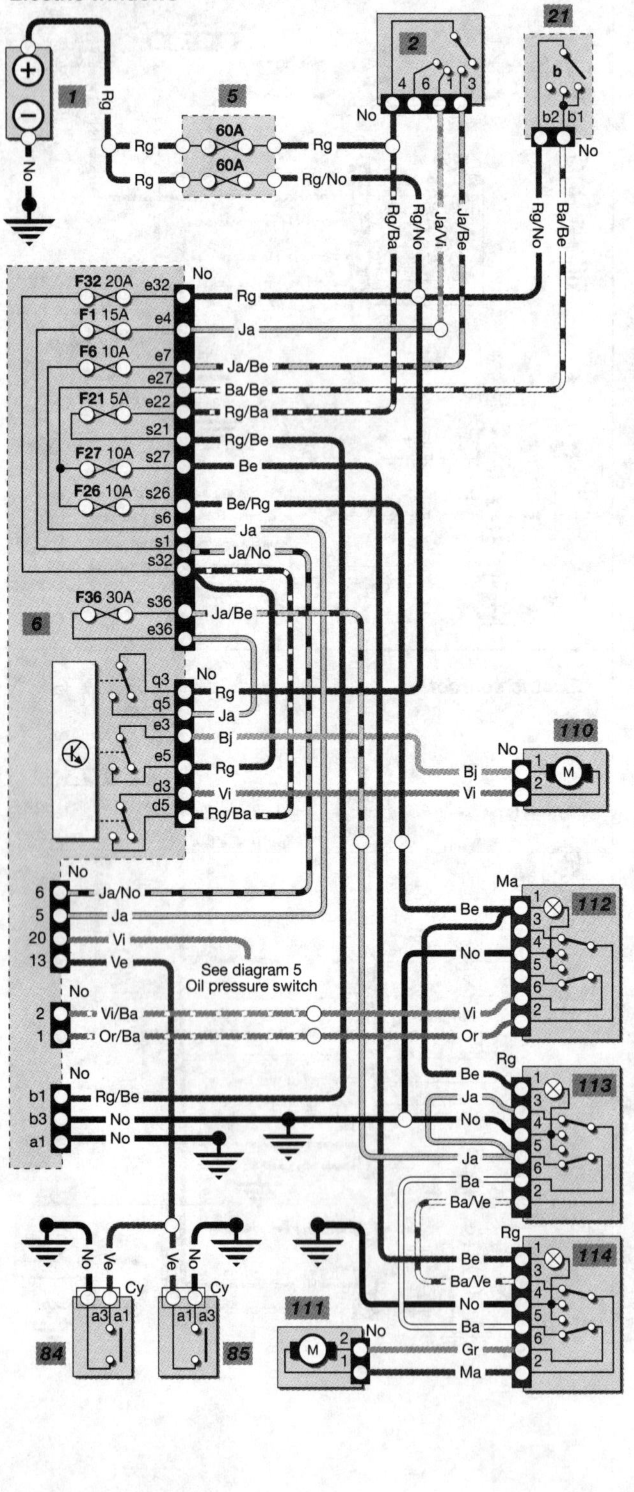

Engine management (typical Diesel model)

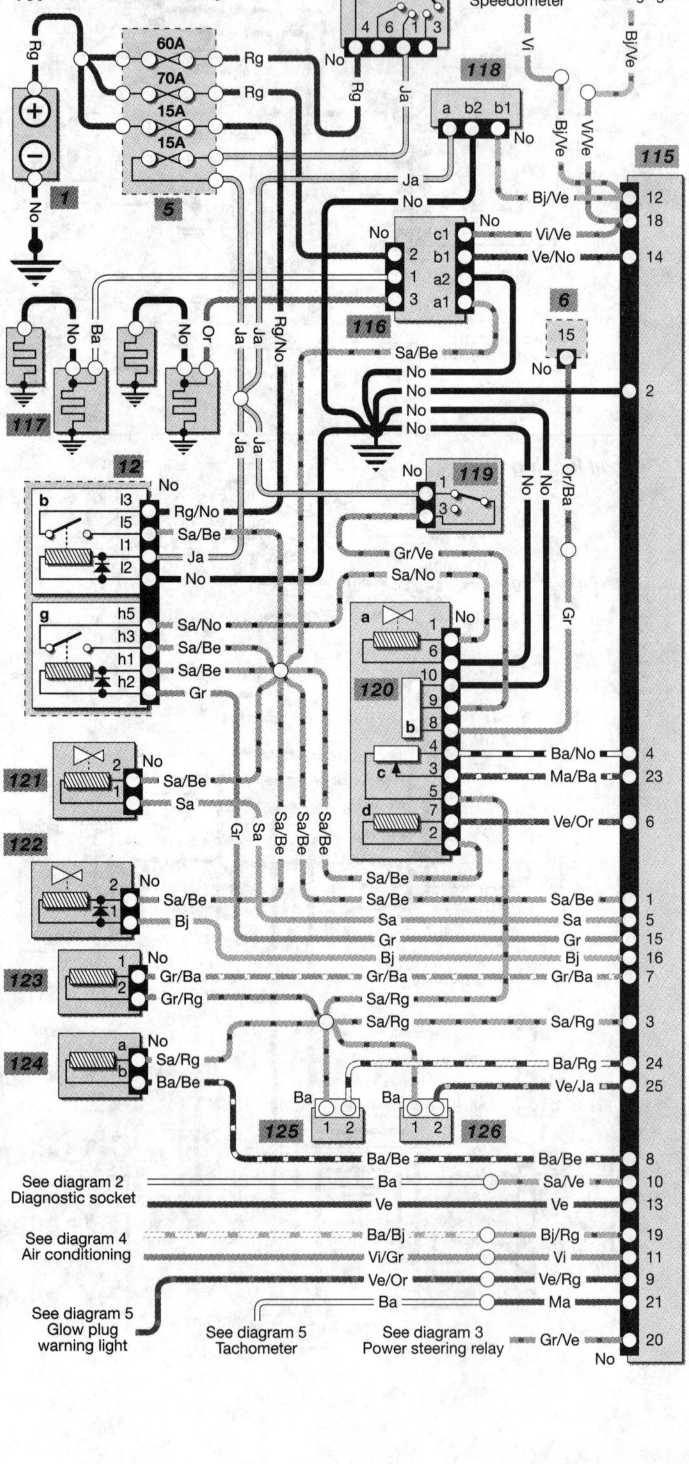

Wire colours

Ba	White	**No**	Black
Be	Blue	**Or**	Orange
Bj	Beige	**Rg**	Red
Cy	Clear	**Sa**	Pink
Gr	Grey	**Ve**	Green
Ja	Yellow	**Vi**	Mauve
Ma	Brown		

Key to items

Diagram 11

1 Battery
2 Ignition switch
5 Engine fusebox
6 Passenger fuse/relay/ /multi-timer unit
12 Engine compartment relay unit
b = injection locking relay
h = fuel pump relay
36 Fuel gauge sender unit/fuel pump
115 Engine management control unit
118 Speed sensor
119 Inertia switch
124 Speed threshold sensor
125 Air temp. sensor
126 Coolant temp. sensor
130 Ignition coil module
131 Suppressor
132 Fuel injector
133 Throttle unit
134 Power steering pressure switch
135 Knock sensor
136 MAP sensor
137 Oxygen sensor
138 EVAP valve
139 Throttle potentiometer

H32318

Fuel injection (typical D7F 720 model)

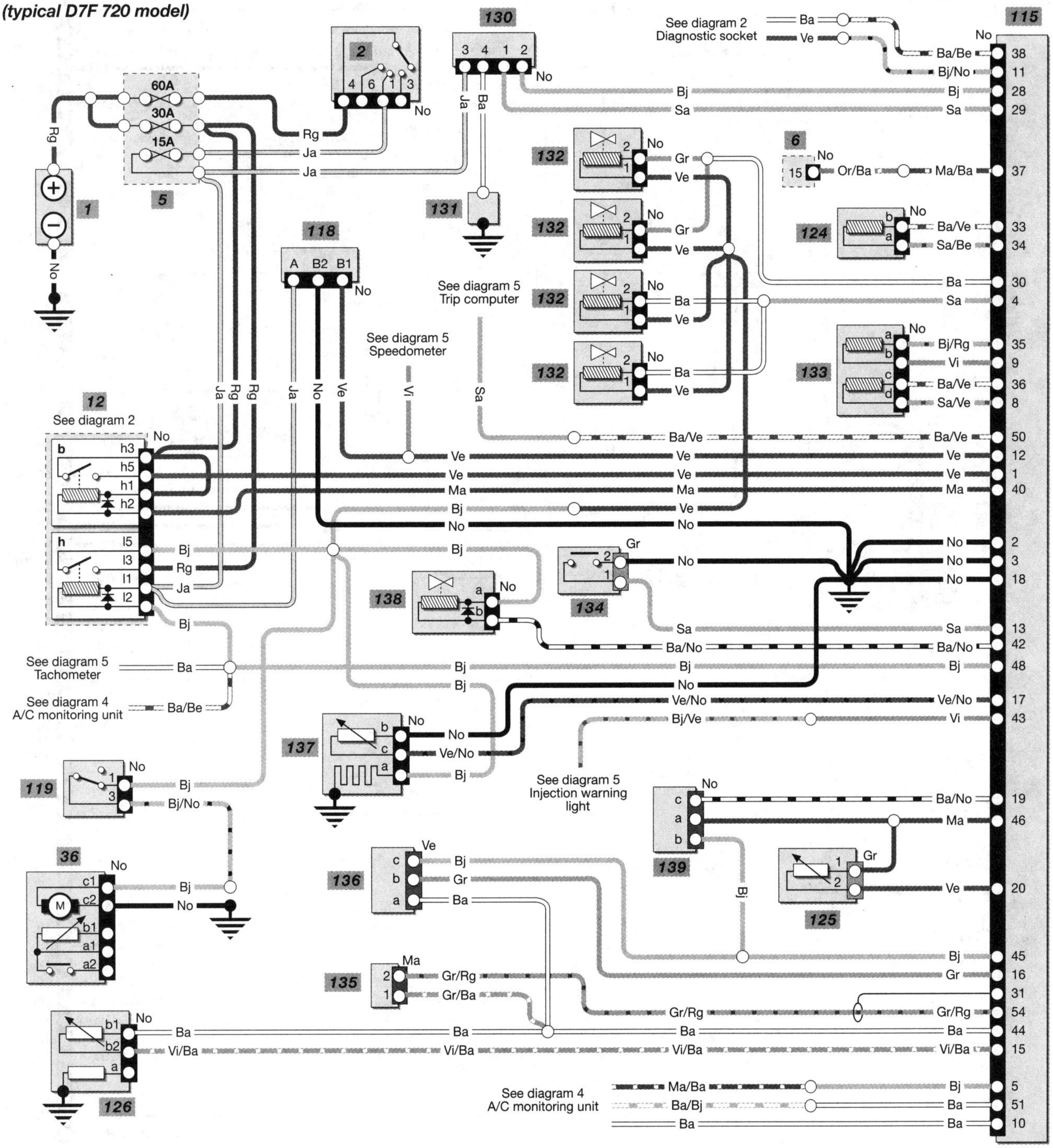

Diagram 12

Wire colours

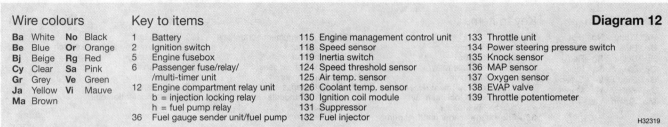

Ba	White	**No**	Black
Be	Blue	**Or**	Orange
Bj	Beige	**Rg**	Red
Cy	Clear	**Sa**	Pink
Gr	Grey	**Ve**	Green
Ja	Yellow	**Vi**	Mauve
Ma	Brown		

Key to items

1 Battery
2 Ignition switch
5 Engine fusebox
6 Passenger fuse/relay/ /multi-timer unit
12 Engine compartment relay unit
 b = injection locking relay
 h = fuel pump relay
36 Fuel gauge sender unit/fuel pump
115 Engine management control unit
118 Speed sensor
119 Inertia switch
124 Speed threshold sensor
125 Air temp. sensor
126 Coolant temp. sensor
130 Ignition coil module
131 Suppressor
132 Fuel injector
133 Throttle unit
134 Power steering pressure switch
135 Knock sensor
136 MAP sensor
137 Oxygen sensor
138 EVAP valve
139 Throttle potentiometer

H32319

Fuel injection (typical D7F 726 model)

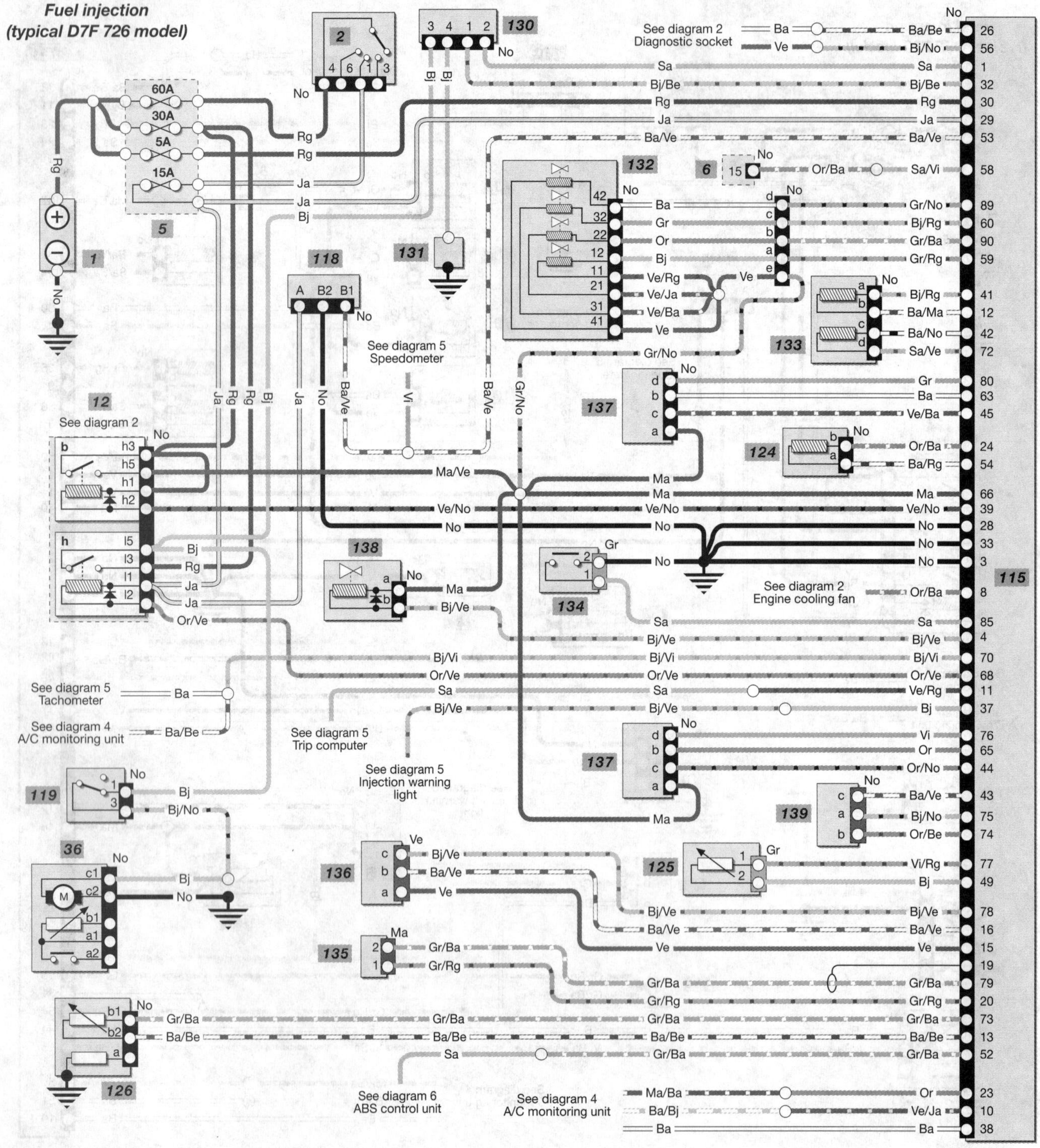

Wire colours

Ba	White	**No**	Black
Be	Blue	**Or**	Orange
Bj	Beige	**Rg**	Red
Cy	Clear	**Sa**	Pink
Gr	Grey	**Ve**	Green
Ja	Yellow	**Vi**	Mauve
Ma	Brown		

Key to items

1 Battery
2 Ignition switch
5 Engine fusebox
6 Passenger fuse/relay/ /multi-timer unit
12 Engine compartment relay unit
b = injection locking relay
h = fuel pump relay
36 Fuel gauge sender unit/fuel pump
115 Engine management control unit
118 Speed sensor
119 Inertia switch
124 Speed threshold sensor
125 Air temp. sensor
126 Coolant temp. sensor
131 Suppressor
132 Fuel injector
133 Throttle unit
134 Power steering pressure switch
135 Knock sensor
136 MAP sensor
137 Oxygen sensor
138 EVAP valve
139 Throttle potentiometer
140 Ignition coil

Diagram 13

H32320

Fuel injection (typical E7J 780/K7M 744 models)

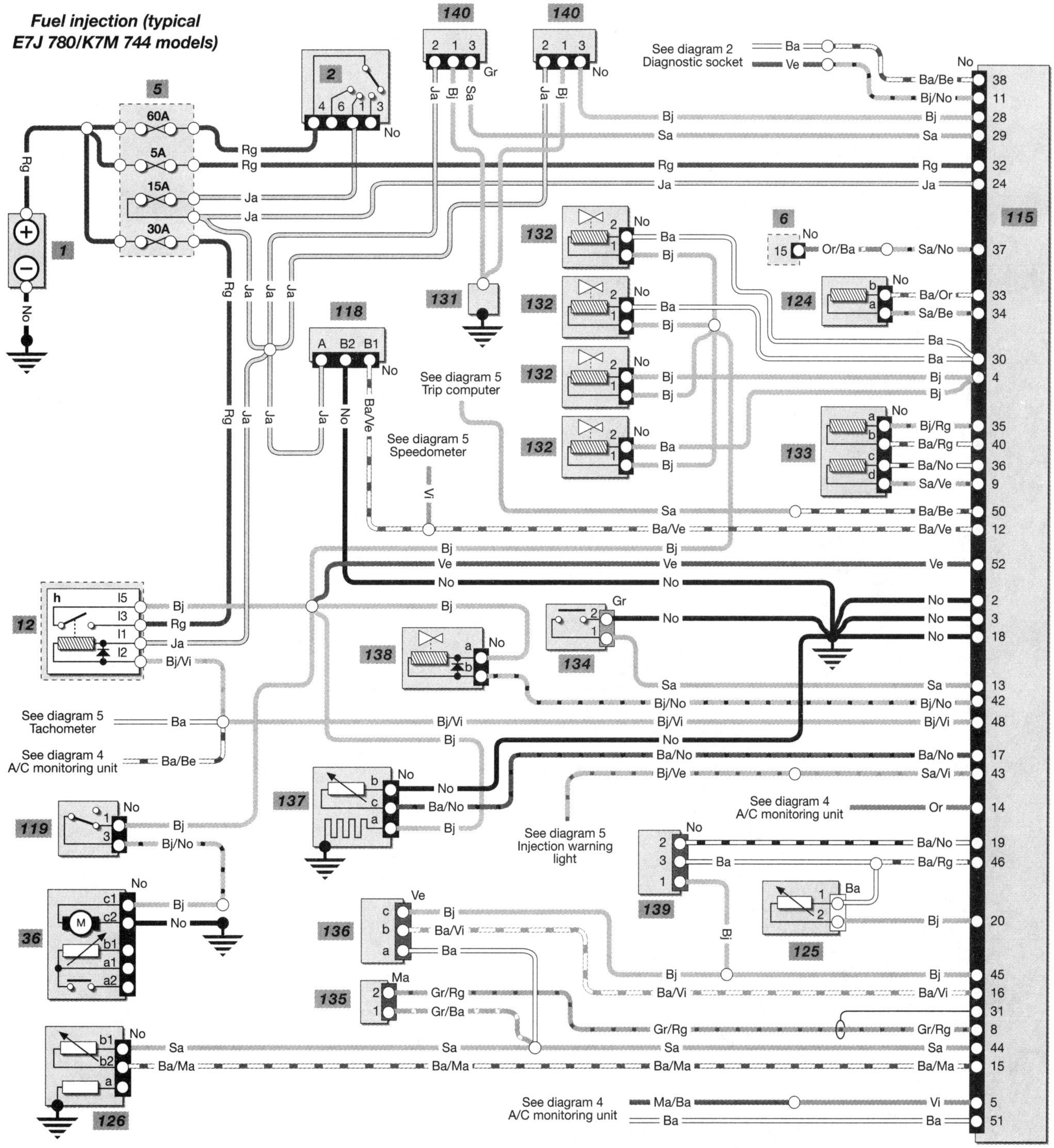

Dimensions and weights

Note: *All figures are approximate and may vary according to model. Refer to manufacturer's data for exact figures.*

Dimensions

Overall length	3773 mm
Overall width (including door mirrors)	1940 mm
Overall height (unladen)	1417 mm
Wheelbase	2472 mm
Front track	1406 mm
Rear track	1385 mm
Turning circle (between walls)	10.7 or 11.2 metres (according to equipment level)

Weights

Kerb weight:	
1.2 litre 3-door models	880 kg
1.2 litre 5-door models	900 kg
1.4 litre manual 3-door models	940 kg
1.4 litre manual 5-door models	960 kg
1.4 litre automatic 3-door models	965 kg
1.4 litre automatic 5-door models	985 kg
1.6 litre manual 3-door models	965 kg
1.6 litre manual 5-door models	985 kg
1.6 litre automatic 3-door models	980 kg
1.6 litre automatic 5-door models	1000 kg
1.9 litre 3-door models	975 kg
1.9 litre 5-door models	995 kg
Maximum gross vehicle weight:	
1.2 litre models	1565 kg
1.4 litre manual	1605 kg
1.4 litre automatic	1625 kg
1.6 litre manual	1605 kg
1.6 litre automatic	1635 kg
1.9 litre models	1645 kg
Maximum roof rack load (all models)	70 kg
Maximum towing weight:	
1.2 and 1.4 litre 3-door models	850 kg
1.2 litre 5-door models	800 kg
1.4 litre 5-door models	850 kg
1.6 and 1.9 litre manual 3-door models	900 kg
1.6 automatic 3-door models	950 kg
1.6 litre 5-door models	900 kg

Conversion factors

Length (distance)

Inches (in)	x 25.4	= Millimetres (mm)	x 0.0394	= Inches (in)
Feet (ft)	x 0.305	= Metres (m)	x 3.281	= Feet (ft)
Miles	x 1.609	= Kilometres (km)	x 0.621	= Miles

Volume (capacity)

Cubic inches (cu in; in^3)	x 16.387	= Cubic centimetres (cc; cm^3)	x 0.061	= Cubic inches (cu in; in^3)
Imperial pints (Imp pt)	x 0.568	= Litres (l)	x 1.76	= Imperial pints (Imp pt)
Imperial quarts (Imp qt)	x 1.137	= Litres (l)	x 0.88	= Imperial quarts (Imp qt)
Imperial quarts (Imp qt)	x 1.201	= US quarts (US qt)	x 0.833	= Imperial quarts (Imp qt)
US quarts (US qt)	x 0.946	= Litres (l)	x 1.057	= US quarts (US qt)
Imperial gallons (Imp gal)	x 4.546	= Litres (l)	x 0.22	= Imperial gallons (Imp gal)
Imperial gallons (Imp gal)	x 1.201	= US gallons (US gal)	x 0.833	= Imperial gallons (Imp gal)
US gallons (US gal)	x 3.785	= Litres (l)	x 0.264	= US gallons (US gal)

Mass (weight)

Ounces (oz)	x 28.35	= Grams (g)	x 0.035	= Ounces (oz)
Pounds (lb)	x 0.454	= Kilograms (kg)	x 2.205	= Pounds (lb)

Force

Ounces-force (ozf; oz)	x 0.278	= Newtons (N)	x 3.6	= Ounces-force (ozf; oz)
Pounds-force (lbf; lb)	x 4.448	= Newtons (N)	x 0.225	= Pounds-force (lbf; lb)
Newtons (N)	x 0.1	= Kilograms-force (kgf; kg)	x 9.81	= Newtons (N)

Pressure

Pounds-force per square inch (psi; lbf/in^2; lb/in^2)	x 0.070	= Kilograms-force per square centimetre (kgf/cm^2; kg/cm^2)	x 14.223	= Pounds-force per square inch (psi; lbf/in^2; lb/in^2)
Pounds-force per square inch (psi; lbf/in^2; lb/in^2)	x 0.068	= Atmospheres (atm)	x 14.696	= Pounds-force per square inch (psi; lbf/in^2; lb/in^2)
Pounds-force per square inch (psi; lbf/in^2; lb/in^2)	x 0.069	= Bars	x 14.5	= Pounds-force per square inch (psi; lbf/in^2; lb/in^2)
Pounds-force per square inch (psi; lbf/in^2; lb/in^2)	x 6.895	= Kilopascals (kPa)	x 0.145	= Pounds-force per square inch (psi; lbf/in^2; lb/in^2)
Kilopascals (kPa)	x 0.01	= Kilograms-force per square centimetre (kgf/cm^2; kg/cm^2)	x 98.1	= Kilopascals (kPa)
Millibar (mbar)	x 100	= Pascals (Pa)	x 0.01	= Millibar (mbar)
Millibar (mbar)	x 0.0145	= Pounds-force per square inch (psi; lbf/in^2; lb/in^2)	x 68.947	= Millibar (mbar)
Millibar (mbar)	x 0.75	= Millimetres of mercury (mmHg)	x 1.333	= Millibar (mbar)
Millibar (mbar)	x 0.401	= Inches of water (inH$_2$O)	x 2.491	= Millibar (mbar)
Millimetres of mercury (mmHg)	x 0.535	= Inches of water (inH$_2$O)	x 1.868	= Millimetres of mercury (mmHg)
Inches of water (inH$_2$O)	x 0.036	= Pounds-force per square inch (psi; lbf/in^2; lb/in^2)	x 27.68	= Inches of water (inH$_2$O)

Torque (moment of force)

Pounds-force inches (lbf in; lb in)	x 1.152	= Kilograms-force centimetre (kgf cm; kg cm)	x 0.868	= Pounds-force inches (lbf in; lb in)
Pounds-force inches (lbf in; lb in)	x 0.113	= Newton metres (Nm)	x 8.85	= Pounds-force inches (lbf in; lb in)
Pounds-force inches (lbf in; lb in)	x 0.083	= Pounds-force feet (lbf ft; lb ft)	x 12	= Pounds-force inches (lbf in; lb in)
Pounds-force feet (lbf ft; lb ft)	x 0.138	= Kilograms-force metres (kgf m; kg m)	x 7.233	= Pounds-force feet (lbf ft; lb ft)
Pounds-force feet (lbf ft; lb ft)	x 1.356	= Newton metres (Nm)	x 0.738	= Pounds-force feet (lbf ft; lb ft)
Newton metres (Nm)	x 0.102	= Kilograms-force metres (kgf m; kg m)	x 9.804	= Newton metres (Nm)

Power

Horsepower (hp)	x 745.7	= Watts (W)	x 0.0013	= Horsepower (hp)

Velocity (speed)

Miles per hour (miles/hr; mph)	x 1.609	= Kilometres per hour (km/hr; kph)	x 0.621	= Miles per hour (miles/hr; mph)

Fuel consumption*

Miles per gallon, Imperial (mpg)	x 0.354	= Kilometres per litre (km/l)	x 2.825	= Miles per gallon, Imperial (mpg)
Miles per gallon, US (mpg)	x 0.425	= Kilometres per litre (km/l)	x 2.352	= Miles per gallon, US (mpg)

Temperature

Degrees Fahrenheit = (°C x 1.8) + 32

Degrees Celsius (Degrees Centigrade; °C) = (°F - 32) x 0.56

** It is common practice to convert from miles per gallon (mpg) to litres/100 kilometres (l/100km), where mpg x l/100 km = 282*

Spare parts are available from many sources, including maker's appointed garages, accessory shops, and motor factors. To be sure of obtaining the correct parts, it will sometimes be necessary to quote the vehicle identification number. If possible, it can also be useful to take the old parts along for positive identification. Items such as starter motors and alternators may be available under a service exchange scheme – any parts returned should be clean.

Our advice regarding spare parts is as follows.

Officially-appointed garages

This is the best source of parts which are peculiar to your car, and which are not otherwise generally available (eg, badges, interior trim, certain body panels, etc). It is also the only place at which you should buy parts if the vehicle is still under warranty.

Accessory shops

These are very good places to buy materials and components needed for the maintenance of your car (oil, air and fuel filters, light bulbs, drivebelts, greases, brake pads, touch-up paint, etc). Components of this nature sold by a reputable shop are usually of the same standard as those used by the car manufacturer.

Besides components, these shops also sell tools and general accessories, usually have convenient opening hours, charge lower prices, and can often be found close to home. Some accessory shops have parts counters where components needed for almost any repair job can be purchased or ordered.

Motor factors

Good factors will stock all the more important components which wear out comparatively quickly, and can sometimes supply individual components needed for the overhaul of a larger assembly (eg, brake seals and hydraulic parts, bearing shells, pistons, valves). They may also handle work such as cylinder block reboring, crankshaft regrinding, etc.

Tyre and exhaust specialists

These outlets may be independent, or members of a local or national chain. They frequently offer competitive prices when compared with a main dealer or local garage, but it will pay to obtain several quotes before making a decision. When researching prices, also ask what 'extras' may be added – for instance fitting a new valve and balancing the wheel are both commonly charged on top of the price of a new tyre.

Other sources

Beware of parts or materials obtained from market stalls, car boot sales or similar outlets. Such items are not invariably sub-standard, but there is little chance of compensation if they do prove unsatisfactory. in the case of safety-critical components such as brake pads, there is the risk not only of financial loss, but also of an accident causing injury or death.

Second-hand components or assemblies obtained from a car breaker can be a good buy in some circumstances, but this sort of purchase is best made by the experienced DIY mechanic.

Vehicle identification numbers

Modifications are a continuing and unpublicised process in vehicle manufacture, quite apart from major model changes. Spare parts manuals and lists are compiled upon a numerical basis, the individual vehicle identification numbers being essential to correct identification of the component concerned.

When ordering spare parts, always give as much information as possible. Quote the car model, year of manufacture, body and engine numbers as appropriate.

The *Vehicle Identification Number (VIN)* plate is located on the door pillar behind the driver's door. The plate carries the VIN number, chassis number, vehicle weight information and various other information, depending on territory **(see illustrations)**.

The *engine number* is located on a metal plate attached to the front of the engine **(see illustration)**.

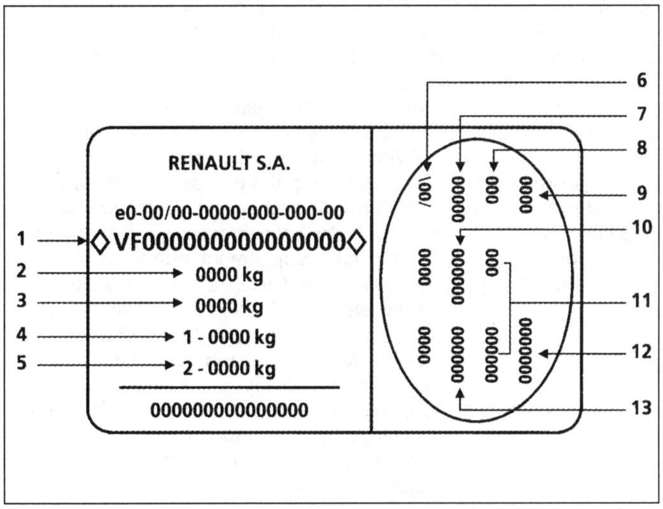

VIN plate information

1 *Type and chassis number*
2 *Maximum permissible all-up weight*
3 *Maximum permissible total train weight*
4 *Maximum permissible front axle loading*
5 *Maximum permissible rear axle loading*
6 *Technical specifications*
7 *Paint code*
8 *Equipment level*
9 *Vehicle type*
10 *Trim code*
11 *Additional equipment code*
12 *Fabrication number*
13 *Interior matching trim code*

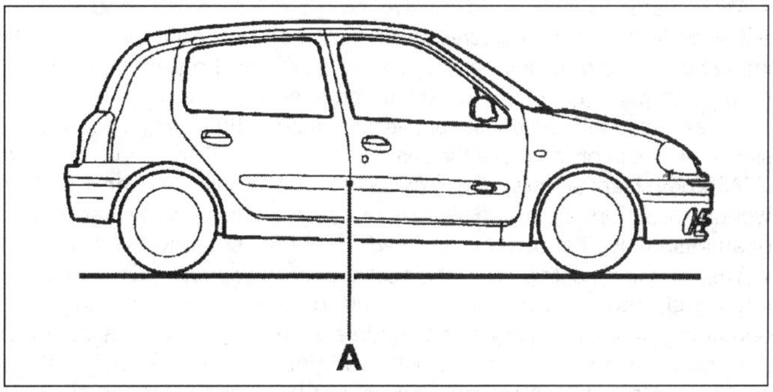

VIN plate location on the door pillar (A)

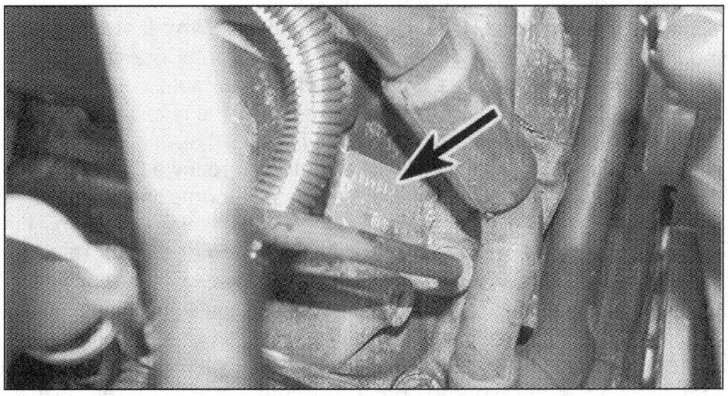

Engine number plate – diesel engine

Whenever servicing, repair or overhaul work is carried out on the car or its components, observe the following procedures and instructions. This will assist in carrying out the operation efficiently and to a professional standard of workmanship.

Joint mating faces and gaskets

When separating components at their mating faces, never insert screwdrivers or similar implements into the joint between the faces in order to prise them apart. This can cause severe damage which results in oil leaks, coolant leaks, etc upon reassembly. Separation is usually achieved by tapping along the joint with a soft-faced hammer in order to break the seal. However, note that this method may not be suitable where dowels are used for component location.

Where a gasket is used between the mating faces of two components, a new one must be fitted on reassembly; fit it dry unless otherwise stated in the repair procedure. Make sure that the mating faces are clean and dry, with all traces of old gasket removed. When cleaning a joint face, use a tool which is unlikely to score or damage the face, and remove any burrs or nicks with an oilstone or fine file.

Make sure that tapped holes are cleaned with a pipe cleaner, and keep them free of jointing compound, if this is being used, unless specifically instructed otherwise.

Ensure that all orifices, channels or pipes are clear, and blow through them, preferably using compressed air.

Oil seals

Oil seals can be removed by levering them out with a wide flat-bladed screwdriver or similar implement. Alternatively, a number of self-tapping screws may be screwed into the seal, and these used as a purchase for pliers or some similar device in order to pull the seal free.

Whenever an oil seal is removed from its working location, either individually or as part of an assembly, it should be renewed.

The very fine sealing lip of the seal is easily damaged, and will not seal if the surface it contacts is not completely clean and free from scratches, nicks or grooves. If the original sealing surface of the component cannot be restored, and the manufacturer has not made provision for slight relocation of the seal relative to the sealing surface, the component should be renewed.

Protect the lips of the seal from any surface which may damage them in the course of fitting. Use tape or a conical sleeve where possible. Lubricate the seal lips with oil before fitting and, on dual-lipped seals, fill the space between the lips with grease.

Unless otherwise stated, oil seals must be fitted with their sealing lips toward the lubricant to be sealed.

Use a tubular drift or block of wood of the appropriate size to install the seal and, if the seal housing is shouldered, drive the seal down to the shoulder. If the seal housing is unshouldered, the seal should be fitted with its face flush with the housing top face (unless otherwise instructed).

Screw threads and fastenings

Seized nuts, bolts and screws are quite a common occurrence where corrosion has set in, and the use of penetrating oil or releasing fluid will often overcome this problem if the offending item is soaked for a while before attempting to release it. The use of an impact driver may also provide a means of releasing such stubborn fastening devices, when used in conjunction with the appropriate screwdriver bit or socket. If none of these methods works, it may be necessary to resort to the careful application of heat, or the use of a hacksaw or nut splitter device.

Studs are usually removed by locking two nuts together on the threaded part, and then using a spanner on the lower nut to unscrew the stud. Studs or bolts which have broken off below the surface of the component in which they are mounted can sometimes be removed using a stud extractor. Always ensure that a blind tapped hole is completely free from oil, grease, water or other fluid before installing the bolt or stud. Failure to do this could cause the housing to crack due to the hydraulic action of the bolt or stud as it is screwed in.

When tightening a castellated nut to accept a split pin, tighten the nut to the specified torque, where applicable, and then tighten further to the next split pin hole. Never slacken the nut to align the split pin hole, unless stated in the repair procedure.

When checking or retightening a nut or bolt to a specified torque setting, slacken the nut or bolt by a quarter of a turn, and then retighten to the specified setting. However, this should not be attempted where angular tightening has been used.

For some screw fastenings, notably cylinder head bolts or nuts, torque wrench settings are no longer specified for the latter stages of tightening, "angle-tightening" being called up instead. Typically, a fairly low torque wrench setting will be applied to the bolts/nuts in the correct sequence, followed by one or more stages of tightening through specified angles.

Locknuts, locktabs and washers

Any fastening which will rotate against a component or housing during tightening should always have a washer between it and the relevant component or housing.

Spring or split washers should always be renewed when they are used to lock a critical component such as a big-end bearing retaining bolt or nut. Locktabs which are folded over to retain a nut or bolt should always be renewed.

Self-locking nuts can be re-used in non-critical areas, providing resistance can be felt when the locking portion passes over the bolt or stud thread. However, it should be noted that self-locking stiffnuts tend to lose their effectiveness after long periods of use, and should then be renewed as a matter of course.

Split pins must always be replaced with new ones of the correct size for the hole.

When thread-locking compound is found on the threads of a fastener which is to be re-used, it should be cleaned off with a wire brush and solvent, and fresh compound applied on reassembly.

Special tools

Some repair procedures in this manual entail the use of special tools such as a press, two or three-legged pullers, spring compressors, etc. Wherever possible, suitable readily-available alternatives to the manufacturer's special tools are described, and are shown in use. In some instances, where no alternative is possible, it has been necessary to resort to the use of a manufacturer's tool, and this has been done for reasons of safety as well as the efficient completion of the repair operation. Unless you are highly-skilled and have a thorough understanding of the procedures described, never attempt to bypass the use of any special tool when the procedure described specifies its use. Not only is there a very great risk of personal injury, but expensive damage could be caused to the components involved.

Environmental considerations

When disposing of used engine oil, brake fluid, antifreeze, etc, give due consideration to any detrimental environmental effects. Do not, for instance, pour any of the above liquids down drains into the general sewage system, or onto the ground to soak away. Many local council refuse tips provide a facility for waste oil disposal, as do some garages. If none of these facilities are available, consult your local Environmental Health Department, or the National Rivers Authority, for further advice.

With the universal tightening-up of legislation regarding the emission of environmentally-harmful substances from motor vehicles, most vehicles have tamperproof devices fitted to the main adjustment points of the fuel system. These devices are primarily designed to prevent unqualified persons from adjusting the fuel/air mixture, with the chance of a consequent increase in toxic emissions. If such devices are found during servicing or overhaul, they should, wherever possible, be renewed or refitted in accordance with the manufacturer's requirements or current legislation.

OIL CARE – FOLLOW THE CODE

OIL BANK LINE
0800 66 33 66
www.oilbankline.org.uk

Note: It is antisocial and illegal to dump oil down the drain. To find the location of your local oil recycling bank, call this number free.

The jack supplied with the car should only be used for changing the roadwheels – see *Wheel changing* at the front of this manual. When carrying out any other kind of work, raise the vehicle using a hydraulic trolley jack, and always supplement the jack with axle stands positioned under the vehicle jacking points.

When using a hydraulic jack or axle stands, always position the jack head or axle stand head under one of the relevant jacking points **(see illustrations)**.

Do not jack the vehicle under any other part of the sill, sump, floor pan, or any of the steering or suspension components. With the vehicle raised, the axle stands should be positioned beneath the vehicle jack location points on the sill.

Warning: Never work under, around, or near a raised car, unless it is adequately supported.

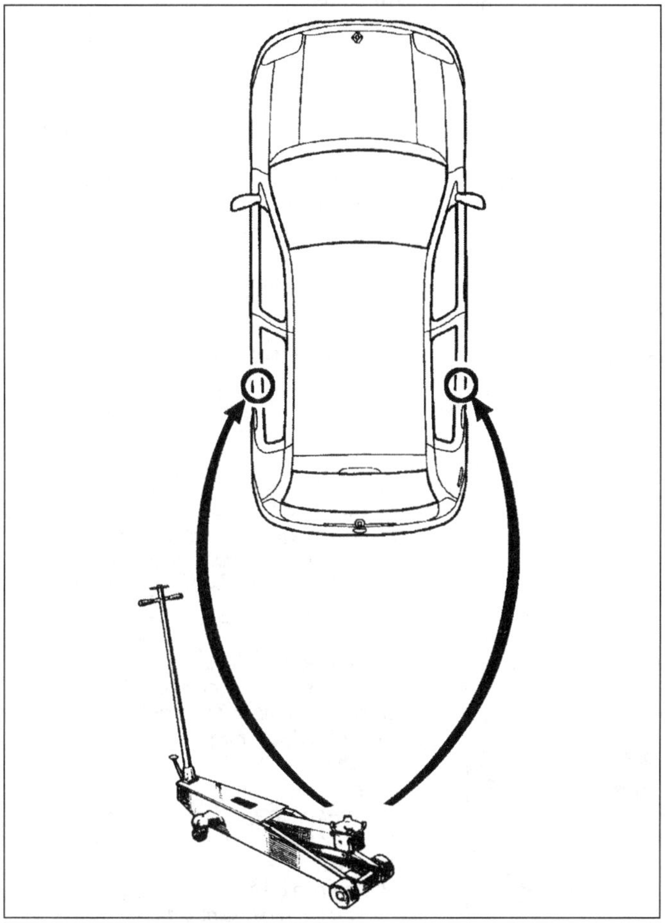

Rear jacking point for use with trolley jack

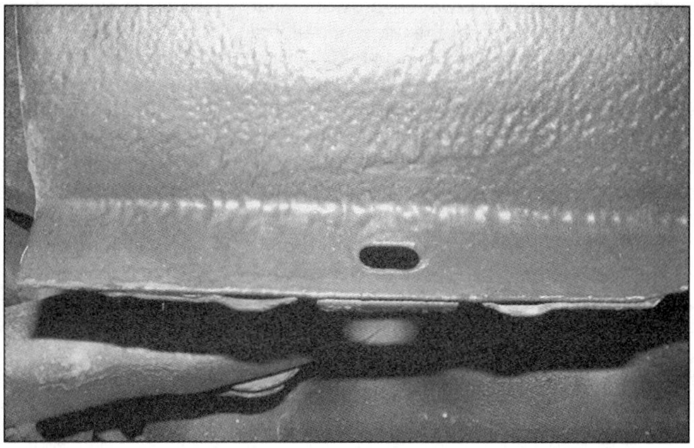

The jacking points are indicated by an arrow on the sill

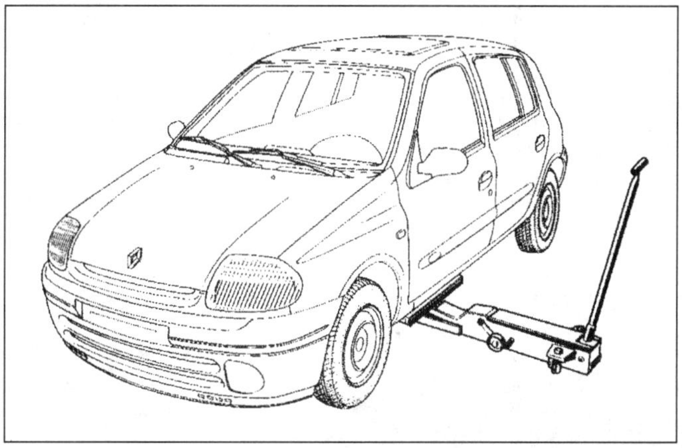

Use a piece of wood between the jack head and sill when jacking the side of the vehicle

Disconnecting the battery

Several systems fitted to the vehicle require battery power to be available at all times, either to ensure their continued operation (such as the clock), or to maintain electronic memory settings which would otherwise be erased. Whenever the battery is to be disconnected, first note the following points, to ensure there are no unforeseen consequences:

a) First, on any vehicle with central door locking, it is a wise precaution to remove the key from the ignition, and to keep it with you, so that it does not get locked in if the central locking engages when the battery is reconnected.

b) If a security-coded audio unit is fitted, and the unit and/or the battery is disconnected, the unit will not function again on reconnection until the correct security code is entered. Details of this procedure, which varies according to the unit fitted and vehicle model, are given in the vehicle owner's handbook. Where necessary, ensure you have the correct code before you disconnect the battery. If you do not have the code or details of the correct procedure, but can supply proof of ownership and a legitimate reason for wanting this information, a Renault dealer may be able to help.

c) On vehicles equipped with an original equipment anti-theft alarm system, before disconnecting the battery, de-activate the alarm siren, using the dedicated key. When reconnecting the battery, as soon as the battery is reconnected, the alarm is automatically activated. Use the remote control transmitter to turn off the alarm, then activate the alarm siren using the dedicated key.

Devices known as 'memory-savers' or 'code-savers' can be used to avoid some of the above problems. Precise details of use vary according to the device used. Typically, it is plugged into the cigar lighter socket, and is connected by its own wiring to a spare battery; the vehicle battery is then disconnected from the electrical system, leaving the memory-saver to pass sufficient current to maintain audio unit security codes and other memory values, and also to run permanently-live circuits such as the clock.

Warning: Some of these devices allow a considerable amount of current to pass, which can mean that many of the vehicle's systems are still operational when the main battery is disconnected. If a 'memory-saver' is used, ensure that the circuit concerned is actually 'dead' before carrying out any work on it!

Introduction

A selection of good tools is a fundamental requirement for anyone contemplating the maintenance and repair of a motor vehicle. For the owner who does not possess any, their purchase will prove a considerable expense, offsetting some of the savings made by doing-it-yourself. However, provided that the tools purchased meet the relevant national safety standards and are of good quality, they will last for many years and prove an extremely worthwhile investment.

To help the average owner to decide which tools are needed to carry out the various tasks detailed in this manual, we have compiled three lists of tools under the following headings: *Maintenance and minor repair*, *Repair and overhaul*, and *Special*. Newcomers to practical mechanics should start off with the *Maintenance and minor repair* tool kit, and confine themselves to the simpler jobs around the vehicle. Then, as confidence and experience grow, more difficult tasks can be undertaken, with extra tools being purchased as, and when, they are needed. In this way, a *Maintenance and minor repair* tool kit can be built up into a *Repair and overhaul* tool kit over a considerable period of time, without any major cash outlays. The experienced do-it-yourselfer will have a tool kit good enough for most repair and overhaul procedures, and will add tools from the *Special* category when it is felt that the expense is justified by the amount of use to which these tools will be put.

Maintenance and minor repair tool kit

The tools given in this list should be considered as a minimum requirement if routine maintenance, servicing and minor repair operations are to be undertaken. We recommend the purchase of combination spanners (ring one end, open-ended the other); although more expensive than open-ended ones, they do give the advantages of both types of spanner.

- ☐ *Combination spanners:*
  Metric - 8 to 19 mm inclusive
- ☐ *Adjustable spanner - 35 mm jaw (approx.)*
- ☐ *Spark plug spanner (with rubber insert) - petrol models*
- ☐ *Spark plug gap adjustment tool - petrol models*
- ☐ *Set of feeler gauges*
- ☐ *Brake bleed nipple spanner*
- ☐ *Screwdrivers:*
  Flat blade - 100 mm long x 6 mm dia
  Cross blade - 100 mm long x 6 mm dia
  Torx - various sizes (not all vehicles)
- ☐ *Combination pliers*
- ☐ *Hacksaw (junior)*
- ☐ *Tyre pump*
- ☐ *Tyre pressure gauge*
- ☐ *Oil can*
- ☐ *Oil filter removal tool*
- ☐ *Fine emery cloth*
- ☐ *Wire brush (small)*
- ☐ *Funnel (medium size)*
- ☐ *Sump drain plug key (not all vehicles)*

Repair and overhaul tool kit

These tools are virtually essential for anyone undertaking any major repairs to a motor vehicle, and are additional to those given in the *Maintenance and minor repair* list. Included in this list is a comprehensive set of sockets. Although these are expensive, they will be found invaluable as they are so versatile - particularly if various drives are included in the set. We recommend the half-inch square-drive type, as this can be used with most proprietary torque wrenches.

The tools in this list will sometimes need to be supplemented by tools from the *Special* list:

- ☐ *Sockets (or box spanners) to cover range in previous list (including Torx sockets)*
- ☐ *Reversible ratchet drive (for use with sockets)*
- ☐ *Extension piece, 250 mm (for use with sockets)*
- ☐ *Universal joint (for use with sockets)*
- ☐ *Flexible handle or sliding T "breaker bar" (for use with sockets)*
- ☐ *Torque wrench (for use with sockets)*
- ☐ *Self-locking grips*
- ☐ *Ball pein hammer*
- ☐ *Soft-faced mallet (plastic or rubber)*
- ☐ *Screwdrivers:*
  Flat blade - long & sturdy, short (chubby), and narrow (electrician's) types
  Cross blade – long & sturdy, and short (chubby) types
- ☐ *Pliers:*
  Long-nosed
  Side cutters (electrician's)
  Circlip (internal and external)
- ☐ *Cold chisel - 25 mm*
- ☐ *Scriber*
- ☐ *Scraper*
- ☐ *Centre-punch*
- ☐ *Pin punch*
- ☐ *Hacksaw*
- ☐ *Brake hose clamp*
- ☐ *Brake/clutch bleeding kit*
- ☐ *Selection of twist drills*
- ☐ *Steel rule/straight-edge*
- ☐ *Allen keys (inc. splined/Torx type)*
- ☐ *Selection of files*
- ☐ *Wire brush*
- ☐ *Axle stands*
- ☐ *Jack (strong trolley or hydraulic type)*
- ☐ *Light with extension lead*
- ☐ *Universal electrical multi-meter*

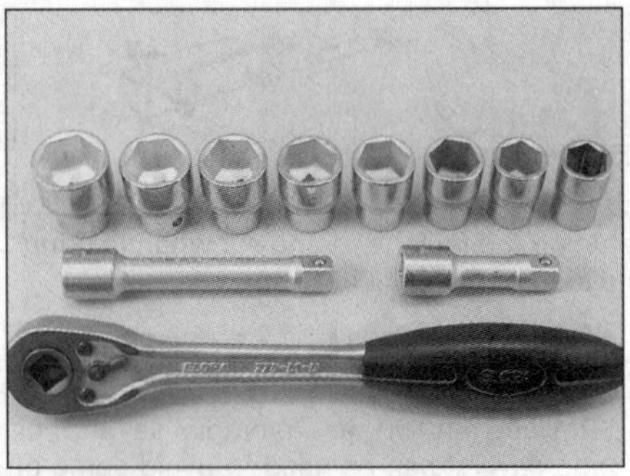

Sockets and reversible ratchet drive

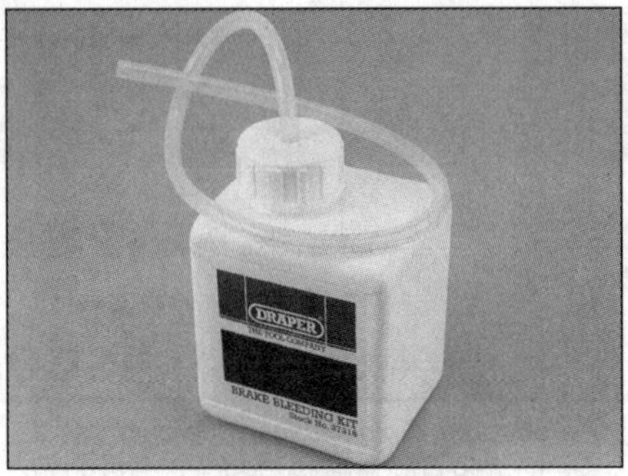

Brake bleeding kit

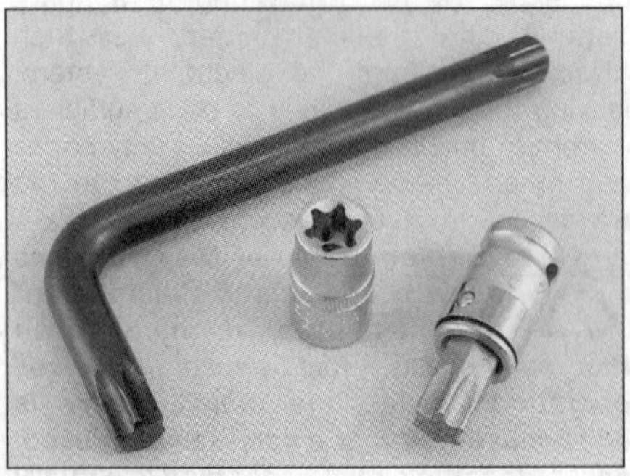

Torx key, socket and bit

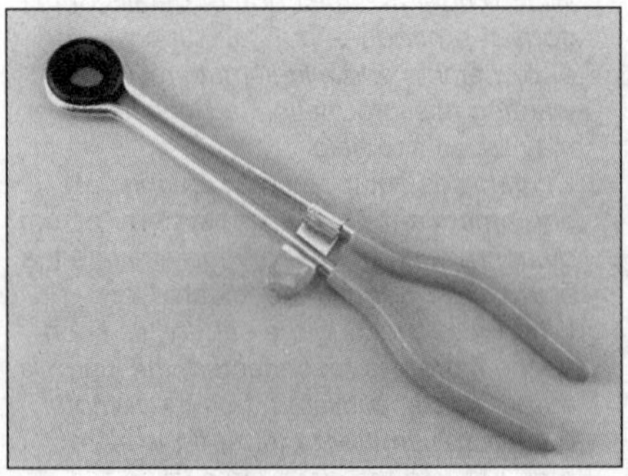

Hose clamp

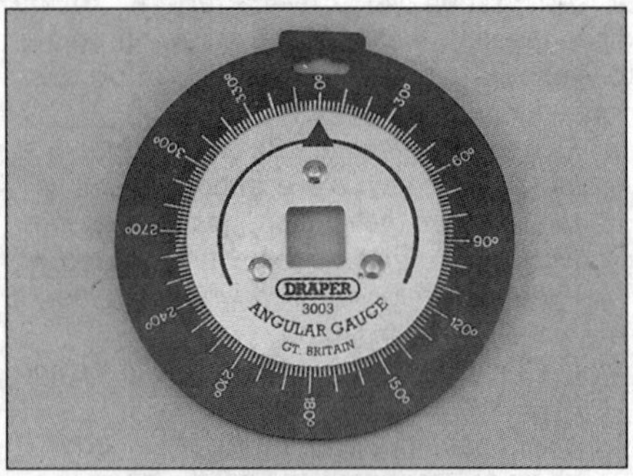

Angular-tightening gauge

Special tools

The tools in this list are those which are not used regularly, are expensive to buy, or which need to be used in accordance with their manufacturers' instructions. Unless relatively difficult mechanical jobs are undertaken frequently, it will not be economic to buy many of these tools. Where this is the case, you could consider clubbing together with friends (or joining a motorists' club) to make a joint purchase, or borrowing the tools against a deposit from a local garage or tool hire specialist. It is worth noting that many of the larger DIY superstores now carry a large range of special tools for hire at modest rates.

The following list contains only those tools and instruments freely available to the public, and not those special tools produced by the vehicle manufacturer specifically for its dealer network. You will find occasional references to these manufacturers' special tools in the text of this manual. Generally, an alternative method of doing the job without the vehicle manufacturers' special tool is given. However, sometimes there is no alternative to using them. Where this is the case and the relevant tool cannot be bought or borrowed, you will have to entrust the work to a dealer.

- ☐ *Angular-tightening gauge*
- ☐ *Valve spring compressor*
- ☐ *Valve grinding tool*
- ☐ *Piston ring compressor*
- ☐ *Piston ring removal/installation tool*
- ☐ *Cylinder bore hone*
- ☐ *Balljoint separator*
- ☐ *Coil spring compressors (where applicable)*
- ☐ *Two/three-legged hub and bearing puller*
- ☐ *Impact screwdriver*
- ☐ *Micrometer and/or vernier calipers*
- ☐ *Dial gauge*
- ☐ *Stroboscopic timing light*
- ☐ *Dwell angle meter/tachometer*
- ☐ *Fault code reader*
- ☐ *Cylinder compression gauge*
- ☐ *Hand-operated vacuum pump and gauge*
- ☐ *Clutch plate alignment set*
- ☐ *Brake shoe steady spring cup removal tool*
- ☐ *Bush and bearing removal/installation set*
- ☐ *Stud extractors*
- ☐ *Tap and die set*
- ☐ *Lifting tackle*
- ☐ *Trolley jack*

Buying tools

Reputable motor accessory shops and superstores often offer excellent quality tools at discount prices, so it pays to shop around.

Remember, you don't have to buy the most expensive items on the shelf, but it is always advisable to steer clear of the very cheap tools. Beware of 'bargains' offered on market stalls or at car boot sales. There are plenty of good tools around at reasonable prices, but always aim to purchase items which meet the relevant national safety standards. If in doubt, ask the proprietor or manager of the shop for advice before making a purchase.

Care and maintenance of tools

Having purchased a reasonable tool kit, it is necessary to keep the tools in a clean and serviceable condition. After use, always wipe off any dirt, grease and metal particles using a clean, dry cloth, before putting the tools away. Never leave them lying around after they have been used. A simple tool rack on the garage or workshop wall for items such as screwdrivers and pliers is a good idea. Store all normal spanners and sockets in a metal box. Any measuring instruments, gauges, meters, etc, must be carefully stored where they cannot be damaged or become rusty.

Take a little care when tools are used. Hammer heads inevitably become marked, and screwdrivers lose the keen edge on their blades from time to time. A little timely attention with emery cloth or a file will soon restore items like this to a good finish.

Working facilities

Not to be forgotten when discussing tools is the workshop itself. If anything more than routine maintenance is to be carried out, a suitable working area becomes essential.

It is appreciated that many an owner-mechanic is forced by circumstances to remove an engine or similar item without the benefit of a garage or workshop. Having done this, any repairs should always be done under the cover of a roof.

Wherever possible, any dismantling should be done on a clean, flat workbench or table at a suitable working height.

Any workbench needs a vice; one with a jaw opening of 100 mm is suitable for most jobs. As mentioned previously, some clean dry storage space is also required for tools, as well as for any lubricants, cleaning fluids, touch-up paints etc, which become necessary.

Another item which may be required, and which has a much more general usage, is an electric drill with a chuck capacity of at least 8 mm. This, together with a good range of twist drills, is virtually essential for fitting accessories.

Last, but not least, always keep a supply of old newspapers and clean, lint-free rags available, and try to keep any working area as clean as possible.

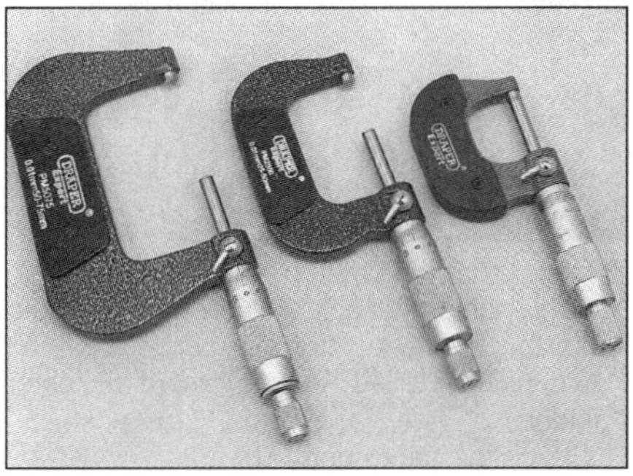

Micrometers

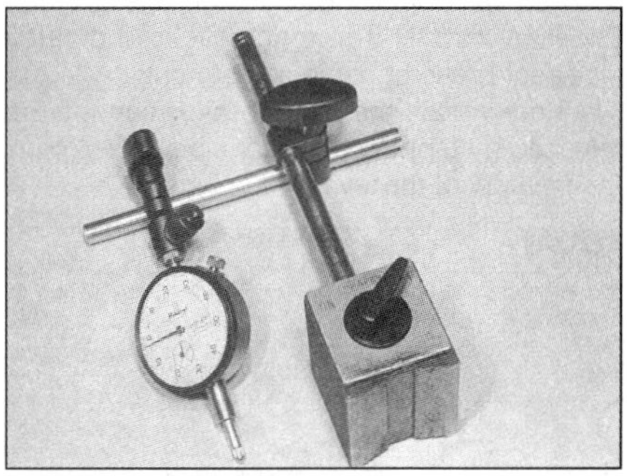

Dial test indicator ("dial gauge")

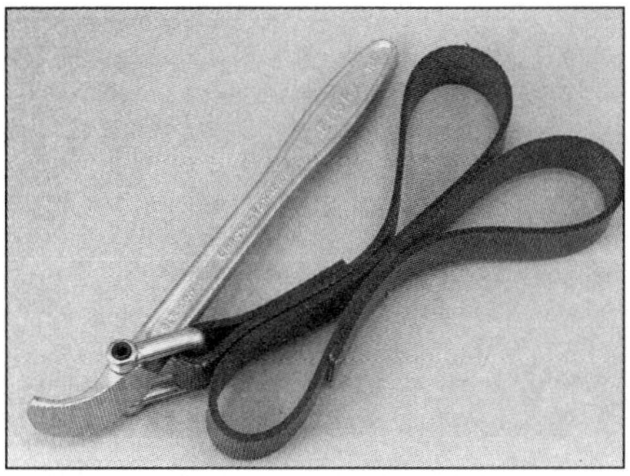

Strap wrench

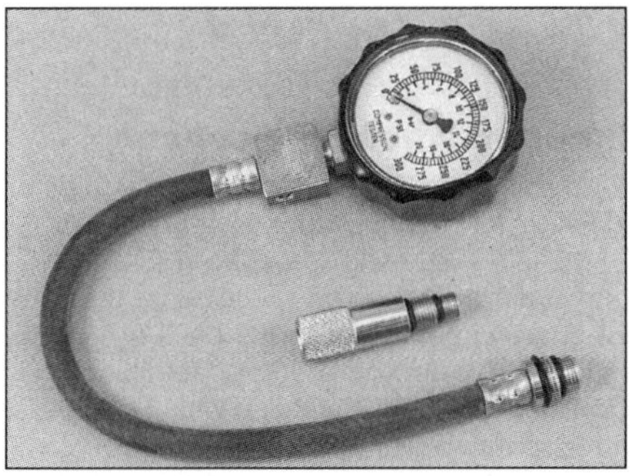

Compression tester

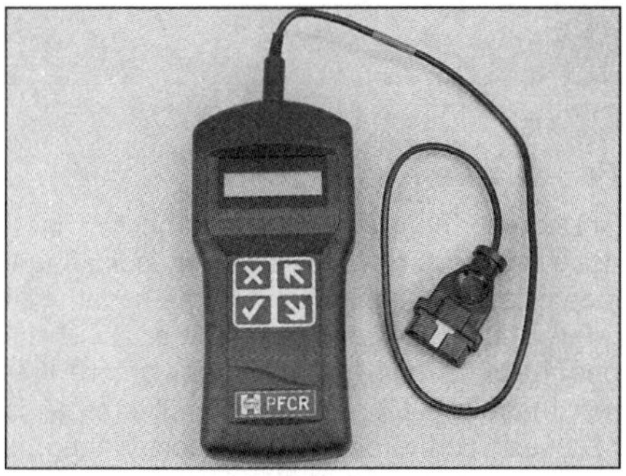

Fault code reader

This is a guide to getting your vehicle through the MOT test. Obviously it will not be possible to examine the vehicle to the same standard as the professional MOT tester. However, working through the following checks will enable you to identify any problem areas before submitting the vehicle for the test.

Where a testable component is in borderline condition, the tester has discretion in deciding whether to pass or fail it. The basis of such discretion is whether the tester would be happy for a close relative or friend to use the vehicle with the component in that condition. If the vehicle presented is clean and evidently well cared for, the tester may be more inclined to pass a borderline component than if the vehicle is scruffy and apparently neglected.

It has only been possible to summarise the test requirements here, based on the regulations in force at the time of printing. Test standards are becoming increasingly stringent, although there are some exemptions for older vehicles.

An assistant will be needed to help carry out some of these checks.

The checks have been sub-divided into four categories, as follows:

1 Checks carried out **FROM THE DRIVER'S SEAT**

2 Checks carried out **WITH THE VEHICLE ON THE GROUND**

3 Checks carried out **WITH THE VEHICLE RAISED AND THE WHEELS FREE TO TURN**

4 Checks carried out on **YOUR VEHICLE'S EXHAUST EMISSION SYSTEM**

1 Checks carried out FROM THE DRIVER'S SEAT

Handbrake

☐ Test the operation of the handbrake. Excessive travel (too many clicks) indicates incorrect brake or cable adjustment.

☐ Check that the handbrake cannot be released by tapping the lever sideways. Check the security of the lever mountings.

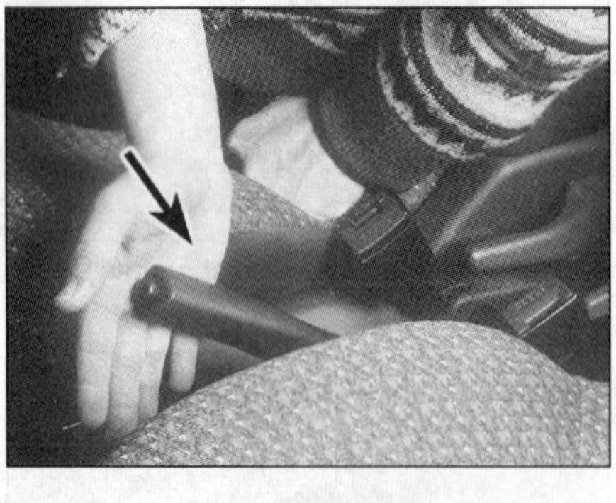

Footbrake

☐ Depress the brake pedal and check that it does not creep down to the floor, indicating a master cylinder fault. Release the pedal, wait a few seconds, then depress it again. If the pedal travels nearly to the floor before firm resistance is felt, brake adjustment or repair is necessary. If the pedal feels spongy, there is air in the hydraulic system which must be removed by bleeding.

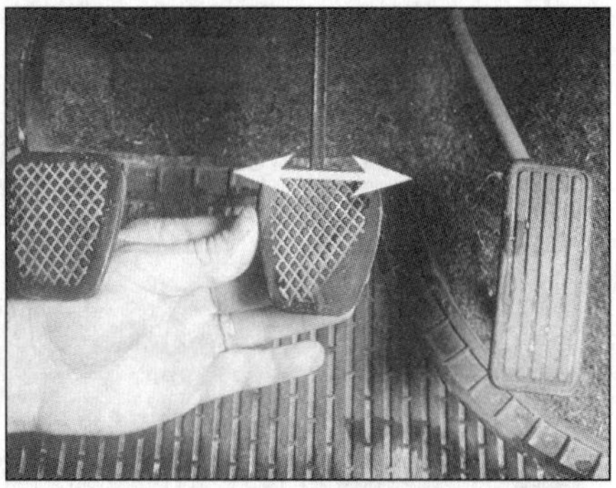

☐ Check that the brake pedal is secure and in good condition. Check also for signs of fluid leaks on the pedal, floor or carpets, which would indicate failed seals in the brake master cylinder.

☐ Check the servo unit (when applicable) by operating the brake pedal several times, then keeping the pedal depressed and starting the engine. As the engine starts, the pedal will move down slightly. If not, the vacuum hose or the servo itself may be faulty.

Steering wheel and column

☐ Examine the steering wheel for fractures or looseness of the hub, spokes or rim.

☐ Move the steering wheel from side to side and then up and down. Check that the steering wheel is not loose on the column, indicating wear or a loose retaining nut. Continue moving the steering wheel as before, but also turn it slightly from left to right.

☐ Check that the steering wheel is not loose on the column, and that there is no abnormal

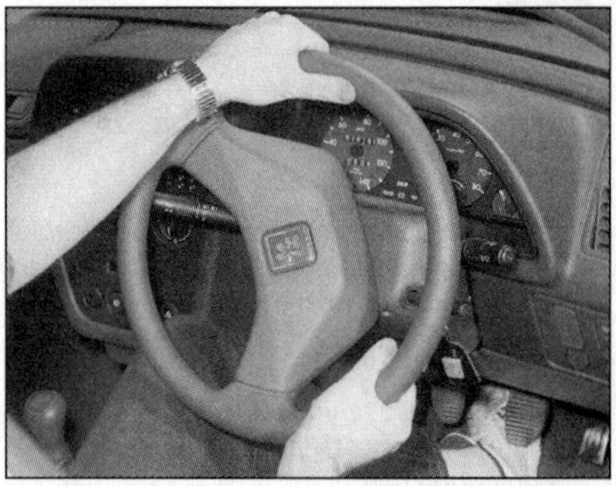

movement of the steering wheel, indicating wear in the column support bearings or couplings.

Windscreen, mirrors and sunvisor

☐ The windscreen must be free of cracks or other significant damage within the driver's field of view. (Small stone chips are acceptable.) Rear view mirrors must be secure, intact, and capable of being adjusted.

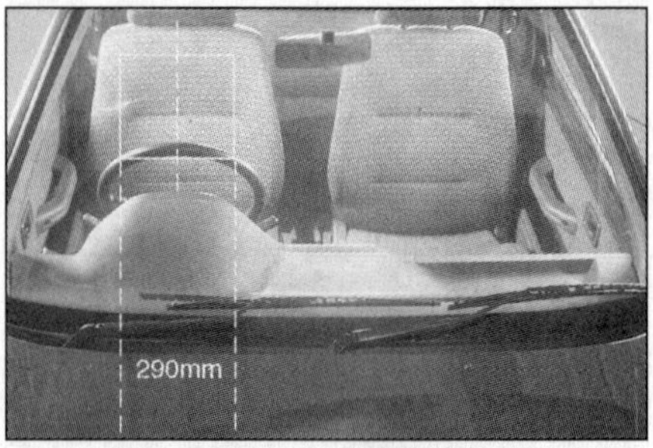

☐ The driver's sunvisor must be capable of being stored in the "up" position.

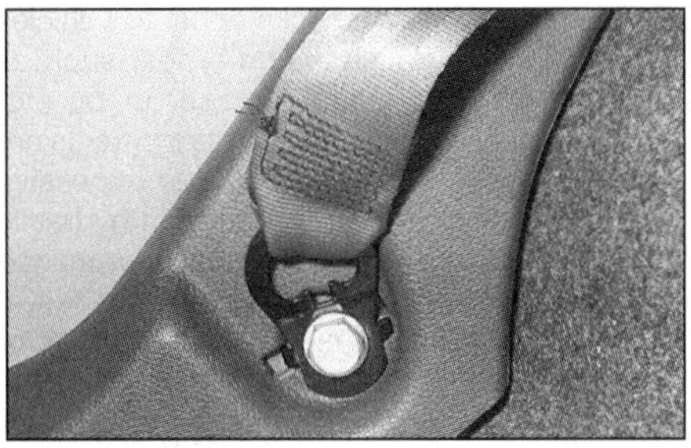

Seat belts and seats

Note: *The following checks are applicable to all seat belts, front and rear.*

□ Examine the webbing of all the belts (including rear belts if fitted) for cuts, serious fraying or deterioration. Fasten and unfasten each belt to check the buckles. If applicable, check the retracting mechanism. Check the security of all seat belt mountings accessible from inside the vehicle.

□ Seat belts with pre-tensioners, once activated, have a "flag" or similar showing on the seat belt stalk. This, in itself, is not a reason for test failure.

□ The front seats themselves must be securely attached and the backrests must lock in the upright position.

Doors

□ Both front doors must be able to be opened and closed from outside and inside, and must latch securely when closed.

2 Checks carried out **WITH THE VEHICLE ON THE GROUND**

Vehicle identification

□ Number plates must be in good condition, secure and legible, with letters and numbers correctly spaced – spacing at (A) should be at least twice that at (B).

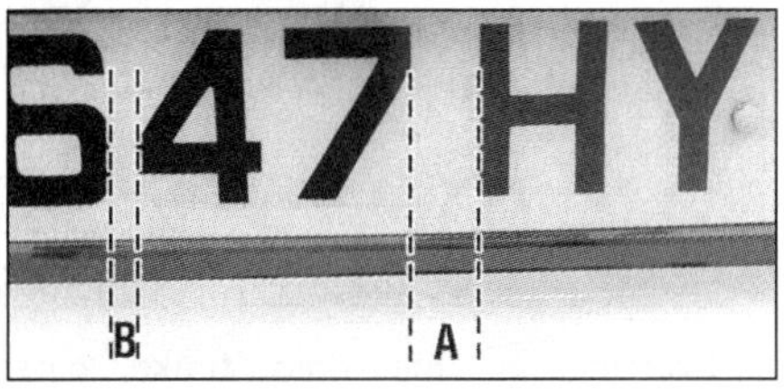

□ The VIN plate and/or homologation plate must be legible.

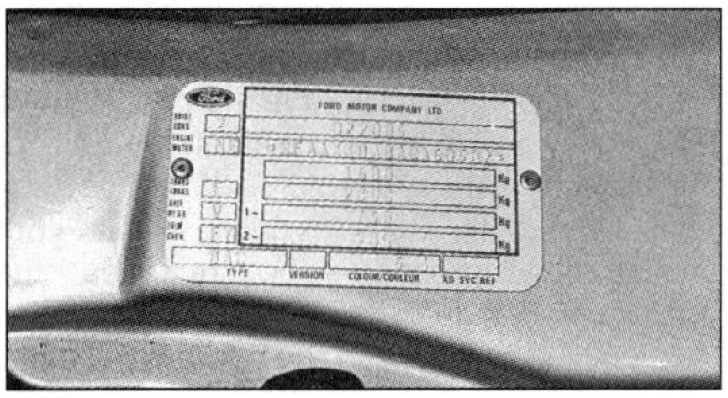

Electrical equipment

□ Switch on the ignition and check the operation of the horn.

□ Check the windscreen washers and wipers, examining the wiper blades; renew damaged or perished blades. Also check the operation of the stop-lights.

□ Check the operation of the sidelights and number plate lights. The lenses and reflectors must be secure, clean and undamaged.

□ Check the operation and alignment of the headlights. The headlight reflectors must not be tarnished and the lenses must be undamaged.

□ Switch on the ignition and check the operation of the direction indicators (including the instrument panel tell-tale) and the hazard warning lights. Operation of the sidelights and stop-lights must not affect the indicators - if it does, the cause is usually a bad earth at the rear light cluster.

□ Check the operation of the rear foglight(s), including the warning light on the instrument panel or in the switch.

□ The ABS warning light must illuminate in accordance with the manufacturers' design. For most vehicles, the ABS warning light should illuminate when the ignition is switched on, and (if the system is operating properly) extinguish after a few seconds. Refer to the owner's handbook.

Footbrake

□ Examine the master cylinder, brake pipes and servo unit for leaks, loose mountings, corrosion or other damage.

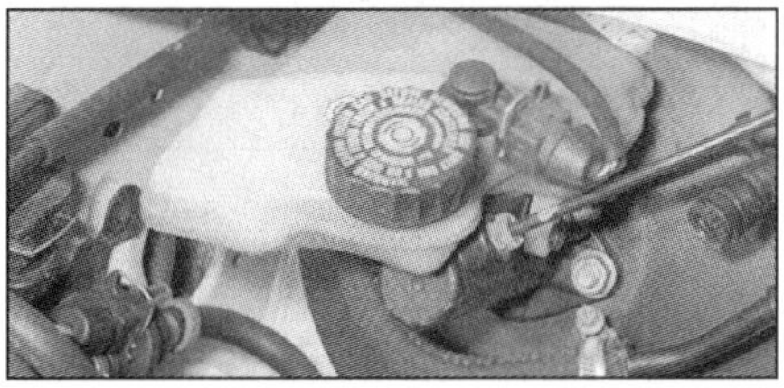

□ The fluid reservoir must be secure and the fluid level must be between the upper (**A**) and lower (**B**) markings.

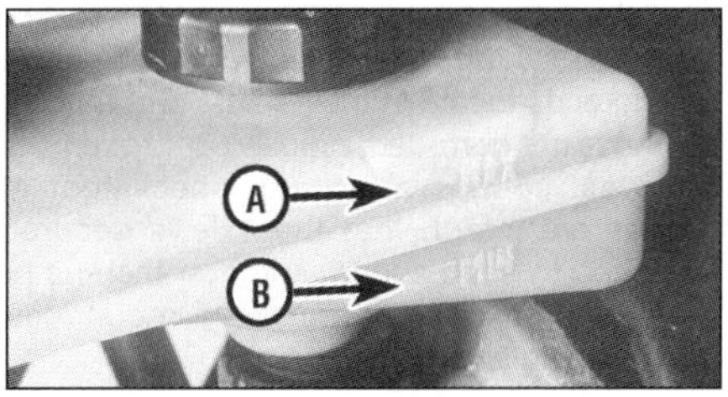

□ Inspect both front brake flexible hoses for cracks or deterioration of the rubber. Turn the steering from lock to lock, and ensure that the hoses do not contact the wheel, tyre, or any part of the steering or suspension mechanism. With the brake pedal firmly depressed, check the hoses for bulges or leaks under pressure.

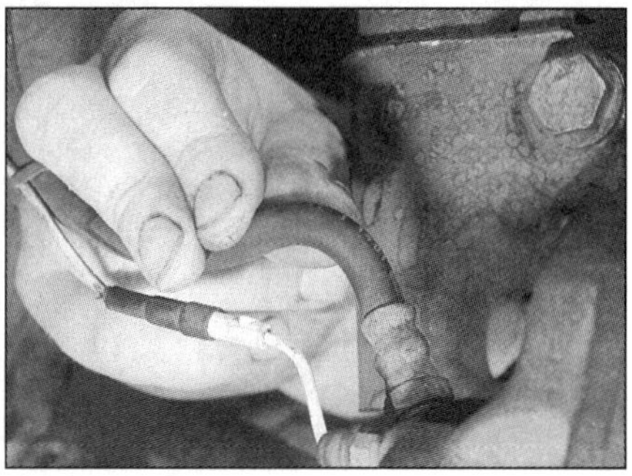

Steering and suspension

□ Have your assistant turn the steering wheel from side to side slightly, up to the point where the steering gear just begins to transmit this movement to the roadwheels. Check for excessive free play between the steering wheel and the steering gear, indicating wear or insecurity of the steering column joints, the column-to-steering gear coupling, or the steering gear itself.

□ Have your assistant turn the steering wheel more vigorously in each direction, so that the roadwheels just begin to turn. As this is done, examine all the steering joints, linkages, fittings and attachments. Renew any component that shows signs of wear or damage. On vehicles with power steering, check the security and condition of the steering pump, drivebelt and hoses.

□ Check that the vehicle is standing level, and at approximately the correct ride height.

Shock absorbers

□ Depress each corner of the vehicle in turn, then release it. The vehicle should rise and then settle in its normal position. If the vehicle continues to rise and fall, the shock absorber is defective. A shock absorber which has seized will also cause the vehicle to fail.

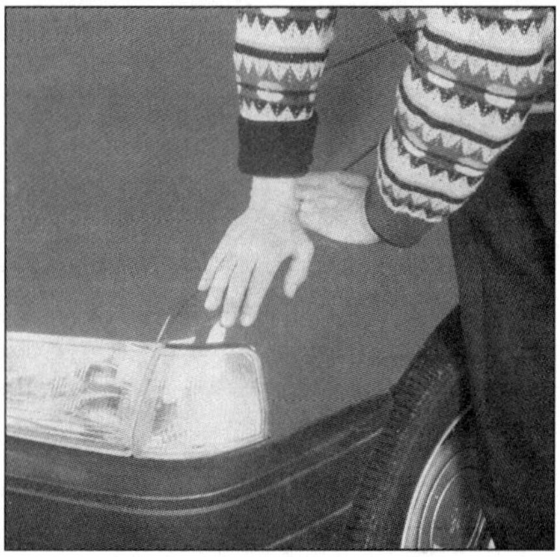

Exhaust system

☐ Start the engine. With your assistant holding a rag over the tailpipe, check the entire system for leaks. Repair or renew leaking sections.

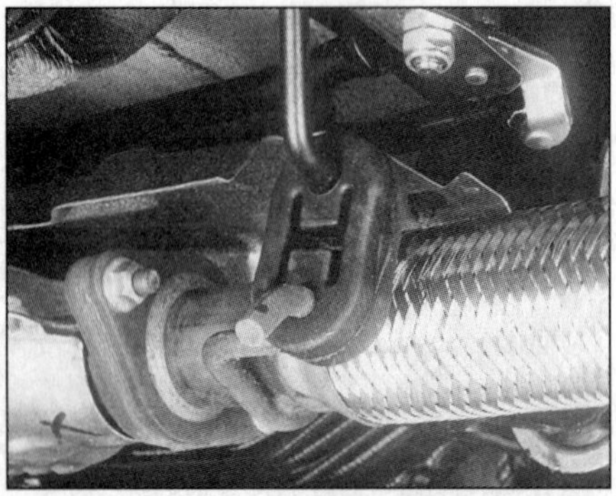

3 Checks carried out WITH THE VEHICLE RAISED AND THE WHEELS FREE TO TURN

Jack up the front and rear of the vehicle, and securely support it on axle stands. Position the stands clear of the suspension assemblies. Ensure that the wheels are clear of the ground and that the steering can be turned from lock to lock.

Steering mechanism

☐ Have your assistant turn the steering from lock to lock. Check that the steering turns smoothly, and that no part of the steering mechanism, including a wheel or tyre, fouls any brake hose or pipe or any part of the body structure.

☐ Examine the steering rack rubber gaiters for damage or insecurity of the retaining clips. If power steering is fitted, check for signs of damage or leakage of the fluid hoses, pipes or connections. Also check for excessive stiffness or binding of the steering, a missing split pin or locking device, or severe corrosion of the body structure within 30 cm of any steering component attachment point.

Front and rear suspension and wheel bearings

☐ Starting at the front right-hand side, grasp the roadwheel at the 3 o'clock and 9 o'clock positions and rock gently but firmly. Check for free play or insecurity at the wheel bearings, suspension balljoints, or suspension mountings, pivots and attachments.

☐ Now grasp the wheel at the 12 o'clock and 6 o'clock positions and repeat the previous inspection. Spin the wheel, and check for roughness or tightness of the front wheel bearing.

☐ If excess free play is suspected at a component pivot point, this can be confirmed by using a large screwdriver or similar tool and levering between the mounting and the component attachment. This will confirm whether the wear is in the pivot bush, its retaining bolt, or in the mounting itself (the bolt holes can often become elongated).

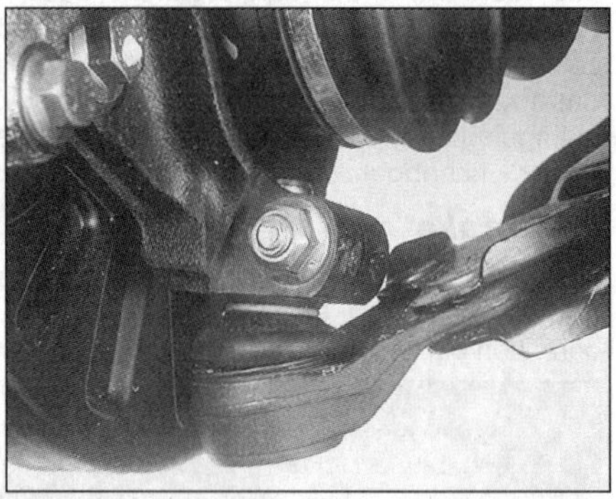

☐ Carry out all the above checks at the other front wheel, and then at both rear wheels.

Springs and shock absorbers

☐ Examine the suspension struts (when applicable) for serious fluid leakage, corrosion, or damage to the casing. Also check the security of the mounting points.

☐ If coil springs are fitted, check that the spring ends locate in their seats, and that the spring is not corroded, cracked or broken.

☐ If leaf springs are fitted, check that all leaves are intact, that the axle is securely attached to each spring, and that there is no deterioration of the spring eye mountings, bushes, and shackles.

☐ The same general checks apply to vehicles fitted with other suspension types, such as torsion bars, hydraulic displacer units, etc. Ensure that all mountings and attachments are secure, that there are no signs of excessive wear, corrosion or damage, and (on hydraulic types) that there are no fluid leaks or damaged pipes.

☐ Inspect the shock absorbers for signs of serious fluid leakage. Check for wear of the mounting bushes or attachments, or damage to the body of the unit.

Driveshafts (fwd vehicles only)

☐ Rotate each front wheel in turn and inspect the constant velocity joint gaiters for splits or damage. Also check that each driveshaft is straight and undamaged.

Braking system

☐ If possible without dismantling, check brake pad wear and disc condition. Ensure that the friction lining material has not worn excessively, (A) and that the discs are not fractured, pitted, scored or badly worn (B).

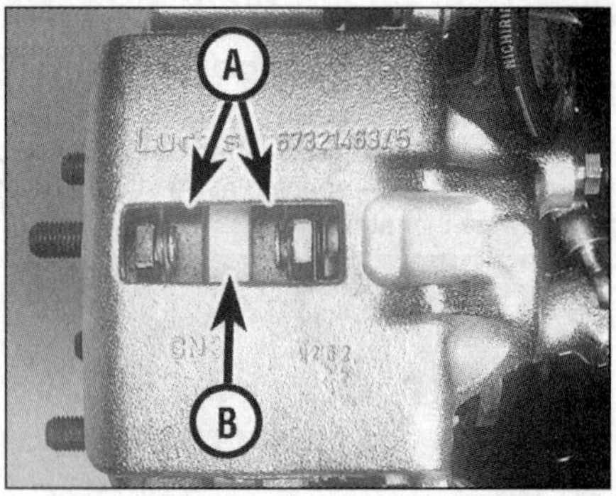

☐ Examine all the rigid brake pipes underneath the vehicle, and the flexible hose(s) at the rear. Look for corrosion, chafing or insecurity of the pipes, and for signs of bulging under pressure, chafing, splits or deterioration of the flexible hoses.

☐ Look for signs of fluid leaks at the brake calipers or on the brake backplates. Repair or renew leaking components.

☐ Slowly spin each wheel, while your assistant depresses and releases the footbrake. Ensure that each brake is operating and does not bind when the pedal is released.

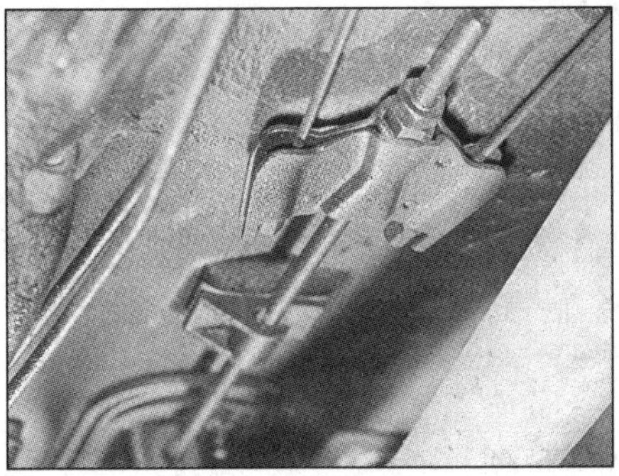

☐ Examine the handbrake mechanism, checking for frayed or broken cables, excessive corrosion, or wear or insecurity of the linkage. Check that the mechanism works on each relevant wheel, and releases fully, without binding.

☐ It is not possible to test brake efficiency without special equipment, but a road test can be carried out later to check that the vehicle pulls up in a straight line.

Fuel and exhaust systems

☐ Inspect the fuel tank (including the filler cap), fuel pipes, hoses and unions. All components must be secure and free from leaks.

☐ Examine the exhaust system over its entire length, checking for any damaged, broken or missing mountings, security of the retaining clamps and rust or corrosion.

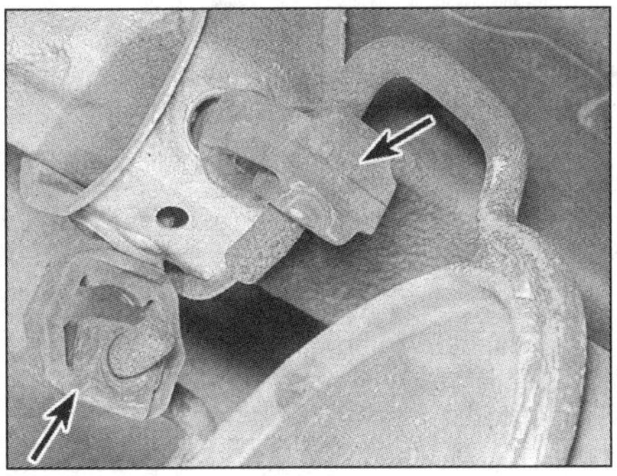

Wheels and tyres

☐ Examine the sidewalls and tread area of each tyre in turn. Check for cuts, tears, lumps, bulges, separation of the tread, and exposure of the ply or cord due to wear or damage. Check that the tyre bead is correctly seated on the wheel rim, that the valve is sound and properly seated, and that the wheel is not distorted or damaged.

☐ Check that the tyres are of the correct size for the vehicle, that they are of the same size and type on each axle, and that the pressures are correct.

☐ Check the tyre tread depth. The legal minimum at the time of writing is 1.6 mm over at least three-quarters of the tread width. Abnormal tread wear may indicate incorrect front wheel alignment.

Body corrosion

☐ Check the condition of the entire vehicle structure for signs of corrosion in load-bearing areas. (These include chassis box sections, side sills, cross-members, pillars, and all suspension, steering, braking system and seat belt mountings and anchorages.) Any corrosion which has seriously reduced the thickness of a load-bearing area is likely to cause the vehicle to fail. In this case professional repairs are likely to be needed.

☐ Damage or corrosion which causes sharp or otherwise dangerous edges to be exposed will also cause the vehicle to fail.

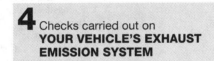

4 Checks carried out on YOUR VEHICLE'S EXHAUST EMISSION SYSTEM

Petrol models

☐ Have the engine at normal operating temperature, and make sure that it is in good tune (ignition system in good order, air filter element clean, etc).

☐ Before any measurements are carried out, raise the engine speed to around 2500 rpm, and hold it at this speed for 20 seconds. Allow the engine speed to return to idle, and watch for smoke emissions from the exhaust tailpipe. If the idle speed is obviously much too high, or if dense blue or clearly-visible black smoke comes from the tailpipe for more than 5 seconds, the vehicle will fail. As a rule of thumb, blue smoke signifies oil being burnt (engine wear) while black smoke signifies unburnt fuel (dirty air cleaner element, or other carburettor or fuel system fault).

☐ An exhaust gas analyser capable of measuring carbon monoxide (CO) and hydrocarbons (HC) is now needed. If such an instrument cannot be hired or borrowed, a local garage may agree to perform the check for a small fee.

CO emissions (mixture)

☐ At the time of writing, for vehicles first used between 1st August 1975 and 31st July 1986 (P to C registration), the CO level must not exceed 4.5% by volume. For vehicles first used between 1st August 1986 and 31st July 1992 (D to J registration), the CO level must not exceed 3.5% by volume. Vehicles first used after 1st August 1992 (K registration) must conform to the manufacturer's specification. The MOT tester has access to a DOT database or emissions handbook, which lists the CO and HC limits for each make and model of vehicle. The CO level is measured with the engine at idle speed, and at "fast idle". The following limits are given as a general guide:

At idle speed -
CO level no more than 0.5%
At "fast idle" (2500 to 3000 rpm) -
CO level no more than 0.3%
(Minimum oil temperature 60°C)

☐ If the CO level cannot be reduced far enough to pass the test (and the fuel and ignition systems are otherwise in good condition) then the carburettor is badly worn, or there is some problem in the fuel injection system or catalytic converter (as applicable).

HC emissions

☐ With the CO within limits, HC emissions for vehicles first used between 1st August 1975 and 31st July 1992 (P to J registration) must not exceed 1200 ppm. Vehicles first used after 1st August 1992 (K registration) must conform to the manufacturer's specification. The MOT tester has access to a DOT database or emissions handbook, which lists the CO and HC limits for each make and model of vehicle. The HC level is measured with the engine at "fast idle". The following is given as a general guide:

At "fast idle" (2500 to 3000 rpm) -
HC level no more than 200 ppm
(Minimum oil temperature 60°C)

☐ Excessive HC emissions are caused by incomplete combustion, the causes of which can include oil being burnt, mechanical wear and ignition/fuel system malfunction.

Diesel models

☐ The only emission test applicable to Diesel engines is the measuring of exhaust smoke density. The test involves accelerating the engine several times to its maximum unloaded speed.

Note: *It is of the utmost importance that the engine timing belt is in good condition before the test is carried out.*

☐ The limits for Diesel engine exhaust smoke, introduced in September 1995 are:

Vehicles first used before 1st August 1979:
Exempt from metered smoke testing, but must not emit "dense blue or clearly visible black smoke for a period of more than 5 seconds at idle" or "dense blue or clearly visible black smoke during acceleration which would obscure the view of other road users".

Non-turbocharged vehicles first used after 1st August 1979: $2.5m^{-1}$

Turbocharged vehicles first used after 1st August 1979: $3.0m^{-1}$

☐ Excessive smoke can be caused by a dirty air cleaner element. Otherwise, professional advice may be needed to find the cause.

Engine

- ☐ Engine fails to rotate when attempting to start
- ☐ Engine rotates, but will not start
- ☐ Engine difficult to start when cold
- ☐ Engine difficult to start when hot
- ☐ Starter motor noisy or rough in engagement
- ☐ Engine starts, but stops immediately
- ☐ Engine idles erratically
- ☐ Engine misfires at idle speed
- ☐ Engine misfires throughout the driving speed range
- ☐ Engine hesitates on acceleration
- ☐ Engine stalls
- ☐ Engine lacks power
- ☐ Engine backfires
- ☐ Oil pressure warning light illuminated with engine running
- ☐ Engine runs-on after switching off
- ☐ Engine noises

Cooling system

- ☐ Overheating
- ☐ Overcooling
- ☐ External coolant leakage
- ☐ Internal coolant leakage
- ☐ Corrosion

Fuel and exhaust systems

- ☐ Excessive fuel consumption
- ☐ Fuel leakage and/or fuel odour
- ☐ Excessive noise or fumes from exhaust system

Clutch

- ☐ Pedal travels to floor – no pressure or very little resistance
- ☐ Clutch fails to disengage (unable to select gears)
- ☐ Clutch slips (engine speed increases, with no increase in vehicle speed)
- ☐ Judder as clutch is engaged
- ☐ Noise when depressing or releasing clutch pedal

Manual transmission

- ☐ Noisy in neutral with engine running
- ☐ Noisy in one particular gear
- ☐ Difficulty engaging gears
- ☐ Jumps out of gear
- ☐ Vibration
- ☐ Lubricant leaks

Automatic transmission

- ☐ Fluid leakage
- ☐ Transmission fluid brown, or has burned smell
- ☐ General gear selection problems
- ☐ Transmission will not downshift (kickdown) with accelerator fully depressed
- ☐ Engine will not start in any gear, or starts in gears other than Park or Neutral
- ☐ Transmission slips, shifts roughly, is noisy, or has no drive in forward or reverse gears

Driveshafts

- ☐ Clicking or knocking noise on turns (at slow speed on full-lock)
- ☐ Vibration when accelerating or decelerating

Braking system

- ☐ Vehicle pulls to one side under braking
- ☐ Noise (grinding or high-pitched squeal) when brakes applied
- ☐ Excessive brake pedal travel
- ☐ Brake pedal feels spongy when depressed
- ☐ Excessive brake pedal effort required to stop vehicle
- ☐ Judder felt through brake pedal or steering wheel when braking
- ☐ Pedal pulsates when braking hard
- ☐ Brakes binding
- ☐ Rear wheels locking under normal braking

Suspension and steering systems

- ☐ Vehicle pulls to one side
- ☐ Wheel wobble and vibration
- ☐ Excessive pitching and/or rolling around corners, or during braking
- ☐ Wandering or general instability
- ☐ Excessively-stiff steering
- ☐ Excessive play in steering
- ☐ Lack of power assistance
- ☐ Tyre wear excessive

Electrical system

- ☐ Battery will only hold a charge for a few days
- ☐ Ignition/no-charge warning light remains illuminated with engine running
- ☐ Ignition/no-charge warning light fails to come on
- ☐ Lights inoperative
- ☐ Instrument readings inaccurate or erratic
- ☐ Horn inoperative, or unsatisfactory in operation
- ☐ Wipers inoperative, or unsatisfactory in operation
- ☐ Washers inoperative, or unsatisfactory in operation
- ☐ Electric windows inoperative, or unsatisfactory in operation
- ☐ Central locking system inoperative, or unsatisfactory in operation

Introduction

The vehicle owner who does his or her own maintenance according to the recommended service schedules should not have to use this section of the manual very often. Modern component reliability is such that, provided those items subject to wear or deterioration are inspected or renewed at the specified intervals, sudden failure is comparatively rare. Faults do not usually just happen as a result of sudden failure, but develop over a period of time. Major mechanical failures in particular are usually preceded by characteristic symptoms over hundreds or even thousands of miles. Those components which do occasionally fail without warning are often small and easily carried in the vehicle.

With any fault-finding, the first step is to decide where to begin investigations. Sometimes this is obvious, but on other occasions, a little detective work will be necessary. The owner who makes half a dozen haphazard adjustments or replacements may be successful in curing a fault (or its symptoms), but will be none the wiser if the fault recurs, and ultimately may have spent more time and money than was necessary. A calm and logical approach will be found to be more satisfactory in the long run. Always take into account any warning signs or abnormalities that may have been noticed in the period preceding the fault – power loss, high or low gauge readings, unusual smells, etc – and remember that failure of components such as fuses or spark plugs may only be pointers to some underlying fault.

The pages which follow provide an easy-reference guide to the more common problems which may occur during the operation of the vehicle. These problems and their possible causes are grouped under headings denoting various components or systems, such as Engine, Cooling system, etc. The Chapter and/or Section which deals with the problem is also shown in brackets. Whatever the fault, certain basic principles apply. These are as follows:

Verify the fault. This is simply a matter of being sure that you know what the symptoms are before starting work. This is particularly important if you are investigating a fault for someone else, who may not have described it very accurately.

Don't overlook the obvious. For example, if the vehicle won't start, is there fuel in the tank? (Don't take anyone else's word on this particular point, and don't trust the fuel gauge either!) If an electrical fault is indicated, look for loose or broken wires before digging out the test gear.

Cure the disease, not the symptom. Substituting a flat battery with a fully-charged one will get you off the hard shoulder, but if the underlying cause is not attended to, the new battery will go the same way. Similarly, changing oil-fouled spark plugs for a new set will get you moving again, but remember that the reason for the fouling (if it wasn't simply an incorrect grade of plug) will have to be established and corrected.

Don't take anything for granted. Particularly, don't forget that a 'new' component may itself be defective (especially if it's been rattling around in the boot for months), and don't leave components out of a fault diagnosis sequence just because they are new or recently-fitted. When you do finally diagnose a difficult fault, you'll probably realise that all the evidence was there from the start.

Engine

Engine fails to rotate when attempting to start

- ☐ Battery terminal connections loose or corroded (*Weekly checks*).
- ☐ Battery discharged or faulty (Chapter 5A).
- ☐ Broken, loose or disconnected wiring in the starting circuit (Chapter 5A).
- ☐ Defective starter solenoid or switch (Chapter 5A).
- ☐ Defective starter motor (Chapter 5A).
- ☐ Starter pinion or flywheel ring gear teeth loose or broken (Chapters 2A, 2B, 2C and 5A).
- ☐ Engine earth strap broken or disconnected (Chapter 5A).

Engine rotates, but will not start

- ☐ Fuel tank empty.
- ☐ Battery discharged (engine rotates slowly) (Chapter 5A).
- ☐ Battery terminal connections loose or corroded (Chapters 1A or 1B).
- ☐ Ignition components damp or damaged – petrol models (Chapters 1A, 1B and 5B).
- ☐ Broken, loose or disconnected wiring in the ignition circuit – petrol models (Chapters 1A, 1B and 5B).
- ☐ Worn, faulty or incorrectly-gapped spark plugs – petrol models (Chapter 1A).
- ☐ Preheating system faulty – diesel models (Chapter 5C).
- ☐ Fuel injection system fault – petrol models (Chapter 4A).
- ☐ Stop solenoid faulty – diesel models (Chapter 4B).
- ☐ Air in fuel system – diesel models (Chapter 4B).
- ☐ Major mechanical failure (eg camshaft drive) (Chapter 2A, 2B or 2C).

Engine difficult to start when cold

- ☐ Battery discharged (Chapter 5A).
- ☐ Battery terminal connections loose or corroded (Chapter 1A or 1B).
- ☐ Worn, faulty or incorrectly-gapped spark plugs – petrol models (Chapter 1A).
- ☐ Preheating system faulty – diesel models (Chapter 5C).
- ☐ Fuel injection system fault – petrol models (Chapter 4A).
- ☐ Other ignition system fault – petrol models (Chapters 1A and 5B).
- ☐ Fast idle valve incorrectly adjusted – diesel models (Chapter 4B).
- ☐ Low cylinder compressions (Chapter 2A, 2B or 2C).

Engine difficult to start when hot

- ☐ Air filter element dirty or clogged (Chapter 1A or 1B).
- ☐ Fuel injection system fault – petrol models (Chapter 4A).
- ☐ Low cylinder compressions (Chapter 2A, 2B or 2C).

Starter motor noisy or rough in engagement

- ☐ Starter pinion or flywheel ring gear teeth loose or broken (Chapters 2A, 2B, 2C and 5A).
- ☐ Starter motor mounting bolts loose or missing (Chapter 5A).
- ☐ Starter motor internal components worn or damaged (Chapter 5A).

Engine starts, but stops immediately

- ☐ Loose or faulty electrical connections in the ignition circuit – petrol models (Chapters 1A and 5B).
- ☐ Vacuum leak at the throttle body or inlet manifold – petrol models (Chapter 4A).
- ☐ Blocked injector/fuel injection system fault – petrol models (Chapter 4A).

Engine idles erratically

- ☐ Air filter element clogged (Chapter 1A or 1B).
- ☐ Vacuum leak at the throttle body, inlet manifold or associated hoses – petrol models (Chapter 4A).
- ☐ Worn, faulty or incorrectly-gapped spark plugs – petrol models (Chapter 1A).
- ☐ Uneven or low cylinder compressions (Chapter 2A or 2B).
- ☐ Camshaft lobes worn (Chapter 2A, 2B or 2C).
- ☐ Timing belt incorrectly tensioned (Chapter 2A, 2B or 2C).
- ☐ Blocked injector/fuel injection system fault – petrol models (Chapter 4A).
- ☐ Faulty injector(s) – diesel models (Chapter 4B).

Engine misfires at idle speed

- ☐ Worn, faulty or incorrectly-gapped spark plugs – petrol models (Chapter 1A).
- ☐ Faulty spark plug HT leads – petrol models (Chapter 1A).
- ☐ Vacuum leak at the throttle body, inlet manifold or associated hoses – petrol models (Chapter 4A).
- ☐ Blocked injector/fuel injection system fault – petrol models (Chapter 4A).
- ☐ Faulty injector(s) – diesel models (Chapter 4B).
- ☐ Ignition fault – petrol models (Chapter 5B).
- ☐ Uneven or low cylinder compressions (Chapter 2A, 2B or 2C).
- ☐ Disconnected, leaking, or perished crankcase ventilation hoses (Chapter 4C).

Engine (continued)

Engine misfires throughout the driving speed range

- ☐ Fuel filter choked (Chapter 1A or 1B).
- ☐ Fuel pump faulty, or delivery pressure low – petrol models (Chapter 4A).
- ☐ Fuel tank vent blocked, or fuel pipes restricted (Chapter 4A or 4B).
- ☐ Vacuum leak at the throttle body, inlet manifold or associated hoses – petrol models (Chapter 4A).
- ☐ Worn, faulty or incorrectly-gapped spark plugs – petrol models (Chapter 1A).
- ☐ Faulty spark plug HT leads – petrol models (Chapter 1A).
- ☐ Faulty injector(s) – diesel models (Chapter 4B).
- ☐ Distributor cap cracked or tracking internally – petrol models (where applicable) (Chapter 5B).
- ☐ Faulty ignition coil – petrol models (Chapter 5B).
- ☐ Uneven or low cylinder compressions (Chapter 2A, 2B or 2C).
- ☐ Blocked injector/fuel injection system fault – petrol models (Chapter 4A).

Engine hesitates on acceleration

- ☐ Worn, faulty or incorrectly-gapped spark plugs – petrol models (Chapter 1A).
- ☐ Vacuum leak at the throttle body, inlet manifold or associated hoses – petrol models (Chapter 4A).
- ☐ Blocked injector/fuel injection system fault – petrol models (Chapter 4A).
- ☐ Faulty injector(s) – diesel models (Chapter 4B).

Engine stalls

- ☐ Vacuum leak at the throttle body, inlet manifold or associated hoses – petrol models (Chapter 4A).
- ☐ Fuel filter choked (Chapter 1A or 1B).
- ☐ Fuel pump faulty, or delivery pressure low – petrol models (Chapter 4A).
- ☐ Fuel tank vent blocked, or fuel pipes restricted (Chapter 4A or 4B).
- ☐ Blocked injector/fuel injection system fault – petrol models (Chapter 4A).
- ☐ Faulty injector(s) – diesel models (Chapter 4B).

Engine lacks power

- ☐ Timing belt incorrectly fitted or tensioned (Chapter 2A, 2B or 2C).
- ☐ Fuel filter choked (Chapter 1A or 1B).
- ☐ Fuel pump faulty, or delivery pressure low – petrol models (Chapter 4A).
- ☐ Uneven or low cylinder compressions (Chapter 2A, 2B or 2C).
- ☐ Worn, faulty or incorrectly-gapped spark plugs – petrol models (Chapter 1A).
- ☐ Vacuum leak at the throttle body, inlet manifold or associated hoses – petrol models (Chapter 4A).
- ☐ Blocked injector/fuel injection system fault – petrol models (Chapter 4A).
- ☐ Faulty injector(s) – diesel models (Chapter 4B).
- ☐ Injection pump timing incorrect – diesel models (Chapter 4B).
- ☐ Brakes binding (Chapter 9).
- ☐ Clutch slipping (Chapter 6).

Engine backfires

- ☐ Timing belt incorrectly fitted or tensioned (Chapter 2A, 2B or 2C).
- ☐ Vacuum leak at the throttle body, inlet manifold or associated hoses – petrol models (Chapter 4A).
- ☐ Blocked injector/fuel injection system fault – petrol models (Chapter 4A).

Oil pressure warning light illuminated with engine running

- ☐ Low oil level, or incorrect oil grade (*Weekly checks*).
- ☐ Faulty oil pressure sensor (Chapter 5A).
- ☐ Worn engine bearings and/or oil pump (Chapter 2A, 2B or 2C).
- ☐ High engine operating temperature (Chapter 3).
- ☐ Oil pressure relief valve defective (Chapter 2A, 2B or 2C).
- ☐ Oil pick-up strainer clogged (Chapter 2A, 2B or 2C).

Engine runs-on after switching off

- ☐ Excessive carbon build-up in engine (Chapter 2A, 2B or 2C).
- ☐ High engine operating temperature (Chapter 3).
- ☐ Fuel injection system fault – petrol models (Chapter 4A).
- ☐ Faulty stop solenoid – diesel models (Chapter 4B).

Engine noises

Pre-ignition (pinking) or knocking during acceleration or under load

- ☐ Ignition system fault – petrol models (Chapters 1A and 5B).
- ☐ Incorrect grade of spark plug – petrol models (Chapter 1A).
- ☐ Incorrect grade of fuel (Chapters 1A or 1B).
- ☐ Vacuum leak at the throttle body, inlet manifold or associated hoses – petrol models (Chapter 4A).
- ☐ Excessive carbon build-up in engine (Chapter 2A, 2B or 2C).
- ☐ Blocked injector/fuel injection system fault – petrol models (Chapter 4A).

Whistling or wheezing noises

- ☐ Leaking inlet manifold or throttle body gasket – petrol models (Chapter 4A).
- ☐ Leaking exhaust manifold gasket or pipe-to-manifold joint (Chapter 4A or 4B).
- ☐ Leaking vacuum hose (Chapters 4A, 4B or 4C, 5B and 9).
- ☐ Blowing cylinder head gasket (Chapter 2A, 2B or 2C).

Tapping or rattling noises

- ☐ Worn valve gear or camshaft (Chapter 2A, 2B or 2C).
- ☐ Ancillary component fault (water pump, alternator, etc) (Chapters 3, 5A, etc).

Knocking or thumping noises

- ☐ Worn big-end bearings (regular heavy knocking, perhaps less under load) (Chapter 2C).
- ☐ Worn main bearings (rumbling and knocking, perhaps worsening under load) (Chapter 2C).
- ☐ Piston slap (most noticeable when cold) (Chapter 2C).
- ☐ Ancillary component fault (water pump, alternator, etc) (Chapters 3, 5A, etc).

Cooling system

Overheating

- ☐ Insufficient coolant in system (*Weekly Checks*).
- ☐ Thermostat faulty (Chapter 3).
- ☐ Radiator core blocked, or grille restricted (Chapter 3).
- ☐ Electric cooling fan or thermostatic switch faulty (Chapter 3).
- ☐ Inaccurate temperature gauge sender unit (Chapter 3).
- ☐ Airlock in cooling system (Chapter 3).
- ☐ Expansion tank pressure cap faulty (Chapter 3).

Overcooling

- ☐ Thermostat faulty (Chapter 3).
- ☐ Inaccurate temperature gauge sender unit (Chapter 3).

External coolant leakage

- ☐ Deteriorated or damaged hoses or hose clips (Chapters 1A or 1B).
- ☐ Radiator core or heater matrix leaking (Chapter 3).
- ☐ Pressure cap faulty (Chapter 3).
- ☐ Coolant pump internal seal leaking (Chapter 3).
- ☐ Coolant pump-to-block seal leaking (Chapter 3).
- ☐ Boiling due to overheating (Chapter 3).
- ☐ Core plug leaking (Chapter 2A, 2B or 2C).

Internal coolant leakage

- ☐ Leaking cylinder head gasket (Chapter 2A, 2B or 2C).
- ☐ Cracked cylinder head or cylinder block (Chapter 2A, 2B or 2C).

Corrosion

- ☐ Infrequent draining and flushing (Chapters 1A or 1B).
- ☐ Incorrect coolant mixture or inappropriate coolant type (Chapters 1A or 1B).

Fuel and exhaust systems

Excessive fuel consumption

- ☐ Air filter element dirty or clogged (Chapters 1A or 1B).
- ☐ Fuel injection system fault – petrol models (Chapter 4A).
- ☐ Faulty injector(s) – diesel models (Chapter 4B).
- ☐ Ignition system fault – petrol models (Chapters 1A and 5B).
- ☐ Tyres under-inflated (*Weekly checks*).

Fuel leakage and/or fuel odour

- ☐ Damaged or corroded fuel tank, pipes or connections (Chapter 4A or 4B).

Excessive noise or fumes from exhaust system

- ☐ Leaking exhaust system or manifold joints (Chapters 1A, 1B, 4A or 4B).
- ☐ Leaking, corroded or damaged silencers or pipe (Chapters 1A, 1B, 4A or 4B).
- ☐ Broken mountings causing body or suspension contact (Chapters 1A or 1B).

Clutch

Pedal travels to floor – no pressure or very little resistance

- ☐ Badly stretched or broken cable (Chapter 6).
- ☐ Leak or other fault in clutch hydraulic system – where applicable (Chapter 6).
- ☐ Incorrect clutch adjustment (Chapter 6).
- ☐ Broken clutch release bearing or arm (Chapter 6).
- ☐ Broken diaphragm spring in clutch pressure plate (Chapter 6).

Clutch fails to disengage (unable to select gears)

- ☐ Incorrect clutch adjustment (Chapter 6).
- ☐ Clutch friction plate sticking on gearbox input shaft splines (Chapter 6).
- ☐ Clutch friction plate sticking to flywheel or pressure plate (Chapter 6).
- ☐ Faulty pressure plate assembly (Chapter 6).
- ☐ Clutch release mechanism worn or badly assembled (Chapter 6).

Clutch slips (engine speed increases, with no increase in vehicle speed)

- ☐ Clutch friction plate linings excessively worn (Chapter 6).
- ☐ Clutch friction plate linings contaminated with oil or grease (Chapter 6).
- ☐ Faulty pressure plate or weak diaphragm spring (Chapter 6).

Judder as clutch is engaged

- ☐ Clutch friction plate linings contaminated with oil or grease (Chapter 6).
- ☐ Clutch friction plate linings excessively worn (Chapter 6).
- ☐ Faulty or distorted pressure plate or diaphragm spring (Chapter 6).
- ☐ Worn or loose engine or gearbox mountings (Chapter 2A, 2B or 2C).
- ☐ Clutch friction plate hub or gearbox input shaft splines worn (Chapter 6).

Noise when depressing or releasing clutch pedal

- ☐ Worn clutch release bearing (Chapter 6).
- ☐ Worn or dry clutch pedal pivot (Chapter 6).
- ☐ Faulty pressure plate assembly (Chapter 6).
- ☐ Pressure plate diaphragm spring broken (Chapter 6).
- ☐ Broken clutch friction plate cushioning springs (Chapter 6).

Manual transmission

Noisy in neutral with engine running

- ☐ Input shaft bearings worn (noise apparent with clutch pedal released, but not when depressed) (Chapter 7).*
- ☐ Clutch release bearing worn (noise apparent with clutch pedal depressed, possibly less when released) (Chapter 6).

Noisy in one particular gear

- ☐ Worn, damaged or chipped gear teeth (Chapter 7).*

Difficulty engaging gears

- ☐ Clutch fault (Chapter 6).
- ☐ Worn or damaged gear linkage (Chapter 7).
- ☐ Worn synchroniser units (Chapter 7).*

Jumps out of gear

- ☐ Worn or damaged gear linkage (Chapter 7).
- ☐ Worn synchroniser units (Chapter 7).*
- ☐ Worn selector forks (Chapter 7).*

Vibration

- ☐ Lack of oil (Chapters 1A or 1B).
- ☐ Worn bearings (Chapter 7).*

Lubricant leaks

- ☐ Leaking oil seal (Chapter 7).
- ☐ Leaking housing joint (Chapter 7).*

**Although the corrective action necessary to remedy the symptoms described is beyond the scope of the home mechanic, the above information should be helpful in isolating the cause of the condition, so that the owner can communicate clearly with a professional mechanic.*

Automatic transmission

Note: *Due to the complexity of the automatic transmission, it is difficult for the home mechanic to properly diagnose and service this unit. For problems other than the following, the vehicle should be taken to a dealer service department or automatic transmission specialist. Do not be too hasty in removing the transmission if a fault is suspected, as most of the testing is carried out with the unit still fitted.*

Fluid leakage

- ☐ Automatic transmission fluid is usually dark in colour. Fluid leaks should not be confused with engine oil, which can easily be blown onto the transmission by airflow.
- ☐ To determine the source of a leak, first remove all built-up dirt and grime from the transmission housing and surrounding areas using a degreasing agent, or by steam-cleaning. Drive the vehicle at low speed, so airflow will not blow the leak far from its source. Raise and support the vehicle, and determine where the leak is coming from. The following are common areas of leakage:

a) Oil pan (Chapter 1A and 7B).
b) Dipstick tube (Chapter 1A and 7B).
c) Transmission-to-fluid cooler pipes/unions (Chapter 7B).

Transmission fluid brown, or has burned smell

- ☐ Transmission fluid level low, or fluid in need of renewal (Chapter 7B).

General gear selection problems

- ☐ Chapter 7B deals with checking and adjusting the selector cable on automatic transmissions. The following are common problems which may be caused by a poorly-adjusted cable:

a) Engine starting in gears other than Park or Neutral.
b) Indicator panel indicating a gear other than the one actually being used.
c) Vehicle moves when in Park or Neutral.
d) Poor gear shift quality or erratic gear changes.

- ☐ Refer to Chapter 7B for the selector cable adjustment procedure.

Transmission will not downshift (kickdown) with accelerator pedal fully depressed

- ☐ Low transmission fluid level (Chapter 1 and 7B).
- ☐ Incorrect selector cable adjustment (Chapter 7B).

Engine will not start in any gear, or starts in gears other than Park or Neutral

- ☐ Incorrect starter/inhibitor switch adjustment (Chapter 7B).
- ☐ Incorrect selector cable adjustment (Chapter 7B).

Transmission slips, shifts roughly, is noisy, or has no drive in forward or reverse gears

- ☐ There are many probable causes for the above problems, but the home mechanic should be concerned with only one possibility – fluid level. Before taking the vehicle to a dealer or transmission specialist, check the fluid level and condition of the fluid as described in Chapters 1A, 1B or 7B, as applicable. Correct the fluid level as necessary, or change the fluid and filter if needed. If the problem persists, professional help will be necessary.

Driveshafts

Clicking or knocking noise on turns (at slow speed on full-lock)

- ☐ Lack of constant velocity joint lubricant, possibly due to damaged gaiter (Chapter 8).
- ☐ Worn outer constant velocity joint (Chapter 8).

Vibration when accelerating or decelerating

- ☐ Worn inner constant velocity joint (Chapter 8).
- ☐ Bent or distorted driveshaft (Chapter 8).
- ☐ Worn right-hand driveshaft intermediate bearing – where applicable (Chapter 8).

Braking system

Note: *Before assuming that a brake problem exists, make sure that the tyres are in good condition and correctly inflated, that the front wheel alignment is correct, and that the vehicle is not loaded with weight in an unequal manner. Apart from checking the condition of all pipe and hose connections, any faults occurring on the anti-lock braking system should be referred to a Renault dealer for diagnosis.*

Vehicle pulls to one side under braking

- ☐ Worn, defective, damaged or contaminated front or rear brake pads/shoes on one side (Chapters 1A, 1B and 9).
- ☐ Seized or partially-seized front or rear brake caliper/wheel cylinder piston (Chapter 9).
- ☐ A mixture of brake pad/shoe lining materials fitted between sides (Chapter 9).
- ☐ Brake caliper or rear brake backplate bolts loose (Chapter 9).
- ☐ Worn or damaged steering or suspension components (Chapters 1A, 1B and 10).

Noise (grinding or high-pitched squeal) when brakes applied

- ☐ Brake pad or shoe friction lining material worn down to metal backing (Chapters 1A, 1B and 9).
- ☐ Excessive corrosion of brake disc or drum – may be apparent after the vehicle has been standing for some time (Chapters 1A, 1B and 9).

Excessive brake pedal travel

- ☐ Faulty rear drum brake self-adjust mechanism (Chapter 9).
- ☐ Faulty master cylinder (Chapter 9).
- ☐ Air in hydraulic system (Chapter 9).
- ☐ Faulty vacuum servo unit (Chapter 9).
- ☐ Faulty vacuum pump – diesel models (Chapter 9).

Brake pedal feels spongy when depressed

- ☐ Air in hydraulic system (Chapter 9).
- ☐ Deteriorated flexible rubber brake hoses (Chapters 1A, 1B and 9).
- ☐ Master cylinder mountings loose (Chapter 9).
- ☐ Faulty master cylinder (Chapter 9).

Excessive brake pedal effort required to stop vehicle

- ☐ Faulty vacuum servo unit (Chapter 9).
- ☐ Disconnected, damaged or insecure brake servo vacuum hose (Chapters 1A, 1B and 9).
- ☐ Faulty vacuum pump – diesel models (Chapter 9).
- ☐ Primary or secondary hydraulic circuit failure (Chapter 9).
- ☐ Seized brake caliper or wheel cylinder piston(s) (Chapter 9).
- ☐ Brake pads or brake shoes incorrectly fitted (Chapter 9).
- ☐ Incorrect grade of brake pads or brake shoes fitted (Chapter 9).
- ☐ Brake pads or brake shoe linings contaminated (Chapter 9).

Judder felt through brake pedal or steering wheel when braking

- ☐ Excessive run-out or distortion of brake disc(s) or drum(s) (Chapter 9).
- ☐ Brake pad or brake shoe linings worn (Chapters 1A, 1B and 9).
- ☐ Brake caliper or rear brake backplate mounting bolts loose (Chapter 9).
- ☐ Wear in suspension or steering components or mountings (Chapters 1A, 1B and 10).

Pedal pulsates when braking hard

- ☐ Normal feature of ABS – no fault

Brakes binding

- ☐ Seized brake caliper piston(s) or wheel cylinder piston(s) (Chapter 9).
- ☐ Incorrectly-adjusted handbrake mechanism or linkage (Chapter 9).
- ☐ Faulty master cylinder (Chapter 9).

Rear wheels locking under normal braking

- ☐ Seized brake caliper piston(s) or wheel cylinder piston(s) (Chapter 9).
- ☐ Faulty brake pressure regulator (Chapter 9).

Steering and suspension

Note: *Before diagnosing suspension or steering faults, be sure that the trouble is not due to incorrect tyre pressures, mixtures of tyre types, or binding brakes.*

Vehicle pulls to one side

- ☐ Defective tyre (Chapter 1A or 1B).
- ☐ Excessive wear in suspension or steering components (Chapters 1A, 1B and 10).
- ☐ Incorrect front wheel alignment (Chapter 10).
- ☐ Accident damage to steering or suspension components (Chapters 1A, 1B and 10).

Wheel wobble and vibration

- ☐ Front roadwheels out of balance (vibration felt mainly through the steering wheel) (Chapter 10).
- ☐ Rear roadwheels out of balance (vibration felt throughout the vehicle) (Chapter 10).
- ☐ Roadwheels damaged or distorted (Chapter 10).
- ☐ Faulty or damaged tyre (*Weekly Checks*).
- ☐ Worn steering or suspension joints, bushes or components (Chapters 1A, 1B and 10).
- ☐ Wheel bolts loose (Chapter 10).

Excessive pitching and/or rolling around corners, or during braking

- ☐ Defective shock absorbers (Chapters 1A, 1B and 10).
- ☐ Broken or weak coil spring and/or suspension component (Chapters 1A, 1B and 10).
- ☐ Worn or damaged anti-roll bar or mountings (Chapter 10).

Wandering or general instability

- ☐ Incorrect front wheel alignment (Chapter 10).
- ☐ Worn steering or suspension joints, bushes or components (Chapters 1A, 1B and 10).
- ☐ Roadwheels out of balance (Chapter 10).
- ☐ Faulty or damaged tyre (*Weekly Checks*).
- ☐ Wheel bolts loose (Chapter 10).
- ☐ Defective shock absorbers (Chapters 1A, 1B and 10).

Excessively-stiff steering

- ☐ Lack of steering gear lubricant (Chapter 10).
- ☐ Seized track rod end balljoint or suspension balljoint (Chapters 1A, 1B and 10).
- ☐ Broken or incorrectly adjusted auxiliary drivebelt (Chapters 1A or 1B).
- ☐ Incorrect front wheel alignment (Chapter 10).
- ☐ Steering rack or column bent or damaged (Chapter 10).

Steering and suspension (continued)

Excessive play in steering

- ☐ Worn steering column universal joint(s) (Chapter 10).
- ☐ Worn steering track rod end balljoints (Chapters 1A, 1B and 10).
- ☐ Worn rack-and-pinion steering gear (Chapter 10).
- ☐ Worn steering or suspension joints, bushes or components (Chapters 1A, 1B and 10).

Lack of power assistance

- ☐ Broken or incorrectly-adjusted auxiliary drivebelt (Chapters 1A or 1B).
- ☐ Incorrect power steering fluid level (*Weekly Checks*).
- ☐ Restriction in power steering fluid hoses (Chapter 10).
- ☐ Faulty power steering pump (Chapter 10).
- ☐ Faulty rack-and-pinion steering gear (Chapter 10).

Tyre wear excessive

Tyres worn on inside or outside edges

- ☐ Tyres under-inflated (wear on both edges) (*Weekly Checks*).
- ☐ Incorrect camber or castor angles (wear on one edge only) (Chapter 10).
- ☐ Worn steering or suspension joints, bushes or components (Chapters 1A, 1B and 10).
- ☐ Excessively-hard cornering.
- ☐ Accident damage.

Tyre treads exhibit feathered edges

- ☐ Incorrect toe setting (Chapter 10).Tyres worn in centre of tread
- ☐ Tyres over-inflated (*Weekly Checks*).

Tyres worn on inside and outside edges

- ☐ Tyres under-inflated (*Weekly Checks*).
- ☐ Worn shock absorbers (Chapters 1A, 1B and 10).

Tyres worn unevenly

- ☐ Tyres out of balance (*Weekly Checks*).
- ☐ Excessive wheel or tyre run-out (Chapters 1A or 1B).
- ☐ Worn shock absorbers (Chapters 1A, 1B and 10).
- ☐ Faulty tyre (*Weekly Checks*).

Electrical system

Note: *For problems associated with the starting system, refer to the faults listed under Engine earlier in this Section.*

Battery will only hold a charge for a few days

- ☐ Battery defective internally (Chapter 5A).
- ☐ Battery electrolyte level low – where applicable (*Weekly Checks*).
- ☐ Battery terminal connections loose or corroded (*Weekly Checks*).
- ☐ Auxiliary drivebelt worn – or incorrectly adjusted, where applicable (Chapters 1A or 1B).
- ☐ Alternator not charging at correct output (Chapter 5A).
- ☐ Alternator or voltage regulator faulty (Chapter 5A).
- ☐ Short-circuit causing continual battery drain (Chapters 5A and 12).

Ignition/no-charge warning light remains illuminated with engine running

- ☐ Auxiliary drivebelt broken, worn, or incorrectly adjusted (Chapters 1A or 1B).
- ☐ Alternator brushes worn, sticking, or dirty (Chapter 5A).
- ☐ Alternator brush springs weak or broken (Chapter 5A).
- ☐ Internal fault in alternator or voltage regulator (Chapter 5A).
- ☐ Broken, disconnected, or loose wiring in charging circuit (Chapter 5A).

Ignition/no-charge warning light fails to come on

- ☐ Warning light bulb blown (Chapter 12).
- ☐ Broken, disconnected, or loose wiring in warning light circuit (Chapter 12).
- ☐ Alternator faulty (Chapter 5A).

Lights inoperative

- ☐ Bulb blown (Chapter 12).
- ☐ Corrosion of bulb or bulbholder contacts (Chapter 12).
- ☐ Blown fuse (Chapter 12).
- ☐ Faulty relay (Chapter 12).
- ☐ Broken, loose, or disconnected wiring (Chapter 12).
- ☐ Faulty switch (Chapter 12).

Instrument readings inaccurate or erratic

Instrument readings increase with engine speed

- ☐ Faulty voltage regulator (Chapter 12).

Fuel or temperature gauges give no reading

- ☐ Faulty gauge sender unit (Chapters 3, 4A or 4B).
- ☐ Wiring open-circuit (Chapter 12).
- ☐ Faulty gauge (Chapter 12).

Fuel or temperature gauges give continuous maximum reading

- ☐ Faulty gauge sender unit (Chapters 3, 4A or 4B).
- ☐ Wiring short-circuit (Chapter 12).
- ☐ Faulty gauge (Chapter 12).

Horn inoperative, or unsatisfactory in operation

Horn operates all the time

- ☐ Horn contacts permanently bridged or horn push stuck down (Chapter 12).

Horn fails to operate

- ☐ Blown fuse (Chapter 12).
- ☐ Cable or cable connections loose, broken or disconnected (Chapter 12).
- ☐ Faulty horn (Chapter 12).

Horn emits intermittent or unsatisfactory sound

- ☐ Cable connections loose (Chapter 12).
- ☐ Horn mountings loose (Chapter 12).
- ☐ Faulty horn (Chapter 12).

Electrical system (continued)

Wipers inoperative, or unsatisfactory in operation

Wipers fail to operate, or operate very slowly

- ☐ Wiper blades stuck to screen, or linkage seized or binding (*Weekly Checks* and Chapter 12).
- ☐ Blown fuse (Chapter 12).
- ☐ Cable or cable connections loose, broken or disconnected (Chapter 12).
- ☐ Faulty relay (Chapter 12).
- ☐ Faulty wiper motor (Chapter 12).

Wiper blades sweep over too large or too small an area of the glass

- ☐ Wiper arms incorrectly positioned on spindles (Chapter 12).
- ☐ Excessive wear of wiper linkage (Chapter 12).
- ☐ Wiper motor or linkage mountings loose or insecure (Chapter 12).

Wiper blades fail to clean the glass effectively

- ☐ Wiper blade rubbers worn or perished (*Weekly Checks*).
- ☐ Wiper arm tension springs broken, or arm pivots seized (Chapter 12).
- ☐ Insufficient windscreen washer additive to adequately remove road film (*Weekly Checks*).

Washers inoperative, or unsatisfactory in operation

One or more washer jets inoperative

- ☐ Blocked washer jet (Chapter 12).
- ☐ Disconnected, kinked or restricted fluid hose (Chapter 12).
- ☐ Insufficient fluid in washer reservoir (*Weekly Checks*).

Washer pump fails to operate

- ☐ Broken or disconnected wiring or connections (Chapter 12).
- ☐ Blown fuse (Chapter 12).
- ☐ Faulty washer switch (Chapter 12).
- ☐ Faulty washer pump (Chapter 12).

Washer pump runs for some time before fluid is emitted from jets

- ☐ Faulty one-way valve in fluid supply hose (Chapter 12).

Electric windows inoperative, or unsatisfactory in operation

Window glass will only move in one direction

- ☐ Faulty switch (Chapter 12).

Window glass slow to move

- ☐ Regulator seized or damaged, or in need of lubrication (Chapter 11).
- ☐ Door internal components or trim fouling regulator (Chapter 11).
- ☐ Faulty motor (Chapter 11).

Window glass fails to move

- ☐ Blown fuse (Chapter 12).
- ☐ Faulty relay (Chapter 12).
- ☐ Broken or disconnected wiring or connections (Chapter 12).
- ☐ Faulty motor (Chapter 12).

Central locking system inoperative, or unsatisfactory in operation

Complete system failure

- ☐ Blown fuse (Chapter 12).
- ☐ Faulty relay (Chapter 12).
- ☐ Broken or disconnected wiring or connections (Chapter 12).

Latch locks but will not unlock, or unlocks but will not lock

- ☐ Faulty switch (Chapter 12).
- ☐ Broken or disconnected latch operating rods or levers (Chapter 11).
- ☐ Faulty relay (Chapter 12).

One motor fails to operate

- ☐ Broken or disconnected wiring or connections (Chapter 12).
- ☐ Faulty motor (Chapter 11).
- ☐ Broken, binding or disconnected lock operating rods or levers (Chapter 11).
- ☐ Fault in door lock (Chapter 11).

A

ABS (Anti-lock brake system) A system, usually electronically controlled, that senses incipient wheel lockup during braking and relieves hydraulic pressure at wheels that are about to skid.

Air bag An inflatable bag hidden in the steering wheel (driver's side) or the dash or glovebox (passenger side). In a head-on collision, the bags inflate, preventing the driver and front passenger from being thrown forward into the steering wheel or windscreen.

Air cleaner A metal or plastic housing, containing a filter element, which removes dust and dirt from the air being drawn into the engine.

Air filter element The actual filter in an air cleaner system, usually manufactured from pleated paper and requiring renewal at regular intervals.

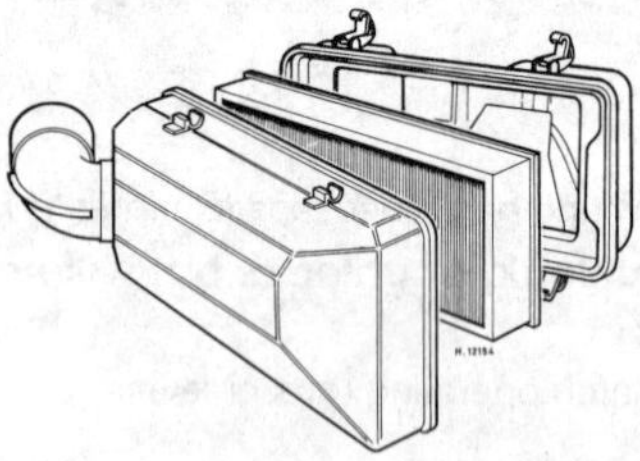

Air filter

Allen key A hexagonal wrench which fits into a recessed hexagonal hole.

Alligator clip A long-nosed spring-loaded metal clip with meshing teeth. Used to make temporary electrical connections.

Alternator A component in the electrical system which converts mechanical energy from a drivebelt into electrical energy to charge the battery and to operate the starting system, ignition system and electrical accessories.

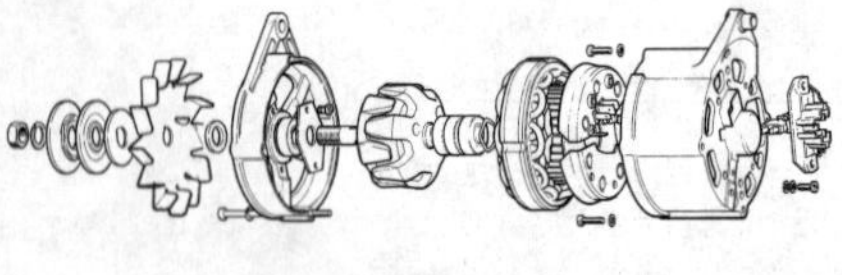

Alternator (exploded view)

Ampere (amp) A unit of measurement for the flow of electric current. One amp is the amount of current produced by one volt acting through a resistance of one ohm.

Anaerobic sealer A substance used to prevent bolts and screws from loosening. Anaerobic means that it does not require oxygen for activation. The Loctite brand is widely used.

Antifreeze A substance (usually ethylene glycol) mixed with water, and added to a vehicle's cooling system, to prevent freezing of the coolant in winter. Antifreeze also contains chemicals to inhibit corrosion and the formation of rust and other deposits that would tend to clog the radiator and coolant passages and reduce cooling efficiency.

Anti-seize compound A coating that reduces the risk of seizing on fasteners that are subjected to high temperatures, such as exhaust manifold bolts and nuts.

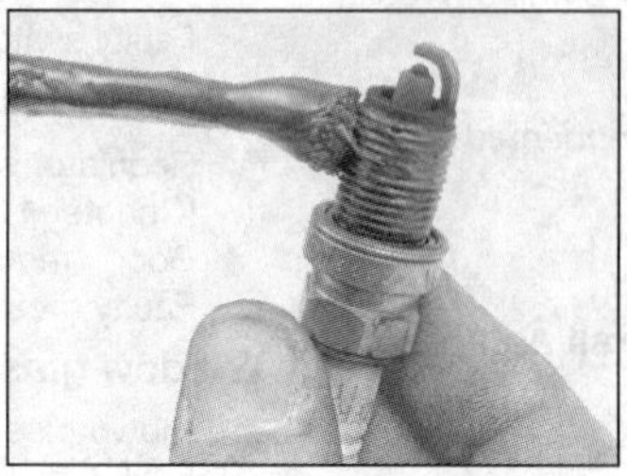

Anti-seize compound

Asbestos A natural fibrous mineral with great heat resistance, commonly used in the composition of brake friction materials. Asbestos is a health hazard and the dust created by brake systems should never be inhaled or ingested.

Axle A shaft on which a wheel revolves, or which revolves with a wheel. Also, a solid beam that connects the two wheels at one end of the vehicle. An axle which also transmits power to the wheels is known as a live axle.

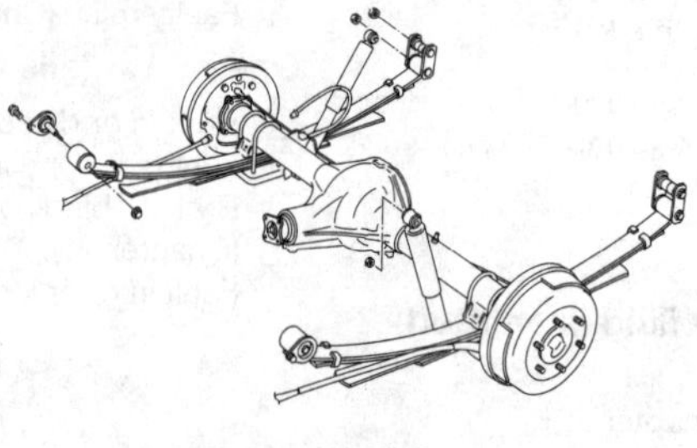

Axle assembly

Axleshaft A single rotating shaft, on either side of the differential, which delivers power from the final drive assembly to the drive wheels. Also called a driveshaft or a halfshaft.

B

Ball bearing An anti-friction bearing consisting of a hardened inner and outer race with hardened steel balls between two races.

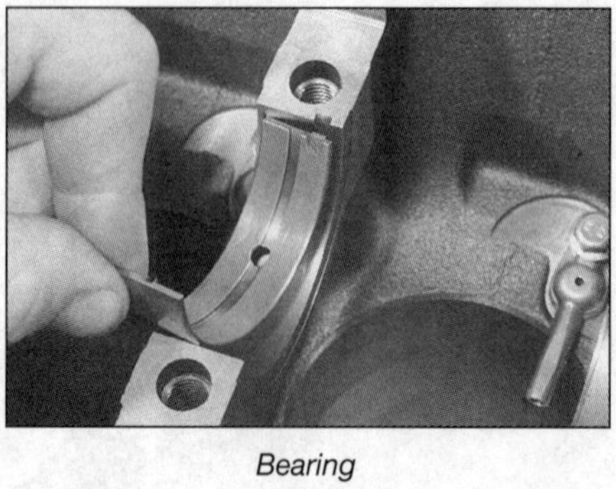

Bearing

Bearing The curved surface on a shaft or in a bore, or the part assembled into either, that permits relative motion between them with minimum wear and friction.

Big-end bearing The bearing in the end of the connecting rod that's attached to the crankshaft.

Bleed nipple A valve on a brake wheel cylinder, caliper or other hydraulic component that is opened to purge the hydraulic system of air. Also called a bleed screw.

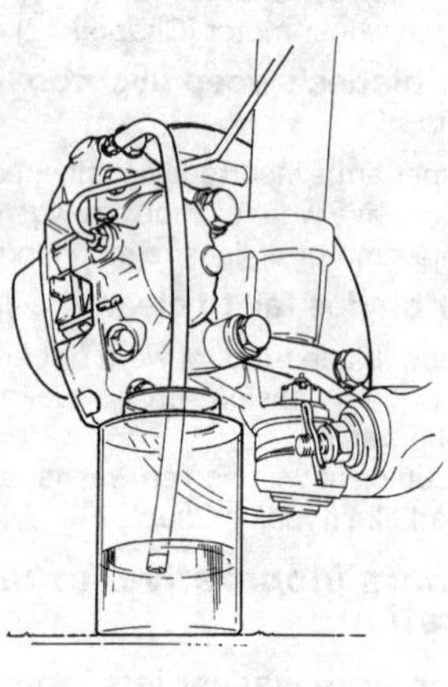

Brake bleeding

Brake bleeding Procedure for removing air from lines of a hydraulic brake system.

Brake disc The component of a disc brake that rotates with the wheels.

Brake drum The component of a drum brake that rotates with the wheels.

Brake linings The friction material which contacts the brake disc or drum to retard the vehicle's speed. The linings are bonded or riveted to the brake pads or shoes.

Brake pads The replaceable friction pads that pinch the brake disc when the brakes are applied. Brake pads consist of a friction material bonded or riveted to a rigid backing plate.

Brake shoe The crescent-shaped carrier to which the brake linings are mounted and which forces the lining against the rotating drum during braking.

Braking systems For more information on braking systems, consult the *Haynes Automotive Brake Manual*.

Breaker bar A long socket wrench handle providing greater leverage.

Bulkhead The insulated partition between the engine and the passenger compartment.

C

Caliper The non-rotating part of a disc-brake assembly that straddles the disc and carries the brake pads. The caliper also contains the hydraulic components that cause the pads to pinch the disc when the brakes are applied. A caliper is also a measuring tool that can be set to measure inside or outside dimensions of an object.

Camshaft A rotating shaft on which a series of cam lobes operate the valve mechanisms. The camshaft may be driven by gears, by sprockets and chain or by sprockets and a belt.

Canister A container in an evaporative emission control system; contains activated charcoal granules to trap vapours from the fuel system.

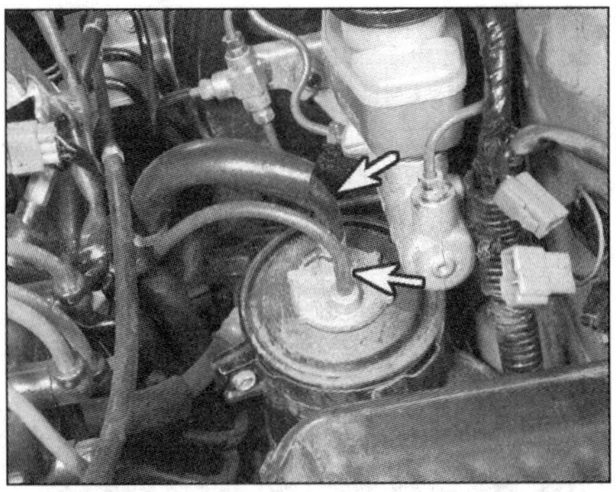

Canister

Carburettor A device which mixes fuel with air in the proper proportions to provide a desired power output from a spark ignition internal combustion engine.

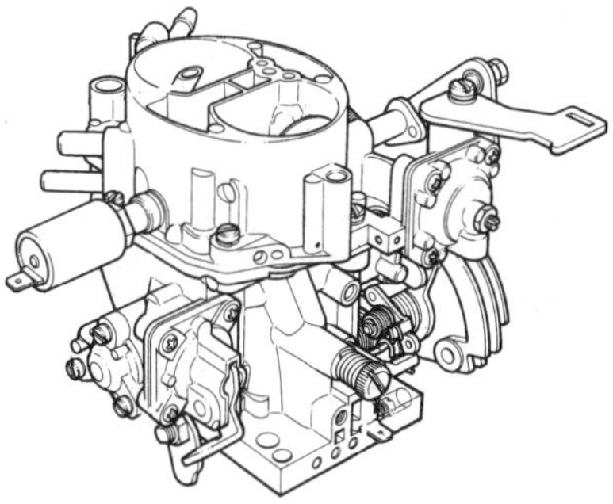

Carburettor

Castellated Resembling the parapets along the top of a castle wall. For example, a castellated balljoint stud nut.

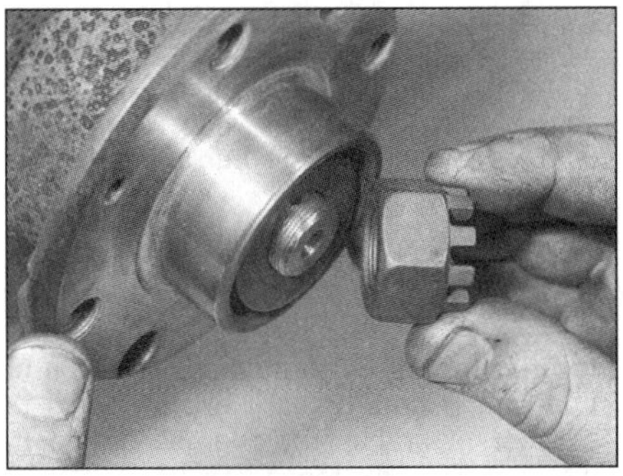

Castellated nut

Castor In wheel alignment, the backward or forward tilt of the steering axis. Castor is positive when the steering axis is inclined rearward at the top.

Catalytic converter A silencer-like device in the exhaust system which converts certain pollutants in the exhaust gases into less harmful substances.

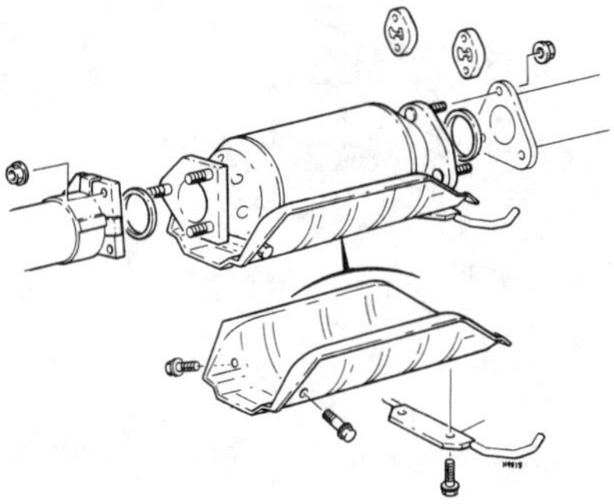

Catalytic converter

Circlip A ring-shaped clip used to prevent endwise movement of cylindrical parts and shafts. An internal circlip is installed in a groove in a housing; an external circlip fits into a groove on the outside of a cylindrical piece such as a shaft.

Clearance The amount of space between two parts. For example, between a piston and a cylinder, between a bearing and a journal, etc.

Coil spring A spiral of elastic steel found in various sizes throughout a vehicle, for example as a springing medium in the suspension and in the valve train.

Compression Reduction in volume, and increase in pressure and temperature, of a gas, caused by squeezing it into a smaller space.

Compression ratio The relationship between cylinder volume when the piston is at top dead centre and cylinder volume when the piston is at bottom dead centre.

Constant velocity (CV) joint A type of universal joint that cancels out vibrations caused by driving power being transmitted through an angle.

Core plug A disc or cup-shaped metal device inserted in a hole in a casting through which core was removed when the casting was formed. Also known as a freeze plug or expansion plug.

Crankcase The lower part of the engine block in which the crankshaft rotates.

Crankshaft The main rotating member, or shaft, running the length of the crankcase, with offset "throws" to which the connecting rods are attached.

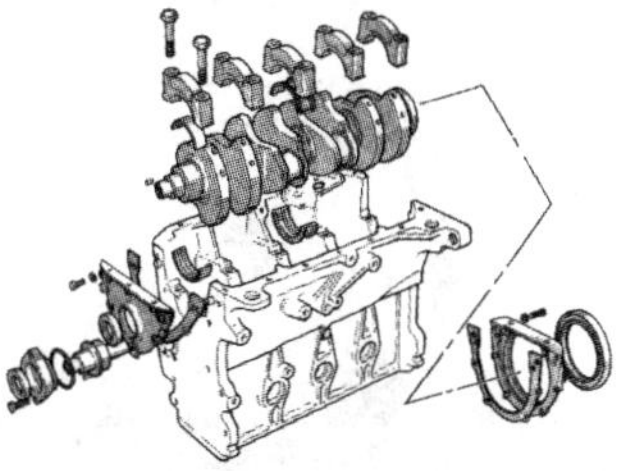

Crankshaft assembly

Crocodile clip See Alligator clip

D

Diagnostic code Code numbers obtained by accessing the diagnostic mode of an engine management computer. This code can be used to determine the area in the system where a malfunction may be located.

Disc brake A brake design incorporating a rotating disc onto which brake pads are squeezed. The resulting friction converts the energy of a moving vehicle into heat.

Double-overhead cam (DOHC) An engine that uses two overhead camshafts, usually one for the intake valves and one for the exhaust valves.

Drivebelt(s) The belt(s) used to drive accessories such as the alternator, water pump, power steering pump, air conditioning compressor, etc. off the crankshaft pulley.

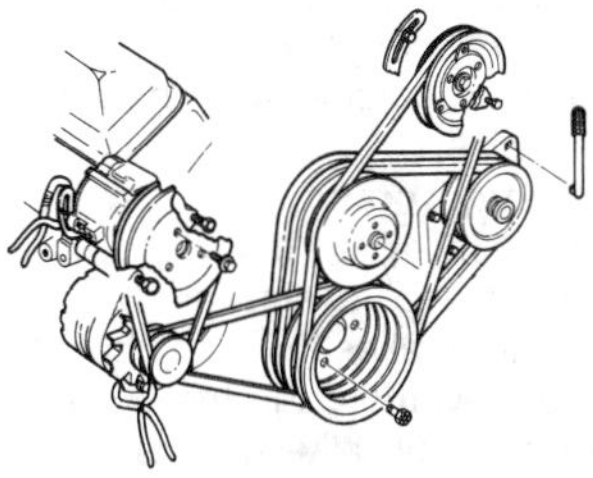

Accessory drivebelts

Driveshaft Any shaft used to transmit motion. Commonly used when referring to the axleshafts on a front wheel drive vehicle.

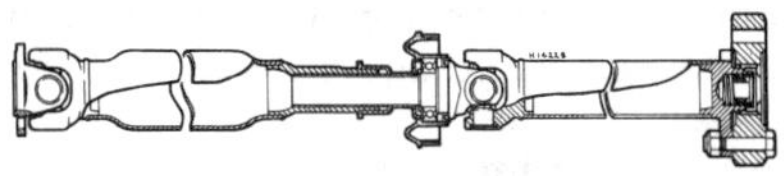

Driveshaft

Drum brake A type of brake using a drum-shaped metal cylinder attached to the inner surface of the wheel. When the brake pedal is pressed, curved brake shoes with friction linings press against the inside of the drum to slow or stop the vehicle.

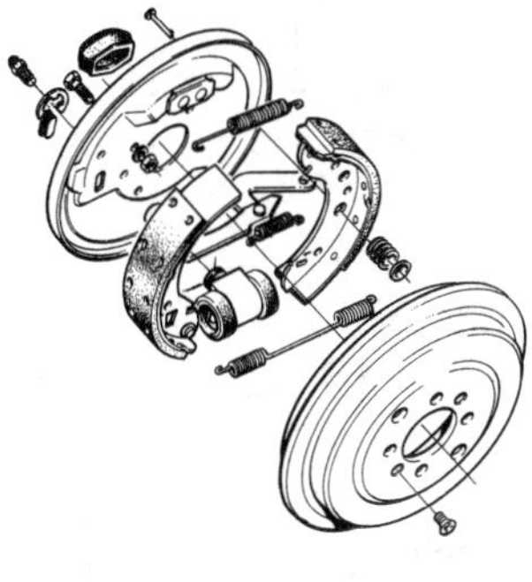

Drum brake assembly

E

EGR valve A valve used to introduce exhaust gases into the intake air stream.

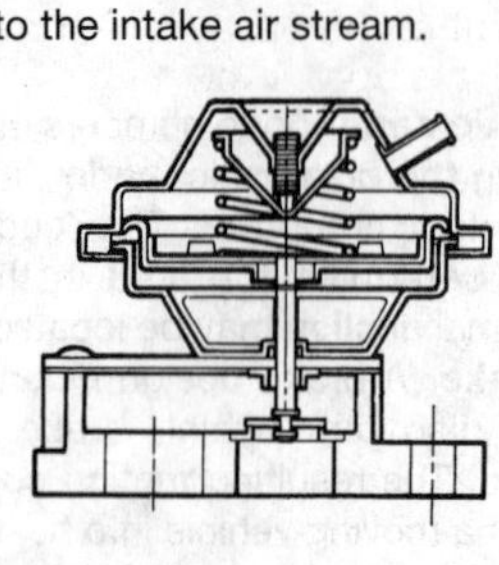

EGR valve

Electronic control unit (ECU) A computer which controls (for instance) ignition and fuel injection systems, or an anti-lock braking system. For more information refer to the *Haynes Automotive Electrical and Electronic Systems Manual.*

Electronic Fuel Injection (EFI) A computer controlled fuel system that distributes fuel through an injector located in each intake port of the engine.

Emergency brake A braking system, independent of the main hydraulic system, that can be used to slow or stop the vehicle if the primary brakes fail, or to hold the vehicle stationary even though the brake pedal isn't depressed. It usually consists of a hand lever that actuates either front or rear brakes mechanically through a series of cables and linkages. Also known as a handbrake or parking brake.

Endfloat The amount of lengthwise movement between two parts. As applied to a crankshaft, the distance that the crankshaft can move forward and back in the cylinder block.

Engine management system (EMS) A computer controlled system which manages the fuel injection and the ignition systems in an integrated fashion.

Exhaust manifold A part with several passages through which exhaust gases leave the engine combustion chambers and enter the exhaust pipe.

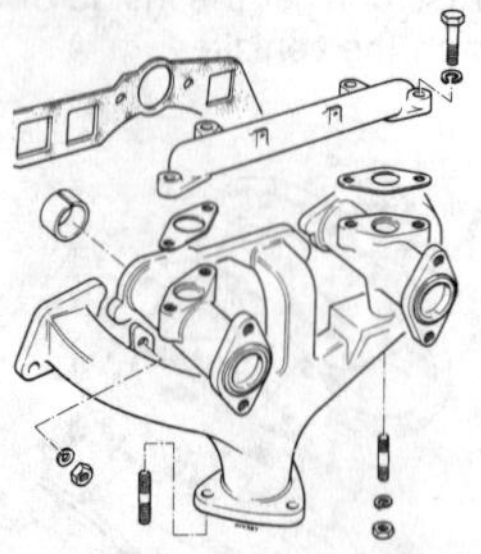

Exhaust manifold

F

Fan clutch A viscous (fluid) drive coupling device which permits variable engine fan speeds in relation to engine speeds.

Feeler blade A thin strip or blade of hardened steel, ground to an exact thickness, used to check or measure clearances between parts.

Feeler blade

Firing order The order in which the engine cylinders fire, or deliver their power strokes, beginning with the number one cylinder.

Flywheel A heavy spinning wheel in which energy is absorbed and stored by means of momentum. On cars, the flywheel is attached to the crankshaft to smooth out firing impulses.

Free play The amount of travel before any action takes place. The "looseness" in a linkage, or an assembly of parts, between the initial application of force and actual movement. For example, the distance the brake pedal moves before the pistons in the master cylinder are actuated.

Fuse An electrical device which protects a circuit against accidental overload. The typical fuse contains a soft piece of metal which is calibrated to melt at a predetermined current flow (expressed as amps) and break the circuit.

Fusible link A circuit protection device consisting of a conductor surrounded by heat-resistant insulation. The conductor is smaller than the wire it protects, so it acts as the weakest link in the circuit. Unlike a blown fuse, a failed fusible link must frequently be cut from the wire for replacement.

G

Gap The distance the spark must travel in jumping from the centre electrode to the side electrode in a spark plug. Also refers to the spacing between the points in a contact breaker assembly in a conventional points-type ignition, or to the distance between the reluctor or rotor and the pickup coil in an electronic ignition.

Adjusting spark plug gap

Gasket Any thin, soft material - usually cork, cardboard, asbestos or soft metal - installed between two metal surfaces to ensure a good seal. For instance, the cylinder head gasket seals the joint between the block and the cylinder head.

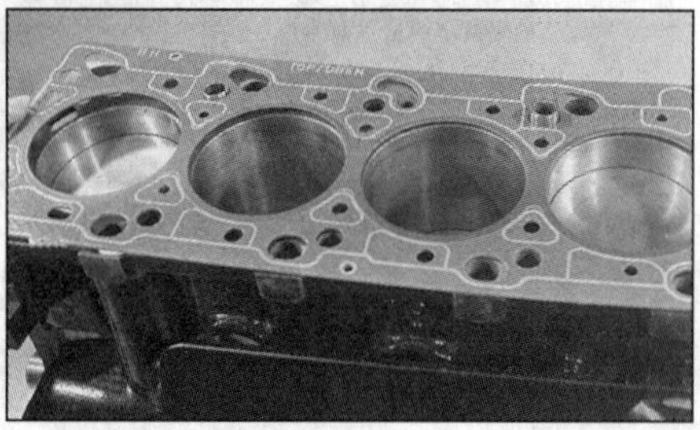

Gasket

Gauge An instrument panel display used to monitor engine conditions. A gauge with a movable pointer on a dial or a fixed scale is an analogue gauge. A gauge with a numerical readout is called a digital gauge.

H

Halfshaft A rotating shaft that transmits power from the final drive unit to a drive wheel, usually when referring to a live rear axle.

Harmonic balancer A device designed to reduce torsion or twisting vibration in the crankshaft. May be incorporated in the crankshaft pulley. Also known as a vibration damper.

Hone An abrasive tool for correcting small irregularities or differences in diameter in an engine cylinder, brake cylinder, etc.

Hydraulic tappet A tappet that utilises hydraulic pressure from the engine's lubrication system to maintain zero clearance (constant contact with both camshaft and valve stem). Automatically adjusts to variation in valve stem length. Hydraulic tappets also reduce valve noise.

I

Ignition timing The moment at which the spark plug fires, usually expressed in the number of crankshaft degrees before the piston reaches the top of its stroke.

Inlet manifold A tube or housing with passages through which flows the air-fuel mixture (carburettor vehicles and vehicles with throttle body injection) or air only (port fuel-injected vehicles) to the port openings in the cylinder head.

J

Jump start Starting the engine of a vehicle with a discharged or weak battery by attaching jump leads from the weak battery to a charged or helper battery.

L

Load Sensing Proportioning Valve (LSPV) A brake hydraulic system control valve that works like a proportioning valve, but also takes into consideration the amount of weight carried by the rear axle.

Locknut A nut used to lock an adjustment nut, or other threaded component, in place. For example, a locknut is employed to keep the adjusting nut on the rocker arm in position.

Lockwasher A form of washer designed to prevent an attaching nut from working loose.

M

MacPherson strut A type of front suspension system devised by Earle MacPherson at Ford of England. In its original form, a simple lateral link with the anti-roll bar creates the lower control arm. A long strut - an integral coil spring and shock absorber - is mounted between the body and the steering knuckle. Many modern so-called MacPherson strut systems use a conventional lower A-arm and don't rely on the anti-roll bar for location.

Multimeter An electrical test instrument with the capability to measure voltage, current and resistance.

N

NOx Oxides of Nitrogen. A common toxic pollutant emitted by petrol and diesel engines at higher temperatures.

O

Ohm The unit of electrical resistance. One volt applied to a resistance of one ohm will produce a current of one amp.

Ohmmeter An instrument for measuring electrical resistance.

O-ring A type of sealing ring made of a special rubber-like material; in use, the O-ring is compressed into a groove to provide the sealing action.

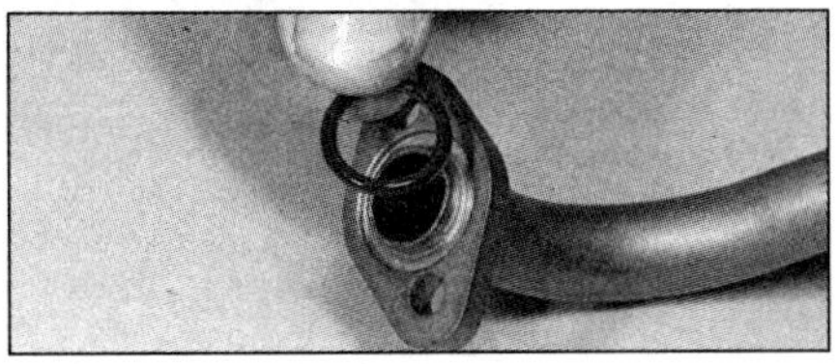

O-ring

Overhead cam (ohc) engine An engine with the camshaft(s) located on top of the cylinder head(s).

Overhead valve (ohv) engine An engine with the valves located in the cylinder head, but with the camshaft located in the engine block.

Oxygen sensor A device installed in the engine exhaust manifold, which senses the oxygen content in the exhaust and converts this information into an electric current. Also called a Lambda sensor.

P

Phillips screw A type of screw head having a cross instead of a slot for a corresponding type of screwdriver.

Plastigage A thin strip of plastic thread, available in different sizes, used for measuring clearances. For example, a strip of Plastigage is laid across a bearing journal. The parts are assembled and dismantled; the width of the crushed strip indicates the clearance between journal and bearing.

Plastigage

Propeller shaft The long hollow tube with universal joints at both ends that carries power from the transmission to the differential on front-engined rear wheel drive vehicles.

Proportioning valve A hydraulic control valve which limits the amount of pressure to the rear brakes during panic stops to prevent wheel lock-up.

R

Rack-and-pinion steering A steering system with a pinion gear on the end of the steering shaft that mates with a rack (think of a geared wheel opened up and laid flat). When the steering wheel is turned, the pinion turns, moving the rack to the left or right. This movement is transmitted through the track rods to the steering arms at the wheels.

Radiator A liquid-to-air heat transfer device designed to reduce the temperature of the coolant in an internal combustion engine cooling system.

Refrigerant Any substance used as a heat transfer agent in an air-conditioning system. R-12 has been the principle refrigerant for many years; recently, however, manufacturers have begun using R-134a, a non-CFC substance that is considered less harmful to the ozone in the upper atmosphere.

Rocker arm A lever arm that rocks on a shaft or pivots on a stud. In an overhead valve engine, the rocker arm converts the upward movement of the pushrod into a downward movement to open a valve.

Rotor In a distributor, the rotating device inside the cap that connects the centre electrode and the outer terminals as it turns, distributing the high voltage from the coil secondary winding to the proper spark plug. Also, that part of an alternator which rotates inside the stator. Also, the rotating assembly of a turbocharger, including the compressor wheel, shaft and turbine wheel.

Runout The amount of wobble (in-and-out movement) of a gear or wheel as it's rotated. The amount a shaft rotates "out-of-true." The out-of-round condition of a rotating part.

S

Sealant A liquid or paste used to prevent leakage at a joint. Sometimes used in conjunction with a gasket.

Sealed beam lamp An older headlight design which integrates the reflector, lens and filaments into a hermetically-sealed one-piece unit. When a filament burns out or the lens cracks, the entire unit is simply replaced.

Serpentine drivebelt A single, long, wide accessory drivebelt that's used on some newer vehicles to drive all the accessories, instead of a series of smaller, shorter belts. Serpentine drivebelts are usually tensioned by an automatic tensioner.

Serpentine drivebelt

Shim Thin spacer, commonly used to adjust the clearance or relative positions between two parts. For example, shims inserted into or under bucket tappets control valve clearances. Clearance is adjusted by changing the thickness of the shim.

Slide hammer A special puller that screws into or hooks onto a component such as a shaft or bearing; a heavy sliding handle on the shaft bottoms against the end of the shaft to knock the component free.

Sprocket A tooth or projection on the periphery of a wheel, shaped to engage with a chain or drivebelt. Commonly used to refer to the sprocket wheel itself.

Starter inhibitor switch On vehicles with an automatic transmission, a switch that prevents starting if the vehicle is not in Neutral or Park.

Strut See MacPherson strut.

T

Tappet A cylindrical component which transmits motion from the cam to the valve stem, either directly or via a pushrod and rocker arm. Also called a cam follower.

Thermostat A heat-controlled valve that regulates the flow of coolant between the cylinder block and the radiator, so maintaining optimum engine operating temperature. A thermostat is also used in some air cleaners in which the temperature is regulated.

Thrust bearing The bearing in the clutch assembly that is moved in to the release levers by clutch pedal action to disengage the clutch. Also referred to as a release bearing.

Timing belt A toothed belt which drives the camshaft. Serious engine damage may result if it breaks in service.

Timing chain A chain which drives the camshaft.

Toe-in The amount the front wheels are closer together at the front than at the rear. On rear wheel drive vehicles, a slight amount of toe-in is usually specified to keep the front wheels running parallel on the road by offsetting other forces that tend to spread the wheels apart.

Toe-out The amount the front wheels are closer together at the rear than at the front. On front wheel drive vehicles, a slight amount of toe-out is usually specified.

Tools For full information on choosing and using tools, refer to the *Haynes Automotive Tools Manual.*

Tracer A stripe of a second colour applied to a wire insulator to distinguish that wire from another one with the same colour insulator.

Tune-up A process of accurate and careful adjustments and parts replacement to obtain the best possible engine performance.

Turbocharger A centrifugal device, driven by exhaust gases, that pressurises the intake air. Normally used to increase the power output from a given engine displacement, but can also be used primarily to reduce exhaust emissions (as on VW's "Umwelt" Diesel engine).

U

Universal joint or U-joint A double-pivoted connection for transmitting power from a driving to a driven shaft through an angle. A U-joint consists of two Y-shaped yokes and a cross-shaped member called the spider.

V

Valve A device through which the flow of liquid, gas, vacuum, or loose material in bulk may be started, stopped, or regulated by a movable part that opens, shuts, or partially obstructs one or more ports or passageways. A valve is also the movable part of such a device.

Valve clearance The clearance between the valve tip (the end of the valve stem) and the rocker arm or tappet. The valve clearance is measured when the valve is closed.

Vernier caliper A precision measuring instrument that measures inside and outside dimensions. Not quite as accurate as a micrometer, but more convenient.

Viscosity The thickness of a liquid or its resistance to flow.

Volt A unit for expressing electrical "pressure" in a circuit. One volt that will produce a current of one ampere through a resistance of one ohm.

W

Welding Various processes used to join metal items by heating the areas to be joined to a molten state and fusing them together. For more information refer to the *Haynes Automotive Welding Manual.*

Wiring diagram A drawing portraying the components and wires in a vehicle's electrical system, using standardised symbols. For more information refer to the *Haynes Automotive Electrical and Electronic Systems Manual.*

Note: *References throughout this index are in the form* **"*Chapter number • Page number*"**

Haynes Manuals - The Complete List

Title	Book No.
ALFA ROMEO	
Alfa Romeo Alfasud/Sprint (74 - 88) up to F	**0292**
Alfa Romeo Alfetta (73 - 87) up to E	**0531**
AUDI	
Audi 80 (72 - Feb 79) up to T	**0207**
Audi 80, 90 (79 - Oct 86) up to D & Coupe (81 - Nov 88) up to F	**0605**
Audi 80, 90 (Oct 86 - 90) D to H & Coupe (Nov 88 - 90) F to H	**1491**
Audi 100 (Oct 82 - 90) up to H & 200 (Feb 84 - Oct 89) A to G	**0907**
Audi 100 & A6 Petrol & Diesel (May 91 - May 97) H to P	**3504**
Audi A4 (95 - Feb 00) M to V	**3575**
AUSTIN	
Austin A35 & A40 (56 - 67) *	**0118**
Austin Allegro 1100, 1300, 1.0, 1.1 & 1.3 (73 - 82) *	**0164**
Austin Healey 100/6 & 3000 (56 - 68) *	**0049**
Austin/MG/Rover Maestro 1.3 & 1.6 (83 - 95) up to M	**0922**
Austin/MG Metro (80 - May 90) up to G	**0718**
Austin/Rover Montego 1.3 & 1.6 (84 - 94) A to L	**1066**
Austin/MG/Rover Montego 2.0 (84 - 95) A to M	**1067**
Mini (59 - 69) up to H	**0527**
Mini (69 - Oct 96) up to P	**0646**
Austin/Rover 2.0 litre Diesel Engine (86 - 93) C to L	**1857**
BEDFORD	
Bedford CF (69 - 87) up to E	**0163**
Bedford/Vauxhall Rascal & Suzuki Supercarry (86 - Oct 94) C to M	**3015**
BMW	
BMW 1500, 1502, 1600, 1602, 2000 & 2002 (59 - 77)*	**0240**
BMW 316, 320 & 320i (4-cyl) (75 - Feb 83) up to Y	**0276**
BMW 320, 320i, 323i & 325i (6-cyl) (Oct 77 - Sept 87) up to E	**0815**
BMW 3-Series (Apr 91 - 96) H to N	**3210**
BMW 3- & 5-Series (sohc) (81 - 91) up to J	**1948**
BMW 520i & 525e (Oct 81 - June 88) up to E	**1560**
BMW 525, 528 & 528i (73 - Sept 81) up to X	**0632**
CITROEN	
Citroën 2CV, Ami & Dyane (67 - 90) up to H	**0196**
Citroën AX Petrol & Diesel (87 - 97) D to P	**3014**
Citroën BX (83 - 94) A to L	**0908**
Citroën C15 Van Petrol & Diesel (89 - Oct 98) F to S	**3509**
Citroën CX (75 - 88) up to F	**0528**
Citroën Saxo Petrol & Diesel (96 - 01) N to X	**3506**
Citroën Visa (79 - 88) up to F	**0620**
Citroën Xantia Petrol & Diesel (93 - 98) K to S	**3082**
Citroën XM Petrol & Diesel (89 - 98) G to R	**3451**
Citroën Xsara Petrol & Diesel (97 - Sept 00) R to W	**3751**
Citroën ZX Diesel (91 - 98) J to S	**1922**
Citroën ZX Petrol (91 - 98) H to S	**1881**
Citroën 1.7 & 1.9 litre Diesel Engine (84 - 96) A to N	**1379**
FIAT	
Fiat 126 (73 - 87) *	**0305**
Fiat 500 (57 - 73) up to M	**0090**
Fiat Bravo & Brava (95 - 00) N to W	**3572**
Fiat Cinquecento (93 - 98) K to R	**3501**
Fiat Panda (81 - 95) up to M	**0793**
Fiat Punto Petrol & Diesel (94 - Oct 99) L to V	**3251**
Fiat Regata (84 - 88) A to F	**1167**
Fiat Tipo (88 - 91) E to J	**1625**
Fiat Uno (83 - 95) up to M	**0923**
Fiat X1/9 (74 - 89) up to G	**0273**
FORD	
Ford Anglia (59 - 68) *	**0001**

Title	Book No.
Ford Capri II (& III) 1.6 & 2.0 (74 - 87) up to E	**0283**
Ford Capri II (& III) 2.8 & 3.0 (74 - 87) up to E	**1309**
Ford Cortina Mk III 1300 & 1600 (70 - 76) *	**0070**
Ford Cortina Mk IV (& V) 1.6 & 2.0 (76 - 83) *	**0343**
Ford Cortina Mk IV (& V) 2.3 V6 (77 - 83) *	**0426**
Ford Escort Mk I 1100 & 1300 (68 - 74) *	**0171**
Ford Escort Mk I Mexico, RS 1600 & RS 2000 (70 - 74)*	**0139**
Ford Escort Mk II Mexico, RS 1800 & RS 2000 (75 - 80)*	**0735**
Ford Escort (75 - Aug 80) *	**0280**
Ford Escort (Sept 80 - Sept 90) up to H	**0686**
Ford Escort & Orion (Sept 90 - 00) H to X	**1737**
Ford Fiesta (76 - Aug 83) up to Y	**0334**
Ford Fiesta (Aug 83 - Feb 89) A to F	**1030**
Ford Fiesta (Feb 89 - Oct 95) F to N	**1595**
Ford Fiesta (Oct 95 - 01) N-reg. onwards	**3397**
Ford Focus (98 - 01) S to Y	**3759**
Ford Granada (Sept 77 - Feb 85) up to B	**0481**
Ford Granada & Scorpio (Mar 85 - 94) B to M	**1245**
Ford Ka (96 - 99) P to T	**3570**
Ford Mondeo Petrol (93 - 99) K to T	**1923**
Ford Mondeo Diesel (93 - 96) L to N	**3465**
Ford Orion (83 - Sept 90) up to H	**1009**
Ford Sierra 4 cyl. (82 - 93) up to K	**0903**
Ford Sierra V6 (82 - 91) up to J	**0904**
Ford Transit Petrol (Mk 2) (78 - Jan 86) up to C	**0719**
Ford Transit Petrol (Mk 3) (Feb 86 - 89) C to G	**1468**
Ford Transit Diesel (Feb 86 - 99) C to T	**3019**
Ford 1.6 & 1.8 litre Diesel Engine (84 - 96) A to N	**1172**
Ford 2.1, 2.3 & 2.5 litre Diesel Engine (77 - 90) up to H	**1606**
FREIGHT ROVER	
Freight Rover Sherpa (74 - 87) up to E	**0463**
HILLMAN	
Hillman Avenger (70 - 82) up to Y	**0037**
Hillman Imp (63 - 76) *	**0022**
HONDA	
Honda Accord (76 - Feb 84) up to A	**0351**
Honda Civic (Feb 84 - Oct 87) A to E	**1226**
Honda Civic (Nov 91 - 96) J to N	**3199**
HYUNDAI	
Hyundai Pony (85 - 94) C to M	**3398**
JAGUAR	
Jaguar E Type (61 - 72) up to L	**0140**
Jaguar MkI & II, 240 & 340 (55 - 69) *	**0098**
Jaguar XJ6, XJ & Sovereign; Daimler Sovereign (68 - Oct 86) up to D	**0242**
Jaguar XJ6 & Sovereign (Oct 86 - Sept 94) D to M	**3261**
Jaguar XJ12, XJS & Sovereign; Daimler Double Six (72 - 88) up to F	**0478**
JEEP	
Jeep Cherokee Petrol (93 - 96) K to N	**1943**
LADA	
Lada 1200, 1300, 1500 & 1600 (74 - 91) up to J	**0413**
Lada Samara (87 - 91) D to J	**1610**
LAND ROVER	
Land Rover 90, 110 & Defender Diesel (83 - 95) up to N	**3017**
Land Rover Discovery Petrol & Diesel (89 - 98) G to S	**3016**
Land Rover Series IIA & III Diesel (58 - 85) up to C	**0529**
Land Rover Series II, IIA & III Petrol (58 - 85) up to C	**0314**
MAZDA	
Mazda 323 (Mar 81 - Oct 89) up to G	**1608**
Mazda 323 (Oct 89 - 98) G to R	**3455**
Mazda 626 (May 83 - Sept 87) up to E	**0929**

Title	Book No.
Mazda B-1600, B-1800 & B-2000 Pick-up (72 - 88) up to F	**0267**
Mazda RX-7 (79 - 85) *	**0460**
MERCEDES-BENZ	
Mercedes-Benz 190, 190E & 190D Petrol & Diesel (83 - 93) A to L	**3450**
Mercedes-Benz 200, 240, 300 Diesel (Oct 76 - 85) up to C	**1114**
Mercedes-Benz 250 & 280 (68 - 72) up to L	**0346**
Mercedes-Benz 250 & 280 (123 Series) (Oct 76 - 84) up to B	**0677**
Mercedes-Benz 124 Series (85 - Aug 93) C to K	**3253**
Mercedes-Benz C-Class Petrol & Diesel (93 - Aug 00) L to W	**3511**
MG	
MGA (55 - 62) *	**0475**
MGB (62 - 80) up to W	**0111**
MG Midget & AH Sprite (58 - 80) up to W	**0265**
MITSUBISHI	
Mitsubishi Shogun & L200 Pick-Ups (83 - 94) up to M	**1944**
MORRIS	
Morris Ital 1.3 (80 - 84) up to B	**0705**
Morris Minor 1000 (56 - 71) up to K	**0024**
NISSAN	
Nissan Bluebird (May 84 - Mar 86) A to C	**1223**
Nissan Bluebird (Mar 86 - 90) C to H	**1473**
Nissan Cherry (Sept 82 - 86) up to D	**1031**
Nissan Micra (83 - Jan 93) up to K	**0931**
Nissan Micra (93 - 99) K to T	**3254**
Nissan Primera (90 - Aug 99) H to T	**1851**
Nissan Stanza (82 - 86) up to D	**0824**
Nissan Sunny (May 82 - Oct 86) up to D	**0895**
Nissan Sunny (Oct 86 - Mar 91) D to H	**1378**
Nissan Sunny (Apr 91 - 95) H to N	**3219**
OPEL	
Opel Ascona & Manta (B Series) (Sept 75 - 88) up to F	**0316**
Opel Ascona (81 - 88) *(Not available in UK see Vauxhall Cavalier 0812)*	**3215**
Opel Astra (Oct 91 - Feb 98) *(Not available in UK see Vauxhall Astra 1832)*	**3156**
Opel Astra & Zafira Diesel (Feb 98 - Sept 00) *(See Astra & Zafira Diesel Book No. 3797)*	
Opel Astra & Zafira Petrol (Feb 98 - Sept 00) *(See Vauxhall/Opel Astra & Zafira Petrol Book No. 3758)*	
Opel Calibra (90 - 98) *(See Vauxhall/Opel Calibra Book No. 3502)*	
Opel Corsa (83 - Mar 93) *(Not available in UK see Vauxhall Nova 0909)*	**3160**
Opel Corsa (Mar 93 - 97) *(Not available in UK see Vauxhall Corsa 1985)*	**3159**
Opel Frontera Petrol & Diesel (91 - 98) *(See Vauxhall/Opel Frontera Book No. 3454)*	
Opel Kadett (Nov 79 - Oct 84) up to B	**0634**
Opel Kadett (Oct 84 - Oct 91) *(Not available in UK see Vauxhall Astra & Belmont 1136)*	**3196**
Opel Omega & Senator (86 - 94) *(Not available in UK see Vauxhall Carlton & Senator 1469)*	**3157**
Omega (94 - 99) *(See Vauxhall/Opel Omega Book No. 3510)*	
Opel Rekord (Feb 78 - Oct 86) up to D	**0543**
Opel Vectra (Oct 88 - Oct 95) *(Not available in UK see Vauxhall Cavalier 1570)*	**3158**
Opel Vectra Petrol & Diesel (95 - 98) *(Not available in UK see Vauxhall Vectra 3396)*	**3523**

* Classic reprint

Title	Book No.
PEUGEOT	
Peugeot 106 Petrol & Diesel (91 - 01) J to X	**1882**
Peugeot 205 Petrol (83 - 97) A to P	**0932**
Peugeot 206 Petrol and Diesel (98 - 01) S to X	**3757**
Peugeot 305 (78 - 89) up to G	**0538**
Peugeot 306 Petrol & Diesel (93 - 99) K to T	**3073**
Peugeot 309 (86 - 93) C to K	**1266**
Peugeot 405 Petrol (88 - 97) E to P	**1559**
Peugeot 405 Diesel (88 - 97) E to P	**3198**
Peugeot 406 Petrol & Diesel (96 - 97) N to R	**3394**
Peugeot 505 (79 - 89) up to G	**0762**
Peugeot 1.7/1.8 & 1.9 litre Diesel Engine (82 - 96) up to N	**0950**
Peugeot 2.0, 2.1, 2.3 & 2.5 litre Diesel Engines (74 - 90) up to H	**1607**
PORSCHE	
Porsche 911 (65 - 85) up to C	**0264**
Porsche 924 & 924 Turbo (76 - 85) up to C	**0397**
PROTON	
Proton (89 - 97) F to P	**3255**
RANGE ROVER	
Range Rover V8 (70 - Oct 92) up to K	**0606**
RELIANT	
Reliant Robin & Kitten (73 - 83) up to A	**0436**
RENAULT	
Renault 4 (61 - 86) *	**0072**
Renault 5 (Feb 85 - 96) B to N	**1219**
Renault 9 & 11 (82 - 89) up to F	**0822**
Renault 18 (79 - 86) up to D	**0598**
Renault 19 Petrol (89 - 94) F to M	**1646**
Renault 19 Diesel (89 - 95) F to N	**1946**
Renault 21 (86 - 94) C to M	**1397**
Renault 25 (84 - 92) B to K	**1228**
Renault Clio Petrol (91 - May 98) H to R	**1853**
Renault Clio Diesel (91 - June 96) H to N	**3031**
Renault Clio (May 98-01) R-reg onwards	**3906**
Renault Espace Petrol & Diesel (85 - 96) C to N	**3197**
Renault Fuego (80 - 86) *	**0764**
Renault Laguna Petrol & Diesel (94 - 00) L to W	**3252**
Renault Mégane & Scénic Petrol & Diesel (96 - 98) N to R	**3395**
ROVER	
Rover 213 & 216 (84 - 89) A to G	**1116**
Rover 214 & 414 (89 - 96) G to N	**1689**
Rover 216 & 416 (89 - 96) G to N	**1830**
Rover 211, 214, 216, 218 & 220 Petrol & Diesel (Dec 95 - 98) N to R	**3399**
Rover 414, 416 & 420 Petrol & Diesel (May 95 - 98) M to R	**3453**
Rover 618, 620 & 623 (93 - 97) K to P	**3257**
Rover 820, 825 & 827 (86 - 95) D to N	**1380**
Rover 3500 (76 - 87) up to E	**0365**
Rover Metro, 111 & 114 (May 90 - 98) G to S	**1711**
SAAB	
Saab 90, 99 & 900 (79 - Oct 93) up to L	**0765**
Saab 95 & 96 (66 - 76) *	**0198**
Saab 99 (69 - 79) *	**0247**
Saab 900 (Oct 93 - 98) L to R	**3512**
Saab 9000 (4-cyl) (85 - 98) C to S	**1686**
SEAT	
Seat Ibiza & Cordoba Petrol & Diesel (Oct 93 - Oct 99) L to V	**3571**
Seat Ibiza & Malaga (85 - 92) B to K	**1609**
SKODA	
Skoda Estelle (77 - 89) up to G	**0604**
Skoda Favorit (89 - 96) F to N	**1801**
Skoda Felicia Petrol & Diesel (95 - 99) M to T	**3505**
SUBARU	
Subaru 1600 & 1800 (Nov 79 - 90) up to H	**0995**
SUNBEAM	
Sunbeam Alpine, Rapier & H120 (67 - 76) *	**0051**
SUZUKI	
Suzuki Supercarry/Bedford/Vauxhall Rascal (86 - Oct 94) C to M	**3015**
Suzuki SJ Series, Samurai & Vitara (4-cyl) (82 - 97) up to P	**1942**
TALBOT	
Talbot Alpine, Solara, Minx & Rapier (75 - 86) up to D	**0337**
Talbot Horizon (78 - 86) up to D	**0473**
Talbot Samba (82 - 86) up to D	**0823**
TOYOTA	
Toyota Carina E (May 92 - 97) J to P	**3256**
Toyota Corolla (Sept 83 - Sept 87) A to E	**1024**
Toyota Corolla (80 - 85) up to C	**0683**
Toyota Corolla (Sept 87 - Aug 92) E to K	**1683**
Toyota Corolla (Aug 92 - 97) K to P	**3259**
Toyota Hi-Ace & Hi-Lux (69 - Oct 83) up to A	**0304**
TRIUMPH	
Triumph Acclaim (81 - 84) *	**0792**
Triumph GT6 & Vitesse (62 - 74) *	**0112**
Triumph Herald (59 - 71) *	**0010**
Triumph Spitfire (62 - 81) up to X	**0113**
Triumph Stag (70 - 78) up to T	**0441**
Triumph TR2, TR3, TR3A, TR4 & TR4A (52 - 67)*	**0028**
Triumph TR5 & 6 (67 - 75) *	**0031**
Triumph TR7 (75 - 82) *	**0322**
VAUXHALL	
Vauxhall Astra (80 - Oct 84) up to B	**0635**
Vauxhall Astra & Belmont (Oct 84 - Oct 91) B to J	**1136**
Vauxhall Astra (Oct 91 - Feb 98) J to R	**1832**
Vauxhall/Opel Astra & Zafira Diesel (Feb 98 - Sept 00) R to W	**3797**
Vauxhall/Opel Astra & Zafira Petrol (Feb 98 - Sept 00) R to W	**3758**
Vauxhall/Opel Calibra (90 - 98) G to S	**3502**
Vauxhall Carlton (Oct 78 - Oct 86) up to D	**0480**
Vauxhall Carlton & Senator (Nov 86 - 94) D to L	**1469**
Vauxhall Cavalier 1300 (77 - July 81) *	**0461**
Vauxhall Cavalier 1600, 1900 & 2000 (75 - July 81) up to W	**0315**
Vauxhall Cavalier (81 - Oct 88) up to F	**0812**
Vauxhall Cavalier (Oct 88 - 95) F to N	**1570**
Vauxhall Chevette (75 - 84) up to B	**0285**
Vauxhall Corsa (Mar 93 - 97) K to R	**1985**
Vauxhall/Opel Corsa (Apr 97 - Sept 00) P to W	**3921**
Vauxhall/Opel Frontera Petrol & Diesel (91 - Sept 98) J to S	**3454**
Vauxhall Nova (83 - 93) up to K	**0909**
Vauxhall/Opel Omega (94 - 99) L to T	**3510**
Vauxhall Vectra Petrol & Diesel (95 - 98) N to R	**3396**
Vauxhall/Opel 1.5, 1.6 & 1.7 litre Diesel Engine (82 - 96) up to N	**1222**
VOLKSWAGEN	
Volkswagen 411 & 412 (68 - 75) *	**0091**
Volkswagen Beetle 1200 (54 - 77) up to S	**0036**
Volkswagen Beetle 1300 & 1500 (65 - 75) up to P	**0039**
Volkswagen Beetle 1302 & 1302S (70 - 72) up to L	**0110**
Volkswagen Beetle 1303, 1303S & GT (72 - 75) up to P	**0159**
Volkswagen Beetle (Apr 99 - 02) W-reg onwards	**3798**
Volkswagen Golf & Bora Petrol & Diesel (April 98 - 00) R to X	**3727**
Volkswagen Golf & Jetta Mk 1 1.1 & 1.3 (74 - 84) up to A	**0716**
Volkswagen Golf, Jetta & Scirocco Mk 1 1.5, 1.6 & 1.8 (74 - 84) up to A	**0726**
Volkswagen Golf & Jetta Mk 1 Diesel (78 - 84) up to A	**0451**
Volkswagen Golf & Jetta Mk 2 (Mar 84 - Feb 92) A to J	**1081**
Volkswagen Golf & Vento Petrol & Diesel (Feb 92 - 96) J to N	**3097**
Volkswagen LT vans & light trucks (76 - 87) up to E	**0637**
Volkswagen Passat & Santana (Sept 81 - May 88) up to E	**0814**
Volkswagen Passat Petrol & Diesel (May 88 - 96) E to P	**3498**
Volkswagen Polo & Derby (76 - Jan 82) up to X	**0335**
Volkswagen Polo (82 - Oct 90) up to H	**0813**
Volkswagen Polo (Nov 90 - Aug 94) H to L	**3245**
Volkswagen Polo Hatchback Petrol & Diesel (94 - 99) M to S	**3500**
Volkswagen Scirocco (82 - 90) up to H	**1224**
Volkswagen Transporter 1600 (68 - 79) up to V	**0082**
Volkswagen Transporter 1700, 1800 & 2000 (72 - 79) up to V	**0226**
Volkswagen Transporter (air-cooled) (79 - 82) up to Y	**0638**
Volkswagen Transporter (water-cooled) (82 - 90) up to H	**3452**
Volkswagen Type 3 (63 - 73) *	**0084**
VOLVO	
Volvo 120 & 130 Series (& P1800) (61 - 73) *	**0203**
Volvo 142, 144 & 145 (66 - 74) up to N	**0129**
Volvo 240 Series (74 - 93) up to K	**0270**
Volvo 262, 264 & 260/265 (75 - 85) *	**0400**
Volvo 340, 343, 345 & 360 (76 - 91) up to J	**0715**
Volvo 440, 460 & 480 (87 - 97) D to P	**1691**
Volvo 740 & 760 (82 - 91) up to J	**1258**
Volvo 850 (92 - 96) J to P	**3260**
Volvo 940 (90 - 96) H to N	**3249**
Volvo S40 & V40 (96 - 99) N to V	**3569**
Volvo S70, V70 & C70 (96 - 99) P to V	**3573**
AUTOMOTIVE TECHBOOKS	
Automotive Air Conditioning Systems	**3740**
Automotive Brake Manual	**3050**
Automotive Carburettor Manual	**3288**
Automotive Diagnostic Fault Codes Manual	**3472**
Automotive Diesel Engine Service Guide	**3286**
Automotive Electrical and Electronic Systems Manual	**3049**
Automotive Engine Management and Fuel Injection Systems Manual	**3344**
Automotive Gearbox Overhaul Manual	**3473**
Automotive Service Summaries Manual	**3475**
Automotive Timing Belts Manual – Austin/Rover	**3549**
Automotive Timing Belts Manual – Ford	**3474**
Automotive Timing Belts Manual – Peugeot/Citroën	**3568**
Automotive Timing Belts Manual – Vauxhall/Opel	**3577**
Automotive Welding Manual	**3053**
In-Car Entertainment Manual (3rd Edition)	**3363**

* Classic reprint

CL12.10/01

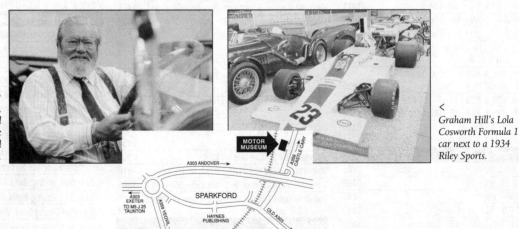